Enforcement of European Union Environmental Law

Legal Issues and Challenges

2nd Edition

Offering a detailed account of the various legal arrangements at European Union level, this book is an ideal reference tool for practitioners and legal scholars. As well as examining the principal sources of EU environmental law enforcement, it also contributes to the legal and political debates that surround the subject.

Spanning three parts, the author examines the practical impact of the legal arrangements at Union level that are used to uphold EU environmental norms. Offering a comprehensive account of the current state of EU environmental law enforcement and the developments affecting it, Martin Hedemann-Robinson explores the role of the European Commission, the possibilities for private law enforcement, and the responsibilities of member state national authorities.

Key legal developments that have occurred since the first edition have been incorporated, including new statutory developments and case law. Particular attention is paid to the impact of the 2007 Lisbon Treaty on foundational EU treaty provisions enabling the European Commission to take legal action against EU member states infringing Union environmental law, the establishment of a new legal architecture at Union level on the topic of environmental criminal policy, as well as increased EU legislative intervention in the area of environmental inspections. The impact of the 1998 Århus Convention on EU environmental law enforcement is also addressed in detail, including the influence of recommendations of the Århus Convention's Compliance Committee.

Martin Hedemann-Robinson is a Senior Lecturer in Law at Kent University, Canterbury, UK.

Enforcement of European Union Environmental Law

Legal Issues and Challenges

2nd Edition

Martin Hedemann-Robinson

Routledge
Taylor & Francis Group
LONDON AND NEW YORK

Second edition published 2015
by Routledge
2 Park Square, Milton Park, Abingdon, Oxon, OX14 4RN

and by Routledge
711 Third Avenue, New York, NY 10017

Routledge is an imprint of the Taylor & Francis Group, an informa business

First edition published by Routledge-Cavendish 2007

British Library Cataloguing in Publication Data
A catalogue record for this book is available from the British Library

Library of Congress Cataloging-in-Publication Data
Hedemann-Robinson, Martin, author.
   Enforcement of European Union environmental law / Martin
Hedemann-Robinson. — Second edition.
      pages cm
   Includes bibliographical references and index.
   1. Environmental law—European Union countries.   I. Title.
   KJE6242.H43 2015
   344.2404'6—dc23
   2014041272

ISBN: 978-0-415-65959-8 (hbk)
ISBN: 978-0-203-07484-8 (ebk)

Typeset in Baskerville
by Apex CoVantage, LLC

For Sam, Freya and Jocelyn,
Ute Ruth and Alan,
as well as
Ludwig Krämer and all my other former colleagues in
DG ENV.

Contents

PART II

The role of private persons in enforcing EU environmental law

Section 1   Taking action at national level

9A Private enforcement of EU environmental law at EU institutional level (1A): access to environmental information (on website)

10 Private enforcement of EU environmental law at EU institutional level (2): administrative complaints procedures and other possibilities   481

PART III
The role of member states in enforcing EU environmental law

11 Enforcement of EU environmental law by national authorities (1): general principles and environmental inspection responsibilities

All eResource chapters can be accessed online at http://www.routledge.com/books/details/9780415659598/

Preface

Without their proper enforcement, governmental commitments to improving the state of the environment are prone to remain but 'greenspeak'. Over the last 40 years and more, the European Union has developed a raft of legislation intended to enhance standards to protect the environment. The main purpose of this book is to provide an overview of the current principles and provisions of the European Union (EU) legal order concerning the enforcement of Union environmental law. It aims to examine the subject of EU environmental law enforcement by providing a detailed account of the various legal arrangements that may be used for the purpose of upholding EU environmental norms as well as a critical appraisal of the practical impact of those arrangements, considering in particular issues of efficacy and accountability. Spanning three parts, the book focuses on the principal modes of EU environmental law enforcement: namely, the role of the European Commission, possibilities for private law enforcement and the role of national authorities.

In Part I, in addition to detailing the key legal considerations that affect the European Commission's prosecution of infringement proceedings against member states acting in violation of EU environmental law, the author also draws from his own professional experience within the Commission's Environment Directorate-General of the practical and systemic limitations faced by this EU institution. In Part II, the author seeks to appraise the possibilities available under EU law for private individuals to enforce EU environmental law, in particular taking account of legal principles developed by the Court of Justice of the Union, EU legislative instrumentation (such as that on environmental damage and access to environmental information) as well as EU institutional systems of support. In Part III, the book examines the requirements and structures in place at EU level which may serve to assist national authorities involved in environmental protection to utilise EU environmental law.

It is hoped that this monograph, now in its second edition, will continue to provide a useful reference point of key information as well as a platform for ongoing legal and political discourse at academic and legal professional levels concerning the state of EU mechanisms intended to assist with enforcement of EU environmental law.

Since the first edition of this book, it is fair to say that there are heartening signs regarding the long-term prospects of the legal arrangements relating to EU environmental law enforcement. These include notably the recent opening up of possibilities for civil society to play a more active and serious legal role in supervision of EU environmental law, in large part due to the Union's commitment to implementing the 1998 UNECE Århus Convention. In addition, recent EU legislative initiatives have sought to crystallise EU member state authorities' enforcement role and responsibilities more precisely, including with respect to the key area of environmental inspections. One could also point to the recent reforms within the European Commission to try to focus its existing limited resources for law enforcement more effectively, in particular by concentrating more on ensuring that member states transpose their obligations in EU environmental directives, the main legislative tool used in EU environmental policy, into national law correctly and on time.

Nevertheless, challenges still remain. For instance, there is a strong case for enhancing the limited current enforcement role of the European Commission, particularly in the areas of inspection and investigations. National authorities are crucially important actors in relation to EU environmental law enforcement. Yet it is apparent that the quality of law enforcement work carried out at national authority level across the Union varies considerably. This is an area that warrants attention at EU level, in order to ensure that a floor of minimum standards applies with respect to essential aspects of law enforcement agency work concerning resourcing, inter-agency co-ordination and planning of environmental investigations and inspections.

The EU has made great strides in recent years towards developing a more coherent and effective strategy for overseeing the implementation of Union environmental law. Efforts have been made and are continuing to be made to enhance the roles of civil society and national authorities in relation to law enforcement work, so as to complement the important but ultimately limited capabilities of the European Commission in this area. However, the journey is far from complete and will require sustained effort at EU level and, in particular, by member state governments to ensure that resources are effectively utilised to craft a suitably comprehensive framework that meets the challenges of EU environmental law enforcement.

I have intended the book to be up to date as at the end of September 2014.

Martin Hedemann-Robinson

Canterbury, October 2014

Table of cases

Court of Justice of the European Union
(General Court and Court of Justice)

(All CJEU judgments may be inspected on the Court's website (InfoCuria database): http://curia.europa.eu/)

Key: Page numbers in bold refer to endnotes; page numbers in brackets refer to position of notes within the main text

Table of treaties and environmental legislation

TREATIES

European Union

Founding Treaties:

Other primary EU Law sources:

Council of Europe

Other multilateral agreements

ENVIRONMENTAL LEGISLATION

European Union

EU Regulations:

EU Directives:

EU Recommendations:

Other selected EU policy instruments:

Table of abbreviations

AEI	access to environmental information
AG	Advocate General of the Court of Justice
AJEM	access to justice in environmental matters
Århus Convention	1998 UNECE Convention on Access to Information, Public Participation in Decision-making and Access to Justice in Environmental Matters
BATNEEC	best available technology not entailing excessive cost
BSE	bovine spongiform encephalopathy
BWD	EU Bathing Water Directive
CFI	Court of First Instance
CFP	Common Fisheries Policy
CJEU	Court of Justice of the European Union
CFSP	Common and Foreign Security Policy
CITES	Convention on International Trade in Endangered Species 1973
CLJ	*Cambridge Law Journal*
CML Rev	*Common Market Law Review*
CoE	Council of Europe
CoJ	Court of Justice
COM	European Commission document
COR	Committee of the Regions
CPECL	Council of Europe Convention of the Protection of the Environmental through Criminal Law
Crim LR	*Criminal Law Review*
CSDP	Common Security and Defence Policy
DG	Directorate-General
DG ENV	Environment Directorate-General (European Commission)
EAP	Environmental Action Programme
EC	European Community (European Community Treaty if placed immediately after a treaty article)
ECB	European Central Bank
ECGAB	EU Code of Good Administrative Behaviour
ECHA	European Chemicals Agency

ECHR	European Convention on Human Rights and Fundamental Freedoms 1950, of the Council of Europe
ECI	European Citizens' Initiative
ECJ	European Court of Justice
ECSC	European Coal and Steel Community
EEA	European Environment Agency, also European Economic Area (Agreement 1992)
EEB	European Environmental Bureau
EEC	European Economic Community
EEEL Rev	*European Energy and Environmental Law Review*
EI	environmental inspection
EIA	environmental impact assessment
ECI	EU Citizens' Initiative
EIB	European Investment Bank
ELD	EU Environmental Liability Directive 2004/35
ELJ	*European Law Journal*
ELM	*Environmental Law & Management Journal*
EL Rev	*European Law Review*
EMSA	European Maritime Safety Agency
ENV	Environment
Env Liability	*Environmental Liability Journal*
Env LRev	*Environmental Law Review*
EO	European Ombudsman
EP	European Parliament
EPL	*European Public Law Journal*
EPER	European Pollutant Emission Register
E-PRTR	European Pollutant Release and Transfer Register
ESC	Economic and Social Committee
EU	European Union
EU	Treaty on European Union (prior to the 2007 Lisbon Treaty) – when used in conjunction with an Article reference
EUC	European Union Constitution (Treaty establishing a Constitution for Europe 2004)
EUCFR	EU Charter of Fundamental Rights 2000
EU15	European Union of 15 Member States (before 1 May 2004)
EU25	European Union of 25 Member States (as at 1 May 2004)
Euratom	European Atomic Energy Community (Treaty)
Eur Const L Rev	*European Constitutional Law Review*
Eur J Crime, Crim L & Crim Justice	*European Journal on Crime, Criminal Law and Criminal Justice*
Fordham Int LJ	*Fordham International Law Journal*
GA	General Assembly
GAP	general and persistent (infringement)
GC	General Court of the Court of Justice

GMOs	genetically modified organisms
HWD	(Former) EU Hazardous Waste Directive 91/689
ICLQ	*International Comparative Law Quarterly*
IED	Industrial Emissions Directive 2010/75
ILM	International Legal Materials
IMPEL	EU Network for the Implementation of Environmental Law
IPPC	integrated pollution prevention and control
JEL	*Journal of Environmental Law*
JHA	Justice and Home Affairs
J Pl & Env Law	*Journal of Planning & Environment Law*
LFN	letter of formal notice
LIEI	*Legal Issues of Economic Integration Journal*
LIFE	EC Financial Instrument for the Environment
LQR	*Law Quarterly Review*
Lugano Convention	1993 Council of Europe Convention on civil liability resulting from activities dangerous to the environment
Maastricht Treaty	Treaty on European Union 1992
MEP	Member of the European Parliament
MJ	*Maastricht Journal of European and Comparative Law*
MLR	*Modern Law Review*
NGO	non-governmental organisation
NGEO	non-governmental environmental organisation
NIMBY	not in my back yard
Nordic JIL	*Nordic Journal of International Law*
ODS	ozone depleting substance
ODSR	EU Ozone Depleting Substance Regulation 1005/2009
OJ	Official Journal of the European Union
OOPEC	Office for Official Publications of the EC, L-2985 Luxembourg
OPI	overriding public interest
p.e.	population equivalent
PECL	protecting the environment through criminal law
PRP	preliminary ruling procedure
QMV	qualified majority voting
RECIEL	Review of European Community and International Environmental Law
RMCEI	Recommendation 2001/331 on minimum criteria for environmental inspections
RO	reasoned opinion
RP	rules of procedure
SCI	Site of Community Importance
SEA	Single European Act 1986
SEC	European Commission internal working paper
SMEs	small and medium-sized enterprises

SPA	Special Protection Area
TEU	Treaty on European Union
TFEU	Treaty on the Functioning of the European Union
ToA	Treaty of Amsterdam 1997
ToN	Treaty of Nice 2001
VAT	value added tax
UN	United Nations
UNECE	United Nations Economic Commission for Europe
UNTS	United Nations Treaty Series
WEEE	waste electrical and electronic equipment
WFD	Waste Framework Directive
YEL	*Yearbook of European Law*
YEEL	*Yearbook of European Environmental Law*

1 Introduction

Without question, environmental policy of the European Union (EU) has, over the last 40 years,[1] evolved into being an important integral component within the wide range of the regional international organisation's economic and political objectives. Until the mid 1980s, though, the constitutional framework of the EU did not formally provide itself with a mandate to develop a policy on the environment. Specifically, this came about by virtue of the Single European Act (SEA) 1986,[2] a treaty agreed between the EU's member states which served to amend the Union's original founding treaties and include protection of the environment amongst its official objectives and tasks. The entry into force of the SEA signalled an important shift in relation to the identity, purpose and direction of supranational European integration. Hitherto, the EU had predominantly, if not exclusively, been founded upon the objective of establishing a common market between its constituent member states, principally through the elimination of trading barriers between them as well as other distortions to competition.

At the inception of the Union in the early 1950s, the project of realising a common market was intended to serve as the principal mechanism of achieving the core, broader ambitions of the founding treaties, namely the former 1951 European Coal and Steel Community (ECSC) Treaty, former 1957 European Economic Community (EEC) Treaty and the 1957 European Atomic Energy Community (EAEC/Euratom Treaty). The original principal founding treaty, namely the former EEC Treaty, envisaged most notably the laying of the 'foundations of ever closer union among the peoples of Europe', 'to ensure the economic and social progress' of the member states and the 'constant improvement of the living and working conditions' of the member states' populations.[3] Those goals still form an essential part of the constitutional fabric of the contemporary legal framework of the Union.[4]

However, it was not until 1986, by virtue of treaty amendment through the SEA, that the EU specifically included within its mandate the development of a common environmental protection policy. The specific inclusion of an environmental protection policy in the constitutional make-up of the EU confirmed and brought with it a profound change to the political nature of the regional international organisation. Notably, the EU was now no longer an organisation predominantly focused on achieving closer economic integration between its constituent member countries, but one that also aspired to achieve a high level of environmental protection. The environmental protection commitment remains entrenched amongst the various policy objectives of the Union, as contained in Article 3 of the current version of the Treaty on European Union (TEU). Specifically Article 3(3) TEU cites the 'sustainable development of Europe' as well as 'a high level of protection and improvement of the quality of the environment' amongst the objectives of the Union. This is complemented by the inclusion of provisions within the EU treaty framework enabling the adoption of measures for the development of a common environmental policy at EU level.[5] Since 1986, the Union's constitutional commitment to environmental protection has been further strengthened through additional treaty amendments, most significantly by the incorporation of a stipulation within the foundational EU treaty framework that environmental protection requirements must be incorporated within the definition and implementation of the entire range of its economically related policies and activities.[6]

Since the inauguration of an environmental protection dimension to the EU's policy portfolio, a substantial number of legislative instruments have been adopted at Union level on the environment. Over 200 legislative measures have been passed by the EU concerning environmental protection issues.[7] It is true that EU rules on environmental protection account for only part of the legal framework that constitutes environmental law from the perspective of EU member states. For them, the subject of environmental law also comprises rules binding on them passed at national and other international levels. However, it is fair to say that the material range and depth of EU environmental legislation is both wide and deep. In 2013, the European Commission estimated that some 80 per cent of environmental legislation of the Union's member states derives from EU instruments.[8] Although member states share competence with the EU in relation to the area of environmental policy,[9] national rules that conflict with the requirements of environmental measures adopted at Union level are required to be set aside, in order to respect the principle of the supremacy of EU law over national law.[10] Accordingly, EU environmental law constitutes a very significant element in the overall package of measures adopted by member states to protect the environment.

Notwithstanding the now long-standing constitutional commitment on the part of the EU to develop a common environmental policy, the implementation of that promise into practice has faced considerable challenges at various levels, political as well as legal. First, from a purely political perspective, moves to adopt environmental protection measures have faced resistance from various quarters, public and private. Concerns are constantly raised about the impact of the perceived level of 'economic cost' of environmental measures intended to introduce enhanced systems for the protection of the environment, particularly from certain industrial lobby groups and member state governments. This tension is part and parcel of the constant struggle that faces the Union, and indeed all systems of contemporary political governance, on determining the extent to which regulation is required in order to address anthropogenic impacts on the state of the environment. Ultimately, it is a battle of ideas and interests over the means of changing societal behaviour so as to render a sustainable relationship between society and the environment, including decisions over allocation of governmental resources to assist in this endeavour. This challenge is essentially a political struggle, in respect of which there are no scientifically objective or otherwise clear-cut solutions. The EU treaty framework reflects this approach to decision-making, in that its environmental provisions allow for broad interpretation by the incumbent EU legislature (composed fundamentally of the European Parliament (EP) and Council of the EU) whose hands are effectively free from any significant legally enforceable constitutional constraints over policy content.

Secondly, the EU has faced difficulties in securing the proper implementation of its adopted policies relating to environmental protection. Specifically, it has been confronted with a number of problems in ensuring that its legislation on environmental protection is actually implemented fully and on time by Union member states, notwithstanding the legally binding force of such measures. Implementation of agreed policy is a problem shared by several international organisations, not only the EU. In general, the writ of international law does not run readily or easily within the internal legal systems of nation states. The standard principles of international law do not provide legal tools through which legally binding accords agreed between subjects of international law (nation states and international organisations) may be enforced. Under international law, contracting parties to an international environmental agreement must agree to specific mechanisms in the agreement to enhance the implementation and supervision of implementation of its obligations. Such mechanisms (ranging from reporting, peer review, arbitration, referral to an international court such as the International Court of Justice, independent monitoring through to the adoption of financial incentives and sanctions) have been slow to emerge and develop effectively in international practice as far as multilateral environmental agreements are concerned.[11]

However, as will be discussed in detail later on in this book, the EU has developed its own special legal order, radically different from that which applies between international organisations and their respective contracting parties. The EU's legal order, as developed notably at the hand of the Union's judicial institution, the Court of Justice of the European Union (CJEU), involves the existence of a special legal relationship between the EU and its member states, whereby there are several possibilities for various actors to take steps to enforce provisions adopted at Union level that are intended to be binding on the EU institutions, member states and/or private persons. Notwithstanding these legal possibilities, the record of several member states on ensuring proper implementation of Union legislative measures on environmental protection has been a relatively poor one. The responsibility of member states to internalise the environmental measures agreed at EU level and apply them within their respective jurisdictions has been a difficult legal and political pill for many of them to swallow.

The focus of this book is to consider the second of the major challenges identified above that confront the EU in its aims to deliver its environmental protection commitments, namely the task of securing effective implementation. The question as to what extent the Union, in developing its environmental protection policy, has achieved an appropriate balance between the relevant interests involved and affected by its environmental measures is open to debate as a political question and is not the concern of this book. Instead, this book aims to consider the various Union legal mechanisms and principles through which EU environmental law may be enforced effectively at the level of the member state as well as at EU institutional level. Specifically, it will look in detail at the particular legal principles and mechanisms that exist under EU law to assist in ensuring that binding measures adopted by the Union on environmental protection are actually adhered to, both in terms of the letter of the law as well as in practice. In addition, where appropriate, the relevant EU legal machinery will be placed into its broader political context.

Just as the content of environmental policy (including legislation) at EU level is subject to change and innovation in line with developments in science and political pressures, a non-static picture applies equally with regard to the area of EU environmental law enforcement. Since the turn of the millennium, in particular, the EU legal area concerning EU environmental law enforcement has been transformed and, at the time of writing, is still undergoing a series of significant alterations. This has been due in substantial part to the EU's membership of the United Nations Economic Commission for Europe's (UNECE) Convention on Access to Information, Public Participation in Decision-making and Access to Justice in Environmental Matters, agreed on 25 June 1998 in Århus, Denmark (referred to as the 'Århus Convention').[12] The Århus Convention has important ramifications for the EU, in terms of the extent to which private persons, in particular environmental non-governmental organisations (NGOs), may have an input and influence in supervising the implementation of EU environmental law. The Union is still very much in the process of completing the internalisation of legal commitments entered into by it under the Convention. A significant part of this book[13] will be devoted to considering its impacts at EU level.

This book seeks to explore the subject of EU environmental law enforcement from the perspectives of the three principal stakeholders involved in law enforcement work, namely the European Commission of the EU, member state authorities engaged in environmental protection as well as civil society (primarily but not exclusively non-governmental environmental organisations (NGEOs)). Historically, supervision of implementation of EU environmental law has been viewed as a responsibility principally resting with the executive institution of the Union, namely the European Commission. Supervision of the implementation of EU law has always been one of the Commission's tasks. The original founding treaties of the Union imposed a specific duty on the Commission to ensure the application of the treaty provisions and secondary measures taken at EU level[14] and this core duty continues under the aegis of the current EU treaty framework.[15] In addition, from the outset they provided the Commission with specific powers to take legal proceedings against member states in the event of its detecting that the latter had breached the law of the EU.[16] These treaty powers have been subsequently fortified in the current Union legal framework.[17] The involvement of other actors in the area of EU law enforcement, notably in relation to the environmental sector, has materialised only relatively recently in terms of EU history. As far as civil society is concerned, a combination of the evolving jurisprudence of the CJEU together with recent legislative developments have served to provide private persons with a range of rights relevant to area of enforcement of EU environmental law. The potential for civil society to become effectively engaged in supervisory tasks has not, though, yet been fully harnessed, in no small part due to the fact that a number of pieces of EU legislation intended to internalise within the EU's legal order the access to environmental justice and information provisions of the Århus Convention have only relatively recently been adopted or are still pending legislative endorsement. Finally, member states through their national (environmental) authorities play a seminal role in the enforcement area, shouldering key legal obligations under EU law[18] to ensure that the Union's environmental protection legislation is properly implemented within their respective territories and within the deadlines foreseen.

However, in practice, over the years there have been numerous instances of failures on the part of member states to show diligence in ensuring that national law and practice are aligned with the environmental obligations entered into by them at EU level. Until relatively recently, it would be fair to assess the general approach of member states towards the issue of compliance with EU environmental obligations as being low key, sluggish and minimalist. The poor state of implementation of EU obligations by member states was the principal reason for the Union in 1992 to introduce the possibility of financial sanctions being imposed by the CJEU in relation to infringement actions prosecuted by the European Commission against persistent non-compliant states. To a large extent, the EU has in the past been unduly reliant on the Commission's supervisory work to detect and follow up breaches of EU environmental law by member states, whether committed by governments, other public authorities and/or the private sector located within their respective territories. Since the turn of the millennium, though, the picture has begun to change. Notably, recent EU legislative initiatives on environmental inspections, civil and criminal environmental liability foresee a far greater and more effective role to be played by national authorities to ensure that legally binding EU environmental protection standards are adhered to within their respective territories.

There are a number of reasons to account for the gradual but steady transformation of the legal picture of EU environmental law enforcement, which is moving from a situation originally dominated by one stakeholder (namely the European Commission) to one that is becoming subject to the influence of three types of players (Commission, member state authorities and civil society). Law enforcement is becoming genuinely three-dimensional. From the perspective of resources alone, it has been evident for a considerable number of years that the Commission has faced often overwhelming challenges to meet its supervisory duties as enshrined in the EU treaty framework. Since its inception, EU membership has expanded from 6 to 28 countries. The number of member states is to set to rise further in the coming years.[19] It is now an even less realistic proposition than it ever was to consider the Commission's services, comprising essentially a legal team of around two lawyers dealing with environmental law enforcement issues in each member state, to be able to monitor each and every breach of EU environmental legislation. Moreover, the Commission's services have never been endowed with the requisite legal or financial resources to undertake routine and non-routine inspections and investigations, with a view to checking for compliance. Accordingly, from the perspective of efficiency, it has never been a satisfactory position to consider placing primary responsibility on the shoulders of the Commission to ensure due implementation of EU environmental legislation at the national level. Recent efforts at EU level to require member state authorities to take a more active role in enforcement of EU environmental law tie in with long-standing concerns about the limited effectiveness of relying upon the Commission alone to ensure due compliance by member states with their EU obligations. Efforts have also been made in other Union policy sectors to decentralise responsibility for law enforcement for similar reasons, most notably in the fields of competition,[20] consumer protection[21] and the internal market.[22] The advent of moves to include the participation of civil society, notably NGEOs, within the sphere of EU environmental law enforcement policy has its roots in moves since the early 1990s to render the decision-making processes of the EU and its impact both more transparent and accountable to the general public. This development was entrenched with the Union signing the 1998 Århus Convention and becoming a contracting party in 2005. Notwithstanding the fact that several changes have been made, it is still fair to say at this stage the Commission still constitutes the dominant actor in matters relating to enforcement of EU environmental law. The legislative changes made, as well as those in the pipeline, will take a considerable period of time to bed down in practice as well as be appreciated for the major cultural shift that they collectively represent in terms of legal practice.

To take account of the three-dimensional nature of the subject of EU environmental law enforcement, this book is divided into three parts. Part I (Chapters 2–5) examines the role of the European Commission in enforcing EU environmental law. It will first examine in detail the various legal provisions and principles that govern the operation of the particular legal proceedings that the Commission may institute against member states over suspected infractions of EU environmental protection legislation. After a brief overview of the relevant treaty provisions in Chapter 2, Chapters 3 and 4 will assess the operational rules underpinning the Commission's right to take legal action against member states under the infringement procedures contained in Articles 258 and 260 of the Treaty on the Functioning of the European Union (TFEU). A number of cases have ultimately led to financial penalties being imposed on member states by the CJEU in respect of failings to comply with their environmental protection obligations. Subsequent to detailed legal analysis of the law attending to these proceedings, Chapter 5 takes stock and offers some critical reflections on the supervisory role of the Commission.

Part II of the book (Chapters 6–10) focuses on the role of and rights accorded to civil society in being able to assist in the supervision the implementation of EU environmental law. It is divided into two sections, in order to take account of the bi-dimensional nature of private sector enforcement of the EU's environmental protection legislation, namely supervision of implementation at national level as well as supervision of the decision-making processes conducted at EU level that may affect environmental protection issues. The first section of Part II (Chapters 6–8A) considers to what extent the EU has developed a body of rules that serve to assist private persons in taking legal steps to ensure that the Union's environmental protection legislation is properly implemented and adhered to in practice at national level. It commences in Chapters 6 and 7 with an analysis of the important general legal principles that have emerged from the CJEU's case law, which has served to establish a floor of rights for private persons to be able to enforce certain norms of EU law before national courts, including those relating to the environment. Chapter 8 examines the extent to which the Union has taken steps to enhance rights of access to justice at national level in alignment with the requirements of the Århus Convention. Chapter 8A (available on website) considers the Union's adoption of legislation to provide a right of access to environmental information in member states, a right that may be seen as one that complements the enhancement of law enforcement by civil society.

The second section of Part II (Chapters 9–10) turns to consider the extent to which private persons are vested with legal powers under Union law to hold EU institutions to account in respect of the decisions they make affecting the environment. Chapter 9 considers in detail the various rights that private persons have to take legal proceedings against those EU institutions they consider have breached requirements of EU environmental law. Chapter 9A (available on website) assesses their EU rights to gain access to information on the environment held by Union institutional actors, information that may well throw light on the extent of justification underpinning decision-making processes at Union level which civil society (e.g. an NGEO) may wish to subject to legal challenge. Consequent to this examination of judicially enforceable mechanisms available to private persons, Chapter 10 provides an analysis of the various non-judicial complaints procedures open to civil society to use to seek review of controversial EU decisions on the environment, including the complaints process before the European Ombudsman and petitions system of the EP about contested decisions of the Commission to refrain from taking infringement action against member states.

Part III of the book (Chapters 11–13) considers the role and responsibilities of the member states of the EU and their public authorities involved in overseeing implementation of EU environmental protection controls. Chapter 11, in examining this issue from a general perspective, assesses the impact of broad EU legal obligations on member states in relation to enforcement of EU environmental legislation. In addition, it looks at the evolution of measures taken at Union level since the early 2000s to develop benchmarks and minimum standards for environmental inspections of installations and activities that represent significant risks or threats to the quality of the environment. The shaping of these latter arrangements have been influenced, in particular, by an informal forum comprising representatives of the EU member states (with representation from the Commission) known as the EU Network for the Implementation of Environmental Law (or IMPEL). Chapters 12 and 13 consider the impact of two important relatively recent EU legislative initiatives intended to enhance the performance of member states in fulfilling their EU environmental obligations. Specifically Chapter 12 examines the legislation addressing the area of environmental civil liability at national level, specifically the provisions of the EU's Directive 2004/35 on environmental liability with regard to the prevention and remedying of environmental damage.[23] Chapter 13 considers the nature and impact of the EU's legislation on environmental criminal liability, notably Directive 2008/99, on the protection of the environment through criminal law.[24] In both cases, the EU legislative instruments concerned seek to place central responsibility for applying the liability rules with the competent national authorities charged with implementing environmental protection policy. Finally, the book closes in Chapter 14 with some reflections on the actual and prospective state of the EU's legal and administrative machinery for enforcing its environmental protection legislation. It is intended that this second edition of the book will provide a reasonably up-to-date and comprehensive analysis of the current and prospective state of environmental law enforcement mechanisms provided under EU law as at the end of September 2014.

Before proceeding to examine the three elements of EU environmental law enforcement, it is first worth incorporating within this first chapter some introductory comments about the general nature and terminology of the law of the EU. This is, in part, intended to be of assistance to readers who may not be readily familiar with the evolving legal and political structures of the Union.

1.1 Legal architecture and terminology of the EU: a brief overview

Fundamental to any analysis of the enforcement of EU environmental law is a clear understanding of the core legal structures and provisions of the Union's constitutional arrangements.[25] The current legal framework of the Union, as crafted by the 2007 Lisbon Treaty,[26] is contained in three principal treaties, namely:

- the 1992 Treaty on European Union (TEU), as amended[27]
- the 2009 Treaty on the Functioning of the European Union (TFEU)[28]
- the 1957 Euratom Treaty, as amended.[29]

The primary or founding treaties comprise the TEU and TFEU, with the Euratom Treaty serving as a specialist treaty (*lex specialis*) concerning the regulation of civil nuclear energy within the Union. In broad terms, the TEU sets out the general tenets of the Union as a whole, including notably its values and objectives as well as key institutional structures. The TFEU provides more detail on the constitutional structure of the Union, including notably the legal bases for the development of the vast majority of its several common policies such as environmental protection.[30] The following sections summarise the principal features of the legal framework of the Union, as evolved since its inception in the early 1950s.

1.1.1 *Overview of the Union's constitutional development*

An important part in understanding the nature of the legal status and impact of the EU is to appreciate how its framework has evolved since its origins in the 1950s. Since its inception in 1957, the Union has developed substantially, both in terms of range of policies falling within its remit as well as in terms of its legal impact upon the national legal systems of the member states.

1.1.1.1 *Phase I (1951–92): the three European Communities*

Originally, the EU was a regional international economic organisation comprised formally of three framework treaties that established three distinct Communities, each with its own distinct sets of norms. These were the 1951 ECSC Treaty, 1957 EEC Treaty and the 1957 Euratom Treaty. Whereas the coal, steel and atomic energy sectors of the economies of the Communities' member states were to be addressed principally by the ECSC and Euratom Treaties, the EEC Treaty constituted the legal framework that would serve as the basis for developing greater integration of the economies of the member states, principally by fostering completion of a common market area comprising the territories of the states concerned. The Communities were served by a common institutional framework by the late 1960s. The body of rules in the EEC Treaty together with the measures adopted under its auspices as judicially interpreted by the CJEU, comprised EEC law. Over time the EEC acquired a range of policy competences whose scope transcended the original core economic priorities set down in 1957 of establishing a common market and customs union. Successive amending treaties agreed between the member states, notably the Single European Act (SEA) 1986,[31] TEU 1992 (or Maastricht Treaty),[32] the Amsterdam Treaty 1997 and Nice Treaty 2001, broadened the remit of the initial European integration project, amending the scope of the original EEC Treaty to include new common policy agendas on areas such as the environment, consumer protection, public health, education, culture and justice and home affairs. As a symbolic recognition of this process towards a greater depth and range of Community co-operation, the 1992 TEU (Maastricht Treaty) determined that references in the 1957 treaty to 'EEC' should be replaced by 'EC'. Accordingly, the terms 'EC Treaty' and 'EC law' superseded the 'EEC'.

1.1.1.2 *Phase II (1993–2009): the establishment of a three-pillar framework of the EU*

The 1992 TEU (or Maastricht Treaty) constituted an important milestone in the Union's evolution. By virtue of the TEU, which amended the foundational framework, the regional international organisation's general name was formally changed to 'European Union'. This change signalled, in particular, that the original regional compact of the 1950s no longer simply focused on forging closer economic integration through common rules on inter-state trade but included a greater range of common policy objectives, some of which were overtly political in nature such as in relation to foreign policy, justice and home affairs and economic and monetary union. In incorporating a wider range of policy objectives and platforms into the EU's constitutional fabric, the TEU established a complex legal framework that served to underpin the reformed regional international organisation's activities. Specifically, the framework comprised three main elements or 'pillars' as they were commonly known, each reflecting the degree of intensity of European political integration with which the member states agreed to proceed in relation to particular policy areas.

Collectively, the three pillars were to embody the 'European Union', an entity founded on the European Communities and supplemented by the policies and forms of intergovernmental co-operation introduced by the TEU, with a set of common overarching objectives.[33] The first pillar comprised the original Community treaties and law. Given that the ECSC Treaty elapsed in 2002,[34] this meant that the first pillar ended up including the body of rules and policies developed under the aegis of the EC and Euratom Treaties. In addition to amending the original Community treaties, the TEU introduced a set of rules on mutual co-operation in two broad areas of policy that would be governed wholly outside the legal frameworks of the Community treaties. These related to provisions on a common foreign and security policy (CFSP) and on co-operation in the field of justice and home affairs (JHA) respectively.[35]

Key reasons why pillars two and three were developed outside the auspices of the Community treaty framework was that not all the member states were prepared to accept that co-operation measures agreed in the policy sectors covered by those pillars should be subject to the supranational decision-making type processes and legal effects characteristic of the first pillar (namely European Community law). Specifically, member states were not prepared collectively to engage in a process of majority voting on decisions in such matters. Accordingly, rules established under the TEU preserved sovereign powers of member states by incorporating intergovernmental decision-making processes (i.e. safeguarding the principles of unanimity and national veto as well as preserving the right of initiative for member states). In addition, member states were collectively unwilling to craft foreign and security as well as justice and home affairs measures in the legal form of Community measures, given that the CJEU had established in its jurisprudence that Community law could have special legal effects within the individual legal systems of the member states.

The CJEU, in a long line of jurisprudence tracing back to the seminal cases of *Van Gend en Loos*[36] and *Costa/ENEL*[37] in the early 1960s, established some fundamental principles pertaining to Community norms that had a profound bearing on the relationship between national and EC law: namely supremacy and direct effect. In *Costa/ENEL* and in subsequent cases, the CJEU established that Community law was supreme over conflicting national laws and that national governments and authorities were obliged under the EC Treaty to ensure that domestic rules were suitably amended and/or repealed in order to ensure due compliance with Community obligations. In addition, it held that national courts were obliged to set aside rules of national law that conflicted with sources of Community law. In *Van Gend* the CJEU ruled that under certain conditions, private individuals may enforce certain Community norms directly before national courts without the need for those norms to have been formally transposed into national law such as by way of rules promulgated by domestic parliaments. This became known as the doctrine of direct effect, where the CJEU established in a substantial body of case law that private individuals would be able to rely directly upon Community treaty and legislative provisions before national courts of the member states where the sources of EC law were sufficiently precise, clear and unconditional. This particular judicial interpretation of the legal effect of Community law represented a radical departure from the then mainstream analysis of its legal effects, which viewed the legal ramifications of the Community through the lens of classic tenets of international law. Under international law, agreements struck between states do not confer rights or obligations automatically on private individuals insofar as this is not specifically agreed to; instead, ratification and implementation measures at national level are required for this to occur. The Community treaties did not expressly provide for the principles of direct effect or supremacy. However, in a long line of cases starting with *Van Gend*, the CJEU established that Community law constituted a new legal order of international law, in which member states had limited their sovereign rights within particular fields and the subjects of which comprised not only member states, but also individuals.

Pillars two and three under the TEU were established with a view to ensuring that they would not be affected by the unique supranational legal quality accorded to Community norms outlined above. The powers of the CJEU to be able to interpret and rule on the validity of measures adopted under the aegis of the second and third pillars were deliberately curtailed for this purpose.[38] Subsequently, by virtue of treaty amendment (1997 Amsterdam Treaty) the material scope of the second and third pillars was revised to comprise provisions on a common foreign and security as well as on police and judicial co-operation respectively. The member states agreed to transfer immigration and asylum policy matters to be regulated under the first pillar, albeit with special derogations applying to the UK, Ireland and Denmark.

Measures that could be taken under the second and third pillars were qualitatively different in form and nature than those adopted under the first pillar, in retaining an intergovernmental as opposed to supranational character. The fact that the EU was described at the time of the tripartite pillar framework's inception as having a common set of objectives and being served by a single institutional framework could not mask the fact that the norms emanating from the Union did not possess a single common set of underlying legal principles. The legal system of the European Union was bifurcated into two distinct legal structures, namely the pillar-one framework (commonly referred to as the *acquis communautaire*) on the one hand, and the second and third pillars, on the other. Whereas pillar-one measures were subject to the full range of supranational legal consequences in accordance with the existing jurisprudence of the CJEU on Community law deriving from the EC and Euratom Treaties, pillar-two and -three measures were essentially of an intergovernmental nature with very limited jurisdiction vested in the European Commission[39] and CJEU[40] for the purposes of supervising policy implementation.

1.1.1.3 Phase III (December 2009–): unification of the EU legal order

The constitutional framework of the EU underwent a further radical overhaul by virtue of the 2007 Lisbon Treaty, which entered into force on 1 December 2009. A major achievement of Lisbon was to establish a single unified legal order to the EU. Together with the replacement of the EC Treaty by the TFEU, the Lisbon Treaty ended the tripartite pillar framework. Both the TEU and TFEU stipulate that the Union is founded on both treaties which have the 'same legal value'.[41] The principles of the former first pillar, notably including the jurisprudence of the CJEU relating to direct effect and supremacy, have been carried forward so as to apply to the new unified EU legal order, insofar as the treaties do not provide for any qualifications or restrictions.[42] The Lisbon Treaty secured many of the aspirations underpinning the earlier failed 2004 Treaty establishing a Constitution for Europe (EU Constitutional Treaty),[43] which had been rejected in 2005 as a result of negative referenda held in France and in the Netherlands.

As mentioned at the outset of this section, the new foundational treaty framework that has emerged from the 2007 Lisbon Treaty comprises: the TEU as amended, the TFEU and the Euratom Treaty as amended. Each treaty has a distinct structural role to play. The TEU sets out the EU's essential values[44] and objectives,[45] principles of governance,[46] the remit of its institutions,[47] enhanced co-operation[48] and the general provisions on external action[49] as well as specifically concerning the CFSP.[50] Some qualifications have been made under the revised TEU with respect to the CFSP, so that no legislative measures may be adopted in this policy area and the CJEU's jurisdiction is limited to being able to review whether acts adopted under the aegis of the CFSP have encroached unlawfully on the legal terrain of other common policy areas and vice versa.[51] The intergovernmental character of CFSP decision-making has also been preserved, with unanimity amongst member states being the basic ground rule for the adoption of measures unless otherwise agreed.[52] The TFEU provides the foundational legal framework concerning parameters of Union competence,[53] other general principles relating to Union action,[54] non-discrimination and EU Citizenship,[55] other common policies[56] of the Union including in relation to the environment[57] as well as institutional decision-making[58] and budgetary matters.[59] The Euratom Treaty continues to serve as a specialist treaty on civil nuclear energy matters.

One particularly important constitutional innovation introduced by the Lisbon Treaty was to incorporate the Charter on Fundamental Rights of the EU,[60] adopted originally as a political document in 2000, into the constitutional fabric of the Union, specifically making it legally binding under the TEU as a source of primary Union law.[61] Hitherto, the development of fundamental rights protection in EU law was solely down to the CJEU's jurisprudence relating to the general unwritten principles of EU law. Of particular interest from an environmental perspective is the fact that the Charter contains a specific clause devoted to environmental protection. Specifically, Article 37 of the Charter stipulates:

> Article 37 *Environmental protection*
> A high level of environmental protection and improvement of the quality of the environment must be integrated into the policies of the Union and ensured in accordance with the principle of sustainable development.

To what extent this particular provision may be of direct assistance in relation to the enforcement of EU environmental law is not clear. Whilst legally binding and a source of primary (i.e. the highest level) Union law, Article 37 is generally worded and does not appear to ground a self-standing, distinct right of environmental protection. The clause does not establish a general basic right to a clean environment. Instead, it reaffirms the integration principle already enshrined in the TFEU[62] and requires the Union to 'ensure' a high level of environmental protection in accordance with the sustainable development principle. Accordingly, Union policy-makers are effectively granted a wide margin of discretion in crafting common policies and actions so as to respect the environment, it being unlikely that this provision could be triggered unless the EU manifestly disregards its broadly worded requirements. It appears evident that this clause was intended to underpin trust in the EU's political decision-making process in fulfilling its general objective of achieving a high level of protection for the environment. The scope and impact of this human rights clause remains to be fully clarified by the CJEU.

1.2 The EU's institutional framework

Before proceeding to consider the specific treaty provisions that underpin the EU's environmental policy structures in more detail, it is useful at this stage to take stock of the Union's institutional framework. Aside from the growth of a multiplicity of substantive tasks undertaken by the EU, it is important to note that the Union is endowed with a supranational institutional framework designed to develop as well as enforce policies agreed at Union level. Such a decision-making framework is unique in the sphere of international relations. Various supranational institutions and other organs at EU level have particular responsibilities and powers affecting the shaping of EU environmental law and policy, each with distinct and complementary roles. Article 13 TEU specifies that seven entities are vested with the legal status of Union institution, namely the EP, European Council, Council of the EU, European Commission, CJEU, European Central Bank (ECB) and Court of Auditors. The latter two institutions, which have particular financial-related responsibilities with respect to monetary policy and auditing of Union expenditure, are not considered in any detail for the purposes of this book.

The first four institutions constitute the key decision-makers in terms of the EU's political developments. The European Council, composed of the Heads of State or government of the member states together with its president[63] and the president of the European Commission, provides the Union with its overall political direction and priorities.[64] Meeting usually at least twice every six months, the European Council clarifies its positions on internal and external matters affecting the Union in the form of published Conclusions. Most key substantive decisions are taken on the basis of consensus being achieved between the member state representatives.[65] As far as environmental matters are concerned, the European Council usually only comments on certain environmental issues it considers being of majority political priority, which have tended to concern chiefly in recent years matters related to climate change and energy policy. In practice, the European Council defers to the Council of the EU (formerly known as the Council of Ministers) to represent member state interests in relation to specific environmental policy aspects and developments.

The Council of the EU has various configurations to cover particular Union policy sectors. The Environment Council[66] is the configuration addressing environmental policy matters, in which member states are represented by the environmental ministers of their respective national governments. The EP, Council of the EU and the European Commission constitute the key decision-makers in terms of the Union's development of its common policies, including that relating to the environment. Notably, all three institutions play an integral role in the adoption of legislative measures in relation to common policies falling under the aegis of the TFEU (i.e. excluding CFSP). Whereas the Commission is vested essentially with a monopoly over deciding whether to propose legislation based on the TFEU's common policy provisions, the EP and Council of the EU are the actors responsible for determining whether any specific draft legislative measure should be passed.

In the context of EU environmental policy, the EP and Council of the EU have for the most part equal powers in relation to legislative decision-making. Apart from a limited range of areas, Union environmental policy measures (legislative and non-legislative) are adopted on the basis of the so-called 'ordinary legislative procedure'[67] under which both institutions take decisions on the basis of defined majority voting.[68] This legislative procedure predicates the adoption of measures upon the consent of both the EP and Council.[69] Certain aspects of environmental policy are, though, subject to a different decision-making process, according to which the Council must decide by way of unanimity and the EP has only a consultative role. These concern fiscal measures, measures affecting town and country planning, quantitative water resources management and land use (except waste management) and measures significantly affecting a member state's choice between different energy sources and the general structure of energy supply.[70] It should be noted that the EU treaty framework contains a range of common policies other than the general Union environmental policy, the development of which may well have a significant bearing on environmental protection matters, such as in particular civil nuclear energy,[71] agriculture and fisheries,[72] energy,[73] transport,[74] single market[75] and external trade.[76] Insofar as EU level policy proposals fall essentially within these other sectors, then the relevant common policy provisions in the TFEU apply with regard to determining the appropriate EU institutional decision-making. Particular legal considerations apply for determining the correct legal basis for decision-making (see section 1.3.1 below).

The European Parliament[77] shares legislative decision-making power with the Council of the EU in respect of most Union environmental policy matters. Composed of 751 elected members (MEPs) the EP has established over time a strong influence on the shaping of Union environmental legislation, particularly since it was vested with genuinely equal decision-making power with the Council of the EU in the late 1990s.[78] As part of its co-legislative role, it scrutinises the activities of the European Commission, the Union's chief executive institution, in various ways. Notably, the EP may require the Commission to answer questions,[79] often posed through parliamentary committee,[80] and ultimately has a right in plenary to issue the Commission with a motion of censure which, if passed by at least a two-thirds majority of votes cast, would require the dismissal of the entire College of Commissioners.[81] In addition, the European Ombudsman (EO), who is appointed by the EP, has responsibility to investigate instances of alleged institutional maladministration at EU level. From an EU environmental law enforcement perspective the EO's role is particularly significant, as the Ombudsman may undertake administrative review of Commission decisions to take or desist from taking legal action against member states over fulfilment of their EU environmental obligations. The EO's and EP's roles in relation to EU environmental law enforcement are addressed in Chapter 10 of this book.

The European Commission,[82] the chief executive institution of the Union, is vested with a plurality of very important tasks in relation to Union common policy matters covered by the TFEU, including environmental policy. In particular, the Commission has a high degree of institutional responsibility for developing policy. It is charged with the promotion of the general Union interest and to take 'appropriate initiatives to that end'.[83] Notably, it has exclusive power to propose legislative measures unless the EU treaty framework otherwise prescribes.[84] As far as environmental policy is concerned, it has a monopoly over crafting legislative initiatives to be considered by the EU legislature. It also executes the Union's budget, manages programmes as well as exercises co-ordinating, executive and management functions. In addition to its executive role, the Commission has also a prosecutorial role. Specifically, it has responsibility for overseeing the due application of Union law under the control of the CJEU.[85] The Commission's law enforcement responsibilities with respect to EU environmental legislation are considered in detail in Part I of this book.

The CJEU[86] constitutes the Union's judicial institution. The Court comprises two branches, namely the Court of Justice (CJEU) and General Court (GC). The GC was formerly known as the Court of First Instance (CFI) until December 2009. Whereas the CJEU hears disputes brought before it by the EU institutions, member states or national courts of the member states, the GC adjudicates cases brought by private persons against certain EU institutions. An appeal lies to the CJEU from the GC on points of law.[87] Self-evidently, the CJEU has a major role to play in relation to the subject of EU law and is the subject of considerable attention throughout this book concerning its contribution to the development of rules and principles underpinning the enforcement of EU environmental law. The TEU stipulates that the CJEU has responsibility to ensure that 'in the interpretation and application of the [EU founding] Treaties the law is observed'.[88] Under the EU treaty system, the CJEU is vested with exclusive power to provide definitive interpretation of Union law as well as determine the validity and interpretation of acts adopted under the TFEU.[89] Notably, it has the power to issue financial penalties in proceedings brought by the Commission against member states for violating their Union obligations.[90] Unlike the International Court of Justice, the triggering of jurisdiction of the CJEU is not dependent upon the consent of states party to litigation and the CJEU's judgments are enforceable through national civil procedural rules within the jurisdictions of those states.[91] Over the last half century, development of the EU has also witnessed unprecedented legal innovations and developments, many of which have had and do have important ramifications relating to the enforcement of EU environmental law. Jurisprudence from the CJEU has confirmed that Union law represents a special and unique source of public international arrangement. Unlike traditional forms of treaty-based organisations, the rules and norms that go to form the EU may, depending on their particular structure and legal base, in certain circumstances have special legal effects within the jurisdictions of the member states without the need for individual ratification at national level and/or the enactment of a domestic statute. This has opened up possibilities for individuals to seek to rely upon and enforce those EU norms vested with those particular legal qualities. As this book will explore in some detail in Part II, this judicial development has had some impact on how EU environmental legislation may be enforced.

Over and above the seven EU institutions, various other supranational bodies exist at EU level to assist in various ways in the promotion and delivery of Union policies and activities. Of particular note from an environmental policy perspective is the European Environment Agency (EEA),[92] an agency set up in the early 1990s in order to collate and disseminate statistical data relating to the state of Europe's environment.[93] Once mooted in some quarters as having a potential role to play in connection with law enforcement of EU environmental legislation, the EEA's mandate has, to date, been limited to focusing on appraising scientific, administrative and other sources of factual information concerning developments in environmental quality across Europe as well as in relation to the state of national implementation of key obligations of EU environmental legislation. Mention should also be made of two Union organs which have consultative powers in relation to EU environmental policy, namely the Economic and Social Committee (ESC)[94] and Committee of the Regions (COR).[95] Both bodies must be consulted by the Commission on draft environmental policy proposals by virtue of Article 192 TFEU. The ESC is composed of representatives drawn from socio-occupational interest groups (employer associations and trade unions) and other groups from civil society, so as to try to assemble a collective view from these civic interest groups on draft Union measures. COR's membership is drawn from representatives of the various regions of the member states. Members of both organs are appointed by the Council of the EU for terms of five years. Whilst the opinions of both advisory entities may exercise some degree of influence, decisive decision-making power in the context of EU environmental decision-making ultimately rests with the EP and Council of the EU.

1.3 EU environmental policy and law

The principal EU treaty provisions concerning the Union's common environmental policy are currently housed within Title XX (Environment) of Part Three (Union policies and internal actions) of the 2009 Treaty on the TFEU, specifically Articles 191–3 TFEU. These foundational treaty sources complement other more general provisions contained in the TEU and TFEU grounding environmental protection as an integral component of the EU's constitutional fabric. Notably Article 3(3) TEU expressly confirms that the Union's objectives include working for sustainable development in Europe and attainment of a high level of protection and improvement of the environment. Article 11 TFEU stipulates that environmental protection requirements must be integrated into the definition and implementation of all Union policies and activities, in particular with a view to promoting sustainable development.

Title XX TFEU contains the relevant framework provisions relating to the aims, principles and decision-making processes involved in crystallising binding as well as well as non-binding agreements forged by the EU political institutions intended to address environmental protection issues. Article 191 TFEU fleshes out a range of general principles to be referred to and applied in order to fashion the Union's common policy on the environment. Specifically, Article 191(1) TFEU requires Union environmental policy to contribute towards pursuit of a range of environmental objectives, specifically: preserving, protecting and improving environmental quality; protecting human health; prudential and rational use of natural resources; as well as promoting international measures to address regional or global environmental problems, such as climate change. Article 191(2) TFEU stipulates the common policy must aim at a high level of environmental protection taking into account regional diversity within the Union. In addition, EU environmental policy is required to be based on the principles of precaution, that preventive action should be taken, rectification of environmental damage at source (proximity) and that the polluter should pay. Article 191(3) TFEU requires the EU to take into account a range of specific factors when preparing policy: namely available scientific and technical data, regional environmental conditions in the Union, potential costs and benefits of EU (in)action as well as the Union's economic and social development as a whole and the balanced development of its regions. Article 191(4) TFEU confirms the Union's competence to develop an external dimension to its environmental policy, in terms of co-operating with third countries and competent international organisations according the respective spheres of legal competence of the Union and member states.[96] Given the open-textured nature of these treaty provisions, with none of the environmental principles being defined, Article 191 TFEU effectively gives a very wide margin of discretion to the EU's policy-making institutions with respect to the precise development and intensity of Union action in relation to environmental protection issues.

Article 192 TFEU sets out various ground rules concerning the delivery of Union environmental policy, notably concerning decision-making procedures and elaboration of general action programmes. Article 192(1)–(2) TFEU sets out the EU institutional decision-making procedures to be applied for the common policy's development. Whereas the default decision-making procedure regarding the adoption of EU environmental policy measures is the ordinary legislative procedure under Article 294 TFEU (involving joint decision-making between the EP and Council of the EU based on majority voting),[97] for certain environmental matters EU measures may only be adopted by the Council of the EU unanimously[98] (see section 1.2 above for details).

Article 192(3) TFEU confirms that the Union must adopt general action programmes setting out the environmental priority objectives to be attained. The Union has adopted seven such programmes, the first of which was adopted in 1973,[99] each setting out a list of topics and measures to be addressed and adopted respectively within the period set for the particular programme. The Seventh Environment Action Programme (EAP7)[100] was adopted in 2013 and runs until 2020. In recent years, issues relating to enhancement of implementation and enforcement of EU environmental legislation have received close attention in the Union's action programmes. For instance, a strategic objective of the Sixth Environment Action Programme (EAP6) (2002–12)[101] was to encourage more effective implementation and enforcement of EU environmental legislation,[102] including development of rules on environmental liability[103] and ensuring access to environmental justice as required by the Århus Convention.[104] EAP7 contains within the context of its Priority Objective 4 on maximising benefits of EU environmental legislation by improving implementation[105] a commitment to guarantee Union citizens effective access to environmental justice,[106] extending binding criteria for effective national environmental inspections.[107]

Article 193 TFEU provides an important qualification to the general rule that member states may not adopt measures unilaterally in relation to a matter of environmental policy that is already subject to Union legislative regulation. Specifically, member states retain the right to maintain or introduce more stringent protective measures, so long as compatible with the EU founding treaties.

1.3.1 Legal basis for the adoption of EU environmental measures

As was mentioned earlier (in section 1.2) the EU's activities covers a range of policy areas, a number of which may directly or indirectly affect environmental protection concerns. Under the EU constitutional framework, the founding Union treaties (principally the TFEU) contain sets of provisions providing the legal basis for decision-making in relation to specific common policy areas. Where a proposed policy measure concerns more than one policy sector, the question arises as to which legal basis applies in relation to its adoption. If the Union adopts a measure on an incorrect legal basis, the measure is vulnerable to being legally challenged before the CJEU and declared void by the Court.[108] In relation to environmental matters, policies affecting the environment can also concern a range of Union common policy areas (including civil nuclear energy, transport, energy, single market and common commercial policy). The position is made all the more acute if (potential) legal bases for Union action prescribe differing degrees of power for Union legislative institutions.

The CJEU has provided through its jurisprudence a number of legal principles to assist Union policy-makers in ensuring that the correct legal basis for EU policy action on the environment is selected. As a starting point the choice of the legal basis must be founded on objective factors which are amenable to judicial review and include, in particular, regard to the aim and content of the measure.[109] The CJEU has developed a 'centre of gravity' test as the principal legal tool for ascertaining which legal basis is to be selected in the event that more than one alternative appears to exist. Specifically, the CJEU has clarified that Article 192 TFEU will be the appropriate legal basis for a Union environmental policy measure if its provisions relate principally to the environmental field.[110] Accordingly, where the environmental aspects are ancillary or merely incidental to the main policy objectives of the particular measure, then the measure will not fall under the aegis of Title XX TFEU.[111] Particular difficulties concerning determination of the correct legal basis have arisen in the environmental policy context where a draft measure seeks to regulate trade (whether internally within the single market and/or externally) for environmental reasons. It is not necessarily straightforward to ascertain whether the measure should be deemed to be essentially a trade or environmental measure.[112] Where the aim of an EU measure containing environmental protection requirements is intended to fulfil equally essential environmental and non-environmental policy goals, with neither being the predominant objective, the CJEU has ruled that such measures may be adopted in principle on a joint legal basis,[113] subject to the decision-making procedures foreseen in both legal bases as being essentially similar. Where the decision-making procedures are materially different from one another (i.e. give materially different degrees of influence to individual EU institutions involved in the legislative process), the CJEU has favoured an approach that gives preference to using the legal basis according to which the EP's decision-making powers are strongest.[114] The likelihood of substantially differing levels of institutional power arising has receded considerably over time as the 'ordinary legislative procedure' (under Article 294 TFEU) involving equal decision-making between EP and Council of the EU has become the standard decision-making procedure for most Union policy areas, although there are some notable exceptions and variations.

A notable example in the recent past of a lengthy dispute over legal basis in relation to Union environmental policy arose in relation to the promulgation of measures in the field of environmental crime. When the dispute arose in the early 2000s, the tripartite pillar system was still in force. Specifically, the Council of the EU and the European Commission disagreed as to whether a policy measure on environmental crime could be legally adopted under the aegis of the first pillar's common environmental policy framework, namely the Title XIX to the former EC Treaty (ex Article 175 EC). Whereas the Commission considered that the European Community had implied power to adopt such an instrument under Article 175 EC, the Council considered that the third-pillar framework provisions on police and judicial co-operation in criminal matters (former Title VI TEU)[115] should constitute the appropriate legal basis instead. Accordingly, provisions in both the first and third pillars of the EU legal framework (prior to the Lisbon Treaty changes) presented themselves as potential legal bases for the promulgation of measures designed to develop environmental criminal law at national level.

Several member states were opposed to moves on the part of the European Commission, supported in particular by the EP, to introduce any degree of harmonisation of national laws on environmental crime under the auspices of the first pillar. They maintained a strong preference, on grounds of preserving national sovereignty, to retain exclusive competence to enact measures in the criminal law field. The Council of the EU, in support of this position, asserted that Title VI TEU was the appropriate legal framework, on the grounds essentially that member states had clearly determined to structure the EU treaty framework in operation at the time so that any matters concerning co-operation in criminal policy field should be decided in the intergovernmental context of the third pillar and that historically Community law had proceeded on the basis that member states remained ultimately competent and sovereign to determine the means by which they ensure compliance with pillar-one obligations. This analysis also resonated with growing concerns of a number of member state governments since the 1990s to foster and entrench principles pertaining to subsidiarity within the framework of EU governance.[116] Former Title VI to the TEU on co-operation in the fields of police and criminal matters required unanimous voting within the Council of the EU for the adoption of policy measures at Union level with no substantive powers for the EP. In contrast, environmental policy measures adopted under the first pillar (Article 175 EC) applied the equivalent to the ordinary legislative procedure (co-equal powers of decision-making between EP and Council). In addition, the use of the first pillar as a legal basis would entitle the Commission to take infringement proceedings[117] against those member states failing to implement the policy measure. No powers of law enforcement for the Commission existed with respect to third-pillar measures. Accordingly, any suggestion of a joint legal basis was out of the question.

The matter eventually came before the CJEU which, in a landmark ruling in September 2005,[118] confirmed that the European Community had implicit legal competence to pass measures intended to require member states to punish breaches of Community environmental legislation under the auspices of former Article 175 EC. The judgment paved the way for the EU ultimately to adopt a measure addressing environmental crime under the aegis of the former first pillar. This came in the form of Directive 2008/99 on the protection of the environment through criminal law,[119] which remains in force. The entry into force of the Lisbon Treaty in December 2009 led to the establishment of new provisions concerning the development of a common policy on combating crime in the form of Chapter 4 (Judicial co-operation in criminal matters) of Title V (Area of freedom, security and justice) of the TFEU, specifically Articles 82–6. Article 83 TFEU provides a legal basis for the adoption of approximation of national criminal law considered essential to ensure effective implementation of Union policy in an area which has been subject to harmonisation measures. By virtue of that treaty provision, though, individual member states have the right to block any such legislative proposal if they deem this would affect fundamental aspects of its criminal justice system.[120] In the absence of CJEU clarification it is a moot point as to whether now any new EU legislative proposals concerning environmental crime should be based either on Article 83 TFEU or Article 192 TFEU. A joint legal basis would appear impossible given the fact that Article 192 TFEU does not allow individual member states to block draft EU environmental legislative initiatives. The development of EU intervention in matters relating to combating environmental crime is discussed in detail in Chapter 13.

1.3.2 *Types of EU environmental legislative measures*

Title XX (Environment) of the TFEU is not specific about which types of EU norms may be used to further Union objectives in relation to environmental protection. Notably, Article 192(1) TFEU stipulates that the European Parliament and Council, acting in accordance with the ordinary legislative procedure and after consulting the Economic and Social Committee and Committee of the Regions, 'shall decide what action is to be taken' in order to achieve the objectives set out in Article 191. Accordingly, the Union policy-makers are not constrained by the EU treaty framework as to the type of measures selected for crystallising policy agreements into legislative or non-legislative format.

1.3.2.1 *Environmental policy instruments*

An indicative list of the range of measures that may be adopted for the development of Union policies enshrined within the TFEU is provided in Article 288 TFEU. Article 288 refers to the following types of policy instruments: regulations, directives, decisions, recommendations and opinions. Recommendations and opinions are technically non-binding and serve as instruments of guidance.[121] The first three types of normative measures listed in Article 288 are, in contrast, legally binding measures. Regulations and directives are designed to serve as Union legislative measures, so as to be capable of affecting the public community at large. Decisions, on the other hand, are measures more suited to impose obligations on specific persons (e.g. particular member states or private persons). Whilst the CJEU has clarified that the list of instruments contained in that provision is not exhaustive,[122] in practice regulations and directives are used as the principal legal means at Union level in order to crystallise environmental policy into minimum standards across the territory of the European Union.

EU regulations are used relatively infrequently as measures to enact Union environmental policy, not least given the lack of involvement of national parliamentary bodies in relation to completion of the promulgation process. Article 288(2) TFEU defines a regulation as having 'general application' and being 'binding in its entirety and directly applicable in all Member States'. CJEU case law has established that where a regulation is used as the mechanism to enact EU legislation, then it is automatically taken to be a constituent part of the national legal orders of the member states without the need for national parliamentary bodies having to pass any local measures in order to implement its contents.[123] In addition, the CJEU has confirmed that regulations may be capable under its doctrine of direct effect (see Chapter 6) of being enforced by private individuals directly before national courts.[124] Only a few EU environmental regulations have been enacted, given that member states have been reluctant to develop substantive policy without local legislative involvement, a factor that a Union directive is designed to take on board. A number of the Union's environmental regulations passed to date relate to international trade affecting the environment, such as controls on transboundary waste shipments,[125] transboundary movements in substances that deplete the ozone layer[126] and on the importation/sale of endangered species.[127] Given the often very detailed and inherently transboundary nature of these instruments, it would make little sense if a further legislative process at national level was required. A single legislative document is of benefit to all concerned in order to facilitate certainty of normative application in each national jurisdiction, where often several national authorities and traders liaise with each other over permit requirements on a frequent basis. However, under the current EU treaty framework there is no formal limitation or hard-and-fast rules on the use of the regulation as a policy implementation instrument, and it has been used on a number of occasions in the environmental protection context.[128]

In practice, though, the vast majority of legislative instruments that are adopted at Union level in relation to environmental protection are crafted in the form of directives. Article 288(3) TFEU defines a directive as 'being binding, as to the result to be achieved, upon each Member State to whom it is addressed, but shall leave to the national authorities the choice of form and methods'. In essence, this means that where the EU decides to use the instrument of a directive to establish environmental protection standards, the legislative process does not stop at the adoption of the directive but goes on to require a second decision-making stage, specifically the promulgation of national rules designed to implement the directive's provisions within the national legal systems of the individual member states. EU member states have the choice as to how they implement obligations entered into under a directive, subject to the mode of implementation being legally binding rules (e.g. civil, administrative and/or criminal measures promulgated by the appropriate relevant legislative or other decision-making bodies according to domestic constitutional law). Accordingly, Union directives, unlike regulations, are not designed to be self-executing instruments, but are intended to involve a two-stage legislative process: first, the adoption of the directive itself by the EU legislature, and secondly, the adoption by member states of binding national implementation measures. The entire legislative process, as envisaged under Article 288(3), is accordingly only fully completed when the addressees of the directive, namely the member states, have enacted specific implementing measures at national level in accordance with domestic constitutional procedural requirements.

Where the TFEU is silent on the choice of legislative instrument that should be used in any given instance by the EU legislature, over time it is has become evident that the directive has become the standard preferred legislative vehicle for enacting EU-wide binding standards. This practice also applies in relation to the Union's environmental policy, in respect of which the vast majority of the 200 or so EU measures adopted to date are directives. From the perspective of member state governments, enactment of Union policy through the form of the directive offers a number of advantages. Notably, by specifically including member state legislative participation in the process, in terms of determining how Union obligations should be implemented at local level, the directive accords with the subsidiarity principle which mandates the Union to act only if and insofar as is necessary.[129] Moreover, where local legislative action is foreseen, substantial periods are frequently granted to member states under the terms of each directive for them to ensure that steps are taken to ensure that their respective domestic laws are in compliance with the Union instrument's provisions. The period allowed by a directive for transposing its obligations into national law is generous, usually at least two years or sometimes longer where the case for lengthier transition times has been persuasive for the EU legislature. In contrast, no standard transposition period is in principle foreseen where Union regulations are used, given that they are intended to be directly applicable in their entirety in all member states upon entry into force. Nevertheless, given that supplemental national measures are usually required to implement the obligations of EU regulations on the ground (such as establishment of local institutional mechanisms and supervisory measures) periods of grace for implementation are also commonly foreseen by regulations.

1.3.2.2 Implementing and delegated Union acts

By virtue of the 2007 Lisbon Treaty, the EU treaty framework now makes a distinction between legislative, delegated and implementing Union legislation. The changes have been made to introduce a greater degree of transparency and accountability into the area of delegated power generally at Union level. As with other common policies, the development of EU environmental policy has been supported through the adoption of a substantial amount of detailed measures delegated to the European Commission by the principal EU legislative institutions, namely the EP and Council of the EU. Such detailed measures are intended to implement the main essential Union legislative obligations as defined by the EU legislature in a framework or other principal statutory instrument. Often technical in nature, such secondary 'micro' measures have been seen as being more suited to be the responsibility of the European Commission, subject to there being adequate safeguards and oversight mechanisms in place to ensure that the Commission does not adopt decisions that conflict with or contradict the main tenets of primary legislation agreed to by Parliament and Council. The changes introduced by the Lisbon Treaty establish mechanisms by which the EU legislative bodies can maintain oversight of the Commission's exercise of delegated power or power to adopt implementing instruments. In particular the role of parliamentary oversight is effectively enhanced.

Article 290 TFEU specifically foresees that an EU legislative act may delegate to the Commission power to adopt non-legislative acts of general application to supplement or amend certain non-essential elements of the legislative act. The parameters and conditions to which the delegation is subject are to be set out in the legislative instrument.

By way of complement to Article 290, Article 291 TFEU deals with implementing acts. Under this treaty provision, where uniform conditions for implementing legally binding Union acts are required, those acts are to confer implementing powers on the Commission (or to the Council in the context of the CFSP). Article 291(2) TFEU provides the European Parliament and Council of the EU with the power to enact rules and general principles concerning mechanisms for control by member states of the Commission's exercise of implementing powers. This has been done with the adoption of Regulation 182/2011,[130] which provides two main alternative decision-making procedures for the purpose of adoption of implementing acts (with a separate special procedure reserved for cases of urgency), namely the advisory and examination procedure. The examination procedure applies in respect of the Union's environmental policy field.[131] Under the examination procedure, the Commission must submit a draft of its proposed implementing act before a committee composed of member state representatives chaired by the Commission. The Committee must give its opinion on the proposal within a deadline set by the Commission, the Commission having the power to amend the draft in light of Committee discussions prior to the latter issuing its opinion. The implementing act will be adopted if the Committee adopts a positive opinion, voting in accordance with the rules for qualified majority voting foreseen for the Council in Article 16 TEU. Where a negative opinion is expressed by the Committee, the draft measure may not be adopted. Where the Committee is unable or unwilling to express an opinion, the Commission may not adopt the draft measure if *inter alia* the proposal concerns the protection of health or safety of humans, animals or plants, the main legislative act blocks adoption where no opinion is delivered or a simple majority of Committee members is against it.[132]

Currently, the examination committee procedure envisaged by Regulation 182/2011 is being rolled out across the spectrum of EU environmental legislation; the EU regulation contains specific provisions on transition.[133] What appears evident is that the new examination committee procedure places more control in the hands of member states, in the sense that in practice only those draft implementing measures of EU environmental legislation will be adopted that have positive committee approval. That has not been the case under the old 'comitology' arrangements[134] prior to those introduced by Regulation 182/2011, such as those applicable in relation to EU legislation concerning genetically modified organisms,[135] which have allowed Commission proposals to be adopted in the event that committees have not been able to express an opinion (having failed to reach a qualified majority vote).

Notes

1   The first environmental legislative instruments adopted by the EU were in 1975, notably including measures such as the former Directive 75/439 on waste oils

(OJ L194/23) and former Directive 75/442 on waste (OJ 1975 L194/26). Both have now been superseded by Directive 2008/98 on waste (OJ 2008 L312/3). See Krämer (2011), pp. 4–5.

2　OJ 1987 L169.

3　As set out in recitals 1–3 of the former EEC Treaty 1957 (Treaty of Rome).

4　See recitals 1–3 of the Treaty on the Functioning of the European Union (TFEU).

5　Specifically within Arts. 191–3 TFEU.

6　Now enshrined in Art. 11 TFEU, superseding counterpart provisions in the former Treaty of Rome in 1987 and 1993 (ex Art. 6 EC/Art. 130r (2) EEC).

7　See Morghera (2014), p. 652.

8　Environment Directorate General (DGENV), European Commission: *Management Plan 2013* (14 January 2013), p. 17 (Ref ARES(2013) 416906).

9　As confirmed by Art. 4(2)(e) in conjunction with Arts. 191–3 TFEU.

10　Art 193 TFEU stipulates, by way of exception to the supremacy principle, that member states are entitled to maintain or introduce 'more stringent protective measures' than those adopted at EU level, so long as they comply with other EU treaty requirements. Such measures must be notified to the Commission.

11　See e.g. Ch. 5 of Sands and Peel (2012); Birnie, Boyle and Redgwell (2010), pp. 257 *et seq.*; and Brown Weiss and Jacobsen (2000) esp. Chs. 1 and 5.

12　United Nations, Treaty Series, Vol. 2161, p. 447. The text of the Convention is accessible on the following UNECE website: www.unece.org.

13　Specifically in Part II, esp. Chs. 8–11.

14　By virtue of former Art. 211 EC (ex Art. 155 EEC).

15　Art. 17 TEU.

16　Former Art. 226 EC (ex Art. 169 EEC).

17　Arts. 258 and 260 TFEU.

18　Art. 4(3) TEU, superseding former Art. 10 EC (ex Art. 5 EEC).

19　As at the time of writing, the candidate countries which have applied for EU membership include Albania, Iceland, Montenegro, FYROM, Serbia and Turkey. In September 2014, the Ukraine also signalled its intention to apply to accede to the Union.

20　Regulation 1/2003 on the implementation of the rules of competition laid down in Articles 81 and 82 of the Treaty (OJ 2003 L1/1).

21　Regulation 6/2004 on co-operation between national authorities responsible for the enforcement of consumer protection laws (the Regulation on Consumer Protection co-operation) (OJ 2004 L354/1).

22　Commission Recommendation 2005/309 on the transposition into law of directives affecting the internal market (OJ 2005 L98/47).

23　OJ 2004 L143/56.

24　OJ 2008 L328/28.

25　For a more detailed analysis of the general EU legal and institutional structures concerning the development of EU environmental law and policy, see e.g. Krämer (2011) esp. Chs. 1–3.

26　OJ 2007 C306/1.

27　Consolidated version available in the EU's Official Journal: OJ 2012 C326/13.

28　Consolidated version: OJ 2012 C326/47.

29　Consolidated version: OJ 2012 C327/1 (formally known as the European Atomic Energy Community (EAEC) Treaty).

30　Title XX TFEU (Arts. 191–3 TFEU).

31　OJ 1987 L169.

32　OJ 1992 C191.

33　See the former Title I of the original version of the TEU (OJ 1992 C191).

34　Art. 97 ECSC, specifying that the Treaty would remain in force for fifty years.

35　See TEU, Titles V and VI.

36　Case 26/62 *Van Gend en Loos*.

37 Case 6/64 *Costa/ENEL*.
38 See Art. L of the original version of the TEU (OJ 1992 C191).
39 See e.g. Art. 13(3), third sentence of the original TEU (OJ 1992 C191) which charged the Council of the EU, as opposed to the Commission, with ensuring 'unity, consistency and effectiveness of action by the Union' in pillar-two matters. Similarly, the Commission had no specific enforcement role with respect to pillar-three instruments in Title VI TEU. Instead, the Commission was simply to be 'fully associated' (i.e. informed) of work under the auspices of the second and third pillars (see Arts. 27 and 36(2) of the original version of the TEU). The Commission had a supervisory role in the negative sense, in that it had responsibility to ensure that pillar-two and -three work did not interfere with jurisdiction already conferred to the EU in pillar one, as required by Art. 47 of the original TEU. Art. 211 EC (now replaced by Art. 17 TEU) required the Commission to ensure that the provisions of the EC Treaty and measures taken thereunder by the EC institutions were applied.
40 Art. 46 of the original TEU (OJ 1992 C191).
41 See Art. 1 TEU and Art. 1 TFEU.
42 See notably Declaration (No. 17) concerning primacy annexed to the TEU/TFEU which recalls that in accordance with 'well settled case law of the [CJEU] the Treaties and the law adopted by the Union on the basis of the Treaties have primacy over the law of the Member States, under the conditions laid down by the said case law' (OJ 2012 C326/C327).
43 OJ 2004 C310. For a brief discussion of the 2004 Treaty establishing a Constitution for Europe, see the first edition of this book (Ch. 1).
44 Art. 2 TEU.
45 Ibid., Art. 3.
46 Ibid., Arts. 9–12.
47 Ibid., Arts. 13–19.
48 Ibid., Art. 20 in conjunction with Arts. 326–34 (ibid).
49 Art. 21 TEU.
50 Ibid., Arts. 21–46.
51 See Art. 24 in conjunction with Art. 40 (ibid.).
52 Ibid., Art. 31(1).
53 Arts. 2–6 TFEU.
54 See Ibid., Arts. 7–17.
55 See Ibid., Arts. 18–25.
56 Ibid., Arts. 26–222.
57 Ibid., Arts. 191–3.
58 Ibid., Arts. 223–309.
59 Ibid., Arts. 310–32.
60 Consolidated version: OJ 2010 C83/2.
61 By virtue of Art. 6 TEU.
62 Art. 11 TFEU.
63 The current incumbent is the former Polish premier Donald Tusk, who succeeded Herman van Rompuy with effect from 1 November 2014.
64 Art. 15(1) TEU. European Council website: http://www.european-council.europa.eu.
65 Ibid., Art. 15(4). A notable exception is the convening of intergovernmental summits for the purpose of formally triggering a political review process of the existing EU Treaty framework, in respect of which the EU Council decides by way of simple majority (ibid., Art. 48(1)). See also Art. 236 TFEU.
66 See Environment Council website: http://www.consilium.europa.eu/policies/env?lang=en.
67 Art. 192(1) TFEU.
68 The Council adopts measures under this procedure essentially by way of qualified majority voting or 'QMV' (see Art. 16(3)–(4) TEU in conjunction with Art. 294(13)

TFEU) although it is required to be unanimous if wishing to approve EP amendments at second reading stage in the face of a negative Commission opinion (see Art. 294(9) TFEU). As from 1 November 2014 QMV in the Council is defined as at least 55 per cent of the Council members (one representative from each member state) comprising at least 15 members and representing at least 65 per cent of the Union's population and not being subject to a 'blocking minority' which must be composed of at least four Council members (see Art. 16(4) TEU). The EP acts by a majority of the MEP votes cast (see Art. 231 TFEU in conjunction with Art. 294(13) TFEU).

69 Art. 294 TFEU.
70 Ibid., Art. 192(2).
71 1957 Euratom Treaty, as amended.
72 Title III (Arts. 38–44) of Part Three of the TFEU.
73 Ibid., Title XXI (Art. 194).
74 Ibid., Title VI (Arts. 90–100).
75 Ibid., Chapter 3 of Title VII (Arts. 114–18).
76 Ibid., Title II (Arts. 206–7) of Part Five.
77 See EP website: http://www.europarl.europa.eu/.
78 By virtue of the 1997 Treaty of Amsterdam (ex Art. 175 EC).
79 Art. 230 TFEU.
80 The EP's Committee on Environment, Public Health and Food Safety (ENVI) has responsibility for environmental aspects of EU policy. See ENVI website: http://www.europarl.europa.eu/committees/en/envi/home.html#menuzone.
81 Art. 234 TFEU. The EP is not entitled to require the dismissal of individual Commissioners.
82 See Art. 17 TEU. See the general European Commission website: http://ec.europa.eu/index_en.htm.
83 Ibid., Art. 17(1).
84 Ibid., Art. 17(2).
85 Ibid., Art. 17(1) in conjunction with Arts. 258 and 260 TFEU.
86 CJEU website: http://curia.europa.eu/.
87 Art. 256 TFEU.
88 Art. 19(1) TEU.
89 See Art. 267 TFEU.
90 Ibid., Arts. 258 and 260. The infringement procedures are considered in detail in Part I of this book.
91 Ibid., Arts. 280 and 299.
92 EEA website: http://www.eea.europa.eu/.
93 See Regulation 401/2009 on the European Environment Agency and the European Environment Information and Observation Network (OJ 2009 L126/13). Based in Copenhagen, the EEA began operations in 1993.
94 Section 1 (The Economic and Social Committee) of Ch. 3 (The Union's advisory bodies) of Title I (Institutional provisions) of Part Six (Institutional and financial provisions) of the TFEU: Arts. 301–4 TFEU. ESC website: http://www.eesc.europa.eu/.
95 Section 2 (The Committee of the Regions) of Ch. 3 (The Union's advisory bodies) of Title I (Institutional provisions) of Part Six (Institutional and financial provisions) of the TFEU: Arts. 305–7 TFEU. COR website: http://cor.europa.eu/en/Pages/home.aspx.
96 According to Art. 4(2)(e) TFEU the Union and member states share competence in environmental matters. To the extent that the Union has not adopted measures addressing an issue not falling with the exclusive competence of the Union, member states in principle retain competence to act unilaterally (see Case 22/70 *Commission v Council (ERTA)*). This is subject to the qualification that, by virtue of Art. 193 TFEU, member states retain the right to adopt stricter environmental protection measures than those agreed at Union level.

97 Ibid., Art. 192(1).
98 Ibid., Art. 192(2).
99 OJ 1973 C112/10.
100 Decision 1386/2013 on a General Union Environment Action Programme to 2020 'Living Well, within the Limits of our Planet' (OJ 2013 L354/171).
101 Decision 1600/2002 laying down the Sixth Community Environment Action Programme (OJ 2002 L242/1).
102 Ibid., Art. 3(2).
103 Ibid., Art. 3(8).
104 Ibid., Art. 3(9).
105 Paras. 56–65 of Annex to EAP7 (Decision 1386/2013 (OJ 2013 L354/171)).
106 Ibid., para. 62.
107 Ibid., para. 65(iii).
108 Notably, either by way of annulment proceedings brought directly before the General Court under Art. 263 TFEU or through the use by a national court or tribunal of the preliminary ruling procedure under Art. 267 TFEU.
109 Case 45/86 *Commission v Council (Generalised System of Preferences)*.
110 See e.g. Case C-155/91 *Commission v Council (Waste Shipment Regulation)*, and Joined Cases C-164–5/97 *EP v Council (Forest Protection)*.
111 See e.g. Case C-281/01 *Commission v Council (Energy Star)* and Case C-70/88 *EP v Council (Radioactively contaminated foodstuffs)*.
112 Compare for instance the CJEU rulings in Opinion 2/00 *(Cartagena Protocol)* and Case C-94/03 *Commission v Council (Rotterdam Convention)*. Whereas the CJEU considered that the EU's decision to accede to the 2000 Cartagena Protocol on Biosafety to the 1992 UN Biodiversity Convention regulating the transboundary movement of living modified organisms resulting from biotechnology should be based on Art. 192 TFEU, it took the view that the Union's decision to join the 1998 Rotterdam Convention on the Prior Informed Consent Procedure for certain hazardous chemicals and pesticides in international trade should be based jointly on Arts. 192 and 207 TFEU.
113 See e.g. Case C-94/03 *Commission v Council (Rotterdam Convention)*.
114 See e.g. Case C-300/89 *Commission v Council (Titanium Dioxide)*.
115 Specifically, on the basis of Arts. 29, 31(e) and 34(2)(b) of former Title VI TEU.
116 See former Art. 5 EC (now superseded by Art. 5(3) TEU) introduced in 1993 by virtue of the Maastricht Treaty and former Protocol No. 30 annexed to the former EC Treaty on Subsidiarity and Proportionality, added by virtue of the 1997 Amsterdam Treaty.
117 By virtue of former Arts. 226 and 228 EC (now superseded by Arts. 258 and 260 TFEU).
118 Case C-176/03 *Commission v Council*.
119 OJ 2008 L328/28.
120 Art. 83(3) TFEU.
121 This does not mean, however, they are completely devoid of having any legal effect. The CJEU has, for example, confirmed that member state courts may refer to it for advice on the interpretation and validity of such measures (see e.g. Case C-322/88 *Grimaldi*).
122 See e.g. Case 22/70 *Commission v Council (ERTA)*.
123 See e.g. Case 34/73 *Variola*.
124 See e.g. Case 50/76 *Amsterdam Bulb BV*.
125 Regulation 1013/2006 on shipments of waste (OJ 2006 L190/1) as amended. Consolidated versions of EU legislation are available for inspection via the Union's EUR-LEX web portal: http://eur-lex.europa.eu/homepage.html.
126 Regulation 1005/2009 on substances that deplete the ozone layer (recast) (OJ 2009 L286/1).

127 Regulation 338/97 on the protection of species of wild fauna and flora by regulating trade therein (OJ 1997 L61/1) as amended.
128 The failed 2004 Treaty on a Constitution for Europe (OJ 2004 C310) sought to specify with more precision which types of Union act could be used for legislative and non-legislative purposes for the development of Union policies (see Arts. I-32–4 EUC) but this initiative was not followed through by the 2007 Lisbon Treaty.
129 See Art. 5(3) TEU in conjunction with Protocol (No. 2) on the Application of the Principles of Subsidiarity and Proportionality (OJ 2012 C326).
130 Regulation 182/2011 laying down the rules and general principles concerning mechanisms for control of the Commission's exercise of implementing powers (OJ 2011 L55/13).
131 Ibid., Art. 2(2)(b)(iii).
132 See ibid., Art. 5(4).
133 See ibid., Arts. 12–13. Notably, existing EU legislation that employs the so-called regulatory scrutiny procedure (under Art. 5a of Decision 1999/468 laying down procedures for the exercise of implementing powers conferred on the Commission (OJ 1999 L184/23) as amended) will be unaffected by Regulation 182/2011 unless made subject to legislative revision.
134 Former Decision 1999/468 laying down procedures for the exercise of implementing powers conferred on the Commission (OJ 1999 L184/23) as amended by Decision 2006/512 (OJ 2006 L200/11).
135 Directive 2001/18 on the deliberate release into the environment of genetically modified organisms and repealing Council Directive 90/220/EEC (OJ 2001 L106/1) as amended.

2 EU institutional enforcement of EU environmental law
The general legal framework

The aim of this chapter is to provide an overview of the core legal machinery set down in the EU's foundational framework to enforce the proper application of EU environmental law by EU member states. In particular, it will consider the general framework of Articles 258–60 of the Treaty on the Functioning of the European Union (TFEU)[1] which provide the possibility, *inter alia*, for the European Commission or a member state to be able to take legal proceedings against member states considered by them to have infringed EU law, including environmental protection legislation enacted under the relevant TFEU provisions relating to the environmental policy sector.[2] In addition, this chapter considers the types of infringement these law enforcement procedures seek to address. The provisions relevant to the enforcement of the rules contained in and adopted under the European Atomic Energy Community Treaty 1957 in relation to the civil nuclear sector are briefly considered at the end of this chapter (section 2.5). Chapters 3 and 4 proceed to examine in more detail the legal principles applicable to infringement proceedings under Articles 258–60 TFEU, before Chapter 5 takes a critical look at their impact and effectiveness.

The EU treaty provisions vesting the Commission with the power to take legal action against EU member states over alleged failings to adhere to their EU legal obligations, namely Articles 258 and 260 TFEU, have traditionally constituted very significant – indeed arguably the most significant – EU legal mechanisms for securing proper implementation by member states of EU law. Entrusted with these prosecutorial powers since the Union's inception of the EU, the European Commission has come to be perceived as the entity primarily responsible for enforcing the proper implementation of EU norms at national level. Whilst later chapters of this book will seek to explore the enforcement role of other actors and question the appropriateness of this widely held perception, it is fair to state that this view is still held today in several quarters, including by many member states, that the issue of EU environmental law enforcement is essentially a task for the Commission. In recent years, the Commission has made substantial and increasing ongoing efforts to decentralise responsibilities for EU environmental law enforcement to the national level, notably but not only to national public authorities in the environment sector. This is illustrated most recently in the EU's recent decision to establish a Seventh EU Environment Action Programme (EAP7), in which it emphasises the importance of enhancing implementation supervision systems at national level as an integral component of one of its EAP priority objectives, namely the maximisation of the benefits of EU environmental legislation.[3] This development is examined in detail in Chapter 6. In recognition of the Commission's central position in the area of EU environmental law enforcement, the first part of this book focuses on the nature and impact of its role.

Article 259 TFEU provides for the possibility of an EU member state bringing infringement proceedings against another member state on grounds that the latter is considered to have violated EU law. This particular type of infringement action, complementary to proceedings able to be pursued by the European Commission, is considered in section 2.4 below. In practice, its impact is relatively minimal, given that very few member states decide to initiate litigation through this procedure.

The entry into force of the 2007 Lisbon Treaty[4] on 1 December 2009, in amending the EU's foundational legal architecture, has resulted in some substantial alterations being made, intended to streamline and enhance the impact of the treaty provisions concerning infringement proceedings. The changes are considered in section 2.3 below. As far as substantive coverage is concerned, the EU's treaty architecture maintains a basic division between the civil nuclear and non-nuclear aspects of EU environmental law. The 1957 European Atomic Energy Community (EAEC/Euratom) Treaty, as amended, provides the legal basis for Union measures relevant to the regulation of the civil nuclear sector, with the TFEU constituting the legal foundation for the development of the Union's common environmental policy in all other environmental matters. Member state breaches of EU environmental legislation, whether covered by the Euratom Treaty or TFEU, are addressed under the aegis of the TFEU's general infringement action procedures (namely Articles 258–60 TFEU) insofar as the Euratom Treaty does not provide for specific infraction procedures in relation to particular Euratom obligations. The details on the infringement procedures applicable to the Euratom sector are set out in section 2.5 below.

The former tripartite pillar structure that characterised the legal framework of the EU prior to the Lisbon Treaty's entry into force was organised in part with a view to curtailing the Commission's powers to undertake infringement proceedings in certain policy sectors. Specifically, whilst the bulk of EU environmental legislative measures were subject to Commission oversight, if legally based upon the former European Community (EC) Treaty (first pillar) provisions relating to the Union's common environmental policy (i.e. based upon the former Article175 EC), certain other policy measures affecting the environment, such as in relation to the area of justice and home affairs, could not be subject to Commission infringement proceedings if based upon the pre-Lisbon former Title VI to the Treaty on European Union on police and judicial co-operation in criminal matters (third pillar). Prior to the changes effected by the Lisbon Treaty, a considerable amount of uncertainty existed concerning the extent of first- and third-pillar powers in relation to the development of EU legislative initiatives intended to assist in the combating of environmental crime. This resulted in a protracted legal dispute between the Commission and the Council of the EU,[5] as highlighted in the previous chapter.[6]

The dissolution of the former pillar structure and unification of the EU's founding constitutional framework (composed of the TFEU and the Treaty on the European Union (TEU)) has expanded the scope of application of Articles 258–60 TFEU infringement proceedings. Specifically, they cover not only EU legislative instruments adopted specifically under the aegis of the Union's common environmental policy (Articles 191–3 TFEU) but also all measures passed in the spheres of police and judicial co-operation in criminal matters relating to environmental crime (Articles 82–9 TFEU). As was the case before the entry into force of Lisbon, EU measures adopted under the auspices of the Common Foreign and Security Policy (CFSP) in Title V TEU (formerly, the second pillar) are not capable of being the subject of Commission infringement proceedings. In practice, though, the CFSP has little if any direct or indirect bearing currently on environmental policy issues. The EU's international relations with respect to environmental affairs, with the exception of the civil nuclear sector, is primarily conducted under the auspices of its specific common environmental policy framework (Articles 191–3 TFEU) or other EU policy areas covered by the TFEU. Measures adopted by the EU in the sphere of international relations under the TFEU, such as the decision by the Union to participate in international environmental protection conventions, are capable being supervised by the Commission through infringement action.[7]

2.1 The role of the European Commission as primary law enforcer

When addressing the subject of enforcing EU environmental law, it is important to be clear about the distinction that needs to be made between implementation and enforcement at national level. The Union's foundational treaty provisions place legal responsibility with the member states for ensuring that EU norms are correctly implemented within their respective national legal systems. This duty is laid down in general terms in Article 4(3) TEU[8] and is broad in scope. Specifically, Article 4(3) states:

> 3. Pursuant to the principle of sincere co-operation, the Union and Member States shall, in full mutual respect, assist each other in carrying out tasks which flow from the Treaties.
>
> The Member States shall take any appropriate measure, general or particular, to ensure fulfilment of the obligations arising out of the Treaties or resulting from the acts of the institutions of the Union.
>
> The Member States shall facilitate the achievement of the Union's tasks and refrain from any measure which could jeopardise the attainment of the Union's objectives.

Of particular importance is the stipulation set out in the second subparagraph to Article 4(3) TEU, requiring member states to take all appropriate measures to ensure fulfilment of their EU treaty obligations and measures derived from them. Fundamentally, this particular obligation embraces the requirement to ensure that national laws are wholly in alignment with EU rules. This is reaffirmed more specifically in Article 291(1) TFEU with respect to the role of member states in ensuring that their legal systems adhere to EU legislative requirements:

Article 291

1.   Member States shall adopt all measures of national law necessary to implement legally binding Union acts.

That the legal responsibility for implementation of EU law rests with member states reflects a fundamental division of the balance of powers and jurisdiction struck between the EU and member states under the EU's constitutional framework. As a matter of general principle, member states have competence to determine the means by which EU norms are implemented at national level (e.g. whether through civil or criminal procedures and/or sanctions). This retention of legislative involvement at national level in relation to EU policy development serves to meet a concern on the member states' part to ensure that decisions are taken as locally as possible to the citizen. This concern is crystallised in the EU treaty provisions incorporating the principle of subsidiarity (Article 5 TEU).[9] From a practical perspective, there are sound reasons for having member states shoulder the burden of implementing their EU obligations, as opposed to the Union. Only member states command the necessary financial and administrative resources necessary to ensure that the rule of EU law is adhered to on the ground in a sufficiently comprehensive manner.

The duty of implementation also embraces a requirement to ensure that the law is adhered to in practice by all persons operating within a member state's territory. Article 4(3) TEU reflects the general principles existing in international law that states are required to take steps to ensure that internationally binding norms are respected and adhered to. Accordingly, law enforcement of EU norms has always constituted an integral part of the member states' responsibilities that inhere in EU membership. However, in practice, member states have been reluctant to undertake this particular dimension of their implementation obligations seriously. In general terms, they have not readily internalised their legal responsibility to ensure that EU law is properly enforced, but have tended to focus on ensuring that the terms of their respective domestic laws accord with EU rules of law.

The EU's founding treaty framework, namely TEU and TFEU, also addresses the issue of enforcement from the perspective of the Union's own institutions. Collectively, they provide the European Commission with both powers and responsibility for overseeing the performance by member states of their obligations to ensure timely and full implementation of EU law at national level. The EU's treaty architecture has, since its inception in the 1950s, conferred on the European Commission the task of ensuring that Union treaty provisions and measures taken by the EU institutions thereunder are correctly 'applied'.[10] This responsibility of guardianship co-exists with the Commission's other executive functions and powers, including principally the role of proposing EU policy and legislative initiatives.[11] The task of implementation is therefore one shared between the member states and Commission, the latter having an ancillary part to play in overseeing that member states fulfil their Union implementation obligations at national level, in practice as well as on paper.

The European Commission's duty to oversee the correct application of EU law covers environmental protection measures promulgated under the auspices of Title XX of the TFEU (Articles 191–3). The principal mechanisms with which the Commission holds member states to account in respect of their duty to ensure timely and complete implementation of EU environmental norms are the provisions contained in Articles 258 and 260 TFEU, which provide the possibility for the Commission to bring member states before the Court of Justice of the EU (CJEU) in the event of the latter failing to fulfil this obligation, ultimately with the possibility of financial penalties being imposed on an unsuccessful defendant. The Commission is entitled to bring proceedings against a member state in the event of a violation of EU environmental law occurring within the latter's territory. For the purposes of Articles 258 and 260 TFEU, the member state's national government is legally responsible for due implementation of EU supranational commitments within its borders. It is irrelevant that a violation is carried out by a third party, such as a private person, and not perpetrated by a state agency. The obligations assumed by member states under EU law, in particular by virtue of Article 4(3) TEU, mean that they are held accountable for failures to supervise and take effective action against entities that breach binding EU environmental requirements.

The conferral in the TFEU of specific law enforcement tools to the Commission has provided this EU institution with a high-profile role in the area of EU law enforcement. Member states' obligations to secure enforcement of EU norms within their respective territories are less obviously visible within the provisions of the treaty and are to be drawn out from the general requirements imposed on them to implement such norms. Over time, these factors have contributed to a general occlusion of law enforcement responsibilities incumbent on member states. The TFEU does, however, now make specific reference to the connection between law enforcement and member states. Notably, the second subparagraph of Article 19(1) TEU stipulates that:

> Article 19
>
> 1. ...
>   Member states shall provide remedies sufficient to ensure effective legal protection in the fields covered by Union law.

This generally worded provision has recently been incorporated within the core EU treaty structure by virtue of the 2007 Lisbon Treaty. Whilst it undoubtedly requires member states to ensure that private individuals have effective redress before national courts and tribunals as a result of breaches of their EU law rights, it also includes the obligation for member states to ensure that their national legal orders provide adequate judicial procedures for national public authorities to ensure that breaches of EU norms are held to account. In addition, Article 259 TFEU provides member states with the power to bring infringement proceedings.

2.2 Types of breaches of EU environmental law

Before proceeding to consider the legal structure of the infringement proceedings provisions contained in the EU treaty framework, including the CJEU's case law, it is perhaps useful at this stage first to be clear about the types of breaches of EU environmental law with which the Commission is typically confronted. In order to do this, it is first necessary to be clear about the sources of EU environmental law involved and how their implementation into the national legal order is to be secured by individual member states. Legal proceedings taken by the European Commission against member states' failures to adhere to EU environmental norms are most commonly triggered as a result of member states' failure to complete the implementation process at national level in respect of directives, as is required under EU law.

Breaches of EU environmental law that may give rise to the Commission deciding to take legal proceedings against member states under Articles 258 and 260 TFEU may be divided up broadly into two distinct categories: namely 'non-transposition' and 'bad-application' cases. They address different types of failure on the part of member state authorities to ensure that EU environmental legislative instruments are properly implemented within the state's territorial jurisdiction covered by the EU Treaties. This typology has been used by the relevant legal units dealing with infringements within the Commission's Environment Directorate-General (DG ENV) when drawing up implementation reports with respect to EU environmental legislation, as well as for regularly updating and liaising with member states on the state of infringement proceedings in the environmental sector.[12]

2.2.1 Non-transposition cases

'Non-transposition' relates to instances where member states have failed to adopt legislative measures to transpose into national law an EU environmental directive within the deadline set down in its provisions (commonly referred to as the transposition deadline). The most serious instance of non-transposition is where a member state fails to communicate to the European Commission the national implementing rules within the set transposition deadline. These are referred to as 'non-communication' cases by the Commission. It is standard legislative practice for a provision to be included in each EU directive requiring member states to notify national implementing rules to the Commission. Non-communication may involve a member state failing to notify the Commission of any legislative measures intended to ensure that its domestic provisions are duly amended so as to be in alignment with a particular EU directive (referred to as 'total' non-communication).

A non-communication infringement case also includes the scenario where a member state notifies the Commission of national legislative measures which only partially transpose the particular EU directive into national law or cover only part of the member state territory (known as 'partial' non-communication). Occasionally, a member state may take the view that its existing rules already satisfy the terms of a directive, so no transposition steps need to be taken, but this is rarely the case and needs careful review as well as checking with the Commission. In any event, the member state is obliged to communicate its implementing rules, whether in force before or after adoption of the particular directive concerned.

A partial failure in non-communication is a shortcoming not infrequently encountered in member states with highly devolved constitutional settlements and as a consequence providing for regional devolution in respect of environmental policy. In such countries, the involvement of a number of local, regional and/or national legislative bodies may lead to implementation delays and/or fragmentation of policy approach. The federal government of the member state concerned, though, bears legal responsibility for nationwide implementation of EU (environmental) directives, and this is not affected if it transpires that a regional as opposed to the federal government is to blame for incomplete geographical coverage of implementation.

Non-communication cases are considered by the Commission as being the most serious type of infringement of EU (environmental) law, as the lack of transposition will usually mean a significant delay in implementation of EU legislative commitments at national level. Moreover, the prescribed transposition deadlines set down in EU legislation are usually quite substantial, meaning that there is little or no justification for delays in the adoption of national implementing measures. Collectively, the EU member states themselves have acknowledged the gravity of this type of breach of EU law as being particularly serious, in having introduced an amendment to the EU treaty provisions on infringement actions in Article 260(3) TFEU so as to enable the Commission to apply to the CJEU for a financial penalty to be imposed on offending member states at a relatively early stage, where the member states have failed to notify the Commission of transposition measures in relation to EU measures passed through a legislative procedure.[13] The special infringement procedure in relation to non-communication cases is discussed in section 2.3.1.

Non-transposition also includes situations where a member state has failed to adopt measures in order to implement part or all of a directive correctly (referred to as 'nonconformity' cases by the Commission). Transposition deficiencies of this kind may either be essentially substantive or geographical in nature, the former being usually more serious, given that such a deficiency would normally affect the entire country. Substantive nonconformity involves situations where, although the member state concerned has adopted national transposition measures, these do not transpose correctly one or more elements contained in an EU environmental directive's provisions, such as a minimum protection standard or definition over material scope of application of the directive (such as a definition of an activity, area or species). Such breaches may arise in practice for a number of reasons, ranging from a false assumption that the norm is already in force under national law, misinterpretation of the directive, administrative oversight, through to outright hostility to agreed EU environmental policy.

2.2.2 'Bad-application' cases

'Bad application' is the label commonly attached to the scenario where a member state has failed to ensure that EU environmental legislation has been respected in practice. It is important to note that under the EU founding treaties, as reflected particularly in Articles 4(3) TEU and 291(1) TFEU, it is the legal responsibility of member states to ensure that EU (environmental) law is implemented within their respective territories. Article 4(3) TEU lays down the general duty incumbent on member states to ensure fulfilment of the obligations arising out of the EU founding treaties or resulting from actions taken by the Union's institutions under the auspices of that treaty (namely legislative measures), whereas Article 291 TFEU reaffirms this obligation with respect to the implementation of Union acts (e.g. legislation). Accordingly, mere transposition of a directive into national law is *per se* inadequate for the purposes of meeting a member state's implementation commitments under the TFEU. Member states are obliged in addition to ensure that directives are duly adhered to in practice by the national community, by force of law. This legal responsibility to ensure practical in addition to formal legislative implementation applies to all forms of legally binding environmental commitments entered into by the member states at EU level, not just directives. Accordingly, the same considerations apply, for instance, with respect to EU decisions (e.g. to accede to an international environmental convention) and EU regulations.

In several of its annual reports on implementation and enforcement of EU environmental law, the European Commission has focused on instances of 'horizontal bad application' by member states. These cases refer to situations where a number of member states have failed to implement obligations contained in EU environmental directives which serve to create the necessary administrative infrastructure needed for their implementation: e.g. drawing up plans, designating sites/installations, adopting programmes, filing monitoring data/reports. They are 'horizontal' in the sense that they involve the infraction of basic implementation provisions shared in common by all member states. Horizontal bad application is likely to be detected by the Commission on its own initiative, not least given that the implementation of the environmental legislative provisions in question is most likely to be subject to a clear timetable supervised by the Commission under the relevant directive and carried out through distinct and readily verifiable decision-making and drafting procedures. In contrast, the Commission most usually is going to be heavily reliant on complaints from members of the public and non-governmental organisations in order to take up other instances of bad application, such as failures on the part of local environmental protection authorities to ensure territorial integrity of a legally protected habitat, to ensure delivery of an environmental impact assessment in relation to a particular development project or to ensure that individual industrial installations comply with EU emission requirements.

Recent reports carried out by the Commission on implementation and enforcement of EU environmental law have revealed widespread deficiencies in implementation on the part of member states. Specifically, 17 non-communication, 79 nonconformity and 199 bad-application cases were reported by the DG ENV of the Commission as being the subject of Article 258 TFEU infringement proceedings that it was addressing as at 19 November 2012 with a total of 304 open infringements overall.[14] These do not include the 61 open infringement cases concerning non-compliance with EU climate change legislation which were being managed by the Commission's Directorate-General for Climate Action (DG CLIMA) as the end of 2011.[15] Significant numbers of nonconformity and bad-application cases continue to be prosecuted by the Commission. Collectively, environment infringement cases comprise a significant amount of all infringement cases taken up by the Commission against member states, as has been the case for several years. For 2011, the Commission reported the environment sector to be the most infringement-prone EU policy sector.[16] The environmental sector represents one of the most litigious policy areas as far as state implementation is concerned. However, it is questionable whether the EU's official statistics alone are capable of providing a fully accurate picture of the actual state of conformity with EU environmental legislation at national level.

One of the principal reasons for this doubt lies with the very limited scope of investigatory powers available to the Commission. For some types of cases, though, such powers are not necessary or vital. The Commission is able in the main to detect several basic and obvious implementation failings on the part of member states to adopt measures in order to establish a framework for law enforcement at local level. These cases tend to relate to instances of failure to adopt and communicate to the Commission domestic legislation suited to implement EU environmental directives (non-communication/nonconformity). Due notification of transposition measures to the Commission is a standard requirement inserted into several environmental directives. Similarly, the Commission is likely to be able to follow up cases of bad horizontal application, as it will be able to chase member states for omissions in adopting measures designed to be an integral part of the framework for implementing a particular directive's aims and objectives, such as reports, plans and itemised lists (e.g. protected sites or targeted industrial installations). Notification of adoption of such measures within a certain deadline is usually stipulated to be a standard requirement in EU environmental legislative instruments. Given that assessment by the Commission as to whether there is compliance with EU environmental law in these cases is based wholly on the presence and precision of nationally adopted measures (i.e. correct transposition), investigatory powers are not in principle usually required in order to garner evidence of a breach of law.

However, on the other hand, detection of other types of infringements of EU environmental law often depend on the Commission (and/or national authorities) being vested with appropriate powers to investigate allegation of non-compliance. These cases typically concern complaints (e.g. made by the general public or nongovernmental organisations) that an activity at a specific location breaches EU environmental legislation and that no action has been taken at national level to remedy the situation. Common examples include complaints about uncontrolled fly-tipping contrary to EU waste management legislation, failures to establish an environmental impact assessment in relation to project development contrary to EU environmental impact assessment rules and unlawful encroachment of protected habitats contrary to EU nature protection laws. Complaints concerning specific breaches of EU environmental legislation are frequently communicated to the Commission. In 2011, 604 complaints (usually either from members of the public or non-governmental organisations) were lodged with the Commission concerning alleged infringements of EU environmental legislation, which represented over 19 per cent of all complaints filed to the Commission concerning suspected breaches of EU law.[17] For these types of cases, the Commission is not in a strong position to be able to detect a breach by itself or ensure that member state authorities apply EU environmental legislation in specific cases. The Commission has no specific powers to require member states to provide EU officials engaged in law enforcement access to sites for the purpose of obtaining information and evidence concerning compliance issues. Neither does it have powers to require member state authorities to carry out investigations. Instead, the relationship between Commission and member states over EU environmental law enforcement in instances of alleged bad application is currently structured on the footing that member state authorities are deemed to be primarily responsible for day-to-day implementation of EU environmental legislation. The Commission has no specific legal powers to follow up these complaints with mandatory investigations of its own, such as surprise 'dawn raid' site inspections to verify whether EU environmental standards have been breached. Instead, it has to rely upon the national authorities to do this and supply it with information in order to place it in a position to assess whether or not there is sufficient evidence to proceed with an infringement action.

This state of affairs contrasts sharply with the administrative legal position adopted in some other EU policy sectors. For instance, in the field of EU antitrust policy, both the Commission as well as member state authorities are specifically vested with substantial powers to investigate and fine companies suspected of breaches of EU competition rules.[18] One of the reasons for the difference in approach to enforcement lies in the fact that substantive EU competition rules, as opposed to many EU environmental legislative requirements, are directly binding upon individuals as well as member states under EU law. The direct applicability of key competition norms such as Article 101 TFEU (prohibition of anticompetitive agreements), Article 102 TFEU (prohibition of abuse of a dominant position) and the EU's Merger Regulation 139/2004[19] (mandatory assessment of concentrations of a Union dimension) serve to legitimise the basis for constructing a direct and robust relationship of law enforcement between the Commission and private entities. In contrast, much of EU environmental law does not possess the same legal quality of direct obligation upon the general public. The bulk of EU environmental legislation is passed in the form of a directive, an instrument which is specifically addressed only to member states.

2.3 Enforcement proceedings brought by the European Commission: Articles 258 and 260(2) TFEU

The relevant TFEU provisions which provide the legal framework for the Commission's law enforcement role that cover the environmental sector are Articles 258 and 260 TFEU. These provisions divide up the system of enforcement by the Commission into two distinct basic types of infringement actions, commonly referred to as 'first-round' and 'second-round' proceedings. First-round proceedings are set out in Articles 258 and 260(3) TFEU, and second-round proceedings in Article 260(2) TFEU. Both types of proceedings are linked to one another in a temporal sense, in that second-round legal action may only be brought subsequent to the completion of first-round proceedings. Where the Commission initially detects a breach of EU law, it may decide to take enforcement proceedings under the auspices of Article 258 TFEU ultimately before the CJEU for a declaratory ruling of non-compliance and, in non-communication cases, a financial penalty. If, subsequent to CJEU judgment finding against a defendant member state, it transpires that the state persists with the particular breach of EU law at hand, then subsequent follow-up legal action can be taken by the Commission in the form of proceedings brought under Article 260(2) TFEU. Second-round proceedings enable the Commission ultimately to be able to request the CJEU to impose financial penalties on the defendant member state in addition to the court making a further judicial declaration of non-compliance.

First-round infringement proceedings enable the Commission to bring proceedings against a member state where it considers for the first time that a particular state has breached a norm of EU law. Article 258 TFEU envisages the possibility of such a dispute being brought before the CJEU for the purpose of obtaining a declaratory judgment from the Court on whether a breach has been committed. The principal aim underpinning Article 258 TFEU, though, is to seek a non-judicial resolution, namely a friendly settlement on the matter between the Commission and defendant member state. Referral to the CJEU is seen only as a last-resort mechanism and in practice the vast majority of enforcement proceedings, including those relating to environmental protection disputes, are settled before the matter comes before the CJEU for definitive judgment.[20]

Prior to entry into force of the 2007 Lisbon Treaty it was only possible for the Commission to request a financial penalty from the CJEU at the stage of second-round proceedings. First-round proceedings did not foresee any possibility of pecuniary sanctions being imposed. However, since 1 December 2009 the position has changed with the inclusion of Article 260(3) TFEU, which envisages the possibility of a financial penalty being sought in those first-round cases involving non-communication of national measures to implement an EU directive adopted under a legislative procedure. This change was first envisaged in the 2004 Treaty on a Constitution for Europe (EUC),[21] which failed to enter into force on account of being rejected by French and Dutch referenda in 2005.

Second-round infringement proceedings under Article 260 TFEU may be brought by the Commission if a defendant member state fails to take necessary measures to remedy a breach of EU environmental law, as prescribed by a first-round judgment of the CJEU under Article 258 TFEU. As with Article 258, second-round proceedings are designed with a view to achieving an out-of-court settlement of the dispute through negotiation between Commission and defendant member state. However, a notable difference lies in the fact that with all second-round actions the CJEU is entitled to impose one or more financial penalties on the member state in the event of finding that the defendant state has failed to take the necessary remedial measures in order to comply with its initial first-round judgment. Second-round legal action is a relatively recent feature of the system of EU law enforcement, having been inserted into the former Treaty of Rome (EC Treaty) by virtue of the 1992 Treaty of Maastricht (Treaty on European Union). The member states agreed to introduce this supplemental enforcement mechanism into the system of EU law enforcement, having taken account of the poor record of compliance by a number of member states with Union legislation over the years, including with respect to environmental legislation. The inclusion of a financial penalty was perceived to introduce a much needed element of deterrence in the arrangements for implementation supervision.

2.3.1 Structure and format of Article 258 TFEU proceedings

This section focuses in more detail on the structure and organisation of first-round infringement proceedings, with reference to the specific text of the TFEU provisions. The primary provision of Article 258 TFEU is considered first, followed by an examination of Article 260(3) TFEU which applies to non-communication casework.

2.3.1.1 General points

Article 258 TFEU states:

> If the Commission considers that a Member State has failed to fulfil an obligation under the Treaties, it shall deliver a reasoned opinion on the matter after giving the State concerned the opportunity to submit its observations.

> If the State concerned does not comply with the opinion within the period laid down by the Commission, the latter may bring the matter before the Court of Justice of the European Union.

The brevity of the text belies the often complex, unpredictable and prolonged nature of first-round proceedings in practice. Article 258 TFEU contains two principal stages: namely the pre-litigation and litigation phases. The pre-litigation phase, cited in the first paragraph of Article 258, is a requisite first step to be taken in the course of (first-round) legal action. Also known as the non-contentious phase of proceedings, it is designed in particular to achieve two things: to assist the Commission in seeking to verify the factual position concerning state of compliance with EU law, and to facilitate a dialogue with the defendant member state with a view to reaching a friendly settlement of the dispute if the Commission considers there to be a proven breach of law (i.e. avoiding the need to litigate before the CJEU). The descriptions of 'pre-litigation' and 'non-contentious' reflect the main underlying purpose of the first phase of the proceedings, namely to seek an out-of-court settlement, where the Commission assesses this to be possible within a reasonable time-frame. The pre-litigation comprises two formal stages: namely the issuing of a letter of formal notice (LFN) and a reasoned opinion (RO) to the defendant member state by the Commission. The LFN constitutes a first official communication from the Commission to a member state which sets outs the essential lines of argument that lead the Commission to consider that the member state has breached EU law. In essence, the LFN constitutes a first official warning to a member state to address the issues raised by the Commission (and is commonly referred to as a first written warning).

In cases where the Commission has clear evidence of non-compliance with EU environmental legislation by a member state, such as where a member state fails to enact domestic legislation in order transpose a directive into national law within the stipulated deadline, it is usually prepared to issue an LFN without the need for further preparatory work prior to commencing proceedings. However, in respect of complaints sent to it from the public about allegations of specific instances of improper application of EU environmental legislation (e.g. uncontrolled deposition of waste contrary to the Waste Framework Directive 2008/98[22] or failures to hold an environmental impact assessment for a particular development project in accordance with the Environmental Impact Assessment Directive 2011/92)[23] the Commission will normally first raise the matter informally with the member state to enable more detailed disclosure of factual evidence prior to triggering the formal commencement of Article 258 infringement proceedings. This informal correspondence may take the form of what is known as a pre-letter of formal notice (pre-LFN). Whilst no formal legal implications run from non-compliance with a pre-LFN by a member state, in that the letter does not formally constitute the commencement of enforcement proceedings, such a letter indicates a degree of seriousness which the Commission attaches to the subject matter and conveys the message that proceedings may well be taken up in the event of a non-co-operative attitude on the part of the member state concerned in dealing with the issues raised by the pre-LFN.

Article 258 TFEU does not stipulate a minimum or maximum period which the Commission should set member states for sending observations on the alleged breach(es) of EU law set out in a formal LFN. For several years, it was usual for the Commission to afford member states at least up to six months or more to issue observations. However, since the turn of the millennium the Commission has sought to shorten the deadline for member state responses to LFNs in environmental cases to two months where possible, with a view to speeding up the processing of infringement actions. Where the Commission has clear evidence of a breach of EU environmental law, such as where national law appears not to conform with EU legislative requirements, the imposition of a two-month deadline is now standard practice.

If the Commission is not satisfied that the member state's observations disprove the allegation of non-compliance, it may then go on to issue a formal RO which will set out in precise detail the legal grounds underpinning the Commission's view that EU law has been violated. Article 258 TFEU is silent as to how much time should be afforded to member states to comply with the RO, which is in effect a second – and usually final – official warning. For environmental cases, it used to be common and established practice for the Commission to grant member states a substantial period to respond to the RO and set out for the Commission how it would arrange a pathway (administrative/legislative) towards compliance, usually at least another six months before the Commission would set about initiating the next step of the infringement procedure, namely the litigious phase before the CJEU. However, in recent years the practice of the Commission has been to issue member states with tighter deadlines for RO responses when deemed possible. Specifically, the Commission now seeks to impose a two-month response time to ROs in cases involving nonconformity of national law with EU environmental legislation, namely where it is clear that a basic breach has occurred. In other types of case, the Commission may determine a deadline for response in accordance with what it may deem a reasonable period for the defendant member state to arrange for either full compliance or a credible pathway to achieving conformity with EU legislative requirements.

The Commission may also seek to impose very short time-frames for responses to an LFN and RO in cases of urgency, for instance where the Commission is minded on the existing evidence available to it to consider that a bad breach of EU environmental law has occurred and that injunctive relief needs to be secured from the CJEU against the defendant state, in order to prevent the breach leading to irremediable environmental damage. Under the current TFEU framework an injunction may only be applied for from the CJEU in the context of the infringement procedure after pre-litigation phase has been completed.[24]

The second phase, known as the litigious or contentious phase of Article 258 proceedings commences where the Commission decides to refer the dispute to the CJEU for judgment. Reference to the Court follows where a member state fails to comply with the RO within a reasonable time period set by the Commission in the circumstances of the particular case. Once the file has been registered with the CJEU, it may take up to on average 17–20 months before the Court issues its ruling.[25] Prior to the judgment, the CJEU will have had the opportunity to consider a formal detailed legal opinion on the case issued by a member of the Court, namely from one of the Advocate Generals who are specific legal advisers of the CJEU, acting as *amicus curiae*. Whilst an Advocate General's opinion is not binding upon the Court and is of persuasive value only, it is usually the case that the views of the Advocate General are followed by the judges. However, one should be guarded about make any generalisations here, particularly where legal interpretation of EU law may be open to a number of differing but equally valid constructions. With the exception of non-communication cases, for which Article 260(3) TFEU provides that it is open for the CJEU to impose a pecuniary penalty, the principal role of the Court is to provide a definitive declaratory judgment as to whether or not the defendant member state in question has acted or failed to act in breach of EU law.

2.3.1.2 *Non-communication cases and Article 260(3) TFEU*

As mentioned earlier, the Lisbon Treaty introduced an important amendment to the EU's treaty provisions on first-round infringement proceedings, namely the possibility of member states being subject to fines over failures to notify the Commission of national legislative measures intended to transpose EU directives adopted through a legislative procedure. Article 260(3) TFEU states:

> Article 260
>
> [. . .]
>
> 3. When the Commission brings a case before the Court pursuant to Article 258 on the grounds that the Member State concerned has failed to fulfil its obligation to notify measures transposing a directive adopted under a legislative procedure, it may, when it deems appropriate, specify the amount of the lump sum or penalty payment to be paid by the member State concerned which it considers appropriate in the circumstances.
>
> If the Court finds that there is an infringement it may impose a lump sum or penalty payment on the Member State concerned not exceeding the amount specified by the Commission. The payment obligation shall take effect on the date set by the Court in its judgment.

The inclusion of the possibility of financial penalties being imposed at first-round stage for non-communication cases reflects recognition on the part of member states, when revising the EU founding treaties, of the seriousness of this particular type of breach of EU law. In the environmental sector, EU policy is heavily dependent upon the use of directives in order to crystallise and implement political commitments entered into by the member states. The vast majority of EU environmental legislative instruments are directives. Failure on the part of member states to transpose their environmental obligations contained in EU directives into national law on time may quickly serve to undermine the credibility of EU environmental policy. For without their proper implementation at national level, EU directives will remain effectively paper provisions and theoretical commitments. It is standard legislative practice for each directive to commit member states to complete the transposition of its provisions into national law and communicate this to the Commission by a specified deadline.[26] A failure on the part of member states to comply with transposition obligations represents an elemental and fundamental breach. There is usually no justification for member states missing the deadline, given that this involves a relatively straightforward task of providing in a timely fashion the basic administrative resources necessary to draft national implementing legislation and organising steerage through the appropriate national parliamentary channels. The Commission has interpreted Article 260(3) TFEU as applying to situations of total as well as partial non-communication, namely where a member state either has failed to notify the Commission of it having adopted any legislative measures in order to transpose an EU directive into national law (total non-communication) or where the member state has notified the Commission of national legislative measures that only partially transpose the EU directive into national law.[27] The fact that partial transposition is also covered by Article 260(3) TFEU means that the treaty provision is far more potent in being able to capture a far wider range of non-compliance situations than simply total failure to communicate national transposition measures, and will serve to place considerable pressure on member states (post-Lisbon Treaty) to ensure that national law is fully in alignment with EU environmental legislation.[28] The Commission is making full use of this opportunity.[29]

It should be emphasised that transposition obligations are not the same animal as obligations to implement the substantive commitments agreed in EU directives. Depending on the severity of environmental problem addressed by an EU environmental directive, it may take several years for member states to be able to comply with minimum environmental quality requirements set out and this is reflected in the EU legislation itself, with often substantially lengthy deadlines allowed for implementation at national level.[30] Transposition merely provides the national legal framework for the substantive implementation of EU environmental legislation and is therefore relatively straightforward to comply with. A specific fast-track for imposing penalties in non-communication cases was already envisaged in the failed 2004 EU Constitution.[31]

The CJEU has confirmed that, in certain circumstances, the provisions of EU directives may have direct legal effects within the national legal orders of the member states after the transposition deadline has elapsed. This aspect is considered later in this book in Chapter 6. In particular, the CJEU has confirmed in a number of cases that national authorities, as emanations of the state, are bound by the obligations contained in directives. In addition, the Court has also confirmed that private individuals may rely upon and enforce those norms of EU directives against member state authorities which are sufficiently precise and unconditional (principle of vertical direct effect). However, notwithstanding these general legal implications they do not detract from the central importance of individual member states adopting specific legislative measures designed to ensure transposition of EU environmental directives into national law. Without transposition legislation in place, national authorities will not be able to identify their specific role in the implementation process. The terms set down in an EU directive leave it up to individual member states to determine which of its national authorities will be designated as responsible for overseeing implementation and in what respects, the specific powers (under civil, administrative and/or criminal law) to be vested in national authorities for overseeing implementation of EU environmental directive obligations as well as how administrative supervision at national level is to be resourced.

The new penalty mechanism in Article 260(3) TFEU vests distinct powers in the Commission and the CJEU in managing infringement cases involving non-communications. As is evident from the first subparagraph of Article 260(3), it is the Commission which has power to determine whether to launch the second-round procedure and request a financial sanction be imposed by the CJEU. In addition, the Commission has the task of specifying to the CJEU what it considers to be an appropriate level of fine to be paid. As is the case for second-round proceedings under Article 260(2) TEU (considered in section 2.3.2), the type of financial sanction may include a one-off payment in the form of a lump sum or a series of penalty payments to be levied until the defendant member state secures compliance with EU law. Where the CJEU finds that an infringement has occurred, Article 260(3) specifies that it may then impose a lump sum or penalty payment, but the level of pecuniary sanction must not exceed that proposed by the Commission. This restriction on the power of the CJEU does not apply in the context of second-round proceedings, for which the CJEU has power to determine the level of any fine wholly independently. One other notable distinct feature of Article 260(3) TFEU is that it specifies that the CJEU may determine the date from which any penalty payment may take effect, whereas Article 260 TFEU is silent on this point in respect of second-round proceedings. The Commission has interpreted this to mean that the CJEU may set the relevant date as being either on the day of the judgment or a subsequent date.[32] However, this interpretation is, arguably, overly narrow. The CJEU could conceivably stipulate that a penalty payment is to run from an earlier point in time, such as from the end of the deadline for responding to the RO or from the moment at which the CJEU was seised of the case. Such an interpretation would arguably be more in keeping with the aim of deterrence underpinning the treaty provision.

Given the fact that Article 260(3) TFEU only came into force relatively recently, there has been relatively little opportunity so far to assess the impact of this fast-track penalty mechanism. It does not apply to legal proceedings not already pending before the CJEU as at 1 December 2009,[33] but covers all new infringement proceedings commenced after that date or cases referred to the CJEU after that point in time. In 2011, the Commission published a Communication[34] providing some initial indicative guidance on the impact of Article 260(3) TFEU and its approach to applying the treaty provision. Certainly, the Commission has not shied away from making full use of the procedure in the environment sector and has applied short two-month deadlines for member states to respond to LFNs and ROs. Whilst it may well be too early at this stage to tell definitively whether the new procedure is having an impact, there are signs that it may be concentrating member states' minds on ensuring the needs for timely compliance. Statistical data released by the Commission on the number of non-communication cases handled by DG ENV appear to show that these have reduced steadily and considerably since the special fast-track financial penalty procedure came on stream as from December 2009 by virtue of entry into force of the Lisbon Treaty. Specifically, the Commission reports the following numbers of non-communication cases in relation to EU environmental legislation between the years 2008–12: 88 (2008), 212 (2009), 115 (2010), 41 (2011) and 17 (2012).[35] Only time will tell if this trend continues. However, a major factor affecting matters will no doubt be the prospect of a defendant member state having to face substantial levels of penalties for transposition breaches if a non-communication dispute comes before the CJEU. Member states are most likely to wish to settle disputes out of court and thus ensure that the transposition process is completed. There is also little doubt that the Commission will have to deal with significant numbers of non-communication cases in the future, taking into particular account that Article 260(3) TFEU captures partial transposition scenarios as well as total failures on the part of a member state to adopt transposition measures on time.

2.3.1.3 Compliance with first-round judgments

By virtue of Article 260(1) TFEU, member states are explicitly obliged to take the necessary measures to comply with the CJEU's judgment if the latter finds, in the context of first-round infringement proceedings, a member state has failed to fulfil an obligation under the TFEU. The text of Article 260(1) TFEU has remained essentially unaltered since the signing of the initial founding European Economic Community (EEC) Treaty in 1957:

> Article 260
>
> 1. If the Court of Justice of the European Union finds that a Member State has failed to fulfil an obligation under the Treaties, the State shall be required to take the necessary measures to comply with the judgment of the Court.

It makes express what is implicitly required in the founding EU Treaties, namely that CJEU rulings should be respected by member states, as representing the definitive interpretation on what amounts to the correct interpretation and application of EU law.[36] However, it is important to note that the force of a declaratory judgment by the Court does not necessarily mean in practice that member states always take the appropriate steps to ensure that the position is changed within their respective borders. For the first 40 years of its existence, the EU's three founding treaties (ECSC, EEC and Euratom Treaties) only provided for the possibility of declaratory judgments being handed down by the CJEU in the context of infringement proceedings. The absence of a sanction accompanying a judicial declaration of non-compliance on the part of member states has, over time, proved to be a clear disadvantage of infringement proceedings and was a principal reason why second-round proceedings with penalty sanctions were introduced into the EU treaty framework by virtue of the 1992 Treaty on European Union. By the end of the 1980s, a number of states were failing to follow up and adhere to condemnatory declaratory judgments of the CJEU. Whilst the Commission could decide to take such states before the CJEU again through the old infringement procedure, for their having failed to adhere to the duty set out in the (predecessor to) Article 260(1) TFEU to adhere to an CJEU ruling, the end result would once again only lead to a declaration of illegality, without any specific sanction such as a penalty or judicial order being imposed.

This state of affairs brought into question the authority of the CJEU itself, mandated to ensure that the rule of law is observed.[37] By virtue of the TEU, the former Treaty of Rome was amended so as to introduce the power for the Commission to bring additional law enforcement proceedings against any member state failing to comply with a CJEU judgment against it, ultimately leading to a possibility of the Court imposing a financial penalty on the defaulting state. These additional proceedings are set out now in Article 260(2) TFEU.[38] The penalty procedure was strengthened further by virtue of the 2007 Lisbon Treaty, by introducing the fast-track procedure for non-communication cases through Article 260(3) TFEU as well as streamlining the second-round action.

2.3.2 *Structure and format of Article 260(2) TFEU second-round proceedings*

Article 260(2) TFEU states:

> Article 260
>
> [. . .]
>
> 2. If the Commission considers that the Member State concerned has not taken the necessary measures to comply with the judgment of the Court, it may bring the case before the Court after giving that State the opportunity to submit observations. It shall specify the amount of the lump sum or penalty payment to be paid by the Member State concerned which it considers appropriate in the circumstances.
>
> If the Court finds that the Member State concerned has not complied with its judgment it may impose a lump sum or penalty payment on it.
>
> This procedure shall be without prejudice to Article 259.

When originally introduced into the EU treaty framework by virtue of the TEU in 1993, the structure to second-round infringement proceedings introduced under the aegis of former Article 228(2) EEC was similar to that applicable to first-round enforcement proceedings. Specifically, a pre-litigation phase, comprising LFNs and ROs, was to be followed by a litigation phase before the CJEU. Accordingly, the emphasis was still very much on seeking a friendly settlement as far as possible, with appearance before the CJEU viewed as a last resort. However, a notable difference lay in the fact that the proceedings ultimately could culminate in the imposition of a financial penalty on the defendant member state. Subsequent structural reform of the second-round procedure by virtue of the 2007 Lisbon Treaty has shortened the pre-litigation phase so as to include a single written warning (LFN) needed from the Commission prior to referral to the CJEU. The need for an RO has been terminated. Should now a defendant state fail to reply to the allegations set out in the second-round LFN within the set deadline to the Commission's satisfaction, the latter has the power to refer the member state to the CJEU. The effect of this change will be to accelerate the processing of second-round disputes, which have in the past often taken several years to complete.[39] In particular, the elimination of the RO is intended to act as a spur or incentive of defaulting member states to comply more quickly with CJEU rulings and accordingly improve the process of implementation of EU law. The treaty amendment reflects recognition on the part of stakeholders, including member states, that the inclusion of both an LFN and RO made the pre-litigation phase unduly protracted and overly generous for the defendant. To what extent this relatively minor adjustment will, though, have a significant impact on the behaviour of member states in terms of accelerating compliance with EU environmental obligations remains to be seen. For, overall, the length of time before a member state faces the immediate prospect of a financial penalty for breaches of EU environmental legislation remains substantial, with the exception of non-communication cases where penalties may now be imposed at the first-round stage under Article 260(3) TFEU.

Article 260(2) TFEU makes it clear that, whilst the Commission's role in bringing proceedings ultimately before the CJEU is to propose to the Court the particular nature and level of fine that might be imposed, it is for the Court to decide whether to impose any pecuniary sanction and what form this might take. The text refers to the pecuniary sanction taking the form of either a 'lump sum' (a single one-off payment), or a 'penalty payment' (a fine of a periodic nature, for instance, payable on a daily basis pending compliance). In contrast to the situation applicable to the sanctioning regime applicable to non-communication cases under Article 260(3) TFEU, in which the CJEU may not impose a financial penalty higher than that proposed by the Commission, the CJEU has complete autonomy to determine the level of a fine on a defendant member state in the context of second-round proceedings governed by Article 260(2) TFEU. Notably, the CJEU may, if it considers this appropriate, decide to impose a higher level of financial penalty than that proposed by the Commission. The cap set in Article 260(3) reflects the difference in terms of the relative length and gravity of the two infringement procedures, with member states in second-round actions being in the aggravated position of having failed to honour the terms of a CJEU judgment made against them.

Since the entry into force of the second-round infringement procedure on 1 October 1993, the Commission has published a series of guidelines on how it is to set about framing proposals for penalties under Article 260(2) TFEU in individual cases. The original Commission guidelines, adopted in the mid 1990s,[40] have been subsequently replaced, in part to take into account the emerging case law of the CJEU and in part to assist in ensuring that financial penalties adjust broadly in line with economic developments, notably rates of inflation across the Union. Currently, the relevant Commission guidelines are contained in a package of instruments, specifically in a series of Commission Communications dating from 2005.[41] This guidance documentation will be examined in detail in Chapter 4, which focuses on the structure and impact of second-round infringement proceedings. As more litigation involving the penalty procedure has begun to emerge in recent years, it appears that the CJEU has broadly endorsed the Commission's evolving guidelines as being a suitable starting basis for penalty assessment and determination by the Court. As at the end of September 2014 the CJEU had delivered 21 second-round judgments. Out of those, seven involved the CJEU imposing pecuniary sanctions on member states under the auspices of Article 260(2) TFEU concerning failures to adhere to EU measures relating to environmental protection.[42]

It should be pointed out by way of general comment that, although its existence within the EU legal framework has spanned over two decades,[43] the full legal implications of Article 260(2) TFEU proceedings are far from having been fully clarified. The absence of definitive guidance in the treaty text and the relatively limited number of second-round actions brought before the CJEU inevitably mean that it will take a considerable period of time for the legal parameters of Article 260(2) to be settled. As a consequence, an element of uncertainty will surround the operation of its penalty procedures probably for some time to come. Given the considerable length of time (often several years) for a second-round case to come before the CJEU, on account of the structure and practice underpinning infringement proceedings, it is no surprise that by the end of 2005 only three CJEU second-round judgments had been handed down. However, more recent practice of the Commission services involved in environmental casework is to seek a faster turnaround of proceedings at second-round stage, in particular with the introduction of shorter time limits for member state responses to pre-litigation communications. In respect of environmental cases, it is now standard practice for Commission services to confine member states to relatively short periods (usually two months) for issuing communications in the early part of the pre-litigation stage. However, it is questionable to what extent this tightening up will, in practice, have a significant bearing on ensuring a meaningful reduction in the overall length of time that currently transpires between initial detection of infringement of EU law and eventual penalty. So long as two sets of infringement actions are required (first and second round) for all breaches apart from non-communication cases, this will mean inevitably that a considerable amount of time will be required before any financial penalty is imposed on a defendant state. Chapter 5 takes a detailed critical look at the temporal aspects to first- and second-round infringement proceedings under Articles 258 and 260 TFEU.

2.4 Enforcement proceedings brought by a Member State: Article 259 TFEU

Article 259 TFEU states:

> A Member State which considers that another Member state has failed to fulfil an obligation under the Treaties may bring the matter before the Court of Justice of the European Union.

> Before a Member State brings an action against another Member state for an alleged infringement of an obligation under the Treaties, it shall bring the matter before the Commission.

> The Commission shall deliver a reasoned opinion after each of the States concerned has been given the opportunity to submit its own case and its observations on the other party's case both orally and in writing.

If the Commission has not delivered an opinion within three months of the date on which the matter was brought before it, the absence of such an opinion shall not prevent the matter from being brought before the Court.

The above-mentioned provision provides a mechanism enabling member states to take legal action against one another over alleged breaches of European Union law, including EU environmental law. Such proceedings may be brought independently of any action taken by the Commission under the auspices of Articles 258 and 260(2) TFEU. So much is made expressly clear in the final sentence to Article 260(2). A potentially radical and far-reaching dimension in Article 259 TFEU in the context of international relations is that the treaty provision vests member states with the power to initiate enforcement proceedings, irrespective of whether the plaintiff state has suffered any loss or damage within its particular borders as a result of the infringement committed by another member state. In practice, though, this European public interest dimension to Article 259 remains a theoretical possibility, with each member state government in practice taking a self-oriented narrow viewpoint of the national interest, i.e. to what extent is any violation having specific effects within its immediate frontiers. In any event, member states considering making use of Article 259 need to take into account to what extent might they expect to face reprisal action from the defendant state in some form, whether this be a counter-prosecution or, more likely, hostility in the context of deliberations within the European Council and/or Council of the EU on Union policy decisions.

The legal framework of Article 259 TFEU bears some resemblance to the powers enjoyed by the Commission under Article 258 TFEU. The process is, however, distinct and qualitatively different in nature. The proceedings involve four distinct phases. First, Article 259 stipulates that where a member state considers that another EU country has violated an obligation under the EU's founding treaties (TFEU and TEU) it must first bring the matter to the attention of the Commission before it may bring an action before the CJEU. The second phase, set out in Article 259(3), then involves the Commission taking up the matter with the defendant and plaintiff member states, providing them with the opportunity to submit their own case and observations on the plaintiff state's case both orally and in writing. The oral phase of the process is an aspect which is not formally enshrined as an integral part of the earlier phases of Article 258 proceedings. In practice, though, the relevant legal unit within the Commission's Environment Directorate-General, charged with administering the progress of first-round environmental infringement casework, engages in informal oral bilateral talks and discussions with each member state for Article 258 cases. Usually held at least twice a year, these discussions are referred to as 'package meetings', where substantive legal issues are discussed between the Legal Unit and counterpart national officials on the current list of infringement actions against the member state concerned. The third phase of Article 259 proceedings focuses on the Commission's reaction to the parties' submissions. Specifically, Article 259(3) requires the Commission to draw up an RO as to the merits of the particular allegation(s) of EU law infringement(s) made by the plaintiff state. The fourth and final phase concerns the decision of the plaintiff state whether to refer the matter to the CJEU for definitive adjudication. If the Commission fails to deliver an opinion within three months of the matter having been brought to its attention, the TFEU provides the possibility of the plaintiff state being able to bring proceedings before the CJEU (Article 259(4) TFEU).

Whilst it has not yet been tested before the CJEU and is not specifically addressed in the text within Article 259 TFEU, it appears fairly evident from the provision as a whole that a plaintiff state may decide to take proceedings before the CJEU even if a Commission's RO considers there to be no breach of EU law.[44] Article 259(1) stipulates that a member state 'may bring the matter before the Court of Justice' which establishes as a matter of principle that an independent right of referral to the CJEU exists, a right that may not be abrogated by a third party, such as through Commission intervention.

In practice, however, it is clear that Article 259 proceedings have remained a theoretical legal remedy for addressing breaches of EU environmental law. To date, no cases have been brought to the CJEU involving environmental protection issues, and hardly any cases in other policy sectors have been adjudicated upon by the CJEU. The absence of litigation supports the view that member states are careful not to arouse political and diplomatic ill-feeling or tit-for-tat counter-litigation amongst their counterparts in the Council of the EU, even in situations which are perceived to damage the immediate national interest. Given that domestic electoral pressures and vested interests do not normally revolve around environmental issues, it would be an unusually grave set of circumstances for a member state to decide to pursue Article 259 proceedings. Conceivably, a member state government might decide to take such proceedings if the effects of a breach were felt within its territorial borders (e.g. cross-border air/water pollution) and the effects were of a significant magnitude. The concept of extraterritorial responsibility for environmental protection does not feature on diplomatic agendas of member states, unless there clear potential or actual adverse effects to be felt within domestic borders resulting from an activity taking place extraterritorially. It is as if there is an unwritten concord between member states that they are each exclusively responsible for the state of the environment within their particular frontiers unless the pollutant effects of a breach of EU environmental law by a member state spills over into the national territory of another EU country. Environmentally responsibility appears to be compartmentalised on a national basis.

It is accordingly no real surprise that no member state has yet taken legal action under Article 259 against other states in respect of pollution incidents located within the other's territory. No doubt it would be perceived to be an act of unwarranted political interference in the internal affairs of another state, notwithstanding the concept of the European Union is defined by the EU's founding treaties as common and shared internal space deserving of a high level of environmental protection and notwithstanding widespread awareness of the political artificiality of drawing up national borders for the purposes of environmental protection issues. Even in circumstances of cross-border pollution, where a member state's own territory is affected by illicit pollution carried out in another state, it is most likely that the latter state may well prefer the Commission to take up the case itself and prosecute under Article 258 TFEU. A state could lobby the Commission to take up a case on its behalf, thereby defusing any question of national bias in relation to the actual prosecution of litigation. In addition, persons suffering loss and/or injury as a result of a breach of EU environmental legislation perpetrated by a polluter located in another EU member state have the possibility under EU conflicts-of-laws rules (the so-called 'Rome II' Regulation)[45] to file civil claims either in their home state or the state in which the breach of law occurred on the same terms as nationals of the latter state.[46] Member state governments are wary of and reluctant to use Article 259 TFEU, being aware of the need to avoid making adversaries within the Council of Ministers as far as possible. Each state has to bear in mind the requirement to find sufficient numbers of allies amongst fellow member states in order to secure qualified majorities for approving favoured EU policy proposals as well as the need to be mindful of avoiding being outvoted on policy initiatives that it may not approve of. Notably, for instance, the principle of the single member state veto no longer applies for the majority of measures adopted under the aegis of the EU's common environmental policy decisions.[47]

Accordingly, it would be fair to suggest that to date Article 259 proceedings are viewed only as a legal mechanism of last resort by member states. The prospect of the Commission, in its constitutional capacity as legal guardian of the EU Treaties, of taking up legal proceedings is much preferred no doubt in order to defuse potential diplomatic confrontation. A well-known example of this approach was the UK government's strategy of preferring to let the Commission undertake legal proceedings against French government policy to restrict the importation of British beef products in the wake of concern over BSE.[48] In some respects, though, one could argue that allowing the Commission to take charge of the prosecution of infringement proceedings under Article 258 TFEU may serve to place a mask over the continuation of inter-member state legal battles. It is not uncommon, for instance, for one or more member states to take sides once a case has been brought by the Commission under Articles 258 and 260(2) TFEU before the CJEU, particularly where the legal position is not clear-cut. Under the Statute of the Court of Justice,[49] member states[50] have the automatic right as interveners to make legal submissions in cases filed before the CJEU. Such interventions are treated by the CJEU in the same manner as any pleadings submitted in legal proceedings. The right given to member states to make interventions in proceedings before the CJEU may therefore serve as an informal proxy for Article 259 proceedings and may well account for the lack of inter-state litigation.

On occasion, the facility provided for member state interventions in enforcement proceedings brought by the Commission can also expose sharp divisions between the states on policy as well as on legal grounds. Member states may wish to intervene in support of or against a defendant, even though the activities taking place on the defendant's territory do not directly interfere with the intervener's current legal practice. One example has been over the issue of waste definition under Article 1 of the EU's Waste Framework Directive.[51] Several member states have clashed over their individual interpretations as to how broadly the material scope of the definition of waste should be defined.[52] In this type of context, the facility provided for member state interventions has frequently been used to provide additional legal arguments in support of either party, with a view to defending current or potential domestic practice. Interventions before the CJEU are made, though, with the member state's attention firmly focused on upholding a current domestic political agenda, as opposed to the geographical locus of the alleged breach of law.

2.5 The European Atomic Energy Community Treaty and infringement proceedings

Whilst the vast majority of the European Union's environmental legislation is adopted under the aegis of the TFEU,[53] the Union has a distinct set of rules pertaining to its organisation and development of a common policy in the sphere of the civil nuclear sector, namely those contained within and adopted under the 1957 Treaty establishing Euratom, as amended.[54] As such, the Euratom Treaty acts as *lex specialis* in the field of civil nuclear matters, with the consequence that the EU's core general founding treaties, namely the TEU and TFEU, do not in principle apply in this policy area. The Euratom Treaty sets out a mandate for the Union to develop the growth of the civil nuclear energy industry amongst its member states[55] and stipulates a number of EU tasks for this purpose,[56] including notably, from an environmental protection perspective, the establishment of uniform safety standards to protect the health of workers and the general public and ensure that they are applied,[57] as well as make certain by appropriate supervision that nuclear materials are not diverted to purposes other than those for which they are intended.[58]

The Euratom Treaty contains a number of provisions relating to the supranational supervision of its rules. These include a number of treaty clauses that establish the possibility of infringement proceedings being brought against member states which fail to adhere to their Euratom obligations. The treaty contains both generally applicable infringement proceedings akin to those found in the TFEU (and discussed earlier in this chapter) as well as specific types of infraction procedures tailored to address particular breaches of Euratom law.

As far as general infringement procedures are concerned, by virtue of the Lisbon Treaty 2007, the Euratom rules have now been melded with those in the TFEU. Specifically, by virtue of Protocol 2 to the Lisbon Treaty,[59] Articles 258–60 TFEU now apply to the Euratom Treaty as general infringement procedures to be used by the Commission and member states to supervise compliance with the Euratom rules.[60] The effect of this change is to terminate the former separate general Euratom infringement procedures[61] and introduce a single set of general infringement procedures applicable in principle to all EU founding treaties, with the exception of the common and foreign security policy field contained in the TEU.[62] Accordingly, since the entry into force of the Lisbon Treaty on 1 December 2009, the first- and second-round proceedings clauses contained in Articles 258–60 TFEU are now applicable for the purposes of Euratom law enforcement.

Apart from general infringement procedures, the Euratom Treaty also contains certain specific infraction proceedings that apply when the Commission considers that certain Euratom treaty obligations have been breached. Specifically, these concern Article 38 of the Euratom Treaty concerning health and safety standards and Articles 82–3. Articles 38 and 82 of the Euratom Treaty empower the Commission to accelerate the prosecution of infringement action by enabling it to issue directives to member states it considers have violated basic standards and/or regulations on health and safety relating to ionising radiation or breached minimum requirements on maintaining operating records in order to account for ores, source materials or special fissile materials used, produced or transported in connection with civil nuclear energy activities. Should a member state fail to comply with the Commission directive by the set deadline, the Commission is empowered (in derogation from Articles 258–9 TFEU) to refer the matter to the CJEU directly. The Commission is greatly assisted in its supervisory duties by a guaranteed right of access to member state civil nuclear energy facilities so as to ensure effective, regular monitoring of levels of ambient radioactivity[63] as well as a Commission-recruited inspectorate responsible for obtaining and verifying operating records.[64] Such powers of access and inspection are not guaranteed in relation to the supervision of the EU's environmental legislation adopted under the aegis of its common environmental policy enshrined in Title XX of the TFEU. Moreover, the Commission has the power to decide to impose specific sanctions on persons or undertakings that it finds guilty of infringing any obligations binding on them under Chapter 7 of the Euratom Treaty on safeguards (Articles 77–85). The range of sanctions available to the Commission, which are directly enforceable in the member states, vary in their severity and may include: a warning; the withdrawal of special benefits such as financial or technical assistance; the placing of an undertaking for up to four months under a new administration set up jointly by the Commission and member state in which the sanctioned person/undertaking is located; or total or partial withdrawal of source materials or special fissile materials.[65] Sanctioning decisions may be the subject of appeal before the CJEU, which shall have suspensory effect with regard to the decision unless this is successful contested by the Commission before the CJEU.[66] By way of comparison, such powers of sanction are not vested in the Commission with respect to violations of EU environmental legislation adopted under the TFEU. Finally, the Commission has the power under Article 45 of the Euratom Treaty to call upon a member state to impose sanctions in accordance with its national law in cases where the Commission considers that a person/undertaking has infringed the Euratom Treaty but in respect of which Article 83 of that treaty does not apply. Should the member state fail to comply with the Commission's request within a deadline set by the Commission, the Commission may then bring an action before the CJEU to have the infringement established.

Notes

1 Superseding predecessor provisions contained in the former Treaty of Rome: Arts. 226–88 EC, Arts. 169–71 EEC.

2 Arts. 191–3 TFEU.

3 See sections 54–63 (Priority Objective 4) of the Annex of Decision 1386/2013 on a General Union Environment Action Programme to 2020 'Living Well, within the Limits of our Planet' (OJ 2013 L354/171).

4 Treaty of Lisbon amending the Treaty on European Union and the Treaty establishing the European Community (OJ 2007 C306).

5 See notably Case C-176/03 *Commission v Council* and Case C-440/05 *Commission v Council.*

6 A more detailed examination of this former unduly complex and unpredictable legal framework is provided in the first edition of this book. See Chs. 1, 2 and 13 of the first edition.

7 See Case C-239/03 *Commission v France (Etang de Berre)* and Hedemann-Robinson (2012).

8 Successor provision to former Art. 10 EC.

9 Succeeding former Art. 5 EC.

10 As stipulated in Art. 17(1) TEU, successor to Art. 211 EC.

11 The sensitive constitutional issues that arise in relation to the state of plurality of functions assumed by the Commission, with particular reference to how these affect its ability and credibility on carrying out its enforcement duties, will be considered during the course of this book.

12 This is usually done by way of information briefings in so-called 'package meetings' held jointly between Commission services and Member State representatives. Such meetings are usually held at least twice a year.

13 See Art. 289 TFEU for an overview of types of EU legislative procedures.

14 As reported on the *Statistics on Environmental Infringements* webpage of the Commission's Environment Directorate-General (DG ENV): http://ec.europa.eu/environment/legal/law/statistics.htm.

15 See p. 46 of Annex to COM(2012)714, Commission Report, *29th Annual Report on Monitoring the Application of EU Law*, 30 November 2012. Available for inspection at: http://ec.europa.eu/eu_law/infringements/infringements_annual_report_29_en.htm.

16 See ibid., p. 12.

17 See ibid., pp. 9 and 51 for the relevant complaints data.

18 See Regulation 1/2003 on the implementation of Articles 81 and 82 EC (now Arts. 101 and 102 TFEU) (OJ 2003 L1/1) and Regulation 139/2004 on the control of concentrations between undertakings (OJ 2004 L24/1).

19 OJ 2004 L24/1.

20 See e.g. COM(2002)725, Commission Communication on better monitoring of the application of Community law, which estimates that around 10% of infringement cases are referred to the CJEU (see p. 3).

21 See Art. III-362(3) EUC.

22 OJ 2008 L312/3.

23 OJ 2012 L26/1, as amended.

24 See, in particular, Art. 279 TFEU which stipulates that the CJEU 'may in any cases before it prescribe any necessary interim measures'. In the context of infringement proceedings under Art. 258 TFEU, a case does not come before the CJEU until completion of the pre-litigation phase (namely after issuance of the LFN and RO and a reasonable time allowed for the defendant state to respond to both).

25 See the CJEU's *Annual Report 2011 Synopsis of the Work of the Court of Justice, the General Court and the Civil Service Tribunal*, p. 111 which indicated the following average number of months required for completion by the CJEU of the judicial phase of infringement proceedings (referred to as 'direct actions' in the Report) between 2007–11: 2007 (18.2), 2008 (16.9), 2009 (17.1), 2010 (16.7) and 2011 (20.2). The Report is accessible on the CJEU's website at: http://curia.europa.eu/jcms/jcms/Jo2_7000/.

26 Directives commonly stipulate around two years from entry into force as a transposition deadline.

27 Commission Communication, *Implementation of Article 260(3) of the Treaty* (OJ 2011 C12/1), section II.19.
28 See also Wennerås (2012), p. 167.
29 For instance, in 2013 the Commission took action against a number of member states (Bulgaria, Estonia and the UK) over partial transposition of EU energy market legislation (Directive 2009/72 and Directive 2009/73 (OJ 2009 L211/94 and 155 respectively)): Commission Rapid Press Release IP/13/42.
30 There are several examples of this in EU environmental law. For instance, the Water Framework Directive 2000/60 adopted at the turn of the millennium sets a 2015 deadline for member states achieving good ecological status for their domestic waters. The 1999 Landfill Directive 99/31 (OJ 1999 L182/1) sets a deadline of 2009 by which landfills in existence prior to the directive's entry into force are required to be in compliance with the EU legislation's requirements. The 1991 Urban Waste Water Directive 91/271 (OJ 2001 L135/40) prescribes a 2005 deadline for member states to ensure that all agglomerations with a population equivalent (p.e.) of more than 2,000 are provided with collecting systems for urban waste water and that, prior to entering collecting systems, urban waste water is subject to secondary treatment. In the area of air quality law, the EU through Directive 2008/50 on ambient air quality and cleaner air for Europe provides for the possibility of member states extending the existing deadlines set in 1999 for complying with minimum quality standards in relation to nitrogen dioxide and benzene from 2010 to 2015, recognising that several member states have particular difficulties in achieving compliance with the limit value deadlines. The list goes on. Specific and often longer implementation deadlines are often negotiated with accession member states.
31 See Art. III-362 EUC.
32 Commission Communication, *Implementation of Article 260(3) of the Treaty* (OJ 2011 C12/1), para. 29.
33 See ibid., section VII, para. 31.
34 Ibid.
35 As reported on the Commission's DG ENV following webpage: http://ec.europa.eu/environment/legal/law/statistics.htm.
36 In particular, two treaty provisions are especially relevant in this regard. Specifically, Art. 19 TEU invests the CJEU with the task of ensuring that 'the law is observed' in the interpretation and application of the TFEU and TEU and Art. 267 TFEU specifies that the CJEU has jurisdiction to give preliminary rulings to national courts and tribunals on the interpretation of those treaties as well as EU acts adopted under their auspices.
37 As set out in Art. 19 TEU (ex Art. 220 EC).
38 Succeeding the former treaty provision of Art. 228(2) EC (ex Art. 171(2)).
39 The Commission has estimated that this treaty change will reduce the duration of second-round proceedings by some 25%, namely to between 8–18 months as compared with between 12–24 months prior to Lisbon (para. 3 of the 2011 Commission Communication, *Implementation of Article 260(3) of the Treaty* (OJ 2011 C12/1)).
40 Specifically, the 1996 Commission Memorandum on applying Article 228 of the EC Treaty (OJ 1996 C 242/7) and the 1997 Commission Communication on the method of calculating the penalty payments provided for pursuant to Article 228 of the EC Treaty (OJ 1997 C 63/2).
41 SEC(2005), Commission Communication, *Application of Article 228 of the EC Treaty*; SEC(2010)1371, Commission Communication, *Implementation of Article 260(3) TFEU*; and SEC(2011)1024, Commission Communication, *Updating of Date Used to Calculate Lump Sum and Penalty Payments to be Proposed by the Commission to the Court of Justice in Infringement Proceedings*. These documents may be inspected on the following European Commission website: http://ec.europa.eu/eu_law/infringements/infringements_260_en.htm.

42   Specifically, Cases C-387/97 *Commission v Greece*, C-278/01 *Commission v Spain*, C-304/02 *Commission v France*, C-121/07 *Commission v France*, C-374/11 *Commission v Ireland*, C-533/11 *Commission v Belgium* and C-576/11 *Commission v Luxembourg.* These CJEU judgments will be examined in detail in Ch. 4.

43   Entry into force of the TEU was 1 November 1993.

44   See in support of this view e.g. Craig and de Búrca (2011), p. 402.

45   Regulation 867/2007 on the law applicable to non-contractual obligations (OJ 2007 L199/40).

46   See ibid., Arts. 4 and 7. See also Case 21/76 *Handelskwekerij GJ Bier*.

47   As confirmed by Art. 192(1) (in conjunction with Art. 294) TFEU. Each member state retains a veto, though, to block policy proposals in certain environmental matters as specified in Art. 192(2)(a)–(c) TFEU and in relation to environmental crime under Art. 83 TFEU.

48   Case C-1/00 *Commission v France*.

49   See Art. 40 of the Protocol (No. 3) on the Statute of the Court of Justice, as annexed to the TFEU (OJ 2010 C83). See also Art. 93 of Rules of Procedure of the Court of Justice of 25 September 2012 (OJ L265, 29 September 2012), as amended on 18 June 2013 (OJ L173, 26 June 2013) issued on the basis of Art. 266 TFEU (ex Art. 223 EC).

50   In addition, under Art. 40(3) of the CJEU Statute, EFTA states party to the 1992 European Economic Area Agreement (Iceland, Norway and Liechtenstein) have the right to make submissions in cases before CJEU where one of the fields of the Agreement is concerned. Environmental policy (apart from marine fish stock management) is a field covered by the EEA Agreement.

51   Directive 2008/98 (OJ 2008 L312/3) (superseding former Directives 2006/12 (OJ 2006 L114/9) and 75/442 (OJ 1975 L194/39).

52   See e.g. Case C-9/00 *Palin Granit Oy*.

53   Specifically, Title XX *Environment* (Arts. 191–3) of the TFEU.

54   OJ 2010 C84/01.

55   Art. 1 Euratom Treaty.

56   Ibid., Art. 2.

57   Ibid., Art. 2(b) in conjunction with Ch. 3 Health and safety (Arts. 30–9).

58   Ibid., Art. 2(e) in conjunction with Ch. 7 Safeguards (Arts. 77–85).

59   Protocol (No. 2) amending the Euratom Treaty, annexed to the Lisbon Treaty 2007 (OJ 2007 C306/199).

60   See Art. 106a Euratom Treaty (inserted by Protocol (No. 2)).

61   Namely, former Arts. 141–3 Euratom (pre-Lisbon).

62   See Art. 24(1) TEU, second subpara.

63   Art. 35 Euratom Treaty.

64   Ibid., Art. 82.

65   Ibid., Art. 83(1).

66   Ibid., Arts. 83(2) and 144.

3 Enforcement action brought by the European Commission (1)

Article 258 TFEU and 'first-round' infringement proceedings

This chapter together with Chapter 4 will focus on the legal principles under-pinning the particular provisions enabling the European Commission to take legal action against those member states failing to implement EU environmental measures correctly under the auspices of the Treaty on the Functioning of the EU (TFEU). Collectively, those provisions are Articles 258 and 260(2) TFEU. As explained in the previous chapter, Commission infringement actions concerning breaches of environmental norms based on the TFEU may be divided up into two types: namely 'first-round' and 'second-round' actions. Article 258 TFEU pro-vides the legal basis for the Commission to take action against particular violations when they first arise (first-round action), ultimately bringing the defendant mem-ber state of the EU before the Court of Justice of the European Union (CJEU) for a definitive ruling as to whether or not a breach of EU law by the defendant has transpired. Article 260(2) TFEU (second-round action) enables the Commission to take subsequent legal action against the same member state where the latter fails to respect a judgment against it by the CJEU laid down in the first-round legal proceedings under Article 258 TFEU.

Currently, the types of rulings that may be delivered by the CJEU differ between those handed down in the context of first- and second-round proceedings. Specifi-cally, in the context of Article 258 TFEU proceedings, the CJEU has the power to issue a judicial declaration on the question of compliance by a member state with respect to its obligations under EU law. For particular types of cases, namely non-communication cases (discussed in the previous chapter), the Commission may also request the CJEU to impose penalties on a member state which fails to adopt and communicate to it national measures intended to transpose an EU directive passed under a Union legislative procedure.[1] In relation to Article 260(2) proceed-ings, the CJEU has the power to levy fines against a member state it finds guilty of having failed to comply with an earlier judgment it has had made against it under the auspices of Article 258 TFEU.

This chapter will consider the various legal steps involved in the context of first-round proceedings. Chapter 4 will focus on Article 260(2) TFEU. Particular emphasis will be placed on the relevant case law of the CJEU which has assisted in interpreting the scope of the relevant provisions. This jurisprudence has set down important markers relating to the scope of the Commission's investigatory powers as well as assisted in identifying the parameters of the various procedural rights of defendant member states faced with such legal action. The legal principles discussed in this chapter are pertinent to all first-round proceedings. Where appropriate, any differences applicable to non-communication cases will be noted.

3.1 Detection of breaches of law

Infringement proceedings commenced by the Commission under Article 258 TFEU may be triggered usually in one of two ways: either by way of own initiative or on the basis of third-party information (typically complaints submitted by private persons or other non-governmental entities). The Commission will be able to initiate legal action on its own account in cases where national laws fail to implement EU environmental norms as required. Typically, this type of case might well involve a failure on the part of a member state to transpose an EU environmental protection directive into national legislation within the deadline prescribed by the directive. Tracking of compliance is relatively easy for the Commission in such a case, as directives are drafted so as to contain a standard obligation for member states to notify the Commission of their transposition measures. However, the Commission is far less likely, of its own initiative, to uncover instances of incorrect application or implementation of EU environmental norms in respect of specific practical situations (e.g. non-compliance with minimum binding environmental quality standards as enshrined in EU legislative instrumentation). Instead, any enforcement action launched by the Commission in respect of member states failing to ensure that EU environmental norms are respected in practice is most likely to stem from information garnered from members of the general public, including non-governmental organisations (NGOs). Given that no formal powers are vested in the Commission to investigate potential or alleged breaches of EU environmental law (other than in a few areas such as the civil nuclear[2] or fisheries sectors),[3] this is not particularly surprising. The Commission has published a model complaints form for complainants to complete and send to it when filing allegations of infringements.[4] The form is designed to assist the Commission receiving details and evidence of the particular case at hand. It is not binding, though, and members of the public may send in complaints in any particular format they choose.

The means available to law enforcement agencies in securing detection of breaches of environmental law is a matter that is central to any assessment of the relative effectiveness of a system of environmental law enforcement. The range of tools available to the Commission for detecting actual or suspected infringements of EU environmental law is, in general, pretty limited. In practice, other than in relation to civil nuclear and fisheries sectors for which the EU has established particular supranational inspection procedures, the Commission is reliant upon the general public for referring to it specific instances of breaches of EU environmental law. Even when the Commission has received a complaint, it has no general powers to investigate any particular site, either by dispatching its own officials to relevant sites or instructing national environmental protection agencies to carry out an inspection on its behalf. Instead, it is wholly reliant upon the defendant member state to supply it with site-specific environmental information and evidence. The balance of power between prosecution and defence in relation to the garnering factual evidence lies heavily in the defendant member state's favour. The recent EU treaty reforms to the structure of infringement proceedings made by the 2007 Lisbon Treaty has left this important issue untouched. This state of affairs raises a number of questions about the efficacy and scope of Commission law enforcement powers, in particular to what extent they represent a satisfactory means of holding member states to account in meeting their obligations to ensure that EU environmental norms are adhered to within their respective territories. It is relatively straightforward to understand why it is the case that the vast majority of proceedings taken by the Commission in environmental disputes relate to transposition-type issues, given that the question of alleged non-compliance in these cases may usually be resolved by way of simple examination of usually publicly accessible legal documents (i.e. comparing national implementing measures with those required to be in place by EU legislation).

3.2 Overview of core elements of Commission infringement proceedings

Both first- and second-round infringement proceedings undertaken by the Commission under Articles 258 and 260(2) TFEU[5] respectively are composed of a distinct set of steps leading from initial decision to launch legal action through to eventual judgment by the CJEU. The steps may be described as falling into two broad stages of legal action: namely the pre-litigation and litigation phases. Given that both first- and second-round infringement proceedings are designed essentially to encourage friendly out-of-court settlement of disputes between the Commission and defendant member state, in practice a significant period of time has often been taken up by the respective parties in the pre-litigation phase. This phase essentially involves an exchange of correspondence and views between the Commission and defendant member state, undertaken with a view to seeking a negotiated settlement where possible. The CJEU has described the purpose of the pre-litigation phase as enabling a member state to have an opportunity to comply with EU obligations as well as avail itself of the right to defend itself against the Commission's charges of non-compliance.[6] In recent years, the Commission has take steps to shorten the amount of time taken up in the pre-litigation phase, with a view to placing greater urgency and pressure on defendant member states to secure compliance with EU law.

3.2.1 General remarks regarding first-round proceedings under Article 258 TFEU

3.2.1.1 Pre-litigation phase and the EU Pilot system

The nature of the pre-litigation phase for Article 258 TFEU proceedings involves the Commission aiming, in particular, to achieve two things. First and foremost, the Commission is charged with the task of following up lines of enquiry with a defendant member state in order to verify whether or not any allegations or concerns of a breach of law occurring within the state's territory are borne out. The second principal task comes into operation if the Commission is satisfied that a breach of law has occurred. This involves the Commission seeking ways of ensuring that the defendant state takes appropriate remedial action. If a satisfactory solution can be found, further pursuit of legal proceedings will be unnecessary. Where the breach is an ongoing violation of environmental provisions, action on the part of the defendant state to require a cessation of the breach might be sufficient remedial action in certain cases for environmental protection purposes. An example could be a member state ordering the cessation of illegal hunting methods of protected species in a special conservation area, as required under EU nature protection legislation.

However, in a number of other cases cessation of illegal activity would be an insufficient remedy, such as where a protected habitat site has been the subject of unlawful development or where uncontrolled fly-tipping has led to a situation of ongoing pollution to the environment. In these situations appropriate remedial action on the part of the defendant member state requires additional steps to be taken in order to tackle the effects generated by illicit activities, namely positive restorative measures. In other instances, it may not be possible to unravel the environmental consequences of certain illegal acts. The prosecution of legal proceedings may nevertheless be necessary for other reasons, such as deterrence and/or holding a defendant state to account at law.

The pre-litigation phase envisaged in Article 258 TFEU involves the European Commission issuing two formal written warnings to the defendant member state to institute corrective action, namely a letter of formal notice (LFN) followed by a reasoned opinion (RO). In practice, these written warnings are issued only after the Commission is satisfied that the strength of evidence before it indicates that a breach of EU environmental law is likely to have occurred. Cases involving allegations that a member state has failed to transpose EU environmental directives (or other legislative instrumentation, as required) correctly into national law are usually relatively straightforward to investigate and assess, with the Commission usually being able to determine the position without needing to liaise with national authorities for detailed information. The question concerning state of compliance with EU law in incorrect transposition cases is usually evident from the state of national implementing measures available for inspection by the Commission services. Accordingly, in these types of cases relatively little time needs to be spent by the Commission prior to launch of formal infringement proceedings in verifying factual matters. It is standard procedure for Commission services to track the progress of transposition of individual EU directives into national law of the member states in the run-up to the transposition deadline set by each EU directive. Each directive requires, as a standard obligation, for member states to notify the Commission of national implementation measures. Accordingly, the Commission has been keen to reduce the amount of time taken up by its services in assessing non-compliance in transposition cases. Notably, the Commission has set itself a benchmark of seeking to ensure that the length of the pre-litigation phase for non-communication cases should not exceed 12 months.[7]

By way contrast, the pre-litigation phase involving allegations of bad application of EU environmental law may take a substantially longer period of time to assess by the European Commission, given the need usually to verify a considerable amount of factual information relating to events and practices on the ground. In the past, the Commission used to pursue allegations of bad application and non-conformity initially through a series of administrative letters between itself and the member state concerned (commonly referred to as pre-letters of formal notice or pre-LFN). Since April 2008, the Commission has streamlined the manner in which it handles these types of cases through a system known as EU Pilot.[8]

In cases involving allegations by the European Commission or by any person or body who files a complaint to the Commission of incorrect implementation or transposition of EU environmental law by member states, it is now standard practice since mid 2008 for the Commission (Environment Directorate-General's Legal Unit) as a general rule to engage the so-called EU Pilot system. This involves referring the incorrect implementation allegation to the member state authority concerned with a view to seeing whether recourse to formal infringement procedures may be possibly avoided and the dispute satisfactorily resolved at a relatively early stage.[9] The EU Pilot scheme may be traced back to the Commission's 2007 Communication, *A Europe of Results – Applying Community Law*,[10] in which it proposed the initiation of a project to involve closer co-operation between the Commission and member states in ensuring a correct understanding and application of EU law. Specifically, the Communication proposed that, unless urgency would require commencement of formal enforcement action immediately and so long as the Commission considers that contact with the member state would contribute to an efficient resolution of the complaint, then the member state concerned should be given a short deadline to provide the necessary clarifications, information and solutions directly to the complainant concerned and inform the Commission of its response. If the case were to involve a breach of EU law, the Communication envisaged that the member state contact would be expected to remedy, or offer to remedy, the breach within set deadlines. If no informal solution could be found, then the Commission would consider undertaking follow-up action, reserving the right to initiate formal infringement proceedings under Article 258 TFEU where it deems this to be appropriate.[11]

Since the 2007 Communication, the Commission has now rolled out the EU Pilot project with a view to it being used as a standard reference procedure for handling complaints or Commission-initiated cases concerning alleged instances of incorrect implementation of EU law by member states,[12] including EU environmental law. The majority of files are usually generated by private parties registering complaints or enquiries with the Commission, whilst the Commission undertakes a number of cases generated within its services[13] (so-called 'own-initiative' casework). A confidential online database has been created under the EU Pilot scheme for communication between the Commission services and the member state authorities. A network of contacts has been established at Commission and member state levels to operate the EU Pilot system, so that case files entered into the database reach their correct destination and for the purposes of monitoring progress and use of the scheme. Complainants, whose files are registered under the Commission's internal IT tool known as CHAP ('Complaint handling/Accueil des plaignants'),[14] are informed that the EU Pilot is to be used. Whilst the EU Pilot envisages direct communication by the member state authority to the complainant whenever appropriate to simplify and shorten the time to process files, this communication will in practice often be channelled through the Commission services which will provide the complainant and member state with its evaluation of the member state's response. A general 20-week deadline has been set for responses to be provided in respect of the allegation of non-compliance, which means ten weeks for the member state authorities followed by ten weeks for the relevant Commission service overseeing the handling of the case file. The Commission has committed itself, as a general rule, to come to a decision as to whether or not to proceed to formal launch of infringement proceedings under Article 258 TFEU within one year of the date of registration of the file, whether initiated by complainant or Commission.[15]

The Commission has produced annual evaluation reports concerning the operation of the EU Pilot system.[16] Whilst the scheme has not yet had that much time to bed down, the Commission has reported that initial results so far have been encouraging. In 2011 it reported that 80 per cent of member state responses were assessed by the Commission to be acceptable, enabling the case file to be closed without the need to launch an infringement procedure under Article 258 TFEU.[17] The remaining 20 per cent of files went on to be the subject of formal infringement proceedings.

3.2.1.2 Litigation phase

If the pre-litigation phase proves unsuccessful in resolving matters to the satisfaction of the Commission, then the Commission may decide to bring proceedings before the CJEU. At the point when a case is filed before the CJEU by the Commission, the litigation phase of infringement proceedings under Article 258 TFEU commences. During this phase, handling of the case will take place under the stewardship of the CJEU in accordance with its procedural rules.[18] Filing of court papers and all correspondence from the parties is conducted through the CJEU. The litigation phase is completed once the CJEU has issued a declaratory judgment as to whether a member state has infringed EU law and, in non-communication cases, once the CJEU has determined whether a penalty should be imposed on the defendant state.

3.2.2 General remarks regarding second-round proceedings under Article 260(2) TFEU

Only a few general and introductory comments need to be made at this point about the second-round infringement procedure under Article 260(2) TFEU, as

Chapter 4 will address the procedure in detail. In many respects the legal framework of second-round infringement proceedings is similar to that applicable to those under the aegis of Article 258 TFEU. They are composed formally of pre-litigation and litigation phases. However, the nature of the dispute in second-round actions is profoundly different. The object of Article 260(2) proceedings is to hold member states to account should they fail to take suitable steps to adhere to a first-round CJEU judgment made against them under Article 258 TFEU. Whilst the EU treaty framework is silent on the length of time allowed for defendant states to comply with first-round judgments,[19] CJEU case law has clarified that the importance of immediate and uniform application of Union law means that the process of compliance must be initiated at once and completed as soon as possible.[20]

In practice, the second-round pre-litigation phase is often not as protracted as for first-round proceedings, given that the zone of conflict between Commission and member state at second-round stage is quite clearly defined by the terms and findings of the first-round judgment handed down by the CJEU. In addition, by virtue of the changes introduced by virtue of the 2007 Lisbon Treaty, the pre-litigation phase in second-round actions has been shortened so as to involve only one written warning from the Commission to the defendant, namely an LFN. The principal tasks for the Commission in the pre-litigation stage of Article 260(2) proceedings are to verify whether the member state has taken appropriate steps to comply with the Court's findings within a reasonable period of time after the first-round judgment and, if not, that the state takes corrective measures as warranted. These responsibilities of the Commission are assisted significantly by the fact that it is for the defendant member state to satisfy the Commission that compliance has been achieved, not the other way around. In practice, within a relatively short time of the first-round CJEU judgment (usually within one to two months) the Commission contacts the member state concerned for the purpose of elucidating the latter's timetable for instituting remedial measures. Should the Commission consider that the member state has submitted an unsatisfactory response to its request for setting out a timetable for achieving compliance, for instance because it considers the pace of remediation is unduly slow and/or the suggested programme for remedial measures to be incomplete, it will issue the state with an LFN. Legal pressure is placed accordingly upon the defendant to set about implementing the first-round judgment as soon as practicable. The Commission has set itself a benchmark of seeking to ensure that the length of the pre-litigation phase for second-round proceedings should not exceed between 12 and 24 months, subject to any exceptional circumstances that may arise in particular cases.[21]

3.2.3 *Tables highlighting procedure and typical length of Article 258 TFEU infringement actions*

For ease of reference, Tables 3.1–3.5 below indicate the various legal stages involved in the context of first-round infringement proceedings taken by the Commission under Article 258 TFEU. Tables 3.1 and 3.2 concern the management of first-round proceedings, divided up between the handling of non-communication cases (Table 3.1) and non-conformity and bad-application cases (Table 3.2). Non-communication casework is subject to particular internal management procedures and deadlines. An indication of the current notional length of each stage is provided in respect of what the Commission now anticipates should be involved generally in application of the procedures for first- and second-round proceedings. The times noted in Tables 3.1–3.2 are intended to indicate the period of time that would be usually earmarked for management of a case through to completion, namely through to judgment by the CJEU. These timescales may well vary in practice, though, depending on the nature and degree of complexity of each particular case as well as the degree to which the EU Pilot system is able to operate efficiently. In addition, in certain instances the CJEU may decide to shorten its proceedings where it deems this appropriate in straightforward, relatively uncontroversial cases (e.g. by deciding to expedite the proceedings upon request by a litigant,[22] by not requiring the delivery of an advisory opinion by an Advocate General where no new point of EU law is in issue[23] or by issuing a judgment by default as a result of a failure by the defendant member state to file a timely defence in the proper form).[24]

The management of the litigation phase of infringement proceedings has also been made easier and swifter since 2011 with the decision to allow court procedural documentation to be submitted electronically by member states and EU institutions (known as the 'e-Curia' system).[25] In addition, whilst the CJEU is obliged to state the reasons on which its judgments are based and to disclose the names of the judges involved in the Court's deliberations[26] as well as to disclose judgments in open court,[27] the official case reports of the full judgments of infringement cases not involving new points of EU law may now frequently be published[28] in a restricted number of language versions (namely the CJEU working language of French and the language of the defendant member state), with summaries made available in other official Union languages.[29] The restriction on the use of language versions serves to assist in optimising the use of CJEU translation resources and reducing the overall time needed to generate official court reports.

Tables 3.3–3.5 provide an overview of the average duration of first-round infringement proceedings for those cases that have actually culminated in a CJEU judgment between 2010–12. These tables provide some insights into how first-round infringement procedures are being currently managed in practice, taking into account the treaty changes introduced by the Lisbon Treaty 2007 as well as the initial impact of other recent reforms introduced by the Commission and CJEU to assist in streamlining and accelerating case management of environmental infringement casework.

Looking at the Tables it is possible to appreciate the considerable length of time that is often taken up in practice by the prosecution of infringement proceedings under Article 258 TFEU before a judgment is handed down by the CJEU. This is notwithstanding the introduction of a range of initiatives and reforms, as outlined earlier, introduced by the Commission at pre-litigation stage and the CJEU

Table 3.1 Article 258 TFEU (first-round) proceedings environmental disputes – anticipated duration of non-communication cases

A. Pre-litigation phase	
Maximum time envisaged: 12 months*	
1. Letter of Formal Notice (LFN)	• LFN issued within 2 months after end of deadline for transposition of EU Directive • Normally 2 months' deadline given for member state response to the LFN • Normally up to 2–6 months for Commission to assess member state response
2. Reasoned Opinion (RO)	• Normally 2 months' deadline given for member state response to RO • Normally up to 2–6 months for Commission to assess response to RO

B. Litigation phase	
Approximate anticipated duration: up to 10 months** (if Advocate General Opinion is not used)	
1. Case papers registered with CJEU	Approx. within 2–6 months of end of RO deadline
2. Hearing	Approx. within 6–9 months after case filed with CJEU
3. Advocate General's (AG) Opinion (rarely used given no new points of law involved)	Approx. 9–12 months after case filed with CJEU
4. CJEU judgment with possible penalty	Approx. up to 10 months after case is filed with the Court
Total approx. duration of proceedings envisaged:	Up to 22 months

* Benchmark set by Commission Communication, *A Europe of Results – Applying Community Law* (COM(2007)502).
** See Table 3.4 below, which indicates the average times researched by the author for environmental cases culminating in a CJEU judgment between 2010 and 2012.

Table 3.2 Article 258 TFEU (first-round) proceedings: environmental disputes – anticipated duration of non-conformity and bad-application cases

A. Pre-litigation phase	
Approximate timescale varies, usually anticipated to be at least approx. 20–8 months	
1. EU Pilot system (for complaints/Commission own-initiative cases concerning bad application of/non-conformity with EU environmental law)	20 weeks as a benchmark* (10 weeks each for member state and Commission responses after file is registered in EU Pilot)
2. Letter of Formal Notice (LFN)	• Decision to proceed to LFN stage made within 12 months after registration of case file in EU Pilot • Approx. up to 2 months' deadline given for member state to respond to LFN • Approx. up to 6 months for Commission to analyse member state response to LFN

(Continued)

Table 3.2 (Continued)

A. Pre-litigation phase
Approximate timescale varies, usually anticipated to be at least approx. 20–8 months

3. Reasoned Opinion (RO)	• Approx. up to 2 months' deadline given for response to RO • Approx. up to 6 months for Commission to respond to member state response to RO

B. Litigation phase
*Approximate duration: 20+ months**

1. Case papers registered with CJEU	Approx. within 2–6 months of end of RO deadline
2. Hearing	Approx. within 6–9 months after case filed with CJEU
3. Advocate General's (AG) Opinion (although this may be dispensed with by the CJEU esp. where no new points of law involved)	Approx. 9–12 months after case filed with CJEU
4. CJEU judgment	Approx. up to 15 months after case is filed with the CJEU
Total approx. duration of proceedings envisaged:	Usually more than 40 months

* Member states may request a time extension from the Commission, which may or may not accept this according to its assessment of particular circumstances. Likewise, the Commission may indicate a shorter member state response time than 10 weeks is warranted in the circumstances: see SEC(2011)1629/2 at section 2 (Working Method), p. 3.

** Figure based on the average time recorded by the CJEU of 20.2 months taken for it to process direct actions filed before it, as published in the CJEU's 2011 Annual Report (*Annual Report 2011 – Synopsis of the work of the Court of Justice, the General Court and the Civil Service Tribunal* (2012 OOPEC) at p. 110. The CJEU's annual reports may be found at http://curia.europa.eu/jcms/jcms/Jo2_7000/.

Table 3.3 Article 258 TFEU (first-round) infringement proceedings: environmental cases 2010–12

Pre-litigation phase
Average duration in months

Year of CJEU environmental judgments	*Non-Communication cases*	*Non-conformity cases*	*Non-implementation/ bad-application cases*	*Average duration of pre-litigation phase for all types of cases*
2010	17.9	30.9	30.5	28.4
2011	12.3	51.3	29.8	33.3
2012	–	63.7	26.6	41.5

Table 3.4 Article 258 TFEU (first-round) infringement proceedings: environmental cases 2010–12

| | **Litigation phase** | | | |
| | *Average duration in months* | | | |
Year of CJEU environmental judgments	*Cases without an Advocate General Opinion*	*Cases with an Advocate General Opinion*	*Non-communication cases*	*Average duration of litigation phase for all types of cases*
2010	12.4	24.3	7.4	14.9
2011	13.7	25	7	15.8
2012	12.9	28	–	14

Table 3.5 Article 258 TFEU (first-round) infringement proceedings: environmental cases 2010–12

| | **Average total duration of proceedings** | | | |
| | *Average duration in months* | | | |
Year of CJEU environmental judgments	*Average duration of pre-litigation phase for all types of cases*	*Average duration of litigation phase for all types of cases*	*Average total duration of Art. 258 TFEU proceedings (from LFN to judgment)*	*Number of Art. 258 TFEU environmental judgments*
2010	28.4	14.9	43.3	29
2011	33.3	15.8	49.1	22
2012	41.5	14	55.5	14

at litigation stage in order to accelerate the management of case work. From Tables 3.3–3.5 above considering the environmental cases decided between 2010 and 2012, it appears that the minimum amount of time for the completion of first-round proceedings through to judgment would currently be expected to be in the region of around 22 months for non-communication cases, 63 months for non-conformity cases and 44 months for non-implementation/bad-application cases. The average length of first-round proceedings for environmental cases overall amounts to around 49 months, so just over four years. Whilst these timescales are considerable, they compare relatively favourably with the times taken up by infringement proceedings in earlier times, such as the 1990s. Specifically, it has been calculated that on average the time span between the Commission's decision to issue an LFN and application to file an action before the CJEU in environmental cases was 35 months during 1992–4, 33 months during 1995–7, 48 months during 1998–9 and 59 months during 2000–1.[30] In addition, it has been calculated that in respect of the environmental cases decided between 1998 and 1999, the litigation phase took on average 20 months, with the entire Article 258 TFEU action lasting 68 months, over five and a half years.[31]

In practice, the time taken up by infringement proceedings may often be considerably longer than the official EU institutional benchmarks envisaged, with the European Commission frequently having provided – and reserving the right to provide – extended deadlines to member states for compliance during pre-litigation phases in first-round environmental infringement actions under Article 258 TFEU. In addition, the litigation phase may take considerably longer than anticipated, there being no hard-and-fast rules about turnaround times for judicial pronouncements on any particular case. The CJEU is in sole control of handling each case through the various stages in the litigation phase of infringement proceedings. However, the CJEU's turnaround time for casework is relatively impressive, in particular in respect of non-communication cases.

Whilst some useful insights may be gained on the state of case management of environmental infringement proceedings through the use of general statistical data, it should be noted that statistics do not necessarily reveal the full picture. In particular, it should be noted that relatively recently the Commission has begun to develop the practice of filing a specific new type of infringement action which aims to establish a general and persistent (GAP) practice of non-compliance by a member state where the latter has engaged in or failed to prevent widespread similar breaches of EU (environmental) law.[32] Such an infringement action will cover several instances of infractions by a defendant member state, not just a single breach. The GAP proceedings will be registered as one legal action against a particular member state (instead of several separate proceedings), and case title and reference numbering will not reflect how widespread and serious a particular infraction of EU environmental law is within the defendant state. Moreover, the length of individual proceedings may well be affected by the fact that a case involves several separate violations, all of which have to be monitored by the Commission under one formal case file.

With the recent substantial increase in the number of states acceding to the EU within recent times, the timescale involved in the case management of infringement proceedings is not expected to shorten in the near future. Thirteen new member states have joined the Union between 2004 and 2013 alone, representing an almost doubling of member numbers since the beginning of 2004. It may be anticipated that, not simply down to an increase in size of the Union, the Commission and CJEU will be likely to face an increased infringement caseload. Specifically, a sizeable number of the most recent member states are likely to continue to experience significant financial, political as well as technical challenges in meeting the full range of EU environmental legislative obligations, notwithstanding the availability of various sources of Union financial assistance such the Cohesion and Structural Funds. In addition, it is evident that certain other pre-2004 member states continue to be confronted by a number of long-standing environmental compliance problems due to a lack of long-term of infrastructural investment and supervision required for enhancing environmental quality. For instance, it is clear that a number of states, particularly but not only in the Mediterranean area, have struggled in particular to ensure adherence to EU legislative requirements relating to the management of waste water and solid waste. Moreover, the EU as a whole is facing a long-standing challenge in being able to address air quality management, particularly as a result of particulate pollution, nitrate pollution of water basins as well as stemming and reversing deterioration in biodiversity. These are just some of the multifarious ongoing long-term environmental problems and challenges likely to confront the EU for the years ahead.

The remaining sections of this chapter will examine the provisions and jurisprudence concerning the various legal stages to Article 258 TFEU proceedings in more detail, with a view to exploring their practical impact on the handling of environmental cases.

3.3 The pre-litigation phase in Article 258 TFEU infringement proceedings

As already mentioned, Article 258 infringement proceedings are essentially divided into two distinct phases: pre-litigation and litigation. The pre-litigation phase, constituting the first part of an enforcement action, involves the European Commission placing a member state on notice that it considers a breach of EU law to have occurred within its territory, the responsibility falling on the defendant state to effect a remedy within a reasonable period of time. The notification of a breach takes the form of two consecutive written warnings, each with independently set deadlines for compliance: a letter of formal notice (LFN) followed by a reasoned opinion (RO) after the member state has had an opportunity to submit its observations. An RO is issued if the Commission considers that the member state has failed to take steps for the purpose of remedying the alleged breach of law or prove to the Commission's satisfaction that the allegation is in fact unfounded. The purpose of the pre-litigation phase has been summed up by the CJEU in the following terms in an action against the Netherlands over implementation failures regarding the Wild Birds Directive:[33]

> The aim of the pre-litigation procedure is . . . to give the member state an opportunity to justify its position or, as the case may be, to comply of its own accord with the requirements of the [TFEU]. If that attempt to reach a settlement proves unsuccessful, the member state is requested to comply with its obligations as set out in the reasoned opinion which concludes the pre-litigation procedure provided for in Article [258 TFEU] within the period prescribed in that opinion.[34]

Put another way, the purpose of the pre-litigation procedure is to provide the member state concerned, on the one hand, with a real opportunity to remedy the position before the matter is brought before the CJEU and, on the other, of putting forward its defence.[35] The Court has made it clear that the Commission is obliged to ensure proper respect for the essential rights of the defendant during this phase, in particular by ensuring that the member state is informed precisely about the exact extent and nature of any allegation of illegal (in)activity within its frontiers or other breaches of EU law. In any event, by the time the Commission comes to issuing an RO to the defendant, that will constitute the definitive subject matter of any legal action it wishes to bring before the CJEU during the subsequent phase, namely the litigation phase of proceedings.

3.3.1 Evidence and onus of proof

One of the central features of Article 258 TFEU proceedings is that the onus of proof is placed upon the Commission to demonstrate that there has been an infringement of EU law in respect of which a particular member state is responsible.[36] The Commission, in discharging its responsibility of supervising due application of EU law within the constituent member states, may not enter into any presumptions of culpability on the part of national authorities, but must provide evidence of sufficient probative value in order to back up its statement(s) of claim.[37]

The CJEU has had occasion to comment on the onus of proof in a case brought against Germany[38] over failure to implement correctly the first EU directive on access to environmental information.[39] In that case the European Commission submitted that German legislation had omitted to include national courts, as well as criminal prosecution and disciplinary authorities within the scope of the national implementing legislation, arguing that these bodies may well obtain or have obtained environmental information not necessarily through their judicial activities and would be obliged to disclose such information to the public upon request (e.g. statistical information on the environment).[40] The CJEU held that the Commission had failed to discharge its onus of proof in this case, having relied on a presumption that such entities would have responsibilities derived from the EU directive in addition to those when they acted normally in the exercise of their judicial powers. In addition, it had not come forward with any evidence to show that such authorities were in possession of environmental information obtained by them outside their judicial functions.

In non-transposition cases, namely where the European Commission alleges that a member state has failed to transpose an EU environmental directive correctly within the time period set by the legislative instrument, the issue of evidence does not usually arise as a problem for the Commission. The defective state of implementation will be evident from the wording of the national legislation itself. In an important judgment against Ireland[41] the CJEU has confirmed that in a non-transposition case the Commission does not have to prove that non-compliance with an EU environmental directive exists in practice in addition to having to show that national law fails to adhere to the requirements of the directive on paper. The CJEU upheld the Commission's claim that Ireland had failed to transpose the Environmental Impact Assessment (EIA) Directive[42] accurately into national law in failing, *inter alia*, to ensure that certain development projects would be subject to an EIA in accordance with the terms of the directive (including peat extraction, afforestation, use of uncultivated land as well the cumulative impact of small projects). It was immaterial according to the CJEU that the Commission had not presented it with any evidence to show that in practice any of these deficiencies had actually materialised. Incorrect transposition of an environmental directive into national law is accordingly sufficient on its own to constitute an infringement for the purposes of Article 258 TFEU proceedings. This is an important judgment, as it prevents member states from being able to abuse their position by taking advantage of the lack of investigatory powers vested in the Commission. It also enables the Commission to take preventive action, in that it is not bound to wait until defective national legislation bears out to be the cause of harmful effects to the environment.[43]

It should be pointed out, however, that although as a principle the onus of proof rests with the European Commission to make out its legal case, that evidentiary burden may be displaced as soon as the Commission has amassed sufficient evidence that points towards probability of liability on the part of the defendant member state.[44] Once it has gleaned information and evidence of a sufficiently specific and concrete nature indicating in all likelihood that a breach of EU environmental law has occurred (e.g. through photographic, documentary, physical and/or witness evidence) this should be enough for the burden of proof to be shifted to the defendant member state to account for these circumstances. Accordingly, it is not for the Commission to prove liability in an absolute sense. This relates directly to the fact that Article 258 and 260(2) proceedings are of a civil and not criminal nature, so the standard of proof required has been recognised by the CJEU to be below that of beyond all reasonable doubt. The requisite legal standard referred to by the Court appears to be based upon a test of the balance of probabilities, a test broadly similar to that one would expect to be applied generally in disputes at national level involving civil or administrative law. The standard of proof set for Article 258 infringement proceedings may in practice be crucial in assisting the Commission to hold member states to account for failures to ensure due implementation of EU environmental law. This is particularly so for cases concerning alleged bad application of EU environmental legislation, given the fact that the Commission's legal teams in such casework rely for the most part upon local sources of information. The Commission has no legal powers to initiate an independent investigation of its own over bad-application complaints, nor to require member states to do so on its behalf. Moreover, the Commission has neither the requisite financial nor administrative resources as things currently stand to supervise the management of on-site investigations of bad-application claims.

A good example of the importance of application of the onus-of-proof principle may be taken from the *San Rocco* valley waste case.[45] In this case, the Commission had pursued a complaint concerning illegal depositions of hazardous hospital waste into a quarry in the San Rocco valley near Naples. The Commission sent an LFN to Italy in June 1990, setting out a number of heads of infringement of EU waste legislation that it had identified, in particular a number of provisions of the original version of the Waste Framework Directive (WFD)[46] and the former Hazardous Waste Directive[47] (HWD). In particular, the Commission considered that the requirements of the WFD incumbent on member states to ensure that waste is recovered or disposed of without endangering human health and without using processes or methods which could harm the environment had been breached by Italy.[48] The Commission received a reply from the Italian government in 1992, which admitted that the San Rocco valley had been used for illegal waste dump-ing, including the disposal of biological and chemical waste from a local general hospital. It informed the Commission that a particular quarry in the local area used for waste dumping had been sequestrated in May 1990, only to be subse-quently reused as a fly-tip again in 1991 with the site operator consequently being prosecuted for breaching national waste management legislation.

Given that it did not receive any information from the Italian authorities about any follow-up measures intended to restore the San Rocco riverbed environment in conformity with EU environmental legislative (WFD and HWD) requirements relating to waste management safety, the European Commission decided in 1996 to issue Italy with an RO. By way of reply, the Italian government notified the Commission in 1997 of various initiatives that had been taken to restore the local environment, including: the sequestration of a number of sites in the valley pre-viously used for fly-tipping, the rechannelling of waste waters discharged by a local general hospital to a municipal sewer as well as the appointment of a spe-cial taskforce to draw up a plan for restoring the valley's riverbed. Subsequently, the Commission undertook checks to assess whether or not these initiatives were capable of restoring the environment in conformity with the WFD. In the light of a report it received from the municipality of Naples in 1997, it decided to press ahead with legal action and filed infringement proceedings before the CJEU. The Neapolitan report confirmed that pollution of the valley riverbed had intensi-fied and concluded that remedial measures were urgently required. As part of its defence, the Italian government submitted that the WFD had not been breached, on the grounds that at the time of the deadline for compliance with the RO the Commission had been unable to show that biological and chemical waste was still being discharged into the riverbed.

The CJEU dismissed the Italian government's arguments in defence, by effec-tively reversing the burden of proof in this instance. Given that the Commission had amassed sufficient evidence to prove that in the early 1990s hospital waste had been discharged into the San Rocco valley, including information to that effect gleaned from the Italian Environment Ministry's on-the-spot investigations in 1991–2, the CJEU held that it was for the Italian government to prove that the position had changed subsequently, namely to show that the riverbed was being fouled only by municipal waste water which is a waste stream not covered by the WFD and is addressed under separate EU legislation.[49] Accordingly, it found that that the Commission had established to the requisite legal standard that waste discharged into the valley did not solely comprise waste waters.

However, the CJEU has also established limits to which it will be prepared to accept *prima face* evidence of an infringement of EU law from the Commission. Specifically, it is not in principle prepared to allow the Commission to base its case upon what it terms a 'presumption' of fact. Each head of infringement must normally be based upon sufficient evidence. In environmental investigations, the distinction between a presumption of fact and an inference of fact that might be made logically from available evidence may be a very fine one to draw, and even an unrealistic one given the very real practical and legal challenges facing the Commission to be able to prove its case successfully. Nevertheless, the CJEU has held that presumptions of illegality are inadmissible, even where they may appear to be quite plausible in the circumstances. A good illustration of this difficulty may be taken again from the *San Rocco* case. In its statement of claim, the Commission had submitted that, given that the valley concerned had been subject to illicit dumping of waste in contravention of the WFD's provisions on waste management safety, it was reasonable to assume that the Italian authorities had also failed to organise supervision of undertakings involved either in the transport, collection, storage, tipping or treating their own waste or in the collection or transportation of waste on behalf of third parties in contravention of other WFD provisions.[50] However, the CJEU held that the Commission was barred from making what it termed to be such a presumption; instead, specific evidence needed to be garnered by the Commission that illicit dumping of waste in the area had been carried out by an undertaking or undertakings subject to supervision by the national authorities.

It appears questionable whether the conclusions drawn by the European Commission were unreasonable in the circumstances. The Commission submitted that it was not in a position to verify the identity of individuals involved in the fly-tipping, not least given the absence of investigatory powers and resources vested in its services for this purpose. In addition, the Court had already accepted that on the evidence illicit dumping of hospital waste had been carried out in the valley. It was highly unlikely that unauthorised entities had been solely responsible for all the damage caused, not least given that the type of waste found in the valley was hazardous medical waste, the management of which has been required to be subject to close supervision by national authorities under EU waste legislation since the end of the 1970s.[51] One could have expected the CJEU to shift the onus of proof to the Italian authorities to show that fly-tipping had been solely carried out by unsupervised entities, bearing in mind that the Commission was successful in proving its case that illegal dumping of waste had occurred. The CJEU's decision here might be explained by an overly cautious attitude on its part towards making judicial conclusions that could serve to impute culpability indirectly upon particular identifiable individual operators concerned with the management of hospital waste in the area. However, if that caution existed it was misplaced. From the available evidence, it was logical to conclude that the Italian authorities had failed to ensure adequate supervision of a particular hazardous waste stream, which the member states are obliged under EU law to carry out. Culpability of any individual operators involved in the collection, transportation and management of that waste would be a matter settled exclusively under national law, as directives do not have binding effects upon private individuals.

It should be noted in this context that the CJEU has relatively recently moved to relax the burden of proof on the Commission in certain cases where the latter has already provided ample evidence of widespread serious and persistent infringements of a similar nature in a defendant state. The CJEU will be prepared to conclude that a GAP breach of EU law exists in a defendant state upon production of proof from the Commission of the occurrence of several instances of similar types of infringements. If the CJEU makes such a judicial conclusion, the defendant state has the onus of demonstrating that the GAP state of affairs has been addressed for the purpose of successfully defending second-round infringement proceedings under Article 260(2) TFEU. GAP cases are considered below in section 3.4 of this chapter. This judicial development does not, however, remove the fundamental difficulties and challenges confronting the Commission in being able to verify allegations bad application of EU environmental law.

3.3.2 Investigations and the role of Article 4(3) TEU: duty of co-operation

Whilst the evidentiary burden is firmly on the Commission to prove its case, member states are under a general legal duty to co-operate with investigations and proceedings carried out under the auspices of Article 258 TFEU. The CJEU has confirmed that this obligation derives from the general provision on co-operation contained in Article 4(3) of the Treaty on European Union (TEU). Article 4(3) TEU, which has superseded Article 10 of the former European Community (EC) Treaty,[52] states:

> Article 4
>
> [. . .]
>
> 3. Pursuant to the principle of sincere co-operation, the Union and the member States shall, in full mutual respect, assist each other in carrying out tasks which flow from the Treaties.
>
> Member States shall take any appropriate measures, general or particular, to ensure fulfilment of the obligations arising out of the Treaties or resulting from the acts of the institutions of the Union.
>
> The Member States shall facilitate the achievement of the Union's tasks and refrain from any measure which could jeopardise the attainment of the Union's objectives.

This wide-ranging set of treaty provisions contains both a positive as well as negative element. Specifically, member states are obliged not only to desist from activities that would undermine the implementation of law and objectives existing under the auspices of the EU's founding treaties (negative component), but also to take active steps to ensure that legal obligations arising under the treaty are duly fulfilled (positive component). This duty of co-operation has come to the aid of the Commission in the context of a number of infringement proceedings, including environmental cases. For instance, in *Commission v Netherlands*[53] the CJEU found that the Netherlands had been guilty of infringing (the predecessor provision to) Article 4(3) TEU in failing to co-operate adequately with the Commission in the context of an investigation over implementation of the original Bathing Water Directive (BWD).[54] Specifically, the Netherlands had failed to provide the Commission with information about any steps taken to transpose the BWD. Article 12 of the original BWD required member states to notify the Commission within two years of its entry into force of those national laws, regulations and provisions designed to transpose the directive's norms into its national law. In its defence, the Dutch government submitted that implementation had been fulfilled, in that the relevant local authorities responsible for Dutch water management were directly bound by the provisions of the BWD. The CJEU dismissed this argument, underlining that member states are under a positive duty in accordance with Article 4(3) TEU to facilitate the achievement of the Commission's responsibility[55] to ensure that the EU's treaty provisions are applied. In this case, the duty of co-operation was crystallised in the form of a notification obligation contained in the directive itself. A failure to fulfil that obligation would entitle the Commission to commence Article 258 TFEU proceedings against the member state concerned.

The general duty of co-operation under Article 4(3) TEU has been of assistance to the Commission in the course of investigating suspected breaches of EU environmental law. A good example is the *San Rocco* case.[56] The CJEU took into account the former good faith provision contained in Article 10 of the EC Treaty in its judicial findings regarding the relevant responsibilities involved at national and supranational levels during the investigation of alleged breaches of EU environmental law. Specifically, the Court commented:

> [I]t is primarily for the national authorities to conduct the necessary on-the-spot investigations, in a spirit of genuine co-operation and mindful of each Member State's duty under . . . Article 10 EC to facilitate attainment of the general task of the Commission, which is to ensure that the provisions of the Treaty, as well as provisions adopted thereunder by the institutions, are applied.[57]

This judgment underlines the particular importance of the provisions in Article 4(3) TEU in securing active as well as passive assistance from member states in connection with the Commission's task to secure due application of EU environmental law. Passive assistance involves member states desisting from taking any steps that may obstruct Commission infringement investigations or proceedings; active assistance requires member states to ensure that they take steps to help the Commission determine the veracity of allegations of illegal conduct. In the absence of powers of investigation specifically vested in the Commission for the purposes of uncovering and following up alleged breaches of environmental norms, the general duties incumbent on each member state under Article 4(3) to take the necessary steps to ensure full implementation of EU law cannot be underestimated.

The CJEU has established that a number of duties on member states arise in connection with the detection and prosecution of infringements of EU law in accordance with Article 4(3) TEU. The Court has confirmed that the duty of co-operation in this context requires member states to ensure that they proceed in respect of EU law infringements with the same diligence as that which they bring to bear in implementing corresponding national laws.[58] In holding that

Article 4(3) TEU requires member states to take all measures necessary to guarantee the application and effectiveness of EU law, the CJEU has established that this includes ensuring that infringements of EU law are penalised effectively. This point was illustrated in *Commission v Ireland*,[59] where the Commission took infringement proceedings against Ireland for failing to legislate for adequate penalties for the purpose of enforcing particular animal welfare requirements required by EU legislation on animal experimentation for scientific purposes.[60] Whilst the relevant EU directive did not include any specific provisions on penalty provisions, Ireland had introduced pecuniary fines for breaches of the directive's requirements significantly below the threshold it set for other animal cruelty scenarios (some 200 per cent less). Notwithstanding the omission of specific provisions on penalty clauses in the directive, the CJEU confirmed that member states had a legal obligation under Article 4(3) TEU to ensure that infringements of EU law are penalised under conditions and terms analogous to the handling of infringements of national law of a similar nature and importance. The Court confirmed that, in any event, member states were obliged to ensure that the penalties laid down in respect of breaches of the EU legislative instrument were effective, proportionate and dissuasive. Thus, whilst the CJEU recognised that member states in principle retain choice over the particular mode of implementing an EU directive, it also ruled that the particular means used by states to deter, detect and sanction breaches of EU legislation is subject to the residual caveat that it must be an effective enforcement mechanism. The autonomy of member states in Article 288(3) TFEU (ex Article 249(3) EC) over the methods used to transpose EU directives into national law is thereby made subject to notable qualifications. This jurisprudence of the CJEU is particularly important in the context of EU environmental law, where effective sanctions are especially needed, not least given the marked lack of private interest, resources and possibilities to tackle infringements of EU environmental provisions through private law remedies. This latter point will be explored in Part II of this book.

3.3.3 European Commission discretion in deciding to take legal action

A key feature of the various powers vested in the European Commission under the TFEU in taking infringement proceedings against member states for breaches of EU law is that, as interpreted by the CJEU, the Commission has complete discretion in determining whether or not to commence or continue with legal action against a member state. The TFEU accordingly confers upon the Commission a certain amount of political leverage which it may use in deciding whether or not – or how far – to prosecute any particular case. It also enables the Commission to have some purchase on seeking to manage its own finite legal, administrative and financial resources as efficiently as possible in tackling instances of breaches of EU law.

This autonomy has enabled the European Commission in recent years to make the decision to set priorities for the purpose of managing suspected cases of breaches of EU law. In 2007, the Commission indicated in a Communication[61] that it would from now on in general be refocusing its infringement casework under Articles 258 and 260 TFEU to categories of breaches it considered represented 'the greatest risks, widespread impact for citizens and businesses and the most persistent infringements confirmed by the Court [of Justice of the EU]'.[62] It identified these as being:

- non-communication of implementing measures;
- breaches of EU law, including non-conformity cases, raising issues of principle or having particularly far-reaching negative impact for citizens, such as those concerning the application of EU treaty principles and main elements of framework EU regulations and directives; and
- failure to comply with CJEU judgments declaring the existence of infringements.

By way of follow-up, in 2008 the Commission announced[63] that it would apply this prioritisation with respect to the management of environmental infringements. This clarification of infringement strategy by the Commission was drawn up in the wake of prolonged internal debate within the Commission's services over possible moves towards decentralising the enforcement of EU environmental law so that, in particular, member state authorities would assume greater responsibility in respect of supervising its proper implementation. Relatively recently, two EU legislative initiatives have emerged addressing the subjects of civil and criminal liability for breaches of EU environmental law, which involve the imposition of specific responsibilities on national competent authorities to enforce EU environmental legislation. These are discussed in detail in Chapters 12 and 13. The European Commission has been less successful so far, though, in being able to promote greater access to justice for the public (including notably NGOs) at national level in order to assist in the implementation of EU environmental law.[64] This aspect is considered in Chapter 8.

The wide degree of discretionary power afforded to the European Commission over the launch of Article 258 TFEU proceedings is a double-edged sword, in that it may well bring with it problems of accountability and inefficiency, not least as the Commission has a monopoly over whether or not to launch and/ or continue with any proceedings. Moreover, whether or not the Commission decides to take infringement action in any given case may be crucial in terms of the relevant EU environmental legislative norm(s) being enforced, given that the possibilities for legal actions by private persons or national authorities may be limited. For instance, one might contrast the position regarding enforcement of EU environmental law with the legal and institutional infrastructure in place with respect to EU competition law, where EU legislation stipulates specific law enforcement obligations to national authorities whilst providing for the retention of far-reaching investigative and sanctioning powers for the Commission.[65] These issues are discussed in Chapter 5.

3.3.3.1   Legal justification needed for bringing an action before the CJEU

The CJEU has confirmed that success of any particular infringement action will be determined according to whether objectively there has been a breach of EU law by the close of the deadline set to reply to the Commission's final written warning, namely the deadline set for responses to the RO. All other factors are in principle irrelevant to the outcome of such litigation.

The Court has confirmed that the motives for the Commission's legal action are irrelevant in assessing its legitimacy. This was illustrated in *Commission v UK*,[66] in which the Commission took legal proceedings against the UK over alleged failures to implement EU legislation[67] on value added tax (VAT). The Commission considered that the UK had provided zero-rating on VAT in respect of certain services for various social reasons not permitted under the terms of Union rules. The UK countered by submitting that the Commission was seeking to use infringement proceedings for political reasons, namely to bypass the requirement of a unanimous vote in the Council of the EU which would be needed for an amendment to the rules on VAT exemption. The CJEU dismissed the UK's arguments, confirming that it was not for the Court to comment upon the particular objectives pursued for the purposes of infringement proceedings, only to determine whether or not the member state had failed to comply with its EU obligations, the launch of Article 258 TFEU proceedings being at the discretion of the Commission.[68] This line of jurisprudence leaves the Commission effectively free to prioritise particular types of cases, for legal or policy reasons. As mentioned earlier in this section, in 2008 the Commission decided[69] to introduce a system of focusing infringement casework on certain types of cases, partly in order to ensure that the caseload remained within Commission resource capabilities but also to devolve greater responsibility to member states for addressing bad-application complaints.

The CJEU has also confirmed that it is no defence to an infringement charge that not all member states have been treated equally from an enforcement perspective. For instance, this was confirmed in another infringement case against the UK[70] in which the Commission claimed that the UK had violated EU common fisheries rules in having unilaterally extended its fishing exclusion zones. The UK authorities submitted that the infringement action should be struck out on the basis that the Commission had previously failed to take legal proceedings against other member states for similar infractions. The CJEU held that it is for the Commission alone to assess whether or not it is appropriate to commence an enforcement action. In practice, though, the Environment Directorate-General of the Commission, which has overall responsibility for managing environmental infringement casework, has made it clear on a number of occasions that litigation against member states will be conducted upon an equal treatment basis. In particular, each member state's record on transposing EU environmental directives into national law is tracked and monitored on an equal basis. League tables are regularly published by the Commission to indicate relative performance between the member states on transposition performance across environmental legislative sectors. The Commission has on a number of occasions launched infringement proceedings against several member states simultaneously, where it finds that states have failed to honour a particular transposition deadline. Recent notable examples include action taken against several member states over failures to communicate transposition[71] of the EU Ambient Air Quality Directive[72] and over non-implementation of key aspects of the EU Water Framework Directive,[73] such as the cost recovery principle[74] and establishment of national water management plans.[75]

The above case law provides the Commission with a good deal of flexibility when deciding to take infringement proceedings against any particular member state, allowing it to use litigation as a last resort if other channels of dispute resolution of a faster and more informal nature may be found.

3.3.3.2 *Temporal aspects: delays in taking legal action and historical breaches*

Article 258 TFEU does not prescribe any specific deadline by which the Commission must decide whether or not to commence infringement action. The CJEU has also confirmed that there are no express or implied limitation periods which apply. Accordingly, as a matter of legal principle there are no specific deadlines by which the Commission must decide whether or not to take legal action. Even where the Commission has taken a considerable period of time (months, even years) either to decide to launch proceedings or to process the pre-litigation phase, the Court has dismissed arguments from defendant member states that an action should be barred on grounds that such substantial delay is tantamount to procedural impropriety on the part of the Commission.

For instance, in *Commission v France*[76] the Commission had decided to take action against France on account of its failures to abide by fishing quota restrictions allocated to it for the years 1988 and 1990 under the auspices of the Common Fisheries Policy (CFP). Specifically, the Commission submitted that France had failed to monitor the quota level and had omitted to take penal measures against French enterprises contravening those conservation measures. By the time the matter came to Court, some ten years had elapsed. This was largely due to the Commission having taken some seven years to complete the pre-litigation stage of proceedings. The French government pleaded that the action should be declared inadmissible, submitting that such a delay on the Commission's part in handling the proceedings deviated from the objective of Article 258 TFEU to secure compliance with EU law. However, the CJEU dismissed this argument, holding that the rules pertaining to the operation of Article 258 did not oblige the Commission to act within a specified period.[77]

In the absence of any evidence to show that the unusual length taken in processing the case during pre-litigation stage undermined the rights of the defendant, the CJEU has confirmed that the admissibility of the action will not be put into question.[78] There is no specific statute of limitations that applies in respect of Article 258 TFEU proceedings. This was underlined in *Commission v Belgium*[79] where the Commission decided to initiate Article 258 TFEU proceedings against Belgium in March 1981 over failures in transposing the Sixth VAT Directive.[80] The Commission's legal action was launched over three years after the time

(December 1977) when the Belgian government had notified its national rules intended to implement the EU tax rules. Whilst it had communicated its objections by informal letter in November 1979, the Commission had waited until the directive entered into force for all member states before examining compatibility issues. The CJEU ruling underlines that the Commission will not be estopped from taking action even if a significant period of time elapses between when it is informed of a breach and when it formally launches litigation.[81] This element of flexibility is useful in allowing the Commission a broad opportunity to be able to negotiate with a member state behind the scenes with a view to achieving, where possible, a workable friendly settlement. Not only does this bring the advantage of avoiding the embarrassing publicity of legal proceedings for the state concerned, it also allows the Commission to be able to prioritise its resources on targeting and processing proceedings on the most serious infractions. Given the large number of complaints over member states' failure to protect the environment that are regularly sent to the Commission, it is important that the Commission has the possibility of following up these appropriately. In some instances, an immediate LFN will not be warranted, for instance because of lack of verification of the statement of complaint, the real prospect that the member state may offer a solution without the need for recourse to litigation or the fact that a case on a key legal point is currently being adjudicated upon by the CJEU.[82] In these circumstances, more time may well be needed before a definitive view may be taken on whether Article 258 TFEU proceedings are required.

The CJEU's case law also confirms that the Commission is not *per se* barred from taking action against breaches of EU law that are purely historical, namely infringements that are not ongoing at the time when the proceedings are commenced and/ or when the matter is brought before the Court. The general position established by the CJEU is that a member state will be held liable for a breach of EU law if it has not remedied the position by the time the deadline set by the Commission's RO has elapsed.[83] One might consider that this principle might render legal proceedings taken against member states for historical breaches of EU law problematic. However, the CJEU has confirmed that the Commission may take states to court for such breaches so long as the Court is presented with objective evidence of an infringement having taken place at some point in time. For instance, in *Commission v Greece*[84] infringement proceedings were taken against Greece over failures by the state to supply the Commission with information relating to fishery prices during a particular time period. Such information was necessary for the Commission to establish an EU guide price for fish products imported into the Union for the purposes of the CFP. The Greek government argued that the infringement should be considered inadmissible on grounds of being of merely of historical interest, given that an entirely new time period was in place for managing the current CFP at the material time when legal proceedings were brought before the CJEU. The CJEU rejected that submission, holding that it was for the Commission alone to assess whether it was appropriate to launch infringement proceedings in any given case, bearing in mind the Commission's discretionary power to decide whether or not to institute such proceedings for a declaration of illegality on the part of the member state concerned.[85]

On the other hand, the European Commission will not continue to pursue proceedings against a member state where the EU legislation concerned has been repealed prior to the case coming to court so that the relevant provisions are no longer in force in some form or another. However, if the relevant legislative provisions have simply been included without changes into new successor legislation, then the pleadings simply have to be amended accordingly without proceedings having to be commenced afresh. These points arose in the *San Rocco* litigation,[86] where during the course of the proceedings legislative amendments had been made to the EU's original Waste Framework Directive (WFD).[87] The CJEU confirmed that the Commission would be able to continue to rely on the WFD's provisions cited at the commencement of its action so long as their scope had not been altered by the amendment made to the Union directive, even if they may have been relocated in the amended legislation so as to have different article numbers. The CJEU has confirmed in a case against Portugal concerning a failure to implement the former EU Waste Oils Directive[88] that the Commission is barred from relying upon any legislative requirements that have arisen since the initiation of the Article 258 TFEU procedure against a defendant state, given that this would extend the material scope of the infringement claim retrospectively.[89] Accordingly, the Commission is obliged to commence a fresh infringement action in the event of non-compliance by a member state with Union legislation which has been introduced to amend existing EU legislation, (even) where the state is already subject to ongoing infringement proceedings on account of its alleged failure to adhere to the existing EU legislative requirements.

In an environmental protection context, that the Commission retains the right to bring an action against member states for historical breaches of EU environmental law is an important factor. It may be the case, for instance, that a particular incident of illicit pollution that member states fail to address in accordance with their EU legislative obligations may have been cleared up or have dissipated prior to the Commission being notified of its existence (e.g. dumping of waste in the marine environment, failing to supervise emissions from a particular installation over a specified period properly). This would be no bar to the Commission being able to take legal action once appraised of the facts and evidence of an infringement. If member states were able to avail themselves of a defence of the breach being a 'historical' infringement, this would potentially undermine the scope and potency of Article 258 TFEU proceedings in relation to bad-application cases. Member states would effectively be able to excuse themselves from failing to take measures to prevent or address breaches of environmental law, however serious, by submitting that they had subsequently taken remedial measure to rectify the position. The CJEU case law would appear to confirm that the Commission may seek to bring an action in order to uphold provisions of EU law as a matter of legal principle. It may be the case that the Commission might wish to take a member state to court in respect of a particularly serious breach of environmental legislation, which may have long-term adverse impacts for public health and/ or the environment. An example would be, for instance, failures on the part of a member state to take steps to minimise the effects of an oil or chemical spillages in marine environs. A case in point would appear to be the 2002 sinking of the *Prestige* oil tanker in the Bay of Biscay near Spain and Portugal. Both countries, fearing for the safety of their local fishery reserves, ordered the tanker out to sea away from their coastlines, notwithstanding that the ship's crew had appealed for emergency assistance after reporting leakages of oil and a failed engine. In the event, the tanker sank a few days later some 200 miles away in the Atlantic, with a total loss of oil cargo. Wind and tidal forces soon forced the spill to land onto the Galician and French coastlines with severe effects on coastal marine life, particular wild birds, as well as local fishing and tourist sectors. Within the Environment Directorate-General of the Commission, the question arose as to whether legal action should be initiated against Spain and Portugal for failing to minimise oil pollution waste in accordance with the terms laid down in the EU's Waste Framework Directive,[90] such as taking the oil tanker into a local port as advised by the expert salvage team on location at the time. In the event the Commission services decided not to bring legal proceedings, preferring to take action instead to subsidise those governments' coastline clean-up operations. The Commission, however, would have been perfectly entitled to take action even though the steps taken by the member states were not of an ongoing nature.

On the other hand, not all historical breaches of EU environmental law may be caught. In particular, if a member state manages to prove the absence of or remedy to an infringement of EU environmental law before the elapse of the deadline for compliance within the RO set by the Commission, then the action will fail. In *Commission v Germany*[91] the Commission had taken action against Germany over failures in various parts of its territory to adhere to minimum environmental protection standards prescribed by the EU's original Bathing Water Directive.[92] The German government sought to defend itself before the CJEU by arguing that, by the time the action had come before the Court for a hearing, the various bathing sites alleged to have infringed the directive had either been sufficiently cleaned up in accordance with the terms of the directive or closed. Due to the fact that these steps had not occurred within the deadline set by the RO, the Court held that they did not cure the infringement.[93] However, had the German government completed these measures before that deadline, then the outcome would have been different. Thus, although the state of the environment on a closed beach would not have met agreed environmental protection standards, the member state would have been able to avoid liability.

3.3.3.3 *Collegiality and Commission decision-making*

Another significant element that goes to make up the wide degree of discretion afforded to the Commission in relation to Article 258 infringement proceedings is the very limited degree of scrutiny in law and practice that its internal decisions concerning case management have been subjected to. At a formal level, though, this would not appear to be the case from inspection of the constitutional position.

Under the TFEU system, Commission decisions over whether or not to commence, progress or terminate legal proceedings against a member state are formally taken at College level, namely by the Commissioners themselves acting on a collective basis. Specifically, it is foreseen in the treaty that Commission decisions are to be taken on the basis of a majority of the Commissioners (Article 250 TFEU); action pursued by the Commission on any other footing would be *ultra vires*. Accordingly, each stage of the litigation process has to be ratified by the College of Commissioners.[94] That the College itself, as opposed to the Commission's services (namely Directorates-General), is invested with the responsibility of decision-taking is a particular crystallisation of the principle of political accountability and balance of institutional powers crafted into the legal framework of the Union. The Commissioners are made accountable to the other key political EU institutions (principally the European Parliament (EP), European Council and Council of the EU) in various ways under the EU treaty system notably by virtue of: the quinquennial appointments process of the Commission controlled by the European Council and EP (Article 17(3) and (7) TEU); European Parliamentary powers to subject Commissioners to questions, to receive and assess annual reports from the Commission of its activities as well as to censure and force resignation of the College (Articles 230, 233 and 234 TFEU respectively); and power by the Council of the EU to force compulsory retirement of individual Commissioners in the event of the latter's misconduct or incapacity to perform duties (Article 247 TFEU).

However, in practice, most infringement case management is processed, to all intents and purposes, far from the collegiate level of Commissioners and instead within the internal European civil service system of the Commission itself. Environmental casework is principally handled within the relevant legal units within the Commission's Environment Directorate-General (DG ENV), which at the time of writing are housed within Directorate D (Implementation, Governance and Semester).[95] Infringement cases concerning EU climate change, the 1957 European Atomic Energy Community (Euratom) Treaty law and legislation are similarly processed by legal teams within the relevant DGs, namely the Directorate-General for Climate Action (DG CLIMA)[96] and Energy Directorate-General (DG ENER)[97] respectively. The various legal teams within the Commission's services focusing on environmental infringement casework assess which next steps should be taken regarding the litigation process in individual cases; their proposals are then forwarded through the administrative hierarchy to College level for ratification. In practice, Commission officials handling infringement cases are in regular contact with desk officers responsible for oversight and development of specific EU environmental policy areas, for the purpose of liaising on specific issues and information arising in connection with interpretation as well as national implementation of EU environmental law.

Substantive legal analysis of casework is accordingly conducted more or less exclusively at the level of the DG. The Commission College rarely, if ever, conducts its own legal assessment on proposals forwarded to it on infringement decisions. In practice, such proposals are usually adopted on the nod at collegiate level without independent verification or substantive debate amongst Commissioners. However, occasionally the Legal Service of the Commission may be referred to for advice in the event of any internal dispute amongst or within Commission services over whether a member state has violated EU law. The Legal Service is attached to the Secretariat of the Commission, a Commission service independent of any particular DG and falling under the direct supervision of the Commission's Presidency. The view taken by the Legal Service is usually regarded as definitive and final. Its legal opinions, just like those of the Commission's services in general, are not considered by the Commission open to review by the public[98] and there is no formal way of knowing if its services for a second legal opinion have been requested or knowing to what extent its opinions prevail in any particular case.

Whilst on paper the Commissioners must authorise European Commission legal action on the basis of a majority vote, it is rare for this to happen in practice. The vast majority of formal Commission decisions over Article 258 and 260(2) TFEU litigation are made without any substantive debate or exchange of views at Commissioner level. Such decisions are channelled upwards through the Commission service hierarchy ultimately to the Commission's Secretariat General, before being classified usually as items on the agenda of a College meeting not requiring oral debate. They are normally subject to a purely 'written procedure' and are signed off on paper only by the College without substantive debate. The internal decision-making practices of the College of Commissioners are not open to public scrutiny; all that appears on the public record is that a College decision has been reached. However it appears fairly clear from available (mostly anecdotal) evidence that the principle of majority voting is not applied or expected to be applied, particularly in the context of decisions over infringement proceedings. Instead, a culture of consensus appears to prevail in terms of College decision-making. First, there appears to be a basic working presumption that, bar special or unusual circumstances, issues concerning infringement proceedings are anticipated to be outwith the sphere of usual political negotiation and that Commissioners with portfolio for the particular policy sector concerned are to take a lead role. Hence, the practice has developed to favour a written procedure classification for litigation items. Secondly, if a major dispute does arise within the Commission over whether to pursue legal action against a member state, a culture of consensus has appeared to surface traditionally at collegiate level so that effectively a minority within the college may hold sway and block litigation. However, given the secrecy that attends Commission voting procedures, it is nigh impossible to analyse the political dynamics involved in such cases or to make any safe generalisations that policy factors do not interfere with decisions on individual cases. What comment may be made safely is that the element of voting coupled with the fact the fact the Commission is also responsible for policy development at EU level is a combination that is inappropriate for the purposes of law enforcement. Some decisions over litigation may actually or potentially become susceptible to compromise by unrelated broader political considerations (e.g. trade-offs in relation to current/pending policy initiatives or instruments). Whilst it may be argued that such conflicts of interest are remote from surfacing in practice, it is nevertheless the case that the current institutional set-up remains vulnerable to the accusation that it is unable to establish a system of ensuring consistent impartiality of decision-making on law enforcement issues. More work and reflection needs to be done here on ensuring that there is a clearer and more accountable functional separation made within the Commission between decisions on policy development and individual operational decisions on law enforcement.

The manner in which the European Commission has come to process infringement proceedings has itself been questioned before the CJEU. From a formal perspective, the CJEU has confirmed that decision-making on the part of the Commission in relation to law enforcement under Articles 258 and 260(2) TFEU necessarily implies equal participation on the part of Commissioners, collective deliberation and no possibility of decisions being delegated (e.g. to individual Commissioners).[99] However, the case law has also made it clear that collective decision-making on the part of the Commission may also be passive in nature. For instance, in litigation over compliance with the original version of the Bathing Water Directive,[100] the German government submitted that the principle of collegiality at Commissioner level had been breached when the College came to issue Germany with an RO.[101] Specifically, Germany considered that the RO had been issued *ultra vires* in that the Commission was unable to demonstrate that all the Commissioners had been aware of the operative part of or the reasons underpinning the draft Commission decision to issue Germany with an RO, at the time when the College met to decide how it should proceed. Collegiality, in the German government's view, implied active collective deliberation. In contrast, the CJEU employed a more flexible test of collegiality, holding that this principle would be observed as long as the members of the College had available to them all the information that would assist them in adopting a decision to issue an RO. Whether and to what extent individual Commissioners followed up this information at the College meeting was accordingly immaterial. This judgment effectively legitimises the practice within the Commission for the College to leave, in most instances, active responsibility for case management decisions in the hands of individual Commissioners according to political portfolio, with passive endorsement from the rest of the College. Whilst the form suggests collegiality, the substance indicates legitimisation of *de facto* delegated responsibility.

In fact, it is not even clear that individual Commissioners necessarily have command over the processing of infringement proceedings concerning EU legislation falling within their particular policy area portfolio. As far as environmental casework is concerned, all proposals for next steps in litigation matters are made at the level of the legal units and/or teams dealing with infringements at Directorate-General level. In practice, for instance, the Environment Commissioner is rarely in any position to query proposals for next steps made by DG ENV, not least given the fact that s/he does not usually have the time or resources to do this. The Commissioner's group of advisers (cabinet) is not staffed with a team dedicated to inspect litigation issues, and in any event the Commissioner's primary agenda is usually filled with considerations pertaining to policy development. Reliance is placed in practice upon the Commission's services, in this case the legal and relevant technical units within DG ENV, to do the day-to-day job of monitoring member state implementation of EU environmental law and following this up where necessary. The author knows of no initiative for proposing litigation against a member state over contravention of EU environmental legislation that has originated from a Commissioner's office.

3.3.3.4 Commission immunity from judicial review proceedings

A central feature of the discretionary nature of Articles 258 and 260(2) TFEU proceedings is the degree of legal immunity afforded to the Commission vis-à-vis any legal challenges launched against decisions on its part either to commence or desist from taking action against a member state. Legal challenges have been made in the past on the basis principally of two types of legal proceedings set down in the EU treaty framework, namely annulment proceedings (Article 263 TFEU) and action for a failure to act (Article 265 TFEU). The position of the CJEU has been robust in seeking to safeguard the discretionary power of the Commission as to whether to launch an infringement action, by minimising the rights of defendants or third parties to interfere with a Commission decision. Accordingly, in principle any Commission decision over the commencement of infringement proceedings will not be subject to judicial review, either at national or supranational levels.[102] The Commission is vested with sole control over determining whether or not to take legal action under either Articles 258 or 260(2) TFEU. This legal area is considered in detail in Chapter 9, which assesses the various rights available to private persons under EU law to subject Commission environmental decision-making to independent scrutiny.

The jurisprudence from the CJEU which provides the European Commission with judicial immunity is problematic. From a legal perspective, the narrow judicial interpretation adopted by the Court does not accord with the fact that the Commission has a definitive obligation set out in Article 17(1) TEU for the Commission to ensure that its provisions and measures are duly applied. The jurisprudence of the CJEU though effectively provides the Commission with little or no risk of its decisions over law enforcement being held to account. It is highly questionable whether those drafting the original EU Treaties intended that infringement provisions (such as now Article 258 TFEU) should have this effect. It is also difficult to see how the CJEU's case law complies with the obligations set down for it under the foundational EU treaty framework to ensure that the rule of law is maintained, specifically those set out in Article 19 TEU which stipulate the Court of Justice 'shall ensure' that the 'law is observed' in the application and interpretation of the EU Treaties. The legal position as it stands places a great deal of trust in the Commission to be able to follow up infringements of EU environmental law objectively, without political factors interfering with its management of Article 258/260(2) cases. Such trust may be misplaced, given that the Commission has overtly political functions to fulfil in its capacity as an EU institution. The stance taken by the CJEU over immunity is even more questionable when one considers that the Commission has concurrent responsibility for the development of policy as well as enforcement. Under the interpretation provided by the Court, the Commission may not be held to account for purely political decisions to desist from taking legal action against a member state.

The jurisprudence of the CJEU, as has been outlined in this section, confirms that the Commission is vested with a good deal of flexibility and power when deciding to take infringement proceedings against any particular member state, allowing it to use litigation as a last means of resort if other channels of dispute resolution of a faster and more informal nature may be found. However, in certain respects the fact that the Commission retains a monopoly over triggering infringement proceedings and discretion over determining the individual circumstances required to justify such action is problematic. These factors raise questions about whether the Commission is sufficiently accountable, both legally and politically, for its actions on the litigation front. Given that the Commission has a considerable degree of responsibility also for the development of environmental policy and legislation at Union level (having a monopoly over proposing environmental legislative initiatives under the EU treaty framework), it is questionable whether the Commission should also be granted the executive responsibility of law enforcement from a separation-of-powers perspective. The legal system provides little in the way of safeguards for preventing the Commission taking or, more importantly, desisting from taking infringement proceedings for predominantly political reasons.

3.3.4 Letter of Formal Notice (LFN): the first written warning

The LFN constitutes the first formal stage in infringement proceedings under Article 258 TFEU. Essentially the LFN is an initial formal written warning from the Commission to a particular member state, placing the latter on notice that the Commission considers on the evidence made available to it that there has been a violation of EU law within its territory. Whilst Article 258 does not refer specifically to the LFN as being the starting point of legal proceedings, this may be deduced logically from the wording of that provision. The text only refers to the Commission's RO. However, the RO may only be issued 'after giving the State concerned the opportunity to submit its observations'; logically, this means that the Commission has to place the member state on formal notice of its views and provide a genuine opportunity to address them prior to the delivery of the RO. The LFN fulfils this function.

3.3.4.1 Purpose and degree of precision of the LFN

The LFN constitutes the formal commencement of legal proceedings under Article 258 TFEU. Effectively, it is the trigger for the commencement of legal action that ultimately may result in a declaration of illegality from the CJEU under Article 258 TFEU and, if the case concerns non-communication of a national transposition measure of a legislative directive, even financial penalties for the defendant member state concerned.[103] Failure to comply with an Article 258 judgment may also ultimately lead to the imposition of financial penalties via second-round infringement proceedings under Article 260(2) TFEU. The potential consequences for defendants are therefore serious, in terms of implications for their reputations relating to upholding the rule of law and credibility in defending EU agreed policy but also from a financial perspective. Bearing this in mind, the CJEU has carved out a number of important legal principles that underpin the workings of Article 258 TFEU proceedings, in particular specifying particular legal consequences that flow from the issuing of an LFN.

The CJEU has established that the LFN constitutes the basic legal document that serves to frame the scope of the legal action itself. Case law confirms that the letter must delimit the subject matter of the legal dispute, convey this information to the member state concerned and invite the latter to submit its observations. Accordingly, the LFN must be drafted with sufficient clarity and precision in order to enable the defendant state to prepare for its defence.[104] This means that the Commission not only has to be sufficiently precise about its allegations of illegality, delineating facts and relevant EU norms that it alleges have been breached, it is also barred from extending the material scope of its action at a subsequent stage in the same proceedings. This is so even if it finds new evidence of related breaches at a later stage. In that event the Commission is obliged to commence a separate legal action with respect to any new allegations of infringements. Failure to comply with these elemental requirements will inevitably result in the action being declared inadmissible by the CJEU if the matter comes to court. The chief concern of the CJEU is to ensure that the defendant has had sufficient opportunity to address each legal challenge raised by the Commission, and not be surprised by any new heads of infringement presented at a late stage in proceedings. The Court is particularly strict on safeguarding the procedural rights of the defence.

Accordingly, the Commission has to take care when drafting the terms of the LFN to ensure that its allegations are neither too vague nor too narrow. In certain environmental cases this should not pose a problem, namely cases where a member state fails to transpose EU environmental norms into national law where this is required (notably in the case of EU environmental protection directives). The Commission must, though, ensure that its LFN covers the particular dispute. For instance, in an action against the UK[105] over alleged failure to implement the original version of the Drinking Water Directive),[106] the UK argued that the Commission had drawn up the terms of infringement in the LFN as focusing only on the standard of water quality in private water supplies. Given that subsequent to the issuance of the LFN the CJEU had ruled in a judgment[107] that private water supply was a matter excluded from the remit of the directive, the UK submitted that the action should be ruled inadmissible. However, the CJEU agreed with the Commission's counter-submission that the LFN had in fact made a general complaint concerning non-implementation of the directive by the UK, and had not restricted itself to addressing the subject of private water supply, which was mentioned in the letter only by way of example. Accordingly, the action was ruled admissible, although the particular heads of infringement referring to private water supply would have to be dropped. The point clarified here by the CJEU is that the Commission is not entitled to extend the scope of its legal action beyond that which it sets out in the LFN. Specifically, the RO and/or subsequent court proceedings must not include heads of infringement which have not already been referred to or are otherwise covered within the terms of the LFN.[108] The CJEU has also confirmed that usually the Commission is obliged to specify in its LFN the particular provisions of EU law it considers have been breached. In one infringement case against Denmark[109] the Commission had simply referred to a failure by the member state to transpose a particular EU directive into national law in the LFN. Exceptionally, the action was declared admissible on account of the fact that in pre-litigation correspondence the member state had received advice from the Commission of its particular concerns, with relevant details of the directive's provisions alleged not to have been transposed into Danish law.

In certain types of environmental disputes between the European Commission and a member state, the details of the infringement will be self-evident. These are the so-called non-transposition cases, where the Commission finds that a state has failed to ensure that an EU environmental protection directive has been properly transposed into national law. The defects of the national implementing measures will usually be evident from their texts (such as ambiguous wording, wording which only partially transposes an environmental directive or wording which overtly contradicts EU legislative requirements). As already mentioned, the CJEU has confirmed that the Commission need not prove in practice as well as in form that implementation of a directive has been defective.[110] In non-transposition cases, the drafting of a sufficiently clear and detailed LFN will usually be a relatively straightforward affair.

However, in cases where the Commission considers that a member state has failed to ensure respect for EU environmental norms in practice (instances of 'bad application'), it usually is far more challenging for the Commission to be in a position to provide precise details of breaches of EU environmental legislation by the time it wishes to issue an LFN. The Commission has no independent mandatory investigatory powers either to follow up and verify complaints of particular incidents of environmental pollution notified to it from the general public or to launch own-initiative inspections or site investigations binding on national authorities or private entities it may consider needed as a result of information gleaned elsewhere (e.g. scientific reports or journal articles). It may receive information from an external source that is incomplete or otherwise yet unsuited to constitute sufficient evidence to prosecute a particular member state. Notably, the information received from the general public may be very general and/or short on substantial detailed evidence. Hard evidence on the source and/or nature of pollution may be difficult to come by. Pollutants may be difficult to identify and source without specialist knowledge, equipment and/or powers to search sites such as industrial premises. The Commission is, accordingly, in most instances fundamentally reliant on the co-operation of national environmental authorities and ministries of the defendant member state concerned to assist it in its investigation of allegations of factual non-compliance with EU environmental law. It may well be faced with a situation at LFN stage where it considers that there might have been a breach of EU environmental legislation in light of the information it has received, but is not in a position to completely verify all the details of the instant case and accordingly requires further investigation and explanation to be carried out at local level by the member state authorities which are responsible for implementation of EU law at national level.[111]

If the LFN in a bad-application case had to detail in precise terms all the specific details of alleged infringements of EU environmental law, this would effectively place the Commission in a catch-22 situation. Such a precise account would in practice only be feasible with the active co-operation of national investigatory authorities. However, those authorities would only be required to deliver this information if they were faced with a specific case to answer (i.e. an LFN). This issue was addressed to some extent in the *San Rocco* case,[112] where the Italian government submitted that the Commission had provided an insufficiently clear description of alleged illegal waste dumping activities in its LFN, with the consequence that it was unable to prepare its defence. The Commission countered by submitting that it had issued a sufficiently precise statement of claim in referring to the general location of pollution (the upper San Rocco valley), the manner of its generation (uncontrolled fly-tipping) and relevant EU environmental provisions that had been breached. The CJEU agreed with the Commission, holding that the LFN in general may not be subject to equivalent strict requirements of precision as is the case with the RO, given that the initial warning cannot contain anything other than an initial brief summary of the complaints concerned. According to the Court, an LFN would satisfy the degree of precision required if it identifies the factual circumstances and relevant specific EU norms relating to a state's alleged non-compliance so as to enable the defendant to present a defence against the infringement claim.[113] This important judgment underlines the requirement of active participation that is incumbent upon member states to verify instances of alleged infringements of EU (environmental) law; they may not simply sit back and wait for the Commission to provide definitive proof. The *San Rocco* case effectively confirms that the Commission is able to trigger environmental infringement proceedings on the basis of information that points towards a *prima facie* case of non-compliance, whereupon it is up to the member states to demonstrate satisfactorily to the Commission that proceedings are unwarranted (e.g. by showing that the allegations are factually inaccurate or satisfying the Commission that adequate steps have been taken to rectify the situation).

It may be the case that as proceedings develop, more information and evidence comes to light that may require a refinement of the original statement of claim filed by the Commission in its LFN. The CJEU has confirmed that the Commission is entitled to further delimit (i.e. narrow down) its claims of infringement as proceedings progress, but not the other way around.[114] A delimitation may be warranted for a variety of reasons. For instance, the defendant member state may alter its behaviour so as to comply with certain provisions of EU environmental legislation, which may well render redundant the need to continue to pursue a particular head or heads of infringement. For instance, in the *San Rocco* case the Commission abandoned its initial claims of non-compliance with Article 7 of the original version of the EU Waste Framework Directive[115] after Italy had taken steps to establish a waste management plan for the region as required by that provision. Likewise, proceedings will have to be refined if the

EU legislation concerned is substantively amended or repealed during the course of pre-litigation with the effect that a specific legislative obligation no longer pertains in its current form.[116]

3.3.4.2 Defendant's observations regarding the LFN

It is a formal procedural requirement of Article 258 and 260(2) TFEU proceedings that the defendant member state has a genuine opportunity to submit to the European Commission observations on the LFN. Essentially, the observations stage provides the defendant member state with the first real opportunity to prepare and deliver any available lines of defence in response to the charges of illegality alleged by the Commission. Whilst the treaty text does not specify a specific deadline by which defendants must reply, the CJEU has held that the Commission is implicitly obliged to allow the defendant a reasonable period to reply to the LFN, this to be determined in the light of the particular circumstances of the case.[117] Accordingly, very short periods may be justified in certain circumstances, especially where there is an urgent need to remedy a breach or where the defendant state is fully aware of the Commission's views long before the pre-litigation procedure is actually commenced.[118] However, the Commission is not entitled to allege that there is an urgent situation when it is partially or fully responsible for failing to take action earlier.

The possibility available to the Commission of being able to process legal proceedings expeditiously brings with it several potential benefits for the purposes of enhancing the effectiveness of EU environmental law enforcement. For non-transposition cases, the CJEU's case law would appear to suggest that relatively short deadlines could be provided to defendants to require relevant changes to be made to national law so that the latter would come into alignment with the particular environmental directive(s) in issue. Typically, member states are provided with a substantial period of time between formal adoption of an environmental directive and the deadline it stipulates by which transposition has to have occurred into national law. Given that such directives commonly contain clauses requiring member states to provide the Commission with details of implementation measures, it is quite likely that a state will know in advance of the transposition deadline the Commission's views as to whether its national implementation measures are in conformity with the particular EU environmental directive. Substantial periods of time granted for transposition of directives is a key factor that points in favour of allowing the Commission to be able to provide defendant states with relatively short deadlines to reply to an LFN and an RO in non-transposition cases.

Occasionally, the Commission may be confronted with a particularly urgent situation in a bad-application case that requires fast-tracking of litigation. For instance, this could involve a situation where a planned project development threatens to encroach upon a protected habitat. Unless the Commission is able to turn around legal proceedings relatively swiftly, the development may have already completed the planning process and be constructed or in the process of being constructed, with all the irrevocable consequences that this may bring to a particular habitat of protected wild species.

Until fairly recently the practice of the Commission was not to set particularly rigorous deadlines for responses to the LFN and RO during the pre-litigation stage of most environmental cases. Typically six months was usually the minimum period allowed by it for a defendant to reply to an LFN for Article 258 environmental cases until around the turn of the millennium, and not infrequently this could have been up to one year. However, current practice of the Commission now sets a tighter standard time limit of two months for a response to either an LFN or RO. In addition, the Commission has also the possibility to apply to the CJEU for interim relief in urgent cases, a procedure which is discussed below in section 3.6.

The CJEU has clarified that any observations sent by member states must be taken into account by the Commission if the latter decides to progress to the next stage of pre-litigation, namely the RO stage. Accordingly, even if a state has failed to meet the deadline set for observations on an LFN and sends in belated submissions to the Commission, these will nevertheless have to be taken into account in the RO. A fresh RO will have to be issued if the existing one does not take the state's observations on board, even if the Commission considers that the submissions do not provide any convincing defence to the alleged heads of infringement.[119]

3.3.5 *Reasoned Opinion (RO): the second written warning*

The issuing of an RO by the Commission to a defendant member state constitutes the most significant step of the pre-litigation phase of Article 258 TFEU infringement proceedings. It is designed to be a second and final written warning to a defendant member state to take the necessary measures to rectify a breach of EU law in the member state's territory within a deadline set by the Commission. Typically, the breach may be ongoing (e.g. defective implementation of a directive). Alternatively, it might be historical due to the unsatisfactory state of implementation or enforcement of EU law at national level, in which case the Commission's interest in taking any action is in seeking to prevent a reoccurrence in the future. The issuing of an RO signals that there is a final opportunity for the defendant to take steps to avoid having to face proceedings before the CJEU and thereby arrive at a friendly resolution of the dispute. In contrast with the LFN, the RO bears more distinct and significant legal consequences in the event of a failure by a member state to heed its admonitions. Specifically, if a defendant member state fails to take remedial measures in respect of the complaints set out in the RO within the deadline set by the Commission, then the defendant will be liable if the facts and evidence are borne out before the CJEU at the subsequent stage in proceedings.

For both parties the RO represents a cornerstone of the entire litigation. The RO stage may be divided essentially into two parts: namely the issuing of the opinion followed by a window of opportunity for the member state to take action in response. If the defendant member state accepts the Commission's arguments that a breach has occurred, it must seek to take measures within the deadline set by the Commission for a satisfactory response in order to ensure that the proceedings will be dropped against it. Alternatively, the defendant state may consider the Commission's case ill-founded, in which case it must submit its defence (known as 'observations') to the Commission within the set deadline. If the defendant member state fails to provide the Commission with a satisfactory defence to the complaints within the set period, the Commission may decide to apply to the CJEU for a ruling on the matter.

3.3.5.1 *General requirements and effects of the RO*

The RO constitutes a key legal document for the purposes of infringement proceedings and the European Commission needs to pay particular care to draft its contents with sufficient precision. Failure by the Commission to crystallise its statement of complaint in the RO in accordance with legal requirements is liable to render an application to the CJEU inadmissible and set back a successful prosecution of litigation a considerable period of time. In this sense the RO may be contrasted with the LFN, which need only set out the Commission's complaint of breach in basic and general terms.

CONTENT OF THE RO

The CJEU has confirmed that it is the RO, and not the LFN, which constitutes the formal foundation of the legal action and is to crystallise the specific subject matter of any proceedings brought before it under Article 258 TFEU.[120] Accordingly, all the various heads of infringement of EU environment law identified by the Commission in a particular case need to be set out definitively and precisely in the RO. The CJEU has confirmed that it must contain a coherent exposition of the reasons that have led the Commission to conclude that the defendant member state has failed to fulfil an obligation under the TFEU. Whether or not an action is well founded will ultimately turn upon an objective finding of a failure to fulfil an EU legal obligation on the defendant's part. Liability is strict in the sense that the Commission need not have to demonstrate specific intention or negligence on the part of the State in jeopardising or omitting to effect due implementation of EU law.[121] Accordingly, a member state may not be able to shrug off blame for a breach of EU environmental law on account of internal difficulties, such as constitutional problems associated with decentralisation of responsibility for environmental affairs at sub-national level or lack of parliamentary time to enact national transposition legislation.

The central task of the Commission is to prove ultimately to the satisfaction of the CJEU on the balance of probabilities that the defendant member state has committed a breach of EU law and has not remedied the particular legal defects concerned within the deadline set for compliance in the RO. The CJEU has confirmed that it is not incumbent upon the Commission to specify to the defendant in the RO or elsewhere the necessary measures required in order to remedy the breach of law. Instead, the duty to identify and carry out remediation falls squarely upon the shoulders of the defendant who must seek to convince the Commission that further pursuit of infringement proceedings is no longer warranted.[122]

DEADLINE FOR COMPLIANCE

Culpability will ultimately turn upon whether there in fact is a breach of EU law committed as at the time when the opportunity for the defendant member state to deliver observations on the RO has elapsed. It is, therefore, no defence for a member state to assert after this point in time that the breach has been remedied; the legal action will not fail on this ground. As a matter of fundamental legal principle, the European Commission is entitled to bring an action to the CJEU under Article 258 TFEU to obtain a judicial declaration that a member state has failed to adhere to EU law by end of the deadline set for responses to an RO.[123] For instance, in a case against Germany over its failure to ensure that environmental impact assessments would be carried out in relation to extensions of thermal power stations in contravention of the Union's environmental impact assessment legislation,[124] the CJEU dismissed the German government's submission that the proceedings were devoid of purpose on the grounds that, subsequent to the RO, German legislation had been introduced to remedy the particular deficit in national implementation rules. The Court held that the Commission is alone competent to determine whether it would be appropriate to pursue court action against a member state. It need not have to demonstrate any specific special interest in bringing proceedings before the CJEU in such circumstances. Effectively, the Court has recognised the legitimate role of the Commission in holding member states to account for any failure to remedy a defective state of national implementation of EU law after the defendant concerned has been sent two formal warnings and has not responded in sufficient time.

The LFN and RO need not necessarily be identical to one another. There is nothing to prevent the European Commission setting out in the RO in more detail the general complaints it initially registers in the LFN, such as specifying particular provisions of the EU legislation identified as being in issue or setting out more precise legal argumentation.[125] With respect to environmental cases involving a failure to transpose legislation correctly, in practice there will not be any significant difference between the contents of an LFN and RO, for the Commission will be seised of all the relevant information in order to be able to set out its case at first written-warning stage. However, in cases involving bad application of EU environmental legislation, it may well be the case that the Commission will need to receive and assess the information to be gleaned from the defendant's observations to the LFN and other available investigatory work before being in a suitable position to issue a definitive statement of complaint in the form of an RO. Requiring the LFN and RO to be identical would constitute an unreasonable procedural hurdle for the Commission to overcome. Given that the Commission has no powers to investigate instances of practical breaches of EU environmental legislation, it is often heavily reliant upon the co-operation of the member state

and its environmental authorities to submit to it the particular details and information about the activities occurring at national level which have been placed in
question. Frequently, the only realistic way of inducing member states to assist in
investigatory work on behalf of the Commission is to compel them to act by virtue
of opening Article 258 TFEU proceedings. As mentioned earlier, the CJEU has
recognised that member states are under a general legal duty to co-operate with
the due enforcement of EU law under Article 4(3) TEU.

TAKING INTO ACCOUNT EU MEMBER STATE RESPONSES TO THE LFN

As a matter of general principle, the European Commission is obliged to take
into account replies filed by member states to LFN when drawing up the terms
of the RO. Where the Commission fails to do this, it is at risk of rendering
further pursuit of legal action inadmissible. This is especially the case where the
member state's response the LFN has a clear bearing on assisting the Commission to delimit the subject matter of the case. For instance, in one case against
Spain[126] the Commission had sent an LFN to Spain in August 1993 on account
of its failure to ensure timely transposition of a particular telecommunications
directive.[127] The Spanish government sent to the Commission by registered post
a reply in October 1993 notifying it of imminent fulfilment of certain provisions
of the EU legislation. Due to what the Commission later described as communication problems, the RO, issued in February 1994, failed to respond to the Spanish observations and stated that the Commission had received no formal reply
from Spain. The Commission decided to pursue proceedings to the next stage,
by applying to the CJEU for a ruling, notwithstanding another reply from Spain
in March 1994. The Commission contended before the CJEU that in the event
no procedural irregularity on its part had been committed, given that it took into
account the Spanish replies to the RO in the course of the judicial stage of proceedings (through the reply and rejoinder). Moreover, the Commission submitted
that the defendant's replies failed in any case to exculpate the member state from
the charge of failing to transpose the directive into national law. In its view, the
replies only referred to partial transposition of the EU legislation. However, the
CJEU ruled the action inadmissible, on the grounds that the definition of the subject matter of the dispute had only been clarified during the course of the judicial
stage of proceedings and not in the RO. According to the Court, the Commission
should have examined the Spanish responses and then delivered a second RO
specifying the complaints it intended to maintain.[128]

A special situation may arise in non-transposition cases where the defendant
member state notifies the Commission of newly adopted national legislation
intended to address the Commission's complaints. Whilst the Commission is
obliged to consider whether the defendant's new measures satisfactorily address
the alleged breaches of EU law, the fact that the member state may have repealed
earlier national legislation identified as source of the breach(es) does not *per se*
mean that the proceedings are blocked from progressing to the litigation phase.
The Commission remains entitled to pursue the infringement action to the next

phase if the more recent succeeding national legislation fails to ensure correct transposition; the change of legislative source will not be deemed to have effect an alteration to the subject matter of the legal dispute between Commission and defendant.[129] If it were otherwise, as recognised by the CJEU, member states would be able to halt the progress of litigation and require the Commission to start proceedings afresh simply by notifying a slight amendment to existing national law during the course of the pre-litigation phase. This is a sensible judicial clarification that serves to remove any prospect of an abuse of process by defendant member states using unwarranted stalling tactics. The CJEU[130] has confirmed that this principle also applies with respect to second-round infringement proceedings under Article 260(2) TFEU, which are discussed in detail in Chapter 4.

SUBSEQUENT AMENDMENTS OF THE RO

After issuing the RO, the Commission may not amend its complaint at a later stage in pleadings before the CJEU to include additional related allegations and arguments concerning infringements, even if evidence is available to support additional claims of illegality. The subject matter of an application brought before the CJEU is determined by the RO and both legal documents must be founded upon the same grounds and submissions.[131] As a matter of principle any extension to the scope of legal proceedings must be conducted by way of fresh litigation, namely by issuing a separate LFN. Accordingly, any discovery by the Commission of additional new heads of complaints which are related to the instant legal proceedings against a member state after the RO has been issued may not be included in the same action at a later stage.[132]

On the other hand, in the relatively rare event that the Commission is able to launch or finance its own on-site investigation of a complaint, this step may be used to check the veracity of a member state's defence and/or bring itself up to date on the factual state of a particular site prior to progressing further with litigation. This may be particularly useful where proceedings become protracted. An example of this was in the *San Rocco* litigation[133] where the Commission took Article 258 TFEU proceedings against Italy in 1990 over failures to prevent illegal depositions of hazardous and non-hazardous waste taking place in the San Rocco valley near Naples, contaminating local riverbeds in contravention of EU waste management legislation. In 1992 the Italian government replied to the initial LFN by stating that the site area had been sequestrated in 1990, before being reused as a waste tip whereupon the operator concerned had been prosecuted. The Commission received no communication from the Italian authorities for some four years about progress on implementation of measures to rehabilitate the site in accordance with the requirements of the EU's waste management legislation.[134] In July 1996 the Commission issued Italy with an RO. In January 1997 Italy replied with a list of measures that it had undertaken to deal with the fly-tipping problem, including establishment of a waste management plan for the area, further sequestration of the site in September 1996 and establishment of a local taskforce. Not satisfied with this reply, the Commission decided to organise its own independent investigation in 1997 to verify the state of the site area. The investigation confirmed that Italy still had not complied with the Commission's original complaints. The CJEU held that, in such circumstances, the findings of the investigation did not constitute a fresh complaint for the purposes of enforcement litigation under Article 258 TFEU.

3.3.5.2 Defendant's observations regarding the RO

It is an integral part of the RO stage that the defendant member state be afforded an opportunity to submit to the European Commission a formal response to the complaints laid out in the Commission's opinion (known as observations). In effect, the time limit set for a response constitutes a deadline for achieving compliance on the part of the defendant member state. The response filed by the member state will be with a view to seeking to settle the dispute, if possible, out of court. The nature of the legal framework underpinning Article 258 TFEU infringement proceedings provides the possibility for plaintiff and defendant to work towards a friendly 'out of court' settlement of the dispute. Accordingly, even where a member state may be clearly in breach of a provision of EU law and not be in a position to remedy the defective state of national implementation of the EU norm, it is within the power of the Commission to decide nevertheless to desist from further legal action if it considers that the member state will secure compliance at a later date. Alternatively, it may decide to suspend proceedings until compliance actually materialises. In practice, the Commission will follow the latter option where, for instance, the member state promises that national implementing rules are forthcoming or in a legislative pipeline. By suspending as opposed to closing proceedings the Commission will seek to keep up the pressure by maintaining the 'live' status of legal action, as and until it is satisfied that compliance at national level has in actual fact occurred. This may, for instance, be by way of issuing the defendant state with a second RO, if the period for response to the first RO has elapsed.

PERIOD FOR OBSERVATIONS TO BE SUBMITTED

Just as in the case with respect to the LFN, Article 258 TFEU does not specify a particular maximum or minimum period by which time a defendant member state must submit observations in relation to an RO. The treaty wording is open-ended and has always been so. Case law of the CJEU, though, has established a general principle that the time afforded for a response should be a reasonable period, this to be determined in accordance with the circumstances of the particular case at hand.[135]

The European Commission services usually set a time limit of two months now in the context of a first-round environmental action. Prior to the turn of the millennium, though, time limits were usually substantially longer, typically six months, and it was not uncommon for a period of a year or longer to elapse before the proceedings progressed to the next stage, in the event of an unsatisfactory response to the statements of complaint set out in the RO. According to CJEU case law there is no reason why the time limit set by the Commission for observations may not be relatively short. This may be so where the defendant member state has already had a substantial period to ensure that national legislation is compliant with EU law. A couple of examples serve to illustrate this point. In one case Portugal[136] had failed to transpose an open tender procedure for a particular public sector telephone exchange contract in accordance with a 1977 directive.[137] Upon receiving an LFN in September 1987 two years after it had joined the EU, it disputed that the particular contract (supply to airport traffic control agency) fell within the scope of the relevant EU legislation. The ensuing RO, issued in November 1988, requested Portugal within one month to bring its national implementing rules into compliance with the terms of the directive. The CJEU confirmed that, in the circumstances, one month was not an unreasonable deadline, given that the Commission had brought the matter to the defendant's attention already one year previously and that Portugal had disputed liability from the outset. In another case Luxembourg[138] contested the reasonableness of a four-month deadline set by the Commission in an RO. Luxembourg was in breach of the EU treaty provisions on the free movement of workers[139] in reserving a number of civil servant positions exclusively for its own nationals. Aware of the problem at least since the early 1980s, by virtue of a Commission Communication on the subject[140] as well as a number of related rulings from the CJEU, the state nevertheless failed to take any action. An LFN was issued in March 1991, giving Luxembourg six months to reply. Luxembourg replied almost a year later, submitting that it had already applied the free movement provisions in a wide range of fields. The RO, issued in July 1992, gave the defendant state four months to comply. When the dispute came before the CJEU, Luxembourg submitted that the four months' compliance period set out in the RO was unreasonably short in the circumstances, given that it would have to enact a series of legislative measures at national level in order to bring its domestic legal system into compliance with EU law and that this would take a considerable period of time. In dismissing the defendant member state's arguments, the CJEU took into account the length of time that Luxembourg had known of the Commission's position, the fact that Luxembourg had made it clear that it was not going to undertake legislative reform and that the four-month period was double the length of the standard period for observations granted by the Commission.

In recent years, the Commission appears to have begun to put more effort into accelerating the deadlines it sets for defendant member state responses to its formal warnings in the pre-litigation phase. This is particularly so with respect to non-transposition cases, in respect of which the legal and evidential issues are usually relatively unproblematic from the Commission's perspective and where there is no justification for any lengthy deadline period.

The case law of the CJEU has made it clear that the Commission may even impose shorter time limits than two months for compliance with an RO. The Court has established that very short time periods may be justified in particular circumstances, especially where there is an urgent need to remedy a breach or where the member state is fully aware of the Commission's position long before the commencement of legal proceedings. In one case where Austria had failed to ensure public tendering procedures were in place as required by EU legislation,[141] the CJEU held that periods of one week to reply to an LFN and two weeks to comply with an RO were justified given that a number of relevant public tender contracts were yet to be awarded by the Austrian authorities which fell under the auspices of the EU tendering rules. In another case, the Republic of Ireland[142] was given just five days after receipt of an RO to terminate its ban on imports of poultry meat and other products from EU countries that vaccinated their livestock. The Irish Republic had employed a non-vaccination policy on poultry meat since 1938. The RO was issued less than two months after the initial LFN. Even though the CJEU voiced disapproval of the Commission's conduct as being unreasonable in principle, the Court nevertheless held the infringement action to be admissible as the Commission had in fact taken in to account the Irish government's observations which were submitted some time after the five-day deadline (in fact one and three months). Had the Commission in fact only allowed five days for compliance, the proceedings would have been held inadmissible, as this would have meant that the Commission could have demanded immediate amendment to national legislation notwithstanding the fact that it had neither seen fit to signal its concerns regarding the legality of Irish legislation beforehand nor shown that this was an exceptionally urgent case.

The admissibility of very short time limits may be valuable in certain types of environmental cases where urgency may be a prevalent factor. Specifically, in cases where EU environmental law has been identified by the Commission as having been incorrectly implemented in practice (i.e. bad application), a very short time limit for compliance specified in the RO (and LFN) may be useful in inducing a defendant member state to introduce measures so as to minimise or eradicate pollution arising from a breach or to prevent activities that may have irrevocable consequences for the environment. Examples of particular urgency in an environmental protection context could include member state failures to carry out an environmental impact assessment prior to development on a particular site in accordance with the Environmental Impact Assessment Directive 2011/92,[143] or failures to respect habitat protection norms under the Habitats Directive 92/43.[144] Failures to control or restrict illicit activities on protected habitat sites may have irrevocable adverse consequences for wildlife, such as the undermining or destruction of breeding areas and/or food resources.

Articles 258 and 260(2) TFEU of themselves do not provide the European Commission with specific powers to require the cessation of particular illicit activities. However, pending the delivery of a judgment under Articles 258 and 260 TFEU, the Commission may seek to obtain interim relief from the CJEU in order to require a defendant member state to cease illegal activity. This particular legal procedure is discussed in section 3.6 below. There is some evidence to suggest that the Commission has been prepared, relatively recently, to use interim relief in urgent cases involving suspected infringements of EU nature protection legislation,[145] such as in relation to illicit hunting of protected bird species. The efficacy of this mechanism is heavily dependent upon the Commission being informed in good time about prospective or actual illicit conduct. The lack of investigatory powers afforded to the Commission coupled with lack of direct co-ordination between environmental protection authorities at national and EU levels may often mean that infringement proceedings are commenced at a relatively late stage, hindering the chances of using Article 258 TFEU proceedings as a means effectively to prevent the commencement or continuation of illicit activity.

The CJEU has made it clear that the reasonableness of the time limit set for submission of observations will depend upon the circumstances. In particular, the conduct of the Commission in steering proceedings is relevant in this regard, as underlined by the Court in a case against Belgium over discriminatory university tuition fees.[146] In this case, in the wake of preliminary ruling in *Gravier*[147] in February 1985 holding the Belgian rules on tuition fees to be contrary to EU treaty provisions prohibiting discrimination on grounds of nationality, the Commission sought belatedly to follow up this ruling by obtaining a declaration from the Court confirming the illegality of the Belgian fee system prior to the commencement of the academic year 1985/6. The Belgian system was slightly amended with new rules promulgated in mid June 1985. However, these amendments merely required reimbursement of fees charged to non-Belgian students who had brought legal proceedings prior to the *Gravier* judgment. Having issued its LFN in July 1985, the Commission sought to justify very short response deadlines given to the defendant state on grounds of urgency (eight days to reply to LFN and 15 days to submit observations in respect of the RO). However, when the matter came before the CJEU, the Court held the action to be inadmissible on the grounds that the brevity of the time limit for observations was unjustified in the circumstances; the Commission could have commenced legal proceedings immediately after the *Gravier* judgment, i.e. long before July 1985. Neither had it indicated unequivocally to Belgium before July 1985 that it considered the Belgian rules as amended to be contrary to EU law, and thus the defendant could not be said to be sufficiently aware of the Commission's view in advance. In addition, the Commission had failed to respond to a request from the Belgian government for an extension to the set time limit for responding to the LFN. The fact that the Commission considered these deadlines in practice not to be absolute and would have taken into account any replies from the defence was irrelevant for the CJEU.

TAKING INTO ACCOUNT THE MEMBER STATE'S OBSERVATIONS

Once the European Commission has received a response from a defendant member state to the complaints set out in the RO, it will seek to take them on board before deciding whether to pursue the infringement proceedings to the next level, namely the judicial phase. The object of the pre-litigation phase is to provide an opportunity for the two parties to come to an out-of-court settlement by achieving a mutually acceptable solution, where this is possible. Not infrequently, however, member states submit observations after the deadline stipulated in the RO. The question arises as to whether the Commission is obliged nevertheless to take such submissions into account prior to filing an application for a declaration before the CJEU. The CJEU has confirmed that the Commission is entitled to proceed to the judicial phase in these circumstances, where an opportunity is provided for the defendant's submissions to be heard.

This issue arose in an environmental infringement action taken against the Netherlands,[148] where the latter had failed to notify the Commission of sufficient number of special protection areas (SPAs) for the purposes of the EU's Wild Birds Directive.[149] A dispute arose between the parties as to whether the observations had been submitted by the defendant out of time, the Commission having claimed not to have received them within the two-month time limit it had specified. Nevertheless, the Commission argued that it had taken them on board when crafting its application to the CJEU, in particular recognising that three new SPAs had been included within the Dutch total. The Commission maintained, however, that the defendant's observations did not have a material bearing on the complaints set out in the RO. The CJEU rejected the Dutch claims of inadmissibility on this point, in holding that the defendant's fundamental procedural guarantees of a fair hearing had not been undermined, given that the Dutch government had ample opportunity to raise its arguments during the litigation phase of proceedings and for them to be assessed by the Court itself. Ideally, the Commission should have issued another RO, but the fact that it did not do so did not vitiate the proceedings. One may compare this judgment with the relatively stricter approach taken by the Court in relation to belated replies to an LFN, where the Court has held that these must be taken into account by the Commission if they have a bearing on the Commission's ability to delimit the complaints of non-compliance set out in the RO.[150] On the other hand, the case law may be explained by the fact that the elapse of the deadline for responses to an RO is qualitatively different from that applicable to an LFN. Notably, the former constitutes the point in time where any future remedial action on the part of the defendant has no effect upon the outcome of proceedings. If the defendant member state is in breach of EU law by the time the period for observations to the RO has expired, then automatically the Court will make a finding of illegality when the matter comes to the contentious phase in proceedings.[151]

3.4 The litigation phase: application to the CJEU

The pre-litigation phase is terminated once the period for submitting observations in respect of an RO has elapsed. The Commission must then take a decision (formally speaking it is the College of Commissioners to decide) whether or not to proceed to the next phase of proceedings. The filing of an infringement case application to the CJEU by the Commission constitutes the commencement of the second and final phase of Article 258 TFEU infringement proceedings known as the litigation phase.

3.4.1 Contents of the Court application

As with the RO, the application to the CJEU must meet basic requirements of precision and completeness. Article 21 of the Statute of the CJEU[152] stipulates that the application must contain, *inter alia*, the subject matter of the dispute, the relevant submissions and a brief statement of the grounds upon which it is based. Failure to meet these formal requirements will render the action inadmissible, and a cross-reference to the contents of the LFN or RO will not suffice.[153] The complaints set out by the Commission in the application must be those specified together with relevant evidence as submitted at RO stage. The case law of the CJEU has confirmed that no new legal claims may be filed by the Commission before the CJEU after the termination of the pre-litigation phase. The application to the Court for a declaration of illegality must mirror the terms of the RO, or more precisely must not extend beyond the remit of the complaints set out in the RO.[154] The Commission is not entitled to add related complaints to the action during the litigation phase, even in situations where this may not have been possible so to do at an earlier stage. Accordingly, even if it elucidates evidence of a breach of EU environmental law distinct from other complaints it has already specified in an RO in relation to a particular site, it is barred from incorporating such evidence and new claim of a violation of EU environmental law into its application to the Court. The CJEU has applied this procedural principle with particular vigour.

This point may be illustrated in a number of environmental cases. One example involved action taken against the Netherlands[155] over transposition failures concerning the EU Wild Birds Directive.[156] The complaint set out in the RO had focused solely on the fact that the defendant had failed to notify a sufficient number of special protection areas for wild birds to the Commission as required by the Union legislation. The CJEU held it to be inadmissible for the Commission to introduce fresh submissions at the court application stage that the dimensions to particular SPAs notified to the Commission were inadequate from an ornithological perspective (specifically the extent of notified fresh water lakes, marshes and moorland). Such heads of complaint of a qualitative nature should have been specifically crystallised already in the RO together with those concerning quantitative-type compliance failures, with a view to enabling the defendant to respond at pre-litigation stage to these particular allegations. The Court was unmoved by the Commission's submission that the qualitative aspects of its complaint against the defendant state only served to underline its contention that a breach of the EU directive had been committed, namely a failure to notify a sufficient number of SPAs. On the other hand, the CJEU did not question the admissibility of the Commission specifying only at application stage two particular sites that should have been notified as SPAs. Although references to these sites did not appear in the RO, the Court considered that they were merely examples of the failure of the defendant to classify a sufficient total area of SPAs.

In another environmental protection case, the Court confirmed that any evidence that the Commission may glean from investigations carried out on its or a third party's behalf regarding the environmental state of a site after delivery of the RO may only be used to confirm the veracity of a specific complaint set out in the RO itself.[157] If the investigation reveals evidence of a separate head of infringement, then the Commission must commence separate infringement proceedings.[158] The reasoning of the Court here is rather unconvincing and formalistic to say the least, given that it is inconceivable that most of the key measurements if not the findings of a major study of this kind would not in all probability have been extrapolated prior to the period running up to the delivery of the RO[159] and taking into account that the defendant state would have had the opportunity to respond to the study's findings during the litigation phase. However, the CJEU has demonstrated its keenness to uphold to the letter the principle it has established that the application must not introduce distinctly new evidence or legal complaint into the proceedings.

Where the Commission has referred to a particular complaint sufficiently clearly in the pre-litigation stage, and most importantly in the RO, then it will be able to carry this through to the contentious phase. In a case against the Republic of Ireland over the original version of the EIA Directive[160] (Case C-392/96 *Commission v Ireland*), the Commission submitted that the defendant had transposed the directive in a defective manner. Specifically, it asserted that by applying absolute minimum thresholds in relation to the regulation of certain types of development projects (peat extraction, afforestation and use of uncultivated land), Ireland had failed to ensure that its domestic rules respected the requirements of the directive, which stipulates that projects having significant effects on the environment must be subject to an impact assessment. Part of the Commission's complaints concerned the fact that the Irish rules on implementing the directive failed to address the problem of cumulative impact of small development projects located in the same area. However, the RO did not expressly refer to the issue of cumulative impact. According to the CJEU, though, this particular head of complaint was nevertheless ruled admissible in the application to the CJEU, given that the Commission had addressed this particular issue clearly in the text of the RO as part of the general problem resulting from threshold setting. The fact that it had not specifically used the words 'cumulative effects of projects' was accordingly immaterial.

3.4.1.1 *Applications for a finding of general and persistent (GAP) breaches of EU law*

Where the European Commission is taking legal action in relation to a series of similar types of bad-application infringements with a member state, the CJEU has recognised that the Commission may seek to claim a general and persistent (GAP) practice of non-compliance by a member state, thereby relieving the Commission of having to provide details of every single instance of alleged violation in the court application. This was first recognised in 2005 by the CJEU in its ruling in *Irish Waste*.[161] In that case the Commission had filed an infringement action against the Republic of Ireland over a number of instances of fly-tipping contrary to EU waste management legislation.[162] In its judgment, the CJEU held that, in addition to being able to declare non-compliance in relation to each specific instance of EU law having being violated, the Court has jurisdiction to declare (at the request of the Commission) in parallel a finding of non-compliance because member state authorities have adopted a general practice of a repeated and persistent failure to adhere to one or more specific obligations under Union law.[163] As with all infringement claims, the Commission shoulders the burden of proof and may not rely on any presumptions of illegality,[164] in this context having to show to the satisfaction of the CJEU that there is evidence of either repeated breaches of EU law or that the defendant member state authorities have engaged in a repeated and persistent practice of breaching Union law.[165]

This judicial development has, though, enabled the Commission to ratchet up the pressure on member states to address systemic failures to ensure compliance with EU (environmental) law. Significantly, a GAP declaration in an Article 258 judgment by the CJEU is a distinct judicial finding of non-compliance in itself, requiring a defendant member state to take steps to address it in order to avoid the prospect of a second-round action being launched against it under Article 260(2) TFEU. That task is arguably far more challenging than having to deal with individual instances of bad application of EU law. The fact that a member state may be able to solve a few instances of breaches of EU law after first-round judgment may not be sufficient to demonstrate it has overcome a general and persistent state of non-compliance. In order to be successful in proving to the CJEU that a GAP state of affairs for the purposes of a second-round infringement action under Article 260(2) TFEU, the Commission is required to show sufficient evidence of the continuation of repeated breaches of EU law or of the defendant member state authorities having maintained a repeated and persistent practice of breaching Union law.[166] That need not involve having to show that individual violations of EU law identified in the first-round judgment persist. Instead, evidence of continuation of a GAP breach could conceivably be illustrated by the occurrence of a number of breaches arising after the date of the first-round judgment. Accordingly, a defendant member state seeking to address a GAP first-round ruling must show to the satisfaction of the Commission and ultimately the CJEU that, subsequent to the (first-round) Article 258 TFEU judgment it has taken measures to ensure that instances of non-compliance are no longer widespread or systemic. As has been noted elsewhere,[167] the development of GAP rulings may come to have a significant deterrent effect on member states being prepared to tolerate widespread breaches of particular EU environmental legislative obligations, given the fact that member states face considerable evidentiary challenges to disprove the continuation of GAP breaches for the purposes of second-round infringements (when financial penalties may be imposed).

The innovation of GAP rulings also introduces a welcome degree of flexibility as well as realism into the management of first-round infringement cases involving claims of serial offending by a member state. In particular, the CJEU has confirmed that the fact that a defendant member state may have remedied one or more specific examples of violations prior to delivery of the CJEU judgment under Article 258 TFEU does not (necessarily) affect the subject matter of the dispute as being characterised as a general and persistent failure to comply with EU law.[168] Moreover, the CJEU has confirmed that the Commission is entitled to adduce in the litigation phase fresh evidence of non-compliance in order to underpin its case of a GAP breach by the defendant state.[169] It will not be barred from so doing, merely on the grounds that this specific allegation was not cited in the RO.

Subsequent to the ruling in *Irish Waste* the Commission brought a number of infringement cases against member states in the environmental sector[170] and other sectors[171] in which the CJEU has confirmed GAP breaches. The GAP ruling is set to become an important legal tool in the Commission's armoury against infringements of EU environmental law, notably against instances of systemic non-compliance by a particular member state.

3.4.2 Temporal aspects of the litigation phase

Logically, one might expect that the litigation phase should not take up a significant amount of time, bearing in mind that both parties will have already had ample opportunity in the pre-litigation phase to prepare and present their legal arguments in relation to the substance of the case and that liability arises when the period for submission of observations to the RO has elapsed. However, until relatively recently environmental infringement proceedings were almost invariably subject to a relatively elaborate litigation phase that served to draw out the processing of litigation considerably. For instance, Krämer has calculated that the average time taken for the litigation phase for environmental infringement cases brought before the CJEU in 1998–9 was some 20 months.[172] In its annual report on proceedings for 2013,[173] the CJEU stated that the average duration for the litigation phase applicable in general to direct actions (the vast majority of which include Article 258 TFEU proceedings) filed before it in 2012 and 2013 was 19.7 months and 24.3 months respectively.

The principal reason why a particular infringement action may take several months in the litigation phase is usually accounted for by the fact that the phase will have been subject to the maximum number of procedural stages envisaged under the relevant CJEU rules of procedure.[174] The full procedure at litigation phase encompasses a number of steps. First, it is envisaged that both parties have the opportunity to engage in a further exchange of legal argument in the litigation phase (by way of a reply and rejoinder to the court application). Secondly, an oral hearing is usually expected to be convened before the Court in plenary session after this written correspondence. Other member states are vested with automatic legal standing to act as interveners during this phase. Specifically, they may submit legal arguments relating to the case at hand, which may be taken up by the CJEU in its assessment of the dispute; however, they will not be entitled to raise a plea of inadmissibility which has not already been set out in the forms of order sought by the defendant.[175] Thirdly, if the full litigation procedure envisaged for infringement cases is followed, an advisory opinion is issued by one of the Advocate Generals assigned to the case prior to the CJEU's definitive judgment. Such opinions, which are not formally binding on the CJEU, are usually issued some months after the oral hearing. Whilst the opinion is technically not binding, in practice the majority of CJEU judgments concur with the Advocate General's submissions. If all the above procedural features are deployed, they will accumulate and contribute to a considerable period of time being used up by the litigation phase. As the date in Table 3.4 above (section 3.2.3) indicates in relation to environmental infringement cases brought before the CJEU between 2010–12, where Advocate General opinions are used in environmental infringement cases the litigation phase may take in the region of 25 months or more.

However, the overall situation has become more nuanced in recent years as the CJEU has increasingly sought to reduce the number of procedural stages within the litigation phase where possible. Specifically, the CJEU has now managed to reduce the time taken for the litigation phase considerably for those cases which do not involve complex or novel points of law. This has been achieved in a number of ways. Notably, the CJEU has made increasing use of its power to proceed without recourse to an Advocate General's opinion in appropriate cases, notably in cases not involving contested points of legal interpretation.[176] As Table 3.4 shows, the absence of such an opinion reduces the litigation phase considerably to around 12 months. The reduction in use of Advocate General opinions in environmental casework has resulted in a reduction overall in the average turnaround time for all environmental infringement cases determined by the CJEU. Table 3.4 indicates this to be around 15 months (taking into account data on CJEU judgments made between 2010–12). The CJEU has also used other means at its disposal to reduce the litigation phase, including questioning the parties as to whether they consider it necessary to have an oral hearing[177] as well as determining judgments which are subsequently published in summary form. Typically, a CJEU judgment on an environmental infringement case which has no novel points of law (e.g. questions of legal interpretation) may usually be expected now to be published only in summary form as a court report.[178] Initially, judgments will be published in the CJEU's official *Curia* website[179] only in a few official EU languages, notably the working language by the Court (French) and the language of the case (language of the defendant member state)[180] before eventually being published subsequently in all the official languages in the European Court Reports. These procedural innovations have been no doubt instrumental in the Court achieving an average of around seven months for the litigation phase in non-transposition cases involving the environmental sector, as indicated above in Table 3.4.

3.5 Common defence submissions in environmental infringement proceedings

The range of legal defences available to a member state in the context of Article 258 TFEU constitutes a fundamental component of the legal structure underpinning infringement proceedings at EU level. To what extent the scope of legitimate defences is defined will have an impact in terms of contributing to the degree of stringency and overall effectiveness of legal proceedings. From an environmental protection perspective, the deterrence value of law enforcement is an important factor that goes hand in glove with the aim of securing due implementation of EU environmental norms by member states within their respective jurisdictions. The more likely infringement proceedings are to be conducted efficiently and swiftly with an effective result at the end of the legal process, the more likely

it is that member states will prioritise resources into implementing their environmental commitments correctly in the first place.

There is, however, a sensitive and sometimes difficult balancing of interests to
be weighed in this context, namely ensuring on the one hand that law enforcement action represents a real and effective response to illegitimate conduct on the
part of member states whilst on the other hand upholding the basic rights of the
defendant to a fair hearing and due process. In the context of environmental protection disputes between the Commission and member states under Articles 258
and 260(2) TFEU, the body of law that has been developed on this front has been
principally developed by the CJEU. The TFEU and EU environmental legislation
are, to all intents and purposes, mostly silent on the issue of defences to complaints
of breaches of EU environmental law. This situation may be contrasted with the
legal framework concerning some other key policies of the EU, such as in relation
to free movement of the factors of production, competition or common commercial policy where the EU treaty framework expressly provides instances of possible
lines of defence (see e.g. Articles 36, 52, 62, 72, 106–7 TFEU). The CJEU has
developed its body of jurisprudence on the rights of the member state defendant
in Article 258 TFEU proceedings broadly in line with the evolution of fundamental rights recognised as being an inherent necessary safeguard in the context
of litigious processes. The 1950 European Convention on Human Rights and
Fundamental Freedoms (ECHR) has been influential in this regard. The CJEU
has focused on the need to uphold in particular basic procedural rights of the
defendant member state, such as the right to a fair hearing and the right not to
be subject to retrospective prosecution. Such rights have received constitutional
recognition in the form of the Charter of Fundamental Rights of the European
Union,[181] now an integral component of the legal fabric of the EUs constitutional
framework by virtue of Article 6 TEU as amended by the 2007 Lisbon Treaty.
The EU's institutions are bound by the Charter as are the member states, the latter insofar as when they 'are implementing Union law'.[182]

In the context of Article 258/260(2) TFEU infringement actions, the CJEU has
stressed the need for the European Commission to observe high standards of procedural propriety and for there to be a genuine opportunity for the member state
to be in a position to raise a comprehensive defence to the statement of complaint
set out by the Commission. We have already seen above that the Court has taken
a strict view of the need for adherence to procedure and form by the Commission
during the pre-litigation stage. The Court has adopted a more lenient position in
relation to defendant member states. For instance, the CJEU has recognised that
it is admissible for a member state to raise a fresh line of argument to defend an
action at a relatively late stage, namely during the litigation phase of proceedings (i.e. when the case has been filed with the Court for hearing). The Court has
justified the need for allowing the possibility of belated defence pleas on the basis
that otherwise the general principle respecting the rights of the defence would be
undermined.[183]

In contrast, the European Commission may not raise a new line of legal argument which has not been set out already in its RO, which the CJEU has stated

must contain a clear, coherent and full statement of complaint founding the subject matter of the legal action. Consequently, the RO and the application to the CJEU must be identical, in that both must be founded on the same grounds and submissions.[184] Notwithstanding the fact that the member state has a number of opportunities to defend itself in relation to any refinements of Commission submissions made after the RO stage (e.g. during the written submissions and oral hearing stages of the litigation phase), the CJEU has adhered strictly to its view that the Commission's grounds of attack must be crystallised already at pre-litigation phase in the form of the RO. One might question whether the principle that parties should bear an equality of arms in terms of fighting their case is respected here, particularly given the time that infringement proceedings take before judicial resolution is obtained.

In some environmental cases this had led to problems for the Commission in being unable to address all dimensions to a particular case in one set of proceedings. In one case where the Commission brought an action against the Netherlands for failing to provide sufficiently complete lists of special protection areas as required by the EU Wild Birds Directive,[185] the defendant alleged inconsistencies had occurred between the Commission's position at pre-litigation and litigation phases. *Inter alia*, the Dutch government objected to the fact that the Commission had submitted only at court application stage that certain areas actually notified by the Netherlands failed to fulfil the qualitative criteria required by the directive. The Court agreed, holding that the original complaint contained in the Commission's LFN and RO was quantitative in nature, namely focusing on the insufficient number of SPAs recognised by and notified to it from the defendant. It concluded that quantitative nature of the Commission's complaint could not implicitly subsume or cover the complaint that certain notified Dutch SPA sites were deficient, even where the problem lay with insufficient size of particular notified sites. In addition, the Court barred the Commission from using a 1994 ornithological study as evidence in support of its complaint, given that the study could not be shown to have related to a period prior to the expiry of the RO deadline. In another case against Ireland[186] the Commission had taken action against Ireland for having set up thresholds in relation to certain development projects before environmental impact assessments would be required (peat extraction, afforestation, uncultivated land use). The Commission submitted that the thresholds contravened the EIA Directive which requires impact assessments to be held in the event of a project having significant effects on the environment. Ireland defended itself in part by submitting that the Commission had only filed one of its particular objections at application stage, namely that the threshold system would ignore the cumulative effect of small projects upon the environment. The CJEU held that although the Commission had not specifically used the words 'cumulative effects of projects' at pre-litigation stage, it was clear nevertheless that the Commission had addressed the issue in substance in the RO by referring to the problem or danger of developers avoiding impact assessments by splitting projects into small parcels of development in order to evade EIA scrutiny. Accordingly, it appears that the substance of all material submissions made by the Commission must be made at pre-litigation stage, as the Court has emphasised that the subject matter of the action is delimited at this point in the Article 258 procedure.[187]

Over the years, the CJEU has considered and ruled on a great number of legal submissions from member states presented in order to justify why they have been unable to implement EU legislation at national level. The case law reveals that the CJEU has taken a relatively strict viewpoint over compliance, accepting only a very narrow range of exculpatory arguments to justify implementation failures. This has been a particularly important development from the perspective of EU environmental law enforcement. The jurisprudence of the Court has confirmed that member states are fundamentally and strictly bound to the task of implementing their legislative commitments undertaken at EU level. It would not be inaccurate to describe member states as being essentially strictly liable for the state of implementation of EU environmental law within their respective borders. The following examples of defence submissions raised by member states in the context of infringement proceedings underline the importance recognised by the CJEU of holding them to account for failures to fulfil their responsibilities to implement EU environmental norms.

3.5.1 Internal problems facing an EU member state

The CJEU has confirmed on a number of occasions that member states are barred from pleading domestic internal problems within their own jurisdictions as being factors that may have the effect of justifying failures on their part to secure due implementation of EU (environmental) law within their own sovereign borders. The Court has taken the view that liability is strict here for member states. Even where it may be shown that a national government or central administration is not to blame for a delay in correct implementation, the member state concerned nevertheless must shoulder full legal responsibility for any implementation failure. Accordingly, it has been held, for instance, that member states may not be able to plead serious or emergency economic domestic circumstances,[188] internal constitutional problems,[189] failures by domestic legislatures to adopt implementing measures,[190] internal technical problems[191] or overriding domestic priorities[192] as mitigating factors. Even if it may be shown that draft national implementation measures are currently being drafted or undergoing internal scrutiny through its internal legislative system, liability will be strict if those measures have not been passed as at the elapse of the deadline for compliance with the RO.[193]

The factor of internal circumstances may be particularly evident in environmental disputes between the Commission and member states. Specifically, the defendant state may wish to plead that internal local opposition to new environmental regulatory or structural changes as being responsible for failures to implement EU environmental law. This may be particularly the case in waste management and water treatment cases, where local inhabitants may raise objections to planning consents for landfill sites, recycling plants or sewage treatment works sought to be introduced in order to meet improved environmental protection standards agreed at Union level. The CJEU has made it clear that defendant member states are not entitled to rely on the factor of NIMBY-ism as a justification for delaying proper implementation of EU obligations.[194] Constitutional settlements within a member state that devolve decision-making powers on the environment at sub-national level may not be pleaded in order to abrogate the member state from its supranational responsibilities.

3.5.2 *The element of fault on the part of the defendant member state*

Crucially, the CJEU has not interpreted from Article 258 (or 260(2)) TFEU that the element of fault on the part of the defendant member state is relevant for the purposes of infringement proceedings. Thus, where it is clear that a member state neither intended to breach EU environmental law nor was negligent in taking steps to ensure timely implementation of its EU environmental obligations, the defendant state will nevertheless be held liable for any implementation failures. It is irrelevant, for instance, that under domestic constitutional law, responsibility for environmental protection matters is devolved at regional or sub-regional level; the federal government assumes full responsibility for nationwide adherence to legally binding EU environmental standards.[195] Similarly, it is no defence for a member state to argue that it has undertaken what it considers to be all reasonable or practicable measures to implement EU environmental protection requirements, unless this defence is expressly woven into the text of the Union legislation. The CJEU made this clear, for instance, in the context of infringement proceedings taken against the UK[196] over breaches of the aquatic pollution limit values contained in the original version of the Bathing Water Directive[197] relating to waters around Blackpool, Formby and Southport. The Court held that that the directive's provisions required compliance with its pollution limit values within a specified transposition deadline of ten years; the only exceptions to these obligations were and could only be set out in any express derogations contained in the legislative instrument. Were this strict approach by the CJEU to be relaxed, it would be relatively easy to see how the credibility of the rule of law could be challenged by virtue of member state claims that it would be reasonable in the light of circumstances that they require more time than agreed in order to implement EU environmental protection obligations. It is of course a slippery slope to begin to accept arguments based on reasonableness or practicability in terms of implementation. The result is that the legal certainty and enforceability pertaining to environmental protection obligations becomes fatally undermined.

3.5.3 *Breach by another member state*

The CJEU has also consistently rejected arguments to the effect that a breach by a member state of its EU obligations may be justified on account of a failure by another or other member state(s) to adhere to the same obligations. The Court has confirmed that under the EU treaty system, a member state may not under any circumstances be entitled to adopt trade measure unilaterally to mitigate or respond to breaches alleged to be perpetrated by another member state.[198] In this sense the system of EU law enforcement may be contrasted with the rules of enforcement adopted by the World Trade Organization, which are predicated ultimately upon traditional international norms of reciprocity of obligation. At EU level, the infringement procedures under Articles 258–60 TFEU provide for a supranational form of legal action with the CJEU ultimately imposing final judgment (with the possibility of sanctions in certain situations)[199] on any particular case. In a similar vein, the CJEU has also clarified that member states may not be entitled to plead that the European Commission must institute enforcement action equally between member states; what is material is whether the defendant in question has failed to adhere to its EU legal obligations.[200]

3.5.4 De minimis-*type arguments*

On more than one occasion, member states have sought to overturn infringement proceedings taken against them on the grounds that the particular subject matter disputed before the CJEU is of a minor or insignificant nature seen from a EU perspective. Such arguments have succeeded in relation to other EU policy areas, where jurisdiction of the Union to intervene over infractions of its norms has been confined to being applicable to situations where more than one member state is involved. Notably, the traditional core areas of law underpinning the EU legal system, namely the rules pertaining to the realisation of the internal market, have always been founded upon this jurisdictional principle. For instance, the free movement provisions in the TFEU pertaining to goods and services are predicated upon the existence of an impact on inter-state trade patterns.[201] Rules on the free movement of capital and persons are likewise triggered in situations involving cross-border scenarios or dimensions.[202] The CJEU has confirmed such provisions to be inapplicable where the effects are felt simply within the borders of a single member state or where the inter-statal connection is too tenuous or remote. Another example is competition policy, where the jurisdiction of the EU to control anti-competitive practices has been similarly limited.[203] Traditionally, then, the EU has developed on the basis that its policies and laws should apply in the context of regulating member states' trading relationships with one another, leaving states free to develop and enact policies autonomously that are not considered to be of a significant direct threat to the establishment of an internal market area. The principle of subsidiarity, enshrined in the EU treaty system[204] originally by virtue of the TEU, was inserted into the EU legal framework as a fundamental principle to accommodate concerns perceived by certain member states that the development of EU law and policies should not intervene in areas that could not be 'sufficiently achieved by the member states', with reference to the scale and effects of any proposed action.

Member states have in the past sought to raise *de minimis*-type arguments as a means of escaping liability for instances of bad application of EU environmental law. In particular, they have attempted to undermine the possibility of EU control where it appears that adverse impacts on the environment flowing from breaches of EU environmental law have been felt within a relatively small geographical area within their own borders. The CJEU has dismissed such arguments consistently and robustly. For instance, in the *San Rocco* litigation,[205] where the Commission took legal action against Italy over illicit dumping of waste in the San Rocco valley near Naples, the Italian government submitted that the limited territorial extent of the case rendered the action inadmissible. The CJEU rejected this argument, holding that the question of finding of non-compliance with the directive is not determined upon whether it takes place in a small part of the national territory.[206] Similarly, in an infringement case against Germany over failures to implement the limit values contained in the Bathing Water Directive in five of its regional states (*Länder*), the German government's argument that the infractions in question were relatively minor given that the bathing waters concerned represented under 5 per cent of bathing waters in Germany as a whole, was held to be irrelevant by the Court as regards the question of compliance by that state with the directive.[207]

The position taken by the Court is fully justified. It would be a false and dangerous argument to suggest that a particular breach of EU environmental law could be purely local affair on account of its 'minor' impact, and thus fall outside the scope of supranational jurisdiction. By definition, any breach of an EU norm has a supranational dimension. Whilst any particular instance of breach of EU environmental legislation might appear to be confined to a relatively small area, the discovery of such a practice might be indicative of a number of implementation failures in the particular member state. Moreover, the instance of pollution may well have less obvious but real international dimensions: adverse impact on migrant bird populations, foreign nationals (e.g. tourists residing in the immediate area) and distortion of the internal market (e.g. 'environmental dumping' by a particular member state either by design or default) to name but a few examples. It is also impossible to be clear about what may amount to an insignificant instance of illicit pollution for the purposes of applying a *de minimis* construct in any given case. The CJEU has rightly adhered to its position of asserting that evidence of a breach of EU environmental law, irrespective of the degree of adverse impact involved, is sufficient for prosecution of a case under the auspices of Article 258 TFEU. Any other judicial approach would undermine not only legal certainty and equity in terms of law enforcement, but also the very legal commitments stipulated by the EU legislature itself on environmental protection matters and crystallised into EU legislative obligations.

3.5.5 Adequacy of implementation of EU environmental law

The CJEU has confirmed on a number of occasions that it is fundamental for member states to ensure that they implement their supranational legal obligations at national level unequivocally and comprehensively, in both substance as well as form. This approach by the CJEU has been important from an environmental law enforcement perspective, given that many member states have sought to take a number of shortcuts or only soft measures in order to internalise EU environmental norms.

A number of problems have been encountered with the transposition of EU environmental directives into national law. For various reasons, member states have frequently failed to ensure that binding national implementing legislation is in place as at the deadline stipulated in the directive, notwithstanding that often substantial periods of time are provided for transposition of the EU instrument into national law. According to Article 288(3) TFEU, which defines the legal nature of EU directives, a directive shall be binding as to the result to be achieved upon each member state to which it is addressed, but shall leave to the national authorities the choice of form and methods. The Court has construed from this TFEU provision that national implementing legislation alone fulfils the requirements of proper transposition prescribed by this provision, notwithstanding the fact that the provision allows a distinct element of choice and discretion for national authorities over the means to achieve the objectives set out in the EU norm. Two factors in particular would seem to have influenced the CJEU's approach here: the need to respect the legally binding nature of directives and the need to ensure that their transposition is carried out in a publicly transparent manner. The requirement of having to adopt national legislation as the mechanism for transposing EU environmental directives serves to sustain the legally binding nature of the provisions contained in the EU directive and more specifically ensure that the terms of the directive are enforceable publicly at national level, namely via the respective national judicial systems and throughout the entire territory of the EU. Secondly, the promulgation of national legislation offers a transparent means of introducing the directive's terms into the national domain, ensuring that all stakeholders (from enforcement authorities through to members of the public) are aware of the requirements to adhere to them.

Accordingly, it is well established by the CJEU that administrative measures alone will not suffice for the purposes of transposing and implementing requirements set down in an EU environmental directive. In one case (Case 96/81 *Commission v Netherlands*), the Commission had taken action against the Netherlands for having failed to implement the Bathing Water Directive into national law within a two-year time period set by the directive. The Dutch government sought to defend itself by arguing that in practice the terms of the directive were being observed at national level; the decentralised nature of water quality management in the Netherlands meant that the local and regional water authorities were directly bound by the terms of the directive. The CJEU dismissed this argument, holding that the delegation of responsibilities by central government to domestic local or regional authorities does not release the member state itself from the basic duty to enact national provisions of binding nature serving to transpose the terms of the EU directive concerned. Specifically, the CJEU justified this requirement by underlining that 'mere administrative practices which by their nature may be altered at the whim of the administration, may not be considered as constituting the proper fulfilment of the obligations deriving from that directive'.[208] For similar reasons, informal measures adopted at central government level designed to instruct or guide local authorities, such as ministerial circulars[209] or multiannual programmes,[210] are likewise deficient means of transposing EU directives given their non-binding status.

The reason for the Court's strict approach on the need for national legislative measures to be adopted in order to fulfil the transposition obligation is readily understandable from a number of perspectives. First, national legislation is beneficial in terms of assisting in securing proper enforcement by all member states of agreed specific EU environmental legislative standards. In particular, where specific parameters on pollutant emissions are agreed between member states, such as a maximum permissible amount of discharge of a particular substance into the environment, it is obviously important that these are seen to be respected and enforced by each member state within their respective jurisdictions on an equal footing. If the enforcement of thresholds were to depend upon the relative efficacy and good faith of administrative practice and discretion in each constituent country, this could easily lead to an undermining of general confidence in the feasibility and credibility of effective enforcement. Member state governments would understandably be hesitant to commit resources to local implementation measures in a situation where it would be difficult to scrutinise the state of implementation in other EU countries. In particular, such an approach would effectively open up the EU legal system to 'environmental dumping' by member states, namely practices which tolerate non-observance of environmental protection measures for the purpose of lowering compliance costs for local industries. The principle that member states are to refrain from engaging in protectionist-type measures vis-à-vis one another is axiomatic in the context of an internal market, which is predicated upon the abolition of obstacles to free circulation of goods, services, labour and capital and anti-competitive constraints. Member states would be also wary of investing in implementation measures in environmental protection that could be undermined on account of neighbouring laxity in implementation of EU environmental norms (measures designed to address cross-border pollution scenarios).

Secondly, where EU directives aim to create certain substantive or procedural rights and/or obligations for individuals, these have to be similarly expressed in national law in order to ensure that they are enforceable at national level, under national law. The CJEU has confirmed that it is no defence for a member state to argue that an EU norm is directly effective according to EU law, namely one that confers rights on individuals which is directly enforceable before national courts, and therefore is not in want of transposition. Even if certain provisions in EU directives are directly effective, this does not exempt a member state from its transposition obligations rooted in Article 288(3) TFEU; direct effect only constitutes a minimum legal guarantee arising from the binding nature of a particular type of supranational obligation.[211] It is in practice often debatable whether a particular EU environmental provision may have direct effect, namely where it is sufficiently precise clear and unconditional so as to entitle individuals to enforce it before national courts. This underlines the need for transposition measures to be in place, in order to obviate unnecessary legal uncertainty and litigation costs that would otherwise focus on this issue. It is also no defence for a member state to argue that because provisions of an EU environmental directive do not have direct effect, they need not as a consequence be implemented by national authorities in practice prior to the date when the directive is actually transposed into national law. That line of argument was raised unsuccessfully in a case taken by the Commission against Germany[212] over partially defective implementation of EU environmental impact assessment legislation.[213] The CJEU held that the material question over compliance under Article 258 TFEU was whether the development project concerned (thermal power station) should have been subject to an environmental impact assessment in accordance with the terms of the directive, an entirely separate question from whether individuals were able to rely upon its provisions directly before a national court. The impact of the direct effect doctrine in the area of EU environmental law enforcement is explored in detail in Chapter 6.

The need for ensuring comprehensive local enforcement of EU environmental directives that stipulate minimum protection measures has been emphasised by the CJEU's focus on developing the general principle that member states are required to ensure that domestic transposition measures contain effective means to attain their goals. In particular, the Court has stressed the need for member states to ensure that national transposition measures are underpinned by genuinely effective penalties in the event of any violations. As a basic legal principle, in the absence of EU rules it is a matter for the member states to stipulate the type and measure of penalty that should apply in the event of an infringement of an EU norm. The mode of procedure used to secure implementation of EU law is presumed essentially to rest within the exclusive competence of the member state insofar as the Union has not agreed to harmonise the process of implementation. This is underpinned by the fact that most EU environmental protection measures are crafted in the form of a directive, which specifically stipulates that it is for the individual state addressed by the directive to determine the form and methods by which it will attain compliance with the substantive requirements set out in the legislative instrument (see Article 288(3) TFEU). This leaves it up to member states to decide what type of law enforcement measure is appropriate to apply in respect of infringements of environmental protection standards set at EU level (e.g. administrative sanctions such as cease and desist orders, or criminal sanctions such as fines and/or custodial punishment for offenders).

Nevertheless, the CJEU has confirmed that member states do not have complete autonomy over the means used to fulfil EU obligations. Specifically, it has construed that a general obligation flows from Article 4(3) TEU requiring member states to guarantee the effectiveness and application of EU law. For that purpose, they are obliged to ensure that infringements of Union law are penalised under conditions, both procedural and substantive, which are analogous to those applicable to infringements of a similar nature and importance and which, in any event, make the penalty effective, proportionate and dissuasive.[214] This legal requirement was illustrated in a case against the Republic of Ireland[215] over the state's failure properly to implement animal welfare safeguards contained in EU legislation on animal experimentation.[216] The Commission had taken action on account of the fact that Irish law had introduced a relatively modest financial penalty in the event of breaches of the directive's terms (which was at the time 50 Irish pounds), whereas commensurate animal cruelty offences in the Irish Republic at the time were backed up by much stiffer penalty provisions (at the time 1,000 Irish pounds). The EU directive itself was silent as to how its provisions should be enforced. The CJEU held that penalties established under Irish law to implement the directive were incompatible with the minimum requirements under (the predecessor provision) to Article 4(3) TEU[217] with regard to fulfilment of member state obligations under EU law.

That national implementing measures should be in place to provide for effective penalties of minimum standards set out in EU environmental norms is further underpinned by a human rights argument. It is a well-established basic principle recognised at national and international levels that no one shall be held guilty of an offence which has not been already prescribed by the law (*nullum crimen sine lege*). Article 7 of the ECHR specifically enshrines this principle in the form of a fundamental human right. The EU legal system, principally through the case law of the CJEU, and most recently under the auspices of Article 49 of the Charter of Fundamental Rights of the EU,[218] also recognises the importance of this legal principle.

Bearing this principle in mind, the CJEU has had occasion to prevent member state environmental authorities from seeking to enforce obligations contained in an EU environmental directive against individuals, where no national legislation had been passed to transpose the particular directive. In the case of *Luciano Arcaro*[219] Italian authorities had sought to rely directly upon the former 1976 directive on dangerous discharges of pollutants into the aquatic environment[220] in order to bring a criminal prosecution against a precious metal plant owner Arcaro for discharges of cadmium into a river system. Article 3 of the former directive contained a basic prohibition against discharges of certain pollutants, including cadmium, into aquatic environments within the EU. The CJEU held that, although the deadline for the directive's transposition had elapsed, the national authorities concerned were not entitled to rely upon the terms of a directive against a private individual in the context of a criminal prosecution, either directly or indirectly (e.g. in order to construe existing national law so that it would include a criminal sanction that would otherwise not apply under national legislation). Instead, the directive had to have been transposed expressly into national law in order to provide the appropriate clear basis for individual liability. This is underlined by the fact that only member states are the addressees of EU directives, and not private persons. In other words, whilst it may undoubtedly have been the intention of the EU directive that there should be a comprehensive public ban on cadmium discharges into aquatic environments, no formal legal obligation arose on the part of individuals as and until national publicly applicable legislation crystallised this intention into obligations specifically targeted at private persons in the form of criminal law. The Court has underlined that it is most reluctant to see a member state taking advantage, as it sees it, of any failure to comply with EU law in this way, namely by taking shortcuts in the formal implementation process to determine or aggravate liability of individuals.[221]

Thirdly, the need for national implementing measures in the form of legislation assists greatly in ensuring that the process of transposition and implementation becomes transparent, more accountable and legally certain. It enables the Commission to monitor member states' formal steps to implement EU environmental directives, and to intervene if basic conceptual errors are made over the interpretation of the material or personal scope of obligations underpinning the directive's provisions. Moreover, the requirement to provide for binding national implementation measures ensures that the public and national/local authorities are in a suitable position to be cognisant of the entire reach and effect of the legal obligations that run from the terms of the EU directive concerned. These factors were clearly illustrated in two environmental infringement cases. In Case C-392/99 *Commission v Portugal* the defendant member state was held to have failed to provide interested parties with a sufficiently clear and precise legal implementation of the former Waste Oils Directive,[222] in not having made it clear that adoption of certain health protection measures was a precondition for the grant of a licence to manage waste oils. The national legislation merely enabled the authorities to establish that appropriate health measures were present. In a case taken against Germany[223] the member state failed to transpose the terms of the original version EU legislation on access to environmental information[224] sufficiently clearly, by not making it clear whether national authorities would be obliged to disclose any information at all in circumstances where they would be justified in refusing to disclose part of the information requested. The CJEU has elevated the principle of state transparency to be a fundamental prerequisite of national transposition measures. Accordingly, even if under national law it would be illegal for a public authority to deviate from the terms of a nationwide administrative practice or policy document that aligns itself fully to implementing a particular EU directive, this will not suffice for the purposes of proper transposition of the latter into national law. As the Court has confirmed, such a state of affairs would nevertheless leave the position insufficiently transparent for individuals to discover their rights and rely on them before national courts if required.[225]

Adequate implementation of EU environmental law requires, of course, that at national level systems are in place to ensure that compliance is respected in practice as well on paper. It is one thing for member states to ensure that the letter of their domestic laws reflect the requirements of EU environmental directives within the relevant time limit prescribed by the latter. Correct transposition of directives into national law is an important integral component of the implementation process. However, national transposition does not constitute by any means the entirety of a member state's legal obligation. On the contrary, it merely constitutes completion of the initial process of ensuring that the requisite domestic legal framework is in place, so that the relevant legal tools are in place at national level in order to assist local authorities in the fundamental task of upholding the requirements laid down in EU environmental directives. Crucially, member states are also held to account under EU law if they fail to ensure that action is taken in order to apply those legal tools. Without active and effective systems of public agency enforcement in place, any national transposition legislation is most likely to be wholly ineffective, especially if, as is the case in the vast majority of environmental protection instruments, the enforcement process is largely dependent upon member state authority involvement.

Similar considerations apply to EU regulations. In the rare event that these instruments are used in order to promulgate EU environmental legislation, it is in practice of relatively little consequence that they are at the time of entry into force directly applicable and generally binding within each of the legal systems of the member states (Article 288(2) TFEU). Individual states are required to enforce the requirements contained in each regulation actively and effectively in order to meet their ongoing duty of due and correct implementation of EU law.[226] Accordingly, where the Commission has obtained evidence of the failure within a member state to respect the requirements of EU environmental legislation, it has the opportunity to take legal proceedings against the member state government under Article 258 TFEU. It is irrelevant in this instance whether the state concerned has adopted domestic legislation designed to implement EU environmental protection standards (e.g. Case C-337/89 *Commission v UK*) or whether private parties have been directly responsible for the illicit pollution incident(s) and not the member state itself or its agencies.

The latter point is well illustrated in various actions that the Commission has brought against member states in respect of failures to take steps to clean up incidents of fly-tipping perpetrated by unknown third parties.[227] Each member state is held legally responsible for implementation within their particular sovereign territory in practice as well as under national law. The CJEU has thus confirmed that infringement proceedings under Article 258 TFEU may be used as a means to pierce the veil of formal compliance with EU environmental norms and enable the Commission to hold member states accountable for substantive compliance with legislative commitments on minimum environmental standards. In this sense, Article 258 TFEU enables the EU Commission to engage a far more in-depth and comprehensive legal scrutiny of member state compliance than would be expected under traditional rules of public international law. The classic principal role of international organisations involved in developing international environmental protection standards is to consider whether or not a member country of its organisation that has signed up to a particular international environmental agreement has actually adopted internal legislative measures to ratify it. Few international organisations are vested with specific powers to scrutinise *de facto* compliance with international law and/or take legal or disciplinary action in respect of non-compliance in particular instances.

3.5.6 Temporal arguments

A not infrequent claim raised by member states in the context of Article 258 TFEU proceedings is that they have been provided insufficient time to comply with EU environmental legislation after the European Commission initiates legal action. In cases where the Commission is confident of having obtained sufficiently persuasive evidence of an infringement and has decided relatively early on to move to judicial resolution of the dispute, unless it is satisfied of moves on the part of the defendant to ensure compliance with the EU environmental norms in question, it may well see little reason to engage in prolonged phases of attempting to secure an out-of-court friendly settlement of the dispute during the pre-litigation phase. In such circumstances, the Commission may wish to set relatively short time limits for the defendant member state to respond to the LFN and RO. The Commission is aware of the fact that Article 258 TFEU proceedings may often take a considerable number of months to culminate in a judgment from the CJEU, even in the cases with short pre-litigation phases (see Table 3.1 in section 3.2.3). This situation is far from satisfactory in many environmental implementation disputes, such as where illicit pollution may well be an ongoing situation as opposed to a one-off event. Defendant member states may seek to lever for more time to comply with the environmental requirements or to negotiate an alternative workable settlement with the Commission during the pre-litigation phase. They have, on occasion, sought to resist attempts, as they see it, by the Commission to shortcut the pre-litigation phase and impose unreasonably short deadlines for legislative compliance.

The CJEU has been wary of member state attempts to abuse the pre-litigation phase by stringing out the length of proceedings. The terms of Article 258 do not specify the minimum length of time which the Commission should allow member states to be able to respond to the LFN and RO. The CJEU has refused to stipulate absolute minimum periods, holding instead that the response times should be reasonable in length, account being taken of the circumstances in each case. In practice, the Commission usually sets as a standard deadline of two months for a defendant's response to materialise, although as discussed earlier, it has set tighter deadlines which the CJEU has endorsed in urgent cases. An important case dealing with this temporal element in environmental actions was the UK Bathing Waters case,[228] in which the UK submitted that the two months' compliance deadline set out in the Commission's RO was unreasonable, given that it was not physically possible to ensure implementation of pollution limit values prescribed by the original 1976 Bathing Water Directive[229] in respect of its bathing waters around Blackpool and adjacent to Southport and Formby. The CJEU dismissed this argument as irrelevant in the circumstances, noting that the Commission in fact had pointed out its concerns regarding the particular bathing waters some two years earlier and that the UK could have prohibited bathing in the areas concerned. The Court could also have underlined the fact that member states are provided often with substantial periods for compliance in the relevant EU environmental legislation, as negotiated and agreed by the EU legislative institutions. Ten years were provided for implementation of the original Bathing Water Directive.

The purpose of the LFN and RO is not principally to provide sufficient time for the member state to comply, but instead to have sufficient opportunity to provide a detailed response to the statements of complaint raised in those documents. In other words, the defendant state is entitled to be provided with a fair hearing at pre-litigation as well as litigation phases. That the pre-litigation phase may be and is in many instances used by the Commission together with defendant to engineer a friendly settlement should not lead to any inference being drawn that such an outcome is a mandatory requirement of the pre-litigation phase. Article 258 TFEU proceedings are there to ensure that EU law is enforced, ultimately with a view to obtaining a judicial declaration in the event of an infringement having occurred.

Another type of temporal-based defence raised by member states is where they allege that the Commission has delayed in bringing proceedings to the point where it would be unfair to bring an action. This issue has been discussed earlier in this chapter (see section 3.3.3.2). Suffice it to say that the CJEU has in general not implied any general limitation period as being applicable to Article 258 (or 260(2)) TFEU. It has consistently held that Article 258 does not oblige the Commission to act within any given period.[230]

3.6 Interim relief and Article 258 TFEU proceedings

A key factor that has to be borne in mind when considering the nature and efficacy of environmental law enforcement systems is the extent to which emergency measures may be applied or requested by an enforcement agency against a defendant in order to prevent or minimise prospective or actual environmental damage. Given the fact that it may take a considerable period of time before the substantive legal issues underpinning an environmental enforcement dispute are heard and adjudicated upon by a judicial body, the responsibilities of the disputing parties pending final judicial resolution of the case may be a real issue from an environmental protection perspective. This may be of particular significance if the contested conduct of the defendant is active and ongoing in nature. In particular, the question then arises to what extent it may be possible to require a defendant to refrain from continuing with certain activities considered by the enforcement agency to be infracting environmental protection law. In certain situations, the availability of emergency measures for the purposes of enforcement may be even more important than the final legal outcome of the case itself. For instance, if a particular disputed building development is permitted to proceed within a particularly sensitive ecological area containing protected wildlife species and habitats pending the outcome of environmental litigation, judicial confirmation of a breach of law may come too late in order to provide effective safeguards against their deterioration or even eradication; the environmental damage may well have become irreversible by that stage. The saying 'justice delayed is justice denied' resonates particularly strongly here.

The issues at stake in respect of environmental law enforcement under the auspices of Articles 258 (and 260(2)) TFEU are no different. Mention has already been made earlier in this chapter concerning the considerable length of time it may take in practice from start to completion of a first-round environmental enforcement action. The average time taken for environmental infringement cases from LFN through to CJEU judgment under Article 258 TFEU is 49 months (see Table 3.5 in section 3.2.3 which is based on case management data extrapolated from CJEU judgments determined between 2010 and 2012).

Whilst it is conceivable, as discussed also earlier,[231] that very short pre-litigation deadlines (i.e. member state response times in relation to the LFN and RO) may be stipulated by the Commission in urgent cases, this alone does not solve the problem that a considerable period of time is often taken up between court application and judgment, ranging from seven months in non-transposition cases to 20 months or over in other types of cases (see Table 3.4 in section 3.2.3). In any event, the Commission often takes a considerable legal risk in setting very tight pre-litigation deadlines, as it is not necessarily sufficiently clear in any particular case what deadline the CJEU would consider reasonable in the circumstances. It has been rare in general for the Commission to have set very short deadlines in the context of Article 258 TFEU proceedings. A response deadline deemed unreasonable by the Court would, as already outlined earlier, render the action inadmissible. If the Commission wished to continue to pursue the matter, it would have to commence first-round proceedings afresh, resulting in considerable delays before a judicial declaration could be obtained. This would, of course, fatally undermine the key purpose of securing speedy resolution of the dispute and minimisation of environmental damage.

A more fundamental problem with Article 258 (and 260(2)) TFEU infringement proceedings in being able to address situations requiring urgent intervention is that they do not have suspensory effect, as is made expressly clear in the EU treaty framework by virtue of Article 278 TFEU (ex Article 242 EC).[232] This means that the commencement of the infringement procedure by the European Commission does not have the automatic effect of obliging member states to ensure that activities claimed by the Commission as being contrary to EU environmental law are ceased pending outcome of the CJEU's judgment. Accordingly, on its own the basic legal framework underpinning infringement proceedings under Article 258 TFEU is unsuitable for dealing with situations that require urgent remedial measures. The question as to whether the Commission is able to take distinct emergency measures vis-à-vis a member state may, though, be a particularly core issue in the context of bad-application cases, namely where the defendant state has failed to ensure that EU environmental legislation is respected in practice within its borders. The Commission is required to take additional, complementary legal action in order to require any immediate suspension of a targeted activity within a member state prior to the first-round judgment.

3.6.1 Legal and institutional framework for securing interim measures

The EU treaty framework does provide the European Commission with the possibility to request emergency measures from the CJEU. Specifically, Article 279 TFEU (ex Article 243 EC) provides that the CJEU is entitled to prescribe 'in any cases before it any necessary interim measures'. These judicial powers apply in relation to the entire range of legal actions that may be brought before the CJEU, including infringement actions (Articles 258 and 260(2) TFEU). Accordingly, it is possible for injunctive relief to be obtained pending delivery of a definitive infringement judgment as to whether a breach of EU environmental law has been committed by a defendant member state. It is the Commission that shoulders the principal responsibility of initiating steps to secure emergency relief measures from the CJEU. The framework underpinning Article 258 (and 260(2)) places the onus upon the Commission to prove to the satisfaction of the CJEU of the need to for special interim measures. The fact that the TFEU rules out Article 258 (or 260(2)) proceedings having any automatic immediate suspensory effect underlines this point. There is an in-built presumption within Article 258 (and 260(2)) TFEU that the defendant's actions or inaction are to be considered lawful until final decision of the CJEU.

It is to be noted from Article 279 TFEU that it is the CJEU which has authority to decide upon the issue of granting any interim relief; the Commission is not vested with any such powers in the context of infringement proceedings. One may contrast this with the express powers vested in the Commission to adopt interim measures in the context of other EU administrative law procedures, such as applicable in the field of competition law.[233] Evidently, the current state of EU administrative law reflects a long-standing institutionalised and cultural bias that resources are prioritised to prevent or minimise monetary as opposed to environmental damage flowing from breaches of EU law. This position reflects a narrow perception about the parameters, concerns and values underpinning the Union's single market economy. Nevertheless, Article 279 TFEU effectively confirms that it is in principle open to the Commission to seek to persuade the Court of the need for injunctive relief in the context of an environmental enforcement action. It is not clear from the treaty text what scope of interim relief under Article 279 TFEU is available. However, it would appear reasonable to conclude from its deliberately generally worded terms – and this is also borne out in CJEU case law – that Article 279 TFEU should be construed broadly so as to cover a wide range of interim remedies. This construction would be in alignment with the essential mandate of the CJEU itself, as set out in Article 19 TFEU, which is 'to ensure that in the interpretation and application of the [EU founding] treaties the law is observed'. An overly narrow view of interim relief could undermine that mandate, something the drafters of the EU treaty framework clearly did not envisage or intend to be the case. The range of interim measures could accordingly include, for instance, judicial orders directed to the defendant, pending final judgment, to require the cessation of particular conduct carried out by public authorities or private persons within the defendant's territory or to require the defendant state to take restorative measures vis-á-vis the effects generated by certain activities commenced after the commencement of infringement proceedings.

The Statute of the CJEU together with the Rules of Procedure (RP) of the Court of Justice, established under the auspices of Article 253 TFEU, provide specific details concerning the relevant procedures involved for applications for interim measures.[234] As is made clear from those legal sources, it is the President of the Court (or Vice-President in certain circumstances) who is invested with the power to issue interim measures[235] and these take the form of reasoned order, from which no appeal lies.[236] Article 160 RP provides that such an application shall state the subject matter of the proceedings, the circumstances giving rise to urgency and the pleas of fact or law establishing a *prima facie* case for the interim measures applied for. Applications to the Court for interim relief may only be submitted by the parties to legal proceedings and in respect of that case.[237] In the context of Article 258 TFEU cases involving infringements of EU environmental law, this means that it is exclusively the Commission that may file an application against a defendant member state. Third parties who may be interested in taking or supporting enforcement action, such as complainants to the Commission (e.g. individuals or environmental NGOs who may have alerted it of the infringement) or other entities who may be seised of the facts of the case such as local authorities, have no opportunity to file an application in the event that the Commission decides not to do so. Third parties interested in obtaining emergency interim measures are wholly dependent upon any legal proceedings and remedies available to them for this purpose provided under national law. Member states would also be able apply to the CJEU for interim relief in conjunction with infringement proceedings they might bring against a fellow member state under Article 259 TFEU. However, given the well-established and marked reluctance of member states to assume such a prosecutorial role, this remains only a theoretical possibility.

Whilst it is the case that interim measures are available as a legal enforcement tool at EU level in conjunction with Article 258 TFEU proceedings, in practice they have until relatively recently been rarely used by the Commission in the context of environmental disputes.[238] A number of reasons may serve to explain the relative paucity of cases to date.

One of the reasons may lie in the fact that neither the Commission nor any other Union body such as the European Environment Agency[239] has independent powers under EU law to investigate suspected instances of misapplication of EU environmental law within a member state. Specifically, the Commission has no powers to investigate any particular sites without the prior consent of either the relevant member state or site owner, to seize and copy relevant documents, or to interview witnesses. The availability of such powers would be of considerable use in assisting the Commission in being able to meet the legal requirements that attend the granting of interim measures. Not only would such powers enable the Commission to launch a search for evidence at an early stage in proceedings but also enable it to have the advantage of launching an investigation without the defendant or site owner having prior notice, thus maximising possibilities for evidence of any breaches to be identified. In respect of the supervision of other EU policy areas, notably EU competition law, the Commission has been vested with such investigative powers, notably for the purpose of tackling anti-competitive practices contrary to Articles 101–2 TFEU.[240] One could certainly make the case that such powers are implicit from Article 4(3) TEU, which obliges member states to take steps to ensure fulfilment of their EU obligations and 'facilitate achievement of the Union's tasks'.[241] However, in practice such an argument remains tenuous and prone to arguments of legal uncertainty without specific EU legislation adopted in order to crystallise specific investigative powers vested in the Commission. In addition, given that any on-site inspections should be allowed to access privately as well as publicly owned property, the issues concerning rights of the defence and third parties need to be addressed carefully and in detail. The general 'good faith' obligations contained in Article 4(3) TEU simply do not address this dimension.

In the absence of specific investigative powers, the Commission is wholly reliant upon third-party evidence for the purposes of building a case against a member state suspected of failing to secure adherence to or implementation of EU environmental legislative obligations on the ground. Frequently, information is initially gleaned from complainants (e.g. members of the public or NGOs). It may, in certain circumstances, be difficult to obtain sufficient evidence sufficiently speedily from such sources for the purposes of securing interim relief. In particular, complainants may be up against technical, financial and/or legal constraints at national level in being able to gain access to sufficiently detailed information pertinent to the case. The existing range of EU legislative instruments intended to facilitate or enhance public access to environmental information may be of some, if limited, use for detection purposes in specific cases.[242] In recent years the Commission has also established some publicly accessible data systems that provide greater levels of information on the state of the environment in specific sectors, such as with the E-PRTR (European Pollutant Release and Transfer Register)[243] providing information on certain industrial installation emissions as well as an online database on European bathing water site quality.[244] However, whilst these initiatives may well be helpful in providing more focused and up-to-date information on environmental quality, in terms of law enforcement there is often no effective substitute for site-specific investigations designed to root out evidence material to allegations facts of illicit pollution.

In practice, the European Commission frequently has to rely upon the pre-litigation procedure underpinning Article 258 TFEU in order to seek to substantiate factual matters on alleged instances of bad application of EU environmental legislation through the defendant member state authorities. Accordingly, it usually has to negotiate through the cumbersome and often lengthy interchanges involved in the pre-LFN, LFN and RO stages as a means of garnering further information from the defendant member state. There is no small irony in the fact that, whilst the Commission is supposed to be in charge of the management of pre-court infringement procedure, it may be vulnerable to being substantially reliant upon defendant member state authorities for detailed factual explanations, data and other information relating to an alleged instance of bad application of EU environmental law.

Another factor which may well account for the relative lack of interim relief cases at EU level is the limited amount of human resources at the Commission's disposal for the purposes of environmental law enforcement. Usually there have been no more than two legal officers in DG ENV charged with responsibility for managing environmental infringement cases relating to an entire member state; for some countries, less than two officials are involved. This has been and remains a long-standing issue in connection with the management of environmental cases in general. Without more legal staff being employed, it is simply inconceivable in practical terms that the Commission could manage the workload involved for securing interim measures. One could, though, imagine that the enlistment of co-ordinated assistance from national environmental protection authorities could be most helpful in this regard. However, there is no legal framework at EU level providing for an integrated network of European environmental enforcement authorities. In particular, there is no effective mechanism which ensures that any relevant information and evidence gleaned by a national authority may be disseminated (quickly) to the Commission. Nor are there any specific requirements laid down at EU level that national environmental authorities are obliged to enforce EU environmental law or are to be endowed with relevant investigative (and injunctive) powers to assist them in this purpose. In the context of environmental disputes, the Commission is not empowered to address national environmental authorities directly without the member state's prior approval. In practice, this never happens in the context of Article 258 or 260(2) proceedings where the dialogue is solely between the Commission and member state government. Once again, the position with respect to EU competition law is radically different, where a special dedicated network of (competition) enforcement authorities has been formally established for some years with specific responsibilities to offer mutual assistance in the context of law enforcement.[245] In the field of EU competition law, casework responsibility concerning infringements of Articles 101–2 TFEU has been heavily decentralised and devolved to national authority level with the Commission maintaining an overall supervisory role and key role in infringements affecting more than one state. In large part, institutional decentralisation in the competition policy sector was taken as recognition of the practical difficulties experienced in seeking to maintain centralised law enforcement through the Commission.

3.6.2 *Interim measures and environmental casework*

There have been very few occasions in which the CJEU has issued interim measures against member states in the context of environmental infringement proceedings.[246] Prior to 2007 there had been only one reported instance of the Commission having sought interim relief in an environmental case (the *Leybucht* litigation (see below)) with the Commission showing considerable reluctance to utilise the interim relief procedure.[247]

The first instance that the Commission tried to obtain emergency interim measures in an environmental enforcement action proved to be unsuccessful before the CJEU. This was in the context of infringement proceedings taken against Germany, commonly known as the *Leybucht* litigation.[248] The legal dispute between Commission and member state concerned certain coastal defence works that the Commission considered to infringe the requirements of the original Wild Birds Directive[249] in having encroached upon a designated wild bird SPA in the northern German coastal bay area known as Leybucht, specifically the 'Wattenmeer' of Lower Saxony. The German authorities justified the project on the grounds of health and safety, submitting that coastal defences needed strengthening in order to protect local coastal communities against flooding from storm tides that had breached the existing dikes in the past. From the Court's file, the Commission had been informed by certain environmental and nature NGOs in September 1984 that the project constituted a potential threat to protected bird habitats, affecting such species as the avocet. Works commenced on the coastal defence project in 1986, following its formal drawing up in September 1985. The Commission considered that the German authorities had breached the terms of the EU directive in failing to have ensured that the SPA would only be subjected to the minimum degree of deterioration necessary for the purposes of dike strengthening. Accordingly, it issued an LFN in August 1987, followed up by an RO almost a year later in July 1988. Infringement proceedings were then filed with the CJEU in February 1989.[250] Subsequently in July 1989 the Commission applied to the CJEU for interim measures, seeking an injunction from the Court in order to compel Germany to cease commencement of the final phase of the project, known as Stage IV.[251] Some two-thirds of the defence works had already been completed by this time. The Commission submitted that completion of this phase could result in the disappearance of the habitat of bird species meant to be protected, disrupting some 10 per cent of breeding pairs established in the Leybucht area.

The President of the CJEU, responsible for hearing such applications for interim measures, dismissed the Commission's application, identifying a number of problems with the latter's contention of the need for interim measures in the case. A major issue concerned the factor of urgency, one of the elements required to be shown in order to justify an application. The CJEU President noted that the Commission had only filed its request for interim relief after two-thirds of the works had already been completed. In listing the chronology of events, with specific reference to the time taken for the Commission's processing of its complaints, the CJEU President clearly understood the situation as being one where the Commission could have applied for interim relief at a much earlier stage. Nevertheless, he did not formally use this point to undermine the Commission's case. In fact, the CJEU President considered that an application for an injunction against commencement of Stage IV of the project could have been theoretically granted had the Commission been able to convince it that there would be the prospect of serious harm to birds resident in the Leybucht area.[252] In coming to this decision, he took into account three factors: the nature of the Stage IV works, which did not reduce the size of the bay but constituted a dike extension into the sea, the statistical evidence proffered by the regional Land authorities which indicated that the coastal defence project had not affected resident avocet populations (a steady fall in avocet numbers had occurred since 1984 – before the project began – stabilising somewhat in 1987); and the inability of the Commission to substantiate evidence concerning development of mass tourism in the immediate area.

For several years after the *Leybucht* litigation, the Commission appeared to show a marked reluctance to seek interim relief in environmental infringement casework. Relatively recently, however, the Commission has signalled a marked change in its approach towards the subject of interim relief measures in the context of infringement proceedings in the environmental sector. Specifically, in a number of cases since 2006 the Commission has, through the legal mechanism of interim relief, been successful in forcing member states to halt the development of various construction projects and authorisation of hunting of wild fauna considered by it to be in breach of EU environmental legislation. The Commission has been motivated to intervene in this manner where it is convinced that the consequences of a particular project could prove to have permanent and irremediable damage to the environment. The utilisation of the interim relief procedure by the Commission has been pivotal in determining an ultimately successful outcome to its legal action, in making sure that defendant member states do not actively or passively permit illicit activity to go ahead prior to the date of the substantive judgment of the Court of Justice on the case as to whether a breach of EU environmental law has actually occurred. Three cases serve to illustrate this new enforcement tack taken by the Commission.

The first two cases concern instances of illicit hunting of wild birds in Italy and Malta. In the *Ligurian Bird Hunting* case[253] the Commission decided to take infringement proceedings against Italy on account of the Region of Liguria having passed local legislation which authorised the hunting of birds in contravention of Article 9 of the Wild Birds Directive. The origin of the problem dated back to 2001, when the Commission received a complaint that the Italian Region of Liguria had adopted legislation legitimating the hunting of wild birds protected under the directive, principally as a means of preventing damage to olive groves. Initially, the Commission took up the complaint in the standard way through the pre-litigation procedure. Whilst this led to some legislative changes at national level, it was apparent that by October 2006, and the end of the set deadline for compliance with the RO, regional Ligurian law had still not fully complied with the terms of the EU directive allowing a derogation to the hunting ban in time for the 2006/7 hunting season. Ligurian legislation adopted in 2006 authorised the hunting of starlings *(sturnus vulgaris)*. Mindful of the need to take action as swiftly as possible in order to prevent the Italian regional legislation having the effect of authorising hunting for the impending 2006/7 hunting season, on 13 December 2006 the Commission sought interim measures from the CJEU against Italy, at the same time as referring the substantive infringement proceedings against the member state to the CJEU. The Commission requested the Court to suspend the operation of the 2006 Ligurian law for the 2006/7 hunting season, and also requested that the Court's President ensure that an interim order was imposed for this purpose prior to hearing the defendant member state's observations under Article 84(2) RP, presumably in order to ensure that a judicial decision on an interim measure was arrived at before the commencement of the 2006/7 hunting season in earnest.

The Court's reaction to the Commission's request was swift. Six days after the Commission's request for judicial support, the President of the Court of Justice on 19 December 2006 issued an interim order under Article 4(2) RP, requiring the suspension of the 2006 Ligurian law until the Court delivered an order terminating the interim measure's effects. The President held that the legal requirements for an interim measure had been fulfilled. As regards the criterion of urgency, he recognised that the 2006 regional law risked causing serious and irreparable harm to protected wild bird species, given that on previous occasions the Court had made it clear that bird hunting is being fully capable of disturbing wildlife and impacting upon species conservation adversely. As regards the balance of interests in the case, the Court President considered that, whereas the risk of serious and irreparable harm had been proved, it did not appear that the suspension of the operation of the Italian legislation would seriously compromise or undermine its objects, which were to ensure that the requirements of Article 9 of the Wild Birds Directive were complied with. In particular, the 2006 law did not specify with sufficient precision the need for a derogation from the hunting ban, as required by the EU legislation.

Ultimately, the Commission proved to be successful also in its substantive infringement proceedings with the CJEU declaring on 15 May 2008 that Italy had breached Article 9 of the Wild Birds Directive with respect to the adoption of the 2006 Ligurian law. Given that the definitive judgment in the main proceedings was made a significant amount of time after the Commission initially referred the matter to the Court of Justice, namely some 17 months later and over a year after the 2006/7 hunting season had ended, it was patently obvious that the Commission's strategy of seeking to secure an emergency interim injunction against the Italian state had proven to be a pivotal success. Without the delivery of an interim order from the CJEU, no other step could have been taken in practice at European Union level to force the suspension of illicit bird hunting.

Subsequent to its success in *Ligurian Bird Hunting*, the Commission used the interim relief procedure to good effect also in *Maltese Bird Hunting* litigation.[254] After Malta joined the EU, the Commission had commenced infringement proceedings against the member state on account of the latter's authorisation of hunting of quail (*coturnix coturnix*) and turtle dove (*streptopelia turtur*) contrary to EU nature protection law. Specifically, whilst Malta had secured a special concession during accession negotiations that allowed it to hunt both wild bird species under the auspices of Article 7 of the Wild Birds Directive, this particular derogation from the general bird hunting ban contained in Article 5 did not permit it to authorise hunting during the breeding season. Nor had Malta supplied the Commission with any information that might justify the hunting of the species during the breeding season under Article 9 of the directive, the other gateway permitting a derogation from the hunting ban. As a result, the Commission opened an infringement case and issued a final warning to Malta in the form of an RO in October 2007 that it was in breach of Article 9 of the EU directive. By way of response, in January 2008 the Maltese government failed to commit itself to guaranteeing the prohibition of hunting during the breeding season 2007/8. The Commission was mindful of the need to act swiftly, as it had done previously in *Ligurian Bird Hunting*, in order to pre-empt any attempt on the part of the Maltese authorities to authorise spring hunting of quail and turtle dove. Accordingly, on 21 February 2008 the Commission applied under Article 84(2) RP to the CJEU for interim measures, requesting that the defendant state be directed not allow hunting during the 2008/9 breeding season. This request was filed at the same time as the Commission's referral of its main infringement action to the Court, similar to its practice in previous cases. In finding for the Commission and issuing an interim order against Malta, the CJEU President provided a fully reasoned decision which provides an excellent overview of the key legal issues to be weighed regarding applications for emergency relief in infringement cases concerning breaches of EU environmental law.

Malta submitted a number of procedural as well as substantive grounds in support of its case for dismissing the Commission's request for interim measures. First, it put forward three reasons supporting its view that that the Commission's request was inadmissible. All three grounds were dismissed by the Court's President. Specifically, Malta argued that the Commission would have to await the national reports on implementation, required to be notified to it under Article 9(3) of the directive, and take it into account under Article 9(4), which requires the Commission to assess whether derogations utilised by member states on the basis of Article 9(1) are in conformity with its requirements. The Court President, in dismissing this ground, held that such a complaint questioned the admissibility of the main enforcement action and should therefore be examined at that stage, as opposed to the stage of interim proceedings which must not prejudge the outcome of the main infringement action.[255] Malta also argued that the interim measure request was inadmissible in that it sought to prejudge the outcome of the main infringement action, which would determine the legal merits of the Commission's claim that the Wild Birds Directive had been breached. In dismissing this particular argument, the CJEU President noted that request for interim relief had simply sought to guard against the deterioration of the conservation status of the wild bird species in question during the breeding seasons pending outcome of the main legal proceedings.[256] Finally, the Maltese government submitted that the request for interim measures should be declared inadmissible on grounds that it was premature, given that there was, at the material time, no national measure capable of being suspended. In dismissing also this particular objection, the CJEU President set out the distinct purposes of the principal relevant EU treaty provisions on interim relief, namely (the then equivalent to) Articles 278–9 TFEU, both of which had been relied upon by the Commission. Whereas he confirmed that Article 278 TFEU provides the Court with power to suspend any measure contested in the main action, he also underlined that Article 279 TFEU enables the Court to issue other types of interim measures, such as issuing directions to a party on a provisional basis (e.g. to desist from taking specified action).

As regards the substantive elements needing to be fulfilled in order to justify the imposition of an interim measure, the CJEU President provided a detailed legal analysis of the relevant requirements and found in favour of the Commission in respect of the immediate 2008 hunting season. With reference to case law,[257] he confirmed that three essential cumulative key requirements needed to be proved by the applicant to the satisfaction of the Court for the issuance of interim measures: namely that such a judicial measure is justified *prima facie* in fact and in law, that the situation requires urgent action in order to avoid serious and irreparable harm to the applicant's interests that would otherwise prior to judgment in the main legal proceedings and that a weighing up of the interests involved is adjudged to balance in the applicant's favour.[258] Turning to the individual criteria in turn, the Court President first held that the Commission had established a *prima facie* case of a breach of Article 9 of the Wild Birds Directive. Specifically, Maltese legislation had authorised the possibility for spring hunting in the period 2004–7, there being nothing to indicate that a similar measure might not also be adopted with respect to 2008. The Maltese authorities had neither shown the absence of alternative measures to spring hunting as required by Article 9. Even if, as Malta contended, insufficient numbers of the bird species were present during the autumn period, the CJEU President considered this factor irrelevant having regard to the protective framework of the EU directive and given that hunting during this alternative period would be possible. In addition, he noted that Malta had failed to demonstrate why and with regard to what needs the autumn take of birds should be deemed to be insufficient.[259]

As far as the element of urgency was concerned, the Court President affirmed it was fulfilled in the light of existing precedent. He identified that the alleged presence of urgency had to be appraised in the light of the need of an interim order being able to prevent the occurrence of serious and irreparable harm to the party seeking emergency judicial relief, as well as taking into account the purpose of interlocutory proceedings to guarantee maximum effectiveness of the definitive judicial ruling in the main action. In having the onus of demonstrating the element of urgency, the applicant had to show that such damage was likely to occur with a sufficient degree of probability (as opposed to being an absolute certainty).[260] The CJEU President proceeded to consider the opposing arguments of the parties regarding this factor. On the one hand the Commission submitted that spring hunting would have a devastating impact on bird populations suffering from unfavourable conservation status, and that the fact that a certain amount of bird fatalities would arise as a result would be sufficient to prove irreparable damage. On the other hand, the Maltese government contended that the Commission's claims of potential adverse impact were vague, general and even contradictory. It submitted that the onus was on the Commission to provide clear proof that spring hunting would create a devastating impact on the species concerned. The Court President indicated that it was necessary to steer a course between the parties' polarised positions, laying down a couple of general points of guidance to assist in the appraisal of factual submission and counter-submission by the parties. First, he confirmed that the purpose of the interim procedure was not to engage in establishing the veracity of detailed and contested facts presented to the Court, given the limited means and time at the disposal of the Court to carry out such an examination. Secondly, he affirmed in accordance with judicial precedent[261] that EU legislation on wild birds is required to be interpreted in accordance with the precautionary principle, one of the foundations of EU environmental policy under Article 191 TFEU.[262] In light of the above general points, he then took into account a number of specific factors to consider whether the element of urgency had been satisfied in the present proceedings. In acknowledging that the system of wild bird protection under the EU legislation required individual member states to oversee its implementation, he underlined that any hunting activity is liable to disturb wild fauna and may affect its conservation status, irrespective of the extent to which it reduces species' populations. He took into account that it had not been disputed by Malta that the turtle dove and quail are assessed as having unfavourable conservation status in Europe. In addition, with a view to the broader context of the case, he noted the fact that the Maltese government had submitted that the Wilds Bird Directive accommodated the possibility of spring hunting, a practice which the Commission disputed as undermining basic principles of bird conservation policy. Finally, the Court President indicated that the cumulative effect of turtle dove and quail spring hunting in Malta in previous years would be taken into account as well as the fact that the national authority responsible for making hunting recommendations to the Maltese government had decided to suspend its decision pending a decision by the Court of Justice. In light of the above factors, the Court President held that the Commission's application for emergency judicial relief measures could not be dismissed for want of urgency as regards the then current bird hunting season (2008), although he considered the Commission's claim for the subsequent 2009 season as not made out. His reasoning revealed a relatively close affinity with the Commission's approach to the issue of urgency, in line with previous case law. In particular, it was highly relevant that the Court President emphasised that conservation status could be seriously jeopardised, even where species numbers are not depleted in large numbers.

The CJEU President then turned to consider the third and final key element needed to be satisfied by the Commission in order to justify the imposition of interim judicial relief measures, namely whether that the balance of interests weighed in the applicant's favour. Taking account of the need to ensure that interlocutory proceedings must not prejudice the resolution of the dispute in the main action, he compared the ecological interests of the Commission alongside the hunting priorities expressed by the Maltese government. In finding that the Commission's interest in upholding the observance of the Wild Birds Directive outweighed the Maltese government's interests in supporting its hunting lobby, the Court President noted that a ban on spring hunting would not have conflicted with any acquired rights of hunters or even a legitimate expectation of engaging in hunting in 2008, an activity he defined as being more aptly categorised as a leisure activity as opposed to a type of occupation.[263] Just as in *Ligurian Bird Hunting*, subsequent to the Court of Justice's interim order suspending the operation of the Maltese hunting legislation, the Commission proved to be successful in the main action. On 10 September 2009, the Court of Justice declared that Malta had infringed the Wild Birds Directive in providing for the possibility of permitting the spring hunting of turtle doves and quails. The Court underlined that the fact that only relatively few bird numbers could be captured in the autumn season did not justify the legitimation of spring hunting without qualification.

The Commission has also used the interim relief procedure recently for the purposes of halting the execution of construction projects deemed contrary to EU environmental legislation, as illustrated in infringement action against Poland in the *Rospuda River Valley* case.[264] In this case, the Commission decided to apply to the CJEU for injunctive relief against the Polish government over the latter's failure to ensure that two proposed road developments did not breach the Habitats Directive 92/43.[265] The dispute concerned a decision by the Polish government to authorise construction of two road bypass projects along the E67 route (the Via Baltica) between Warsaw and Helsinki, circumventing the towns of Augustów and Wasilków. The proposed bypass traversed areas within the Rospuda river valley, a unique type of natural area in Europe containing primeval forest and wetland. Both developments were projected to encroach upon a number of areas falling under the auspices of the Habitats Directive: two designated special protection areas (SPAs) as well as a potential Site of Community Importance (SCI) of Ostoja Augustowska. In addition, a related afforestation project, intended as a measure to compensate for the interference with these SPAs, cut across a potential SCI. The Commission originally sent Poland an initial LFN concerning the proposed developments in December 2006.

The Commission considered that both bypasses breached the terms of the Habitats Directive. As far as the 17.1 km-long Augustów bypass was concerned, the Commission assessed that Poland had violated the terms of the EU Habitats Directive in failing to take appropriate measures to avoid habitat deterioration and significant species disturbance of the SPA (Puszcza Augustowska) lying south-west of the town. It considered that the bypass would affect some 41 protected wild bird species located within the SPA and 21 habitat types and nine fauna (including a priority species of wolf) and eight flora species protected under the EU directive located within the potential SCI. Notwithstanding that the authorisation procedure for the Augustów bypass had preceded Poland's accession to the EU, the Commission took the view that this proposed development breached particular provisions of the directive (notably Article 6(2) in conjunction with Article 7) which require member states to take appropriate steps to avoid the deterioration of natural habitats and habitats of species in SCAs, as well as to avoid significant disturbance of the species for which the areas have been designated in relation to the EU Directive's objectives. Specifically, the Commission assessed that the road scheme, by virtue of it damaging habitats and disturbing species for which the Puszcza Augustowska SPA was classified, would be liable to cause irreversible environmental harm and lead to the deterioration of the unique and exceptional ecosystem of Rospuda valley. It considered that the Polish authorities overseeing the particular bypass project had failed to take into account alternative solutions, and therefore would not be able to rely on any defence based on an overriding public interest.[266] With regard to the project's negative impact on the potential SCI of Ostoja Augustowska, the Commission opined that the Habitats Directive was applicable and had been breached, in light of the case law of the Court of Justice relating to similar circumstances.[267]

As regards the intended 5.2 km-long Wasilków bypass, which would cut across the Puszcza Knyszńska SPA affecting 37 protected wild bird species covered under Annex I of the EU Wild Birds Directive, the particular legal objections of the Commission were different. It considered that the Polish authorities had breached Article 6(3) in conjunction with Article 7 of the Habitats Directive. Specifically, it considered that Article 6(3) had been breached on the grounds that the impact assessment carried out in relation to the bypass project had been defective, the Polish authorities having failed to consider alternative solutions properly and not having raised the issue of compensatory measures with respect to the area of land destroyed by the bypass. An additional complaint filed by the Commission in this case was the fact that the Polish authorities had failed to ensure that their intended measures to compensate for the incursions into the two SPAs did not fall foul of EU nature protection law. Specifically, the Commission considered that a particular afforestation project earmarked to be carried out to account for the ecological losses sustained by the Augustów bypass scheme not only failed to compensate adequately for such losses but also encroached unlawfully on a potential SCI site (site of Pojezierze Sejneńskie). It was of the view that the afforestation scheme would have led to a substantial part of the potential SCI being deforested as part of the overall measures envisaged by the road project investor to compensate for habitat damage caused by construction of the Augustów bypass. As a consequence, the Commission concluded that the proposed compensatory measures had breached the provisions of the Habitats Directive, on a footing similar to that of the Augustów bypass scheme.

The initial LFN sent by the Commission against Poland in December 2006 under (then equivalent to) Article 258 TFEU appeared to have little in the way of deterrent effect. Subsequently, on 28 February 2007 the Commission subsequently issued an RO against the member state, by way of response to information it had received that the national authorities had provided development contractors with permission to commence works on the road projects earlier in February 2007. Tree-felling had actually commenced on the Wasilków bypass on 15 February. In its press release[268] about its reasoned opinion, the Commission made clear that it considered the possibility of resorting to emergency relief measures if necessary, as it did in the *Ligurian Bird Hunting* case. As a consequence of the Polish authorities' unsatisfactory response to the Commission's two pre-litigation phase warnings, in particular by virtue of a definitive decision on 9 March 2007 by the Polish Environment Ministry to permit the commencement works on the sites, the Commission then decided to refer Poland to the CJEU. At the same time it sought interim measures from the CJEU with a view to securing immediate suspension of the afforestation project which the Polish authorities had confirmed they wished to have seen completed by end of June 2007.[269] The Polish authorities apparently, though, were prepared unilaterally to suspend commencement of the construction works relating to the bypasses pending final judgment of the Court of Justice on the legality of the bypass schemes.[270]

The Commission's decision to apply for interim measures ultimately had the desired effect and ultimately led to the settlement of litigation in the Commission's favour. On 18 April 2007, the President of the CJEU issued an interim order[271] requiring Poland to desist from and suspend works immediately relating to the afforestation scheme until it had an opportunity to declare a definitive judgment on whether the Habitats Directive had been breached in this case. The interim order was subsequently withdrawn in July 2007 when the Polish government confirmed that the afforestation project would not be started pending final adjudication of the legal dispute by the Court.[272] During the early summer of 2007, contradictory messages appeared to be coming from Polish sources as to whether road construction works would be allowed by the Polish authorities to be continued after the ending of the breeding season on 31 July 2007. Ultimately, though, the matter was cleared up by the CJEU, which obtained official confirmation from the Polish government on 2 and 31 August 2007 that works would not commence prior to the Court issuing its definitive judgment on the case. By virtue of these assurances from the defendant member state, the Commission informed the CJEU[273] that it would desist from continuing to request for the imposition of interim measures. As a result, the Court's President subsequently ordered removal of the interim proceedings from the Court's register in January 2008.[274] Notwithstanding its initial strong stance in defending its position in favour of the bypass projects[275] and receipt of official support from certain other member states,[276] by the beginning of 2008 it appeared that Poland had begun to reconsider matters. First, the Polish Environment Ministry opened a series of meetings with stakeholders in the spring of 2008 to assist in the process of finding alternative road routes which would avoid encroaching on protected nature sites. The Polish government then decided in the spring of 2009 to abandon the two original bypass schemes and opt for an alternative new route for the E67 (called the 'Raczki variant') located outside any Natura 2000 sites, which led to the Commission announcing on 14 April 2009 that it would withdraw all legal proceedings in the case.[277]

Accordingly, it may be seen that interim measures constitute a potentially valuable legal tool for the Commission in the context of environmental disputes that require immediate intervening steps. In practice, the Commission may often not be in a strong position to be able to meet the relevant requirements set out in the CJEU's RP, not least when it can only be seised of the facts and supporting evidence attending to the particular matter over a lengthy period of time. However, the CJEU has demonstrated that it is prepared to countenance injunctive relief where the Commission is able to show convincingly that without such relief serious environmental harm may be caused prior to a formal judgment being declared under Article 258 TFEU and does appear to be generally supportive of Commission efforts to seek emergency injunctive action in environmental cases. In particular, the CJEU has not undermined a case for urgency simply on account of the fact that for whatever reason the Commission has brought the matter to the Court's attention at a relatively late stage, namely where the disputed conduct has already been taking place for a period of time. What appears material for the CJEU, already made apparent in its judgment in *Leybucht*, is to consider whether the Commission is able to show prospective immediate serious harm prior to the definitive declaratory judgment been made.

Notwithstanding these positive developments, it is important to appreciate the significant limits of the interim relief procedure. In particular, the procedure may only be used if it is evident that conduct (whether act or omission) on the part of the defendant member state concerned would result in irreparable environmental harm occurring in the period prior to delivery of the CJEU's substantive judgment in relation to the particular infringement action. This effectively rules out the possibility of interim relief being accessible in a number of contexts which may otherwise be fairly described as urgent from an environmental protection and/or public health perspective (e.g. breaches of EU air quality legislation and EU legislation intended to combat water eutrophication).

Notes

1 Art. 260(3) TFEU.
2 See Art. 35 Euratom Treaty.
3 See Regulation 1224/09 establishing a Community control system for ensuring compliance with the rules of the common fisheries policy (OJ 2009 L343/1) in conjunction with Implementing Regulation 404/2011 laying down detailed rules for the implementation of Council Regulation 1224/2009 (OJ 2011 L112/1).
4 OJ 1999 C119/5. The form may be accessed from the Commission's Secretariat General website: http://ec.europa.eu/eu_law/your_rights/your_rights_forms_en.htm. In addition, a special form has been prepared for complaints relating to alleged non-compliance with EU nature protection legislation and may be accessed from the Commission's Environment Directorate-General's website: http://ec.europa.eu/environment/legal/law/complaints.htm.
5 The texts of Arts. 258 and 260 TFEU are reproduced in the previous chapter.
6 Case C-160/08 *Commission v Germany*.
7 COM(2007)502, Commission Communication, *A Europe of Results – Applying Community Law*, section III.3 (seeking a more efficient management of infringements), p. 10.
8 The EU Pilot system is explained on the Commission's Secretariat-General's website at: http://ec.europa.eu/eu_law/infringements/application_monitoring_en.htm.
9 The EU Pilot does not involve non-communication cases, which the Commission addresses directly through formal infringement procedures: see SEC(2011)1629/2, Commission Report, *Second Evaluation Report on EU Pilot*, p. 6, n. 9.
10 COM(2007)502 final, 5 September 2007.
11 See section 2.2 (Improving working methods) in COM(2007)502.
12 When originally launched in 2008, the EU Pilot involved 15 member states. By the time of the Commission's second annual evaluation report on the EU Pilot, which was published in November 2011, it had been extended to include 25 member states, with Malta anticipated to join soon and negotiations continuing with Luxembourg (SEC(2011)1629/2, Commission Report, *Second Evaluation Report on EU Pilot*, p. 2).
13 The Commission's second annual evaluation report on the EU Pilot system states that, as between April 2008 and September 2001 a total of 2,121 files were processed through EU Pilot. Of these, 49% originated from complaints, 7% from enquiries and 44% Commission own-initiative cases: SEC(2011)1629/22, Commission Report, *Second Evaluation Report on EU Pilot*, section 3 (Evaluation), p. 5.
14 For information on the handling of complaints under the CHAP system, see COM(2012)154 final, Commission Communication, *Updating the Handling of Relations with the Complainant in Respect of the Application of Union Law*, 2 April 2012.
15 See COM(2010)70, Commission Report, *EU Pilot Evaluation Report*, p. 5.
16 Ibid. and SEC(2011)1629/2, Commission Report, *Second Evaluation Report on EU Pilot*, 21 December 2011.
17 SEC(2011)1629/2, Commission Report, *Second Evaluation Report on EU Pilot*, section 3 (Evaluation), p. 6.
18 These are set down in Protocol (No. 3) on the Statute of the Court of Justice (OJ 2010 C83) and Rules of Procedure (RP) of the Court of Justice of 25 September 2012 (OJ L 265, 29 September 2012), as amended on 18 June 2013 (OJ L 173, 26 June 2013) available for inspection on the CJEU's website at: http://curia.europa.eu/jcms/jcms/Jo2_7031/.
19 Art. 260(1) TFEU simply stipulates that the defendant state 'shall be required to take the necessary measures to comply with the judgment of the Court'.

20   See e.g. Case C-278/01 *Commission v Spain* (para. 27 of judgment).
21   COM(2007)502, section III.3, p. 10
22   As foreseen by Arts. 133–6 of the CJEU RP.
23   As foreseen by Art. 20 of the Statute of the Court of Justice (Protocol 3 to the TFEU/ TEU) (OJ 2010 C83/1). In its 2011 Annual Report, the CJEU reported that 50% and 46% of its judgments were delivered with an AG opinion in 2010 and 2011 respectively (*Annual Report 2011 – Synopsis of the Work of the Court of Justice, the General Court and the Civil Service Tribunal* (2012 OOPEC), p. 11).
24   As foreseen by Art. 41 of the Statute of the Court of Justice (OJ 2010 C83/1) and Art. 152 of the CJEU RP.
25   Summary details on e-Curia are available on the CJEU's website at: http://curia. europa.eu/jcms/jcms/P_94806/.
26   As required by Art. 36 of the Statute of the Court of Justice (OJ 2010 C83/1).
27   As required by ibid., Art. 37.
28   Official publication of CJEU judgments are made in the *European Court Reports* series as well as via the CJEU's online case search database (Info Curia) accessible at: http:// curia.europa.eu/jcms/jcms/j_6/.
29   E.g. the full judgment in Case C-508/09 *Commission v Italy*, decided on 3 March 2011, which concerned Italy's failure to ensure Sardinian legislation complied with the prohibition on hunting in Art. 9 of the Wild Birds Directive 2009/147 (OJ 2009 L20/7), is published only in French and Italian.
30   See Krämer (2002a), p. 423.
31   Ibid., p. 424.
32   See e.g. Case C-494/01 *Commission v Ireland (Irish Waste)*. For analysis of the impact of this judgment, see Wennerås (2007), pp. 262 *et seq.*
33   Directive 2009/147 (OJ 2010 L20/7), replacing Directive 79/409 (OJ 1979 L103/1).
34   Case C-396/96 *Commission v Netherlands* (para. 16 of judgment).
35   See e.g. Case C-74/82 *Commission v Ireland*.
36   See e.g. Cases 96/81 *Commission v Netherlands*, C-217/97 *Commission v Germany*, C-300/95 *Commission v UK*, C-365/97 *Commission v Italy*.
37   See e.g. C-300/95 *Commission v UK*, C-365/97 *Commission v Italy*.
38   Case C-217/97 *Commission v Germany*.
39   Namely former Directive 90/313 (OJ 1990 L158/56), which has been superseded by Directive 2003/4 (OJ 2004 L41/26).
40   The former Directive 90/313 excluded public authorities from information disclosure obligations where acting in a judicial or legislative capacity (Art. 2(b)). It also excluded from its scope information affecting matters *sub judice*, under enquiry or the subject of preliminary investigation proceedings (Art. 3(2) second indent).
41   Case C-392/96 *Commission v Ireland*.
42   Directive 2011/92 (OJ 2012 L26/1) as amended, superseding former Directive 85/337 (OJ 1985 L175/40). (A consolidated version of the directive is available on the Union's EUR-Lex website: http://eur-lex.europa.eu/en/index.htm.)
43   See e.g. Case C-392/96 *Commission v Ireland* (paras. 61–2 of judgment).
44   See e.g. Case 272/86 *Commission v Greece*.
45   Case C-365/97 *Commission v Italy*.
46   Former Directive 75/442 (OJ 1975 L194/47) as amended, superseded by Directive 2008/98 (OJ 2008 L312/3).
47   Former Directive 78/319 (OJ 1978 L84/43) as amended, which has now been replaced and superseded by Directive 2008/98.
48   See Art. 13 of Directive 2008/98, which contains the same safety requirements regarding waste management as Art. 4 of the original WFD (Directive 75/442).
49   See Art. 2(2) of Directive 2008/98 in conjunction with Directive 91/271 on urban waste water treatment (OJ 1991 L135/40) as amended. (A consolidated version of Directive 91/271 is available on the Union's EUR-Lex website: http://eur-lex. europa.eu/en/index.htm.)

50 Now contained in Art. 15 of Directive 2008/98, which supersedes the requirements contained in Art. 13 of the predecessor Directive 75/442.

51 Namely, former Directive 78/319 on toxic and dangerous waste (as subsequently succeeded by the former Hazardous Waste Directive 91/689 (OJ 1991 L377/20) and then replaced by Directive 2008/98).

52 The 'good faith' treaty article was originally enshrined in Art. 5 of the former EEC Treaty.

53 Case 96/81 *Commission v Netherlands.*

54 Former Directive 76/160 (OJ 1976 L31/1) subsequently superseded by Directive 2006/7 (OJ 2006 L64/37).

55 As set out in Art. 17(1) TEU (ex Art. 211 EC).

56 Case C-365/97 *Commission v Italy*.

57 Para. 85 of judgment.

58 Case 68/88 *Commission v Greece* (esp. paras. 23–4 of judgment).

59 Case C-354/99 *Commission v Ireland.*

60 Former Directive 86/609 (OJ 1986 L358/1) has now been replaced by Directive 2010/63 on the protection of animals used for scientific purposes (OJ 2010 L 276/33).

61 See COM(2007) 502 final, Commission Communication, *A Europe of Results – Applying Community Law*, 5 September 2007.

62 Ibid., section 3 'Seeking a More Efficient Management of Infringements'.

63 COM(2008)773 final, Commission Communication, *Implementing EC Environmental Law*, 18 November 2008

64 Notably, the Commission's 2003 proposal for a directive on access to justice in environmental matters (COM(2003)624) has lain dormant for over a decade on account of marked reluctance by the Council of the EU to contemplate legislation at EU level in this area.

65 See Reg. 1/2003 (OJ 2003 L1/1/).

66 Case 416/85 *Commission v UK.*

67 Specifically, Directive 77/388 (OJ 1977 L145/1) as amended.

68 Case 416/85 *Commission v UK* (para. 9 of judgment).

69 COM(2008)773 final, Commission Communication, *Implementing EC Environmental Law*, 18 November 2008.

70 Case 146/89 *Commission v UK.*

71 See Commission RAPID press releases concerning infringement action against several member states: e.g. IP/11/169, Brussels, 16 February 2011; IP/11/172, Brussels, 16 February 2011; IP/11/435, Brussels, 6 April 2011; IP/11/596, Brussels, 19 May 2011.

72 Directive 2008/50 (OJ 2008 L152/1).

73 Directive 2000/60 (OJ 2000 L327/1).

74 See Commission RAPID press releases concerning infringement action against several member states: e.g. IP/11/1433, Brussels, 24 November 2011; IP/11/1101, Brussels, 29 September 2011; IP/11/1264, Brussels, 27 October 2011.

75 See Commission RAPID press releases concerning infringement action against a number of member states: e.g. IP/11/438, Brussels, 6 April 2011.

76 Case C-333/99 *Commission v France.*

77 This may be contrasted with the time restrictions imposed in other types of enforcement actions set out in the TFEU (e.g. single market supervision under Art. 114(6) TFEU, Council of Ministers involvement in state aid supervision under Art. 108(2) TFEU, and supervision of mergers under Regulation 139/2004 (OJ 2004 L24/1)).

78 Case C-333/99 *Commission v France* (para. 25 of judgment).

79 Case 342/82 *Commission v Belgium.*

80 Directive 77/388 (OJ 1977 L145) as amended.

81 See also Case C-287/03 *Commission v Belgium*, where three years had elapsed before the Commission decided to take Art. 258 TFEU proceedings against the defendant state over the latter's infringement of the freedom to provide services guaranteed under EU law.

82 See e.g. Case C-96/89 *Commission v Netherlands.*
83 Case C-392/96 *Commission v Ireland.*
84 Case C-200/88 *Commission v Greece.*
85 Case C-200/88 *Commission v Greece* (para. 9 of judgment).
86 Case C-365/97 *Commission v Italy.*
87 Specifically, the former original 1975 WFD (Directive 75/442) had been subject to legislative amendments in 1991 by virtue of former amending Directive 91/156 (OJ 1991 L78/32).
88 Former Directive 75/439 (OJ 1975 L194/23) subsequently repealed and replaced by the current Waste Framework Directive 2008/98 (OJ 2008 L312/3).
89 Case C-392/99 *Commission v Portugal.*
90 Notably, Art. 4 of the former Directive 75/442 (OJ 1975 L194/47), now replaced by Directive 2008/98 (OJ 2008 L312/3).
91 Case C-198/97 *Commission v Germany.*
92 Former Directive 76/160 (OJ 1976 L31/1) subsequently replaced by Directive 2006/7 (OJ 2006 L64/37).
93 Case C-198/97 *Commission v Germany* (para. 33 of judgment).
94 Under Art. 17(4) TEU the Commission appointed until 31 October 2014 shall consist of one Commissioner per EU member state. However, as from 1 November 2014 the number of Commissioners will correspond to two-thirds of the number of member states, unless the European Council, acting unanimously, decides otherwise (Art. 17(5) TEU).
95 The complete organisation chart (organigram) of DG ENV is set out at the following website for public inspection: http://ec.europa.eu/dgs/environment/directory.htm.
96 The relevant legal team is housed in DG CLIMA section 003 (Administrative and Legal Support, Liaison with the Shared Resources Directorate) within the Director-General's Office. A full DG CLIMA organisation chart may be inspected at the following website: http://ec.europa.eu/dgs/clima/chart/index_en.htm.
97 Compliance with Euratom law is monitored within DG ENER Directorate D (Nuclear Safety and Fuel Cycle) and Directorate E (Nuclear Safeguards) of DG ENER. Both Directorates are based in Luxembourg, making them geographically distinct from the DG's principal base in Brussels. A full DG ENER organisation chart may be inspected at the following website: http://ec.europa.eu/dgs/energy/index_en.htm.
98 On the basis of Art. 4 of Regulation 1049/01 (OJ 2001 L145/43). For criticism of this, see e.g. Krämer (2011), p. 138.
99 Case C-191/95 *Commission v Germany* and Case 272/97 *Commission v Germany.*
100 Directive 76/160 (OJ 1976 L31/1) subsequently replaced by Directive 2006/7 (OJ 2006 L64/37).
101 Case C-198/97 *Commission v Germany.*
102 See e.g. Case 247/87 *Star Fruit.*
103 By virtue of Art. 260(3) TFEU.
104 Case 211/81 *Commission v Denmark* and Case C-145/01 *Commission v Italy.*
105 Case C-337/89 *Commission v UK.*
106 Former Directive 80/778 (OJ 1980 L229/11 subsequently replaced by Directive 98/83 (OJ 1998 L330/32).
107 Case C-42/89 *Commission v Belgium.*
108 See Case 193/80 *Commission v Italy.*
109 Case 211/81 *Commission v Denmark.*
110 Case C-392/96 *Commission v Ireland.*
111 See, in particular, Arts. 4(3) TEU and 288(3) TFEU.
112 Case C-365/97 *Commission v Italy.*
113 Para. 27 of judgment in Case C-365/97 *Commission v Italy.*
114 See e.g. Case C-191/95 *Commission v Germany.*

115 Former Directive 75/442 (OJ 1975 L194/47), now superseded by Directive 2008/98 (OJ 2008 L312/3).
116 See e.g. Case C-365/97 *Commission v Italy* and Case C-145/01 *Commission v Italy*.
117 See e.g. Case 293/85 *Commission v Belgium*.
118 Ibid. (para. 14 of judgment).
119 Case C-362/01 *Commission v Ireland*.
120 The position is different with respect to second-round infringement proceedings under Art. 260(2) TFEU, as discussed in Ch. 4. Since the 2007 Lisbon Treaty eliminated the need for an RO in second-round proceedings, the LFN constitutes the foundation of the legal action in Art. 260(2) TFEU.
121 See e.g. Case 301/81 *Commission v Belgium*.
122 See e.g. Case C-247/89 *Commission v Portugal* and Case C-328/96 *Commission v Austria*.
123 See e.g. Case 7/61 *Commission v Italy*, Case 240/86 *Commission v Greece* and Case 200/88 *Commission v Greece*.
124 Case C-431/92 *Commission v Germany*.
125 Case 74/82 *Commission v Ireland*.
126 Case C-266/94 *Commission v Spain*.
127 Directive 92/44 on open network leased telecommunication lines (OJ 1992 L165/27).
128 Case C-266/94 *Commission v Spain* (paras. 22–3 of judgment).
129 Case C-203/03 *Commission v Austria*.
130 Case C-177/04 *Commission v France*.
131 Case 211/81 *Commission v Denmark*.
132 See Case 124/81 *Commission v UK* and Case C-160/08 *Commission v Germany*.
133 Case C-365/97 *Commission v Italy*.
134 At the material time this was Art. 4 of former Directive 75/442 (OJ 1975 194/47), as amended. The safety obligations are now housed in Art. 13 of the current version of the Waste Framework Directive 2008/98 (OJ 2008 L312/3).
135 See e.g. Cases 293/85 *Commission v Belgium* and C-473/93 *Commission v Luxembourg*.
136 Case C-247/89 *Commission v Portugal*.
137 Directive 77/62/EEC co-ordinating procedures for the award of public supply contracts (OJ 1977 L13/1), as amended.
138 Case C-473/93 *Commission v Luxembourg*.
139 Art. 45 TFEU (ex Art. 39 EC).
140 OJ 1988 C72/2.
141 Case C-328/96 *Commission v Austria*.
142 Case 74/82 *Commission v Ireland*.
143 OJ 2012 L26/1.
144 OJ 1992 L206/7, as amended.
145 See notably Case C-503/06 *Commission v Italy*, Case C-193/07 *Commission v Poland* and Case C-76/08 *Commission v Malta*.
146 Case 293/85 *Commission v Belgium*.
147 Case 293/83 *Gravier*.
148 Case C-3/96 *Commission v Netherlands*.
149 Former Directive 79/409 (OJ 1979 L103/1), subsequently replaced by Directive 2009/147 (OJ 2009 L20/7).
150 See e.g. Case C-266/94 *Commission v Spain*.
151 Case C-365/97 *Commission v Italy (San Rocco)*.
152 Protocol (No. 3) on the Statute of the CJEU annexed to the TFEU/TEU (OJ 2010 C83), as amended. See also Arts. 57–8 of the CJEU RP.
153 Case C-43/90 *Commission v Germany*.
154 See e.g. Case C-431/92 *Commission v Germany* and Case 211/81 *Commission v Denmark*.
155 Case C-3/96 *Commission v Netherlands*.
156 Former Directive 79/409 (OJ 1979 L103/1), subsequently replaced by Directive 2009/147 (OJ 2009 L20/7).

157 See Case C-365/97 *Commission v Italy (San Rocco)*.
158 See also Case C-3/96 *Commission v Netherlands* where the Commission was barred from using a 1994 ornithological study in support of its case (1994 edition of the Inventory of Important Bird Areas in the Community) as there was no evidence to show that its information related to a situation covering the period prior to the elapse of the period for compliance with the RO (i.e. before 14 June 1993).
159 This is all the more likely given the previous edition to the study was compiled in 1989.
160 Directive 85/337 (OJ 1985 L175/40) subsequently replaced by Directive 2011/92 (OJ 2012 L26/1).
161 Case C-494/01 *Commission v Ireland (Irish Waste)*.
162 For a detailed overview of this area, see e.g. Wennerås (2006).
163 Case C-494/01 *Commission v Ireland* (para. 27 of judgment).
164 Para. 41 of judgment. See also Case C-287/03 *Commission v Belgium*.
165 Case C-494/01 *Commission v Ireland* (para. 47 of judgment).
166 By analogy with the burden of proof for first-round proceedings as set out in Case C-494/01 *Commission v Ireland* (para. 47 of judgment).
167 Wennerås (2010), p. 43.
168 Case C-431/01 *Commission v Ireland* (para. 32 of judgment).
169 Ibid., para. 37.
170 See Case C-502/03 *Commission v Greece*, Case C-423/05 *Commission v France*, Case C-135/05 *Commission v Italy* and Case C-248/05 *Commission v Ireland*.
171 See e.g. Case C-160/08 *Commission v Germany*.
172 See Krämer (2002a), p. 424.
173 Court of Justice of the EU Annual Report 2013. See the report at: http://curia.europa.eu/jcms/jcms/Jo2_7000/.
174 Specifically, as set out in Protocol (No. 3) on the Statute of the CJEU annexed to the TFEU/TEU (OJ 2010 C83), as amended, and the CJEU RP.
175 Case C-13/00 *Commission v Ireland*.
176 See Art. 20 final paragraph of Protocol (No. 3) on the Statute of the CJEU annexed to the TFEU/TEU. For example, see Case C-259/09 *Commission v UK* (case involving non-transposition of the Mining Waste Directive 2006/21 (OJ 2006 L102/15)).
177 See Art. 76 of the CJEU RP.
178 E.g. see the official CJEU report of its Art. 258 TFEU ruling in Case C-508/09 *Commission v Italy* (case involving illicit authorisation of bird hunting contrary to the original version of the Wild Birds Directive 79/409 (OJ 1979 L103/1). The summary report, as published in the European Court Reports, only provides the operative part of its judgment, without displaying its reasoning.
179 Namely, curia.eu.europa.
180 See Ch. 8 (Languages) of the RP (esp. Art. 36).
181 OJ 2010 C83/2. See esp. Arts. 47–50 (Ch. VI. Justice).
182 See Art. 51 of the Charter.
183 See e.g. Case C-414/97 *Commission v Spain*.
184 Case 211/81 *Commission v Denmark*.
185 Case C-3/96 *Commission v Netherlands*.
186 Case C-392/96 *Commission v Ireland*.
187 See also e.g. Cases 232/78 *Commission v France*, C-279/94 *Commission v Italy* and C-247/89 *Commission v Portugal*.
188 See e.g. Case 7/61 *Commission v Italy* and Case 232/78 *Commission v France*.
189 See e.g. Case C-337/89 *Commission v UK*.
190 See e.g. Case 7/68 *Commission v Italy* and Case 77/69 *Commission v Belgium*.
191 See e.g. Case C-200/88 *Commission v Greece*.
192 See e.g. Case 160/82 *Commission v Netherlands*.
193 See e.g. Case C-123/99 *Commission v Greece*, Case C-354/99 *Commission v Ireland* and Case C-13/00 *Commission v Ireland*.

194 See e.g. Case C-41/92 *Commission v Germany*.
195 See e.g. Cases C-347/97 *Commission v Belgium*, C-71/97 *Commission v Spain*.
196 Case C-56/90 *Commission v UK*.
197 Directive 76/160 (OJ 1976 L31/1) subsequently replaced by Directive 2006/7 (OJ 2006 L64/37).
198 Case 232/78 *Commission v France*.
199 Namely, in non-transposition cases (Art. 260(3) TFEU) and second-round infringements (Art. 260(2) TFEU).
200 Case C-146/89 *Commission v UK*.
201 See Arts. 34–6 and 56 TFEU.
202 See ibid., Arts. 63 and 45.
203 Ibid., Arts. 101 on anti-competitive agreements and 102 on abuses of dominance apply in so far as the outlawed practices 'may affect trade between Member States'. EU law prescribing competition controls over mergers and acquisitions is limited in principle to tackling concentrations of a 'Community dimension' (see Art. 1 of Regulation 139/2004 (OJ 2004 L 24/1)). Exceptionally, the European Commission may also come to scrutinise concentrations that fall below this quantitative threshold involving either at least three member states or, whilst affecting only one member state, nevertheless affect trade between member states (see Arts. 4(5) and 22 of the regulation).
204 Art. 5(3) TEU. See also Protocol (No. 2) on the application of the principles of subsidiarity and proportionality (OJ 2010 C83).
205 Case C-365/97 *Commission v Italy*.
206 Ibid., (para. 70 of judgment).
207 Case C-198/97 *Commission v Germany*.
208 Case 96/81 *Commission v Netherlands* (para. 12 of judgment).
209 See e.g. Case C-262/95 *Commission v Germany*.
210 See e.g. Case 96/81*Commission v Netherlands*.
211 Case C-301/81 *Commission v Belgium*.
212 Case C-431/92 *Commission v Germany*.
213 Directive 85/337 (OJ 1985 L175/40) subsequently replaced by Directive 2011/92 (OJ 2012 L26/1) as amended.
214 See e.g. Cases 68/88 *Commission v Greece* and C-354/99 *Commission v Ireland*.
215 Case C-354/99 *Commission v Ireland*.
216 The litigation concerned former Directive 86/609 (OJ 1986 L358/1) subsequently replaced by Directive 2010/63 (OJ 2010 L276/33).
217 Namely, former Art. 10 EC.
218 OJ 2010 C83/2.
219 Case C-168/95 *Luciano Arcaro*.
220 Directive 76/464 (OJ 1976 L129/23) as phased out and now replaced by the Water Framework Directive 2000/60 (OJ 2000 L327/1).
221 See e.g. Case 80/86 *Kolpinghuis*.
222 Former Directive 75/439 (OJ 1975 L194/23), now superseded by the general Waste Framework Directive 2008/98 (OJ 2008 L312/3).
223 Case C-217/97 *Commission v Germany*.
224 Former Directive 90/313 (OJ 1990 L156/58), superseded by Directive 2003/4 on public access to environmental information and repealing Directive 90/313 (OJ 2003 L41/26).
225 See Case C-29/94 *Aubertin*.
226 In most cases, EU regulations do not provide the detailed rules by which national authorities are to enforce its requirements. The specific national authorities responsible for enforcement, their investigative powers as well as the sanctions that they are to enforce are, in conformity with standard practice and orthodox understanding, set out under national legislation.

227 See e.g. Cases C-45/91 *Commission v Greece (Kouroupitos I)*, C-365/97 *Commission v Italy (San Rocco)* and C-387/97 *Commission v Greece (Kouroupitos II)*.
228 Case C-56/90 *Commission v UK*.
229 Former Directive 76/160 (OJ 1976 L31/1) subsequently replaced by Directive 2006/7 (OJ 2006 L64/37).
230 See e.g. Cases 7/71 *Commission v France* and C-96/89 *Commission v Netherlands*.
231 See section 3.3.5.2.
232 Art. 278 TFEU states: 'Actions brought before the Court of Justice of the European Union shall not have suspensory effect. The Court may, however, if it considers that circumstances so require, order that application of the contested act be suspended.' The second sentence is only relevant to actions taken in respect of EU measures, so irrelevant to infringement proceedings.
233 See e.g. Art. 8 of Regulation 1/2003 on the implementation of the rules on competition laid down in Articles [101 and 102 TFEU] (OJ 2003 L1/1).
234 Specifically, Art. 39 of Protocol 3 on the Statute of the CJEU annexed to the TEU/TFEU (OJ 2010 C83/1) and Ch. 10 (Suspension of Operation or Enforcement and Other Interim Measures) of Title IV (Direct Actions) to the CJEU RP.
235 See Art. 39 CJEU Statute.
236 Art. 162(1) CJEU RP.
237 Ibid., Art. 160(2).
238 For a recent overview, see Hedemann-Robinson (2010).
239 Set up under the auspices of Regulation 1210/1990 (OJ 1990 L120/1), as amended. The European Environmental Agency (EEA), which came into operation in November 1993, produces general and sectoral reports on the state of the Union's environment.
240 Regulation 1/2003 (OJ 2003 L1/1).
241 See Krämer (1993), p. 405.
242 See notably Directive 2003/4 on public access to environmental information (OJ 2003 L41/26), which repealed Directive 90/313 on the freedom of access to information on the environment (OJ 1990 L158/56) with effect from 14 February 2005. One could also mention here Directive 85/337 on environmental impact assessment (OJ 1985 L175/40) as amended, the Water Framework Directive 2000/60 (OJ 2000 L327/1), Directive 2001/42 on the environmental assessment of certain plans and programmes on the environment (OJ 2001 L197/30), Directive 2003/35 on public participation in respect of the drawing up of certain plans and programmes relating to the environment and amending Directives 85/337 and 96/61 (OJ 2003 L156/17), as well as Directive 2010/75 on industrial emissions (permitting) (OJ 2010 L334/17) which in various ways also enable the public to gain access to information on certain actual or planned activities that may or do have impacts on the environment.
243 The E-PRTR is intended to fully implement the 2003 UNECE (Kiev) Protocol on Pollutant Release and Transfer Registers (agreed under the aegis of the 1998 The UNECE Convention on Access to Information, Public Participation in Decision-making and Access to Justice in Environmental Matters) and whose members include the EU, Iceland, Norway, Liechtenstein, Serbia and Switzerland. The EU has implemented the E-PRTR scheme through Regulation (EC) No. 166/2006 (OJ 2006 L33/1). Succeeding the former EPER (European Pollutant Emission Register) and operational since 2007, the E-PRTR requires national authorities to maintain inventories of emission data from specified industrial sources from and to report emissions from individual industrial facilities, covering some 65 economic sectors (and at the time of writing including some 28,000 industrial sites). The reported data are made accessible in the E-PRTR, a public register. See the E-PRTR website: http://prtr.ec.europa.eu/Home.aspx.
244 See EEA website: http://www.eea.europa.eu/themes/water/status-and-monitoring/state-of-bathing-water/state/state-of-bathing-water.
245 Reg 1/03 (OJ 2003 L1/1).

246 Namely, the interim relief orders secured in the *Liguria Bird Hunting* case (Case C-503/06R *Commission v Italy*), the *Rospuda River Valley* case (Case C-193/07R *Commission v Poland*) and the *Maltese Bird Hunting* case (Case C-76/08R *Commission v Malta*). The case proceedings are available for inspection on the Court's website: www.curia.eu.int.

247 See Krämer (2002a), p. 432 where he provides a telling insight into Commission legal appraisal of the factor of urgency in a contaminated drinking water case (Case C-42/89 *Commission v Belgium*). He comments that in the case 'there was a serious contamination of drinking water with lead in the Belgian city of Verviers. This had even led to fatalities. The Commission considered asking the Court for interim measures, but refrained from that, since the fatal cases dated several years back. The legal advice was that interim measures would be possible if a new fatal accident occurred!'

248 Joined Cases C-57/89 and C-57/89R *Commission v Germany (Leybucht)*.

249 Former Directive 79/409 (OJ 1979 L103/1), subsequently superseded by Directive 2009/147 (OJ 2009 L20/7).

250 Case C-57/89 *Commission v Germany (Leybucht)*.

251 Case C-57/89R *Commission v Germany (Leybucht)*.

252 Ibid., para. 18 of the judicial order.

253 Case C-503/06 *Commission v Italy*.

254 Joined Cases C-76/08R and Case C-76/08 *Commission v Malta*.

255 Para. 15 of CJEU order in Case C-76/08R *Commission v Malta*.

256 Ibid., para. 17.

257 Case C-404/04P *Technische Glaswerke v Commission*.

258 Paras. 21–2 of judicial order in Case C-78/08R *Commission v Malta*.

259 Ibid., paras. 28–9.

260 Ibid., paras. 31–2.

261 Case C-127/02 *Waddenvereniging (Waddenzee)*.

262 Paras. 36–7of judicial order in case C-76/08R *Commission v Malta*.

263 Ibid., para. 48.

264 Case C-193/07R *Commission v Poland*, Court of Justice Presidential Orders of 18 April 2007 and 18 July 2007; Case C-193/07 *Commission v Poland* (OJ 2010 C11/19). The case proceedings are available for inspection on the Court's website: www.curia.eu.int.

265 Directive 92/43 (OJ 1992 L206/7), as amended. A consolidated version of the directive is available for inspection on the European Union's EURLEX website: http://eur-lex.europa.eu/en/index.htm.

266 The Polish government sought to justify the development on grounds of improvement to road safety (as reported in the European Commission RAPID press release IP/07/263, Brussels, 28.2 2007).

267 Specifically, the judgments in Cases C-117/03 *Società Italiana Dragaggi SpA* and C-244/05 *Bund Naturschutz in Bayern*.

268 European Commission RAPID press release IP/07/263, Brussels, 28 February 2007, 'Poland: Commission takes urgent action to protect threatened wildlife habitats'.

269 Case C-193/07 *Commission v Poland*, reported pleadings of 5 April 2007.

270 See also European Commission RAPID press release IP/07/369, Brussels, 21 March 2007, 'European Commission takes Poland to court to protect threatened wildlife habitats'.

271 Case C-193/07R *Commission v Poland*, interim order of 18 April 2007. Decision available for inspection on the Court of Justice's website: www.curia.eu.int. As was the case with *Ligurian Bird Hunting*, the Court President is reported to have heard an Advocate General (Kokott) in accordance with Art. 85 of the CJEU RP prior to his decision on interim measures, whose opinion has not been published.

272 Case C-193/07R *Commission v Poland*, decision to remove case from CJEU register on 18 July 2007. Decision available for inspection on the Court of Justice's website: www.curia.eu.int.

273 In accordance with Art. 78 CJEU RP.

274   Case C-193/07R-2 *Commission v Poland*, decision to remove case from CJEU register of 25 January 2008. Decision available for inspection on the Court of Justice's
website: www.curia.eu.int.
275   On 25 May 2007, the Polish government sought to apply for an accelerated procedure in relation to the case under Art. 62a CJEU RP, a request which was rejected
as unfounded by the Court on 18 July 2007: see Case C-193/07 *Commission v Poland*
judicial order on an accelerated procedure request of 18 July 2007. Decision available
for inspection on the Court of Justice's website: www.curia.eu.int.
276   The Lithuanian, Slovak and Estonian governments applied to the Court of Justice in
the autumn of 2007 to intervene in the case in order to be able to issue observations in
support of Poland. See Case C-193/07 *Commission v Poland*, CJEU decisions on intervention applications of 7 December 2007 and 30 January 2008. The Court's decisions
are available for inspection on the Court of Justice's website: www.curia.eu.int.
277   European Commission RAPID press release IP/09/566, Brussels, 14 April 2009,
'Environment: Commission closes two nature cases against Poland'. See also Case
C-193/07 *Commission v Poland*, removal of case from register, 25 August 2009 (OJ 2010
C11/19).

4 Enforcement action brought by the European Commission (2)

Article 260 TFEU and 'second-round' infringement proceedings

This chapter focuses on the provisions contained in Article 260 of the Treaty on the Functioning of the European Union (TFEU) that enable the European Commission to take legal action against an EU member state that fails to adhere to the terms of a judgment of the Court of Justice of the European Union (CJEU), such as one made under the auspices of Article 258 or 259 TFEU.[1] Such legal action may be brought by the Commission under Article 260(2) TFEU, known as 'second-round' proceedings. Since their integration within the EU's treaty system in the early 1990s, these particular proceedings have developed over time, gradually at first, into establishing themselves as an important source of law relating to the enforcement of EU law generally, including the environmental sector. Whether or not the second-round procedure succeeds in becoming a genuinely effective tool in relation to the enhancement of due implementation of EU environmental law on the part of member states remains an open question, and this issue is discussed in further depth in Chapter 5.[2] The purpose of this particular chapter is to consider the legal components of the second-round procedure under the aegis of Article 260 TFEU, in the light of the evolving CJEU jurisprudence and Commission practice.

4.1 Introduction

As noted in previous chapters, the second-round infringement action was initially introduced into the EU legal system by virtue of the 1992 Maastricht Treaty (namely the Treaty on European Union (TEU)) as a means of providing the possibility for financial penalties to be imposed on those member states guilty of persistently failing to adhere to their EU legal obligations, and notwithstanding having received a condemnatory judgment from the CJEU. With the exception of non-communication cases, namely those cases involving a member state failing to notify the Commission on time of measures intended to transpose EU directives into national law, first-round infringement proceedings under Articles 258–9 TFEU culminate solely with a reasoned judicial declaration by the CJEU as to whether or not a defendant member state has breached EU law. The 2007 Lisbon Treaty introduced a special treaty provision (Article 260(3) TFEU) enabling the Commission to request the CJEU to impose financial penalties in non-communication cases. Accordingly, save for non-communication cases, the CJEU has no powers under Articles 258–9 TFEU to subject defendant member states to financial sanctions as a means of inducing them to rectify instances of defective implementation of EU environmental law when the matter of non-compliance is first brought before the Court.

However, such powers are vested in the CJEU under the aegis of Article 260(2) TFEU when the same matter of non-compliance is brought before the Court on a subsequent occasion. Article 260(2) TFEU provides the possibility for the Commission to take legal action in the event that a member state fails to adhere to the terms of a ('first-round') CJEU judgment made under Articles 258–9 TFEU. Such second-round legal action taken by the Commission under Article 260(2) may ultimately lead to the CJEU imposing one or more financial penalties on the member state concerned if it finds that the terms of its first-round judgment have been breached. The financial penalty may take the form of a periodic penalty payment and/or a lump sum payment, depending on the particular circumstances of a case. In broad terms, penalty payments will be imposed as a means of inducing member states to continue addressing a breach of their EU obligations, whereas lump sum payments are intended to reflect the degree of admonition the CJEU wishes to impose in respect of the adverse impact(s) that it perceives have been generated as a result of the defendant's non-compliance between first- and second-round judgment.

Given that the second-round infringement procedure was only introduced into the EU treaty system not that long ago in Union history (with effect from 1 November 1993) and that it takes a relatively lengthy period of time before second-round judgments are delivered, it is not that surprising that the infringement procedure under Article 260(2) TFEU has only recently begun to gain some degree of legal maturity. As at the end of September 2014, the CJEU had delivered 21 judgments[3] under the aegis of the second-round infringement procedure, with only three judgments having been handed down by the end of 2005. Of those 21 judgments, eight had been handed down by the CJEU concerning the application of Article 260(2) TFEU involving the environmental sector.[4] All of the cases involved instances where member states received substantial fines in respect of failing to adhere to Article 258 TFEU CJEU rulings, which had found them to be in breach of EU law concerning environmental protection. The cases are examined in detail in Chapter 4A (available on website).

Five of the eight second-round environmental rulings involved instances of bad application, with the other three concerning issues relating to non-transposition. In the first case, in 2000 the CJEU imposed a daily penalty of €20,000 on Greece in respect of the failure by its competent authorities to ensure compliance with the terms of the original version of the EU Waste Framework Directive[5] in relation to a waste disposal site at Kouroupitos on the island of Crete (Case C-387/97 *Commission v Greece* hereafter referred to as '*Kouroupitos (2)*'). The second ruling involved the imposition by the CJEU in 2003 of an annual penalty payment of €624,150 against Spain in respect of each 1 per cent of the latter's inshore bathing areas continuing to fail to comply with the terms of the initial version of the

Bathing Water Directive[6] (Case C-278/01 *Commission v Spain* hereafter referred to as '*Spanish Bathing Waters (2)*'). In 2005, the CJEU imposed on France a penalty payment of €57,761,250 for each six months it continued to fail to adhere to an earlier first-round judgment against it relating to implementation of EU measures requiring the imposition of conservation measures in the fishing industry as well as a lump sum fine of €20m (Case C-304/02 *Commission v France*, hereinafter referred to as '*French Fishing Controls (2)*'). In 2008 the CJEU imposed a lump sum fine of €10m on France as a result of the non-conformity of its national law with EU legislation on the propagation of genetically modified organisms (Case C-121/07 *Commission v France*, hereinafter referred to as the '*French GMO Controls (2)*' case). In December 2012 the CJEU imposed a lump sum fine of €1.5m on Ireland on account of its failure to correctly transpose into national law on time EU legislative requirements on environmental impact assessment (EIA) of certain development projects[7] (Case C-279/11 *Commission v Ireland*, hereinafter referred to as the '*Irish EIA 2*'case). The most recent wave of second-round environmental infringement CJEU judgments to emerge up to the time of writing (in September 2014) have concerned three infringements of the EU's legislative rules on waste water management, namely Directive 91/271.[8] One case concerned a shortcoming over transposition, specifically Case C-374/11 *Commission v Ireland* (hereafter referred to as '*Irish Waste Water (2)*'). The CJEU imposed on the Irish government a €12,000 daily penalty payment and a €2m lump sum fine as a result of the member state having failed to transpose the EU waste framework legislation fully into national law. The two other cases concerned failures to implement various environmental protection requirements regarding discharges of waste water, specifically Case C-533/11 *Commission v Belgium* (hereafter referred to as '*Belgian Waste Water (2)*') and Case C-576/11 *Commission v Luxembourg* (hereinafter referred to as '*Luxembourg Waste Water (2)*'). Both member states received substantial penalties from the CJEU. Belgium had to pay a daily penalty payment of €859,404 on a six-monthly basis as well as a lump sum fine of €10m, whilst Luxembourg was required to pay a daily penalty payment of €2,800 and a lump sum fine of €2m.

The substantial amounts of the fines involved in the environmental and other second-round cases have undoubtedly raised the profile of the Article 260(2) infringement procedure considerably amongst member states. This is illustrated by the fact that no fewer than 16 member states elected to supply the CJEU with observations in *French Fishing Controls (2)* regarding the extent of the CJEU's sanctioning powers under Article 260(2) TFEU.[9]

4.1.1 Duration of second-round infringement procedure

It should be borne in mind that, owing to the considerable length of time it has taken in most cases for the combination of first- and second-round infringement litigation to be completed (several years in all cases), to date the CJEU has had relatively limited opportunity to clarify in depth the legal principles and parameters underpinning Article 260(2) TFEU. However, the picture is changing as more cases are now reaching judicial adjudication stage.

A notable feature of Article 260(2) TFEU proceedings to date has been the fact that more often than not they have taken a substantial period of time, in several cases years, before judicial resolution. A considerable amount of information regarding duration of second-round litigation may be gleaned from the CJEU's reported judgments, which relay details about the various milestones of proceedings. From these reports the author has calculated that the average amount of time taken between the letter of formal notice (LFN) issued by the Commission in first-round proceedings to the date of the second-round judgment across all EU policy sectors was 131 months overall (10 years and 11 months). The length of litigation has varied significantly, though, depending on the type of infringement involved. Far longer times have been required in general for bad-application cases to reach second-round judgment. Specifically, an average of 108 months (nine years) was taken up in non-transposition cases[10] and an average of 148 months (12 years and 4 months) needed to complete bad-application cases. Timescales may vary considerably, though, even within distinct types of infringement action, this being largely down to the degree of urgency applied by the Commission to processing each case. Specifically, the author found the shortest length of infringement litigation to complete both first- and second-round proceedings in non-transposition cases was 66 months (5.5 years), with the longest being 126 months (10.5 years). The shortest length of litigation to complete first- and second-round proceedings in bad-application cases was 78 months (6.5 years), with the longest being incredibly 275 months (20 years and 11 months)!

The average length of time taken in environmental infringement cases has also been considerable to say the least. Specifically the average length of time needed to complete first- and second-round litigation in all environmental cases was 142 months (11 years and 10 months). Table 4.2 below indicates that the average time required for the four environmental infringement cases to reach second-round judgment between 2010 and 2013 was 126.5 months (over 10.5 years). So far there does not appear to be any notable trend towards any significant shortening of the duration of litigation involving second-round infringement proceedings overall. The elimination of the need for a reasoned opinion (RO) during the pre-litigation phase of Article 260(2) TFEU (by virtue of the 2007 Lisbon Treaty) may be expected to have only a relatively limited beneficial impact in reducing the length of proceedings. In any event, the time periods involved underline how significant a delay is generated by virtue of the requirement of having two consecutive infringement proceedings needing to be completed prior to the imposition of financial sanctions (for non-conformity and bad-application cases).

As was discussed in Chapter 3, since the amendments introduced by the Lisbon Treaty, financial sanction may be imposed in non-communication cases at first-round stage (Article 260(3) TFEU) which will usually eliminate the need for a second-round action to be launched. For non-communication cases, the average length of first-round proceedings is now around 22 months[11] and this is evidently going to have a significant beneficial impact in reducing litigation times for this type of infringement action.

For ease of reference, and by way of complement to the discussion on Article 258 TFEU in the previous chapter, Tables 4.1 and 4.2 below provide an overview of key aspects of the second-round infringement action under Article 260(2) TFEU. Table 4.1 focuses on the management of second-round infringement proceedings, with a view to assessing the anticipated duration of each stage of the legal procedure from pre-litigation through to completion of the judicial phase. Table 4.2 contains data on the average time taken in the years 2010–13 for second-round proceedings involving non-compliance with EU environmental law to be completed.

Table 4.1 Article 260(2) TFEU (second-round) proceedings: environmental disputes – anticipated duration

A. Pre-litigation phase
Maximum time usually envisaged: 12–24 months after issuance of LFN*

1. Commission assessment of member state response to first-round judgment	• Commission to contact member state within usually 2 months of first-round judgment to request information on national programme of remedial measures • Commission assesses member state response to its informal enquiry: approx within 6 months after CJEU first-round judgment. (Usually quicker where member state fails to communicate any remediation plan.)
2. Letter of Formal Notice (LFN)	• Approx. 1–2 months' deadline given for member state response to LFN • Approx. up to 6 months for Commission to assess and act upon member state response to LFN

B. Litigation phase
Approximate anticipated duration: 20 months**

1. Case papers registered with CJEU	Approx. within 2 months of end of LFN deadline
2. Hearing	Approx. within 6–9 months of case registration
3. Advocate General's Opinion (although this may be dispensed with by the CJEU esp. where no new points of law involved)	Approx. within 9–12 months of case registration
4. CJEU judgment (with possible penalty)	Approx. within 9–18 months after AG Opinion
Total approx. duration of proceedings envisaged:	Usually, approx. 32 months

* Benchmark set in COM(2007)502 Commission Communication, *A Europe of Results – Applying Community Law*, section III.3 (Seeking a more efficient management of infringements).
** Figure based on the average time recorded by the CJEU of 20.2 months taken for it to process direct actions filed before it, as published in the CJEU's 2011 Annual Report (*Annual Report 2011 – Synopsis of the Work of the Court of Justice, the General Court and the Civil Service Tribunal* (2012 OOPEC) at p. 110. The CJEU's annual reports may be found at: http://curia.europa.eu/jcms/jcms/Jo2_7000/.

Table 4.2 Article 260(2) TFEU (second-round) infringement proceedings: environmental cases 2010–13

	Average duration in months			
Year of second-round CJEU environmental judgments (and numbers of judgments)	Duration of pre-litigation phase	Duration of litigation phase	Total duration of second-round case (i.e. time between LFN and judgment)	Total duration of first- and second-round case (i.e. time between first LFN and second-round judgment)
2010 (0)	–	–	–	–
2011 (0)	–	–	–	–
2012 (2)	13	16	28	113.5
2013 (2)	58	23	86.5	139.5

Table 4.1 above considers the anticipated duration of each phase in the second-round infringement action, in line with current Commission practice. Notwithstanding the fact that, by virtue of the fact that the 2007 Lisbon Treaty has curtailed the pre-litigation phase by eliminating the need for an RO, the author estimates that the anticipated duration of Article 260(2) proceedings is likely to involve a considerable period of time, specifically around 32 months for straightforward cases (typically non-transposition cases). However, this timeline is liable to become extended considerably where the individual circumstances render the case more complex (e.g. bad-application casework where there are particular evidential challenges or where EU obligations require long-term infrastructural investment). The total period for second-round proceedings may be shortened somewhat where the CJEU decides that an opinion from the Advocate General is unnecessary (notably in cases not involving novel legal issues).

Information gleaned by the author from CJEU judgments on the duration of the second-round procedure reveal that Article 260(2) TFEU proceedings in general are relatively lengthy. Table 4.2 above provides a contemporary snapshot of the duration of second-round environmental infringement proceedings. It considers those cases which resulted in a judgment in the years 2010–13.

Between 2010–13 there were four second-round judgments involving EU environmental law,[12] all of which were delivered in 2012–13. The average duration of the second-round litigation for those cases was some 57 months (4.75 years). Placed in a broader temporal context, the author's research revealed that the average duration of those cases from start to finish in total (i.e. total length of first- and second-round litigation was 126.5 months (over 10.5 years).

From the author's own further research of second-round infringement cases, it was found that the average duration of the second-round procedure across all EU policy sectors (namely the period between the second-round LFN and judgment) was 48 months (four years) in non-transposition cases and 59 months (approx. five years) in bad-application cases. For environmental cases the average duration of second-round action for non-transposition and bad-application cases was

32 (two years and eight months) and 77.4 months (approx. six and half years) respectively. It should be noted that these averages to some extent mask the considerable fluctuations in time that may arise between individual cases. So, for example, the shortest and longest duration of second-round proceedings in environmental non-transposition cases was 24 and 40 months respectively. The shortest and longest duration of second-round proceedings in bad-application environmental cases was 47 and 110 months respectively.

The information available from CJEU case reports reveals that second-round casework involving instances of bad application of EU law takes a considerably longer period in practice to be resolved than other types of breaches. This is not really surprising given that the Commission is usually faced with far more complex evidential questions in such cases than in relation to non-transposition and non-conformity casework, in which the sole focus of evidence of non-compliance relates to the current state of national law which the Commission may be able to assess relatively straightforwardly. As with all second-round cases, the Commission will have to trace and appraise the degree to which a member state has taken steps to adhere to a first-round judgment. However, this evidential task may be particularly complicated, not least because the Commission in being devoid of investigative powers will in practice be heavily reliant upon member state authorities for updated information on the state of play. In addition, the Commission may have to take on board the impact and implications of incremental improvements made to the state of implementation of EU law notified to it by defendant member states, which may have the effect of slowing down the processing of formal proceedings.[13] The Commission may be willing to slow down the pace of proceedings, depending on whether the defendant member state is perceived to be taking sufficiently serious steps to bring about a state of compliance with EU law as quickly as may be deemed reasonably feasible in the circumstances. Whether a defendant member state is deemed to be responsible for (unwarranted) delays in progress towards ensuring adherence to a first-round judgment is ultimately a matter for the Commission to determine. The Commission will not hesitate to trigger the next stage in formal proceedings if it considers that a defendant member state is engaging in, tolerating or approving unjustified delays in steps to ensure compliance with the first-round CJEU judgment. The Commission has taken a stricter line in non-conformity and non-transposition cases, unwilling to be deflected by promises of or appearances of draft legislation notified by defendant member states.

The 2007 Lisbon Treaty introduced an amendment to the second-round procedure designed to shorten the pre-litigation phase. Specifically, Lisbon reduced from two to one the number of formal written warnings to be given by the Commission to a defendant member states in the pre-litigation phase. The Commission has estimated that this will serve to reduce the length of proceedings by between 4 and 6 months.[14] In addition, the Commission's operational practice with Article 260(2) TFEU appears to have been tightened up with quicker follow-up of first-round judgments. As a result of these changes, there appears to have been a general trend towards a reduction in the time taken to process second-round proceedings, and whilst it is difficult in the absence of further evidence to predict with certainty what this may be, a reasonably cautious estimate would be to expect that in the medium term second-round proceedings should settle down to take around two to three years between LFN and judgment stage (possibly shorter or longer depending on the complexity of the particular case involved).[15] However, even with a shortening of the period required for the second-round procedure, the entirety of the infringement action process (encompassing both first- and second-round proceedings) is set to continue to run into several years (at least five or more years) under the auspices of the current EU treaty arrangements.

Notwithstanding the relatively protracted nature of the infringement litigation process, the CJEU has now been able to establish a core set of important legal principles applicable to the second-round infringement procedure. The CJEU's jurisprudence has been assisted and complemented by a series of published guidance documents issued by the Commission, which have been intended to provide transparency to the principles and factors relating to the Commission's calculation of financial penalties that it may request to be imposed by the CJEU in individual cases.

The remainder of this chapter will consider the various key aspects that underpin the law and practice pertaining to the operation of the second-round infringements procedure. Section 4.2 will first reflect on the evolution of the general legal framework underpinning the second-round procedure, namely the treaty text of Article 260 TFEU as well as relevant general procedural features as recognised by the CJEU in the course of its case law. Section 4.3 then focuses on the relevant guidance and principles relating to the imposition of financial sanctions under the aegis of Article 260(2) TFEU, as developed by both the Commission and CJEU. Finally, Chapter 4A (available on website) reflects on specific second-round judgments that have involved breaches of EU environmental law.[16]

4.2 General legal framework of the second-round infringement action (Article 260 TFEU)

Article 260 TFEU contains the various provisions dealing with the obligations and procedures that relate to enforcement of first-round judgments. Article 260 contains three paragraphs, only the first two of which are relevant to second-round proceedings.[17] Article 260(1) TFEU lays down a basic legal duty on member states to take the necessary measures to comply with a judgment of the CJEU, whereas Article 260(2) outlines the various key stages and requirements of the second-round proceedings taken by the Commission in order to enforce a finding of the Court that a member state has breached EU Law.

Until the entry into force of the TEU on 1 November 1993, the EU treaty framework did not provide for the possibility of the Commission being able to seek second-round proceedings with a view to requesting the imposition of a financial penalty from the CJEU. The original founding framework of the Union, namely the 1957 Treaty of Rome (European Community (EC) Treaty) simply referred to the basic duty of member states to adhere to CJEU judgments that found that they had breached EC law,[18] a duty now contained in Article 260(1) TFEU. A distinct second-round infringement procedure did not exist in the original founding EU treaty provisions. Prior to the amendments introduced to the former EC Treaty by the 1992 TEU, in the event of the Commission finding that a member state was not adhering to the terms of a judgment made against it in infringement proceedings under the aegis of the predecessor to Article 258 TFEU (namely former Article 226 EC), the only further legal action that the Commission could take was to initiate by way of follow-up further legal proceedings, again on the basis of Article 258 TFEU. However, the sole judicial remedy that could be provided at the end of the day by the CJEU was simply a further judicial declaration.

Under the terms of the former EC Treaty, financial sanctions were only available for the enforcement of specifically prioritised sectors of policy, such as competition rules.[19] Enforcement of environmental law fell under the auspices of the general provisions on proceedings that may be taken by the Commission or a member state against an infracting member state,[20] under which no specific definitive sanctions could be employed in order to induce defendants to comply with their obligations. Whereas the EC Treaty specifically determined that decisions of the CJEU against persons other than states were to be made enforceable,[21] this to be governed according to national civil procedural rules, it was silent on the question of enforceability against defendant member states until the amendments introduced by the TEU. The EC Treaty implicitly trusted that the member states would fulfil their obligations ultimately on the basis of a legal finding being declared by the CJEU, namely the rule-of-law principle, without the need of any coercive penalties. Its framework did contain the facility for secondary legislation being passed in order to introduce specific sanctions in order to provide some teeth to judicial findings against defendant member states.[22] However, these were not followed up and it fell to a treaty amendment under the TEU in 1992 to effect a step change.

By the time the TEU was being negotiated by the member states in the early 1990s, it was clear that the credibility of the framework of EU law enforcement was coming under increasing pressure. It was evident that in the early 1990s the Commission was undertaking an increasing number of repeated infringements actions on account of failures by member states to adhere to CJEU judgments. Its annual reports on the monitoring of the implementation of EU law provided evidence of a growth in this type of case, indicating that member states were failing in their basic duty to uphold the rule of law. The environmental sector was a good example of this unfortunate trend. Krämer[23] has provided a useful survey of the increasing number of instances where the Commission had decided to initiate follow-up enforcement action in the 1980s and early 1990s against member states who were failing to carry out decisions of the CJEU confirming breaches of EU legislative obligations. He notes that the Commission reported the following number of environmental cases being taken up by the Commission on the grounds that member states were failing to adhere to the basic duty contained in (the then equivalent to) Article 260(1) TFEU, based on the annual reports filed by the Commission on the monitoring of the application of EU law: 1984 (1 case);

1985–7 (2 cases); 1988 (8 cases); 1989 (8 cases); 1990 (13 cases); 1991 (21 cases).[24] This data reveals that the number of instances in which member states were prepared to defy CJEU rulings against them in the environmental sector were steadily increasing, placing the credibility of the writ of EU environmental legislation in some doubt. Similar law enforcement problems were being encountered in other EU policy sectors.

The TEU's introduction of second-round proceedings with the possibility of pecuniary sanctions being imposed by the CJEU in 1993 was brought about specifically with a view to enhancing the performance of member states in implementing their EU legislative obligations. The threat of a real penalty was recognised as being a necessary supplement to reliance on trust and goodwill alone that the rule of law would be respected. The member states decided initially in 1992 to retain the 'declaratory' infringement procedure, in existence since the inception of the Union, and introduce the prospect of financial sanctions being applied by the CJEU in the context of an ancillary or second-round infringement procedure. The second-round procedure would apply in the event of a member state's failure to adhere to the terms of an earlier declaratory judgment from the Court.

The EU member states could have chosen to be more ambitious in their treaty reform in 1992, by introducing the possibility of financial sanctions being applied by the CJEU in a single infringement procedure. This would have introduced a considerably greater degree of deterrence and effectiveness into the infringement procedure system, avoiding the complexity and time taken up with two rounds of legal action for each case. It would have focused member states' attention on the core goal underpinning infringement proceedings, namely to ensure that member states are to be held accountable for proper implementation and application of EU law at national level. The focus of the second-round infringement action is primarily about holding states accountable for disrespecting CJEU judgments, which is a separate if related aspect. However, it was evident at the time of the Maastricht Treaty negotiations in the early 1990s that member states had insufficient collective political will to agree to establish a single infringement penalty procedure; most if not all appeared to be relatively satisfied at that stage with the introduction of a second-round infringement procedure as being an appropriate enhancement to the system of EU law enforcement.

Over two decades have elapsed since the second-round infringement procedure was first introduced into the EU treaty framework on 1 November 1993, when the TEU originally entered into force. Since that time, particularly within the last few years and since the first edition of this book (in 2006), the second-round infringement procedure has been subject to a number of substantial changes, both in terms of law and practice. From a legal perspective, the procedure has evolved through treaty amendments made by the Lisbon Treaty 2007 as well as clarification through an increasingly substantial body of case law of the CJEU. The Commission's practice of managing the prosecution of its casework has also been subject to a substantial amount of alteration and refinement over the years, in part not least due to the necessity of ensuring that its approach to second-round prosecutions remains in alignment with the CJEU's interpretation of the relevant treaty provisions.

Two significant changes were introduced to the EU treaty provisions on infringements by virtue of the Lisbon Treaty 2007,[25] which have a direct as well as indirect impact on the second-round procedure. Both of these changes share a common aspect, namely recognition on the part of the member states that the completion of the infringement procedures (first and second round) needed to be accelerated so as provide a more effective deterrent against member state failures to correct instances of breaches of EU law identified by the Commission. One of the Lisbon amendments shortened the pre-litigation phase in the second-round procedure, by eliminating the need for the Commission to issue an RO. The Commission is now only required under Article 260(2) TFEU to issue a single written warning (LFN) to a defendant member state prior to referring the case to the CJEU. According to the Commission, this change is likely to reduce the time used in the pre-litigation phase of second-round proceedings to between 8 and 18 months in practice.[26] The other alteration made by virtue of Lisbon has had a more indirect, but arguably more profound influence on the future operation of the second-round procedure. Specifically, the Lisbon Treaty introduced a new treaty clause (Article 260(3) TFEU) establishing the possibility for the first time of financial penalties being imposed at first-round infringement proceedings stage in relation to a certain class of infringement, namely cases involving failures by member states to notify the Commission of any measures to transpose EU legislative directives into national law (so-called 'non-communication cases'). This type of case was discussed in detail in the previous chapter. The intention behind this innovation is to provide a faster track for penalising member states that fail to take any steps to transpose EU directives into national law by the set deadline, a breach regarded as particularly serious and warranting a high level of deterrence built into the law enforcement framework.

This particular recent set of treaty amendments raises the question whether in the long term the decision in the 1990s to introduce the second-round procedure will prove to be an insufficient deterrent to instances of persistent failings on the part of member states to respect the writ of EU law and, in particular, whether the EU treaty framework on infringement actions should ultimately become recast into a single, one-stage procedure. Whether this may happen will ultimately depend on whether the member states consider that too many cases begin to reach second-round stage and that the two-stage process effectively licenses a significant delay in compliance with Union law. It remains to be seen whether the recent reforms introduced to the management of first- and second-round infringement procedures are successful in addressing these concerns.

The next two sections consider the particular clauses within Article 260 TFEU relevant to the prosecution of the second-round infringement procedure, namely Article 260(1)–(2) and underlying general procedural features clarified in light of the evolving case law of the CJEU.

4.2.1 *Article 260(1) TFEU*

Under the first paragraph of Article 260 TFEU, each member state is obliged to take the necessary measures to comply with a judgment of the CJEU that finds it has failed to fulfil an obligation under the EU's founding treaties. This basic duty has been enshrined in the EU's treaty framework since its inception,[27] and the Court has had a number of opportunities to clarify a range of aspects regarding the scope and application of this legal obligation.

One aspect of notable significance concerning Article 260(1) TFEU that has needed to be clarified by the CJEU is the question of how long a member state may be permitted in order to take the necessary measures. The treaty text has always been silent on the point. On a number of occasions, including in environmental cases, member states have sought to argue that the Commission has been unduly hasty in taking second-round legal action, not allowing them sufficient time in order to carry out the findings of the Court made against them in a previous judgment. The thrust of their defence has been to argue that Article 260(1) implicitly provides a member state with a reasonable opportunity to effect compliance with a CJEU ruling, so that in effect the Commission should be regarded as being obliged to allow for a period of time appropriate to the circumstances before deciding whether or not to initiate legal action to enforce the CJEU's first-round judgment.

The CJEU has set out some general principles concerning the temporal dimension to the duty set out in Article 260(1) TFEU. Whilst noting that the treaty provision does not stipulate specific time limits by which a member state is to comply with a particular judgment, such as one made under the aegis of either Articles 258 or 259 TFEU, the CJEU has consistently held that it is in the interest of a direct and uniform application of EU law that measures be taken immediately and come into effect without delay by the state involved.[28] The CJEU has emphasised the obligations of the defendant member state to ensure swift compliance with its first-round judgments, rather than laying down general time limits that must be observed by the Commission prior to its decision to launch a second-round infringement action. The Court itself has declared that it has no power under Article 260(1) to grant a member state a specific period of grace in order to comply with its judgment.[29] Instead, the decision as to when legal action should be taken in order to compel a member state to comply with a previous CJEU ruling lies in practice essentially with the Commission itself.

The CJEU has given little guidance, though, on the length of time that should be afforded by the Commission in order to comply with a first-round judgment. This is understandable and welcome, given that the nature of infringements may vary considerably as does the time in respect of which compliance may be achieved. The position is no different as regards cases involving failures to implement EU environmental legislation.

Cases involving non-conformity of national law with EU obligations have been treated by the CJEU as infringements whose remediation may be relatively quick and straightforward, as it noted in *French GMO Controls (2)*.[30] In *Irish Waste Water (2)* the CJEU held that even where implementation of a first-round ruling involved complex operations in terms of ensuring that national law fully complied with EU rules, this did not qualify the basic duty incumbent on the member state to ensure that the process of securing compliance was set in train immediately and completed as soon as possible. In that case the period between the first-round judgment and referral to the CJEU for the second time spanned 21 months. However, the CJEU rejected the Irish government's argument that this relatively short timescale reflected that the Commission's legal action was premature and allowed insufficient time for Ireland to ensure that deficiencies with its national law could be corrected with the appropriate degree of expert scrutiny and care.[31] In a recent Article 260(2) TFEU judgment against Sweden[32] which involved a failure to transpose EU legislation on retention of electronic data[33] the CJEU noted that 27 months had elapsed between the first-round infringement ruling and the date of compliance. The Court appraised this as being a 'significant period of time',[34] underlining by implication that relatively swift follow-up action on the part of the Commission in non-conformity-type cases through second-round proceedings would be unlikely to be subject to admissibility queries. The approach of the CJEU in supporting swift legal action on the part of the Commission may be endorsed on a number of fronts. Specifically, not only are non-conformity problems usually readily detectable by the Commission and national authorities: the corrective changes that need to be effected are usually clear and relatively straightforward, namely the adoption of amending legislative instrumentation. The Commission need not be expected to wait that long before it may be able expect such changes to be made to national law. The practice of the Commission in relation to situations involving persistent incorrect transposition of EU legislation, historically a relatively common issue in environmental cases, is now to expect to open enquiries regarding compliance with the member state concerned within couple of months at most after the first-round judgment and afford a deadline of two months for filing observations in response to an LFN. A swift follow-up in non-conformity scenarios is all the more justifiable, given that instances of non-communication of EU legislative directives are dealt with by a single infringement penalty procedure under Article 260(3) TFEU since entry into force of the Lisbon Treaty on 1 December 2009.

In contrast with infringements involving non-conformity of national law, cases involving bad application of EU environmental law may require corrective steps that take a considerable period of time before a state of conformity with the law is achieved. In particular, this may be the case where the legal dispute involves a member state failing to attain a minimum set environmental standard within a prescribed legislative deadline that requires large-scale and long-term infrastructural investment (e.g. relating to water or air quality). The question then arises whether the Commission should take this into account when deciding the appropriate time to commence second-round litigation.

A case in which this issue arose was in the *Spanish Bathing Waters (2)* litigation,[35] where the Commission took second-round infringement proceedings against Spain concerning the state's failure to comply with the water quality limit values under the original EU Bathing Water Directive[36] in respect of its inland bathing waters. One of the Spanish government's arguments raised in defence to the legal action was that it had received insufficient time from the Commission to carry out meaningful improvements to its inland bathing waters prior to the launch of second-round proceedings. Some 31 months elapsed between the date of the first CJEU judgment and close of the pre-litigation phase of second-round proceedings. The Advocate General, as *amicus curiae* to the CJEU, opined that the Commission's action should be declared inadmissible on grounds that it had failed to take into account in particular technical difficulties faced by the defendant member state in attaining conformity within that timescale with the directive's water quality requirements.[37] The appraisal of the CJEU, though, differed markedly from the Advocate General's legal assessment by finding in favour of the Commission, taking a strict approach to the issue of processing second-round cases. Whilst noting that Article 260(1) TFEU does not specify the period within which a first-round judgment should be complied with, the CJEU stressed instead the importance of defendant member states initiating the process of compliance at once and having this completed as soon as possible for the purpose of securing immediate and uniform application of EU law.[38] The determinative factor for the CJEU was whether, at the expiry of the deadline set by the Commission's final warning in second-round proceedings, the defendant had failed to take the necessary steps to adhere to the CJEU's first-round judgment.[39] The CJEU did not specifically engage in any assessment of weighing up the reasonableness of the period allowed by the Commission for compliance; by implication the judgment signalled that even if compliance called for relatively complex and long-term infrastructural operations to improve bathing water quality and if a defendant had taken some remedial steps, this would not constitute a bar to the Commission utilising Article 260(2) TFEU as a means of maintaining the pressure on a member state to ensure complete compliance with EU obligations. Accordingly, the second-round action was not struck out as inadmissible on grounds of a failure to allow the defendant member state a reasonable period to take steps to comply with the first judgment.

The difference between the approach taken by the Advocate General and CJEU in *Spanish Bathing Waters (2)* raises an important issue in relation to the management of second-round proceedings, an issue that has not completely been resolved. On the one hand, the Advocate General's position posits the existence of an implicit duty incumbent on the Commission underpinning Article 260(1) TFEU that before it pulls the trigger in launching second-round infringement action it needs to ensure that that the defendant member state is afforded a reasonable opportunity to be able to comply with the first-round judgment. How long that opportunity should be would depend on the particular circumstances of the case at hand, and is therefore difficult to specify, but a reasonable inference one might draw from Article 260(1) TFEU would be that the Commission is obliged to ensure that any compliance timelines it sets for defendant member state are realistically achievable. On the other hand, the CJEU's position as implied (although not expressly set out) in *Spanish Bathing Waters (2)* and not rebutted in subsequent case law is that in principle the relative length of time afforded to defendants to achieve compliance with a first-round judgment should be regarded as immaterial. This approach resonates with the consideration that by the time member states come to face the music in the form of a second-round judgment they have already had a very substantial period of time (usually years) beyond the original deadline for complying with the relevant EU environmental legislation in order to honour their Union legal obligations. Weaving in a factor of reasonableness with the respect to the time period allowed for adhering to a first-round judgment would only serve to increase the possibilities for delaying compliance with EU law on the part of the defendant member state as well as undermine legal certainty of second-round proceedings. Viewed in that context, it appears that the CJEU's reluctance to be drawn into arguments concerning the alleged reasonableness or unreasonableness of the period allowed to member states to adhere to first-round judgments is well-founded.

The CJEU has in practice preferred to take into account member state claims concerning alleged undue haste on the part of the Commission to prosecute and complete second-round proceedings when assessing the questions of whether financial sanctions should be imposed and, if so, how severe these should be. This as well as other legal principles pertaining to the operation of the second-round infringement procedure under Article 260(2) TFEU will be explored in the next section.

4.2.2 Article 260(2) TFEU

Article 260(2) TFEU provides the European Commission with the possibility of taking legal action against any EU member state that fails to take the appropriate corrective measures to remedy one or more breaches of Union law confirmed by a judgment of the CJEU, such as a judgment declared as a result of Article 258 TFEU (first-round) infringement proceedings having been brought by the Commission. The second-round infringement procedure shares some key elements with those applicable to the first-round infringement action, with some notable differences. The principal difference is that the Commission has the possibility of requesting the CJEU in any second-round case that one or more financial penalties to be imposed on the defendant member state, this being only possible at first-round stage in relation to non-communication cases by virtue of Article 260(3) TFEU.

Second-round infringement proceedings may ultimately lead to the following judicial decisions being delivered by the CJEU:

* a judicial declaration of in/compatibility with a previous (first-round) judgment of the CJEU;
* a penalty payment being imposed on the defendant member state; and/or
* a lump sum fine being imposed on the defendant member state.

Article 260(2) TFEU stipulates that the CJEU 'may' decide that a financial penalty is warranted. Accordingly, it is important to note that it is the CJEU and not the Commission which has the power to decide whether any particular financial penalty should be imposed in any given situation, the role of the Commission being to provide it with non-binding requests and suggestions for specific monetary fines in individual cases.

The case law of the CJEU has underlined the central role of the Court in terms of both developing as well as applying the procedural and substantive principles governing the second-round infringement procedure. The CJEU has, through its emerging jurisprudence on Article 260(2), developed a series of fundamental principles underpinning the operation of the second-round infringement procedure during pre-litigation and litigation phases. These principles have served to provide greater levels of certainty and predictability on a variety of key issues as well as to underline the ultimate authority of the CJEU as recognised by EU law[40] to provide a definitive interpretation of the relevant EU treaty framework.

4.2.2.1 *Procedural aspects of Article 260(2) TFEU*

As is the case with first-round proceedings, the procedure under Article 260(2) TFEU requires completion of a pre-litigation phase prior to the Commission referring the matter to the CJEU. Prior to the treaty amendments introduced by the Lisbon Treaty 2007, the pre-litigation phase required the Commission to issue two formal written warnings, namely an LFN and RO. However, since the entry into force of those amendments on 1 December 2009, the pre-litigation phase has been shortened so that only one formal written warning must be sent, namely the LFN.[41]

The CJEU has confirmed that the Commission must adhere to a number of essential requirements during this particular phase, which mirror the standards of procedural fairness it has interpreted to apply in connection with the operation of first-round proceedings. Notably, the CJEU has had occasion to emphasise the importance of the Commission ensuring that it does not extend the scope of the legal complaint beyond that identified in its formal pre-litigation correspondence with the defendant member state. This point was illustrated in *Commission v Portugal*,[42] where the Commission brought an action against Portugal for failing to adhere to a previous judicial ruling condemning the member state for breaching EU free movement of goods rules in connection with its domestic approval procedures for marketing polyethylene pipes used in the water industry. The CJEU ruled the action inadmissible on grounds that the Commission had introduced new complaints before the CJEU not previously raised in the pre-litigation correspondence with the defendant member state.

The CJEU has confirmed on several occasions that the date upon which liability is determined for the purpose of Article 260(2) TFEU is the end of the deadline stipulated by the Commission in its final written warning for the purposes of the pre-litigation phase,[43] which is now that set by the LFN since entry into force of the 2007 Lisbon Treaty.[44] Accordingly, if a member state decides to inform the Commission of a change in legal or factual circumstances after this particular date, they will have no bearing on the question of the existence of liability. This issue arose in *Commission v France*,[45] a case in which France had previously been adjudged by the CJEU to have failed to transpose the EU Product Liability Directive[46] correctly into national law. The French government submitted that the Commission's action should be ruled inadmissible on the grounds that it had notified Brussels of new transposition legislation, albeit after the Commission had referred the case to the CJEU. The Commission decided nevertheless to continue with the case and refer to the CJEU, opining that the new legislation only partially transposed the EU legislation correctly. The CJEU held that, whilst the Commission is under a duty to ensure that the subject matter of its legal action remained limited to that identified at the culmination of the pre-litigation phase,[47] an alteration in national legislation subsequent to that time did not of itself amount to effecting a change in the subject matter of litigation.[48] Accordingly, the Commission was perfectly entitled in this case to continue with its action on the grounds of non-compliance with the first-round judgment. It is not obliged to restart the second-round infringement procedure each time a member belatedly adopts fresh national legislation in order to comply with a previous judicial ruling. The CJEU has also confirmed that even if a member state manages to effect compliance with a first-round judgment subsequent to the elapse of the deadline for a reply to the LFN set by the Commission, the second-round action will not be deemed to be devoid of purpose. Instead, the Commission retains the right to maintain its legal action before the CJEU and the Court has power to adjudicate upon the case, including deciding to impose a financial penalty upon the defendant member state if it deems this appropriate in the particular circumstances of the case.[49]

If a defendant member state provides the Commission with new factual and/or legal information prior to the LFN deadline, just as is the case with first-round infringement actions, the Commission is obliged to appraise their legal impact before any referral to the CJEU. In practice, if the Commission considers the member state's response is still unsatisfactory it will typically issue the defendant state with a supplementary LFN setting out its reasons for continued dissatisfaction and setting the defendant state with a fresh deadline for reply.

The CJEU has indicated that the principles relating to the burden of proof in second-round infringement proceedings effectively mirror those applicable to first-round actions. Accordingly, it is the Commission which has the legal responsibility to provide sufficient evidence to show that the breach of EU law confirmed in the first-round ruling of the Court has persisted in order to be able to utilise Article 260(2) TFEU.[50] As with first-round proceedings, the burden of proof is of a civil as opposed to criminal legal standard, so essentially based upon the balance of probabilities. There is no automatic presumption that the breach persists after the first-round judgment is delivered. Once the Commission has elicited sufficient evidence of non-compliance with the first-round judgment as at the end of the LFN deadline, the burden of proof then switches to the defendant member state to challenge in a detailed manner the substantive content of that evidence.[51]

The approach adopted by the CJEU to construe that the same principles of burden of proof apply as in relation to Article 258 TFEU is questionable. First, it is clear that the second-round proceedings are substantially different, in that it has already been proven to the satisfaction of the CJEU that an infringement has occurred; the Commission should not have to repeat the exercise. In fairness, the onus should fall automatically to the defendant state to prove that it has taken the requisite steps to address the breach(es) of EU law in question within a reasonable period after the first-round judgment. Secondly, the placing of the burden of proof on the Commission may be in practice particularly and unduly onerous in relation to certain bad-application cases, taking into account the fact that the

Commission has a lack of investigatory powers and resources to verify the situation on the ground. Typically, these include most environmental casework (apart from fisheries and the civil nuclear sector in respect of which the Commission has certain investigatory powers). It may be the case, though, as is evident from some of the recent case law pertaining to first-round litigation discussed in the previous chapter, that the CJEU may contemplate a relatively low threshold of factual information having to be met by the Commission in order to displace the burden of proof, bearing in mind the lack of investigatory tools available to the Commission. Further case law of the CJEU is needed to clarify this area.

4.2.2.2 *Defences under Article 260(2) TFEU*

As in the case of first-round actions under Article 258 TFEU, the CJEU has adopted a strict approach with respect to attempts by defendant member states to justify failures on their part to comply with their EU obligations. Notably, the CJEU has given short shrift to defendants raising internal domestic difficulties as explanations for delays in complying with a previous Court judgment. It has held that these do not provide a valid defence to a second-round action. For instance, the CJEU has confirmed in a series of Article 260(2) TFEU second-round infringement actions over instances of failure to transpose specific pieces of EU legislation that second-round action against them by the Commission could not be found to be inadmissible on grounds of internal political difficulties or legislative delays, such as resulting from a change of national government, suspension of national parliamentary elections or intense and lengthy internal parliamentary scrutiny and debate over implementation.[52] Partial completion and evidence of good faith on the national government's part to seek to adhere to a first-round judgment will also not act as a bar to the Commission launching second-round proceedings in the event of compliance not being effected as soon as possible.[53]

The CJEU has also confirmed that national systems of property ownership, including property rights of third parties that might be adversely affected by compliance with a previous CJEU ruling, do not constitute valid reasons to defend a second-round case. Specifically, in one infringement action taken against Germany[54] the German government sought unsuccessfully to assert the protection of third-party property rights as a defence in second-round proceedings taken against it over the failure to comply with EU public procurement legislation in the award of two public tender contracts, specifically for the collection of waste water in Bockhorn and the management of waste in Braunschweig. The CJEU held that member states may not rely on principles relating to the sanctity of contracts[55] in order to evade compliance with EU law, in this case implementation of a previous CJEU judgment. According to the Court,[56] member states may neither exempt national systems of property ownership from EU rules nor plead domestic law in order to justify non-implementation of a CJEU judgment, notwithstanding the existence of Article 345 TFEU.[57] In this particular ruling the CJEU applied long-established principles derived from its jurisprudence on the relationship between nationally protected property rights and the free movement of goods[58] to the context of infringement proceedings. This second-round judgment has important implications for casework in the environmental sector, where the Commission may well be confronted with the situation of contracts or real-property transfers having been agreed and/or executed in contravention of EU environmental legislation (e.g. waste disposal licences being granted in contravention of EU waste management legislation, development contracts in contravention of EIA legislation, carbon emission allowances granted in breach of EU climate change legislation).

4.2.2.3 Interim relief and second-round infringement actions

To date there have been no reported cases of the European Commission having applied for interim relief pending the delivery of a second-round judgment from the CJEU. However, it is evident from the EU treaty framework that such relief is (theoretically at least) technically available, should the Commission and ultimately the CJEU consider this necessary and justified. The relevant treaty rules on interim relief[59] apply to all legal actions brought and pending before the CJEU.

As discussed in the previous chapter, the availability of interim relief measures may be highly relevant in certain kinds of environmental infringement cases brought by the Commission under the auspices of Article 258 TFEU, where urgent action may be required to be taken in order to prevent potential and actual irrevocable specific environmental damage occurring prior to the date when the CJEU may first be able to deliver a definitive judgment on whether a breach of EU environmental law has been committed. Typically, these may involve instances of bad application of EU law, such as a failure to adhere to EU nature protection legislation in which specific protected flora or fauna species and/or their habitats may be subject to an ongoing or imminent illicit encroachment (e.g. a development that has not been subject to an appropriate EIA or uncontrolled hunting). As is the case with first-round proceedings, the Commission is entitled to apply to the CJEU for interim relief in such urgent cases arising under the aegis of Article 260(2) TFEU, as soon as the pre-litigation phase has elapsed. For second-round proceedings, this will be as soon as the deadline for the reply set by the Commission in respect of the LFN has passed.

With the introduction of a single-round infringement penalty procedure now being applicable in respect of non-communication cases by virtue of Article 260(3) TFEU, the question of interim relief in relation to casework involving non-transposition scenarios is arguably less of an issue. As was indicated in the previous chapter, in practice the Commission is usually able now to complete the pre-litigation phase in these types of case fairly swiftly under the aegis of Article 258 TFEU so as to be able to request a financial penalty from the CJEU within a relatively short period of time.[60]

4.3 Financial penalties under Article 260(2) TFEU

Article 260(2) TFEU stipulates that the CJEU may decide to impose two types of financial penalty on a defendant member state that it finds guilty of failing to comply with one of its previous judgments. Specifically, the treaty text refers to the possibility of a penalty payment or lump sum being imposed by the CJEU. No definitions or conditions relating to the application of these financial penalties have ever been set out in the relevant EU treaty framework, specifically neither in the TFEU nor the preceding EC Treaty. Ultimately, it has fallen principally to the CJEU to put legal flesh on the bare bones of the treaty provisions so as to clarify when and how such financial sanctions may be deployed; for the CJEU has power to provide a definitive interpretation of the sources of Union law.[61] Whilst the Commission has adopted and developed some guidance documentation on financial penalties covered by the second-round infringement action under Article 260(2) TFEU as well as non-communication cases under Article 260(3) TFEU, this guidance is ultimately not legally binding on the CJEU and in practice only of a relatively limited degree of assistance in predicting the degree of liability of a defendant in any given case.

In terms of clarifying the purposes of a penalty payment and lump sum fine, the CJEU has approved of a basic distinction suggested by the Commission in its original guidance on second-round penalties between the different types of financial sanction available under Article 260(2) TFEU. Specifically, the CJEU has verified that the penalty payment is particularly suited as a sanction for inducing a defendant member state to change its current conduct that has been identified as an ongoing failure to comply with a previous Court judgment.[62] Typically, the CJEU will construct the penalty payment to be in the form of an obligation placed on the defendant to pay a series of regular payments to be made from the date of the second-round judgment until compliance has been attained. In this sense, the sanction of the penalty payment is designed essentially (if not exclusively) to address the prospective dimension of the breach of EU law. By way of distinction, a lump sum fine is viewed by the Commission and the CJEU as having an essentially separate (albeit related) function in taking into account historic aspects of the second-round infringement. Specifically, both EU institutions view the lump sum as a means to reflect the effects of the breach of EU obligations by the defendant member state that have already occurred in relation to public and private interests, in particular in considering the length of time that the breach has persisted since the first-round judgment.[63]

This particular section of the chapter will explore how, in their respective roles, the Commission and CJEU have proceeded to establish clarity concerning both the purposes and bases for calculating the two types of financial penalty under Article 260(2) TFEU. It will first consider the guidelines set out and developed over time by the Commission relating to the modalities for calculating fines it wishes to request from the CJEU in individual second-round infringement actions. Subsequently, it will analyse the definitive general and particular principles developed by the CJEU in its case law relating to the imposition of financial sanctions.

4.3.1 *European Commission policy on financial penalties under Article 260(2) TFEU*

The European Commission plays an important, if ultimately inferior, role to the CJEU with respect to the financial penalty framework underpinning Article 260(2) TFEU. As the CJEU has reiterated in its case law consistently, under the

TFEU it is the Court and not the Commission that determines the level of fines in individual cases, the Court not being legally bound to accede to requests submitted to it from the Commission as prosecution agency.[64] Whilst that is true, it is nevertheless also clear that the Commission has had – and continues to exercise – a significant amount of influence on the conceptual as well as operational development of the penalty system underpinning Article 260(2) TFEU. This may be traced to the fact that it is the Commission, and not the CJEU, which is the EU institution having a specific responsibility to flesh out a detailed framework for the purposes of determining how to calculate penalties in individual cases. In its prosecutorial capacity under Article 260(2) TFEU, the Commission is required to 'specify the amount of the lump sum or penalty payment to be paid by the member state concerned which it considers appropriate in the circumstances'. The Commission considered that in order to be able to fulfil this obligation in a sufficiently transparent, proportionate and equitable manner, it needed to establish some clear and detailed criteria for the purpose of informing its calculations. Accordingly, relatively soon after the introduction of the second-round infringement procedure and prior to the first case being referred to the CJEU, the Commission published guidance in the mid 1990s, which it has subsequently periodically updated.

The original guidance documentation published by the Commission was published in 1996 and 1997. Specifically, this included the 1996 Commission Memorandum on applying Article 171 of the EC Treaty[65] and the 1997 Commission Communication on the method of calculating the penalty payments provided for pursuant to Article 171 of the EC Treaty.[66] Both instruments, which are discussed in detail in the first edition of this book and need not be reviewed here, have been replaced with new guidelines. The current set of criteria used by the Commission for the purposes of calculating second-round penalties is now contained in SEC(2005)1658 Commission Communication, *Application of Article 228 of the EC Treaty*[67] (hereafter referred to as the '2005 Communication'). The 2005 Communication, which came into effect at the beginning of 2006,[68] replaced the Commission's original 1996/97 guidance and other accompanying internal instrumentation[69] with a view to consolidating and updating its guidelines. The Commission has also published ancillary instrumentation[70] to the 2005 Communication, used essentially for the purpose of ensuring that the EU institution's fining calculations are adjusted in line with inflation.

The CJEU has welcomed the adoption of this information by the Commission, broadly endorsing what it sees as 'guidelines' as a suitable starting basis for assessment already at an early stage in its case law on the second-round penalty procedure.[71] At the same time, however, it has also been keen to emphasise that such guidelines are not to be considered as binding on the Court, and that it retains autonomy in determining whether fines should be imposed and their amount in each case.[72] From the Commission's perspective, it is clear that it views itself as being essentially committed to the criteria it has set out,[73] although the text of the 2005 Communication does provide for the possibility of the institution deviating from these under certain conditions.[74]

As the CJEU's case law on the second-round enforcement procedure has increased over time, the Commission's guidelines have been revised periodically with a view to ensuring that the Commission continues to align itself with the CJEU's interpretation of principles underpinning Article 260(2) TFEU. One key example of this has been the change of Commission policy, as indicated in the 2005 Communication,[75] to request the CJEU to impose both a lump sum fine and penalty payment in respect of cases involving ongoing failures by a defendant member state to adhere to a first-round judgment. Prior to the 2005 judgment in *French Fishing Controls (2)*, which confirmed the possibility of the CJEU being able to impose both types of penalty in individual cases, the Commission had opted to request only penalty payments from the Court. This had led, as the Commission itself recognised, to situations where a defendant member state might escape the imposition of a financial penalty being imposed if it ensured compliance with its EU obligations at the eleventh hour prior to the Court delivering its second-round judgment.[76] It is anticipated that future revisions of the Commission's guidelines will continue on a similar basis, so that periodically they will be consolidated chiefly in order to take on board developments in the CJEU's approach towards assessing financial penalties.[77]

The Commission's guidelines have been published for a number of reasons, in particular with a view to enhancing the level of transparency[78] and accountability of EU decision-making in this legal area. In particular, the Commission has been keen to establish, as far as is feasible, clear and objective criteria for the purposes of applying the EU treaty powers on financial sanctions against defaulting member states. It should not be underestimated how little in the way of guidance has been laid down in the relevant EU treaty provisions since the introduction of the second-round procedure in the 1992 Maastricht Treaty. From a legal perspective, it is evident that a key priority for both Commission and CJEU has been to flesh out in detail through treaty interpretation the main operative principles underpinning Article 260(2) TFEU to be used to calculate the amount of financial sanctions appropriate to each case. The Commission guidelines have provided both institutions with a core set of criteria which have laid the foundations for calculations to be made on a clear, consistent and proportionate basis. The detailed framework set out in the guidelines has served to ensure that the EU institutions involved in the second-round penalty procedure, in particular the Commission, do not fall foul of the charge that member states are not treated equitably and equally. In addition, in shining a light on the Commission's analytical work in relation to the second-round enforcement procedure, it has also assisted in enhancing the level of predictability of the Commission's proposals and accordingly the degree of legal certainty attached to the proceedings. At the same time, the drawing up of guidelines may be viewed as complementing a long-standing and broader political process dating back to the adoption of the 1992 Maastricht Treaty, in which member states have demanded greater transparency in relation to EU institutional decision-making.[79]

The 2005 Communication constitutes the Commission's core reference tool for the purpose of calculating the amount of financial sanctions that it should request from the CJEU in response to a failure on the part of a member state to adhere to a first-round ruling of the Court within a reasonable period of time, as required by Article 260 TFEU. The document is divided into five parts, the most important of which are Parts II–IV which are discussed below.

Part II of the 2005 Communication sets out key general principles that apply in respect to all financial penalties under the second-round enforcement procedure. Here the Commission identifies that the calculation of penalties should be based on three 'fundamental' criteria: namely (1) the seriousness of the infringement, (2) its duration and (3) the need to ensure that the penalty acts as a deterrent to further infringements.[80] The Commission also refers to a range of principles intended to be used in general terms as assisting in its task to determine the level of any financial penalty. These include, in particular, the principles of proportionality, equality of treatment and effectiveness,[81] all of which have been endorsed in the CJEU's case law and discussed in section 4.3.2 below. Part II of the Communication also provides some amplification on how the Commission is to take on board the proportionality principle, in light of the CJEU's evolving case law.[82] The Commission cites four specific consequences to be drawn from the proportionality principle. First, where it considers that there are clear and objective grounds for so doing, the Commission proposes to request distinct sanctions for each head of infringement in cases involving multiple breaches. The Commission notes that this approach will enable the Commission to propose a reduction of the volume of sanctions in line with the degree to which the defendant complies with a first-round judgment.[83] Secondly, the Commission indicates that in respect of cases involving so-called 'result-based' EU legislative obligations, namely those that involve long-term implementation duties such as those in the original Bathing Water Directive 76/160 litigated in *Spanish Bathing Waters (2)*, it will propose a calculation formula to the CJEU that seeks to take account of progress by the defendant in complying with those obligations.[84] Thirdly, the Commission also commits itself to ensuring that where the degree of implementation with EU obligations may only be assessed at periodic intervals, as exemplified in *Spanish Bathing Waters (2)* and *French Fishing Controls (2)*, it will ensure that it takes care to propose that any penalty payment is not crafted so as to impose a fine over periods when the infringement has in fact ended. In such a situation, the Commission may consider recommending a time reference period longer than the standard daily basis (e.g. six months or one year).[85] Fourthly, the Commission notes that it may in special circumstances be appropriate to provide for the suspension of a financial penalty, namely where a defendant member state affirms that all necessary measures have been undertaken but this may take a period of time to verify.[86]

Parts III and IV of the 2005 Communication focus on establishing the modalities for determining the amount of penalty payment and/or lump sum to be paid in any given case. These will be discussed in turn below.

4.3.1.1 Commission guidance on calculating penalty payments

Part III of the 2005 Communication focuses on establishing the modalities for determining the amount of penalty payment to be imposed in individual cases. From the outset, the Commission's guidance has interpreted from the EU treaty framework that the penalty payment is the financial sanction most appropriate to addressing those failures to adhere to first-round judgments of the CJEU that are still ongoing by the time the CJEU comes to hear the second-round action. The CJEU has endorsed this interpretation in the ensuing case law. The 2005 Communication confirms that, unless exceptional circumstances indicate that a periodic payment is more appropriate,[87] the Commission will request that penalty payments be imposed on a daily basis running from the date of the second-round judgment until the defendant complies with the first-round judicial ruling.[88] The Communication stipulates that the Commission is to propose penalty payments to the Court on the basis of a calculation formula using the following four core components:

- a standard basic flat-rate amount for the penalty payment (Bfrap);
- a co-efficient representing the relative seriousness of the infringement (Cs);
- a co-efficient representing the duration of the infringement (Cd); and
- a factor taking into account the relative ability of the defendant member state to pay (factor 'n').

With reference to the above-mentioned components, the penalty payment is calculated by two multiplications. First, the basic flat rate is multiplied by the co-efficients for seriousness and duration. Subsequently, the result is then multiplied by the 'n' factor. Accordingly, the standard method of the Commission's calculation for determining the daily penalty payment may be expressed[89] as follows:

$$(\text{Bfrap} \times \text{Cs} \times \text{Cd}) \times \text{n} = \text{daily penalty payment}$$

Part III of the 2005 Communication proceeds to elaborate on each of the four components, namely the flat-rate amount and three multiplier co-efficients.

The flat-rate amount applies as a basic starting component for each calculation and is the same in each case. Since the time of the 2005 Communication's adoption the amount has been subject to regular review[90] and normally on an annual basis in order to take into account periodic changes to inflation. The flat rate is calculated so that the Commission retains a broad margin of discretion when applying the co-efficient for seriousness; the amount is 'reasonable and viable for all' member states and, when multiplied by the Cs, is 'high enough to maintain sufficient pressure' on the defendant member state concerned as a means of inducing compliance.[91] As at September 2014, the daily flat-rate amount was set at €660.[92]

As regards the seriousness co-efficient (Cs), the 2005 Communication fleshes out a number of relevant factors that will assist the Commission in determining a multiple for the purposes of the overall calculation.[93] Two parameters are considered especially relevant: namely (1) the importance of the EU rules breached and (2) the impact of the infringement on general and particular interests. In evaluating the first parameter, the Commission is to take into account their nature and extent rather than their relative normative hierarchy. The Cs is set between a minimum of 1 and maximum of 20 depending on the relative gravity of infringement (with the least serious cases allocated the lowest number).[94]

The following are noted as examples of serious infringements in the 2005 Communication: violation of (i) the non-discrimination principle, (ii) fundamental rights and (iii) the four fundamental internal market freedoms.[95] In addition, it specifies that account should be taken of whether the first-round ruling forms part of well-established case law of the CJEU and the relative clarity of the rule breached.[96] The 2005 Communication also specifies that the Commission should factor in the degree to which the defendant has taken any steps to comply with the first-round judgment, and that it may consider a lack of full co-operation in the pre-litigation procedure as an aggravating factor.[97]

The 2005 Communication also provides some clarification of the second parameter of the Cs, namely the impact upon general and particular interests.[98] The parameter as a whole is to be assessed on a case-by-case basis, with the Communication providing a non-exhaustive list of factors that should be taken into account:[99]

- adverse impact on EU budget (loss of EU own resources);
- impact on functioning of the Union;
- serious or irreparable damage to human health or the environment;
- harm (economic or non-economic) sustained by persons, including intangible consequences such as personal development;
- any possible financial advantage gained by the defendant from non-compliance with first-round judgment;
- relative importance of the infringement, taking into account turnover or added value of the economic sector concerned in the defendant state;
- population size affected by the breach (seriousness could be considered less if the infringement does not affect the entire defendant state);
- EU's responsibility in relation to non-member countries; or
- whether the breach is a 'one-off' or a repeat of an earlier infringement (such as repeated delay in transposing directives in a particular sector).

Whilst it is apparent that several of the above factors may be relevant to any given environmental case, a few are of heightened importance in practice for environmental casework. The reference to serious environmental damage in the third bullet is of special significance for both bad-application and non-conformity infringement casework. In addition, the factors relating to the undermining of fair competition within the single market (on account of operators within the defendant state being able to evade EU environmental obligations)[100] and recidivism (repeat compliance failures by a defendant state)[101] may also be highly relevant in practice in environmental casework. The 2005 Communication specifies that the purpose of calculating the impact on particular interests is not to obtain redress for specific damage and/or loss sustained by natural or legal persons as a consequence of an infringement, given that such compensation may be obtained through proceedings before national courts. Instead, the aim is to consider the effects of a breach upon the public more generally, including impacts felt by particular social groups or cohorts.[102]

As far as the duration co-efficient (Cd) is concerned, the 2005 Communication offers relatively brief guidance,[103] part of which is in need of revision in the light of subsequent case law. The 2005 Communication specifies that, for the purpose of calculating the penalty payment, the period taken into account for the Cd is the duration of the breach from the date of the first-round judgment until the Commission decides to refer the matter to the CJEU for a second-round ruling. However, the CJEU in Case C-70/06 *Commission v Portugal* has subsequently confirmed that the period of duration runs further than this, namely until the CJEU assesses the facts in the second-round action (i.e. at the date of the judicial hearing of the parties).[104] The CJEU has also confirmed that the penalty payment may only be relevant if it is established by the CJEU that the breach was still live as at the time it assessed the facts of the case.[105] The 2005 Communication confirms that the Cd is a multiplier between 1 and 3, calculated at a rate of 0.10 per month from the date of the first-round judgment. The scaling of 1–3 leaves the Commission some discretion to raise or lower the co-efficient according to its view of the relative gravity of the period of non-compliance involved.

The 2005 Communication also provides some useful explanatory information and guidance regarding the final component, the requirement to take into account the relative ability of the defendant member state to pay.[106] This component has two main functions, specifically to ensure that the amount of penalty payment requested to be imposed by the CJEU is proportionate as well as dissuasive. In order to be effective, the element of dissuasion or deterrence is recognised in the Communication as needing to ensure that compliance is more (financially) beneficial to the defendant than a state of continued infringement and that the defendant does not repeat the same offence. The component is crystallised into a special 'n' factor, defined as the geometric mean based partly upon the gross domestic product (GDP) of the state concerned and partly upon the weighting of the defendant's voting rights in the Council of the EU.[107] The resulting mathematic formula produces varied co-efficients for each member state. The co-efficients are now updated annually[108] in line with inflation and GDP movements. As at September 2014, the lowest figure applied to Malta (0.35) and the highest to Germany (21.22).[109]

4.3.1.2 *Commission guidance on calculating lump sum fines*

Part IV of the 2005 Communication establishes the modalities for determining the amount of lump sum to be requested by the Commission in individual cases.[110] The lump sum is essentially broken down into two principal elements, namely (1) the setting of a minimum fixed lump sum and (2) a calculation method based on a daily amount multiplied by the number of days the infringement persists between the date of the delivery of the first-round judgment until the infringement desists or, failing that, until the date of the second-round judgment.[111]

In each case referred to the CJEU, the Commission is to propose at least the imposition of the first option, namely the sanctioning of a minimum fixed lump sum. Based upon the special 'n' factor used in relation to the penalty payment, the fixed minimum lump sum is updated every three years in line with inflation.[112] It is intended to ensure that each instance of non-compliance with a CJEU judgment is subject to 'real sanction', so as to reflect the seriousness of the breach as an attack on the rule-of-law principle and to avoid the imposition of purely symbolic amounts that might have little or no deterrence effect.[113] As at September 2014, the lowest and highest minimum lump sum amounts set were €193,000 (Malta) and €11.703m (Germany).[114]

The second type of calculation (multiplication of a daily amount by the number of days of infringement) only applies where the minimum fixed lump sum is exceeded.[115] The Communication notes that, in line with CJEU jurisprudence, the daily payment is to be calculated from the date of delivery of the first-round judgment. Although it concedes that a reasonable period of time must be granted to the defendant state to comply with the judgment, the Commission posits that should it appear that full compliance has not been achieved at the end of this period then the state is to be considered as having failed to fulfil its obligation under Article 260(1) TFEU to start the process of compliance immediately and have this completed as soon as possible.[116]

The daily amount for determining the lump sum is calculated on the basis of the following four core components:

- a standard basic flat-rate amount for the lump sum (Bfals);
- a co-efficient representing the relative seriousness of the infringement (Cs);
- a factor taking into account the relative ability of the defendant member state to pay (factor 'n'); and
- the number of days the infringement persists up until the second-round ruling (dy).

In some respects, the modalities for calculating the lump sum on a daily payment basis bears strong similarities with that applicable to penalty payments. Specifically, the co-efficients for seriousness and the special 'n' factor are exactly the same.[117] However, there are significant differences. First, the basic flat-rate amount is set deliberately at a far lower level than for penalty payments (one-third less), given that the penalty payment should take into account that the defendant will have failed to comply with EU law notwithstanding the declaration of two CJEU judgments.[118] The standard flat-rate amount is adjusted every three years to adjust for inflation[119] and as at September 2014 the amount was set at €220 per day.[120] Secondly, a specific co-efficient for duration is not used, given that the duration of the infringement is taken into account by multiplying the daily amount by the number of days the infringement persists. Accordingly, the standard method of the Commission's calculation for determining the daily amount for the lump sum may be expressed[121] as follows:

$$Bfals \times Cs \times n \times dy = \text{lump sum}$$

4.3.2 The CJEU's principles relating to financial sanctions under Article 260(2) TFEU

The emerging case law of the CJEU on second-round infringement proceedings under Article 260(2) TFEU has established a range of general (unwritten) principles regarding the imposition of financial penalties on defendant member states. These principles have served to carve out the essential legal parameters of both the Commission's and CJEU's powers in this area, and are of pre-eminent importance in assessing whether any particular sanctions are warranted in individual second-round infringement cases. As judicial interpretation of the relevant EU treaty text contained in Article 260(2) TFEU, the principles developed by the CJEU are legally binding[122] and have the same legal status as primary EU law (i.e. equivalent to EU treaty status). Accordingly, their legal status is extremely powerful, given that they may only be subject to adjustment via express treaty amendment (a process which has to be agreed to and ratified by all the EU member states).[123] The principles as developed by the CJEU in its case law to date may be subdivided into three sets, namely those that apply: (1) in common to all financial penalties, (2) to penalty payments and (3) to lump sum fines. They shall be considered in turn below.

4.3.2.1 *General common principles developed by the CJEU on penalty payments and lump sum fines*

The CJEU has over time established a number of general basic principles pertinent to its considerations of whether to hand down financial penalties in the context of Article 260(2) TFEU infringement proceedings. These particular basic principles are relevant to the imposition of penalty payments and lump sum fines.

One of the most important general principles has been the CJEU's consistent assertion of its autonomous and discretionary power to decide whether fines should be applicable in any given case and, if so, at what level they should be set. Whilst the CJEU recognises that the Commission has a role foreseen in Article 260(2) TFEU to make proposals on the amount of financial penalty to be paid, the CJEU has underlined that ultimately the decision over fining is one for the Court to make independently.[124] The CJEU has based its authority on the fact that the wording in Article 260(2) TFEU specifies that it 'may' impose a financial penalty. The CJEU has affirmed on a number of occasions that it is not bound by any proposals on levels of fines suggested by the Commission in second-round infringement proceedings.[125] The Court has also established that it may decide to impose a particular financial penalty, even where this has not been specifically requested to be done by the Commission.[126] At the same time, the Court has accepted that the Commission's guidance and suggestions to it constitute a useful non-binding reference point,[127] contributing as it sees it to ensuring that the Court's decisions are transparent, foreseeable and consistent with legal certainty.[128] In practice, it may be argued that the CJEU has broadly followed the Commission's suggested approach towards the calculation of penalty payments. In contrast, the Court's reasoning has been rather opaque to say the least with respect to the imposition of lump sum fines.

The substantial degree of control exercised by the CJEU in relation to determining the application and extent of second-round fines under Article 260(2) TFEU may be contrasted with the more limited degree of judicial power conferred under the auspices of Article 260(3) TFEU in relation to the imposition of financial sanctions for first-round 'non-communication' cases. The latter EU treaty provision specifically restricts the CJEU from imposing any fine in excess of that requested by the Commission.[129]

The CJEU has also established some important general principles relating to the relevant factors it takes into account when determining the amount of a financial penalty in the context of second-round infringement proceedings. Two key themes appear to be particularly prominent in the Court's thinking, namely the need for it to ensure that any financial penalty is effective to meet the second-round procedure's objective as well as be proportionate in nature. The CJEU considers that the Article 260(2) TFEU infringement procedure's principal objective is to induce compliance by the defendant member state, so that the penalty payment and lump sum fine are to be considered as legal tools to be used to this end.[130] Neither type of financial penalty is intended, according to the CJEU, to be used to compensate for damage having occurred as a result of a breach of EU law. Instead, the CJEU considers the two penalties to be legal mechanisms to be used as a means of placing economic pressure on a defendant member state to change its behaviour (or others within its jurisdiction) in order to attain a situation of compliance.[131] The levels of financial penalty imposed in individual cases are set according to the amount of persuasion required to change the defendant's conduct from a state of non-compliance to legality.[132] The CJEU has confirmed that, in setting a financial penalty, it will exercise its discretion in a manner that appears to it appropriate to the particular circumstances, in proportion to the nature of the breach and in proportion to the ability of the member state to be able to pay.[133] As regards the latter factor, the CJEU has relied very heavily on the Commission's published criteria on member states' relative ability to pay (discussed above in section 4.3.1).

One important general legal issue to arise relatively early on in the case law of the CJEU was whether a penalty payment as well as a lump sum could be imposed cumulatively on a defendant. This issue first arose in *French Fishing Controls (2)*, which is discussed in detail in Chapter 4A (available on website). The relevant treaty text in Article 260(2) TFEU might appear to indicate, from a literal interpretative perspective, that a choice has to be made in imposing either a penalty payment or a lump sum fine in any given case. However, the CJEU has held that the reference to the word 'or' in the final sentence of Article 260(2) TFEU allows for a linguistic interpretation of the text so that it may impose the penalties cumulatively. In addition, the CJEU has stated that cumulative imposition of penalties would not infringe the general legal principle of *non bis idem*, taking into account the distinct functions served by the two types of penalties.[134] The possibility of the CJEU imposing one or more financial penalties on a defendant member state is accordingly now well established.[135]

One element that has not so far received much attention or focus so far in the development of the principles underpinning the system of financial penalties in the second-round procedure is the factor of deterrence. In a general sense, one might argue that the very reason for the establishment of financial penalties in the Union's law enforcement regime originally by the 1992 Maastricht Treaty was to serve as a strong incentive for member states to adhere to their implementation obligations in relation to EU law in a correct and timely manner. However, the way in which the financial penalty system was initially constructed served to create a relatively weak form of deterrence. Specifically, prior to the entry into force of the Lisbon Treaty in December 2009 it was only after a member state had failed to comply with a judgment of the CJEU that the possibility of financial sanctions could be contemplated. Lisbon introduced the possibility of the Commission being able to apply to the Court in first-round cases for penalties where a member state has failed to notify measures intended to transpose an EU legislative directive into national law. However, the majority of non-compliance casework still has to be funnelled through a second-round infringement procedure before financial sanctions may be imposed.

As a result, litigation has tended to be a very lengthy affair to date, and has provided defendants with opportunities to delay the process for achieving compliance with EU obligations. Notably, if a defendant state is able to secure compliance before the close of the pre-litigation phase in the second-round procedure, it will escape having to pay any penalties entirely, notwithstanding the fact that several months even years may have elapsed since the deadline set for implementing the particular set of EU normative obligations in question and the first-round judgment of the CJEU. These factors tend to undermine the extent to which the law enforcement procedure in Article 260(2) TFEU may have a serious deterrent effect against defective implementation of EU law at national level. It remains to be seen whether and to what extent the CJEU over time will seek to strengthen the principle of deterrence that implicitly underpins the framework of the second-round infringement procedure.

4.3.2.2 *CJEU principles applicable specifically to penalty payments*

The CJEU has fleshed out a number of principles specifically relevant to the penalty payment in second-round proceedings. These have been useful in providing some degree of transparency regarding the criteria used by the CJEU in determining whether this type of financial sanction is appropriate in individual cases. The Court has accepted that penalty payments are inherently best suited to addressing situations where the breach is adjudged to be a continuing problem. Typically, it will impose a penalty payment in the form of a regular series of payments to be made by the defendant state commencing from the date of the second-round judgment until compliance has been verified by the Commission as having been achieved.

In practice, the CJEU is likely to be minded to impose a daily penalty payment in cases where it is relatively straightforward to ascertain whether or not compliance has been attained, whether this is a matter of involving non-conformity of national law with EU law[136] or involving an instance of bad application[137] of Union law.

By way of contrast, where the case requires a certain amount of time and assessment to verify whether a series of related breaches have been rectified and where the remedial measures required take a substantial period of time to take effect, the CJEU may prefer to set a longer time period between each penalty payment to allow for such assessment to be completed. So, for example, in *Spanish Bathing Waters (2)* the CJEU set a penalty payment to be payable each six-month period after the second-round judgment based upon the percentage of Spanish beaches identified by the Commission at that point as continuing to fall short of EU bathing water legislation.[138] The CJEU has confirmed[139] that the penalty payment becomes available as a possible sanction if it is established that the defendant's failure to adhere to the first-round judgment was continuing as at the time when the CJEU considered the facts[140] relating to the Article 260(2) TFEU infringement. By way of complement, CJEU case law has also established that the option of a penalty payment is closed if the defendant manages to effect compliance with the first-round judgment prior to that point in time.[141]

The CJEU has set out three primary factors or criteria it takes into account for the purpose of ensuring that penalty payments have sufficient coercive force on a defendant member state to rectify an ongoing breach and ensure that EU law is applied uniformly and effectively: namely (1) the duration of the breach of EU law since the first-round judgment, (2) the seriousness of the breach and (3) the relative ability of the defendant to pay.[142] It is these three key factors that assist the Court in determining the appropriate level of penalty payment, specifically in appraising whether it is prepared to accept or adjust the Commission's suggested amount for a penalty in any given case. All three criteria also feature as integral components in the formulation of lump sum fines. However, whereas the criteria of seriousness and ability to pay are treated interchangeably in respect of both types of financial penalty, the element of duration is calculated by the Commission on a different basis for each penalty. Specific details on calculating the weighting of each criterion are contained in the Commission's detailed published guidance on the application of Article 260(2) TFEU (considered above in section 4.3.1).

Whilst the Commission's guidance on calculating penalty payments for the purposes of Article 260(2) TFEU has been broadly endorsed in broad terms by the CJEU on a number of occasions, it is important to stress that the Court reserves the right to deviate from the formulae set down in the Commission's guidance in individual cases. Whereas the Commission has sought to employ a detailed calculation system that is intended to quantify in a clear, proportionate and equitable manner each penalty it sees as required for a defendant state, the CJEU's approach towards penalty assessment has ultimately been to distance itself from being tied to mathematical models and instead to emphasise the element of its discretionary power in determining the level of fines in individual cases. In particular, the application of the Court's three principal criteria outlined above is subject fundamentally to the CJEU's own assessment of how significantly they should be weighted in a given case according to the particular circumstances. Accordingly, the co-efficient used by the CJEU to weight each criterion may differ from that calculated by the Commission in accordance with its guidance.

This disparity between Commission and CJEU penalty assessment has been evident on a number of occasions, in particular in relation to the relative weighting of the factors of duration and seriousness. In practice, the Commission has endeavoured to align itself with the evolving case law when differences of approach appear to emerge between the two EU institutions. A couple of points may be noted here regarding the distinctive approach of the CJEU. With respect to the criterion of seriousness, the emerging case law indicates that the CJEU is most likely to treat non-compliance with a first-round judgment as particularly serious where it involves a substantive as opposed to a merely technical breach of Union law. This will result in the Court applying a heavier weighting being applied to this factor in the calculation of the penalty, which will serve to increase the level of the fine being imposed. In particular, this may occur when the defendant's conduct has served to undermine a key aspect of EU policy which has been crystallised into legal obligation. By way of example, the CJEU has identified that where the case has involved a breach of EU environmental legislation likely to harm the environment and public health, such a breach may be classified as a one of 'particularly serious nature'.[143] Similarly, breaches of other substantive norms of Union law, particularly in relation to the operation of the single market, have been identified as examples of serious violations.[144] On the other hand, technical or other breaches of Union law that may be considered to have a relatively minor adverse impact upon the operation of EU rules in practice are most likely to attract a lower weighting to the seriousness criterion.[145] However, it will not necessarily always be able to distinguish between minor and major ongoing breaches with first-round judgments, and there have already been a number of instances of divergence between Commission and CJEU as to the quantification of seriousness in individual cases.

The CJEU has also tended to approach the criterion of duration slightly differently to that followed by the Commission in penalty payment calculations. Specifically, whereas the Commission seeks to quantify this particular element precisely according to the length of non-compliance with the first-round judgment, the Court's approach has been to apply a heavy weighting to this criterion after a certain period of time has elapsed. For instance, in *Commission v France*[146] the Court considered that the highest weighting on the scale used by the Commission should be used to calculate the duration criterion, taking into account that four years had elapsed since the first-round judgment and the nature of the breach of Union law was relatively straightforward to rectify (non-transposition).[147] These differences between the Commission and CJEU over the application of the duration and seriousness criteria in specific cases highlight the genuine autonomy of the Court in determining financial penalty calculations as well as the inherently subjective, discretionary nature of assessing defendant member states' behaviour in relation to the criteria. Ultimately, it makes it difficult to predict with any certainty the level of penalty payment that the CJEU is likely to impose in any given case. One interesting trend in the second-round infringement case law so far has introduced one element of apparent predictability, though. Specifically, the experience to date on second-round infringement litigation has shown that the CJEU has consistently awarded lower levels of penalty payment than those requested by the Commission. This may be a reflection of the Court being in practice more open than the Commission to consider taking into account mitigating factors and/or being sympathetic to the difficulties facing member states in meeting their compliance challenges. The reasons for this judicial trend are not really clear, not least because the CJEU does not provide a detailed explanation of the reasoning underpinning its calculations. Whether this trend continues will depend entirely on the CJEU's evolution of its views on how best to employ its discretionary power in meeting the objectives underpinning Article 260(2) TFEU.

4.3.2.3 *CJEU principles specifically applicable to lump sum fines*

The CJEU has assisted in carving out a distinct role for the lump sum fine that may be imposed under the aegis of Article 260(2) TFEU. In particular, the Court has affirmed that this type of penalty is particularly suited to rendering defendant member states accountable for the problems arising as a result of substantial delay that has already occurred in respecting the first-round judgment. Its focus is essentially retrospective in nature, namely to assess the adverse effects on public and private interests that have arisen as at the conclusion of the second-round pre-litigation phase.[148] In this sense, the lump sum fine's principal role is to seek to hold the defendant member state accountable for a substantial and unjustified delay in adhering to the terms of a first-round judgment and in implementing EU obligations.

In addition, the CJEU has also confirmed that part of the general function of the lump sum fine, as with the penalty payment, is to seek to induce member state compliance with its judgments. Like the penalty payment, the object of the lump sum is not to provide compensation for damage sustained but to place a defendant under economic pressure to bring an end to an infringement with EU obligations.[149] In a general sense, the CJEU recognises the lump sum fine as having in part a coercive role to play to induce compliance. However, in cases where the infringement persists as at the time the Court examines the factual circumstances relating to the case, the CJEU has confirmed that the element of coercion becomes exclusively key for the application of the penalty payment, which is more suited to being tailored to induce a change in a defendant's current behaviour.[150]

At the same time, the CJEU has been keen to emphasise the discretionary nature of its power with respect to lump sum fines. Specifically, it has confirmed that the imposition of such a fine is not an 'automatic' decision,[151] taking into account the fact that Article 260(2) TFEU expressly stipulates that the Court 'may' impose a penalty payment or lump sum. The CJEU's emphasis on the element of discretion has often made it especially difficult to predict how the Court will react in individual cases, not least because the judicial reasoning of the CJEU with regard to the determination of a lump sum award has on a number of occasions been extremely brief and accordingly very difficult to analyse. In particular, the CJEU has preferred to avoid providing a mathematical explanation of its fining calculations. Attention to detail here is wanting. This is often especially the case where the CJEU has decided to impose a penalty payment concurrently on a defendant. Typically, the CJEU will devote far more space to providing an analysis of its judicial decision with respect to a request from the Commission for a penalty payment than for a lump sum fine, which may be the subject of a few lines at the end of the judgment.

The CJEU has confirmed in a series of cases a number of key factors that it will appraise in each case when assessing whether a lump sum fine is an appropriate sanction. Specifically, the CJEU has held that it will consider all relevant factors relating, first, to the nature of the infringement and, secondly, to the individual conduct of the defendant member state.[152] Of particular importance in this regard for the Court is to consider the relative duration of the breach of EU law and the private and public interests adversely affected.[153] Whilst it is not required that a certain minimum number of relevant factors need to be present in order for a lump sum to be imposed by the CJEU, it is apparent that the greater the number of factors pertinent to a case, the greater the likelihood of such a fine being sanctioned by the Court and its financial magnitude.

As regards the element of duration of a breach of EU law, the Court has adopted a relatively strict approach towards failures on the part of defendant member states to ensure that their national laws comply on time with the evolving legal requirements of EU law. Notably, the CJEU has consistently viewed transposition of EU directives into national law as a relatively straightforward obligation to fulfil, and accordingly has been generally dismissive of arguments submitted by defendant member states to the effect either that insufficient time has been provided by the Commission for compliance or that the duration of non-compliance at has been relatively short so rendering imposition of a penalty unwarrantable in the circumstances.[154] The Court takes on board that a specific period (often substantial) is provided in EU legislation to allow for transposition to be carried out. For instance, in *Commission v Sweden*[155] the CJEU imposed a €3m lump sum award on Sweden for having failed to transpose an EU directive on data retention in national law, notwithstanding that compliance had been achieved prior to the second-round judgment, that transposition had been delayed on account of an intense and lengthy internal national parliamentary debate about the legislation and that Sweden had an otherwise unblemished record on compliance with EU obligations. The key factor for the Court ultimately was the fact that 'a significant period of time' (27 months) had elapsed subsequent to the first-round CJEU ruling.[156] Similarly, the CJEU has come down heavily on member states where it considers they have failed to ensure compliance with EU obligations of a procedural nature that do not require substantial investment in terms of either finances or administrative supervision. Accordingly, in *Commission v Greece*,[157] where a €3m lump sum was imposed on the Greek state, the CJEU specifically took into account that the breach of EU law, namely the failure to notify to the Commission national legislation needing to be scrutinised for compliance with internal market rules,[158] had continued for a 'long period'[159] (31 months) since the first-round infringement ruling.[160]

In terms of appraising the degree to which private and/or public interests are affected by the failure to adhere to the first-round judgment, the CJEU takes into particular account to what extent the breach of EU law in question may be categorised as serious in nature. Whilst the case law is still in need of clarification in this area, the CJEU has given some indications of what would be relevant to consider here. Specifically, factors that would be relevant in identifying seriousness include considering whether the breach involved violation of substantive norms or merely technical or procedural errors, and whether the infringement concerns a key area of EU policy. The Court has confirmed that breaches of EU rules affecting the operation of the internal market (e.g. free movement of goods norms[161] or EU legislation designed to protect health and/or the environment)[162] may be regarded as instances of violations that have actually or potentially significant adverse consequences for private or public interests. In *French GMO Controls (2)*, the CJEU held that where failure to comply with a judgment of the Court is likely to harm the environment and endanger human health, the protection of which is one of the Union's environmental policy objectives, such a breach is to be regarded as 'of a particularly serious nature'.[163]

The conduct of the defendant member state's government or authorities will also be a highly relevant factor in the mix for a judicial decision over a lump sum. In particular, the CJEU will look closely at the extent to which the defendant member state has co-operated with the Commission in seeking to implement a first-round judgment of the Court. For instance, in *French GMO Controls (2)*, the CJEU was critical of the French government having only adopted the first of its measures intended to transpose EU legislation on GMOs (Directive 2001/18) over a year after the elapse of the Commission's final written warning in second-round proceedings.[164] In addition, the CJEU will also consider the defendant's conduct in a broader context, where it deems the case at hand to be illustrative of a wider or even systemic compliance problem confronting the member state concerned. The CJEU has confirmed that a record of repeated unlawful conduct on the part of a defendant state in a specific sector may be an indication that effective prevention of future recidivist behaviour may require the adoption of a lump sum payment as a dissuasive measure. For example, in the environmental cases *French GMO Controls (2)*[165] and *Irish Waste Water (2)*[166] the CJEU considered as relevant that both defendant states had been subject to a number of other recent first-round actions and judgments for failures to comply with EU legislation in the particular policy sector concerned. In *Commission v Italy*[167] the CJEU noted that the Italian government had already been subject to a number of adverse judgments confirming its illicit use of state aid and underlined that effective prevention of similar infringements could be considered to be an indication that a lump sum fine is warranted.[168]

Notwithstanding the fact that the CJEU has, as outlined above, set out in general terms the core factors used by it to appraise Commission requests for lump sum fines in second-round proceedings, in practice it has been difficult to glean from the Court's reasoning how it calculates fines in specific cases. So far, there has been a distinct lack of transparency on the part of the Court in divulging how it precisely quantifies lump sum fines. Where the Commission has requested the imposition of both a penalty payment request and a lump sum, typically the CJEU has devoted relatively little space for analysis of the lump sum request after having provided its judicial reasoning with respect to the penalty payment claim. It is as if the CJEU's consideration of the lump sum request in these cases constitutes a significantly ancillary and inferior matter, almost an afterthought in the case. For instance, in *French Fishing Controls (2)*, the Court devoted only three paragraphs to the issue of a lump sum fine (paragraphs 114–16), compared with 17 paragraphs on the penalty payment (paragraphs 98–113). Such imbalance of judicial attention between penalty payment and lump sum fine is also reflected in other cases,[169] and has served to restrict insight into the CJEU's approach to quantifying lump sum fines. Even where the specific litigation at hand has been focused solely on the lump sum as a penalty, the CJEU has not elaborated on how the various principles it has developed have had a specific bearing on quantifying the fine it ultimately imposes on a defendant state.[170]

Accordingly, the root of the problem lies not so much with brevity of judicial analysis or lack of cases[171] as with the fact that CJEU does not show how the general core factors, which are supposed to serve as a framework for its analysis, actually feed into specific lump sum calculations. By way of contrast, the European Commission has set out in published guidelines the modalities by which it calculates proposals for lump sum fines (as well as penalty payments) in individual cases. These guidelines have served to inject a considerable amount of transparency and legal certainty into the Commission's role of presenting the Court with suggestions for financial penalties that may be possibly imposed on defendant member states. If the case law to date had been showing the CJEU in broad terms adhering to the Commission's suggested amounts for lump sum fines, one might have been able to impute from the Court that the Commission's guidelines could be treated as essentially authoritative. However, practice has shown otherwise.

Frequently, the CJEU has determined significantly different amounts for lump sum fines compared to those suggested by the Commission, without the Court offering any clear explanation to justify the difference. A case in point is *French GMO Controls (2)*. Whilst the Commission's suggested calculation for a lump sum fine in that case would have amounted to some €69m[172] the CJEU imposed instead a lump sum of €10m. Another example is *Commission v Greece*,[173] in which the Commission suggested imposing a lump sum that would have amounted to around €8.75m, whilst the CJEU determined that instead €1m was appropriate. Admittedly, the CJEU did indicate in general terms that there were factors relating to the conduct of the defendants in both cases that in its view lessened the degree of seriousness attached to the failure to adhere to the first-round judgment.[174] However, rather frustratingly, the Court fails to provide any specific details as to how it arrives at its final lump sum calculation in each case. Moreover, the CJEU fails to provide any convincing explanation as to why the conduct of the defendant member states served as significant mitigating factors, bearing in mind that the litigation had been protracted resulting a situation of non-compliance by both defendants for several years.[175] In *French Fishing Controls (2)*, the CJEU baldly decided that 'the specific circumstances of the case are fairly assessed by setting the amount of the lump sum which the French Republic will have to pay at EUR 20,000,000',[176] without offering any breakdown of this figure and notwithstanding that the Commission had not proposed any lump sum fine for this case.

The overall impression one gains from the available case law on lump sum fines under Article 260(2) TFEU is that the CJEU appears particularly keen to reserve its independence of judgment on determining both the application and amount of this type of financial penalty. On a number of occasions the CJEU has expressly underlined that Article 260(2) TFEU confers upon it a 'wide discretion' with respect to lump sum fines.[177] The CJEU has acknowledged that the factors of deterrence and co-operative conduct on the part of defendant, both of which are very difficult to quantify objectively and are not specifically taken into account in the Commission's framework for analysis, are integral components in the Court's appraisal for lump sum awards. These may be key underlying reasons why the CJEU has shied away from providing detailed mathematical analyses of its lump sum decisions. Moreover, the Court has indicated that it prefers to make decisions that are not subject to any precise or detailed calculation formula. This is underpinned by the fact that all of its judgments on lump sum fines to date have been expressed in figures rounded to one or more millions of euros.[178]

In sum, the CJEU appears to favour using a relatively broad-brush approach in dealing with lump sum fines, whilst preferring to deliver a far more precise and detailed judgment of in respect of penalty payments. This has resulted in inconsistency on the Court's part in applying the rules on financial penalties under Article 260(2) TFU. It is difficult to see what justification the Court has in refusing to provide detailed reasoning for its lump sum decisions as it has done so with respect to penalty payments. Even if some factors may be difficult or well-nigh impossible to quantify objectively, nevertheless the CJEU should provide a greater amount of information on its calculations in the interests of promoting transparency and legal certainty, both of which it has recognised as general principles of EU law. Just as the Commission has provided a system to explain its calculation decisions, the CJEU should do the same, specifically setting out the relevant numerical weighting it attaches to each co-efficient in individual cases. The trend of the CJEU's case law so far though has been regressive, undermining transparency, accountability and certainty of judicial decision-making in this sensitive area. Defendant member states facing financial penalties under Article 260(2) TFEU, which may of course be often substantial, should be entitled to understand in sufficient detail, as far as is feasible, the bases upon which such decisions are made.

4.3.2.4 *Collection of financial penalties*

Under the EU treaty system there is a division of supranational institutional labour shared between the CJEU and the Commission regarding the management of financial penalties levied in infringement proceedings. The functional distinction is not clearly set down in the relevant treaty provisions and, as in so many instances of the development of EU law on environmental law enforcement, the CJEU has had a seminal role in clarifying the roles of both institutions.

One the one hand, the CJEU has jurisdiction to determine whether one or more financial penalties are to be imposed on a defendant member state and, if so, its quantum. This exclusive jurisdiction, confirmed by the CJEU itself from the outset of its case law on second-round infringements,[179] is apparent from the text of Article 260(2) TFEU applicable to second-round proceedings. Similarly, Article 260(3) TFEU applicable to first-round proceedings relating to non-communication cases expressly provides the CJEU with ultimate and exclusive power to sanction a defendant member state.

On the other hand, the Commission has responsibility to ensure that fines are collected from the defendant member state once these have been imposed by the CJEU in a ruling. Whilst this particular role is not expressly set out in the EU treaty provisions, a number of reasons point to this being implicitly the case, and the CJEU has confirmed relatively recently that the Commission has competence to carry out this function.[180] All fines are to be paid into the general budget (own resources) of the European Union. Under Article 317 TFEU the Commission is required to implement the Union's budget in accordance with regulations adopted in accordance with Article 322 TFEU. The EU's Financial Regulation,[181] which provides the legislative framework for implementation of the Union's budget, confirms the authority and procedures for the Commission as authorising officer for implementing revenue to establish entitlements to be recovered and issuing recovery orders.[182]

The competence of the Commission over collection of fines was the subject of spin-off litigation to emerge from the *French Fishing Controls (2)* judgment,[183] one of the CJEU's rulings on second-round penalties involving EU environmental legislation and discussed in detail in the next section. The French government disputed the power of the Commission to adopt a decision requiring France to pay a tranche of the penalty payment set down in the CJEU's second-round ruling. The CJEU had ordered the member state to pay to the Commission into the Union's budget an immediate lump sum fine of €20m as well as a penalty payment of €57,761,250 for each period of six months after delivery of its second-round judgment if it was found that the terms of its first-round ruling had still not been complied with. Subsequent to a request for information about compliance measures taken and five inspections carried out by its officials, the Commission adopted a decision confirming that the terms of the second-round ruling regarding the penalty payment had been breached and requiring France to pay the amount of €57,761,250. Prior to adopting that decision, the Commission had provided the French authorities with copies of the inspection reports. The French government brought proceedings against the Commission before the General Court of the CJEU under Article 263 TFEU seeking an annulment of the decision on a number of grounds, alleging lack of competence on the Commission's part, a breach of the rights of the defence in that the defendant was not offered a hearing prior to the decision, that the Commission had incorrectly assessed measures taken to implement the second-round judgment and that the Commission should have reduced the level of fine imposed.

The General Court dismissed the annulment action and found in favour of the Commission.[184] First, it confirmed that the Commission had competence to recover the penalty payment as part of its mandate to implement the Union budget, and accordingly was not required to refer back to the CJEU for confirmation that payment was due in the circumstances.[185] Secondly, the Court held that the absence of a prior hearing did not breach the defendant's rights. Whilst it recognised that the Commission was obliged under Article 4(3) TEU to seek a constructive dialogue with the defendant state in determining whether the first-round CJEU ruling had been complied with by the deadline set by the CJEU's second-round judgment, this did not extend beyond that requirement.[186] Thirdly, the Court held that, whilst the Commission is obliged to take steps in order to verify whether the complaints upheld by the second-round judgment still apply prior to recovering a deferred penalty payment, in this case France failed to show that the Commission had breached that obligation.[187] Notably, the Commission had carried out a number of inspections confirming the continuation of inadequate controls by French authorities to implement EU Common Fishery Policy requirements on minimum size of fish catches. Finally, the Court confirmed that the terms of the CJEU second-round judgment did not oblige the Commission to reduce the level of penalty payment in taking into account efforts by the defendant state to comply with the second-round ruling. Specifically, the General Court noted that the CJEU in *Fishing Controls (2)* had imposed a set penalty payment, not a gradually decreasing payment as it had done in *Spanish Bathing Waters (2)*. Accordingly, notwithstanding that some progress had been made by the French authorities to comply with the second-round ruling by the end of the six-month deadline, the Commission was obliged to recover the full penalty payment in accordance with its institutional responsibility to adhere to penalty terms set by the CJEU.[188] The General Court also confirmed it had no express or implied authority under the EU treaty system to reduce the penalty itself set by the CJEU.[189] The General Court's judgment makes a significant contribution to the development of the law in ensuring that member states may not seek to draw out litigation still further beyond second-round ruling stage with a view to delaying implementation of their EU environmental obligations. The French government has not appealed the ruling.

4.4 Some concluding remarks on the second-round infringement procedure

As may be seen from the above analysis, the relatively few judgments so far from the CJEU on Article 260(2) TFEU have already managed to clarify several key legal issues surrounding the application of that procedure. As one might expect, though, a number of important legal issues remain as yet unanswered. One outstanding issue of particular note concerns the procedure for determining when payments should finally cease. The text in Article 260(2) is silent as to how matters should be conducted. For instance, no specific arbitration/appeal procedure is provided in the event the Commission and defendant clash over whether the necessary measures have been eventually taken to comply with the first-round ruling of the CJEU. Logically, it should be the Court to decide this, given that it alone has formal powers to impose a fine. It might well be the case that the Court would consider that it has either implied or inherent jurisdiction to hear pleadings in such an instance, as a means of upholding basic procedural rights of litigants to enjoy a fair hearing and be able to defend their legal interests.[190]

In the wake of *Kouroupitos (2)*, the Commission determined in mid 2001 that Greece had taken sufficient measures in order to comply with the first-round judgment and decided that it would no longer require payments to be made to it. Under the terms of the CJEU's second-round ruling, the penalty payments were to be paid to the Commission, into the EU's own resources budget.[191] One might wonder whether the Commission should not first have clarified whether it had the authority unilaterally (i.e. without formal approval from the CJEU) to decide that payments into the EU's budget should cease, for the Commission was instructed to act effectively as 'trustee' of the monies paid to it by Greek government. This issue was all the more important, given the fact that within the Commission itself the decision to suspend the requirement to make payments was highly controversial from a legal perspective (as is discussed in greater detail in the next chapter, which considers the various shortcomings of the current law enforcement framework of Articles 258 and 260(2) TFEU). In his Opinion in *Spanish Bathing Waters (2)*, Advocate General Mischo made some interesting comments on this particular issue which were not taken up by the CJEU in its judgment. He opined that requiring the parties to apply to the Court for adjustments to its financial penalty decisions in a straightforward non-transposition case would be an unreasonably formalistic requirement. In his view, the Commission should be allowed instead to determine cessation of the need to pay in the event of appropriate transposition measures being forthcoming. However, in respect of other types of cases such as those involving bad application of EU law (for example *Kouroupitos (2)* and *Spanish Bathing Waters (2)*, he appeared to question whether the Commission would have the legal authority without prior approval from the CJEU to adjust penalty payment in order to reflect steps taken to ensure compliance with a first-round judgment.[192] Further case law from the CJEU is required to provide clarity on the proper procedures that should be adopted in order to effect an amendment to a penalty payment decision of the Court.

Notes

1   It is important to note that the second-round infringement procedure applies as a follow-up to instances of member states failing to adhere to CJEU judgments in proceedings other than Arts. 258–9 TFEU. An example would be state aid proceedings under Art. 108 TFEU, in respect of which there have been some second-round judgments: see Cases C-369/07 *Commission v Greece* and C-496/09 *Commission v Italy*. However, Arts. 258–9 TFEU constitute the core relevant first-round procedures from the perspective of EU environmental law enforcement. By virtue of the 2007 Lisbon Treaty (Protocol 2 amending the Treaty establishing the European Atomic Energy Community (Euratom)), the first and second-round infringement procedures set out in Arts. 258–60 TFEU apply to the obligations contained in the 1957 Euratom Treaty, as amended (see Art. 106a Euratom). The second-round infringement procedure also applies as a follow-up with respect to other special Euratom infringement procedures applicable to the civil nuclear sector (namely Arts. 38 and 82 Euratom).

2 For a recent appraisal of the second-round infringement procedure, see e.g. Wennerås (2012).
3 Specifically, Case C-387/97 *Commission v Greece (Kouroupitos 2)*, Case C-278/01 *Commission v Spain (Spanish Bathing Waters (2))*, Case C-304/02 *Commission v France (French Fishing Controls (2))*, Case C-177/04 *Commission v France*, Case C-119/04 *Commission v Italy*, Case C-503/04 *Commission v Germany*, Case C-70/06 *Commission v Portugal*, Case C-121/07 *Commission v France (French GMO Controls (2))*, Case C-568/07 *Commission v Greece*, Case C-109/08 *Commission v Greece*, Case C-369/07 *Commission v Greece*, Case C-457/07 *Commission v Portugal*, Case C-407/09 *Commission v Greece*, Case C-496/09 *Commission v Italy*, Case C-610/10 *Commission v Spain*, Case C-374/11 *Commission v Ireland (Waste Water Treatment Systems(2))*, Case C-270/11 *Commission v Sweden*, Case C-279/11 *Commission v Ireland (Irish EIA (2)*, Case C-95/12 *Commission v Germany*, Case C-533/11 *Commission v Belgium (Waste Water Treatment Systems)* and Case C-576/11 *Commission v Luxembourg (Waste Water Treatment Systems)*.
4 Specifically, Case C-387/97 *Commission v Greece (Kouroupitos 2)*, Case C-278/01 *Commission v Spain (Spanish Bathing Waters (2))*, Case C-304/02 *Commission v France (French Fishing Controls (2))*, Case C-121/07 *Commission v France (French GMO Controls)*, Case C-279/11 *Commission v Ireland (Irish EIA (2)*, Case C-374/11 *Commission v Ireland (Waste Water Treatment Systems)*, Case C-533/11 *Commission v Belgium (Waste Water Treatment Systems)* and Case C-576/11 *Commission v Luxembourg (Waste Water Treatment Systems)*.
5 Specifically, former Directive 75/442, now superseded by Directive 2008/98 (OJ 2008 L312/3).
6 Specifically, former Directive 76/160 subsequently superseded by Directive 2006/7 (OJ 2006 L64/37).
7 Now Directive 2011/92 (OJ 2012 L26/1) as amended, which superseded former Directive 85/337 (OJ 1985 L175/1) as amended.
8 OJ 1991 L135/40.
9 Art. 40 of the Statute of the Court of Justice (Protocol 3 to the TEU/TFEU) permits member states to intervene in cases before the CJEU.
10 Namely, cases involving non-communication of transposition measures or non-conformity of national law with EU legislative rules.
11 Based on information to be derived from Tables 3.3 and 3.4 in Chapter 3.
12 Case C-279/11 *Commission v Ireland (Irish EIA (2))*, Case C-374/11 *Commission v Ireland (Irish Waste Water (2))*, Case C-533/11 *Commission v Belgium (Belgian Waste Water (2))* and Case C-576/11 *Commission v Luxembourg (Luxembourg Waste Water(2))*.
13 For instance, in Case C-610/10 *Commission v Spain*, the Commission engaged in over seven years of correspondence with the defendant member state over the extent to which illicit state aid was being repaid by the recipient corporate group after the first-round judgment was declared in July 2002, before ultimately issuing an LFN under Art. 260(2) TFEU in November 2009.
14 See para. I.3 of Commission Communication, *Implementation of Article 260(3) of the Treaty* (OJ 2011 C12/1) published on 15 January 2011.
15 This ties in with the Commission's estimate of 8–18 months to be taken up by the pre-litigation phase for second-round actions in future. See para. I.3 of Commission Communication, *Implementation of Article260(3) of the Treaty* (OJ 2011 C12/1) published on 15 January 2011 in conjunction with COM(2007)502, Commission Communication, *A Europe of Results – Applying Community Law* of 5 September 2007.
16 As at the time of writing, there were five second-round infringement rulings concerning breaches of EU environmental law.
17 Art. 260(3) TFEU, as discussed in the previous chapter, concerns the management of the so-called non-communication cases in first-round proceedings.
18 Former Art. 171 EEC.
19 Since 1962, the European Commission has been vested with powers under EU legislation to impose financial penalties on undertakings which breach the prohibitions

contained in Arts. 101–2 TFEU concerning particular anti-competitive practices. See Regulation 17/1962 (OJ 1962 L13/204) which was superseded by Regulation 1/2003 (OJ 2003 L1/1).

20 Namely, former Arts. 169–71 of the EEC Treaty.

21 Former Arts. 244 and 256 EC (ex Arts. 187 and 192 EEC), superseded by Arts. 280–1 TFEU.

22 See former Art. 229 EC (ex Art. 72 EEC), now superseded by Art. 261 TFEU, which provides the possibility for regulations to be adopted at EU level to give the CJEU unlimited jurisdiction with respect to any penalties provided for in such regulations. Other provisions in the former EC Treaty indicated that the Council had jurisdiction to vest the Commission with powers to issue sanctions in the event of breaches of EU Law (notably, Arts. 211 and 308 EC (ex Arts. 155 and 235 EEC) and now superseded by Art. 17 TEU and Art. 352 TFEU respectively). The fourth indent of former Art. 211 EC (ex Art. 155 EEC) specifically obliged the Commission as one of its tasks to exercise the powers given to it by the Council for the purpose of implementation of rules laid down by the Council. Art. 308 EC (now replaced by Art. 352 TFEU) provided the possibility for the Council on the basis of unanimity to take appropriate measures if action by the EU should prove necessary to attain one of its objectives and the Treaty has not provided the necessary powers for so doing.

23 Krämer (1993), pp. 430–2.

24 Ibid., pp. 429–35.

25 These changes were already envisaged in the failed 2004 European Union Constitution (Art. III-362 of the Treaty establishing a Constitution for Europe (OJ 2004 C310, 16 December 2004).

26 See para. I.3 of Commission Communication, *Implementation of Article 260(3) of the Treaty* (OJ 2011 C12/1) published on 15 January 2011.

27 See former Treaty of Rome provisions Art. 171 EEC and Art. 228(1) EC.

28 As emphasised by the CJEU, e.g. in *French GMO Controls(2)* (Case C-121/07 *Commission v France*) (para. 21 of judgment). This general principle is well established in the Court's case law. See also e.g. *Spanish Bathing Waters (2)* (Case C-278/01 *Commission v Spain*) (para. 27 of judgment), Case C-374/11 *Commission v Ireland (Waste Water Treatment Systems(2))* (para. 21 of judgment), as well as Case C-270/11 *Commission v Sweden* (para. 56 of judgment).

29 See Case C-473/93 *Commission v Luxembourg*.

30 Case C-121/07 *Commission v France* (para. 70 of judgment).

31 Case C-374/11 *Commission v Ireland (Waste Water Treatment Systems(2))* (para. 22 of judgment).

32 Case C-270/11 *Commission v Sweden*.

33 Directive 2006/24 on the retention of data generated or processed in connection with the provision of publicly available electronic communications services or of public communications networks and amending Directive 2002/58/EC (OJ 2006 L105/54).

34 Case C-270/11 *Commission v Sweden* (para. 58 of judgment).

35 Case C-278/01 *Commission v Spain*. The case is discussed in detail in section 4.3 below.

36 Former Directive 76/160 (OJ 1976 L31/1), subsequently replaced by Directive 2006/7 (OJ 2006 L64/37).

37 See paras. 16–71 of Advocate General (AG) Mischo's Opinion in Case C-278/01 *Commission v Spain (Spanish Bathing Waters (2))*.

38 *Spanish Bathing Waters (2)* (para. 27 of judgment).

39 Ibid., paras. 28–9.

40 See Art. 19 TEU and Art. 267 TFEU.

41 In Case C-610/10 *Commission v Spain*, the CJEU confirmed that this treaty amendment covers second-round infringement proceedings commenced both before and after 1 December 2009. Spain complained unsuccessfully to the Court that an RO had not been issued even though the Art. 260(2) TFEU infringement action had been launched (with the issuing of an initial LFN) already on 23 November 2009.

42 Case C-457/07 *Commission v Portugal.*
43 The CJEU has reiterated this principle on several occasions in second-round cases: e.g. Case C-119/04 *Commission v Italy* (para. 27 of judgment), Case C-503/04 *Commission v Germany* (para. 19 of judgment), Case C-121/07 *Commission v France* (para. 22 of judgment) and Case C-496/09 *Commission v Italy* (para. 27 of judgment).
44 As confirmed by the CJEU, e.g. in Case C-610/10 *Commission v Spain* (para. 67 of judgment), Case C-374/11 *Commission v Ireland* (para. 19 of judgment) and Case C-270/11 *Commission v Sweden* (para. 16 of judgment).
45 Case C-177/04 *Commission v France.*
46 Directive 85/374 (OJ 1985 L210/29) as amended by Directive 1999/34 (OJ 1999 L141/20).
47 Case C-177/04 *Commission v France* (para. 37 of judgment).
48 Ibid. (para. 39 of judgment).
49 Case C-503/04 *Commission v Germany* (para. 22 of judgment). Belated compliance will usually effect a significant reduction in the amount of any financial penalty imposed (see e.g. Cases C-568/07 *Commission v Greece* and C-407/09 *Commission v Greece* where only a lump sum and no penalty payment was imposed on the defendant).
50 See e.g. Case 119/04 *Commission v Italy* (para. 41 of judgment) and Case C-369/07 *Commission v Greece* (para. 75 of judgment).
51 Ibid.
52 See Cases C-70/06 *Commission v Portugal* (para. 21 of judgment), C-407/09 *Commission v Greece* (para. of 36 of judgment) and C-270/11 *Commission v Sweden* (para. 54 of judgment).
53 Case C-387/97 *Commission v Greece.*
54 Case C-503/04 *Commission v Germany.*
55 Such as legal certainty, legitimate expectations, *pacta sunt servanda* and the right to property: ibid. (para. 36 of the judgment).
56 Ibid. (paras. 36–8 of judgment).
57 Art. 345 TFEU states: 'The Treaties shall in no way prejudice the rules in member states governing the system of property ownership.'
58 See e.g. Case 78/70 *Deutsche Grammophon.*
59 Arts. 278–9 TFEU.
60 The author has calculated from CJEU reported cases that the average time for completing the pre-litigation phase in non-communication cases in the environmental sector lasted on average just over 12 months in 2011: see Table 3.4.
61 See Art. 19 TEU in conjunction with Art. 267 TFEU.
62 See e.g. Case C-304/02 *Commission v France (French Fishing Controls (2))*, paragraph 81 of judgment.
63 See e.g. Case C-121/07 *Commission v France* (para. 58 of judgment) and Case C-568/07 *Commission v Greece* (para. 45 of judgment).
64 See e.g. Case C-270/11 *Commission v Sweden* (para. 41 of judgment).
65 96/C 242/07.
66 97/C 63/02.
67 Adopted on 13 December 2005 (OJ 2007 C126) and which may be inspected on the following EU Commission website: http://ec.europa.eu/eu_law/infringements/infringements_260_en.htm.
68 Part V.25 of SEC(2005)1658.
69 Notably, former Commission Decision PV(2001)1517/2 on definition of the duration co-efficient, 2 April 2001.
70 SEC(2005)1616/2, Commission Communication, *Empowerment for the Adoption of Decisions Updating Certain Data Used to Calculate Lump Sum and Penalty Payments under the Commission's Policy Regarding the Application of Article 228 of the EC Treaty*, 13 December 2005. At the time of writing, the most recent annual updating of calculation data was set out in the following document: C(2014)6767 final Commission Communication, *Updating of Data Used to Calculate Lump Sum and Penalty Payments to be Proposed by the Commission to*

the Court of Justice in Infringement Proceedings, 17 September 2014. These documents are available for inspection on the following EU Commission website: http://ec.europa.eu/eu_law/infringements/infringements_260_en.htm.

71 See e.g. Case C-278/01 *Spanish Bathing Waters (2)* in which the CJEU describes the Commission guidelines as a 'useful point of reference' (para. 41 of judgment).

72 See e.g. Case C-387/97 *Kouroupitos (2)* (para. 89 of judgment).

73 Part I.4 of SEC(2005) 1658 stipulates that the Communication constitutes a statement of the criteria that the Commission 'intends to apply to indicate to the Court the amount of financial sanctions it considers appropriate in the context'. See also the comments of AG Colomer at para. 100 of his Opinion in Case C-387/97 *Kouroupitos (2)*.

74 Specifically, the second sentence of Part I.5 of SEC(2005)1658 stipulates:

> The case-by case application of the rules and general criteria explained below and developments in the case law of the Court of Justice will enable the Commission further to develop its policy after adoption of this Communication. As each financial sanction must always be tailored to the specific case, the Commission reserves the right to use its discretion and to depart from these rules and general criteria, giving detailed reasons, where appropriate in particular cases, including recourse to the use of the instrument of the lump sum.

This proviso confirms, in particular, that the Commission is able to adjust its penalty requests in line with any requirements set out by the CJEU in case law subsequent to the Communication. The Commission has also ensured that the Communication is effectively updated in line with economic developments (relative GDP of member states and inflation). Accordingly, the proviso ensures that the Commission is not bound in an unduly rigid and inflexible way to the Communication's guidelines by virtue of the general principle of legitimate expectations in EU law. See e.g. Case C-313/90 *CIRFS v Commission*.

75 See Part II. A (The Lump Sum Payment) of Commission Communication SEC(2005)1658, specifically at point 10.3

76 Ibid., Part II.A. (at point 10.1).

77 See ibid., Part I.5. The 2005 Commission Communication is ripe for updating, so as to take on board EU treaty and accession changes (the Communication refers to pre-Lisbon treaty numbering and to only 25 member states) as well as recent judicial developments on the calculation of financial penalties discussed later below (see Case C-70/06 *Commission v Portugal*).

78 The 2005 Communication specifically refers to the 'interests of transparency' as a key ground for publication of guidelines: see Part I.4 of SEC(2005)1658.

79 See Craig and de Búrca (2011), pp. 541–9.

80 Part II.6 of SEC(2005)1658.

81 See Part II.7–8 of SEC(2005)1658. In addition, Part II.13 provides some amplification of how the Commission should have regard to the proportionality principle, in light of the CJEU's evolving jurisprudence (with specific reference to the rulings in Case C-387/97 *Commission v Greece (Kouroupitos (2))*, Case C-278/01 *Commission v Spain (Spanish Bathing Waters (2))* and Case C-304/02 *Commission v France (French Fishing Controls (2))*, all of which are considered in detail below in the final section of this chapter).

82 Art. II.B (The Principle of Proportionality) of SEC(2005)1658, points 13–13.4

83 Ibid., Part II.B.13.1.

84 Ibid., Part B.II.13.2.

85 Ibid., Part II.B.13.3.

86 Ibid., Part II.B.13.4. Although the Commission does not specifically state it in the 2005 Communication, this was a key issue in the Case C-387/97 *Commission v Greece (Kouroupitos (2))* litigation, when some months after the second-round judgment the

Greek authorities maintained that they had fulfilled their EU waste management obligations with respect to the illicit landfill site in Chania, Crete. Without providing sufficient time and resources for a comprehensive investigation of the site, and notwithstanding there was internal disagreement with the Commission's services in light of available evidence as to whether compliance with the first-round judgment had been achieved, the Commission decided in the summer of 2001 to close the case, thereby terminating the need for further penalty payments to be paid by Greece. However, the Commission subsequently discovered that the Kouroupitos dumping site had failed to be adequately managed in accordance with EU waste management law, and opened fresh first-round proceedings. Of course, financial sanctions could not be immediately reimposed. This would have to wait until the delivery of another second-round judgment, which would have taken several years and in the event did not materialise.

87 As set out in the general principles laid out in Part II.B.13 of SEC(2005)1658 and referred to above at 4.3.
88 Ibid., Part III.14.
89 As confirmed ibid., Part III.18.2.
90 See n. 13 to Part III.15 of SEC(2005)1658.
91 Ibid., Part III.15.
92 See section III(2) of Commission Communication C(2014)6767 final, 17 September 2014.
93 Part III.B.16 (Application of the Coefficient for Seriousness) of SEC(2005)1658.
94 Ibid., Part III.B.16.6.
95 Ibid., Part III.B.16.1.
96 Ibid., Part III.B.16.2.
97 Ibid., Part III.B.16.3.
98 Ibid., Part III.B.16.4–5.
99 Ibid., Part III.B.16.4.
100 See the second, fourth, sixth and seventh bullets of the list.
101 See tenth bullet of the list.
102 The Commission Communication provides the example of a state failing to transpose a directive on recognition of professional qualifications correctly, a breach that 'would undermine the interests of entire profession' (Part III.B.16.5).
103 Ibid., Part III.C.17 (Application of the co-efficient for duration).
104 Case C-70/06 *Commission v Portugal* (para. 45 of judgment).
105 Ibid. (para. 37 of judgment).
106 Part III.D.18 (Taking into account the member state's ability to pay) in SEC (2005)1658.
107 The geometric mean is calculated by taking the square root of the product of the factors based on the individual member state's GDP and weighting of votes in the Council of the EU relative to those of Luxembourg. See SEC(2005)1658, p. 9, n. 18.
108 See Commission Communication SEC(2010)923/3.
109 Commission Communication C(2014)6767 final, 17 September 2014.
110 Part IV.19–24 (Fixing the amount of the lump sum payment) of SEC(2005)1658.
111 Ibid., Part IV.19 and 21.
112 Ibid., Part IV.20, n. 19.
113 Ibid., Part IV.20.
114 See section III(4) of Commission Communication C(2014)6767, 17 September 2014.
115 Part IV.21 of SEC(2005)1658.
116 Ibid., Part IV.22.
117 Ibid., Part IV.23.1.
118 Ibid., Part IV,23.2.
119 See ibid., Part IV.23.2, n. 23.
120 Section III (2) of Commission Communication C(2014)6767 final, 17 September 2014.

121 As confirmed ibid., Part IV.24.

122 It should be noted that the CJEU's interpretation of the sources of EU law including provisions of the founding EU treaties is definitive and legally binding. See Art. 19 TEU and Art. 267 TFEU.

123 See Art. 48 TEU.

124 See e.g. Cases C-177/04 *Commission v France* (para. 58 of judgment), C-70/06 *Commission v Portugal* (para. 31 of judgment).

125 See e.g. Cases C-387/97 *Commission v Greece* (paras. 88–9 of judgment), C-278/01 *Commission v Spain* (para. 41 of judgment) and C-304/02 *Commission v France* (para. 103 of judgment).

126 Specifically, in Case C-304/02 *Commission v France* (*French Fishing Controls (2)*) the CJEU imposed a lump sum fine of €20m on France, notwithstanding that the Commission had requested imposition solely of a penalty payment in that case. The Commission had erroneously interpreted the treaty text on second-round enforcement proceedings (at the time Art. 228(2) EC) as barring it from requesting both types of financial penalty in one and the same case.

127 See e.g. Case C-496/09 *Commission v Greece* (para. 37 of judgment) and Case C-610/10 *Commission v Spain* (para. 116 of judgment).

128 See Case C-70/06 *Commission v Portugal* (para. 34 of judgment).

129 Specifically, as set down in the first sentence of the second subpara. of Art. 260(3) TFEU.

130 See Case C-304/02 *Commission v France* (para. 80 of judgment).

131 See e.g. Case C-177/04 *Commission v France* (para. 60 of judgment), Case C-70/06 *Commission v Portugal* (para. 35 of judgment), Case C-109/08 *Commission v Greece* (para. 28 of judgment) and Case C-496/09 *Commission v Italy* (para. 36 of judgment).

132 Ibid.

133 See e.g. Case C-374/11 *Commission v Ireland* (paras. 36 and 50 of judgment).

134 Case C-304/02 *French Fishing Controls (2)* (esp. paras. 81–3 of judgment).

135 See Case C-496/09 *Commission v Italy* (para. 82 of judgment), Case C-610/10 *Commission v Spain* (para. 140 of judgment) and Case C-374/11 *Commission v Ireland* (para. 46 of judgment).

136 See e.g. Cases C-177/04 *Commission v France*, C-109/08 *Commission v Greece* and C-70/06 *Commission v Portugal*.

137 See e.g. Cases C-387/97 *Kouroupitos (2)* and C-369/07 *Commission v Greece*.

138 See also Case C-533/11 *Belgian Waste Water (2)*.

139 See e.g. Cases C-177/04 *Commission v France* (para. 21 of judgment), C-304/02 *Commission v France* (para.31 of judgment), C-119/04 *Commission v Italy* (para. 33 of judgment), C-369/07 *Commission v Greece* (para. 59 of judgment), C-496/09 *Commission v Italy* (para. 42 of judgment), C-610/10 *Commission v Spain* (para. 96 of judgment) and C-374/11 *Commission v Ireland* (para. 33 of judgment).

140 This will in practice be considered to be the date of the oral hearing when held before the CJEU.

141 See Cases C-503/04 *Commission v Germany* (para. 40 of judgment), C-121/07 *French GMO Controls (2)* (para. 27 of judgment), C-568/07 *Commission v Greece* (para. 43 of judgment) and C-407/09 *Commission v Greece* (paras. 28–9 of judgment). See also Case C-279/11 *Irish EIA (2)*.

142 See e.g. Case C-70/06 *Commission v Portugal* (para. 39 of judgment), Case C-610/10 *Commission v Spain* (para. 119 of judgment).

143 See Cases C-387/97 *Kouroupitos (2)* (para. 94 of judgment), C-278/01 *Spanish Bathing Water (2)* (para. 57 of judgment), C-121/07 *French GMO Controls (2)* (para. 77 of judgment) and C-374/11 *Irish Waste Water (2)* (para. 38 of judgment).

144 See second-round cases involving violation of one of the four freedoms underpinning the single market (Case C-568/07 *Commission v Greece* (para. 54 of judgment, freedom of establishment), Case C-109/08 *Commission v Greece* (para. 33 of judgment,

free movement of goods and services). See also cases concerning breaches of EU rules relating to competition (Case C-496/09 *Commission v Italy* (para. 60 of judgment) and Case C-610/10 *Commission v Spain* (para. 125 of judgment, state aid rules).

145 For example, in Case C-177/04 *Commission v France* the French government's belated transposition of the EU Product Liability Directive 85/374, which occurred after the matter had been referred to the CJEU, was recognised by the Commission and Court as having served to reduce the state of non-compliance to a degree that could not, in practice, be adjudged to constitute a serious interference with the directive's objectives or with public and private interests (see para. 66 of judgment). Accordingly, the CJEU set a low weighting to the seriousness co-efficient (a factor of 1 on a scale from 1 to 20).

146 Case C-177/04 *Commission v France.*

147 See paras. 68–73 of judgment. See also Case C-70/06 in which the CJEU adjudged that a weighting of 2 should apply to the coefficient scale for duration, as opposed to a factor of 1 proposed by the Commission, on the grounds that the failure to comply with the first-round judgment had persisted for over three years.

148 See e.g. Case C-304/02 *French Fishing Controls (2)* (para. 81 of judgment), C-121/07 *French GMO Controls (2)* (para. 58 of judgment) and C-270/11 *Commission v Sweden* (para. 42 of judgment).

149 Case C-304/02 *French Fishing Controls (2)* (paras. 59–60 of judgment) and Case C-121/07 *French GMO Controls (2)* (para. 57 of judgment).

150 See e.g. Case C-121/07 *French GMO Controls (2)* (para. 56 of judgment).

151 See e.g. Case C-121/07 *French GMO Controls (2)* (para. 63 of judgment) and Case C-568/07 *Commission v Greece* (para. 63 of judgment).

152 Case C-121/07 *French GMO Controls (2)* (para. 62 of judgment). See also Case C-568/07 *Commission v Greece* (para. 44 of judgment), Case C-109/08 *Commission v Greece* (para. 51 of judgment), Case C-407/09 *Commission v Greece* (para. 30 of judgment) and Case C-496/09 *Commission v Italy* (para. 83 of judgment).

153 Case C-304/02 *French Fishing Controls (2)* (para. 114 of judgment), Case C-121/07 *French GMO Controls (2)* (para. 58 of judgment), Case C-568/07 *Commission v Greece* (para. 45 of judgment), Case C-109/08 *Commission v Greece* (para. 52 of judgment) and Case C-407/09 *Commission v Greece* (para. 28 of judgment).

154 See e.g. Case C-121/07 *French GMO Controls (2)* (para. 70 of judgment).

155 Case C-270/11 *Commission v Sweden.*

156 See also Case C-407/09 *Commission v Greece* where the CJEU decided that a €3m lump sum fine on Greece over its failure to ensure due transposition of an EU directive on compensation for crime victims (Directive 2004/80) was justified on the grounds that the Greek government had failed to even propose implementation legislation a year after the Commission's reasoned opinion had been issued (see para. 33 of judgment).

157 Case C-109/08 *Commission v Greece.*

158 Required by the EU's Notification Directive 98/34 (OJ 1998 L204/37).

159 Para. 53 of judgment.

160 An extreme case of delayed compliance concerned the state aid litigation of Case C-496/09 *Commission v Italy*, the seriousness of which the CJEU underlined in its judgment (see paras. 84–5 of judgment). The defendant member state had failed for over seven years after first-round judgment to define the aid needed to be recovered and had failed to take any measures to recover illicit state aid payments for two years after that initial judgment. The CJEU imposed a €30m lump sum fine on Italy.

161 See e.g. Case C-568/07 *Commission v Greece* (para. 54 of judgment, freedom of establishment). See also Case C-121/07 which involved a breach of Directive 2001/18 on deliberate release of genetically modified organisms (GMOs), the purpose of which the CJEU acknowledged was in part to facilitate the free movement of goods (see para. 78 of judgment). The CJEU has also referred to the 'vital nature' of EU competition rules in assessing the criterion of seriousness in connection with application of a penalty payment: see Case C-496/09 (para. 60 of judgment).

162 Case C-121/07 *French GMO Controls (2)* (para. 77 of judgment). See also C-374/11 *Irish Waste Water (2)* (paras. 38 and 47 of judgment).

163 Ibid.

164 Case C-121/07 (para. 71 of judgment).

165 See ibid. (paras. 66–9 of judgment).

166 See ibid. (paras. 48–9 of judgment).

167 Case C-496/09 *Commission v Italy.*

168 See ibid. (para. 89 of judgment).

169 See e.g. Case C-109/08 *Commission v Greece*, in which the CJEU devoted 29 para-
     graphs to address the request from the Commission for a penalty payment (paras.
     18–46 of judgment) and 9 paragraphs with respect to the request for a lump sum
     fine (paras. 47–55 of judgment) and Case C-369/07 *Commission v Greece*, in which
     the CJEU used 17 paragraphs to assess the amount of the penalty payment (paras.
     111–27 of judgment) as compared with 7 paragraphs devoted to the request for a
     lump sum fine (paras. 144–50 of judgment). See also Case C-503/04 *Commission v
     Germany* where the CJEU failed to explain why it considered that a lump sum fine
     was not appropriate in that case, notwithstanding that the defendant member state
     took over two years to comply fully with the first-round judgment (which was after
     the point at which the Commission had referred second-round proceedings to the
     Court).

170 As at June 2013, there were four second-round cases in which the CJEU imposed solely
     a lump sum, namely Cases C- 121/07 *French GMO Controls (2)* (€10m), C-568/07 *Com-
     mission v Greece* (€1m), C-407/09 *Commission v Greece* (€3m) and C-270/11 *Commission v
     Sweden* (€3m).

171 Until the judgment in *French Fishing Controls (2)* on 12 July 2005 the Commission con-
     sidered that it had no power to file a cumulative request for a penalty payment and
     lump sum fine before the Court in individual cases.

172 Expressed as €43,660 per day between the first and second-round judgments
     (52 months). The suggested daily amount was calculated by the Commission on the
     basis of multiplying a basic sum (€200) by co-efficients for seriousness and relative
     ability to pay.

173 Case C-568/07 *Commission v Greece.*

174 In Case C-121/07 *French GMO Controls (2)* the CJEU, in noting that this case was
     not one involving a situation where the defendant had not taken any implementing
     measures, held that several provisions of Directive 2001/18 did not call for specific
     measures to be taken by the French government and that within a month of the case
     being referred to the Court only three provisions of the EU directive required imple-
     mentation. The Court also noted that after the hearing and before the second-round
     judgment, proper transposition of the directive was achieved in June 2008. Moreover
     the Court accepted that there had not been any breach of good faith or deliberate
     delaying tactics in this case. In Case C-568/07, the CJEU took into account the fact
     that the Greek government had taken measures which had led to partial compliance
     with EU law prior to the first-round judgment and had subsequently introduced leg-
     islative changes over time which ultimately achieved full compliance with EU law
     within one year after the Commission referring to the matter to the Court for second-
     round judgment.

175 Over five years elapsed between the Commission's first-round RO and second-round
     judgment in *French GMO Controls (2)* and over ten years elapsed between the Commis-
     sion's first-round LFN and second-round judgment in Case C-568/07 *Commission v
     Greece.*

176 Case C-304/02 (para. 115 of judgment).

177 See e.g. Cases C-374/11 *Irish Waste Water (2)* (para. 47 of judgment) and C-270/11
     Commission v Sweden (para. 40 of judgment).

178 As at September 2014, the following lump sum fines had been imposed by the CJEU: €20m (in Case C-304/02 *French Fishing Controls (2)*), €10m (in Case C-121/07 *French GMO Controls (2)*), €1m (in Case C-568/07 *Commission v Greece*), €3m (in Case C-109/08 *Commission v Greece*), €2m (in Case C-369/07 *Commission v Greece*), €3m (in Case C-407/09 *Commission v Greece*), €20m (in Case C-610/10 *Commission v Spain*), €2m (in Case C-374/11 *Irish Waste Water (2)*), €3m (in Case C-270/11 *Commission v Sweden*), €1.5m (in Case C-279/11 *Irish EIA (2)*), €10m (in Case C-533/11 *Belgian Waste Water (2)*) and €2m (in Case C-576/11 *Luxembourg Waste Water (2)*).
179 See Case C-387/97 *Commission v Greece (Kouroupitos (2))* (para. 89 of judgment).
180 Case T-139/06 *France v Commission.*
181 Regulation 966/2012 on the financial rules applicable to the general budget of the Union and repealing Council Regulation 1605/2002 (OJ 2012 L298/1) as amended.
182 See esp. Chapters 3 and 6 of Regulation 966/2012.
183 Case C-304/02 *Commission v France.*
184 The case took over five years to be resolved by the Court, far longer than an annulment action would usually be expected to take. This might be taken as an indication that the General Court may have found this to be a difficult case to resolve internally. However, it should also be noted here that a change of composition of the chambers of the Court, which occurred during the litigation, may have contributed to the delay: Case T-139/06 *France v Commission* (para. 18 of judgment).
185 Ibid., (para. 37 of judgment).
186 Ibid., para. 44.
187 Ibid., para. 55.
188 Ibid., paras. 79–80.
189 Ibid., para. 81.
190 Consider e.g. Case C-70/88 *European Parliament v Council*, where the CJEU accepted that the European Parliament had an implicit right of standing to bring an action for annulment in order to be able to protect its prerogatives, notwithstanding that the relevant EU Treaty provision on judicial review at the time (ex Art. 173 EEC) did not accord the Parliament with such privileged access to the Court. (The Parliament has subsequently been accorded automatic legal standing to bring annulment actions under by virtue of treaty amendment, now consolidated in Art. 263 TFEU.)
191 See Order of the Court (item 2 of its ruling in Case C-387/97 *Kouroupitos (2)*).
192 See paras. 82–5 of his Opinion in Case C-278/01 *Spanish Bathing Waters (2)*.

5   Enforcement action brought by the European Commission (3)

Some critical reflections

Following on from the discussion in the previous two chapters of the legal framework underpinning Articles 258 and 260 of the Treaty on the Functioning of the European Union (TFEU), this chapter seeks to reflect on the broader context and effect of these particular tools of environmental law enforcement at EU level. At a basic level, their importance for EU environmental policy should not be underestimated. As has been noted with good reason elsewhere, the credibility of policy is undermined unless there is due and effective supervision and enforcement of transposition of legally binding commitments entered into by the constituent member states.[1] Whilst member states have a clear unambiguous duty under the EU treaty framework to secure the proper implementation of EU environmental law and legislation,[2] in practice this obligation has proven insufficient to ensure that the writ of EU environmental norms are respected at national level. The threat of legal action from the Commission in the form of infringement proceedings provides an important tool to use where necessary in order to provide sufficiently strong incentives for member states to comply with their Union-level legal obligations. The introduction and development of financial sanctions within the infringement proceedings system by virtue of the 1992 Maastricht Treaty and 2007 Lisbon Treaty have significantly enhanced the potency of the threat of law enforcement litigation under Articles 258 and 260 TFEU.

In many respects these particular enforcement proceedings remain the most important legal weapons that the Commission holds in order to assist it in its role as the EU institution charged with responsibility for ensuring that EU environmental law is applied correctly by and within the member states under Article 17(1) of the Treaty on European Union (TEU).[3] The Commission itself is effectively charged with the duty of upholding the environmental obligations undertaken by member states at EU level. That role becomes all the more important, when one considers in practice how relatively isolated the Commission stands in shouldering this responsibility.[4] As Krämer aptly points out, the environment has no 'vested interest defender'.[5]

Member states' record on compliance with EU environmental law over the years indicates that it is unsafe to rely on their promises to fulfil their environmental obligations. It is evident that the state of political and financial resources invested into EU environmental law enforcement at national level in some member states leaves a lot to be desired. Budgeting for delivery on environmental protection has not traditionally been a political priority for several member state governments, as compared with the efforts placed to secure economic benefits to be gleaned from the single market. Very few member states ensure that EU environmental directives are transposed into national law on time. The environmental inspections regimes within member states remain patchy and often under-resourced. The Union has only relatively recently begun to address the shortcomings in this area in earnest under the aegis of the Seventh EU Environmental Action Programme (EAP7).[6] At the same time, member states' records on facilitating the possibilities of the public, notably non-governmental environmental organisations (NGEOs), becoming involved and assisting in EU environmental law enforcement, as endorsed by the Union's membership of the 1998 UNECE Convention on Access to Information, Public Participation in Decision-making and Access to Justice in Environmental Matters (Århus Convention), is very mixed.

Moreover, it is also evident that there are relatively few powerful actors outside of government interests in civil society which are prepared and/or able to shoulder the responsibility of EU environmental law enforcement. The mainstream within the business sector has little if any vested economic interest in ensuring that environmental norms are upheld, unless it is apparent that non-compliance with specific environmental norms by competitors offers the latter a distinct unfair economic advantage. In contrast, large elements within this sector have been and are established crucial players in terms of assisting in the enforcement of the laws pertaining to the single market, through such methods as taking civil action before national courts as well as reporting of instances of violations of EU law to the Commission or to national governmental support contacts such as those under the SOLVIT[7] system. This is not surprising, of course, when one considers that the enforcement of single market law is a means of enhancing market and therefore profit opportunity for several businesses, particularly those with international presence. This leaves ordinary citizens and NGEOs, the latter in practice constituting important actors in environmental law enforcement. However, there are several well-known significant legal, financial and technical challenges facing citizens and NGEOs interested in pursuing (EU) environmental law enforcement. These range from being able to secure the legal right to act on behalf of the environment to take action against polluters in any given case (legal standing issue), being able or entitled to secure evidence of a principal cause of illicit pollution (causation issue), to having the financial resources to be able to be in a position to take legal action (legal costs issue). The ability of the private individuals and associations to undertake EU environmental law enforcement work will be considered later in more detail in Part II of the book.

Accordingly, there is little doubt that Articles 258 and 260 TFEU will continue to retain an important role in terms of assisting in EU environmental law enforcement across the Union. Taking into account the lack of priority member state governments attach to environmental protection as compared with economic policies and limited scope for civil society to be involved in upholding environmental policy (e.g. frequent, significant practical hurdles involved in mounting legal action to enforce environmental protection standards) it is evident that the Commission's supranational supervisory controls under the EU treaty framework will remain key tools in its task to ensure due application of Union environmental law at national level.

At the same time it is also widely understood and recognised from Commission and commentators alike that Article 258 and 260 legal proceedings suffer from a number of significant problems and limitations, many of which are not easily soluble. There are several issues concerning the current structure of infringement proceedings which constitute serious checks on the capability of the Commission to carry out its task to ensure that EU environmental law is upheld within the Union. The problems range from the technical inadequacies and shortcomings of the legal machinery itself to more profound issues concerning the inherent limitations posed for a centralised model of law enforcement. In particular, it is important ultimately to recognise the resource limits that constrain the ability of the EU infringement system to serve as an environmental law enforcement system and, as a consequence, to acknowledge the importance of the need to ensure that Articles 258 and 260 TFEU are appropriately supported by complementary law enforcement mechanisms at national level.

This chapter seeks to identify and reflect on these aspects, with a view to discussing possible ways and means of improving the current position and, in particular, how the Commission itself has sought to address some of the problems and challenges involved. Tables are provided at the end of the chapter containing some statistical data on the case management of environmental infringements by the Commission services.

5.1   Investigation and detection of infringements

A significant area of weakness associated with infringement proceedings brought under Article 258 TFEU is the pre-judicial process, namely the initial period of investigation carried out by the Commission.[8] In a number of important respects the Commission is hampered from the outset in certain types of cases when trying to ascertain whether or not a violation of law has occurred, in not having suitable powers or resources to verify complaints or launch own-initiative enquiries.[9] These are the so-called 'bad-application' cases, where the Commission suspects that EU environmental law has failed to be applied properly in a particular member state. For cases which involved scrutinising whether a member state has transposed its environmental obligations into national law as required by an EU environmental legislative instruments (non-communication and non-conformity casework) this particular problem does not arise, as legal analysis of these cases is entirely document based.

5.1.1   Investigatory and inspection tools

Article 258 TFEU does not provide the Commission with any powers to investigate cases where a member state is alleged or suspected of failing to ensure that

EU environmental law is applied in practice (the so-called bad-application cases). The allegation could embrace a situation where a member state authority is suspected of infringing an environmental norm itself or of tolerating an infringement on its territory by a third party. In either case, the Commission is not vested with any legal powers under Article 258 to be able to require relevant sites to be subject to mandatory inspection by its officials or those of the relevant environmental authorities within the member state concerned. As a result, the Commission has in practice been virtually dependent upon outsiders for the delivery of information and evidence for each bad-application case, whether from the member state authorities or from a complainant. In the vast majority of cases, EU environmental legislation does not incorporate provisions that specifically address the subject of EU level inspection.[10] Article 4(3) TEU, the treaty provision imposing a general duty of co-operation by member states in connection with the activities of the Union, is too vague and general in nature to constitute any clear or firm legal basis on its own for requiring member states to subject themselves to supranational investigations of suspected violations of law or to carry out systematic inspections of installations and sites. For this to occur, specific EU legislation would need to be adopted in order to crystallise the definitive obligations of member states and powers of the Commission for the purposes of conducting EU-led investigations. Historically, though, the majority of member states have been steadfastly reluctant to be amenable to the idea of facilitating or constructing a system enabling the Commission to spearhead infringement investigations. Currently, there is no clear, effective legal or administrative structure at EU level to enable the Commission to be in a position to make systematic checks on member states through the mechanism of investigations.[11]

In the past, the Commission has occasionally dispatched officials and/or contracted scientific investigation teams to carry out site inspections in the context of Article 258 casework. However, it should be noted that this is only possible where the defendant member state has agreed in advance or is in a position to be able to accept Commission site scrutiny. If the member state and/or site owner refuses to submit to an inspection, the Commission may not carry out on-site investigation. In practice, such investigations are rare and in any event lack the element of surprise. On each occasion a suspected defendant is forewarned of an investigation request. Even where the Commission decides in the highly unusual event to send out an environmental inspection team, it is not that straightforward internally within the Commission to find the necessary funds for the investigation.[12] For instance, in the aftermath of the *Kouroupitos (2)* litigation,[13] I recall during my period as an administrator dealing with legal issues in the Commission's Environment Directorate-General (DG ENV) technical unit responsible for waste management[14] there being a situation of uncertainty and financial wrangle in mid 2001 as to which Directorate within DG ENV would actually be responsible for funding the investigation of the waste sites suspected of breaches of EU waste management legislation in Chania, Crete. An inspection was considered necessary by the technical unit dealing with waste management issues to verify whether or not the Greek authorities had taken sufficient measures to implement the second-round judgment of the Court of Justice of the European Union (CJEU). Given the lack of a clear framework for the organisation of Commission environmental inspections, it was in any event difficult to access EU funding for such an inspection as there was no specific EU budgetary line for such work. Accordingly, whilst it may be the case that member state refusals to accede to an EU-level environmental inspection are rare,[15] this matters little, given the relative paucity of genuine powers and resources at the disposal of the Commission to launch such investigations in appropriate cases.

The lack of investigatory powers afforded to the Commission reflects a long-standing scepticism and resistance by the majority of member states into contemplating any independent EU environmental inspectorate for the purposes of assisting in EU environmental law enforcement. The matter of environmental inspection in general has been considered predominantly by member states to be a domain exclusively reserved to the national as opposed to supranational level, any attempts to introduce EU-level initiatives resisted as unwarranted incursions into matters perceived to be sovereign internal issues. Accordingly, the majority have resisted attempts by the Commission, for instance, to develop a supranational and independent dimension to inspections of installations.[16] This has been rightly criticised[17] as the emotionalising of sovereignty and subsidiarity principles, not least given that several other sectors of EU policy envisage EU-level inspectors, including notably in the areas of competition,[18] veterinary health,[19] fisheries[20] and customs policy.[21]

The absence of investigatory powers afforded to the Commission in enforcement work raises the prospect of the Commission having in practice to be substantially if indeed not overly reliant on the co-operation of member state administrations for supplying information on suspected violations and state of environmental legislative implementation.[22] This raises a clear potential conflict of interest, which may materialise where national or sub-national public authorities are reluctant or insufficiently resourced to carry out inspections or enforcement activities on account of non-environmental reasons or pressures.[23] For instance, the *Kouroupitos* litigation[24] was protracted and made particularly difficult not least because of the unreliability of information supplied by the local administration on the subject of compliance with EU waste management legislation. The lack of supranational oversight capabilities into bad-application cases also raises questions as to whether there are adequate systems in place to ensure that the implementation of EU environmental law is applied consistently across the Union. It is a core EU treaty mandate that the Union should aim for a high level of environmental protection.[25] This fundamental (constitutional) obligation applies across the geographical space of the combined territories of the Union's member states and an inability to ensure a comparable level of national implementation of EU environmental protection legislation serves only to undermine this essential legally binding commitment. Furthermore, a failure to ensure that member states are providing comparable levels of effort and effectiveness regarding implementation of Union law opens up the prospects of damaging competitive distortions arising within the single market, with enterprise in certain member states being subject in practice to less rigorous law enforcement regimes than others.

The incorporation of effective investigatory powers for the Commission has in the past attracted some degree of support from a number of quarters.[26] It has also been mooted in the not so distant past that the European Environment Agency (EEA), founded in 1990,[27] might expand its remit to be able to engage as an independent environmental inspectorate.[28] Currently, its core function is to provide information concerning the state of the environment, and this is based heavily on the supply of environmental data it receives from national authorities. Its original legal framework provided for a review to be conducted within two years of its inception as to whether it should be granted a role in the monitoring of EU environmental law.

Notwithstanding initial support from the European Parliament (EP) in favour of developing a monitoring role in the early 1990s, both the Commission and Council of the EU were not persuaded that a change in the EEA's functions was warranted. The Commission and Council decided to opt for a more informal process of encouraging better inspection standards at national level, rejecting the idea of a supranational role of the Commission in being directly involved in supervisory or operational aspects of environmental inspections. Both institutions considered that inspections should be considered essentially a national responsibility, whether these were routine checks or related to investigations of suspected breaches of Union environmental law. The Commission was at that stage initially reluctant to promote the idea for an EU-level environmental auditing body.[29] Rejecting the EP's call for a binding supranational legislative instrument setting common minimum standards on inspections, the Council of the EU adopted in 2001 instead a recommendation[30] establishing some non-binding minimum criteria regarding the organisational aspects of inspections at national level. No operational role is envisaged for the Commission (or other EU-level supranational entity such as the EEA) under the soft law instrument, which currently remains in place. The 2001 Recommendation's remit is confined to a limited area addressed by EU environmental legislation, specifically industrial installations covered by the EU's regime on integrated pollution prevention and control. In 2007 the Commission completed a first a review[31] of the recommendation's implementation, which expressed criticism about its narrow coverage and limited impact. Nevertheless, at that time the Commission concluded that the non-binding status of the instrument should not be hardened into an EU legislative measure.

However, most recently the Commission appears to be changing its views and assumed a renewed level of interest in the area of environmental inspections. The Seventh EU Environment Action Programme (EAP7) (2013–20)[32] specifies, in the context of one of its priority objectives,[33] that the EU is to extend binding requirements on inspections and surveillance to the wider body of EU environmental law, complementing these with an EU-level capacity that can address situations where there is due reason for concern.[34] The Commission is currently in the process of proposing a revision to the current EU legislative framework, with a view to establishing a minimum set of legally binding requirements. The subject of environmental inspections at national level is considered in more detail in Chapter 11 of this book.

Member states are also in practice vested with exclusive responsibility for reporting on the state of implementation of EU environmental legislation within their respective territories. It is a standard requirement[35] placed in EU environmental legislation that member state authorities are obliged to provide the Commission with basic information via questionnaires on the implementation of EU environmental legislation within their respective territories. It is apparent that this system of reporting has had a number of drawbacks. One obvious disadvantage is the in-built conflict of interest set up by this type of scheme, where member states are clearly going to be reluctant to spell out implementation shortcomings in full knowledge that this will attract potential litigation.[36] Implementation reports have also taken in practice a considerable time to be completed by a number of member states, which has hampered the Commission in being able to draw up sectoral reports on an EU-wide basis.[37] The questionnaires are also limited in the sense that they do not necessarily elicit all information pertinent to implementation problems. For instance, in respect of EU waste management legislation, questionnaires are designed principally to derive only relatively basic information from the member states on how they have put in place requisite infrastructure in order to implement the legislation (such as registration systems and waste plans). Important though that is, they do not require member states to report in detail on their experience in implementing environmental protection standards vis-à-vis the wider community (e.g. steps taken to tackle illicit waste dumping scenarios). It is rare, if at all, that EU environmental legislation requires member states to report on the degree of effectiveness of the implementing measures they have taken.[38]

The Commission's own periodic reporting on the state of implementation of specific EU legislative instruments, foreseen in practice as a standard requirement in EU environmental legislation, often takes a considerable period of time to be drawn up and published, being predicated and reliant upon information submitted to it from the member states. For example, the Commission reports on implementation of the EU waste framework legislation for 2007–9 and the 1991 Urban Waste Water Directive for 2009–10 were only published in 2013.[39] Delayed publication may render the information contained in the Commission implementation reports vulnerable to challenges of being out of date.

One judicial development to emerge from the CJEU's case law that is likely to be of some degree of assistance in the investigation and particularly prosecution of systemic breaches of EU environmental law by the Commission is the establishment of the category of 'general and persistent' (GAP) infringement by virtue of the *Irish Waste* case,[40] as discussed in Chapter 3. In that case the CJEU held that the Commission had proven that Ireland was guilty of a GAP infringement of EU waste management legislation in having failed to address a number of instances of fly-tipping. The GAP status of the breach meant that the defendant state was obliged to address the systemic underlying problem identified by the case of failing to ensure that its implementation policy of EU waste legislation was sufficiently effective in practice, without any opportunity to shut down EU legal scrutiny by only addressing the symptoms of failure through closure of particular illicit dumping sites.[41] At the same time, the evidential burden on the Commission is eased once it is able to provide sufficient proof of widespread failure to honour EU obligations; the GAP status of proceedings will not be affected by measures taken by a defendant state to address one or a few instances of non-compliance and the CJEU confirmed that additional evidence of similar breaches could be referred to by the Commission after the pre-litigation phase has been completed. Moreover, the development of a category of GAP breaches has potentially beneficial implications for the prosecution of second-round proceedings. First, from an evidential perspective, the Commission will not be faced with the potential collapse of a second-round case if a member state demonstrates that compliance has been achieved in only one or a few instances. Secondly, given the seriousness of a member state being found guilty of a GAP breach of EU environmental law, the CJEU has the opportunity to impose a far higher level of financial sanction than for instances of single or isolated breaches, although at the time of writing the CJEU had yet to confirm this to be the case and how this would be factored into its calculation framework for financial sanctions.[42]

5.1.2 Resources issues

A long-standing problem facing the Commission has been the question of a lack of resources internally to deal with the number of environmental cases under Articles 258 and 260 TFEU.[43] In terms of personnel charged with the principal responsibility of following up complaints, own-initiative enquiries into suspected violations and preparing case dossiers (including letters of formal notice and reasoned opinions), the relevant legal units[44] dealing with infringements within the DG ENV of the Commission has been staffed with relatively few personnel for much of the DG's history.

Until fairly recently, the number of legal officers barely exceeded one per member state.[45] For the years 2002 and 2004, for example, there were reportedly 18 and 16 full-time desk officers respectively to cover the then 15 EU member states.[46] In more recent times, matters do not have appeared to have improved. As at October 2013, the information available from the Commission's Staff Directory indicated that 25 case handlers and infringement support staff were in post to service infringement casework for the 28 member states, though some of these appear to be on part-time contractual arrangements.[47] In the past, the law enforcement teams within DG ENV have been hampered by not infrequent staff turnover, often compounded by the fact that a number of personnel have been supplied by member states on temporary secondments. Borzsák notes that in recent years the situation has stabilised somewhat with Commission staff postings lasting usually for a minimum of two years.[48] Nevertheless, the current position pans out to fall considerably short of two full-time desk-officers per member state, an informal benchmark that the Commission services aimed to achieve for a considerable number of years, and serves to underline the point that the Commission remains stretched in terms of personnel to take on the number of environmental infringement cases involved.

Figures from the Commission's annual reports on monitoring the implementation of EU environmental law show that the environmental sector accounts for, on average, the largest proportion of Article 258 TFEU casework. Specifically, between 2002–12 the proportion of infringement actions concerning EU environmental legislation opened annually by the Commission has averaged just under a quarter (23 per cent) of the total number of first-round case pursued by the institution (see Table 5.3 at the end of this chapter). Over the same period, the Commission reported in its annual surveys monitoring the application of EU law that the environmental sector has accounted for the largest number of case investigations of alleged EU law infringements in any given sector. As at the end of 2012, there were 296 live environmental infringement cases, representing some 20 per cent of all Article 258 TFEU casework[49] (see Table 5.3).

The reader is referred to the statistical tables at the end of the chapter for further information on infringement case numbers. Against this backdrop, it is not difficult to see that the question of allowing on-site investigations becomes particularly challenging from a Commission perspective.

5.1.3 Complainants as sources of information on environmental law enforcement

It has been evident for a number of years now that complaints to the Commission have proven to be an important source of information on EU law implementation matters. It has been noted generally that complainants are of significant value to the Commission in assisting it in carrying out its supervisory functions under Articles 258 and 260 TFEU, particularly in fields such as environmental policy where the Commission has not been vested with any specific monitoring powers.[50] For the environment sector, the complaints system presents itself as an opportunity for ordinary citizens and particularly environmental and other non-governmental organisations (NGOs) to seek to trigger legal action without having to incur legal costs that they would normally have to shoulder if they decided to take civil action before the national courts

Annual monitoring reports of the Commission on the application of EU law have for several years disclosed a consistently high number of complaints filed by the public with Commission services concerning alleged instances of member state non-compliance with EU environmental law. The number of environmental complaints rose quite rapidly in the 1980s, reflecting with increase in environmental legislation adopted at EU level. Whilst in the early part of the 1980s environmental complaints numbered around 10 a year, by the end of that decade this had increased to around 500.[51] Since then, the Commission (DG ENV) has continued to address a considerable amount of environmental complaints. Between 2002–13, for instance, the average number of complaints filed annually from the general public with the Commission about alleged instances of infringements of EU environmental law was 380, representing approximately one-fifth (20.7 per cent) of the total amount of complaints filed across all EU policy sectors (see Table 5.1 below). For the overwhelming majority of that period the environmental sector accounted for the largest proportion of complaints. Whilst the number of environmental complaints has varied over the previous decade and appeared to have decreased in the mid 2000s, it is evident that the quantity of complaints has been substantial in most recent years. There were 666, 604, 588 and 520 complaints registered with the Commission annually between 2010 and 2013[52] (see Table 5.1). With the recent accession of a number of Central and Eastern European countries to the EU, many of which face considerable challenges in meeting and maintaining EU environmental protection standards, notwithstanding the provision of transitional relief and structural funding assistance, it is unlikely that use of the complaint system will diminish significantly in the near future.

Analysis of recent Commission reports and data on monitoring the application of EU environmental law suggest that information from complainants has been useful and has led to the triggering of a substantial proportion of environmental infringement actions. However, it appears that the relative significance of complaints as sources for the launch of infringement action has decreased in recent times.[53] Whereas DG ENV has reported some 50 per cent of environmental infringement proceedings could be traced back to a complaint, by 2011 this proportion had decreased to around 28 per cent (see Table 5.2 below). These figures may well underestimate their significance in the prosecution of bad-application cases, taking into account that the Commission has no supranational powers to undertake on-site investigations in such cases.

Notwithstanding the continuing importance of complainants as a source of information for the Commission services, a note of caution also needs to be sounded. It is perhaps too easy to run away with a complacent view that complainants may serve effectively as watchdogs on member state implementation of EU environmental law. Their involvement depends on a number of factors. In particular, the degree of legal, technical and/or financial capability of the potential complainant may often be crucially significant for it to be able to garner information and evidence. In addition, the parameters of environmental interest of a complainant will serve to determine the range of legislation covered. For instance, Grohs notes that few complaints are filed affecting the chemicals, noise and air quality sectors. She suggests that this may be down to the fact that the legislation concerning the first two sectors is focused on delivering product norms and less at involving the wider public, whilst EU air quality legislation has provided few enforceable standards.[54] She also notes that far more complaints are filed affecting nature conservation issues (Habitats, Wild Birds and EIA Directives), which relate to standards the public can readily understand. This may also have something to do with a number of well-known NGEOs tending to specialise in wildlife protection and conservation issues.

5.2 Limitations of legal structures underpinning Articles 258 and 260 TFEU

The procedures envisaged for the prosecution of infringement actions, and especially those concerning EU environmental law, suffer from a number of serious shortcomings. The central core legal framework relating to infringements, namely

Article 258 TFEU, has remained essentially unchanged since its inception in the 1950s under the aegis of the original Union Treaty framework (former Treaty of Rome 1957 or E(E)C Treaty). True, the 1992 Maastricht Treaty did introduce the possibility for the first time of financial penalties being imposed via second-round infringement proceedings (now Article 260(2) TFEU) and the 2007 Lisbon Treaty enabled the Commission to request penalties from the CJEU in first-round proceedings in respect of non-communication cases.[55] However, these changes have had a relatively limited impact in terms of making the prosecutorial tools more effective for the Commission. For a good deal of the infringement caseload, the infringement procedures remain cumbersome and essentially wedded to the traditional approach that leans towards reaching resolutions out of court as far as possible, through negotiations between Commission and defendant member states.[56] It may be questioned whether this structure is suited to providing the Commission with an effective legal mechanism in order to assist in its mandate to 'ensure the application of the Treaties'.[57]

Whilst the Commission has sought in recent years to introduce some practical changes to the handling of its environmental casework, there is relatively little that can be done until the legal structures of the infringement process, and particularly those relating to Article 258, are amended. This would require unanimous approval from the member states which, although a difficult task, has not proved impossible in the past when they agreed to the TEU in 1992 introducing changes to the infringement structures by incorporating the second-round penalty procedure in the form of Article 260(2) TFEU. The following sections explore some of the key problem areas.

5.2.1 *Temporal aspects*

A major drawback of both first- and second-round infringement actions governed by Articles 258 and 260 TFEU is the considerable length of time it takes on average for the Commission to be able to arrive at a legally binding resolution to a particular case.[58] This is a factor that offers a distinct advantage to defendant member states whose authorities may be able effectively to play for extra time without penalty in sorting out implementation difficulties. This raises questions about the (adequacy of) deterrence value attached to the current infringement action frameworks.

5.2.1.1 *Length of infringement proceedings*

With the exception of non-communication cases, whenever a member state is determined to resist the Commission's view that it has failed to implement EU environmental law correctly, the scene is often set for a lengthy litigious battle. Whilst treaty amendments introduced by virtue of the 2007 Lisbon Treaty as well as changes in case management practice by both the Commission and CJEU have made some improvements, the position overall remains challenging with many cases taking a long time to be concluded.

The introduction of the element of financial penalties at first-round stage in relation to non-communication cases by virtue of the Lisbon Treaty (Article 260(3) TFEU) without doubt has had a positive impact in terms of speeding up the resolution of casework for this type of infringement case. As Table 3.1 in Chapter 3 indicates, the anticipated timescale for completion of infringement proceedings in respect of non-communication cases (from letter of formal notice (LFN) to CJEU judgment) can be expected to be around 22 months, and even shorter if the Advocate General decides it unnecessary to provide the CJEU with an advisory opinion in the case at hand. The author's own research into the average time taken for non-communication cases to be completed during 2010–11 found this to be 22.3 months (see Tables 3.4 and 3.5 of Chapter 3). In addition, it should be pointed out that the Commission's approach in the administrative phase has become stricter in recent years, shortening the time period from six to two months for defendant member state responses. The Commission also has no qualms about launching a formal infringement procedure straight away in such cases, thus bypassing the practice employed in other types of infringement case of engaging with the member state behind the scenes informally prior to issuing an LFN.

However, the position continues to be significantly different for other types of infringement cases, namely those dealing with non-conformity and bad-application situations. Both types of infringement action comprise the bulk of environmental infringement casework, some 85 per cent of cases between 2010 and 2012 (see Table 3.5 of Chapter 3). The author's research into the handling of environmental infringement actions completed between 2010 and 2012 indicates that the average length of time of the infringement action (from LFN to CJEU judgment) for non-conformity and bad-application cases took just over five years (63 months) and just under four years (44 months) respectively (see Tables 3.4 and 3.5 in Chapter 3). The average length of time for the completion of environmental infringement actions in total (across all types of cases) was just over four years (49 months). It is important to remember that these time lengths covered only first-round proceedings under Article 258 TFEU, where the outcome would only lead to a judicial declaration from the CJEU (with no possibility of a financial penalty being imposed at that stage). The deployment of second-round infringement proceedings under Article 260(2) TFEU for the purpose of obtaining a financial sanction via the CJEU serve to extend the overall litigation time by several months. The author's own research, gleaned from information obtainable from CJEU case reports, reveal that the average combined length of first- and second-round infringement proceedings of environmental cases resulting in second-round judgments between 2010 and 2013 averaged 126.5 months (10.5 years) (see Table 4.2 of Chapter 4). The substantial lengths of time involved have been a long-standing problematic feature of environmental infringement proceedings and for infringement actions in general under Article 258 TFEU. The picture is not dissimilar to the position recorded over the past two decades or so. For instance, Krämer has assessed the average number of months taken as follows in the following time periods: 2004–5 (47 months); 2002–3 (45 months); 2000–1 (59 months); 1998–9 (68 months); 1995–7 (47 months); and 1992–4 (57 months).[59]

The current amount of time taken by Article 258 TFEU proceedings is considerable by any standards, but especially drawn out when considered in the context of environmental litigation.[60] Without the possibility of the Commission being able to secure effective and relative speedy legally binding measures to ensure correction of an implementation failure on the part of member states, the utility of environmental litigation may be severely compromised or even defunct in certain cases where time may be of the essence. As Grohs aptly points out, 'much polluted water may have flowed under the bridge' before the Commission obtains a court ruling.[61] One should be careful when making generalisations about length of proceedings, in the sense that environmental cases differ considerably in terms of the level of difficulty and temporal nature of complying with EU obligations.[62] In some instances, it might be argued a slower pace of prosecuting a defendant member state may be warranted to achieve compliance within a realistically attainable time-frame according to particular circumstances facing member states. For instance, obligations on member states to improve environmental infrastructure (e.g. installation and upgrading of sewage treatment works) require considerably more time and investment than the adoption of transposition legislation. However, recognition of such gradations in difficulty should be recognised and woven into the fabric of the relevant EU environmental legislative instrument as a result of political negotiation, rather than being accommodated in the law enforcement phase. It is standard practice for very considerable implementation periods to be foreseen in legislation involving long-term structural reforms and innovations.[63]

In many respects, the core problem of drawn-out proceedings derives from the fact that the legal framework contained in Articles 258 and 260 TFEU, notwithstanding recent reforms, is ill-suited to dealing with the challenges thrown up by environmental litigation. Their design has not been changed fundamentally since their inception, which is to encourage informal and discreet resolution of disputes between the Commission and member states out of court and out of the public's gaze if at all possible. This reflected a perception widely held in the early years of the EU that it would be considered a considerable political and diplomatic embarrassment for a member state to be hauled up before the CJEU. Over time, the infringement procedure has no longer been seen as a means of last resort and is now a commonplace enforcement tool mechanism.[64] Yet no specially tailored infringement procedure for the environment sector has been established to substitute Article 258. The result has been to deny the Commission the possibility of taking swift legal action in order to ensure due implementation of EU environmental legislation.

Under the Article 258 procedure, it is the CJEU and not the Commission which has the power to determine the issue of compliance. The Commission has no powers to issue a defendant state with any binding instruction or penalty in the form of correcting an implementation failure. The CJEU has interpreted its powers as enabling it to issue a declaration as to whether a member state has failed to comply with EU law. In contrast, under the auspices of the former European Coal and Steel (ECSC) Treaty 1951, the Commission was vested with powers to take binding decisions against a member state it considered to have violated ECSC law

and initiate a process to suspend the payment of ECSC funds as a means of applying pressure on a defendant to effect compliance with the law (Article 88 ECSC).
A member state retained the right to appeal through annulment proceedings in
the usual way if it were ever minded to object to such a Commission decision.
This particular legal procedure was never in fact used by the Commission. Such
a procedure would have significant advantages if employed in an environmental
infringement context, in terms of having the potential to effect a swift, binding
resolution to a dispute and carrying a strong element of pressure and deterrence.[65]
The power to issue a decision would enable the Commission to tailor binding
instructions to the defendant on corrective action, as warranted by the particular
case at hand. It would also be more suited than Article 258 to addressing implementation failures of a more short-term nature as well as cases requiring urgent
action.

Some commentators, though, have expressed concern that such a procedure
would not be welcome in placing the Commission in the invidious position of
being accuser, judge and executioner.[66] Such concerns are unfounded, as the
defendant member state would have the standard automatic right of appeal by
way of judicial review under Article 263 TFEU to the CJEU which would have
the power to annul a decision it considered on any of the grounds listed in the
provision. In any event, such a procedure has been applied for many years in
other law enforcement contexts at EU level, such as in the field of competition
law,[67] without such concerns being raised by member states. However, the member states have so far shown no willingness to alter the current structuring of
Article 258 by way of treaty amendment. The changes introduced by virtue of the
TEU to the infringement provisions in 1992 with the introduction of the second-
round infringement procedure (Article 260(2) TFEU) confirmed the deep-rooted
view held by member states that the proceedings should retain in essence their
status as a tool for negotiating as opposed to imposing resolutions in respect of
compliance disputes. Likewise the subsequent Lisbon Treaty changes effectively
reaffirmed this paradigm. The penalty envisaged in the second-round procedure
in Article 260 TFEU may only be imposed by the CJEU after there has been an
attempt to reach a friendly settlement through a pre-litigation process.

As matters currently stand, then, even in a clear-cut case of non-communication
of an environmental directive, the relatively cumbersome pre-litigation and litigation phases in Article 258 have to be complied with before a binding decision may
be made on the issue of alleged non-compliance. Specifically, this will involve
initially two written warnings from the Commission (namely an LFN and reasoned opinion (RO)) with opportunities for the defendant to be able respond on
each occasion, as well as completion of the judicial phase when the case is then
referred to the CJEU. The internal workings of the Commission ensure that in
practice it is rare for such a case to be fast-tracked. The hierarchical nature of the
decision-making process requires that the College of Commissioners has responsibility to decide each formal step taken in each proceedings. Moreover, the parties
in infringement cases are not subject to any legally binding deadlines for completing the pre-judicial phase under either Article 258 or 260 TFEU proceedings.

Thus, there is the possibility for a member state to be able to drag out proceedings by, for instance, refusing to disclose information on a suspected infringement in a timely manner, without being subject to any penalty in so doing.[68] Accordingly, there have been calls for revision to the current EU treaty provisions such as through clear procedural rules to be adopted under the auspices of Article 337 TFEU (ex Article 284 of the European Community (EC) Treaty) as a means of eliminating this tactic.[69] In particular, some have argued for mandatory short time limits to be imposed on member states when responding to formal Commission written warnings in the pre-litigation phase.[70] However, no such rules have been proposed, notwithstanding that they have been enacted in other Commission law enforcement contexts, such as competition law.

The current position applicable to the environmental sector effectively tolerates a member state being able to build in a substantial amount of extra time for attaining compliance, over and beyond that foreseen and prescribed by EU environmental legislation. For instance, if the Commission decides to take an infringement action against a member state on account of its failure to implement an EU environmental directive into national law, and that member state then gets round to notifying the Commission of transposition legislation before the expiry of the deadline for responding to the reasoned opinion, then the proceedings terminate without any penalty falling on the defendant for disrespecting the original implementation deadline prescribed by the legislation. Similarly, in second-round infringement proceedings a member state will be able to avoid incurring a penalty if it secures compliance before the deadline set by the final written warning, although it should be pointed out that possibilities for abuse of this kind have been significantly reduced with the elimination of the need for an RO under Article 260(2) TFEU by virtue of Lisbon as well as the practice introduced by the Commission in the mid 2000s of requesting from the CJEU a lump sum penalty if a member state fails to honour the deadline set by the final written warning (LFN) but secures belated compliance prior to the time when the CJEU gives its second-round judgment.[71] Nevertheless, the treaty system effectively still builds in a very substantial time period before judgment is handed down, which has led to calls, for instance, for the second-round procedure to be curtailed.[72]

It should be pointed out, though, as outlined earlier in Chapter 3, the Commission has in recent years taken steps in order to streamline and speed up its handling of casework during the pre-litigation phase of first-round infringement proceedings. These changes, introduced in the wake of the Commission's 2007 review of EU law implementation,[73] have brought some benefits. Specifically, the establishment of the EU Pilot system[74] has meant that national authorities are now given early warning of and opportunity to resolve complaints that are sent to the Commission, prior to any decision being made by the Commission whether or not to launch formal infringement proceedings. Where complaints are unable to be resolved via the EU Pilot within 20 weeks, the Commission then may move to open proceedings formally if it considers the complaint meritorious and a priority case. The Commission has reported that under the EU Pilot generally the vast majority of complaints may be expected to be resolved at an informal stage.[75]

For 2012 and 2013, the Commission reported resolution rates of 68.34 per cent and 70.22 per cent respectively.[76] In addition, in recent years the Commission has also taken steps with a view to shortening the formal pre-litigation phase of the Article 258 first-round infringement procedure. Whilst up to the early 2000s it was not uncommon for the Commission to provide the defendant member state with six months or more to respond to individual formal written warnings, current standard practice of the Commission has reduced this now to two months. Other techniques have also been employed to streamline the process, such as the practice of joining similar breaches together into a single action against a particular member state.

The relative informality of the pre-litigation phase of the Article 258 procedure does appear to be beneficial in some respects. For a considerable number of years, several commentators have noted that the vast majority of infringement disputes are resolved without going to court.[77] Estimates have fluctuated over the years, but it appears that around only10 per cent of Article 258 disputes culminate in being referred to the CJEU for judicial resolution.[78] Commission annual reports on monitoring EU law indicate that a substantial number of cases are resolved at pre-judicial stage and settled out of court. The annual rate of referrals to the CJEU has been consistently and markedly lower than the number of infringement proceedings in motion (open infringement cases). Over the period 2000–10, for instance, the average annual rate of total court referrals was 18.6 per cent of the number of open cases. For environment cases the position has been broadly similar, although the out-of-court settlement rate appears not to have been as impressive as the overall position across the entire spectrum of EU sectors. During 2000–10 the average annual rate of court referrals in environmental cases was 25.4 per cent of the number of proceedings opened annually.

Some commentators may feel ready to assume from these statistics that the high number of pre-trial case closures indicates a significant degree of efficiency and that member states view the procedure as a deterrent.[79] However, the picture is more complex. There is little in the way of hard evidence to suggest that member states consider the infringement procedures as such to be a major deterrent, not least in the environment sector. Were that the case, one would expect to see relatively few infringement actions being launched by the Commission.

However, the Commission's annual monitoring reports on the application of EU law have revealed that the number of environmental infringement cases has remained relatively high over a period of several years now. As Table 5.6 at the end of this chapter indicates, in all but two years over the period 2002–10 the environment sector accounted for the largest proportion of infringement cases to reach the final warning stage under Article 258 TFEU across all EU policy sectors (averaging 27 per cent of the caseload). Similarly, the environment sector accounted for the most referrals to the CJEU in infringement actions during the same period except for one year (averaging 32 per cent of the caseload to have reached CJEU referral stage). Reports from the DG ENV on EU environmental law implementation at national level reveal that as at the end of 2012 and 2013 there were respectively 296 and 353 live infringement proceedings in the environmental sector. Out of these, bad-application cases constituted the vast majority of cases: 197 (66 per cent) and 192 (54 per cent) by the end of 2012 and 2013 respectively. Non-conformity cases amounted to 77 (26 per cent) and 63 (18 per cent) of the live environmental infringement cases by the end of 2012 and 2013 respectively. Non-communication cases in the environmental sector have recently increased in number. By the end of 2012 and 2013 environmental non-communication cases amounted to 13 (4.3 per cent) and 92 (26 per cent) of the total number of live environmental infringement proceedings.[80] Over the period 2002–12, the environment sector also accounted on average for 44 per cent of the total number second-round infringement cases being pursued by the Commission, by far the largest number amongst EU sectors as a whole (see Table 5.8 at the end of this chapter).

A key reason why there remains considerable room for improvement with regard to the state of member state implementation of EU environmental legislation lies with the legal structures underpinning the infringement action framework as contained in Articles 258 and 260 TFEU. Notwithstanding some modifications made to them by virtue of the Lisbon Treaty 2007, the EU treaty infringement provisions remain deficient in providing member states with effective incentives to ensure timely compliance with Union environmental protection obligations. Given the length of time it takes to complete first-round proceedings, there is little in the way of pressure upon them to ensure that national law is in conformity with Union environmental legislative requirements by the time the relevant implementation deadline expires. Member state governments are fully aware that they have in practice a considerable amount of time thereafter to achieve compliance before a CJEU ruling or financial sanction imposed (which except for non-communication cases may only be made in second-round proceedings). Unsurprisingly it is indeed rare to see member states achieving compliance within the time period envisaged by EU environmental legislation.

That being said, there appears to be evidence that indicates that compliance rates are significantly enhanced if the threat of financial sanctions is brought forward to an earlier stage in the infringement process. Specifically, it is evident that since the Lisbon Treaty changes introduced the possibility of financial penalties for non-communication cases at first-round stage,[81] the number of non-communication cases has dropped significantly. DG ENV reports on annual implementation of EU environmental law[82] indicate that for the period 2001–9 non-communication cases represented on average of one-third of all environment infringement cases, whereas for the period 2010–12 this figure had fallen to an average of 14 per cent of the infringement caseload. For 2012, only 4.53 per cent of environment infringement cases concerned non-communication breaches. In terms of absolute numbers, this meant a reduction from an average of 120 open infringements each year during 2001–9 to 56 such cases annually during 2010–12 (with just 13 as at the end of 2012).

Leaving aside the factor of out-of-court settlements, it is clear that the Commission is currently not vested with adequate tools to effect a satisfactory legal outcome to an infringement of EU environmental law in the face of intransigence on the part of a member state. The legal structure underpinning Articles 258 and 260 TFEU is such that the enforcement system is effectively still heavily reliant upon member states' preparedness to adhere to the principle of the rule of law. Were the member states to agree to establish a single infringement procedure leading to the possibility for the CJEU to impose financial penalties in all types of breaches of EU environmental law, not simply non-communication cases as is the current position, this would be likely to have a major beneficial impact in reducing the length of infringement proceedings and enhancing the deterrent effect of the infringement provisions. As has been pointed out elsewhere, any significant change to the structure of the infringement system would need to be supported with appropriate levels of staff resourcing within the Commission (and where appropriate the CJEU) for the purposes of ensuring that a swifter case management could be delivered.[83]

5.2.1.2 *Interim measures*

The possibility of securing interim measures in the context of Article 258 proceedings was discussed in Chapter 3. The subject is of considerable importance when dealing with bad-application scenarios that require particularly urgent action. The case law of the CJEU has confirmed that it is legally possible for the Commission to be able to secure interim measures under Article 279 TFEU (ex Article 243 EC) in the context of Article 258 proceedings, subject to it being able to demonstrate to the Court that it has a *prima facie* case, that the matter is urgent and that a failure to grant relief would effect serious and irreparable damage to the legal interest sought to be protected by the Commission if the parties waited until the date of judgment.[84] Significantly the CJEU has rejected the need for the Commission to submit a financial security when filing a request for emergency measures before the Court,[85] something that would otherwise be expected in a civil action where a party pleads for injunctive relief pending judgment.[86] The CJEU has instead waived such a requirement on the grounds that the Commission does not present it with a risk of non-payment due to insolvency.

In practice, though, the Commission has rarely sought to apply for such relief measures in the context of environmental litigation. It was not until 2006 when the Commission was able to deploy the interim measures procedure successfully in an environmental infringement case, namely in *Ligurian Bird Hunting*.[87] Prior to that case the Commission had shown little interest or confidence in the possibilities of applying to the CJEU for interim measures. One of the key reasons for the Commission's lack of appetite stems from the setback it sustained in the *Leybucht* infringement case,[88] discussed in Chapter 3. In *Leybucht*, the Commission had failed to meet the test of urgency according to the CJEU. A substantial amount of works had already been carried out on the particular coastal site host to wild birds in respect of which the Commission sought emergency measures from the Court. The Commission was adjudged to have left it too late to apply for injunctive relief against Germany for the purposes of requiring a cessation of building activity. The case highlights the need for the Commission to have access to a good source of information and evidence at a relatively early stage in any bad-application dispute which might require interim measures (such as the need to order a cessation of unlawful development with actual or potential adverse impacts on a protected nature site or on EU environmental quality standards). As has already been pointed out earlier, taking into account in particular its lack of investigatory powers and other resources, the Commission is not really in a ready or suitably independent position to be able to present a plea to the Court for such types of measure.

Matters are made more difficult given the fact that it is the CJEU and not the Commission that has the power to issue interim relief measures. A plea for interim measures may only be made to the CJEU in relation to an action pending before the Court. Accordingly, the pre-litigation requirements of Article 258 TFEU have to be completed before the Commission may approach the CJEU for interim relief, a process that may take some time.[89] However, as was noted in Chapter 3, the CJEU has accepted the imposition of tight deadlines in Article 258 actions for responding to formal written warnings from the Commission (LFNs and ROs) so the legal hurdles do not seem insuperable in an appropriate case. Indeed, the Commission was able to apply successfully to the CJEU for interim measures in a few environmental cases since 2006, without having to accelerate the pre-litigation phase unduly.[90] In addition, there do not appear to be any internal structural problems that may bar the convening of emergency inter-service meetings between the Commission's DG ENV and its Legal Service to arrange for an expedited processing of a case warranting interim relief, even though there may appear to be a lack of clarity on specific internal procedures.[91] The key appears to be the Commission being in timely receipt of information and evidence of a bad-application breach. For the interim relief procedure is only suited to addressing those types of bad-application infringement cases which are able to be processed speedily within the pre-litigation phase of Article 258 TFEU.

5.2.2 *Legal sanctions*

Another major problem concerning the Article 258 and 260 TFEU infringement procedures is their lack of provision for the imposition of effective sanctions. This traces back to the origins of the infringement procedure, which was designed at the outset to secure if possible a friendly settlement outcome and minimise unnecessary tension between member states with regard to the evolving European Union integration process. The position also reflects the degree of political and diplomatic sensitivity involved with the establishment of an international court, in terms of the degree of its 'reach' into what may be perceived in orthodox international law terms to be within the sovereign internal domain of a nation state. In international relations, it is rare for nation states to agree to submit to the jurisdiction of an international court on a mandatory basis, as is the case with the EU member states and the CJEU under Articles 258 and 260 TFEU. It is rarer still for an international court to be issued with powers to impose sanctions as a means of enforcing its rulings. Accordingly, from a broader public international legal context, EU infringement proceedings may be viewed in a relatively positive light as being a relatively effective set of law enforcement tools.[92] However, this does not detract from the reality that without genuinely effective sanctions, EU infringement procedures remain overly reliant on the goodwill and co-operation of member states to adhere to their environmental obligations.

5.2.2.1 Sanctions and Article 258 TFEU

With the possible exception of the special procedure applicable for dealing with non-communication cases which foresees the imposition of financial penalties,[93] the first-round infringement procedure under Article 258 TFEU is a rather weak form of litigation tool in terms providing inducements for member states to comply with their EU obligations. An effective outcome depends to a great extent upon the co-operation of the defendant, particularly in bad-application cases. As has already been mentioned, the Commission has no power of its own motion to take decisions in the area of environmental policy to issue binding instructions to member states, as it does in other fields of law such as competition. Neither does it have powers to impose pecuniary-type penalties, as was the case with respect to the coal and steel sector until the lapse of the former ECSC Treaty in July 2002.[94] Moreover, it has no power of its own motion to order interim measures, unlike in other areas of EU administrative law such as competition law.[95]

The CJEU may only issue a judicial declaration under Article 258 TFEU, save for the special exception of non-communication cases for which it may decide to impose financial penalties. The Court's position is that member states are obliged as a matter of EU law to give effect within their domestic legal systems to its rulings on whether EU law has been infringed, and it has refused to grant interim relief against member states which default on implementing its judgments. In its view, an interim relief measure would simply duplicate what has been already required to be carried out by its Article 258 judgment.[96] However, it is clear that the system of declaratory judgments by the end of the 1980s was having little deterrent effect, with many member states being on the receiving end of supplementary infringement actions on account of failing to implement CJEU judgments. The Court has taken the approach of avoiding issuing defendant member states with definitive instructions as to what they should do to achieve a state of compliance ('*arrêt educatif*') and instead simply affirm whether or not the defendant has perpetrated a violation of EU law. It has been mooted that the issuing of instructions would be within its current jurisdiction.[97] As has been pointed out elsewhere, the issuing of instructions or guidance from the Court might be particularly useful in those environmental cases where it is not self-evident what the appropriate remedial action is from a legal perspective. Winter takes the example of the *Santona Marshes* cases,[98] where it was not clear whether the effect of the ruling of the Court was that building works carried out on an area that should have been designated as a special protection area (SPA) contrary to the EU Wild Birds Directive[99] should be removed or allowed to stay.[100]

5.2.2.2 Sanctions and Article 260(2) TFEU

As has already been discussed in the Chapter 4, the second-round penalty infringement procedure Article 260(2) TFEU was incorporated into the EU legal order by virtue of the TEU with a view to enhancing the record of member state implementation of EU law and in particular the levels of compliance with CJEU judgments. Prior to that amendment, the only legal means available to the Commission to try and seek to induce a member state which had failed to implement an Article 258 ruling was to launch a fresh infringement action. Krämer notes that whereas in 1984 there was but one reported instance involving the environment where the Commission had decided to take such action, by 1991 this had risen to 21 repeat infringement actions.[101] However, even though the second-round penalty infringement procedure (now under Article 260(2) TFEU) has introduced a marked change, in that the CJEU is now vested with power to impose pecuniary sanctions on a member state that defaults over implementing a first-round judgment, it appears that the new second-round infraction procedure has not brought significant improvements in terms of speeding up member state compliance rates, and this also applies to the environmental sector. It should be noted, of course, that the 2007 Lisbon Treaty assisted in reducing the length of the pre-litigation phase of Article 260(2) proceedings by eliminating the need for an RO.

Since its inauguration by virtue of the 1992 Maastricht Treaty, the second-round procedure (Article 260(2) TFEU) has not appeared in practice to have deterred member states significantly from continuing to fall short when it comes to implementing EU law, including EU environmental legislation. Even with the recent Lisbon Treaty amendments, the second-round infringement procedure does not appear to have induced member states to ensure that they meet transposition or implementation deadlines stipulated in EU environmental legislation notably any quicker. Specifically, the Commission remains frequently confronted by situations in which several member states fail to comply with EU environmental legislative obligations on time, notwithstanding the fact that substantial transitional periods are built into EU environmental directives to allow member states to adopt national transposition and/or implementation legislation. For instance, in respect of the Water Framework Directive 2000/60[102] none of the member states had complied with the directive's 22 December 2003 transposition deadline, and by the beginning of 2005 infringement actions had been launched against six member states. Other more recent examples of widespread non-compliance abound. For instance, in 2010 Commission press releases[103] reported that the Commission had decided to launch infringement action against nine member states over failures to transpose the Ambient Air Quality Directive 2008/50.[104] In 2011 the Commission issued 8, 14 and 13 member states with final written warnings (ROs) on account of failure to transpose correctly the Marine Strategy Framework Directive 2008/56,[105] Waste Framework Directive 2008/98[106] and Environmental Crime Directive 2008/99[107] respectively. In the same year, infringement proceedings were commenced against eight member states in respect of transposition failings regarding a 2009 amendment to the Ship Source Pollution Directive

2005/35.[108] In 2013 infringement action was started against four member states over failures to transpose the Energy Efficiency in Buildings Directive 2010/31.[109] Other examples of recent 'horizontal' infringement action in relation to non-compliance with EU environmental legislation includes the launch of proceedings in 2010 against 17 member states over failure to implement environmental quality obligations contained in the Air Quality Directive 2008/50.[110] In the same year, 12 member states received final written warnings under Article 258 TFEU on account of their failure to comply with management plan requirements contained in the Water Framework Directive 2000/60.[111]

The environmental sector has accounted for the largest proportion of ongoing Article 258 infringement cases for several years. As at the end of 2013, some 25.6 per cent (334) of all live first-round infringement proceedings concerned EU environmental law (see Table 5.3 at the end of this chapter). Moreover, it appears from Commission annual reports on the monitoring of EU law that several member states are still failing to implement CJEU judgments within a reasonable time period (as required under Article 260(1) TFEU) and as a result face the prospect of second-round infringement action. Specifically, as at the end of 2013 the Commission was prosecuting 40 second-round environmental infringement cases, representing some 35 per cent of all live Article 260(2) TFEU proceedings (see Table 5.9 at the end of this chapter). Table 5.9 shows that the position has remained fairly consistent for a number of years now, with the environment sector regularly having the highest proportion of second-round infringement actions across all EU policy sectors. Given that the Lisbon Treaty amendments came into effect relatively recently in December 2009, it is probably too early to make definitive conclusions about the impact of the reduction to a single warning in the pre-litigation phase. However, the early data to have emerged from Commission monitoring reports are not particularly encouraging, in that they do not appear to indicate at the time of writing any notable let-up in the number of live second-round proceedings being opened by the Commission. In the long-term, though, the introduction of penalties for first-round actions relating to non-transposition cases by virtue of the Lisbon Treaty is likely to have some effect in terms of reducing the number of second round environmental proceedings.

It is not that difficult to find reasons to explain why the effect of Article 260(2) has thus far appeared to have been relatively minimal. A prime concern is the fact that the second-round procedure does not reduce the length of the infringement procedure system itself.[112] Before a member state is faced with the prospect of receiving any penalty, the Commission is obliged to carry out a pre-judicial negotiation process akin to that applicable to first-round infringement proceedings under Article 258 TFEU, albeit this has been somewhat shortened by the Lisbon Treaty as a result of the elimination of the need for a second written warning from the Commission. This means that it may be several months after the initial judgment before a member state may face a pecuniary fine. In respect of the eight environmental cases that have, at the time of writing, culminated in a second-round judgment under Article 260(2) TFEU, the average time taken between initial Article 258 LFN and court fine imposed in a second-round judgment has been

142 months (11 years and 10 months). The lack of will on the part of the Commission to seek to secure a quick legal outcome after a member state has defaulted on a court ruling has been sharply criticised in the past.[113] It should be noted, though, more recent practice of the Commission has been more assertive in terms of curtailing pre-litigation phase case management, with the results of this change yet to feed through statistically into the court reports. It should also be noted that under the EU treaty framework the Commission has also been vested with discretion as to whether to prosecute a second-round action, for the wording relating to the pre-litigation phase in Article 260(2) TFEU is identical to that contained in Article 258 TFEU. However, this interpretation has been disputed in some quarters.[114]

The nature of the sanctions available under the second-round procedure is not really appropriately geared or tailored to securing implementation of EU environmental legislation. The pecuniary sanctions were introduced instead principally as a means of fining member states in terms of their disrespect of the CJEU, not the EU norms in question.[115] The second-round procedure is in large degree a contempt of court procedure, as opposed to a legislative enforcement mechanism.[116] However, the CJEU has considered the procedure to share the same purpose as Article 258 TFEU in ensuring the effective application of EU law.[117] As was seen in the previous chapter the Commission has sought to infuse the calculation methods applicable to second-round penalties with criteria that relate also to the nature and severity of the original legislative infringement.[118] Under the second-round procedure, a pecuniary penalty may only be applicable from when a member state has been provided with a reasonable opportunity to implement the Article 258 TFEU court ruling. The second-round procedure might have had more effect if it had employed the principle of being able to sanction a member state as from the date the Commission originally issued an LFN to it under the Article 258 procedure. Such an approach has been applied for many years in the EU competition law sector. A fine which is imposed on a company for anti-competitive behaviour for breaching Articles 101 and 102 TFEU may run from the date the defendant is put on notice by the Commission by way of a statement of objections that it considers there has been a breach of Articles 101 and 102 TFEU and not only from the later date when an official decision is issued against the defendant after the hearing stage.[119] Accordingly, the pecuniary sanction system contained in Article 260(2) TFEU is not designed to punish past illicit conduct.[120]

Several commentators have criticised the sanctioning mechanism under Article 260(2) TFEU as being ill-suited to addressing the implementation failings of a defendant member state. In an environmental context, it appears rather an unsatisfactory approach to seek to try to quantify environmental damage (wholly) in monetary terms; a more effective sanction would be to impose an obligation to remediate the damage caused.[121] Currently, the infringement procedure does not provide for the recovery or suspension of any EU environmental fund payments to the defendant member state concerned, a sanction option that might well be more tailored and effective in securing compliance from the defendant.[122] Moreover, unless the CJEU actually imposes a sufficiently high periodic penalty, there is the danger that the pecuniary sanction system may fall into the trap of becoming a *de facto* tax on pollution.[123] It has been queried by some whether the levels of pecuniary sanctions are adequate to serve as an effective deterrent.[124] It is apparent, for instance, that the CJEU has often imposed lower lump sum fines than those recommended by the Commission and at the same time does not usually provide any indication of the criteria it uses to calculate the final amount.[125] Brian Jack makes the point that the co-efficients recommended by the Commission and used by the CJEU to calculate fines have not been appropriately applied to acknowledge the severity of adverse environmental impact.[126] He cites the example of a far higher seriousness co-efficient being recommended in a free movement of persons case against Italy as compared with the one applied by the CJEU failure by France to adhere to fishing conservation measures.[127] In addition, he questions whether the criterion of relative voting strength should feature in the calculation framework.[128]

One step taken to strengthen the impact of the second-round procedure, though, has been the CJEU's clarification[129] that it may impose more than one type of financial sanction in a given case. Whilst the text of Article 260(2) and (3) TFEU refers to the CJEU having the power to impose a lump sum 'or' a penalty payment, the wording does not exclude the possibility of cumulative fines. As Prete and Smulders point out, if the CJEU were confined to imposing only one type of financial sanction, namely a lump sum for those states complying before second-round judgment and a penalty payment for defendants still in breach at that time, this would lead to a number of unjust scenarios arising as well as a dampening of the deterrent effect underpinning the second-round procedure.[130] In particular, they note that, under a single fining system, perversely a defendant state might receive a much smaller fine if compliance were achieved very shortly after second-judgment than before it.

Finally, there is still some uncertainty as to whether and how the CJEU may enforce collection of pecuniary sanctions under Article 260(2) in the face of an intransigent member state. Thus far, there does not appear to be any indication that a member state is likely to decide to refuse to pay any or part of fines imposed on it by the CJEU. As was discussed in the previous chapter, in the follow-up to the *French Fishing Controls (2)* case, the French government did dispute the legal competence of the Commission to require collection of a deferred penalty payment. However, that issue has been resolved by the General Court[131] in the Commission's favour and not contested by France or other member states. Nevertheless, it is not out of the question that a member state might dispute the legitimacy of the level of a fine imposed and refuse to pay and, in that event, it appears unlikely the CJEU has jurisdiction to force the issue by ordering the withholding of EU funds until payment of fines are fulfilled.[132] Ultimately due payment of fines, as is the case with effecting due compliance with EU law, is a matter principally for member states and depends upon their preparedness to uphold the rule of law.[133]

Eight of the 21 second-round judgments under Article 260(2) TFEU to have been handed down by the CJEU (so far as at the time of writing in September 2014) have concerned environmental legislation.[134] These judgments undoubtedly have had some psychological impact in terms of promoting member states' awareness of the ultimate powers of the CJEU to impose pecuniary sanctions. It appears, though, that Article 260(2) TFEU has had to date but a limited deterrent effect on member states. This is borne out by the fact noted earlier that there are a large number of unimplemented first-round judgments, including in the environmental sector. In its annual monitoring report on the application of EU law for 2012, the Commission has reported that as at the end of 2012 it had opened 35 formal second-round proceedings involving breaches of first-round environmental judgments, representing the highest number of second-round infringements across all EU sectors (27 per cent) (see Table 5.8 at the end of this chapter). The low number of second-round judgments (only 21 after over two decades of Article 260(2) TFEU being operational) indicates that member states will probably eventually wish to settle a dispute out of court with the Commission to avoid a fine.[135]

European Commission reports on the monitoring of EU law have noted that the vast majority of second-round infringement proceedings come to be settled after the point in which the Commission has referred a case to the CJEU and determined the level of penalty it wishes to request from the Court. As at the end of 2003, 76 per cent of cases for which a penalty request to the CJEU had been made had been settled before judgment (22 out of 29 cases). However, it also appears that settlement is often reached at a relatively late stage, with some evidence of defendants drawing out proceedings until the moment when liability cannot be avoided.[136] This problem was more acute in the past when the Commission pursued a practice of not requesting a financial penalty from the CJEU if a defendant managed to comply with the terms of the first-round judgment prior to the second-round judgment[137] and when the pre-litigation phase was longer than present in requiring two Commission warnings. If, as the evidence suggests, member states' minds are seriously concentrated on correcting implementation failures only during the latter part of second-round proceedings, this raises questions as to whether the first-round infringement proceeding is but perceived little more than a trivial inconvenience or banal exercise by defendants.[138] The recent introduction of the availability of penalties in first-round proceedings for non-communication cases may well have some deterrent impact for this type of breach, although more time is required to assess the evidence for this.

5.3 The European Commission and conflicts of interest

It is the Commission which is vested with the exclusive responsibility of deciding whether or not to prosecute an infringement case under Articles 258 and 260(2) TFEU. As confirmed by the CJEU on a number of occasions, the Commission has unfettered discretion in deciding whether or not to pursue an infringement case. A decision by the Commission not to prosecute a case is immune from legal challenge from a third party such as a private individual interested in seeing infringement proceedings commenced, either through annulment proceedings under Article 263 TFEU (ex Article 230 EC) or by way of an action for failure to act under Article 265 TFEU (ex Article 232 EC).[139] The Commission has a particularly important and powerful position in this regard. In the environmental policy context, the Commission's responsibility and power as principal monitor of EU environmental law under Article 17 TEU (ex Article 211 EC) is all the more enhanced, given the range of difficulties and challenges (legal, technical and financial) that other stakeholders have in terms of being in a position to enforce environmental obligations.

At one basic level, one can understand the reasons of those that drafted the EU treaty framework in having accepted that the Commission should be vested with exclusive power to initiate enforcement proceedings under Article 258 TFEU. The Commission was seen to be in a suitable position to act as an independent and impartial arbiter as between member states, an actor that would be placed at arm's length to supervise the implementation of the process of European legal integration as promised by the constituent member states. The Commission's tasks, as set out in Article 17 TEU, underpin its supranational status. It is charged effectively with defending a collective interest ultimately expressed in the EU's founding treaties and derivative legislation, as opposed to representing any minority viewpoint such as a particular national interest on behalf of which an individual member states would normally be expected to negotiate.

However, the decision to vest the Commission with the exclusive responsibility and role of seeking to ensure that member states apply EU law has not been an unproblematic one. It is not so clear in practice whether the elements of independence and impartiality are adequately safeguarded. A major cause of concern is the fact that the Commission is charged with the responsibility of not only enforcing policy but also being responsible for its development as well. Since the EU's inception in 1957, the Commission has retained a principal role in the legislative decision-making process of the Union. For the vast majority[140] of policy matters falling within the purview of the EU, including environmental matters, the Commission is vested with a monopoly of proposing legislative initiatives. The EP still only has a relatively weak proposal function in this regard, virtually unused in practice to date, in being able only to request the Commission to present legislative proposals (Article 225 TFEU).[141] The Commission also has significant powers at later stages during the EU legislative process, including those in relation to environmental matters. Specifically, in the context of the ordinary legislative procedure (as set out in Article 294 TFEU) applicable to most EU environmental policy decisions,[142] the Commission has the power to be able to force the Council of the EU to vote on a unanimous basis in respect of any amendments tabled by the EP with which it disagrees.

The multiplicity of tasks of the Commission, which cross over into executive, quasi-judicial and legislative territories, raise questions as to whether the institution is in a suitable position to be able to shoulder its law enforcement responsibilities under Articles 258 and 260 TFEU in a sufficiently impartial manner. The lack of a clear demarcation between enforcement and policy position of the Commission has raised concerns of a lack of accountability in infringement procedure decision-making.[143] The conflation of policy innovation and law enforcement roles potentially leads the Commission into situations where decisions to launch or terminate infringement proceedings may become particularly vulnerable to the influence of political as opposed to enforcement motivations.

5.3.1 College of Commissioners

As a matter of principle, decisions over infringement matters must be channelled through and approved at the collegiate level of the European Commission. Thus, any decision to commence infringement proceedings must receive the approval of the College, as is the case for subsequent legal steps in the proceedings (LFN, RO and referrals to the CJEU). In that sense, the EU infringement procedures may be characterised as being policy-sensitive as opposed to constituting a purely technocratic process, given that formal decisions are not taken by a body exclusively charged with law enforcement responsibilities. Although on paper, decisions taken by the College are to be taken on the basis of an absolute majority of the members,[144] it is understood that in practice a consensual approach usually has been adopted. Access to information on College decisions regarding infringements is not made public, so no hard evidence has ever been gleaned as to the particular dynamics, political or otherwise, that go to underpin a decision as to whether an action should commenced or taken to the next step.[145]

However, it has been suggested in the past that the system has been vulnerable to individual Commissioners blocking proposals to launch infringements on political grounds, although proof has been difficult to come by to substantiate this.[146] Alleged problems are said to have arisen where, for instance, an infringement action would interfere with the political portfolio or remit of a particular or a number of Commissioners. Krämer has stated that the Commission decided to close an infringement case against Germany over breaches of the EU Wild Birds Directive[147] in the wake of political interference by the German Chancellor sending a letter to the Commission President.[148] Williams, for instance, cites the example of a report in *The Independent* newspaper in August 1992 alleging that the then Commissioner for the Internal Market, Martin Bangemann, had provided assurances to the UK Home Secretary that no action would be taken in respect of the UK's policy on border controls at the time carried out with respect to EEA citizens and that the then UK Secretary of State, John MacGregor, had also secured a deal for the Commission to refrain from taking legal action under the auspices of the EIA Directive in the M3 motorway development of Twyford Down although being unable to secure an agreement over Oxleas Wood.[149] She also cites another report in *The Independent* newspaper of 30 June 1992 which reported having been briefed that the former Commission President Delors was responsible for the early retirement of the Environment Commissioner at the time Mr Ripa di Meana, on account of the latter's willingness to press for a number of environmental infringement actions. The report indicated that the move was taken in order to facilitate ratification of the 1992 Maastricht Treaty (TEU). Concerns over the Commission's decision-making process at College level are set to continue for as long as it is charged with carrying out both policy development and law enforcement functions in respect of its decisions over law enforcement.

To some extent concerns could be addressed if the Commission were to apply a distinctive decision-making procedure to law enforcement matters. In particular, one notable improvement could be the introduction of a process unique to law enforcement decisions which would guarantee that only purely legal reasons should be able to be raised for discussion at College level if a proposal for an infringement action were to be doubted by any Commissioner. Such concerns would logically have to be raised prior to a meeting of the College through the Commission Presidency, which is responsible for managing the Commission's Legal Service.

5.3.2 The level of Directorate General

It is important to realise that in substance the vast majority of administrative work relating to infringement actions is taken below collegiate level within the European Commission. In practice, the vast majority of infringement cases are effectively 'rubber stamped' at College level where there is no dispute of any substance between Commissioners over a case or its implications, and in that (frequent) scenario no oral discussion takes place. Instead, proposals over infringement decisions are channelled through a written procedure up to the College from the level of the Directorate-General. Commissioners do not usually get to see the details of cases at College meetings, but are usually provided access to a brief résumé (or 'fiche') of the dispute. As was discussed in Chapter 3, this practice has been challenged unsuccessfully before the CJEU. Specifically, in infringement proceedings brought against it the 1990s, Germany claimed that the Commission, as formally composed of the College of Commissioners, had acted *ultra vires* in having failed to take genuinely informed decisions as to the processing of the legal action.[150] Controversially, the CJEU held that the practice of making information on individual cases available to Commissioners, if they so wished to access it, was an adequate basis for the College to be able to proceed in making formal decisions over the Commission's next steps on the case(s) in question.[151]

Each particular Directorate-General which has responsibility for a particular EU policy field within the Commission is usually vested with its own legal unit and/or teams dedicated to preparing infringement dossiers. For environmental cases, the relevant unit or units dealing with infringements within the DG ENV have the task of organising the day-to-day case management of infringement proceedings.[152] It is the legal units, in liaison with the Commission's Legal Service, which in principle determine whether or not a proposal should be made to go before the College that infringement proceedings should be commenced.

It is possible that political considerations may come to influence law enforcement casework at this level. For instance, one criticism in the past has been that the legal units have not been vested with sufficient independence within DG ENV. Specifically, such units have been housed in the past in a particular environmental directorate that has also accommodated units responsible for environmental policy development. On certain occasions conflicts of interest might arise between units within the same directorate over infringement cases; some policy units may not wish to see an infringement action launched if it might result in an incursion into policy development (e.g. if an infringement action might be directed against a member state whose vote might be key in securing approval for EU legislation at Council level, or where an infringement action might have the effect of depriving funds for environmental projects in a particular member state). Williams has rightly raised the concern that such a situation may well lend itself to a Director being in a difficult position in adjudicating over the units' rival positions.[153] A more suitable organisational position would be to ensure that the legal units are contained within a directorate devoid of policy units or under direct supervision of the Director-General of DG ENV, in order to avoid the possibility of such problems arising. Currently, the legal units are housed within Directorate D of DG ENV (Implementation, Governance and Semester), which spreads legal teams across three units which also deal, *inter alia*, with cohesion policy issues.[154]

It is also possible that on occasion political considerations interfere with the decision-making process of the legal units themselves. In practice, the office holder of Head of Unit of the relevant DG ENV unit in which law enforcement teams operate is in a pivotal position to determine which cases should be processed to the next level or withdrawn. Technically, it is possible that their opinion could be overridden either by the Director of the particular directorate in which the unit is located, Director-General or the Commission's Legal Service. However, whilst possible, this rarely happens, which means that the Head of Unit usually has a particularly strong position in relation to decisions concerning the prosecution of infringements. There is nothing inherently objectionable with this, so long as the work of the Head of Unit (or Director) is not subject to non-law enforcement considerations, namely political interference. However, the experience of DG ENV in this respect has not been without disturbing incidents. For instance, it has been alleged that a former Head of the Legal Unit in the mid 1990s was removed from his post for reasons of political expedience, on account of being perceived to be overly active in initiating environmental infringement action.[155]

In the more recent past, there have been instances where there appear to have been shortcomings within the Commission to safeguard the principle of political independence of the office holder of Head of Unit. In 2002, the European Ombudsman was very critical of the Commission and found it guilty of maladministration in the handling of an environmental infringement case where it had failed to intervene vis-à-vis a senior DG ENV official in charge of overseeing infringement matters who had maintained a senior political position within a national party of a member state which was at the time the subject of infringement proceedings.[156] The position of Head of the Legal Unit is particularly important when seen in the context of access to EU funds allocated to relatively poorer parts of the Union, notably the Cohesion Funds and Structural Funds. As a matter of principle, a member state will not be able to access such funding to support particular environmental projects in a sector in respect of which a member state is considered to be in breach of EU rules.[157] Accordingly, a decision as to whether an infringement case should be commenced or withdrawn may take on an especially significant financial dimension, in addition to its immediate environmental protection context. The safeguarding of the independence of office holder Head of Unit overseeing law enforcement staff is, therefore, of substantial importance. The EU[158] and the Commission[159] has instituted a legal framework that should address these issues. To what extent this machinery has been implemented in practice remains questionable, though.[160]

Whilst working within DG ENV between 2001 and 2003, I came across a memorable situation which demonstrated to me that, on occasion, political considerations may interfere with the work of law enforcement. I was an official working within the unit at the time responsible for waste management policy, dealing with legal issues. The matter in question arose in connection with the sinking of the *Prestige* oil tanker in November 2002. The vessel had come into difficulties in heavy weather off the Galician coast on 13 November 2002 before starting to leak fuel oil. A specialist salvage team was commissioned to seek to take control of the vessel and bring her under control. Media reports indicated that both the Spanish and Portuguese authorities had ordered the salvage team to tow the *Prestige* out into the Atlantic, contrary to the advice and request of the salvage team, which wished the tanker to be allowed to be taken into calmer waters port for repair. At one time the tanker was reported to be as close 3 miles from the Galician coast. Between 14 November and the date of its breaking up in the Atlantic on 19 November 2001, the salvage team were reportedly refused access to the nearest available Spanish and Portuguese ports. In following up those reports, I managed to gain confirmation of these events from a representative of the salvage company. His assessment was that there was a much better chance for the oil pollution to be limited if the salvage could be undertaken in the relative shelter of port as opposed to on the high seas in rough weather (at the time weather reports indicated a 30-knot SW wind and heavy rain). He reported to me that the Portuguese authorities were 'very clear in their opinion', in dispatching a navy vessel to the location of the *Prestige* and ordering the tanker to 'go in a westerly direction'. In the event, the tanker broke into two parts in the heavy seas and sank releasing its cargo of 77,000 tonnes of heavy fuel oil into the Atlantic Ocean, resulting in substantial pollution of the Atlantic coastlines of France, Spain and Portugal.

In my view this testimony pointed to there being a case for pursuing legal action against the Spanish and Portuguese authorities on grounds that there had been a failure to apply the basic duty of care enshrined in EU Waste Framework Directive,[161] which requires member states to take the necessary measures to ensure that waste (in this case the leaking fuel oil) is recovered or disposed of without endangering human health and without using processes or methods which could harm the environment. The response from senior management of the DG ENV legal unit to the request for legal action was quite revealing, not least in terms of the overt reference to political considerations that underpinned its analysis of the situation:

Subject: 'Prestige' accident and WFD

Importance: High

. . .

As regards the Prestige case I would like to bring your attention to the following considerations:

1) From a legal point of view it can be argued that an infringement of the Waste directive has occurred. The fact that this was accidental is not

relevant for the application of the directive, although Spain could invoke as a defence the 'force majeure' which is a general principle of EU law. The decisive argument for pursuing this case is that it has now become an 'infraction consommé' (see note in Annex of the LS on the relevant case law).

2) The Commission has always the possibility to ask member states to provide information on cases which might constitute potential infringements. In the present case this should have been done during the days following the 13th November (day of the accident). Sending such a letter now could raise expectations and in any case it would be considered as a 'post mortem' reaction.

3) Needless to say that this case has a strong political sensitivity and cannot be dealt with as a 'business as usual' case.

4) Nevertheless, I believe that, since such accidents may occur in the future, it could be useful to send all the maritime MS[162] a letter stressing the dimension of the WFD as a lesson to learn from this accident.

In the event, no infringement action was brought against the member states involved. The matter was never deliberated beyond Director-General level; the College of Commissioners therefore had no control over whether or not legal action should be brought. A number of important and interesting issues are illustrated by this particular case. Point 3 of the email revealed that political considerations were considered to be important in terms of how the DG ENV legal unit was advised to proceed, although no justification is offered for this. The correspondence highlights the issue concerning the importance of being able to secure information and evidence quickly in emergency cases, a matter that the Commission is not usually in a position to be able to do (point 2). It also raises doubts that legal action might have been allowed to proceed on the basis that it would be an 'infraction consommé'. The issue of the Commission taking action in respect of historical breaches was discussed in Chapter 3. Although not clear-cut, the available case law suggests that the CJEU will not determine that an action is inadmissible where a member state has not taken the appropriate steps to remedy a breach. In this case, an appropriate remedy on the part of the defendant might be considered only to have been achieved when appropriate systems would have been put in place to ensure that appropriate assistance to stricken vessels are offered in similar future cases. Whilst one may debate the legal issues pertaining to the particular case and the question of admissibility, what is most important here is to consider the sensitivity recognised in the correspondence to political factors which appear to have influenced in part the recommendation to desist from taking legal action, and those factors were not even addressed by the politicians themselves (i.e. Commissioners). Interestingly, a Galician High Court in November 2013, some 11 years after the event and investigation by Spanish authorities, has been reported to have found there to be insufficient evidence to convict the former head of Spain's merchant marine department, Jose Luis Lopez-Sors, of crimes against the environment in relation to the affair.[163]

The spectre of conflicts of interest arising within the Commission has caused some commentators to propose conferring responsibility for monitoring EU environmental law enforcement upon a body other than the Commission or otherwise by setting up systems to ensure that law enforcement activities are separated from policy considerations.[164] A number of possibilities could be considered. For instance, as far as a separate body is concerned, the remit of the European Environment Agency could be altered to take on more enforcement responsibilities. Alternatively, a special EU environmental law task force could be set up within the Commission services under a legal framework suitable to guarantee it immunity from outside political interference and foster a more rigorous culture of independence of decision-making on case management decisions.

5.4 Prioritisation of cases and reform of the monitoring process

A major issue which has confronted the Commission for a substantial period of time now has been the question of how best to deal with the substantial amount of cases referred to it under Article 258 TFEU. The Commission has a relatively small team of lawyers charged with responsibility to oversee the implementation of EU environmental law, which has averaged out at around two lawyers for each of the larger member states. The overseeing or monitoring duty covers three broad areas: checking that member states have notified the Commission of national legislation designed to implement EU environmental legislation (non-communication casework); checking that such obligations have been correctly transposed into national legislation (non-conformity casework); as well as responding to complaints and other evidence which indicates that EU environmental legislation has not been applied correctly on the ground (bad-application casework). As has already been mentioned, the environmental sector accounts for the largest number of infringement cases of a particular EU policy sector managed by the Commission (334 live cases as at the end of 2013 accounting for 25.6 per cent of the total Article 258 caseload – see Table 5.3 at the end of this chapter). Complaints of suspected member state infringements of EU environmental law are amongst the highest filed for any EU policy sector (520 in 2013 representing 14.83 per cent of all complaints filed with the Commission – see Table 5.1 at the end of this chapter).

The sheer quantity of environmental infringement casework alone has placed a great strain on the Commission's services employed to carry out the monitoring functions assigned to the institution.[165] In many respects, the relatively high caseload underlines the reality that the Commission is never really going to be able to be in a position to shoulder on its own the responsibility of monitoring and enforcing due implementation of EU environmental law.[166] Not only does it command a relatively small number of legal staff assigned to the subject of law enforcement, the Commission is not vested with any powers to carry out investigations of suspected cases of bad application of the law. Moreover, the core functions and work of the Commission, which tend to focus on broad picture policy issues and agendas of inter-state relations do not lend themselves to addressing issues which are predominantly local in nature. The primary responsibility lies with the member states to ensure that norms pertaining to the European legal integration process are duly applied within their own frontiers; they are not only best placed to ensure that this occurs, they also have ultimate legal responsibility to realise compliance at national level.[167] Accordingly, the Commission services are not in a position to offer a complete quality control service as far as ensuring due implementation of EU environmental law.[168]

As a consequence, the approach originally fostered by the Commission since the 1980s to encourage complainants to come forward to the Commission has subsequently come under scrutiny and review. A number of commentators expressed the view that the Commission needed to engage in a prioritisation of cases it investigated. Some were concerned with the prospect of the Commission enforcement work otherwise drifting towards being reactive as opposed to being strategic in outlook in terms of which infringement issues need to be addressed most.[169] Various suggestions were made. Some suggested that the Commission should concentrate on the cases that it is best suited to address, namely those that essentially revolve around transposition issues (non-communication and non-conformity).[170] As we have seen, cases of non-communication and non-conformity are often the most straightforward infringement case to deal with from the Commission's perspective, given that the investigation is 100 per cent document based and need not involve on-site investigation. These cases are more suited in another sense to be addressed by the Commission, as they relate more closely to the Commission's core overall functions which are in ensuring that inter-state relations are compatible from the perspective of the EU project. Specifically, in ensuring that member states have adopted the appropriate legal frameworks at national level to implement EU environmental legislation, the Commission addresses two key supranational objectives of the Union. It assists in ensuring that all member states are in a position to contribute commensurately towards achieving a high level of environmental protection, in line with fundamental environmental policy objectives and tasks specified in Article 3(3) TEU and Article 191 TFEU. In addition, it assists in ensuring that member state legal systems are not liable to be in a position to distort competition within the single market on account of individual state failures to implement agreed environmental norms into national legislation. Accordingly, non-conformity and non-communication cases lend themselves to be addressed by the Commission, as they raise issues primarily of a federal–structural as opposed to local nature.

The argument that the Commission's environmental infringement casework should be prioritised so as to concentrate on transposition disputes would mean, as a direct consequence, a reduction in the number of bad-application cases investigated by the Commission. Demmke suggested that Commission resources in the environmental sector should be focused on addressing only the worst bad-application cases which come to its attention, namely those where there is evidence to indicate deliberate flouting of environmental norms and repeat-offender scenarios.[171] Others pointed out that, in any event, the Commission is in too remote a position geographically and from other perspectives to be able to tap into the relevant local knowledge required to address such types of implementation dispute as a rule.[172]

However, a prioritisation strategy raises particular problems as far as environmental law enforcement work is concerned. By restricting the number of bad-application cases it is prepared to investigate, the Commission raises the prospect of narrowing the opportunities for private individuals to have access to environmental justice.[173] The avenues available for stakeholders other than the Commission to take legal action to uphold EU environmental law have been and remain limited, which means that the complaints system which currently feeds into the functioning of Articles 258 and 260 TFEU in the environmental sector takes on a particular heightened degree of importance. The aspect of access to environmental justice for civil society is discussed in greater detail in Part II of this book. Suffice it to say at this stage that private individuals and bodies concerned to uphold EU environmental obligations such as NGEOs have a number of difficult legal and other problems to overcome in seeking to rely upon EU environmental law themselves in order to seek to have it implemented and applied correctly at national level. For instance, in many instances, they will not be vested with legal capacity to rely upon EU environmental norms before national courts (the so-called direct effect doctrine). The case law of the CJEU has recognised that individuals may only be able to rely directly upon such norms where they are clear, precise and sufficiently unconditional in nature. In many instances, these criteria may not be fulfilled in the environmental sector where standards may be general or imprecise in nature – e.g. very general duties pertaining environmental stewardship, requirements to establish plans/programmes, provisions being subject to other open-ended conditions such as best available technology not entailing excessive cost (BATNEEC).[174] Even if environmental provisions are found to be directly effective, there are limits to their reach within the internal legal order of a member state depending on the legislative instrument in which they are contained. Notably, no person may be able to enforce directly effective provisions contained in EU environmental directives against a private individual, as the CJEU has barred the possibility of any horizontal or inverse direct effect of directives.[175] With some exceptions, the EU directive remains the standard form of legislative instrument that the Union legislature uses when introducing EU-wide binding environmental standards. In the absence of a directly effective norm upon which an individual may rely in a given case, it may be particularly difficult for private individuals to have legal standing (*locus standi*) to take legal proceedings in order to enforce EU environmental law, whether against other private parties, national authorities or even EU institutions. Aside from all the legal hurdles that lie in the way of legal action that might be pursued at national level by private entities, one should not forget also the often not inconsiderable technical and practical problems that may arise for private bodies considering environmental litigation as an option (e.g. the legal costs involved, difficulties connected with securing of requisite evidence of non-compliance such as causation issues). In general, access to environmental justice at local level has been a major issue confronting the EU for a considerable period of time, a subject with which the Union has only relatively recently begun to introduce initiatives to try to address. These will be examined in Part II.

It has also been suggested that it might well also be a false economy for the Commission to try and limit the number of suspected bad-application cases which are brought to its attention. Such cases may lead to uncovering useful and more profound insights into the state of implementation of EU environmental law, which would not be gleaned simply through document-based transposition checks. The state of transposition of EU environmental law into the national laws of a member state says little if anything about the state of actual practical implementation of those norms.[176] The possibility of individuals being able to complain to the Commission about the ineffective level of response of a local environmental authority offers the opportunity for the Commission to follow up allegations of deficiencies in practical implementation at local level (information function) as well as providing the basis for a meaningful fall-back response against ineffective local environmental authority protection mechanisms (deterrence element). In addition, as pointed out by Winter, supervision by the Commission of bad-application cases may lead it to be able to canvass the guidance of the CJEU on the interpretation of key points of environmental law that may be crucial for development of policy as well as to detect more profound differences in the state of implementation of EU environmental policy and law by the member states.[177] Accordingly, any decision to restrict the number of bad-application case investigations undertaken by the Commission carries with it a number of implications that may not be that easy to reconcile with the mandate provided to the Commission as guardian of the EU founding treaties under Article 17 TEU.

5.4.1 *Commission responses to the issue of casework prioritisation*

The European Commission has for some time been alive to the problems and limitations posed by the Article 258/260 TFEU infringement procedures and has decided over the last decade or so to take certain steps to improve the handling and management of enforcement casework as well as to introduce alternative routes to securing better implementation records on the part of member states. It is to the examination of these steps that we now turn.

5.4.1.1 *Recognition of the limits to Articles 258 and 260 TFEU and decentralisation of enforcement*

The Commission's 1996 Communication, *Implementing Community Environmental Law*[178] was the first time that the Union institution took stock of the issue of implementation, taking the opportunity to reflect upon the limits of the Article 258 TFEU infringement procedure as far as the environmental sector was concerned. The Commission quite rightly drew attention to the inherent limitations of the infringement procedure as a means of ensuring that member states adhered to their EU environmental obligations. Amongst others, the following factors were

noted by the Commission as limiting the efficacy of EU-level infringement procedures as far as environmental casework was concerned: the lengthy and formal
nature of the procedure and lack of its being attuned to dealing with environmental cases; the practical impossibility for all infractions to be addressed through
Article 258/260 procedures; the issue that infringement procedures may only be
targeted against central governments which may not be immediately or directly
responsible for implementation shortcomings in questions (such as in federal states
where environmental protection competence is devolved to regional/local levels);
the absence of an EU-level inspection system; and wide disparity in and often
poor level of delivery of national/regional/local inspection and environmental
reporting mechanisms.[179]

In recognising the inherent limitations posed by the Article 258/260 infringement procedures, the Commission chose to focus on alternative routes and methods
in its 1996 Communication to enhance the state of member state implementation
of EU environmental law. In particular, the Commission was keen to stimulate
work on developing better tools at national level to effect changes. These included
developing minimum criteria across the EU on environmental inspections to be
carried out by well-resourced national environmental authorities, the provision
of more effective opportunities for the public to become involved in assisting law
enforcement work and delivery of more effective sanctions at national level against
persons perpetrating violations of EU environmental standards. With respect to
the point concerning greater public involvement, the Commission indicated that
it was keen to see more possibilities for the public to be able to register complaints
within the member states at suitable contact points as well as to be assured of
greater possibilities of securing access to local courts to enforce environmental
legislation. We shall examine in Part II of the book to what extent the Commission
has developed greater opportunities for more effective decentralised enforcement
of EU environmental law.

What is important to note at this point is that the Commission chose, from the
outset of its 1996 examination of EU environmental law implementation, not
to go about seeking ways to enhance the existing infringement structures in any
profound way. In many respects, that is to be regretted as the procedures could be
improved in a number of ways, as the problems with the procedures highlighted in
this and earlier chapters indicate. The Commission could have pressed for reform
of the current infringement procedures alongside its calls for an expansion of
decentralised routes to EU environmental law enforcement. One example could
have been to request competence to be able to take action against sub-national
authorities within federal states, to take account of constitutional devolution of
responsibility for the environment.[180]

The call for achieving a greater decentralisation of responsibilities and roles
associated with the enforcement of EU environmental law as advocated by
the Commission's 1996 Communication raised a number of important issues.
In many respects, the Commission's 'reality check' approach, in placing the
infringement procedures in their practical context, was a welcome development. It reminded stakeholders that the fundamental responsibilities for

implementing Union law rests with the member states, and not with the Commission; it is after all, the member states who have undertaken to carry out EU environmental legislative commitments within their respective territories. In underlining how unrealistic it would be to expect a single supranational institution in the form of the Commission to be in a practical position to be primarily responsible for ensuring complete correct application of environmental obligations set at EU level, the Communication also brought home the importance of harnessing all other viable means to assist in this task. In particular, the pivotal importance of the capacities of local stakeholders (in particular environmental authorities and NGEOs) to affect compliance behaviour is appropriately highlighted. A shift on the Commission's part towards enhancing decentralisation of EU environmental law enforcement received widespread support, for a wide variety of reasons, including notably: the Commission's own limitations in being able to carry out enforcement work and local actors' potential or actual superior position in terms of familiarity with and access to locally relevant knowledge;[181] the factor of local accountability; and sovereignty–subsidiarity concerns with the prospect of the Commission being perceived as an outsider interfering with internal matters.[182]

However, the case for decentralisation has a number of limits as well. For instance, an overly relaxed or restricted view of Article 258/260 TFEU enforcement could risk the objective of attaining commensurate levels of environmental protection systems within member states, and undermine the aims of achieving a uniformly high level of environmental protection across member states and absence of a distortion of competitive conditions as between those states.[183] Demmke has taken the idea of decentralisation to the level of suggesting that the Commission should only look to intervene where a member state fails in practice to comply with EU environmental law, namely to bring infringement proceedings where it is found that a member state has breached substantive legal requirements. In particular, he suggests that the Commission should not take action where, for instance, a member state has elected to implement EU environmental legislative instruments in an informal manner, such as through administrative circular. Accordingly, any legal action to insist upon formal transposition of EU environmental obligations as contained in a directive into national legislation would, in his view, be an ineffective use of Commission resources if it could be shown that in practice implementation was in place.[184] However, as has been pointed out elsewhere such confidence in the national position would be misplaced. Unless a national authority as well as all other stakeholders operating within each member state are subject to clear, legally binding obligations that serve to implement minimum EU environmental protection standards, it is far from apparent how those standards may be enforced with any degree of certainty or efficacy. For instance, as stated by the CJEU on a number of occasions, it is always possible for a public authority to be able to alter its commitment to environmental protection at a whim if it is faced with only an administrative circular containing recommendations or guidance.[185] Moreover, attempts to implement legislation through more informal means such as (administrative circulars, codes of conduct or environmental agreements) serve to undermine the rights of individuals that may be intended to be derived under the legislation conceived at EU level.[186]

5.4.1.2 *Prioritising and improving handling of infringement casework*

By the end of the 1990s, the Commission had decided to take certain steps to improve the case management of its infringement actions. Following on from the requests set out in the European Council's conclusions at its meetings Amsterdam[187] and Cardiff[188] in June 1997 and 1998 respectively for prompter action in monitoring of the application of EU law (particularly in the area of the single market), the Commission responded by adopting some internal measures and practices to improve its working methods in relation to infringement proceedings. These were set out in a 1998 internal Communication document[189] issued by the Commission's Secretariat General, under whose auspices the Commission's Legal Service is based. The Communication set out a number of general changes that would be effected to the Commission's procedures. These included speeding up case handling, making Commission decisions more transparent and improving relations with the complainant. The latter two aspects will be discussed more fully in the next section of this chapter. As regards the aspect of speed, the Commission decided to ensure that in principle in future it would take a maximum of only one week to implement its decisions on infringement matters, as in many instances this had been allowed to drift so as to delay processing cases to the next procedural step. In the document the Commission made clear its intention to foster the practice of developing regular bilateral 'package' meetings between the Commission services and individual member states, in order to assist in resolving disputes as far as possible out of court in an informal, potentially quicker and perhaps more meaningful manner than through the distant and formal means of communication of pre-litigation correspondence of LFN, RO and member state observations. The practice was also developed in which LFNs would from now on be processed more quickly, so that as a rule the individual Commissioner together with Commission President are responsible for arranging for this step to be carried out. In 2002 the Commission indicated its intention to apply a similar practice with respect to the RO stage.[190]

With the publication of its *White Paper on European Governance* in 2001,[191] the Commission made clear its intentions to bring forward more radical changes to the handling of infringement cases. Notably, it set out a general programme for prioritising infringement casework. The Commission envisaged that it would target its law enforcement resources as from 2002 to addressing the following types of EU law infraction scenarios: transposition failures; cases involving fundamental principles of EU law; cases seriously affecting Union interests or the interests that EU legislation had intended to protect; repeated implementation problems; as well as cases involving the payment of EU funds. The White Paper also envisaged various flanking measures at national level as a means to enhance EU law enforcement. Specifically, these included promoting better dialogue with member states on enforcement issues, encouraging the establishment of twinning arrangements between older and new member states in order share best practice on implementation, fostering a change of perception held at national level by key players such as national authorities of the still widely held perception that EU law is 'foreign' law and the establishment by member states of networks of national bodies capable of dealing with disputes involving citizens and EU law.

Several of the ideas outlined in the White Paper were fleshed out more fully in a follow-up 2002 Commission Communication, *Better Monitoring of the Application of Community Law*.[192] It clarified a number of details concerning the Commission's future strategy on law enforcement. With respect to first-round infringement actions the Communication identified in more detail three priority areas for the Commission to concentrate on: infringements that undermine the foundations of the rule of EU law; infringements undermining the smooth functioning of the EU's legal system; and infringements consisting of transposition failures. As regards the first identified priority area, the 2002 Communication signalled that this would include Commission action against member state challenges to (1) the principles of primacy and uniformity of application of EU law, (2) breaches of fundamental rights and freedoms of individuals protected under EU law including environmental damage scenarios having implications for human health as well as (3) situations where the Union's financial interests are damaged (including violations of EU law in relation to projects receiving EU funding). As regards the second area of priority, the Commission noted that this would embrace the following infringement scenarios: violation of the EU's exclusive powers, repetition of infringements in the same member state and cross-border infringements. Infringements falling outside the three priority areas would be deemed to be 'lower priority' areas not usually warranting the commencement of infringement proceedings. Instead, the Commission would seek to introduce what it would perceive to be 'complementary' mechanisms to seek to deal with disputes. Included within these complementary mechanisms would be the potential for greater scope for negotiation with member states in order to arrive at out of court settlements: e.g. package meetings, establishment of *ad hoc* contact points and dispute resolution mechanisms at national level to deal with complaints about alleged instances of non-compliance with EU law; development of independent and specialised national authorities; and initiatives to foster greater access to national courts for complainants. The 2002 Communication also indicated that the Commission would be keen to introduce more preventative strategies in the field of law enforcement, with a view to obviating the need to rely on the traditional reactive and often cumbersome strike of an infringement action.[193]

In the environmental sector, it appeared that a number of measures identified in these early Commission general strategic documents on handling of infringement procedures were taken on board within the DG ENV of the Commission. In particular, the Fifth Annual Survey on the Implementation and Enforcement of Community Environmental Law (2003),[194] drafted by DG ENV, reported that the Commission services had invested more resources in a number of preventative-type steps including issuing implementation guidance documentation to accompany new legislation,[195] the holding of implementation seminars with national authorities on particularly complex legislative instruments, entrenchment of bilateral package meetings with individual member states, publication of scoreboards of compliance records, a commitment to ensuring delivery of more effective reporting on implementation of environmental legislation as well as fostering information exchange between implementing national authorities. As regards the latter aspect, the Annual Survey indicated that support would be channelled through IMPEL, the network for the Implementation of Environmental Law established as an informal mechanism between the Commission and member states since 1992. The work of IMPEL is discussed in detail in a later chapter (Chapter 11). Finally, the Annual Survey also referred to the initiatives undertaken by the EU to improve access to environmental justice for the public taken in alignment with developments at international level under the auspices of the 1998 Århus Convention. These initiatives will be also discussed in detail in later chapters (chapters 8–9A).

However, it was far less clear how DG ENV's law enforcement teams would seek to introduce any changes in terms of prioritising infringement cases. Whilst the prioritisation agenda outlined in the 2001 White Paper and follow-up 2002 Commission Communication, *Better Law Monitoring*, indicated that the Commission would continue unabated its work in tackling transposition failings (non-communication and non-conformity), it was less clear what was going to happen in practice in relation to the future handling of bad-application cases in the environment sector, the majority of which stem from information issued to the Commission by complainants.[196] The issue was recognised as acutely important given the danger that application of a prioritisation agenda could leave a gap in terms of the Commission's abilities to fulfil its responsibilities of ensuring proper implementation of EU environmental law, taking account of the access to environmental justice problems noted earlier.[197]

The Commission's emerging prioritisation strategy for infringement cases appeared to indicate confining Article 258 TFEU intervention to the following environmental infraction scenarios: grave violations of fundamental environmental norms with implications for human health; systematic and repeat infringements in the same member state; deliberate breaches of EU environmental law by state authorities; breaches of EU financial rules in connection with environmental projects; and breaches of a cross-border nature (e.g. waste shipment violations, inter-state-related pollution incidents). It began to be apparent that if the prioritisation agenda would be rolled out to apply to environmental casework, bad-application cases would in future have to meet a notional level of seriousness/gravity before being allowed to proceed to the status of an infringement investigation. As was readily recognised, though, unless complainants had a realistic chance of securing recourse to legal action at national level, the application of a prioritisation agenda could lead in effect to a denial of environmental justice and an abrogation of the Commission's responsibilities under the EU treaty framework (Article 17 TEU).[198]

Until the Commission intensified its prioritisation agenda in 2007–8, it was not clear that practice in case management of environmental infringements altered significantly, though. For instance, Grohs writing in 2004 indicated that DG ENV practice at the time did not make it apparent that the volume of case management was being decreased, and that cases falling within lower priority areas were still being handled in accordance with standard practice regarding responses to complaints.[199] However, things were about to change quite fundamentally, which would see to it that the Commission's original 'open door' approach to taking up complaints about member state non-compliance with EU environmental law would be permanently closed. Instead, cases would be selected according to perceived order of priority.

With the publication of the Commission's 2007 Communication, *A Europe of Results – Applying Community Law*,[200] the Commission provided definitive clarification about its general strategy to improve the effectiveness of its law enforcement work across EU policy sectors under the auspices of Article 258 TFEU. As with its 2002 follow-up to the 2001 White Paper, the 2007 Communication underlined the need for the Commission services to devote increased attention to preventive measures, namely those which enhanced the prospects for member state compliance with new EU legislation and assist where possible in avoiding the need to resort to formal infringement litigation. These included the promotion of the following: development of guidelines (e.g. on legislative interpretation and expected operational practice); sustaining enhanced dialogue with member states (e.g. through bilateral package meetings and holding expert group meetings on transposition issues); reviews of existing EU legislative instruments in light of implementation difficulties; use of correlation tables setting out member state transposition measures in respect of specific EU legislative obligations; and promoting EU law training for national civil servants and judiciary.[201] The major focus of the 2007 Communication, though, was on elaborating a strategy seeking to limit the focus of the Commission's infringement casework to certain 'priority' cases.[202] Specifically, the Commission outlined that priority should be attached to the following types of infringement cases, which it considered to represent the greatest risks, most widespread impact for citizens and businesses, as well as the most persistent infringements: (1) non-communication cases; (2) failures to respect CJEU judgments; and (3) cases involving breaches of EU law raising issues of principle or having a particularly far-reaching impact on citizens.

The Commission underlined that a key motivation underpinning this new prioritisation strategy was to achieve a swifter and better focused addressing of member state breaches of Union law. It has been mindful of the fact that a lack of formal prioritisation of casework has not assisted the Commission legal services in addressing the worst kind of infringements as vigorously could have been expected, bearing in mind that the average time for resolving cases had been relatively slow.[203] What was clear from the 2007 document was that infringement casework would be scaled back, notably with respect to bad-application cases. However, it was not clear how this scaling-back would be applied in detail within the environmental sector. Subsequently, the Commission published a further Communication in 2008 on detailing how this guidance is to be applied in relation to the management environmental infringement cases (2008 Communication, *Implementing EC Environmental Law*).[204]

The 2008 Communication constitutes currently the principal official document setting out the Commission's strategy on enhancing EU member states' implementation of EU environmental legislative commitments, fleshing out application of the supervisory principles identified in the general 2007 Communication. In essence, it sets out the Commission's approach towards fulfilling its mandate under the EU treaty framework[205] in ensuring the proper application of Union law by member states as regards the environmental sector. By way of complement to the 2007 Communication, key elements of the 2008 document concern the promotion and development of measures to assist in minimising or preventing member state breaches of EU environmental legislation as well as adoption of a prioritisation strategy regarding the management of infringement cases.

With respect to the issue of prevention of breaches, the Commission identifies a number of activities services are to pursue or reinforce as good practice. These include notably the following measures to be introduced and/or entrenched by Commission services (DG ENV):

- effective information-gathering to be secured on the state national transposition and implementation (e.g. assessment of national implementation reports);
- performance scoreboards to be publicised to compare relative member state compliance with Union legislation ('name and shame');
- ensuring appropriate use of EU funds (including pre-accession funding) to support national environmental protection and implementation efforts;
- Commission guidance documents to be developed to assist in avoiding interpretative disputes over Union legislation;
- Commission support of structured dialogue with member state authorities (e.g. bilateral package meetings, meetings through expert networks such as IMPEL and other stakeholder groups);
- Commission funding of judicial training in EU environmental law and liaison with judicial networks (such as European Forum of Judges for the Environment);
- establishment of permanent network points between Commission and member states in all new legislative initiatives, with a view to facilitating information exchange (advice/experience) on ways and means of attaining full and timely implementation of EU environmental legislative obligations.

At the heart of the 2008 Communication, though, lies its prioritisation strategy with respect to future handling of infringement casework. Specifically, the Communication confirms that the Commission is to focus its attention on the three types of infringements identified in its 2007 *A Europe of Results* Communication. Crucially, it provides specific information and guidance on the sorts of environmental cases that are to be considered as falling under the third infringement case type, namely those involving breaches of EU environmental legislation that are considered by the Commission services to raise either issues of principle or having a particularly far-reaching negative impact for citizens. It specifies that this priority type includes situations where, on a significant scale or repeatedly, people are exposed or may in the future become exposed to direct harm or serious detriment to their quality of life as a result of non-compliance with EU environmental legislative requirements. Where any harm sustained might be classified as irreversible, this is to be identified as a prioritisation factor.[206] The Commission identifies four criteria to be used for the purposes of identifying the most important instances of the third priority type of infringement case.[207] Specifically, these involve assessing whether one of the following four types of infraction are present:

(1) non-conformity of key legislation presenting a significant risk for correct implementation of EU environmental rules;
(2) systemic breaches of environmental quality norms or other requirements presenting serious adverse consequences or risks for human health and well-being or for aspects of nature that have a high ecological value;
(3) breaches of core strategic obligations upon which fulfilment of other EU environmental obligations depends; or
(4) breaches concerning big infrastructure projects or interventions involving EU funding and/or significant adverse impacts.

The 2008 Communication provides some additional brief guidance on the scope of each criterion. As regards the first, the range of non-conformity cases to be caught is intended to be limited to those EU directive provisions that set out the main framework for environmental protection. This would cover defective national (transposition) legislation that either significantly limits the scope of the EU legislation's application or otherwise compromises the results to be achieved by the Union legislation. The second criterion relates to situations where there is repeated or significant contravention of substantive 'state of the environment' obligations (e.g. maximum pollutant thresholds) or of key procedural or operational-related obligations (e.g. permit or management requirements). The emphasis is to be on addressing widespread (systemic) non-compliance issues within and/or across member states. The third criterion refers to shortcomings on meeting designation, planning, programming and reporting obligations, intended to provide a fundamental framework for other legislative requirements (e.g. nature protection site networks, waste management plans). The fourth criterion covers scenarios where EU funding is involved (e.g. EU Cohesion/Structural Funds) in relation to a project in breach of EU environmental law or where very serious ecological damage resulting from a breach is deemed to have occurred. The Commission also indicates that in urgent cases falling under this criterion it may be appropriate to seek interim measures from the CJEU.

   The introduction of a prioritisation strategy on environmental infringement casework has long-term and potentially profound implications on law enforcement in relation to EU environmental law. On the one hand, it is evident that the Commission has turned to focus on what it might consider to be its core area of casework and work within its resource capabilities. In the context of a seemingly ever-enlarging Union this appears to reflect a sound realism that the Commission cannot possibly be expected to monitor all types of infringements of EU environmental law. It neither has the personnel nor legal investigative powers to be able to monitor compliance with Union obligations on the ground at national level. Moreover, it is the member states themselves who have primary responsibility in ensuring proper implementation of EU legislative requirements at national level. Accordingly, it is not surprising that the Commission has sought to rein in and streamline its supervisory role under Article 258 TFEU.

However, there is no doubt that this reorientation will potentially have some negative impacts on the degree of effectiveness and impact of environmental law enforcement if other measures are not introduced to mitigate them. It is apparent that the prioritisation strategy most likely will result in fewer cases being pursued by the Commission, particularly those in relation to bad application of Union obligations, for the Article 258 TFEU procedure will be increasingly earmarked or reserved for scenarios involving widespread and/or very serious breaches of key legislative obligations. Consequently, it is vitally important that other stakeholders interested in environmental law enforcement (notably NGEOs and national authorities) are vested with effective powers and resources, financial and legal (investigative powers as well as appropriate access to justice), to be able to ensure that all EU environmental obligations may be effectively monitored and enforced.[208] One suggestion has been that the Commission should provide more contact points at national level through its representative offices for the public to raise complaints about non-compliance with EU environmental law.[209] The complementary role of these actors in the area of law enforcement will be considered in detail in the subsequent parts of this book.

Given that the changes to prosecutorial practice under Article 258 TFEU have been only introduced (officially at least) relatively recently, it is perhaps premature to pass judgment on their impact. What is clear, though, is that these changes in law enforcement activities and policy by the Commission's services require very careful handling in order to avoid falling into the trap of creating an environmental implementation strategy that is counterproductive and lessens pressures on member states to fulfil their environmental obligations.

5.5 Accountability and infringement proceedings

One aspect of the Article 258/260 TFEU infringement procedures that has come in for considerable criticism is the extent to which they remain closed and effectively elite dispute resolution processes, with relatively limited possibilities for public scrutiny and participation. Under the EU treaty framework the Commission is invested with primary responsibility for overseeing the management of the infringement system. Specifically, the Commission has exclusive powers in determining whether proceedings are formally launched and in acting as the prosecuting agency. Effectively, it is tasked with the responsibility of upholding the Union interest with respect to infringement litigation. It remains a key feature of the infringement provisions in Articles 258 and 260 TFEU that the Commission has autonomy in deciding on whether or how to proceed in any given case. The element of autonomy reflects the evident intention of the EU treaty drafters to underpin the infringement proceedings with the principle of impartiality, namely that the Commission should be able to discharge its prosecutorial functions free from external interference (notably from member states).

The autonomous role of Commission action in relation to infringement proceedings runs in tension with the EU's principles of transparency and open decision-making that have evolved in recent years within the constitutional fabric of the Union. The current treaty framework builds on earlier tentative political steps taken in the 1990s to move towards opening up EU decision-making processes.[210] The principal provision in the EU treaty framework is Article 15 TFEU (ex Article 255 EC), which may be traced back to its introduction in the EU legal order through the 1997 Amsterdam Treaty. Article 15 TFEU, which stipulates that the Union institutions and other organs must conduct their operations 'as openly as possible', provides for the following specific right in its third paragraph:

> 3. Any citizen of the Union, and any natural or legal person residing in or having its registered office in a Member State, shall have a right of access to the Union institutions, bodies, offices and agencies, whatever their medium, subject to the principles and the conditions to be defined in accordance with this paragraph.

The basic position in paragraph 3 is qualified. Each EU institution is to elaborate its own Rule of Procedure regarding access to documents. The specific rules regarding public access to EP, Commission and Council documents have now been established under Regulation 1049/2001.[211] The Commission has published further implementing rules in its Rules of Procedure with respect to access to Commission documentation.[212] A right of access to documents is also entrenched within the EU's Charter of Fundamental Rights.[213]

The infringement system is effectively a 'closed' system in the sense that the Commission's decisions over whether to commence, suspend or terminate legal action are essentially barred from public scrutiny. The general public, including notably complainants, have no power over the determination of whether a particular case is formally prosecuted. Whilst complainants are recognised to constitute a key information source for the Commission in terms of its abilities to carry out its mandate to supervise implementation of EU law, they have been granted historically relatively few rights in terms of challenging Commission inaction or in accessing Commission documentation relating to the management of the infringement procedures themselves. These rights will be discussed in detail in later chapters (Chapters 9–9A); however, some general points on this subject may be usefully made at this point in relation to the way in which the Commission handles complaints and liaises with complainants.

A matter closely related to the general issue of transparency in the context of infringement proceedings under Articles 258 and 260 TFEU is the question of the extent of participatory rights of complainants. Whilst the issue of complainants' rights will be dealt with in more detail in Part II of the book as part of its focus on the role of private individuals in the enforcement of EU environmental law, it is useful to set out a few key points in brief here. As already mentioned, complainants constitute an important source of information for the Commission with regard to suspected infringements. In 2012, for instance, the Commission received 588 complaints of suspected environmental infringements, 18.72 per cent of all complaints registered with the Commission and the highest number for a particular EU policy sector. Their information is particularly important in the context of bad-application cases, in respect of which the Commission has few if any effective resources to investigate suspected infringements. Notwithstanding their significance in terms of enabling the Commission to undertake a degree of supervision in this area, complainants are afforded relatively few participatory rights in the conduct of the infringement process itself. The position has improved somewhat, though, in recent years with the Commission's new system of handling complaints.

Originally, the complainant was totally marginalised in the processing of infringement actions by the Commission. Historically, this may be explained by the fact that Article 258 TFEU was conceived on the basis of an essentially inter-governmental perspective of how disputes concerning implementation failures relating to international law should be handled. The aim of the process was to secure member state compliance if possible in a discreet, relatively speedy, infor-mal way, negotiated behind closed doors at international level. It was not designed to protect the position of complainants.[214] However, perceptions of the function of the Commission and the infringement procedure – and in particular how it should be conducted – have changed considerably over time as the principle of transparency became woven within the legal fabric of the EU treaty. With the rise and recognition of the importance of the complainant as an information source on compliance issues coupled with the development of a principle of transparency within the unfolding legal order of the EU by virtue of the Maastricht Treaty, by the 1990s the traditional workings of the infringement procedure had come under strain.

As a result, the Commission introduced changes to its operational procedures in terms of handling complaints about suspected violations of Union law by member states. Changes have been driven in part due to pressure from the Euro-pean Ombudsman investigating cases of maladministration by the Commission in handling complaint files. In 2002 the Commission introduced a number of reforms,[215] which have recently been consolidated and updated in a 2012 Com-munication *Updating the Handling of Relations with the Complainant in Respect of the Application of Union Law.*[216] The Commission has also published a standard com-plaints form,[217] which it recommends, but does not require, complainants to use. More recently, DG ENV has created a special complaints form relating to nature protection cases.[218] Some basic information concerning the infringement proce-dure is contained in an explanatory memorandum in the form. Complaints are to be filed first with the Commission's Secretariat General, which will then process the matter internally and distribute files to be handled by the law enforcement teams in the Directorate-General responsible for the policy sector concerned by the complaint.

The Commission's current policy on complaints handling affords the complainant some basic procedural rights in relation to the management of an infringement procedure. These are listed within the 2012 Communication. They include maintaining an open approach as to who may lodge a complaint. Anyone may file a complaint free of charge, and without being required to show a specific legal or other particular interest connected with the dispute.[219] The complaint must be submitted in writing and in one of the EU's official languages to the Commission, and need not be submitted in any particular format although the Commission recommends use of its standard complaints form in order to assist in speeding up the process.[220] All complaints are now recorded on the IT central application system for the registration of complaints (CHAP database), unless they are deemed to be non-investigable.[221] Until October 2009 the Commission operated a system under which an initial evaluation was made of complaints to determine whether there was sufficient evidence or information of a potential breach of EU law to justify registration of a complaint. This generated some concerns that some valid complaints were failing to be registered by the Commission.[222] Non-investigable complaints are defined in the 2012 Communication as including those: from anonymous correspondents; which fail to specify a particular member state to which an allegation may be attributed; which denounce actions of private persons unless the complaint reveals involvement or omissions to intervene by public authorities; which fail to set out a grievance; which set out grievances in respect of which the Commission has adopted a clear, public and consistent position which is also to be disseminated to the complainant; or which refer to a grievance that falls outside the scope of EU law. [223] The complainant is to receive an acknowledgement of receipt of the complaint within 15 working days of the Commission having received the complaint, including confirmation of the registration number to be used in all correspondence.[224] The complainant is guaranteed anonymity, namely that their identity will not be revealed to a third party such as the defendant member state unless they agree to disclosure.[225] Subsequent to registration, complaints may be examined in co-operation with the member state concerned, and the Commission will inform the complaint of this in writing.[226] Complainants may request at their own expense to arrange a meeting with Commission officials to provide a supplementary oral explanation of the grounds of their case.[227] A general target time limit of one year is set by the Commission for it to come to a decision whether or not to open proceedings formally with a formal LFN.[228] In the past, the so-called one-year rule came in for criticism as being arbitrary, vulnerable to delaying tactics by member states prepared to stall co-operation on disclosing information about suspected bad-application environmental infringements as well as not allowing for sufficient time to ascertain facts in complex cases.[229] However, the 2012 update to the complaints procedure has made the system more flexible, clearly envisaging scenarios where more time may be required.

The complainant is afforded a basic minimum of information as to the development of the case file, as is confirmed by the 2012 Communication. The Commission is to inform the complainant of the reasons for deciding not to register a complaint on grounds of non-investigability.[230] They are also to be informed after formal decisions have been taken in the infringement procedure of the steps taken in relation to their case.[231] If the Commission intends to propose no further action be taken with respect to a complaint or file, unless there are exceptional circumstances (not defined), the Commission will provide the complainant with prior notice setting out its grounds, inviting the complainant to respond within four weeks.[232] The Communication makes it very clear that at all stages the Commission retains complete discretion as to deciding matters relating to the complaint, in particular the desirability of opening or terminating proceedings.[233] In practice it is the legal teams of the individual Commission Directorate-Generals that are in substantive control of decisions to close files and not the Commission College. In the case of the environment sector this is the law enforcement teams of DG ENV dealing with infringements. The system underpins the strategic role played by the Head of the relevant unit(s) housing the law enforcement teams in relation to the handling of environmental complaints.

The 2012 Communication on complaints handling offers little in the way of helpful guidance on the question of complainants' rights to access documents in infringement cases. The Communication simply refers to the legislation (notably Regulation 1049/2001)[234] governing access to documents, without providing details as whether if any documents in Article 258/260 TFEU proceedings may or are as a rule to be disclosed.[235] Article 4(2) of Regulation 1049/2001 specifically provides that EU institutions shall refuse access to documents where disclosure would undermine the protection of the court proceedings and legal advice as well as the purpose of investigations, unless there is an overriding public interest in disclosure. Current practice of the Commission has not appeared to diverge from its traditional view of maintaining confidentiality of decisions regarding the management of alleged or suspected infringements of EU law by member states (such as internal legal advice, LFNs, ROs and court pleadings) insofar as a particular case has not yet been definitively completed or, although completed, is related to pending legal action. On the other hand, Commission administrative practice does in principle foresee the disclosure of historic infringement files, namely those which have been terminated, completed or considered devoid of ongoing issues or links with live proceedings.[236] The area of access to environmental information held at EU level, including that relating to legal proceedings, is considered in Chapter 9A (available on website).

The Commission has also changed its complaints handling procedures in other respects with a view to enhance the speed and efficiency of the initial (pre-LFN) investigation phase. Specifically, since 2008 the Commission has been rolling out a new handling system called EU Pilot, subsequent to its 2007/8 review of the infringement process. EU Pilot,[237] discussed in detail in Chapter 3, is intended to provide complainants with quicker responses and also ensure more effective communication between the Commission's law enforcement teams and its Directorate-Generals and national authorities responsible for addressing non-compliance issues. Under EU Pilot, any allegation of member state non-compliance from the public is forwarded by the Commission to the relevant member state designated contact point with the aim of establishing the factual details and seeing whether any resolution may be achieved informally at an early stage without the need for recourse to formal infringement proceedings. A deadline of 20 weeks is set for both the member state authority and Commission to respond to the complainant. This represents a significant improvement as compared with the previous position, in which there were no structures in place to require responses from member states within a set deadline and where the Commission would often close a case on the grounds of insufficient evidence obtained if it did not hear from the member state concerned within a year of the complaint.

5.6 Statistical information on EU environmental infringement cases

The Commission publishes two reports annually which provide information on recent developments concerning the state of implementation of and its monitoring of EU environmental law. Specifically, each year the Commission provides a formal and comprehensive report on its activities in relation to Articles 258 and 260 TFEU concerning the previous calendar year. This is known as the Commission's Report on monitoring the application of Union Law and several reports have been published, all accessible on the Commission's Secretariat General's website.[238] At the time of writing, the Commission's had published its latest (31st) annual monitoring report covering the year 2013 on 1 October 2014. Each annual report contains a summary of infringement actions commenced and pursued for each EU policy sector, including the environment, as well as information on the numbers of infringement actions brought (e.g. per member state as well as per policy sector).

Since 1996, these reports have been complemented with annual surveys and then online summary information carried out by the DG ENV on the state of implementation of EU environmental law in the member states. Seven annual surveys have been published covering the years until 2005, accessible from the Commission's Environment Directorate General's website.[239] Subsequently, DG ENV has focused on providing statistical overviews and has discontinued its annual surveys. Overall, the information to be gleaned from these reports has been relatively limited, with little provided in the way of strategic analysis on key implementation problem trends.[240]

5.6.1 *European Commission annual reports on monitoring the application of EU law*

Each annual report of the Commission includes a sectoral analysis of infringement cases, so as to incorporate basic data and summary assessment of the state of casework affecting individual EU policy areas including EU environmental policy. The European Commission's annual reports, compiled by the Commission's Secretariat General, may be accessed from the following EU website: http://ec.europa.eu/eu_law/infringements/infringements_annual_report_en.htm.

The reports and their Commission document references are as follows:

16th Report (1998):   (COM(1999)301)
17th Report (1999):   (COM(2000)92)
18th Report (2000):   (COM(2001)309)
19th Report (2001):   (COM(2002)324)
20th Report (2002):   (COM(2003)669)
21st Report (2003):   (COM(2004)839)
22nd Report (2004):   (COM(2005)570)
23rd Report (2005):   (COM(2006)416)
24th Report (2006):   (COM(2007)398)
25th Report (2007):   (COM(2008)777)
26th Report (2008):   (COM(2009)675)
27th Report (2009):   (COM(2010)538)
28th Report (2010):   (COM(2011)588)
29th Report (2011):   (COM(2012)714)
30th Report (2012):   (COM(2013)726)
31st Report (2013):   (COM(2014)612)

5.6.2 European Commission annual surveys and other annual publications on the implementation and enforcement of EU environmental law

Since the mid 1990s the DG ENV of the European Commission has published information on the annual management of infringement casework concerning EU environmental law on its website in the form of annual surveys as well as statistical information. Since 2006 this source information has been compressed into a summary format providing essentially simply an outline statistical analysis of casework.

- *Annual surveys on EU environmental infringements 1996–2005*

  First Annual Survey (Oct. 1996–Dec. 1997): (SEC(1999)592)
  Second Annual Survey (1998–9):   (SEC(2000)1219)
  Third Annual Survey (2000–1):   (SEC(2002)1041)
  Fourth Annual Survey (2002):   SEC(2003)804)
  Fifth Annual Survey (2003):   SEC(2004)1025
  Sixth Annual Survey (2004):   SEC(2005)1055
  Seventh Annual Survey (2005):   SEC(2006)1143

The above annual surveys may be located on the following European Commission website: http://ec.europa.eu/environment/legal/law/implementation.htm.

- *Statistical information on EU environmental infringements (2006–)* Since 2006, the practice of the DG ENV of the European Commission has been to discontinue the annual surveys and replace them with annual publication of statistical overviews of environmental infringement proceedings on the Commission's Environmental Directorate-General's website: http://ec.europa.eu/environment/legal/law/statistics.htm.

Since 2010 the European Commission's data on environmental infringements has been organised on the basis that information on infringements in the area of climate change policy is reported separately from those on environmental infringements. This change has been made to reflect the fact that a separate Directorate-General within the European Commission was established in February 2010 for EU climate change policy (Directorate-General for Climate Action (DG CLIMA)). Accordingly, the following set of tables does not take into account data on infringement action relating to EU legislation on climate change from 2010 onwards.

5.6.3 Statistical tables on EU environmental complaints and infringement cases

The tables below provide statistical information on recent developments in environmental infringement actions based on information derived from the above-mentioned European Commission sources (annual monitoring reports, surveys and other online sources of information).

5.6.3.1 Complaints to the European Commission concerning non-compliance with EU environmental law

Table 5.1 below indicates the number of complaints from the public filed with the European Commission in a given year concerning allegations of non-compliance with EU environmental law. It also shows the proportion of environmental complaints relative to the total number of complaints sent to the Commission across all EU policy sectors.

5.6.3.2 EU environmental infringement cases (Articles 258 and 260(2) TFEU)

ARTICLE 258 TFEU CASES

Table 5.2 below provides a breakdown of Article 258 TFEU environmental infringement cases according to particular type of case, whether based on a complaint, relating to non-communication of a directive or otherwise initiated by the Commission. (No official data available for 2012/13.)

Table 5.3 below indicates the number of Article 258 TFEU environmental infringement cases that had been formally opened and which were live as at the end of a given year.

Table 5.4 below provides a breakdown of Article 258 TFEU infringement cases according to particular environmental sector which were live as at the end of a given year.

Tables 5.5a and 5.5b below indicate the proportion of Article 258 TFEU environmental infringement cases which were live as at the end of a given year.

Table 5.1 Complaints about suspected EU member state violations of EU environmental law

Year	Environmental non-compliance complaints		Total number of complaints across all EU policy sectors
	Quantity	Percentage across all EU policy sectors	
2002	555*	38.78	1,431
2003	505*	39.15	1,290
2004	336*	29.32	1,146
2005	275*	23.83	1,154
2006	167	15.92	1,049
2007	113	11.80	958
2008	87	8.38	1,038
2009	143	18.15	788
2010	666*	19.77	3,368
2011	604*	19.39	3,115
2012	588*	18.72	3,141
2013	520	14.83	3,505

Key (*): Denotes highest proportion of complaints across all EU policy sectors.

Table 5.2 Origins of Article 258 TFEU infringement cases in environment sector

As at end of year	Origins of EU environmental infringement cases under examination (Article 258 TFEU)					
	Complaint-based		Own-initiative		Non-communication	
	%	Quantity	%	Quantity	%	Quantity
2004	56.97	286	14.54	73	28.49	143
2005	57.89	462	26.94	215	15.16	121
2006	54.16	371	38.98	267	6.86	47
2007	41.30	306	52.09	386	6.61	49
2008	36.27	243	50.75	340	12.99	87
2009	30.20	164	55.99	304	13.8	75
2010	27.03	120	47.07	209	25.90	115
2011	28.09	84	58.19	174	13.71	41

Table 5.3 Article 258 TFEU environmental infringement cases opened

As at end of year	EU environmental infringement procedures opened (Article 258 TFEU)	
	Quantity	Percentage across all EU sectors
2002	505*	29.79
2003	508*	27.39
2004	568	21.19
2005	489*	23.01
2006	421*	21.01
2007	480*	22.51
2008	480*	23.54
2009	452*	24.37
2010	394*	23.59
2011	339*	17
2012	272*	20
2013	334*	25.6

Key: (*) Denotes highest proportion of Article 258 TFEU actions across all EU policy sectors.

Table 5.4 Article 258 TFEU environmental infringement cases by sector (percentage breakdown)

As at end of year	EU environmental infringement cases by sector – percentage breakdown (Article 258 TFEU)					
	Nature (%)	Water (%)	Waste (%)	Air (%)	EIA (%)	Other (%)
2001	26.3	13.9	20.6	13.3	9.4	9.6
2002	30.4	15.4	21.5	7.3	11.5	8.7
2003	15.6	19.3	21.6	24.6	7	8.3
2004	24.4	15.1	25.1	16.8	12.3	3.3
2005	23.7	14.7	22.5	13.1	15.1	10.8
2006	28	18	19	16	15	4
2007	25	16	19	17	12	11
2008	22	20	23	14	10	11
2009	20	20	19	16	11	14
2010	20	30	15	13	9	13
2011	22	24	22	10	13	9
2012	23	27	19	13	11	7
2013	18	23	32	12	8	7

Tables 5.5a and 5.5b Article 258 TFEU environmental infringement case types

Tables 5.5a

As at end of year	Types of EU environmental infringement cases (Article 258 TFEU)					
	Non-communication cases		Non-conformity cases		Horizontal bad-application cases	
	%	Quantity	%	Quantity	%	Quantity
2001	42	126	29	86	30	89
2002	38	97	35	89	27	70
2003	29	88	39	118	32	95

Note: For the year 2004 onwards the European Commission has disclosed figures on all live bad-application cases, not simply those which involve legal proceedings taken against several member states ('horizontal' cases). This makes statistical comparisons with earlier years challenging. The Commission has not published data for the years 2006–7.

Table 5.5b

As at end of year	Types of environmental infringement cases (Article 258 TFEU)					
	Non-communication cases		Non-conformity cases		Bad-application cases	
	%	Quantity	%	Quantity	%	Quantity
2004	30.35	173	18.07	103	51.58	294
2005	25.36	124	17.59	86	57.06	279
2006	–	–	–	–	–	–
2007	–	–	–	–	–	–
2008	18.30	88	31.80	153	49.90	240
2009	49.65	212	17.56	75	32.79	140
2010	26.08	115	20.63	91	53.29	235
2011	12.24	41	22.99	77	64.78	217
2012	4.53	13	26.83	77	68.64	197
2013	26.51	92	18.16	63	55.33	192

Table 5.6 indicates the number of case management decisions that had been made as at the end of a given year and which were live cases. It appears that as from 2011 the annual reports from the Commission have been changed so as to no longer provide information on the amount and distribution of pending reasoned opinions and referrals to the CJEU.

Table 5.7 indicates which EU member states were subject to the most environmental infringement cases which were live as at the end of a given year. (Prior to 2004 the European Commission only disclosed data regarding horizontal and not individual bad-application environmental cases.)

Table 5.6 Article 258 TFEU environmental infringement case management decisions

As at end of year	Case management decisions for environmental infringement cases (Article 258 TFEU)			
	ROs (reasoned opinions)		Referrals to CJEU	
	Environmental sector: Quantity (% in brackets)	Total number for all EU policy sectors	Environmental sector: Quantity (% in brackets)	Total number for all EU policy sectors
2002	323 (32.30)*	1,000	149 (41.27)*	361
2003	311 (31.13)*	999	146 (35.52)	411
2004	309 (31.06)*	995	142 (31.28)*	454
2005	306 (26.91)*	1,137	128 (32.65)*	392
2006	244 (22.02)*	1,108	118 (32.87)*	359
2007	230 (24.03)	957	111 (31.27)*	355
2008	236 (24.71)	955	109 (27.53)	396
2009	225 (25.71)*	875	100 (28.33)*	353
2010	219 (25.83)*	848	92 (31.62)	291

Key: (*): Denotes highest proportion of case management decisions across all EU policy sectors.

Table 5.7 EU member states subject to most Article 258 TFEU environmental infringement cases

As at end of year	EU member state with most reported EU environmental infringement cases (Article 258 TFEU)					
	Highest	2nd highest	3rd highest	4th highest	5th highest	Total env'l cases
2004	Italy (75)	Spain (66)	Ireland (51)	France (50)	Greece (41)	570
2005	Italy (77)	Spain (57)	Ireland (45)	Greece (36)	Portugal (35)	489
2006	Italy (61)	Spain (40)	Ireland (38)	UK (33)	Greece (30)	421
2007	Italy (60)	Spain (42)	Ireland (34)	UK (33)	France (32)	479
2008	Italy (45)	Spain (37)	Ireland (35)	France (34)	UK (31)	481
2009	Spain (40)	Italy (35)	Ireland (34)	France, UK & Czech Rep. (26)	Greece (24)	451
2010	Italy (46)	Spain & Greece (33)	Poland & Portugal (26)	Ireland (25)	France (19)	445
2011	Italy (40)	Spain (27)	Greece (25)	Portugal (24)	Poland & Czech Rep. (21)	339
2012	Spain (32)	Italy (25)	Greece (22)	Poland (19)	Portugal (17)	296
2013	Spain (29)	Italy/Gr. (25)	Greece (22)	Poland (19)	France (19)	353

Table 5.8 Article 260(2) TFEU environmental infringement cases

As at end of year	Second-round environmental infringement cases (Article 260(2) TFEU)		Total number of Article 260(2) TFEU proceedings formally opened across all policy sectors
	Number of active env'l cases (number of new proceedings opened)	*Percentage of env'l cases out of all second round infringement proceedings opened*	
2002	33 (33)	53.22*	62
2003	40 (40)	57.97*	69
2004	20 (37)	50.68*	73
2005	77 (36)	36.00*	100
2006	66 (37)	39.36*	94
2007	77 (33)	39.29*	84
2008	61 (41)	48.24*	85
2009	61 (40)	40.40*	99
2010	62 (37)	51.39*	72
2011	56 (36)	46.75*	77
2012	54 (35)	27.34*	128
2012	54 (35)	27.34*	128
2013	40	35.39*	113

Key: (*): Denotes highest proportion of cases across all EU policy sectors.

ARTICLE 260(2) TFEU SECOND-ROUND CASES

Table 5.8 above indicates the number of second-round environmental infringements actively pursued by the DG ENV of the Commission, as well as the number of Article 260(2) TFEU proceedings formally opened for environmental cases which were live as at the end of a given year. It also shows the proportion of live environmental cases amongst all second-round infringements formally opened across EU policy sectors as at the end of a given year.

5.7 Some brief concluding remarks

Notwithstanding its limitations and drawbacks, there is little doubt that the infringement procedures set out in Articles 258 and 260 TFEU have been the subject of some notable improvements in recent years, legal as well as operational. The Lisbon Treaty changes to the first-round procedure in relation to the prosecution of non-communication cases have been particularly important. Under Article 260(3) TFEU the Commission does not need to negotiate its way through two lengthy infraction proceedings before the possibility of a financial sanction arises in respect of this type of case. Instead fines may be requested from the CJEU in a relatively short period of time in a single procedure. The treaty change appears already to be having a significant effect as the early evidence since the change has come into force indicates a significant decline in the number of non-communication judgments. There are compelling reasons to extend this recent treaty change so as to cover all types of EU environmental infringement, and also to lift the current cap on CJEU financial sanctions currently in place in Article 260(3) TFEU. Such an amendment would provide a significant additional element of deterrence to the current infringement framework and assist in ensuring that member states adhere to their EU environmental legislative commitments in a full and timely manner.

The Commission has through its 2007/8 internal review of infringement case management finally begun to rise to the challenge of prioritising its caseload in order to focus its limited resources on breaches of more strategic importance for the implementation of EU environmental law. However, it is also apparent that more measures and care are needed to ensure that this transition is not made at the expense of complainants or other stakeholders (such as national authorities) finding themselves otherwise unable at national level to secure access to environmental justice for legal or financial reasons. It is not apparent that the Commission has taken into account sufficiently the adverse impacts that its prioritisation strategy may have either in the short or longer term on the prospects for the public, and NGEOs in particular, in being able meaningfully to continue to assist in ensuring the upholding of legally binding Union obligations in the environmental sector.

There are other changes that also need to be made to the current infringement regime which would be highly beneficial in enhancing its effectiveness. Notably, powers of inspection should be granted to the Commission so as to enable it to investigate the veracity of claims of bad application of EU environmental law and not have to rely on often unreliable information supplied by national governments or authorities and NGEOs (which do not have investigatory powers). In addition, the Commission needs to address long-standing staffing resource problems in order be able to address its environmental infringement caseload effectively. The benchmark of two desk officers per (large) member states is wholly inadequate.

In summary, it would be overly optimistic to depict the recent evolution of the infringement procedures as having 'come of age', to coin a phrase used recently in the literature,[241] with respect to the EU environment sector. A number of profound improvements are required to be made to both the legal framework and operational practice relating to case management. However, it may be fair to say that the Union has perhaps begun now to set itself on a course potentially towards meaningful reform of the Article 258/260 TFEU procedures, a position which the author assesses to be far more positive than at the time of completing the first edition of this book but a few years ago in 2006.

Notes

1 See e.g. Demmke (2003), p. 354; Johnson and Corcelle (1995), p. 482; Krämer (2003), p. 377.
2 By virtue of Art. 4 (3) TEU.

3 Formerly Art. 211 EC.
4 See Macrory (1992), p. 348 and also more generally Rawlings (2000), p. 28.
5 Krämer (2003), p. 378.
6 Decision No. 1386/2013/EU of the European Parliament and of the Council of 20 November 2013 on a General Union Environment Action Programme to 2020 'Living Well, within the Limits of our Planet' (OJ 2013 L354/171) (within Priority Objective 4: To maximise the benefits of EU environment legislation). For a recent assessment of member state environmental inspection systems sponsored by the Commission, see e.g. Bio-Intelligence, *Service Study on Possible Options for Strengthening the Commission's Capacity to Undertake Effective Investigations of Alleged Breaches in EU Environment Law*, Final Report, 4 January 2013 (accessible at: http://ec.europa.eu/environment/legal/law/inspections.htm).
7 SOLVIT is an online network of contact points in EU member states (and EFTA countries part of the 1992 European Economic Area Agreement), which was established in 2002 by the EU and is co-ordinated by the European Commission. It was set up in order to assist in resolving complaints from the public about instances of non-compliance by national authorities with single market rules. Details may be obtained from the SOLVIT website: http://ec.europa.eu/solvit/site/about/index_en.htm.
8 See comments e.g. by Somsen (2003a), p. 418.
9 See Jack (2011), p. 75.
10 One notable exception is the Ozone Regulation 1005/09 (OJ 2009 L286/1) which provides for the possibility of the Commission providing assistance to national authorities in inspections (see Art. 28). See also comment by Jans (2000), p. 160.
11 See Wägenbaur (1990–1), p. 462.
12 See Grohs (2004), p. 30.
13 Case C-387/97 *Commission v Greece (Kouroupitos (2))*. The case is discussed at length in Ch. 4.
14 At the time of writing, waste management issues were now being addressed by Unit A.2 (Waste Management and Recycling) within Directorate A (Green Economy) of DG ENV.
15 Jans (2000), p. 169.
16 See e.g. Demmke (2001), p. 29 and Grohs (2004), p. 38.
17 Krämer (2003), p. 381.
18 Regulation 1/2003 (OJ 2003 L1/1).
19 Directive 2010/63 on the protection of animals used for scientific purposes (OJ 2010 L276/33).
20 Regulation 1224/09 establishing a Community control system for ensuring compliance with the rules of the common fisheries policy (OJ 2009 L343/1).
21 Regulation 2185/96 concerning on-the-spot checks and inspections carried out by the Commission in order to detect fraud and irregularities affecting the EC's financial interests (OJ 1996 L292/2).
22 See e.g. Demmke (2001), p. 5.
23 See Winter (1996), p. 711 and Krämer (1993), p. 395.
24 Case C-387/97 *Commission v Greece (Kouroupitos(2))*, discussed in Chapter 4.
25 Art. 3(3) TEU and Art. 191(2) TFEU.
26 See e.g. UK House of Lords EU Select Committee Report 1991; Macrory (1992); and Winter (1996).
27 Regulation 1210/90 (OJ 1990 L120/1), as amended.
28 See e.g. Wägenbaur (1990–1), p. 472; House of Lords EU Select Committee Reports (1991) and (1997).
29 COM(1996)500, para. 9.
30 Recommendation 2001/331 providing for minimum criteria for environmental inspections in the member states (OJ 2001 L118/41).

31 COM(2007)707 Commission Communication on the review of Recommendation 2001/331 and accompanying Annex (SEC(2007)1493 Commission Staff Working Paper), 14 November 2007.
32 Decision No. 1386/2013/EU of the European Parliament and of the Council of 20 November 2013 on a General Union Environment Action Programme to 2020 'Living Well, within the Limits of our Planet' (OJ 2013 L354/171).
33 'Priority Objective 4: To maximise the benefits of EU environmental legislation' (paras. 54–63 of the 7EAP).
34 Paras. 58 and 63(c) second subpara. of COM(2012)710.
35 Reporting requirements for several pieces of EU environmental protection legislation have been crafted on the basis of Directive 91/692 standardising and rationalising reports on the implementation of certain Directives relating to the environment (OJ 1991 L377/48) as amended by Regulation 1882/03 (OJ 2003 L284/1).
36 van den Bossche (1996), p. 388.
37 See Krämer (2003), p. 380.
38 See Demmke (2003), p. 334.
39 COM(2013)6, *Commission Report on the Implementation of EU Waste Legislation (2007–9)*, 17 January 2013; COM(2013)574, *Commission 7th Report on the Implementation of Urban Waste Directive 91/271*, 7 August 2013.
40 Case C-494/01 *Commission v Ireland (Irish Waste)*.
41 See e.g. Lenaerts and Gutiérrez-Fons (2011), p. 10; Prete and Smulders (2010), p. 24; Schrauwen (2006), p. 292.
42 Schrauwen (2006), p. 294.
43 See e.g. Macrory (1992), p. 363; Jack (2011), p. 75; Borzsák (2011), pp. 128–9.
44 Currently the units are based within Directorate D Implementing Governance and Semester (ENV D.1, D.2 and D.3).
45 Borzsák (2011), p. 128.
46 See Hattan (2003), p. 285; Grohs (2004), p. 33.
47 See Commission weblink: ec.europa.eu/dgs/environment/directory.htm.
48 Borzsák (2011), p. 129.
49 See COM(2013)726, *30th Commission Annual Report on Monitoring the Application of EU Law*, 22 October 2013 in Part II (Policies), p. 55.
50 Craig and de Búrca (2011), p. 410.
51 See Krämer (2002), p. 177; Wägenbauer (1990–1), p. 462.
52 See the Commission's annual monitoring reports on the application of EU law for 2010 (COM(2011)588), 2011 (COM(2012)714), 2012 (COM(2013)726) and 2013 (COM(2014)612) respectively.
53 Kingston (2011), p. 7.
54 Grohs (2004), p. 31. See also Krämer (2003), p. 273.
55 By virtue of Art. 260(3) TFEU.
56 See also comments by Lenaerts and Gutiérrez-Fons (2011), p. 4.
57 Art. 17(1) TEU, second sentence.
58 See e.g. Krämer (2006a), p. 414; Jack (2011), p. 91; Lenaerts and Gutiérriez-Fons (2011), p. 4.
59 Krämer (2006a), p. 407 and (2003), p. 388.
60 Williams (1994), p. 368.
61 Grohs (2004), p. 26.
62 See comments by Jack (2011), p. 93.
63 For instance, consider the lengthy times granted for reducing the dumping of biodegradable waste into landfills in the Landfill Directive 99/31 (OJ 1999 L182/1) and long implementation timeline (15 years) regarding the attainment of good surface water status under the aegis of the Water Framework Directive 2000/60 (OJ 2000 L327/1).
64 Audretsch (1987), p. 842; Barav (1975), p. 369; Bonnie (1998); Weatherill and Beaumont (1999), p. 214.

65 See also Wägenbaur (1990–1), p. 473.
66 See e.g. Dashwood and White (1989), p. 413.
67 For example, Article 106(3) TFEU on state monopolies.
68 Ibáñez (1998a), para. 2.1.4.
69 See e.g. Gaffney (1998), p. 126 and Ibáñez (1998a).
70 For instance, Audretsch has suggested curtailing the maximum response time to Commission writing warnings in the pre-litigation phase to one month: Audretsch (1986), p. 380. The EP has also endorsed introducing strict time limits for responses: EP Resolution P6 TA(2006)202 (at para. 24).
71 A practice effectively endorsed by the CJEU, e.g. in Case C-121/07 *Commission v France (French GMO Controls (2))*. See comments from Lenaerts and Gutiérrez-Fons (2011), p. 8; Jack (2011), p. 82.
72 For instance, Borzsák suggests eliminating the second-round pre-litigation phase: Borzsák (2011), p. 239.
73 COM(2007)502, Commission Communication, *A Europe of Results – Applying Community Law*, 5 September 2007.
74 The EU Pilot system, discussed in Ch. 3, is explained on the Commission's Secretariat General's website at: http://ec.europa.eu/eu_law/infringements/application_ monitoring_en.htm.
75 See SEC(2011)1629/2, Commission Report, *Second Evaluation Report on EU Pilot*, section 3 (Evaluation), p. 6 where the Commission reported that 80% of cases are resolved without formal infringement proceedings being opened..
76 See COM(2014)612, *31st Commission Annual Report on Monitoring the Application of EU Law* (1 October 2014), p. 10.
77 See e.g. Barav (1975), p. 383; Audretsch (1987), p. 842; and Dashwood/White (1989), p. 413.
78 See e.g. COM(2002)725, Commission Communication, *Better Monitoring of the Application of Community Law*, p. 3; Prete and Smulders (2010), p. 11.
79 See e.g. comments by Dashwood and White (1989), p. 413.
80 See DG ENV summary report at: http://ec.europa.eu/environment/legal/law/sta tistics.htm.
81 By virtue of Art. 260(3) TFEU.
82 See DG ENV websites: http://ec.europa.eu/environment/legal/law/statistics.htm and http://ec.europa.eu/environment/legal/law/pubs.htm.
83 Borzsák (2011), p. 239.
84 See Macrory (1992), p. 357; Gray (1979).
85 See e.g. Case C-195/90R *Commission v Germany*.
86 See Hartley (2003), p. 313.
87 Case C-503/06 *Commission v Italy*.
88 Joined Cases C-57/89R and 57/89 *Commission v Germany*.
89 See Grohs (2004), p. 26; Krämer (2003), p. 392.
90 Namely, the interim relief orders secured in the *Liguria Bird Hunting* case (Case C-503/06R *Commission v Italy*), the *Rospuda River Valley* case (Case C-193/07R *Commission v Poland*) and the *Maltese Bird Hunting* case (Case C-76/08R *Commission v Malta*). The case proceedings are available for inspection on the Court's website: www.curia.eu.int.
91 Williams (1994), p. 369.
92 See Audretsch (1987), p. 854; Dashwood and White (1989), p. 388.
93 By virtue of Art. 260(3) TFEU.
94 By virtue of former Art. 88 ECSC.
95 See Arts. 101–2 TFEU in conjunction with Art. 8 of Regulation 1/2003 (OJ 2003 L1/1).
96 See Joined Cases 24 and 97/80R *Commission v France*.
97 See e.g. Audretsch (1987), p. 842; Mertens de Wilmars (1970), p. 404.
98 Case C-355/90 *Commission v Spain*.

99 Directive 2009/147 (OJ 2010 L20/7), replacing former Directive 79/409 (OJ 1979 L103/1).

100 Winter (1996), p. 715.

101 Krämer (1993), pp. 430–3.

102 OJ 2000 L327/1.

103 Via the EU RAPID press release system, available for inspection at: http://europa. eu/rapid/latest-press-releases.htm.

104 OJ 2008 L152/1. The member states concerned were the Czech Republic, Estonia, Finland, Greece, Hungary, Luxembourg, Romania, Slovenia and Spain. (See summary reports in the EU Current Survey sections of the *Environmental Liability* law journal covering the months of November–December 2010.)

105 OJ 2008 L164/19. The member states concerned were Cyprus, Estonia, Finland, France, Greece, Ireland, Malta and Poland. (See summary reports in the EU Current Survey sections of the *Environmental Liability* law journal covering the months of January–May 2011.)

106 OJ 2008 L312/3. The member states concerned were Belgium, Bulgaria, Cyprus, Estonia, Finland, France, Greece, Hungary, Latvia, Luxembourg, Poland, Romania, Slovakia and Slovenia. (See summary reports in the EU Current Survey sections of the *Environmental Liability* law journal covering the months of February, March, July, September and October 2011.)

107 OJ 2008 L328/28. The member states concerned were Austria, Cyprus, Czech Republic, Finland, Greece, Italy, Lithuania, Malta, Portugal, Romania, Slovenia and the UK. (See summary reports in the EU Current Survey sections of the *Environmental Liability* law journal covering the months of July, September and October 2011.)

108 Directive 2009/123 (OJ 2009 L280/52). The member states concerned were the Czech Republic, Finland, Greece, Italy, Lithuania, Portugal, Romania and Slovakia. (See summary reports in the EU Current Survey sections of the *Environmental Liability* law journal covering the months of July 2011.)

109 OJ 2010 L153/13. The member states concerned were Bulgaria, Greece, Italy and Portugal. (See summary reports in the EU Current Survey sections of the *Environmental Liability* law journal covering the months of January–February 2013.)

110 The member states concerned were Austria, Belgium, Cyprus, Czech Republic, France, Germany, Greece, Hungary, Italy, Poland, Portugal, Romania, Slovakia, Slovenia, Spain, Sweden and the UK. (See summary reports in the EU Current Survey sections of the *Environmental Liability* law journal covering the months of March–June, September and October 2010.)

111 OJ 2000 L327/1. The member states concerned were Belgium, Cyprus, Denmark, Greece, Ireland, Lithuania, Malta, Poland, Portugal, Romania, Slovenia and Spain. (See summary reports in the EU Current Survey sections of the *Environmental Liability* law journal covering the months of May and June 2010.)

112 See Wennerås (2012), pp. 173–4.

113 See e.g. Macrory and Purdy (1997), p. 43; Rawlings (2000), p. 23; Craig and de Búrca (2003), p. 401.

114 See Bonnie (1998), pp. 537 *et seq.*; Theodossiou (2002), pp. 25 *et seq.*

115 Bonnie (1998), pp. 537 *et seq.*

116 By way of exception, this 'contempt of court' factor no longer applies to non-communication cases, which since the Lisbon Treaty may be the subject of fines at first-round stage (see Art. 260(3) TFEU).

117 See e.g. para. 26 of the General Court's judgment in Case T-139/06 *Commission v France.*

118 Notably, SEC(2005)1658 Commission Communication, *Application of Article 228 of the EC Treaty* of 13 December 2005 (OJ 2007 C126) which may be inspected on the following EU Commission website: http://ec.europa.eu/eu_law/infringements/ infringements_260_en.htm.

119 See Regulations 1/2003 (OJ 2003 L1/1) and 773/2004 (OJ 2004 L123/18) as amended.
120 Theodossiou (2002), pp. 25 *et seq.*
121 Winter (1996), p. 716; more generally Rawlings (2000), p. 23 and Theodossiou (2002), pp. 25 *et seq.*
122 See e.g. Winter (1996), p. 716; Krämer (2003), p. 391.
123 See comments by Tesauro (1992), p. 489.
124 Demmke (2003), p. 354.
125 See comments by Prete and Smulders (2010), p. 54; Jack (2011), p. 83 and Wennerås (2012), p. 165. See also discussion in Ch. 4 on second-round CJEU judgments.
126 Jack (2011), p. 88, commenting that the maximum duration co-efficient applied by the CJEU (3) may be insufficient to address long-term breaches.
127 The Commission recommended a seriousness co-efficient of 14 in the free movement of workers Case C-119/04 *Commission v Italy* (the CJEU did not impose a fine in the event for lack of evidence) and the CJEU applied a seriousness co-efficient of only 10 in Case C-304/02 *French Fishing Controls (2)*.
128 Jack (2011), p. 90.
129 In Case C-304/02 *Commission v France (French Fishing Controls (2))*.
130 Prete and Smulders (2010), p. 53. For an opposing viewpoint, see Kilbey (2007).
131 Case T-139/06 *France v Commission*.
132 See Tesauro (1992), p. 488.
133 See also comments by Jack (2011), p. 91.
134 Specifically: Case C-387/97 *Commission v Greece (Kouroupitos 2)*; Case C-278/01 *Commission v Spain (Spanish Bathing Waters (2))*; Case C-304/02 *Commission v France (French Fishing Controls (2))*; Case C-121/07 *Commission v France (French GMO Controls)*; Case C-279/11 *Commission v Ireland (Irish EIA (2))*; Case C-374/11 *Commission v Ireland (Waste Water Treatment Systems)*; Case C-533/11 *Commission v Belgium (Belgian Waste Water (2))*; and Case C-576/11 *Commission v Luxembourg (Luxembourg Waste Water (2))*.
135 Krämer (2002b), p. 181.
136 Hedemann-Robinson (2006).
137 This practice was changed after the CJEU confirmed in 2005 in Case C-304/02 *French Fishing Controls (2)* that the CJEU could impose a lump sum as well as a periodic penalty payment.
138 See e.g. Tesauro (1992), p. 489.
139 See e.g. Case 48/65 *Lütticke* and Case 247/87 *Star Fruit*.
140 The Common Foreign and Security policy area (Chapter 2 of Title V TEU) is a notable exception to this general rule of thumb, in respect of which the EU member states have retained a substantial degree control over powers to submit policy proposals at Union level, with the Commission having a parallel and qualified role in conjunction with the High Representative of the Union for Foreign Affairs and Security Policy (see Art. 30 TEU).
141 The Commission is only obliged to inform the EP of its reasons if deciding to reject a legislative request from the latter institution. Likewise, the Commission is not bound to adhere to a request for a legislative proposal from a citizens' initiative (petition backed by at least a million EU citizens from a significant number of member states): see Art. 11 TEU in conjunction with Art. 24 TFEU and Regulation 211/11 (OJ 2011 L65/1).
142 See Art. 192 TFEU.
143 See Williams (1994), p. 352; Williams (2002), p. 271; Hattan (2003), p. 275.
144 Art. 250 TFEU (ex Art. 219 EC).
145 See Ch. 9 for discussion on the EU's access to information rules with respect to information held by EU institutions.
146 Macrory and Purdy (1997), p. 35.

147 Directive 2009/147 (OJ 2010 L20/7), replacing former Directive 79/409 (OJ 1979 L103/1).
148 Krämer (2006a), p. 409.
149 Williams (1994), p. 354.
150 Case C-198/97 *Commission v Germany.*
151 See critical comments from Weatherill and Beaumont (1999), p. 222.
152 At the time of writing, the relevant units are located within Directorate D (Implementation, Governance and Semester) of DG ENV. Periodically, their location may change as organisational changes may be made to each Directorate-General.
153 Williams (1994), p. 364.
154 At the time of writing, Directorate D contains four units: D1–D3, Enforcement, Cohesion Policy and European Semester (Clusters 1–3) and D.4 Compliance Promotion, Governance and Legal Issues (see weblink at: http://ec.europa.eu/dgs/environment/directory.htm).
155 See Williams (1994), p. 358; Scott (1998), p. 151.
156 European Ombudsman Decision 1288/99/OV against the Commission (cited in the EO's Annual Report 2002, p. 98).
157 Regulation 1303/2013 laying down common provisions on the European Regional Development Fund, the European Social Fund, the Cohesion Fund, the European Agricultural Fund for Rural Development and the European Maritime and Fisheries Fund and laying down general provisions on the European Regional Development Fund, the European Social Fund, the Cohesion Fund and the European Maritime and Fisheries Fund and repealing Council Regulation (EC) No. 1083/2006 (OJ 2013 L347/320). See notably Art. 6 of Regulation 1303/2013 which stipulates that release of EU funding is conditional on this being in compliance with Union law.
158 The right to good administration from the EU's political institutions is enshrined within Art. 41 of the EU's Charter of Fundamental Rights (OJ 2010 C83/2).
159 See notably the Commission's 2002 Code of Good Administrative Behaviour for Staff of the European Commission in relations with the public, of 13 September 2000 (OJ 2000 L267). (See weblink: http://ec.europa.eu/transparency/code/index_en.htm; http://ec.europa.eu/transparency/code/_docs/code_en.pdf.) Section 2 of the Code stipulates that Commission staff must act objectively and impartially, and ensure that their conduct is not guided by personal or national interests or political pressure. Disciplinary measures against infracting staff may be taken under the aegis of the Commission's Staff Regulations (Regulation 21/62/EEC and Regulation 11/62/EAEC (OJ 1962 L45/1385) as amended).
160 Subsequent to European Ombudsman's report the official served as a Head of Unit and a Director within DG ENV. The official concerned remains in a senior post within DG ENV at the time of writing.
161 Now Art. 13 of Directive 2008/98 (OJ 2008 L312/3), previously Art. 4 of former Directive 75/442 (OJ 1975 L194/39).
162 'MS' signifies 'member states'.
163 See *The Guardian* newspaper report 'Spanish Government Cleared of Blame for Prestige Oil Tanker Disaster' of 13 November 2013 (http://www.theguardian.com/world/2013/nov/13/spanish-prestige-oil-tanker-disaster). The Spanish judge presiding over the case, Judge Juan Luis Piá is reported to have said in his judgment:

> Nobody knows exactly what might have been the cause of what happened, nor what would have been the appropriate response to the emergency situation created by the *Prestige*'s breakdown.

164 Williams (1994), pp. 398–9.
165 Demmke (2003), p. 344.
166 The point that the Commission is not capable of being able to pursue every infringement is well acknowledged; see e.g. Prete and Smulders (2010), p. 17; Kingston (2011), p. 7.

167 Art. 4(3) TEU.
168 Grohs (2004), p. 31.
169 See e.g. Macrory and Purdy (1997), p. 43; Macrory (1996).
170 Demmke (2003), p. 344; Ibáñez (1998a), section 2.7.2.2.
171 Demmke (2003), p. 344. See also Ibáñez (1998a), section 2.7.2.2; and Grohs (2004), p. 31.
172 Jans (2000), p. 169.
173 See e.g. Kingston (2011), p. 7.
174 Best available technique not exceeding excessive cost.
175 Namely the enforcement of directives between private individuals (horizontal direct effect scenario) and the enforcement of directives by public authorities against private individuals (inverse direct effect scenario).
176 Demmke (2001), p. 15.
177 Winter (1996), p. 706.
178 COM(1996)500.
179 COM(1996)500, pp. 4 *et seq.*
180 See e.g. Macrory and Purdy (1997), p. 43; Ibáñez (1998a), section 2.7.
181 See e.g. Jans (2000), p. 169; Hattan (2003), p. 286.
182 Demmke (2003), p. 338.
183 See e.g. Harding (1997), p. 14.
184 Demmke (2003), p. 15.
185 Case C-131/88 *Commission v Germany*.
186 See e.g. Krämer (1993), p. 121; Krämer (2003), p. 375.
187 European Council Doc. SN00150/97.
188 European Council Doc. SN00150/1/98 REV1.
189 SEC(1998)1733.
190 COM(2002)725 Commission Communication, *Better Monitoring of the Application of Community Law*, 11 December 2002, section 3.5.
191 COM(2001)428 Commission Communication, *European Governance – A White Paper*, 27 May 2001.
192 COM(2002)725 Commission Communication, *Better Monitoring of the Application of Community Law*, 11 December 2002.
193 For details see Ch. 5 in the first edition of this book.
194 SEC(2004)1025.
195 The Report gives the example of this being used in respect of Directive 2001/42 on the assessment of the effects of certain plans and programmes on the environment (Strategic Environmental Assessment) OJ 2001 L197/30.
196 See Grohs (2004), p. 37.
197 See Hattan (2003), p. 279.
198 Ibid., p. 279.
199 Grohs (2004), p. 31.
200 COM(2007)502, Commission Communication, *A Europe of Results – Applying Community Law*, 5 September 2007.
201 Ibid., section 1 (Prevention), pp. 12 *et seq.*
202 Ibid., section 3 (Seeking a more efficient management of infringements).
203 The average time taken by the Commission to process infringements over the period 1999–2007, from opening of a file to applying to the Court under Art. 258 TFEU was 24 months (COM(2009)675, *26th Annual Report of the Commission on Monitoring the Application of Community Law* (2008), 15 December 2009, p. 2.
204 COM(2008)773 final, *Commission Communication on Implementing European Community Environmental Law*, 18 November 2008.
205 Art. 17 TEU.
206 Ibid., section 3.3, p. 8.
207 Ibid., pp. 8–9.
208 See also Kingston (2011), p. 7, pointing out the dangers of prioritisation in having a marginalisation effect on complainants.

209 Jack (2011), p. 78.
210 See e.g. Declaration 17 on the Right of Access to Information, attached to the Treaty on European Union 1992. See also the 1993 Inter-Institutional Declaration on Democracy, Transparency and Subsidiarity agreed between the three EU institutions involved in the legislative process.
211 OJ 2001 L145/43.
212 Commission Decision 2001/937 (OJ 2001 L345/94), Annex. The rules on access to documents and accompanying case law of the CJEU are examined in detail in Chapter 9A (online).
213 See Art. 42 of the EU Charter of Fundamental Rights guaranteeing a right of access to EU institutional documentation (OJ 2010 C83/2).
214 See Rawlings (2000), pp. 8 *et seq.*
215 COM(2002)141, Communication, *Relations with the Complainant in Respect of Infringements of Community Law.* The Commission undertook some earlier changes on complainant relations in 1998 (see SEC(1998)1733, *Improvement to the Commission's Working Methods in Relation to Infringement Proceedings*, 15 October 1998).
216 COM(2012)154 Communication, *Updating the Handling of Relations with the Complainant in Respect of the Application of Union Law*, 2 April 2012.
217 OJ 1999 C119/5. Accessible also online from the Commission's Secretariat General's website: http://europa.eu.int/comm/secretariat_general.
218 Accessible on the DG ENV website at: http://ec.europa.eu/environment/legal/law/complaints.htm.
219 Para. 2 (General principles) of COM(2012)154.
220 Ibid., para. 5. Complaints may be sent by post to the Commission's Secretariat General Brussels postal address (1049 Brussels) or to one of the Commission's representative offices in the member states. Alternatively, a complaint may be sent by email to: SG-PLAINTES@ec.europa.eu.
221 Ibid., para. 3.
222 See comments in COM(2010)538, *Commission's 27th Annual Report Monitoring the Application of EU Law*, 1 October 2010, p. 7.
223 COM(2012)154, para. 3.
224 Ibid., para. 4.
225 Ibid., para. 6.
226 Ibid., para. 7.
227 Ibid.
228 Ibid., para. 8.
229 Williams (1994), p. 369.
230 Para. 4 of COM(2012)154.
231 Ibid., para. 9.
232 Ibid., para. 10.
233 Ibid., para. 9.
234 Regulation 1049/2001 regarding public access to European Parliament, Commission and Council documents (OJ 2001 L145/43) as implemented by the provisions set out in the Annex Commission Decision 2001/937 (OJ 2001 L345/94).
235 Para. 12 of COM(2012)154.
236 SEC(2003)260/3, *Commission Working Paper on Public Access to Documents Relating to Infringement Proceedings*, 28 February 2003.
237 Information on EU Pilot may be obtained from the following Commission website: http://ec.europa.eu/eu_law/infringements/application_monitoring_en.htm.
238 http://europa.eu.int/comm./secretariat_general/sgb/infringements.
239 http://europa.eu.int/comm/environment.
240 See comments by Krämer (2006a), p. 421.
241 Prete and Smulders (2010) refer to the 'coming of age' of infringement procedures in general in their article.

6 Enforcement of EU environmental law at national level by private persons

General legal principles

Part II of this book focuses on the rights of private persons under EU law to engage in the enforcement of EU environmental legislation and is divided into two sections. Section 1 comprises Chapters 6–8, which consider the impact of these rights at the level of the EU member state. Section 2 contains Chapters 8A–9 and examines the extent of private persons' rights to enforce such legislation against EU institutions. This particular chapter will focus on the general legal principles established by the Court of Justice of the EU (CJEU) that are of relevance in creating possibilities for private persons to enforce EU environmental law before national courts of the member states. Unlike the European Commission, private persons have not been vested with express powers under the EU treaty framework to enforce legal commitments entered into by member states at EU level. However, as will be discussed below, the CJEU has developed a body of jurisprudence since the early 1960s confirming that private persons may, in certain circumstances, take legal steps to enforce certain norms established under the auspices of the EU treaty framework. The Court has confirmed that the EU treaty framework system has implicitly established a legal order in which individuals as well as member states are integral constituents. As the CJEU case law has evolved, it has become increasingly clear that the Court's judicial development of rights for private persons to enforce EU norms before national courts and tribunals of the member states has significant implications for the EU environmental sector.

The jurisprudence of the CJEU on enforceable rights for private persons extends in principle right across the spectrum of EU norms under the aegis of the foundational treaties, except for those few policy areas in respect of which supranational legally binding effects are restricted. These include notably the fields of the Common Foreign and Security Policy (CFSP) and Common Security and Defence Policy (CSDP) of the Union, the legal framework for which is set out in Title V of the Treaty on European Union (TEU) (notably Articles 23–45).[1] The 2007 Lisbon Treaty, in abolishing the tripartite 'pillar' framework that previously underpinned the legal framework of the Union, has effectively increased the material scope of the CJEU jurisprudence on enforceable supranational rights. Under the 'pillar' system, as referred to in more detail in Chapter 1, certain EU policy fields were essentially intergovernmental in nature and outside the supranational framework (first pillar) of the then European Community legal order (specifically CFSP (second pillar) as well as justice and home affairs (third pillar)).[2] Private persons were not vested with any supranational-inspired rights to enforce the norms falling within the second and third pillars. However, under Lisbon the fragmented state of the EU legal order was terminated with the revised foundational treaty framework of the Union in the form of the Treaty on the Functioning of the Union (TFEU) and amended TEU stipulating that the provisions contained in those two treaties shall have the equivalent legal value.[3] From an EU environmental policy perspective, the unification of the Union's legal order has a profound (long-term) impact for the development of measures to combat environmental crime, an area discussed in Chapter 13.

In Part I we considered the legal tools available to the European Commission to enforce EU environmental law. As discussed, the Commission is vested with specific powers in the EU treaty framework under Articles 258 and 260 TFEU to take legal action against member states in respect of failures to implement its obligations under EU law within its national legal system, and these include environmental legislative instruments passed under the auspices of the provisions contained in Title XX of the TFEU on a common environmental policy (specifically, on Article 192 TFEU). Notwithstanding a number of significant problems connected with Articles 258 and 260(2) TFEU and their application in practice, it is clear that the Commission is a key actor responsible for ensuring the due adherence by member states to their legal commitments under the EU treaty framework. Not only is the Commission vested with a clear legal mandate to ensure that the proper application of EU law is respected by member states, it is also endowed with institutional means to follow up this commitment in the form of an internal law enforcement network comprised principally within its Environment Directorate General and Legal Service. The costs of legal action taken by the Commission are readily absorbed within its budget and, in practice, are not a factor influencing whether or not an action should be initiated. If the Commission's legal teams are agreed on the legal merits of a case and it falls within the criteria of a priority case,[4] so long as there are no special political issues that might interfere, there is usually no bar to an infringement action being launched.

It is evident that private persons contemplating civil litigation to enforce environmental law at national level, notably non-governmental environmental organisations (NGEOs), are faced with considerably greater practical and financial hurdles. Of pre-eminent concern may be the factor of costs of taking legal action, the plaintiff having to bear in mind that, in the event of losing the case, under national rules of civil procedure they will usually have to shoulder the legal costs of both parties. The amount of costs to pursue litigation may well represent not only a considerable but also relatively prohibitive financial burden for a private plaintiff to shoulder.[5] These include not only legal and court fees, but also expenditure necessary to obtain, analyse and present often complex scientific evidence. For instance, NGEOs may have to make difficult decisions over the allocation of scarce budgetary resources to further their policy goals; litigation may well have to compete with other political strategies to enhance environmental protection and awareness.

Moreover, given the lack of a specific power in the EU treaty framework or its secondary legislation for individuals to enforce EU norms at national level, private litigants are reliant upon the often ambiguous and open-ended state of the CJEU's case law regarding the extent of their EU law rights. As will be evident from the discussion in the chapters of this first section to Part II, EU environmental law is affected by this legal state of affairs. Private litigants may have to take on board the risk of not knowing whether a particular EU environmental legislative obligation contained in a Union directive or other legislative instruments endows them with any legal rights to enforce it. Two important related legal issues arise in this context. First, there is the question of whether private persons may be entitled to rely upon a provision contained in EU environmental legislation before a national court in the context of legal proceedings, with the purpose of invoking it against another party (public or private entity). Secondly, there is the issue as to what extent private persons are entitled to access national courts to rely upon such norms, namely the extent and terms of their access to national courts to seek environmental justice. This chapter will focus on the first of those issues, with a view to clarifying the existing CJEU case law on the rights of private persons to rely upon EU environmental norms before national judicial bodies. Chapters 7 and 8 will consider the second issue, focusing on the extent to which case law of the CJEU and recent EU legislative initiatives provide rights to private persons to bring legal action before the national judiciary with a view to enforcing EU environmental law.

The uncertainty surrounding the extent of legal rights for private persons under EU law has exacerbated the subordinate role that private civil litigation has traditionally had to play in terms of environmental law enforcement.[6] In addition, private litigants also are hampered by the fact that they have no rights to investigate or inspect sites where they suspect violations of EU environmental law have occurred. Neither are they currently endowed with any rights to force environmental protection agencies (whether national or supranational) to utilise any inspection powers that they might have at their disposal. Finally, it should be noted that the personal scope of the private sector to engage in environmental enforcement issues is always going to be relatively limited on grounds of self-interest. Economic self-interest, the motivation that underpins most civil litigation, is a blunt and ineffective instrument for assisting in environmental law enforcement. Unless a violation of EU environmental law adversely affects a person's immediate property rights, physical personhood and/or economic interests, it is usually unlikely that they will be motivated and/or in a suitable financial position to undertake legal action. The important exception to this is, of course, the presence of NGEOs. However, as will be discussed later, even where NGEOs are keen to litigate in order to promote law enforcement, it is by no means certain that they will necessarily have the right to take civil action in a particular case, given that a number of member states employ restrictions on legal standing to pursue a case, confining standing to sue to those deemed to be immediately affected by the defendant's (in)activities.

By way of contrast, the 'economic interest' factor is a far more effective influence in other fields of EU law related to the realisation of the single market (such as the free movement of goods, competition and state aids law). Business communities are far more likely to be ready to undertake legal action in order to enforce these areas of law, given that the norms will often coincide with their perceived fundamental economic interests. Carefully tailored, though, the dynamic of self-interest may have a useful if limited role to play in environmental law enforcement. For instance, a business organisation complying with certain environmental protection standards has an obvious economic interest to see that other business entities in competition with it located within the EU do the same, namely to ensure that other businesses do not get a free ride or engage in environmental dumping practices. Whether that economic interest is sufficiently great to crystallise into action of some sort depends on a number of factors, including the value placed by society on the protection standards expressed in terms of cost to business organisations and the degree to which a compliant business entity may be able to detect environmental standards cheating by others.

All these factors, amongst others, serve to underline the importance of placing private enforcement of EU environmental law into its proper practical context. Notwithstanding the gradual and not insignificant steps that have been made to date towards enhancing individuals' rights to enforce EU environmental norms, it is still fair comment to say that private litigation remains of limited value as a law enforcement tool. The Commission, in its mid 1990s review of securing better implementation of EU environmental law enforcement, quite rightly recognised these challenges as limiting expectations and qualifying the potential of the private sector to be engaged in the law enforcement process.[7]

On the other hand, it would be wrong to dismiss the potential of private litigation altogether as a complementary means of EU environmental law enforcement. Indeed, private litigation offers a number of advantages over the traditional reliance on the European Commission's infraction proceedings under Articles 258 and 260(2) TFEU, particularly when it comes to instances of specific violations of EU environmental law within a member state, namely, 'bad-application' cases.[8] Often the presence of individuals close to the site in question means that the plaintiff will be able to have more detailed and quicker knowledge of the environmental issues involved, although the absence of investigatory powers represents an obvious and serious limitation. Private plaintiffs are not affected by internal political conflicts over the pursuit of litigation that may arise within the European Commission, an institution which is vested with the task of promoting or accommodating often conflicting policy goals and interests. Moreover, civil litigation (notably, judicial review proceedings) is unlikely to be as protracted as infringement proceedings brought by the Commission under Articles 258 and 260 TFEU. In the past, the Commission has been sometimes slow or incapable of using its powers to secure timely implementation of EU environmental instruments by member states,[9] although (as discussed in Chapter 5) recent changes to infringement case management have committed the Commission to strive for faster response times to allegations of member state breaches of EU environmental law. Private litigants may well have better prospects of securing interim relief against defendants than the Commission, which considers the opportunities for obtaining injunctions in the context of infringement proceedings as a limited possibility. Moreover, as will be seen in later chapters, since the early 2000s the EU has adopted a number of legislative instruments and proposals with a view to furthering and enhancing possibilities of private sector EU environmental law enforcement, notably by means of the EU Environmental Liability Directive 2004/35[10] as well as other legislative initiatives intended to implement the 1998 UNECE Convention on Access to Information, Public Participation in Decision-making and Access to Justice in Environmental Matters (Århus Convention) within the EU legal order. Several of these legislative initiatives are relatively recent and will take some time to bed down; others are awaiting legislative endorsement or in the pipeline. They will be considered in later sections of this book. It is appropriate, though, first to consider the impact of the general precepts and principles of EU law on the enforceability of Union norms by individuals.

6.1 Direct effect and EU environmental law

6.1.1 General introduction

The CJEU has been the EU institution primarily responsible for establishing and developing rights for private individuals to enforce Union norms at national level. The EU treaty framework itself is silent on the question of whether individuals may derive rights from its treaty provisions, secondary legislation and other legal sources.[11] The orthodox understanding and approach in international law is to consider that only nation states and not their citizens may be considered to be subjects of such an international agreement, not least where the agreement does not make any express provision to the contrary. However, the CJEU has interpreted the legal framework underpinning the first pillar of the EU, namely the law pertaining to the EU treaty framework, as encompassing individuals as well as member states as integral constituents within its remit. Its ground-breaking early judgment in *Van Gend en Loos*[12] in 1963 constituted a key moment in the evolution of the EU's legal system. The Court declared that it is implicit within the EU treaty framework system that individuals may, in certain circumstances, derive rights under the treaty and enforce them directly before the national courts of the EU member states. The Court rejected the argument supported by observations of three member states (the Netherlands, Germany and Belgium) that individuals would be only able to enforce EU obligations under the auspices of national laws that have implemented international obligations entered into by member states at EU level. The radical doctrine of 'direct effect' of EU law had been born.

The case of *Van Gend* is one of the most important in EU law, as it constituted a radical departure from traditional understandings concerning the legal effects of an international agreement. It created the possibility for individuals to assert new rights gleaned from an internationally created system. From an environmental policy perspective, this jurisprudence has only relatively recently in the EU's history begun to have significant implications. As the doctrine of direct effect has been developed and refined by the CJEU since *Van Gend*, it has opened up possibilities for individuals, in addition to the European Commission, to enforce legally binding EU environmental commitments entered into by member states.

The *Van Gend* ruling remains a leading CJEU judgment on the doctrine of direct effect. The case involved a dispute between the Dutch authorities and a private freight delivery company, Van Gend en Loos, over the imposition of a Dutch customs tariff unilaterally introduced in 1960. The company contested the legality of the tariff, which had been imposed on the import of a consignment of formaldehyde from Germany, and appealed to the relevant appellate body, the Dutch Tarifcommissie. Van Gend submitted before the Tarifcommissie that the tariff was contrary to Article 12 of the former European Economic Community (EEC) Treaty (now superseded by Article 30 TFEU), which prohibits member states from introducing new tariffs after the entry into force of the EU treaty framework (i.e. after 1 January 1958 in respect of the six original member states). The Tarifcommissie decided to request a preliminary ruling from the CJEU on whether Article 12 EEC had direct application within the territory of a member state, with the effect of providing individual rights to be protected by the national courts. The preliminary ruling procedure, as governed by Article 267 TFEU,[13] is a judicial procedure whereby national courts and tribunals may, and in certain circumstances must, seek the guidance of the CJEU on questions of EU law during the course of national legal proceedings. It stipulates that the CJEU has competence to provide preliminary rulings on questions concerning the interpretation of the EU treaty framework, the validity and interpretation of acts of EU institutions, bodies, offices and agencies. Article 267 also stipulates that, whereas lower national courts and tribunals have discretion to refer such questions to the CJEU, those courts and tribunals acting as final appellate bodies at national level are required to refer such questions raised in a case pending before them to the CJEU. Although there is no space here to dwell in any great detail on this particular procedure, suffice it to say in brief that it has proved to be a critically important vehicle for the CJEU to develop its jurisprudence on the impact of EU law in the member states.[14] Not only has it provided the principal forum for the Court to declare the fundamental legal principles underpinning EU law, notably the possibilities for individuals to assert their rights under EU law before national courts, it also has enabled the CJEU to construct a hierarchical relationship between EU law and national legal orders and between itself and national courts. Specifically, it has been via the preliminary ruling procedure that the CJEU has declared the principle of supremacy,[15] according to which EU law takes precedence over conflicting national rules and is to be respected by the national courts.

In *Van Gend* the CJEU affirmed that Article 12 EEC produced direct effects and created individual rights which the member state courts must protect. The Court arrived at this conclusion by considering the spirit, general scheme and wording of provisions of the EU treaty framework (at the material time this was the EEC Treaty). It held that the objective of the EU treaty framework to establish a common market, the functioning of which is of direct concern to many interested private parties in the territory of the Union, implies that the treaty framework was more than an agreement which simply created mutual obligations between the contracting parties.[16] The Court drew the following conclusion, which provides an underpinning of the direct effect doctrine in constitutional terms:

> The conclusion to be drawn from this is that the [European Union] constitutes a new legal order of international law for the benefit of which the states have limited their sovereign rights, albeit in limited fields, and the subjects of which comprise not only member states but also their nationals. Independently of the legislation of member states, [Union] law therefore not only imposes obligations on individuals but is also intended to confer upon them rights which become part of their legal heritage. These rights arise not only where they are expressly granted by the Treaty, but also by reason of obligations which the Treaty imposes in a clearly defined way upon individuals as well as upon the member states and upon the institutions of the [Union] . . .[17]

The CJEU set out some criteria to assist in determining whether Article 12 EEC could have direct effect. The Court referred to the clear and unconditional nature of the prohibition contained in Article 12 EEC, as well as the fact that it was a negative obligation. Specifically, the provision was not qualified by the fact that its implementation was conditional upon a positive legislative measure enacted under national law.

Subsequent jurisprudence of the Court has refined the test for direct effect of the first pillar of EU law to comprise two principal elements, namely that the norm in question must be sufficiently clear and unconditional in nature. The 'negative obligation' criterion has been dropped. In addition, it is clear also in the light of subsequent and well-established CJEU jurisprudence that it is not necessary for an EU norm to expressly or implicitly confer individual rights in order for it to have direct effect.[18] This is important from an EU environmental law enforcement perspective, given that a wide range of EU environmental legislation contains obligations that protect general or diffuse public interests. Limiting the scope of direct effect to cover solely provisions specifically intended to protect individual rights, such as those focusing on public health or consumer protection, would have the effect of severely restricting the possibilities of private persons being able to enforce EU environmental norms before national courts.[19]

Elsewhere in its jurisprudence, the CJEU has developed the principle of supremacy of EU law starting with the case of *Costa v ENEL*,[20] according to which obligations under the EU treaty framework have precedence over conflicting national rules. In subsequent case law the CJEU, has clarified that national courts are obliged to apply Union law in its entirety, protect rights which the latter confers on individuals and must set aside any provision of national law which conflicts with it, irrespective of whether the national rule was promulgated prior to or subsequent to the EU rule.[21] The combination of direct effect and supremacy provides individuals with the primary legal tools needed to assert their legal interests under EU law, including those under EU environmental law. However, as the subsequent discussion aims to show, these judicial developments have only so far led to a partially effective means for the public to utilise EU environmental law in the context of litigation conducted before national courts.

Given that the bulk of legally binding EU environmental obligations is contained within the legislative instrument of the Union directive, this chapter will focus predominantly on how the CJEU has developed a core of rights for individuals to enforce provisions housed in the form of a directive. However, it is worth noting first that other sources of EU environmental law, primary and secondary, may also be able to be relied upon directly as of right by private individuals. The primary sources of EU law include, notably, provisions contained in the EU foundational treaties, international agreements concluded by the Union and unwritten general principles of the Union. Secondary sources of EU law include, notably, legally binding measures adopted by the EU legislative institutions other than directives, such as regulations and decisions, as defined in Article 288 TFEU. These sources will be considered briefly in turn.

It is true that the EU treaty framework itself contains a number of important general commitments on the part of the EU in respect of environmental protection. These include notably: Article 3 TEU and Article 191(2) TFEU, first sentence (promotion of a high level of protection and improvement of the quality of the environment); Article 11 TFEU (environmental protection requirements to be integrated into the definition and implementation of Union policies and activities with a view to promoting sustainable development); and Article 191(2) TFEU, second sentence (EU environmental policy to be based upon the principles of precaution, preventive action, rectifying environmental damage at source and that the polluter should pay). However, it is apparent from the terms of these provisions that they are drafted in broad terms and primarily designed to be political objectives for the purpose of assisting in the crafting of environmental policy at EU level, and therefore ill-suited in the main to be utilised in the context of enforcement litigation. A considerable margin of appreciation is afforded to the EU and its constituent member states in respect of the manner of the implementation of these broadly worded and policy-oriented provisions. Accordingly, it is doubtful whether any of the environmental policy provisions in the EU treaty framework meet with the criteria of sufficient precision and unconditionality necessary for the application of the direct effect doctrine.[22] The extent to which the environmental principles set out in the EU treaty framework's provisions may be otherwise used as legal tools to ensure that EU environmental law is enforced is a matter which so far has received relatively little judicial attention. The existing case law from the CJEU sheds relatively little light on the legal effects that such principles have for the purposes of environmental law enforcement at national level. However, the CJEU has provided some general indications that they may well be relevant as important residual interpretative tools in assisting analysis of whether member states have adhered to EU environmental commitments.[23] Undoubtedly, further case law is required for judicial light to be shed on the legal impact of EU treaty framework environmental provisions.

International agreements concluded by the Union are binding upon both member states and the Union institutions, as stipulated by Article 216 TFEU. The

CJEU has also confirmed that, in certain circumstances, provisions of international agreements concluded by the EU[24] may be capable of having direct effect so that individuals may be able to rely upon them directly as of right before the national courts of the member states. This was exemplified in *Pêcheurs de l'étang de Berre*[25] which involved application of the 1980 Protocol for the protection of the Mediterranean Sea against pollution from land-based sources adopted under the auspices of the 1976 Barcelona Convention on the protection of the Mediterranean Sea against pollution.[26] Both international instruments had been ratified by the EU (at the time the former European Community) by way of Council decisions,[27] but the Union had not adopted any detailed secondary legislation to implement these international commitments internally. A syndicate of French fishermen took action before the French courts to challenge the legality of failures by French authorities to prevent the eutrophic pollution of a saltwater marsh (Etang de Berre) through the discharge of freshwater and alluvia into the marsh as a result of operations of an upstream hydro-electric plant. The syndicate relied upon certain requirements[28] contained in the 1980 Protocol which stipulate that contracting parties should ensure that discharges into protected marine areas are subject to prior authorisation. In a preliminary ruling, the CJEU confirmed that the relevant provision of the Protocol was directly effective and that the fishermen were entitled to rely upon it in the context of judicial proceedings before the French courts. The fact that the international agreement concerned was a mixed agreement for EU legal purposes, namely one falling within the scope of a policy field in respect of which both the Union and member states shared competence, did not affect the possibility of its norms having direct effect if they met the relevant requirements for direct effect to exist. The CJEU has consistently confirmed that in order for a provision of an international agreement concluded by the Union to be capable of having direct effect, a broader set of factors need to be considered than those applicable to other sources of EU law. In particular, the CJEU has referred to the need to consider the 'purpose and nature' of the agreement, in addition to considering whether the statutory wording is clear, precise and unconditional.[29] This broader and more uncertain test has made it in practice more challenging to assess whether or not a particular agreement may be capable of being direct effective. In recent years, attempts have been made to invoke direct effect in relation to the 1998 Århus Convention, in respect of which the Union is a contracting party.[30] Whilst at the time of writing these particular attempts have proven so far to be unsuccessful, the CJEU has at the same time confirmed that the Union's commitment to Århus requires national courts of the member states, in accordance with Article 4(3) TEU, to ensure as far as possible that national law is interpreted in accordance with the international agreement's requirements.[31]

The CJEU has also confirmed that unwritten general principles of EU law, another source of primary Union law, are capable of being directly effective. The Court has developed its jurisprudence on these general principles over several years,[32] affirming their existence through the reference to 'general principles common to the laws of the member states' contained in the EU treaty provision on non-contractual liability of the Union (Article 340 TFEU). Over time, the CJEU has clarified that a large range of principles are caught under the category of unwritten general principles. These include, notably, principles of proportionality, legal certainty, non-discrimination, fundamental rights, legitimate expectations, the precautionary principle as well as the principle of effectiveness. On a number of occasions, recourse to general principles of EU law have been of considerable use to private persons in seeking to challenge the manner in which member states[33] or private persons[34] have implemented or failed to implement their obligations under Union law. The impact of general principles has also been of relevance to the environmental sector, as will be considered in a later section of this chapter.

Brief mention should also be made of the fact that the CJEU has confirmed that the doctrine of direct effect is applicable to secondary legislative instruments other than the directive. Article 288 TFEU[35] lists the various instruments that the EU may use in order to implement policies included in the EU treaty framework. In addition to directives, Article 288 TFEU refers to regulations and decisions as measures having binding effects. A regulation is defined in this provision as having 'general application', being 'binding in its entirety and directly applicable in all member states'. A decision is defined as being 'binding in its entirety upon those to whom it is addressed'. The CJEU has confirmed that both instruments are capable of having direct effect, subject to the standard criteria of sufficient precision, clarity and unconditionality being fulfilled.[36] The CJEU has also confirmed that directly effective provisions of regulations may be enforced against both individuals as well as member state authorities, given their legal characteristic of being 'generally binding'.[37] For the purposes of EU environmental policy implementation, the instruments of regulation and directive are most relevant where the EU legislature wishes to enact general binding legislation.

Article 192 TFEU, which provides the legal basis for the implementation of EU environmental policy, does not limit the range of legislative instruments that may be chosen for this purpose. Article 192 refers to 'action', 'provisions' and 'measures' which may be adopted. Notionally, then, the EU legislative decision-making bodies have the legal possibility to elect between regulations and directives as legislative alternatives. However, whilst regulations are occasionally used to pass EU environmental legislation, they are used relatively infrequently. As a legislative tool, they are designed in principle to be a self-contained source of obligations for the implementation of policy. The CJEU has confirmed that the definition of regulation contained in Article 288 TFEU implies that member states are not required to transpose regulations into their national legal systems by way of domestic implementing rules unless provisions within the particular regulation require additional legislative action at national level.[38] A regulation is intended, as a matter of principle, to be a self-executing instrument. From a political perspective, the use of the form of a regulation has proved to be a sensitive issue, member states being fully aware that national parliaments are effectively bypassed in the legislative process, given that a regulation has the equivalent legal force to a national parliamentary statute.

This may be contrasted with the legislative instrument of the EU directive, which requires the member states themselves to enact national implementing legislation after a directive has been passed in order to complete the legislative process (Article 288(3) TFEU). The member states' strong preference for EU legislation to take the form of directives where possible was expressed in a formal protocol attached to the EU treaty framework by virtue of the Treaty of Amsterdam 1997.[39] Occasionally, member states have agreed to the enactment of environmental policy under the auspices of Union regulations. The underlying reason for the adoption of a regulation is usually traced to the fact that the measure is closely related to matters affecting the transboundary movement of goods and/or services within the EU, a matter that falls within the core competence of the Union. A regulation serves to provide a single set of rules for traders, so as to ensure that distortions to competition that might otherwise arise by virtue of the existence of differing trading standards set at national level are avoided. Notable examples include the regulations on waste shipments,[40] ozone depleting substances[41] and on trade in endangered species.[42] Directives, though, remain overall the favoured legislative instrument in general when it comes to the enactment of EU environmental legislation.

EU decisions are rarely, if ever, employed for the crystallisation of Union environmental policy, given that such instruments are intended to be addressed to particular entities, public or private. They are more suited to be used as administrative tools to lend support to the implementation of a policy already clearly defined at EU treaty framework or legislative level. As mentioned in Chapter 5, the EU treaty framework does not provide the European Commission with the power to issue decisions against persons infracting EU environmental law, although this would be possible to arrange if the member states so wished to amend the EU treaty framework. The Commission has such a power in the sector of competition policy.[43] The EU has enacted legislation in order to enable the Commission to issue binding decisions against private persons acting in contravention of its competition rules under the auspices of Article 103 TFEU.[44]

6.1.2 Criteria for direct effect and EU environmental directives

Given the preponderance of EU environmental legislation being crafted using the legislative form of the Union directive, the rest of this chapter will consider the CJEU case law on direct effect of directives in more detail. It was not until the mid 1970s that the CJEU in the *Van Duyn* case[45] confirmed that the doctrine of direct effect applied to provisions contained in directives. Article 288(3) TFEU, the treaty provision which provides a basic definition of a directive and which has not been altered since its inception in the original EU treaty framework (1957 Treaty of Rome), is silent on the issue of direct effect. As is the case with other sources of EU law, there is no mention of whether the EU treaty framework authors intended there to be rights for individuals to enforce directives. Article 288(3) TFEU states:

> A directive shall be binding, as to the result to be achieved, upon each member state to which it is addressed, but shall leave to the national authorities the choice of form and methods.

In theory, the issue of direct effect should not need to come into play in the case of directives. The directive itself should not in principle be required to constitute a source of rights and obligations for individuals and public authorities operating within the territories of the member states. For it is evident from the legislative framework and scheme set out in Article 288(3) TFEU, that the rules adopted at national level intended to implement a directive will be best suited to crystallising the requirements of the latter into enforceable rights and obligations against individuals and state authorities. In effect, this treaty provision would appear to imply that the EU directive itself constitutes an instrument which clarifies the commitments entered into by the member state national governments, it being the governments' task to decide upon and ensure the adoption of national rules to give concrete effect to the supranational commitments entered into. The reference to 'choice of form and methods' in Article 288(3) TFEU indicates that member states have discretion to decide upon the type of national law and administrative procedures necessary to ensure the directive's objectives are adhered to. They may use, for example, civil, criminal and/or public law mechanisms to construct specific duties and rights for individuals as means for transposing the requirements of directives into national law.

However, in practice, the issue of direct effect of directives is a very real issue, not least in the sector of environmental policy, where member states have a poor record on ensuring that national implementing rules have been passed by the relevant transposition deadline stipulated in each directive and ensuring that they accord with the directive's requirements.[46] The CJEU has been confronted with several cases referred to it from national courts where member states have failed to implement a directive correctly by the end of the transposition deadline and where individual claimants have sought to rely on particular provisions of the directive within the national legal order before the national courts. Until the *Van Duyn* judgment, several member states were sceptical about the possibility of individuals being able to apply the doctrine of direct effect to provisions of directives, on the grounds that Article 288(3) TFEU arguably implies that legal effects for individuals are to be derived solely from national implementation rules, the directive being an instrument solely binding upon member states. However, the CJEU has rejected this interpretation of the provision. In affirming the capability of directives to have direct effects, the Court has underpinned its jurisprudence on this issue by its so-called 'estoppel' reasoning. Specifically, the Court has expressed the view consistently that a member state may not rely upon its failure to implement a directive correctly on time against individuals.[47] The CJEU's central argument has been that member states should be prevented from taking advantage of their failures to adhere to a directive, and this is a theme that has influenced the development of its subsequent case law and served to define the reach of the direct effect doctrine into the context of application of EU directives.[48] In essence, the CJEU has considered the legal position from a pragmatic and contextual interpretative perspective, determining the impact of Article 288(3) TFEU in light of the overall spirit, scheme and context of the EU treaty framework as opposed to its literal meaning. The teleological approach of the Court to treaty interpretation used to unpack the legal meaning and effects of EU law has been well documented and is now clearly established in practice as a constituent element of the legal foundations of EU law. It has been noted that the doctrine of direct effect developed by the CJEU has served as a means to enhance the effectiveness of EU law,[49] underpin the principle of the supremacy of EU law over conflicting national rules[50] as well as to promote its practicability and feasibility.[51]

It is appropriate at this stage to turn to consider the criteria identified by the CJEU that need to be fulfilled in order for a provision of a directive to have direct effect, so that private persons may be able to rely upon it before national courts. The CJEU has sought to strike a balance between the legitimate interests of both individuals and member states in developing its jurisprudence on direct effect. Notably, the CJEU has limited the scope of direct effect to those EU norms (whether located in the EU treaty framework, in secondary EU legislation or in international agreements concluded by the Union) which have suitable legal characteristics to be relied upon directly by individuals. Specifically, only those provisions of EU law, including those contained in directives, which are sufficiently clear, precise and unconditional are directly effective.[52] As applied in the context of enforcing directives, the standard formula used by the CJEU is exemplified by the following extract applied in one of the leading environmental cases on direct effect, namely the *Difesa della Cava* case,[53] which shall be considered in more detail later:

> The [CJEU] has consistently held . . . that wherever the provisions of a directive appear, as far as their subject-matter is concerned, to be unconditional and sufficiently precise, those provisions may be relied upon by an individual against the State where the State fails to implement the directive in national law by the end of the period prescribed or where it fails to implement the directive correctly.[54]

The criteria for direct effect will be considered below in turn, although it should be recognised that to some extent they overlap with one another.

6.1.2.1 Sufficient precision

The criterion of sufficient precision has been included in the legal test for direct effect in order to exclude provisions which are ambiguous or too vague and general in nature to lend themselves to judicial application. Reference has already been made above to the difficulties of arguing application of direct effect to EU treaty framework provisions on the environment, given that they have been crafted in general and often open-ended terms. The CJEU's motivation here has been to ensure as far as possible that only those provisions of directives may have direct effects which clearly and unambiguously express the specific will of the EU legislature, without there being any significant room for competing interpretations of the relevant provisions. The CJEU has clarified that the criterion of sufficient precision is fulfilled where the material provision is 'set out in unequivocal terms'.[55]

In essence, the provision in question must express a clear and precise requirement which does not afford member states discretion in terms of what definitive result to achieve in any given case.[56] Applied to an EU environmental legal context, only relatively few provisions of EU environmental directives meet with these requirements. Examples of such provisions in environmental directives have been suggested in the literature as including very specific and self-contained environmental protection requirements imposed on member states such as environmental quality controls (emission restrictions in the form of limit values, maximum allowable concentrations, product bans and industrial process prohibitions)[57] as well as specific prior consultation requirements in relation to activities affecting the environment.[58] The Court has provided some support to this analysis, albeit rather indirectly, by indicating in the context of Article 258 TFEU infringement proceedings taken against a member state that emission limits set down in EU environmental in respect of groundwater,[59] sulphur dioxide in ambient air[60] and lead in air[61] set out precise and detailed rules intended to create rights and obligations for individuals.

However, for various reasons, relatively few EU environmental provisions contained in directives, especially those passed in recent years, meet the criteria of adequate clarity and sufficient precision. A key factor is that member states have become increasingly wary, on grounds of economic cost, to agree to be subject to specific and quantitatively identifiable legal commitments on environmental protection or improvement within the standard two-year time period envisaged by the European Commission by for the transposition of directives.[62] Unsurprisingly, member state governments are frequently concerned about the impact of EU environmental legislation and the ability of companies within their territories to be able to meet economic costs of compliance with additional environmental quality controls. As a consequence, open-ended economic cost-related qualifications may become woven into legislative commitments on environmental protection, such as the term 'best available technology not entailing excessive cost' or similar phrases.[63] The effect of such clauses is to undermine clarity and precision from an enforcement perspective, whether by the European Commission or through litigation pursued by individuals. Other reasons also explain why relatively few clear and precise substantive environmental protection provisions exist in directives. For instance, in many instances the crystallisation of environmental policy is decentralised, with member states provided with substantial discretion over the contents of policy implementation. An example of this includes requirements under a directive to develop plans or programmes to enhance a general environmental objective. Such broad commitments reflect a degree of political sensitivity on the part of member states to the issue of national sovereignty (such as expressed in the principle of subsidiarity in Article 5(3) TEU),[64] where EU involvement in environmental matters without an overtly obvious international dimension may receive a hostile reaction from member states, as well as a recognition of the often long-term nature of being able to introduce improvements to the quality of environmental media. Finally, it should be noted since the 1990s, the EU has turned increasingly to consider the application of other forms of environmental policy implementation in the wake of criticism that traditional so-called 'command and control' techniques of mandatory stipulations in directives may be less effective than economic or market-oriented instruments in stimulating environmental improvements (such as local environmental taxes, trading permit schemes, voluntary ecological accreditation schemes).

6.1.2.2 Unconditionality

The criterion of unconditionality serves to complement the first element in the direct effect test of sufficient precision. Its essential purpose is also to ensure that the reach of the doctrine of direct effect only applies to provisions of a directive that are unambiguous and provide no margin of discretion to member states in their application. The presence of conditionality renders a provision wholly unsuited to be relied upon directly before a judicial authority, otherwise the latter would be in the untenable position of having to presume specific policy decisions yet to be made by other authorities designated to do this task. The CJEU has defined the criterion of unconditionality as being where the provision in question are 'not subject, in its implementation or effects, to the taking of any measure either by the EU institutions or by member states'.[65] In other words, the Court has stressed the importance of the provision being a self-contained norm, whose requirements may be derived from its terms alone without being dependent upon further measures taken either at EU or national levels.

The CJEU has sought to clarify the parameters of the unconditionality criterion in a number of cases. Specifically, it has clarified that where it is possible to discern from the directive's provision in question a clear minimum legal guarantee, then the criterion of unconditionality will be satisfied. A brief example serves to illustrate the point. Unconditionality was an issue in the *Becker* case,[66] a case involving the application of the sixth VAT Directive 77/388[67] which Germany had failed to transpose into national law by the requisite deadline set out in the EU instrument. Under the directive, member states were required to exempt from VAT transactions involving the granting and negotiation of credit 'under conditions which they shall lay down for the purpose of ensuring the correct and straightforward application of the exemptions and of preventing any possible evasion, avoidance or abuse'. The German tax authorities had refused to waive VAT liability in respect of Ursula Becker, a person trading in the grant and negotiation of credit. When called upon by the German Finance Court adjudicating the tax dispute to provide an interpretation of the effects of the provision of the directive via the preliminary ruling procedure, the CJEU refused to concur with the German government's submission that it was not unconditional in nature. It held that the conditions attached to the provision, namely measures to be taken by member states to prevent tax fraud, did not affect the definition of the subject matter or the exemption conferred in the provision; the tax exemption requirement, owing to its particular subject matter, could be severed from the 'general body of provisions and applied separately'.[68] The analysis of the CJEU of the unconditionality criterion was clearly underpinned by its 'estoppel' reasoning. Specifically, it held that Germany could not plead its own omission in taking precautionary anti-fraud measures in order to refuse to grant to a taxpayer an exemption.[69]

However, the principles set out in this particular line of jurisprudence are not free from ambiguity. The carving out of a distinct minimum guarantee from within a particular provision of a directive may not be straightforward in practice, as exemplified in the *Francovich* case.[70] This case involved the failure on the part of the Italian state to transpose former Directive 80/987 on protection of workers in the event of insolvency.[71] The directive required member states to ensure that employees of insolvent firms should be entitled to receive compensation for outstanding payments owed to them by the insolvent employer. Member states had a choice to implement a range of formulae to calculate the maximum level of compensation. The member state could elect, from three dates, the one prior to which payments had to be made. Depending upon the date chosen, member states were entitled to restrict liability to periods of three months or eight weeks. In addition, member states were entitled to set a ceiling on the level of liability as well as to introduce anti-fraud measures. Notwithstanding these array of options afforded to member states, the CJEU held that they did not exclude the fact that a minimum guaranteed level of payment could be gleaned from the terms of the directive. However, the Court held that the relevant provisions of the directive on minimum insolvency entitlement were not directly effective for other reasons, notably that they were conditional on member states establishing the particular entities responsible for providing the guaranteed payments to affected employees. The Court held that, in the absence of the particular entities being established, the terms of the directive were insufficiently precise to confer direct effect. It refused to hold that the member state concerned should be construed to be directly liable as guarantor in the event of a transposition failure. The Court was not prepared to apply its 'estoppel' reasoning to this extent. However, the reasons for it not doing so are not explained. The case has the added special novelty, though, of being responsible for introducing the remedy of state liability for persons suffering loss as a result of failures by member states to transpose directives correctly. This may explain the decision of the Court to limit application of a 'minimum guarantee' analysis. We return to examine the *Francovich* case in Chapter 7, when considering the remedy of state liability for breaches of EU environmental directives.

6.1.2.3 *Sufficient precision and unconditionality applied to environmental cases*

Two environmental cases illustrate the considerable challenges often faced by plaintiffs seeking to claim that provisions in environmental directive have direct effects. These are the judgments of the CJEU in *Difesa della Cava*[72] and in *Enichem Base*,[73] both of which are examples of unsuccessful attempts to enforce different provisions contained in the general EU Waste Framework Directive.[74] *Difesa della Cava* involved an Italian NGEO and several individuals seeking to overturn before the Italian courts a decision of the Region of Lombardy to site a waste tip. During the course of judicial review proceedings, the Italian administrative tribunal decided to stay proceedings and request a preliminary ruling from the CJEU. It had doubts whether Italian law and practice providing for the management of solid urban waste exclusively by method of disposal (namely, landfilling) was compatible with the general minimum safety provisions contained with the directive, at the time Article 4 of former Directive 75/442. The terms of Article 4 of Directive 75/442, which spread over two paragraphs, were as follows:

> Member states shall take the necessary measures to ensure that waste is recovered or disposed of without endangering human health and without using processes or methods which could harm the environment, and in particular:
>
> - without risk to water, air, soil and plants and animals,
> - without causing a nuisance through noise or odours,
> - without adversely affecting the countryside or places of special interest.
>
> Member states shall also take the necessary measures to prohibit the abandonment, dumping or uncontrolled disposal of waste.

The current version of the Waste Framework Directive (Directive 2008/98)[75] has incorporated similar successor provisions to Article 4 of former Directive 75/442.[76] Amongst the questions referred to the CJEU from the Italian tribunal, was whether Article 4 of former Directive 75/442 conferred individual rights which the national courts had to protect. The CJEU held that Article 4 did not provide directly effective rights for individuals, the criteria of sufficient precision and unconditionality not being fulfilled. The Court held that Article 4 essentially indicated a programme of environmental improvements to be followed by member states, setting out objectives which they had to observe in the performance of more specific obligations contained in the directive elsewhere on planning, supervision and monitoring of waste disposal undertakings. It merely constituted, according to the CJEU, a provision defining the framework for action on waste treatment and did not require the adoption of specific measures or a particular method of waste disposal.

To the extent that the CJEU reached the correct legal outcome in respect of the specific circumstances of the case in *Difesa* is not in serious doubt. Article 4 of former Directive 75/442 and its successor provisions in the current version of the EU Waste Framework Directive 2008/98 do not set down any clear-cut obligations to ensure that waste management is conducted so as to minimise disposal operations. Its general safety requirements cannot be construed so as to imply a required hierarchy or prioritisation of waste management techniques to be applied in practice by member states.

However, the CJEU was incorrect in *Difesa* to conclude that Article 4 of former Directive 75/442 as a whole was devoid of direct effects. Specifically, the criteria of sufficient precision and unconditionality appear to be fulfilled with respect to the prohibition on abandonment, dumping or uncontrolled disposal of waste contained in the second paragraph to Article 4 (now superseded by Article 36(1) of Directive 2008/98).[77] With regard to the Court's own established jurisprudence, the legal analysis of the CJEU should have made clear that its findings would be without prejudice to the question as to whether the second paragraph of Article 4 of former Directive 75/442, clearly being not of a programmatic nature, could have been severed from the rest of the provision in accordance with its approach in *Becker*.[78] Subsequently, the CJEU appears to have modified its position somewhat in the wake of illicit dumping of waste cases taken by the Commission against Italy and Greece.[79] In those cases the Court recognised that Article 4 of Directive 75/442 contained an enforceable legal obligation on member states to ensure that waste was not disposed of in an uncontrolled fashion. Specifically, it held in these cases that in principle a 'significant deterioration in the environment over a protracted period when no action has been taken by the competent authorities' would be an indication of a breach of Article 4.[80] Had the provision been entirely of a programmatic character as held earlier in *Difesa*, the Commission's action would not have succeeded. However, the fact that the Court in these cases made the caveat that a protracted period of illicit behaviour is required before liability under Article 4 could be deemed to have triggered, introduced an unnecessary and unhelpful element of uncertainty to the legal position as far as private litigants are concerned. It is not yet clear whether the CJEU has discontinued its apparent outright rejection in *Difesa* of direct effects in respect of the general safety requirements contained in the Waste Framework Directive. If the CJEU has now impliedly accepted that the basic safety provisions of the directive (as now enshrined in Articles 12–13 and 36 of Directive 2008/98) may have direct effects in limited circumstances, it is unclear in practice as to when a protracted period of illicit behaviour will have elapsed. In addition, the introduction of the element of a lengthy of period of illicit pollution is detrimental from an environmental protection perspective and certainly not in accordance with the environmental objectives underpinning the directive, given that a single instance of uncontrolled dumping of hazardous waste may have profound, potentially even irremediable, adverse environmental effects.

Another environmental case which highlights difficulties that private litigants may encounter in practice when seeking to utilise the doctrine of direct effect is *Enichem Base*.[81] In this case a dispute arose over the legality of a decision made by the Italian municipality of Cinisello Balsamo to introduce a ban on the supply to consumers of non-biodegradable bags and other containers except those intended to collect waste. Article 3(2) of the original version of the Waste Framework Directive (Directive 75/442) required member states to inform the Commission over any measures they intend to take to achieve the aims set out in the first paragraph of Article 3, which obliged them to take appropriate measures to encourage the prevention, reduction and recovery of waste as well as its use as a source of energy. In this case, the ban on sale of plastic bags had not been notified to the Commission. One of the questions referred to the CJEU by the Italian administrative tribunal adjudicating the dispute was whether Article 3(2) conferred a right on individuals enforceable before national courts to annul or suspend national measures which conflicted with its terms. At first sight that question might be considered worthy of an answer in the affirmative, given that the requirement contained in the provision appears to fulfil the criteria of sufficient precision and unconditionality. However, the CJEU rejected that view, drawing its conclusion by using a broader contextual analysis of its overall function. It considered that the purpose of Article 3(2) was for member states to inform the Commission in good time of any draft rules within the scope of the provision, without there being any procedure for monitoring its application or making implementation of the planned rules conditional upon agreement by the Commission or its failure to object. The CJEU further held that neither the wording nor the purpose of the provision provided support for the view that failure by the member states to observe their obligation renders unlawful the rules adopted.[82]

With respect, the reasoning of the CJEU is rather weak. It is perfectly plausible for an opposing interpretation of the directive's provision to apply. In particular, it should be noted that Article 3(2) makes reference by way of analogy to the Transparency Directive[83] which lays down a procedure for the provision of information in the field of technical standards and regulations. The EU Transparency Directive requires member states to notify to the Commission the draft of any measures which might constitute barriers to inter-state trade contrary to the EU treaty framework, notably Articles 34–6 TFEU on the free movement of goods within the single market. Under the directive, there is a minimum stand-still period of three months[84] during which member states are required to abstain from introducing such measures into national law whilst the Commission and other member states have an opportunity to assess the proposals. The CJEU has held in a number of cases, starting with the *CIA Security* judgment,[85] that individuals may rely upon the stand-still provision of the directive and enforce it before national courts with the latter being required to disapply measures that have been introduced without being notified in advance or applied in conformity with the terms of the directive (see section 6.1.4.4 below). Admittedly, as the CJEU notes in its judgment in *Enichem Base*, Article 3(2) of former Directive 75/442 did not provide for a detailed stand-still formula. However, that in itself should not detract from the clear implication indicated in the provision, that the prior notification obligation contained in Article 3(2) should be considered as being closely linked with the function of the prior notification obligation as contained in the Transparency Directive. By virtue of its revision in 2008, the old notification provision has now been removed from the EU Waste Framework Directive, which contains a number of distinct obligations relating to notifying information to the Commission.[86]

The cases above highlight the degree of legal uncertainty often faced by individual litigants when seeking to prove to national courts that the core criteria of direct effect (sufficient precision and unconditionality) of provisions contained in environmental directives are fulfilled. In particular, plaintiffs shoulder the burden of being able to prove that the material provision(s) in question are unconditional in the sense of constituting a severable minimum guarantee of conduct on the part of member states as well as being able to satisfy the CJEU that the legal context in which the provision is situated does not disqualify it from being suitable for the application of the direct effect doctrine.

6.1.2.4 Transposition deadline and direct effect

In principle, EU directives are not capable usually of having any direct effect until the elapse of the deadline provided by them for transposition of their requirements into national law. The CJEU confirmed this basic principle in one of the first environmental cases to come before it, namely in *Ratti*.[87] The case involved an Italian trader of solvent and varnish products who wished to rely upon two directives concerning mandatory labelling of certain chemical products as a defence to criminal charges brought against him by Italian authorities: Directive 73/173[88] on labelling of solvents and Directive 77/728[89] on labelling for varnishes. Italy had failed to implement either directive. Existing Italian legislation at the time required information to be provided on product labels additional to that required by the two directives. By the time the case came to be litigated before the Italian courts, the transposition deadline pertaining to the 1973 directive on solvents labelling had elapsed. The CJEU confirmed in a preliminary ruling that individuals may not be able to rely upon the doctrine of direct effect before the end of the transposition deadline where the member state in question had not enacted any legislation to implement a particular directive.

In its more recent jurisprudence, the CJEU has refined its position in cases where member states have enacted internal legislation intended to implement a directive prior to the transposition deadline and which is contrary to the directive's requirements. This issue arose in the *Inter-Environnement Wallonie* case.[90] Inter-Environnement Wallonie (IEW), an NGEO based in the Wallonian Region of Belgium, sought to annul a Wallonian legislative order enacted to give effect to a 1991 directive[91] amending the original version of the Waste Framework Directive. IEW submitted that the order infringed the directive,[92] in that it automatically excluded certain installations from being required to obtain a waste permit, namely those who operated waste collection, pre-treatment, disposal or recovery as an integral part of an industrial process. The case reached the Belgian Conseil D'Etat on appeal, which considered that the order was not in compliance with the terms of EU waste management legislation.[93] The national court questioned the CJEU as to what extent, if at all, a member state was entitled to adopt legislation contrary to the terms of a directive before the elapse of the transposition deadline. The CJEU held that it follows from the duties of co-operation set out in Article 4(3) TEU that member states are obliged to refrain from taking any measures 'liable seriously to compromise the result prescribed' by a Union directive.[94] The national court would have to assess the individual circumstances and consider whether the measures in question purport to constitute a full transposition of the directive, taking into account their effects in practice and of their duration in time. If a national legislative measure purported to constitute a full transposition of a particular EU directive, the national court would have to consider whether the measures might give rise to the presumption that the result required by the directive will not be achieved on time.[95] The CJEU also held that, conversely, a national court should recognise that member states have a right to adopt transitional measures or implement the directive in stages; in such cases, incompatibility of such measures with the terms of a directive would not necessarily compromise the result required to be attained by the latter instrument.[96] It should be borne in mind that national courts form a constituent part of the concept of 'member state' and are obliged according to well-established CJEU jurisprudence, as part of the general obligations contained in Article 4(3) TEU, to set aside national measures pleaded before them which contravene EU law.

The CJEU has confirmed that the direct effect doctrine may be relied upon in two main types of scenario after the transposition deadline of a directive has elapsed. First, the classic application of direct effect is where the member state has failed to pass any national legislation to implement a directive by the transposition deadline. Secondly, the CJEU has also confirmed that the doctrine applies also where member states have adopted transposition legislation but the latter is incomplete and/or in conflict with the terms of the directive in question.[97] Accordingly, the CJEU has confirmed that the directive will have residual legal effects, so long as a member state has failed to implement its EU legal obligations accurately.

6.1.2.5 *Subjective individual rights and direct effect*

It has been a long-standing debate, still not clearly resolved in the CJEU's case law, as to whether the doctrine of direct effect may only be used where the material provisions contained in directives purport, expressly or impliedly, to grant substantive rights for the benefit of individuals. The debate has sometimes been referred to in terms of a distinction between subjective and objective direct effect. Subjective direct effect envisages that, in addition to the criteria of sufficient precision and unconditionality, the EU legislative provision(s) in question must, impliedly or expressly, grant particular rights to the benefit of individuals. Objective direct effect, in contrast, envisages a position whereby persons are entitled to utilise the direct effect doctrine where the criteria of sufficient precision and unconditionality are fulfilled, it being irrelevant whether or not they are intended to derive personal substantive rights under the provision(s) concerned. The issue is of crucial importance to a policy field such as environmental law, where several EU directives on environmental protection contain no or only an indirect connection to individual personal rights.[98] Classic examples include directives on nature protection, such as the Wild Birds Directive[99] and Habitats Directive,[100] whose provisions are principally intended to benefit wildlife conservation, as opposed to any specific anthropogenic interests.

The debate has close links with the issue of the evolution of discussions concerning legal standing (*locus standi*) in administrative proceedings.[101] In judicial review proceedings, whether it be in the context of national proceedings or proceedings at EU level, the issue of deciding how to set an appropriate limit to the personal scope of potential plaintiffs in any given dispute is an important as well as politically sensitive subject. On the one hand, arguments grounded in safeguarding an adequate level of democratic accountability in state decision-making point towards constructing a judicial review framework which provides for a relatively flexible and open system for allowing interested citizens to seek annulment of measures they consider to be contrary to the law. On the other hand, arguments grounded in ensuring that the democratically elected governments should not be unduly constrained in implementing policy point in favour of ensuring that the range of persons who should be entitled to seek legal review of state decision-making should be confined to those with clearly identified personal legal interests. Technically the issues of direct effect and legal standing are legally distinct matters and should not be confused with one another,[102] as was done in the judgment of the High Court concerning the dispute over the failure to apply the EIA Directive[103] in relation to the motorway project at Twyford Downs in the UK.[104] Whereas the subject of direct effect determines whether or not an individual may rely on a particular EU norm in the context of legal proceedings brought either by them or against them (whether civil, criminal or administrative), the issue of legal standing is a matter which determines whether or not a particular person has a legal right to bring an action before a court (such as judicial review or a civil action against a decision of the state or public authority). The doctrine of direct effect does not in itself determine who may bring a particular action in order to enforce EU law. That is primarily a matter to be determined by the laws of the member states, although the CJEU has in its more recent jurisprudence provided some important new legal innovations in this regard, as will be discussed towards the end of this chapter.

The jurisprudence of the CJEU to date has not satisfactorily resolved the issue as to whether substantive individual rights should feature in the direct effect doctrine. On the one hand, there are a number of indications that the CJEU would reject a narrowly defined doctrine of direct effect, namely confined to instances where EU law confers subjective rights for individuals. The criteria established by the CJEU itself to determine direct effect do not specifically include reference to a subjective legal interest dimension, the Court having consistently referred to the elements of sufficient precision and unconditionality as the integral elements to the direct effect doctrine. The inclusion of a subjective rights element to the doctrine would run counter to the overall approach of the CJEU in working to ensure that the legal framework underpinning the EU treaty framework is effective in terms of ensuring that the legal commitments entered into by member states are adhered to. Such a limitation would also undermine the 'estoppel' line of reasoning employed by the CJEU in relation to directives.

In addition, in at least one environmental case, the CJEU has appeared to have rejected the argument that directives must be intended to confer subjective rights on individuals. Specifically, in the *Grosskrotzenburg* case[105] the CJEU rejected the German government's submission that the direct effect of the provisions of directives could only materialise where they confer rights on individuals.[106] The case arose in the wake of a complaint to the Commission that certain public authorities in Germany had acted in breach of the Environmental Impact Assessment (EIA) Directive[107] by failing to carry out an environmental impact assessment prior to the construction of an extension to an existing thermal power station. Consequently, the Commission brought an infringement action against Germany, submitting that various provisions[108] of the directive had been breached. Germany had, at the time, failed to transpose the EIA Directive by the requisite deadline stipulated in the directive. The German government submitted that irrespective of whether those particular provisions in the directive were sufficiently precise and unconditional, the German authorities were not obliged to apply them directly because none of them were intended to confer rights on individuals. Article 2 lays down a general obligation for member state authorities to undertake an EIA in relation to certain projects; Article 3 sets out the content of the EIA and lists the factors to be taken into account by the relevant authorities whilst leaving some discretion regarding the manner of carrying out assessments in individual cases; whilst Article 8 requires national authorities to take on board information obtained in the course of the assessment for the purposes of appraising whether or not to grant development consent. The German government was effectively arguing that its national authorities were not obliged to adhere to the terms of those particular provisions in the absence of national transposition legislation, and would only be bound by national implementing legislation which transposed the particular terms of the directive. The CJEU rejected this submission, holding that the particular provisions of the EIA Directive unequivocally imposed an obligation on the national authorities responsible for granting development consent and obligation to carry out an impact assessment.[109] The CJEU did not find it necessary to comment on whether the particular provisions in fact were directly effective. Nevertheless, it is clear from this judgment that member state authorities are, just as member state governments, bound by EU directives irrespective of whether they have direct effects or not.

However, the case of *Associazione Italia per il WWF v Regione Veneto*[110] would appear to lend clearer support for the view that the CJEU favours the objective as opposed to subjective conception of direct effect. In this environmental case, certain Italian NGEOs took legal action against the regional authority for Veneto in order to annul its decision to fix the hunting calendar for the 1992/3 on a basis which they submitted contravened the terms of the EU Wild Birds Directive.[111] By way of derogation from the general hunting ban contained in Article 5 of the directive, Article 7 of the directive stipulates that member states under certain conditions may authorise the hunting of bird species listed in its Annex II. In addition, member states may exceptionally authorise the hunting of other birds under strict conditions set out in Article 9 of the directive. The plaintiffs submitted that the calendar for the Veneto region had authorised the hunting of species not listed in Annex II of the directive, without complying with the conditions of Article 9. In its preliminary ruling in relation to the case, the CJEU confirmed, in relation to one of the conditions under which Article 9 of the directive authorises member states to derogate from the hunting ban set out in Articles 5 and 7, that individuals would be able to rely upon sufficiently precise and unconditional provisions of a directive against any authority of a member state where the state has failed to implement the directive in national law by the end of the transposition period or implements it in incorrectly.[112] This advice to the national referring court gave a strong indication that the doctrine of direct effect was pertinent to a case even where, as in this one, anthropocentric legal interests were not at stake.

Commentators seem, though, somewhat divided over whether the direct effect doctrine is based on a 'subjective' or 'objective' basis. Krämer, for instance, has argued that the CJEU has indicated that the express or implied inclusion of individual substantive rights in an EU norm are a prerequisite for the capacity of private persons being able to utilise the direct effect doctrine.[113] The case of *Enichem Base*, discussed above, might appear to lend support to that argument. However, Jans disagrees with this analysis, holding that the CJEU has not stated that this is to be a requirement, whilst also making the point that the assertion of direct effect is easier if the relevant provision is closely linked to the protection of clearly defined individual interests such as public health protection or free trade.[114] Lackhoff and Nyssens submit that in the light of the *Grosskrotzenburg* case, the CJEU has clarified that the direct effect doctrine is based on an objective as opposed to subjective basis.[115] Others have registered uncertainty regarding the CJEU's position.[116]

Notwithstanding the current relative state of controversy and confusion that surrounds this issue, it appears that the CJEU has recently begun to introduce new elements to its jurisprudence which may now have effectively bypassed or side-stepped the debate over subjective and objective direct effect, as well as arguably the core criteria traditionally associated with direct effect. Specifically, the CJEU appears to have developed its jurisprudence so as to focus more on the duties of national courts to uphold directives relied upon by individuals, as a means of ensuring that EU law, and in particular EU environmental law, is upheld. The leading case in this significant new judicial approach is the *Kraaijeveld* case,[117] which will be explored later in this chapter (in section 6.1.3.3). The next two sections will examine the various persons and entities against whom individuals may enforce directly effective provisions of EU environmental directives before national courts and tribunals.

6.1.3 *Applying direct effect of directives against public authorities*

6.1.3.1 *General points*

One of the key limitations developed by the CJEU in relation to the application of the direct effect doctrine as applied to provisions of directives is the range of persons and entities against whom the doctrine may be relied upon before national courts. The Court has made a basic distinction between enforcement of directives against public authorities, on the one hand, and against private persons, on the other. Whereas it has confirmed that individuals may directly rely upon provisions of directives which meet the criteria for direct effect against state authorities (so-called 'vertical' direct effect) it has ruled out the possibility of the direct effect doctrine being used by individuals against other individuals (so-called 'horizontal' direct effect)[118] or by the state authorities against individuals (so-called 'inverse' direct effect).[119]

The principal reason for this limitation may be traced to the CJEU's understanding of the legal nature and purpose of the directive as an EU legislative instrument as well as its 'estoppel' reasoning referred to earlier. The CJEU's analysis of the legislative process envisaged in Article 288(3) TFEU, when the EU selects a directive in order to crystallise policy into a legally binding format, interprets from this provision that directives are not intended as a matter of principle to be addressed to individuals. The provision refers to directives being binding upon the member states to whom it is addressed. It is evident from the wording and structure of Article 288(3) that the treaty authors saw the completion of the entire legislative process finalised only when national legislation is adopted in order to implement the requirements of a directive into national law, particularly when one compares the provision with the description of the impact of regulations described in Article 288(2) TFEU. National implementing legislation is clearly required from the wording in Article 288(3) TFEU to translate the directive's requirements into rights and responsibilities for the general public of each member state. As already noted, the Court has developed the doctrine of direct effect in the context of directives as a means of ensuring that member states are not in a position to take advantage of the fact that they have failed to implement their EU obligations correctly and/or on time. However, it has refused to extend the doctrine to encompass directly effective obligations for individuals, on grounds that the latter are not expected to take responsibility for the fact that a member state has failed to honour its supranational legal commitments.[120]

As will be discussed below, it is evident that recent jurisprudence from the CJEU has begun to blur the distinction between vertical and horizontal effects of directives, which has important ramifications for the prosecution of civil litigation by individuals with the purpose of altering behaviour of private individuals so as to ensure that legally binding commitments contained in EU environmental directives are upheld.

6.1.3.2 *Vertical direct effects*

As noted above, the CJEU has laid down the general principle that EU member states are not entitled to rely upon their failure to transpose directives into national law in order to evade legally binding commitments contained in directives which are couched in sufficiently precise and unconditional terms. Accordingly, the CJEU has confirmed that individuals may rely upon such provisions in defence against member state government agencies which seek to enforce domestic legislation which conflicts with the directly effective terms of a directive.[121] Since then, the CJEU's case law has expanded considerably the range of situations that may be described as vertical direct effect scenarios.

Notably, the CJEU has confirmed that the *ratione personae* of what may be deemed the 'member state' should be construed broadly. In a number of cases, the Court held that individuals could rely upon directly effective provisions in directives against a series of public authorities, not only those located at the heart of central government such as government departments (as was the case in *Van Duyn*,[122] the first case on direct effect of directives). For instance, the CJEU has accepted that direct effect could be evoked in disputes against local authorities,[123] even where such an authority acted in its capacity as employer as opposed to public policy decision-maker,[124] police authorities[125] and universities.[126] It had become clear in a relatively few years after its initial case on the subject of direct effect of directives that emanations of the state as well as its central branches were subject to the doctrine.

The Court set out a basic test for determining the parameters to the definition of 'member state' for the purpose of vertical direct effect of directives in the *Foster* case.[127] That case concerned a dispute between an employee of British Gas plc and the company, which had been recently privatised at the time. The employee, Ms Foster, sought to challenge the legality of the company's policy to require compulsory retirement of women at 60 and men at 65. Specifically, the employee submitted that the policy contravened the EU's Sex Equality in Employment Directive,[128] which requires that member states ensure that the principle of equal treatment between men and women is applied in relation to workplace terms and conditions for employees. A key question was whether or not the employee could rely upon the directive against a privatised utility company (British Gas plc). The CJEU set out the following framework for the national court adjudicating the dispute to apply to determine the issue:

> (18) [T]he Court has held in a series of cases that unconditional and sufficiently precise provisions of a directive could be relied on against organisations or bodies which were subject to the authority or control of the State or had special powers beyond those which result from the normal rules applicable between individuals.
>
> [. . .]
>
> (20) It follows . . . that a body, whatever its legal form, which has been made responsible, pursuant to a measure adopted by the State, for providing a public service under the control of the State and has for that purpose special powers beyond those which result from the normal rules applicable in relations between individuals, is included in any event among the bodies against which the provisions of a directive capable of having direct effect may be relied upon.

This judgment makes it clear that privatised utilities are most likely to fall within the definition of an emanation of the state for the purposes of direct effect. This has important ramifications for the environment sector where in several member states privatisation of utilities affecting environmental quality has been completed or is being actively considered, such as in the water, energy and transport sectors.

From an environmental sector perspective, it has been particularly significant that the CJEU acknowledged that local or regional authorities are to be considered a constituent part of the member state for the purposes of vertical direct effect, given that it is common to find a strong element of devolution or decentralisation in terms of environmental policy decision-making within member states. It meant that authorities were provided with a definitive legal obligation under EU law to ensure that unambiguous and self-contained environmental commitments entered into at EU level and enshrined in directives were enforced at local level, insofar as those commitments fell within their field of jurisdiction at national level. As will be addressed in the final part to this chapter, the CJEU has gone further to confirm that a general legal obligation on member state authorities flows from Article 4(3) TEU to ensure that they apply EU law and legislation which falls within the scope of the jurisdiction allocated to them under national law, irrespective of whether or not the provisions of the directive in question are directly effective (see e.g. the *Grosskrotzenburg* and *Kraaijeveld* cases referred to earlier).[129] This dimension to the CJEU's jurisprudence has profound implications, given that the duty arises irrespective of whether an individual takes legal action against the relevant authority or whether the norm in question meets the standard criteria of direct effect of sufficient precision and unconditionality.

It has been argued that the credibility of the 'estoppel' line of reasoning so heavily used by the Court to justify its jurisprudence on conferral of direct effect of directives has been stretched to the limit with the expanded notion of the member state.[130] Specifically, one might question whether a local council, for instance, should be expected to assume legal responsibility for the failure on the part of a relatively remote central government of the member state in question to carry out its obligations in promulgating correct transposition legislation on time. A far more convincing line of argument to support the imposition of direct effect on public authorities would be to focus on the CJEU's understanding of the EU treaty framework as having created a unique supranational legal order comprising both member states and resident individuals coupled with the need to enhance the effectiveness of the enforcement and supremacy of EU law within member states territories as far as possible, whilst at the same time recognising that the argument of *effet utile* (securing the practical effectiveness of EU law) should not go so far so as to introduce obligations for individuals who have no immediate links with nor represent the exercise of state authority.

6.1.3.3 Limited member state discretion and 'vertical' effects of directives

Within the last decade, the CJEU appears to have developed a new dimension to its traditional jurisprudence on direct effect in the context of directives. Specifically, the Court has confirmed in a number of cases that member state courts have been obliged to apply provisions of EU environmental directives relied upon by individuals in the context of national legal proceedings against state entities, even though the provisions would not appear to meet the standard core criteria for direct effect, namely sufficient precision and unconditionality. The cases have involved disputes as to whether national authorities have exceeded the limits of discretion accorded to member states under the auspices of EU environmental directives. In these particular cases, the Court has usually avoided references to the direct effect doctrine in its legal analysis, choosing instead to focus on determining under what circumstances such discretion may be exceeded so as to be incompatible with the requirements of EU legislation. In particular, these cases have emphasised the responsibility of member states not to fetter a national authority's discretion in a manner that would limit the impact of an environmental directive's requirements.

The leading case in this particular line of CJEU jurisprudence is the *Kraaijeveld* case.[131] That case involved a failure by Dutch authorities to adhere to the terms of the EIA Directive[132] in relation to a particular construction project. Specifically, certain private companies including Aannermersbedrijf P. K. Kraaijeveld BV sought to annul the decision by the South Holland Provincial Executive to approve a zoning plan siting the reinforcement of certain dyke works designed to protect inland areas from storm tides. An effect of the planned dyke works would have been the closure of access by Kraaijeveld to navigable waterways, upon which its business operations were dependent. Under Dutch law at the time, no environmental impact assessment was carried out because the size of the works fell below the minimum[133] set by national legislation for an environmental impact assessment to be mandatory. Kraaijeveld, supported by the European Commission, submitted that omission of an impact assessment contravened the terms of the directive.

The legal backdrop to the case involved a rather nuanced understanding of the EIA Directive's provisions. The particular project in question fell within the remit of Annex II to the EIA Directive,[134] in respect of which member states are afforded a certain amount of discretion in determining the organisation of impact assessment procedures. Specifically, Article 4(2) of the directive stipulates that member states are competent to determine whether Annex II listed projects should be subject to an impact assessment.[135] Article 4(1), in conjunction with Annex I to the directive, specifies projects in respect of which an impact assessment is mandatory. Article 2(1) of the directive contains a distinct obligation in relation to all prospective projects likely to have significant effects on the environment. Article 2(1) states:

> Member states shall adopt all measures necessary to ensure that, before consent is given, projects likely to have significant effects on the environment by virtue inter alia of their nature, size or location are made subject to a requirement for development consent[136] and an assessment with regard to their effects. These projects are defined in Article 4.

The Dutch court adjudicating the dispute referred a number of questions to the CJEU under the preliminary ruling procedure in Article 267 TFEU. Specifically, the national court enquired whether Article 2(1) in conjunction with Article 4(2) imposed an impact assessment obligation on each member state in respect of projects covered by Annex II which would have significant effects on the environment, notwithstanding that such projects fall below minimum thresholds set by a member state for an impact assessment to be required. In addition, it also requested the CJEU to confirm whether such an obligation is directly effective.

The CJEU answered the first question in the affirmative. It considered in essence that the effect of Article 2(1) was to limit member states' discretion conferred in Article 4(2) of the directive. Specifically, it ruled that a member state's legislation having the effect of exempting automatically certain dyke construction projects from the requirement of an EIA would exceed the limits of the member state's discretion conferred under Articles 2(1) and 4(2) of the directive, unless all projects excluded could, when viewed in their entirety, be regarded as not being likely to have significant effects on the environment.[137]

However, the Court did not address the issue of direct effect in clear or specific terms. Instead, it referred in general terms to the conduct of judicial review proceedings to be carried out by the adjudicating national court, given the circumstances presented to it. The CJEU first reiterated its previous jurisprudence confirming the obligation upon member states to take all necessary measures to achieve the result prescribed by a directive set out by Article 288(3) TFEU as well as the particular directive itself. Following on from that initial general position, the CJEU underlined that the duty to take all appropriate measures, whether general or particular, is binding on all the authorities of the member states including, for matters within their jurisdiction, the national courts.[138] The CJEU stated, in accordance with previous jurisprudence, that it would be incompatible with the binding effect attributed to a directive under Article 288 TFEU to exclude, in principle, the possibility that the obligation which it imposes may be invoked by the individuals concerned. The Court underlined that the effectiveness of directives would otherwise be undermined:

> In particular, where the [Union] authorities have, by directive, imposed on member states the obligation to pursue a particular course of conduct, the useful effect of such an act would be weakened if individuals were prevented from taking it into consideration as an element of [Union] law in order to rule whether the national legislature, in exercising the choice open to it as to the form and methods for implementation, has kept within the limits of its discretion set out in the directive.[139]

Finally, the CJEU addressed the element of discretion afforded to the member state authorities in relation to Articles 2(1) and 4(2) of the EIA Directive. From an orthodox standpoint, the margin of discretion conferred to member states in those provisions appears arguably too wide to fulfil the criteria of sufficient precision and unconditionality inherent in the test of direct effect. For instance, the reference to 'significant effects on the environment' in Article 2(1) is not legally defined in the directive and inherently involves elements of political judgment by competent authorities in each case (i.e. at what particular point the threshold of 'significance' is reached). In addition, there is a strong element of discretion contained in Article 4(2), which stipulates that member states are competent to determine whether Annex II-type projects are to be subject to an impact assessment. Nevertheless, crucially, the CJEU did not consider the presence of considerable discretionary powers on the part of member states to be a bar or relevant consideration for the national court to take into account when carrying out its duties under Article 288(3) TFEU:

> The fact that in this case the member states have a discretion under Articles 2(1) and 4(2) of the directive does not preclude judicial review of whether the national authorities exceeded their discretion . . .[140]

[. . .]

If that discretion has been exceeded and consequently the national provisions must be set aside in that respect, it is for the authorities of the member state, according to their respective powers, to take all the general or particular measures necessary to ensure that projects are examined in order to determine whether they are likely to have significant effects on the environment and, if so, to ensure that they are subject to an impact assessment.[141]

There is little doubt that the CJEU in *Kraaijeveld* extended the range of possibilities for individuals to be able to enforce EU (environmental) directives. It is clear that the Court requires the national court in this instance to ensure, in the context of annulment proceedings brought by individuals against a state authority, that the core minimum legal duty set down in the directive is adhered to. In this case, the legal duty distilled by the Court from the directive's provisions was a duty on the part of the member state and its competent authorities to ensure that any project which would generate significant environmental effects would be subject to an impact assessment. The CJEU effectively recognised the enforceability by individuals of a public law duty imposed on member state authorities under Articles 2(1) and 4(2) of the directive. Not only did the relevant local planning authorities have a duty to ensure that an assessment would be carried out, but also national courts had a concomitant legal duty to set aside decisions taken by such authorities which exceeded the margins of their discretion under those provisions. Scott has aptly described this judgment of the Court in terms of the CJEU creating a 'public law effect' to directives, in respect of which individuals have new legal rights to uphold.[142] Several commentators have speculated whether the CJEU has created a new source of legal enforceability of directives, to apply alongside direct effect. Some intimate that this recent line of jurisprudence might be best described as being outside the realm of direct effect, having in effect constituted a new and distinct legal doctrine.[143] Other commentators opine that the CJEU has extended the doctrine of direct effect to include a new branch of legal principle which precludes member states from exceeding limits to discretion as set out in EU law.[144] Others remain uncertain of the Court's position, noting that the CJEU did not comment on the impact of its judgment in relation to existing direct effect jurisprudence.[145]

Whatever the correct position, it is clear that the CJEU has moved the legal discussion pertaining to private enforcement of EU (environmental) directives beyond a purely individual rights context.[146] Specifically, it is evident from the judgment that individuals may rely on the *Kraaijeveld* case in order to enforce legal duties enshrined in directives intended to benefit society as a whole, as opposed to specific or exclusively individual legal interests. Moreover, the CJEU has also clarified that legal duties set out in directives containing substantial elements of discretion afforded to member states may be enforced by individuals where the national authorities have failed to exercise the discretion within the legal boundaries set by the directive. There has been some disquiet in some quarters concerning the implications of the judgment. Wyatt, for instance, doubts the conclusions reached by the Court on the grounds that the decision as to whether or not an impact assessment should be carried out in relation to Annex II projects involves a complex analysis of factors and policy choices and is ill-suited to judicial adjudication.[147] However, the implications of the judgment may not necessarily be intended to encroach upon the area of policy-making in this way. In *Kraaijeveld* itself, the basic criticism pointed to the fact that the national legal position did not ensure that an EIA would be carried out in respect of projects having significant environmental effects. If the CJEU is referring to the exceeding of discretion in this narrow manner, and there are grounds in its reasoning to suggest that this is the case, the judgment in *Kraaijeveld* arguably is not that far removed from classic conceptual lines of thought in relation to direct effect. According to this reading of the CJEU's ruling it has effectively distilled a minimum legal guarantee contained in the terms of a directive, which is not conditional on further measures at national or supranational level: the guarantee that a legal framework is in place to ensure that projects likely to have significant legal effects should be subject to an impact assessment. As a consequence, any national rule or practice which restricts or blocks an impact assessment taking place in relation to such projects must be set aside.

Since the *Kraaijeveld* judgment, the CJEU has fortified the range of possibilities for individuals to rely upon directives before national courts in order to enforce member state obligations designed to promote public as opposed to individual interests. For instance, the CJEU reiterated in *Linster*[148] the general point that national courts would be entitled to take the provisions of the EIA Directive into account in order to review whether the national legislature had kept within the limits of discretion afforded to it under the terms of the directive.[149] That particular case involved the failure on the part of Luxembourg to ensure that an impact assessment and public consultation was carried out in relation to a motorway project, a project falling under Annex I to the EIA directive. The CJEU's subsequent judgment in *WWF v Bozen*[150] was more significant, in developing the scope of application of the CJEU's *Kraaijeveld* ruling. In that case, the Italian branch of the World Wildlife Fund NGEO sought judicial review before the Italian courts of a planned construction project intended to extend the length of an existing airport runway in the northern Italian region of Bozen (Bolzano). The length of the runway fell short of the minimum requirement in the EIA Directive for a mandatory impact assessment as an Annex I project.[151] Instead, the project fell within ambit of Article 4(2) and Annex II of the directive as a project which member states had a certain degree of discretion as to whether or not to require an impact assessment. The relevant Italian planning rules applicable to the project provided for a simplified impact study to be considered by conference of the Italian region's directors, a procedure not envisaged in the EIA Directive. The study failed to carry out an investigation into the impact of the project in terms of noise and atmospheric changes, elements that would have to be incorporated into an impact assessment within the meaning of the EIA directive.[152] Neither did the national procedure involve a consultation of the public as required under Article 6 of the directive. The Italian administrative court which was charged with hearing the case referred a number of questions to the CJEU under the preliminary ruling procedure, including (1) whether, in the case of a project requiring an impact assessment under the directive, Article 2 of the directive permitted the use of an impact assessment procedure other than envisaged in its provisions and (2) whether individuals would be able to rely upon Articles 2(1) and 4(2) of the directive directly before the national court in order to set aside national rules or decisions which conflicted with the terms of the directive.

The CJEU's replies in *WWF v Bozen* to the two questions were clear and emphatically in favour of the plaintiff's case. First, the Court confirmed that where a project required an impact assessment under the terms of the EIA directive, a procedure different from the one envisaged in the directive would not be permitted, otherwise it would undermine the environmental protection objective underpinning the directive.[153] The CJEU's response to the second question served to underline and entrench its analysis and findings in the *Kraaijeveld* case in relation to the possibility of private enforcement of Articles 2(1) and 4(2) of the directive. It held:

> Articles 4(2) and 2(1) of the directive are to be interpreted as meaning that, where the discretion conferred by those provisions has been exceeded by the legislative or administrative authorities of a member state, individuals may rely on those provisions before a court of that member state against the national authorities and thus obtain from the latter the setting aside of the national rules or measures incompatible with those provisions. In such a case, it is for the authorities of the member state to take, according to their relevant powers, all the general or particular measures necessary to ensure that projects are examined in order to determine whether they are likely to have significant effects on the environment, and if so, to ensure that they are subject to an impact assessment.[154]

The judgment underlines that individuals are indeed entitled to rely upon the provisions of a directive before a national court to ensure that a national authority is held to account in the event that it exceeds the limits of discretion afforded to it by the directive when actively exercising its judgment as to whether and what type of steps or measures are to be taken in a particular case. Accordingly, individuals were entitled in *WWF v Bozen* to rely upon Articles 2(1) and 4(2) of the EIA Directive before the national courts in the context of judicial review proceedings in order to have set aside the application of an imperfect impact assessment procedure conducted in relation to the Bozen airport runway extension. The judgment in *WWF v Bozen* served to extend the reach of the *Kraaijeveld* judgment. *Kraaijeveld* concerned a situation where national rules did not provide for an impact study to be carried out for certain types of projects. The CJEU made clear that this automatic block to the application of an impact assessment procedure would be contrary to the terms of the directive, unless it meant that the exclusion from assessment viewed as a whole would not include projects likely to have significant environmental effects. The *WWF v Bozen* case involved a distinctly different set of circumstances and issues. Specifically, it concerned whether individuals could utilise the directive's provisions to challenge the legality of a particular impact assessment procedure undertaken under the auspices of national rules, on the grounds that the process constituted exceeding the discretionary limits afforded to member state authorities by the EIA directive.

The CJEU's legal reasoning in *Kraaijeveld* and *WWF v Bozen* has also has been echoed and affirmed in other EIA cases.[155]

Another recent judgment of the CJEU, also involving the environmental policy sector, appears to have confirmed the more expansive approach taken by it in *Kraaijeveld* when determining the parameters of legal effects that may be construed from provisions of EU directives. Specifically, in the *Waddenzee* case[156] two environmental associations sought judicial review before the Dutch courts to annul a decision taken by Dutch authorities to grant fishing permits to persons wishing to engage in mechanical cockle fishing in an inland water zone known as the Waddenzee, an area designated as a protected nature site. The plaintiffs submitted that the decision infringed both the Wild Birds Directive (now Directive 2009/147) and Habitats Directive 92/43, given that cockle fishing would disturb specific protected breeding sites and food sources for oystercatchers and other wild wading birds. The Dutch court handling the dispute referred a number of legal questions to the CJEU, including whether the key provision relevant to the case, Article 6(3) of the Habitats Directive, had direct effect. Article 6(3) of the directive, which had not been transposed into Dutch law, specifies that:

> Any plan or project not directly connected with or necessary to the management of a site but likely to have a significant effect thereon, either individually or in combination with other plans or projects, shall be subject to appropriate assessment of its implications for the site in view of the site's conservation objectives. In the light of the conclusions of the assessment of the implications for the site and subject to the provisions of paragraph 4, the competent authorities shall agree to the plan or project only after having ascertained that it will not adversely affect the integrity of the site concerned and, if appropriate, after having obtained the opinion of the general public.

The CJEU's appraisal of the question of direct effect resonated with the one applied by it in its ruling in *Kraaijeveld*, with the Court emphasising the responsibilities of the national court in applying EU legal obligations. The Court interpreted the question of direct effect as essentially being whether a national court may examine whether the limits of discretion made available to the competent national authority under national rules of law were in accordance with the requirements of the relevant EU directive. It answered in the affirmative,[157] having confirmed that national courts, as integral parts of the member states, were obliged under Article 288 TFEU(3) as well as the individual directive concerned to take all measures, general and particular, necessary to achieve the result prescribed by the directive for matters falling within their jurisdiction:

> As regards the right of an individual to rely on a directive and of the national court to take it into consideration, it would be incompatible with the binding effect attributed to a directive by Article [288 TFEU] to exclude, in principle, the possibility the obligation which it imposes may be relied on by those concerned.

In particular, where the [Union] authorities have, by directive, imposed on member states the obligation to pursue a particular course of conduct, the effectiveness of such an act would be weakened if individuals were prevented from relying on it before their national courts, and if the latter were prevented from taking into consideration as an element of [Union] law in order to rule whether the national legislature, in exercising the choice open to it as to the form and methods of implementation, has kept within the limits of its discretion set by the directive (see *Kraaijeveld and others*, paragraph 56). That also applies to ascertaining whether, failing transposition into national law of the relevant provision of the directive concerned, the national authority which has adopted the contested measure has kept within the limits of its discretion set by that provision.[158]

In holding that these considerations applied to Article 6(3) of the directive, the CJEU did not address the factors of sufficient precision or unconditionality as being relevant to its analysis of the extent of legal effects flowing from the provision. Notwithstanding the imprecise nature of the provision's terms, in particular the reference to 'likely' in the first sentence of Article 6(3), the Court confirmed that individuals could rely on it before national courts to challenge national authority decision-making.

Another case illustrating the CJEU's expansive approach to private law enforcement of EU environmental directives arose in the *Janecek* case.[159] The CJEU confirmed that Dieter Janecek, a resident in Munich, was entitled to rely upon certain requirements contained in EU air ambient quality legislation before the national courts, notwithstanding that the relevant EU legislative provision endowed national authorities with a certain amount of discretion. Specifically, the case turned on whether Article 7(3) of former Directive 96/62[160] on ambient air quality assessment could be relied upon in judicial review proceedings against local authorities which had failed to draw up a plan to indicate the measures needed to be taken in order to reduce the risk of exceeding EU air quality limit values, with particular reference to limit values set for particulate matter. The element of discretionary power accorded to national authorities in relation to fulfilment of the legislative provision's requirements did not undermine the right of Janecek to be able to rely upon it as of right before national courts. The CJEU held:

It must be noted in this regard that, while the Member States thus have a discretion, Article 7(3) of Directive 96/62 includes limits on the exercise of that discretion which may be relied upon before the national courts (see, to that effect, Case C-72/95 *Kraaijeveld and Others* [1996] ECR I-5403, paragraph 59), relating to the adequacy of the measures which must be included in the action plan with the aim of reducing the risk of the limit values and/or alert thresholds being exceeded and the duration of such an occurrence, taking into account the balance which must be maintained between that objective and the various opposing public and private interests.[161]

The CJEU has also reaffirmed its approach to appraising the boundaries of national authority discretion in its *Djurgården* judgment.[162] In that case the municipality of Stockholm had concluded a contract with an electric company to build a 1-km tunnel for housing electric cables with a view to replacing overhead high-tension cables in a part of the city area (north Djurgården). The engineering project required the abstraction of groundwater seeping into the tunnels as well the construction of facilities designed to draw off water and have this recharged into the ground as a means of addressing any reduction in groundwater amounts. In 2006 the municipality was granted development consent for the project. However, a local environmental association appealed against the decision granting development consent. Its appeal was ruled inadmissible by the Swedish court hearing the appeal on the grounds that under Swedish law environmental associations had no legal standing to bring an appeal unless they could show that they had at least 2,000 members. The environmental association brought an appeal against that judicial decision, submitting that the Swedish rules contravened the provisions contained in the Union's EIA Directive on access to justice.[163]

At the material time the relevant access-to-justice provisions were housed in Article 10a of former EIA Directive 85/337.[164] The provisions, which have not been changed in substance, are now enshrined in Article 11 of the current codified version of the EIA Directive (Directive 2011/92).[165] The EIA Directive's access-to-justice provisions stipulate that member states are to ensure, *inter alia*, that members of the public having either a 'sufficient interest' or alternatively maintaining the impairment of a right, where national administrative procedure law requires this as a precondition, are to be ensured access to a review procedure before a court of law or other independent and impartial body established by law to challenge the substantive or procedural legality of decisions, acts or omissions subject to public participation provisions enshrined in the directive.[166] The directive's provisions also provide for a significant amount of discretion and competence to member states in implementing this commitment. Notably, the directive provides that member states are to determine at what stage such conduct may be challenged.[167] In addition, the directive expressly confirms that the member states have competence to determine what constitutes a sufficient interest and impairment of right, subject to such competence being exercised 'consistently with the objective of giving the public concerned wide access to justice'.[168] As regards non-governmental organisations which promote environmental protection, the EIA Directive specifies that those 'meeting any requirements under national law' are to be regarded as either having a sufficient interest or having a right which is capable of being impaired by projects falling within the scope of the directive.[169]

Whilst accepting that the EIA Directive's access-to-justice provisions essentially defer to member states' legislatures the task of determining conditions required for NGEOs to have a right of appeal, the CJEU qualified this discretion by underlining that national rules must secure a wide access to justice under terms of the directive as well as ensure that the directive's provisions on judicial remedies are fulfilled. As a consequence, the CJEU held that:

> Accordingly, those national rules must not be liable to nullify [Union] provisions which provide that parties who have a sufficient interest to challenge a

project and those whose rights it impairs, which include environmental protection associations, are to be entitled to bring actions before the competent courts.[170]

In this particular case, according to the Court, Sweden had transposed the requirements of the EIA Directive incorrectly in having established a requirement that NGEOs must have at least 2,000 members in order to be entitled to secure access to justice, taking into particular account that the directive concerns projects of more limited size than a national or regional scale in respect of which locally based environmental associations are better placed to deal with than larger counterparts.[171] The Court also rejected the Swedish government's arguments that the impact of the national minimum threshold on membership numbers would not have a detrimental impact on access to justice in practice given that small NGEOs were given the right to express their views in the participatory phase of decision-making procedures relating to project development consent and that they could seek to lobby larger NGEOs to take legal action if they wished to pursue an objection through the courts. Specifically, the CJEU underlined that the EIA Directive does not legitimate access-to-review procedures being restricted, on grounds that the persons concerned have been granted rights to express views in the participatory phase; it also pointed out that lobbying another NGEO would not necessarily guarantee that an appeal against development consent would be brought.[172] In essence, the CJEU's judgment in *Djurgården* re-emphasised the point that private persons (such as NGEOs) will be able to rely upon the provisions of EU environmental directives against national authorities where the latter exceed the parameters of discretion set down in the Union legislation. National authorities are unlikely to be able to block such judicial review on the grounds that a particular norm contained in a directive does not technically meet one or more of the requirements of direct effect, such as unconditionality.

6.1.4 Reliance upon directives against private persons

Whereas the CJEU has been prepared to hold that rights for individuals may exist to enforce EU directives, so far it has resolutely refused to contemplate the possibility of individuals deriving obligations directly from their provisions. The essential reasons for this limitation to the application of direct effect have been outlined above (see section 6.1.3.1). The consequences of this judicial position are far-reaching in terms of a brake being placed on the possibility of enforcement action taken either by public authorities or by private legal persons against non-state actors in order to uphold EU environmental legislation. The scope of the term 'private person' includes natural persons as well as business and non-profit private legal entities, the latter of which may take a number of legal forms, including limited and public limited companies, partnerships, sole traders and trusts.

6.1.4.1 Inverse vertical effects of directives

In line with its position of ruling out the possibility of the doctrine of direct effect being able to confer obligations on private persons, the CJEU has confirmed on a number of occasions that state authorities are barred from relying upon provisions of directives against private persons in order to ensure that the instrument's requirements are respected within the member states. Such a scenario is often referred to as one envisaging an inverse effect of a directive, namely the possibility of legal obligations contained in directives being enforced against individuals by public authorities as opposed to the other way round, which is the classical situation of vertical direct effect. The Court has stuck to its basic initial position constructed in the 1980s when the issue first arose[173] that the legal characteristics of a directive implicitly rule out such a legal effect occurring, noting in particular that the definition of a directive in Article 288(3) TFEU speaks only of such instruments being binding on their addressees, namely member states, as to the result to be achieved.

There have been several instances where national authorities have sought to rely on EU environmental directives against private persons with a view to ensuring that binding minimum environmental protection standards are upheld. National courts have frequently referred questions to the CJEU as to whether they may refer to environmental directives for this purpose. In a long line of cases, commencing with the *Pretore di Salò* case[174] the Court has continued to rule this out as a possibility. Most of the cases concern whether public authorities may use environmental directives in the context of criminal investigations and prosecutions targeted at instances of illicit acts of pollution. Such authorities have on occasion sought to rely on provisions in environmental directives in order to establish, confirm or enhance criminal liability of private persons in respect of their activities. In *Pretore di Salò*, an Italian investigating magistrate referred a number of questions to the CJEU concerning the interpretation of former Directive 78/659 on fresh water quality,[175] as part of the magistrate's judicial investigation into various acts disrupting the course and quality of the Chiese river (erection of dams and instances of discharges). On its own initiative, the CJEU made it clear that the EU directive could not be considered to be a source of legal obligation on the part of private persons in the context of criminal liability, where the directive had not been transposed into national law:

> [. . .] Directive 78/659 of 18 July 1978 cannot, of itself and independently of a national law adopted by a member state for its implementation, have the effect of determining or aggravating the liability in criminal law of persons who act in contravention of the provisions of that directive.[176]

One of the key reasons why the CJEU has rejected the possibility of inverse direct effect of EU directives has been the awareness that this might have particular adverse consequences for private individuals faced with criminal proceedings at national level. It is a well-established principle in EU law,[177] inspired by protection contained in the European Convention on Human Rights,[178] that individuals should not be subject to retrospective criminal legislation (*nulla poene sine lege*). Specifically, without a restriction on application of the direct effect doctrine, a national authority might otherwise be able to use the doctrine in order to establish or aggravate criminal liability under existing national law by relying upon obligations in a Union directive that might not have been first transposed into the national legal system by way of national implementation legislation. Such a scenario would give rise to the prospect of a retrospective imposition of criminal liability, in that the national parliament would not have specifically promulgated for criminal liability and at the same time it would be effectively bypassed if inverse direct effect were allowed to stand. Under Article 288(3) TFEU, which provides the definition of a directive, it is for the member states to determine the 'form and choice of methods' by which they transpose Union directives into national law.

On other occasions, the CJEU has expressly barred the utilisation of the direct effect doctrine by public authorities against private persons. For instance, in a series of waste management-related cases, the Court has confirmed that environmental protection authorities may not rely on EU waste directives in order to prosecute polluters.[179] In *Traen*,[180] for instance, three criminal actions had been taken against operators of waste disposal companies as well as a driver, for having disposed of waste in fields without being in possession of a permit. The accused had been charged of infringing a Belgian 1981 decree of the Flanders Region which was intended to implement the original (former) 1975 Waste Framework Directive (Directive 75/442).[181] The Belgian court, unsure as to whether Flemish legislation was compatible with particular provisions of the directive, referred a number of questions relating to the interpretation of the directive to the CJEU for a preliminary ruling. The directive's provisions in question stipulated that member states had to establish a system of supervision and control over waste disposal activities. Notably, Article 8 stipulated that any undertaking treating, storing or tipping waste on behalf of third parties had to obtain a permit from the national competent authorities[182] and Article 12 provided that undertakings were required to supply certain information to such competent authorities.[183] In particular, the Belgian court wished to know whether an undertaking carrying waste and an owner of land receiving waste from third parties were required to obtain a waste permit from the competent national authorities by virtue of these provisions of the former directive. In addition, the court wished to know whether the terms of the directive could apply directly to undertakings or whether its provisions were dependent on, *inter alia*, the adoption of implementing rules. The CJEU confirmed that the directive could not of itself impose obligations on individuals,[184] drawing from its general position in *Marshall (1)*[185] that a directive may not of itself impose obligations on individuals.

By way of exception to the general rule excluding inverse direct effects of EU directives, the CJEU has confirmed that the requirements of a directive may be relied upon by national authorities against individuals where those requirements are contained within a Union regulation. Specifically, in *Viamex*[186] the CJEU held that German authorities were justified in refusing to pay export refunds for live animals under the auspices of an EU regulation[187] which had made payment subject to the condition that the requirements of a particular directive[188] on animal welfare controls had been complied with. The CJEU qualified this exception by confirming that it would only apply if general principles of EU law, including legal certainty, are observed.[189] In theory, this judgment could have some important implications for the future operation of the general rule against inverse effects of EU directives. However, in the field of EU environmental policy its potential impact is likely to remain pretty minor, given that regulations are rarely used for the purposes of implementing policy.

6.1.4.2 Horizontal direct effect and directives

The CJEU has also ruled out the possibility of private persons being able to enforce directives against other individuals before national courts. In the leading case of *Marshall (1)*[190] the CJEU held that the doctrine of direct effect could not be utilised in the context of litigation fought out between two private parties. That case concerned a breach of EU employment legislation, namely the Sex Equality in Employment Directive.[191] Ms Marshall, an employee of local health authority in the UK, had been required to retire from her place of employment at the age of 60. The authority's policy was to apply a different retirement age for male staff (65), which did not appear to contravene national law at the time. Marshall took legal action before an industrial tribunal, submitting that her dismissal from employment violated the terms of the EU directive, which requires member states to ensure that the principle of equal treatment between the sexes as regards working conditions is adhered to within their respective territories. Whilst the CJEU, in a preliminary ruling, held that Marshall could rely upon the directive against organs of the state (which included, for this purpose a local authority) it clarified that a directive may not of itself impose obligations on individuals. The Court held that it was irrelevant in what capacity the organ of state was acting in the material case at hand (e.g. as employer or as public authority), holding that vertical direct effect could not be confined to situations where state-controlled authorities were simply taking decisions on behalf of the state.

The CJEU has confirmed the exclusion of horizontal direct effects of directives in a number of judgments subsequent to *Marshall (1)*.[192] It is clear that the position adopted by the Court limits the range of possibilities of EU environmental legislation being enforced in the member states.[193] Neither environmental protection authorities nor private persons (such as NGEOs) may be able to rely on the requirements set out in directives in order to enforce them directly against private persons acting in violation of those legal commitments. Given the clarity and steadfastness of the CJEU's position, it is no surprise that a case on horizontal direct effect of an environmental directive has yet to appear before the Court.

The case law has come in for a certain amount of criticism from certain quarters. For instance, in *Marshall (1)* the UK government opined that if the plaintiff were able to use direct effect against her public employer, this would mean that the application of the doctrine of direct effect as applied to norms contained in directives would result in some arbitrary results. Specifically, in the employment sector, employees of the private sector would be granted fewer rights under EU law than their counterparts working in public sector jobs. The CJEU responded to that point by noting that a member state should not be allowed to take advantage of its failure to transpose directives with such an argument, and was in a position to rectify such a state of affairs by properly transposing its obligations into national law.[194] Others have not been convinced by the Court's reasoning and have suggested that its denial of horizontal direct effects flowing from directives is ill-founded[195] as well as the opinions of three former Advocate Generals, namely Van Gerven, Jacobs and Lenz.[196] A number of reasons have been put forward to suggest a rethink on the 'horizontal' issue and apply horizontal direct effect to directives. Several of the key arguments are set out in Craig's seminal commentary[197] and which may be briefly referred to here. Specifically, he raises the point that the interpretation of the Court regarding Article 288(3) TFEU appears rather formalistic; the provision does not specifically rule out the possibility of directives binding individuals other than its addressees. In addition, he notes that the conferral of horizontal direct effect would not serve to collapse the distinction between directives and regulations, given that the former need not be addressed to all member states. Furthermore, since the entry into force of the TEU all EU directives are now required to be published in the Official Journal of the EU, so that individuals may have full knowledge of their contents from the outset of their entry into force; the principle of *nulla poena sine lege* is arguably no longer relevant to the debate. In addition, it is clear that the CJEU's case law has stretched its 'estoppel' line of reasoning to breaking point, in that public authorities derive obligations under the existing direct effect doctrine notwithstanding the absence of any culpability on their part in terms of the member state's failure to enact transposition legislation accurately reflecting the requirements of a directive and/or on time.[198] Finally, he correctly points out that the CJEU has conferred horizontal direct effects to certain EU treaty framework norms which specifically contain instructions directed solely at member states.[199] Other commentators have criticised the CJEU for applying the direct doctrine at all to directives, given the fact they are not, unlike regulations, described in the EU treaty framework as directly applicable.[200]

The coherence of the well-established position of the CJEU on excluding the possibility of directives creating legally enforceable obligations against in individuals has come into further question on account of judicial developments to have emerged since the 1990s. Specifically, as will be explored below, the Court has appeared to confirm in particular limited situations individuals may be burdened by the reliance upon directives by other individuals.

6.1.4.3 'Triangular' situations and indirect inverse effects of EU directives

One of the instances in which individuals may be subject to clear and foreseeable adverse implications as a result of reliance upon a directive is the situation often referred to as 'triangular'. A triangular scenario involves three players: a plaintiff who is a private individual, a defendant who is a state organ and a third party who is a private person. Typically, in such a situation, the plaintiff is ultimately aiming to alter the conduct of a private third party, and is able to achieve this by seeking to rely upon an EU directive against a state authority in order to achieve this result. This litigation technique may prove to be a very effective way in order to evade the CJEU's exclusion of horizontal direct effect for directives. In the environmental sector, a triangular situation may arise in a number of contexts where state authorities are involved in the licensing of the targeted activity as required by EU environmental legislation, such as in relation to building development or the approval of certain industrial activities such as waste management operations (e.g. landfilling of waste or waste incineration operations).

An interesting example of this arose in the recent case of *Delena Wells*.[201] In this case Wells, a private landowner, contested a decision by the UK Secretary of State for Transport, Local Government and the Regions to approve the grant of planning consent for the operation of a neighbouring quarry mine in Conygar, Wales, without having undertaken a prior environmental impact assessment. Under UK legislation at the material time, an impact assessment was not required in respect of old mines whose operations dated back before entry into force of the original version of the EIA Directive 85/337,[202] namely before 3 July 1988. The Conygar mine had originally been granted planning permission in 1947. It then fell into disuse for some 37 years before the site operators wished to revive operations by securing renewal of planning permission. Wells sought judicial review of the Secretary of State's decision not to revoke or modify the planning permission granted by the mineral planning authority in view of the fact that the planning permission process had not undergone an environmental impact assessment. The High Court of Justice of England and Wales, hearing the case, referred a number of legal questions to the CJEU under the preliminary ruling procedure, including whether such a project would have to be subject to an impact assessment under the EIA Directive and, if so, whether it would be open for a private person to rely upon the EIA Directive in this case, bearing in mind the limitations imposed by the CJEU in its jurisprudence in relation to the application of direct effect of directives in horizontal situations.

By way of initial comment the CJEU confirmed that that there is an obligation under Article 2(1) in conjunction with Article 4(2) of the EIA Directive to subject the reopening of a disused quarry mine to an impact assessment. It held that this was not a situation where key planning permission decision was decided before the entry into force of the directive; instead, the renewal of planning permission which was taken after that point served to replace the terms and substance of the initial original consent. This left the question as to whether Wells could be allowed to invoke the directive against the Secretary of State's decision, notwithstanding the foreseeable adverse consequences that would arise for another private person if she was successful in so doing. Specifically, an annulment of the approval of consent would render the planning permission decision void and bar the mining operator from commencing quarrying activity. The CJEU held that legal certainty did prevent directives from creating obligations for individuals,[203] including the situation where there is a state obligation directly linked to the performance of another obligation falling under the directive on a third party.[204] However, the Court made a distinction and exception where the invocation of direct effect against a state authority had 'mere adverse repercussions on the rights of third parties, even if the repercussions are certain'.[205] This was the case with respect to Wells's legal action against the Secretary of State, the adverse economic effects of which would be felt by the mining operators. As the CJEU pointed out, similar situations had already arisen in other cases which had come before it, such as the effects of its rulings in *Costanzo*[206] and *WWF v Bozen*,[207] both of which have been referred to earlier in this chapter. One could also mention in this context another case discussed earlier, namely the *Waddenzee* case,[208] which also involved potentially adverse repercussions for businesses which had applied to Dutch authorities to engage in cockle fishing in the inland water area known as the Waddenzee.

There is some considerable debate in the literature as to whether this body of jurisprudence developed by the CJEU is tantamount to the establishment of horizontal direct effect of directives through the back door in limited circumstances. Certainly, the rationale of the Court appears to tread a very fine line in distinguishing between vertical and horizontal case situations. On the one hand it appears to rule out the reliance upon directives by individuals against state authorities in order to enforce the latter to secure the fulfilment of specific duties envisaged in the directive for private persons. Such was the case for instance in *Daihatsu*[209] where the CJEU held that a plaintiff company could not rely upon a provision in the former First Companies Directive 68/151[210] in order to apply to a competent authority (a local court) to impose penalties upon a private person who had failed to ensure full disclosure of its annual accounts, a duty that member states had been required to ensure be carried out under the terms of the directive. On the other hand, the Court has, as discussed above, desisted from intervening against the use of vertical direct effect against state authorities in cases where clear adverse repercussions are likely to materialise as a result for private third parties, but who are not envisaged as having any specific obligations under the directive's terms.

This distinction appears to be a rather fine one and arguably is essentially arbitrary in nature. In particular, in the context of EU environmental legislation, it is evident that some licensing arrangements required by environmental directives may fall either side of the distinction made in *Delena Wells*. For instance, it would appear in the light of that judgment that individuals would be able to invoke the impact assessment requirements contained in the EIA Directive[211] as well site development procedures contained in the Habitats Directive[212] against state authorities in order to seek a cessation of development plans and projects wished to be carried out by a private person. This is notwithstanding that the EIA Directive envisages certain duties for the developer in relation to the EIA procedure (e.g. see Article 5(1)). However, it appears doubtful from the judgment in *Delena Wells* that an individual would be able to take legal action against a state authority and rely on the terms of the EU Waste Framework Directive[213] in order to restrain the activities of a waste management operator who has failed to obtain a waste permit from the authorities in accordance with the directive's requirements, given that the terms of the directive specifically refer to duties of such operators to obtain a permit. In a similar vein, it has also been argued that, in light of CJEU jurisprudence such as *Delena Wells*, direct effect may not apply in respect of certain aspects of the Environmental Liability Directive 2004/35 which are intended to result in obligations being imposed on operators of sites causing environmental damage.[214]

Arguably, the position adopted by the CJEU should be the exact reverse, given that the consequences envisaged for private individuals are spelled out clearly in the case of directives such as the Waste Framework Directive and are thus more transparent than those whose 'side effects' for individuals are less predictable. The literature appears somewhat divided on the issues surrounding triangular situations. Jans, for instance, has disputed that inverse effects emanating from vertical direct effect case scenarios should be equated with horizontal direct effect, given that the direct effects flow from the rights which the plaintiff derives and burdensome effects emanate from the failure of the member state authorities to fulfil their EU obligations.[215] Wyatt also agrees that the situations cannot be equated with one another.[216] However, Colgan supports the contrary opinion, focusing in particular on the fact that it is usually the case in such triangular situations that a private person, as opposed to a state authority, is subject *de facto* to a penalty, which runs counter to the 'estoppel' reasoning of the CJEU.[217] Lackhoff and Nyssens also submit that triangular situations involving adverse consequences for third parties are equivalent to horizontal direct effect scenarios, bearing in mind that the litigation concerned is motivated to seek the same result: namely the cessation of activities of one or more identifiable private persons.[218]

Apart from the academic controversy that surrounds the CJEU's evolution of indirect horizontal effects of directives through cases such as *Delena Wells*, it is clear that this body of jurisprudence does have potentially some implications for limiting possibilities for the enforcement of some elements of EU environmental legislation by private persons. The horizontal effects of directives effectively tolerated by the CJEU in situations like *Wells* do not appear to encompass those environmental directives which specifically envisage member states crystallising into national legislation specific duties for individuals. This limitation runs counter to the otherwise consistent approach of the CJEU not to allow member states to pray in aid the distortional effects that may be generated on the market as a result of a person being allowed to invoke a provision of a directive against a state authority.[219] In principle, it should not matter whether any reference to duties of individuals are contained in directives. If a norm in a directive meets the criteria of direct effect or sets down limits on the exercise of member state discretion for specific scenarios, then in accordance with the reasoning underpinning much of the CJEU's case law on legal effects of directives, individuals should be entitled to enforce such provisions before national courts against competent authorities that have failed to ensure that they are adhered to in matters falling within their jurisdiction. Inevitably, there will be some adverse economic consequences for some private persons if a competent authority is taken to court to ensure that EU environmental legislative requirements are respected. However, that is in essence a factor which does not have any substantial bearing on the legal position, given that adverse economic effects are going to result for various sectors of the economy and in society whenever public policy is executed. Opportunities for commercial and/or industrial activity are going to be curtailed in some fashion or other. In line with the comments made by Jans noted above, the root of the problem lies with member states failing to uphold their EU obligations, a situation that may be

readily resolved by them. It does not lie with the fact that the direct effect jurisprudence of the CJEU may give rise to individual burdens as well as rights.[220]

6.1.4.4 *Incidental horizontal effects*

A brief reference should also be made to another branch of the CJEU's case
law on legal effects of directives that appears to undermine its orthodox position
on ruling out horizontal effects of directives. In a few cases since the 1990s, the
CJEU has appeared to create an exception to the rule and endorsed the possibility of individuals being able to enforce certain types of directives against other
private persons before national courts. The cases have been commonly referred to
as those which the CJEU has appeared to legitimate 'incidental' horizontal effects
between private parties engaged in a civil legal dispute before a national court or
tribunal. This emerging body of case law may be distinguished from the triangular situation described in the previous section, where an individual seeks to effect
changes to conduct of another private person by bringing legal action against a
state authority. However, it is far from clear what the long-term implications of
this 'incidental effects' jurisprudence are on the main body of case law on direct
effect. Too few judgments have so far emerged which give a clear indication of its
parameters.

The leading case in this branch of jurisprudence is the *CIA Security* case.[221]
The plaintiff, a Belgian company called CIA Security, brought libel proceedings
against two rival Belgian companies which alleged that one of its security alarm
products failed to adhere to Belgian legislative requirements. The defendants
brought counterclaims, including a request for an order to restrain CIA Security
from continuing to operate as a trader in alarm systems in view of the fact that
CIA had not been granted authorisation as a security firm and had not received
approval for its security alarm product as required under Belgian legislation. The
Liège Commercial Court hearing the case decided to refer a number of questions
to the CJEU concerning the compatibility of the material Belgian legislation with
the EU Transparency Directive,[222] which lays down a procedure for the provision of information in the field of technical standards and regulations. Under the
terms of the Transparency Directive,[223] member states are required to notify the
Commission and other member states of draft technical regulations containing
technical specifications laying down mandatory characteristics of products other
than those implementing EU legislation. Member states are required to refrain
from adopting the draft regulations for a three-month standstill period, during
which the Commission and member states have an opportunity to assess whether
they might have adverse implications for the free movement of goods within
the EU. The standstill period is extended to six months in the event that either the
Commission or a member state is of the opinion that the draft measures must be
amended in order to eliminate or reduce barriers to trade that they might create,
or up to one year where the Commission indicates its intention to come forward
with legislative proposals or where a Union proposal is already before the Council of the EU. Effectively, the directive constitutes a mechanism through which

the Commission is able to monitor the legislative activities of member states that might interfere with the core principles of the internal market, namely the fundamental principle of free circulation of goods within the Union.

In the *CIA Security* case, the Belgian legislation in question had not been notified to the Commission prior to its promulgation, as required by the directive. A key question referred to the CJEU by the Belgian court was whether it was required to refuse to apply a national technical regulation not communicated to the Commission in accordance with the Transparency Directive. The CJEU held that the notification provisions in the directive met the criteria of direct effect, being sufficiently precise and unconditional. The Court affirmed that national regulations which contravened the notification provisions of the directive are inapplicable against individuals, notwithstanding the absence of an express provision to this effect in the EU legislative instrument.[224] In coming to this conclusion, it took particular account of the core aim of the directive to protect the freedom of goods by preventive control and that notification was essential to fulfil that purpose. It contrasted this position with that of the notification procedures envisaged in the (original version of the) Waste Framework Directive,[225] which it had held in the *Enichem Base* case[226] as not supporting an intention to render national rules unlawful which had not been notified prior to their enactment.[227] Finally, the CJEU made use of its *effet utile* reasoning in order to assist in the justification of its conclusions; specifically, the Court referred to the point that the effectiveness of EU controls over technical regulations of member states would be enhanced if the breach of notification obligations contained in the directive were to be interpreted as meaning that a substantial procedural defect had occurred so as to render the regulations inapplicable against individuals.[228]

Although the CJEU's judgment itself formally steers clear of engaging in the issues associated with horizontal direct effect, it is clear that the effect of its decision is to legitimise the enforcement of a directive by an individual against another before a national court. In so doing, the Court makes use of the principle of *effet utile* and stresses the interpretative duties of the national court, instead of referring to its traditional 'estoppel' reasoning. This is not surprising because it is difficult to see how in the case before it the Belgian state, as opposed to private litigants, is seeking to take advantage of a position that contravenes an EU directive. In *Unilever Italia*[229] the Court extended the reach of its judgment in *CIA Security* by confirming that the failure to adhere to the standstill period in the Transparency Directive is sufficient to render a national technical regulation inapplicable against individuals, even though the measure may have been notified to the Commission. The case involved a contractual dispute between two parties over the supply of a quantity of olive oil to Italy, which was in conformity with EU but not Italian labelling rules. The Italian rules had entered into force prior to the elapse of the standstill period envisaged under the directive. The CJEU held that national courts were obliged, in the context of civil proceedings between individuals, not to apply a national rule in contravention of the directive's notification procedures. It sought to differentiate the EU Transparency Directive from other directives so as to constitute a special legal situation, in which the standard rule on horizontal direct effect did not apply. The CJEU pointed out in this context that, unlike most other directives, the Transparency Directive does not envisage transposition of its requirements into national law and has concluded that as such it does not create substantive rights or obligations for individuals. The directive simply entitles individuals to invoke it in order to have national law in conflict with it set aside.[230]

The CJEU has, however, appeared to set limits as to the possibilities of individuals being able to invoke the Transparency Directive to the detriment of other private persons. Specifically, in the *Lemmens* case[231] the CJEU ruled out the possibility of a private individual relying upon the directive in order to render inapplicable a measure that did not hinder the use or marketing of a product within the internal market. It held that the failure to notify national regulations did not have the effect of rendering unlawful the use of the product in conformity with the national regulations.[232] In that case, a Dutch national had sought to undermine the evidence of his criminal conviction for drink driving by submitting that the Dutch legislation on breathalyser apparatus had not been notified to the Commission. The CJEU thereby made clear that the purpose of its judgment in *CIA Security* was to enhance the effectiveness of the principle of free movement of goods as furthered by the directive. One may contrast the approach of the CJEU in *CIA Security* and *Lemmens* with the *Enichem Base* case[233] discussed earlier in this chapter, where the Court refrained from utilising the effectiveness principle in coming to its legal conclusions in that case.

A few other cases involving different EU policy areas have had the effect of legitimising enforcement of certain directives as between individuals. One such example is the *Bernaldez* case.[234] The case concerned the extent of civil liability under the auspices of former Directive 72/166 on motor vehicle insurance.[235] As in *Lemmens*, the case involved an instance of drink driving; a Spanish driver had caused property damage to a third party whilst driving under the influence of alcohol. In the context of criminal proceedings brought against the driver (Bernaldez), the Spanish criminal court referred the case to the CJEU for advice on whether Spanish insurance rules were in compliance with the directive. Spanish insurance law purported to absolve a car insurer from liability in respect of property damage caused by an intoxicated driver. Article 3(1) of the 1972 directive stipulated that, subject to certain derogations not covering the subject matter addressed by the Spanish legislation, member states were obliged to take all appropriate measures to ensure that civil liability in respect of the use of vehicles was covered by insurance. That obligation has been developed and refined further by directives subsequent to the 1972 directive, to include compulsory cover specifically in respect of personal injury and property damage sustained in the event of a motor vehicle accident. The CJEU held that Article 3(1) of the 1972 directive, as amended, precluded an insurer from being able to rely upon national statutory provisions or contractual clauses to refuse to compensate third-party victims of an accident caused by the insured vehicle.[236] Another example is the *Panagis Pafitis* case[237] in which original shareholders of a Greek bank brought a civil action against the bank and new shareholders in respect of a decision to raise capital. The decision, which had been sanctioned under the auspices of Greek legislation

(Presidential Decree), had failed to respect the terms of former Directive 77/91[238] which required the convention of a general shareholders' meeting to decide such a capital increase. In a preliminary ruling, the CJEU held that the directive precluded national rules which permitted an increase in capital. Similarly, in *Smith-kline Beecham*[239] the CJEU held, in the context of a dispute between two private parties over the marketing of a brand of toothpaste, that a 1976 directive on the marketing of cosmetics[240] prevented the application of national legislation restricting particular types of toothpaste marketing in contravention of the directive's requirements.

The emergence of a number of cases involving 'incidental' horizontal effects of directives in the context of legal disputes between individuals has caused a good deal of confusion as well as speculation in the literature as to whether the CJEU is in effect beginning to retreat from its orthodox position against horizontal direct effect of directives. It appears that so far it has done so clearly only in relation to the application of the Transparency Directive, by virtue of its jurisprudence in the *CIA Security* and *Unilever* cases. Some, however, have questioned whether this might be genuinely the case, on the basis that had the competent authorities in this line of cases sought to enforce their national rules against persons such as CIA Security, the latter would be able to utilise the concept of vertical direct effect to shield themselves from liability under national law.[241] Hilson and Downes have sought to reconcile the case law with the CJEU's traditional position by pointing to the 'public law' elements evident in the cases; namely that one of the private parties to the dispute was seeking to enforce national, public statutory rules.[242] Other commentators have pointed out that a common feature of the cases appears to be that the CJEU is keen to prevent private persons from being able to exercise an unfair advantage over others, as a result of a failure on the part of a member state to adhere to its obligations under directives which do not directly impose obligations on individuals. The provisions of national rules which conflict with such EU directives are set aside with the result that a private person is subject to a liability or disadvantage which they would not otherwise have escaped but for the conflicting national legislation.[243] This interpretation of judicial developments has close links with Advocate General Leger's analysis in his Opinion in the *Linster* case[244] in which he has made the distinction between a directive being invoked by an individual in order to substitute as opposed to exclude a rule of national law in conflict with a directive.[245] However, the CJEU has so far not adopted that distinction.

The above-mentioned interpretations of the CJEU's case law have not, however, managed to square the circle and find a credible distinction between the incidental horizontal effect cases and orthodox judgments on horizontal direct effect of directives. For instance, the 'public law' analysis has been criticised for failing to account for the instances where a private party has sought to enforce contractual obligations on another.[246] The 'substitution–exclusion' distinction floated by Advocate General Leger does not provide a comprehensive account of the case law. The CJEU has not taken up the 'substitution–exclusion' formulation, although having been provided the opportunity to do so. For instance, as was discussed earlier in the chapter, the CJEU failed to apply such a distinction in the *Enichem Base* case,[247] a case where the CJEU had an opportunity to apply its 'incidental effects' reasoning. The judgment in *El Corte Ingles*[248] provides another example, where the CJEU did not instruct the national court to disapply the part of the Spanish Civil Code which prevented her from securing an appropriate remedy against a finance company in line with the rights envisaged under the terms of the directive in question, but instead held to the line that directives could not have horizontal direct effects. Even if adopted by the Court at some stage, the application of a 'substitution–exclusion' test would, in any event, generate an arbitrary and unfair division between success and failure in terms enforcing directives by private parties within the member states. Whereas individuals would not be able to enforce their rights against private persons in those member states which had not adopted any legislation to implement a directive, individuals in other member states which had adopted (conflicting) national rules would potentially be in a more advantageous position in potentially being able to ensure that the directive could be enforced (albeit in a limited sense) by having the conflicting national rules set aside by national courts. Finally, the case law on incidental horizontal effects appears to run counter to the CJEU's traditional instructions to member state courts on the issue of interpreting national legislation in line with directives (indirect effect). This area will be addressed in section 6.2 of this chapter.

The above outline of the CJEU's case law on the incidental effect of directives indicates that it has delivered some recent judgments which are most difficult to reconcile with traditional principles pertaining to the direct effect of directives. Of particular concern appears to be the level of uncertainty as to when the Court will be prepared to instruct a national court to disapply a national rule in conflict with a directive, where the case referred to it from the national court concerns a legal dispute between private litigants. The only element of certainty appears to be its preparedness to apply a different set of criteria consistently in relation to the Transparency Directive. It is difficult to see how this particular line of cases may or will assist in the private law enforcement of EU environmental directives against private persons which contravene environmental protection requirements contained in such legislative instruments. The state of the law in light of these judicial developments is at an uncertain and unclear stage. In principle, though, it would now appear at least conceivable that a private individual or entity might be able to use the judgments in *Bernaldez*, *Pafitis* and *Smithkline Beecham* as precedents for the purpose of assisting the pursuit of civil action[249] or, where permitted under national law, a private prosecution against companies whose activities have been legitimised by national rules in conflict with EU environmental legislation. However, given the fact that environmental law enforcement in general is heavily dependent, from both a technical as well as practical perspective, upon the ability of public law agencies to intervene to uphold legally binding environmental protection standards, any legal opportunities facilitating the possibility for private actors to enforce (EU) environmental law against private operators is likely to have a relatively slight impact in practice for the foreseeable future terms of enhancing the state of compliance with the law. Factors such as legal costs, length of proceedings, complexity of subject matter, paucity of powers to obtain and/or search for hard evidence of non-compliance all serve to make the horizontal enforcement scenario of EU environmental directives in the form of a legal action between private disputants a pretty rare event. Instead, private enforcement of environmental directives via the 'triangular' route described in section 6.1.4.3 above would appear to be much more of a fruitful course of action to undertake.

6.1.4.5 Impact of unwritten general principles of EU law

One other significant qualification to the general rule against horizontal direct effect of directives has been the impact of general principles of EU law (as outlined in section 6.1.1 above), which individuals have on a number of occasions been able to rely upon directly before national courts of the EU member states. This was exemplified in the *Mangold* case[250] in which a German employee was able to invoke the general principle of non-discrimination against his employer, who had required his dismissal on grounds of age. The CJEU confirmed that the German court adjudicating the employment dispute should set aside any national provisions that conflicted with the EU principle of non-discrimination on grounds of age, notwithstanding that the deadline for transposing the EU's Framework Employment Directive 2000/78,[251] which specifically prohibited ageism in employment relations, had at the material time not yet expired. The general principles of EU law have also been of service to private entities, such as NGEOs, in seeking to enforce EU environmental obligations. The general principles of effectiveness as well as precaution have been significant in this respect.

For instance, in the *Lesoochranárske zoskupenie VLK* case[252] the CJEU confirmed that the principle of effectiveness requires national courts of the member states to ensure that national law is interpreted as far as possible in line with the requirements of Article 9(3) of the 1998 Århus Convention regarding access to environmental justice for members of the public.[253] In *Lesoochranárske zoskupenie VLK* an NGEO considered that Slovakian authorities had breached the requirements of the Habitats Directive 92/43 on prohibition of hunting of protected wild fauna by permitting the hunting of brown bears. The NGEO wished to challenge the decision by way of judicial review before the Slovakian courts; however under rules of Slovakian law at the time it was denied the possibility of having the requisite legal standing to seek a judicial review of the authority's decision. A question arose as to whether the NGEO could rely upon the requirements of Article 9(3) of the Århus Convention as a matter of EU law, given that the Union is a contracting party. No secondary EU law had been adopted (and at the time of writing still has not been adopted) to implement the requirements of Article 9(3) of the Århus Convention in relation to decisions taken at member state level. The CJEU confirmed that the requirements of the Convention constitute a source of Union law, given that the EU ratified the international agreement. Notwithstanding that the Court considered that Article 9(3) did not fulfil the requirements of direct effect, it nevertheless held that the provision has residual legal impact in the sense that the principle of effectiveness applied with respect to it. Accordingly, the CJEU held that individuals are able to utilise the general principle of effectiveness as a means of ensuring that national courts interpret national rules

on access to justice as far as possible in accordance with the requirements of Article 9(3). This translates to mean that if it is possible for a national court to construe
national rules on access to justice in line with Århus in accordance with national
rules on the interpretation of national law, then the national court is obliged to
apply such an interpretation. The judgment of the CJEU in *Lesoochranárske zoskupenie
VLK* is similar in approach to the requirements it has set down for national courts in
construing national law in line with EU directives (so-called 'indirect effect' doctrine)
which is considered in the next section.

In the *Waddenzee* case[254] the legal impact of the precautionary principle came
under scrutiny. Specifically, a Dutch court raised the question with the CJEU by
way of a preliminary ruling request as to what extent the precautionary principle,
one of the environmental protection principles mentioned in Article 191 TFEU,
was applicable in terms of the operation of the Habitats Directive. Two environmental associations had claimed that an authorisation of cockle fishing in the
Waddenzee inland water zone had failed to comply with the impact assessment
requirements set out in Article 6(3) Habitats Directive. Article 6(3) predicates the
obligation to carry out an impact assessment on the project or plan in question
being 'likely to have a significant effect' on the site's management. A question
arose as to what extent Article 6(3) should be read in light of the precautionary
principle, notwithstanding the absence of an express legal reference to the principle and its specific application in the directive.

The CJEU confirmed that the competent national authorities had an implicit
obligation to respect the principle in connection with exercising judgment over
the application of Article 6(3) of the Habitats Directive. The CJEU referred to
the principle as one of the foundations underpinning the commitment to a high
level of environmental protection governing EU environmental policy, in accordance with Article 191(2) TFEU. Notwithstanding the absence of an express legal
reference to the principle in the EU directive, the Court was prepared effectively
to interpret that it was necessarily an integral part of the construction and component of the directive, given that the legislative instrument was predicated upon
the environmental principles that formed core elements of EU environmental
policy. Accordingly, competent authorities were obliged to apply Article 6(3) in
light of the principle. The CJEU considered that such authorities were obliged
to carry out an impact assessment in the case of there being either a probability or a risk that the project/plan would have significant effects.[255] In assessing
the factor of risk, the precautionary principle would be applicable, so that an
authority would have to make a finding that a risk was present if significant effects
could not be excluded on the basis of objective information such as scientific studies. Specifically, in cases of doubt as to absence of significant effects, an impact
assessment would have to be carried out. Such an interpretation, the Court held,
was consonant with the promotion of the biodiversity objective underpinning the
directive.[256] The Court used similar reasoning to require incorporation of the
precautionary principle into the authorisation criteria specified in the second sentence of Article 6(3). Only where no 'reasonable scientific doubt' existed over the
absence of adverse effects to the integrity of the site would authorisation for the

plan/project be granted.[257] Elsewhere, the Court has held that the precautionary principle is implicitly incorporated into the obligations contained in environmental directives. An example is the *Fornasar* case,[258] where the CJEU held the principle to be an implicit part of the basic safety obligations contained in Article 4 of the original version of the Waste Framework Directive (Directive 75/442).[259] By implication, other environmental principles specified in Article 191(2) TFEU are relevant in this regard. Effectively, the CJEU has enhanced the potentiality of these principles to be enforced at national level, in that their incorrect application may be subject ultimately to judicial scrutiny in the context of judicial review proceedings brought by private in respect of planning decisions made by national authorities covered, *inter alia*, by the EIA, Habitats and/or Wild Birds Directives, or indeed in respect of any decisions involving discretionary assessment coming under the auspices of EU environmental legislation

6.2 Indirect effect and EU environmental law

Distinct from its direct effect jurisprudence, the CJEU has developed a body of case law intended to assist individuals as well as public authorities in being able to secure proper enforcement of EU directives at national level. Specifically, the Court has established that a basic legal duty under EU law befalls the national courts, in particular derived from the general obligations flowing from both Article 4(3) TEU and Article 288(3) TFEU, to seek to construe national law in line with the requirements of EU directives insofar as is possible so to do under national law. This body of precedent established by the CJEU has become known as the legal doctrine of 'indirect effect' or 'sympathetic interpretation' in EU law. The doctrine has traditionally been relevant and of some use to individuals who have been unable to utilise the doctrine of direct effect, on account of the fact that provisions of the material directive they wish to enforce may not fulfil the standard criteria of sufficient precision and unconditionality.

6.2.1 General points

The doctrine of indirect effect, as it has become known, was first clearly applied by the CJEU in the case of *Von Colson*.[260] The case involved application of the Sex Equality in Employment Directive[261] which requires that member states ensure that equal working conditions for men and women are respected by employers. Specifically, Ms von Colson, had suffered discrimination on grounds of sex in having been rejected for a position as a social worker in a German male prison on account of her being a woman. She sought to claim compensation through civil action before the German courts. Article 6 of the original 1976 version of the EU directive (former Directive 76/207), the relevant provision on remedies in respect of breaches of equal treatment principles set out in the directive, was couched in general terms requiring member states to ensure that claimants are enabled 'to pursue their claims by judicial process after possible recourse to other competent authorities'. Notably, the provision did not specify a particular remedy or range of remedies that must be afforded to a claimant; this matter was left to the member states to determine.[262] Von Colson's judicial remedy available under German law at the time appeared to be based upon traditional principles of compensation relating to tortious claims, namely the right to claim for losses on a retrospective basis (i.e. those losses actually sustained as a result of the illicit act until judgment). Compensation in respect of loss of employment opportunity was potentially ruled out, although the national court hearing the case considered the national legal position to be ambiguous. If compensation would be construed on an actual loss basis, von Colson would have merely been entitled to reimbursement of the travel and postal expenses involved in securing an interview. The national court referred to the CJEU for a preliminary ruling, requesting, *inter alia*, advice on the nature of judicial remedy required to be afforded to victims of sex discrimination under Article 6 of former Directive 76/207. The CJEU initially confirmed that Article 6 was insufficiently precise a provision to have direct effects. It held though that it contained an implicit obligation on member states to ensure that judicial remedies afforded to victims of discrimination were to be effective so as to constitute a sufficient deterrent to employers not to engage in discriminatory practices and policies in the working environment. The Court proceeded to hold that the national courts were obliged under a basic duty of EU law to construe national legislation and in particular its provisions intended to implement the directive 'in the light of the wording and purpose of the directive in order to achieve the result referred to in [Article 288(3) TFEU]'.[263] However, later in its judgment it added an important qualification to the duty, namely that a national court is obliged to construe national law to be in accordance with the terms of directives 'in so far as it is given discretion to do so under national law'.[264]

The CJEU has further refined the general principles of the indirect effect doctrine since the *Von Colson* case. Specifically, in *Marleasing*[265] it confirmed that the doctrine applies also to cases involving exclusively private litigants, so that individuals are able to utilise the doctrine to their advantage against other private persons. That case also confirmed that the doctrine applied irrespective of when national legislation is passed, specifically whether it is has been enacted either before or after the directive's entry into force. The CJEU has thereby confirmed that the legal effect of a directive cannot be negated by any existing national constitutional principles which stipulate that later statutes shall take precedence over earlier ones.[266] In *Pfeiffer*, the CJEU clarified the broad scope of the indirect effect doctrine in requiring national courts to consider whether national law as a whole, not simply the provisions of any implementing national legislation, may be construed so as to ensure conformity with a directive's requirements.[267]

However, the principles of indirect effect elaborated in the case law of the CJEU have had less impact on the operation of national law than the direct effect doctrine. This is for the reason that, as far as indirect effect is concerned, the Court has qualified the application of the supremacy principle in the context of indirect effect. Specifically, it has made the application of indirect effect conditional upon the extent to which the law of a member state permits its courts to construe national legislation in line with the terms of directives.[268] For instance, under rules of construction of national legislation applied by the UK courts, it appears that the judiciary are not prepared to distort the meaning of a statute so that it be in accordance with an EU directive where this would conflict with the ordinary meaning of the national legislation.[269] Exceptions though may be made to this rule where the national legislation is clearly intended to transpose a directive.[270] Whilst the UK courts have indicated that they will be prepared to accommodate the indirect effect doctrine in cases where the national legislation is ambiguous or otherwise open to interpretation, it is clear that they will not interpret a statute *contra legem*, as this would be a step tantamount to undermining the fundamental UK constitutional principle of parliamentary sovereignty.

Accordingly, it can be seen that the case law of the CJEU on indirect effect doctrine does not impose an absolute duty upon national courts to construe national law in line with EU directives, but one conditional upon the requirements of member state's rules on statutory construction. Although the indirect effect doctrine therefore serves to underpin the general principle of supremacy of EU law,[271] it invokes a softer enforcement of that principle than the direct effect doctrine. The indirect effect doctrine does, however, have the advantage over the doctrine of direct effect of being able to be used in order to assist in the enforcement of non-directly effective provisions of directives. It may also be utilised by both private persons as well as state authorities; however, as will be evident from the next section, the latter have in practice only limited possibilities to apply it in order to enforce directives against individuals in criminal law contexts.

6.2.2 Indirect effect and liability under criminal or administrative law

In a series of judgments the CJEU has clarified that there are specific limits on the extent to which the indirect effect doctrine may be used in order to enforce the requirements contained in directives against private persons. This issue has arisen on a number of occasions, directly and indirectly, in connection with criminal prosecutions taken against individuals in respect of failures to adhere to particular minimum environmental protection standards. A primary example is the *Arcaro* case.[272] The case concerned the prosecution of a the legal representative of a precious metals company in connection with the violation of Italian criminal law on industrial discharges of dangerous substances into a river. The Italian criminal legislation in question had been enacted with a view to implementing a number of EU directives on dangerous substance discharges, including former Directive 76/464 on pollution caused by certain dangerous substances discharged into the aquatic environment[273] as well as former Directive 83/513 on limit values and quality objectives for cadmium discharges.[274] Arcaro was prosecuted under the Italian law for failing to apply for a discharge authorisation in respect of his company's operations. Article 3 of Directive 76/464 provided that all discharges of substances listed in its Annex 'shall require prior authorisation of the competent authority concerned'. However, the Italian legislation made a distinction regarding authorisations between new plants and those existing before its entry into force (old plants). Exceptionally, old plants would not have to apply for authorisation for discharges until the adoption of specific ministerial decrees on emission limits, which had not yet been passed. Arcaro submitted that his plant was an old plant for the purposes of the Italian law and would not be obliged to obtain a discharge authorisation until adoption of ministerial decrees on emission limits pertaining to such plants. The Italian magistrates' court hearing the case, decided to refer to the CJEU for advice on whether Directive 76/464 was directly effective and whether any other method of procedure could be used to achieve elimination from national legislation of provisions incompatible with EU law.

On the issue of direct effect, the Court reiterated its established position from earlier cases[275] that the doctrine of direct effect could not be used to secure criminal liability of individuals:

> [T]he Court has also ruled that a directive cannot, of itself and independently of a national law adopted by a member state for its implementation, have the effect of determining or aggravating the liability in criminal law of persons who act in contravention of the provisions that directive . . .[276]

Turning to the national court's second question, the CJEU noted initially that no method of procedure under EU law existed allowing a national court to eliminate national rules contrary to a directive. However, it then confirmed the specific interpretative obligations under EU law that national courts were to fulfil when construing national law. Specifically, it confirmed the general principle set out in *Marleasing* that national courts, called upon to interpret national law, are required to do so, as far as possible, in the light of the purpose and wording of the directive in order to achieve the result pursued by that directive.[277] The CJEU then held that there was a limit to that particular duty:

> However, that obligation of the national court to refer to the content of the directive when interpreting the relevant rules of its own national law reaches a limit where such an interpretation leads to the imposition on an individual of an obligation laid down in a directive which has not been transposed or, more especially, where it has the effect of determining or aggravating, on the basis of the directive and in the absence of a law enacted for its implementation, the liability in criminal law of persons who act in contravention of that directive's provisions.[278]

Accordingly, *Arcaro* confirmed that EU directives may not be relied upon in order to establish or aggravate criminal liability before national courts.[279] The Court's position is in alignment and is consistent with the one adopted by it in relation to the issue of inverse direct effect discussed in section 6.1.4.1 above.

The impact of the *Arcaro* judgment with regard to the issue of enforceability of EU environmental directives against private persons is significant. The Court has effectively ruled out the possibility of either a private person or state authority using the doctrine of indirect effect in order to require national courts to interpret national environmental legislation in line with EU environmental directives so as to compel individuals and private legal persons to adhere to legislative obligations enshrined in those directives. This limitation to the application of indirect effect also applies where national law is ambiguous, namely a situation where an interpretation in accordance with the terms of the directive would not constitute a distortion to the ordinary meaning of the national provision(s) concerned. The judgment may also appear, given its broad terms, to exclude the possibility of state authorities applying the indirect effect doctrine to determine or aggravate liability under national administrative law in respect of breaches of environmental standards stipulated in EU environmental directives. If the aim of legal action at national level is to achieve enforcement of an obligation under a directive, the mode of enforcement should not affect the basic position favoured by the CJEU in general that obligations for individuals should not flow from directives, but instead from national implementing legislation. Subsequent to *Arcaro* the CJEU has also confirmed that it would not be permissible for a national court to interpret national tax law in light of an EU directive where this would be tantamount to the imposition of an obligation set out in the directive itself.[280] This indicates that the principles set down by the CJEU in *Arcaro* also apply in the context of administrative law, not only criminal law. Accordingly, it would not be permissible for a national environmental authority to seek to rely upon a minimum environmental standard contained in an EU environmental directive against a private person (whether a corporate entity or a natural person).

It would appear, though, that outside the context of criminal and administrative liability, the application of the indirect effect doctrine may be utilised with the consequence of private persons being subject to a detriment of some kind.[281] Notably, the CJEU has appeared to confirm that the indirect effect doctrine may be used quite effectively in contractual disputes. This was illustrated in the *Centrosteel*[282] case where an Italian company, Centrosteel, sued for payment under a commercial agency contract from Adipol, an Austrian company. Adipol claimed that the contract should be deemed void on the grounds that Centrosteel had failed to comply with Italian legal requirements of compulsory registration of commercial agents. Centrosteel counter-claimed that the Italian legal requirements, being contrary to an EU directive's[283] stipulation that a commercial agency agreement only needs to be in written form, should be disapplied by the Italian court adjudicating the dispute. In a preliminary ruling the CJEU held that the national court should interpret the national law in light of the EU directive, with the result that the contract would be enforceable against Adipol.[284] This line of CJEU jurisprudence may well have implications for the environmental sector, particularly in the context of contractual arrangements between national authorities and service providers that are struck for the purpose of fulfilling particular requirements of EU environmental directives. The case law implies, for instance, that a national authority would be able to rely upon the terms of a directive in accordance with EU principles of interpretation and enforce these against a service provider even where the application of domestic civil law principles might lead to a different result.

Overall, though, the state of the CJEU's jurisprudence on the rules underpinning the doctrine of indirect effect remains rather unclear and would appear to be in a state of flux. On the one hand, the Court has for the most part stuck to the general proposition that the indirect effect doctrine is not absolute in requiring national courts to interpret national rules of law in line with the requirements of EU directives. The obligation applies in the words of the CJEU 'in so far as possible', namely to the extent that national rules on interpretation of legal sources would permit this. In addition, the CJEU has also confirmed that the indirect effect doctrine may not lead to the creation or aggravation of a private person's liability under national criminal or administrative law. On the other hand, the CJEU has also introduced some qualifications and exceptions to this approach, notably with respect to the impact of EU directives with regard to how they might affect a private person's liability under national civil law as indicated in cases such as *Centrosteel*. Within the Court itself there have also been calls effectively for the development of a stricter approach concerning the duties incumbent on national courts with respect to interpreting national law in line with EU directives. Notably, Advocate General Saggio has requested the CJEU to modify and simplify the existing principles of indirect effect by requiring national courts in general to exclude the application of national rules which conflict with provisions in EU directives, whilst not substituting them with the contents of the conflicting provisions of directives unless these are directly effective in relation to the case at hand.[285] The CJEU has, though, so far not (expressly at least) adopted the 'exclusion–substitution' formula. Such a proposal would, however, if accepted result in liabilities and burdens arising for private individuals which would not otherwise be envisaged under national law,[286] not that different in substance from the adverse impact of a statutory obligation being imposed.

There are also strong grounds for the CJEU to develop possibilities for national authorities and/or private persons such as NGEOs pursuing (non-criminal) public interest litigation against private persons to be able to utilise the indirect effect doctrine as a means of ensuring that EU (environmental) directives are adhered to notwithstanding that existing national rules of law may be in conflict with a particular directive. Such a development would render the indirect effect doctrine more effective from the perspective of EU environmental law enforcement. The fact that a defendant in administrative or civil law proceedings is a private person should not make any difference with respect to the upholding of EU legislation, such as an environmental directive, which is intended to be applicable to the public at large not just with respect to national authorities.

6.3 Concluding remarks

The above exploration of the CJEU's case law reveals that the Court has developed some important legal principles concerning the rights and responsibilities of stakeholders involved in the enforcement of EU environmental law.

Significantly, the doctrine of direct effect in combination with the principle of EU law supremacy has established the possibility for private individuals to be able to rely upon sufficiently precise and unconditional provisions of environmental directives which guarantee minimum public health standards or environmental protection standards directly against member state public authorities in environmental matters falling within their particular remit of responsibility. The case law on the direct effect of directives has been further refined by the CJEU to enable private persons (such as NGEOs) to rely upon provisions in directives that limit the scope of discretion afforded to public authorities regarding their decisions affecting the environment, as demonstrated in cases such as *Kraaijeveld*. This line of jurisprudence has effectively opened up new possibilities for judicial review of environmental decision-making, such as in the area of environmental impact assessment where member state authorities are obliged to ensure that a project listed in Annex II of the EIA Directive[287] is subject to prior impact assessment where it is likely to have 'significant effects' on the environment. The CJEU has confirmed that private persons may rely upon such provisions in EU directives before national courts in order to ensure that the exercise of discretion by public authorities has not been exceeded. The Court's jurisprudence has also confirmed that national courts are obliged under Article 4(3) TEU to construe national legislation in line with EU directives insofar as this is possible to achieve under national law (so-called 'indirect effect' doctrine) as confirmed in cases such as *Marleasing*.

Whilst opening up actual and potential avenues in terms of enabling private persons to enforce EU environmental legislation, the CJEU's case law has, at the same time, some notable limitations. In relation to the direct effect doctrine, the CJEU has ruled out (for the most part) the possibility of directives imposing obligations on individuals, with the notable exception of the EU Transparency Directive.[288] The CJEU's rejection of horizontal effects of EU directives has the consequence of restricting the possibilities of state agencies as well as private persons being able to enforce requirements in EU environmental directives against private polluters who fail to adhere to those requirements where the member state has not implemented the requirements of the directives correctly into national law and/or by the requisite deadline (issues of inverse and horizontal direct effect). In relation to the indirect effect doctrine, the CJEU has curtailed its application so as to exclude the possibility of allowing it to be used in national courts in order to determine or aggravate criminal or administrative liability on the part of a private person. Once again, this places a brake on the possibility of EU environmental law being enforced more effectively against private polluters. In addition, the restrictions on direct and indirect effects of EU directives may raise difficulties in situations where private entities, contracted to carry out projects or tasks on behalf of public authorities, fail to adhere to an EU environmental directive's requirements where the directive has not yet been correctly transposed into national law. The jurisprudence of the CJEU appears to rule out the possibility of any direct imposition of obligations contained in directives on private persons in this type of scenario, unless they may be deemed to be an 'emanation of the state' in the sense of the *Foster* judgment.[289] In the wake of increased privatisation and contracting out of public service provision in a number of EU states, this limitation on effects of directives may come to have a more prominent impact in future.

Overall, the CJEU's stance against horizontal and inverse direct effect of directives appears difficult to justify and warrants review. The arguments in favour of excluding the possibility of private persons being subject directly to obligations under EU directives are ultimately no longer compelling (for this author at least). One might argue that, at its root, an EU directive is a legislative instrument addressed to member states and not to private individuals (as defined in Article 288(3) TFEU) and accordingly responsibility for ensuring that the requirements of directives are carried out fall primarily on the shoulders of member states and their representative governments, not on private individuals. By contrast, an EU regulation is defined in Article 288(2) TFEU as being 'directly applicable' and 'generally binding', without the need for further legislative implementation at national level (unless its terms so require). So, in the event of a failure on the part of member state to transpose a directive's requirements correctly into national law, one might at first sight have some sympathy with the CJEU's reluctance to displace the legal responsibility for that transposition failure onto private individuals and companies.

However, those concerns are misplaced for a variety of reasons. Notably, the EU treaty definition of a directive in Article 288(3) TFEU does not expressly rule out horizontal effects. Moreover, affirmation of horizontal direct effect for directives would not collapse the distinction between EU regulations and EU directives, given that they may be still distinguished from each other by the fact that a directive need not be addressed to all member states. The CJEU's own jurisprudence has recognised the possibility of EU treaty provisions having horizontal direct effects notwithstanding that they are expressed, on the face of it, as being addressed to member states (e.g. as in the *Defrenne (2)* case).[290] The Court has also contradicted its own position in having established an exception to the rule with respect to the Transparency Directive in 'incidental effects' cases such as *CIA Security*, in respect of which the CJEU has failed to provide a convincing justification. In addition, in a number of other exceptional cases the CJEU has appeared to confirm that private persons may be entitled to rely upon directives in the context of 'horizontal' disputes with other private persons with the result that the latter may suffer a detriment of some kind (e.g. being unable to rely upon national rules where they conflict with an EU directive as in *Centrosteel*). In other instances, the CJEU has occasionally made use of unwritten general principles of EU law as a means of evading the problem of the rule against horizontal direct effects of directives, as in the *Mangold* case.[291] Finally, it is important to note that directives are instruments that are publicly debated and disclosed legislative instruments; it would be a specious argument to suggest that directives are measures determined far removed from public scrutiny and decided in essence through intergovernmental negotiations behind closed doors. Since the 1992 Maastricht Treaty, it has been obligatory for all EU directives to be published in the Union's Official

Journal.[292] The legislative process underpinning the adoption of EU directives, such as that applicable to the environmental sector, involves three readings by the European Parliament. Throughout the legislative process, including even before the Commission comes forward with draft proposals, there are ample opportunities for lobbying and stakeholder consultation. In the environment sector, it is standard procedure for the Commission to consult with stakeholders in the civic sector (such as European business associations as well as NGEOs). Throughout the legislative process, details of legislative proposals, amendments and final measures are published in real time on the EU's *europa* website. Accordingly, it is not tenable to suggest that the public at large (particularly commerce and industry affected) may not be deemed to have constructive knowledge of their contents or that recognition of directly effective obligations for individuals under directives would be tantamount to a retrospective application of legislation. With the entry into force of the 2007 Lisbon Treaty, the CJEU has an opportunity to change course. In particular, Lisbon has introduced a specific new commitment in the EU's foundational treaty framework within Article 19(2) TEU, namely the obligation on member states 'to provide remedies sufficient to ensure effective judicial protection in the fields covered by Union law'. Arguably, seen from a broad teleological perspective, this new treaty provision would justify a move by the CJEU to terminate its long-standing rejection of horizontal direct effect of directives as a means of assisting in the fulfilment of the requirements underpinning Article 19(2) TEU.

Whilst one might query the CJEU's decisions on the limits of legal effects of EU directives, there is little doubt that the root problem lies with the ambiguities inherent in the definition of directives as set out in Article 288(3) TFEU. Directives are defined as being 'addressed' to member states and requiring transposition into national law at national level where national legislatures are to choose the 'form and methods' of transposition. At the same time, the EU treaty provision stipulates that directives are 'binding, as to result to be achieved'. This definition raises questions and doubts as to whether Union directives are designed or intended to enable individuals to rely upon them and enforce them directly before national courts prior to the national legislative implementation phase has been completed. The CJEU has had to wrestle with these textual ambiguities and has evolved its own conclusions regarding legal problems thrown up by failures on the part of member states to implement EU directives fully and/or on time. Some of its conclusions have facilitated the possibilities for private law enforcement of EU environmental law, notably the affirmation that directives may be capable of having vertical direct effects. Other conclusions are more questionable and have potentially served to undermine greater involvement of the private sector (notably NGEOs) in EU environmental law enforcement, in particular the rejection by the CJEU of directives being capable of imposing directly effective obligations on private polluters (in non-criminal proceedings).

The difficulties and limitations surrounding the extent of enforceability of EU directives that stem from their statutory definition raise the question as to whether the legislative instrument of a directive is the most appropriate legal form in which to house EU environmental protection requirements. The element of national transposition foreseen for EU directives is arguably a major weakness, rather than strength, not least seen in an environmental context. As was discussed in Part I of this book, the infringement procedures in Articles 258 and 260 TFEU continue to be used very frequently by the European Commission in response to shortcomings on the part of member states in transposing EU environmental directives. As has been appraised in this chapter, the writ of the directive is limited when it comes to enforcement of its obligations against private polluters. Accordingly, there is a strong argument for the European Union institutions involved in the legislative process (Commission, European Parliament and Council of the EU) to review their current preference for the directive as a legislative vehicle for EU environmental policy. Instead of the directive, the appropriate instrument of first choice should be the regulation, which is recognised by the CJEU as being capable of horizontal direct effect, and in respect of which a transposition phase is not foreseen in its statutory definition in Article 288(2) TFEU (but which may stipulate the need for national implementing rules where appropriate). The Commission currently uses the format of regulation relatively rarely in the EU environmental policy area, primarily for economic[293] as opposed to environmental protection reasons. What is the justification, though, from an environmental protection perspective, for housing minimum binding standards on the trade in endangered species in a legal framework that is more effective from a law enforcement perspective than minimum standards on air or water quality? The EU needs to ensure that its choices of legislative instrument for the delivery of its environmental policy meet its constitutional commitment to ensure a 'high level of protection and improvement of the quality of the environment' throughout the Union.[294] That commitment must surely support the use of the most effective legislative instruments available to the Union for the purposes of assisting in the due enforcement of EU environmental protection obligations.

Notes

1 See Art. 24 TEU which rules out adoption of legislative acts and limits the jurisdiction of the CJEU to scrutinising whether CFSP acts are *ultra vires* in encroaching upon on other areas of EU policy.
2 Under the 1992 Maastricht Treaty the sectors of non-EU national migration as well as co-operation in criminal matters (so-called 'third-pillar' matters) were under the aegis of Title VI TEU. Direct effect for third-pillar measures was expressly ruled out (Art. K.6(2) TEU). By virtue of the 1997 Amsterdam Treaty the material scope of the third pillar was reduced to including the area of co-operation in criminal matters (former Arts. 29–42 TEU), with immigration being transferred to the supranational first pillar of the former EC Treaty (Title IV of the former EC Treaty).
3 Art. 1 TEU and Art. 1 TFEU.
4 As set out in COM(2008)773 final, Commission Communication, *Implementing European Community Environmental Law*, 18 November 2008. See discussion on prioritisation in Ch. 5.
5 Somsen (2001), p. 326.
6 Krämer (1991), p. 48.

7 COM(96)500, p. 11.
8 Somsen (2001), p. 311.
9 Grant, Matthews and Newell (2000), p. 72.
10 Directive 2004/35 on environmental liability with regard to the prevention and remedying of environmental damage (OJ 2004 L143/56).
11 Such as international agreements entered into by the Union.
12 Case 26/62 *Van Gend en Loos.*
13 Formerly Art. 234 EC and Art. 177 EEC.
14 See e.g. Craig and de Búrca (2011), Ch. 13; Hartley (2003), Ch. 9.
15 Case 6/64 *Costa v ENEL.*
16 The Court referred to other factors in support of this analysis, such as the reference in the treaty preamble to peoples and not only governments, the establishment of supranational institutions endowed with sovereign rights as well as the involvement of nationals of the member states in the Community's functioning via the European Parliament and the Economic and Social Committee.
17 [1963] ECR 1, pp. 12–13.
18 See e.g. Case C-72/95 *Kraaijeveld.*
19 See Lenaerts and Gutiérrez-Fons (2011), p. 27.
20 Case 6/64 *Costa v ENEL.*
21 See e.g. Case 106/77 *Simmenthal.* The principle of supremacy has been affirmed in a declaration annexed to the TFEU and TEU: Declaration 17 concerning primacy (OJ 2010 C83).
22 Krämer (1996a), p. 113.
23 See e.g. Case C-2/90 *Commission v Belgium (Wallonian Waste)* and Case C-293/97 *ex parte Standley* on application of the principle of rectification of environmental damage at source.
24 It is well established in the case law of the CJEU that an international agreement concluded by the Union may have direct effect if, regard being had to its wording and to the purpose and nature of the agreement, the provision contains a clear and precise obligation which is not subject, in its implementation or effects, to the adoption of any subsequent measure (see e.g. para. 44 of judgment in Case C-240/09 *Lesoochranárske zoskupiene*).
25 Case C-213/03 *Syndicat professional coordination des pêcheurs de l'étang de Berre et de la région v EDF.*
26 Both international environmental instruments may be accessed on the Ecolex website: http://www.ecolex.org/ecolex/ledge/view/SimpleSearch.
27 Council Decisions 77/585 (OJ 1977 L240/1) and 83/101 (OJ 1983 L67/1).
28 Art. 6 of the 1980 Protocol.
29 Case C-213/03 *Pêcheurs de l'étang de Berre* (para. 39 of judgment).
30 The Union signed the UNECE Convention in 1998 but only ratified its participation in international agreement in 2005 by virtue of Council Decision 2005/370 (OJ 2005 L124/1).
31 See Case C-240/09 *Lesoochranárske zoskupenie VLK.*
32 For a detailed analysis of the general principles of EU law see e.g. Tridimas (2006), Craig (2006) and Schwarze (2006).
33 See e.g. Case C-285/98 *Kreil.*
34 See e.g. Case C-144/04 *Mangold.*
35 Formerly Art. 249 EC and Art. 189 EEC.
36 See e.g. Cases 34/73 *Variola*, 43/71 *Politi* (regulations) and 9/70 *Grad* (decisions).
37 See Case C-253/00 *Muñoz.*
38 See Case 39/72 *Commission v Italy* and Case 50/76 *Amsterdam Bulb BV.*
39 Para. 6 of the Protocol on the application of the principles of subsidiarity and proportionality (OJ 1997 C340).
40 Regulation 1013/06 (OJ 2006 L190/1) as amended.

41 Regulation 1005/09 (OJ 2009 L286/1).
42 Regulation 338/97 (OJ 1997 L61/1), as amended.
43 See e.g. Arts. 103 TFEU (rules applying to undertakings) and 108 TFEU (rules on state aids).
44 See notably Regulation 1/2003 on implementation of the rules on competition laid down in Articles [101] and [102] of the [TFEU] (OJ 2003 L1/1).
45 Case 41/74 *Van Duyn.*
46 See e.g. Jack (2011), 74.
47 See Case 148/78 *Ratti* (para. 22 of judgment).
48 Krämer (1991), p. 40 and (1996a), p. 112.
49 Ibid.
50 Lenz (2000), p. 509.
51 Hartley (2003), p. 202.
52 See e.g. Cases 8/81 *Becker* and C-194/94 *CIA Security.*
53 Case C-236/92 *Difesa della Cava.*
54 Para. 8 of judgment.
55 Case C-236/92 *Difesa* (para. 10 of judgment).
56 Krämer (1996a), p. 108.
57 See e.g. Krämer (1991), p. 46.
58 See e.g. Sunkin, Ong and Wight (2002). p. 13; Jans (1996), p. 51.
59 Case C-131/88 *Commission v Germany* (para. 7 of judgment).
60 Case C-361/88 *Commission v Germany* (para. 16 of judgment).
61 Case C-59/89 *Commission v Germany.*
62 See e.g. Bell and McGillivray (2000), Ch. 7.
63 See e.g. the definition of 'best available techniques' in Art. 3(10) of the IPPC Directive 2010/75 (OJ 334/17) which refers to the criteria of economic viability and costs and advantages.
64 See also Protocol (No. 2) on the application of the principles of subsidiarity and proportionality annexed to the TEU and TFEU (OJ 2010 C83).
65 See Case C-236/92 *Difesa* (para. 9 of judgment).
66 Case 8/81 *Becker.*
67 Directive 77/388 (OJ 1977 L145/1) as amended.
68 Paras. 29 and 32 of judgment.
69 Para. 33 of judgment.
70 Joined Cases C-6 and 9/90 *Francovich and Bonifaci.*
71 Former Directive 80/987 (OJ 283/23) has been repealed and superseded by Directive 2008/94 (OJ 2008 L283/36).
72 Case C-236/92 *Difesa della Cava.*
73 Case 380/87 *Enichem Base.*
74 Directive 2008/98 (OJ 2008 L312/3) which has superseded the original version of the Waste Framework Directive, namely Directive 75/442 (OJ 1975 L194/23) as amended.
75 OJ 2008 L312/3.
76 The relevant basic safety provisions are now contained in Arts. 12–13 and 36(1) of Directive 2008/98, which are basically similar in nature to the original safety provision contained in the original version of the Waste Framework Directive (Art. 4 of Directive 75/442).
Art. 12 of Directive 2008/98 stipulates:

Disposal
Member States shall ensure that, where recovery in accordance with Article 10(1) is not undertaken, waste undergoes safe disposal operations which meet the provisions of Article 13 on the protection of human health and the environment.

Art. 13 of Directive 2008/98 states:

Protection of human health and the environment
Member States shall take the necessary measures to ensure that waste management is carried out without endangering human health, without harming the environment and, in particular:

(a)   without risk to water, air, soil, plants or animals;
(b)   without causing a nuisance through noise or odours; and
(c)   without adversely affecting the countryside or places of special interest.

Art. 36(1) of Directive 2008/98 states:

Enforcement and penalties
1. Member States shall take the necessary measures to prohibit the abandonment, dumping or uncontrolled management of waste.

77   There is support in the academic literature for the proposition that this legislative stipulation fulfils the requirements of direct effect: see e.g. Krämer (1996a), p. 122; Holder (1996), p. 324; Hedemann-Robinson (2003), p. 100.
78   In similar vein, see Jans (1996), p. 59.
79   Cases C-365/97 *Commission v Italy (San Rocco)* and C-387/97 *Commission v Greece (Kouroupitos (2))*, as discussed notably in Chs. 3 and 4.
80   Case C-387/97 *Commission v Greece (Kouroupitos (2))* (para. 56 of judgment).
81   Case 380/87 *Enichem Base.*
82   Ibid. (paras. 21–2 of judgment).
83   Now Directive 98/34 (OJ 1998 L204/37) as amended, replacing former Directive 83/189 (OJ 1983 L109/8) (which was in force at the material time of the case).
84   Under Directive 98/34 this standstill period may be extended to six months where the Commission or a member state considers the draft national measures may generate barriers to intra-EU trade or up to one year where the Commission indicates its intention to come forward with legislative proposals or where a Union proposal is already before the Council of the EU.
85   Case C-194/94 *CIA Security.*
86   Notably, the notification obligations contained in Art. 6 (cessation of waste), Art. 25 (exemption from waste treatment permit requirements), Art. 33 (waste plans and prevention programmes) and Art. 37 (reporting) of Directive 2008/98 (OJ 2008 L312/3). The member states are required to use the Transparency Directive procedures when unilaterally determining when a specific waste substance ceases to be waste (see Art. 6(4) of Directive 2008/98).
87   Case 148/78 *Ratti.*
88   OJ 1973 L189/7.
89   OJ 1977 L303/23.
90   Case C-129/96 *Inter-Environnement Wallonie.*
91   Former Directive 91/156 (OJ 1991 L78/32).
92   Specifically, Art. 11 of former Directive 91/156.
93   In addition to considering that Wallonian legislation did not comply with Art. 11 of Directive 91/156, the Conseil d'Etat also considered that there was a breach of Art. 3 of former Directive 91/689 (OJ 1991 L226/3) on hazardous waste, which stipulated special EU level application procedures in order for an exemption to be granted.
94   Case C-129/96 *Inter-Environnement Wallonie* (para. 45 of judgment).
95   Ibid. (paras. 47–8 of judgment).
96   Ibid. (para. 49 of judgment).
97   See Case 51/76 *Verbond* and Case C-118/94 *Regione Veneto.*
98   See e.g. Davies (2004), p. 102.

99 Directive 2009/147 (OJ 2009 L20/7).
100 Directive 92/43 (OJ 1992 L206/7).
101 See e.g. comments by Sunkin, Ong and Wright (2002), p. 16.
102 See Jans (1996), p. 77.
103 Now Directive 2011/92 (OJ 2011 L26/1) repealing former Directive 85/337 (OJ 1985 L175/40) as amended.
104 *Twyford Parish Council v Secretary of State for the Environment and another* (1992) 1 CMLR, 286–8.
105 Case C-431/92 *Grosskrotzenburg.*
106 Ibid. (paras. 24–5 of judgment).
107 Former Directive 85/337 (OJ 1985 L175/40), subsequently replaced by Directive 2011/92 (OJ 2011 L26/1).
108 Specifically, Arts. 2, 3 and 8 of former Directive 85/337.
109 Case C-431/92 *Grosskrotzenburg* (para. 40 of judgment).
110 Case C-118/94 *Associazone Italia per il WWF v Regione Veneto.*
111 Directive 2009/147 (OJ 2009 L20/7) superseding former Directive 79/409 (OJ 1979 L103/1).
112 Case C-118/94 *Associazone Italia per il WWF* (para. 19 of judgment).
113 Krämer (2011), p. 406; (1996a), p. 109 and (2003), p. 386.
114 Jans (1996), pp. 62 and 79.
115 Lackhoff and Nyssens (1998), p. 396.
116 See e.g. Davies (2004), p. 102.
117 Case C-72/95 *Kraaijeveld.*
118 See e.g. Case 152/84 *Marshall (1).*
119 See e.g. Case 80/86 *Kolpinghuis.*
120 See e.g. Case C-91/92 *Dori.*
121 See e.g. Case 8/81 *Becker* and Case 148/78 *Ratti.*
122 Case 41/74 *Van Duyn.*
123 Case 103/88 *Costanzo.*
124 Case 152/84 *Marshall (1).*
125 Case 222/84 *Johnston.*
126 Case C-419/92 *Scholz.*
127 Case C-188/89 *Foster.*
128 Directive 2006/54 (OJ 2006 L204/23) superseding former Directive 76/207 (OJ 1976 L39/40).
129 Cases C-431/92 and C-72/95 respectively.
130 See e.g. Hartley (2003), p. 216.
131 Case C-72/95 *Kraaijeveld.*
132 At the time former Directive 85/337 (OJ 1985 L175/40), subsequently replaced by Directive 2011/92 (OJ 2011 L26/1) as amended.
133 Under 5 km in length with a cross-section of at least 250m².
134 Annex II para. 10(e) of former Directive 85/337 (canalisation and flood relief works), now superseded by Annex II para. 10(f) of Directive 2011/92 (inland-waterway construction not included in Annex I, canalisation and flood-relief works).
135 Art. 4(2) of the former 1985 version of the former EIA Directive 85/337 states that Annex II projects are to be subject to an impact assessment 'where member states consider that their characteristics so require' and 'to this end could specify certain types of projects as being subject to an assessment or may establish the criteria and/or thresholds necessary' to determine which projects are likely to be subject to an assessment. The current version of Art. 4(2) of the EIA Directive 2011/92 specifies that member states are to make that determination by way of a case-by-case examination and/or through the use of thresholds or criteria.
136 At the material time of the case Art. 2 (1) in former Directive 85/337 did not contain a requirement for development consent.

137 Case C-72/95 *Kraaijeveld* (para. 53 of judgment).
138 Ibid. (para. 55 of judgment).
139 Ibid. (para. 56 of judgment).
140 Ibid. (para. 59 of judgment).
141 Ibid. (para. 61 of judgment).
142 Scott (1998).
143 Somsen (2001), p. 341; Krämer (2002a), p. 68.
144 See e.g. Jans (1996), p. 50.
145 See e.g. Hilson (1999), p. 133; Davies (2004), p. 174.
146 Prechal and Hancher (2002), p. 94.
147 Wyatt (1998), p. 18.
148 Case C-287/98 *Linster.*
149 See para. 38 of judgment.
150 Case C-435/97 *WWF v Bozen.*
151 Minimum length of 2.1km (para. 7 of Annex I of the EIA Directive).
152 As set out in Arts. 3, 5–10 of the EIA Directive respectively.
153 Para. 53 of judgment. The Court also considered that the exemption provided in Art.
     1(5) of the directive in respect of national legislative acts was not applicable in this
     case, given that the Italian law approving regional development of the airport exten-
     sion did not include the elements necessary to assess the environmental impact of the
     project.
154 Para. 71 of judgment.
155 See e.g. Case C-2/07 *Abraham and others,* Case C-75/08 *Mellor* and Case C-427/07
     Commission v Ireland.
156 Case C-127/02 *Waddenzee.*
157 Ibid. (para. 65 of judgment).
158 Ibid. (para. 66 of judgment).
159 Case C-237/07 *Janecek.*
160 Former Directive 96/62 (OJ 1996 L296/55) as subsequently repealed and superseded
     by Directive 2008/50 on ambient air quality assessment and management (OJ 2008
     L152/1).
161 Case C-237/07 *Janecek* (para. 46 of judgment).
162 Case C-263/08 *Djurgården-Lilla Värtans.*
163 Directive 2011/92 (OJ 2011 L26/1) which repealed and superseded former Directive
     85/337 (OJ 1985 L175/40). At the time of the relevant access-to-justice provisions
     were contained in Art. 10a of the former Directive 85/337. These particular provi-
     sions, which have not changed in substance, are now contained in Art. 11 of Directive
     2011/92.
164 Former Directive 85/337 (OJ 1985 L175/40).
165 Directive 2011/92 (OJ 2011 L26/1)
166 Ibid., Art. 11(1).
167 Ibid., Art. 11(2).
168 Ibid., Art. 11(3).
169 Ibid., Art. 1(2)(e).
170 Case C-263/08 *Djurgården* (para. 45 of judgment).
171 See para. 50 of judgment.
172 Ibid. (paras. 48–51 of judgment).
173 Case 152/84 *Marshall (1).*
174 Case 14/86 *Pretore de Salò.*
175 Directive 78/659 (OJ 1978 L22/1), as subsequently codified in former Directive
     2006/44 (OJ 2006 L264/20). The 1978 directive has been repealed by virtue of Art.
     22 of the EU Water Framework Directive (OJ 2000 L327/1), 13 years after the latter's
     entry into force (22 December 2013).
176 Para. 20 of judgment.

177 See e.g. Case 63/83 *R v Kent Kirk* and Joined Cases C-74 and 129/95 *Procura della Republica v X*. See also Art. 49 of the EU Charter of Fundamental Rights (OJ 2010 C83/2).
178 Art. 7 ECHR, which states: 'No one shall be held guilty of any criminal offence on account of any act or omission which did not constitute a criminal offence under national or international law at the time when it was committed. Nor shall a heavier penalty be imposed than the one that was applicable at the time when the criminal offence was committed.'
179 See Joined Cases 372–4/85 *Traen*, Case C-168/95 *Arcaro*, Joined Cases C-304 *et al.*/95 *Tombesi*, Case C-235/02 *Saetti* and Case C-457/02 *Niselli*.
180 Joined Cases 372–4/85 *Traen*.
181 Former Directive 75/442 (OJ 1975 L194/23) as amended was repealed and superseded by Directive 2008/98 (OJ 2008 L312/3).
182 Obligation now enshrined in Art. 23 of Directive 2008/98.
183 Obligation now enshrined in Art. 35 (ibid.).
184 Paras. 24–6 of judgment.
185 Case 152/84 *Marshall (1)*.
186 Joined Cases C-37 and 58/06 *Viamex*.
187 Regulation 615/98 laying down specific detailed rules of application for the export refund arrangements as regards the welfare of live bovine animals during transport (OJ 1998 L82/19).
188 Former Directive 91/628 on the protection of animals during transport (OJ 1991 L340/17) as subsequently repealed by Regulation 1/2005 (OJ 2005 L3/1).
189 The judgment has been criticised for not adhering to the principle of legal certainty, on the grounds that the EU regulation made a general reference to the directive without specifying which requirements had to be complied with: Craig and de Búrca (2011), p. 215.
190 Case 152/84 *Marshall (1)*.
191 Directive 2006/54 (OJ 2006 L204/23) superseding former Directive 76/207 (OJ 1976 L39/40).
192 See e.g. Case C-91/92 *Dori*, Case C-192/94 *El Corte Ingles* and Case C-97/96 *Daihatsu*.
193 See e.g. Krämer (2003), p. 386.
194 See Case 152/84 *Marshall (1)* (para. 51 of judgment).
195 See e.g. Craig (1997b), Lackhoff and Nyssens (1998) and Tridimas (1994).
196 See the three Advocate Generals' (AG's) opinions in Cases C-271/91 *Marshall (2)*, C-316/93 *Vaneetveld* and C-91/92 *Dori* respectively.
197 Craig (1997b).
198 See also Tridimas (1994).
199 Consider e.g. Case 43/75 *Defrenne (2)* in which the CJEU held that Art. 119 of the former EEC Treaty (now superseded by Art. 157 TFEU) on equal pay for male and female workers was horizontally directly effective.
200 Hartley (2003), p. 206.
201 Case C-201/02 *Delena Wells*.
202 Former Directive 85/337 (OJ 1985 L175/40) subsequently superseded by Directive 2011/92 (OJ 2011 L26/1).
203 As confirmed in Case 152/84 *Marshall (1)*.
204 As in Case C-97/96 *Daihatsu*.
205 Case C-201/02 *Delena Wells* (para. 57 of judgment).
206 Case 103/88 *Costanzo*.
207 Case C-435/97 *WWF v Bozen*.
208 Case C-127/02 *Waddenzee*.
209 Case C-97/96 *Daihatsu*.
210 Directive 68/151 (OJ 1968 L65/8) as repealed by Directive 2009/101 (OJ 2009 L258/11).
211 Directive 2011/92 (OJ 2011 L26/1).

212 Directive 92/43 (OJ 1992 L206/7).
213 Directive 2008/98 (OJ 2008 L312/3).
214 Wennerås (2007), p. 49; Jans and Vedder (2008), p. 193.
215 Jans (1996), p. 68.
216 Wyatt (1998), pp. 15–16.
217 Colgan (2002), p. 556.
218 Lackhoff and Nyssens (1998), pp. 405–6.
219 See e.g. Case 152/84 *Marshall (1)*.
220 Jans (1996), p. 68.
221 Case C-194/94 *CIA Security*.
222 Directive 98/34 (OJ 1998 L204/37) which superseded former Directive 83/189 (OJ 1983 L109/8). Information on the application of the Transparency Directive may be obtained from the following European Commission 'TRIS' (Technical Regulations Information System) website: http://ec.europa.eu/enterprise/tris/index_en.htm.
223 See esp. Arts. 8–9 of the directive.
224 Case C-194/94 *CIA Security* (para. 54 of judgment).
225 Former Directive 75/442 (OJ 1975 L194/23).
226 Case 380/87 *Enichem Base*.
227 As discussed above (section 6.1.2.3.), this conclusion of the CJEU is debatable.
228 Case C-194/94 *CIA Security* (para. 48 of judgment).
229 Case C-443/98 *Unilever Italia*.
230 Ibid. (para. 51 of judgment).
231 Case C-226/97 *Lemmens*.
232 Para. 35 of judgment.
233 Case 380/87 *Enichem Base*.
234 Case C-129/94 *Bernaldez*.
235 Former Directive 72/166 (OJ 1972 L103/1) which has been repealed and superseded by Directive 2009/103 (OJ 2009 L263/11).
236 Case C-129/94 *Bernaldez* (para. 20 of judgment).
237 Case C-441/93 *Panagis Pafitis*.
238 Former Directive 77/91 (OJ 1977 L16/1) repealed by Directive 2012/30 (OJ 2012 L315/74).
239 Case C-77/97 *Smithkline Beecham*.
240 Directive 76/768 (OJ 1976 L262/169) as amended.
241 See Hartley (2003), p. 214.
242 Hilson and Downes (1999), p. 127.
243 Craig and de Búrca (2011), pp. 207 *et seq.*; Arnull (1999), p. 1.
244 Case C-287/98 *Linster*.
245 See also AG Saggio's opinion containing similar remarks in Case C-240/98 *Océano*.
246 Craig and de Búrca (2003), p. 225.
247 Case 380/87 *Enichem Base*.
248 Case C-192/94 *El Corte Ingles*.
249 For example, a nuisance action in the context of disputes between neighbouring landowners.
250 Case C-144/04 *Mangold*.
251 OJ 2000 L303/16.
252 Case C-240/09 *Lesoochranárske zoskupenie VLK (WOLF Forest Protection Movement) v Slovakian Environment Ministry*.
253 Art. 9(3) of the 1998 Århus Convention states:

> In addition and without prejudice to the review procedures referred to in paragraphs 1 and 2 above, each Party shall ensure that, where they meet the criteria, if any, laid down in its national law, members of the public have access to administrative or judicial procedures to challenge acts and omissions by private persons

328   *Enforcement of European Union Environmental Law*

and public authorities which contravene provisions of its national law relating to the environment.

254 Case C-127/02 *Waddenzee.*
255 Ibid. (para. 43 of judgment).
256 See ibid. (paras. 44–5 of judgment).
257 See ibid. (para. 59 of judgment).
258 Case C-318/98 *Fornasar.*
259 Ibid. (para. 37 of judgment).
260 Case 14/83 *Von Colson.*
261 Directive 2006/54 (OJ 2006 L204/23) superseding former Directive 76/207 (OJ 1976 L39/40).
262 The current version of the Sex Equality in Employment Directive (Directive 2006/54) is more specific in requiring in Art. 26 that member states establish 'effective, proportionate and dissuasive' penalties applicable to breaches of its terms.
263 Case 14/83 *Von Colson* (para. 26 of judgment).
264 Ibid. (para. 28 of judgment).
265 Case C-106/89 *Marleasing.*
266 See also on this point Cases C-91/92 *Dori*, C-334/92 *Wagner Miret* and C-54/96 *Dorsch Consult.*
267 Joined Cases C-397–403/01 *Pfeiffer and others* (para. 115 of judgment).
268 The CJEU confirmed in *Marleasing* that the national court's duty to interpret national law in line with EU directives applies 'in so far as possible', signalling that national rules of (statutory) interpretation have the final word: see Case C-106/89 *Marleasing* (para. 8 of judgment).
269 See e.g. the UK Supreme Court's (former House of Lords) judgments in *Duke v Reliance* (1987) and *Webb v EMO* (1995).
270 See UK Supreme Court (former House of Lords) judgment in *Litster* (1990).
271 See Krämer (1996a), p. 122.
272 Case C-168/95 *Arcaro.*
273 Former Directive 76/464 (OJ 1976 L129/23) was initially superseded by former Directive 2006/11 (OJ 2006 L64/52). The directive has now been repealed by the Water Framework Directive (OJ 2000 L327/1) 13 years after entry into force of the latter directive (22 December 2013).
274 Former Directive 83/513 (OJ 1983 L291/1) has been superseded by Directive 2008/105 on water quality standards in the field of water policy (OJ 2008 L384/84) as amended.
275 Such as in Case 80/86 *Kolpinghuis* and Case 14/86 *Pretore di Salò.*
276 Case C-168/95 *Arcaro* (para. 37 of judgment).
277 Ibid. (para. 41 of judgment).
278 Ibid. (para. 42 of judgment).
279 See also Case C-105/03 *Pupino.*
280 Case C-321/05 *Kofoed.*
281 See notably Case C-456/98 *Centrosteel* and Case C-240–244/98 *Océano*. See analysis by Craig and de Búrca (2011), p. 204.
282 Case C-456/98 *Centrosteel.*
283 Directive 86/653 (OJ 1986 L382/17).
284 AG Jacobs opined that the rule in *Arcaro* should be construed as being confined to the context of criminal proceedings: see paras. 31–5 of his Opinion in Case C-456/98 *Centrosteel.*
285 See his Opinion in Case C-240–244/98 *Océano.*
286 See Craig (2003), p. 218.
287 Directive 2011/92 (OJ 2011 L26/1).
288 Directive 98/34 (OJ 1998 L204/37).

289 Case C-188/89 *Foster.*
290 Case 43/75 *Defrenne (2).*
291 Case C-144/04 *Mangold.*
292 Art. 297 TFEU.
293 In particular, where the Commission considers that a single set of binding rules is important for avoiding distortions to the operation of the single market that might arise by virtue of the existence of differing national rules of the member states, such as in relation to inter-statal movements of goods (e.g. see Waste Shipment Regulation 1013/06 (OJ 2006 L190/1) and Regulation 338/97 on trade in endangered species (OJ 1997 L61/1), as amended).
294 As set out in Art. 3(2) TEU. See also Art. 191(2) TFEU.

7 Access to justice at national level for breaches of EU environmental law (1)

The role of the Court of Justice of the EU

As was explored in the previous chapter, the Court of Justice of the EU (CJEU) has developed several possibilities for private individuals to be able to rely upon EU norms before national courts, with a view to enforcing these against persons whose conduct infringes the legal requirements stipulated in those norms. Specifically, it has confirmed that in principle individuals may rely upon EU rules of law that are sufficiently precise and unconditional before national courts of the EU member states (direct effect doctrine), in the context of litigation either prosecuted or defended by them. The CJEU has also confirmed that individuals may be entitled to require national courts to enforce EU norms which, although providing member state authorities with a considerable degree of discretion, are found to have been infringed by virtue of a state authority having exceeded the limits of discretion afforded under the EU provisions concerned.[1] In addition, the CJEU has clarified that national courts are under a general duty, so far as is possible, to interpret national legislative rules in line with the requirements of EU treaty and secondary legislative provisions covering the same subject matter (doctrine of indirect effect). However, the above-mentioned legal principles are of relatively limited practical use in themselves without there being a clear legal framework in place to facilitate access of individual claimants to national courts and tribunals as well as to ensure the provision of an effective judicial remedy in the event of the individual's legal action being successful.

The purpose of this and the next chapter is to explore and assess the ways and means by which EU law has been developed in order to provide the foundations of a framework for guaranteeing effective access to justice for private persons (such as NGEOs) seeking to enforce EU obligations at national level. This chapter focuses specifically on the role that the CJEU has played in developing a body of general procedural rights for individuals engaged in litigation before national courts as well as the responsibilities of member state authorities (including judicial fora) to secure remedies in the event of breaches of EU law, including EU environmental norms. In addition to the general legal principles established by its case law in shaping the basic legal rights of private persons as well as obligations of state authorities under EU law (principally the doctrines of direct and indirect effect as well as the supremacy principle), over time the CJEU has developed through case law a corpus of rules that has served to shape the scope and nature of national judicial remedies made available to individuals for the purpose of upholding EU law. The next chapter will look beyond the contribution that the CJEU has made in terms of developing procedural rights and remedies for private individuals and consider the impact and implications of recent EU environmental legislative measures and initiatives which have emerged since the early 2000s and are intended to bolster access to environmental justice within Union member states. These particular EU legislative innovations have come principally as a means of implementing an important recent international environment agreement, namely the 1998 United Nations Economic Commission for Europe (UNECE) Århus Convention on Access to Information, Public Participation in Decision-making and Access to Justice in Environmental Matters, of which the European Union is a contracting party.[2]

7.1 General principle of procedural autonomy under EU law

The starting point for analysing judicial remedies at national level from the perspective of general principles developed by the CJEU is to recognise that the Union's original foundational treaties, principally the former EEU treaty framework, were clearly not devised with any specific view to providing or altering the conditions for access to courts and legal remedies as afforded to individuals under the law of the member states. For several years after the launch of the European Economic Community there were no treaty provisions expressly addressing the issue of administration of justice at national level, insofar as this affected the practical application of EU norms. For a considerable period it was widely assumed that the member states had retained exclusive competence in matters of determining the availability of rights of action as well as remedies for private plaintiffs to enforce EU law at national level. It also appears that the CJEU initially accepted this to be a correct interpretation of the constitutional settlement agreed between member states and the former European Community. For some 20 years or so after the entry into force of the former 1957 EEU treaty framework, the CJEU held in various cases that it was for the particular national legal systems of the member states to determine the extent to which private persons should have access to justice before national courts to enforce EU norms, including notably the setting controls on legal standing to sue and the range of remedies available to successful private plaintiffs. Evidently, in its early years the Court considered its broad mandate under Article 220 of the former EEU treaty framework to ensure observance of the law in the interpretation and application of Community law could not be construed as justifying its judicial appraisal of the adequacy of judicial remedies provided within the national legal systems of the member states.[3] The CJEU confirmed initially that member states had in essence retained autonomy in terms of how they determined to set up legal procedures at national level in order to safeguard private persons' rights enshrined in EU law.[4] Whilst the CJEU was initially prepared to develop the scope of individual rights under EU law in terms of whether or not a particular EU norm conferred direct legal benefits or burdens on individuals (in/direct effect doctrines), it was reluctant to interfere with aspects of civil and criminal procedure under national law.

However, over time the CJEU clarified that the principle of procedural autonomy recognised by EU law was not absolute. Instead, having regard to the general duties of co-operation incumbent on member states under Article 4(3) of the Treaty on European Union (TEU)[5] to ensure fulfilment of the legal obligations derived from the EU's foundational treaties (now the Treaty on the Functioning of the European Union (TFEU) and TEU), the CJEU qualified the basic position favouring national autonomy in relation to access to justice and remedies with two important general principles: namely, the guarantee of non-discrimination and the assurance that the exercise of EU legal rights must be made a genuine possibility in practice.[6] The current position of the Court on the general meaning of procedural autonomy may be summed up by reference to the following extract from one of its more recent judgments:

> In the absence of [Union] rules governing the matter, it is for the domestic legal system of each member state to designate the courts and tribunals having jurisdiction and to lay down the detailed procedural rules governing actions for safeguarding rights which individuals derive from the direct effect of [Union] law. However, such rules must not be less favourable than those governing similar domestic actions nor render virtually impossible or excessively difficult the exercise of rights conferred by [Union] law.[7]

Since the initial clarification made by the CJEU of those twin qualifications to the principle of member state autonomy in relation to the national legal procedures, the EU has expanded its remit on a number of fronts. In particular, the CJEU has developed its jurisprudence on the role and responsibilities of authorities of the member states, judicial as well as administrative in nature, with regard to the question of affording appropriate remedies for individuals whose EU rights have been breached. This case law will be examined more closely in section 7.2 below.

More recently still, the CJEU has broken away from the traditional position of procedural autonomy in a more radical fashion, in having established the right for private individuals in certain circumstances to seek compensation in respect of loss sustained as a result of a serious breach of EU law by a member state (state liability). This relatively recent legal innovation is considered in section 7.3 below, with a view to exploring its implications for private enforcement of EU environmental law at national level.

Before considering the CJEU's case law in detail it is worth noting that the 2007 Lisbon Treaty, in amending the EU's foundational treaty framework, introduced a new treaty clause expressly referring to the subject of national provision of remedies. Specifically, this is the second sentence of Article 19(1) TEU which states:

> Member States shall provide remedies sufficient to ensure effective legal protection in the fields covered by Union law.

This particular innovation serves to underpin the CJEU's case law which has clarified that a number of legally binding principles are incumbent upon on member states, including national courts, when determining outcomes in relation to instances of breaches of Union law. It is notable that the current EU treaty framework does not specifically address the more general issue of adequacy of access to justice at national level for individuals seeking to enforce Union obligations. The treaty provisions have in this sense still to catch up and reflect the CJEU's case law, which has not refrained from appraising national rules on access to justice in light of Article 4(3) TEU.

7.2 Remedies at national level: general principles developed by the CJEU

Notwithstanding its reticence in the early years of European supranational integration to interfere in the area of 'procedural autonomy', the CJEU has subsequently developed a number of general legal principles pertaining to member state responsibilities in remedying breaches of EU law. Mention has already been made in the previous section of the obligations confirmed by the Court that member states have to ensure that their national rules which afford remedies to individuals in respect of breaches of EU law must meet the requirement of equal treatment (i.e. the procedures must be equivalent to those applicable in respect of analogous situations involving breaches of national law) as well as ensure that the national procedures concerned offer a genuine opportunity for a claimant to uphold their EU rights (i.e. must not be in such a state as to render it in practice virtually impossible to secure a remedy). However, the CJEU has moved beyond these two important qualifications and developed other general principles on remedies drawn out from the general duties of good faith under Article 4(3) TEU.

7.2.1 Duties on national courts to provide remedies

One area of development in the CJEU's case law on remedies has been to expand the extent to which national courts and tribunals are required under EU law to ensure that effective remedies are provided to plaintiffs who are successful in claims that EU law has been breached. Notably, it appears that in a number of cases the CJEU has established that national courts are obliged, in certain circumstances, to take steps to provide individuals with adequate judicial remedies in order to enable them to uphold their directly effective rights.

Specifically, the Court has required national courts to set aside national rules preventing claimants from being able to secure effective remedies in respect of breaches of directly effective norms of EU law, where but for those rules a suitable remedy would be available under national law. A few examples serve to illustrate this point. In *Marshall (2)*[8] for instance, a sex discrimination case concerning adequacy of compensation under Article 6 of the former original 1976 version of the Sex Equality in Employment Directive (Directive 76/207)[9] the CJEU held that national courts were obliged without qualification to construe national legislation in line with Article 6 in order to ensure that an individual employee received an adequate remedy in respect of a breach by her state employer of her directly effective rights to equal treatment under other provisions of the directive. Article 6 contained a general obligation on member states to ensure that measures are introduced into their national legal systems necessary to enable claimants of sex discrimination within the workplace to pursue their claims by judicial process after possible recourse to other competent authorities. Article 6 was itself clearly not directly effective, given that it was imprecise and conditional upon the adoption of member state measures.[10] In Marshall's case, UK law at the time imposed a ceiling of £6,250 on the amount of damages that could be awarded by a UK employment tribunal in respect of a claim of unequal treatment on grounds of sex. In contrast, no such ceilings applied with respect to the jurisdiction of the English High Court in awarding compensation for other types of civil wrong. In its preliminary ruling to the employment tribunal hearing the employment dispute, the CJEU considered the fixing of an upper limit of damages to be in conflict with the requirements of Article 6, and required the national tribunal to set aside the limit when awarding damages. This represented a significant shift from its previous jurisprudence on Article 6, where it had held that national courts were only under a duty 'so far as possible' to construe national law to be in line with the EU legislative provision.[11] A similar approach was adopted by the CJEU in the case of *Factortame (1)*[12] in which it held that the UK courts were bound under Article 4(3) TEU to set aside a statutory rule in UK law at the time excluding the possibility of persons being able to obtain interim injunctions against national government authorities which infringed the directly effective right of freedom of establishment under the EU treaty framework (Article 49 TFEU).[13] The CJEU has therefore developed a general principle that courts are under a general duty to afford the maximum range of generally available remedies under national law to persons relying upon directly effective EU rights in disputes heard by them (adopt a 'maximalist' position when it comes to the question of judicial remedies in the event of such a person whose directly effective rights have been breached).

However, the CJEU has not usually applied the same approach in situations where the provision of EU law relied upon by a private litigant is not directly effective. The discussion in the previous chapter on the doctrine of indirect effect revealed that traditionally the Court will only require national courts to interpret national law in line with a non-directly effective provision of EU Directives insofar as is possible under the rules of national law on statutory interpretation.[14] In these situations, the CJEU has not deduced from Article 4(3) TEU that national courts are, as a matter of basic principle, under duties to take steps to secure effective judicial remedies for breaches of non-directly effective provisions of EU directives, where national law precludes the possibility of its rules being interpreted in line with a non-directly effective provision of a directive. By way of exception, and as was discussed in Chapter 6, the CJEU has held that individuals may rely upon provisions in EU Directives directly against state authorities before national courts, notwithstanding that the provisions may not necessarily fulfil the traditional criteria of direct effect (sufficient precision and unconditionality), as has been the case with respect to Articles 2(1) and 4(2) of the Environmental Impact Assessment (EIA) Directive,[15] as discussed in the previous chapter.[16]

It is also clear that the CJEU has not interpreted the duties incumbent on the national courts and tribunals of Union member states under Article 4(3) TEU (to take steps to ensure adequate remedies are provided in respect of breaches of EU law) to be an absolute and automatic obligation in all instances. Instead, the general duty of co-operation in good faith under Article 4(3) is qualified by the principle of procedural autonomy, which means that national courts and tribunals have to operate as far as possible in accordance with national rules governing the procedures and outcomes on applications for judicial remedies. With the notable exception of the CJEU's jurisprudence on state liability,[17] the aim of the CJEU's jurisprudence has not been to establish remedies *de novo*. The principle of procedural autonomy sets limits on the extent to which courts and tribunals are required to apply EU law as well as secure effective remedies in relation to its breach. The following example serves to illustrate this point. The CJEU has held that national courts and tribunals which are not in general empowered under national rules of judicial procedure to raise points of EU law of their own motion are not required to consider or apply the relevance of EU law to the case at hand where the parties to a dispute have not themselves raised them in court.[18] On the other hand, the CJEU has also confirmed that where national law obliges or entitles a court or tribunal to raise of its own motion pleas in law based on a binding national law, then those judicial bodies are obliged to examine of their own motion whether the legislative or administrative authorities of the member state have acted lawfully according to the requirements of EU law in the context of a legal dispute concerning the legality of the relevant authorities' behaviour.[19] Both rulings of the CJEU may lead to a fracturing of responsibilities of courts and tribunals in relation to EU law in the various member states, insofar as they enable member states to confer different levels of procedural rights to private persons for the purpose of civil litigation. This does not assist in the EU's project of securing the means to achieve a high level of environmental protection throughout the EU. On the other had, the rulings are nevertheless compatible with one another when considered in the context of the procedural autonomy principle fostered by the Court. The effect of these rulings is to signal acknowledgement of the independence of member states to determine whether its judicial bodies are to be invested with passive (adversarial based) or active (investigative) roles and responsibilities, these to be determined solely in accordance with local legal heritage and tradition.

It should, though, be borne in mind that the CJEU has set clear limits on the principle of procedural autonomy. These qualifications, underpinned by principles of equivalence and effectiveness developed by the Court, ultimately require courts and tribunals to take steps to intervene and set aside national rules on access-to-justice matters (e.g. rules relating to access to courts and the provision of judicial remedies) where they impede a person being able to address breaches of EU law in two types of scenario. First, the procedural autonomy principle does not apply where national rules are of a less favourable nature than those provided in respect of similar situations but which are purely internal to the member state and do not concern Union law (equivalence principle). Secondly, procedural autonomy no longer applies where national rules render it impossible or excessively difficult in practice for a person to be able to secure a remedy for a breach of EU law (effectiveness principle).[20]

The principle of effectiveness may be of particular relevance in the context of private enforcement of EU environmental law, where plaintiffs may encounter a number of procedural hurdles which may be unreasonable in the circumstances for them to shoulder. One notable example of this arising may be seen from the *Janecek* case,[21] in which the CJEU confirmed that an individual was entitled to rely upon certain obligations contained in EU air quality legislation against national authorities before the national courts. Dieter Janecek, a resident in Munich living near its central ring road, the Landshuter Allee, objected to the fact that the local authorities had not adhered to EU air quality legislative requirements (at the time Article 7(3) of former Directive 96/62 on ambient air quality assessment),[22] in not having drawn up a plan indicating measures to be taken in the short term where there is a risk of the EU legislative limit values and/or alert thresholds being exceeded. At the time, the EU limit values relating to particular matter (PM10) (as set out by former Directive 1999/30)[23] had been exceeded in the local area. In confirming that Article 7(3) of former Directive 96/62 contained a directly effective obligation, the CJEU held that private persons directly concerned by a risk of limit value exceedance 'must be in a position to require the competent authorities to draw up an action plan where such a risk exists, if necessary by bringing an action before the competent courts'.[24] In the case, the referring national court disputed any personal right existing for private persons under Article 7(3) of former Directive 96/62 to have an action drawn up. Directive 96/62 did not contain any specific provisions relating to access to justice at national level,[25] yet this was not material for the CJEU. Effectively, the CJEU's judgment confirmed that access to the national courts had to be guaranteed so that the plaintiff would be able to assert the directly effective EU legislative provision in an effective manner.

The importance of the issue of access to environmental justice was also highlighted in the *Lappel Bank* litigation[26] where a UK NGEO (the Royal Society for the Protection of Birds (RSPB)) sought judicial review of a decision by the UK Secretary of State for the Environment to exclude an area of inter-tidal mudflats known as Lappel Bank from falling within a designated local special protection area (SPA) for the purposes of the EU Wild Birds Directive.[27] Pending the outcome of the judicial review proceedings, the RSPB sought interim relief from the High Court of England and Wales by way of an injunction or judicial declaration to prevent development of a port on the mudflats. Under English law, as confirmed by the subsequent UK House of Lords' judgment in the case, a financial guarantee (cross-undertaking in damages) is to be usually provided by the plaintiff in order to cover loss of profit incurred by the defendant as a result of such relief being granted pending final judgment, this being recoverable if the plaintiff's case ultimately proves successful. In the case, however, the RSPB was not in a financial position to be able to offer such an undertaking, with the result that the purpose of litigation effectively collapsed, the site not being required to be preserved until final judgment. In the course of legal proceedings, the CJEU confirmed in a preliminary ruling to the House of Lords that the UK had violated the terms of the Wild Birds Directive in having failed to classify the mudflats within the ambit of the SPA. That proved to be pyrrhic victory, given that development had already commenced on the mudflat area. The national procedural requirement of a cross-undertaking in damages effectively meant that the RSPB was unable to secure an appropriate remedy in respect of a breach of EU environmental law. It has been argued that the jurisprudence of the CJEU on remedies would not go as far as to require a national court to set aside require-ments for a financial deposit to be required where interim relief is requested.[28] However, it is also arguable that the CJEU's case law on procedural autonomy requires, by virtue of Article 4(3) TEU, a national court to set aside the applica-tion of such a rule where national law provides the national court with discretion to require a deposit of financial security and the plaintiff has fulfilled the other core requirements attending requests for interim relief, these being essentially that the plaintiff has made out a *prima facie* case that an infringement of law has occurred and the matter is proven to be urgent with a substantial risk of the plaintiff's case being rendered meaningless unless interim relief is granted. The requirement to put down a cross-undertaking in damages in this case effectively rendered the prosecution of civil action by the RSPB impossible. The *Lappel Bank* case should now be seen in light of more recent jurisprudence of the CJEU on the impact of written sources of EU law on access to environmental justice, such as the EU's ratification of the Århus Convention. This will be considered in the next chapter.

7.2.2 Duties of non-judicial national authorities to provide adequate remedies

Another branch of the jurisprudence of the CJEU on remedial responsibilities has now established as a matter of general principle that it is incumbent on all emana-tions of the member states, not simply the national courts and tribunals, to remedy breaches of EU law. In the context of a number of environmental disputes the CJEU has made reference to this general legal principle, which it has concluded is an implicit obligation under EU law to be drawn from Article 4(3) TEU.[29] As the Court confirmed in the *Delena Wells* case:

> [I]t is clear from settled case law that under the principle of co-operation in good faith laid down in Article 4(3) TEU the member states are required to nullify the unlawful consequences of a breach of [Union] law . . . Such an obligation is owed, within the sphere of its competence by every organ of the member state concerned.[30]

In *Delena Wells*, referred to in the previous chapter in relation to the direct effect doctrine, a private plaintiff sought judicial review before the High Court of England and Wales of a decision by the UK Secretary of State for Transport,

Local Government and the Regions to authorise planning consent in respect of a request resume mining operations at a quarry that had laid dormant for a considerable period. Under UK planning legislation, plans for the resumption of operations in old dormant mines and quarries were, in certain circumstances, exempt from any requirement to undergo an impact assessment. The High Court referred a number of questions concerning the interpretation of the EIA Directive[31] to the CJEU under the preliminary ruling procedure in Article 267 TFEU, including whether the directive precluded such development from being excluded from an impact assessment and, if so, whether the UK was under a duty to remedy its failure to adhere to the terms of the directive. In affirming that such an exemption amounted to a breach of the directive, the CJEU set out some general principles regarding the obligations of national authorities involved in the application of EU rules concerning environmental impact assessment procedures to rectify the consequences of their decisions which breach EU rules:

> [I]t is for the competent authorities of a member state to take, within the sphere of their competence, all the general or particular measures necessary to ensure that projects are examined in order to determine whether they are subject to an impact assessment . . . Such particular measures include, subject to the limits laid down by the procedural autonomy of the member states, the revocation or suspension of a consent already granted, in order to carry out an assessment of the environmental effects of the project in question as provided for by [the EIA] Directive.
>
> The member state is likewise required to make good any harm caused by the failure to carry out environmental impact assessment.[32]

What is to be concluded from this line of jurisprudence of the CJEU is that Article 4(3) TEU imposes a general legally binding duty on member states, including emanations of the state such as local authorities as well as national or regional government departments and agencies, to ensure that breaches of EU law falling within their particular area of jurisdiction are remedied. Accordingly, a state authority competent to issue licences to persons to engage in industrial and/or commercial activities is required under Article 4(3) TEU to take steps to remedy the situation where it has applied licensing conditions in contravention of EU environmental law. A state authority charged with the responsibility of overseeing the compliance by private and public entities with environmental standards prescribed by law is obliged under Article 4(3) TEU to take steps to remedy a situation where it has failed to ensure that the requirements of EU environmental law are adhered to. Although such an authority may not, as was discussed in the previous chapter, invoke the requirements of EU environmental directives against private persons where these have not been transposed correctly into national law (no 'inverse vertical direct effect' of directives), the state authority is nevertheless required to seek other ways and means of ensuring that the requirements of EU law be fulfilled. In particular, it is obliged to take steps to remedy breaches of EU law that arise as a result of its own decision-making or actions.

For example, it would be incumbent on a public authority under Article 4(3) TEU to refuse to issue a licence or permit required for the execution of a particular activity (e.g. development project or industrial operation) where the proposed activity would contravene the requirements of an EU environmental directive, even where existing national rules would deem authorisation to be lawful. This would not contravene the rule in *Marshall*,[33] discussed in the previous chapter, that obligations contained in EU directives may not be imposed on individuals. For the national authority would not be actively imposing EU directive requirements on a private person but instead ensuring that a private person would not be able to compel it to commit an act contrary to Union law. The authority is obligated under Article 4(3) to ensure that it issues any authorisation document only in conformity with EU legislative requirements. Likewise if a national authority discovers that it has issued a licence or permit in contravention of EU environmental law, it would be obligated to take steps on its own initiative to remedy the situation as soon as feasible. Although adverse effects of an amendment or revocation of a licence issued in contravention of EU law may well be sustained by the licensee, this should not be considered in legal terms to constitute a situation of a public authority seeking to enforce a directive directly against a private individual. Instead, it would be a scenario where action is taken to ensure that a public authority's activities are in compliance with EU environmental legislation. The effects felt by the licensee would be ancillary, an inevitable consequence of the measures taken to render the actions of a public authority in conformity with EU requirements, and therefore not blocked by the principle that directives may not have direct effects against private persons.[34]

The duty of co-operation imposed on public authorities under Article 4(3) TEU is thus both wide-ranging and profound. In an environmental protection context, the CJEU has clarified in cases such as *Kraaijeveld* and *Delena Wells*, that competent authorities of the member states responsible for protecting the environment or taking decisions affecting the environment in areas covered by EU law are to take all necessary measures to ensure fulfilment of EU environmental legislative obligations falling within their particular area of jurisdiction. This may take any number of forms. For instance, it may include placing pressure on a national and/or regional government to take legislative measures to transpose EU environmental directives. It may include notifying the European Commission of a breach of EU environmental law where law enforcement action is not undertaken at national level to remedy a breach of EU environmental law. The Commission may then commence infringement proceedings against the member state concerned under Articles 258 and 260 TFEU. It is important to recognise that the duty of co-operation incumbent on member state authorities exists as a general legal responsibility and that it is not somehow determined by the extent to which private persons are able to bring legal proceedings against an emanation of the state for failure to enforce EU environmental law in a particular case. Competent state authorities have duties to secure effective remedies to infractions of EU environmental law, irrespective of whether the rules of law in question may be invoked by private individuals against them in a court of law.

The above-mentioned duties under Article 4(3) TEU on member state authorities to ensure due compliance with EU environmental legislation may, accordingly, be used to good effect by private persons engaged in enforcement of EU environmental legislation. Specifically, competent authorities may be reminded of their obligations to take remedial action to correct breaches of EU environmental law that have emanated from decisions and/or activities of public authorities. The various responsibilities of member state authorities in relation to EU environmental law enforcement are addressed in further detail in Part III of the book.

7.3 State liability for breaches of EU environmental law

Until relatively recently, it was thought that the CJEU would refrain from compelling member states to create specific rights of action and/or remedies at national level in order to enable private persons to enforce their EU rights. Consonant with its now well-established principle of procedural autonomy, the initial position of the CJEU was indeed to confirm that the EU treaty framework was not intended to create new remedies in the national courts in order to ensure the observance of EU law other than those already in existence in the respective national legal systems of the member states. It supported its arguments by referring to the absence of any EU treaty provisions establishing such new actions and remedies, contrasting this with the EU treaty provisions expressly conferring rights for individuals to take legal action[35] against EU institutions.[36] The two qualifications to procedural autonomy noted in the previous section require member states, if necessary, to effect changes to their national procedural rules, namely to render them suitable to address breaches of EU law in a fashion equivalent to that afforded already in relation to breaches of national law of a similar nature as well to ensure that private persons have a genuine possibility of enforcing their EU rights. However, until relatively recently, the CJEU's jurisprudence appeared to exclude the creation of specific rights of action grounded in EU law for private persons to use to ensure observance of EU law. However, in its judgment in *Francovich*[37] the CJEU signalled a radical departure from the case law on this issue by specifically establishing an individual's right to bring an action before national courts for compensation in respect of serious breaches of EU law perpetrated by member states (namely, the creation of member state liability). In the wake of this ruling, the Court has proceeded to establish a legal framework on state liability, which national courts are intended to apply in respect of claims brought before them by individuals.[38] Before considering the implications of this case law for the environmental sector (section 7.3.2 below), the key legal principles underpinning state liability in respect of breaches of EU law will be examined.

7.3.1 General legal criteria for proving state liability under EU law

In *Francovich* two private individuals brought civil actions against the Italian Republic in respect of a failure on the latter's part to transpose on time a particular employment rights directive, namely the Employer Insolvency Directive[39] on the protection of employees in the event of insolvency of their employer. Under the terms of the directive, member states are obliged to guarantee that employees are to receive a minimum amount of compensation in respect of outstanding unpaid salary claims against their insolvent employer. The national court hearing the legal dispute referred some questions to the CJEU under the preliminary ruling procedure in Article 267 TFEU, including whether the Italian state was required to pay the plaintiffs the minimum guaranteed payments, notwithstanding the absence of any transposition legislation. By way of initial comment, the CJEU held that the directive's provisions requiring a minimum financial guarantee payment to insolvent employees were not directly effective. Given that the directive specifically vested the member states with discretion as to which entity at national level would be liable to make the relevant payments and how that entity would be financed, according to the Court the criteria for direct effect (i.e. sufficient precision and unconditionality) were not fulfilled. Nevertheless, the CJEU went on to confirm that, notwithstanding the absence of direct effect in the case, the private plaintiffs had a right under EU law to seek compensation from the Italian state through the Italian courts. The Court drew on general findings made in its previous case law about the nature and implications of the EU treaty framework in order to reach this conclusion: specifically, its clarification of the unique and autonomous nature of the EU legal system integrated into the member states' own legal systems and which their national courts are bound to apply, its finding that subjects of the EU legal system comprise individuals as well as member states as well as its previous rulings to the effect that national courts' tasks under EU law include the responsibility to apply EU legal provisions in areas falling within their jurisdiction, ensure that those provisions take full effect and protect the rights which they confer on individuals.[40] The Court then proceeded to utilise the concept of *effet utile* to hold that the principle that a member state should be liable for loss and damage caused to individuals as a result of breaches of EU law for which the state can be held responsible was inherent in the EU treaty system.[41] In addition, the CJEU considered that individuals have a right to reparation[42] in respect of such losses and damage from the state:

> The full effectiveness of [Union] rules would be impaired and the protection of the rights which they grant would be weakened if individuals were unable to obtain redress when their rights are infringed by a breach of [Union] law for which a member state can be held responsible.
>
> The possibility of obtaining redress from the member state is particularly indispensable where, as in this case, the full effectiveness of [Union] rules is subject to prior action on the part of the state and where, consequently, in the absence of such action, individuals cannot enforce before the national courts the rights conferred upon them by [Union] law.[43]

The Court has referred in subsequent cases to the factor of effectiveness as well as other grounds as justification for its interpretation that state liability is implicit in the system of the EU treaty framework. The need to ensure effective rights protection is cited, for instance, in subsequent state liability cases of *Brasserie du Pêcheur*[44] and *Dillenkofer*.[45] Other grounds have included ensuring the need for uniformity of application of EU law within the member states[46] and the requirement in Article 19 TEU incumbent upon the CJEU to ensure that EU law is observed.[47]

In *Francovich*, the CJEU set out the three core elements that constituted collectively the legal criteria to be fulfilled in seeking financial redress in respect of illicit statal conduct. These are as follows: first, that the result prescribed in the particular directive should entail the grant of rights individuals; secondly, that it should be possible to identify the content of the rights on the basis of the directive's provisions; and thirdly, the existence of a causal link between the breach of EU law by the member state and the loss and damage suffered by third parties.[48] The Court thereby set out the framework for national courts and tribunals to apply in respect of individual claims of state liability. Whilst it made clear that member states would be responsible for establishing particular national legal procedures to provide for implementation of the principle of state liability, it held that the member states' discretion in so doing is tempered by the requirements to ensure that the procedures are not less favourable to claimants than those in relation to similar internal claims and are not crafted so as to render it virtually impossible or excessively difficult for a claimant to obtain reparation.[49] Accordingly, it is evident that the principle of procedural autonomy has been heavily curtailed and qualified in *Francovich*; not only are member states required to establish a particular right of action and remedy but also are subject to requirements regarding its fairness and efficacy.

Since *Francovich*, the CJEU has had opportunity to offer further clarification and refinement to the legal elements that need to be fulfilled for state liability to be proved. In the leading case of *Brasserie du Pêcheur*[50] the CJEU confirmed a member state would be liable to pay compensation in respect of loss or damage sustained by an individual on account of any serious breach of EU law by the member state, not simply failures to transpose directives correctly. The Court identified that the conditions for liability were from now on to be understood as follows:

> [Union] law confers a right to reparation where three conditions are met: the rule of law infringed must be intended to confer rights on individuals; the breach must be sufficiently serious; and there must be a direct causal link between the breach of obligation resting on the state and the damage sustained by the injured parties.[51]

The CJEU thereby introduced a qualification to the second component of liability, namely that the breach of law had to be shown to be 'sufficiently serious'. The Court thereby clarified that member states would not be automatically liable in respect of each and every breach of EU law, but only those deemed to be of a sufficiently grave nature. It is clear from the case law on state liability that the CJEU has specifically limited exposure of member states to liability in respect of EU law in a number of ways. Not all breaches of EU law may give rise to a duty on the part of states to provide reparation. In particular, the Court has restricted exposure on three fronts: the EU provision in question must be intended to create individual rights, the breach must be of a sufficiently serious nature and there must be evidence of a direct causal link between the breach by the state and loss or damage sustained by an individual or individuals. The three criteria may be viewed as filter mechanisms, designed to exclude claims not regarded as significantly important by the CJEU to warrant liability on the part of member states. The various legal components to state liability will be now examined in more detail below.

7.3.1.1 *Rule of EU law must be intended to confer rights on individuals*

The first criterion of state liability constitutes perhaps the most significant limitation to the application of the rules on state liability under EU law. The CJEU has confirmed that the EU norm in question that is alleged by a plaintiff to have been infringed must have been intended by its authors to create rights for individuals. The CJEU appears to have confirmed that at least three types of EU provisions fulfil this criterion: namely those which are expressly designed to create new substantive or procedural rights for individuals,[52] those which are directly effective[53] as well as those whose effects will have readily foreseeable and immediate economic benefits for individuals.[54]

It appears from the current CJEU case law that breaches of EU norms which are not intended to confer individual rights will in principle not be caught by the rules on state liability. In particular, breaches of EU norms which are intended to benefit society in general, as opposed to enhancing the welfare of individuals, will not usually be subject to the application of state liability. Some discussion has, however, arisen from the CJEU's judgment in *Wells*, discussed earlier, as to whether the Court may not always apply such a rigid approach to this first criterion. In *Wells* the CJEU commented that the claimant in the case would be entitled to compensation from the UK authorities in the event of her sustaining damage as a result of the latter failing to honour the requirements of the Union's Environmental Impact Assessment (EIA) Directive.[55] Given that the Union's EIA legislation does not stipulate rights intended for individuals, but instead primarily focuses on subjecting decisions authorising certain activities affecting the environment to impact assessment as well as public scrutiny, this judicial statement might appear to indicate a loosening of the requirements for state liability.[56] However, it is not evident from the case law whether the CJEU has intended to mark a change of direction in this area. In any event, the judicial comments made by the CJEU were grounded fundamentally in an individual rights paradigm, in terms of limiting themselves to addressing impacts on an individual's personal sphere (e.g. property rights). There was no question of the CJEU in *Wells* moving beyond the conceptual sphere of the protection of individual human interests towards assessing whether the EU rule of law in question intended to protect environmental interests. The implications of this first criterion on state liability for the environmental sector will be examined further in section 7.3.2 below.

7.3.1.2 Sufficiently serious breach of EU law

In *Brasserie du Pêcheur*[57] the CJEU provided some guidelines and factors to be taken into account by the national courts in individual cases in determining whether a particular member state has in fact perpetrated a sufficiently serious breach:

> the decisive test for finding that a breach of [Union] law is sufficiently serious is whether the member state . . . concerned manifestly and gravely disregarded the limits of its discretion.
>
> The factors which the competent [national] court may take into consideration include the clarity and precision of the rule breached, the measure of discretion left by that rule to the national or [Union] authorities, whether the infringement and the damage caused was intentional or involuntary, whether any error of law was excusable or inexcusable, the fact that the position taken by a [Union] institution may have contributed towards the omission, and the adoption or retention of national measures or practices contrary to [Union] law.[58]

These guidelines and factors have become entrenched as key principles in establishing liability on the part of member states. The CJEU's clarification of the criterion of sufficient seriousness identifies that it is not necessary to establish specific subjective intention on the part of the defendant member state in order to prove a manifest and grave violation of EU law. The test for a finding of fault on the part of a defendant state is focused on an essentially objective as opposed to subjective appraisal of the state's behaviour in the circumstances. As the CJEU made clear in *Brasserie du Pêcheur*, reparation for loss or damage may not be made conditional upon fault (intentional or negligent) on the part of the organ responsible for the breach.[59] Accordingly, some violations of EU law are deemed automatically to be inexcusable, given the clear and uncontroversial nature of the EU legal obligations incumbent on a member state. These include failures to transpose directives into national law on time,[60] failure to respect a basic and fundamental legal requirement of one of the provisions of EU law[61] and failure to respect a legal position settled already by the CJEU in a previous ruling.[62]

In particular, where no discretion is afforded to member states in fulfilling their EU obligations, the criterion of sufficient seriousness is in principle likely to be met. An example of where the issue of discretion arose is the *Hedley Lomas* case.[63] The UK government had decided to restrict the export of live animals to Spain for slaughter, having been convinced that animals were being ill-treated in Spanish slaughterhouses contrary to EU Directive 74/577 on stunning of animals before slaughter.[64] Hedley Lomas (Ireland) Ltd, a company whose business involved live sheep exports from the UK, challenged the legality of a decision of the then Ministry of Agriculture, Fisheries and Food to refuse to issue it with an export licence to Spain. Hedley Lomas submitted that the export ban contravened Article 35 TFEU, which prohibits as between member states quantitative restrictions on exports and measures having equivalent effect. Well-established jurisprudence of the CJEU had already confirmed that the provisions were directly effective, so that persons engaging in cross-border trade encountering export restrictions imposed by national law would be able to rely upon the prohibition directly before national courts and enforce it against the competent authorities of the member state of export. In a preliminary ruling under Article 267 TFEU, the CJEU in *Hedley Lomas* noted the following guideline in assisting in determining the presence of a sufficiently serious breach:

> where, at the time when it committed the infringement, the member state in question was not called upon to make any legislative choices and had only considerably reduced, or even no, discretion, the mere infringement of [Union] law may be sufficient to establish the existence of a sufficiently serious breach.[65]

In concluding that the UK had been guilty of a serious breach of EU law, the CJEU noted that the UK had not been in a position in the particular case to produce any proof of non-compliance with the directive in the country to which the animals for which the export licence was sought were destined. Article 36 TFEU affords member states the opportunity to derogate from the prohibition contained in Article 35 TFEU on grounds, *inter alia*, relating to the protection of the life and health of animals. However, that derogation is subject to the express qualification in Article 36 TFEU that prohibitions or restrictions on inter-state trade 'shall not, however, constitute a means of arbitrary discrimination or a disguised restriction on trade between member states'. In effect the CJEU had concluded from the circumstances that the UK had clearly exceeded its discretion set out under EU law pertaining to the free movement of goods.

On the other hand, where there is ambiguity in EU law in relation to the correct interpretation of an obligation, and a member state authority has adopted a plausible but incorrect interpretation, then the CJEU has indicated that it is unlikely for circumstances to be present in which it may fairly be stated that any breach committed by a member state is to be regarded as 'serious'.[66] For instance, the Court concluded that there was no sufficiently serious breach in the *BT* case[67] where a provision in a telecommunications directive contained ambiguous wording and the UK's implementation of the directive had not been subject to any questioning or legal action by the European Commission.[68]

7.3.1.3 Attribution of liability

Case law subsequent to *Francovich* has confirmed that the right to reparation from a member state under the principle of state liability is not only triggered by illicit conduct on the part of a member state's central government (e.g. in failing to transpose a directive correctly or introducing legislation contrary to EU law). The CJEU has confirmed that state liability may arise in respect of actions and omissions of emanations of the state which contravene requirements of EU law. It has employed a wide definition of 'the state' for this purpose, akin to its approach in the direct effect doctrine discussed in the previous chapter. Accordingly, liability may arise as a result of decisions on the part of public authorities at central or local levels.[69] Recently, the CJEU has even confirmed that state liability may arise on account of a failure on the part of a national court of final appeal to enforce EU law.[70] The CJEU has clarified that, although liability may arise from the conduct of any number of institutions within the public sector (including judicial, executive or legislative branches of government) the member state remains liable as a single entity. Whilst the member state has the responsibility to organise internally how the system of state liability is to operate, it is clear that the national legal proceedings used for this purpose must accord with the standard qualifications to the principle of autonomy regarding the administration of justice at national level. Specifically, they must employ procedures and remedies at least commensurate with existing provisions used to render state authorities legally and financially accountable to individuals; these must neither be impossible or excessively difficult in practice to use.[71]

7.3.1.4 Loss and damage

The CJEU has made clear that it is prepared to adopt a relatively wide interpretation of what may be deemed to be loss or damage sustained by an individual as a result of a breach by member states of EU law. Loss or damage may include any economically quantifiable detriments suffered as a result of a breach, prospective as well as historic in nature. A right to reparation is not confined to losses sustained as a result of physical injury or damage to property as it is in some national civil law systems (e.g. as is the case in respect of the foundations to the law of tort in England and Wales). Accordingly, a private person is entitled to reparation in respect of past and/or future pure economic losses (such as loss of commercial profits) as a result of a failure by the member state to adhere to EU rules of law.[72] The general principle enunciated here by the CJEU is that reparation 'must be commensurate with the loss of damage sustained', albeit that it is for the national legal systems of the member states to set criteria or the extent of reparation.[73] Member states are entitled to limit the extent of reparation in order to take account of whether the plaintiff showed reasonable diligence in mitigating his loss and whether he availed himself of all available legal remedies, although they are not permitted to limit the amount of damages simply to account for losses sustained after judgment finding an infringement.[74]

7.3.1.5 Causation

The CJEU has also developed some important ancillary rules on the determination of the third element to state liability, namely proof of a causal link between member state breach and loss and/or damage sustained. It has, for example, confirmed that a defendant state authority may not plead that there is no direct causal link on account of imprudent conduct by a third party or exceptional or unforeseeable events. In the *Rechberger* case[75] a travel company had failed to anticipate the high level of demand for a particular travel offer sponsored by an Austrian newspaper and as a result applied for bankruptcy proceedings to be initiated against itself, leaving several holidaymakers out of pocket having paid deposits and/or the total costs of travelling in advance. The Austrian government had failed to implement on time Directive 90/314 on package travel, holidays and tours.[76] The directive requires member states to ensure that package travel providers give consumers a guarantee by way of insurance contract or bank guarantee so that, in the event of insolvency of the travel provider, any monies paid by the traveller to it in advance of the holiday are reimbursed. The CJEU confirmed that once a direct causal link has been established by the national court in a particular case between loss or damage sustained and the member state's breach, then state liability may not be precluded by imprudent third-party conduct or by exceptional or unforeseeable results.[77]

The CJEU has also had an opportunity to provide some guidance on state liability situations involving more than one state authority. One such instance was in the *Brinkmann* case.[78] The case involved a German company, Brinkmann Tabakfabriken GmbH, which sold rolled tobacco products known as 'Westpoint' in the European Union, including in Denmark. Unlike ordinary cigarettes, Westpoint tobacco products required the consumer to roll paper around a stick of pressed rolled tobacco. The company took legal action before the Danish courts in respect of a decision taken by the Danish Ministry of Fiscal Affairs (Skatteministeriet) on the basis of a determination by its VAT Board (Momsnævnet) that imports of Brinkmann's rolled tobacco products should be classified as cigarettes for the purposes of VAT classification. Under Directive 79/32 on turnover taxes for manufactured tobacco, cigarettes[79] are defined as 'rolls of tobacco capable of being smoked as they are and which are not cigars or cigarillos'. Brinkmann submitted that its products did not constitute cigarettes for the purposes of VAT classification under the directive, but instead 'smoking tobacco' which would be subject to a lower rate of VAT. Denmark had not transposed the directive into national law. In a preliminary ruling, the CJEU confirmed that the Skatteministeriet had misinterpreted the definition of cigarette in this particular.[80] Of interest in the case from the perspective of state liability was the Court's analysis of the criterion of causal link. Specifically, the CJEU held that in this case it could not be argued that state liability could be founded upon the argument that failure to transpose the directive into national law was the cause of losses sustained by Brinkmann, given that the competent national authorities had sought to give immediate effect to the directive in practice. There was no direct causal link between failure to transpose the directive and breach of its requirements.[81] The CJEU went onto confirm that, although technically the Danish tax authorities had breached the terms of the directive by misconstruing the definition of 'cigarette' for the purposes of VAT classification, the breach in itself was not sufficiently serious, given that their interpretation was not 'manifestly contrary' to the directive's wording. Accordingly, the plaintiff had no grounds to sue for reparation from the Danish state under the EU rules on state liability. The *Brinkmann* judgment of the CJEU is particularly important, because it confirms that state liability may flow from the decisions taken by potentially any state or public authority. A member state is accountable, from a legal perspective, for sufficiently serious breaches of EU law perpetrated from any quarter of the public sector and must offer a genuine opportunity for adversely affected individuals to bring claims for reparation in respect of loss or damage resulting from such breaches. A national government, for instance, will not be able to submit that there is no direct causal link on account of the breach having been taken by a local as opposed to central state authority. It is, though, a matter for the member state's legal system to determine how to apportion liability within the public sector.

7.3.2 *State liability and EU environmental law*

It is evident from the overview provided above of the key legal elements that constitute the rules on state liability under EU law that the current legal framework under the *Francovich* jurisprudence offers but limited opportunities for private persons to use them as tools of environmental law enforcement. In several respects, the current rules on state liability developed by the CJEU do seem ill-suited to providing an effective remedy in respect of breaches of EU environmental legislation.[82] The main reason appears to lie with the inherent anthropocentric bias of the rules themselves, which are tailored to accommodating individual human legal interests as opposed to being capable of supporting environmental protection requirements. This becomes readily apparent when one considers the key criteria for liability in turn, namely that the EU norm must be intended to create individual rights, that the breach must be sufficiently serious and that there must be proof of a direct causal link between breach and damage. It also becomes apparent if one takes into account the nature of remedy to be offered if liability is established.

7.3.2.1 *Rights intended to be created for individuals*

The first criterion of state liability, namely that the EU norm in question must be intended to create rights for individuals, has potentially significant implications for the environmental policy sector. Many, if not most, of the requirements on environmental protection enshrined in EU environmental legislation are designed to benefit the collective good, and are not clearly or specifically targeted at enhancing the legal interests of the individual or particular individuals. For instance, the requirements contained in the EU Waste Framework Directive[83] and other EU waste management legislation for member states to take measures to prevent, reduce and recover waste are designed to improve the ability of society in general to manage its waste more efficiently and safely as well as to assist in conserving resources and preserving natural open spaces. The benefits to be reaped from the attainment of these obligations are to be felt by the public and environment in general, and may not be readily interpreted as enhancing rights of the individual. Other environmental instruments at EU level are not even targeted directly at the welfare of humans, but are designed to protect the natural environment, such as the habitats of wild animal species.[84] Admittedly, there are exceptions in EU environmental legislation which lend themselves to be interpreted in an individual rights context. These include requirements which have a direct connection with human legal interests such as public health (e.g. minimum water quality requirements contained in the Bathing Water Directive)[85] or express guarantees of public consultation in respect of site development (e.g. EIA Directive).[86] They also include provisions in EU law which are directly effective. In the main, though, it may be fairly stated that environmental legislation does not readily lend itself to being depicted as a body of rules intended to uphold individual rights.

However, notwithstanding the clear current limitations of the 'individual rights' criterion, it may be premature for two principal reasons to consider that this will remain such a difficult legal hurdle in the long-term future. One is that there is reason to consider that the case law of the CJEU may in future refine the existing criteria for liability. The second reason lies in the recent development of an environmental dimension to human rights analysis at European level. These will be considered in turn.

One should bear in mind that the CJEU's case law on state liability, as is the case in respect of all of its key principles and doctrines, is subject to evolution in accordance with the changing requirements of the EU treaty framework itself. It is no surprise that the CJEU has focused attention initially on individual rights protection in the context of state liability. Its principal motivation thus far in developing the rules on state liability has been quite evidently to ensure that the EU legal order is respected as effectively as possible within the territories of the member states, an order which the Court has depicted since *Van Gend en Loos*[87] as comprising not only the member states as contracting parties but also the individuals located within the Union affected by the rules underpinning the EU treaty framework. In the previous chapter, we have seen how the CJEU has sought to develop a body of rights for individuals in order to enable them to rely upon EU provisions contained in directives before national courts and tribunals (direct and indirect effect doctrines). The development of rules on state liability has served to enhance the rights of individuals to enforce EU provisions intended to safeguard or promote their specific legal interests. In particular, in relation to EU Directives state liability plugs a gap left open by the direct and indirect effect doctrines. This is evident from the *Francovich* case, in which neither doctrine was of use to the private plaintiffs seeking to rely upon legal commitments entered into by the Italian state under the Employer Insolvency Directive[88] to guarantee them a minimum amount of outstanding salary payments.

It is evident though that the EU treaty system has changed significantly since its original conception in the 1950s. Its original core purpose centred on promoting a specific anthropocentric interest, namely the establishment of a common market. Environmental protection was not cited as a specific goal of the overall aspiration of an 'ever closer union among the peoples of Europe' in the original foundational treaty of the EU, the former 1957 EEC Treaty. However, since the mid 1980s, it is evident that the political priorities of the European Union have been formally amended to take account of new environmental protection aims and objectives of that international organisation. By virtue of successive amendments to the EU's treaty framework (notably by virtue of the Single European Act 1986, Treaty on European Union 1992), the Amsterdam Treaty 1997, the Nice Treaty 2001 and Lisbon Treaty 2007) the EU has steadily developed stronger political commitments and an accompanying legal framework intended to foster European supranational co-operation on environmental protection issues. In particular, the objects clause of the EU foundational treaty structure (Article 3 TEU) has been amended to establish that 'a high level of protection and improvement of the quality of the environment' as well as 'sustainable development' constitute integral political objectives of the European Union.[89] In addition, it is now a fundamental principle of the EU treaty framework that environmental protection requirements are to be integrated into the definition and implementation of Community policies and activities.[90] These constitutional changes to the EU treaty framework indicate that over time the Union's political and legal order has been amended so as to embrace environmental protection requirements as well as interests of immediate economic concern to individuals. It is evident that the contemporary legal architecture of the EU could be described as containing a strong integral environmental dimension within its constitutional framework.[91]

Bearing this in mind, it would appear that the first criterion developed by the CJEU on state liability does not lend itself to assisting in the achievement of the environmental protection dimension underpinning the fundamental treaty objectives of the Union. Much of the case law of the CJEU on individual rights protection (e.g. direct and indirect effect as well as state liability) has been justified on the basis of ensuring that the norms constituting the EU legal order are enforced as effectively as possibly within the territories of the member states. It may therefore be more appropriate for the CJEU in future to focus on reappraising whether its existing legal principles and doctrines pertaining to the proper enforcement of EU law at national level adequately reflect the requirements of a supranational legal order which places environmental protection amongst the fundamental tasks assumed by the Union. In some respects, it may be argued that the CJEU has already undertaken some steps to accommodate environmental protection requirements within the range of rights afforded to individuals to engage in enforcement of EU law. Specifically, as was noted in the previous chapter, the *Kraaijeveld* case[92] appears to have loosened the traditional requirements of the direct effect doctrine in order to enable private persons to enforce adherence to impact assessment requirements contained in the EIA Directive.[93] It may be the case that the CJEU may come to loosen the existing criteria regarding state liability with a view to achieving the same ends.[94]

Even if the CJEU maintains the first criterion as a condition for a finding of state liability, there is a second reason to consider that in the long term it may not constitute such a significant legal hurdle in respect of environmental cases. Specifically, it is submitted that the evolving state of human rights protection within the EU legal order may present interesting possibilities in this regard. Until relatively recently, environmental protection was not considered to form any direct links with the subject of human rights protection. For instance, the environmental protection rights do not feature expressly in any of the classic international human rights instruments, such as the UN Declaration on Human Rights 1948,[95] International Covenant on Economic, Social and Cultural Rights 1966[96] and International Covenant on Civil and Political Rights 1966.[97] Whilst the 1972 UN Declaration on the Human Environment[98] in Stockholm sought to establish an internationally recognised general principle of a human rights dimension to the environment, subsequent international political developments have failed to entrench this into treaty format; indeed the follow-up 1992 UN Declaration[99] at Rio in the UN Conference on Environment and Development refers merely to human 'entitlement' as opposed to any 'right' to a healthy and productive life in harmony with nature. At European level, the central regional human rights instrument, the European Convention on Human Rights and Fundamental Freedoms (ECHR) 1950,[100] similarly does not expressly provide for any human rights with respect to the state of the environment. Likewise, until relatively recently the EU constitutional framework has been devoid of any express commitment to link human rights with respect to the environment.

However, the legal picture has changed with the advent of a new generation of human rights instruments affecting the EU legal order. Specifically, in 2000 the Heads of State of the EU signed a formal declaration on human rights intended to shape the future political decision-making of the Union, namely the Charter of Fundamental Rights of the European Union (EUCFR).[101] Initially a political non-binding instrument, the EUCFR has been eventually[102] woven into the EU treaty fabric by virtue of the 2007 Lisbon Treaty. Specifically, Article 6 TEU confirms that the rights, freedoms and principles set out in the EUCFR have the same legal value as the foundational treaties of the Union (TFEU and TEU). Article 37 EUCFR, housed in Chapter IV (Solidarity) of the instrument stipulates:

Article 37 Environmental Protection

> A high level of environmental protection and the improvement of the quality of the environment must be integrated into the policies of the Union and ensured in accordance with the principle of sustainable development.

Although Article 37 EUCFR does not itself expressly speak in terms of individual rights, it is clear that the EU Heads of State intended to endow its requirements with the fundamental significance of human rights, given that Article 37 is enshrined within a human rights instrument.

Bearing in mind these recent constitutional developments, the role of the CJEU in interpreting their significance is critically important. In the past, the CJEU has shown itself prepared to develop its jurisprudence on human rights protection within the EU legal order, notwithstanding the absence of any specific legal commitment in the EU treaty framework to protect human rights. In a variety of cases tracing back to the 1970s it has confirmed the implicit presence of human rights forming part of the general principles of law underpinning the EU treaty system, partly on the basis that the EU institutions had signed up to human rights declarations, notwithstanding these being of a politically as opposed to legally binding nature, and partly on the basis that all the member states were party to the ECHR 1950.[103] Given that the member states have now committed themselves to ensuring the environment is protected to a high level and is to be treated as being of the nature of a human right (through the EUCFR), it is open for the CJEU to conclude that human rights protection within the EU legal order has a clearly articulated environmental dimension. Specifically, the CJEU could now conclude that the environmental protection legislation passed by the EU is recognised by the member states to have an inherent human rights element or dimension. Accordingly, such an interpretation would enable the CJEU to conclude that all legally binding commitments entered into by the member states to enhance environmental quality are by definition designed, albeit in part, to underpin human rights. As has been pointed out elsewhere,[104] the European Court of Human Rights has, for example, noted the contribution that environmental impact legislation may bring in forging an appropriate balance between public interests and individual rights to privacy and family life as protected under Article 8 ECHR.[105] Seen through the lens of EU human rights protection, the first criterion of the rules on state liability under EU law could be interpreted so as to embrace EU norms intended to protect the environment.

All this, of course, is not to say that the CJEU will definitely shift or otherwise amend the boundaries set by the first criterion to state liability along the lines suggested above. What is pertinent to say is that it would be open for the CJEU to develop its jurisprudence to modify the current appreciation of the first criterion or even abandon it, in a way that would be consonant with its existing approaches to developing new legal possibilities of enforcing EU law by private persons. In so doing, it might also thereby make available legal opportunities for a broader range of stakeholders to hold member states legally accountable for failures to adhere to EU environmental legislation. Specifically, a relaxation or broadening out of the 'individual rights' criterion could make it easier for NGEOs and even public agencies involved in environmental protection to be able to utilise the rules on state liability to ensure that activities damaging to the environment which are in contravention of EU environmental legislation are effectively remedied. At the moment, though, it appears that the 'individual rights' criterion does not appear to anticipate private litigants taking legal action against member states in order to protect the rights of third parties. The current EU framework on state liability appears to expect, if not require, that only personally adversely affected individuals should be entitled to bring legal action before the national courts. As a consequence, in practice only a limited range of persons would appear to have a clear right to be vested with legal standing to pursue a state liability case, namely individual victims of illicit state conduct. Other stakeholders motivated to engage in environmental law enforcement may well, as a result of this procedural requirement on standing, be barred from taking any action under national procedural rules.[106]

Ultimately, the root of the problem lies with the requirement established by the CJEU that state liability may only attach itself to breaches of EU norms intended to create individual rights. However one may be able to stretch this legal element, for instance by incorporating a human rights dimension within it, this will not be sufficient to ensure the appropriate level of legal support to members of the public and/or NGEOs seeking to enforce EU environmental legislation. According to Article 19 TEU member states are required to provide remedies sufficient to ensure effective legal protection in the fields covered by Union law. Given that constitutionally the EU is committed to ensuring a high level of protection and improvement of the quality of the environment,[107] the CJEU should seek to interpret the obligations in Article 19 and its jurisprudence on state liability in a manner suited to ensure effective protection of EU environmental obligations. It is difficult to see how the first criterion serves to fulfil those constitutional commitments.

7.3.2.2 Criterion of a 'sufficiently serious' breach

The second legal component to state liability under EU law, namely that the breach of EU law must be sufficiently serious in order to trigger state liability, also serves to restrict the range of possibilities for legal action to be taken by private persons to enforce EU environmental legislation. The criterion makes clear that only certain types of breaches of EU law, including EU environmental legislation, are potentially open to the possibility of a state liability claim. This confirms that member states are not to be made automatically liable to offer remedies in respect of all infractions of EU environmental legislation; there is no strict liability in the sense of there being an automatic duty to remedy breaches of environmental protection norms under the rules of EU state liability. In its defence, the criterion of 'seriousness' aims to serve a practical purpose in helping to ensure that national courts as well as the CJEU are neither bound to adjudicate on trivial cases nor overwhelmed with casework. However, it is important that the criterion of 'seriousness' is carefully and clearly defined in order to ensure that claimants are not confronted with a legal term lacking in legal certainty and ill-suited to ensuring that meritorious cases succeed.

Depending upon how it is to be interpreted, one might argue with some justification, though, that the introduction of the criterion of sufficient seriousness is prone to falling short of the overall constitutional requirements binding upon the EU in relation to its environmental policy. Specifically, it is important that the criterion is defined sufficiently clearly and strictly so as to be in accordance with the objective of the EU treaty framework of attaining a 'high level' of environmental protection,[108] as well as with other general environmental principles set out in Article 191(2) TFEU, including notably the principles of 'polluter pays', precaution and of preventive action. Otherwise, Union member states might be able to evade responsibility for implementing EU environmental law correctly within their respective territories. This is a plausible scenario if the criterion were to be defined in a broad and/or ambiguous manner by the CJEU. For, as was discussed in Part I of this book, it is unrealistic in practice to expect that the European Commission is able or even willing to launch infringement proceedings under Articles 258 and 260 TFEU in all environmental protection cases. Even if infringement proceedings are launched, they take a substantial length of time (years) before a member state may end up being subject to specific pecuniary sanctions. Whilst environmental authorities at national level may be available to enforce EU environmental legislation, this is not possible where national law has not provided them with the relevant legal powers and resources in order to do this. For instance, a national environmental authority has little or no opportunity to take action against a private polluter whose activities infringe the requirements of an EU environmental directive that has not been correctly implemented into national law (see doctrines of direct and indirect effect discussed in Chapter 6).

The CJEU has, to some extent, sought to accommodate these concerns by confirming that a failure to transpose a directive, whose provisions are unambiguous, correctly into national law constitutes *per se* a sufficiently serious breach for the purposes of state liability. Liability will be automatic in these cases, irrespective of the degree of adverse consequences in practice for the environment. However, the criterion is particularly prone to the charge of legal uncertainty in so-called 'bad-application' cases, where member states and national authorities have failed to discharge their duties to implement the specific environmental protection requirements of an EU directive in practice. Specifically, how much pollution would have to flow under the bridge, so to speak, before a 'sufficiently serious' breach is deemed to have been committed in an individual case? The simple formula of sufficient seriousness is unhelpful in this regard and needs clarification and refinement by the CJEU, in order to assist national courts apply it to the facts of individual instances of detected illicit pollution. Otherwise, the ambiguity of the legal position may well serve to act in practice as a deterrent to persons contemplating enforcement litigation. In accordance with the requirements of attaining a high level of protection of the environment, any breach of EU environmental legislation should be deemed to constitute a 'sufficiently serious' breach for the purposes of state liability.

The dangers of drawing up a vague and loose criterion for state liability have been illustrated elsewhere in the CJEU's jurisprudence. Specifically, a similar problem of interpretation has emerged in the context of the Commission enforcing general requirements of EU waste management law, as discussed in Part I of this book. The CJEU has held that the general and core environmental and public health safety duties contained in the EU Waste Framework Directive[109] may be said to be infringed only where there is a significant deterioration in the environment over a protracted period when no action has been taken by the competent national authorities.[110] The inclusion of the term 'significant deterioration' does nothing to assist in the Commission's task of knowing at what point to intervene with infringement action against a member state under Articles 258/260 TFEU. In addition, the criterion of 'significant deterioration' undermines the object of the preventive action principle set out in Article 191(2) TFEU which mandates the EU institutions and Member states when implementing EU environmental law, *inter alia*, to ensure that action is taken so far as practicable to prevent environmental harm taking place where this is likely to otherwise occur or become worse.

7.3.2.3 *Direct causal link*

In practice, proving a direct causal link between a breach of EU environmental law and damage or loss may prove to be a particularly difficult hurdle for private litigants to overcome in certain types of cases. On the one hand, causation is not a significant issue if the root of the problem lies in a failure to transpose an EU environmental directive on time and/or correctly. Likewise, if a case centres on the failure by state authorities to implement the provisions of directives correctly, it is clear that they may rely neither upon the factor of imprudent third party conduct[111] nor upon the existence of unforeseeable events[112] as a defence to liability. However, in certain types of bad-application cases, the task of the plaintiff to be able to prove a direct causal link may prove very challenging.

In particular, this may arise in so-called 'multiple source' cases where it is not clear from a scientific perspective as to the precise source of loss or damage sustained by the plaintiff. For instance, there may well be a lack of scientifically verifiable evidence that a failure on the part of a member state to implement the requirements of EU air quality legislation designed to curb air pollutant emissions from road vehicles is in fact predominantly or partially to blame for a specific case of ill-health of an individual (e.g. asthma or other lung-related diseases). It may be perfectly plausible to consider a range of causes in respect of a particular medical condition, one of which may include pollutant emissions from road vehicles. It is apparent that in these types of situations the CJEU may well have to accommodate the third criterion of state liability to the requirements of environmental principles recognised in the EU treaty framework such as the precautionary and preventive action principles (Article 191(2) TFEU), in order to do justice to its overall objective and obligation as judicial institution of the Union to see that EU law is applied properly and effectively in the member states.[113]

The CJEU has already acknowledged that member states are required to take account of principles such as the precautionary principle in the context of implementing EU environmental directives. In the *Waddenzee* case[114] the CJEU was required to interpret the meaning of Article 6(3) of the Habitats Directive 92/43,[115] which requires member states to subject a plan or project 'likely to have a significant effect' on the management of a protected habitat site to an environmental impact assessment, even though the plan or project is not directly connected with or necessary to the management of the site concerned. The CJEU proceeded to interpret the meaning of 'likely' (i.e. probability) on the following basis:

> In the light, in particular, of the precautionary principle, which is one of the foundations of the high level of environmental protection pursued by [Union] policy on the environment, in accordance with the first subparagraph of [Article 191(2) TFEU], and by reference to which the Habitats Directive must be interpreted, such a risk exists if it cannot be excluded on the basis of objective information that the plan or project will have significant effects on the site concerned . . . Such an interpretation of the condition to which the assessment of the implications of a plan or project for a specific site is subject, which implies that in case of doubt as to the absence of significant effects such an assessment must be carried out, makes it possible to ensure effectively that plans or projects which adversely affect the integrity of the site concerned are not authorised, and thereby contributes to achieving, in

accordance with the third recital in the preamble to the Habitats Directive and Article 2(1) thereof, its main aim, namely, ensuring biodiversity through the conservation of natural habitats and of wild fauna and flora.[116]

This jurisprudence has potentially profound implications for future interpretation and application of EU environmental legislation. The CJEU has appeared to confirm that the precautionary principle is relevant in relation to the implementation of all environmental legislation adopted under the auspices of Article 192 TFEU. As is the case in respect of the Habitats Directive 92/43, express reference to the principle is not required to be incorporated in the legislation itself; this will be implicit by virtue of the fact that the principle is an inherent part of EU environmental policy under Article 191(2) TFEU. The Court has yet, though, to consider if and how the precautionary principle should be applied in the context of a state liability case involving a breach of EU environmental law. The application of the principle may well prove to be crucial in terms of the degree to which plaintiffs of environmental damage may be able to negotiate successfully the difficulties associated with disputes over the credibility of scientific evidence on a suspected cause of environmental damage.

The requirement to prove a direct causal link between member state and loss or damage, as currently crafted by the CJEU, is challenging from an environmental perspective in other ways in respect of bad-application cases. In particular, a member state government and/or its environmental protection authorities may wish to deny responsibility for environmental damage where the physical damage may be immediately attributed to a third party which is not an emanation of the state. A direct causal link may be legitimately refuted where the member state concerned has correctly transposed relevant minimum EU legislative standards into national law by way of public statute so as to be applicable to all potential and actual polluters located within its territory and which contains adequate enforcement systems such as penalties of a sufficiently deterrent nature.[117] However, it is clear that a causal link may not be denied where a member state has failed to transpose an EU environmental directive into national law and a private company within the member state contravenes the requirements of the directive, given that directives are not legally binding on private persons.

7.3.2.4 Loss, damage and reparation

Two other elements to the current case law on state liability present significant obstacles to private persons being able to utilise the principles of state liability in environmental disputes. These concern the legal specification of loss or damage sustained as well as the type of remedy that may be available to a successful litigant in a state liability action. Both elements are closely interlinked, the root of the problem lying with the CJEU's limitation on the type of remediation that is to be afforded to a successful claimant who has proved that environmental damage has been sustained as a direct result of a breach of EU environmental law by the member state and/or its authorities.

Since its first ruling on state liability in the *Francovich* case the CJEU has appeared to have consistently restricted the nature of the remedy for state liability claims as a monetised and wholly economic conception of remediation. The standard approach of the Court has been to refer to member states' obligation to pay 'reparation' to individuals who have sustained loss or damage. This model of economic remediation is clearly based on an anthropocentric perception of the degree to which legal responsibilities are imposed on member states under EU law. Specifically, the CJEU has predicated its entire approach on the principle of state liability on the basis that individuals should be afforded adequate guarantees in being able to enforce rights that have been agreed at Union level for their specific and immediate economic benefit. It is no coincidence that the case law of the CJEU on state liability has been developed subsequent to its jurisprudence on direct and indirect effect; the state liability principles have been designed quite evidently in order to ensure that individuals are able to uphold EU norms intended to protect their economic interests vis-à-vis the member state authorities before the national courts. In effect, the case law on state liability seeks to provide a minimum remedy for breaches of EU law norms that seek essentially to bring economic benefits for individuals, in particular where the doctrines of direct and indirect effect may not be able to be utilised in a particular case. The CJEU's case law on state liability has accordingly limited the scope of remedy to one of monetary reparation. In addition, it is clear that the CJEU has limited the concept of loss or damage envisaged to being one that may be characterised as personal to the plaintiff and quantifiable in terms of a monetary value. Such legal conceptions of loss, damage and remediation are quite evidently ill-suited to offering private plaintiffs a suitable legal remedy in the cases involving damage to the environment.

REPARATION AS A LEGAL REMEDY IN ENVIRONMENTAL CASES

First and foremost, the remedy of monetary reparation is not usually going to prove to be an effective legal remedy in an environmental protection context. The optimal solution from an environmental perspective is to harness law enforcement procedures so as to secure cessation of damaging activities and restoration of the site concerned to its state prior to being damaged by illicit activity. Any order by a national court or tribunal for the defendant member state authorities to transfer a monetary form of reparation to the plaintiff, who has proven damage resulting from a breach of EU environmental law, is tantamount to a form of taxation for illicit pollution. Taxation effectively legitimises the activities or behaviour of the defendant. Such a remedy obviously does not further environmental protection objectives; the reparation of itself does not require or necessarily result environmentally restorative steps to occur. In addition, the assessment of environmental damage in monetary terms may often be a notoriously difficult if not impossible enterprise to undertake, where the monetary reparation is not going to be calculated on the basis of need to restore the damaged environment and/or where the particular environmental damage is irrevocable. For these reasons, the availability of injunctive relief would prove a far more effective remedy in many instances involving illegal environmental degradation.[118]

In addition, the legal conception of 'loss' or 'damage' appears from the CJEU's case law thus far to be confined to harm personal to the plaintiff, namely to be identified as falling within the plaintiff's exclusive domain. This would typically include loss or damage sustained in respect of the claimant's physical person and/ or legal interests in land or goods. The requirement that harm must be shown to have been perpetrated to the proprietary realm of the plaintiff seriously limits the possibilities for the private sector to seek effective judicial remedies in respect of environmental damage. It effectively excludes the possibility of private entities using the right of action developed by the CJEU in respect of illicit statal conduct to ensure the national courts order a remedy in respect of environmental damage, irrespective of whether the plaintiffs have a legal proprietorial interest in the affected geographical location. The right of action is instead predicated upon the readiness of a legal proprietor, whose property interests may be adversely affected by statal conduct, to launch litigation before the national courts. Accordingly, the possibility of NGEOs and others being able to sue the state for effective remedies in respect of breaches of EU environmental law is severely undermined. The EU rules on state liability developed by the CJEU effectively exclude private entities from being able to sue on behalf of the environment wherever environmental damage may be perpetrated within the EU. They fail to recognise that the environment and the need for its protection are issues which respect neither frontiers nor legal conceptions of ownership. EU environmental legislation is intended to deliver benefits for society as a whole. The breach of such legislation violates the public interest. The CJEU's current rules on state liability for breaches of EU law appear focused, however, on securing remedies for breaches of law intended to further legal interests of individuals as opposed to collective interests. This constitutes a serious limit on the ability of the state liability case law to be capable of delivering the necessary legal tools to enable private entities to uphold EU environmental law at national level.

The CJEU's conception of relevant 'loss' or 'damage' appears also to be restricted in a temporal sense. Specifically, the case law appears to indicate that national judicial remedial assistance in respect of state liability may only be able to be requested at the stage where harm has already been perpetrated. The existing jurisprudence of the Court is firmly rooted in traditional conceptions of tortious liability, where a remedy is to be provided in respect of harm having taken place in the past (*ex post* litigation). This judicial approach by the CJEU means that private litigants are not able to utilise the state liability action to situations where environmental damage is a realistic likelihood or even definite outcome in the future (*ex ante* litigation). Scenarios of loss or damage considered to be material from the current orthodox legal perspective are accordingly limited to instances where environmental harm has occurred. A private party may not initiate action on the basis of a probable future loss or damage to the environment as a result of illicit statal behaviour. This limitation runs counter to fundamental principles of environmental protection grounded in the EU treaty framework, in particular the principles of preventive action and precaution (Article 191(2) TFEU).

In summary, it is evident from the above analysis that the current rules developed thus far by the CJEU on a right of action in respect of state liability for breaches of EU law are, for the most part, essentially ill-suited to the purpose of securing an effective remedy in respect of actual or potential illicit damage to the environment. The origins of the rules are clearly rooted in the CJEU's long-standing quest since the *Van Gend en Loos* case[119] to develop the emerging *sui generis* EU legal order on a footing that encompasses individuals as well as member states. However, the Court has yet to ensure that the rules on state liability adequately reflect the transition of the EU's constitutional framework to one which, since the adoption of amendments such as the Single European Act 1986, now expressly recognises that a high level of environmental protection constitutes a prominent dimension to the process European integration under the aegis of the EU treaty framework. The EU self-evidently is no longer simply an anthropocentric concern.[120]

Bearing in mind these constitutional changes, there is a compelling case on grounds of *effet utile* to argue that the Court should expand the remit of state liability under EU law in order to encompass a requirement that member states are to effect suitable remedies to rectify environmental damage in respect of which they or their competent authorities are responsible. The CJEU has developed a right of action in respect of state conduct under EU law, notwithstanding the absence of any specific or express provision that this is to be provided in the provisions of the EU treaty framework. Rights of action are provided in the EU treaty framework to seek review of illicit conduct on the part of EU institutions[121] but not in respect of activities and omissions by member states that breach EU law. The Court has nevertheless held since *Francovich* that such a right of action is to be implied from the Treaty, principally on the basis of the general 'good faith' provisions contained in Article 4(3) TEU and that the right of action serves to promote the effectiveness of legally binding EU rules, as agreed between member states. Given that the nature of the EU legal order is one in which now contains a clear environmental protection dimension, it would be arbitrary on the Court's part to decide to limit state liability as being a legal mechanism incapable of holding member states to account in respect of those breaches of EU environmental law for which they and/or their national competent authorities are directly responsible. Accordingly, it is incumbent upon the CJEU to shape the state liability rules so that they represent an effective remedy vis-à-vis member states who fail to ensure that EU environmental protection standards are upheld within their territory. Otherwise, the jurisprudence of the CJEU on state liability will fail to ensure that the rights and remedies to be drawn from the EU treaty framework are equipped to be effective in upholding the legally binding guarantees on environmental protection that member states agree to in the form of EU secondary measures.

7.4 Some concluding remarks

From the overview and discussion provided above, there is no doubt that the CJEU has made, and continues to make, significant contributions in terms of developing the scope and depth of private persons' rights and interests to uphold norms of EU law within the Union's member states. The qualifications that it has made to the principle of procedural autonomy have assisted individuals substantially in being able to rely on the doctrines of direct and indirect effect of EU law before national courts. The establishing of state liability by the CJEU in *Francovich* has also ensured that member states are held to account for serious failures on their part to ensure that EU law is implemented, including most notably in situations where direct and indirect effect may not be available as legal tools in specific cases to assist in ensuring that erroneous application of EU law is corrected.

However, it is also clear that the CJEU's jurisprudence has significant limitations when applied in the context of private enforcement of EU environmental law. In particular, the Court's jurisprudence concerning the principle of procedural autonomy suffers from the disadvantage that the legal implications of several of its rulings are uncertain, given that the Court often sets out broad and general precedents in relation to the provision of remedies for breaches of EU law. The reach of the general principles it has set down in previous cases is often difficult to determine and is not in practice readily taken on board by competent member state authorities. Frequently, national courts may have to resort to the time-consuming and, for the litigants, added cost of the preliminary ruling procedure under Article 267 TFEU, in order to gain definitive advice from the CJEU as to the extent of procedural rights and responsibilities of EU law in the material circumstances at hand. The *Lappel Bank* litigation[122] provides a good example of uncertainty as to whether or not the requirement of a national rule of legal procedure exceeds the limits of autonomy given to member states in constructing rules on the administration of justice at national level where these involve administering the application of EU law. The House of Lords in that case did not refer either to the CJEU for advice as to whether EU law would require the national requirement of a cross-undertaking in damages to be set aside, which underlines a separate but important related issue that the preliminary ruling procedure under Article 267 TFEU is not a right of the parties to seek assistance from the CJEU but ultimately a facility for the national courts to use if they consider a point of EU law to be relevant to the case at hand. That litigation also demonstrated another key weakness of the principle of procedural autonomy, namely that it serves to suppress the development by the CJEU of rights of access before and remedies from the national courts, the state liability right of action notwithstanding. Instead, the procedural autonomy principle is predicated upon a fundamental recognition that the member states retain sovereignty to determine the particular legal suits that individuals may bring before the national judiciary and remedies they may claim to effect changes to the conduct of other parties that may be found to be in breach of EU law.

The CJEU's jurisprudence on state liability, as an exception to the procedural autonomy principle, harbours different problems and challenges. Although it does establish a right of a private person to take legal action in order to uphold certain norms of EU law, something that the traditional general legal principles on rights developed by the CJEU did not do (such as the direct and indirect effect doctrines as well as the general principles on procedural autonomy), the right is limited in scope and potential to enhance private enforcement of EU environmental law. The existing legal criteria established for state liability, in being anthropocentric in outlook, do not lend themselves to being appropriate for the context of environmental litigation. Thus far, the CJEU has not crafted the state liability rules so as to provide private persons with an effective right to seek due enforcement of EU environmental norms at national level. Instead, the rules have been shaped so as to provide a personalised remedy in monetary form for individual plaintiffs as opposed to a remedy that upholds EU law for the benefit of society as a whole and as originally intended by the legislator. Whilst EU rules on state liability may provide some assistance in the context of litigation involving breaches of EU environmental law that result in damages to physical health or economic loss to individuals, they offer no help in terms of holding member states to account for breaches of EU environmental law resulting in environmental damage that may not be somehow easily categorised or classified in terms of human legal interests. Thus, the current legal framework for state liability under EU law is therefore of little use in supporting private litigation which seeks to ensure that member states enforce EU environmental legislation on nature protection. In addition, state liability is no assistance in the context of disputes over compliance with EU environmental law where the adverse environmental impact of a breach is not incurred by person's exclusive private sphere (e.g. in relation to a particular geographical location over which they have specific preferential legal entitlement or in relation to their physical well-being).

What is certain is that the CJEU's current case law on procedural rights and remedies is, at best, of limited assistance in practice to private persons seeking to enforce EU environmental law at national level and gain an appropriate remedy from member state judicial and/or non-judicial authorities. The Court has not yet developed its jurisprudence in the areas of access to justice and remedies sufficiently to take account of the fact that the nature of the EU legal order has changed into one in which environmental protection interests feature alongside purely anthropocentric concerns of individuals. Whilst there are signs in the CJEU's jurisprudence that the Court is perhaps beginning to evolve the current body of general legal principles on rights and remedies to a position that emphasises member state responsibilities in upholding EU legally binding commitments, as opposed to focusing principally on the particular interests of claimants in their capacities of individuals, this judicial process is both an uncertain enterprise and one in which legal development is gradual in nature.

This leads appropriately into a discussion of the recent legislative developments at EU level that are intended to establish significant legal reform in the area of private enforcement of EU environmental law. These legislative innovations are discussed in the next chapter.

Notes

1 Case C-72/95 *Kraaijeveld.*
2 The Union signed the UNECE Convention in 1998 and ratified its participation in 2005 by virtue of Council Decision 2005/370 (OJ 2005 L124/1).
3 This broad mandate of the CJEU is now contained in Art. 19(1) TEU.
4 See e.g. Case 6/60 *Humblet* and Case 13/68 *Salgoil.*
5 Superseding predecessor 'good faith' treaty provisions contained in Art. 10 EC/Art. 5 EEC.
6 See e.g. Case 33/76 *Rewe.*
7 Case C-430/93 *Van Schijndel* (para. 17 of judgment).
8 Case C-271/91 *Marshall (2).*
9 Former Directive 76/207 (OJ 1976 L39/40) as subsequently replaced by Directive 2006/54 (OJ 2006 L204/23).
10 The current Sex Equality in Employment Directive 2006/54 contains more detailed requirements regarding the provision of national remedies in relation to breaches of the directive's equality provisions (see esp. Arts. 18 and 25).
11 See in particular Case 14/83 *Von Colson.* See also Case C-180/95 *Draehmpahl,* where the CJEU confirmed unconditional obligations upon national courts flowed from Art. 6 of the former Directive 76/207 so as to preclude the application of national laws imposing ceilings on compensation.
12 Case C-213/89 *Factortame (1).*
13 See also para. 107 of judgment in Case C-416/10 *Križan and others* (judgment of 15 January 2013, not yet reported).
14 See e.g. Case C-106/89 *Marleasing* and Case C-91/92 *Dori.*
15 Directive 2011/92 (OJ 2011 L26/1).
16 See e.g. Case C-72/95 *Kraaijeveld,* Case C-435/97 *WWF v Bozen,* Case C-287/98 *Linster* and Case C-127/02 *Waddenzee.*
17 The major exception is the jurisprudence of the CJEU on state liability, which has created the existence of a right to a specific legal remedy and conditions for its application under EU law in the event of a serious breach of EU rules. This particular legal area and its implications for EU environmental law enforcement will be addressed in the section 7.3 below.
18 Case C-430/93 *Van Schijndel.*
19 See Case C-72/95 *Kraaijeveld* (para. 60 of judgment).
20 See Case C-115/09 *Bund für Umwelt and Naturschutz Deutschland* (para. 43 of judgment); Case C-416/10 *Križan and others* (para. 85 of judgment of 15 January 2013 (not yet reported)).
21 Case C-237/07 *Janecek.*
22 Former Directive 96/62 (OJ 1996 L296/55) as subsequently repealed and superseded by Directive 2008/50 on ambient air quality assessment and management (OJ 2008 L152/1). (See Art. 24 of Directive 2008/50 which is the successor provision to Art. 7(3) of former Directive 96/62).
23 Former Direvctive 1999/30 relating to limit values for sulphur dioxide, nitrogen dioxide, oxides of nitrogen, particulate matter and lead in ambient air (OJ 1999 L163/41) as subsequently repealed and superseded by Directive 2008/50 on ambient air quality assessment and management (OJ 2008 L152/1).
24 Case C-237/07 *Janecek* (para. 39 of judgment).
25 The successor EU directive (Directive 2008/50) is similarly silent on this issue.
26 Case C-44/95 *Lappel Bank.*
27 Directive 2009/147 (OJ 2009 L20/7) superseding former Directive 79/409 (OJ 1979 L103/1) which was in force at the time of the case.
28 Scott (1998), pp. 164–5.
29 See e.g. Cases C-72/95 *Kraaijeveld,* C-318/98 *Fornasar* and C-201/02 *Delena Wells.*

30 C-201/02 *Delena Wells* (para. 64 of judgment).
31 Directive 2011/92 (OJ 2011 L26/1) which replaced former Directive 85/337 (OJ 1985 L175/40) in force at the time of the case.
32 C-201/02 *Delena Wells* (paras. 65–6 of judgment).
33 Case 152/84 *Marshall (1)*.
34 See e.g. Case C-201/02 *Delena Wells*.
35 See Arts. 263, 265 and 268 TFEU (ex Arts. 230, 232 and 235 EC).
36 Case 158/80 *Rewe* (para. 44 of judgment).
37 Joined Cases C-6 and 9/90 *Francovich and Bonifaci*.
38 See e.g Case C-319/96 *Brinkmann* (para. 26 of judgment).
39 Directive 2008/94 (OJ 2008 L312/3) which superseded former Directive 80/987 (OJ 1980 L283/23) which was in force at the time of the case.
40 Joined Cases C-6 and 9/90 *Francovich and Bonifaci* (paras. 31–2 of judgment).
41 Ibid. (para. 35 of judgment).
42 Ibid. (para. 39 of judgment).
43 Ibid. (paras. 33–4 of judgment).
44 Case C-46/93 *Brasserie du Pêcheur* (paras. 20–39 of judgment).
45 Case C-178/94 *Dillenkofer* (para. 22 of judgment).
46 Case C-46/93 *Brasserie du Pêcheur* (para. 33 of judgment).
47 Ibid.
48 Joined Cases C-6 and 9/90 *Francovich and Bonifaci* (para. 40 of judgment). See also C-178/94 *Dillenkofer* (para. 22 of judgment).
49 Joined Cases C-6 and 9/90 *Francovich and Bonifaci* (para. 43 of judgment). See also C-46/93 *Brasserie du Pêcheur* (para. 73 of judgment).
50 Case C-46/93 *Brasserie du Pêcheur*.
51 Ibid. (para. 51 of judgment).
52 See e.g. Joined Cases C-6 and 9/90 *Francovich*, Case C-178/94 *Dillenkofer* and Case C-140/97 *Rechberger*.
53 See e.g. Cases C-46/93 *Brasserie du Pêcheur* and C-48/93 *Factortame (3)*.
54 See e.g. Case C-319/96 *Brinkmann*, a case which involved questions on the interpretation of the second directive on turnover taxes for manufactured tobacco, Directive 79/32 (OJ 1979 L10/8).
55 Case C-201/02 *Wells* (paras. 64 and 66 of judgment).
56 Lenaerts and Gutiérrez-Fons (2011), p. 31; Wennerås (2007), p. 153.
57 Case C-46/93 *Brasserie du Pêcheur*.
58 Ibid. (paras. 55–6 of judgment).
59 Ibid. (para. 80 of judgment).
60 See e.g. Cases C-6 and 9/90 *Francovich* and C-178/94 *Dillenkofer*.
61 See e.g. Case C-48/93 *Factortame (3)*.
62 See e.g. Case C-46/93 *Brasserie du Pêcheur*.
63 Case C-5/94 *Hedley Lomas*.
64 OJ 1974 L316/10.
65 Case C-5/94 *Hedley Lomas* (para. 28 of judgment).
66 See e.g. Case C-392/93 *BT* and Case C-424/97 *Haim (2)*.
67 Case C-392/93 *BT*.
68 See also Case C-319/96 *Brinkmann*, discussed below.
69 See e.g. Case C-424/97 *Haim (2)*, Case C-127/95 *Norbrook*, Case C-319/96 *Brinkmann* and C-118/00 *Larsy*.
70 Case C-224/01 *Köbler*.
71 See Joined Cases C-6 and 9/90 *Francovich* (para. 43 of judgment), Case C-46/93 *Brasserie du Pêcheur* (para. 73 of judgment) and Case C-261/95 *Palmisani* (para. 27 of judgment).
72 Case C-46/93 *Brasserie du Pêcheur* (para. 87 of judgment).
73 Ibid. (para. 90 of judgment).

74 Ibid. (paras. 84–5 and 95 of judgment).
75 Case C-140/97 *Rechberger.*
76 OJ 1990 L158/59.
77 Case C-140/97 *Rechberger* (paras. 75 and 77 of judgment).
78 Case C-319/96 *Brinkmann.*
79 OJ 1979 L10/8.
80 The CJEU noted that both the European Commission and the Finnish government had made representations in the litigation in support of Brinkmann's interpretation of the directive.
81 See Case C-319/96 *Brinkmann* (para. 29 of judgment).
82 So Prechal and Hancher (2002), p. 108.
83 Directive 2008/98 (OJ 2008 L312/3).
84 See e.g. EU's Wild Birds Directive 2009/147 (OJ 2009 L20/7) and Habitats Directive 92/43 (OJ 1992 L206/7).
85 Directive 2006/7 (OJ 2006 L64/37).
86 Directive 2011/92 (OJ 2011 L26/1).
87 Case 26/62 *Van Gend en Loos.*
88 Now Directive 2008/94 (OJ 2008 L312/3).
89 Compare with Art. 2 of the former EEC Treaty which made no reference to environmental objectives of the former Community.
90 Arts. 11 and 191 TFEU.
91 See e.g. Winter (2002).
92 Case C-72/95 *Kraaijeveld.*
93 Directive 2011/92 (OJ 2011 L26/1).
94 As noted earlier in this chapter, there is some discussion as to whether the CJEU may be modifying its approach in light of its judgment in Case C-201/02 *Wells.* However, one swallow does not make a summer, as they say.
95 UN Doc A/811.
96 6 ILM (1967) 360.
97 6 ILM (1967) 368.
98 UN Doc. A/CONF/48/14/REV.1.
99 UN Doc. A/CONF.151/26/REV.1.
100 213 UNTS 221.
101 OJ 2010 C83/2.
102 The 2004 Treaty establishing a Constitution for Europe ('the European Union Constitution') (EUC) incorporated the 2000 EU Fundamental Rights Charter within its legal framework. The Charter's provision on environmental protection was replicated in the Constitutional Treaty as Article II-37 EUC. Due to ratification failures in France and the Netherlands the Constitutional Treaty never entered into force.
103 See e.g. Case 4/73 *Nold,* Case 36/75 *Rutili,* and Case 118/75 *Watson.*
104 Lenaerts and Gutiérrez-Fons (2011), p. 32.
105 See e.g. *Giacomelli v Italy,* ECtHR judgment of 2 November 2006.
106 This issue has arisen in the past in connection with discussions over the range of persons who may utilise the direct effect doctrine in the context of judicial review proceedings in England and Wales. See e.g. the approach taken by McCullough J taken in the Twyford Down dispute: *Twyford Parish Council v Secretary of State for the Environment* (1990).
107 Art. 3(3) TEU.
108 As set down in Art. 3 TEU and Art. 191 TFEU.
109 Principally contained in Arts. 12, 13 and 36 of Directive 2008/98 (OJ 2008 L312/3).
110 See Case C-365/97 *Commission v Italy (San Rocco)* and C-387/97 *Commission v Greece (Kouroupitos (2)).*
111 See Case C-140/97 *Rechberger.*
112 See Case C-319/96 *Brinkmann.*

113 As required under Art. 19 TEU.
114 Case C-127/02 *Waddenzee*.
115 OJ 1992 L206/7.
116 Case C-127/02 *Waddenzee* (para. 44 of judgment).
117 See e.g. Case C-68/88 *Commission v Greece*.
118 See e.g. Prechal and Hancher (2002), p. 108.
119 Case 26/62 *Van Gend en Loos*.
120 For an excellent discussion on anthropocentric values in national and international environmental law, see Gillespie (1997), Ch. 1.
121 See Arts. 263, 265 and 268 TFEU (ex Arts. 230, 232 and 235 EC).
122 Case C-44/95 *Lappel Bank*.

8 Access to justice at national level for breaches of EU environmental law (2)

EU legislation on access to legal review at national level

Several environmental protection legislative initiatives have been adopted at EU level since the millennium, which have introduced important procedural as well as substantive rights for private persons to be able to assist in the enforcement of EU environmental legislation at national level. The initiatives enhance both rights of access to national administrative and judicial appeal procedures as well as rights to access information on the environment. As such, they serve as an important addition to the growing body of jurisprudence of the Court of Justice of the European Union (CJEU) on general procedural and substantive rights that flow from EU law, as discussed in the previous two chapters. The driving force behind these legislative developments emanates largely from the Union's membership of the 1998 United Nations Economic Commission for Europe's (UNECE) Convention on Access to Information, Public Participation in Decision-making and Access to Justice in Environmental Matters, concluded in Århus, Denmark (hereinafter referred to as the 'Århus Convention').[1] The EU has sought, and to some extent struggled, to secure full implementation of the Århus Convention's particular obligations on securing enhanced procedural rights for the public, whether ordinary citizens or other private legal persons such as non-governmental environmental organisations (NGEOs), in order to facilitate their participation in the enforcement of national and EU environmental protection laws.

Broadening access to justice in the environmental protection sphere has been an item on the political agenda of the EU for quite a period of time, dating back to the early 1990s.[2] Before the Århus Convention was agreed in 1998, the European Commission had, for instance, already noted its concern about the relative lack of legal avenues for private persons including NGEOs to seek redress for breaches of EU environmental legislation at national level. This has been exemplified by the restrictive nature of rights of legal standing for private persons to take legal proceedings against acts or omissions by state authorities before an independent court or review body in a number of EU Member states, such rights commonly being predicated upon the plaintiff having to show that they have a distinct legal interest that sets them apart from other members of the public in order to justify their access to court. Arguments in support of such restrictions tend to centre on concerns to avoid courts being flooded with disputes (so-called 'floodgates' argument), and there is often an in-built presumption within national legal systems that a claim is most likely to be unmeritorious where the plaintiff has no specific personal legal interest in its outcome, such as a proprietary right or claim. Such argumentation carries little or no weight in relation to environmental litigation, particularly where it is the case that environmental damage alleged to be illicit has not resulted in adverse legal effects to any particular individual or group of individuals on account of it being diffuse in nature (e.g. air pollution) or having resulted in adverse impacts exclusively on non-anthropocentric matters (e.g. habitat destruction). The position of legal standing is fractured amongst the EU member state's legal systems, with some systems allowing for members of the public or NGEOs to take legal action on behalf of an environmental interest (*actio popularis*) and others adopting more restrictive regimes requiring a plaintiff to demonstrate either an impairment of an individual right or other sufficient interest.[3] Other major hurdles include ones of an essentially evidential nature (access to information), cost of financing litigation as well as possibilities of obtaining interim relief.

The EU first raised concerns about the state of access to environmental justice at national level in earnest in the early 1990s. This initially came in the form of a political commitment incorporated within the EU's Fifth Environmental Action Programme (1993–2000) (EAP5)[4] which affirmed the need to improve the public's access to environmental justice.[5] In its 1996 Communication on the state of implementation of EU environmental law the Commission proposed that policy changes in the area of legal standing were needed to facilitate access of NGEOs in particular to be able to participate in the process of EU environmental law enforcement.[6] The Commission's views were supported both by the Council of the EU[7] and the European Parliament.[8] However, in the event no proposal was officially tabled by the Commission during the lifetime of EAP5.[9] It was not until 2003 before any official legislative proposals were published by the European Commission, in the wake of the EU's signature of the Århus Convention and political commitment for better public participation in environmental issues in the Sixth Environment Action Programme (2001–10) (EAP6).[10]

As far as the area of access to justice is concerned, since 2003 a number of EU measures have been introduced with the purpose of seeking to enhance the rights of individuals and other private entities to access courts and tribunals in the event of disputes over the correct application of EU environmental legislation. The European Commission's original aim, in the early 2000s, of having the Union adopt a principal legislative instrument designed to lay a common basic (default) framework on access to justice across EU environmental policy sectors stalled due to political resistance from member state governments. Instead, what has emerged to date is an incremental implementation of the obligations flowing from the Århus Convention, namely an approach by the Union to implement access-to-justice requirements within the framework of particular EU legislative instruments in certain environmental policy sectors. This has resulted in only partial and delayed compliance with the EU's international obligations to ensure that adequate guarantees on access to environmental justice are secured throughout the EU legal order (namely across the Union's member states as well as at EU institutional level). In figurative terms one might depict the legislative quilt woven so far by the EU to secure implementation of Århus commitments on access to justice as a patchwork affair, full of holes. True, the Union member states have distinct obligations themselves under international law as contracting parties to the Århus Convention (alongside the EU) to ensure that their respective national legal systems comply with the Convention's requirements. The Convention is a 'mixed agreement' in the sense that it involves a policy field in which the Union and member states share competence to contract international obligations.[11] However this does not legally excuse the Union from its duty to ensure that the writ of the Convention runs across the geographical span of the combined territories of its member states.

The original attempt by the European Commission to introduce a principal legislative instrument in order to implement the access-to-justice requirements contained in the Århus Convention at national level within the EU member states' legal systems was the 2003 draft directive on access to justice in environmental matters (hereafter referred to as the Draft AJEM Directive).[12] It was intended to serve as a 'horizontal' measure in the sense of being designed, as a matter of general principle, to apply generally across EU environmental policy sectors. However, insofar as other EU legislative rules on access to justice would arise in relation to specific sectors and contexts, they would operate as *lex specialis* so that the Draft AJEM Directive would not be applicable. The Draft AJEM Directive contains provisions granting rights for individuals and other private entities, in particular NGEOs, to have access to specific types of administrative and judicial review procedures. Such procedures are intended principally to serve as mechanisms to enable private entities to hold member state public authorities to account in relation to administrative acts or omissions in breach of EU environmental legislation. In addition, it also requires member states to grant members of the public rights of access to administrative or judicial review proceedings in order to challenge acts and omissions by private persons in breach of EU environmental legislation. Subsequent to its publication, the Draft AJEM Directive however failed to make legislative headway, with the Council of the EU deciding not to respond to the initiative. It was apparent that a substantial majority of member states considered at the time that the adoption of such an instrument would constitute an excessive encroachment in an area considered to be by them a matter that should rest principally within the competence of individual member states, namely the organisation of judicial procedures before national courts.[13] With the Council deciding not to give the proposal a first reading, the Draft AJEM Directive was placed in the political deep freezer. However, the European Commission never formally withdrew its proposal and it remains a relevant reference point, not least because the EU has most recently signalled in its Seventh Environment Action Programme (2013–20) (EAP7)[14] that the area of access to environmental justice is a matter of renewed political priority. Specifically, the EAP7 requires that the principle of effective legal protection for citizens and their organisations is enhanced by 2020, which includes 'ensuring that national provisions on access to justice reflect the case law of the Court of Justice of the EU'.[15] During his tenure as Environment Commissioner (2009–14) Jan Potočnik was a strong advocate for moves to introduce legislative reform in the area of access to justice, as one of the components needed to be put in place for a more effective implementation of EU environmental law at national level.[16] However, no new EU legislative proposal emerged under his five-year tenure as Commissioner. In tandem with the European Parliamentary elections in May 2014, the College of Commissioners was recomposed in November of the same year. At the time of writing there is a degree of uncertainty as to what degree of priority will be attached by the new incumbent of the post of Environment Commissioner, Karmenu Vella, to the area of access to justice.

Notwithstanding the failure of the EU to adopt a 'horizontal' instrument on access to environmental justice at national level, from 2003 onwards the Union has passed a series of legislative measures intended to enhance access to justice in various areas of EU environmental policy. Notably, the first wave of EU instruments to incorporate access-to-justice clauses included, notably, Directive 2003/4 on public access to environmental information,[17] Directive 2003/35 on public participation in respect of the drawing up of certain plans and programmes relating to the environment (EU Public Participation Directive)[18] and Directive 2004/35 on environmental liability with regard to the prevention and remedying of environmental damage.[19] Subsequently, the EU has consolidated the implementation of the Århus Convention's access-to-justice requirements relating to the second pillar through Directive 2010/75 on industrial emissions[20] and the consolidated Environmental Impact Assessment (EIA) Directive 2011/92.[21] However, a substantial number of EU environmental policy areas remain without Union legislative safeguards on access to justice including, notably, in the water, waste, air quality, noise pollution and nature protection sectors. By way of complement to its focus on access to environmental justice at national level, the EU has also adopted legislation to ensure that Union institutional decision-making accords with the requirements of the Århus Convention. The principal implementation measure in this regard is Regulation 1367/06,[22] the impact of which is assessed later in Chapter 9.

In terms of rights concerning access to information on the environment, the position at EU level has been transformed by Directive 2003/4 on public access to environmental information and repealing Directive 90/313.[23] Directive 2003/4 provides members of the public with rights to access information on the environment held by member state public authorities. It also obliges member states to make available and disseminate to the public a range of legislative, policy and scientific documentation and assessments on the environment. Such information may be particularly useful in gleaning evidence of compliance or non-compliance with EU environmental norms, and as such constitutes an important integral factor in terms of private persons' capabilities of being in a suitable position to pursue legal steps to enforce EU environmental law.

This particular chapter will focus on assessing the contribution that EU legislative instrumentation has made towards implementation of access to environmental justice obligations under the Århus Convention within the EU member states in terms of enhancing of private persons' access to EU member state courts and tribunals. Prior to examining the various individual legislative instruments involved, the chapter will first assess the impact of the Århus Convention on the EU's legal order in general and with specific reference to the access-to-justice area (section 8.1). Given that the Union has ratified the Convention as well as ensured express reference to it in several pieces of environmental legislation, it is important to take on board, in light of CJEU jurisprudence,[24] that the Convention plays an influential role in the emerging field on Union law on access to environmental justice. The chapter then proceeds to assess the content and impact of the various existing EU environmental legislative instruments implementing the requirements of the Århus Convention on the provision of safeguards concerning access to environmental justice (section 8.2). Subsequently, the chapter considers the Draft AJEM Directive, which covers an area of access to justice relating to Århus not yet implemented by the EU (section 8.3), before concluding.

Separate later chapters will consider other aspects of the impact of the Århus Convention on the EU legal order that either directly or indirectly concern or relate to the subject of access to environmental justice. Specifically, Chapter 8A (available on website) considers the EU's implementation of Århus with respect to the subject of access to environmental information, and reflects on the significance of this particular right in serving to complement efforts to enhance public access to environmental justice. Chapter 9 appraises how the EU has made progress on ensuring that EU-level environmental policy decision-making and other institutional action accords with Århus access-to-justice standards.

8.1 The 1998 Århus Convention and its impact on the EU legal order

A good deal of the EU legislation on access to justice has been inspired by and drawn from the Århus Convention,[25] which entered into force on 30 October 2001. As at the time of writing, the Convention has 47 contracting parties.[26] As far as EU participation in the Convention is concerned, the European Union[27] together with all 28 EU member states[28] have ratified the Convention.

8.1.1 Overview of Århus

The Århus Convention seeks to promote the development of individual rights in relation to environmental affairs in three areas, commonly referred to as the three pillars underpinning the Convention: access to environmental information, public participation in environmental decision-making and access to environmental justice.[29] It preserves the right for contracting parties to introduce or maintain measures offering more generous individual rights than those contained in the Convention.[30] As part of its initial efforts to implement the three pillars of the Århus Convention, in October 2003 the European Commission brought forward a package of legislative proposals designed to bind the member states and EU institutions to minimum requirements regarding access to information, public participation in environmental decision-making and access to justice. Three of these particular proposals came to be adopted, namely Directive 2003/4 on public access to environmental information (the AEI Directive), Directive 2003/35 on public participation in environmental decision-making and Regulation 1367/06 on the application of the provisions of the Århus Convention on Access to Information, Public Participation in Decision-making and Access to Justice in Environmental Matters to EU institutions and bodies. However, the draft proposal for a directive on access to justice (the Draft AJEM Directive) was not adopted. Instead, the Union adopted over time a number of access-to-justice provisions within the corpus of certain sectoral EU environmental protection instruments, which has meant that to date the Århus Convention has not yet been fully implemented within the EU legal order.

Before considering the legal impact of the Århus Convention within the Union's legal order, it is perhaps useful first to set out in outline the key principles and obligations of the international instrument. The overall principal aim underpinning the Convention is to enhance the possibilities for the public to understand, influence and challenge decisions taken by national authorities affecting the environment with a view to promoting protection of the environment. It seeks to build upon Principle 10 of the Rio Declaration agreed at the 1992 UN Conference on Environment and Development, which affirms the need for states to enhance citizen involvement in environmental affairs in terms of enhancing access to information, public participation in environmental decision-making and access to judicial and administrative proceedings.[31] The Århus Convention is structured around these three strands or pillars to enhancement of citizen involvement, which crystallises them into a rights-based format. The Convention's approach is to promote involvement of civil society in a broad sense, defining the 'public' to include 'natural and legal persons and, in accordance with national legislation or practice, their associations, organisations or groups'.[32] The rights-oriented approach of the Convention is emphasised by its stated objective in Article 1 of contributing 'to the protection of the right of every person of present and future generations to live in an environment adequate to his or her health and well being'. The emphasis of the Convention is on reconfiguring the relationship between the ordinary citizen and public authorities, taking into account the latter's central importance for the environment in being empowered to stipulate binding levels of protection for the environment. As a consequence, it contains only a very few provisions relating to the issue of accountability of private persons' activities affecting the environment to the general public. Its three pillars will be briefly considered in turn.

The first pillar of the Århus Convention's framework, access to environmental information, is housed within Articles 4–5 of the international instrument. These two provisions focus on public access to environmental information from two main angles, namely active as well as reactive responsibilities of contracting parties. Article 4 sets down a number of minimum requirements relating to establishment of a right of the public to access information of the environment held by public authorities (reactive-type obligations), whilst permitting a limited range of derogations. Article 5 stipulates a number of obligations for contracting parties with a view to ensuring that environmental information is collected on an up-to-date basis as well as disseminated efficiently (active-type obligations). In addition, Article 3 houses some important general requirements related to the subject of access to information, including the right of applicants for information to be free from penalty, persecution or harassment in asserting their Convention rights[33] as well as the right of any person to have access to information as prescribed by the Convention, regardless of their citizenship, nationality, domicile or location of registered seat in the case of a legal person.[34] Moreover, contracting parties are required to ensure that the public receives guidance and assistance when seeking to access environmental information, in the form of education and environmental awareness campaigns as well as help from officials and authorities.[35] The implementation by the EU of the Århus provisions on right of access to environmental information is considered in two later chapters (Chapters 8A and 9A).

The second pillar, focusing on the area of public participation in environmental decision-making, is housed within Articles 6–8 of the Århus Convention. These provisions set out basic rights of citizen involvement in relation to decisions concerning specific industrial projects as well as more general strategic public planning and policy-related decisions. Specifically, Article 6 establishes the right of the public to participate in decisions over the authorisation of specific activities[36] affecting the environment. Key elements of the framework securing effective participation include early and full public disclosure of proposed activities and information on their environmental impact, the right of the public to have their views taken into account on the issue of authorisation as well as dissemination of decisions on authorisation applications and their underlying reasoning. Article 7 extends this framework to include public participation in relation to the preparation of plans, programmes and, 'to the extent appropriate', policies relating to the environment. Finally, Article 8 sets down some rather general and weak obligations on contracting parties 'to strive to promote' effective public participation during the preparation by public authorities of executive regulations and other generally applicable legally binding rules that might have a significant effect on the environment and to take this into account 'as far as possible'.[37]

The third pillar of Århus concerns the area of access to environmental justice and a number of important guarantees and commitments from contracting parties are secured in Article 9 of the Convention. This provision and its follow-up by the EU constitute the particular focus of this chapter (see section 8.2 below). In broad terms, Article 9 of the Convention stipulates that each party is to ensure that in three types of situations the public should have access to independent legal review of decisions, omissions and acts concerning the following areas: access to environmental information (Article 9(1)), public participation in certain decisions relating to the environment (Article 9(2)) and contraventions of environmental law by public authorities or private persons (Article 9(3)). In relation to the first category, Article 9(1) stipulates that persons who consider that their request for access to information has not been addressed in accordance with the requirements of Article 4 is to be granted under national legislation access to a review procedure either before a court of law or another independent and impartial body established by law. Contracting parties are obligated also to make available, where they provide for review before a court, access to an 'expeditious' procedure which is free or 'inexpensive' for reconsideration by a public authority or review by an independent and impartial body other than a court. In relation to the second category, Article 9(2) specifies that the public, subject to having either a sufficient interest or maintaining an impairment of a right where national administrative law requires this as a precondition, are to be provided access under national leg-islation to a review procedure before either a court and/or other independent and impartial body established by law to challenge the substantive or procedural legality of any administrative conduct relating to authorisation decisions covered by Article 6 of the Convention.[38] Contracting parties may require utilisation of a preliminary review procedure and/or the exhaustion of administrative review procedures prior to recourse to judicial review or review by an independent body.[39] Whilst recognising as a matter of principle that contracting parties should determine the parameters of legal standing (*locus standi*) of members of the public to bring forward challenges, Article 9(2) also specifies that this should be done in a manner consistent 'with the objective of giving the public wide access to justice'. In addition, it also stipulates that NGOs promoting environmental protection and meeting any requirements under national law shall be deemed to have a sufficient interest or impairment of right.[40] This provision seeks to promote an enhanced role for NGEOs in enforcing the requirements of Article 6, albeit this role is quali-fied according to rules of recognition stipulated at national level.

In relation to the third category of access to environmental justice, Article 9(3) of the Århus Convention sets out a general obligation on contracting parties to facilitate environmental law enforcement by the public. Article 9(3) stipulates the following general binding commitment:

> 3. . . . [E]ach Party shall ensure that, where they meet the criteria, if any, laid down in its national law,[41] members of the public have access to administra-tive or judicial procedures to challenge acts and omissions by private persons and public authorities which contravene provisions of its national law relating to the environment.

The provision is couched in general terms, leaving a lot of discretion in the hands of contracting parties as to how its requirements are to be implemented by them. In particular, it is important to note that the contracting parties reserved for them-selves the right to determine the specific requirements of legal standing (*locus standi*) to be fulfilled by members of the public in order to be in a position to pur-sue environmental litigation against a private or public defendant. Accordingly, the Convention itself does not, strictly speaking, require the parties to establish a general citizen's right of action or *actio popularis* to enforce environmental law, but instead leaves it to contracting parties to determine the particular *locus standi* requirements in any given case. However, it is evident from the wording of the provision that contracting parties are obliged to facilitate access to justice. The obligation, as crafted, is evidently intended to steer them to introduce systems sympathetic to facilitating access to justice to a wide range of claimants; in par-ticular, this is emphasised by the reference to the words 'if any' in Article 9(3). The Århus Convention Compliance Committee has concluded that the phrase 'where

they meet the criteria, if any, laid down in its national law' does not entitle contracting parties to introduce or maintain so strict criteria on legal standing so that
effectively all or almost all NGEOs would be barred from being able to challenge
administrative conduct that contravene national environmental law.[42] Moreover, it
is also clear that the material scope of Article 9(3) is broad, in covering both substantive as well procedural types of breaches of environmental law. Contracting
parties to the Convention are not entitled to limit the scope of legal review to only
certain types of breaches.[43]

The commitment to access to justice in the Convention is supported by some
common flanking provisions in Article 9(4)–(5) which apply to all three types of
review procedure referred to in Article 9. These provisions contain some generally
worded requirements on the conduct, expense and transparency of procedures.
Article 9(4) stipulates some minimum general requirements that must be respected
by the relevant administrative or judicial review procedures, namely that:

> In addition and without prejudice to the review procedures referred to in
> paragraphs 1 and 2 above, each Party shall provide adequate and effective
> remedies, including injunctive relief as appropriate, and be fair, equitable,
> timely and not prohibitively expensive. Decisions under this article shall be
> given or recorded in writing. Decisions of courts, and whenever possible of
> other bodies, shall be publicly accessible.

Article 9(5) contains two further general obligations, one hard and one soft. First,
it obliges the contracting parties to ensure that the public is provided with access
to information about access to judicial and administrative review procedures.
In addition, contracting parties are required to 'consider' the establishment of
'appropriate' mechanisms to remove or reduce financial and other barriers to
access to justice. Notably, the second commitment falls far short of requiring the
provision of legal aid or other financial assistance mechanisms for the purpose of
facilitating public interest environmental litigation. The information requirement
in Article 9(5) is reinforced more broadly in the general provisions of Article 3
of the Convention, with Article 3(2) obliging contracting parties to 'endeavour'
to ensure that officials and authorities assist and provide guidance to the public
in seeking access to justice, and Article 3(3) requiring parties to 'promote' public
education and awareness, especially on how the public may obtain information
on access to justice. Although these flanking provisions to Article 9(1)–(3) are very
general in nature and leave considerable room for legal interpretation, they contain in essence a core requirement for contracting parties to ensure that their relevant administrative review and judicial procedures are appropriately advertised
and structured so as to ensure that the public is aware of them and is in a genuine
position to be able to use them to good effect without having to face unnecessary
or insurmountable financial or procedural hurdles. Collectively, such provisions
contain an important body of fundamental general legal principles that are to
underpin national implementation of independent legal review mechanisms of
environmental acts or omissions that breach national environmental law.

8.1.2 Legal impact of Århus for the European Union

From the perspectives of both international and EU law the contents of the Århus Convention constitute a legally binding source of obligations for the Union.

Accordingly, notwithstanding the fact that the EU has yet to adopt its full legislative programme of implementing the Convention, this does not mean that Århus is without legal impact in those areas not yet covered by EU internal legislation. In addition, it is important to note that the Convention plays an important residual role regarding the interpretation of EU legislative measures that have been passed in order to implement it within the EU with respect to Union institutional decision-making or with respect to conduct by private persons or public authorities within EU member states. Although amongst the first signatories to the Århus Convention in 1998, the EU took a considerable period of time to become a contracting party. In 2005 the Council of the EU concluded its ratification of the Århus Convention in the usual way by adopting a decision.[44]

As a matter of general international law the Union, as an entity with international legal personality[45] and as contracting party to an international treaty, is obligated to ensure that the provisions of Århus are honoured within its area of jurisdiction; the duty to ensure implementation of treaty obligations normally rests solely with individual contracting parties, insofar as a treaty does not provide other law enforcement mechanisms.[46] Unusually, in addition to the standard and infrequently used modes of inter-state dispute settlement mechanisms employed in multilateral environmental agreements (notably referral to the International Court of Justice and international arbitration),[47] the Århus Convention also foresaw from the outset the establishment of a special mechanism of a 'non-confrontational, non-judicial and consultative nature' for the purpose of reviewing compliance by contracting parties, with the option of considering communications from the public.[48] At the meeting of the parties in 2002 a Compliance Committee structure was established to hear complaints from parties as well as the public on implementation shortcomings.[49] Since its inception, the Compliance Committee has heard a substantial number of complaints, including ones against both EU member states and the Union itself. These have resulted in a number of adverse findings against certain contracting parties, including notably the UK[50] as well as the EU[51] in relation to the Convention's requirements concerning access to justice. Given the non-confrontational nature[52] of the Compliance Committee procedure, no sanctions are able to accompany committee conclusions that a contracting party has defaulted on its Convention obligations. The Compliance Committee may only issue non-binding recommendations, which are considered at the subsequent (biennial) Meeting of Parties (MOP) of the Convention. As Ebbesson notes,[53] with the endorsement of their findings by the MOP, the normative influence of Committee recommendations is further enhanced by being considered valid sources of interpretation of the Convention from the perspective of international law.[54] To what extent, though, the Committee's findings are taken into account by courts of the contracting parties of the Convention is ultimately a matter for the law of the individual contracting parties of the Convention. As far as EU law is concerned, the Committee's findings are to be treated formally as non-binding, although they may be considered as valid reference points to be taken into account for the purposes of judicial deliberation on questions of interpretation of the Convention.[55]

From an EU law perspective, which is the focus of this book, the Århus Convention constitutes a legally binding source of Union law. Under the EU's foundational treaty framework international agreements concluded by the Union are binding upon the Union's institutions as well as the member states as a matter of EU law.[56] In terms of their legal hierarchy within the Union legal system, the CJEU has confirmed that such agreements take precedence over EU secondary law (i.e. EU legislation), and so are akin to primary sources of Union law. However, the CJEU has also confirmed that international agreements concluded by the Union may not override fundamental precepts of the EU's founding treaties, including human rights commitments.[57] Accordingly, as a general tenet of EU law, EU member states are obliged to ensure they comply with the requirements of international agreements entered into by the Union.

The EU legal position is more nuanced and requires further clarification where, as in the case of international agreements concerning the environment sector, the Union and EU member states share competence.[58] Under EU law, the degree of competence of the Union to act in a particular policy sphere is determined by the foundational Union treaty framework, specifically by Title I of the Treaty on the Functioning of the European Union (TFEU) (Articles 2–6 TFEU). The standard types of competence that may be allocated to the Union are in essence exclusive, shared or supplementary in nature. In relation to the environment sector, competence over policy is shared between the Union and member states.[59] Accordingly, this means that EU member states may in principle intervene unilaterally in those environmental policy areas in respect of which the Union has not adopted measures as part of the EU's developing common policy on the environment under the aegis of Title XX of the TFEU (Articles 191–3 TFEU).[60] Where, however, the EU has adopted policy measures in relation to a particular environmental matter, Union member states are then obliged to refrain from acting in the same field unless they wish to enact more stringent environmental protection measures than those adopted at Union level.[61] Such national measures are required to be compatible with the requirements of the founding EU treaties.[62] In other words, the policy competence of the Union is transformed to be virtually exclusive subsequent to the adoption of Union acts, subject to the retention of power by member states to adopt stricter protection measures.

The principles concerning sharing of competence are also reflected to a degree in the context of the Union's external relations (commonly referred to as 'mixity' or 'mixed competence'). In situations of mixity, international agreements involving the EU are anticipated to be concluded by both the Union and the member states. In relation to environmental policy matters, at the international level the TFEU charges the Union and member states to co-operate with third countries and competent international organisations in their respective spheres of competence.[63] The EU treaty framework foresees as a matter of general principle a strengthened presence of the Union in the context of relations with the international community in shared policy areas. The material treaty provision here is Article 3(2) TFEU which stipulates that:

> The Union shall also have exclusive competence for the conclusion of an international agreement when its conclusion is provided for in a legislative act of the Union or is necessary to enable the Union to exercise its internal competence, or insofar as its conclusion may affect common rules or alter their scope.

Exclusive external competence is accordingly vested in the Union in situations additional to the scenario of the member states ceding sovereignty in the event that the Union has adopted legislative rules concerning a particular policy matter (doctrine of pre-emption as first established in the *ERTA* ruling).[64] Article 3(2) TFEU itself consolidates existing CJEU jurisprudence on the general principles of implied exclusive Union competence. For the environment sector, though, member states will almost invariably retain some competence in the external relations sphere of policy given that Article 193 TFEU guarantees them the possibility of taking a more stringent environmental protection position than that adopted by the Union. Accordingly, in practice both the Union and member states share competence in international environmental negotiations arena and both will be expected to sign and conclude any agreements struck between the European Union and third parties. Confirmation that the European Union engages in negotiations on the basis of shared internal competence between Union and constituent member states is often now conveyed to non-EU contracting parties in the form of a declaration of a division of competence, setting out in broad terms clarification of the parameters of the respective external relations powers of the Union and member states, noting that the balance of competence may change over time. Such a declaration[65] was made, for instance, by the EU when ratifying the Århus Convention, which foresees that, in the event of a regional economic integration organisation together with its member states becoming contracting parties, they are to determine their respective responsibilities for performance of the Convention and may not be entitled to exercise their rights under the agreement concurrently.[66]

A number of legal questions have arisen and continue to arise in connection with the legal status and impact of mixed agreements within the EU legal order, such as the Århus Convention. In particular, clarification has been needed about the extent to which such agreements ratified by the Union may be considered as sources of EU law, given the fact that they may concern areas of policy not subject to internal Union legislative regulation and may not have been concluded by all the member states. CJEU case law has, to a significant extent, assisted in clarifying a considerable number of these legal issues. In essence, the Court has confirmed that all the provisions of such mixed agreements are to be considered legally binding sources of EU law upon Union ratification,[67] including the Århus Convention.[68] Such agreements may also be enforced against a Union member state by the European Commission through infringement proceedings under Articles 258 and 260 TFEU irrespective of whether or not a particular EU member state has become a contracting party.[69] In *Etang de Berre*[70] the CJEU confirmed that the Commission had power to take infringement proceedings against France over the latter's failure to adhere to aspects of the 1976 Convention for the protection of the Mediterranean Sea against pollution (Barcelona Convention) and an accompanying 1980 Protocol for the protection of the Mediterranean Sea against pollution from land-based sources,[71] both of which had been ratified by the EU.[72] The CJEU held that both international accords are legally binding on member states as a matter of Union law. In addition, it held that it was irrelevant that the Union had not already adopted internal legislation specifically concerning matters regulated by the international agreements, namely discharges of freshwater into the marine environs, taking into account that the agreements fell 'in large measure' within Union competence, as reflected by the fact that the EU had adopted a number of legislative instruments concerning water quality issues, such as the Water Framework Directive 2000/60.[73]

One particular important legal issue that has arisen in connection with shared or mixed competence status of the Union's relationship with the Århus Convention has been the extent to which the member states retain (sole) competence in relation to the delivery of treaty commitments entered into with respect to the third pillar, in particular the guarantees regarding access to justice under Article 9(3) of the Convention. At the time of the Union's ratification of the Convention in 2005, a statement was made within the EU's declaration on the division of competence between itself and member states accompanying the ratification instrument that the member states and not the Union would remain responsible for the implementation of Article 9(3) in respect of those administrative and judicial procedures concerning challenges to conduct of public authorities and private persons other than EU institutions covered by Article 2(2)(d) of the Convention so long as the EU did not adopt EU legislative measures covering implementation of those Article 9(3) obligations.[74] The thrust of this part of the EU's declaration appeared to imply that the Union did not have legal responsibility for the implementation of Article 9(3) within the Union's member states in the absence of internal EU measures targeted at the national level. Such a position appeared to be held by the European Commission as recently as May 2008, when the Commission published its first implementation report of the Convention.[75] The impact of the adoption of the Environmental Liability Directive 2004/35 appeared not to have made any impact on the division-of-competence issue from the Commission's perspective, notwithstanding this being an internal EU instrument serving to implement, albeit partially, Article 9(3) obligations at member state level. In sum, it was not evident from the European Commission's perspective to what extent EU legal obligations arose in relation to the third pillar of Århus. However, subsequent jurisprudence from the CJEU has clarified that clear EU legal obligations do arise in relation to Article 9(3) of the Convention, as confirmed notably by the judgment in *Lesoochranárske zoskupenie VLK*[76] which is discussed below.

In *Lesoochranárske zoskupenie VLK* the CJEU had occasion to assess the legal impact of Article 9(3) of the Århus Convention on the EU legal order and specifically whether it could be considered to be directly effective. An integral part of an analysis of the legal impact of the Århus Convention with the EU legal order is the assessment of the extent, if at all, private persons are entitled as a matter of EU law to rely as of right upon the provisions of an international agreement concluded by the Union, with a view to enforcing them, where necessary, before the national courts. The CJEU had acknowledged as a general proposition prior to this case that provisions of international agreements concluded by the Union may be capable of having direct effects, depending on the fulfilment of certain criteria, whether falling within the exclusive competence of the Union[77] or subject to shared competence with member states.[78] Specifically, the Court has consistently held that Union agreements concluded with third countries and/or international organisations may have direct effect when, regard being had to the wording, purpose and nature of the agreement, the material provision concerned contains a clear, precise and unconditional obligation.[79] This particular case involved a Slovakian NGEO which wished to seek judicial review of a decision taken by national authorities to authorise the hunting of certain wild fauna, including the brown bear, a species protected under the aegis of the Habitats Directive 92/43.[80] The NGEO considered that such authorisations breached the EU legislation. However, under Slovakian law at the time, private associations were excluded from being able to subject such decisions to judicial review (being only permitted to participate in administrative proceedings). The NGEO challenged the legality of the national rules excluding its legal standing to seek redress before the Slovakian courts by claiming that they breached Article 9(3) of the Århus Convention. As referred to earlier in this chapter, Article 9(3) requires contracting parties to ensure that, where they meet the criteria, if any, laid down in national law, members of the public are to have access to administrative or judicial procedures to challenge acts and omissions by private persons and public authorities which contravene provisions of national law relating to the environment. The Habitats Directive 92/43 itself was of little assistance to the NGEO, in not containing any specific safeguards on access to justice for civil society. The dispute came before the Slovakian Supreme Court on appeal, which sought a preliminary ruling from the CJEU specifically on the question as to whether Article 9(3) had direct effect.

In her opinion to the CJEU, Advocate General Sharpston considered that the Union (and accordingly the CJEU) had no jurisdiction to consider this issue, on the grounds that Article 9(3) did not lie within a sphere falling within the scope of Union law.[81] In support of this view, she noted that the EU had not adopted any specific internal measures to implement Article 9(3) and also the wording of the Declaration on division of competence deposited by the EU upon its ratification of the Convention in 2005 indicates that Union member states are to be deemed responsible for the performance of Article 9(3) obligations in the absence of internal EU legislation implementing those Convention obligations to challenge acts and omissions by private persons and public authorities of the EU member states.[82] Consequently, the Advocate General concluded that it was for national courts of the member states to determine whether Article 9(3) had direct effect within their own internal legal order, whilst opining also that the particular Convention provision failed to meet the standard criteria of unconditionality and sufficient precision required for direct effect to exist.[83]

In contrast with the Advocate General's opinion, the CJEU considered that it had jurisdiction to consider whether Article 9(3) of the Convention was directly effective as a source of EU law. First, the Court affirmed that it had jurisdiction to interpret the Convention on the grounds that it formed an integral part of the EU legal order in accordance with settled case law on mixed agreements.[84] Secondly, the CJEU proceeded to assess whether the field covered by Article 9(3) fell within the competence of the member states rather than the Union. The test used by the Court to determine this issue was whether the Union had exercised its powers and adopted provisions to implement obligations deriving from it. Referring to its ruling in *Etang de Berre*,[85] the Court noted that an issue addressed in an international agreement but not yet subject to specific EU legislation is nevertheless to be deemed to be part of EU law where the issue concerns a field in large measure covered by EU law. Whilst acknowledging the absence of specific internal EU legislation implementing Article 9(3) with respect to the national level of the EU member states, the Court held in this case that the issue did however concern a field in large measure covered by EU law. Specifically, the CJEU considered that coverage was provided in the form of the Habitats Directive 92/43, which under its aegis[86] makes protected species (such as the brown bear) subject to a system of strict protection from which derogations may only be permitted under the terms of the EU directive (Article 16).[87] For the Court it was therefore irrelevant that the EU had only adopted measures to implement Article 9(3) in respect of the conduct of EU institutions (via Regulation 1367/06) and not in respect of the conduct of private persons or public authorities of the member states.[88] On this jurisdictional point, the CFEU underlined that it is 'clearly in the interest' of EU law for a uniform interpretation to be provided in relation to a provision of an international accord falling within the scope of national and EU law, in order to prevent future differences of interpretation arising.[89]

Having affirmed the EU legal status of the Århus Convention and specifically the access-to-justice provision contained in Article 9(3), the CJEU then proceeded to assess the legal effects of the latter. First, the Court considered the question of direct effect. In concurring with the Advocate General on this point, it considered that Article 9(3) fails to fulfil the requirements of precision and unconditionality, since its implementation or effects are predicated upon the promulgation of a subsequent measure. This was an unsurprising conclusion to make, given the open-ended terms of the Convention provision. However, the CJEU did not stop at that point, but proceeded, secondly, to assess whether Article 9(3) procured other legal effects from an EU legal perspective. The Court held that, notwithstanding the absence of direct effect, national courts could not ignore the implications of the Convention provision which, although drafted in broad terms, was 'intended to ensure effective environmental protection'.[90] It recognised, in accordance with settled case law (as considered in Chapter 6), that in the absence of EU rules, as in this instance, it was in principle for the member states to lay down the procedural requirements regarding legal actions for protecting an individual's EU rights such as those under the EU Habitats Directive, so long as the national rules were non-discriminatory and did not render it in practice impossible or excessively difficult to exercise such rights.[91] With reference to the effectiveness principle, the CJEU went onto hold that national courts, in order to ensure effective environmental protection in the fields covered by EU law, are obliged to interpret their national law in a way which, to the fullest extent possible, is consistent with the objectives laid down in Article 9(3) of the Århus Convention.[92]

The CJEU's findings in *Lesoochranárske zoskupenie VLK* are significant in confirming that, as sources of EU law, the provisions of the Århus Convention contain binding obligations for national courts to take into account when interpreting national rules concerning or affecting rights of access to justice of the public seeking to uphold EU environmental legislation.[93] The obligation is, however, somewhat ambiguous in terms of the Court's reference to the phrase 'to the fullest extent possible', which could be interpreted in one of two ways. One interpretation of the CJEU's phrase could be that the Court has thereby implicitly suggested that the national courts' duty is to interpret national procedural rules insofar as is permissible under national law, akin to the doctrine of indirect effect in case law such as *Marleasing*[94] (as considered in Chapter 6). In contrast, the alternative way of interpreting this part of the CJEU's judgment would be that the Court has construed that a far more significant obligation befalls national courts, whereby the latter are under an absolute duty to ensure that members of the public have access to judicial review in line with the requirements of Article 9(3) if existing national procedural rules make it effectively impossible or excessively difficult to secure.[95] It is probable that the CJEU meant the former interpretation, not least given the fact that Article 9(3) does not itself stipulate a self-contained obligation, but defers to national rules to determine the rules on legal standing. The CJEU did not, however, have occasion to consider the legal impact of the complementary provision of Article 9(4)–(5) of the Convention. The former provision is not predicated upon the existence or promulgation of national rules and requires contracting parties to provide 'adequate and effective remedies, including injunctive relief and be fair'. Arguably, the CJEU might consider a far more potent form of the effectiveness principle applying in relation to Article 9(4), akin to the approach taken in the *Janecek* case[96] as discussed in Chapter 6. The text of Article 9(5), similar to Article 9(3), is expressly contingent upon a national decision to take legislative action and consequently would not be expected to contain implicit interpretative duties on national courts.

Elsewhere, the CJEU has consolidated its approach in *Lesoochranárske zoskupenie VLK* by confirming that, where the EU has adopted particular rules implementing the three Århus pillars, the Union secondary legislation must be interpreted in light of the Convention's provisions.[97] This consistent seam of case law confirms the well-established principle of supremacy of international accords concluded by the EU in relation to EU secondary legislative rules[98] as well as recognising the intention of the EU legislative institutions, which typically make a specific reference in the preamble to the Århus Convention as a key or primary source for introducing legislation[99] and/or noting the importance of ensuring that the EU legislative instrument is interpreted in line with the Convention.[100] The CJEU has also confirmed that the implementation guide published by UNECE in relation to the Convention may be taken into consideration but is not to be considered to have any binding force in terms of interpreting the Convention's provisions.[101]

In light of the above-mentioned jurisprudence of the CJEU, it is clear that the Convention has a distinct independent legal impact within the EU legal order as a source of EU law, both directly and indirectly. Its direct impact may be felt through the possible use of infringement proceedings by the Commission or direct reliance by members of the public before national courts on those of its provisions able to fulfil the requirements for direct effect. Its indirect and more residual legal impact may be seen through the deployment by the Court of the principle of effectiveness, according to which national courts are obliged to the fullest extent possible to ensure that national law is interpreted by them to be in alignment with Århus requirements.

8.2 EU legislative implementation of the Århus Convention's obligations on access to environmental justice

Subsequent to its signature of the Århus Convention in 1998, the EU proceeded to take steps to implement the three pillars of the international instrument internally. As already mentioned earlier, however, the Union has so far failed to roll out comprehensive implementation of the third pillar, access to environmental justice, via EU secondary legislation. The Commission's 2003 proposal[102] for a general EU directive in order to assist the public's recourse to judicial review before national courts for the purpose of upholding EU environmental law against public authorities, as well as private persons, stalled at an early stage for want of sufficient political support within the Council of the EU. This initiative has so far not been revived at the time of writing, although the Commission is actively reviewing the possibility of so doing under the aegis of the EAP7.

Notwithstanding the absence of a 'horizontal' EU instrument implementing the third pillar of Århus, the Union has adopted a range of legislative measures in order to promote and introduce certain safeguards for civil society regarding access to environmental justice. Notably, the Union has adopted EU legislation securing access to justice in relation to EU institutional conduct, as well as in respect of the fields of access to environmental information and public participation in environmental decision-making (first and second pillars). It has also adopted access to provisions within a range of other EU legislative instruments concerning certain environmental protection policy fields. However, these initiatives have only led so far to a partial and rather fragmented state of implementation of the third pillar of Århus at the level of the member state. Broad areas of EU environmental law are not yet underpinned by EU secondary legislative guarantees on access to justice, including notably the sectors covering air quality, waste, water, noise and nature protection.

This section will consider the extent to which the Union has implemented through the adoption of legislation its access to environmental justice commitments under Århus, as far as the level of the member state is concerned. The next section (section 8.3) will consider the nature and contents of the Commission's 2003 proposal for a horizontal instrument. Given renewed political focus on the subject of implementation of EU law and access to justice in the context of the EAP7, appraisal of the 2003 proposal is warranted.

8.2.1 Access to justice regarding the first pillar of Århus (environmental information)

As part of its original wave of measures in 2003 to implement the Århus Convention, the EU introduced access-to-justice safeguards with respect to the first pillar of the Convention, namely with respect to the policy area of access to environmental information. These are safeguards housed within Directive 2003/4 on public access to environmental information (the AEI Directive).[103] The substantive rights to information contained in the AEI Directive are considered in a later chapter (Chapter 8A – available on website).

The inclusion of access-to-justice safeguards in the AEI Directive follows directly from the requirements set out in the Århus Convention. Whereas Article 4 of the Convention establishes rights to environmental information, Article 9 underpins this with a complementary right of members of the public to independent review of decisions concerning information disclosure. Specifically, Article 9(1) of the Convention requires contracting parties to ensure that members of the public have access to a review procedure if dissatisfied with the response given by a public authority to a request for information. Article 9(1) stipulates that contracting parties must ensure within their national laws that any person who considers that his or her request for information has been ignored, wrongfully refused (whether in part or in full), inadequately answered or otherwise not deal with in accordance with Article 4 of the Convention, has access to a review procedure before a court of law or another independent and impartial body established by law. The provision also requires that where a party provides for judicial review before a court of law, it must also offer access to a free or 'inexpensive' and 'expeditious' procedure under law for the purpose of either reconsideration by a public authority or review by an independent and impartial body other than a court of law. In addition, decisions by review bodies which are final must be binding on the public authority holding the information and reasons shall be stated in writing, at least where access to information is refused. Article 9(1) of the Convention is also complemented by other more general safeguards regarding access to justice contained in Article 9(4)–(5). These Convention provisions have been considered earlier in section 8.1. Article 9(4) is especially important in this regard, requiring in particular that contracting parties provide 'adequate and effective remedies, including injunctive relief where appropriate', which are 'fair, equitable, timely and not prohibitively expensive'.

The implementation of Article 9(1) of Århus by the AEI Directive offers to some extent more safeguards than required in the Convention. Specifically, whereas the Convention foresees the possibility of a contracting party offering a single (non-judicial) review procedure to information applicants, the AEI Directive requires

EU member states to secure two review channels. The relevant provisions are set out in Article 6 of the directive. First, Article 6(1) of the AEI Directive requires member states to ensure that an applicant for environmental information from competent national authorities has access to an administrative review procedure. Specifically, this is to entail free or inexpensive and expeditious access to a procedure through which contested conduct of the public authority concerned in relation to an information request may be either reconsidered by it or another public authority, or subject to an administrative review by an independent and impartial statutory body.

Secondly, Article 6(2) of the AEI Directive requires member states additionally to ensure that an applicant has access to a court of law or another independent and impartial statutory body, so that the conduct of the public authority concerned may be reviewed and a final decision made. Article 6(2) also provides the option for member states to enable third parties incriminated by information disclosed to have 'access to legal recourse'. By virtue of Article 6(3), final decisions under Article 6(2) are required to be binding on the public authority holding the information concerned. In addition, reasons are to be provided, at least where access to information is refused.

These requirements constitute a significant advance on the position under the former EU legislation preceding the AEI Directive, according to which member states were simply required in broad terms to provide the availability of a 'judicial or administrative review' of any decision by a competent authority regarding access to information requests.[104]

On the other hand, the access-to-justice provisions appear relatively weak in certain other respects. In particular, the right to judicial review or review by an independent body contained in Article 6(2) omits to incorporate the general complementary safeguards contained in Article 9(4)–(5) of the Convention. However, CJEU jurisprudence makes it clear that the EU legislation implementing the Århus Convention must be interpreted in line with the latter,[105] taking into account in particular the express reference in the preamble that EU law provisions 'must be consistent with' the Convention.[106] Accordingly, the access-to-justice safeguards in the AEI Directive are stronger than they may first appear. However, of course, the safeguards contained in Article 9(4) are rather general in nature and open to interpretation. It would have been far better had the AEI Directive incorporated specific obligations on these aspects from the outset. As it is, the directive leaves member states with a substantial amount of discretion in this field,[107] making it unclear as to what amounts to a minimum set of binding obligations with respect to key issues concerning public access to justice.[108]

8.2.2 *Access to justice regarding the second pillar of Århus (public participation in environmental decision-making)*

As with first-pillar issues, the EU introduced access-to-justice protection with respect to the Union's implementation in 2003 of the second pillar of the Århus

Convention concerning public participation in relation to certain decisions relating to the authorisation of specific industrial activities affecting the environment. The original EU implementation instrument was Directive 2003/35 providing for public participation in respect of the drawing up of certain plans and programmes relating to the environment and amending Directives 85/337 and 96/61 (hereafter referred to as the 'EU Public Participation Directive').[109] Subsequently, the access-to-justice provisions contained in the EU Public Participation Directive have been effectively relocated within more recent EU legislation, as will be explained below.

The incorporation of access-to-justice provisions with the EU Public Participation Directive constituted a natural implementation response to the requirements of the Århus Convention. Article 6 of the Convention establishes a series of related rights for members of the public to be able to participate in decisions to be taken by public authorities on whether certain proposed industrial projects listed in the Convention's Annex and other unlisted proposed activities potentially having a significant effect on the environment should be authorised. Article 9(2) of Århus sets out a complementary set of access-to-justice rights for members of the public, with the purpose of enabling them to be able to have recourse to independent review over such decisions where the public considers a decision has breached the requirements of Article 6. Specifically, Article 9(2) requires contracting parties to grant members of the public, subject to certain legal standing (*locus standi*) requirements, a right of access to a review procedure before a court and/ or an alternative independent and impartial statutory body for the purpose of challenging the substantive or procedural legality of the conduct of public authority concerning a matter caught by Article 6 decisions.[110] This right is flanked by supporting protections and guarantees set out in Article 9(4)–(5) and discussed in earlier sections. The right of review contained in Article 9(2) in respect of second-pillar decisions is arguably weaker than its counterpart in Article 9(1) relating to access to information in the sense that Article 9(1) guarantees applicants recourse to a separate, 'free or inexpensive' non-judicial review mechanism where parties also provide for review before a court. Under Article 9(2) of the Convention contracting parties are obliged to ensure that members of the public have access to such a review procedure, either where they have a 'sufficient interest' or 'maintaining an impairment of right' depending upon the administrative procedural legal requirements set by national law. These terms broadly reflect the position commonly adopted by contracting parties with respect to judicial review proceedings, namely in establishing criteria for limiting possibilities of members of the public to have legal standing to bring claims in respect of administrative decisions unless they are able to demonstrate a particular private interest or other special connection in relation to the dispute. The stringency of the criteria vary considerably amongst the legal systems of the contracting parties.

As a matter of general principle, the Århus Convention defers to the law of contracting parties to determine the issue of legal standing. Accordingly, the terms 'sufficient interest' and 'impairment of right' are not terms defined by the Convention itself. However, the Convention at the same time qualifies contracting parties' autonomy in certain important respects. First, Article 9(2) requires parties to ensure generally that the definition of a sufficient interest or impairment of a right defined under national law is consistent with the 'objective of giving the public concerned wide access to justice' within the scope of the Convention.[111] Secondly, the provision also stipulates that NGEOs should be given access to the review procedure, irrespective of whether they are deemed to have either a sufficient interest or an impaired right under national law, if they meet the requirements of Article 2(5) of the Convention. Article 2(5), which defines the term 'the public concerned' and provides for preferential recognition in this context for NGEOs, stipulates:

> 5. 'The public concerned' means the public affected or likely to be affected by, or having an interest in, the environmental decision-making; for the purposes of this definition, non-governmental organisations promoting environmental protection and meeting any requirements under national law shall be deemed to have an interest.

It is evident, though, from this provision that the degree of preferential status of NGEOs remains ultimately dependent upon how each contracting party decides to construct recognition requirements for such organisations. The Convention effectively allows contracting parties a wide margin of discretion in providing for broad or narrow recognition of NGEOs. However, in promoting wide access to justice the Convention also reflects an understanding that the common traditional approach applied in several jurisdictions to limit legal standing of the public to challenge administrative conduct, insofar as claimants are unable to show that their individual rights are unaffected by such conduct, is unsuitable to dealing with situations where public authority behaviour may give rise to or exacerbate diffuse types of environmental damage (e.g. air pollution, habitat loss).[112]

As mentioned above, the EU Public Participation Directive was the original Union legislative instrument to implement the second pillar of Århus. For this purpose, a key aspect of the 2003 directive was its amendment of two key legislative instruments relating to authorisation of industrial activities affecting the environment, namely the former directives on environmental impact assessment (EIA Directive 85/337)[113] and on integrated pollution prevention and control (IPPC Directive 96/61).[114] An integral part of the amendments was the incorporation of access-to-justice provisions in the two former directives.[115] Subsequently, these provisions have been transferred to the most recent versions of the Union legislation on impact assessment and IPPC, namely Article 11 of the codified Directive 2011/92 on the assessment of certain public and private projects on the environment (the 'EIA Directive')[116] and Article 25 of the recast Directive 2010/75 on industrial emissions (integrated pollution prevention and control) (the 'Industrial Emissions Directive').[117] Both provisions contain a virtually literal implementation of the requirements of Article 6 of the Convention. As is the case with the AEI Directive, both legislative instruments make specific reference to the Convention in their preambles and make it evident, as recognised by the CJEU,[118] that interpretation of the EU legislation (e.g. on access to justice) must be interpreted in line with Convention requirements.[119]

Predictably, both sets of access-to-justice provisions contained in the EIA Directive and Industrial Emissions Directive are structured on a similar basis, each with five subparagraphs sharing the same functions and virtually the same wording. Accordingly, it is only necessary to reproduce the access-to-justice provisions of one of the instruments here, those of the EIA Directive being selected. Article 11 of the EIA Directive (as successor to Article 10a of former Directive 85/337) states:

1. Member States shall ensure that, in accordance with the relevant national legal systems, members of the public concerned:

    (a) having a sufficient interest, or alternatively:
    (b) maintaining an impairment of right, where administrative procedural law of a Member State requires this as a precondition;

    have access to a review procedure before a court of law or another independent and impartial body established by law to challenge the substantive or procedural legality of decisions, acts or omissions subject to the public participation provisions of this Directive.

2. Member States shall determine at what stage the decisions, acts or omissions may be challenged.

3. What constitutes a sufficient interest and impairment of a right shall be determined by the Member States, consistently with the objective of giving the public wide access to justice. To that end, the interest of any non-governmental organisation meeting the requirements in Article 1(2)[120] shall be deemed sufficient for the purpose of point (a) of paragraph 1 of this Article. Such organisations shall also be deemed to have rights capable of being impaired for the purpose of point (b) of paragraph 1 of this Article.

4. The provisions of this Article shall not exclude the possibility of a preliminary review before an administrative authority and shall not affect the requirement of exhaustion of administrative review procedures prior to recourse to judicial review procedures, where such a requirement exists under national law.

    Any such procedure shall be fair, equitable, timely and not prohibitively expensive.

5. In order to further the effectiveness of the provisions of this Article, Member States shall ensure that practical information is made available to the public on access to administrative and judicial review procedures.

Since EU legislative implementation of the second pillar of the Århus Convention, the CJEU has had a number of opportunities to provide clarification on various aspects of the accompanying access-to-justice provisions. Notwithstanding the often general nature of the provisions, the Court has made it clear that the EU legislative requirements on access to environmental justice in relation to second-pillar decision-making constitute significant legal constraints on the autonomy of member states to construct their administrative and judicial review systems. The legal terminology employed in the EU legislation not only constitutes part of the autonomous body of norms that collectively form Union law (and so independent and distinct from national legal interpretation), but is also required to be interpreted in line with key objective underpinning the access-to-justice provisions of providing 'wide access' to review.[121] Judicial clarification from the CJEU on various aspects of the EU legislative provisions, provided notably to national courts via the medium of the preliminary ruling procedure under Article 267 TFEU, has resulted in a cementing and greater specification of member state (and consequently national courts') obligations emanating from the EU legislation. To date, the CJEU has already had occasion to consider a range of legal issues arising from the operation of the EU access-to-justice provisions, including notably in relation to legal costs, legal standing requirements, privileged status of NGEOs and interim relief. It should be borne in mind that this emerging seam of case law is relevant to the entire spectrum of EU legislation on access to environmental justice, not simply confined to provisions derived from the EU Public Participation Directive, given the similarity of wording and function of access-to-justice legislative provision. Some of the key aspects and implications of the case law are considered here.

An important part of the emerging jurisprudence of the CJEU has been on the question of legal costs relating to review procedures, namely those relating to court fees as well as, in particular, legal representation. It is apparent that such costs may in practice be substantial for litigants, not least in jurisdictions which apply the principle of legal costs of both sides having to be paid by the loser such as in relation to the courts of the UK and Ireland. Those drafting the Århus Convention recognised that this issue could be a problem in deterring members of the public and/or NGEOs from seeking recourse to judicial review mechanisms as a means of assisting the enforcement of environmental legislation. As a consequence Article 9(4) of the Convention requires contracting parties to ensure that legal costs are not 'prohibitively expensive' and this general requirement has also been incorporated into the EU legislation implementing the international instrument. At the same time, it is evident that this requirement of itself in offers relatively limited assistance to members of the public and NGEOs. Notably, litigants are not entitled to 'free or inexpensive' access to a review procedure as is the case in relation to reviews of access to environmental information decisions under Article 9(1); neither are there any guarantees afforded in relation to legal aid in the Convention. Accordingly, public interest environmental litigation is allowed to remain an expensive and accordingly risky enterprise for members of the public and NGEOs alike.

In a few cases already the CJEU has had occasion to interpret the requirement in relation to prohibitive costs in relation to costs awards being imposed on unsuccessful litigants.[122] The case law has been important in fleshing out the implicit parameters of this obligation. Although neither the Århus Convention nor the EU's implementing legislation defines what 'prohibitively expensive' means, the CJEU has taken note of (whilst not accepting as definitively binding) the Convention's implementation guide in this respect, which indicates that costs must not be so expensive as to prevent persons seeking a review in appropriate cases.[123] The CJEU has confirmed the prohibition broadly to cover all the costs arising from a claimant's participation in legal proceedings,[124] thus including any fees imposed by a court as well as the costs of legal representation.[125] That legal representation fees are covered is particularly important, as they typically constitute the bulk of costs involved in litigation, particularly so in the context of legal disputes conducted in jurisdictions, such as the UK and Ireland, which are based on adversarial approaches to justice and employ costs rules that stipulate as a matter of principle that the loser should bear both parties' costs ('costs follow the event' rule). Moreover, in *Commission v UK* the CJEU held that any imposition of a cross-undertaking in damages required to be paid by an applicant for interim relief is also subject to the prohibition.[126] Again, this is an important development, given that in the not-so-distant past the levying of such undertakings could be so substantial as to have a chilling effect on public interest environmental litigation brought by NGEOs, as in the *Lappel Bank* case.[127]

Whilst the Court has accepted that costs orders relating to costs incurred from participation in the national judicial review procedure may be imposed on unsuccessful litigants,[128] at the same time it has held that member states must ensure that these may never exceed the threshold of being prohibitively expensive. Accordingly, a discretionary practice on the part of national courts not to impose or to impose reduced costs awards on impecunious litigants has been held by the CJEU to violate the requirements of the access-to-justice provisions contained in the EU Public Participation Directive (as now contained in Article 11 of the EIA Directive and Article 25 of the Industrial Emissions Directive).[129] In *Edwards*[130] and *Commission v UK*[131] the CJEU has confirmed that the discretionary practice of UK courts to award protective costs orders[132] contravened the access-to-justice requirements of the EU Public Participation Directive, largely on the basis that such awards constituted an uncertain and therefore insufficient implementation of the duty to ensure against prohibitive costs. The successful infringement action brought by the Commission against the UK followed a previous recommendation by the Århus Compliance Committee[133] in 2010, which concluded that the UK breached, *inter alia*, the requirement in Article 9(4) of the Convention against prohibitively expensive legal costs.[134] The CJEU in *Edwards* and *Commission v UK* also clarified that a legal costs assessment for a litigant by a national court must be undertaken to take into account the interests of the litigant (as rights holder) as well as the public interest in protecting the environment. Accordingly, a costs assessment needs to be seen from both a subjective and objective perspective by national courts. Specifically, not only should the financial situation of the litigant be taken into account but also national courts must consider whether the costs are not unreasonable from an objective standpoint, taking into account that the public and NGOs are entitled to play an active role in defending the environment. For this purpose, the CJEU has acknowledged that national courts could take into account the following factors to assess the level of costs: whether the litigant has a reasonable chance of succeeding; the importance of the case for both litigant and environmental protection; degree of complexity of law and review procedure; and whether the claim is frivolous.[135] Such an assessment must be carried out at all levels of stages of appeals, it being irrelevant whether a claimant has so far been deterred from bringing a legal claim before the national courts.[136] As from April 2013, new rules have been introduced in the UK in order to cap the amount of legal costs that judicial review applicants may face in proceedings subject to the Århus Convention.[137]

The CJEU has also had occasion to consider the ambit of rights of legal standing and associated rights of members of the public and NGEOs to have access to national judicial review procedures. In *Gemeinde Altrip*[138] the Court clarified that, notwithstanding the broad discretion accorded to member states in determining the legal standing of members of the public to seek legal review of second-pillar environmental decisions under the aegis of the access-to-justice provisions of the EU Public Participation Directive, this autonomy was by no means unqualified. In particular, any conditions fixed by members states relating to sufficiency of interest or existence of an impairment of right must accord with the standard principles of equivalence and effectiveness as applicable to national procedural rules governing remedies in relation to the safeguarding to EU legal rights[139] (as discussed in Chapter 7). The Court noted that the latter principle requires that any national requirements relating to *locus standi* must not make it in practice either impossible or excessively difficult to exercise second-pillar rights, in order to give the public concerned 'wide access to justice', with a view to contributing to preserving, protecting and improving environmental quality and public health.[140]

Elsewhere, the CJEU has appraised the privileged legal status afforded to NGEOs under the aegis of the EU Public Participation Directive. In *Arnsberg*[141] the CJEU confirmed that the access-to-justice provisions of the EIA Directive (specifically now Article 11(3)) guarantee a directly effective right to a judicial or independent review process, irrespective of whether or not an NGEO fulfils the requirements of a sufficient interest or impairment of right stipulated by national law for members of the public to have access to such a review in respect of public authority conduct. Accordingly, member states are not entitled simply to assume that they may conflate the standard legal standing requirements applicable to members of the public with those of NGEOs, otherwise this would be, according to the Court, contrary to the principle of effectiveness in not allowing such associations to have access solely on the ground that they protect the environmental public interest.[142] In *Djurgården*[143] the CJEU also underlined that member states must ensure that they construct requirements governing the legal standing of NGEOs in a manner that accords with the general principle of effectiveness and obligation (in Article 11(3) of the EIA Directive) to secure 'wide access' to legal review procedures.[144] In that case, the CJEU held that Swedish law had breached its EU legislative obligations on access to justice under the EIA Directive in having required an applicant NGEO to have at least 2,000 members. The Court considered that national rules may not fix minimum membership levels of NGEOs at a level running counter to the directive's objectives to ensure wide access to justice, which had been the effect of national rules in this instance. It was irrelevant that the NGEO in question had an opportunity to express its views in the participatory phases of the relevant decision by a public authority, or that conceivably the NGEO could have lobbied other larger NGEOs to seek judicial review.[145]

The CJEU has also been instrumental in other respects in entrenching the access-to-justice rights concerning EU implementation second-pillar legislation. In particular, the Court has confirmed that the remedy of interim relief must be available as an implied integral part of the access-to-justice legislative package, notwithstanding the absence of an express requirement to this effect contained in the EU legislative rules. In *Križan*[146] the CJEU confirmed, with reference to its general jurisprudence on national remedies in respect of breaches of Union law,[147] that that the exercise of rights under (the then equivalent to) Article 25 of the Industrial Emissions Directive must include the possibility of requesting a national court to order interim measures for the purposes of preventing pollution, including where necessary by way of temporary suspension of a permit.[148] This judicial conclusion is supported by the obligations contained in the Århus Convention, which in Article 9(4) requires that 'injunctive relief, where appropriate' shall be provided in national review procedures. This is an important recognition that availability of interim relief may be critically important in order to prevent irremediable environmental damage that is liable to arise from an erroneous administrative decision to authorise a particular development project.[149] The CJEU has also made it clear that the utilisation of review procedures in order to uphold EU environmental legislation may not be obstructed *per se* on grounds that a judicial decision arising from such a review interferes with fundamental personal freedoms of an operator. Specifically, in *Križan* the CJEU confirmed that a judicial annulment of a permit granted in breach of second-pillar rights may not be construed as an unlawful interference with property rights guaranteed under Article 17 of the EU Charter of Fundamental Rights. In *Commission v UK*[150] the CJEU condemned the UK government for failing to ensure that UK law ensured that applications for interim relief were not prohibitively expensive as required by the access-to-justice provisions contained in the EU Public Participation Directive. In the UK, an applicant for an interim injunction in the context of environmental judicial review proceedings may be subject to the imposition by a court of a cross-undertaking in damages, the purpose of which is to ensure the party subject to the injunction is compensated if the court ultimately decides the case in its favour and that party suffers a quantifiable financial loss as a result of complying with it. The CJEU found that the UK's procedural rules were insufficiently clear so as to ensure that they complied with the ban against prohibitive costs, the UK government having merely asserted that in practice such financial orders are not always imposed by UK courts and not demanded from impecunious litigants.[151]

8.2.3 *Access to justice regarding the third pillar: environmental law enforcement*

Notwithstanding the Union's efforts to implement the Århus Convention through the adoption of a range of EU legislative instruments, its implementation of the

Convention's requirements relating to access to justice remains incomplete. As discussed above (in sections 8.2.1 and 8.2.2), the Union has taken measures to ensure that legislative safeguards are put in place at national level to ensure that civil society has access to legal review mechanisms in order to ensure that the first two pillars of the Convention (namely the rights of access to environmental information and public participation in environmental decision-making) are respected. However, the Union has so far failed to ensure at national level the complete implementation of the third dimension of access-to-justice requirements under Århus, specifically Article 9(3) of the Convention which requires contracting parties to ensure that the public has access to legal review procedures to challenge conduct of public or private entities which contravene the requirements of environmental law of the contracting parties. Specifically, the EU has not legislated to safeguard a general right of access to justice at national level for civil society to use in order to secure enforcement of EU environmental law. The Commission's original legislative proposal in this regard (the Draft AJEM Directive, which is discussed in section 8.3) has remained on the shelf due to member state resistance expressed within Council of the EU in 2003 when the draft instrument was assessed by the EU legislature. As a consequence, the Union has taken few steps to implement Article 9(3) of the Convention with legislation targeted at the national level (i.e. adherence by EU member states). The notable exception to this omission has been the Environmental Liability Directive 2004/35,[152] which provides access-to-justice safeguards for the public including NGEOs in respect of ensuring that national competent authorities adhere to the directive's requirements regarding remediation of environmental damage generated as a result of breaches of EU environmental law. Overall, though, the result of the EU's failure to adopt the Draft AJEM Directive has meant that there is a significant gap in terms of the coverage of the EU's implementation of its commitments under the third pillar of the Århus Convention. The specific access-to-justice provisions of Directive 2004/35 will be considered below.

8.2.3.1 *Access to justice under Directive 2004/35 on environmental liability (ELD)*

An important source of EU law relating to access to environmental justice is Directive 2004/35 on environmental liability with regard to the prevention and remedying of environmental damage, as amended[153] (hereafter referred to as the 'ELD'). The principal aim of this instrument is to establish, in accordance with the 'polluter pays' principle, a legal framework for the purpose of ensuring that member states are equipped with the requisite legal tools in order to ensure that operators carrying out certain industrial-related activities and causing actual or threatened damage to the environment are legally held to account. The environmental liability regime established under the ELD focuses exclusively on securing the prevention and remediation of damage to the environment. It does not affect existing rights that private persons enjoy under the civil law of the member states to compensation and other remedies in relation to impairment to the environment that causes damage to their personal legal interests (such as physical well-being or property rights in land).[154] The ELD effectively entered into force three years after its adoption in 2004, with member states required to have transposed it into national law by 30 April 2007.[155]

The ELD focuses on the key role that public authorities of the member states are to play in taking requisite action in order to ensure that such operators take appropriate preventive or remedial steps in relation to environmental damage caused or threatened as a result of their activities. Member states are required to designate competent authorities to ensure that the requirements of the ELD are fulfilled (hereinafter referred to as 'competent authorities').[156] Given the fact that the environmental liability requirements contained in the directive are ones principally for the competent authorities to enforce, the contents of the ELD will be considered in detail in Chapter 11 in Part III, covering member state authorities' responsibilities for EU environmental law enforcement. However, it is important also to mention it in the context of law enforcement undertaken by private entities, as the directive provides important procedural rights for individuals. Specifically, Articles 12–13 ELD contain specific rules which confer a distinct law enforcement role on private entities, such as NGEOs. The ELD's provisions on law enforcement mechanisms for civil society are exclusively focused on the review of public authority conduct. Unlike the Århus Convention, the ELD does not provide any specific procedural rights for private entities to seek legal review and redress from other private entities in respect of environmental damage caused or threatened by the latter. The relevant ELD provisions are structured on a two-tier basis: internal and external review. Specifically, (certain) individuals and other private entities are vested with rights to request a competent authority to investigate instances of alleged environmental damage[157] as well as having rights to seek independent legal review of the acts, decisions or omissions of a competent authority.[158] These two provisions will be examined in turn.

RIGHTS OF PRIVATE ENTITIES TO REQUEST ACTION UNDER THE ELD

Article 12 of the ELD provides certain private entities with the right, in certain circumstances, to request a competent authority to undertake action in relation to instances of environmental damage or imminent threat of environmental damage alleged to have occurred in contravention with the directive's requirements. In principle, two criteria must be fulfilled before the competent authority is compelled to undertake a review of such a request, namely those relating to the legal standing of the applicant(s) and the supply of relevant information in support of the request. However, member states are entitled to waive any or all these requirements in relation to cases of imminent threat of damage.[159]

Article 12(1) addresses the aspect of legal standing. By virtue of this provision, only certain private entities are entitled to submit to the competent authority observations relating to alleged cases of actual or threatened environmental damage and file requests for action. Specifically, standing to file a request is granted to natural or legal persons:

(a) affected or likely to be affected by environmental damage or
(b) having a sufficient interest in environmental decision-making relating to the damage or, alternatively,

(c)   alleging the impairment of a right, where administrative procedural law
of a member state requires this as a precondition[.]

Subject to one significant qualification, the ELD specifies that the definitions of
'sufficient interest' and 'impairment of a right' are to be matters left to national
law of the member states.[160] The qualification is in relation to the position of
NGEOs, which are vested with less restrictive rights of standing, as set out in the
third paragraph of Article 12(1):

> To this end, the interest of any non-governmental organisation promoting
> environmental protection and meeting any requirements under national law
> shall be deemed sufficient for the purpose of subparagraph (b). Such organ-
> isations shall also be deemed to have rights capable of being impaired for the
> purpose of subparagraph (c).

The impact of this qualification is to open up the possibility for NGEOs to be able to
file requests for action, even though they or their members' personal legal interests or
assets may not be affected or impaired in some way by the environmental damage.
This is an important clause, as it does not predicate the right of request upon a local
'residency' requirement that may otherwise be set down by national law. The phrase
'meeting any requirements under national law' refers to any particular requirements
laid down by member states' general laws on the incorporation and registration of
bodies that would apply to such NGOs. It is evident from the legislative background
to the ELD that the phrase is not intended to permit member states to establish special standing requirements for NGEOs for filing Article 12 requests.[161] That would be
a misinterpretation of the phrase. It is not clear why standing requirements have had
to be laid down in respect of natural or legal persons. Indeed, it might be thought that
it would be in the interests of competent authorities to be open to receive any well-
founded information on environmental damage, irrespective of the source of that
information, a view held by the Commission in relation to the filing of complaints to
it that may lead it to open Article 258/260 TFEU infringement proceedings against
member states. The view that a filter is needed in order to ensure that competent
authorities are not flooded with ill-founded requests is unconvincing, for – as is discussed below – such authorities are not required to pursue any request other than
those adjudged by them to be plausible. The incorporation of legal standing requirements does not sit well with the EU treaty requirement of ensuring a high level of
environmental protection, nor with the spirit, if not the letter, of the Århus Convention. One could argue that the standing requirements set out under Article 12(1)
ELD contravene the requirements in Article 5(1)(a) of the Convention, which
requires contracting parties to ensure that their public authorities possess and update
environmental information which is relevant to their functions. Standing requirements restrict the possibilities for competent authorities to ensure that they have the
best possible means of securing information pertinent to their areas of responsibility
that is both up to date and comprehensive in scope and depth.[162]

Article 12(2)–(3) ELD stipulates the requirements pertaining to the supply of information that must accompany any request for action. Article 12(2) specifies that the request must contain 'relevant information and data supporting the observations' submitted in relation to environmental damage. Article 12(3) specifies that a competent authority is only obliged to consider observations and requests which 'show in a plausible manner that environmental damage exists'. These provisions confirm that requests must be sufficiently supported by credible information of some kind before a competent authority is under a duty to undertake a review of whether or not to take action. It is important to note that the burden of proof is relatively low, and probably no more onerous than a requirement to show reasonable suspicion of damage. A more onerous burden would be difficult to reconcile with the precautionary and preventive principles,[163] both being fundamental principles of EU environmental policy and law.[164] Significantly, the observations do not have to provide any evidence that of itself determines individual culpability; the persons making the request are required only to provide the authority with plausible information about the existence of damage. This is important, given that private persons filing requests are not usually going to be in any position, legally, technically or financially, to deduce the source of environmental damage. Attribution of liability under the ELD is a matter for competent authorities to establish, not those who file requests for action.

Article 12(3)–(4) ELD contains some general provisions regarding the administrative procedural steps to be taken once an admissible request has been filed with a competent authority. Article 12(3) specifies that the authority is to consider the observations and request for action, and 'give the relevant operator an opportunity' to comment on them. Article 12(4) requires the authority 'as soon as possible' and in accordance with national law to inform the person who filed the request of its decision to accede to or refuse the request for action. The notification must provide the reasons upon which the decision is grounded. Regrettably, no timetable is set down in the provisions of the directive for the completion of these procedures. The ELD does not require competent authorities to meet any specific deadline to react to requests from the concerned public. The Commission's original draft proposal for the ELD had envisaged a four-month deadline.[165] It should also be noted that member states' discretion over timing of public authority responses is limited in general terms also by the safeguards set down in the Århus Convention, specifically Article 9(4) thereof which requires access to environmental justice procedures to be, *inter alia*, both 'effective' and 'timely'. However, the absence of a specific time limit for public authority responses to applicants is a potentially significant shortcoming, liable to cause unnecessary confusion and potential delay in the operation of review procedures as well as national distortions of what is supposed to be a common legal framework for the Union. In cases of imminent threat of environmental damage, the ELD provides that these particular procedural requirements need not apply before an authority decides to take action,[166] namely the obligation to hear the relevant operator(s) involved and notify persons requesting action.

RIGHT TO SUBJECT COMPETENT AUTHORITY'S CONDUCT TO LEGAL
REVIEW UNDER THE ELD

In addition to being granted the right to request action from a competent authority, the ELD also confers a right to persons to seek independent legal review of the authority's conduct. Specifically, Article 13(1) of the ELD states that persons granted the right to file requests for action must also have access to a court or other independent and impartial public body competent to review the procedural as well as substantive legality of decisions, acts or omissions of competent authorities in relation to the requirements of the directive. The right to seek review is accordingly very wide-ranging in that its remit applies to all formal aspects of a designated competent authority's work in relation to carrying out the ELD, not just in respect of its decisions whether or not to act in relation to requests to take action.

Article 13(1) of the ELD is made subject to a rather broad qualification in Article 13(2), to the effect that the ELD is to operate 'without prejudice to any provisions of national law which regulate access to justice' or national provisions that require administrative review procedures to be exhausted prior to recourse to judicial proceedings. At first glance Article 13(2) might appear to offer member states the possibility of adopting or maintaining a restrictive stance on legal standing of private persons seeking judicial review of administrative conduct. However, this would be a misreading of that provision. Instead, Article 13(2) should be seen in the light of the access-to-justice protections offered under the aegis of the Århus Convention which, as a source of EU law, is also a component of 'national law' for the purposes of Article 13(2). Article 9(3)–(4) of the Convention is especially important in this regard. Article 9(3) requires contracting parties to ensure that members of the public have access to administrative or judicial review procedures to challenge conduct by public authorities contravening their national laws on the environment. Article 9(4) requires parties, *inter alia*, to ensure that judicial review procedures 'provide adequate and effective remedies, including injunctive relief as appropriate, and be fair, equitable, timely and not prohibitively expensive'. Accordingly, the amount of discretion provided to member states under Article 13(2) is tempered and qualified by the legal constraints set down in Århus. It would, though, have been more in keeping with the objective of promoting access to environmental justice objective if the access formula contained in Article 12(1) of the directive could have been applied also in Article 13.

IMPACT OF THE ELD ON ACCESS TO ENVIRONMENTAL JUSTICE

Given that the transposition deadline in respect of the ELD has only elapsed relatively recently in 2007[167] and at the time of writing the Commission has yet to issue its first report on the implementation of the directive,[168] it is relatively early to assess the full extent of the practical impact the ELD is set to have with respect to assisting in the enforcement of EU environmental legislation. It is also worth noting in this context that the ELD contains a specific temporal limit as regards the scope of its application. Specifically, it does not apply to damage caused by an emission, event or incident that transpires prior to 30 April 2007 (the implementation deadline) or in respect of any emission, event or incident which, although occurring after 30 April 2007, derives from a specific activity which took place and ended prior to that date.[169] It is fair to say, though, that the ELD did not get off to an auspicious start, with the Commission having to take infringement proceedings in 2008–9 against several member states over failures to transpose the directive into national law.[170] No doubt transposition would have been somewhat swifter had the introduction by the Lisbon Treaty on 1 December 2009 of financial penalties for non-transposition cases been integrated earlier within the first-round infringement procedure system under Article 258 TFEU.

On the one hand, there are a number of features of the ELD that point towards the instrument having a significant contribution to make in relation to enhancement of access to environmental justice for civil society. Notably, it appears that the right to request action and legal review enshrined in Articles 12–13 of the ELD will enable certain members of the public and NGEOs to become more readily involved in the review processes without having to negotiate through unclear or onerous legal standing (*locus standi*) requirements that may exist under some current national procedural rules of member states. It is also evident that member states will have to ensure that persons with standing have the opportunity to subject the conduct of a competent authority to procedural as well as substantive legal scrutiny before an independent body, whose decisions are to be binding upon the competent authority. Such a body must be capable of ensuring that the competent authority not only adheres to procedural rights of private persons filing requests or persons subject to investigation; it must also ensure that the substantive decisions taken by the authority accord with the ELD as well as with other EU environmental legislation. Accordingly, existing legal review procedures under national administrative law may have to be extended where review bodies are unable to conduct a comprehensive legal review as envisaged by the Article 13(1) ELD. To some extent it is also highly probable that the beneficiaries of these provisions will be able to rely upon them before national courts. True, elements of both legislative provisions would appear to rule out direct effect given their conditional and imprecise nature (e.g. the need for member states to establish the relevant competent authority and procedural rules on legal standing). However, there is little doubt in light of CJEU jurisprudence on indirect effect of directives (as discussed in Chapter 6) and on national remedies (as discussed in Chapter 7) that national courts are under a duty, as far as possible, to ensure that their national laws comply with the access to review procedures in Articles 12–13 ELD. This may well lead over time to the amplification of access-to-justice protection under the ELD by way of judicial clarification provided by the CJEU in preliminary rulings to national courts on the interpretation of the extent of the legislative instrument's guarantees.

On the other hand, there are several features of the ELD that give some cause for concern in terms of their impact on access to justice. For instance, the directive does not stipulate any requirements regarding the maximum level of administrative and legal costs that may be levied on persons utilising the review procedures.[171] Member states appear to retain substantial discretion to determine the amount charged in respect of such costs. If set at too high a level, they may well act as a significant deterrent to persons wishing to request action or seek legal review of a competent authority's conduct. However, member states do not have a completely free rein in the sense that they are obliged to adhere to the general requirements of Article 9(4) of the Århus Convention. In addition, the ELD fails to set a clear time-table in respect of the handling of a request for action. The timetable will be set according to national rules and there is no guarantee that these will be sufficiently swift, commensurate with the degree of urgency attached to any particular case. Moreover, given that member states are required to take the step of designating their own competent authorities to carry out the requirements of the ELD, it is doubtful whether either Articles 12 or 13 are sufficiently unconditional in order to qualify as directly effective provisions; individuals will therefore probably not be able to enforce them in the absence of national transposition legislation which designates a competent authority.[172] Accordingly, the effectiveness of the ELD's access-to-justice provisions depends a good deal upon the particular detailed pro-cedural provisions adopted by individual transposition legislation.

8.3 Possibilities for a general EU directive on access to justice in environmental matters at national level

By way of rounding off this chapter on the state of the EU's implementation of the Århus Convention's access to environmental justice obligations, this section reflects on the possibilities that lie ahead for the EU in promulgating a general 'horizontal' legislative instrument on access to environmental justice at national level. It will focus in particular on the European Commission's 2003 Draft AJEM Directive[173] which remains a significant reference point, not least in the light of recent renewed political interest taken by the EU and in this area under the aegis of the EAP7.[174]

Based on Article 192 TFEU (ex Article 175 European Community Treaty), the Draft AJEM Directive constituted part of a package of proposed measures intended to implement the three pillars of Århus into the EU legal order. Whilst other elements of the initial 'Århus package' were either relatively swiftly or even-tually adopted, the Draft AJEM Directive stalled due to political resistance within the Council of the EU. Adoption required a qualified majority vote of approval in the Council of the EU as well as the assent of the European Parliament.[175] The position of the Council was rather contradictory, given that it was prepared to assist in promulgating measures that addressed the subject of access to environ-mental justice from the outset in relation to access to environmental information (Directive 2003/4) and public participation in environmental decision-making relating to integrated pollution prevention and control (Directive 2003/35). Sub-sequently, the Council has also approved as we have seen, together with the Euro-pean Parliament as co-legislator, further extensions in implementation of the third pillar through the adoption of a number of legislative guarantees on access to justice in other particular environmental policy contexts, notably in relation to environmental liability (Directive 2004/35). The EU has also ensured that legislative guarantees on access to environmental justice have been adopted with respect to EU-level institutional conduct.[176]

Whilst the 2003 Draft AJEM Directive has remained effectively on the political shelf for over a decade due to resistance from member states,[177] its relevance has recently re-emerged with a vengeance in the light of renewed EU political appetite in the context of the EAP7[178] to develop enhanced protection for the public in terms of their access to and procedural rights before national courts when seeking to uphold EU environmental legislation. It is apparent that (a number of) member states remain sensitive to and wary of interference from the Union in the field of judicial procedure and protection concerning the operation of national courts and tribunals, an area historically considered to be a matter to be governed principally at national level.[179] It is also clear that the political and legal realities relating to the issue of access to environmental justice have arguably evolved significantly since 2003 to favour the development of a more comprehensive and coherent EU-level approach on securing delivery of the requirements of Århus. Whether this turns out to be the case and EU legislation is ultimately adopted remains, of course, to be seen.

8.3.1 The Seventh EU Environmental Action Programme (EAP7) and access to environmental justice at national level

The EU has recently confirmed in the context of its EAP7[180] that the area of access to environmental justice is to constitute one of the dimensions of its focus on implementation and enforcement. The EAP7 lists nine thematic priority policy objectives for the Union, the fourth of which focuses on the Union enhancing implementation of EU environmental legislation.[181] Listed amongst the measures to be taken under the auspices of 'Priority Objective 4' is a specific commitment to enhance the Union's existing position regarding access to environmental justice at national level. This is contained within paragraph 65 of the Annex to the EU Decision adopting the EAP7, the relevant extracts of which are reproduced below:

> 65. In order to maximise the benefits of Union environment legislation by improving implementation, the EAP7 shall ensure that by 2020:
>
> [. . .]
>
> (e) the principle of effective legal protection for citizens and their organisations is facilitated.
> This requires, in particular:
>
> > [. . .]
>
> > (v) ensuring that national provisions on access to justice reflect the case law of the Court of Justice of the European Union . . .[182]

Interestingly, the EAP7 does not expressly commit to the promulgation of new legislation but this is a possible and plausible inference to be drawn from the

Programme's text. Indeed, the European Commission has been keen to promote a renewed legislative agenda for some time during the preparations and negotiations over the EAP7. In particular, in a 2012 Communication[183] the Commission took note of the recent case law of the CJEU[184] (considered in the previous sections of this chapter) that has confirmed on a number of occasions national courts' responsibilities to interpret national access-to-justice rules in line with the Århus Convention, and has viewed this development as giving rise to legal uncertainty. The Commission considered it appropriate to explore how greater certainty could be achieved for national courts and economic and environmental interests, such as through developing guidance on CJEU case law as well as defining at EU level the conditions for efficient as well as effective access to national courts in respect of all areas of EU environmental law. The European Parliament[185] and Committee for the Regions[186] have both voiced recent support for a directive on access to environmental justice.

At the time of writing the European Commission has taken matters further with moves that indicate a shift in the direction of seriously contemplating EU legislative action. Specifically, the Commission's Environment Directorate-General (DG ENV) has launched a series of initiatives in order to prepare the ground for launching a legislative initiative.[187] In particular, DG ENV has commissioned a number of studies examining member state systems of access to environmental justice as well as a study on economic impacts of possible Commission initiatives. It has also set up an expert consultative working group as well as launching a public consultation questionnaire in 2013.[188] The Commission has also published an explanatory consultation text on its DG ENV website which sets out the range of policy options open to the Union.[189] The document signals that one of the options might be to revisit the Draft AJEM Directive, taking on board European Parliament first-reading amendments, or to launch a completely fresh legislative initiative. Given that the Commission is seriously contemplating the possibility of proposing legislation in this area once more, it is appropriate to consider the contents of the 2003 Draft AJEM directive, which may serve as an influential guide for the Commission's possible legislative reworking of this area.

8.3.2   The 2003 Draft Access to Justice in Environmental Matters (AJEM) Directive

In October 2003, the Commission presented the European Parliament and Council of the EU with a legislative proposal to implement the 'third-pillar' access-to-justice obligations contained in the Århus Convention into the legal systems of the member states. The draft EU legislative initiative took the form of a draft directive (the Draft AJEM Directive).[190] It was primarily designed to enable a broad spectrum of civil society to be endowed with rights to hold public authorities as well as private persons to account by way of taking environmental proceedings at national level in respect of acts or omissions to act in contravention of EU environmental law.[191] Whilst the material scope of the draft initiative is focused essentially on private enforcement of Union environmental legislation, the proposal also provides that member states have the option of transposing its requirements in respect of environmental laws of exclusively national origin, i.e. which have been established independently of EU environmental law.[192]

Based upon the core legal structures and requirements foreseen in the Århus Convention, the Draft AJEM Directive fleshes out, in some respects in general and in others in more detail, how EU member states are to implement the Århus legal principles on widening access to environmental justice as far as the enforcement of EU environmental law is concerned. Specifically, it sets out a wide-ranging legal framework to ensure that members of the public and NGEOs (as 'qualified entities') are able to secure better access to judicial proceedings at national level before the member state courts in order to seek redress in respect of the conduct of private persons or national public authorities they consider to breach EU environmental law. In addition, it also provides such persons with the right to request a public authority to undertake an internal review of conduct alleged to have contravened EU environmental law. Given that the legal basis of the Draft AJEM Directive is Article 192 TFEU, member states are to remain competent to be able introduce or maintain measures more generous than the minimum floor of access-to-justice rights granted in the legislative proposal.[193]

8.3.2.1 Beneficiaries of the Draft AJEM Directive: 'Members of the public' and 'qualified entities'

Addressed to the EU member states, the purpose the Draft AJEM Directive is to establish a set of binding provisions under EU law to ensure access to justice in environmental proceedings for both 'members of the public' as well as 'qualified entities'.[194] The latter concept was introduced in order to enable particular enhanced rights of legal standing for NGEOs to apply in relation to public interest environmental litigation before national courts. Both legal concepts will be examined briefly in turn.

'Members of the public' are defined broadly in the Draft AJEM Directive to mean 'one or more natural legal persons and in accordance with national law, associations, organisations or groups made up by these persons'.[195] This definition embraces a very wide notion of the public, given that it is not predicated on the criteria of nationality, residence, number of persons involved or particular legal forms.

'Qualified entities' are a special category of private persons created by the Draft AJEM Directive vested with distinct enforcement rights. The term 'qualified entities' is defined in Article 2(1)(c) of the Draft AJEM Directive as meaning any association, organisation or group whose objective is to protect the environment and which is recognised by individual member states under a specific procedure set out in Article 9. Article 9(1) stipulates that member states are to adopt a special procedure to ensure an 'expeditious' recognition of such entities, either on a case-by-case basis (ad hoc) or under an advance dedicated recognition procedure, where they fulfil specific requirements as set out in Article 8 of the Draft AJEM Directive. Member states are to set up the procedures involved for recognition, determine the competent authorities responsible for deciding upon recognition as well as ensure that rejections of requests for recognition shall be subject to independent review laid down in law.[196]

Article 8 of the Draft AJEM Directive elaborates the criteria to be used for identifying a 'qualified entity'. It specifies four requirements to be met before a body is to be regarded as a qualified entity, namely: (1) it must be an independent, non-profit-making legal person whose objective is to protect the environment;[197] (2) it must have an organisational structure enabling it to ensure the adequate pursuit of its statutory objectives;[198] (3) it must have been legally constituted and have worked actively for the protection of the environment in conformity with its statutes for a period to be determined by the member state but no longer than three years;[199] and (4) it must have its annual statement of accounts certified by a registered auditor for a period to be determined by the member state in which it is constituted.[200] The Draft AJEM Directive does not, however, address the conditions under which member states may withdraw recognition; no specific safeguards are set out to protect qualified entities from being subject to an arbitrary withdrawal of recognition by a member state. On the other hand, one may reasonably infer from the unconditional terms crafted in Article 8 that qualified entities have a right to maintain their special status, as long as they continue to fulfil the criteria set out in Article 8. Any deviation from this basic right would, in accordance with standard jurisprudential analysis of the CJEU, have to be construed narrowly. Any withdrawal of qualified entity status would have to ensure that it complied with the procedural and substantive general principles of EU law, including notably the right to a fair hearing,[201] equality[202] and proportionality.[203] These principles apply to situations where member states derogate from individual rights protected under EU law.[204] These rights are also safeguarded as part of the body of rights protected under the Charter on Fundamental Rights of the EU (EUCFR),[205] which specifically applies to member states when implementing Union law[206] (in addition to EU institutions' conduct).

It is probable that the provisions in Articles 8–9, in intending to confer specific rights on persons interested in becoming a qualified entity for the purpose of the Draft AJEM Directive, have the capacity to be directly effective so that individuals may be able to rely directly upon them before national courts in the event of their incorrect transposition into national law. For although the terms of these provisions do not appear to meet the standard criteria of sufficient precision or unconditionality, as would normally be expected for the doctrine of direct effect to apply, it is at least arguable from the CJEU's recent case law that their absence would not necessarily be fatal to a claim that individuals should be entitled to rely directly upon them before national courts and tribunals. Specifically, in the *Kraaijeveld* ruling[207] and related CJEU jurisprudence discussed in Chapter 6, the Court has held that private persons are entitled to rely upon provisions in EU environmental directives where it is clear that a member state has exceeded a margin of discretion conferred on it by the terms of an EU legislative instrument, typically an EU directive. A clear exceedance of discretion in this instance would be where a member state has failed to enact legislation to set up a recognition procedure. On the other hand, it would be more doubtful whether a private applicant could rely upon the obligation of expedition to assert that a particular procedure is unduly protracted and in contravention of Article 9(1).

Under the Draft AJEM Directive qualified entities are to have special rights of legal standing, over and above those vested in the members of public, in taking legal steps to enforce EU environmental law. The object behind the creation of a special status of 'qualified entity' is to vest NGEOs with a special role in terms assisting in ensuring that EU environmental law is complied with by public authorities. Effectively, conferral of this status is recognition of their having the requisite organisational capability and experience in relation to environmental protection issues. The proposed rights of such entities to take legal action will be discussed in detail in the next sections.

8.3.2.2 The right to take environmental proceedings

The Draft AJEM Directive envisages a number of situations where members of the public as well as qualified entities are to have specific rights to initiate environmental proceedings in respect of contraventions of EU environmental law. Environmental proceedings are defined as meaning administrative or judicial review proceedings in environmental matters before a court or other independent body established by national law, excluding proceedings in criminal matters, and concluded by a binding decision.[208] The Draft AJEM Directive requires that proceedings should be taken against either private persons or public entities, with more detailed rules set out in respect of action taken in respect of public administrative conduct. In addition, the instrument also contains various important stipulations with respect to recognition of legal standing of members of the public and qualified entities, for the purpose of assisting the latter in accessing possibilities to seek internal administrative as well as judicial review of decisions on the environment taken by public authorities. These elements of the draft initiative will be considered briefly in turn.

8.3.2.3 Environmental proceedings against private persons

In relation to acts and omissions of private persons which are in breach of EU environmental law, Article 3 of the Draft AJEM Directive lays down a very general and qualified obligation on member states to open up access to justice. Specifically, under Article 3 member states are required to ensure that 'where they meet the criteria laid down in national law' members of the public are to have access to environmental proceedings to challenge such conduct. This provision, laying down a requirement for a 'horizontal' right of action in environmental matters, is very broadly worded leaving much discretion to the member states in terms of how they set about implementing it into national law. In particular, the text defers to member states as to how they wish to determine specific and crucial procedural issues such as legal standing, interim relief, burden of proof, evidential disclosure and legal costs. However, it should be noted that such proceedings are subject to the general overarching requirements for all national environmental proceedings stipulated in Article 10 of the Draft AJEM Directive (considered below in section 8.3.2.5). It is also noticeable that no special enforcement rights are granted to qualified entities in (horizontal) environmental proceedings directed against private persons.

The limited and general nature of the Draft AJEM Directive's provisions on access to environmental justice against private persons does no more than reflect the bare essence of the relatively shallow requirements contained in the Århus Convention. Article 9(3) of the Convention[209] defers as a matter of broad principle to contracting parties to determine a plaintiff's rights of legal standing regarding access to justice in horizontal environmental law disputes. At the same time, their discretion is qualified by general parameters laid down in Article 9(4) (considered above in section 8.1). In its Explanatory Memorandum accompanying the Draft AJEM Directive, the Commission refers to the principle of subsidiarity[210] as a reason for it not proposing more detailed EU level obligations on horizontal environmental justice disputes.[211] Although always an important factor to bear in mind, it is questionable again whether the Commission has struck the correct balance between, on the one hand, ensuring as much respect for procedural autonomy of member states over the administration of justice as is reasonably possible against, on the other hand, the need to ensure that EU environmental protection objectives crystallised in the Draft AJEM Directive are going to be sufficiently implemented across the EU in a credibly consistent manner. It is questionable whether the subsidiarity principle should be interpreted as requiring a distinction to be made on the basis of whether a defendant in environmental litigation is a private or public person. Rather, the key issue from a subsidiarity perspective is whether the EU-level legislative initiative is needed to ensure that private persons' access to national courts, for the purpose of securing due enforcement of EU environmental legislation, is supported by effective legally binding safeguards. The legal status of the defendant should have no material bearing on the issue of access to environmental justice.

8.3.2.4 *Environmental proceedings against public entities and enhanced legal standing*

The Draft AJEM Directive provides a far more sophisticated and wide-ranging set of safeguards for private persons seeking to challenge the conduct of national public authorities. The draft proposal does this in a number of key respects. First, it establishes a right for civil society to be able to utilise two types of review mechanism, not simply recourse to the classic forum of a national court. Specifically, it establishes the possibility for members of the public and qualified entities to seek an internal review by a national authority of conduct considered by the former to have breached EU environmental law before having recourse to environmental proceedings. Secondly, the draft proposal also establishes enhanced rights of legal standing (*locus standi*) for members of the public and qualified entities to be able to have access to both review channels (internal review and environmental proceedings).

INTERNAL REVIEW MECHANISM

Article 6 of the Draft AJEM Directive provides an interesting stand-alone procedure designed to assist members of the public and qualified entities to seek review of national public administrative conduct in a far swifter and less expensive way than recourse to the national courts. This is the so-called 'internal review' mechanism, which enables the public to request a national public authority to scrutinise whether a claim of illegality may be upheld, before having to consider the option of judicial review before the national courts. Potentially, this procedure is very significant in terms of its practical benefit in ensuring that civil society is not deterred from challenging national administrative conduct on grounds of high legal costs, length of proceedings and other procedural hurdles (such as legal standing issues) that may well confront them when utilising judicial review proceedings before national courts. In establishing the internal review mechanism the Draft AJEM Directive goes further than the Århus Convention, which requires contracting parties as a minimum to ensure the public's access to administrative or judicial procedures to challenge conduct contrary to environmental law.[212]

Under Article 6 of the Draft AJEM Directive, members of the public as well as qualified entities, who consider that an administrative acts or omission is contrary to EU environmental law, are entitled under this particular provision to make a request for an internal review to a competent public authority, subject to their having legal standing to do so in accordance with Articles 4–5.[213] Member states are free to designate the public authority to be charged with the responsibility of carrying out the internal review; it need not be the state authority responsible for the act or omission. The time limit for submitting internal review requests is to be determined by the member states, but the limit must not be shorter than four weeks following the date of the alleged administrative act or, in the case of an omission to act, after the date when an administrative act was required by law.[214] In practice, given its relative speed, informality and low cost, the internal review mechanism would be likely to be an attractive procedure to use prior to any decision to launch environmental proceedings on the part of a member of the public or NGEO.

Article 6(2)–(4) of the Draft AJEM Directive specifies the format and basic timetable of the internal review procedure to be carried out by the competent public authority. First, unless the request is 'clearly unsubstantiated', the authority is required in principle to make a decision on the matter within a period of no later than 12 weeks after receipt of the request. Specifically, this must be either a written decision on the requisite measure to be taken to ensure compliance with EU environmental law or on its refusal to agree with the request. Addressed to the person having made the request, the decision must explain the reasons for its conclusions.[215] If, however, the authority considers that it is going to be unable to meet the 12-week deadline, it is to inform the applicant as soon as possible and in any event by the end of the 12-week period of the reasons for the delay as well as when it intends to issue a final decision.[216] However, the authority must not confuse the 12-week deadline as being a standard date for delivery of a decision.

It is instead under a general obligation under Article 6(2) to issue a written decision 'as soon as possible' and in any event to strive to meet the deadline with 'due diligence'.[217] Article 6(4) of the Draft AJEM Directive underlines this point in laying down a general obligation on the authority to make a final decision on the request 'within a reasonable timeframe', bearing in mind the nature, extent and gravity of the subject matter in issue. This obligation is clearly intended to induce competent authorities to be alive to considerations of urgency in any given case, where time may be crucially important from an environmental protection perspective (e.g. in bad-application case scenarios). In addition, Article 6(4) stipulates an absolute deadline for the authority to make a decision on the request: within 18 weeks of receipt of the initial request. Finally, the provision stipulates that applicants are to be informed of the decision.

Whilst the Draft AJEM Directive sets out a reasonable and clear timetable framework for the processing of internal reviews, there is some room for further clarification on practical aspects that may arise. In particular, the text does not address whether an authority is able to suspend the running of the 18-week deadline where it considers that it has not received sufficient information from the applicant. Would an authority be entitled to 'stop the clock' in such circumstances? Similar issues have arisen in the past in connection with the timetable procedure for transboundary waste shipments under the aegis of the EU's legislative framework for waste shipments, prior to legislative reform being introduced in 2006.[218] In addition, provision is also made for the event of unspecified requests for access to information on the environment under the auspices of Directive 2003/4 on public access to environmental information.[219] The Draft AJEM Directive may require accompanying interpretative guidance to be published by the Commission on this technical question. Under Article 6(2) of the draft proposal a competent authority is not vested with any power to 'stop the clock' after receiving a sufficiently substantiated request for an internal review. Accordingly, the internal request procedure expressly takes on board the point that an applicant will not be in a position necessarily to disclose all relevant facts relating to a particular environmental case; that will depend upon the degree to which it is able to obtain relevant environmental information in relation to the administrative act or omission in question (an issue which is addressed in section 8.2.1 above). It is incumbent on the competent authority to use its position of authority to verify the true state of affairs, factually and legally and to take into account the fact that the ordinary public will not have privileged access to (all the) detailed information and evidence.[220]

It is apparent that the internal review mechanism has the potential to offer significant practical advantages over the option of formal legal proceedings, from the perspective of members of the public and qualified entities. The major advantages include relative low cost, informality and speed of the procedure compared to a court action. However, the Draft AJEM Directive does not specify to what extent, if at all, applicants are to be required to pay in terms of administrative fees for an internal review; this is a matter left for member states. This is regrettable because, of course, a very high fee could act as a deterrent to meritorious requests.

Inexplicably, the general principles of Article 10 of the draft only extend to the conduct of environmental proceedings. In addition, the internal review process does not guarantee an independent review to be conducted by an authority distinct from that of the authority responsible for a disputed act or omission. The designation of the competent authority is a matter for member states. To a great extent, the effectiveness of the internal review mechanism would depend heavily upon the procedures adopted by member states.

ENVIRONMENTAL PROCEEDINGS AGAINST PUBLIC AUTHORITIES

In addition to providing for an internal review mechanism, the Draft AJEM Directive also affirms the right of civil society to have effective recourse to national courts of the EU member states in respect of the conduct of national public authorities. The draft proposal sets out some important rights and safeguards for the public when seeking judicial review, both in relation to the operation of the internal review mechanism as well as more generally speaking.

As regards legal challenges in relation to the outcome of an internal review, the Draft AJEM Directive contains only limited specific requirements relating to access-to-justice protection in this area. In the event that the internal review mechanism does not lead to a satisfactory outcome from the review applicant's perspective, Article 7 of the draft proposal stipulates that the applicant, having requested an internal review, 'shall be entitled to institute environmental proceedings' where either no review decision is taken within the stipulated time limits (as set down in Article 6(2)–(4)) or the applicant disputes that the decision is sufficient to ensure compliance with EU environmental law. This provision does not stipulate any detailed requirements on procedural guarantees relating to this access-to-justice right. By default, such aspects are addressed by the general provisions on legal standing contained in the draft proposal (Articles 4–5) which address access-to-justice rights of members of the public and qualified entities generally before the national courts. It is to these provisions we now turn.

Articles 4–5 of the Draft AJEM Directive set out the rights of members of the public and qualified entities to have legal standing in order to bring environmental proceedings in respect of national administrative acts and omissions claimed to be in breach of EU environmental law. These access-to-justice rights apply independently of the internal review mechanism contained in Article 6, discussed above. The position adopted by the Commission on legal standing rights in the draft is to seek a balance between two interests. On the one hand, the Commission is keen to enhance the public's rights of access to justice at national level so as to provide a meaningful opportunity for environmental law enforcement to be sponsored by the private sector in line with Århus. On the other hand, it is also desirous not to establish absolute rights of access tantamount to an '*actio popularis*', which the Commission considers would be incompatible with the principle of subsidiarity.[221]

Article 4 addresses the legal standing rights of members of the public. Specifically, it requires EU member states to ensure a right of the public to have access to environmental proceedings, which is to include the availability of interim relief, where such persons either have a 'sufficient interest'[222] or where 'they maintain the impairment of a right' where the administrative procedural law of the member state concerned requires this as a precondition.[223] The Draft AJEM Directive specifies that member states, 'in accordance with the requirements of their law and with the objective of granting broad access to justice', retain competence to determine the fulfilment of either of these criteria (Article 4(2)). Crucially, member states retain significant controls over the structuring of legal standing requirements under the draft legislative provisions. Member state autonomy over *locus standi* is subject to only a general qualification of being required to be 'in accordance . . . with the objective of granting broad access to justice'.[224] It is difficult to see how this qualification could be a significantly meaningful legal obligation in practice, given its very general nature and capacity to be interpreted in any number of ways. For similar reasons, it is questionable to what extent it could be readily enforceable in the context of Article 258/260 TFEU infringement proceedings

Article 5 of the draft legislative instrument specifies the extent to which 'qualified entities' may have legal standing to bring environmental proceedings. Article 5(1) specifies that such entities as recognised by a member state (in accordance with Article 9) may, subject to certain conditions, have access to environmental proceedings. Such proceedings may include those for the purpose of requesting interim relief, even though the entity may not necessarily have a sufficient interest or have a right impaired as would otherwise be required of members of the public under national law when issuing legal proceedings to challenge the legality of public authority conduct as envisaged in Article 4. The conditions for a qualified entity to be able to take proceedings are that the subject matter of the dispute is covered specifically covered by the 'statutory activities' of – as well as within the 'geographical area of activities' of – the qualified entity concerned. Although not expressly stipulated, it appears implicit from the wording and legislative context of the provision that the qualified entity will be responsible for determining the remit of its activities in terms of material scope and geographically. A member state will not be able to interfere in the autonomy of the entity to set its own corporate objectives.[225] The justification of the insertion of the stipulation relating to 'geographical area' of the entity's activities is not clear and appears to conflict with the terms of the Århus Convention, which does not establish this element as a requirement.[226]

Article 5 of the Draft AJEM Directive also provides the possibility of qualified entities being involved in certain types of transboundary disputes. Specifically, Article 5(2) stipulates that a qualified entity recognised in one member state is entitled to submit a request for an 'internal review' in another member state under the conditions of Article 5(1). Effectively, this entitles the entity to be able to bring environmental proceedings in another member state as of right, so long as the subject matter of the dispute falls within the specific geographical and activities of the entity.[227] This particular review procedure is not be confused with the special public authority internal review procedure envisaged in Article 6 of the Draft AJEM Directive, as discussed earlier. Carefully thought through, the mutual recognition principle enshrined in Article 5(2) potentially could be used to excellent effect by NGEOs facing legal standing difficulties in a particular member state. Thus, a qualified entity in one member state would be entitled to legal standing in the relevant courts and/or tribunals competent to carry out independent legal review of public authority action in any other member state, so long as the bringing of such proceedings would fall within the scope of the entity's activities and geographical area (as defined by its statutes). The wording in Article 5(2) appears sufficiently precise and unconditional to satisfy the criteria of direct effect, so all member state authorities including judicial organs would be obliged automatically to recognise legal standing of the entity, even if this were to conflict with any existing national procedural rules that would otherwise block or impede its access to judicial review.

The legal standing rights accorded to members of the public and qualified entities to be able to take environmental proceedings constitutes an important advance on the existing position of procedural rights granted to private persons under EU law. In particular, the important issue of availability of interim relief is addressed in relation to the acts and omissions of public authorities, albeit not in relation to conduct of private defendants. Accordingly, as recognised in the draft proposal's Explanatory Memorandum,[228] the Commission proposal goes further than the Århus Convention, which does contain specific obligations regarding legal standing issues. The rights of qualified entities accorded in the draft text constitute a significant advance in terms of enhancing possibilities of private law enforcement of EU environmental law. Under the Draft AJEM Directive, such entities will be able to take legal proceedings against public authorities acting in breach of EU environmental legal requirements without having to face the traditional procedural hurdles commonly applied under national administrative law of having to prove a direct personal interest in the subject matter of the dispute. Article 5 of the draft is designed to enable them to be vested with legal powers to take either administrative or judicial review proceedings at national level with a view to enforcing EU environmental legislative requirements, as claimants with privileged (automatic) legal standing.

8.3.2.5 *General requirements regarding environmental proceedings*

Reflecting the tenor of the Århus Convention, the Draft AJEM Directive seeks to ensure that environmental proceedings before national courts are subject to general principles of propriety and fairness in the Draft AJEM Directive. Specifically, Article 10 of the Draft AJEM Directive effectively replicates the conditions set out in Article 9(4) of the Convention (referred to in section 8.1 above):

Article 10 Requirements for environmental proceedings

Member states shall provide for adequate and effective proceedings that are objective, equitable, expeditious and not prohibitively expensive.

Decisions under this Directive shall be given or recorded in writing, and whenever possible shall be publicly accessible.

It is notable and regrettable that the Draft AJEM Directive has not fleshed out in more detail the general provisions concerning access to justice contained in Article 9(4)–(5) of the Århus Convention. Article 9(5) of the Convention stipulates contracting parties must ensure that the public is provided with information on access to administrative and judicial review procedures and shall consider establishing 'appropriate assistance mechanisms to remove or reduce financial and other barriers to access to justice'. Whilst Article 10 specifies that decisions in environmental proceedings are to be recorded in writing and made publicly accessible 'whenever possible', it does not provide for the active public dissemination of information about the availability such proceedings. In addition, no provisions are included in the draft proposal concerning financial assistance (e.g. legal aid) or addressing particular procedural requirements that may in practice constitute severe obstacles encountered by private claimants, such as requirements of cross-undertakings in damages in the event of interim relief being requested.[229]

No specific reason is provided why the Draft AJEM Directive's key substantive provisions on access to justice are crafted in such a general manner. However, it is evident from reading the Explanatory Memorandum accompanying the Draft AJEM Directive that the Commission is concerned not to stray into territory that it might consider being within the exclusive purview of member states under the principle of subsidiarity, as set out in Article 5(3) TEU.[230] However, in this instance, it is submitted that the Commission has been excessively deferential to a perception that member states should retain autonomy in this particular area. It is self-evident that without clear-cut minimum standards on the conduct, management and financing of legal proceedings some member states may offer substantially better conditions for private law enforcement than others. Although that is a scenario envisaged generally in terms of EU environmental law, where member states as a matter of principle retain the option of adopting stricter measures in favour of protecting the environment,[231] the position adopted in the Draft AJEM Directive in Article 10 is one where there is a genuine danger of some member states not perceiving any need to take any specific new steps so as to facilitate access to justice when it may be patently obvious that without legislative change the legal procedural requirements in certain member states will continue to act as a *de facto* deterrent to the launch of private law enforcement actions. That outcome would not only undermine the third-pillar project of Århus but also compromise the EU's constitutional commitment[232] to attaining a high level of environmental protection throughout the territory of the Union. It might be the case that, were the Draft AJEM Directive to be eventually promulgated, the Commission might decide to take infringement proceedings in particular instances where it considers member states have failed to take specific action to transpose Article 10. However, the mechanism of Articles 258 and 260 TFEU are hardly the most efficient of mechanisms in this respect, given the factors of legal uncertainty of outcome as well as cumbersome and lengthy procedures involved. Moreover, infringement proceedings are ultimately a relatively blunt tool to use to procure national legislative change. They have an inherent negative quality, in that they are suited to requiring the dismantling of incorrectly transposed EU legislative measures, as opposed to specifying in detail what replacement statutory provisions should entail.

Under Article 11 of the Draft AJEM Directive member states are to report on the experience gained in the application of the directive. This might or might not provide useful information on good and poor practice in this regard. However, the reporting requirements as set out in the draft text are very general and may not address these important practical issues. In addition, there is no Committee structure envisaged within the terms of the Draft AJEM Directive to take up such issues for the purpose of an ongoing review of the instrument. It is submitted, therefore, that at the very least the Commission should issue some detailed recommendations or other soft law guidance to accompany Article 10 from the outset, in order to ensure that member states are fully aware of what is expected. In particular, the term 'not prohibitively expensive' calls out for detailed clarification.

8.3.2.6 The Draft AJEM Directive's impact on the direct effect doctrine

One of the most significant implications of the Draft AJEM Directive concerns its potential impact on the relative importance of the direct effect doctrine in the context of EU environment law enforcement action undertaken by private persons. If adopted and subsequently properly transposed into national law, the effect of the Draft AJEM Directive would be to facilitate the access of private entities to national courts and tribunals for the purpose of enforcing EU environmental protection legislation. Such litigants would then not have to show that the EU legislative norms they seek to enforce are directly effective, given that the Draft AJEM Directive secures for them the right of access to court on the basis of legal standing criteria, not on the basis of whether or not particular provisions of EU environmental law meet the criteria of direct effect.

As outlined previously, the main aim of the Draft AJEM Directive is to provide members of the public and qualified entities with various rights to take action in the event that they suspect a breach of EU environmental law has taken place within a member state. Specifically, the Draft AJEM Directive refers to breaches of 'environmental law', which is defined in Article 2(1)(g) as meaning:

> [Union][233] legislation and legislation adopted to implement [Union] legislation which have as their objective the protection or the improvement of the environment, including human health and the protection or the rational use of natural resources . . .

The provision proceeds to provide a broad, non-exhaustive list[234] of examples of sources of EU environmental legislation, which is clearly intended to indicate the comprehensive nature of the definition. The list comprises the following areas: water protection; noise protection; soil protection; atmospheric protection; town and country planning and use; nature conservation and biological diversity; waste management; chemicals including biocides and pesticides; biotechnology; other emissions, discharges and release in the environment; environmental impact assessment; access to environmental information; and public participation in decision-making. Legislation for these purposes includes EU measures intended to ratify Union participation in international environmental agreements, such as Council Decision 2005/370[235] adopted to conclude Union ratification of the Århus Convention. Under the draft proposal, EU member states have the option of including sources of environmental law that are exclusively internal to their national legal systems with the definition of 'environmental law', i.e. those which are not intended to be implemented or whose material scope is not covered by EU environmental legislation.[236]

As discussed in earlier sections, the rights accorded under Articles 3–6 of the Draft AJEM Directive require EU member states to provide members of the public and qualified entities who fulfil the requisite legal standing requirements to have access to environmental proceedings and/or an internal review procedure in relation to acts and omissions 'in breach of environmental law'. The provisions therefore do not require claimants to demonstrate, in addition to the legal standing requirements, that the EU environmental norms that they consider to be infringed in any given case are directly effective. Instead, they specify that such persons are entitled to challenge the legality of acts or omissions on the grounds simply on the grounds that they are in breach of environmental law. If the Draft AJEM Directive were to be enacted, these provisions would introduce a profound change to the existing system of private law enforcement of EU environmental law; for, as discussed in Chapter 5, hitherto the possibilities for individuals to be able to rely upon norms contained in EU directives before national courts and tribunals have been pre-eminently developed on the basis of the doctrine of direct effect (and allied doctrines such as indirect effect), by virtue of the jurisprudence of the CJEU. From the perspective of environmental law enforcement, the implications of the direct effect doctrine have been largely restrictive as opposed to facilitative. With the exception of norms containing clear self-contained and unconditional obligations, individuals have effectively been denied the opportunity to take legal action to uphold EU environmental law.

However, the Draft AJEM Directive quite rightly removes this unwarranted precondition for law enforcement of EU environmental law. There are good reasons to open up possibilities for private persons to hold state authorities to account wherever the latter fail to adhere to legally binding EU environmental protection obligations. In particular, this means that law enforcement mechanisms are enhanced and made more efficient, as the private sector becomes enabled to be more involved to complement existing casework carried out by public enforcement institutions at national and supranational levels.

The enhancing the effectiveness of the practical application of EU environmental legislation is a key feature underpinning the motivation behind the Draft AJEM Directive.[237] The Commission has for a number of years recognised the lack of existing genuine possibilities at national level in the member states for private persons, including notably NGEOs, to engage actively in enforcement of EU environmental protection legislation.[238] Accordingly, the Draft AJEM Directive's ambition to remove the requirement of direct effect, as a precondition for private law enforcement, may be seen as an integral element of the Commission's long-standing aspiration to facilitating better access to environmental justice at national level.

8.4 Some concluding remarks

There is little doubt that the package of EU measures designed to implement the Århus Convention at national level on access to environmental justice have enhanced the possibilities for civil society to become more involved and influential in the enforcement of EU environmental legislation. Endowed with rights to seek legal review of acts and omissions of member state authorities affecting the environment as well as rights to obtain information on the state of the environment held by public authorities of the member states, private persons are now better equipped than ever with legal tools to hold public authorities to account in respect of their activities affecting the environment.

A significant shortcoming concerning the EU's legal position on access to environmental justice, though, concerns its partial fulfilment of its Århus Convention obligations. The refusal by the Council of the EU to enact a general legal framework based on the Commission's 2003 Draft AJEM Directive has led to a fragmented delivery of safeguards and protections for members of the public engaged in enforcing EU environmental legislation at national level, and specifically before national courts. Whilst the EU has nevertheless adopted a series of legislative measures in the wake of the effective suspension of the Draft AJEM Directive, these have been sectoral in nature leaving gaps in access-to-justice protection across broad areas of EU environmental policy. Notwithstanding the residual legal effects of the EU's 2005 ratification of the Århus Convention in light of CJEU jurisprudence, this has so far proved to be and is likely to remain an inadequate source of legal protection for private persons pursuing public interest environmental litigation in the member states.

At the time of writing the EU is in the process of actively revisiting the policy area of access to environmental justice. The EAP7 has provided the European Commission with a mandate to ensure that improvements are introduced across the piece with a view to ensuring that the public is guaranteed the same floor of procedural rights protection in accessing national courts with respect to all and not just some EU environmental legislative instrumentation. The European Commission's Environment Directorate General has already augmented its environmental governance priorities to include a policy track for developing existing Union level commitments towards access to justice. A stakeholder consultation[239] as well as expert studies have been commissioned.[240] It is probable that at some stage the Commission will publish a new revised proposal for a principal 'horizontal' instrument on access to environmental justice. Whilst no doubt the Draft AJEM Directive may serve as a reference point in this process, there are a number a matters in respect of which the 2003 draft proposal can be improved upon, such as in relation to environmental law enforcement by members of the public and/or NGEOs against private persons.

In summary, in light of the various political as well as technical drawbacks and limitations discussed above, the EU has had a mixed experience in seeking to implement an access-to-justice agenda in response to its membership of the Århus Convention. On the one hand, it has adopted a number of legislative safeguards on access to justice in crucially important areas, including, notably, the fields of access to environmental information, public participation in environmental decision-making and environmental liability. These achievements are without doubt pivotal for the Union in being able to deliver a more solid legal framework to protect and facilitate the development of public interest enforcement of EU environmental law pursued by the public and NGEOs. On the other hand, at the time of writing, its implementation of that agenda is substantially incomplete and has been so for the best part of two decades since its original enthusiastic signing of the Convention back in 1998. Time will tell whether the EU's EAP7 will be able to complete the project of implementing the third pillar of Århus.

Notes

1 2161 UNTS 447. The text of the Convention is accessible on the following UNECE website: www.unece.org.
2 Dette (2004), p.13.
3 Ibid., p. 11.
4 Fifth Environment Action Programme of the European Union: *Towards Sustainability – A European Community Programme of policy and action in relation to the environment and sustainable development* (OJ 1993 C138/5).
5 See entry in Ch. 9 (Implementation and Enforcement) of EAP5 (OJ 1993 C138/82): 'Individuals and public interest groups should have practicable access to the courts in order to ensure that their legitimate interests are protected and that prescribed environmental measures are effectively enforced and illegal practices stopped.'
6 COM(96)500, p. 11.
7 Council Resolution on the drafting, implementation and enforcement of Community environmental law (OJ 1997 C321/1).
8 European Parliament Resolution on a communication of the Commission on implementing Community environmental law (OJ 1997 C167/92).
9 Krämer (2003), p. 144.
10 See Art. 3(9) of Decision 1600/2002 laying down the Sixth Community Environment Action Programme (OJ 2002 L242/1).
11 See Arts. 4(2)(e) and 191(4) TFEU. On the nature and impact of mixed competence in EU law, see e.g. Koutrakos and Hillion (2010); O'Keeffe and Schermers (1983).
12 COM(2003)624final, of 24 October 2003.
13 See Maurici and Moules (2013), p. 1510 and Krämer (2007), p. 160.
14 Decision 1386/2013 on a General Union Environment Action Programme to 2020 'Living Well, within the Limits of our Planet' (OJ 2013 L354/171).
15 See para. 65(e)(v) of the EAP7 (OJ 2013 L354/190–1) (Priority Objective 4: To maximise the benefits of Union environmental legislation by improving implementation).
16 See the Commissioner's speech in 2012 '"The fish cannot go to court" – the environment is a public good that must be supported by a public voice', SPEECH/12/856, Brussels, 23 November 2012 (accessible on the EU RAPID press release site: http://europa.eu/rapid). In that speech the Commissioner stated that a directive on access to justice was 'indispensable'.
17 OJ 2003 L41/26.

18 OJ 2003 L156/17.
19 OJ 2004 L143/56.
20 Art. 25 of Directive 2010/75 (OJ 2010 L334/17).
21 Art. 11of Directive 2011/92 (OJ 2012 L26/1).
22 Regulation 1367/06 on the application of the provisions of the Århus Convention on Access to Information, Public Participation in Decision-making and Access to Justice in Environmental Matters to Community institutions and bodies (OJ 2006 L264/13). See also Regulation 1257/13 on ship recycling and amending Regulation 101/06 and Directive 2009/16 (OJ 2013 L330/1) which will also be considered in Ch. 9.
23 OJ 2003 L41/26.
24 For an overview of recent CJEU jurisprudence on implementation of the Århus Convention, see e.g. Maurici and Moules (2013).
25 2161 UNTS 447. The text of the Convention is accessible on the following UNECE website: www.unece.org/environmental-policy/treaties/public-participation/aarhus-convention.html.
26 The status of ratification may be inspected at: www.unece.org/env/pp/ratification.html.
27 Council Decision 2005/370 of 17 February 2005 on the Conclusion on Behalf of the European Community of the Convention on Access to Information, Public Participation in Decision-making and Access to Justice in Environmental Matters (OJ 2005 L124/1).
28 Ireland was the latest of the 28 EU member state to ratify the Convention, in June 2012.
29 For an overview, see European Commission RAPID press release MEMO/03/210, Brussels, 20 October 2003 as well as the Commission's Environment Directorate-General's webpage on Århus: www.europa.eu.int/comm/env/environment/aarhus/index.htm.
30 See Art. 3(5) Århus Convention.
31 A copy of the Rio Declaration on Environment and Development may be inspected on the UN Environment Programme's website (www.unep.org). The second recital of the Århus Convention specifically refers to Principle 10 of Rio.
32 Art. 2(4) Århus Convention.
33 Ibid., Art. 3(8).
34 Ibid., Art. 3(9).
35 Ibid., Art. 3(2)–(3).
36 An Annex to the Convention contains a list of activities covered by Art. 6.
37 Given that the Convention does not stipulate access-to-justice obligations in relation to the fields covered by Arts. 7–8, these particular aspects to the second pillar will not be considered further for the purposes of this chapter. The Union, in adopting Directive 2001/42 on the assessment of the effects of certain plans and programmes on the environment (OJ 2001 L197/30) (Strategic Environmental Assessment Directive), has effectively taken measures in the area covered by Art. 7 of the Convention. For an assessment on the extent to which the SEA Directive serves to implement Art. 7 of the Convention, see e.g. Mathiesen (2003).
38 No access-to-justice provision is made in respect of the activities covered by Arts. 7–8 of the Convention.
39 Final subpara. of Art. 9(2) Århus Convention.
40 Art. 9(2) in conjunction with Art. 2(5) of the Convention.
41 For the purposes of the Århus Convention, EU law constitutes a source of 'national law' for the EU member states as well as the European Union as contracting parties of the Convention. This was confirmed in the Århus Compliance Committee's Communication ACCC/C/2006/18 (Denmark).

42 ACCC/C/2005/11 (Belgium).

43 So Ebbesson (2011), p. 267.

44 Council Decision 2005/370 on the Conclusion, on Behalf of the EC, of the Convention on Access to Information, Public Participation in Decision-making and Access to Justice in Environmental Matters (OJ 2005 L124/1).

45 Art. 47 TEU.

46 See Arts. 3, 26, 27 and 46 of the 1969 Vienna Convention on Law of Treaties (UNTS Vol. 1155, p. 331).

47 See Art. 16 Århus Convention.

48 Ibid., Art. 15.

49 Decision I/7 of the Meeting of the Parties (October 2002).

50 See Århus Complaints Committee Findings and Recommendations with regard to Communication ACCC/C/2008/33 concerning compliance by the UK, 21 September 2010 (UK's implementation of access to environmental justice requirements). For a recent overview of the UK's implementation of the Convention's access-to-justice obligations see Macrory and Westaway (2011), pp. 315 *et seq.*

51 See e.g. Århus Complaints Committee Findings and Recommendations with regard to Communication ACCC/C/2008/32 concerning compliance by the EU, 24 August 2011 (Client Earth legal standing case). This case will be considered in Chapter 9.

52 See Wates (2011), pp. 393–4.

53 Ebbesson (2011), p. 251.

54 Art. 31(3)(b) of the 1969 Vienna Convention on the Law of Treaties (1155 UNTS 331, 8 ILM 679).

55 See comments by Advocate General (AG) Kokott in her Opinion in Case C-260/11 *Edwards* [2013] CMLR 18. See also Tanzi and Pitea (2011), pp. 379–80.

56 Art. 216(2) TFEU.

57 See e.g. Case C-402/05P *Kadi and Al Barakaat* (para. 326 of judgment) and Joined Cases C-584, 593 and 595/10P *Commission, UK and Council v Kadi* (para. 97 of judgment of 18 July 2013 (not yet published)).

58 Art. 4(2)(e) TFEU.

59 Ibid.

60 Ibid., Art. 2(2).

61 See Art. 2(2) in conjunction with Art. 193 (ibid.).

62 Ibid., Art. 193.

63 Ibid., Art. 191(4).

64 Case 22/70 *Commission v Council (European Road Transport Agreement (ERTA/AETR))*.

65 Declaration by the European Community in accordance with Art. 19 of the Århus Convention (OJ 2005 L124/3).

66 Art. 19(4) Århus Convention.

67 See e.g. paras. 9 and 14 of judgments in Case 12/86 *Demirel* and Case C-13/00 *Commission v Ireland* respectively. This is supported by Art. 216(2) TFEU which, in stating that agreements concluded by the Union are binding on Union institutions as well as the member states, does not make any qualification to this requirement on grounds that an agreement involves the exercise of mixed competence.

68 See Case C-240/09 *Lesoochranárske zoskupenie VLK (WOLF Forest Protection Movement) v Slovakian Government* (para. 30 of judgment). (See also Joined Cases C-128–31, 134–5/09 *Boxus and others* and Case C-182/10 *Solvay* which arguably implicitly confirm this position in advising referring national courts on the Convention's requirements.)

69 Case C-13/00 *Commission v Ireland (Berne Convention)*. For an overview of this area, see Hedemann-Robinson (2012).

70 Case C-239/03 *Commission v France (Etang de Berre)*.

71 The Commission claimed France had breached the terms of the agreements in first having failed to prevent the pollution of a Mediterranean-linked saltwater marsh (Etang de Berre) through the discharge of freshwater and sediment into the marsh

from a hydroelectric plant, with consequences detrimental to aquatic life and to the state of eutrophication of the marsh. Secondly, the Commission complained that France had failed to issue an authorisation for discharges in accordance with terms of 1980 Protocol.

72 Council Decisions 77/585 (OJ 1977 L240/1) and 83/101 (OJ 1983 L67/1).

73 Case C-239/03 *Commission v France (Etang de Berre)* (paras. 27–31 of judgment).

74 Declaration by the European Community in accordance with Art. 19 of the Convention on Access to Information, Public Participation in Decision-making and Access to Justice in Environmental Matters, as annexed to Council Decision 2005/370 (OJ 2005 L124/3).

75 SEC(2008)556, *European Commission Report: Århus Convention Implementation Report – European Community*, 7 May 2008, produced to fulfil the reporting requirements of Decision I/8 of the MOP.

76 Case C-240/09 *Lesoochranárske zoskupenie VLK (WOLF Forest Protection Movement)*.

77 See e.g. Case 104/81 *Kupferberg*.

78 See e.g. Case 12/86 *Demirel*. For an analysis of direct effect of international agreements concluded by the Union and member states (so falling within the category of shared or 'mixed' competence), see e.g. Gáspár-Szilági (2013).

79 See e.g. paras. 21, 82 and 44 of judgments in Case C-265/03 *Simutenkov*, Case C-372/06 *Asda Stores* and Case C-240/09 *Lesoochranárske zoskupenie VLK* respectively.

80 Directive 92/43 (OJ 1992 L206/7).

81 See para. 79 of her Opinion in Case C-240/09.

82 See para. 2 of the Declaration by the European Community in accordance with Art. 19 of the Århus Convention (OJ 2005 L124/3).

83 See paras. 80–8 of AG Sharpston's opinion in Case C-240/09 *Lesoochranárske zoskupenie VLK*.

84 Case C-240/09 *Lesoochranárske zoskupenie VLK* (paras. 29–31 of judgment).

85 Case C-239/03 *Commission v France (Etang de Berre)* (paras. 27–31 of judgment).

86 In particular, Arts. 12 and 16 in conjunction with Annex IV of the Habitats Directive 92/43.

87 Case C-240/09 *Lesoochranárske zoskupenie VLK* (paras. 32–40 of judgment).

88 Ibid., para. 41.

89 Ibid., para. 42.

90 Ibid., para. 45.

91 Ibid., para. 48.

92 Ibid., paras. 50–1.

93 See Reid (2011) and Ebbesson (2011), p. 264.

94 Case C-106/89 *Marleasing*.

95 This interpretation would be akin to the bold approach taken by the Court in cases such as Case C-237/07 *Janecek*, as discussed in Ch. 6, which held that members of the public must be allowed to bring actions before the national courts in order to uphold directly effective obligations contained in EU air quality legislation.

96 Case C-237/07 *Janecek v Bayern*.

97 See e.g. Case C-115/09 *Bund für Umwelt und Naturschutz v Arnsberg (Trianel)* (para. 41 of the judgment) concerning interpretation of Directive 2003/35.

98 See e.g. Case C-308/06 *Intertanko v Secretary of State for Transport* (para. 42 of judgment).

99 See e.g. recital 27 of preamble to Directive 2010/75 on industrial emissions, recitals 18–21 of Directive 2011/92 on the assessment of the effects of certain public and private projects on the environment.

100 See e.g. recital 5 of the preambles to both Directive 2003/4 on access to environmental information and Directive 2003/35 on public participation.

101 See Case C-182/10 *Solvay* (para. 28 of judgment).

102 COM(2003)264.

103 OJ 2003 L41/26.

104 See Art. 5 of former Directive 90/313 on the freedom of access to information on the environment (OJ 1990 L158/56).
105 See in particular Case C-115/09 *Bund für Umwelt und Naturschutz (Trianel)* (para. 41 of judgment).
106 Recital 5 of the preamble to the AEI Directive.
107 As noted also by Ryall (2004), p. 276.
108 In its recently published first report in 2012 on the application of the AEI Directive (COM(2012)774) the Commission did not, however, raise any concerns in relation to the access-to-justice framework of the directive. See COM(2012)774, *Commission Report on the Experience Gained in the Application of Directive 2003/4*, 17 December 2012.
109 OJ 2003 L156/17.
110 Art. 9(2) of the Convention allows for the possibility of contracting parties establishing a preliminary review procedure before an administrative authority or requiring that administrative review procedures must be exhausted prior to recourse to the independent review procedure.
111 See Ebbesson (2011), p. 258.
112 See Lee (2005), p. 139.
113 Former Directive 85/337 on the assessment of the effects of certain public and private projects on the environment (OJ 1985 L175/40).
114 Former Directive 96/61 concerning integrated pollution prevention and control (OJ 1996 L257/26).
115 Specifically, Art. 10a of former Directive 85/337 and Art. 15a of former Directive 96/61 (as introduced by virtue of Arts. 3 and 4 respectively of Directive 2003/35).
116 OJ 2012 L26/1.
117 OJ 2010 L334/17.
118 See Case C-115/09 *Bund für Umwelt und Naturschutz (Trianel)* (para. 41 of judgment), Case C-416/10 *Križan and others* (para. 77 of judgment) and Case C-260/11 *Edwards and Pallikaropoulos* (para. 26 of judgment) in which the CJEU has confirmed access to justice requirements in the EU legislation relating to impact assessment or IPPC need to be interpreted in line with the requirements of the Convention.
119 See recital 27 of the preamble to Directive 2010/75 and recitals 19–21 of the preamble to Directive 2011/92.
120 Art. 1(2)(e) EIA Directive, in implementing Art. 2(5) of the Convention, states:

(e) 'public concerned' means the public affected or likely to be affected by, or having an interest in, the environmental decision-making referred to in Article 2(2). For the purposes of this definition, non-governmental organisations promoting environmental protection and meeting any requirements under national law shall be deemed to have an interest.

An identical definition of NGEOs is contained in Art. 25(3) of the Industrial Emissions Directive.
121 See e.g. paras. 29–31 of judgment in Case C-260/11 *Edwards and Pallikaropoulos*.
122 See notably Case C-427/07 *Commission v Ireland*, Case C-260/11 *Edwards and Pallikaropoulos* and Case C-530/11 *Commission v UK*.
123 See Case C-260/11 *Edwards and Pallikaropoulos* (para. 34 of judgment).
124 See e.g. Case C-427/07 *Commission v Ireland* (para. 92 of judgment) and Case C-260/11 *Edwards* (para. 27 of judgment).
125 Previously, there had been some doubt expressed in some quarters as to whether the term 'costs' under the Convention covered expenditure incurred for legal representation in proceedings (in addition to court fees), such as in the Irish High Court in *Sweetman v An Bord Pleanála and the Attorney General* [2007] IEHC 153.
126 Case C-530/11 *Commission v UK* (paras. 64–71 of judgment).

127 *R v Sec. State for the Environment ex parte RSPB* [1997] Env LR 431.
128 Case C-427/07 *Commission v Ireland* (para. 92 of judgment), Case C-260/11 *Edwards and Pallikaropoulos* (para. 25 of judgment) and Case C-530/11 *Commission v UK* (para. 44 of judgment).
129 See Case C-427/07 *Commission v Ireland* and Case C-530/11 *Commission v UK.*
130 Case C-260/11 *Edwards and Pallikaropoulos.*
131 Case C-530/11 *Commission v UK.*
132 Notably, in *R (Corner House Research) v SSTI* [2005] EWCA Civ 192. For an overview of the UK jurisprudence in this area, see e.g. Bell, McGillivray and Pedersen (2013), pp. 344–6.
133 See Århus Complaints Committee Findings and Recommendations with regard to Communication ACCC/C/2008/33 concerning compliance by the UK, 21 September 2010 (UK's implementation of access to environmental justice requirements).
134 The issue of member state compliance with Art. 9(4) of the Convention was also the subject of a written question from the European Parliament to the European Commission: E-002454/2011 (PE 461.596) (Questions from MEPs Lambert and Bélier).
135 Case C-260/11 *Edwards* (para. 42 of judgment) and Case C-530/11 *Commission v UK* (para. 49 of judgment).
136 Case C-260/11 *Edwards* (para. 43 of judgment) and Case C-530/11*Commission v UK* (paras. 50–1 of judgment).
137 Practice Direction 45 introduced by virtue of the Civil Procedure (Amendment) Rules 2013 (SI 2013 262) sets a costs cap for judicial review applicants in relation to matters covered by the Convention: specifically a cap of £5,000 for individuals and £10,000 for other persons (e.g. companies, NGEOs). For a comment on these changes, see Hart (2012).
138 Case C-72/12 *Gemeinde Altrip and others v Land Rheinland-Pfalz.*
139 Ibid. (para. 45 of judgment).
140 Ibid. (para. 46 of judgment).
141 Case C-115/09 *Bund für Umwelt und Naturschutz v Arnsberg (Trianel).*
142 Ibid. (paras. 45–7 of judgment).
143 Case C-263/08 *Djurgården–Lilla Vättens Miljöskyddsförening v Stockholm.*
144 Ibid. (para. 45 of judgment).
145 See ibid. (paras. 47–51 of judgment).
146 Case C-416/10 *Križan and others.*
147 Case C-213/89 *Factortame.*
148 Case C-416/10 *Križan and others* (paras. 107–9 of judgment).
149 Ebbesson (2011), p. 260.
150 Case C-530/11 *Commission v UK.*
151 Ibid. (paras. 69 and 71 of judgment).
152 Directive 2004/35 on environmental liability with regard to the prevention and remedying of environmental damage (OJ 2004 L143/56) as amended.
153 Directive 2004/35 on environmental liability with regard to the prevention and remedying of environmental damage (OJ 2004 L143/56) as amended by Directives 2006/21 (OJ 2006 L102/15), Directive 2009/31 (OJ 2009 L140/114) and Directive 2013/30 (OJ 2013 L178/66). A consolidated version of the ELD is available for inspection on the EU's EULEX website. Information about the ELD may also be found on the European Commission's DG ENV website at: http://ec.europa.eu/environment/legal/liability/index.htm.
154 See recital 11 to the preamble and Art. 3(3) of the ELD.
155 Art. 19 ELD.
156 Ibid., Art. 11.
157 Ibid., Art. 12.
158 Ibid., Art. 13.
159 Ibid., Art. 12(5).

160 Ibid., Art. 12(1) second para.
161 See the Commission proposal for the ELD (COM(2002)17) which refers to the right of any 'qualified entity' to file a request for action. 'Qualified entities' are defined in the proposal as meaning 'any body or organisation which, according to the criteria, if any, laid down in national law has an interest in ensuring that environmental damage is restored. Bodies and organisations whose purpose, as is shown by the articles of incorporation thereof, is to protect the environment shall be deemed to have an interest.' Similarly, the discussion of recognition of environmental NGO rights in the context Draft AJEM Directive has revolved around the legal status of such an NGO as a corporate body, as opposed to any nexus between it and the subject matter of a particular dispute.
162 In this sense, one could argue that there is a conflict between Art. 12(1) ELD and Art. 8 AEI Directive.
163 As set out in Art. 191(2) TFEU.
164 Indeed, the Commission proposal for the ELD did not refer to any filter requirement based on plausibility (Art. 11 of COM(2002)17).
165 See Art. 11(3) of draft Commission proposal in COM(2002)1. Best practice arguably would be for the authorities to apply in principle the time limits for responding to requests for internal review envisaged under Art. 6 of the Draft AJEM Directive (considered in section 8.3).
166 Art. 12(5) ELD.
167 30 April 2007 (Art. 19(1)) (ibid.).
168 Ibid., under Art. 18(2), the European Commission is required to submit a report on the application of the directive before 30 April 2014 on the basis of individual national reports received from the member states (which are required to have been sent to the Commission by 30 April 2013 under Art. 18(1)).
169 Ibid., Art. 17.
170 Legal action under Art. 258 TFEU culminated in the CFEU handing down judgments against seven member states for failing to take measures to transpose the ELD: Cases C-328/08 *Commission v Finland*, C-330/08 *Commission v France*, C-331/08 *Commission v Luxembourg*, C-368/08 *Commission v Greece*, C-402/08 *Commission v Slovenia*, C-417/08 *Commission v UK* and C-422/08 *Commission v Austria*. Infringement proceedings were launched against Belgium (Case C-329/08) but discontinued in 2009.
171 This may be contrasted with the approach taken in the Draft AJEM Directive (considered in section 8.3) which does stipulate limits on fees.
172 See e.g. Joined Cases C-6 and 9/90 *Francovich and Bonfaci*.
173 COM(2003)624 final, Commission proposal for a directive on access to justice in environmental matters, 24 October 2003.
174 Decision 1386/2013 on a General Union Environment Action Programme to 2020 'Living Well, within the Limits of our Planet' (OJ 2013 L354/171).
175 See Art. 192 in conjunction with Art. 294 TFEU, which sets out the ordinary legislative procedure requiring joint consent of Council and European Parliament (formerly referred to as 'co-decision').
176 Notably though Regulation 1367/06 on the application of the provisions of the Århus Convention on Access to Information, Public Participation in Decision-making and Access to Justice in Environmental Matters to Community institutions and bodies (OJ 2006 L264/13) and Regulation 1257/13 on ship recycling and amending Regulation 101/06 and Directive 2009/16 (OJ 2013 L330/1) whose impact is considered in Ch. 10.
177 Krämer (2007), p. 160.
178 Decision 1386/2013 on a General Union Environment Action Programme to 2020 'Living Well, within the Limits of our Planet' (OJ 2013 L354/171).
179 For instance, during negotiations over the 2007 Lisbon Treaty the then UK Labour government made plain that non-interference with its national judicial processes

constituted one of its so-called 'red lines' (see Ch. 3 of the House of Lords' Constitution Committee's Sixth Report *European Union (Amendment) Bill and the Lisbon Treaty: Implications for the UK Constitution* (Session 2007–8) HL84, available at: http://www.publications.parliament.uk/pa/ld200708/ldselect/ldconst/ldconst.htm).

180 Decision 1386/2013 on a General Union Environment Action Programme to 2020 'Living Well, within the Limits of our Planet' (OJ 2013 L354/171).

181 Priority Objective 4: To maximise the benefits of Union environment legislation by improving implementation (OJ 2013 L354/189–91).

182 OJ 2013 L354/190–1.

183 COM(2012)95 Commission Communication *Improving the delivery of the benefits from EU measures; building confidence through better knowledge and responsiveness*, p. 9 (Objective: Improve access to justice).

184 Notably, Case C-249/09 *Lesoochranárske zoskupenie VLK.*

185 See para. 68 of EP Resolution of 20 April 2012 reviewing EAP6 and the setting of priorities for EAP7 (2011/2194(INI)) available at: http://www.europarl.europa.eu/sides/getDoc.do?type=TA&language=EN&reference=P7-TA-2012-147.

    See also paras. 29–42 of EP resolution of 12 March 2013 on improving the delivery of benefits from EU environment measures: building confidence through better knowledge and responsiveness (2012/104 (INI)) available at: http://www.europarl.europa.eu/sides/getDoc.do?type=PV&reference=20130312&secondRef=ITEM-010-10&format=XML&language=EN.

186 Opinion of the Committee of the Regions of 28–9 November 2012 'Towards a EAP7: Better implementation of EU environmental law' (CDR 591/2013 – ENVE-V-024), available at: https://toad.cor.europa.eu/corwipdetail.aspx?folderpath=ENVE-V/031&id=21898.

187 The activities of DG ENV in relation to access to environmental justice may be inspected on its website at: http://ec.europa.eu/environment/aarhus/index.htm.

188 Commission RAPID press release IP/13/689, *Environment: 'The Fish Cannot Go to Court': Give your Opinion on How to Improve Access to Environmental Justice*, 15 July 2013, available at: http://europa.eu/rapid/press-release_IP-13-689_en.htm. See also DGENV website on the public consultation: http://ec.europa.eu/environment/aarhus/consultations.htm.

189 European Commission's Explanatory Consultation Text regarding the 2013 public consultation on possible EU legislative action on access to environmental justice is available at: http://ec.europa.eu/environment/consultations/pdf/access.pdf.

190 COM(2003)624.

191 See esp. Arts. 1, 3, 6 and 7 of the Draft AJEM Directive (COM(2003)624).

192 See recital 7 and Art. 2(2) in conjunction with Art. 2(1)(g) of the Draft AJEM Directive.

193 By virtue of Art. 193 TFEU.

194 Art. 1 of Draft AJEM Directive.

195 Ibid., Art. 2(1)(b).

196 See Arts. 9(2)–(4).

197 Ibid., Art. 8(a).

198 Ibid., Art. 8(b).

199 Ibid., Art. 8(c).

200 Ibid., Art. 8(d).

201 See e.g. Case 17/74 *Transocean Marine Paint.*

202 See e.g. Joined Cases 117/76 and 16/77 *Ruckdeschel.*

203 See e.g. Case C-285/98 *Kreil.*

204 See e.g. Case 11/74 *Union des Minotiers* and Case 44/79 *Hauer.*

205 OJ 2010 C83/02. See in particular Art. 20 (equality before the law) and Art. 47 (right to effective remedy and fair trial) CFREU.

206 Art. 51 CFREU.

207 Case C-72/95 *Kraaijeveld.*

208 Art. 2(1)(f)) Draft AJEM Directive.
209 Art. 9(3) of the Århus Convention stipulates that 'each Party shall ensure that, where they meet the criteria, if any, laid down in its national law, members of the public shall have access to administrative or judicial procedures to challenge acts and omissions by private persons . . . which contravene provisions of its national law relating to the environment'.
210 As enshrined now in Art. 5(3) TEU.
211 COM(2003)624, p. 12.
212 Art. 9(3) of the Århus Convention.
213 Art. 6(1), first para. Draft AJEM Directive.
214 Ibid., Art. 6(1) second para.
215 Ibid., Art. 6(2).
216 Ibid., Art. 6(3).
217 Ibid.
218 Waste Shipment Regulation 1013/06 (OJ 2006 L90/1) as amended.
219 Art. 3(3) Directive 2003/4 (OJ 2003 L41/26).
220 The position may be contrasted with the regulation of transboundary shipments of waste under Regulation 259/93, where the body required to notify an export of waste is in a suitable position to be cognisant of all the material details of the waste shipment and disclose this to a competent authority of the importing country.
221 COM(2003)634 Explanatory Memorandum, pp. 12–13.
222 See Art. 4(1)(a) Draft AJEM Directive.
223 See ibid., Art. 4(1)(b).
224 Ibid., Art. 4(2).
225 This interpretation is supported by reference to Art. 8 of the Draft AJEM Directive, which refers to the entity's statutes in the possessive mode ('its statutes').
226 See Art. 2(3) of the Århus Convention.
227 See Explanatory Memorandum (COM(2003)624, p. 13.
228 Ibid.
229 As, for example, experienced by the plaintiff NGEO in Case C-44/95 *Lappel Bank*.
230 COM(2003)624, esp. pp. 12–13.
231 The principle is also specifically enshrined in recital 13 of the preamble to the Draft AJEM Directive.
232 Art. 191 TFEU.
233 The references to 'Community' have been substituted to take account of the fact that the EC no longer exists.
234 Art. 2(1)(g) Draft AJEM Directive.
235 Decision 2005/370 on the conclusion, on behalf of the European Community, of the Convention on Access to Information, Public Participation in Decision-making and Access to Justice in Environmental Matters (OJ 2005 L124/1).
236 See Art. 2(2) Draft AJEM Directive.
237 As indicated in the Explanatory memorandum to the legislative proposal (see COM(2003)624, pp. 4–5).
238 See e.g. COM(96)500 Commission Communication on Implementation of EU Environmental Law; Commission's First, Second and Third Annual Surveys on Implementation of EU Environmental Law (SEC(1999)592, SEC(2000)1219 and SEC(2002)1041); and the Council Decision on EC's Sixth Action Programme on the Environment (OJ 2002 L242/1).
239 Between June and September 2013 the European Commission ran a brief stake-holder consultation on the future of access to environmental justice, specifically to consider whether EU legislative action would add value in ensuring effective and non-discriminatory access to justice in environmental matters across the member states. See EU press report IP/13/689, Brussels 15 July 2013 (*Environment: 'The Fish Cannot Go*

to Court': Give your Opinion on How to Improve Access to Environmental Justice), available at: http://europa.eu/rapid/press-release_IP-13–689_en.htm. The results of the consultation may be inspected at: http://ec.europa.eu/environment/aarhus/consultations. htm.

240 The studies are available at: http://ec.europa.eu/environment/aarhus/studies.htm. See e.g. the 2013 report by J. Darpö, *Effective Justice? Synthesis report of the study on the implementation of Article 9.3 and 9.4 of the Århus Convention in the member states of the EU* (2013–10–11/Final) which recommends adoption of an EU directive on access to justice in environmental matters.

9 Private enforcement of EU environmental law at EU institutional level (1)

Access to justice

Alongside the various rights that private persons have in seeking to enforce European Union environmental legislation at member state level, the EU legal system also provides certain rights and administrative procedures for civil society to be able to take steps to ensure that action taken by certain EU institutions also adheres to their legal obligations pertaining to environmental protection. The objective of this and the subsequent chapters in this section of the book is to examine these particular rights and procedures, with a view to assessing their degree of effectiveness in being able to provide private persons, including members of the public and non-governmental environmental organisations (NGEOs), a genuine opportunity to hold to account EU institutional decision-making affecting the environment. This chapter examines the principal sources of related EU law, namely the various core rights of legal action and review available to private persons under EU law for the purpose of holding to account the conduct of non-judicial EU institutions and bodies which have direct impact on the shaping and implementation of EU environmental protection policy. It is complemented by Chapters 9A (available on website) and 10, which assess particular areas of Union law that underpin in various ways the capability of private persons to be able to be undertake effective legal supervision of Union institutional conduct in relation to environmental policy matters. Specifically, Chapter 9A considers the extent to which EU law affords private persons rights to access environmental information held by Union institutions and other bodies. Chapter 10 assesses particular administrative complaints procedures that are in place at EU level for civil society to use in order to monitor and question particular aspects of EU environmental decision-making.

It is important to note from the outset that a major factor to consider in relation to the development of the area of private law enforcement and supervision of Union environmental obligations at EU institutional level is the EU's membership of the 1998 United Nations Economic Commission for Europe's (UNECE) Convention on access to information, public participation in decision-making and access to justice in environmental matters (the 'Århus Convention').[1] The Århus Convention has already been discussed in some detail in Chapters 8 and 8A with regard to its impact on the legal systems of the EU member states through the medium of EU environmental law. As noted in those chapters, the Convention contains three key sets of obligations (known as 'pillars'), namely ensuring that members of the public have adequate access to environmental information held by authorities, effective opportunities to participate in certain types of decision-making affecting the environment as well as effective access to justice ensure that environmental law is respected.

In addition to ensuring that the legal systems of the member states adhere to the Convention's requirements, the EU has also been mindful of the need to make certain that the institutions and bodies of the Union also adhere to the three pillars of the Convention regarding access to environmental information, participation in decisions affecting the environment and access to environmental justice. The Convention foresees the possibility of regional economic integration organisations such as the EU becoming a contracting party.[2]

An important part of the process of integrating the requirements of Århus within the EU's legal order as a whole has been the European Union's ratification of the Convention in 2005.[3] Article 216(2) of the Treaty on the Functioning of the European Union (TFEU) specifies that international agreements concluded by the Union are binding both on the EU member states as well as on the institutions of the EU. This key EU treaty provision, together with well-established case law of the Court of Justice of the European Union (CJEU),[4] confirms that such agreements are to be considered as integral binding sources of Union law at EU institutional level as well as at the level of the member states. The legal impact of Union ratification from the perspective of member states has already been explored in detail in Chapters 8 and 8A. As that analysis demonstrated, it is clear from CJEU case law that whilst the Århus Convention is a binding source of EU law, this does not automatically mean that individuals may rely upon its provisions as of right. For this to occur, they need to show that a particular provision or provisions they wish to invoke against another entity fulfils the specific requirements of direct effect applicable to international accords entered into by the Union.[5] This may be a difficult hurdle to overcome with respect to the Århus Convention, as several of its provisions are generally worded and offer a broad margin of discretion as regards their implementation by contracting parties. This was highlighted by the *Slovak Brown Bear*[6] judgment discussed in Chapter 8, in which the CJEU ruled out Article 9(3) of the Convention on access to environmental justice having direct effect. Where a provision of the Convention is not directly effective, this does not mean though that it is devoid of any legal effect from the perspective of individuals seeking to rely upon it. The CJEU's case law makes clear that, in accordance with the general principle of effectiveness, EU secondary law should be interpreted in line with the Convention's requirements, where possible. The CJEU jurisprudence has implications for EU institutions, not just for member states. Specifically, private individuals may have some possibilities for holding EU institutions, notably the political institutions responsible for implementation matters, to account over non-compliance with the Århus Convention by virtue of Union ratification of the international accord. The degree to which this may be possible is a matter yet to be clarified by the CJEU.

Another important step taken by the Union regarding its commitment to internalising the obligations of the Århus Convention has been its adoption of secondary legislation intended to implement the Convention's three pillars at EU level. Specifically, in 2006 the EU passed a single piece of legislation for this purpose, namely Regulation 1367/2006 on the application of the provisions of the Århus Convention to access to information, public participation in decision-making and access to justice in environmental matters to Community institutions and bodies (commonly referred to as the 'Århus Regulation').[7] The Århus Regulation, which entered into force on 28 June 2007, is designed to ensure that (non-judicial) Union institutions and bodies adhere to the requirements of the Convention's obligations. An important feature of this legislative instrument is its focus on the area of access to justice, as it introduces a novel mechanism that allows certain qualified NGEOs to seek an internal review of EU institutional acts and omissions which they consider to be in violation of EU law. Given that it entered into force only relatively recently, though, its full significance and impact in terms of contributing towards effective compliance of the Convention at Union level is not yet entirely clear and is still unfolding in light of institutional practice as well as judicial scrutiny before the CJEU.

Given that the Union has acceded to the Århus Convention, it is important to note that the international agreement's provisions have a very influential bearing on the interpretation and development of EU norms concerning implementation of the three pillars. Bearing this in mind, it is worth briefly noting the key Convention obligations on access to justice before focusing attention on the various legal review procedures relevant to the third pillar at EU level. Article 9 of the Convention sets out the scope of obligations relating to the third pillar concerning access to justice. Specifically, it obliges contracting parties to ensure that the public have access to a review procedure before the courts or another independent and impartial body established by law to uphold their rights to access environmental information and participation in environmental decision-making (Article 9(1)–(2)). In addition, Article 9(3) stipulates a broader obligation in relation to access to justice in requiring that each contracting party is to provide rights for members of the public to seek legal review of conduct they believe to contravene a party's environmental law. Specifically, Article 9(3) states:

> In addition and without prejudice to the review procedures referred to in paragraphs 1 and 2 above, each Party shall ensure that, where they meet the criteria, if any, laid down in its national law,[8] members of the public have access to administrative or judicial procedures to challenge acts and omissions by private persons and public authorities[9] which contravene provisions of its national law relating to the environment.

Article 9(4) stipulates that contracting parties must ensure that the three access-to-justice obligations are fulfilled so that review procedures are both fair as well effective, notably ensuring that they provide for 'adequate and effective remedies, including injunctive relief as appropriate', and are 'fair, equitable, timely and not prohibitively expensive'. These provisions are particularly important in setting benchmarks for the Union as regards its implementation of access-to-justice obligations. Whilst the Convention allows a relatively wide margin of discretion to contracting parties in determining the requirements entitling a person to seek legal review of conduct that they believe breaches their participation rights under the Convention or a party's environmental law, this discretion over legal standing to sue is not open-ended in that a contracting party must not render it impossible or excessively difficult in practice for members of the public to exercise their Convention rights on access to environmental justice. As will be discussed in the following sections, the Union has had significant difficulties in complying with the terms of Article 9 on account of its very restrictive rules on legal standing for private plaintiffs seeking judicial review in respect of EU institutional conduct.

This chapter now turns to examine the principal legal sources relating to the area of private enforcement of EU environmental law against (non-judicial) EU institutions and other bodies, specifically the various rights under EU law available to the public to be able to seek a formal legal review of acts or omissions of Union organs affecting the development or implementation of EU environmental policy. For this purpose, the remainder of this chapter is divided into two main parts.

The first part concentrates on the various treaty provisions within the TFEU that establish rights of action or other recourse for individuals to seek judicial review and/or recompense in relation to conduct of EU organs considered by the former to be in breach of Union law. As will be discussed below, in practice these legal procedures have provided to date relatively limited opportunities for members of the public to be able to seek effective judicial review of EU level measures alleged to be in breach of Union environmental protection obligations.

The second part of this chapter focuses on the specific provisions introduced by the Århus Regulation in relation to the access to environmental justice pillar (Articles 10–12). Under the regulation provision is made for the possibility of certain NGEOs having the opportunity to seek an internal review of certain administrative acts or omissions adopted by a non-judicial EU institution or other body within the sphere of EU environmental law. In addition, the regulation also stipulates that such NGEOs may institute proceedings before the CJEU if the EU institution/body fails to consider the internal review request as prescribed. These innovative requirements constitute a distinct set of review rights accorded to NGEOs that operate in parallel to the conventional routes of legal review under the TFEU. Their impact on the issue of access to environmental justice at EU level and compliance with third-pillar obligations under the Århus Convention by the Union is only now just beginning to become clarified in the light of CJEU case law, as will be discussed later below. The second part of the chapter will also briefly consider the special internal review procedure imported into the EU regulatory framework intended to implement the 2009 Hong Kong Ship Recycling Convention, prior to concluding with some reflections on the state of implementation of the third pillar of Århus within the EU as far as at EU institutional level decision-making is concerned.

9.1 Access to environmental justice under the EU treaty system

Under the current legal framework of the EU, a number of provisions under the TFEU provide a range of limited possibilities for private persons to take legal action directed against certain EU institutions where such persons consider that an institution has acted in contravention of EU law. To date, and in particular from the perspective of private persons seeking to uphold EU environmental law through litigation, the particular provisions have not been subject to significant amendment since their original incorporation in the 1957 Treaty of Rome, a time when environmental protection policy did not specifically feature within the original political or legal framework of the European Union. Save for a very few relatively minor amendments, the texts of the relevant EU treaty provisions on private individuals' rights to take legal action against the Union have remained essentially unchanged. This has been a major factor that has served to restrict possibilities for the development at EU level of a viable system of access to environmental justice.

The treaty provisions concerned will be examined in detail in this part of the chapter, with a view to assessing their relevance to the environmental policy sector. The relevant treaty provisions include, first, the following rights of action: annulment proceedings under Article 263 TFEU, proceedings in respect of a failure to act under Article 265 TFEU as well as non-contractual liability proceedings under Article 268 in conjunction with Article 340(2) TFEU. In addition, the preliminary ruling reference procedure under Article 267 TFEU is also relevant to consider, which is a judicial mechanism enabling[10] (and in some circumstances requiring)[11] national courts of the member states to refer to the CJEU for a definitive ruling on the interpretation of questions of EU law arising in the context of legal disputes fought at national level. Whilst not a right of action or appeal for individuals as such, the preliminary ruling procedure is particularly relevant to bear in mind when a national court is confronted with a question regarding the validity of an EU norm upon which a disputed national implementing measure is based. The CJEU has confirmed that all national courts and tribunals are obliged to refer to it questions relating to the legal validity of EU measures,[12] which effectively provides a particular route of access to the EU judiciary for private litigants wishing to challenge Union measures considered by them to have been adopted in breach of EU law. The most important TFEU provisions for the purposes of facilitating access to environmental justice at EU level are annulment proceedings and the preliminary ruling procedure set out in Articles 263 and 267 TFEU respectively.

Before referring to the treaty provisions, as interpreted by the case law of the CJEU, it is worth briefly clarifying the role of the EU's judicial institution in relation to this area. As part of its general remit under Article 19 TEU to ensure that EU law is observed correctly in terms of its interpretation and application, the CJEU is vested with jurisdiction under the TFEU to hear claims challenging the legality of EU institutional conduct (whether act or omission). Article 19 stipulates that the CJEU is comprised of a number of judicial branches, namely the Court of Justice (CoJ), the General Court (GC) (formerly known as the Court of First Instance (CFI) until a change of name was introduced by virtue of the 2007 Lisbon Treaty) as well as 'specialised courts'. The first two branches (CoJ and GC) are of relevance in relation to the adjudication by the CJEU on cases relating to the interpretation and application of EU law at EU and member state levels. The latter branch of specialised courts, which currently comprise the Civil Service Tribunal with jurisdiction concerning employment-related disputes concerning EU officials, is not relevant to the area of law discussed in this chapter. The CoJ and

GC have a division of responsibility with respect to hearing cases relating to allegations of illegal conduct on the part of EU institutions and other bodies. Specifically, the GC has jurisdiction to adjudicate on actions brought by private persons under the TFEU against acts or omissions of the European Union's institutions (notably including proceedings brought under Articles 263, 265 or 268 TFEU).[13] The CoJ has jurisdiction to provide rulings on questions of EU law and on the validity of EU measures referred to it by national courts[14] and determine appeals from the GC on points of Union law.[15] Whereas from a general institutional perspective, the CoJ and GC are elements of a single EU institution, namely the CJEU, there is though a clear system of hierarchy between the two judicial branches, underpinned by the fact that the latter may overrule the former on points of EU law. As will be explored below, differences have in the past emerged between the CFI and CJEU over the interpretation of certain treaty provisions concerning private persons' rights to take legal proceedings against EU institutions. At the heart of this difference lies a long-standing legal debate related to the adequacy of these provisions in securing civil society an adequate range of genuine possibilities to seek judicial review of Union acts. This debate has increased in intensity with the accession by the Union to the Århus Convention and adoption of the Århus Regulation 1367/06. The treaty provisions will now be examined in turn.

9.1.1 Article 263 TFEU – annulment proceedings

Article 263 TFEU (formerly Article 230 European Community (EC) Treaty) constitutes the principal mechanism for seeking judicial review of EU institutional decision-making, including those relating to the development and implementation of Union environmental policy. Specifically, Article 263 provides a procedure giving the GC jurisdiction to review the legality of acts taken by the Council of the EU, the European Commission or the European Central Bank (ECB), other than recommendations or opinions.[16] In addition, judicial review is also available in respect of acts of the European Parliament (EP), European Council and bodies, offices or agencies of the Union intended to produce legal effects vis-à-vis third parties.[17] Accordingly, the scope of the procedure is wide-ranging, in principle covering all legally binding measures taken by EU organs, not only those taken by principal EU institutions, under the aegis of the TFEU. From an environmental policy perspective this is significant, as a number of EU bodies and agencies involved in or which affect directly or indirectly the implementation or development of EU environmental policy are now subject to the possibility of judicial review scrutiny, such as the European Chemicals Agency (ECHA), European Fisheries Control Agency (EFCA), European Maritime Safety Authority (EMSA) and European Environment Agency (EEA).[18] The material scope of the procedure has gradually been widened since its inception in the Treaty of Rome 1957 through various treaty amendments. It is evident that Article 263 TFEU is modelled closely on the provisions foreseen for annulment actions in the failed 2004 EU Constitutional Treaty,[19] and its *travaux préparatoires* have been used as a reference by the CJEU for interpreting the scope of the current treaty framework.[20] Whereas

Article 263 concerns judicial review of EU acts, Article 235 TFEU provides a distinct review procedure in relation to omissions by EU bodies alleged to be illegal (this procedure is considered in section 9.1.3 below).

The object of Article 263 proceedings is to seek annulment of acts considered by claimants to be in contravention of EU law. The time limit for filing suit is tight, specifically proceedings must be instituted within two months of the publication of the disputed measure, its notification to the plaintiff or, in the absence thereof, of the day on which it came to their knowledge.[21] The reason for the short time limit, in common with judicial review procedures in general, is to promote legal certainty relating to the EU's decision-making system as far as possible whilst maintaining respect for the right of legitimate legal challenge. Under Article 264(1) TFEU, if an annulment action proves to be well founded, the disputed act(s) shall be declared the void by the GC.[22]

Article 263(2) TFEU sets out the grounds upon which an EU act may be annulled. Specifically, these include lack of competence, infringement of an essential procedural requirement, infringement of the TEU/TFEU and rule of law relating to their application, or misuse of powers. Accordingly, the annulment procedure provides a broad range of grounds, procedural as well as substantive in nature, for testing the legality of EU measures.

A key feature underpinning the annulment procedure is the issue of legal standing (*locus standi*), namely the determination as to who is entitled to bring judicial review proceedings as plaintiff. In practice, this legal aspect has proved to have a fundamental bearing on the possibilities for private law enforcement of EU environmental law (and EU law in general) via judicial proceedings under Article 263 TFEU. Article 263 TFEU employs a system which widens or narrows entitlement to sue depending on whether a plaintiff is deemed to be privileged, semi-privileged or non-privileged. The most generous entitlement to bring proceedings is vested in EU organs and member states. Specifically, under Article 263(2) member states, the EP, the Council of the EU and the European Commission have an automatic right to file suit (so-called privileged status). Under Article 263(3) the Court of Auditors, the ECB and the Committee of the Regions have the right to bring actions for the purpose of protecting their prerogatives, namely where it is alleged by them that their EU legal rights have been unlawfully compromised in some way by virtue of an EU act (so-called semi-privileged status).

By way of contrast, natural and legal persons have only limited legal standing to bring an annulment action. Private persons wishing to bring annulment proceedings before the GC have non-privileged status, in that they must fulfil specific strict conditions in order to have legal standing to sue. The material provision in this respect is Article 263(4) TFEU which states:

> Any natural or legal person may, under the conditions laid down in the first and second paragraphs, institute proceedings against an act addressed to that person or which is of direct and individual concern to them, and against a regulatory act which is of direct concern to them and does not entail implementing measures.

Accordingly, private persons have three types of opportunity to be able to file an action. First, they will have legal standing to sue if the disputed act is addressed to them. Secondly, they have *locus* if they are able to show that they are directly and individually concerned by the act (where it does not address them specifically). Thirdly, they have standing to sue if they are able to show that they are directly concerned by a regulatory act (not addressed to them) which does not entail implementing measures. The third type of *locus* was introduced by virtue of the 2007 Lisbon Treaty, in the wake of widespread criticism that the criteria for legal standing in respect of non-privileged were too narrow.

The key elements of legal standing for natural and legal persons under Article 263 TFEU will be assessed in detail below. By way of preface to this analysis it is important to note that the legal requirements for *locus standi* set for non-privileged plaintiffs have proved in practice to be very restrictive generally and in particular with respect to public interest environmental litigation. As interpreted by the CJEU, the criteria have had the effect of severely curtailing the possibilities of members of the public and/or NGEOs being able to seek review of EU environmental policy decisions. The first type of opportunity to seek review is in practice irrelevant to private persons seeking to challenge EU environmental measures, given that the latter are very rarely addressed to specific persons but are designed to be applicable generally. Accordingly, public interest environmental plaintiffs will need to fulfil the requirements relating to the second or third opportunities on legal standing. With respect to the second opportunity, plaintiffs must demonstrate that they are both directly and individually concerned by the measure in question; as will be discussed below, the criterion of 'individual concern' – as interpreted by the case law – is particularly difficult to satisfy given that it essentially requires the plaintiff to distinguish themselves from other persons affected by the disputed act. The third possibility of securing legal standing applies only in respect of a distinct type of measure, namely a 'regulatory act' without implementing measures that directly concerns the plaintiff. In practice, this covers a limited range of measures adopted at EU level, crucially excluding legislative instruments.

Two key reasons underpin the restrictions imposed on legal standing for private applicants under Article 263 TFEU, which may be traced to the origins of the EU in provisions on judicial review contained in the former founding principal treaties of the EU (ECSC, EEC and EAEC Treaties). First, they reflect a concern to ensure that the legislative system of the Union, as facilitating policy outcomes of democratic deliberation, should not be unduly encumbered by litigation sponsored by interest groups or individuals. Article 263 reflects clear intent on the part of the treaty drafters to ensure that the Union legislature should be able to pass general legislation in the public interest without fear of the possibility of minority interest litigation placing their legal certainty into question. Secondly, there is also little doubt that the stringency of the legal standing rules reflect a concern on the part of the treaty drafters to ensure that the CJEU is not overly burdened by legal challenges against EU measures. Both of these concerns are widely recognised and expressed in various guises in systems of judicial review at national level. Concern about judicial review interference with the democratic legislative process is also reflected in the Århus Convention, which confirms that the definition of 'public authority' excludes 'bodies or institutions acting in a judicial or legislative capacity'.[23] The Convention targets measures of an administrative nature. One of the long-standing problems with the issue of legal standing for private persons within the system of judicial review at EU level has been the fact that the relevant EU treaty provisions on judicial review have failed to make a sufficiently clear distinction between legislative and non-legislative types of EU measures, and, as a consequence, the rules on legal standing to sue by private litigants have been unduly restrictive.

In order to be able to analyse the content and impact of the legal standing criteria contained in Article 263 TFEU, it is first necessary to consider the evolution of the rules on *locus standi* prior to the amendments introduced by the 2007 Lisbon Treaty, as a considerable body of the relevant principles applicable today were first established prior to the date when Lisbon entered into force on 1 December 2009.

9.1.1.1 The position on legal standing prior to the Lisbon Treaty

Prior to the entry into force of the 2007 Lisbon Treaty, the rules on legal standing for private persons to be able to seek annulment of EU measures were governed by Article 230(4) of the former EC Treaty. The provision was narrower in scope than its contemporary counterpart, not foreseeing the third type of possible challenge against regulatory acts now enshrined in Article 263(4) TFEU. However, in other respects it encapsulated much of the essence of its contemporary statutory counterpart. Specifically, Article 230(4) stated:

> Any natural or legal person may, under the same conditions, institute proceedings against a decision addressed to that person or against a decision which, although in the form of a regulation or a decision addressed to another person, is of direct and individual concern to the former.

Accordingly, Article 230(4) EC provided the possibility for natural or legal persons to be able to bring proceedings only against a decision specifically addressed to them or against a decision which, although in the form of a regulation or decision addressed to another person, was of 'direct and individual concern' to them. The provision had remained intact since the inception of the EU in the 1950s under the aegis of the European Community treaties.

In the context of EU environmental law enforcement, the possibilities for private litigants being able to comply with the legal standing requirements in Article 230(4) were very restricted.[24] In practice, private persons wishing to challenge institutional acts on grounds that they contravene EU environmental law were faced with the task of proving that the disputed act concerned was of 'direct and individual concern' to them personally in order to gain access to court, given that disputed acts would most likely not be addressed specifically to them. Typically, the measure in question would most likely be an act of a general nature, such as a legislative instrument relating to or affecting environmental protection standards or an administrative decision concerning the management of a particular environmental site. The criteria of direct and individual concern, undefined in the treaties, have been the subject of substantial judicial interpretation by the CJEU. Both criteria remain embedded within the core structure of EU law under the auspices of Article 263(4) TFEU. Each is examined in turn in light of CJEU case law.

Whilst 'individual concern' has constituted the most challenging hurdle for private litigants to overcome, the impact of the criterion of 'direct concern' is also important to recognise. The CJEU has established that an EU measure will be of direct concern to a plaintiff if it affects the legal position of the litigant and leave no discretion to the addressees of the disputed act, who are entrusted with its implementation.[25] Accordingly, if any margin of discretion or autonomy is entrusted to an entity by virtue of the EU measure, for the purposes of its implementation it is likely that the requirement of direct concern will not be met. In practice, this has meant that a significant proportion of EU environmental policy instruments automatically fall outside the scope of judicial review proceedings, not least given that the vast bulk of EU environmental policy is crystallised through EU directives, which leave a considerable margin of autonomy to national authorities on how their implementation is to be effected.[26]

The criterion of 'individual concern', though, has been the most difficult requirement on *locus standi* for private persons to meet. The principal reason for this has been that the CJEU has interpreted the phrase extremely narrowly. In the (still) leading case of *Plaumann*[27] it defined the term to mean:

> Persons other than those to whom a decision is addressed may only claim to be individually concerned if that decision affects them by reason of certain attributes which are peculiar to them or by reason of circumstances in which they are differentiated from all other persons and by virtue of these factors distinguishes them individually just as in the case of the person addressed.[28]

The *Plaumann* formula, which has remained intact despite considerable academic and judicial criticism, served to restrict most severely the possibilities of private persons seeking to take annulment proceedings under Article 230 EC, particularly in the context of environmental law enforcement. The interpretation provided by the CJEU has required private litigants to demonstrate that they are affected by the act in question in a way that is clearly uniquely different to the effects felt by others. Accordingly, a private person will have no opportunity to seek annulment of a supranational institutional act they consider to infract EU environmental law, unless they are able to demonstrate that its impact affects them in a manner different from other persons. In practice this is almost impossible to prove, as an overview of the key CJEU case law shows. Several unsuccessful attempts were made under Article 230(4) EC to bring annulment proceedings against the European Commission in respect of decisions it made in relation to the management of allegations made against member states of infringements of EU law.

CHALLENGING COMMISSION DECISIONS ON INFRINGEMENT CASES

A number of unsuccessful annulment actions were launched under Article 230 EC in order to seek review of decisions by the European Commission relating to the management of infringement proceedings under the auspices of Article 226 EC (now Article 258 TFEU). Such actions were ruled inadmissible on the grounds that decisions relating to infringement case management, such as the closure or discontinuation of an infringement file by the Commission, are acts that are not deemed to be of direct and individual concern to private persons.[29] That the private person may have been the sole source of information for the Commission in relation to the subject matter of the dispute or that the private person concerned has entered into a dialogue with the Commission services about allegations of illegal conduct on the part of a member state have not been considered to be factors that distinguish the person individually, according to CJEU jurisprudence. Unless either an EU treaty or legislative provision provided persons with specific procedural rights vis-à-vis a Union institution, such as prior consultation as part of the preparatory phase leading to an administrative decision to be taken by that institution, the CJEU has not been prepared to consider that a person entering into a dialogue with the relevant institution will be able to meet the requirement of 'individual concern'.[30] There are some exceptions, however, notably in the areas of EU competition, state aid and anti-dumping law, where third parties are provided with specific procedural rights to register their views with the Commission prior to it taking decisions relating to the anti-competitive status of other persons' business activities, a member state's provision of state aid or an instance of dumping of third-country imports onto the single market.[31]

In confirming the wide discretion afforded to the Commission under the EU treaty framework in deciding whether or not to proceed with a particular infringement case, the jurisprudence of the CJEU has effectively ruled out the possibility of a substantive review of such decision-making under the annulment procedure.[32] This position remains the case under the current legal framework of Article 263 TFEU. Accordingly, there appears to be no possibility under EU law for private persons to challenge Commission decisions relating to the handling of infringement cases. The same consideration applies with respect to decisions relating to 'second-round' infringement procedure under Article 260 TFEU. The clarity of the case law has deterred efforts by private persons such as NGEOs from seeking to use annulment proceedings for this purpose. This was reflected in *An Taisce*[33] when two NGEOs decided to drop part of an annulment action which sought to review the decision by the Commission not to take infringement action against Ireland. The case concerned a decision by the Irish authorities to approve the development of a visitor centre at Mullaghmore, allegedly made in contravention of the terms of the Environmental Impact Assessment (EIA) Directive.[34] The foreclosure of the possibility of the public being able to challenge Commission decisions not to take up infringement proceedings against member states has been questioned. For instance, Krämer has suggested that the current position should be modified so as to afford persons the opportunity to refer infringement cases to the CJEU, where the Commission has decided to reject the possibility of infringement proceedings.[35] As discussed in Chapter 5, the possibility exists that political factors may come to influence Commission decisions on infringement issues, given the plurality of roles of the Commission within the EU's institutional setting. It therefore appears especially problematic to maintain the Commission's monopoly over decisions to prosecute infringement proceedings, given that the legal merits of a case may not always hold sway. Nevertheless, it appears now firmly settled (also under the aegis of Article 263 TFEU) that annulment proceedings are ruled out in relation to infringement case management decisions. It is doubtful that the Århus Convention lends support for this stance, given that it only excludes from its remit public authorities acting in a judicial or legislative capacity.[36]

CHALLENGING EU ENVIRONMENTAL POLICY INSTRUMENTS

Private persons also faced great difficulties in seeking to challenge the legality of Union decision-making affecting environmental protection issues in a policy (as opposed to an infringement case) context under Article 230(4) EC. This was highlighted in a number of cases, most notably starting with *Stichting Greenpeace*.[37]

In *Stichting Greenpeace* a number of local residents as well as the environmental NGO Greenpeace sought to annul a decision taken by the European Commission to agree to co-finance two power station projects in the Spanish Canary Islands, under the auspices of the European Regional Development Funds. The claimants considered that the development projects had been approved at local level in contravention of the requirements of the EIA Directive. Under EU rules, the award of such Union funding is predicated upon a project application being compatible with the requirements of EU law.[38] Greenpeace and other private persons brought an action under Article 230 EC with a view to annulling the decision to award funding from the EU budget. The CFI rejected the action as inadmissible, holding that the applicants had failed to show that they had the requisite legal standing to bring the case. Although the applicants were able to demonstrate a particular personal connection with the immediate geographical area concerned, such as proving personal residency on the islands affected by the projects or local residency on the part of several of their members (Greenpeace), this was insufficient to demonstrate 'individual' concern for the purposes of Article 230(4) EC. The CFI held that the decision to award funding was a measure whose effects impinged upon the local community generally and in the abstract; the applicants were not able to demonstrate that the Commission's act had affected them in a manner different from that felt by the rest of the local community.[39] In the absence of there being specific procedural guarantees set out in either EC Treaty provisions or EU legislation for the benefit of the persons such as the applicants, the CFI held that the applicants could not be deemed to be individually concerned on the basis of their involvement at EU level in making enquiries with the Commission relating to the projects. Accordingly, the fact that the applicants submitted a complaint to the Commission about the projects, filed requests for information concerning the disclosure of information relating to the Commission's decision to award funding and/or entered into a dialogue with Commission services about the subject matter of the dispute were irrelevant factors in this regard.[40] The CFI's decision was upheld on appeal to the CJEU.[41]

In a number of other environmental cases during the 1990s annulment actions brought by private persons to challenge acts by EU institutions were also declared inadmissible on similar grounds of lack of legal standing. These included actions to challenge the legality of Union acts relating to conservation measures required in the fishing industry,[42] the control of transfrontier shipments of waste,[43] as well as allocation of funding under the EU's financial instrument for the environment (the 'LIFE' programme)[44] to a member state for the purposes of establishing an inter-regional nature park.[45] In *Danielsson*[46] an action was brought for the purpose of challenging Commission approval of the testing of French nuclear devices in French Polynesia, as well as the legality of Commission approval under the auspices of the European Atomic Energy Community (Euratom) Treaty of nuclear weapons testing in French Polynesia.[47] The fact that the plaintiffs were Polynesian residents and might be potentially at risk from physical injury as a result of the nuclear testing did not, in the opinion of the CFI, make them individually concerned on the grounds that this factor did not distinguish them from other Polynesian residents.[48]

One of the key criticisms levelled at the CJEU and CFI's approach to the issue of private persons' legal standing to sue under Article 230(4) EC has been that the Court's interpretation of the criterion of 'individual concern' in that provision effectively acted as a block to the possibility of EU acts being subject to effective judicial scrutiny. In the *Stichting Greenpeace* litigation and other cases at the time applicants submitted that, applied in an environmental protection context, the rules on legal standing interpreted in accordance with the standard *Plaumann* formula would mean that realistically no person would ever be in a position to challenge Union acts that contravened EU environmental law. The applicants invited the CJEU to reappraise the legal standing rules and reinterpret them in a light that would reflect the general legal principle set down in earlier cases that the rules underpinning the EU legal order must ensure effective judicial protection for private persons.[49] In *Danielsson* the applicants referred in support of their arguments for a relaxation of the legal standing rules to the *Les Verts*[50] case. In that case, the CJEU had held that a parliamentary grouping was entitled to seek annulment of a decision of the EP, even though Article 173 of the European Economic Community (EEC) Treaty (the predecessor provision to Article 230 EC) did not at the material time include acts of the EP as being within its scope. The CJEU ruled that standing to sue should be granted to the parliamentary grouping, on the grounds that a complete system of legal remedies and procedures was necessary to permit the Court to review the legality of measures adopted by EU institutions. However, In *Danielsson* the CFI rejected submissions to the effect that standing should be extended for private persons seeking to annul Union measures, on the ground that a complete system of remedies is offered for the purpose of challenging such acts. In particular, the CFI pointed to the availability of other direct actions as well as the preliminary ruling procedure at EU level[51] to plaintiffs in order to test the legality of EU measures.[52] The preliminary ruling procedure (as currently enshrined within Article 267 TFEU) is discussed in a later section to this chapter (section 9.1.2). It offers the opportunity for national courts of the member states to refer to the CJEU on questions concerning the correct interpretation and legal validity of EU measures.

That judicial reasoning was reaffirmed in the *Stichting Greenpeace* case by the CJEU on appeal, which held that a legal vacuum had not been created by virtue of the CFI's ruling that the annulment action was inadmissible. The CJEU considered that, in bringing legal proceedings at national level in order to challenge the administrative authorisations granted by the Spanish authorities to the developers, Greenpeace had the possibility of invoking the application of the EIA Directive and thereby protecting rights afforded to it under that EU legislative instrument. If necessary, in the course of those national proceedings, the national court could refer to the CJEU for a question of interpretation of EU law under the auspices of the preliminary ruling procedure. The heart of the CJEU's argument was that the availability of private litigants being able to gain access to it via the mechanism of the preliminary ruling procedure ensured that a complete and effective system of judicial protection was guaranteed.[53] The Court considered that, at root, Greenpeace's legal actions at national and EU levels were concerned with enforcement of the EIA Directive, and accordingly the preliminary ruling procedure offered itself as a judicial mechanism to ensure that the EU judicature would be able to review its correct interpretation and therefore assist in its proper application.

However, for a number of reasons, that judicial argument contains several fundamental flaws, as recognised in the academic literature as well as by certain members of the EU judiciary subsequently. First and foremost, the availability of the preliminary ruling procedure in the *Stichting Greenpeace* litigation would not actually have resulted in a judicial review of the Commission's disputed decision to award EU funds to the two power station projects. National proceedings would simply only have been able to focus on the legality of the administrative decisions taken at national authority level.[54] Secondly, recourse to the preliminary ruling procedure is not necessarily straightforward and presents its own particular procedural difficulties.[55] Notably, whilst it is a mechanism which empowers and to some extent obliges the national courts to refer to the CJEU for definitive advice on questions of EU law, it does not provide any specific rights for individuals to require this to happen. The possibility of invoking the preliminary ruling procedure also depends upon the extent to which the rules on legal standing at national level permit a private litigant to bring proceedings relating to the enforcement of EU environmental law before the relevant national courts, an area in which EU law to a large extent has not developed any clear legal guidance.[56] In addition, in several cases private litigants would only be able to invoke the question of validity of specific EU legislation at national level if they decided to provoke legal action being taken against them by the national authorities by contravening national implementing rules underpinning the EU measure in question. Being effectively forced to take steps that breach national (criminal) law is hardly an effective or fair method of securing a remedy. Moreover, in some instances the preliminary ruling procedure is not available where a disputed EU legislative norm or measure does not involve implementing measures at national level. Such is often the case with EU regulations, which are binding in their entirety and directly applicable in the member states.[57] It also takes a considerably longer period of time for litigants to obtain a judgment on the legal validity of an EU measure from the CJEU using the preliminary ruling procedure than it does using annulment proceedings under the EU treaty framework. This is principally because the preliminary ruling procedure involves litigants having to take an indirect route to the Court of Justice, namely via legal proceedings regulated under national law before a national court or tribunal.

Several of these criticisms were taken up by the CFI in *Jego Quere*,[58] which involved an action for annulment brought by private persons against a Common Fisheries Policy regulation stipulating emergency conservation measures be taken in relation to the fishing of hake in EU waters. The applicant, a French fishing concern, objected to the fact that the regulation prohibited the use of mesh nets with holes under 10 mm in diameter. Under a standard test of individual concern, the action would have been found inadmissible. However, the CFI held that the definition of individual concern should be reappraised, taking the view that the standard interpretation of 'individual concern' in Article 230(4) had the effect of denying in practice effective judicial protection of rights of private persons, such as those relating to the applicant. Particularly, the Court took into account in this regard that the principle of the need to guarantee effective judicial protection had now been expressly endorsed by the EU under Article 47 of the EU's Charter of Fundamental Rights 2000.[59] The CFI considered that the test of individual concern should be widened accordingly, so as to be predicated upon on the ability of an applicant to be able to show that an EU measure 'affects his legal position in a manner which is both definite and immediate, by restricting his rights or by imposing obligations upon him'. The CFI's ruling on admissibility was supported in its view by an opinion provided by Advocate General Jacobs in a separate case,[60] pending before the CJEU on appeal from an earlier judgment of the CFI at the time.

However, in subsequent rulings the CJEU quickly overruled the CFI and held that such a reinterpretation of Article 230(4) EC would not be possible and that any liberalisation of the test of individual concern would require a specific treaty amendment by the member states. This came about in *UPA*[61] and then in the CJEU's subsequent ruling on the appeal in *Jego Quere*.[62] The *UPA* litigation involved a challenge by an association of farmers against an EU regulation amending the common organisation of the olive market. On an appeal from the CFI, the CJEU affirmed the traditional position of the *Plaumann* formula notwithstanding that the Advocate General had opined that continued application of a restrictive interpretation of the criterion of individual concern undermined provision of an effective judicial protection against generally applicable EU measures. The CJEU held that it would not be acceptable to adopt an approach that would lead to assessing whether particular national procedural rules allowed an applicant to utilise the preliminary procedure, as this would involve the CJEU examining national procedural law which would go beyond its jurisdiction when reviewing EU measures.[63] Moreover, whilst the CJEU acknowledged that the test of individual concern enshrined in Article 230(4) EC should be construed in light of the principle of effective judicial protection, this could not lead to an interpretation that would effectively set aside the criterion, something that would be beyond the jurisdiction of the Court. The interpretation by the CJEU that a treaty amendment was required before changes could be made to Article 230(4) EC was rightly criticised as ill-founded by a number of commentators, given that the wording of the provision was sufficiently open-textured to be interpreted along the lines suggested by the CFI in *Jego Quere*.[64]

IMPACT OF EU RATIFICATION OF THE ÅRHUS CONVENTION

When the EU ratified the Århus Convention in February 2005,[65] speculation began to mount about whether the CJEU might change course and adjust its interpretation of Article 230(4) EC in the light of the international accord's requirements on access to environmental justice. In particular, it was evident that the rules on standing for annulment actions at EU level appeared incompatible with the obligations enshrined in Article 9(3) of the Convention. However, a number of cases in the aftermath of the CJEU's *UPA* ruling appeared to make it clear that ratification of Århus did not impact on the CFI or CJEU's jurisprudence in this area. A few examples serve to highlight this.

One early notable example arose in the *EEB and Stichting Natuur en Milieu* annulment litigation,[66] two joined cases decided by the CFI a few months after ratification in November 2005. Two NGEOs (European Environment Bureau (EEB) and the Dutch organisation Stichting Natuur en Milieu) had brought annul proceedings in order to overturn two Commission decisions regarding the phased withdrawal of market authorisations for two plant protection products, atrazine and simazine.[67] The decisions were taken under the auspices of the general EU legislative instrument on plant protection products, namely Directive 91/414,[68] together with ancillary framework legislation.[69] The NGEOs objected to the fact that certain member states were entitled under the Commissions' decisions exceptionally to continue to authorise marketing for some three years after the principal withdrawal date (16 March 2004). The CFI held the action inadmissible on grounds that the plaintiffs lacked legal standing in not being individually concerned by the EU measures. It held that it was immaterial that only certain member states were affected by the extended phase-out, given that the NGEOs were concerned in the objective capacity as NGEOs just like any other person.[70] Neither could the NGEOs claim to be individualised on account of certain national laws accepting they were individually concerned by acts impacting on environmental interests they defended.[71] Moreover, the CFI considered that various consultative rights afforded to the NGEOs under EU environmental legislation, namely under the Habitats Directive 92/43 and Environmental Liability Directive 2004/35, did not serve to distinguish them from other persons. For neither legislative EU instrument provided specific procedural guarantees to the plaintiffs in respect of plant protection products.[72] The CFI also reaffirmed the *UPA* position adopted by the CJEU that EU law offered the applicants a complete system of remedies for the purpose of reviewing EU acts.[73] The CFI also came to a similar judgment in *EEB and others*[74] when a number of NGEOs as well as trades union combined to bring annulment proceedings against the Commission over a 2003 Commission directive[75] to approve the use of paraquat as a herbicide. The plaintiffs considered the Commission's directive to have been passed *ultra vires*, on the basis that it contravened the human and animal health safety requirements and procedures set out under Directive 91/414. However, the CFI ruled that the action was inadmissible, on the grounds that the applicants lack legal standing to bring the case. It found that the measure in dispute affected them in their objective capacity as entities active in the protection of the environment, workers' health and/or as property holders[76] in the same manner as any other person in the same situation. The CFI held that these capacities were not of themselves sufficient to meet the standard requirements of individual concern for the purposes of Article 230(4) EC.[77] In addition, the CFI reaffirmed its position that unless specific procedural guarantees were granted for the benefit of the applicants under EU treaty or legislative provisions, the requirement of individual concern would not be fulfilled. The fact that the EEB had acquired special advisory status within the EU institutions and other applicants had special legal standing rights under Member State systems of administrative law were not relevant in this regard, according to the Court.[78]

Similarly, the CJEU did not amend its position in relation to the construction of Article 230(4) EC in the wake of EU ratification of the Århus Convention, exemplified in the *WWF*[79] and *Azores*[80] cases. The *WWF* case was more significant from a legal perspective, in that legal proceedings had been initiated after the EU had ratified the Århus Convention, whereas the *Azores* litigation (and *EEB* cases before the CFI) had been commenced prior to EU ratification and so technically could be considered solely on the state of EU law at that material point in time, even though the CJEU judgment was determined after ratification had been completed. In *WWF* an NGEO sought to annul part of a Council regulation[81] that fixed certain fishing quotas in EU waters. Specifically, it challenged part of the EU measure that set a total allowable catch for cod of 30,000 tonnes in 2007 notwithstanding that scientific advice from the International Council for the Exploration of the Sea advocated that no catch should be allowed in order to conserve stocks. The plaintiff was a member of the executive regional advisory council (RAC) for the North Sea which had an advisory role to the Council of the EU under the aegis of the Union's Common Fisheries Policy framework.[82] A majority decision of the RAC advised the Council to allow a catch, the plaintiff being an opposing minority. On appeal from the CFI, which dismissed the action as inadmissible, the CJEU agreed with the CFI that the plaintiff was not individually concerned by the EU regulation for the purposes of Article 230(4) EC. Notwithstanding that the Court recognised that the involvement by a person in the procedure leading to the adoption of an EU act could be capable of distinguishing the person individually, it noted that this factor did not apply in this case for two main reasons. First, the CJEU held that only the RAC itself could be deemed to be individually concerned and not its constituent members, in that only the former was vested with procedural guarantees relating to consultation under the CFP regulatory framework.[83] Secondly, the Court held that as a rule a person or entity enjoying a procedural right will not, as a rule, have standing to bring proceedings to contest the legality of an EU measure in terms of its substantive content. In this instance, the RAC was vested with a right to be heard prior to the CFP decision, but the relevant EU legislation did not in the Court's opinion indicate that the RAC should be recognised as having a right to seek a judicial review on the substance.

In the *Azores* litigation a public authority (Autonomous Region of Azores) also sought to annul, in part, a 2003 EU regulation adopted under the Common Fisheries Policy (CFP). Specifically, the EU regulation introduced a new fishing management system for EU waters in the north-east Atlantic area including the Azores, allowing member states to restrict fishing up to 100 nautical miles from the Azores coast, except for EU vessels that traditionally fished in those waters. The plaintiff objected to certain changes, including, *inter alia*, the removal of EU power to determine the maximum fishing effort regarding demersal species as well as the removal of the exclusion hitherto of Spanish tuna fishing vessels from the Azores area. The CJEU, in agreement with the CFI, held the plaintiff had no legal standing to sue the Council of the EU over the regulation, on the grounds that the factual situation of possible harm to marine conservation, the status of the plaintiff under the EU treaty framework as an outermost region of the EU[84] and the reduction of powers of the plaintiff to exercise fishing management controls were insufficient to categorise the plaintiff as being individually concerned.[85] In addition, the *UPA* formula on sufficiency of judicial protection was reaffirmed by the CJEU, even if the plaintiff had no possibility of bringing any action before the national courts and accordingly was unable to make use of the preliminary ruling procedure as a means of accessing the Court.[86]

COMPLAINT FILED WITH THE ÅRHUS COMPLIANCE COMMITTEE (ACCC/C/2008/32)

By way of response to the CJEU's rejection of any attempt to loosen its restrictive interpretation on legal standing in annulment proceedings involving environmental matters, in December 2008 one NGEO (ClientEarth) filed a complaint with the supervisory authority of the Århus Convention submitting that the EU had breached various provisions of the agreement relating to access to justice.[87] Under the Convention, the Compliance Committee has jurisdiction to hear complaints (formally known as 'communications') from members of the public as well as parties[88] and make findings and recommendations for consideration by the Meeting of the Parties. At the heart of the complaint lay the accusation that the EU, with its test of individual concern applied in relation to judicial review proceedings, fell foul of Article 9(2)–(5) of the Convention.[89] In April 2011 the Compliance Committee published its interim report on the complaint.[90] The Committee decided to release the interim report, given that since the filing of the complaint certain recent legal structural changes had taken place at EU level with respect to the area of judicial review (namely the entry into force of the Lisbon Treaty in amending the treaty provision on annulment proceedings (Article 263 TFEU) as well as the entry into force of the Århus Regulation1367/06) and that it was, at the material time, uncertain as to what impact these changes might have in terms of the state of EU compliance.[91] As a consequence, the Compliance Committee decided to focus its interim report on the extent to which the operation of Article 230(4) EC was in alignment with the access to justice provisions of the Convention.

In its 2011 interim report, the Committee was highly critical of the way in which the annulment procedure under Article 230(4) EC, as interpreted in accordance with CJEU case law, had operated. Notably, the Committee considered that the EU's application of its annulment procedure with respect to private plaintiffs did not conform to the requirements of Article 9(3) of the Århus Convention. Whilst it acknowledged that Article 9(3) accorded contracting parties the power to stipulate legal standing requirements in relation to judicial review procedures, the Committee also held that any requirements on *locus standi* needed to avoid being so strict that they effectively served to bar all or almost all environmental organisations or other members of the public from challenging acts or omissions that contravene the contracting party's law relating to the environment.[92] The Committee went on to hold that, whilst the terms of Article 230(4) EC were drafted in a way that could have been interpreted so as to conform with Article 9(3) of Århus, the CJEU had adopted a jurisprudence that rendered the *locus standi* requirements too strictly to meet the requirements of the Convention.[93] The Committee expressed regret that the CJEU had not taken into account the legal impact of the EU having become a contracting party to the Convention in the *WWF* case, given that it was a case in which proceedings had commenced after the EU's ratification of Århus.[94] The Committee also concluded that the preliminary ruling procedure[95] could not compensate for the stringency of the 'individual concern' test set down by the *Plaumann* formula applicable to Article 230(4) EC. The Committee noted that the procedure was not an appellate system and did not did not meet the requirements of Article 9(3) of the Convention.[96] Ultimately, the Committee reserved judgment in its interim report on whether or not EU law overall failed to comply with the Convention's requirements on access to justice, noting that the impact of the treaty changes introduced by the Lisbon Treaty and the Århus Regulation still needed to be clarified by the CJEU. However, in effect the Committee fired a warning shot across the bows of the EU that unless the law of the Union changed course significantly so as to effect a loosening of the requirements of *locus standi* in relation to judicial review proceedings in environmental matters brought by members of the public, the EU would be found to be falling short of its Convention obligations.[97] At the time of writing, the second report of the Committee is still pending.

9.1.1.2 Legal standing after the 2007 Lisbon Treaty

The issue concerning compliance by the EU with the access-to-justice provisions of the Århus Convention effectively had to be considered afresh in the light of the changes made to the EU foundational treaty framework by virtue of the entry into force of the 2007 Lisbon Treaty in December 2009. Specifically, Article 230 EC has been replaced with a new treaty provision on annulment proceedings in the form of Article 263 TFEU (as reproduced in section 9.1 above), and particular changes have been made with regard to the possibilities for private persons commencing judicial review actions. Notably, Article 263(4) TFEU has introduced an additional (third) route for private plaintiffs to be able to access the EU judiciary in Luxembourg, specifically now the General Court (GC) which had replaced the CFI. At the same time, Article 263(4) in essence retains the traditional two legal bases upon which a private person had legal standing to sue for annulment, namely (1) where the person is an addressee of an EU measure and (2) where the person is directly and individually concerned by an EU act. This section explores to what extent Article 263 TFEU is capable of addressing the shortcomings of its predecessor provision in relation to compliance with the Århus Convention.

The new additional basis for legal standing introduced by Article 263(4) TFEU offers a limited extension to the existing standard routes to accessing the GC by private plaintiffs in annulment proceedings. Specifically, the treaty provision provides for the possibility of individuals being able to challenge 'regulatory acts' of direct concern to them and 'does not entail implementing measures'. Significantly, the new route of access to court drops the requirement of individual concern, a criterion that has come in for severe criticism in terms of its compatibility with the Århus Convention, as discussed in the previous section. On the other hand, the new basis for legal standing inheres elements of both uncertainty as well as restrictiveness. First, the treaty provision, and the TFEU as a whole, does not provide for a definition of the term 'regulatory act'. In particular, in the absence of CJEU case law, there was uncertainty as to whether regulatory acts embraced both legislative as well as non-legislative measures.[98] Whereas the reference to regulatory acts was subject to more clarity in the failed counterpart provisions of the 2004 EU Constitutional Treaty, the TFEU is silent on the issue. In the EU Constitutional Treaty a sharp distinction was made between legislative and non-legislative acts,[99] with the consequence that it was evident from that treaty that legal standing relating to regulatory measures concerned only the latter category of acts. Notably, under the 2004 EU Constitutional Treaty regulations would only be able to be adopted as non-legislative acts.[100] Moreover, it appeared evident from the *travaux préparatoires* of the EU Constitutional Treaty that those drafting the treaty considered that limiting the coverage of the additional legal standing basis for individuals to regulatory acts would enable a restrictive approach to be maintained in relation to actions brought by private plaintiffs in relation to EU measures adopted by way of a legislative procedure.[101] However, no such hierarchy of secondary instruments is adopted under the TFEU; a regulation may be adopted either as a legislative or executive measure under the aegis of the current treaty framework, as was the case under the former EC Treaty. Secondly, the new basis is restrictive in the sense that only those regulatory acts may be challenged which have no implementing measures. This would appear to rule out challenges in relation to EU directives, which under the TFEU[102] are defined as foreseeing the need for transposition and implementation of their obligations by member states.[103]

It appears evident that the novel basis for *locus standi* introduced by Article 263(4) TFEU was meant to address long-standing criticisms raised against the stringency of the 'individual concern' criterion interpreted in Article 230(4) EC in relation to its impact on certain economic operators directly affected by EU secondary legislation. In effect, the new treaty provision appears to be a response to the problems raised in cases such as *Jego Quere*[104] and *UPA*,[105] where certain groups of economic operators' legal positions within the single market had been directly affected by EU executive decisions taken in the form of regulations, and yet they had no effective opportunity to seek review of the legality of the EU acts in question either through annulment proceedings under Article 230 EC or via the preliminary ruling procedure (in the absence, in particular, of any implementing national legislation). This state of affairs was compounded by the aspect of inconsistency in the case law, in that in certain instances economic operators were able to bring annulment proceedings through a more relaxed interpretation by the CJEU of the criterion of 'individual concern'.[106] It appears clear that the treaty changes effected by the TFEU on annulment proceedings, modelled essentially on the EU Constitutional Treaty, were not motivated to respond to the impact of EU accession to the Århus Convention.

Accordingly, questions still remained unanswered after the TFEU entered into force as to whether or not the treaty changes introduced in relation to annulment proceedings and the way in which Article 263(4) TFEU as a whole should be interpreted would now meet the requirements on access to justice under the Århus Convention. In the recent case of *Inuit Tapiriit Kanatami*[107] the GC and CJEU had an opportunity to clarify the scope of *locus standi* for private plaintiffs under Article 263 and so shed some significant legal light on these questions. This case involved an annulment action brought by a number of natural and legal persons in 2010 which challenged the legality of a 2009 EU regulation[108] adopted jointly by the EP and Council of the EU which imposed restrictions on trade in seal products within the EU. Specifically, the regulation only permitted the placing on the single market of seal products resulting from hunts traditionally conducted by Inuit and other indigenous communities and contributing to their subsistence. Both the EP and Council, supported by the Commission, disputed the assertion by the plaintiffs that the latter had legal standing to sue. The litigation ultimately came before the CJEU on appeal in 2013, the GC having dismissed the action in 2011 as inadmissible for want of legal standing on the part of the plaintiffs.[109] In an important ruling, the CJEU clarified some important legal issues concerning the operation of Article 263(4) TFEU.

First, the CJEU clarified the meaning of 'regulatory act' in Article 263(4) TFEU. The Court held that the term only covered acts of general application not adopted by way of a legislative procedure at EU level.[110] In coming to this conclusion, the CJEU was persuaded that the term should be construed in a similar way to the counterpart provision in the 2004 EU Constitutional (EUC) Treaty, acknowledging that the TFEU provision had been drawn up in identical terms to that in the Constitutional Treaty (in Article III-365 EUC).[111] Accordingly, the plaintiffs could not rely upon the new basis of acquiring legal standing introduced in Article 263(4) TFEU, given that the contested regulation had been adopted by way of a legislative procedure. Secondly, the CJEU considered whether the plaintiffs could argue they had legal standing to sue under Article 263(4) on the grounds that they were directly and individually concerned by the disputed measure. By way of initial clarification, the CJEU clarified the change brought about to the material scope of annulment proceedings via the TFEU. Specifically, the Court confirmed that the reference to 'act' in Article 263(4) TFEU (as opposed to the later reference of 'regulatory act' in the treaty provision) covered any act adopted by the EU producing binding legal effects. Accordingly, the term 'act' in the treaty provision covers acts of general application, legislative or otherwise, and individual acts.[112] The key legal issue to determine, though, in this case was whether the plaintiffs had fulfilled the criterion of individual concern. The plaintiffs submitted that the CJEU should reinterpret the phrase as meaning 'substantial adverse effect'. However, in agreement with the GC, the CJEU rejected this submission, holding that the meaning of individual concern in Article 263(4) TFEU should be interpreted in the same manner as that set down in the *Plaumann* formula, namely that the contested EU measure must have affected the plaintiffs by reason of certain attributes peculiar to them or by reason of circumstances in which they are differentiated from all other persons, and by virtue of such factors are distinguished individually just as in the case of a person addressed by an EU measure.[113] The CJEU considered that there was no evidence to indicate that the drafters of the 2007 Lisbon Treaty wished to alter the admissibility criterion of 'individual concern', as was the case with the failed 2004 EU Constitutional Treaty provisions on annulment proceedings upon which, according to the CJEU, Article 263 TFEU was based.[114] The CJEU concluded that, in light of this, the plaintiffs failed to meet the requirements of individual concern as the contested regulation was generally worded and applied indiscriminately to any seal product trader falling within its scope.[115] The CJEU also rejected the plaintiffs' submission that the entry into legally binding force of the EU Charter of Fundamental Rights (EUCFR) by virtue of the Lisbon Treaty,[116] in particular Article 47 EUCFR guaranteeing the right to an effective remedy, meant that the CJEU had to change its approach in holding that the EU provided for a complete system of judicial protection regarding review of legality of EU measures. The Court noted that the explanatory guidance to the EUCFR, to which the CJEU is obliged under the TEU to have due regard with respect to the interpretation of the Charter, indicates that Article 47 EUCFR is not intended to change the system of judicial review under the EU treaty framework.[117]

The impact of the CJEU's ruling in *Inuit Tapiriit Kanatami* appears to have significant consequences with respect to the question of EU compliance with the Århus Convention. Although the case did not specifically address the legal impact of the Convention on the interpretation of the annulment procedure, it appears quite clear that the CJEU clarified the key legal issues to make it clear that post-Lisbon the EU treaty framework on judicial review procedure contained in Article 263 TFEU did not result in any change with respect to the criterion of individual concern. Given that the new additional basis for *locus standi* in Article 263(4) with respect to regulatory acts does not cover all types of legally binding EU administrative measures that could concern EU environmental policy matters, it appears that the current TFEU provision on annulment actions (as interpreted by the CJEU) still falls short of the requirements of the Århus Convention, notably Article 9(3) of the international agreement.

Accordingly, it appears that the Århus Compliance Committee when coming to deliver its definitive report on the 2008 ClientEarth communication, will be likely to reaffirm its dissatisfaction with the state of the case law of the CJEU with respect to the degree to which private persons are afforded opportunities to seek judicial review of EU measures on the environment. There is, however, yet another twist to the saga on *locus standi* yet to be resolved definitively. Specifically, an outstanding question is whether the introduction of internal review procedures by virtue of the Århus Regulation 1367/06 might yet save the Union from falling foul of the access-to-justice requirements under the Convention. For the Århus Regulation provides a distinct set of internal review procedures available to NGEOs with regard to EU environmental decisions. The regulation also includes a specific clause on access to the CJEU in the event that an NGEO is dissatisfied with the internal review process. Whilst the regulation is appraised in detail in the second principal part of this chapter (section 9.2), it is appropriate to make a general comment at this stage on the possible impact that the Århus Regulation may have with respect to the issue of compliance with the Convention's third pillar. It is unlikely that the regulation will have a positive impact in terms of improving the Union's case for arguing that it complies with the Convention for a number of reasons, notably because the instrument neither provides an independent review procedure nor does it appear capable, in light of recent case law, of affecting the operation of the legal standing criteria of the provisions within the TFEU on judicial review.[118] TFEU provisions have superior legal status as primary sources of EU law over the Århus Regulation, which as a legislative instrument has secondary legal status within the system of legal hierarchy of norms of EU law under the EU's foundational treaty framework. The latter point has been confirmed in a 2012 ruling by the GC,[119] which is at the time of writing pending an appeal before the CJEU. It is likely that the Århus Compliance Committee will wait for the CJEU to deliver its ruling on the appeal before proceeding to issue its next report on the state of Union compliance with the Convention.

9.1.2 Article 267 TFEU – the preliminary ruling procedure

Although not a right of action akin to the annulment procedure discussed above under Article 263 TFEU, and technically a mechanism by which national courts and the CJEU may interact with one another over questions of interpretation of sources of EU law, in practice the preliminary ruling procedure (PRP) enshrined in Article 267 TFEU (formerly Article 234 EC) is a key judicial procedure used by private litigants as a means of challenging the legality of EU legislative and executive measures. As mentioned in the previous section, the CJEU has referred to the PRP as an integral part of the system of judicial protection for individuals contesting the legality of EU-level decisions.

Essentially, the PRP provides a mechanism through which national courts and tribunals of the member states may be able, and in certain circumstances are required, to refer questions on EU law to the CJEU that may arise in the context of national judicial proceedings. By way of response to the questions referred to it, the CJEU is vested with the power to provide definitive rulings on those legal questions. The CJEU's ruling is referred to in the treaty text as a 'preliminary ruling', which reflects the fact that the ruling is issued prior to the referring national court applying it to the particular case in its final judgment. Whilst formally being a procedure involving solely the national court and the CJEU on points of law, in practice it has for various reasons come to be seen as an alternative means for private persons to seek review of the due application and interpretation of EU law.

Article 267(1) TFEU vests the CJEU with jurisdiction to give preliminary rulings concerning, *inter alia*, the interpretation of the TFEU and TEU[120] as well as the validity and interpretation of acts of the EU institutions, bodies, offices and agencies of the Union.[121] As far as the interpretation of EU law is concerned, it is evident from the discussion in Chapter 6 that the preliminary ruling procedure has had a crucially important role to play in allowing the CJEU to determine the impact of EU law, including EU environmental legislation, within the legal systems of the EU member states.[122] In this respect, the PRP offers opportunities for private litigants to seek to challenge the way in which national authorities interpret and accordingly apply EU environmental legislation, notwithstanding that the European Commission may refuse to take infringement proceedings against a member under Articles 258 and 260 TFEU.[123]

In addition, the preliminary ruling procedure is also relevant in providing the opportunity for judicial review of Union acts affecting the environment. Article 267(1)(b) TFEU specifically endows the CJEU with the authority to determine questions concerning the legal validity of EU measures. Various judgments of the CJEU have served to ensure that the preliminary ruling procedure may be used as a potential means of securing judicial review of Union measures. In order to ensure that the application of EU law is carried out as uniformly as possible within the member states, the CJEU has held that all national courts and tribunals are, as a matter of general principle, required to refer to it questions concerning the validity of Union acts.[124] By way exception, a national court may decide in certain limited circumstances to grant interim relief in respect of the application of EU measures, notably if the national court harbours serious doubts about the validity of the measure, refers the matter to the CJEU, considers the Union interest, adheres to any relevant GC or CJEU judgment relevant to the subject matter of the dispute and if the interim relief is necessary to prevent serious and irreparable damage to the applicant.[125] This jurisprudence qualifies the wording of Article 267 TFEU, which specifies that courts and tribunals, other than those against which there is no judicial remedy, have discretion as opposed to an obligation to refer questions to the CJEU.[126] National courts, against whose decisions there is no further right to appeal under national law, are obliged as a general rule to refer to the CJEU on questions of EU law.[127] This judicial clarification by the CJEU has enabled litigants in national proceedings to ensure that questions concerning the validity of EU measures raised in the course of those proceedings and relevant to the case are referred without exception to the CJEU. National courts and tribunals have no discretion over whether or not to make a reference to the CJEU in such circumstances. The CJEU has also confirmed that its preliminary rulings have legal effects for the whole of the Union legal order, and not just on the referring national court.[128] National courts and tribunals retain, though, the option of referring questions of EU law to the CJEU, even though the CJEU may have provided a previous ruling relating to the subject matter of legal enquiry.[129]

The impact of this CJEU jurisprudence has opened up the possibility of private litigants using the PRP in order effectively to seek judicial review of EU measures affecting the environment before the CJEU. This is also known as an indirect challenge regarding the validity of an EU measure, as opposed to a direct challenge in the form of annulment proceedings via Article 263 TFEU. It has, for instance, been of considerable assistance to persons seeking to challenge the legality of EU measures on environmental protection that have adversely affected their personal economic position and existing legal rights. Accordingly, preliminary rulings have been obtained from the CJEU, for example, on the substantive legality of EU regulations on conservation measures in the fishing industry[130] and Union regulation on ozone depleting substances,[131] where the private litigants concerned would not have had legal standing to take annulment proceedings in respect of those legislative instruments under Article 263 TFEU for want of being able to fulfil the criterion of 'individual concern'. The PRP has accordingly the notable of advantage of enabling private litigants to be able to circumvent the stringent *locus standi* criteria of the annulment procedure.

However, as was outlined in the previous section on Article 263 TFEU, for a number of reasons it is highly questionable to regard the PRP as a judicial mechanism equivalent to the right to take annulment proceedings in respect of Union acts. A number of the key objections may be set out here. First, utilisation of the PRP mechanism is dependent upon the ability of a private litigant to take legal action against another entity at national level involved in some way regarding the application or implementation of the contested EU act, typically a national authority. Notably, where the EU act does not involve the intervention of such an entity at national level, then it will not be possible to utilise the PRP with a view to seeking review of the legality of the act. This limitation was highlighted, for instance, in the *Stichting Greenpeace* litigation[132] discussed in the previous section when the contested act concerned a European Commission decision to release Union funds to support a development project in contravention of EU environmental legislation. Secondly, it is important to note that the PRP is not a right of action for private plaintiffs, in particular it does not provide a guarantee of access to the CJEU. Ultimately, the decision to refer to the CJEU rests with the member state court adjudicating the national legal proceedings in question. Thirdly, access to the PRP is also dependent upon the extent to which private litigants have legal standing in any given case to bring national proceedings before national courts or tribunals to question the application or validity of EU environmental legislation. Rules on standing may vary considerably between EU member states as well as opportunities to be able to bring legal proceedings, which raises issues concerning the degree to which EU environmental legislation may be monitored under sufficiently uniform conditions in the EU at private litigant level. In some cases it may only be possible to commence litigation at national level by the private litigant inviting criminal proceedings to be taken against them in violating national implementation legislation relating to an EU measure, a situation not reflective of an effective system of judicial protection as required by principles of EU law, as pointed out by Advocate General Jacobs in his Opinion in the *UPA* case[133] as well as the CFI in *Jégo Quéré*.[134] Fourthly, the PRP is a relatively costly, circuitous and time-consuming mechanism to use for the purposes of challenging the legality of EU measures. The duration of litigation may be likely to run for a considerable period, and may be several years if appeals are undertaken through the national court system prior to the PRP mechanism being utilised. Legal costs may well be considerable in practice, given that national proceedings as well as the PRP are envisaged to be involved, and this may prove to be a deterrent to a litigant knowing that they may be faced with having to shoulder the opponent's legal costs if they lose the case in civil suits where the national law applies a 'costs follow the event' rule. As was discussed in Chapter 8, action has recently been taken by the European Commission to ensure that member states respect the obligation in Article 9(4) of the Århus Convention that national legal proceedings in environmental disputes are not prohibitively expensive.[135] Nevertheless, substantial if not prohibitive legal costs are still permitted to be imposed at national level. In practice this might well be expected to deter a significant amount of public interest environmental litigation targeting the use of the PRP in order to challenge the legality of EU measures in the environmental sector.

A fifth reason to doubt the adequacy of the PRP as a judicial review procedure to compensate for the deficiencies of Article 263 TFEU is the fact that the CJEU has, in certain circumstances, even refused to issue a preliminary ruling on the legal validity of EU decisions. Notably, the CJEU has made it clear that it will block a preliminary ruling where it considers that the matter could have been addressed by the private litigant earlier via the annulment procedure. The leading case on this point is *TWD*,[136] a state aid case involving a European Commission decision declaring certain financial assistance paid by German authorities to a company to be in breach of EU state aid rules and requiring to be repaid. The German government informed the recipient company involved of the Commission's decision and pointed out that it could challenge the Commission decision under Article 263 TFEU. However, the company failed to institute annulment proceedings within the two-month time limit and refused to pay back the aid, resulting in a legal action being brought against it for repayment at national level. As part of its legal defence, the company submitted that the Commission decision was illegal under EU law, which prompted the national court to invoke the PRP. However, the CJEU refused to issue a preliminary ruling, holding that no indirect challenge would be possible given that the company knew of its rights to sue the Commission under Article 263 TFEU and 'without any doubt' would have had standing to sue. Although this line of case law constitutes an exception to the CJEU's general approach of accepting that the legal procedures in Article 263 and 267 TFEU are distinct from one another[137] and that the *TWD* ruling does not apply where it is unclear whether a private litigant has *locus standi* to sue in annulment proceedings,[138] it does nevertheless further underline the unreliability of the proposition that Article 267 TFEU constitutes a sufficient backstop for the purposes of providing private litigants effective legal recourse to challenge EU decisions they consider to be unlawful under EU law.

9.1.3 Article 265 TFEU – legal proceedings in respect of a failure to act

Like the annulment procedure in Article 263 TFEU, Article 265 TFEU (formerly Article 232 EC) also offers private persons certain limited rights to seek judicial review of EU institutional conduct before the EU judiciary (specifically, the GC). In particular, the latter treaty provision entitles a private plaintiff, subject to specific stringent conditions, to bring an action before the GC where they consider that EU organs have failed to take action as required under EU law. Accordingly, the right of action set down in Article 265 TFEU addresses illicit omissions, whereas the annulment action under Article 263 provides for judicial review of EU acts. By virtue of the 2007 Lisbon Treaty, the material scope of the Article 265 review procedure (just as with the annulment procedure) has been widened beyond the core range of EU institutions involved in policy decision-making (European Council, Council of the EU, EP, European Commission and ECB) to include also any other body, office or agency of the EU.[139] As will be seen below, though, the right of action in relation to a failure to act is of limited practical value for the purposes of private law enforcement of EU environmental law, as it applies only in very limited circumstances.

In a similar vein to the annulment procedure, Article 265 TFEU approaches the issue of legal entitlement to sue by dividing plaintiffs into privileged and non-privileged categories.[140] As is the case with annulment proceedings, EU institutions as well as member states have an automatic right of legal standing to bring an action in relation to a failure to act (privileged plaintiffs).[141] In contrast, natural and legal persons are vested with far lesser rights of *locus standi*, in having to show that the defendant EU organ in question 'has failed to address to that person any act other than a recommendation or an opinion'.[142] The CJEU has interpreted this requirement restrictively, so as to oblige private plaintiffs to demonstrate that the defendant failed to adhere to a specific legal duty to adopt a measure specifically addressed to the plaintiff or a measure that directly and individually concerned the plaintiff.[143] The treaty does not specify a time limit for filing suit, although the CJEU has held that the action must be brought within a reasonable period of time,[144] reflecting a more favourable if uncertain position than the strict two-month time limit enshrined in Article 263(5) TFEU applicable to annulment proceedings. As a prerequisite to bringing an action before the GC, Article 265 requires the plaintiff to have requested the defendant EU organ to act. If within two months the defendant fails to respond, the plaintiff may then bring proceedings before the GC within a further period of two months.[145] So once the defendant has been called to take action and has failed to do so within two months, at that stage the plaintiff is then subject to a specific two-month time limit for filing suit.

Given that EU organs in the EU environmental policy sector are very rarely subject to a legal duty to undertake measures that are either for the specific benefit of private persons or may be said to be of direct and individual concern to private persons, in practice the right of action for failure to act under Article 265 offers very little opportunity for private persons to seek judicial review of those omissions of EU institutions considered by them to contravene EU environmental law. One notable exception concerns the rules underpinning the Århus Regulation 1367/2006, which is discussed further below and in detail in section 9.2.

9.1.3.1 *Challenging failures to take infringement actions against member states*

On a number of occasions private individuals have sought unsuccessfully to use Article 265 TFEU as a basis for overturning decisions on the part of the European Commission not to bring infringement proceedings against a member state under Article 258/260 TFEU. This is an issue of direct relevance to EU environmental law enforcement given that, as was shown in Part I of this book, Article 258/260 proceedings constitute a key legal mechanism at EU level for the purpose of holding member states to account for failures to implement EU environmental legislation correctly. However, the CJEU and CFI have confirmed on a number of occasions that legal action under Article 265 for the purpose of challenging omissions by the European Commission to launch infringement action is inadmissible.[146] The CFI has confirmed that the obligations of the Commission contained in Article 258 TFEU do not require it specifically to take any measures in relation to private persons as 'addressees' in the sense referred to in Article 265 TFEU. Instead, from a legal perspective, the proceedings relating to the application of Article 258 TFEU involve an exclusively bilateral relationship between the Commission and respective defendant member state.[147] Moreover, decisions by the Commission on managing infringement proceedings are inherently discretionary acts, not subject to any legal duty to act.[148] For similar reasons, the EU judiciary have also consistently dismissed as inadmissible actions brought under Article 263 TFEU seeking to annul Commission decisions to refrain from taking infringement action against member states.[149]

One notable example from the available jurisprudence is *Star Fruit*[150] where a Belgian company brought Article 265 proceedings against the Commission for failing to take up its complaint that French import controls on bananas was incompatible with free movement of goods rules under EU law and commence infringement action against France. The CJEU, in rejecting the company's claim, held that according to the scheme of Article 258 TFEU the Commission is not bound to commence proceedings but instead has discretion so to do, which effectively excludes the possibility of interpreting the existence of a right for individuals to require it to adopt a specific position.[151] The CJEU also went further by holding that even where the Commission decides to commence Article 258 TFEU proceedings and issues a reasoned opinion, with which a member state decides not to comply within the set deadline for a response, the Commission has the right but not the duty to apply to the CJEU for a declaration that the alleged breach of EU obligations has occurred.[152] The bold conclusion of the Court that the Commission has total discretion appears somewhat questionable, given the Commission's specific treaty obligation to safeguard the application of EU's foundational treaties[153] as well as the stipulation in Article 258 TFEU itself that the Commission 'shall' deliver a reasoned opinion if it considers a member state has failed to fulfil an obligation under the EU founding treaties (TEU/TFEU).[154] On the other hand, Article 258 also states that the Commission 'may' bring proceedings before the CJEU,[155] which arguably points in favour of an ultimate power of discretion on the Commission's part as to whether it should proceed to the litigation stage of the infringement procedure. The existing treaty wording might appear, accordingly, to indicate a legal duty on the part of the Commission to issue written warnings to a defendant member state, where it finds evidence of a breach of EU law, but confer discretion on the EU institution regarding any decisions to move an infringement case into the litigation phase before the CJEU. The approach taken by the European Court on the position of legal standing of complainants under Article 265 TFEU is, accordingly, in part at least difficult to defend. However, given the well-established position of the CJEU on this matter, it would appear that a specific amendment would have to be made to Article 226 EC in order for a delimitation of discretion on the Commission's part to occur with respect to decisions on infringement case management. With respect to second-round infringement proceedings conducted under Article 260 TFEU, it appears that the treaty text in similar vein to Article 258 indicates a discretionary power on the part of the Commission to take action before the CJEU.[156]

Accordingly, as currently structured and interpreted by the CJEU, Article 265 TFEU effectively blocks the possibility of private persons such as NGEOs challenging failures by the Commission to take infringement action against a member state in respect of breaches of EU environmental law, even where evidence of a breach is incontestable in light of available evidence. In addition, the right of action does not take into account the practical reality that a considerable fraction of the infringement procedure work by the Commission in the environmental sector, especially with regard to instances bad application of EU environmental law, is primarily driven by information provided by private persons alleging breaches of EU law by or within member states. Complaints from the public filed with the Commission concerning suspected infringements of EU environmental law by member states have consistently been recorded as amongst the highest number for any policy sector (see Table 5.1 in Chapter 5). In 2012, the Commission received 588 environmental complaints. Complaints account for a substantial fraction of the infringement cases pursued by the Commission; in 2012 some 28 per cent of cases had originated from the receipt of information and evidence from complainants (see Table 5.2 in Chapter 5). In practice, complaints often constitute an invaluable source of information with respect to the detection of cases of bad application of Union environmental law, given that the Commission is heavily dependent upon the supply of evidence and information of infringements of this type from the general public. Complainants are, therefore, an integral and central element of the practical functioning of the infringement procedures. Therefore, for the CJEU to hold that they have no rights to review Commission omissions to take legal action against member state in the face of information and evidence provided by them is an overly restrictive interpretation to make, and one that does not reflect the realities of casework dynamics or legitimate expectations for transparency in Union decision-making.

Formally speaking then, private persons have no legal rights under Article 265 TFEU to require that any complaints they lodge with the Commission about an alleged breach of law by a member state will be assessed and that a decision on the matter will be provided to them. Articles 258 and 260 TFEU do not provide for any specific procedural rights of complainants in this regard. However, as will be discussed in Chapter 10, complainants have the possibility of eliciting a reasoned response from the Commission by way of filing a complaint against the Commission with the European Ombudsman.

9.1.3.2 *Challenging omissions to act in relation to EU environmental policy*

Given the restrictions on legal standing afforded to private persons under Article 265 TFEU, as outlined above, the opportunities for private litigants to be able to seek judicial review of EU organs' failures to take policy-related measures under EU environmental law are in general very limited. It is rare in the environmental sector for EU organs to have legal duties to adopt acts with respect to members of the public. However, there is a notable exception with the Århus Regulation 1367/06.

The Århus Regulation contains a range of obligations that EU organs are required to fulfil vis-à-vis the public concerning the three pillars of the Århus Convention. Specifically, the regulation sets out obligations for EU organs to provide access to environmental information held at EU level,[157] to facilitate public participation concerning environmental plans and programmes[158] as well as to respond to requests from certain qualified NGEOs to undertake an internal review of particular EU environmental administrative acts and omissions to adopt administrative acts.[159] Should the relevant EU organ fail to comply with these legislative obligations, Article 265 TFEU would be available to members of the public to assist them in ensuring that these particular obligations are fulfilled. As far as law enforcement is concerned, though, the Århus Regulation is likely to prove of limited value in practice to private plaintiffs given that its specific provisions relating to access to justice concern a limited range of beneficiaries (certain qualified NGEOs), do not lead to a genuinely independent review of EU institutional conduct and would not appear in light of recent case law to affect the EU treaty provisions on judicial review procedure (including, notably the rules on legal standing).[160] The Århus Regulation is considered in detail below in section 9.2.

9.1.4 *Articles 268 and 340(2) TFEU – non-contractual liability*

In certain limited circumstances, private persons are entitled to seek compensation from an EU institution where the latter causes damage as a result of a breach on its part of Union law. The relevant EU treaty provisions are contained in Articles 268 and 340(2)–(3) TFEU (formerly Articles 235 and 288(2)–(3) EC) which collectively constitute the legal framework establishing the parameters of non-contractual liability[161] of EU institutions vis-à-vis private persons. Article 340(2), the principal treaty provision, stipulates:

> In the case of non-contractual liability, the Union, shall, in accordance with the general principles common to the laws of the member states, make good any damage caused by its institutions or by its servants in the performance of their duties.

The GC has jurisdiction to adjudicate such claims.[162] In some respects the non-contractual liability procedure may be seen as far more open in general to litigation pursued by private plaintiffs as compared to the judicial review actions under Articles 263 and 265 TFEU. Unlike the latter two actions, the non-contractual liability procedure does not stipulate for any particular legal standing requirements. In addition, the time limit for filing a non-contractual liability action is far more generous, namely an action must be filed with the court within five years from the occurrence of the event giving rise to liability.[163] Moreover, legal proceedings may be pursued in respect of all types of legally binding EU institutional acts, it being irrelevant as to whether they are legislative or regulatory in nature.

One might think, though, perhaps with some justification, that this particular right of action is rarely going to be used in connection with private law enforcement of EU environmental law. Indeed, the author is unaware of any case successfully brought by any litigant under Article 340(2) as a means of holding a Union institution to account in respect of environmental damage and few books on EU environmental law consider its implications.[164] The procedure was evidently conceived originally as a legal means for persons to seek monetary compensation in respect of damage to personal economic (rather than collective ecological) interests sustained as a result of illegal EU decision-making, so as to effectively mirror the provision of civil law remedies provided under national law within the member states in respect of illicit conduct of national authorities. However, the non-contractual liability procedure under Article 340(2) TFEU is nevertheless an integral part of the system of judicial protection afforded by EU law in relation to illicit EU institutional conduct. It is by no means inconceivable that, potentially at least, the non-contractual liability procedure could play an important role in certain circumstances in relation to environmental law enforcement. For example, situations may arise where environmental damage or imminent threats of such damage arise or are exacerbated within EU member states as a result of flawed decisions or omissions at EU level, such as the authorisation of marketing of dangerous chemicals toxic to the environment; the permission for member states to (or continue to) exceed levels of air pollution damaging to health and the environment; the specification of catch limits for the purpose of continued fishing of species known to be endangered; or failures to take infringement action against member states that tolerate, or permit, illicit hunting of protected wild species. Indeed, there have been a number of instances over the years in which such situations have arisen, and private litigants have sought to challenge such EU institutional conduct by way of judicial review proceedings (typically via the annulment procedure under Article 263 TFEU).[165] If judicial review procedures may be invoked as a means of addressing illicit EU decisions and omissions affecting the environment, there is no convincing reason to doubt why non-contractual liability proceedings may not also be considered in principle as a means of holding the Union to account in respect of environmental damage perpetrated as a result of such illicit institutional conduct. Indeed, the EU treaty framework in Article 11 TFEU stipulates as a fundamental general requirement that environmental protection requirements must be integrated into the definition and implementation of Union policies and activities, in particular with a view to promoting sustainable development. Known as the integration principle, Article 11 should be considered as applicable to the interpretation and operation of the non-contractual liability procedure (and the other rights of action provided under EU law) so as to ensure that it constitutes an effective legal tool for the purposes of EU environmental law enforcement. Requiring EU institutions to take steps in order to remediate environmental damage attributed to them as a consequence of any illegal action on their part would be in alignment with the general objective underpinning Article 340(2) actions as recognised by the EU courts, namely to ensure as far as possible that the victim (in this case the environment) is placed in the situation that would have existed had the breach not occurred.[166]

Regrettably, it is fair to say that the non-contractual liability action, as currently interpreted by the CJEU, is ill-suited to assisting in the private enforcement of EU environmental law, notably litigation brought against EU institutions by private entities such as NGEOs in the public interest. Specifically, the substantive conditions applicable to the operation of non-contractual liability actions under the auspices of Article 340(2) TFEU, as developed by the Court, pose considerable difficulties for private persons seeking to hold EU institutions to account in respect of their actions or omissions in relation to the environmental policy sector. The CJEU has confirmed[167] that the conditions for establishing liability under those provisions in respect of EU institutional conduct are the same as the three core requirements in respect of state liability for member states,[168] namely that the EU rule of law infringed must be intended to confer rights on individuals, that its breach is sufficiently serious and that there is a direct causal link between the breach of the obligation by the defendant Union institution and the damage sustained by the injured parties.[169] These substantive requirements for proving liability, particularly the first and third ones, are unlikely to be met by private litigants taking legal action in relation to measures taken at EU level affecting the environment.

The first requirement, which demands that the EU norm breached must be intended to confer individual rights, self-evidently does not cover EU environmental protection norms that have no clear anthropocentric dimension to them. So whereas an EU institutional breach of the duty to adhere to minimum binding EU air quality or chemical standards would be likely to fall within the material scope of Article 340(2) TFEU, given the clear, direct link to public health protection,[170] breaches by EU institutions of EU rules on biodiversity protection would not. A non-contractual liability action brought by a private person to seek compensation on behalf of the environment in respect of an illegal act or omission on the part of the Union would, in the light of existing case law, be most likely to be dismissed as inadmissible on the ground that no personal individual (human) EU right would be at stake. For it is not evident from available CJEU case law that a breach of EU environmental legislation *per se* should be treated as constituting a breach of an individual right. Whilst protection of the environment is included amongst the fundamental rights contained in the EUCFR, the relevant Charter provision on environmental protection is crafted in broad terms without reference to a specific individual right. Article 37 EUCFR stipulates solely that a high level of environmental protection and improvement of the quality of the environment must be integrated into the EU's policies and ensured in accordance with the principle of sustainable development. The statutory text restates general policy-oriented commitments already set out in the existing constitutional fabric of the EU.[171] Accordingly, it is fairly clear that the current EU legal framework does not conceive of environmental protection in terms of protecting individual rights.

The second substantive requirement concerning the sufficiently seriously nature of breach of EU law introduces a degree of uncertainty in assessing which sorts of EU institutional violations of EU environmental law might attract liability. Akin to principles relating to state liability, where the EU institution has some discretion in relation to how it acts or fails to act, the test of sufficient seriousness is only likely to be met if it can be shown that the defendant institution manifestly disregards the limits of its discretion.[172] Only where there is an absence of discretion may mere infringement of a rule of EU (environmental) law be considered to meet the criterion of sufficient seriousness.[173] This requirement is not unreasonable, though, in requiring plaintiffs to prove beyond doubt that a rule of EU law has been breached, so that policy discretion established under democratically endorsed EU statutory frameworks are respected. In any event, the current 'substantial serious breach' test is a major improvement upon the CJEU's earlier and unduly restrictive approach which limited non-contractual liability in respect of EU legislative acts to instances which involved a 'sufficiently flagrant violation of a superior rule of law for the protection of the individual'.[174]

The third substantive requirement, that the plaintiff is to show a direct causal link (chain of causation) between the illegal conduct of the defendant Union institution and the damage sustained, may also prove problematic, in particular where a third party, such as a member state legislative or administrative authority, is also involved in the implementation of the contested EU-level decision. For example, the role of a defendant EU institution (e.g. European Commission) may have been to authorise or require measures carried out by national authorities, such as the licensing of a specific activity (e.g. marketing of a chemical). Where a national authority is directly involved in the implementation of a contested EU decision, the CJEU has held that a private litigant should in principle be expected to sue the national authority concerned rather than the EU institution under Article 340(2) TFEU,[175] unless no action can be brought at national level

against a national authority.[176] Where an EU institution has improperly authorised a measure taken by a national authority which is contrary to EU law, the
CJEU has likewise required legal action to be pursued (at least initially) at national
level.[177] It may also be difficult in environmental cases to demonstrate with sufficient precision for the purposes of Article 340(2), as interpreted hitherto by the
EU courts, damage caused or to be caused imminently by the defendant's conduct. CJEU case law has established that the plaintiff must prove the nature and
extent of damage sustained.[178] Although the wording in Article 340(2) refers to
'any damage', EU courts have yet to clarify whether environmental damage falls
within its scope. To date, the CJEU has confirmed that economic losses sustained
by plaintiffs, including loss of profits, are recoverable and must be identified with
sufficient precision.[179]

Apart from the above-mentioned procedural difficulties associated with
Article 340(2) TFEU, recourse to non-contractual liability litigation at EU level
by environmental interest litigants is problematic in other respects. For it is evident, in light of the EU treaty framework as interpreted hitherto by the CJEU,
that the objective of a non-contractual liability action against an EU institution
is the provision of a remedy in the form of damages (i.e. monetary compensation). However, such a remedy is clearly not suited to addressing environmental
problems that motivate environmental interest litigation. Specifically, monetary
compensation does not of itself necessarily lead to or secure any remediation of
environmental damage sustained as a result of illicit (in)action. The award of
compensation does not mean that such payment should or even may be used
to rectify environmental damage caused as a result of illicit Union institutional
conduct. It is fair to say, though, that this difficulty arises in relation to the environmental effectiveness of non-contractual civil liability actions in general, and
not simply at EU level. As noted above, the wording of Article 340(2) TFEU is
general, stipulating that liability requires the Union to 'make good' any damage
caused. This open-textured wording of the provision might suggest that the GC
may be able to decide upon a range of remedies in order to secure that, as far as
possible, the environment is placed in a situation that resembles as closely as possible the position prior to the breach. However, Article 340(2) also makes it clear
that liability is to be determined 'in accordance with the general principles common to the member states', which indicates that the nature of non-contractual
liability at EU level must essentially reflect that applicable in general at the level of
the EU member states under national law. This latter requirement places a con-
straint on the CJEU being able to develop novel or not widely shared principles of
law in relation to the non-contractual liability action. Accordingly, it is not apparent that Article 340(2) TFEU offers appropriate judicial remedies to secure rectification of environmental damage caused by illegal EU institutional (in)action. It is
interesting to note in this respect that the EU has taken legislative steps to address
the environmental protection shortcomings of existing civil liability mechanisms
at national level through Directive 2004/35 on environmental liability with regard
to the prevention and remedying of environmental damage. This particular measure is discussed in detail in Chapter 12.

9.1.4.1 Non-contractual liability and infringement actions

It is clear that non-contractual liability actions brought in respect of failures to take infringement proceedings against member states under Articles 258 and 260 TFEU are inadmissible in light of CJEU case law. As mentioned earlier in this chapter (in sections 9.1.1 and 9.1.3), the EU judiciary has confirmed on a number of occasions that the European Commission has discretion to institute infringement proceedings against member states over suspected violations of EU law. Even where a member state might be considered objectively to have breached EU environmental legislation, the Commission has no legal duty to bring enforcement proceedings, according to the existing case law.[180] An action for damages based on Article 340(2) TFEU, whilst usually constituting an autonomous form of action, is to be declared unfounded where it seeks to nullify the effects of allegedly unlawful acts an application for the annulment of which under Article 263 TFEU has been declared inadmissible.[181] Accordingly, such a non-contractual liability action would most likely be deemed inadmissible by the GC on the grounds that a breach of EU law would not have been committed on the part of the Commission, given the latter's wide discretion to decide whether or not to launch infringement proceedings.[182] In addition, given that the root of the particular environmental problem in such cases will lie fundamentally with the issue of member state non-compliance with EU environmental law, it will be inherently difficult in any event to show that a Commission failure to take up infringement proceedings constitutes a direct cause of illicit environmental damage.

9.1.4.2 Non-contractual liability and EU institutional conduct in relation to
        EU environmental policy

On account of the general initial points set out in this section, it is unlikely that private persons will be able to use the non-contractual liability action as an effective legal tool for the purposes of assisting in EU environmental law enforcement. In the absence of specific case law from the EU courts on the question of whether, and if so to what extent, environmental damage claims may fall within the scope of Article 340(2) TFEU it is unclear what impact the judicial procedure may have. In practice, in order to gain further clarity on this area, it will most likely be up to NGEOs to bring test case litigation in order to draw out from the EU judiciary the legal boundaries of the treaty provision, in particular interpreted in light of the integration principle set down in Article 11 TFEU as well as the obligation contained in Article 9(4) of the Århus Convention that contracting parties ensure that effective remedies are provided in relation to their access-to-justice commitments.

Brief mention must be made here also of the potential impact of the Århus Regulation 1367/06 on the area of non-contractual liability. The regulation, discussed in detail below in section 9.2, confers a right for certain qualified NGEOs to be able to request internal review of certain administrative acts adopted at EU level. Wennerås has argued that such NGEOs have rights to seek reparation in respect of any damage caused by sufficiently serious infringements occurring as a result of breaches of the internal review procedure or resulting from failures by EU institutions to comply with a GC judgment annulling an internal review decision in accordance with Article 266 TFEU.[183] However, it is difficult to see how the Århus Regulation might have anything significant to add to existing non-contractual liability rights of private persons under Article 340(2) TFEU. It appears clear from the emerging case law of the EU courts that the Århus Regulation, just like any piece of secondary legislation, may not affect the conditions of liability of EU institutions determined by the TFEU.[184] Moreover, it is difficult to see how a flawed internal review procedure could be, to any significant extent, a genuine cause of alleged damage, as this would logically flow from the EU act or omission requested to be internally reviewed. Again, it is likely that these will remain murky legal waters until the CJEU has an opportunity to clarify the impact, if any, of the regulation on environmental non-contractual liability claims pursued against EU institutions.

9.2 The Århus Regulation 1367/06 and access to environmental justice at EU level

With the European Union's signature of the 1998 Århus Convention in 1998 and formal ratification in 2005, it was clear that specific internal legislative changes were required to be introduced to the Union's legal framework in order to ensure that the three pillars of the Convention concerning access to information, participation in environmental decision-making and access to environmental justice were fully applied at EU institutional level.[185] The statutory arrangements existing at the time were deficient, particularly in the area of access to justice as already outlined above in section 9.1. In order to address this, in 2003 the European Commission proposed[186] to arrange legislative implementation via a single legislative instrument in the form of a regulation. Eventually, the legislative process was completed in 2006 with the adoption of the Århus Regulation (Regulation 1367/2006 on the application of the provisions of the Århus Convention on Access to Information, Public Participation in Decision-making and Access to Justice in Environmental Matters to Community institutions and bodies).[187] The Århus Regulation entered into force on 28 June 2007. This section focuses on the regulation's impact with regard to implementation of the Convention's third-pillar requirements on access to environmental justice. The relevant provisions of the Convention have already been considered at the beginning of this chapter.

The Århus Regulation contains a cluster of provisions which introduced some changes to the state of EU rules on rights of private persons to ensure that EU institutions and bodies adhere to EU environmental law. One of its purposes is, in contributing to the full implementation of the Århus Convention, to grant access to justice in environmental matters at EU level.[188] Specifically, Articles 10–12 of the legislative instrument[189] confer specific rights on certain privileged private persons (certain types of NGEO) to be able to invoke a special internal review procedure where they consider that an EU institution or other body, not acting in either a judicial or legislative capacity, has acted or failed to act in contravention of EU environmental legislation. The two key rights may be summarised here. First, qualifying NGEOs may submit a request to a relevant Union organ to undertake an internal review of a measure or omissions they consider to constitute a breach of EU environmental legislation, with the EU organ being obliged to submit a reasoned response within 18 weeks at the latest (Article 10). Secondly, where the NGEO concerned is dissatisfied with the response, the regulation specifies that it may institute proceedings before the GC 'in accordance with the relevant provisions of the Treaty' (Article 12). The Commission has published online an informal, non-binding guide on the operation of the regulation.[190]

A number of important legal questions and issues, as yet not fully answered, have arisen as a result of the Århus Regulation's promulgation. These include most notably whether the regulation adequately compensates for the deficiencies in the scope of judicial protection afforded under the EU treaty, discussed in section 9.1 above, for the purpose of EU compliance with Article 9 of the Convention. As will be seen below, it appears that the Århus Regulation falls short by some distance of being able address the compliance gap problem. The rest of the this section will be divided up into considering various key elements of the regulation in turn, namely its scope and review procedures, as interpreted in light of recent emerging case law of the EU judiciary.

9.2.1 *Material and personal scope of the Århus Regulation's access to justice provisions*

It is important from the outset to be clear about the personal and material scope of the access-to-justice provisions contained within the Århus Regulation. Analysis of this aspect reveals that the legislative instrument opens up review of Union activities affecting environmental matters only to a relatively limited extent.

9.2.1.1 Personal scope

The Århus Regulation specifies that only certain qualifying persons are able to take advantage of the review procedures set out in the instrument's access to justice provisions. The relevant eligibility criteria are set out in Article 11. Specifically, four basic conditions must be fulfilled in order for a private person to be entitled to invoke the review procedure, namely that (1) the person is an independent and non profit-making legal person in accordance with a member state's national law or practice;[191] (2) the person has the primary stated objective of promoting environmental protection in the context of environmental law;[192] (3) the person has existed for over two years and is actively pursuing the above-mentioned environmental protection objective;[193] and (4) that the subject matter of the internal request is covered by the person's objective and activities.[194]

The original Commission proposal had set additional criteria which would have narrowed eligibility still further,[195] although it also made it clear that NGEOs would not have to fulfil the classic requirements of *locus standi* expected in judicial review proceedings at national level (demonstration of a sufficient interest or main-taining an impairment of rights).[196] The Commission had some concerns of being unduly burdened by review requests if eligibility criteria were not set sufficiently tightly in respect of the internal review procedure. It did, however, acknowledge in its explanatory memorandum to the original draft regulation that its concerns were doubted in other quarters.[197] In the event, the additional proposed standing criteria were subsequently dropped in the course of legislative negotiations with the EP and Council of the EU. As envisaged by the regulation,[198] the Commission has adopted rules to ensure transparent and consistent application of the standing criteria.[199]

It is important to note from the above that the Århus Regulation only confers review rights on certain persons within civil society, namely NGEOs able to fulfil the Article 11 criteria. It does not confer review rights on members of the public in general. Accordingly, private persons unable to meet the standing criteria (such as natural persons) will only be entitled to seek legal review of EU acts and omis-sions affecting the environment via the standard judicial procedures contained in the EU treaty provisions. It should be recalled in this context that Article 9 of the Århus Convention obliges contracting parties to ensure that they provide adequate review procedures for members of the public, not just NGEOs. On this point alone the EU would appear clearly to fall short of its obligations in rela-tion to Århus, given that natural persons' as well as commercial legal persons' access-to-justice rights remain confined to the judicial procedures contained in the TFEU.

As far as the range of EU organs covered by the Århus Regulation is concerned, the legislative instrument ensures that it has a wide reach so that 'any public insti-tution, body, office or agency' established by or on the basis of the EU treaty framework (TFEU) may be the subject of an internal review procedure, except for those acting in a judicial capacity or a legislative capacity other than in relation to the field of access to environmental information.[200] Accordingly, the regula-tion quite rightly does not confine itself to the core EU institutions, as a num-ber of other Union bodies may be engaged in environmental decision-making. The exclusion in relation to authorities acting in judicial and legislative capacities reflects the legal parameters set by the Århus Convention, as explained below.

9.2.1.2 Material scope

As far as the material scope of the Århus Regulation is concerned, it is clear from the statutory text that the drafters of the legislative instrument were keen to ensure that the internal review mechanism did not go beyond the minimum requirements of the Århus Convention. The Convention makes it clear that contracting parties are obliged to ensure that legal review mechanisms are provided to the public only in respect of administrative acts and omissions of their public authorities, so that bodies or institutions acting in a judicial or legislative capacity are essentially excluded from its remit.[201] In recognition of this delimitation in the international agreement, the Århus Regulation specifies that only EU-level administrative acts and omissions may fall within the scope of an internal review request. Article 10(1) of the regulation states:

> 1. Any non-governmental organisation which meets the criteria set out in Article 11 is entitled to make a request for internal review to the Community institution or body that has adopted an administrative act under environmental law[202] or, in the case of an alleged administrative omission, should have adopted such an act.

For the purposes of the Århus Regulation, acts by EU organs acting in a judicial or legislative capacity are expressly excluded from the material scope of the legislative instrument.[203] The regulation also excludes measures taken by EU organs when they engage as an administrative review body, such as the European Commission managing infringement proceedings under Articles 258 and 260 TFEU or the European Ombudsman handling citizen complaints of EU institutional maladministration under Article 228 TFEU.[204] Accordingly, the Århus Regulation does not incorporate a specific right of review regarding decisions and failures to act on the part of the Commission with respect to infringement action pursued against member states or where the Commission otherwise pursues legal action under the EU treaty framework. The Commission has already had opportunity to make use of this particular exclusion in the Århus Regulation.[205] However, whether it accords with the Convention is highly questionable, given that the international agreement only excludes acts undertaken by entities performing judicial (and not administrative review) roles.[206] No doubt at some stage this legal point will be subject to scrutiny before the EU courts and/or the Århus Compliance Committee.

The Århus Regulation defines 'environmental law' as meaning EU environmental protection legislation in broad terms. Specifically, Article 2(1)(f) of the instrument states that the term is to mean any Union legislation which, irrespective of its legal basis, contributes to the pursuit of the objectives of EU policy on the environment as set out in the EU treaty framework (now contained in Article 191 TFEU), namely preserving, protecting and improving the quality of the environment; protecting human health; the prudent and rational utilisation of natural resources; and promoting measures at international level to deal with regional or worldwide environmental problems. This broad definition indicates that EU environmental legislation may be based on EU treaty provisions other than Article 192 TFEU and still constitute 'environmental law' for the purposes of the Århus Regulation. Notable examples would include single market measures designed to improve the environmental quality of products or goods,[207] agricultural measures designed to improve ecological standards in farming activities[208] or measures dealing with environmental improvements in the transport sector.[209]

The material scope of the Århus Regulation is, as Article 10 stipulates, focused upon administrative conduct (acts and omissions) of EU organs. Article 2(1) of the regulation provides a definition of administrative conduct. As far as administrative acts are concerned the following narrow definition is provided by Article 2(1)(g):

> (g) 'administrative act' means any measure of individual scope under environmental law, taken by a Community institution or body, and having legally binding and external effects.

Administrative omissions are also defined in a narrow manner in Article 2(1)(h), resulting from the fact that the definition is predicated upon the definition of administrative act. Article 2(1)(h) states:

> (h) 'administrative omission' means any failure of a Community institution or body to adopt an administrative act as defined in (g).

The original Commission proposal did not require that an administrative act would have to be of individual scope, simply requiring that it have legally binding force and external effects.[210] Similarly, the draft regulation applied a wider definition of administrative omission that simply encompassed a failure on the part of an EU organ to take administrative action under EU environmental law where it was legally required to do so.[211]

However, as a result of pressure in particular from the Council of the EU in legislative negotiations, the criterion of 'individual scope' was incorporated within the definition of administrative act.[212] No doubt intended to ensure that the criteria for legal standing relating to internal review requests should mirror as far as possible the rules on *locus standi* under the judicial review procedures within the TFEU (Articles 263 and 265 TFEU), the effect of the requirement of 'individual scope' meant that the range of acts capable of being challenged would be severely limited. Specifically, a requester for an internal review would now have to demonstrate that the contested act was of individual concern to them. At the same time, the added criterion undoubtedly reflected a concern that EU legislative measures of general concern should not be capable of being questioned via the internal review procedure.

The particular problem with the incorporation of the criterion of 'individual scope' is that it imposes a legal standing requirement that is unduly onerous, contrary to obligations underpinning the Århus Convention. Specifically, the criterion has the effect of making it effectively impossible for NGEOs to seek review of the vast majority of administrative acts and omissions affecting EU environmental policy, given that the acts contested or failed to be taken must be structured so as to be of general application and not targeted at specific individuals. The Convention does not provide any justification for the incorporation of standing criteria that automatically block the review of administrative measures or omissions. The Commission's website on Århus internal review requests discloses a considerable list of requests to review Union administrative measures since 2008 that have been rejected as inadmissible on account of the failure of the requesting NGEO to demonstrate that the contested act was of individual concern.[213] These include, for instance, attempts to review EU measures stipulating maximum pesticide levels, authorising the marketing of chemicals and GMO products and approving an extended deadline for a member state to comply with EU air quality requirements.

However, the position has changed quite significantly in the light of recent case law of the GC. Recently, in two judgments decided in 2012 (*Stichting en Milieu & PAN Europe*[214] and *Vereniging Milieudefensie*[215] which are considered in more detail below in section 9.2.3) the GC held that the definition of administrative act adopted in Article 10(1) of the Århus Regulation is invalid, on the grounds of its being contrary to the requirements of the Århus Convention. At the time of writing, the two rulings were the subject of pending appeals before the CJEU. If, as is likely, the CJEU endorses the GC rulings on this point, the application of the 'individual scope' criterion will have to be dropped and the Århus Regulation revised accordingly to ensure that only EU acts adopted in accordance with a legislative procedure would be excluded from the remit of the regulation.

The current definition of 'administrative act' contained in the Århus Regulation may be criticised in other respects, too. Specifically, it is questionable whether the requirements of the act to be legally binding and having external effects accord with the Århus Convention. Specifically, it is not clear whether these requirements are permitted under the Convention, which in Article 9(3) simply obliges each contracting party to ensure that review is provided in relation to acts or omissions which contravene the party's environmental law. It is, for example, possible to envisage that a technically non-binding measure might contravene EU environmental legal requirements and at the same time have serious consequences for the application of EU environmental policy, such as a Commission opinion on questions of overriding public interest relating to proposed development on sites protected under the Habitats Directive 92/43.[216] The fact that non-binding acts may not be capable of being the subject of judicial review proceedings is irrelevant, given that the internal review procedure is a distinct process.[217] Moreover, the requirement of an act needing to have 'external effects', unless construed narrowly to concern only internal or other non-definitive communications of EU organs, may also serve to exclude certain EU measures that have direct influence on the implementation of EU environmental policy. However, the term is not defined in the Århus Regulation and Pallemaerts has noted that the Commission has employed a wider interpretation that has had the effect of denying the possibility of internal review even though an act has legitimised certain activities contested by the requesting NGEO as being in breach of EU environmental law.[218] Specifically, he cites the example of a review request filed by a Czech NGEO (Ekologicky Pravni) in 2008, challenging the Commission's decision to adopt an operational programme for EU funding to be made available to the Czech Republic. The request was rejected as inadmissible on the grounds that the EU decision had no external effects, since the member state remained free to decide upon authorisation of individual projects. In a similar vein, the Commission has also submitted that decisions by it to appeal GC rulings have neither legally binding nor external effects for the purposes of Article 10(1) of the Århus Regulation.[219]

9.2.2 *Review procedures under the Århus Regulation's access-to-justice provisions*

As mentioned earlier, the Århus Regulation's access-to-justice provisions offer NGEOs meeting the instrument's eligibility criteria[220] the opportunity to start a special internal review process in relation to EU administrative acts and omissions which they consider to have occurred in breach of EU environmental legislation. The review process is set out in Article 10 of Title IV of the regulation. The Commission has adopted rules on its general application[221] and has also amended its own Rules of Procedure in order to detail internal procedures in cases where it is charged with conducting a review.[222] This is complemented by a separate clause (Article 12) detailing that requesting NGEOs may institute proceedings before the Court of Justice of the EU 'in accordance with the relevant provisions of the Treaty'. The latter provision was evidently introduced to cater for situations where an NGEO is dissatisfied with the internal review process and to facilitate an appeal process to the EU judiciary.[223] The legislative provisions will be examined in turn.

The internal review process, as detailed in Article 10 of the Århus Regulation, sets out the particular procedural requirements involved. The process is commenced by qualifying NGEOs filing a request for internal review to the relevant EU institution or body which is alleged to have committed the contested act or omission. The request must be made in writing stating the grounds of review and not later than six weeks after the act's adoption, notification or publication, whichever is the later, or not later than six weeks after the date when the act was required in the case of an omission.[224] Upon receipt of a request, the EU organ is obliged to consider it unless 'clearly unsubstantiated', and is in principle to have 12 weeks to make a written reasoned response.[225] The 12-week period may be extended only up to a maximum of 18 weeks in total, the EU organ being obliged to inform the NGEO of the reasons for any delay.[226]

Under the Århus Convention contracting parties must ensure that administrative or judicial procedures established for the purpose of challenging the legality of acts and omissions are 'fair' and 'effective'.[227] It is questionable whether the EU, in vesting the Union organ responsible for the contested conduct with responsibility and power to discharge the internal review process, has complied with these Convention requirements. Under the Århus Regulation, no independent body is required to assess the review request. As far as the European Commission is concerned, its Rules of Procedure, as amended, specifically stipulate that the Director-General or Head of Department within the Commission services responsible for the contested conduct have power to determine the admissibility of review requests,[228] and that it is ultimately for the member of the Commission responsible for the application of the provisions on the basis of which the contested act was adopted or omission occurred to determine whether EU environmental law was breached.[229] The structural conflict of interest established by the review procedures under the aegis of the Århus Regulation raises serious doubts about whether the internal review process is fit for purpose in terms of meeting the Convention's requirements.[230]

If the requesting NGEO is dissatisfied with the internal review response from the EU institution or body concerned, it may decide to attempt to seek recourse to the GC by way of judicial review under Articles 263 and 265 TFEU. The Århus Regulation envisages two types of legal challenge, namely (1) where the NGEO is seeking to challenge the EU's response on the substantive legal merits and (2) where the NGEO seeks to challenge the EU organ's failure to act in compliance with the internal review procedures. The relevant provisions are contained in Article 12 of the regulation which states:

1.   The non-governmental organisation which made the request for internal review pursuant to Article 10 may institute proceedings before the Court of Justice in accordance with the relevant provisions of the Treaty.
2.   Where the Community institution of body fails to act in accordance with Article 10(2) or (3) the non-governmental organisation may institute proceedings before the Court of Justice in accordance with the relevant provisions of the Treaty.

The effect of these provisions have been the source of considerable debate. Specifically, a key legal issue has been whether they provide specific rights of access to judicial review, distinct from the standard provisions set out under the TFEU. The Commission intended with its original legislative proposal's provisions on EU judicial proceedings to ensure that NGEOs eligible to file an internal review request would be conferred legal standing to challenge the EU institutional response on the grounds of its alleged inadequacy to ensure compliance with EU environmental law or on the grounds of its procedural deficiencies.[231] However, on account of resistance from the Council of the EU in the legislative negotiations, the provisions on court proceedings were watered down considerably and resulted in rather ambiguous wording raising doubts as to whether the legislative outcome, in the form of Article 12 of the definitive regulation, intended for there to be guaranteed a distinct right of access to judicial review.[232] Cryptically, the legislative wording appears to lay particular emphasis upon the words 'in accordance with the Treaty'.[233] Moreover, recent case law of the GC has held[234] that the provisions of the Århus Regulation may not have the effect of altering the legal standing requirements for judicial review under the TFEU, a finding that completely contradicts the Commission's original intentions for the legislative provisions on court proceedings. The GC's case law is examined more closely in the next section.

9.2.3 EU case law on the Århus Regulation's impact on judicial review

One of the most important questions concerning the contribution of the Århus Regulation 1367/06 in compliance with the terms of the Århus Convention has been whether its legislative provisions effect an improvement upon the state of access to environmental justice with respect to EU institutional conduct. As noted in section 9.1.1 and 9.1.3 above, the stringency of the rules on legal standing for natural and legal persons applicable to judicial review proceedings under Articles 263 and 265 TFEU have hampered the Union's ability to ensure compliance with the Convention's obligations on access to justice. The establishment of the internal review mechanism under the Århus Convention raised some hopes that matters might take a turn for the better. Ultimately, the reaction of the EU judiciary to the regulation's provisions would prove crucial.

At the time of writing, two cases have arisen which have enabled the GC to be able to provide judicial interpretation of the meaning and effect of key provisions in Title IV of the Århus Regulation concerning internal review and access to justice, namely *Stichting en Milieu & PAN Europe* and *Vereniging Milieudefensie*.[235] Both were decided on the same day (14 June 2012) and were at the time of writing subject to appeals before the CJEU.[236] Both cases address similar legal issues, having involved judicial review challenges brought by NGEOs dissatisfied with the outcome of internal review requests. In *Stichting en Milieu* two NGEOs had requested review of a Commission regulation[237] that amended the Union's legislative instrument[238] on maximum residue levels of pesticides in or on food and feed of plant and animal origin. In *Vereniging Milieudefensie* two NGEOs requested an internal review be undertaken in relation to a Commission decision to grant an extension to the Dutch government to the time limit set down by EU air quality legislation[239] regarding compliance with Union limit values in relation to emissions of nitrogen dioxide and particulate matter (PM10).[240] The Commission, supported by the Council of the EU and the EP, rejected the requests on grounds that the internal review mechanism in Article 10 of the Århus Regulation only applied to administrative acts of individual scope as stipulated in Article 10 in conjunction with Article 2(1)(g) of the regulation, and not measures of general application like the ones contested by the NGEOs.

In both cases the GC, contrary to the views of the political EU institutions, ruled that the NGEOs had legal standing to request that internal reviews be conducted by the Commission as responsible administrative authority. By way of a starting point, the Court affirmed that it was necessary to determine the validity of the requirements of the Århus Regulation in light of the Århus Convention, particularly bearing in mind that under Article 216(2) TFEU the Convention is binding on EU institutions in the wake of ratification of the international agreement[241] and that it was appropriate to assess the validity of the regulation in light of the Convention, given that the regulation was intended to implement the latter.[242] Noting that the scope of the obligations under Article 9(3) of the Århus Convention regarding access-to-justice matters applied to acts and omissions of public authorities, to the exclusion of judicial and legislative measures, the GC held that it was not justified that Article 10(1) of the Århus Regulation (in conjunction with Article 2(1)) delimited its material scope to measures of 'individual scope'. It noted that the reference to 'individual scope' in the regulation meant that certain non-legislative measures of general application would be excluded from the regulation's scope, whereas under the Convention only legislative and judicial acts were outside the scope of review.[243] In the two cases, neither of the contested acts had been adopted by way of one of the legislative procedures[244] foreseen under the TFEU, but were instead instances of measures adopted by the Commission by reason of powers delegated to it from the Union legislature. Accordingly, the GC confirmed that the limitation of the material scope of the term 'administrative act' in Article 10(1) of the Århus Regulation to measures of 'individual scope', as defined in Article 2(1)(g) of the instrument, was invalid under EU law.[245] In both cases the individual decisions rejecting the plaintiffs' internal review requests as inadmissible were duly annulled by the court.

In both of its judgments, the GC also considered the legal significance of the Århus Regulation's provisions on access to the EU judiciary, as set out in Article 12 of the regulation. The GC confirmed that, according to its interpretation of the legislation, Article 12 of the regulation made no impact or change on the standard requirements of *locus standi* applicable to natural and legal persons under the TFEU judicial review procedures (Articles 263 and 265 TFEU). According to the court, whatever the scope of internal review provided under Article 10 of the Århus Regulation, this did not affect the requirement that the conditions for admissibility of actions under Article 263 TFEU had to be always fulfilled if an action is brought before the EU judiciary.[246]

As a result, the GC confirmed effectively that the standard strict requirement of 'direct and individual concern' regarding access to the GC via judicial review proceedings still had to be fulfilled by NGEOs eligible to file internal review requests under the Århus Regulation. The regulation did not produce an automatic right of legal standing as anticipate by the Commission's original legislative proposal for implementing the Århus Convention. The GC appears to make a sharp distinction between standing requirements for internal and judicial review purposes.

An important related legal issue arising (but not clarified) from the GC's rulings in *Stichting* and *Vereniging* is whether participation by an NGEO in an internal review request will render the NGEO individually concerned for the purposes of Article 263 TFEU, so as to enable the NGEO to have legal standing to seek annulment of the contested EU administrative act before the GC. On the one hand, the GC's and CJEU's case law on the effect of participation with respect to *locus standi* requirements applicable to judicial review actions arguably leads one to be sceptical about the possibilities here. Generally the GC and CJEU have not viewed the existence of participatory rights provided under Union legislation as a feature that renders a person individually concerned for the purposes enabling them to instigate annulment proceedings in order to seek review of a contested EU act on substantive grounds. The GC has acknowledged, for example in its *Eurofer* ruling,[247] that participation in a process by which a measure is adopted at EU level may fulfil the requirement of individual concern insofar as the plaintiff seeks to uphold procedural guarantees accorded to them under EU legislation. However, the GC also held that where a person enjoys such a procedural right this will not, as a general rule, endow the person with legal standing to contest the legality of a Union measure in terms of its substantive content.[248] The dispute in *Eurofer* arose in connection with allocations of greenhouse gas emission allowances issued under the aegis of the Union's Emissions Trading (ETS) Directive[249] for the purposes of the third period of the EU's emissions trading scheme. The plaintiffs submitted

that they had legal standing to challenge the legality of the Commission's allocation decision, taking into account, *inter alia*, that the ETS Directive required the
Commission to undertake consultation of stakeholders in defining the allocation
benchmarks for particular industrial sectors. The GC held that any right of the
plaintiffs to be heard does not of itself confer standing to challenge the substantive
legal merits of an act. Nor, in this instance, was it apparent from the ETS Directive
that the plaintiffs should be accorded a right to challenge the substantive content
of any measure passed under the directive's legislative framework.[250] According
to the GC, the precise scope of an individual's right of action against a Union act
depends on his legal position as defined in Union law with a view to protecting the
legitimate interest afforded to him.[251] The GC's narrow interpretation of 'individual concern' effectively reflects earlier case law of the CJEU.[252]

However, it is submitted that in the case of the Århus Regulation, eligible
NGEOs are vested with guarantees that go beyond mere procedural rights. The
very essence of the regulation is to confer upon NGEOs (meeting Article 11
requirements) a right to seek a review of an EU administrative measure on substantive grounds under Article 10. The regulation contains a right vested in the
NGEO to be heard by the relevant EU organ on legal submissions concerning
the legality validity of a specific Union administrative measure on the basis of
its alleged non-compliance with EU environmental law. This is a special feature
of the Århus Regulation that distinguishes it from other pieces of legislation that
grant general consultation rights. Accordingly, it is submitted that the exercise of a
right to request a review under Article 10 of the Århus Regulation should be construed as a factor that leads to identifying the NGEO as individually concerned for
the purposes of annulment proceedings so that the NGEO will have legal standing to test the substantive legality of an EU act. Accordingly, the fact that Article 12 of the Århus Regulation does not indicate that any particular guarantees
are to be provided to NGEOs regarding access to the EU judiciary is not material, given that an NGEO should be considered as being individually concerned
by the fact of its engagement in the internal review process. The situation of an
NGEO having invoked the internal review process should be distinguished from
situations in cases (assessed above) such as *Inuit*,[253] in which the plaintiff could not
be distinguished from other stakeholders, and *Eurofer*,[254] in which the plaintiff was
not vested with legislative rights to test the substance of the contested act. This
important legal issue concerning the impact of the Århus Regulation on the test
of 'individual concern' remains, though, as yet unclarified by the EU courts.

9.3 Internal review under the Ship Recycling Regulation 1257/13

Prior to concluding this chapter, brief mention should also be made of the special internal review procedure housed within the EU's Ship Recycling Regulation
1257/13,[255] which is intended to serve as implementation of the 2009 Hong Kong
International Convention for the Safe and Environmentally Sound Recycling of
Ships (HK Convention).[256] The EU Ship Recycling Regulation 1257/13, which is

due to come into force by the end of 2018, requires, *inter alia*, that owners of ships covered by the HK Convention and flying the flag of a Union member state must ensure that the ships destined to be recycled are only recycled at certain approved recycling facilities, namely those specified in a designated European List.[257] Under the regulation, member states must notify to the Commission those ship recycling facilities which they have authorised as complying with the requirements of environmental and health protection set down in Article 13 of the legislative instrument; the requirements need to be fulfilled in order for a facility to be eligible for entry on the European List.[258] Recycling facilities located in third countries may also be entered on the European List if they fulfil the same requirements.[259] Whilst member states have specific duties to ensure correct implementation of the Ship Recycling Regulation at national level, the Commission has overall responsibility for updating the European List as well as making sure that member states discharge their obligations appropriately.

The Ship Recycling Regulation 1257/13 incorporates an interesting internal review procedure as a means of assisting the Commission in its role of monitoring the adherence by non-EU recycling facilities of the regulation's safety requirements. The review procedure bears similarities with the one incorporated in the Århus Regulation. Under the review procedure certain private persons may request the Commission to take action in relation to alleged breaches of the legislative instrument by non-EU recycling facilities. Action that could be taken by the Commission includes, notably, removal of substandard recycling facilities from the European List and/or liaising with member state authorities which have responsibilities under Article 22 of the regulation to penalise shipowners who violate the regulation's requirements to ensure safe recycling of vessels. Article 23 of the Ship Recycling Regulation entitles the following persons to request action from the Commission in relation to alleged breaches of the regulation's minimum safety requirements by a recycling facility used by EU shipping in a non-EU country: any natural or legal person affected or likely to be affected by such a breach; any natural or legal person having a sufficient interest in environmental decision-making relating to such a breach; or any NGEO fulfilling the eligibility requirements set down in Article 11 of the Århus Regulation.[260] Where the documentation accompanying a particular request for Commission action shows in a plausible manner that a non-EU recycling facility breaches the regulation's safety requirements, the Commission is obliged to consider the request, giving the facility's owners an opportunity to be heard on the matter.[261] The Commission is required then 'without delay' to inform the person(s) filing the request for action of the reasons underlying its decision to accede to or refuse the request.[262] Unlike the Århus Regulation, though, the Ship Recycling Regulation makes no reference to recourse to judicial review proceedings in the event of a person being dissatisfied with the Commission's response to their request. The internal review mechanism is evidently intended to complement the regulation's obligations concerning member state enforcement of the instrument's minimum safety requirements, notably contained in Article 22 on penalties and inter-state co-operation relating to combating circumvention of those requirements.

Article 23 of the Ship Recycling Regulation represents an innovative approach to law enforcement, taking into account in particular the lack of member state jurisdiction to assert oversight of non-EU facilities. Evidently based on the internal review process enshrined in the Århus Regulation, the review procedure in Article 23 to some extent enhances the powers of private person to monitor and influence the Commission in its supervisory role. So, for example, failure on the part of the Commission to respond to a request would entitle the person filing a request to bring an action in respect of a failure to act under Article 265 TFEU against the Commission, given that the latter has a legal obligation to respond to a request. In addition, the requesting party as addressee (and other individually concerned third parties such as the non-EU facility in question) would have legal standing to bring annulment proceedings under Article 263 TFEU against a Commission decision failing to adhere to the procedural requirements foreseen in Article 23. However, just as in the case of the review procedure in the Århus Regulation, the internal review procedure enshrined in the Ship Recycling Regulation does not give the requesting person or other party any right to compel specific action to be undertaken by the Commission; the decision on whether to act and if so, in what form, rests with the Commission.

9.4 Some brief reflections on the impact of the EU's access to environmental justice framework in relation to EU institutional conduct

It is evident from the above exploration of the various EU rights of private persons to seek legal review of EU-level administrative (in)action in relation to the environmental sector that it remains both complex as well as problematic in terms of assessing whether these rights ensure EU compliance with the third-pillar requirements of Århus Convention. It is evident that the various rights of action or other judicial procedures available to natural and legal persons in order to challenge the legality of EU institutional conduct before the EU courts under the TFEU seem inadequate in themselves to meet the requirements of Article 9(3)–(4) of the Convention. Notably, notwithstanding some minor amendments made to the annulment action by virtue of the 2007 Lisbon Treaty, access to the EU judiciary for private persons via this crucial procedure remains very limited under Article 263(4) TFEU. The stringent legal standing test of 'direct and individual concern' remains very much at the heart of Article 263 TFEU proceedings, as confirmed by CJEU case law. Other judicial procedures have remained virtually untouched by Lisbon (i.e. action in respect of a failure to act (Article 265 TFEU), preliminary ruling procedure (Article 267 TFEU) and non-contractual liability proceedings (Article 268 TFEU)) and their contribution towards enhancing access to environmental justice in respect of EU institutional conduct remains in practice similarly very limited.

Whether the Århus Regulation 1367/06 has improved matters remains unresolved, and the initial case law from the GC on its impact is not encouraging. A number of problems and limitations attend the legislative instrument. First, the internal review procedure established by Article 10 of the regulation does not establish a right of review before an entity independent of the EU organ having been responsible for the contested administrative act or omission. Secondly, the internal review procedure is not open to members of the public in general, but only to certain NGEOs. These limitations overshadow the fact that the GC has held that the material scope of the internal review procedure, in line with the terms of the Århus Convention, is not to be confined to administrative acts of an 'individual scope' (as prescribed by the definition in Article 2(1)(g) of the instrument). Thirdly, it is not yet clear what impact the Århus Regulation has in relation to the issue of access to judicial review proceedings for natural and legal persons under Article 263/265 TFEU. On the one hand, the GC has held in *Stichting en Milieu* and *Vereniging* that, irrespective of the scope of measures falling within the remit of the internal review procedure in Article 10 of the Århus Regulation, the conditions of admissibility with regard to rights of action before the GC (such as annulment proceedings under Article 263 TFEU) remain governed by the principles established under the TFEU. Accordingly, the standard legal standing requirements of 'direct and individual concern' applicable to judicial review proceedings pursued by private plaintiffs under Articles 263 and 265 TFEU remain intact. The GC feels supported in its view by the terms of Article 12 of the regulation, which specify that NGEOs may institute proceedings before the Court of Justice 'in accordance with the relevant provisions of the Treaty'. However, what remains unclear is whether participation by an NGEO in an internal review procedure will enable it to fulfil the crucial test of individual concern for the purposes of wishing to seek judicial review of a response to an internal review request with which it is dissatisfied, for the purposes of testing the contested EU institutional conduct on its legal merits. Until that legal issue is resolved by the EU judiciary, compliance with Article 9 of the Convention by the Union will remain a live issue.

Notes

1   2161 UNTS 447. The text of the Convention is accessible on the following UNECE website: www.unece.org.
2   See Art. 19 of the Convention.
3   Council Decision 2005/370 on the conclusion, on behalf of the European Union of the Convention on access to information, public participation in decision-making and access to justice in environmental matters (OJ 2005 L124/1). Ratification by the Union was disappointingly belated, coming seven years after its signature as an original signatory in 1998.
4   Case 181/73 *Haegemann*.
5   The Court has confirmed that in order for a provision of an international agreement concluded by the EU to be directly effective in EU law regard must be had to the wording, nature and purpose of the particular agreement, as well as assessment as to whether the particular provision of the agreement being relied upon is sufficiently precise and unconditional: see e.g. Case 104/81 *Kupferberg*.
6   Case C-249/09 *Lesoochranárske zoskupenie*.
7   OJ 2006 L264/13.
8   References in the Convention to 'national law' include EU law as far as the Union is concerned: see e.g. the Århus Compliance Committee report, *Findings and Recommendations with Regard to Communication*, ACCC/C/2008/32 (Part 1) of 14 April 2011, esp. paras. 77 *et seq.*

9 'Public authority' is defined in Art. 2(2)(d) of the Convention as including the institutions of any regional economic organisation party to the international agreement.

10 See Art. 267(2) TFEU.

11 See notably ibid., Art. 267(3) which requires a reference to be made to the CJEU on questions relating to the interpretation of EU law or on the validity of EU acts from member state courts or tribunals against whose decisions there is no judicial remedy under national law.

12 See esp. Case 314/85 *Foto Frost*.

13 See Art. 256(1) TFEU.

14 Ibid., Art. 256(3) envisages the possibility of the GC being conferred jurisdiction to give preliminary rulings (under Art. 267 TFEU) by virtue of an amendment to the Statute of the Court of Justice. However, this step has not (yet) been taken.

15 See ibid., Art. 256(1), second subpara.

16 Recommendations and opinions have no binding force, as defined by ibid., Art. 288(5). This provides the justification for their being outside the scope of annulment proceedings under Art. 263 (ibid.).

17 See ibid., Art. 263(1).

18 A full list of EU agencies is provided on the following Union website: http://europa. eu/about-eu/agencies/index_en.htm.

19 Art. III-365 EUC (of the Treaty Establishing a Constitution for Europe (OJ 2004 C310).

20 See e.g. Case C-583/11P *Inuit Tapiriit Kanatami and Others* (para. 59 of judgment).

21 Art. 263(6) TFEU.

22 The GC also has power to temper the immediate effects of its judgment, where it considers this necessary, in being able to determine which of the effects of the act declared void shall be considered definitive (ibid., Art. 264 (2)).

23 See final sentence of Art. 2(2) Århus Convention.

24 See e.g. analyses by Lee (2005), Ch. 5; de Lange (2003); Albors-Llorens (1998); Berrod (1999).

25 See e.g. Joined Cases 41–4/70 *NV International Fruit* and Case 222/83 *Municipality of Differdange*.

26 EU directives are defined in Art. 288(3) TFEU as being 'binding, as to the result to be achieved, upon each Member State to whom it is addressed but shall leave to the national authorities the choice of form and methods'. This definition has remained unchanged since the inception of the EU in the 1950s.

27 Case 25/62 *Plaumann*.

28 Ibid. (para. 107 of judgment).

29 See e.g. Case 247/87 *Star Fruit*, Joined Cases T-479 and 559/93 *Bernardi*, Case T-201/96 *Smanor*, as confirmed on appeal to the CJEU in C-317/97P.

30 See e.g. Case T-94/04 *EEB* (para. 57 of judgment).

31 See Arts. 7(2) and 27 of Regulation 1/2003 on the implementation of the rules of competition laid down in Articles 81 and 82 of the Treaty (OJ 2003 L1/1) and e.g. Case 27/76 *Metro (1)*. See Art. 20 of Regulation 659/99 on rules for application of Article 93 of the EC Treaty (OJ 1999 L831/1) and e.g. Case 169/84 *COFAZ*. See Regulation 1225/09 on protection against dumped imports from countries not members of the European Community (OJ 2009 L343/51), and e.g. Case 264/82 *Timex* (but see also Case T-598/97 *British Shoe Corporation*).

32 See e.g. Case C-87/89 *Sonito*.

33 Case T-461/93 *An Taisce*.

34 Directive 2011/92 (OJ 2012 L26/1), at the material time of the litigation former Directive 85/337 (OJ 1985 L175/40).

35 Krämer (1996b), p. 13.

36 Art. 2(2) Århus Convention. It should be taken into account in this context that the Commission is not acting as a court under the aegis of Arts. 258 and 260 TFEU and

it is evident that derogations to the scope of the Convention should be interpreted restrictively.

37 Case T-583/93 *Stichting Greenpeace*, on appeal Case C-321/95P.

38 See Art. 6 of Regulation 1303/13 laying down common provisions on the European Regional Development Fund, the European Social Fund, the Cohesion Fund, the European Agricultural Fund for Rural Development and the European Maritime and Fisheries Fund and laying down general provisions on the European Regional Development Fund, the European Social Fund, the Cohesion Fund and the European Maritime and Fisheries Fund (OJ 2013 L347/320). At the time of the *Stichting Greenpeace* litigation, this obligation was crystallised in Art. 7 of a predecessor Regulation 2052/88 (OJ 1988 L185/9).

39 Case T-583/93 *Stichting Greenpeace* (para. 54 of judgment).

40 See ibid. (esp. paras. 56 and 61 of judgment).

41 Case C-321/95P.

42 See Case C-131/92 *Arnaud* and Case T-138/98 *ACAV*.

43 Case T-475/93 *Buralux SA*, as confirmed on appeal in Case C-209/94P.

44 Governed currently by Regulation 1293/13 on the establishment of a Programme for the Environment and Climate Action (LIFE) (OJ 2013 L347/185).

45 Case T-117/94 *Associazone Agricoltori della Provincia di Rovigo*.

46 Case T-219/95R *Danielsson et al. v Commission*.

47 The provisions on taking annulment proceedings under the auspices the Euratom Treaty (Art. 146 EAEC) mirrored those of former Art. 230 EC.

48 Case T-219/95R *Danielsson et al.* (para. 71 of judgment).

49 See e.g. Case 222/84 *Johnston*.

50 Case 294/83 *Les Verts*.

51 Art. 150 EAEC establishes the preliminary ruling procedure under the aegis of the Euratom Treaty.

52 Case T-219/95R *Danielsson* (para. 77 of judgment).

53 Case C-321/95P *Stichting Greenpeace* (para. 33 of judgment).

54 See e.g. Ward (2001), p. 154; Williams (2002), p. 275.

55 See Craig and de Búrca (2011), pp. 506 *et seq.*

56 See Ch. 7.

57 As defined in Art. 288(2) TFEU.

58 Case T-177/01 *Jego Quere*.

59 See e.g. Case T-177/01 *Jego Quere* (at para. 42 of judgment).

60 Opinion of Advocate General (AG) Jacobs in Case C-55/00P *UPA*.

61 Case C-50/00P *UPA*.

62 Case C-263/02P *Jego Quere*.

63 Case C-50/00P *UPA* (para. 43 of judgment).

64 See e.g. comments by Biernat (2003), p. 41 and Ragolle (2003), p. 101.

65 Council Decision 2005/370 of 17 February 2005 on the conclusion on behalf of the European Community of the Convention on Access to Information, Public Participation in Decision-making and Access to Justice in Environmental Matters (OJ 2005 L124/1).

66 Joined Cases T-236 and 241/04 *EEB and Stichting Natuur en Milieu*.

67 Decisions 2004/247 and 2004/248 (OJ 2004 L78/50 and L78/53).

68 Directive 91/414 concerning the placing of plant protection products on the market (OJ 1991 L230/1).

69 Notably, Regulation 3900/92 (OJ 1992 L366/10), as then amended.

70 Cases T-236 and 241/04 *EEB and Stichting Natuur en Milieu v Commission* (para. 56 of judgment).

71 Ibid. (para. 61 of judgment).

72 Ibid. (paras. 57–60 and 62 of judgment).

73 Ibid. (paras. 65–7 of judgment).

74 Case T-94/04 *EEB, Pesticides Action Network Europe, International Union of Food, Agricultural, Hotel, Restaurant, Catering, Tobacco and Allied Workers' Associations (IUF), European*

Federation of Trade Unions in the Food, Agricultural and Tourism, Stichting Natuur en Milieu and Svenska Naturskyddföreningen v Commission.

75 Directive 2003/112 (OJ 2003 L321/32).
76 One of the environmental NGO applicants (Svenska Naturskyddföreningen) owned a farm in Sweden, arguing that the licensing of paraquat could have an adverse effect on the conservation and other environmental protection objectives it applied to the operation of the farm.
77 Paras. 53–4 of judgment.
78 See paras. 56–9 of judgment.
79 Case T-91/07 *WWF-UK Ltd v Council* and on appeal Case C-355/08P.
80 Case T-37/04 *Autonomous region of the Azores v Council* and on appeal Case C-444/08P
81 Regulation 41/07 (OJ 2007 L15/1).
82 Regulation 2371/02 (OJ 2002 L358/59) in conjunction with Decision 2004/585 (OJ 2004 L256/17).
83 Case C-355/08P *WWF-UK Ltd v Council* (para. 43 of judgment).
84 Art. 349 TFEU (formerly Art. 299(2) EC).
85 See Case C-355/08P *WWF-UK Ltd v Council* (esp. paras. 38–9, 44, 64–6 of judgment).
86 Ibid. (paras. 70–1 of judgment).
87 Specifically, Arts. 3(1), 6 and 9(2)–(5) of the Convention.
88 See Decision I/7 Review of Compliance of the MOP, 21–23.2002 (ECE/MP.PP/2/Add.8) in conjunction with Art. 15 of the Convention.
89 The complaint also submitted that the EU fell short of the Convention in other respects, namely that Regulation 1367/06 failed to allow individuals other than NGOs the right of access to an internal review of EU decisions affecting the environment, in breach of Art. 3(1) and 9(2) of the Convention; that the costs regime applied by the CJEU was uncertain and potentially prohibitive in contravention of Art. 9(4) of the Convention; and that EU institutions had breached Art. 6 of the Convention in failing to provide for public participation and access to justice in relation to certain decisions, specifically financing decisions and decisions on placing products on the market. The Committee ultimately rejected the complaint concerning legal costs, whilst reserving judgment on the other heads of complaint.
90 Report of the Compliance Committee, *Findings and Recommendations with Regard to Communication ACCC/C/2008/32 (Part I) Concerning Compliance by the European Union* (ECE/MP.PP/C.1/2011/4/Add.1), 14 April 2011. For a detailed analysis of the Committee's report see e.g. Marsden (2012).
91 At the material time, litigation was still pending in relation to the operation of the Århus Regulation's review procedures (Case T-338/08 *Stichting en Milieu PAN Europe v Commission*) which potentially could have had an impact on the degree of access afforded to private persons in relation to legal review proceedings at EU level.
92 Report of the Compliance Committee, *Findings and Recommendations with Regard to Communication ACCC/C/2008/32 (Part I)*, paras. 77–8.
93 Ibid., paras. 86–7.
94 See ibid., paras. 86 and 95.
95 Now enshrined in Art. 267 TFEU (and formerly governed by Art. 234 EC prior to the entry into force of the 2007 Lisbon Treaty).
96 See Report of the Compliance Committee, *Findings and Recommendations with Regard to Communication ACCC/C/2008/32 (Part I)*, para. 90.
97 See ibid., esp. para. 94.
98 See e.g. Balthasar (2010) and Craig and de Búrca (2011), p. 508.
99 See Arts. I-33–7 EUC.
100 See Arts. I-35–7 EUC.
101 See Secretariat of the European Convention, *Final Report of the Discussion Circle on the Court of Justice and the High Court* (Doc. CONV 636/03) of 25 March 2003, para. 22 and the cover note to the Praesidium of the European Convention (Doc. CONV 734/03) of 12 May 2003, p. 20.

102 Art. 288(4) TFEU.
103 See Peers and Costa (2012), p. 97.
104 Case T-177/01 and Case C-263/02P *Jego Quere*.
105 Case C-50/00P *UPA*.
106 See e.g. Case C-309/89 *Codorniu* and Case C-358/89 *Extramet*. For an analysis of the case law, see e.g. Craig and de Búrca (2001), pp. 493 *et seq.*; Usher (2003); and Hedemann-Robinson (1996).
107 Case T-18/10 and on appeal Case C-583/11P *Inuit Tapiriit Kanatami and others v European Parliament and Council.*
108 Regulation 1007/09 (OJ 2009 L216/1).
109 Case T-18/10 *Inuit Tapiriit Kanatami.*
110 This endorsed the view of the GC, as taken in e.g. Case T-381/11 *Eurofer v Commission.*
111 See Case C-583/11P *Inuit Tapiriit Kanatami and others* (paras. 58–60 of judgment).
112 See ibid. (para. 56 of judgment). The predecessor treaty provision on annulment proceedings (former Art. 230(4) EC) deployed a less clear and a more narrow material scope in referring to the requirement of the plaintiff being directly and individually concerned by a 'decision which, although in the form of a regulation or a decision addressed to another person'.
113 See Case C-583/11P *Inuit Tapiriit Kanatami and others* (paras. 70–2 of the judgment).
114 Ibid. (para. 70 of judgment).
115 Ibid. (para. 73 of judgment).
116 Art. 6(1) TEU.
117 Case C-583/11P *Inuit Tapiriit Kanatami and others* (paras. 92–6 of judgment).
118 See Case T-338/08 *Stichting en Milieu & Pesticide Action Network Europe* and Case T-396/09 *Vereniging Milieudefensie, Stichting Stop Luchtverontreiniging Utrecht v Commission*. At the time of writing, both cases were subject to pending appeals, namely Case C-405/12P *Council v Stichting Natuur en Milieu & Pesticide Action Network Europe* and Case C-401/12P *Council v Vereniging Milieudefensie, Stichting Stop Luchtverontreiniging Utrecht* respectively.
119 Case T-338/08 *Stichting en Milieu & Pesticide Action Network Europe v Commission.*
120 Art. 267(1)(a) TFEU.
121 Ibid., Art. 267(1)(b).
122 For an overview of the impact of the preliminary ruling procedure in an environmental protection context, see Somsen (2001).
123 See e.g. Joined Cases 80–1/77 *Ramel.*
124 Case 314/85 *Foto Frost.*
125 See e.g. Case C-465/93 *Atlanta*, Joined Cases C-143/88 and 92/89 *Zuckerfabrik Süderdithmarschen* and Case C-334/95 *Krüger.*
126 Art. 267(2) TFEU.
127 Ibid., Art. 267(3). Exceptionally, a national court of last instance for the litigants may decide not to use the PRP in certain situations, notably where the relevant point of EU law is irrelevant to the outcome of the dispute, has already been determined previously by the CJEU (*acte éclairé*) or where the point of law is so obvious to the national court as to leave no reasonable scope for doubt (*acte clair*): see Case 283/81 *CILFIT.*
128 See Case 66/80 *International Chemical Corporation.*
129 See e.g. Joined Cases 28–30/62 *Da Costa and others* [1963] ECR 31.
130 Case C-405/92 *Mondiet.*
131 Case C-341/95 *Bettati.*
132 Cases T-583/93 and C-321/95P *Stichting Greenpeace.*
133 See para. 102 of the AG's Opinion in Case C-50/00P *UPA.*
134 Case T-177/01 *Jego Quere* (para. 45 of CFI judgment).
135 See notably Case C-427/07 *Commission v Ireland* and Case C-530/11 *Commission v UK.*
136 Case C-188/92 *Textilwerke Deggendorf (TWD)*. See also subsequent CJEU judgments in Case C-178/95 *Wiljo* and Case C-239/99 *Nachi.*
137 See e.g. Case 216/82 *Universität Hamburg* and Joined Cases 133–6/85 *Rau.*

138 See e.g. Case C-241/95 *Accrington Beef* and Case C-343/09 *Afton Chemical Ltd.*

139 See Art. 265(1) and (3) TFEU.

140 Ibid., Art. 265 does not provide for a semi-privileged category of plaintiffs, in contrast with Art. 263 (ibid.).

141 Ibid., Art. 265(1).

142 Ibid., Art. 265(3).

143 See e.g. Case C-107/91 *ENU* and Joined Cases T-79/96, 260/97 and 117/98 *Camar and Tico*. The test for direct and individual concern is the same as for Art. 263 (4) TFEU.

144 Case 59/70 *Netherlands v Commission*.

145 Art. 265(2) TFEU.

146 See e.g. Case 4/69 *Lütticke*, Case 247/87 *Star Fruit*, Case C-371/89 *Emrich*, Cases T-479/93 and 559/93 *Bernardi* and Case T-201/96 and C-317/97P *Smanor*.

147 Cases T-479/93 and T-559/93 *Bernardi* (para. 31 of judgment).

148 See e.g. Case 247/87 *Star Fruit*.

149 See e.g. Case T-186/08 *LPN*.

150 Ibid.

151 Ibid. (para. 11 of judgment).

152 Ibid. (para. 12 of judgment).

153 Art. 17(1) TEU (the obligation was formerly contained in Art. 211 EC).

154 Art. 258 TFEU, first sentence.

155 Ibid., second sentence.

156 See ibid., Art. 260(2).

157 See Arts. 3–8 Århus Regulation 1367/06 (OJ 2006 L264/13).

158 See ibid., Art. 9.

159 See ibid., Arts. 10–12.

160 See CFI cases cited in n. 118.

161 Contractual liability of the EU is governed separately by Art. 340(1) TFEU.

162 See ibid., Art. 256(1) in conjunction with Art. 268.

163 Art. 46 of Protocol 3 to the TEU/TFEU on the Statute of the Court of Justice (OJ 2010 C83) as amended.

164 A notable exception is Wennerås (2007), pp. 246 *et seq.*

165 See by way of illustration e.g. Joined Cases T-236 and 241/04 *EEB & Stichting Natuur en Milieu* (concerning the alleged illegal extended authorisation on the part of the Commission of plant products atrazine and simazine), Case C-355/08P *WWF-UK Ltd* (concerning challenge against EU permission of a total allowable catch for cod in the face of scientific advice that a zero catch should be imposed) and Case T-338/08 *Stichting en Milieu & PAN Europe* (concerning a challenge regarding the maximum pesticide residue level set for food and feed). However, as noted in section 9.1.1, such judicial review litigation has often fallen at the first hurdle, held inadmissible on account of a lack of legal standing on the part of the plaintiffs.

166 See e.g. Joined Cases C-104/89 and 37/90 *Mulder* (paras. 51 and 63 of judgment).

167 See e.g. Case C-352/98P *Bergaderm*, Case T-160/03 *AFCon Management* and Case C-198/03P *Commission v CEVA*.

168 As established in Case C-49/93 *Brasserie*.

169 See Case C-352/98P *Laboratoires pharmaceutiques Bergaderm SA et al. v Commission*.

170 See e.g. comments of the CJEU in Case 131/88 *Commission v Germany* in relation to the rights of individuals under the former EU Groundwater Directive 80/68 (para. 7 of judgment).

171 Specifically, see Art. 3(3) TEU and Arts. 11 and 191–2 TFEU.

172 See Case C-352/98P *Laboratoires pharmaceutiques Bergaderm* (para. 43 of judgment).

173 See Case C-390/95P *Antillean Rice Mills* (e.g. paras. 57 *et seq.* of judgment).

174 See Case 5/71 *Schöppenstedt* (para.11 of judgment).

175 See e.g. Case 96/71 *Haegemann* but see also Case 175/84 *Krohn*.

176   See e.g. Case 281/82 *Unifrex* and Case T-167/94 *Nölle*.
177   Joined Cases 5, 7 and 13–24/66 *Kampffmeyer*.
178   See e.g. Case 26/74 *Roquette Frère* and Case T-1/99 *T Port GmbH*.
179   See e.g. Joined Cases 5, 7 and 13–24/66 *Kampffmeyer* and AG Capotorti's Opinion in Case 238/78 *Ireks-Arkady*, p. 2998.
180   Case 247/87 *Star Fruit*.
181   Joined Cases T-479 and 559/93 *Bernardi* (paras. 38–9 of judgment).
182   See Case 4/69 *Lütticke*, Joined Cases T-479 and 593/93 *Bernardi* and Joined Cases T-201/96 and C-317/97P *Smanor*. See also Craig and de Búrca (2011), p. 575.
183   Wennerås (2007), p. 246.
184   See Case T-338/08 *Stichting en Milieu & Pesticide Action Network Europe* and Case T-396/09 *Vereniging Milieudefensie, Stichting Stop Luchtverontreiniging Utrecht v Commission*.
185   See e.g. de Lange (2003).
186   COM(2003)622, Commission proposal for a draft regulation on the application of the provisions of the Convention on access to information, public participation in decision-making and access to justice in environmental matters to EC institutions and bodies, 24 October 2003.
187   OJ 2006 L264/13.
188   Art. 1(d) Århus Regulation 1367/06 (OJ 2006 L264/13).
189   As contained in Title IV Internal Review and Access to Justice of the Århus Regulation.
190   *Access to Information, Public Participation and Access to Justice in Environmental Matters at Community level – A Practical Guide*, accessible from the European Commission's DGENV website: http://ec.europa.eu/environment/Aarhus/requests.htm.
191   Art. 11(1)(a) of the Århus Regulation 1367/06.
192   Ibid., Art. 11(1)(b).
193   Ibid., Art. 11(1)(c).
194   Ibid., Art. 11(1)(d).
195   Specifically, Art. 12 of the original legislative proposal (COM(2003)622 final, 24 October 2003) stipulated that the qualifying legal person had to be active at Union level and have its annual statement of accounts for the two previous years certified by a registered auditor. Furthermore, where a qualifying person was active in the form of several co-ordinated associations or organisations with a structure based on membership, the associations or organisations had to cover at least three member states.
196   See ibid., Art. 10.
197   COM(2003)622, p. 7.
198   Art. 11(2) Århus Regulation.
199   Commission Decision 2008/50 laying down detailed rules for the application of Regulation 1376/06 (OJ 2008 L13/24). The decision specifies that the following documents need to be submitted by the NGEO: statutes/by-laws of the NGO or other document fulfilling the same purpose under the national law of the member state in which the NGO is incorporated; annual activity reports for the previous two years; copy of legal NGO's registration where required under national law in which the NGO is incorporated; and, where relevant, documentation showing that the NGO has previously been acknowledged by a Union organ as being entitled to make an internal review request (see Art. 3 in conjunction with the Annex of Decision 2008/50).
200   See recital 7 and Art. 2(1)(c) Århus Regulation 1367/2006 (OJ 006 L264/13), the latter provision defining the term 'Community institution or body' which appears throughout the legislative text.
201   See Art. 2(2) in conjunction with Art. 9 Århus Convention.
202   The Århus Regulation defines 'environmental law' as meaning EU environmental protection legislation in broad terms. Specifically, Art. 2(1)(f) specifies that:

> 'environmental law' means Community legislation which, irrespective of its legal basis, contributes to the pursuit of the objectives of Community policy on the

environment as set out in the Treaty: preserving, protecting and improving the quality of the environment, protecting human health, the prudent and rational utilisation of natural resources, and promoting measures at international level to deal with regional or worldwide environmental problems.

203 See Art. 2(1)(c) Århus Regulation 1367/06 (OJ 2006 L264/13).
204 By virtue of Art. 2(2) Århus Regulation.
205 Pallemaerts notes that in July 2008 the Commission rejected as inadmissible a request to review the closure of an infringement procedure against Portugal in connection with a dam project: Pallemaerts (2011), p. 282. The Commission's website on internal review requests under the Århus Regulation also refers to a decision by the Commission to reject as inadmissible a request from the NGEO ClientEarth for it to undertake an internal review of its decision to appeal a decision of two judgments of the CFI (Case T-338/08 *Stichting en Milieu & PAN Europe v Commission* and Case T-396/09 *Vereiniging Milieudefensie. Stichting Stop Luchtverontreiniging v Commission*). At the time of writing, the two cases were the subject of pending appeals brought by the Council, Commission and the EP: Joined Cases C-404–5/12P *Council and Commission v Stichting en Milieu & PAN Europe* and Joined Cases C-401–3/12P *Council, EP and Commission v Vereiniging Milieudefensie, Stichting Stop Luchtverontreiniging*.
206 See Wennerås (2007), pp. 231–2; Jans (2008), pp. 215–16; Pallemaerts (2011), p. 280.
207 Based on Art. 114 TFEU.
208 Based on Art. 43 (ibid.).
209 Based on Art 91 (ibid.).
210 COM(2003)622 final, Art. 2(1)(h) of the draft regulation applying the Convention (and see also p. 10 of the explanatory memorandum).
211 Ibid., Art. 2(1)(l) of draft regulation.
212 See common position of the Council (Common Position No. 31/2005 [2005] OJ 264E/18).
213 See http://ec.europa.eu/environment/Aarhus/requests.htm.
214 Case T-338/08 *Stichting en Milieu & Pesticide Action Network Europe v Commission*.
215 Case T-396/09 *Vereniging Milieudefensie, Stichting Stop Luchtverontreiniging Utrecht v Commission*.
216 See Art. 6(4) Habitats Directive 92/43.
217 For a different view, though, see Wennerås (2007), p. 233.
218 Pallemaerts (2011), p. 282.
219 This concerned a 2013 decision by the Commission rejecting an internal review request from the NGEO ClientEarth regarding the Commission's decision to appeal the GC rulings against it in Cases T-338/08 and T-396/09. (The decision may be inspected on the Commission's website which contains a repository of Århus review requests: http://ec.europa.eu/environment/Aarhus/requests.htm.)
220 As set out in Art. 11 Århus Regulation 1367/06 (OJ 2006 L264/13).
221 Commission Decision 2008/50 laying down detailed rules for the application of regulation 1376/06 (OJ 2008 L13/24).
222 Commission Decision 2008/401 amending its Rules of Procedure as regards the detailed rules for the application of Regulation 1367/06 (OJ 2008 L140/22).
223 The review procedures are structured on a similar footing to that applicable in relation to the 2003 draft directive on access to environmental justice with respect to the acts and omissions of member state authorities (COM(2003)624final) as discussed in Ch. 8.
224 Art. 10(1) Århus Regulation 1367/06. The original proposal set a stricter time limit of four weeks (see Art. 9(1) of draft regulation (COM(2003)621 final)).
225 Art. 10(2) Århus Regulation.
226 Ibid., Art. 10(3).
227 Ibid., Art. 9(4).
228 Art. 4 of Decision 2008/50 (OJ 2008 L140/22).
229 Ibid., Art. 5.
230 See criticism expressed also by Pallemaerts (2011), p. 286.

231 See Art. 11 of the draft Århus Regulation and p. 17 of the Commission's Explanatory Memorandum (COM(2003)622 final). See Lee (2005), p. 143.

232 Pallemaerts (2011), pp.287 *et seq.*

233 See also the similar vague wording employed in the legislative preamble, namely recital 21 to the Århus Regulation.

234 See Case T-338/08 *Stichting en Milieu & PAN Europe v Commission* (para. 80 of judgment) and Case T-396/09 *Vereiniging Milieudefensie, Stichting Stop Luchtverontreiniging v Commission* (para. 72 of judgment).

235 Ibid.

236 Joined Cases C-404–5/12P *Council and Commission v Stichting en Milieu & PAN Europe* and Joined Cases C-401–3/12P *Council, EP and Commission v Vereiniging Milieudefensie, Stichting Stop Luchtverontreiniging*

237 Regulation 149/08 (OJ 2008 L58/1).

238 Regulation 396/05 (OJ 2005 L70/1).

239 Directive 2008/50 on ambient air quality and cleaner air for Europe (OJ 2008 L152/1).

240 Specifically, the Dutch government had requested time extensions be granted to nine zones in respect of nitrogen dioxide (until end 2014 for eight zones and end 2012 for one zone) and nationwide in respect of PM10 (until 10 June 2011).

241 Paras. 51 and 52 respectively of judgments in Case T-338/08 *Stichting en Milieu & PAN Europe v Commission* and Case T-396/09 *Vereiniging Milieudefensie, Stichting Stop Luchtveron-treiniging v Commission.*

242 Paras. 59 and 54 respectively of judgments in Case T-338/08 and Case T-396/09.

243 See paras. 65–8 and para. 66 respectively of judgments in Case T-338/08 and Case T-396/09.

244 Namely ordinary and special legislative procedure as defined in Art. 289 TFEU.

245 See paras. 76–83 and 68–77 respectively of judgments in Case T-338/08 and Case T-396/09.

246 See paras. 80 and 72 respectively of judgments in Case T-338/08 and Case T-396/09.

247 Case T-381/11 *Europäischer Witscahftsverband der Eisen- und Stahlindustrie (Eurofer) ASBL v Commission.*

248 See ibid. (paras. 34–5 of judgment). See also Case T-379/11 *Krupp Mannesmann and Others v Commission.*

249 Directive 2003/87 (OJ 2003 L275/32) as amended.

250 Case T-381/11 (para. 35 of judgment).

251 Ibid.

252 See Case C-355/08P *WWF-UK Ltd v Council* (e.g. paras. 42 *et seq.* of judgment).

253 Case C-583/11P *Inuit Tapiriit Kanatami and others.*

254 Case T-381/11 *Europäischer Witscahftsverband der Eisen- und Stahlindustrie (Eurofer) ASBL v Commission.*

255 OJ 2013 L330/1.

256 IMO Doc.SR/CONF/45. The Hong Kong Convention is not yet in force, with only four signatories (France, Netherlands, Italy, Saint Kitts and Nevis and Turkey) and one contracting party (Norway) at the time of writing. It will enter into force two years after ratification by 15 states, representing 40% of global merchant shipping by gross tonnage, the combined maximum annual ship recycling volume not less than 3% of their combined tonnage. Being an international agreement negotiated under the aegis of the IMO, the HK Convention only foresees the possibility of states becoming contracting parties.

257 Art. 6(2)(a) of Regulation 1257/13 (OJ 2013 L330/1).

258 Ibid., Art. 14.

259 Ibid., Art. 15.

260 Ibid., Art. 23(1).

261 Ibid., Art. 23(3).

262 Ibid., Art. 23(4).

10 Private enforcement of EU environmental law at EU institutional level (2)

Administrative complaints procedures and other possibilities

As was seen from the discussion in Chapter 10, the rights of private persons to seek judicial review of EU environmental decision-making are relatively limited in scope and effectiveness. Restrictive rules on legal standing to sue make it difficult in general for private persons to be able to bring judicial review proceedings under Articles 263 and 265 of the Treaty on the Functioning of the European Union (TFEU) (annulment and failure-to-act proceedings) before the General Court (GC). Moreover, the EU courts have ruled out the possibility of Commission decisions concerning commencement or termination of infringement proceedings against member states under Articles 258 and 260 TFEU being subject to judicial review, given the discretion accorded to the EU institution over infringement case management.[1] Review of EU decisions via the preliminary ruling procedure (Article 267 TFEU) may not be available where no national measures are involved or where a national court does not think a reference to the CJEU is warranted. Notwithstanding these limitations, private individuals have possibilities under the EU treaty system to invoke special administrative complaint procedures at EU level to instigate review of EU decisions affecting environmental policy, whose legal or political validity they may wish to question. These administrative procedures serve as an important complement to the various legal proceedings and mechanisms contained in the TFEU relating to judicial review of acts and omissions of EU institutions, as discussed in Chapter 9. Whilst not leading to legally binding outcomes, these appeal routes may in practice prove to be as effective and swifter than recourse to legal proceedings. Moreover, as a rule they are far less costly.

This chapter will outline various complaint procedures open to members of the public seeking to obtain administrative or political review of EU environmental decision-making from non-judicial EU bodies. The most important of these review bodies are the European Ombudsman (EO) and European Parliament (EP), which are considered first. The EO is charged with hearing complaints about maladministration on the part of non-judicial EU institutions and bodies, such as the European Commission. Whereas the previous chapter discussed the role of the EO in relation to complaints concerning lack of access to environmental information held by EU institutions, this chapter will focus on his role more broadly in hearing complaints challenging the legality of or way in which EU decisions affecting the environment have been determined. It will focus in particular on complaints concerning the handling by the European Commission of suspected cases of infringements of EU environmental law. The EP, within the context of its supervisory functions, offers the possibility for members of the public to present it with petitions on EU issues of personal concern to them, included matters relating to non-compliance with EU law. Whilst the first two main sections of this chapter concentrate on the review role of the EO and the EP in connection with complaints in respect of EU institutional conduct concerning environmental decision-making, the final sections consider the extent to which other review channels are open to private persons at EU level for the purpose of scrutinising EU environmental decision-making.

10.1 The European Ombudsman (EO)

The EO constitutes an important institutional resource for private individuals seeking to hold EU organs to account in respect of their decisions affecting EU environmental policy.[2] The office of the EO[3] is a relatively recent institutional innovation at EU level, intended to bolster the rights of the public, and particularly EU citizens, in terms of enabling them to scrutinise EU decision-making. The legal framework of the EO was established in 1993 by virtue of the Treaty on European Union (TEU) amendments made to the EU's founding treaty system. Specifically, the EO's mandate, which is enshrined in Article 228 TFEU, is to address instances of alleged maladministration on the part of EU organs. Article 228(1) TFEU, which sets out the functions of the EO, stipulates:

> 1. A European Ombudsman, elected by the EP, shall be empowered to receive complaints from any citizen of the Union or any natural or legal person residing or having its registered office in a member state concerning instances of maladministration in the activities of the Union institutions, bodies, offices or agencies, with the exception of the Court of Justice of the European Union acting in its judicial role. He or she shall examine such complaints and report on them.
>
> In accordance with his duties, the Ombudsman shall conduct inquiries for which he finds grounds, either on his own initiative or on the basis of complaints submitted to him direct or through a Member of the European Parliament, except where the alleged facts are or have been the subject of legal proceedings. Where the Ombudsman establishes an instance of maladministration, he shall refer the matter to the institution, body, office or agency concerned, which shall have a period of three months in which to inform him of its views. The Ombudsman shall then forward a report to the European Parliament and the institution, body, office or agency concerned. The person lodging the complaint shall be informed of the outcome of such inquiries.
>
> The Ombudsman shall submit an annual report to the EP on the outcome of his inquiries.

Accordingly, the EO has competence to investigate alleged instances of maladministration on the part of a very wide range of EU organs, namely all organs except the CJEU acting in its judicial capacity. This also encompasses the judicial activities of the various courts that comprise the Court of Justice. Accordingly, the GC and Civil Service Tribunal are also covered by the statutory exception in Article 228(1) TFEU. (References to the CJEU in the remainder of this chapter include all judicial branches of the EU Court, unless otherwise specified.) In addition to investigating EU-level maladministration, the EO's remit extends to seeking to enhance the relations between EU institutions and the general public. Part of this mission involves striving to improve standards of service within the EU's administrative apparatus. The officeholder is appointed by the EP after each parliamentary election for the duration of its term of office, namely five years, with the possibility that the incumbent may be reappointed.[4] At the time of writing, there have been three persons appointed to the EO role over the following periods: Jacob Söderman (1995–2003), P. Nikiforos Diamandouros (2003–13) and Emily O'Reilly (2013–).[5] The EO has a dedicated website which hosts a considerable amount of historical, analytical and practical information about the EO's operational activities.[6] The legal framework which governs the functions of the EO is contained principally in Article 228 TFEU and the EP Decision 94/262 on the regulations and general conditions governing the performance of the Ombudsman's duties[7] (hereafter referred to as the 'EO Statute'). The EO has also adopted a complementary decision containing implementing provisions relating to the EO Statute[8] (hereafter referred to as the 'EO Implementing Decision'). The right to complain to the EO has been recently elevated to fundamental rights status by virtue of Article 43 of the EU Charter of Fundamental Rights 2000 (EUCFR),[9] now a legally binding component of the EU constitutional fabric by virtue of the Lisbon Treaty 2007.[10] This provision is underpinned by the fundamental right to good administration enshrined in Article 41 EUCFR.

From the perspective of private enforcement of EU environmental law, the EO constitutes an important source of assistance, in terms of ensuring that EU organs charged with powers and responsibilities for taking decisions directly or indirectly affecting EU environmental policy adhere both to EU rules of law as well as to principles of good administration. In practice, the principal EU institution subject to EO scrutiny is the European Commission, exemplified by the fact that 53 per cent of enquiries from the public to the EO in 2012 concerned activities of or information concerning the Commission.[11] There are several other EU bodies which also may be the subject of an EO investigation, whether having formal EU institutional status or of a lesser rank such as agencies or offices. A range of EU organs having either direct or indirect involvement with or an impact on EU environmental policy decision-making is open to EO scrutiny. Notable examples include the European Investment Bank (EIB)[12] (in respect of its lending practices concerning development projects) and the European Chemicals Agency (ECHA)[13] (in respect of its EU regulatory powers concerning the management of hazardous chemicals). The European Commission is considered the EU organ responsible for the actions of special committees established in EU legislation to take detailed decisions with respect to the implementation of policy (the so-called 'comitology' process).[14]

The EO has undertaken several investigations into alleged maladministration on the part of the Commission in relation to the way in which it has handled complaints from members of the public concerning suspected cases of infringements of EU environmental legislation. As was discussed in Chapter 5, the European Commission receives a substantial number of complaints from private individuals about alleged breaches of environmental law each year. Under the current legal framework of the TFEU, such persons have no specific legally binding procedural or substantive rights to ensure that their particular case is properly assessed by the Commission.[15] Instead, as was discussed in Chapter 5, the Commission has published guidance in the form of a Communication[16] on the way in which it handles complaints by members of the public alleging breaches of Union law by member states. Where a person is dissatisfied with the response of the Commission in relation to the submissions and evidence put forward of alleged infringements of EU environmental law, they may turn to the EO for assistance, subject to the EO accepting that the response of the Commission has been tantamount to maladministration. As considered in section 10.1.1.2 below, maladministration encompasses situations in which the Commission has allegedly failed to interpret or apply EU law correctly or failed to engage seriously and fairly with a complainant in accordance with principles of sound administrative practice. In taking up such a case, the EO's task is then to liaise with the parties involved (complainant and Commission) with a view to finding an appropriate resolution of the dispute, if possible steering towards a friendly settlement outcome. In this respect, the EO constitutes a means for private persons to seek to hold the European Commission to account over shortcomings in relation to its duty to safeguard the application of European Union law, including EU environmental law, under Article 17 TEU. Complaints against the European Commission constitute the bulk of the EO's work, with the Commission being subject to 52.7 per cent of inquiries opened by the EO in 2012.[17] The number of complaints submitted annually to the EO falling within the Ombudsman's mandate has stabilised in recent years to around 700–50.[18]

Whilst formally independent of one another, the EP and EO have close institutional links with one another. The principal TFEU provisions governing the remit of the EO are contained within the relevant chapter concerned with identifying the parameters of the EP's powers and responsibilities.[19] The EP is the EU institution responsible for electing and overseeing the workings of the EO,[20] including inspecting the EO's annual and individual reports on the outcome of his/her inquiries.[21] In addition, the EP is responsible for establishing the rules governing the performance of the EO's duties, subject to Council approval and after gaining the opinion of the European Commission. Ultimately, it is the EP that can trigger a procedure which may lead to the dismissal of the incumbent office holder if they are no longer deemed capable of fulfilling the conditions for performing EO duties or if they are guilty of serious misconduct; the CJEU though decides whether or not the EO may be dismissed.[22] Finally, the seat of the EO is that of the EP.[23] The close nexus between the EO and the EP underline a key constitutional function of the EO, namely to contribute to a greater level of democratic accountability of non-judicial institutions and bodies at EU level engaged in decision-making relating to policy development or application of existing EU rules.

The decision by the member states to amend the EU treaty framework and incorporate an ombudsman regime within the constitutional framework of the Union was part of a broader package of initiatives brought in by the TEU in 1992 to begin to enhance the role, participation and civic rights of individuals in relation to the activities and institutional workings of the Union.[24] Accordingly, the establishment of the EO was accompanied by other treaty amendments now housed within the TFEU designed to construct a clear citizenship dimension to European supranational politics. These include the construction of EU citizenship predicated upon possession of nationality of a member state,[25] and the following rights for EU citizens: to move and reside freely within the member states' territories;[26] active and passive electoral rights in relation to municipal and EP elections irrespective of location of residence within the EU;[27] to receive consular protection in third countries from any other member state where their own member state is not represented in the host third country;[28] to petition the EP on matters coming within the Union's fields of activity;[29] to apply to the EO;[30] and to correspond with EU institutions and bodies in any official language of the Union.[31] The 2007 Lisbon Treaty augmented this package to include a right of citizens' initiative,[32] the impact of which is considered at the end of this chapter.

Amongst the most significant political rights to emerge from this EU citizenship package are the right of complaint to the EO and right of petition to the EP. Unlike other citizenship rights guaranteed under the Union treaty framework, these rights are not confined to persons possessing at least one nationality of the member states of the Union. The relevant TFEU provisions[33] expressly entitle any natural or legal person who is residing or who has its registered office within one of the member states to be able to exercise the rights of complaint and petition.

10.1.1 General remit and powers of the EO

The EO is heavily dependent upon the general public for information on instances of alleged or suspected maladministration within the EU institutions and bodies. In seeking to uncover these, the EO may commence his investigations either on a passive or proactive basis. First, from a passive perspective, the EO must act upon the submission to it of a complaint of maladministration from any EU citizen or any natural or legal person residing or having its registered office within one of the member states.[34] The complaint may be made via the intermediary of a member of the EP if the petitioner agrees,[35] which effectively means that complaints to the EO may be channelled via the mechanism of the right of petition.[36] Secondly, from a proactive perspective, the EO has the power to launch own-initiative investigations with a view to clarifying any suspected maladministration which has come to his attention.[37] Own-initiative inquiries comprise but a minor fraction of the EO's work in practice[38] and only two such inquiries had been commissioned in relation to environmental matters between 1995 and 2012.[39] Own-initiative inquiries may, in particular, be a useful means of following up suspected systematic institutional maladministration, where a response to an individual complaint might well not be suited to addressing underlying administrative problems.[40]

10.1.1.1 Personal scope of the EO's mandate

BENEFICIARIES

The TFEU provides for a broad range of persons eligible to file a complaint of alleged EU institutional maladministration with the EO.[41] Article 228(1) TFEU specifies that the EO is empowered to receive complaints from any EU citizen, namely any person with nationality of a member state, any natural person resident within the Union or from any legal person having its registered office in a member state. Whilst the treaty provision formally excludes non-EU nationals and companies with no physical or corporate presence located within the Union from having a formal right to file a maladministration complaint, the EO has the opportunity to take up such complaints in the form of own-initiative inquiries. The bulk of complaints to the EO are filed by individuals. In 2012, for instance, some 85 per cent of complaints were submitted by natural persons and 15 per cent by corporate entities.[42]

The requirements for submitting a complaint to the EO are relatively straightforward and generous. Notably, the complainant need not show that she/he is personally affected by the matter, so that complaints may be filed on an *actio popularis* basis. Moreover, the complaint need only be submitted to the EO within two years of the date on which the facts on which it is based came to the attention of the person lodging the complaint.[43] It must, however, be preceded by the appropriate administrative approaches to the EU organ concerned.[44] Accordingly, the complainant must be able to demonstrate that they contacted the EU organ for the purpose of seeking a review of the latter's conduct prior to referring to the EO.

EU ORGANS SUBJECT TO SCRUTINY

As stipulated in Article 228(1) TFEU, the EO's mandate to investigate and assess alleged or suspected cases of maladministration extends to scrutinising the activities of practically all EU institutions, agencies and other bodies, except the judicial activities of the CJEU[45] which thereby preserves its judicial independence under the TFEU framework.

The work of the EO does not extend beyond this remit, such as assessing the activities of national authorities involved in the administration and/or application of EU law. This jurisdictional limit has not appeared to have been well understood by the general public; the EO's annual reports testify that the majority of complaints to the EO fall outside his mandate.[46] However, the total number of 'outside mandate' complaints has steadily fallen in recent years,[47] and this has been attributed to better information and guidance provided to the public[48] especially on the EO's website, such as the interactive online guide. Where a complaint is targeted at the activities of a national authority in connection with the implementation of

EU law, the complainant is usually advised as a matter of course by the EO to file a petition to the EP or to apprise the European Commission of the matter.[49]

This situation is to be distinguished, though, from one where an individual is dissatisfied with the response of the European Commission in addressing their submissions that a breach of EU law has occurred within a particular member state; the appropriateness of the response of the Commission is a legitimate subject for EO scrutiny where the individual considers that it amounts to maladministration.

EXCLUSION OF EO FROM LEGAL PROCEEDINGS

Mention has been already of the fact that the EO's remit does not include scrutiny of the judicial activities of the CJEU. This exclusion serves to preserve the exclusive powers of the CJEU to provide definitive interpretations of EU law as well as to respect the Union's existing legal frameworks and systems of ensuring impartiality of its judiciary. Alongside this particular exception to the EO's remit lies a related exclusion, namely the exclusion of the Ombudsman from interfering with legal proceedings.[50] Specifically, Article 228(1) second subparagraph TFEU rules out the possibility of the EO investigating complaints and other cases where the alleged facts are or have been the subject of 'legal proceedings'. The phrase 'legal proceedings' is not defined in the treaty provision, but is taken in practice to include any type of legal proceedings before a court, whether at international[51] or national level. Flanking and complementary provisions are contained in the EO Statute. Article 1(3) of the EO Statute precludes the EO from intervening in cases before courts or questioning the soundness of a court's ruling. Article 2(7) of the EO Statute requires the EO to consider a complaint to it inadmissible and close any enquiries carried out where legal proceedings are 'in progress or concluded' concerning the facts which have been put forward. Similar justifications underpin this particular exclusion, namely the need to ensure that the role of judicial bodies is not undermined by the EO's office.

To a partial extent the 'legal proceedings' exclusion is relevant in relation to complaints concerning the Commission's handling of infringement proceeding under Articles 258 and 260 TFEU. Specifically, the reference to 'legal proceedings' would cover the litigation phase of infringement proceedings, namely the pleadings of the Commission submitted to the CJEU under Articles 258 and 260 TFEU. It will also exclude the EO from scrutinising Commission handling of any infringement complaint where the infringement procedure is still pending.[52] It does not, however, serve to exclude the EO from scrutinising the decision-making of the Commission during the initial administrative phase of the infringement procedure, namely the part of the procedure up until the Commission issues a final written warning (reasoned opinion in first-round cases under Article 258 TFEU and letter of formal notice in second-round cases under Article 260 TFEU) where the particular infringement file has been closed by the Commission.

Accordingly, operational decisions of the European Commission concerning the management of alleged or suspected infringements of EU environmental law fall within the remit of the Ombudsman, so long as the matter is or has not been

referred to the CJEU and so long as the infringement procedure has been terminated. The EO's review procedure will accordingly be available to those persons
whose complaints to the Commission about alleged breaches of EU environmental law have been rejected by the Commission from the outset. In practice, this
will cover the vast majority of complaints against the Commission over issues
concerned with EU environmental law enforcement. The EO has also asserted
quite rightly that he has a mandate to scrutinise cases where the Commission,
after initially deciding to open an infringement file in the wake of a complaint
against a member state, decides to drop infringement action against a member
state at a later stage during the initial administrative phase of the Article 258/260
TFEU procedure.[53]

There are a number of grounds for supporting the EO's assertion of jurisdiction to be able to investigate Commission decision-making throughout the
administrative phase of the infringement procedure. Notably, it is evident that the
exclusion of 'legal proceedings' from the EO's remit is clearly meant to complement the related statutory exception concerning the judicial activities of the EU
courts. Article 1(3) of the EO Statute stipulates that the EO may not intervene in
cases 'before courts' or 'question the soundness of a court's ruling'. Scrutiny by the
EO of Commission decision-making during the initial administrative phases of
the Article 258/260 procedures does not compromise these requirements, given
that the CJEU is not seised of a case at that stage, this being entirely dependent
upon the decision of the Commission subsequent to the issue of a final written
warning. Moreover, the administrative phase of these two infringement procedures cannot be equated with the classic form of legal proceeding, given that their
progress is contingent upon negotiation between Commission and member state
and do not involve judicial adjudication. The Commission, as a political entity
within the EU, is in charge of managing the administrative phase; responsibility
does not lie with the CJEU. Were the Commission able to escape EO scrutiny after
simply issuing a letter of formal notice, this would open up a significant loophole
in the system of maladministration supervision under EU law. Finally, in alignment with well-established general principles of interpretation developed by the
CJEU itself, exceptions to fundamental rights in EU law (in this instance the right
to petition the EO) should be interpreted narrowly in favour of the individual, not
the defendant administrative organ charged with breaches of such rights. As was
noted above, the EUCFR has elevated the EO complaints system[54] and principle
of good administration[55] to the status of fundamental rights.

10.1.1.2 *Material scope of the EO's mandate: the concept of maladministration*

Maladministration is defined neither in the TFEU nor in the EO's Statute. Over
the years, the EO has sought to develop and refine, as fully as possible, a meaningful explanation of the concept. Initially, the EO established a broad working
definition of the term 'maladministration' to mean a situation where a public
body fails to act in accordance with a rule or principle that is binding upon it.[56]
Subsequently, the EO moved to work with the EP to flesh out more effective

and detailed guidance by setting out in codified form a set of general principles concerning minimum acceptable administrative standards for EU officials and servants. Through this, the EO has managed to carve out for itself a normative-making role in seeking to steer through changes in administrative practice of EU organs via soft law instrumentation.[57]

Specifically, in 2001 the EP endorsed[58] a European Code of Good Administrative Behaviour (ECGAB)[59] drafted by the EO, designed to be used by EU organs with a view to seeking to ensure that their administrative systems are suitably structured so as to minimise risks of maladministration arising. Spanning 26 articles, the ECGAB incorporates a range of principles on good administrative conduct to be applied by Union organs[60] and their officials,[61] notably on the following aspects: ensuring lawfulness of decisions;[62] absence of discrimination;[63] proportionality of decisions;[64] absence of abuse or power;[65] application of impartiality and independence;[66] objectivity in decision-taking;[67] respect for legitimate expectations, consistency and tendering advice;[68] acting fairly[69] and being courteous;[70] replying in the official EU language used by the citizen requesting assistance;[71] providing an acknowledgement of receipt and indicating the competent official;[72] obligation to forward correspondence to relevant specialist department(s);[73] respecting the right to be heard and to make statements;[74] ensuring that no more than a reasonable time limit elapses prior to taking decisions;[75] duty to state grounds of decisions;[76] indication of the possibilities of appeal;[77] notification of decisions to persons concerned;[78] adherence to EU rules on data protection;[79] rules on provision of information[80] and access to documents[81] upon request; and keeping of adequate records.[82] In 2012, the EO complemented this with the adoption a set of five key Public Service Principles intended to guide EU civil servants of the ethical standards expected of their office. The five principles include: commitment to the EU and its citizens, integrity, objectivity, respect for others and transparency. The principles, designed to serve as guidance for civil servants particularly in situations which require the exercise of judgment (as opposed to simply implementing specific rules), are published in the current version of the ECGAB.

The ECGAB reflects the EO's very broad understanding of the concept of 'maladministration' and hence his remit to investigate EU institutional conduct. Notably, the ECGAB makes it clear that, as far as the EO is concerned, investigations should not be considered as being confined to considering purely procedural-type problems concerning poor communication between an EU organ and an individual. Essentially, the ECGAB principles clarify that the EO's investigative remit spans two broad areas of review, namely:

1   *Substantive legality review*: under the ECGAB the EO has the ability to assess whether or not an EU organ has complied with legal requirements.[83]
2   *Procedural propriety review*: the bulk of ECGAB principles are designed to test whether the EU organ's interaction with the public is in accordance with certain basic principles of procedural rigour and fairness, as reflected in EU administrative law (e.g. fair hearing) and/or recognised as the bases for sound administration of individual enquiries.

In practice, complaints submitted to the EO span across the broad spectrum of possible manifestations of maladministration. The bulk of complaints centre around the issue of rule-of-law compliance, namely where a complaint alleges an EU organ has failed to apply procedural and/or substantive EU rules correctly. By way of illustration, the types of complaints filed with the EO in 2012 were identified in the EO's annual report for that year as concerning the following main aspects: lawfulness (27.7 per cent); requests for information (12.5 per cent); fairness (10.3 per cent); reasonable time limit for taking decisions (8 per cent); requests for access to documentation (6.7 per cent); duty to state grounds for decisions and possibilities of appeal (6 per cent); non-discrimination (5.2 per cent); and duty of care (4.1 per cent).[84]

The expansive reach of the EO's remit has significant implications for EO investigations into alleged mismanagement by the European Commission of complaints concerning suspected infringements of EU law. As far as complaints against the European Commission over allegations of breaches of EU law (including EU environmental legislation) are concerned, the term 'maladministration' covers two main aspects of the Commission's law enforcement work. These relate to procedural and substantive aspects of the Commission's handling of such allegations. Procedural matters concern the manner in which the European Commission services have addressed a complainant's allegation of a breach of EU environmental law by or within a particular member state in accordance with principles of good administration, as recognised by the EO. Specifically, the EO may assess the timeliness of correspondence with the complainant and the degree to which the Commission has kept the complainant adequately informed of progress in the handling of their file, provided adequate reasoning for a decision on the complaint as well as offering the complaint a genuine opportunity to respond prior to a (definitive) decision being taken.

Substantive issues relate to whether the EO agrees with the Commission's interpretation of EU environmental law and/or evaluation of the relevant evidence made available to the Commission in support of an allegation of a breach of EU law. This latter aspect of the dimension to maladministration is important, given that it effectively provides a complainant with the opportunity to force the Commission to undergo a review of its decision(s) in relation to the complaint. In the past, Commission services have questioned whether the EO has jurisdiction to engage in a substantive review of an infringement complaint, namely to test whether the Commission's interpretation of EU law in a particular case has been correct.[85]

However, the ECGAB principle that EU institutional conduct must be compliant with the rule of law is now well established as part of the corpus of sound administration principles and the EO has undertaken many substantive reviews of Commission legal analysis in infringement complaints. Whilst it is clear that the ultimate determination of points of EU law are to be decided by the CJEU,[86] the EO, just like the European Commission, is entitled to offer legal opinion on the effect of any aspect of EU environmental law. Such opinions may well, and from time to time do, differ from those held by the Commission. If the EO is in agreement with a complainant over the existence of an infraction of EU environmental law, and makes this clear in his report, the effect of this divergence of viewpoint is likely to place the Commission under some pressure to review any previous decision rejecting a complainant's allegation. For, whilst the Commission is not strictly bound to adhere to EO findings,[87] the fact that the EO is a person in possession either of legal qualifications necessary for the highest judicial office in their own member state or has the acknowledged competence and experience to undertake the office of Ombudsman[88] lends a considerable degree of authority to any legal opinions that he may proffer in relation to a particular case. The authority of the EO is further underpinned by the fact that his position is one of complete independence.[89] Unlike the Commission, the EO does not have to weigh up political as well as legal implications of commencing infringement proceedings. As was outlined in Chapter 5, the Commission's position over infringement proceedings may, on occasion, be vulnerable to political influence, not least given that it is vested with responsibility under the TFEU framework for proposing legislation and developing policy. A decision to launch infringement proceedings may or may not have political implications in relation to the Commission being able to push through related policy initiatives. It is not without significance that the EO Statute endows the Ombudsman with the same rank as a judge of the CJEU in terms of remuneration, allowances and pension.[90] Accordingly, it would be an act in contravention of the spirit, if not the letter, of the constitutional framework of the EU if the Commission were not to undertake a thorough review of a case file in respect of which its conclusions differed markedly from that of the EO.

Whilst the ECGAB (together with public service principles) is technically voluntary and not legally binding on non-judicial EU institutions and bodies, in practice it represents a central benchmark for the EO's investigation of cases of suspected maladministration.[91] The EO in the past has indicated a preference to see the Code become a formally legally binding instrument, and thus not merely be a source of optional guidance for Union officials[92] and one code amongst several applicable to the various institutions and bodies.[93] Such a step would constitute a welcome advance on the existing position, given that the EO has no formal legal powers to require administrative changes take place in the wake of a finding of maladministration (see section 10.1.1.3 below).

At the same time, it is also the case that EU organs have instituted minimum codes of administrative conduct in respect of the activities of their officials. In 2000, the European Commission adopted a decision amending its Rules of Procedure[94] so as to introduce a binding *Code of Good Administrative Behaviour: Relations with the Public for its Staff*.[95] Whilst the Commission's Code does not mirror the contents of the ECGAB, it does contain several principles that either reflect or strongly resonate with sound administration principles contained in the ECGAB. Those particularly relevant to the handling of infringement complaints include the following general principles of good administration identified in the Commission's Code: lawfulness (ensuring that the Commission acts in accordance with the law and applies the rules and procedures laid down in EU legislation), non-discrimination and equal treatment, consistency, objectivity and impartiality, provision of information on administrative procedures, listening to all parties with a direct interest, duty to justify decisions and expedient dealing with enquiries from the public.

Notwithstanding the wide scope afforded to the term 'maladministration' by the EO, it is important to recognise its limits. This is particularly important in connection with scrutiny over the exercise of the European Commission's powers in relation to the prosecution of infringement proceedings under Articles 258 and 260 TFEU. The EO has made it clear that complaints to it of a political rather than administrative nature are regarded as inherently inadmissible. Thus, for instance, the EO will not review the merits of legislative action or inaction on the part of the Union's legislative institutions. In addition, it is clear that it is not the task of the EO to undermine the ultimate discretionary power afforded to the European Commission under the TFEU over whether or not to commence infringement proceedings against a member state. As recognised by the CJEU and discussed in the previous chapter, such a decision is a matter for the exclusive prerogative of the Commission. Were the EO to interfere with this discretion, such a move would be tantamount to undermining and interfering in the judicial activities of the CJEU, something that the EO is specifically barred from doing under Article 228 TFEU. In this context, one should also bear in mind that the Commission has moved in relatively recent years to prioritise the types of cases that it considers most eligible for consideration to be pursued under Article 258 TFEU in infringement proceedings, mostly for resource-related reasons to ensure that it is able to address the most serious cases. Specifically, the Commission's 2007 Communication *A Europe of Results – Applying Community Law*[96] identified that infringement proceedings would be centred around the following types of cases: (1) non-communication cases; (2) failures to respect CJEU judgments; and (3) cases involving breaches of EU law raising issues of principle or having a particularly far-reaching impact on citizens. In 2008 the Commission fleshed out what this would mean for the handling of environmental infringement casework.[97] Any challenge by the EO of the Commission's discretion on whether or not to launch infringement proceedings in any given case would also potentially or actually undermine the Commission's prioritisation strategy.

In a recent decision on an environmental complaint,[98] the EO summarised the reach of his jurisdiction in terms of scrutinising alleged instances of maladministration by the Commission in its management of infringement casework in the following general terms:

(46)   At the outset, the Ombudsman recalls that, according to the case law of the Union courts, the Commission has a wide margin of discretion to decide whether or not to bring an action against a Member State for an alleged infringement of EU law. This discretion is not limited to certain areas of EU law nor is its exercise conditional upon a prior statement from the Commission to this effect in a given infringement complaint, as the complainant appears to believe.

(47)   The scope of the Ombudsman's mandate in relation to such complaints, however, is limited to examining whether the Commission acted with diligence in relation to the infringement complaint submitted to it. In this respect, the Ombudsman's review tries to ascertain

whether the Commission: a) complied with the rules and procedures established in the 2002 [Commission] Communication on relations with the complainant in respect of infringements of Community law ('the 2002 Communication'),[99] which aims to establish a clear and transparent framework for the handling of infringement complaints; and b) provided an adequate statement of reasons when responding to infringement complaints submitted to it.

The EO's comments underline the limits of his powers to appraise the Commission's decision-making. Notably, they relay an understanding that whilst the EO may interrogate the legal reasoning of the Commission in its assessment of a complainant's allegation of a breach of EU environmental law by a member state, this is not to be interpreted as meaning that the EO asserts that the Commission should be compelled to take legal action in the event that the Commission is found to have concluded erroneously that a complaint has not established the existence of a breach of EU law. The EO has acknowledged that, even where the Commission considers that EU law has been breached by a member state, the Commission may exercise a wide margin of discretion in determining whether it is appropriate to commence infringement proceedings and, in so doing, to appraise whether such legal action would be against the Union interest because, for example, national courts or authorities would be better placed to deal with the matter.[100]

Were the Commission ever to declare to a complainant that it has made a purely political decision not to take up a particular case, notwithstanding the legal merits of the complainant's submissions, such a decision would ultimately be immune from a charge of maladministration, given that EU rules allow the Commission to adopt such a position. Yet even in this sensitive area, the EO has made some inroads. In the *Lower Saxony Betting Services Ban* complaint[101] the EO found that the Commission had been guilty of maladministration in failing to act with due diligence in the face of a failure by the Commission college to take a decision on whether to commence infringement proceedings on the back of an individual complaint (i.e. effectively to ignore it) because of the perceived political sensitivity of the case. The EO filed a special report to the EP as a result.[102]

In practice the EO is able to scrutinise Commission rejections of complaints of alleged breaches of EU law, given that the reasons proffered by the Commission will be based normally on legal as opposed to political considerations (legal interpretation and/or on weight of supporting evidence). By virtue of the EO's authority, complainants have a right to expect that their submissions of illegal member state conduct are fully and correctly analysed by the European Commission and that the complaints review process undertaken by the Commission is conducted in accordance with principles of procedural propriety and effectiveness as set out in the ECGAB.

10.1.1.3 Legal powers of the EO

The range of legal powers afforded to the EO in order to carry out his work, as principally set out in the EO Statute and EO Implementing Decision, may be characterised as rather inconsistent in terms of strength and depth. On the one hand, the EO's powers of investigation are fairly wide-ranging and with legal teeth. On the other hand, the EO has little in the way of meaningful power to ensure that his findings in inquiries of maladministration are adhered to by EU organs.

INVESTIGATIVE POWERS

The EO has substantial legal powers for the purpose of facilitating his investigations into suspected cases of maladministration.[103] Under the EO Statute, non-judicial EU institutions and bodies are required to disclose to the EO information he has requested and provide him with access to relevant files, unless they are able to prove that disclosure or access should be denied 'on duly substantiated grounds of secrecy'.[104] Similarly, subject to a qualification in relation to documents classified as secret, they are to deliver up to the EO documents originating in a member state, after informing the state concerned.[105] Classified documents originating in a member state may only be divulged to the EO with member state consent.[106] The EO also has powers to require member state authorities to assist with his investigations where the Ombudsman so requests. Specifically, they are under a duty to provide the EO with 'any information that may help to clarify instances of maladministration' on the part of non-judicial EU institutions or bodies, subject again to a qualification where information is classified as secret.[107] The EO is obliged as a matter of general principle to treat documents he obtains in the course of inquiries as confidential and may not as a matter of course disclose their contents to other persons, including complainants.[108] Where either a Union institution or body or a member state authority fails to provide relevant information, the EO must inform the EP, which is under a consequent duty to 'make representations' with a view to securing disclosure.[109] In environmental cases, access to information by the EO has not (to date) proven to be a material issue in the vast majority of instances;[110] experience overall has shown that requests for disclosure of information are essentially respected.[111] Moreover, it should also be noted in this context that the access to environmental information provisions contained in the Århus Regulation 1367/2006[112] in conjunction with the 2001 Access to Documents Regulation[113] (discussed in online Chapter 9A) contain far-reaching obligations on EU organs such as the Commission to disclose information relating to the environment, including on infringement files that have been closed.

The usual course of events in a complaints inquiry is for the EO first to request disclosure of relevant information, documentation and evidence from each party (complainant and EU organ). Where however the EO considers that the EU organ's efforts to disclose material have been inadequate, he has the power to inspect the relevant file held by the EU organ himself and may make copies of the entirety or part of its contents.[114] The power of accessing the file, however, may not be undertaken without prior notification of the EU organ concerned, and some concern has been expressed that the practice of giving prior notice may provide opportunity for document suppression.[115] The EO may also request EU organs to make arrangements for him to pursue his inquiries on the spot.[116] Where considered necessary, the EO may also require EU officials and service staff to be interviewed and give evidence.[117] Such staff remain bound to observe the duty of professional secrecy enshrined within EU Staff Regulations,[118] the Commission having resisted attempts by the EP and EO to require that EU civil service testimony should be provided on the sole basis of 'complete and truthful information'.[119] The EO may also decide, where he deems it appropriate, to commission studies or expert reports in order to assist in the investigation.[120]

LACK OF SANCTIONS FOR NON-COMPLIANCE

One of the notable shortcomings in the legal framework underpinning the office of EO is the fact that the EO's findings of maladministration against an EU organ are neither legally binding nor enforceable.[121] The EO's findings and any accompanying recommendations do not have the force of EU law behind them. Further, the EO has no legal powers to impose sanctions upon non-judicial EU institutions or bodies found guilty by it of maladministration. The absence of any clear, legally binding mechanism for ensuring that instances of maladministration will be actually addressed by the EU institution or body concerned means that ultimately there is no guarantee that errors will be either acknowledged or corrected in the future. In addition, this means also that there is no mechanism for ensuring that successful complainants may be compensated in respect of instances of maladministration.

Where, as a result of an inquiry, the EO considers that an instance or instances of maladministration have been shown to have occurred, after providing the EU organ concerned with three months to respond he must then file a report to the EP.[122] Occasionally, the EO may wish to make a 'further remark' (or more rarely even 'draft recommendations') with respect to a complaint, even though he may consider overall there to be no instance of maladministration, where he may wish to recommend certain changes be made to the EU organ's administrative practice.[123] The complainant is kept informed throughout. As far as possible, the EO will seek to find a 'friendly solution' with the EU organ concerned where the EO considers maladministration to have occurred.[124] If this is achieved, the EO closes the case with a reasoned decision.[125] In the absence of a friendly solution, the EO may proceed to conclude his findings in the written report either with draft recommendations or a critical remark depending on the circumstances. Where the EO considers either that it is possible for the EU organ concerned to correct the instance of maladministration or that the maladministration has no general implications, he may file a report to the EU organ concerned with 'draft recommendations'.[126] The EU organ has three months to respond by way of a 'detailed opinion', indicating to what extent it agrees with the EO's draft recommendations and describing any measures to be taken in order to implement them.[127] If the EO considers the opinion to be inadequate, he may then file a 'special report' to the EP which may contain recommendations.[128] Where the EO considers it is no longer possible to terminate the instance of maladministration and that the maladministration bears no general implications, he may make instead a 'critical remark' in the report.[129] In practice, the EO provides a generous six months for institutions to respond to a critical remark.[130]

Whether the outcome of an inquiry results in draft recommendations or a critical remark, the stark reality is that there is no guarantee that the EU organ receiving them will act upon them. Any decision by the EO has no legally binding value and may not be enforced via the EU courts. The EO may not invoke judicial review proceedings under Articles 263 and 265 TFEU against the EU organ over failures to implement EO findings, given that these legal procedures exclude the possibility of legal action in relation to non-binding recommendations or opinions. If an EU organ fails to comply with the EO's recommendations, the EO may resort to referring the matter to the EP by way of special report. The EO Annual Report 2012 describes the power of the EO to file a special report to the EP as 'the most powerful tool at his disposal'.[131] That is debatable, as there is no guarantee or mechanism to ensure that the EP will take the matter further[132] and the EP has no effective powers to apply legally binding sanctions on the EU organ concerned if it adopts the special report by way of a resolution.[133]

Effectively, bad publicity is the only genuinely credible weapon that the Ombudsman has at his disposal in order to seek to hold non-judicial EU institutions and bodies, such as the European Commission, to account in respect of their administrative conduct. The EO's recommendations are set out in the annual reports of his activities submitted to the EP,[134] which are published in the Official Journal of the EU. The EO's website contains a publicly accessible database[135] of all his previous decisions as well as providing news and updates of the most recent decisions.[136] One might argue that the powers of the EO effectively boil down to 'name and shame'. Whether or not this is effective or sufficient is open to question. Given that the role of the EO is still not that widely known or properly understood by the general public, it would seem questionable at the moment whether the factor of adverse publicity in an annual report is sufficiently effective in ensuring that instances of maladministration are appropriately rectified and lessons are taken on board for the future (deterrence factor). One might argue that, in the absence of a right of appeal from the EO, the absence of EO powers to issue legal sanctions is justified. However, that is not a cogent argument for justifying the absence of sanctioning powers for the EO in perpetuity. Any such increase in legal powers would enhance the Ombudsman's position as independent arbiter and would, as a matter of basic principle, have to be accompanied by appropriate procedural safeguards such as rights of appeal, especially where EO reports make reference to the conduct of specified EC officials or servants.[137]

Notwithstanding the absence of legal force attached to EO findings of maladministration, the EO has reported that in practice EU organs have a good record of compliance. The EO has estimated that the overall rate of compliance by other EU organs with EO findings is high, in the region of 82 per cent.[138] The EO Annual Report 2012 noted that the institutional follow-up to critical and further remarks made in 2011 was 80 and 89 per cent respectively. Tsadiras has assessed, though, that the rate of compliance by EU organs with EO decisions concerning EU environmental policy matters is notably worse than the general average score

(50 per cent as compared with 70 per cent).[139] A number of factors may have contributed to a relatively positive response from EU organs to EO decisions. First and foremost it should be noted that all EU organs, including notably the Commission, have come at some stage to adopt binding codes on administrative conduct for their staff which, if not incorporating all the ECGAB principles, at least contain a core of them. By virtue of these innovations, an administrative culture of sound administration has now begun to embed itself across the EU institutional spectrum, with EU organs having unilaterally bound themselves to ensure that their activities comply with principles good administration. This will make it more straightforward in general terms for the EO to persuade an EU organ to effect changes to administrative procedure and practice in order to rectify instances of maladministration, given that EU organs have subscribed to a good administrative conduct agenda in respect of which the EO is seen as having established a pioneering as well as leadership role.

Secondly, it has been argued in some quarters that the effectiveness of the EO in practice derives from the capacity to engage in constructive moral persuasion as well as to elicit co-operation from other EU organs in a context that is more flexible, informal, less hostile and rigid than one associated with traditional law enforcement.[140] A characteristic feature of the EO's activities is that they are intended to be carried out in a spirit of constructive institutional co-operation, as opposed to adversarial combat. The EO has laid great emphasis on establishing and fostering good general working relationships with other EU organs, which has served to highlight that the entrenchment of principles of sound administration represents a joint enterprise as opposed to being a mission exclusive to the EO.[141] The EO has also taken to publicising and commending instances of good administrative practice revealed during the course of investigations; these are highlighted as 'star cases' in the Ombudsman's annual reports.[142]

Thirdly, the adoption of the ECGAB has skilfully relocated the focus of the EO's mandate towards a normative as opposed to a litigious goal, namely achievement of lasting improvements to EU administrative practice as opposed to the allocation of blame in respect of instances of maladministration. A fourth factor lies no doubt in the degree of rigour, quality and relatively prompt delivery associated with the EO's casework, with each decision being clearly and fully reasoned. It should be noted here that the EO is backed up by a team of currently around 80 supporting staff (including some 30 lawyers directly involved with handling complaints)[143] which, notwithstanding its relatively small size when compared with for example individual Commission Directorate-Generals, has been crucially important in developing credibility and professionalism of the EO's office.

However, notwithstanding the evidence that EU organs in practice clearly treat the EO with respect, this cannot occlude the fact their compliance with EO reports is by no means guaranteed in any given case. Indeed, there have been a number of instances of non-compliance with EO findings of maladministration, including in relation to the environmental sphere.[144] This factor has given rise to concerns expressed from a number of quarters,[145] including former EO Jacob Söderman. During the negotiations in the run-up to the 2004 Treaty on a

Constitution for Europe, the then EO proposed in the Convention on the Future of Europe some treaty changes be made to the office of EO.[146] In particular, he proposed that the EO be granted the power to refer to the CJEU where, after carrying out an inquiry, he considered either a member state or an EU organ had failed to respect a fundamental or human right binding under EU law. Ultimately, the EO's proposal did not receive support from either EU organs or member states and was not incorporated within the final treaty text. Given that the EO has defined maladministration to include failure to adhere to the rule of law, there is a strong case in favour of ensuring that EO findings of illegal conduct should be capable of being followed up by the EO and enforced ultimately before the EU judiciary, either through judicial review or via a preliminary ruling reference procedure. This is not to suggest that all EO findings of maladministration should be capable of being backed up through the mechanism law enforcement. In particular, those instances of maladministration exposed by the EO which involve essentially non-legal issues relating the manner in which interaction between an EU organ and individual has been handled (e.g. issues concerning professionalism and due courtesy) would obviously not be suited to being dealt with through the system of law enforcement. Accordingly, a distinction should be made between law-related and non-law-related types of maladministration in determining which instances of non-compliance with EO findings of maladministration should be capable of review before the CJEU. Söderman's proposal effectively goes some way to making such a distinction, but falls short in only addressing a very limited aspect of illicit EU institutional conduct (namely covering only fundamental rights protection). In the light of the lack of success with the 2002 Söderman initiative, it would be surprising though whether this legal structural issue will be reconsidered by the EO any time soon.

10.1.1.4 *The EO's complaints procedure: key aspects*

The complaints procedure before the EO is relatively informal and straightforward, there being few procedural requirements and steps involved.[147] The EO review process is usually triggered by an individual complainant, although theoretically the EO may initiate investigations on an own-initiative basis. It is not possible to determine accurately how long the entire process of an appeal to the Ombudsman may take; this will depend upon a number of factors, including the complexity of the file and degree of co-operation forthcoming from the relevant non-judicial Union institution or body under the spotlight. However, as a rough estimate, it would appear from the EO annual reports that environmental complaints filed from private individuals against the Commission take in the region of anywhere between one and two years. The EO has recently asserted that 69 per cent of complaints are addressed within a year, and 79 per cent of cases completed within 18 months.[148] The complaints process is usually document-driven, thus involving normally exclusively a written exchange of correspondence between the EO and other parties concerned.[149] As soon as a complaint is received by the EO, he must inform the EU organ concerned immediately.[150]

Upon receipt of the complaint, which is usually acknowledged to the complainant within one week,[151] the EO first determines whether it falls within its mandate and, if this is confirmed, whether the complaint is admissible. In order to ensure that their complaint is admissible, complainants are required to ensure, in particular, that they meet the five principal formal conditions set out below before filing a complaint with the EO. The key criteria of admissibility set out in the EO Statute comprise:

- The author and object of the complaint must be identified.[152] The person lodging the complaint may, though, request that his identity remain confidential.
- The EO would not be intervening in cases before courts or questioning the soundness of a judicial ruling.[153]
- The complaint must have been filed within two years of the date on which the facts on which it is based come to the complainant's attention.[154] From an EU environmental law enforcement perspective, this means that persons must usually file their complaints with the EO within two years of receiving notification of the decision by the Commission rejecting their submissions that a breach of EU environmental legislation has occurred or otherwise definitively closing an existing infringement file. Notwithstanding this temporal requirement, it is open for the EO to pursue an 'out of time' case on the basis of an own-initiative inquiry if he deems that the case warrants an investigation.
- The complaint must have been preceded by appropriate administrative approaches to the EU organ concerned.[155] As far as EU environmental law enforcement complaints are concerned, the responsibilities of the complainant in this regard are straightforward, namely that they should have first contacted the Commission to request an infringement action be commenced or maintained, as appropriate. The EO has held that once a person has lodged a complaint with the Commission about an alleged infringement of EU environmental law, then it is reasonable for that person to expect to be informed as to the progress of that complaint being processed by the Commission services without having to chase after information and updates from the Commission.[156] The complainant must, though, have at least once contacted the Commission and communicated their submission of alleged breach of law in full.
- In the case of disputes between EU civil servants and EU employers, the possibilities of submitting internal administrative requests and complaints must have been already exhausted.[157]

In order to assess whether or not the complaint falls within his mandate and fulfils the admissibility criteria, the EO may request the complainant to submit further information and/or documentation as appropriate.[158] Any determination of a complaint falling outside the mandate or otherwise being inadmissible is communicated to the complainant with the reasons relayed.[159]

If the EO considers that the complaint is admissible, he will then consider within one month whether there are sufficient grounds to open an inquiry.[160]

During this particular part of the preliminary phase of assessment, the EO will assess whether the complaint appears to be supported with sufficient grounds to open an inquiry.[161] It is self-evident that the complainant must also be able to submit relevant and sufficient legal argument and evidence in support of their case to the Ombudsman in order to persuade the latter of the merits of commencing an investigation. If the EO rejects the complaint at this stage, the complainant is duly informed by way of reasoned decision and the file is closed.[162] If the EO considers it appropriate for the purpose of enhancing the quality of the EU organ's administrative practice, he may bring what is known as a 'further remark' to the attention of the EU organ concerned.[163] However, should the EO consider there are sufficient grounds in support of the maladministration allegation, he will then open an inquiry. His first step will be to inform the relevant EU organ concerned (in addition to the complainant), requesting it to provide him with a preliminary opinion (known as a 'first opinion') of its views within three months.[164] Upon receipt of the EU organ's first opinion, the EO will forward a copy to the complainant, who then has the opportunity to provide comments within a time-frame of usually no more than one month.[165] The EO Implementing Decision provides that the EO organ must not include any information or documentation it regards as confidential.[166] This particular provision, however, must be read restrictively in light of the access to environmental information requirements stipulated by the Århus Regulation 1367/2006[167] (as discussed in the previous chapter (9A)).

If, after assessing the first opinion and comments, the EO is minded to consider that there is a case of maladministration, he will endeavour to work to achieve a friendly settlement with the EU organ concerned.[168] This may involve requests from the EO to the Union entity for supplementary explanation of facts. In addition, where the EO considers this necessary, he may exercise his powers of investigation outlined in section 10.1.1.3 above, such as accessing the relevant files of the EU organ or interviewing staff. Where a friendly resolution to the dispute can be achieved, so as to eliminate the maladministration and satisfy the complainant, the EO will close the case with a reasoned decision.[169] In practice a fair proportion of cases are settled this way (21 per cent of the cases closed in 2012).[170] If, however, no such solution can be found, the EO will proceed to close the case with a reasoned decision containing a critical remark or draft recommendations as appropriate.[171] Overall, the proportion of EO findings of maladministration which cannot be resolved by way of friendly solution is relatively small (14 per cent of cases closed in 2012).[172] As mentioned earlier, draft recommendations will be issued where it is still possible to eliminate the maladministration and/or where it is particularly serious and has ongoing general implications; critical remarks are made in respect cases of maladministration which can no longer be eliminated and which have no general implications. The EU organ is afforded three months to submit a 'detailed opinion' in response to any draft recommendations drawn up by the EO[173] and has six months to respond to critical remarks.[174] Unless the Union institution or body takes the necessary steps to resolve the matter in accordance with the EO's draft recommendations, the EO is then obliged to send a report to the EP and Union institution or body concerned, which may contain recommendations.[175] In all cases, the complainant will be informed by the EO of the outcome of his inquiries as soon as possible, and will be informed of the opinions expressed by the Union institution or body as well as the EO's recommendations.[176]

10.1.2 Environmental maladministration complaints

Since its inauguration in 1995, the office of the EO has had the opportunity to consider a number of cases filed to it from private persons against EU organs concerning the implementation of EU environmental policy. The vast majority of allegations against EU organs of maladministration in relation to environment-related matters have so far centred on the European Commission's handling of their complaints about alleged instances of EU environmental law infringements by member states. Some of the maladministration complaints have also more recently begun to concern the activities of other EU organs, notably the EIB in relation to its lending to member states in respect of development projects.[177] Complaints to the EO have challenged both procedural as well as substantive aspects of EU institutional decision-making.

The EO's annual reports between 1995 and 2012 refer to some 50 decisions taken by the Ombudsman in relation to (admissible) maladministration claims and own-initiative inquiries concerning the environmental sector. Table 10.1 (at the end of this chapter) provides a list of these environmental decisions. The vast majority of these have concerned the application of EU environmental impact assessment and nature protection legislation (some 60 per cent). The texts of the individual decisions of the EO, including those relating to environmental issues, may be inspected on the EO's website.[178] As at July 2014, the EO's database case register[179] indicated that he had taken the following types of decisions concerning the EU environmental policy sector: 52 decisions, three draft recommendations[180] and one special report to the EP.[181] Two own-initiative inquiries have been commissioned into EU environmental institutional decision-making.[182]

Tsadiras[183] has recently undertaken a study of the EO's work in relation to the environmental sector and made some interesting general findings. He has calculated that a far higher proportion of complaints are sponsored by legal entities than from natural persons (51 per cent as compared with the general figure of 20 per cent). This is not necessarily that surprising given that one would expect a substantial level of NGEO interest in utilising the procedure and technical expertise (as well as possibly cost-related) factors may well serve to depress the number of complaints from natural persons. He also found that procedural and substantive issues were raised in maladministration complaints in roughly equal measure and often in tandem (in 64 and 59 per cent of individual cases respectively).[184] He also notes the fact that environmental complaints have had, on average, a far higher success rate than compared with complaints in general to the EO (35 per cent as compared with 20 per cent), possibly reflective of the generally high quality of submissions filed to the Ombudsman.[185] It would appear that the proportion of complaints to the EO resolved by way of friendly settlement is broadly similar to the amount of infringement proceedings resolved out of court by the European Commission (namely around 10 per cent).[186]

The remainder of this section explores the various procedural as well as substantive issues that have been raised in connection with maladministration claims submitted to the EO in the wake of dissatisfaction with Commission handling of complaints concerning suspected environmental infringements.

10.1.2.1 *Procedural failings and environmental infringement complaints*

The manner in which the European Commission handles complaints about purported infractions of EU environmental law has been a topic of significant concern to the EO over the years. The issue of procedural propriety on the part of the Commission has taken up a significant part of the EO's work here. As outlined earlier, over time the EO has developed a number of principles of good administration intended to improve the standard of administrative management of complaints concerning breaches of EU environmental law by the European Commission, as broadly consolidated within the ECGAB adopted in 2001. The EO has been an important influence in raising the standards of administrative responses within the Commission regarding complaints against member states over issues relating to compliance with EU law, including EU environmental law.

When the EO first started operational duties in the mid 1990s, the European Commission notoriously provided virtually no basic standards of care and service to persons submitting complaints about member state infractions of EU law. Specifically, a complainant might receive acknowledgement of receipt, confirmation of registration of the complaint and information on the outcome of the Commission's assessment (no time-frame given). Even these basic aspects were not guaranteed, at least initially. No commitment was offered by the Commission to update the complainant on the progress of their complaint, involve the complainant in the Commission's investigations or inform the complainant of the grounds of the Commission's final decision. In several instances, complainants were only informed of a decision after the Commission had issued a press release on the subject. There was no system to ensure that the complainant had a right to offer comment to the Commission about its conclusions prior to a formal decision being taken by the College. Such a state of affairs was unsurprisingly liable to generate mistrust and disillusion with the early approach taken by the Commission in relation to the handling of complaints.[187]

Within a few months of his appointment, the first EO, Jacob Söderman, decided to take steps to ensure that administrative standards were improved in terms of complaints handling by the Commission. In the wake of a series of own-initiative inquiries as well as other cases,[188] the EO persuaded the Commission to make some improvements to its procedures in 1997. Specifically, complainants were enabled to present observations to the Commission before the latter could decide to close a particular file.[189] As noted in Chapter 5, the Commission has sought to take a number of steps to improve the handling of its complaints procedures since the late 1990s.[190] Notable milestones along this journey were the adoption by the Commission in 2000 of a general code on good administrative conduct[191] and, in particular, a 2002 Commission Communication regarding relations with complainants in respect of alleged infringements of Union law.[192] In turn the Commission's handling procedures have now been updated by a 2012 Communication.[193] The procedural commitments for the benefit of complainants set out in the 2012 Communication have been addressed in some detail in Chapter 5 and need not be repeated here.

EO annual reports submitted to the EP have revealed a variety of procedural shortcomings and failings of the Commission in its handling of complaints about alleged breaches of EU environmental law. It is worth noting the various key principles of good administration that the EO has felt necessary to establish and/or confirm when uncovering instances of maladministration by the Commission services responsible for handling infringement files. Most, if not all, of these principles are common-sensical, and it is revealing that these findings have had to be even formally announced by the EO in the context of investigations of maladministration. Most of the worst types of procedural improprieties appear to have been addressed, although basic errors are periodically reported notwithstanding the existence of written codification in the form of the ECGAB (and to some extent reflected in the Commission's own general codes of conduct mentioned above).

RESPONSIBILITY TO ACKNOWLEDGE AND REGISTER INFRINGEMENT COMPLAINT

As a result of a string of adverse EO maladministration decisions in the 1990s, as from 2002 the Commission formally committed to ensuring that receipt of an infringement complaint should be acknowledged within 15 working days[194] and that it should be duly registered on its internal system for dealing with complaints insofar as it fulfils certain standard minimum criteria.[195] The EO has remained vigilant about ensuring that the Commission adheres to these soft law commitments, with a view to ensuring that each complaint is addressed and not avoided, either deliberately or through negligence.[196] A notable recent example has been the EO's decision in 2010[197] to criticise a Commission practice of deciding to register only those complaints which fall within the scope of the types of cases prioritised by it since 2007[198] for the purpose of infringement proceedings. The Commission has subsequently ensured that all complaints are registered onto its IT central application system for the registration of complaints (CHAP database).[199] Where there are multiple complaints filed by members of the public in relation to the same suspected infringement, the EO has endorsed the Commission's policy[200] of issuing communications via the Official Journal and/or press release.[201]

RESPONSIBILITY TO PROVIDE A DECISION ON THE INFRINGEMENT
COMPLAINT WITH A REASONABLE PERIOD OF TIME

The Commission has on a number of occasions been criticised for failing to respond to complainants' submissions within a reasonable period of time. This issue was intended to be addressed in 2002, when the Commission committed to ensuring that Commission services handling complaints of breaches of EU law should decide normally within one year whether formal action should be taken up in relation to the case. However, subsequently there have been instances where the EO has found that the Commission has been guilty of unnecessary delays in handling complaints.[202] One example concerned a complaint about breaches by the Austrian government to adhere to EU legislative limit values on particulate matter (PM10).[203] The EU issued a critical remark against the Commission for failing to exercise its discretion whether to launch infringement proceedings in light of the available evidence. The EO found that, notwithstanding that the Commission had acquired technical confirmation of a breach of EU air quality legislation in the Vienna area through scientific reports 18 months after the complaint was submitted , the Commission had subsequently (erroneously) wished to wait until it adopted a coherent approach on infringements with respect to all member states. The EO has accepted that, in certain situations, the Commission may have justification to exceed the benchmark one-year deadline, especially where the case involves protracted technical and/or evaluative work such as numerous site visits in a case involving assessment of multiple suspected breaches of EU environmental legislation.[204] However, the EO has been critical of instances where the Commission has effectively sat on a file for purely political reasons, such as because the Commission college has refused to make a decision to prosecute owing to the political sensitivity of the case[205] to certain member states or where the Commission no longer considers litigation justified in view of a prospective change of direction in Union policy.[206]

RESPONSIBILITY TO PROVIDE REGULAR INFORMATION AND FEEDBACK TO THE
COMPLAINANT ON THE PROGRESS OF THE COMPLAINT

On a number of occasions, the EO has criticised the Commission for having failed to provide the complainant with regular updates as to how their particular complaint is progressing.[207] On some occasions, it has transpired that months have elapsed without any Commission feedback, notwithstanding regular enquiries on the complainant's part.[208] Since 2002, the Commission's policy has been to ensure that the complainant is informed in writing of each procedural step taken in the case (LFN, RO, referral to the CJEU or case closure),[209] which the EO has essentially endorsed as the minimum to be expected for the purposes of sound administration.[210]

RESPONSIBILITY TO ADDRESS ALL THE SUBMISSIONS MADE BY THE COMPLAINANT

The EO has confirmed that it is good administrative practice for the Commission to respond to each and every point raised by complainants in their submissions to the Commission,[211] including when a complainant purports to present fresh evidence or argument to support an existing complaint.[212]

RESPONSIBILITY TO INVOLVE THE COMPLAINANT IN SITE VISITS AND
OTHER FACT-FINDING EVENTS/MISSIONS

The EO has held that normally complainants should be informed about investigative site visits and be invited to participate in them, unless the site visit is unlikely to be material to a Commission investigation.[213] The EO has acknowledged, though, that the Commission may exclude participation of complainants in bilateral 'package' meetings with member state representatives, meetings which are intended to enable the Commission to engage with the member state in a frank exchange of views and seek a resolution to the dispute.[214]

RESPONSIBILITY TO PROVIDE COMPLAINANT/INQUIRER ACCESS TO DOCUMENTS,
EXCEPT THOSE WHICH ARE SECRET OR DRAWN UP AS PART OF JUDICIAL PROCEEDINGS

The EO has confirmed that the Commission should, as a matter of good administrative practice, provide individuals with access to documents, subject to the caveat of secrecy and where they are pertinent to ongoing judicial proceedings or specific investigations.[215] This area of law is now subject to the requirements of the Access to Documents Regulation 1049/2001 and Århus Regulation 1367/2006, considered in the previous chapter (9A).

RESPONSIBILITY TO PROVIDE COMPLAINANT WITH REASONS WHY
A DECISION IS TAKEN ON THE CASE (E.G. CLOSURE)

The EO has held that the Commission is guilty of maladministration where it refuses to divulge the reasons for rejecting a complaint of a breach of EU environmental law.[216] Moreover, it is incumbent on the Commission to provide sufficient, clear and coherent reasons for its decision.[217] The Commission's own policy on handling complaints confirms that it will provide a complainant with four weeks to respond to any proposal by the Commission to close the file, with closure decisions being notified to the complainant.[218] The EO has encouraged the Commission to refer complainants to other available avenues of redress at national level (whether via courts or other authorities) in the event that the EU institution decides to close a file notwithstanding the probable existence of a breach of Union law.[219]

RESPONSIBILITY TO ADDRESS INDIVIDUAL COMPLAINTS IMPARTIALLY

One of the most extraordinary reports ever to be published by the EO was a case relating to the Union funding of a sewage and biological treatment works project in Parga, Greece.[220] A complaint had been lodged with the Commission that the project had not been subject to an environmental impact assessment in accordance with the EIA Directive.[221] The initial view of the Commission, as expressed to the complainant, was that the project fell within the remit of the EIA Directive and that there had been a violation of that legislation. However, subsequently the position of the Commission services in relation to the case changed without the complainant being informed. The Greek authorities were informed that no infringement action would be taken, the Commission's view being that the development project was not covered by the EIA Directive from a temporal perspective, and moreover that EU cohesion funding would be granted in respect of the project. Subsequently, a letter was sent to the complainant from the Commission indicating that the Commission services had not decided the matter and would continue to consider her submissions. In investigating the case, the EO found that a fundamental conflict of interest underpinned the change of mind of the Commission services. Specifically, a senior Commission official within the Environment Directorate-General (DG ENV) heavily involved in the infringement case was also an active senior member of a Greek political party at the time, which had an interest in seeing that the project gained approval.[222] Ultimately, the EO's reaction was scathing, holding that the management of the case and the inherent conflict of interest arising amounted to a clear case of maladministration. In his 2002 decision on the case, the EO addressed the issue of professional conduct in no uncertain terms:

> The Ombudsman considers that, from the point of view of the complainant, who did not know that the official in question was on annual and later on unpaid leave on personal grounds, and who had moreover recently received a letter signed by the official on 9 December 1998 stating that the case was still being investigated, there appear to be sufficient reasons to mistrust the impartial and proper handling of the case by the Commission and to question that the official in question did not conduct himself solely with the interests of the Communities in mind. In fact it would be difficult for any citizen in any Member State not to doubt the impartiality of the Commission's actions as the Guardian of the treaty if a Commission official who is deeply involved in dealing with an infringement case also holds a post in a political party in the very Member State that the case concerns and acts publicly in that capacity at a time when the case is being dealt with. In the eyes of European citizens, this kind of incident may put at risk the reputation of the Commission as Guardian of the Treaty, responsible for promoting the rule of law.[223]

In the *Parga* case the EO was ultimately prepared to accept that the Commission's new procedures in relation to complaints handling and in the Commission's Handbook for its officials announced in 2001 would mean that such a situation would not arise in the future.[224] Ironically, notwithstanding the fact the EO's report was not disputed in terms of its truth, the official concerned subsequently was able to sue the EO in part successfully for damages (€10,000) via non-contractual liability proceedings under Article 288 TFEU, the GC holding that the Ombudsman was not justified in briefly publishing the official's name in the original version of the EO decision (for two weeks) according to the right to privacy, the principle of proportionality as well as the adversarial principle.[225] The EO's report, in focusing on the question of maladministration on the part of the Commission, did not according to the GC need to expose the identity of the Commission official concerned in order to deal with that question. The Commission's follow-up in relation to the EO's decision and critical remarks was quite telling. In relation to the official concerned, the Commission has never indicated that it has undertaken an outside independent investigation into the individual's conduct.[226]

10.1.2.2 *Substantive review of environmental infringement complaints*

As part of his remit into investigations of maladministration, the EO is entitled to scrutinise the legal interpretation of EU law made by the European Commission in its evaluation as to whether infringement proceedings should be launched against a member state under Articles 258 and 260 TFEU. The EO has consistently confirmed that maladministration includes situations where non-judicial EU institutions and bodies interpret and/or apply EU law incorrectly. This point is emphasised in the ECGAB, which stipulates that Union officials are to ensure that their decisions are lawful in order to meet requirements of sound administration.[227] The environmental sector is no different. Accordingly, the complaints procedure before the EO has effectively offered private individuals an appeal against legal determinations made by the Commission on the correct implementation of EU environmental legislation, which have been material to the Commission's reasons for rejecting a particular individual's allegation of a breach of legislation. The EO is, however, careful to rule out appraising the handling of a case until the Commission has yet to make any final determination on the alleged infringement.[228]

As pointed out earlier, the EO's determinations on points of law are not binding on the Commission and the Commission retains discretion ultimately whether to pursue infringement proceedings, irrespective of whether or not it transpires that a particular breach of EU law by a member state has occurred. However, it is an established part of the EO's role in scrutinising alleged instances of maladministration to be able to test whether the legal reasoning of the Commission in relation to an infringement complaint is sound, namely in accordance with the rule of Union law in light of any available CJEU jurisprudence.[229] That the Commission's legal reasoning may be subject to scrutiny underlines the EO's view that, whilst the Commission has discretion to commence an infringement action, that discretion must be exercised within the sphere of its legal authority and not in an arbitrary fashion.[230]

On a number of occasions the EO has disagreed with the Commission over the latter's interpretations of EU environmental law in the context of infringement complaints. Conflicts between the Commission and the EO have arisen for instance in relation to Union legislation on environmental impact assessment. A notable example in the past has been in relation to assessing the extent to which the original former EIA Directive 85/337 applied to development projects whose origins pre-dated the directive's implementation deadline[231] (so-called 'pipeline' projects). For instance, in the *Parga* case,[232] involving the approval of a sewage works in Greece, the EO criticised the Commission for considering that the particular development project fell outside the scope of the EIA Directive on the ostensible grounds that official approval for its construction was given prior to the 1988 implementation deadline. The EO considered that the legal analysis carried out by the Commission was flawed, given that the national administrative documentation relied upon by the Commission to justify its conclusions did not purport to approve the project specifically, but instead was merely tantamount to a preparatory study. Approval was provided by the member state government much later after the implementation deadline. In *Vienna Airport*[233] the EO found that the Commission had erred in law in considering that a retrospective impact assessment in relation to an airport extension project would be compatible with the EIA Directive, given that there were conflicts of interest involved with the national authority charged to give approval to the project. Aside from the EIA Directive, the EO has also come into conflict with the Commission regarding the latter's interpretation of other areas of EU environmental law, including waste management[234] and nature protection.[235]

The EO has also shown it is prepared to undertake a substantive review of the Commission's assessment of evidence provided by a complainant in relation to an alleged instance of bad application of EU environmental law, whilst having acknowledged that the complainant has the onus of proving the existence of a breach.[236] For instance, in *Athens Tramway*[237] the EO proposed that the Commission re-examine the complainant's submission concerning the adequacy and propriety of the impact assessment provided by the national authorities as well as reconsider whether adequate publicity had been given in respect of the public consultation element.

10.2 The European Parliament (EP)

In addition to the EO, the European Parliament (EP)[238] represents, albeit to a relatively limited extent, a useful point of reference and assistance for private persons seeking to enforce or otherwise improve the state of implementation of EU environmental legislation. In addition to its primary role as supranational legislative institution alongside the Council of the EU, the EP does have a general function to play in supervising the delivery of Union policies. A number of political powers are granted to the EP, with a view to facilitating this particular role. These include being able to require the Commission to reply to parliamentary questions;[239] to discuss in open session the annual general reports submitted by the Commission;[240] a power to decide upon a motion of censure on the activities of the Commission which, if carried by a two-thirds majority of votes cast, will force the College of Commissioners including the High Representative of the Union on Foreign Affairs and Security Policy to resign;[241] receiving and taking up petitions on aspects of Union activities on behalf of private persons;[242] monitoring the work of the European Ombudsman;[243] and establishing temporary Committees of Inquiry to investigate alleged contraventions or maladministration in the implementation of Union law.[244] The degree of political influence that the EP may be able to exercise in relation to other political institutions of the EU such as the Commission as well as in relation to member states may potentially be of some assistance in connection with a private law enforcement campaign, such as raising the political profile and prominence of a particular dispute.

The EP, though, has no specific legal powers to assist in the process of enforcing EU environmental legislation at national level, which makes its role here rather indirect and complementary in nature. In addition, the EP does not have any legal powers to hold the Commission to account in respect of its decisions whether or not to take infringement proceedings against a member state under Articles 258 and 260 TFEU. In relation to complaints about the Commission's conduct over law enforcement issues, the relevant point of reference as far as the EP is concerned is usually in first instance the European Ombudsman.

10.2.1 *Right of petition to the EP*

The right of citizens to contact the EP and request it to take action by way of petition is laid down in the EU's foundational treaty framework.[245] Specifically, the right to petition the EP is set out in Article 24(2) in conjunction with Article 227 TFEU. The principal provision is Article 227 TFEU which states:

> Any citizen of the Union, and any natural or legal person residing or having its registered office in a Member State, shall have the right to address, individually or in association with other citizens or persons, a petition to the European Parliament on a matter which comes within the Union's fields of activity and which affects him, her or it directly.

In common with the right of complaint to the European Ombudsman, the right of petition is extended to a very wide range of persons. The right is not predicated upon possession by the petitioner of nationality of a Union member state,[246] but is conditional upon residency of the petitioner within the EU. In addition, the petitioner must show that they are directly affected by the matter. Accordingly, unlike the maladministration complaints filed with the EO, the petition is not an *actio popularis* given that the petitioner must demonstrate a personal interest. On the other hand, the material scope of petitions is much broader than that applicable to EO maladministration complaints; they may concern any matter coming within the EU's fields of activity. Accordingly, environmental petitions may cover policy or legal issues and/or matters relating to the performance of a Union institution or national authority in connection with the development or implementation of EU environmental law.

The EP's Rules of Procedure[247] set out the rules governing the examination and handling of petitions, which are managed by the EP's Committee on Petitions (PETI).[248] The Committee files annual reports on its work as well as maintaining a regular briefing newsletter *PETI Journal*.[249]

A notable feature of the right of petition is the fact that it does not compel the EP to take action. Discretion is afforded to the EP to determine what steps, if any, it chooses to take upon receipt of a petition. This may be contrasted with the position of the EO, whose position is more circumscribed. The EO is required under the TFEU to undertake inquiries into specific complaints in respect of which 'he finds grounds'.[250] Under the EO Statute he is obliged to 'conduct all the enquiries which he considers justified to clarify any suspected maladministration'.[251] Accordingly, once a complainant presents information and evidence that indicates maladministration has taken place, the EO is under a basic duty to conduct inquiries. No such formal duties apply to the EP in the context of the right of petition.

The EP's website[252] provides information on the procedures involved for submitting petitions and their processing. Petitions, which may be submitted by post or email and in respect of which there is no administrative fee charged, are entered into a special parliamentary register and are announced at plenary sittings of the EP. The title and a summary of each petition is made available in a publicly accessible database, provided the sponsor(s) of the petitioner agree(s). The petitioner(s) may request the EP to preserve the petition's confidentiality, in which case only MEPs will have access to the relevant records of the file kept in the EP. Admissible petitions will be referred to the EP's Committee on Petitions, which will then determine what action, if any, should be taken next. It is envisaged that usually within a period of three months of its receipt, a petition will be registered with the EP and be subject to a preliminary admissibility assessment. A significant proportion of petitions are rejected annually as inadmissible, some 29 per cent in 2011–12[253] (although the position appears to have improved from previous years).[254] This may well be reflective of a continuing widespread lack of understanding of the scope of the right of petition to the EP, although general awareness of the petition process amongst citizens appears to be high.[255] Whilst a petition may be legitimately sponsored by a single person, it is self-evident that the EP's political interest will be more likely to be aroused the more signatures there are attached to a particular petition. A petition involving over a million signatories spread across at least one-quarter of member states has the opportunity to use the recently inaugurated European Citizens' Initiative (ECI) mechanism which is considered in section 10.3 below.

Annual reports of the Committee have noted a steady and notable increase in the yearly number of petitions tabled, no doubt in part due to a recent substantial increase in the numbers of member states from 15 in 2003 to 28 in 2013. Whilst a total of 1,313 petitions were tabled in the 2003/4 parliamentary year,[256] the number of petitions submitted had risen to 2,862 ten years later in 2013.[257] Environmental petitions to the EP have constituted a significant proportion of petitions overall. Between 2009 and 2012 they represented on average around 15 per cent of all petitions submitted, the second-largest policy thematic type of complaint after fundamental rights (which had an average share of around 22 per cent of all petitions submitted during the same period).[258] Table 10.2 at the end of this chapter provides a detailed breakdown of the sorts of environmental petitions filed.

As far as petitions regarding the enforcement of EU environmental legislation are concerned, the Committee on Petitions has a number of options open to it to address the particular matter raised. If the petition concerns an instance of an infringement of EU environmental law within a particular member state, the Committee may refer the matter to the European Commission if the latter has not already been contacted by the petitioner, given that it is the Commission and not the EP that is vested with specific powers and responsibilities under the TFEU for taking legal action to ensure that EU law is duly applied.[259] However, the Committee regularly hears petitions on poor implementation of EU environmental law and is usually keen to take advantage of the European parliamentary right to ask representatives of the Commission's services questions about the matter with a view to the receiving an explanation concerning the Commission's response. If the petition relates to a complaint against the Commission about a failure on its part to investigate an alleged breach of EU environmental law at national level, the Committee will normally seek to refer the matter to the EO, in order to avoid duplication of roles and in recognition of the fact that the EO (unlike the EP) has specific powers to access information and documents relevant to an investigation of a case of suspected maladministration.

The Petitions Committee may wish to take steps to inquire further into alleged serious, widespread and/or systemic violations of EU law brought to its attention, including cases not necessarily taken up by the Commission, with a view to coming back to the Commission at a later date with any new information or evidence it may glean in the interim. It may wish to invite petitioners' representations in person. It may also decide to send a delegation to the member state concerned, with a view to alerting and/or lobbying the relevant authorities on the salient issues.[260] In 2012, for instance the Committee arranged a fact-finding mission to various waste disposal sites in certain Italian regions (notably Lazio and Campania) associated with long-standing issues related to compliance with EU waste management legislation, with the delegation issuing recommendations both to national authorities to improve upon waste management standards as well to the Commission on releasing support funding to assist with improvements in the Naples area.[261] Similar fact-finding visits were conducted in Greece in 2013.[262] Where the Petitions Committee decides to look into specific cases of alleged infringements of EU environmental law, it may accordingly be able to lend some degree of useful political support and pressure to bear on behalf of petitioners as well as raise greater awareness of the issue at hand, although the degree of influence and impact may vary and be difficult to gauge. Another option available to the Committee, but very rarely used in practice, is to recommend the EP to establish a temporary specific committee of inquiry to look into a particular matter. The role of the committee of inquiry is referred in section 10.2.3 below.

Not all environmental petitions may or need relate to a violation of EU law. For instance, in the wake of several hundred petitions against a proposed hydrological project in Spain in 2003,[263] the Committee organised two public hearings in relation to the matter, providing stakeholders with an opportunity to present their assessment of the particular development. By way of a more recent example, in 2012 the Committee convened a workshop on shale gas convened at the EP.[264] These sorts of initiative open up the possibility for greater public and media deliberation on major contemporary issues of public concern concerning the existing and potential application of EU environmental law, including in particular issues concerning regulation as well as Union funding of development projects or plans.

The EP's standing Committee on the Environment, Public Health and Food Safety (ENVI)[265] will not usually address itself to petitions concerning environment matters, which are principally addressed by the Committee on Petitions. The Environment Committee's principal task is to scrutinise environmental policy issues, such as specific legislative initiatives from the Commission. It has, though, on occasion and not on any systematic footing, of its own initiative requested information and explanation from the Commission in relation to the progress on particular infringement files[266] or on more general aspects of infringement proceedings. Private individuals have no specific rights to request this standing committee to take up a petition or other request.

10.2.2 Parliamentary questions

Under the EU's constitutional framework, the EP has the power to file questions at the European Commission. Specifically, under Article 230(2) TFEU the Commission is obliged to reply either orally or in writing to questions put to it either by the EP or individual Members (MEPs). Questions have been submitted to the Commission on a range of environmental policy issues over the years. Just as the right of petition is not absolute in the sense that it does not guarantee the petitioner that follow-up action will take place, there is no enforceable right for private individuals to require that specific questions are tabled by the EP or its MEPs. Instead, the decision whether or not a question is to be put to the Commission rests exclusively with the recipient of the request, namely the EP or individual MEP(s) as appropriate to the particular case.

Not infrequently, parliamentary questions arise which seek to draw the European Commission's attention and response to alleged breaches of EU environmental legislation. Such questions may serve a useful function in galvanising political attention and, to some degree, public awareness of particular instances of implementation failures. However, in themselves, such questions are unlikely to trigger a Commission investigation. Not only are the questions usually very brief, providing all but the barest of details of a case, but they are also usually submitted without accompanying evidence. Without detailed supportive information and evidence, the Commission is unlikely to undertake an investigation and may invite these to be supplied to it by way of response. Accordingly, a written question in itself may well not be sufficient to trigger the opening of an infringement case file under Articles 258 and 260 TFEU by the Commission.

Some parliamentary questions on enforcement-related issues may carry greater practical significance though. In particular, this may be the case where the question relates to questions on the interpretation of EU environmental legislation, such as the scope or definition of specific terms contained in EU environmental directives. Answers provided by the Commission may have some value as creating 'precedents' on the approach taken by it vis-à-vis the enforcement of a particular norm under Articles 258 and 260 TFEU. In addition, the response from the Commission may serve as a useful benchmark for national authorities and others in applying EU environmental legislation.

10.2.3 EP temporary committees of inquiry

Within the particular TFEU section governing the EP's institutional foundations there lies a special procedure for the establishment of a temporary EP committee of inquiry that may inquire into alleged breaches or poor administrative management of implementation of EU law. In contrast with the role of the European Ombudsman, who focuses exclusively on the conduct of non-judicial activities of EU organs, committees of inquiry concern themselves with legal or administrative failures at national level. The principal EU treaty provision concerning the remit of committees of inquiry is Article 226 TFEU which states:

> In the course of its duties, the European Parliament may, at the request of a quarter of its Members, set up a temporary Committee of Inquiry to investigate, without prejudice to the powers conferred by the Treaties on other institutions or bodies, alleged contraventions or maladministration in the implementation of Union law, except where the alleged facts are being examined before a court and while the case is still subject to legal proceedings.
>
> The temporary Committee of Inquiry shall cease to exist on the submission of its report.
>
> The detailed provisions governing the exercise of the right of inquiry shall be determined by the European Parliament, acting by means of regulations on its own initiative in accordance with a special legislative procedure, after obtaining the consent of the Council and the Commission.

The EP's Rules of Procedure contain detailed rules on the convening of a committee of inquiry.[267] If convened, the committee must conclude its inquiry within 12 months, although this may be extended by the EP up to a maximum of six additional months.[268]

Whilst it is then theoretically possible for the EP to set up a temporary committee of inquiry in order to probe into and investigate alleged misapplication of EU environmental norms at national level, a process independent from the Commission's infringement procedures under Articles 258 and 260 TFEU, in practice the facility is rarely utilised. The procedure for establishing such a committee is rather unwieldy. First, as with other EP political rights, the launch of the committee of inquiry process is one predicated upon consent of sufficient numbers within the EP (namely one-quarter of its membership), and may not be commandeered as of right by individual persons. Secondly, the condition of securing consent from at least one-quarter of component MEPs[269] means that it will be rare that sufficient political support will be mustered for the procedure to be engaged, and most unlikely in relation to environmental cases affecting just one member state. Thirdly, a committee of inquiry is not endowed with any specific powers under the TFEU to be able to require any specific steps to be taken on the part of member state authorities.[270] Notably, it has no powers of investigation or sanction. The absence of such powers serves to raise questions over the utility and credibility of such a procedure being employed in the context of environmental infringement disputes. The TFEU instead refers to the committee being required to file a report at the end of its deliberations, which indicates that any recommendations or conclusions contained in committee reports are effectively reliant upon the effect of adverse publicity to ensure that they are adhered to.

The author is not aware of any committee of inquiry having been convened to examine suspected infringements of EU environmental law. Notwithstanding the lack of formal powers of investigation or sanction vested in a committee of inquiry, it is arguable that such a committee may potentially have a useful role to play in addressing certain types of instances of widespread poor implementation of EU environmental law. Specifically, this may be in relation to widespread and systemic cases of seriously deficient application of EU environmental legislation by a number of member states, where the Commission has already brought a range of infringement proceedings successfully against member states over a substantial period that have confirmed endemic problems relating to implementation. Examples could include municipal waste management, air pollution, waste water management and nitrates pollution where several member states have failed for many years to get to grips with the basic minimum environmental protection standards required by EU environmental law. Committees of inquiry into these areas could serve as a useful forum for highlighting and raising awareness of the seriousness of the implementation deficiencies and so add political pressure on defaulting member states to take corrective action. They could also serve to assess in an open and transparent way the broader context underlying implementation difficulties as well as reflect on the relative effectiveness of Commission strategies to assist in addressing these problems (whether through infringement litigation and/or through EU financial assistance).

In the past, temporary committees of inquiry have been set up to investigate suspected instances of breaches or poor application of EU law in relation to bovine spongiform encephalopathy (BSE) in agricultural livestock, the Union's transit system as well the financial crisis surrounding the Equitable Life Assurance Society.[271]

10.2.4 The EP and Article 258/260 TFEU infringement proceedings

The EP has limited legal powers to hold the European Commission to account over decisions whether or not to commence infringement proceedings against member states under Articles 258 and 260 TFEU in respect of suspected breaches of EU environmental legislation. Given that the Commission retains sole discretion under these TFEU provisions to decide whether to launch or close an infringement procedure, its decision-making in this area is effectively immune from judicial review at EU level (in the absence of a manifest abuse of power) via either an annulment action (under Article 263 TFEU) or an action in respect of a failure to act (under Article 265 TFEU). In any event, sufficient parliamentary support from MEPs must be gained prior to the possibility of the EP being able to launch any legal action and this may well be difficult.[272]

Moreover, under the EU treaty framework, the EP has no legal standing to take member states to court over infractions of EU law. This right is reserved for the Commission.

10.3 European Citizens' Initiative (ECI)

A recent innovation of potential relevance to the area of EU environmental law enforcement is the European Citizens' Initiative (ECI). The ECI was integrated with the EU treaty fabric by virtue of the 2007 Lisbon Treaty and provides the possibility for large-scale cross-border political campaigns to exert some influence on EU institutional decision-making over Union policy matters. The principal treaty provision concerned is Article 11(4) TFEU which states:

> 4. Not less than one million citizens who are nationals of a significant number of Member States may take the initiative of inviting the European Commission, within the framework of its powers, to submit any appropriate proposal on matters where citizens consider that a legal act of the Union is required for the purpose of implementing the Treaties.
>
> The procedures and conditions required for such a citizens' initiative shall be determined in accordance with the first paragraph of Article 24 of the [TFEU].

The establishment of the ECI was intended as a means of enhancing the political rights of EU citizens in the context of supranational decision-making conducted at EU level. In particular, akin to particular lobbying rights afforded to the EP[273] and Council,[274] the ECI was introduced in order to provide the opportunity for large-scale citizen-led initiatives to receive a hearing from the European Commission, which has a monopoly over deciding whether EU legislative proposals should be adopted. Whilst the ECI may not force the Commission's hand, it may bring significant political pressure to bear on the EU organ to take action in a particular field.

Two general aspects of the ECI stand out in particular, namely its personal as well as material scope. As far as its personal scope is concerned, it is notable that the ECI is tied to the construct of EU citizenship. The right of initiative may only be invoked by EU citizens, namely those with nationality of a Union member state.[275] Secondly, it is noticeable that, potentially at least, ECIs may have a very broad material reach. Notably, they are not restricted to being focused on campaigns for EU legislative proposals with a view to developing or changing Union policy in a particular sector. Article 11(4) TFEU, in referring to any 'legal act' for the purpose of implementing the objectives of the EU founding treaties, provides the possibility for ECIs to be able to call for a diverse range of measures to be taken at EU institutional level, including action in relation to improving the state of policy implementation as well as policy development. In practice, though, it is likely that most ECIs will focus on substantive policy issues in order to be able to succeed in mustering sufficient support required from citizens. Given that the ECI mechanism has only very recently been instituted, it is not possible to gauge its practical impact at this early stage. At the time of writing, only one campaign has managed to fulfil the requirements to be submitted formally as an ECI, namely the environmental campaign *Right2Water* (discussed later in section 10.3.2).

10.3.1 Eligibility and procedure concerning the ECI

The legal framework of the ECI was completed in 2012, implementing legislation being required under Article 24(1) TFEU in order to specify various conditions of eligibility and organisational arrangements including the minimum number of member states from which supporting citizens must come. Regulation 211/2011 on the citizens' initiative[276] (hereafter referred to as the 'ECI Regulation') was adopted for this purpose. The ECI Regulation provides for a staged procedure according to which proposed ECIs must fulfil certain eligibility requirements in order to be formally registered with and submitted to the Commission, prior to the latter being obliged to issue a formal response.

The first stage of the process is for the Commission to determine whether a proposed ECI should be officially registered. Prior to initiating the collection of citizen statements in support, the organisers of a proposed ECI must apply to register it with the Commission by providing certain information relating to the proposal's subject matter and objectives.[277] Within two months of receipt of this information, the Commission will register the proposal so long as the following eligibility conditions are fulfilled:

- proof of the establishment of a citizens' organising committee, which is to be composed of (at least) seven EU citizens eligible to vote in EP elections members and who are residents in at least seven different member states;[278]
- the ECI proposal does not manifestly fall outside the Commission's powers to propose legal act of EU law for the purpose of implementing the EU founding treaties;[279]
- the ECI proposal is not manifestly abusive, frivolous or vexatious; and[280]
- the ECI proposal is not manifestly contrary to the Union's values as enshrined in Article 2 TEU.[281]

If the ECI proposal is successfully registered, then the second stage commences with the organising committee having 12 months to garner the necessary one million signatories.[282] Signatures must be confirmed in the form of postal or online statements in support,[283] models for which are detailed in the ECI Regulation.[284] The organisers must ensure that sufficient political support for their initiative is gained from across the Union. In particular, they must ensure that the one million supporters are, in addition to being EU citizens and eligible to vote in EP elections,[285] spread across at least one-quarter of all member states and that in at least one-quarter of member states a minimum number of eligible signatories have shown their support.[286] Minimum numbers are specified in Annex I of the ECI Regulation. These particular requirements serve to ensure that ECIs are most likely to address cross-border (European-wide) issues, as opposed to those which are predominantly of relevance to a single or very few member states.

The third stage is the formal submission[287] of the ECI by the organisers to the Commission when sufficient statements in support have been collated. In order to do this, statements in support must be first verified and certified by national competent authorities.[288] Upon receipt of the ECI, the Commission is obliged to publish the ECI in the register and receive the organisers to allow them to explain in detail the matters raised in the initiative.[289] Furthermore, the organisers at this stage are to be given the opportunity to present the ECI at a public hearing, organised at the EP, with representation from the Commission in attendance and other EU organs as may wish to participate.[290] At the time of writing the first ECI public hearing on the initiative *Right2Water* was due to be convened by the EP Committee on Petitions in late 2014.[291]

The fourth and final stage of the ECI procedure concerns the response of the European Commission. Upon receipt of the formal ECI, the Commission has three months to set out in a communication its legal and political conclusions on the ECI.[292] The communication must indicate what action, if any, it intends to take and supply the reasons for its decision to act or refrain from acting. The ECI is not formally binding on the Commission; this respects the traditional 'Community method' of decision-making whereby the Commission is vested with exclusive power to decide whether to initiate an EU legislative process in the areas covered by the TFEU (including EU environmental policy).[293]

It is interesting to note that the ECI mechanism, whilst formally a matter supervised by the Commission, is a matter also of close interest to the EP. This is not surprising bearing in mind that ECIs are in essence large-scale petitions that would otherwise be within the remit of the EP's Committee on Petitions were it not for the *lex specialis* procedure foreseen for them under the ECI Regulation. Sensibly, the EP's Rules of Procedure prescribe that the Committee on Petitions is to remain closely informed of ECI developments. Specifically, the EP's Rules of Procedure require the Committee to ascertain to what extent ECIs may affect its current work and to inform petitioners of related petitions about ECIs.[294] Moreover, should an ECI proposal fail to meet the requisite criteria to be submitted formally to the Commission (e.g. due to a shortfall in citizen statements in support), it may then be examined by the Committee with a view to considering whether the initiative should be examined as a petition under the standard procedures.[295]

10.3.2 Right2Water – *the first ECI*

Right2Water[296] is the first ECI to have met the requirements set out in the ECI Regulation. Co-sponsored by a range of organisations,[297] including trades unions and the environmental NGO the European Environmental Bureau, it was officially submitted to the Commission by its organisers on 20 December 2013, after having received the support of more than 1.8 million Union citizens. The *Right2Water* initiative invited the Commission 'to propose legislation implementing the human right to water and sanitation, as recognized by the United Nations, and promoting the provision of water and sanitation as essential public services for all'. It called for the EU institutions and member states to be obliged to ensure that all inhabitants enjoy the right to water and sanitation, for water supply and management of water resources not to be subject to internal market rules and water services to be excluded from liberalisation, and for the EU to increase its efforts in achieving universal access to water and sanitation.

In March 2014, the Commission issued a Communication[298] in response, setting out in some detail current and future EU environmental policy on drinking water after meeting the initiative's organisers. In the 2014 Communication, the Commission agreed to undertake a broad range of measures with a view to reinforcing its existing water management policy, including increasing the degree of public participation in relation to its policy assessments. Notably, the Commission committed itself to holding an EU-wide public consultation on the EU's Drinking Water Directive[299] in order to assist it in assessing whether any specific legislative amendments should be proposed in order to improve access to water quality in the EU as well as developing a more 'structured dialogue' with stakeholders on the issue of transparency in the water.[300]

It is clear already from the pioneering example set by *Right2Water* that the ECI mechanism has significant potential to flourish in relation to the environmental protection field. There are several well-known environmental issues of long-standing widespread concern to citizens across the Union (including climate change, water and air pollution, waste mismanagement, hunting of endangered species to name but a few). The cross-border nature of many of these protection concerns means that the minimum threshold requirements set by the ECI Regulation are not likely to pose notable obstacles to many environmental campaigns. The international presence, networks and substantial resourcing underpinning several NGEOs will also assist considerably in meeting the not inconsiderable organisational challenges and requirements involved in promoting an ECI campaign, in particular in ensuring that sufficient political support may be gleaned within the 12-month deadline set by the ECI Regulation. Although the bulk of ECI campaigns are expected to focus on substantive issues of policy, as with the *Right2Water* initiative, the ECI mechanism is of some potential interest from an environmental law enforcement perspective. For instance, it is conceivable that an environmental ECI might call upon the Commission to proceed with infringement action in relation to widespread serious violations of EU environmental legislation experienced in a number of member states (e.g. in relation to the areas of air quality and/or waste management) or even in a single member state where the environmental issue resonates sufficiently across borders (e.g. illicit hunting of endangered species). Any decision by the Commission to launch infringement proceedings under Articles 258 and 260 TFEU is clearly a Union 'legal act' 'required for the purpose of implementing the Treaties' within the terms of Article 11(4) TFEU, although the preamble of the ECI Regulation clearly envisages that legislative proposals are to be the predominant focus of ECI campaigns.[301] ECIs might also conceivably encompass campaigns for the development of greater environmental law enforcement-related powers to be vested at EU level (e.g. in relation to inspections and/or investigations) in the event of substantial public disquiet with the existing tier of enforcement controls at national authority level, although it is difficult to envisage such campaigns mustering sufficient public support. This latter type of initiative would, of course, in any event face the added stiff challenge of having to win over a supporting majority within the principal EU legislative organs, namely the EP and Council of the EU, in addition to the approval of the Commission in order to succeed. By way of a concluding remark to this section, it should be noted that environmental ECIs which focus on substantive environmental policy issues may well also have a complementary (if less visible and substantial) law enforcement dimension in a preventative sense. In particular, where successful, an ECI campaign to improve certain minimum EU environmental protection standards (e.g. tightening limit values) may be expected ultimately to be capable of leading to some stimulation towards improvements regarding the quality of implementation adherence and supervision at national level. This could result, for example, from enhanced monitoring requirements integrated within any new EU environmental legislative instrumentation to emerge from an ECI.

10.4 The European Environment Agency (EEA)

Although the European Environment Agency (EEA)[302] is not a body within the EU to which private persons may turn in order assist them in the enforcement of EU environmental legislation, a brief reference to it in this chapter is worth making in order to clarify its particular role in relation to Union environmental policy. At its inception in the early 1990s, there was some discussion as to whether or not it would take on enforcement-related work. Since the end of the 1990s, though, this particular debate has ebbed away within the EU's political institutions in the wake of resistance by member states to the idea of a law enforcement dimension being added to the EEA's remit. However, it may well be possible that discussions may arise again in the future, depending upon there remaining sufficient support from member states with the existing long-standing position enshrined within the EU treaty framework which endows the European Commission with the dual roles of 'guardian' of the EU treaties and Union institution charged with leading the development of EU environmental policy.

Formally established in 1993 with its seat in Copenhagen, the EEA is an EU agency charged with responsibility for providing the Union and member states with reliable scientifically based information on the environment.[303] The provision of this information is, *inter alia*, intended to enable them to be in a position to frame and implement 'sound and effective environmental policies'.[304] From a Union perspective, the EEA's information role is very important in terms of delivering environmental data that covers the entire territory of the EU and which is to be measured in a harmonised fashion at national level. As information provider, the EEA is also required to gather information in order to make it possible to describe the present and foreseeable state of the environment, from the perspectives of environmental pressures, quality and sensitivity.[305] In order to be able to glean the relevant information, the EEA draws upon the support of the relevant national authorities of the member states which collate information on the environment. Under its founding regulation, the EEA is charged with establishing a European environment information and observation network (EIONET),[306] which is the inter-institutional structure intended to deliver the relevant scientific information. Collectively, the EEA and the 'national focal points' that co-ordinate and transmit information to be supplied to the agency at national level constitute the essential foundations of the EIONET. The EEA has its own dedicated website which contains links to its published information on the state of the European environment.[307]

In the early 1990s there was some support for the development of an independent European environmental inspectorate, endowed with specific powers to be integrally involved in the supervision of adherence to EU environmental legislative requirements. Both the European Commission and EP considered that the establishment of the EEA could open up the possibility for an independent supranational entity becoming involved in supervisory work relating to EU environmental legislative implementation. However, the Council of the EU did not agree to the inclusion of such a mandate for the EEA's list of functions. The Union legislation setting up the EEA did, though, specifically refer to the possibility at a later date of supervisory functions being assigned to the EEA.[308] The Commission has not taken up this issue in subsequent years when submitting draft amendments to the EEA's statutes.[309] In 1997, the Council restated its clear rejection of the establishment of a system of centrally and supranational organised system of European environmental inspectors.[310] As a consequence, the statutes governing the operations of the EEA have so far not extended into the domain of environmental law enforcement.

The EEA does, however, host an electronic tool on its website that is set to be increasingly useful in connection with enforcement of EU environmental legislation, namely the European Pollutant Release and Transfer Register (E-PRTR).[311] E-PRTR is a free online database system providing details of emissions from a wide range of pollution sources and industrial activities located across the Union and in some neighbouring regions. Further details on E-PRTR are provided in online Chapter 9A.

10.5 The Council of the EU and individual member states

Whilst the Council of the EU has a key joint legislative role alongside the EP in the development of EU environmental policy,[312] it does not exercise any specific supervisory function in relation to the enforcement of EU environmental law. This is not that surprising, given that it is the Council which represents the interests of member states in Union affairs, as distinct from the general interest of the Union which is the mandate set for the Commission.[313]

As is the case with the EP, the Council of the EU has no legal standing (under Articles 258 and 260 TFEU) to take legal action against individual member states that have infringed EU environmental law. As was outlined in Chapter 2, individual member states are vested with legal power to bring enforcement proceedings against other member states over infractions of EU law before the CJEU under Article 259 TFEU. However, in practice this legal power is rarely if ever used, member states usually strongly preferring to defer to the Commission to take legal action rather than risk losing support within the Council over policy initiatives they may be keen to promote. To the author's knowledge, no infringement action has ever been launched by a member state against another on account of a breach of EU environmental law. This is not at all surprising, as member states will in practice only resort to infringement litigation in the last instance in order to defend clear domestic economic or political interests.

For political reasons alone, it is virtually inconceivable that the Council of the EU would ever seek judicial review under Articles 263 and 265 TFEU of a Commission decision to commence or refrain from pursuing infringement proceedings against a member state over an alleged breach of EU environmental law. It would not be in keeping with the Council's general mandate to defend the member states' interests within the scheme of political power relations foreseen under the EU legal framework. Moreover, such a step would risk destabilising goodwill and actual and potential political alliances between member states concerning (unrelated) policy issues to be debated at Council level. In any event, the large degree of autonomy and discretion accorded to the Commission in relation to infringement case management places this area from a legal perspective virtually outside the reach of judicial review (see section 10.2.4 above).

Accordingly, neither the Council of the EU nor individual member states constitute appropriate bodies within the EU legal system for private persons to turn to for assistance in connection with the practical enforcement of EU environmental law.

10.6 Some concluding remarks

Notwithstanding the fact that there are a number of EU institutions and bodies other than the European Commission involved in the development of environmental policy at EU level, with the exception of the EO none of them involve themselves to any significant extent in the task of supervising due enforcement of EU environmental legislation. Even the EO's role here is relatively limited, being ultimately unable to take legal action himself in relation to any breach of EU environmental law or to compel others to take steps. Both of the complaint systems employed by the EO and the EP, which offer some scope for receiving and addressing private individual complaints about non-compliance with EU law, are essentially reactive in nature. Neither Union body is really equipped to address compliance issues on a proactive or systematic basis, although both EU organs in their different ways do or may be able to make some inroads and contributions on this front. The EO and the EP's Committee of Petitions have, for instance, launched own-initiative-type inquiries on occasion into areas where widespread non-compliance is either suspected or already known as a result of the number of complaints received. The EP's mechanism of a temporary committee of inquiry has the potential to be far more widely used for the purpose of proactive investigation into serious systemic failures concerning implementation of EU environmental law, but remains at the moment dormant. Accordingly, in practice, persons seeking to request the EU to take action in relation to suspected infringements of EU environmental law are very largely dependent upon the European Commission's services for assistance in this regard.

There is little doubt, though, that the EO has exercised a notable degree of influence on the development of the European Commission's internal practice and procedures regarding the management of complaints from the public concerning alleged member state infractions of EU environmental legislation. Without the EO's scrutiny of the Commission, there is little doubt that the Commission would not have come to revise its procedures for the handling of complaints in a more transparent, fair and accountable manner. In general, a good deal of the principles of good administration elaborated by the EO in its decisions have usually been taken up and adopted by the Commission and other EU organs concerned directly or indirectly with the development of EU environmental policy, although it is fair to say that this process has taken a considerable amount of time to bed down in practice and shortcomings, glaring or otherwise, appear to persist.

For the future, a significant test will be whether the EU will decide to take steps to ensure that the EO's *European Code of Good Administrative Behaviour* becomes formally enshrined in Union law so as to be formally binding upon non-judicial EU institutions and bodies such as the Commission. In addition, an important issue still remains to be convincingly resolved in determining whether the EO should be vested with legal powers to refer to the CJEU in instances where the Ombudsman considers that a (non-judicial) EU organ has breached a rule of Union law. A legally binding code of conduct will not only then be enforceable by the EO, but also by complainants who will have specific legal EU rights that they will be able to defend. The current position is unsatisfactory, not least that there appears to be no clear mechanism for ensuring that non-judicial EU institutions and bodies actually adhere to recommendations and act on critical remarks made in respect of their conduct by the Ombudsman. The EO has accordingly acquired an important, albeit ancillary, role within the existing Union's legal framework for assisting private individuals in seeking to persuade the Commission to pursuing instances of violations of EU environmental law against infracting member states. It remains to be seen whether the current system of auditing EU administrative conduct for maladministration will be enhanced in the future.

To what extent the EP has been able to influence the course of management of EU environmental law enforcement, whether at either Union or national level, remains unclear. Its impact has been more diffuse and diverse in nature. The mandate with which it has been provided under the TFEU for investigating alleged instances of poor implementation of EU rules of law at national level in the form of temporary committees of inquiry has been rarely invoked and arguably underused. The EP's Committee on Petitions, though, does regularly attend to queries and requests submitted by members of the public in relation to Union environmental matters, including in particular in relation to the issue of (mis)application of EU environmental legislation. However, the work of the Committee on environmental matters concerns itself with a very wide range of petitions of a non-legal as well as litigious nature. The Committee also operates on the basis that it is not intended to duplicate work or functions carried out by other EU bodies. Accordingly, complaints it receives against the Commission are normally referred to the EO and petitions relating to instances of alleged breaches of EU law at national level are passed onto the Commission. Finally, the mechanism of parliamentary questions directed at the Commission is of limited assistance in the field of law enforcement.

The other EU organs with notable roles in Union environmental policy development have little or no formal involvement in supervision of the due application of EU environmental law. These include the EEA and the Council of the EU. It remains to be seen whether political interest will re-emerge at EU level for the expansion of the current remit of the EEA into the area of law enforcement. It is interesting to note that the emerging E-PRTR database system housed within the EEA's website is intended at least in part to be a useful tool in connection with law enforcement, namely the close monitoring of an individual installation's environmental performance and compliance with EU environmental legislation. However, a specifically overt law enforcement role is not likely to be vested in the EEA any time soon (such as an inspection or prosecutorial role), given the absence of sufficient political will within the Council of the EU (i.e. amongst member states) to address the conflicts of interest inherent in the multiple roles accorded to the Commission in EU affairs, namely legislative,[314] executive[315] and law enforcement.[316]

As for the European Citizens' Initiative (ECI) mechanism, it is fair to say that for the moment it remains an unknown quantity having commenced operations only very recently. It is also apparent, though, that the ECI mechanism has significant potential as a political tool for the purpose of encouraging greater institutional awareness and focus at Union level, particularly within the Commission, on promoting greater levels of environmental protection. The *Right2Water* initiative has already demonstrated that cross-border environmental campaigns may be capable of garnering sufficient political support for the purposes of the ECI Regulation. Whether campaigners, notably through the sponsorship and assistance of NGEOs, will seek to and/or succeed in promoting ECIs in the area of EU environmental law enforcement remains an open question.

Table 10.1 Environmental complaints and own-initiative inquiries addressed by the European Ombudsman 1995–2012 (as noted in the EO annual reports)

EU environmental legislative sector	Quantity	EO decisions (Note: some EO decisions concern complaints relating to more than one legislative sector)
Environmental Impact Assessment (EIA)	21	132/21.9.95/AH/EN *M40 Motorway* (UK)
		206/27.10.95/HS/UK *Newbury Bypass* (UK)
		472/6.3.96/XP/ES/PD *Itoiz dam* (ESP)
		106/97/PD *RCF Lake District* (UK)
		1288/99/OV *Parga wastewater treatment plant* (GR)
		493/2000/ME *Skälderviken railway* (S)
		767/2001/GG *Athens–Marathon road* (GR)
		39/2002/OV *Anglesey Motor Racing Track* (UK)
		2725/2004/(PB)ID *Alqueva Dam and Reservoir* (PT)
		789/2005/(GK)ID *Athens tramway project* (GR)
		1962/2005/IP *Riva del Garda bypass* (I)
		244/2006/(BM)JMA *High-speed railway link* (ESP)
		962/2006/OV *Rhede wind farm project* (NL)
		1779/2006/MHZ *National Road Fund Programme* (POL)
		1807/2006/MHZ *Flood Damage Reconstruction* (POL)
		3254/2006/ID *Chalkidiki motorway project* (GR)
		1512/2007/JMA *Seville port access project* (ESP)
		1532/2008/(WP) GG *Vienna Airport* (A)
		80/2009/BU *R52 Motorway* (CZ)
		846/2010/PB *Copenhagen-Ringsted railway* (DK)
		2591/2010/GG *Special Report – Vienna Airport* (A)

(Continued)

Table 10.1 (Continued)

EU environmental legislative sector	Quantity	EO decisions (Note: some EO decisions concern complaints relating to more than one legislative sector)
Nature protection	17	472/6.3.96/XP/ES/PD *Itoiz dam* (SP)
		701/3.7.96/JE/UK/KT *Newbury Bypass* (UK)
		298/97/PD *Southport shoreline sea defence* (UK)
		596/97/JMA *Montes Obarenes-Tolono Mine* (SP)
		1062/97/OV *Zakynthos sea turtles* (GR)
		813/98/(PD)/GG *Southport shoreline costal road* (UK)
		271 and 277/2000/(IJH)MA *UK waste reports* (UK)
		493/2000/ME *Skälderviken railway* (S)
		2183/2003(TN)(IJN) *Botniabanan railway* (S)
		2725/2004/(PB)ID *Alqueva Dam and Reservoir* (PT)
		3660/2004/PB *Ballybrown wetland* (IRL)
		OI/2/2006/JMA *Granadilla industrial harbour* (ESP)
		1437/2006 /(WP) BEH *Elze site Hildesheim (Hamsters)* (D)
		885/2007/JMA *Granadilla industrial harbour* (ESP)
		80/2009/BU *R52 Motorway* (CZ)
		846/2010/PB *Copenhagen-Ringsted railway* (DK)
		1561/2010/(MB)FOR *Picris Willkommii, Guadiana River* (ESP)
Access to information	11	396/99/IP *Enichem site* (I)
		271,77/2000/(IJH)MA *UK waste reports* (UK)
		2183/2003(TN)(IJN) *Botniabanan railway* (S)
		2229/2003 *San Roman de la Vega waste processing centre* (ESP)
		2821/2004/OV *Zakynthos EU mission report (sea turtles)* (GR)
		582/2005/PB *WTO GMO Dispute* (EU)
		1463/2005/TN *Greenhouse gas emission allowances* (UK, F, SK)
		355/2007/(TN)FOR *Granadilla industrial harbour* (ESP)
		OI/3/2009/MHZ *Recording of complaints* (EU)
		2587/2009/JFR *Irish implementation of EU environmental acquis* (IRL)
		2073/2010/AN *Vera and Rambla de Mojácar* (ESP)
Waste management	5	271,77/2000/(IJH)MA *UK waste reports* (UK);
		2229/2003 *San Roman de la Vega waste processing centre* (ESP)
		791/2005/(IP)FOR *Malagrotta landfill* (I)
		1528/2006/(GG)WP *German waste oil recycling* (D)
		1956/2007/(SAB)VIK *Greenore landfill* (IRL)
European Investment Bank	4	1338/98/ME *EIB funding of Hungarian M0 orbital motorway* (HUN)
		244/2006/(BM) JMA *High-speed railway link* (ESP)
		1779/2006/MHZ *National Road Fund Programme* (POL)
		1807/2006/MHZ *Flood Damage Reconstruction* (POL)
Co-financing of environmental projects	3	1288/99/OV *Parga wastewater treatment plant* (GR)
		250/97/OV *Kalamitsi sewage works* (GR)
		1152/97/OV *Welsh wind farm project* (UK)
Water management	1	2073/2010/AN *Vera and Rambla de Mojácar* (ESP)
Chemicals	1	512/2012/BEH *Neonicotinoids* (EU)
Bathing water quality	1	235/16.11.95/JMC-fr *Blue flag status* (PT)
Air pollution	1	706/2007/(WP)BEH *Viennese PM10 pollution* (A)

Table 10.2 Environmental Petitions 2009–12 (with percentage shares of total number of petitions registered)

Petition type	2009	2010	2011	2012
Environment	**229 (11.9%)**	**256 (14.9%)**	**260 (18.4%)**	**279 (14.1%)**
EIA	40 (2.1%)	43 (2.6%)	26 (1.8%)	23 (1.2%)
Pollution	53 (2.8%)	48 (2.9%)	49 (3.5%)	57 (2.9%)
Protection and preservation	48 (2.5%)	62 (3.7%)	38 (2.7%)	31 (1.6%)
Waste	18 (0.9%)	25 (1.5%)	25 (1.8%)	37 (1.9%)
Water	11 (0.6%)	14 (0.8%)	19 (1.3%)	24 (1.2%)
All petitions	1924	1655	1414	1986

(Source: *Report on the activities of the Committee on Petitions 2012* (2013/2013(INI) of 24 September 2013)

Notes

1 See e.g. Case 247/87 *Star Fruit*, Joined Cases T-479 and 559/93 *Bernardi*, Case T-201/96 *Smanor* (confirmed on appeal to the CJEU in C-317/97P) and Case T-461/93 *An Taisce*.
2 Bonnor (2000).
3 The official title of the post is 'Ombudsman of the European Union'. However, in practice the office holder is referred to as the 'European Ombudsman'.
4 Art. 228(2) TFEU, first subpara.
5 Confirmed by the EP to continue to be the EO subsequent to the May 2014 EP elections.
6 Namely http://www.ombudsman.europa.eu/home.faces. This website contains, *inter alia*, the EO's decisions, annual reports, standard complaint form and rules pertaining to the EO's activities.
7 OJ 1994 L113/15, as amended by EP decisions of 14 March 2002 (OJ 2002 L92/13) and of 18 June 2008 (OJ 2008 L189/25). The consolidated text of the EO Statute may be inspected on the EO's website at http://www.ombudsman.europa.eu/en/resources/statute.faces. See also Art. 228(4) TFEU.
8 Decision of the European Ombudsman of 8 July 2002 adopting implementing provisions, as amended by EO decisions of 5 April 2004 and 3 December 2008. The consolidated text of the Implementing Decision may be inspected on the EO's website at http://www.ombudsman.europa.eu/en/resources/provisions.faces.
9 OJ 2010 C83/02.
10 See Art. 6 TEU.
11 See the EO's Annual Report 2012: available for inspection on EO website (see n. 6 above).
12 See Arts. 308–9 TFEU. See EIB website http://www.eib.org/.
13 See ECHA website http://echa.europa.eu/.
14 See Arts. 290–1 TFEU regarding delegated and implementing acts and Regulation 182/2011 on general principles concerning mechanisms for control by member states of the Commission's exercise of implementing powers (OJ 2011 L55/13). For an excellent overview of the comitology process as it applies to the EU environmental sector, see e.g. the Institute for European Environmental Policy's Report *New Comitology Rules: Delegated and Implementing Acts* (2011 IEEP) available for inspection at http://www.ieep.eu/publications/2011/10/the-new-comitology-rules-delegated-and-implementing-acts.

15 This is in contrast with specific rights of appeal granted to complainants in other sectors, notably in the competition field as developed by the CJEU. See notably, Art. 27 of Regulation 1/03 on the implementation of the rules of competition laid down in Articles 81 and 82 of the Treaty (OJ 2003 L1/1) and Art. 18 of Regulation 139/04 on the control of concentrations between undertakings (OJ 2004 L24/1).

16 COM(2012)154 Commission Communication, *Updating the handling of relations with the complainant in respect of the application of Union Law*, 2 April 2012.

17 EO's Annual Report 2012, p. 25.

18 The average number of complaints submitted within the period 2003–12 falling within the EO's mandate was 777 out of a total number of complaints submitted annually averaging 2,282 (based on data disclosed in the EO Annual Reports 2003–12).

19 Specifically: Section 1 (The EP) of Chapter 1 (The Institutions) of Title I (Institutional Provisions) of Part Six (Institutional and Financial Provisions) of the TFEU: Arts. 223–34 TFEU.

20 Art. 228(2) TFEU, first subpara.

21 Ibid., Art. 228(1) second and third subparas. Art. 3(7)–(8) EO Statute.

22 Ibid., Art. 228(2) second subpara.

23 Art. 13 EO Statute. Accordingly, the EO is located in Strasbourg. His office is at 1, avenue du Président Robert Schuman, B.P.403, 67001 Strasbourg Cedex, France.

24 See, in particular, Part Two of the TFEU (Non-discrimination and Citizenship of the Union): Arts. 18–25 TFEU.

25 Ibid., Art. 20 TFEU.

26 Ibid., Arts. 20(2)(a) and 21.

27 Ibid., Arts. 20(2)(b) and 22.

28 Ibid., Arts. 20(2)(c) and 23.

29 Ibid., Arts. 20(2)(d) and 24, second subpara.

30 Ibid., Arts. 20(2)d) and 24, third subpara.

31 Ibid., Arts. 20(2)(d) and 24, fourth subpara.

32 Ibid., Art. 24(1). See Regulation 211/2011 on the citizens' initiative (OJ 2011 L65/1) as amended. For general information see http://ec.europa.eu/citizens-initiative/public/basic-facts.

33 Ibid., Arts. 227–8.

34 Ibid., Art. 228(1) and Art. 2(2) EO Statute.

35 Ibid., Art. 228(1), second subpara. See also EO Annual Report 1995 (OOPEC 1996), section II.2.1.

36 Ibid., See Art. 227.

37 Ibid., Art. 228(1), second subpara. and Art. 3(1) EO Statute.

38 E.g. in 2012 the EO launched 15 own-initiative enquiries, as compared with opening 450 complaints inquiries (3.2% of the total) (EO's Annual Report 2012, Table 1.1, p. 18).

39 As noted by Tsadiras (2013), p. 153. The own-initiative inquiries concerned: OI/2/2006/JMA *Granadilla Industrial Harbour Development* (in which the EO had received a number of complaints concerning a particular development project suspected to have been approved of in breach of EU environmental impact law) and EO Decision OI/3/2009/MHZ *Infringement Complaint Registration* (concerning DG ENV's former policy of failing to register infringement complaints without adequate reasoning). The EO's reports on these inquiries may be inspected on the EO website at http://www.ombudsman.europa.eu/en/cases/home.faces.

40 E.g. in 2012, 5 of the 15 own-initiative inquiries launched by the EO concerned instances of suspected systemic problems within EU institutions (EO's Annual Report 2012, p. 15).

41 For an overview, see e.g. Tsadiras (2007a).

42 EO Annual Report 2012, p. 29.

43 Art. 2(4) EO Statute.

44 Ibid.
45 This encompasses also the judicial activities of the various courts that comprise the Court of Justice. Accordingly, the GC and Civil Service Tribunal are also covered by the statutory exception in Art. 228(1) TFEU.
46 The percentage of complaints not within the EO's mandate, as revealed in the EO's annual reports to the EP, has been as follows (rounded up to the nearest integer): 1996 (65%), 1997 (73%), 1998 (69%), 1999 (73%), 2000 (72%), 2001 (71%), 2002 (72%), 2003 (75%), 2004 (74.8%), 2005 (77%), 2006 (77%), 2007 (73%), 2008 (76%), 2009 (77%), 2010 (73%), 2011 (73%) and 2012 (70%).
47 In 2004 and 2012 the number of complaints outside the EO's mandate was 2,729 and 1,720 respectively.
48 See EO introduction to the EO Annual Report 2012, p. 5.
49 EO Annual Report 1995 (OOPEC 1996), section II.2.2.
50 See Tsadiras (2007b).
51 The EO has rejected a Commission claim that WTO dispute resolution procedures may be considered as court proceedings for the purpose of the Access to Documents Regulation 1049/2011: see EO Decision 582/2005/PB (*WTO GMO Dispute*).
52 See e.g. the following: EO decisions OI/2/2006/MA (*Granadilla Harbour*), 706/2007/ (WP)BEH (*Viennese PM10 pollution*) and 1532/2008/GG (*Vienna Airport*).
53 See e.g. EO decisions 995/98/OV (*Macedonian Metro*) and 128/99/OV (*Parga*).
54 Art. 47 EUCFR.
55 Ibid., Art. 41.
56 EO Annual Report 1997 (OOPEC 1998).
57 See Bonnor (2000), p. 39.
58 European Parliament Resolution of 6 September 2001.
59 *The European Code of Good Administrative Behaviour* (EO Document 2013, EU). Available for inspection on EO website http://www.ombudsman.europa.eu/en/resources/ code.faces#/page/1.
60 The Code applies to EU institutions, bodies, offices and agencies: Art. 2(4) of the Code.
61 The Code applies to all officials and other servants to whom the EU Staff Regulations and the conditions of employment of other servants apply: Art. 2 of the Code.
62 Art. 4 ECGAB.
63 Ibid., Art. 5.
64 Ibid., Art. 6.
65 Ibid., Art. 7.
66 Ibid., Art. 8.
67 Ibid., Art. 9.
68 Ibid., Art. 10.
69 Ibid., Art. 11.
70 Ibid., Art. 12.
71 Ibid., Art. 13.
72 Ibid., Art. 14.
73 Ibid., Art. 15.
74 Ibid., Art. 16.
75 Ibid., Art. 17. The provision stipulates a two-month period as a general rule. Where for reasons of complexity, a matter cannot be determined within that time period, the official is to inform the person requesting assistance of that fact 'as soon as possible', with a definitive decision to be made thereafter 'in the shortest time'.
76 Ibid., Art. 18.
77 Ibid., Art. 19.
78 Ibid., Art. 20.
79 Ibid., Art. 21.
80 Ibid., Art. 22.

81 Ibid., Art. 23.
82 Ibid., Art. 24.
83 Art. 4 ECGAB.
84 EO Annual Report 2012, p. 26. The remaining 31.6% of complaints concerned various other (unspecified) types of alleged maladministration.
85 See e.g. Smith (2009), p. 187.
86 Art. 267 TFEU. This is also made clear in the EO Statute: see Arts. 1(3) and 2(1) EO Statute. In addition, the EO takes care to make this clear when providing legal opinions on particular complaints in the EO annual reports.
87 In practice, in relation to legal issues concerning environmental cases, the European Commission will usually defer to the legal analysis of the Legal Unit of the Environment Directorate-General (DG ENV) and/or the Commission's Legal Service. Where there is a dispute within DG ENV over a particular point of law (e.g. between the Legal Unit and one or more technical units), then occasionally the matter may be referred to the Commission Legal Service for 'arbitration', unless the Director-General of DG ENV decides that the matter is to be determined internally within DG ENV (which may well mean in practice that the view of the Legal Unit holds sway).
88 Art. 6(2) EO Statute.
89 Art. 228(3) TFEU and Art. 9 EO Statute.
90 Art. 10(2) EO Statute.
91 *European Code of Good Administrative Behaviour* (EO Document, 2013), p. 4.
92 Currently, it would appear that Art. 22 TFEU could constitute the appropriate legal basis for adoption of a legislative proposal designed to enact the Code (although this requires unanimity in the Council of the EU and ratification at Member State level). Prospectively, Art. III-398 of the EU Constitution would appear to provide a more straightforward legal basis, if and when the Constitution enters into force (requires instead only a qualified majority vote in the Council).
93 The EP's Committee on Petitions has also strongly recommended the Commission to adopt the *European Code of Good Administrative Behaviour* (A6-027./2005). See also EO Annual Report 2004 of 29 February 2005.
94 Commission Decision 2000/633 amending its Rules of Procedure (OJ 2000 L267/63).
95 The Code may be located on the European Commission's website at http://ec.europa.eu/transparency/code/index_en.htm.
96 COM(2007)502, Commission Communication, *A Europe of Results – Applying Community Law*, 5 September 2007.
97 COM(2008)773 final, *Commission Communication on Implementing European Community Environmental Law*, 18 November 2008.
98 EO Decision 2409/2010/RT *(Glebelands landfill)*.
99 COM(2002)141 as subsequently superseded by COM(2012)154, Commission Communication, *Updating the Handling of Relations with the Complainant in Respect of the Application of Union Law*, 2 April 2012.
100 See e.g. (point 1.4 of) EO Decision 1512/2007/JMA *Seville port access project*.
101 See EO Decision 289/2005/GG.
102 EO Special Report of to the EP of 30 May 2006 following the EO Decision 289/2005/GG.
103 See Tsadiras (2008).
104 Art. 3(2) EO Statute, first subpara.
105 Ibid., third subpara.
106 Ibid., second subpara.
107 Ibid., Art. 3(3). The member state may disclose the information provided the EO undertakes not to divulge it.
108 Art. 339 TFEU (ex Art. 287 EC). See also Art. 4(1) EO Statute. Exceptionally, under Art. 4(2) EO Statute, the EO is obliged to contact competent national authorities where he learns of facts which he considers might infringe criminal law of a member

state as well as, if appropriate, the Union institution or body responsible for the relevant official(s) involved in maladministration. The EO likewise may notify the Union institution or body responsible for an official whose conduct may be questioned from a disciplinary perspective.

109 Art. 3(4) EO Statute.

110 A notable exception has been the *Parga* complaint EO Decision 1288/99/OV, referred to in section 10.1.2 of this chapter.

111 The EO's annual reports to date do not reveal any instance of Art. 3(4) EO Statute needing to be invoked in relation to environmental inquiries.

112 Regulation 1367/2006 on the application of the provisions of the Århus Convention to Access to Information, Public Participation in Decision-making and Access to Justice in Environmental Matters to Community institutions and bodies (OJ 2006 L264/13).

113 Regulation1049/2001 regarding access to European Parliament (EP), Council and Commission documents (OJ 2001 L145/43).

114 Art. 3(2) EO Statute and Art. 5(2) EO Implementing Decision.

115 See e.g. Tsadiras (2008), p. 765.

116 See Art. 5(4) EO Implementing Decision.

117 See Art. 3(2) EO Statute and Art. 5(3) EO Implementing Decision.

118 Regulation 31/62/EEC and Regulation 11/62/EAEC laying down the Staff Regulations of Officials and the Conditions of Employment of Other Servants of the European Economic Community and the European Atomic Energy Community (OJ 45, 14 June 1962, p. 1385) as amended.

119 Smith (2009), p. 196.

120 Art. 5(5) EO Implementing Decision.

121 See Tsadiras (2013a).

122 Art. 228(1) TFEU.

123 For examples of further remarks, see e.g. EO Decision 244/2006/(BM)JMA *High-speed railway link* in which the EO made some suggestions to the EIB about its practice of recording impact assessments and EO Decision 791/2005/(IP)FOR *Malagrotta landfill* in which the EO made suggestions concerning future Commission monitoring of compliance by Italian authorities with the Landfill Directive 1999/31 in respect of the landfill site in issue. See also EO Decision 1512/2007/JMA *Seville port access project* in which the EO suggested that the Commission inform complainants of various possibilities open to them to enforce EU law besides the infringement complaint route. A further remark may also be made as part of a finding of maladministration: see e.g. EO Decision 80/2009/BU *R52 Motorway* in which the EO made suggestions for improving the Commission's approach regarding the provision of information concerning handling of complaints. For an example of the EO issuing draft recommendations, notwithstanding the absence of maladministration, see EO Decision 846/2010/PB *Copenhagen-Ringsted railway* in which the EO recommended better clarification of its decision on the infringement complaint and consideration by the Commission of a revised guidance on the Strategic Environmental Assessment Directive 2001/42 (OJ 2001 L197/30).

124 Art. 6(1) EO Implementing Decision.

125 Ibid., Art. 6(2). All EO decisions are published on the EO's website at http://www.ombudsman.europa.eu/en/cases/home.faces, and are referred to in the EO's annual reports published in the Official Journal and on the EO's website at http://www.ombudsman.europa.eu/en/activities/annualreports.faces.

126 See Art. 3(6) EO Statute in conjunction with Art. 8 EO Implementing Decision.

127 Art. 8(3) EO Implementing Decision.

128 Ibid., Art. 8(4).

129 Ibid., Art. 7.

130 EO Annual Report 2012, p. 33.

131 Ibid., p. 35.
132 The EO considers decisions by the EP (and/or its Committee on Petitions) on follow-ing up EO special reports to be of a political nature and outside the mandate of the EO (see EO Annual Report 2012, p. 35).
133 The Commission is required to reply orally and in writing to EP or MEP questions put to it (Art. 230 TFEU). Whilst in theory the EP also has the 'nuclear option' of passing a motion of censure against the Commission under Art. 234 TFEU, forcing the entire college and High Representative of the Union on Foreign Affairs and Security Policy EP to resign, it is basically inconceivable that this power would be used in connection with an instance of maladministration (unless the matter was very serious and involved more than one college member and/or the Commission President).
134 Art. 228(1) TFEU in conjunction with Art. 3(7) EO Statute.
135 See http://www.ombudsman.europa.eu/en/cases/home.faces.
136 See http://www.ombudsman.europa.eu/en/press/pressreleases.faces.
137 See Art. 47 EUCFR.
138 This is based upon studies commissioned by the EO to consider follow up to EO deci-sions made in the 2011–12 period (see EO Annual Report 2012, p. 7).
139 Tsadiras (2013b), p. 159.
140 See Tsadiras (2013a), pp. 63 *et seq.*, who comments that the introduction of legally binding remedies would markedly transform the EO into a 'litigious entity, largely duplicating the role of courts and timidly functioning under the shadow of its Luxem-bourg masters'. See also Tsadiras (2013b).
141 See the EO Report 2012, which notes the regular meetings organised bilaterally between the EO and other EU organs as well as periodical inter-institutional events relating directly or indirectly to the theme of good governance.
142 See e.g. EO Annual Report 2012, p. 36.
143 The organisational structure of the EO may be inspected on the EO's website at http://www.ombudsman.europa.eu/en/atyourservice/team.faces.
144 See e.g. EO decisions 789/2005/(GK)ID (*Athens Tramway*) and 2591/2010/GG (*Vienna Airport*).
145 See e.g. Smith (2009), Hedemann-Robinson (2007).
146 CONV 221/02 CONTRIB 76. The document may be inspected at http://european-convention.europa.eu/pdf/reg/en/02/cv00/cv00221.en02.pdf.
147 A summary of the complaints procedure is set out in the EO Annual Reports (see e.g. EO Annual Report 1995, section I.3). Guidance on EO complaints procedure is also provided on the EO website.
148 EO Annual Report 2012, p. 29.
149 The EO has established an online system for the submission of allegations of EU institutional maladministration. See the EO website at https://secure.ombudsman.europa.eu/en/atyourservice/secured/complaintform.faces.
150 Art. 2(2) EO Statute.
151 EO Annual Report 2012, p. 15. See also Art. 2 EO Implementing Decision.
152 Art. 2(3) EO Statute.
153 Ibid., Art. 1(3).
154 Ibid., Art. 2(4).
155 Ibid.
156 EO Decision 596/97/JMA (*Montes Obarenes-Tolono Mine*).
157 Art. 2(8) EO Statute.
158 Art. 3(1) EO Implementing Decision.
159 Ibid., Art. 3(2).
160 EO Annual Report 2012, p. 15. See also Art. 3 EO Implementing Decision.
161 Art. 4(1) EO Implementing Decision.
162 Ibid., Art. 4(2).

163 EO Annual Report 2012, p. 30. In practice, the EO gives six months for the EU organ to respond to a further remark (see p. 33 of EO Annual Report 2012).
164 Art. 228(1) TFEU, second subpara. See also Art. 4(3) EO Implementing Decision.
165 Art. 4(6) EO Implementing Decision.
166 Ibid., Art. 4(4).
167 OJ 2006 L264/13.
168 Art. 3(5) EO Statute in conjunction with Art. 6 EO Implementing Decision.
169 Art. 6(2) EO Implementing Decision.
170 EO Annual Report 2012, p. 30.
171 Art. 6(3) EO Implementing Decision.
172 EO Annual Report 2012, p. 30.
173 Art. 3(6) EO Statute and Art. 8(3) EO Implementing Decision.
174 EO Annual Report 2012, p. 33.
175 Art. 228(1) TFEU second subpara. and Art. 3(7) EO Statute.
176 Art. 228(1) TFEU second subpara. and Arts. 2(9) and 3(7) EO Statute.
177 See EO Decisions 1338/98/ME *EIB funding of Hungarian M0 orbital motorway*, 244/2006/(BM) JMA *High-speed railway link*, 1779/2006/MHZ *National Road Fund Programme* and 1807/2006/MHZ *Flood Damage Reconstruction*.
178 EO cases may be accessed at http://www.ombudsman.europa.eu/en/cases/home.faces
179 Ibid.
180 EO Decisions 846/2010/PB *Copenhagen-Ringsted railway*, 2591/2010/GG *Viennese Airport* and 1528/2006/(GG)WP *German waste oil recycling*.
181 EO Special Report 2591/2010/GG.
182 Namely, OI/2/2006/JMA *Granadilla industrial harbour* and OI/3/2009/MHZ *Recording of complaints*.
183 Tsadiras (2013b).
184 Ibid., pp. 156–7.
185 Ibid., p. 158.
186 Ibid.
187 Williams (1994), p. 359.
188 See e.g. EO Decision 995/98/OV *Macedonian Metro Joint Venture* .
189 European Commission, *Fifteenth Report on Monitoring the Application of European [Union] Law* (1997) (OJ 1998 C250/1), p. 10.
190 The Commission undertook some earlier changes on complainant relations in 1998 (see European Commission document SEC(1998)1733, *Improvement to the Commission's Working Methods in Relation to Infringement Proceedings*, 15 October 1998.
191 European Commission, *Code of Good Administrative Behaviour – Relations with the Public* (OJ 2000 L267).
192 COM(2002)141.
193 COM(2012)154, Commission Communication, *Updating the Handling of Relations with the Complainant in Respect of the Application of Union Law*, 2 April 2012.
194 See ibid., point 4.
195 See ibid., point 3. Specifically, the minimum criteria are that the complaint (i) has not been submitted anonymously, (ii) refers to a member state and not a private person as allegedly breaching EU law and (iii) sets out a grievance in respect of which the Commission has not adopted a clear public and consistent position and which does not clearly fall outside the scope of EU law.
196 See e.g. EO Decision 80/2009/BU *R52 Motorway* (whilst the Commission acknowledged receipt, it only informed the complainant one year later of its intention not to register the latter's correspondence as a complaint).
197 EO Own-Initiative Investigation OI/3/2009/MHZ (*Infringement Complaint Registration*).
198 See COM(2007)502, Commission Communication: *A Europe of Results – Applying Community Law*, 5 September 2007.

199 See point 3 of COM(2012)154.
200 See ibid., point 7.
201 See e.g. EO Decision 706/2007/(WP)BEH *Viennese PM10 pollution.*
202 See e.g. EO Decisions 2229/2003 *San Roman de la Vega waste processing centre* (three- year delay before decision to issue a LFN), 789/2005/(GK)ID *Athens tramway project* (nine-month delay before Commission contacted national authorities).
203 EO Decision 706/2007/(WP)BEH *Viennese PM10 pollution.*
204 See e.g. EO Decision 1956/2007/(SAB)VIK *Greenore landfill* in which the EO held it had not been unreasonable for the Commission to take 30 months to decide to commence second-round infringement proceedings against Ireland by way of follow-up to the multiple first-round action Case C-494/01 *Commission v Ireland.*
205 See e.g. EO Decision 995/98/OV *Macedonian Metro.*
206 See e.g. EO Decision 1528/2006/(GG)WP *German waste oil recycling.*
207 See e.g. EO Decision 596/97/JMA *Montes Obarenes-Tolono Mine.*
208 See e.g. EO Decisions 250/97/OV *Sewage works Kalamatsi* and 962/2006/OV *Rhede wind farm project* (42 months before complainant heard from Commission about its decision).
209 See point 7 of COM(2012)154.
210 See e.g. EO Decision 1956/2007/(SAB)VIK *Greenore landfill.*
211 See e.g. EO Decision 39/2002/OV *Anglesey Motor Racing Track.*
212 See e.g. EO Decision 1437/2006 /(WP) BEH *Elze site Hildesheim (Hamsters).*
213 See e.g. EO Decisions 298/97/PD *Southport shoreline sea defence*, 1956/2007/(SAB)VIK *Greenore landfill* and 846/2010/PB *Copenhagen-Ringsted railway.*
214 See e.g. EO Decision 846/2010/PB *Copenhagen-Ringsted railway.*
215 See e.g. EO Decisions 271,277/2000/(IJH)MA *Access to UK waste reports*, 2183/2003(TN) (IJN) *Botniabanan railway link* , 2821/2004/OV. 2229/2003 *San Roman de la Vega waste processing centre*, 2821/2004/OV *Zakynthos EU mission report (sea turtles)*, 355/2007/(TN)FOR *Granadilla industrial harbour* and 2073/2010/AN *Vera and Rambla de Mojácar.*
216 See e.g. EO Decisions 132/21.9.95/AH/EN *M40 Motorway* , 472/6.3.96/XP/ES/ PD *Itoiz Dam* (EO Annual Report 1998), 106/97/PD *RCF Lake District* and 493/2000/ ME *Skälderviken.*
217 See e.g. EO Decisions 1962/2005/IP *Riva del Garda bypass* and 846/2010/PB *Copenhagen-Ringsted railway.*
218 Point 9 of COM(2012)154.
219 See e.g. EO Decision 1561/2010/(MB)FOR Picris Willkommii, Guadiana River.
220 EO Decision 1288/99/OV *Parga wastewater treatment plant.*
221 Now Directive 2011/92 (OJ 2012 L26/1) as amended.
222 Under EU Staff Regulations any official who accepts a political appointment is required to take leave from the Commission during the appointment. It transpired that the official concerned remained active in their capacity as a Commission civil servant whilst on leave at the material time.
223 Ibid., p. 104.
224 Art. 4(2) EO Statute obliges the Ombudsman, *inter alia*, to notify immediately the competent national authorities via the Permanent Representations of the member states and, if appropriate, the Union institution with authority over the official or servant concerned with a view to waiving any existing diplomatic-type immunity, if he learns of facts which he considers 'might relate to criminal law', such as fraudulent activity. In this case, though, the EO did not consider it necessary to make any reference to this provision in his report.
225 Case T-412/05 *M v Commission*. The GC rejected the official's claim for €150,000 damages (including dismissing the official's claim for compensation for alleged injury to personal health and to close family members).
226 The official has remained in a senior position within DG ENV.
227 Art. 4 ECGAB.
228 See e.g. EO Own-Initiative Investigation OI/2/2006/JMA *Granadilla industrial harbour.*

229 The EO has asserted that it may assess the Commission's legal analysis of an alleged infringement according to the same standard of review employed by the CJEU: see para. 60 of EO Decision2073/2010/AN *Vera and Rambla de Mojácar.*

230 See para. 58 of EO Decision 791/2005/(IP)FOR *Malagrotta landfill.*

231 Namely 3 July 1988.

232 EO Decision 1288/99/OV *Parga wastewater treatment plant.*

233 EO Special Report 2591/2010 GG *Vienna Airport.*

234 See EO Decision 1528/2006/(GG)WP *German waste oil recycling* in which the EO disagreed as to whether a decision by the German legislature to continue to exempt waste oils used for heating from a mineral excise duty contravened the former Waste Oils Directive 75/439 (OJ 1975 L194/25) and flouted an infringement ruling of the CJEU against Germany (Case C-102/97 *Commission v Germany*).

235 See EO Decision 813/98(PD)/GG *Southport shoreline coastal road.* The EO disagreed with the Commission's position that certain provisions of the Habitats Directive 92/43 would only become operational to a habitat site once a member state formally notifies that site under the Natura 2000 network notification scheme, the reasoning of the EO being that the deadline for meeting the obligation to draw up a list of protected sites contained in the directive had already elapsed.

236 See EO Decisions 2725/2004/(PB)ID *Alqueva Dam and Reservoir* and 3660/2004/PB *Ballybrown wetland.*

237 EO decision 789/2005/(GK)ID (*Athens Tramway*).

238 The EP's website is www.europarl.eu.int.

239 Art. 230 TFEU. Questions may be submitted either by the EP collectively or by individual MEPs.

240 Ibid., Art. 233.

241 Ibid., Art. 234.

242 Ibid., Art. 227.

243 Ibid., Art. 228.

244 Ibid., Art. 226.

245 For an overview of the workings of the petitions system , see A5–0088/2001, Committee on Petitions' Report on the institution of the petition at the dawn of the 21st century, 19 March 2001 (Doc. PE 232.710).

246 The right is, though, stated in the TFEU to be one of a catalogue of rights afforded of EU citizens under Part Two (Non-Discrimination and Citizenship of the Union) of the TFEU, namely Art. 24(2) TFEU.

247 Title IX (Petitions) (Arts. 215–17) of the European Parliament Rules of Procedure, 8th parliamentary term (July 2014). The Rules of Procedure may be accessed on the EP website at http://www.europarl.europa.eu/aboutparliament/en/0025729351/Organisation-and-work.html.

248 See website, http://www.europarl.europa.eu/committees/en/peti/home.html.

249 *PETI Journal* may be accessed at http://www.europarl.europa.eu/committees/en/peti/newsletters.html.

250 Art. 228(1) TFEU, second subpara.

251 Art. 3(1) EO Statute.

252 See notably the following reference point on the EP's website, https://www.secure.europarl.europa.eu/aboutparliament/en/petition.html.

253 *Report on the Activities of the Committee on Petitions 2012* (2013/2013(INI) of 24 September 2013, p. 29. Rapporteur E. Macmillan-Scott. EP Doc. A7–0299/2013:PE508.200v04–00.

254 Over 40% of petitions were declared inadmissible in 2009–10. See ibid.

255 According to a spring 2013 *Eurobarometer* survey 89% of EU citizens questioned were aware of the EP petition process.

256 EP Doc. A6–0040/2005, Committee on Petitions, *Report on its Deliberations during the European Parliamentary Year 2003–4*, 11 February 2005, p. 16.

257 See EP Doc. PE526.099v03.00, *Draft Report on the Activities of the Committee on Petitions 2013* (2014/2008 (INI)) of 30 January 2014 (Rapporteur J. L.Wałesa).

258 See *Report on the Activities of the Committee on Petitions 2012* (2013/2013(INI)) of 24 September 2013, p. 30.

259 Art. 17 TEU in conjunction with Arts. 258 and 260 TFEU.

260 E.g. in petition 1106/2002 concerning risks of pollution of the Toce river and Lake Maggiore from the former Enichem de Pieve Vergonte industrial plant in Italy, a delegation of the Committee was dispatched to meet with representatives of the Italian Ministry of the Environment (reported in EP Doc. A6–0040/2005, Committee on Petitions, *Report on its Deliberations during the European Parliamentary Year 2003–4*, 11 February 2005.

261 See *Report on the Activities of the Committee on Petitions 2012* (2013/2013(INI)) of 24 September 2013, p. 20.

262 See *Draft Report on the Activities of the Committee on Petitions 2013*(2014/2008 (INI)) of 30 January 2014, p. 8.

263 Committee on Petitions, *Report on its Deliberations during the European Parliamentary Year 2003–2004*, 11 February 2005(A6–0040/2005), p. 13 (Spanish Hydrological Plan diverting River Ebro).

264 See *Report on the Activities of the Committee on Petitions 2012* (2013/2013(INI)) of 24 September 2013, p. 22.

265 See website at http://www.europarl.europa.eu/committees/en/envi/home.html.

266 E.g. in spring 2001 the Committee was keen to probe the Commission services about the state of progress by Greece to comply with the CJEU's judgment in the Kouroupitos case (Case C-387/97).

267 See Rule 198 of the EP's Rules of Procedure, 8th parliamentary term (July 2014).

268 Ibid., Rule 198(4).

269 Currently, this would require the consent of 188 MEPs (out of 751). See Art. 14(2) TEU.

270 Indeed, as a general point the EP is not vested with any specific powers under the TEU/TFEU to control member state activities in connection with implementation of EU policies.

271 The reports of these former committees of inquiry may be inspected on the archive pages of the EP's website http://www.europarl.europa.eu/parlArchives.

272 See Rule 141 of the EP's Rules of Procedure, 8th parliamentary term (July 2014).

273 See Art. 225 TFEU.

274 See ibid., Art. 241.

275 It is clear that corporate entities, such as NGEOs, trades unions and companies, may assist and sponsor ECI campaigns. Indeed, their resources, financial, technical and organisational (including number of subscribers/contacts), may be crucial for the success of several if not most ECIs. The success of the *Right2Water* campaign (discussed below) owes no doubt a great deal to these supportive factors.

276 OJ 2011 L65/1.

277 Art. 4 in conjunction with Annex II of the ECI Regulation. Annex II specifies that the relevant information must include: the title, subject matter and brief description of the objectives of the ECI proposal; the provisions of the TEU/TFEU considered relevant; details of the members of the organising committee; as well as all sources of support and funding.

278 Art. 4(2)(a) in conjunction with Art. 3 ECI Regulation.

279 Ibid., Art. 4(2)(b).

280 Ibid., Art. 4(2)(c).

281 Ibid., Art. 4(2)(d).

282 Ibid., Art. 5(5).

283 Ibid., Arts. 5–6.

284 Ibid., Annex III.

285 Ibid., Art. 3(4).
286 Ibid., Art. 2(1) in conjunction with Art. 7.
287 Ibid., Art. 9.
288 Ibid., Art. 8.
289 Ibid., Art. 10(1)(a)–(b).
290 Ibid., Art. 11.
291 See *PETI* Journal (April 2014), p. 1.
292 Art. 10(1)(c) ECI Regulation.
293 By way of exception, the European Council, High Representative of the Union on Foreign Affairs and Security Policy as well as the Council of the EU feature predominantly in terms of rights of initiative in relation to the EU's Common Foreign and Security Policy under the aegis of Title V TEU. The Commission has minimal rights here (e.g. Art. 22(2) TEU).
294 Rule 218 (Citizens' Initiative) of the EP's Rules of Procedure, 8th parliamentary term (July 2014).
295 Ibid.
296 http://www.right2water.eu.
297 The organisations include: Aqua Publica Europea (APE), European Environmental Bureau (EEB), European Anti Poverty Network (EAPN), European Public Health Alliance (EPHA), European Federation of Public Service Unions (EPSU), European Trade Union Confederation (ETUC), Public Services International (PSI), The Social Platform, and Women in Europe for a Common Future (WECF). See http://www.right2water.eu/who-we-are-organizations.
298 COM(2014)177, European Commission, *Communication on the European Citizens' Initiative 'Water and Sanitation Are a Human Right! Water Is a Public Good, not a Commodity!'*, 19 March 2014.
299 Directive 98/83 on the quality of water intended for human consumption (OJ 1998 L330/32). For an overview of the legislation, see the following European Commission website http://ec.europa.eu/environment/water/water-drink/legislation_en.html.
300 The other Commission commitments in the Communication include: reinforced implementation of its water quality legislation; building on the undertakings in the 7th Environment Action Programme and the EU Water Blueprint; improved transparency for urban waste water and drinking water data management and exploration of the idea of benchmarking water quality; co-operation with existing initiatives to provide a wider set of benchmarks for water services; stimulation of innovative approaches for development assistance (e.g. support to partnerships between water operators and to public–private partnerships); promotion of sharing of best practices between EU member states (e.g. on solidarity instruments) and identification of new opportunities for cooperation; and advocacy of universal access to safe drinking water and sanitation as a priority area for future Sustainable Development Goals under the aegis of the UN process.
301 See recital 1 of ECI Regulation.
302 The EEA's website is www.eea.eu.int.
303 See Regulation 1210/90 on the establishment of the European Environment Agency and the European environment information and observation network (OJ 1990 L120/1).
304 Ibid., Art. 2(ii).
305 Ibid., Art. 3.
306 See ibid., Arts.1, 2(i) and 4.
307 http://www.eea.europa.eu/.
308 See Art. 20 of Regulation 1210/90 on the establishment of the European Environment Agency and the European environment information and observation network (OJ 1990 L120/1), as amended by Regulation 93/1999 (OJ 1999 L117/1).
309 As published in the Official Journal of the EU: OJ 1997 C255/9 and OJ 1998 C123/6.

310 OJ 1997 C321/1. This position was endorsed in recital 5 of Recommendation 2001/ 331 providing for minimum criteria for environmental inspections in the member states (OJ 2001 L118/41).

311 Regulation 166/2006 concerning the establishment of a European Pollutant Release and Transfer Register and amending Council Directives 91/689 and 96/61 (OJ 2006 L33/1).

312 Art. 192 TFEU confirms that but for a few specific areas, the ordinary legislative procedure (as enshrined in Art. 294 TFEU) applies with respect to the enactment of EU environmental legislation. The ordinary legislative procedure requires the joint consent of the EP and Council of the EU for the adoption of a legislative measure and Council consent is secured by way of a qualified majority (Art. 16(4) TFEU in conjunction with Art. 238 TFEU). Art. 192(2) TFEU specifies that the Council has to consent by way of unanimity in order for measures in certain areas to be adopted: (a) provisions primarily of a fiscal nature; (b) measures affecting town and country planning, quantitative water resource management or affecting the in/direct availability of such resources, land use (with exception of waste management); or (c) measures significantly affecting a member state's choice between different energy sources and the general structure of its energy supply.

313 Art. 17(1) TEU.

314 The Commission's legislative role in environmental affairs relates to its monopoly over presenting legislative proposals (see Art. 192 TFEU) as well as power to alter the balance of power within the legislative process under the so-called 'co-decision' procedure (as set out in Art. 294 TFEU) which is applicable to the environmental sector. (If the Commission issues a negative opinion on EP proposed amendments to its proposal, the Council of the EU may only adopt them by way of unanimity.) See Art. 17(2) TEU.

315 The executive dimension to the Commission's activities lie principally in its predominant role in the shaping of Union policies as well as strategic position in relation to the passage of delegated and implementing legislation. See Art. 17(1) TEU third and forth sentences, and Arts. 290–1 TFEU.

316 The law enforcement role of the Commission in the environmental sector manifests itself in the fact that it is the Commission which has the responsibility to ensure the application of EU treaty as well as legislative rules (see Art. 17(1) TEU). In addition, under Arts. 258 and 260 TFEU it has the power to bring legal proceedings against member states over infractions of EU law.

11 Enforcement of EU environmental law by national authorities (1)

General principles and environmental inspection responsibilities

This final part of the book considers the legal role and responsibilities of EU member state authorities in enforcing EU environmental legislation. The particular national authorities charged by their member states with the task of overseeing the practical implementation of environmental protection legislation are crucially important actors involved in monitoring and ensuring due compliance with such legislation. For it is national authorities which, ultimately, have the requisite legal powers as well as resources to enforce binding EU environmental standards on the ground.

In the first two parts of the book, the enforcement roles of the European Commission and civil society were considered. For various reasons, it is evident that neither the Commission nor the public (including NGEOs) are ever going to be best placed to serve as the most important or effective source for overseeing compliance with EU environmental law within the Union's member states.

As a centralised institution vested with limited legal and human resources, it is wholly unrealistic to expect the European Commission alone to be able to enforce EU environmental law across the Union, which spans currently 28 states and is likely to continue to expand its membership.[1] As discussed in the first part of this book, the Commission is, of course, endowed with legal powers under Articles 258 and 260 of the Treaty on the Functioning of the European Union (TFEU) to take legal proceedings against member states guilty of infringing EU law; these proceedings may ultimately culminate in a defendant member state being fined. The infringement action has been, and remains, a crucially important tool in ensuring that member states' national rules of law and administrative practice accords with EU legal requirements. The Commission is best placed to monitor the correct transposition of EU legislation into national law, given that such monitoring is essentially based on evaluating publicly available documentation in the member states (i.e. transposition legislation) and, bearing in mind its legislative role, the Commission is able to command an in-depth understanding of the parameters of particular EU legislative requirements. Moreover, the enforcement by a single institution, where feasible, aids consistency of approach in terms of law enforcement.

However, given the fact that the Commission has no general statutory powers to carry out its own investigations of suspected cases of breaches of EU environmental law on the ground, there is in practice limited scope for it to be able to address specific instances of non-observance of Union environmental legislative requirements (so-called 'bad-application' cases). It is not vested with powers to access affected sites or require persons suspected of being involved to disclose information. Moreover, as things stand it does not have sufficient personnel or financial resources to be able to develop a significant inspection role for itself. The Commission is essentially dependent upon the public (as complainants) and member state authorities for information and evidence relating to cases of bad application of EU environmental legislation.

For a variety of reasons, it is to be expected that private individuals and organisations are never likely to have more than a useful ancillary or complementary role in terms of assisting in EU environmental law enforcement. Participation by the commercial/industrial sector in law enforcement activities is likely to be very limited, notably in view of the general lack of clear personal economic motivation for engagement in active peer-review involvement. Whilst some sectors of civil society may well be interested in engaging in supervision-related activity (notably some NGEOs) the range of requisite resources at their disposal to be able to do so may well be seriously limited or absent (namely powers to inspect premises, technical expertise to assess compliance and financial backing to absorb enforcement costs).

As was discussed in detail in Chapters 8–9A, the EU has been keen in various ways to promote the role of civil society in the field of EU environmental law enforcement, notably following up the lead undertaken by the 1998 UNECE Århus Convention concerning access to environmental information, public participation in environmental decision-making and access to environmental justice. Notwithstanding the significance of the emergence of the promotion by the EU of a greater supervisory role for civil society in connection with the delivery of EU environmental policy, it is clear that this cannot mask the fundamental importance of the tasks performed by national authorities to secure adherence to legislative environmental protection commitments, whether these be of Union or national origin.

Compared with the European Commission and private individuals, the national environmental protection authorities of the member states appear best placed for a number of reasons to undertake the bulk of law enforcement work in relation to specific cases of 'bad application' of EU environmental legislation. First, they are better placed geographically than the Commission to oversee compliance and understand its particular challenges within their particular jurisdictions. Secondly, given that the authorities are established by virtue of national legislation, their structures are underpinned by a strong sense of local legitimacy and democratic accountability. Thirdly, such authorities are commonly specifically vested with the purpose, resources and powers to oversee compliance with environmental legislation. Fourthly, given the third point, it is evident that such authorities have usually acquired considerable experience and expertise in environmental law enforcement matters at local level. All these reasons underline the seminal importance of national public authorities in environmental law enforcement work in general, not only in relation to EU environmental legislation.

Of course, the relative efficacy of national authorities is conditional upon their being suitably resourced and independent from external interference that might otherwise raise conflicts of interest. Traditionally and until relatively recently, for reasons associated largely with national sovereignty, the EU has been reluctant to interfere with member state decisions on the structuring and resourcing of national authorities designated with environmental law policing roles. The classic presumption in international law that nation states should be regarded as primarily and independently responsible for the implementation of their international treaty commitments has cast a long shadow over the development of EU (environmental) law. However, the traditionally deferential approach adopted by the EU regarding member state autonomy over implementation matters has gradually eroded over time in light of the experience that several member states have failed to take the necessary steps in order to be able to fulfil their supervisory responsibilities adequately. There is widespread recognition now, also amongst (most) member states, that shortcomings in national supervisory frameworks risk undermining the achievement of key objectives underpinning Union environmental legislation. Accordingly, it is of direct interest to the EU (i.e. a Union issue and matter) that minimum standards of resourcing (in terms of legal powers, finance, technical expertise, staffing and equipment) are properly invested into the national authorities charged by member states with overseeing the adherence to environmental protection requirements enshrined in EU environmental law.

In this third and final part of the book, Chapters 11–13 explore the extent to which the EU has developed specific responsibilities of member states and their public authorities to undertake law enforcement duties in respect of EU environmental legislation. By way of introduction, this chapter provides an overview of general aspects as well the area of environmental inspection powers and responsibilities. Specifically, it focuses on the various general duties that arise under EU law for member states and their authorities engaged in environmental protection to implement and enforce EU environmental norms. In addition, it examines the various policy developments that have emerged at EU level so far in relation to discussions on establishing minimum criteria for environmental inspections at national level. Chapters 12 and 13 focus on EU legislative initiatives introduced to impose particular common minimum requirements at national level concerning civil as well as criminal liability of persons found to have perpetrated serious violations of binding EU environmental protection standards.

11.1 General implementation duties of national authorities under EU law

It is evident from earlier chapters in this book that member states, including their national authorities, have certain general duties under EU law to take the necessary steps to ensure that the legally binding commitments entered into under the EU treaty framework, including notably by virtue of EU legislation, are fulfilled. These implementation duties, based upon general provisions contained in the EU's foundational treaty framework, have been developed by the jurisprudence of the Court of Justice of the European Union (CJEU) over a number of years and are in a process of continual, gradual evolution as well as crystallisation into policy sector contexts. This section of the chapter reflects upon the extent to which these duties devolve also to national authorities of the member states, specifically those entrusted with the task of protecting the environment. These duties may be analysed in terms of the extent to which they require national authorities to take positive steps to ensure that EU environmental law is properly applied (referred to here as active responsibilities) and to which they require them to respond to requests to take action by third parties (passive responsibilities).

11.1.1 Active legal responsibilities of national authorities under EU law

As far as EU environmental legislation is concerned, the most basic implementation obligation concerns the duty to ensure that EU environmental directives, the preferred legislative tool for the passage of environmental legislation at EU level, are properly transposed on time into national law by way of appropriate national implementing legislation. This duty flows directly from Article 288(3) TFEU and is the responsibility of the member states, as represented by their respective national governments. Public authorities, such as national and regional environmental agencies and municipal authorities, do not carry any responsibility for the transposition of directives. Instead, this is a matter for national governments to secure via the relevant domestic legislative processes required to achieve this under the auspices of the particular constitutional legal arrangements of each member states.

However, EU law also imposes an additional and more wide-ranging implementation obligation on member states other than transposition, namely the general duty to ensure that in practice EU law is respected and therefore applied within their respect territories. This general legal obligation is enshrined in Article 4(3) of the Treaty on European Union (TEU) which stipulates that:

> 3. Pursuant to the principle of sincere co-operation, the Union and Member States shall, in full mutual respect, assist each other in carrying out tasks which flow from the Treaties.[2]
>
> The Member States shall take any appropriate measure, general or particular, to ensure fulfilment of the obligations arising out of the Treaties or resulting from the acts of the institutions of the Union.
>
> The Member States shall facilitate the achievement of the Union's tasks and refrain from any measure which could jeopardise the attainment of the Union's objectives.

Commonly known as the 'good faith' or 'sincere co-operation' clause, the current version of this treaty provision was introduced by virtue of the 2007 Lisbon Treaty, thereby superseding the predecessor treaty article contained in the former European Community Treaty (EC) Treaty (Article 10 EC). Article 10 EC[3] contained a more general formulation of the implementation responsibilities of member states, but essentially Article 4(3) TFEU consolidates the pre-Lisbon understanding of the EU duty of good faith as interpreted in light of long-standing CJEU jurisprudence.

The CJEU has established that a number of obligations flow from the good-faith provision enshrined in the EU treaty framework, currently Article 4(3) TEU. In particular, the Court has consistently held that the general implementation responsibilities flowing from this provision are binding not only on member state governments but also upon all national authorities, judicial as well as administrative, including notably those charged with the task of supervising implementing of policy as crystallised into national law.[4] It has been the CJEU which has confirmed that foundational Union treaty framework, in particular by virtue of the good-faith provision as currently enshrined in Article 4(3) TEU, requires member states to ensure practical as well as legal implementation of EU rules of law within their respective territories. In particular, member states governments and competent authorities are required according to the Court's established case law to take active measures to ensure that EU measures falling within their area of jurisdiction is correctly applied. The CJEU has confirmed, for example, that the duty of co-operation requires member states to ensure that they proceed in respect of EU law infringements with the same diligence as that which they bring to bear in implementing corresponding national laws.[5] This implies that member states must ensure that inspection and monitoring systems employed by national authorities to detect infringements of national environmental legislation must also be applied in relation to the supervision of binding EU environmental legislative obligations. The CJEU has established that the sincere co-operation duty under EU law includes ensuring that infringements of EU law are penalised effectively at national level, so that effective, proportionate and dissuasive sanctions are used.[6] Member state governments and their competent authorities are also obliged to afford assistance to the European Commission in connection with the assessment of complaints made to the Commission concerning alleged violations of EU law, with a view to enabling the Commission to be in a suitably informed position to decide whether or not to bring infringement proceedings against a member state.[7]

However, the duties arising under Article 4(3) TEU on member states and competent authorities to take active steps to ensure that EU environmental legislation is adhered to in practice are subject to significant qualifications. Given that the vast majority of EU environmental legislation is passed in the form of EU directives, it is important to note the importance of member states adopting timely and accurate transposition legislation. In the absence of an EU directive being transposed correctly into national law, the national environmental protection authorities have practically no possibility of enforcing their terms against the public at large. For, as was discussed in Chapter 6, the CJEU has held that EU directives do not have binding effects on private persons.[8] Accordingly, in line with judicial reasoning, the Court has confirmed that national competent authorities may not rely upon the doctrine of direct effect in order to enforce provisions of EU directives against private persons.[9]

In addition, authorities may not seek to use the doctrine of indirect effect in order to punish individuals for transgressing norms of EU directives. It will be recalled from Chapter 6 that the doctrine of indirect effect, which emanates from the CJEU's case law, is in essence a duty on emanations of the member states (including courts as well as government departments and authorities) to interpret national legislation in alignment with EU law covering the same policy field, insofar as this is possible.[10] However, in the *Arcaro* case[11] the CJEU ruled out that national courts were obliged under Article 4(3) TFEU to interpret national legislation in line with an EU environmental directive wherever such an interpretation would have the effect of determining or aggravating, on the basis of the directive and in the absence of a law enacted for its implementation, the liability in criminal law of persons who act in contravention of that directive's provisions. It is for these reasons that, to a great extent, national authorities charged with the task of environmental protection are dependent upon national law endowing them with suitable powers to ensure that EU environmental rules may be enforced at local level. Their general responsibilities under Article 4(3) TEU do not extend to using EU environmental directives in order either to determine or aggravate liability of persons in respect of breaches of EU directives.[12] The position is different in relation to EU regulations, which are defined as directly applicable and generally binding under Article 288(2) TFEU. National authorities are entitled to rely upon directly effective provisions of EU environmental regulations against private persons. However, the instrument of the EU regulation is used relatively rarely in the context of EU environmental law, although there are some important examples in relation to environmental policy areas closely connected with international trade.[13]

Notwithstanding these limitations, this does not mean that member states and competent authorities acting in the environmental protection area may not take any active steps to assist in the enforcement of EU environmental legislation where these have not been transposed correctly into national law. The duty of co-operation under Article 4(3) TEU requires member state governments and competent authorities to undertake all steps possible to supervise implementation of such legislation, subject to the qualifications mentioned above in relation to the doctrines of direct and indirect effect. This means that national environmental protection authorities are obliged under EU law, at the very least, to take active steps to ensure that they may verify whether or not a suspected breach of an EU environmental norm has taken place, using their existing powers of inspection granted under national law, notwithstanding that the EU norm has not been correctly transposed into national law. In such a case, the competent authority would be under a duty at least to inform the European Commission of the facts and evidence as well as notify its concerns over transposition to the appropriate national government department responsible for environmental affairs. The Commission would then be in a position to pursue the matter further with the member state government, using the leverage of infringement proceedings under Articles 258 and 260 TFEU where necessary. Whilst the national authority would not have been able to take action specifically against the person(s) responsible for breaching

EU environmental standards, it would – by referring the matter to the Commission and its national government – be fulfilling its implementation responsibilities as far as is possible in accordance with Article 4(3) TFEU. Accordingly, national authorities are not powerless to act in the absence of legislation transposing EU environmental directives; they have concrete independent legal duties to assist in implementation under the EU treaty framework.

However, the author is not aware that these obligations have been made standard operational in practice at national authority level. National authorities of the member states in general do not appear to be appraised of their distinct legal responsibilities relating to implementation of EU environmental law by either the European Commission or member states. A communication from the European Commission to this effect would be appropriate in the circumstances.

In Chapters 12–13, two recent EU legislative initiatives will be discussed which are specifically intended to introduce specific obligations on member state environmental protection authorities to take steps to enforce EU environmental legislation. These are Directive 2004/35 on environmental liability with regard to the prevention and remedying of environmental damage[14] and Directive 2008/99 on the protection of the environment through criminal law.[15] The objective underpinning these legislative instruments is to ensure that member states structure their legal systems so to as provide national competent authorities with responsibilities to impose effective civil and criminal sanctions respectively on persons found to have breached certain minimum legally binding EU environmental protection standards.

11.1.2 Passive legal responsibilities of national authorities under EU law

There are a number of other general and specific EU legal duties on national authorities in connection with implementation matters, which are more of a passive or a reactive character. Specifically, EU law contains a set of legal obligations on member state competent authorities requiring them to assist third parties in various ways who decide to take either administrative or legal action in order to enforce EU environmental law.

At a general level, it is important to note that individuals are able to invoke a number of important general principles of EU law against national environmental protection authorities. Notably, the CJEU has confirmed private persons may rely upon directly effective provisions of EU directives against public authorities,[16] as discussed in Chapter 6. In its more recent case law, the Court has expanded this line of jurisprudence to include the right of private individuals to hold national authorities to account where they fail to carry out responsibilities assigned to them, which involve the exercise of discretion. The right of individuals to be able to rely upon certain provisions of EU environmental directives was used to good effect in the case of *Kraaijeveld*[17] in order to assist in the enforcement of an EU environmental directive. In that case, the CJEU held that a private individual could rely upon the Environmental Impact Assessment (EIA) Directive[18] in order to seek rectification of a failure on the part of a competent national authority to assess whether or not a particular development should be subject to an environmental impact assessment. The Court ruled that the authority concerned was obliged to undertake such a review, notwithstanding that national law did not provide it with specific jurisdiction so to do. Where an EU environmental directive provides member states with duties involving the evaluation of various factors, and therefore incorporates a strong element of discretion or choice on the part of national authorities, the CJEU has ruled that private individuals may rely on them before the national courts in order to ensure that national authorities do carry out those duties, irrespective of whether national law specifically provides them with jurisdiction so to do.[19]

Even where measures taken by a national authority to fulfil requirements of directly effective obligations contained in an EU directive results in specific disadvantages arising for particular persons, the CJEU has held that a national authority must nevertheless apply the directly effective provision concerned. The Court has rejected the view that such a situation is tantamount to enforcing directives against private individuals. This legal point was confirmed in the *Delena Wells* case,[20] also discussed earlier in Chapter 6. That case involved a private person being able to rely upon requirements in the EIA Directive in order to challenge the legality of a grant of planning permission to a private mining company to reopen a dormant quarry. Similar considerations apply in relation to the application of indirect effect. Specifically, where a person is able to use the indirect effect doctrine in order to amend the conduct or policy of a national authority so as to be alignment with EU environmental legislation, it is immaterial from a EU legal perspective whether the adverse effects of that amendment of conduct or policy, as a result of the litigation taken against the public authority, leads to any adverse implications for specific private persons.

In addition to the doctrines of direct and indirect effect, member state authorities are also subject to the legal disciplines of the rules on state liability under EU law. Accordingly, as was discussed in Chapter 7, authorities are liable to pay compensation to individuals in respect of damage caused to them as a direct result of breaches by the authorities of requirements in EU law entailing the grant of individual rights.[21] Given that most EU environmental legislation does not entail the grant of individual rights, though, the potential impact of state liability rules of EU law on environmental protection authorities appears to be limited in the light of the current rules on liability set out in current CJEU jurisprudence.

There are interesting possibilities for national authorities to be able to adapt these passive duties onto a more active footing. For instance, it would be legitimate and appropriate for national authorities to amend their existing policies and practices to the extent needed in order to avoid possible legal action against them for failing to invoke EU environmental legislative rules. In particular, an authority would be perfectly entitled to amend its environmental decision-making practices (e.g. planning application, waste licensing, discharge permitting) in order to accord with EU environmental legislative requirements irrespective of whether or not national transposition legislation required this to happen, as has been clarified by the CJEU in its case law. Although any such amendments may well involve, actually or potentially, certain detrimental consequences for specific individuals, in that an amendment might well require a stiffening of existing environmental protection requirements set locally, it is submitted that this would not fall foul of the CJEU's case law barring the invocation of directives against individuals. Instead, such a move on the part of an authority would be to ensure that private persons could not seek to require it to evade its responsibility to apply EU rules to the fullest extent possible as required under Article 4(3) TEU. However, it is unlikely that many authorities would be keen to take on the risk of employing such a policy without firmer legal foundations (i.e. set out in a specific legislative text). For, notwithstanding the fact that the EU duty of sincere co-operation undoubtedly incorporates particular legal obligations for national authorities involved in implementing EU rules of law, it is apparent that this legal source of EU law is really too general and vague of itself to establish a sufficiently clear set of implementation and enforcement obligations for national authorities.

Recently, the EU has introduced a number of legislative initiatives intended to impose specific responsibilities of a passive or reactive character on member state environmental protection authorities. A notable example is in relation to access to environmental information and access to environmental justice. As was discussed in Chapters 8–8A, the EU has recently enacted a number of legislative instruments designed to confer specific rights of a procedural nature to persons seeking to monitor and/or enforce implementation of EU environmental legislation at national level. Under Directive 2003/4[22] on public access to environmental information and repealing Directive 90/313 designated national authorities are responsible for divulging information relating to a wide variety of environmental matters held by them upon request. Under other EU legislative instrumentation, member state authorities are obliged to act upon complaints or requests to act in relation to suspected violations of EU environmental law, notably Directive 2004/35 on environmental liability with regard to the prevention and remedying of environmental damage[23] which confers specific rights to private persons to access particular administrative legal review procedures.[24]

11.1.3 The principle of subsidiarity

An important factor in debates over the extent to which EU law should intervene to regulate the activities of member state authorities involved in implementing EU norms at national level is the principle of subsidiarity. The principle was first formally incorporated into the EU treaty framework by virtue of the 1992 TEU,[25] and is currently enshrined in Article 5(3) TEU. The principle is intended to ensure that the appropriate level of governing authority (EU or national level) is selected for the purpose of decision-making, but is also widely perceived as a means of checking the extent to which the EU may develop its common policies and encroach upon areas considered by member states to be within the exclusive domain of the nation state. Article 5(3) TEU states:

> Under the principle of subsidiarity, in areas which do not fall within its exclusive competence, the Union shall act only if and in so far as the objectives of

the proposed action cannot be sufficiently achieved by the Member States, either at central level or at regional and local level, but can rather, by reason of the scale or effects of the proposed action, be better achieved at Union level. The institutions of the Union shall apply the principle of subsidiarity as laid down in the Protocol on the application of the principles of subsidiarity and proportionality.[26] National Parliaments ensure compliance with the principle of subsidiarity in accordance with the procedure set out in that Protocol.

The subsidiarity principle has had considerable influence on the course of discussions at EU level over the extent to which the Union should harmonise standards in relation to the aspect of implementation and enforcement of EU environmental law. Until recently, the dominant opinion within the EU has been that member states should retain in principle autonomy over the means and manner in which they implement EU rules of law, including EU environmental legislation. This position has resonances with the CJEU's approach to the issue of judicial remedies discussed in Chapter 7, where the Court has recognised a principle of procedural autonomy of member states reflected in the EU legal framework. Whether or not one agrees with this view is essentially a political question, predicated upon the degree to which one accepts that the Union should have competence to act in a specific policy area.

Recently, this particular viewpoint, held in particular by most of the member states, has been significantly qualified with the recent adoption at EU level of two environmental legislative instruments specifically are designed to regulate the implementation activities of national authorities charged by the member states with environmental protection roles. These are Directive 2004/35 on environmental liability with regard to the prevention and remedying of environmental damage[27] and Directive 2008/99 on the protection of the environment through criminal law[28] which are discussed in detail in Chapters 12 and 13.

The remainder of this chapter will consider the political developments at EU level over to what extent there should be closer co-operation amongst member states over issues connected with administrative implementation and enforcement of EU environmental law at national level.

11.2 The IMPEL network

Since its origins in the early 1990s, the European Union Network for the Implementation and Enforcement of Environmental Law (known as the 'IMPEL network')[29] has had an increasingly significant role to play in developing initiatives at EU level to foster co-operation between the competent authorities of various European countries, including those in particular of the EU, charged with the responsibility of implementing and enforcing EU environmental legislation. As an international non-profit association based in Brussels, IMPEL is an informal network of European environmental policy regulators established as a forum principally for regulatory authorities of the EU member states concerned with the implementation and enforcement of Union environmental law legislation.

Whilst formally speaking it is independent of the European Union and its institutional structures, it maintains close links with Union institutions involved in EU environmental policy development, notably the European Commission[30] and to a lesser extent the European Parliament's Committee on the Environment, Public Health and Food Safety (ENVI). Over time its role has steadily become increasingly influential in relation to EU policy developments in the area of implementation.

11.2.1 Origins and initial development of IMPEL

In order to fully appreciate the extent to which the IMPEL network has gained in political significance, actually and prospectively, within the context of EU policy concerning implementation and enforcement of its common environmental policy, it is useful to reflect first on the key initial milestones and debates that have been associated with the network's establishment. Originally established as a forum principally for national regulatory authorities of EU member states to meet to discuss issues connected with implementation and enforcement of European environmental legislation, the IMPEL network has not always operated in close partnership with the European Commission. Its very inception was marked with controversy. At the time when the network was formally launched in 1992 under the auspices of the then UK Presidency of the European Council, the Commission had indicated very different ideas about who should be vested with the formal task of discussing and developing ideas on securing a more effective manner of implementation of EU environmental law at national level of the member states.

Specifically, in the early 1990s the European Commission had appeared to favour the development of a European environmental inspectorate, endowed with specific powers to be integrally involved in the supervision of adherence to EU environmental legislative requirements. The idea of establishing a central European supervisory body is not without precedent elsewhere in EU administrative law, notably in the field of competition where the Commission has been vested since 1962 with extensive powers to investigate business premises, access corporate documentation and impose fines on persons found guilty of breaching rules of Union competition law.[31]

Indeed, the establishment of the European Environment Agency (EEA) in 1993 opened up a genuine possibility for this particular Union organ to become involved in implementation and enforcement aspects. However, the European Parliament and Council could not agree on this issue at the commencement of the EEA's operations. By way of compromise, the EU legislation setting up the EEA specifically referred to the possible development of supervisory functions being assigned to it at a later date.[32] The Commission, though, did not take up this issue in subsequent years when submitting amendments to the EEA's statutes,[33] presumably owing to continued stiff resistance on the part of the Council of Ministers who could block any such development. In 1997, the Council reaffirmed its clear disapproval of the establishment of a centrally and supranationally organised system of European environmental inspectors.[34] As a consequence, the statutes governing the operations of the EEA have not been expanded into the sector of law enforcement.

Until 1993, the European Commission had no formal involvement in the workings of the emerging independent and loose intergovernmental-based network of European environmental regulators that would later form IMPEL. At its first official meeting in Chester, UK, in November 1992, the network of national environmental authorities (so-called 'Chester network') convened without the Commission being an official participant. It had been encouraged to be set up on an informal basis by the EU Environment Council at its meeting in October 1991. The Commission adopted an observer role, reflecting on how to proceed to fulfil its particular mandate under the auspices of the then Fifth Environmental Action Programme (1993–2000) to establish an implementation and enforcement network of environmental inspectors and enforcement bodies of the member states and the Commission, with assistance as necessary from the EEA.[35] During the initial months of the network's operations, an informal and consensus-based culture of decision-making was established, one that was grounded according to the wishes of its participant member state representatives. Its core task was to provide a mechanism for the exchange of information and experience between environmental agencies in the EU in order to address issues of mutual concern and to enhance the quality of the environment.

By the time that the European Commission decided to participate in the operations of the network in December 1993,[36] network members were reportedly wary of Commission involvement. For instance, in his paper on IMPEL's history Allan Duncan of the English Environment Agency notes that member state representatives were keen to retain the informal and facilitative nature of the entity, and avoid the introduction of new elements that might transform it into a body that would undertake an auditing role of the member states' national authorities.[37] The Commission's participation did appear to effect a temporary broadening of the remit of the network to include focus on ways to ensure better implementation and enforcement by national authorities, including: the elaboration of national legislation and action programmes as required by EU environmental legislation; the administrative and technical tasks of translating environmental standards into specific requirements such as permitting; and the monitoring of compliance with and enforcement of environmental requirements.[38]

In 1997 the organisational structure of IMPEL was subject to amendment again,[39] notably in the wake of a Council Resolution[40] which was adopted in response to a 1996 Commission Communication on implementing EU environmental law.[41] The Council Resolution, whilst endorsing the existing work of the network, at the same time called for a broadening of the scope of its mandate to include giving advice on Commission legislative proposals for EU legislation, in particular where the input of practical experience is necessary. By 1999, IMPEL had settled its organisational arrangements, reaffirming its initial informal and flexible nature and focus on project-based activities.

Since the early 2000s IMPEL's advisory and research role on implementation aspects of EU environmental law has become strengthened, not least through formal recognition of a supportive role in the Commission's work in relation to delivery of particular implementation-related objectives contained in the Union's recent environmental policy programmes since the turn of the century, namely the Sixth Environment Action Programme (2001–12)[42] and Seventh Environment Action Programme (2013–20).[43] The increasing importance of its role in support of Commission involvement in the areas of implementation and enforcement are explored in the next section.

11.2.2 Overview of IMPEL's current organisational structure and activities

11.2.2.1 Organisational structure

The rules regarding IMPEL's membership, mandate and internal organisational structure are set out in its internal statute, namely articles of association[44] as well as accompanying IMPEL internal rules.[45]

According to its statutes, a member of the IMPEL network may be any environmental authority[46] or association of environmental authorities which is according to national law a legal entity or part of a legal entity and is based in either an EU member state, a potential/actual candidate or acceding country to the EU or an EEA or European Free Trade Area (EFTA) member country.[47] Since its inception, the IMPEL network has expanded its membership considerably to cover a wide range of European countries. Whereas it originally had eight founding members including the UK,[48] by 2014 its membership had increased to 47 members from 33 countries encompassing all 28 EU member states as well as FYROM,[49] Turkey, Iceland, Switzerland and Norway. IMPEL membership is likely to increase in line with greater EU enlargement and negotiation of closer association over time with its neighbouring countries, political circumstances allowing of course. The members of each country designate a national co-ordinator and have the option also to choose a high-level representative for representation on the principal decision-making body of the association, namely the General Assembly.[50] The members of each country are represented in the General Assembly by their national co-ordinator or national representative. A number of observers have been admitted to IMPEL with consultative status, including certain international organisations and networks with close links to IMPEL activities.[51] The European Commission has a special working relationship forged with IMPEL, crystallised in a non-binding 2009 memorandum of understanding,[52] the Commission represented by its Environment Directorate-General (DG ENV). Under the memorandum of understanding, the Commission may attend most IMPEL meetings as observer apart from those relating to internal management of IMPEL. The memorandum also specifies that the Commission is to inform IMPEL of new plans and initiatives, as well as invite the association to expert meetings and conferences relevant to IMPEL's remit.

As far as its mission is concerned, IMPEL's objective is in essence to contribute to environmental protection through the promotion of effective implementation and enforcement of EU environmental law. The IMPEL statute sets out a number of tasks for the association to achieve this goal, specifically to:

- promote exchange of information and experience between environmental authorities competent for the implementation and enforcement of EU environmental law;
- promote development of national networks of environmental authorities with special concern for the co-operation between these authorities at all government levels;
- promote mutual understanding of the common characteristics and differences of national regulatory systems;
- undertake joint enforcement projects;
- support capacity building and training of environmental inspectors and enforcers;
- identify and develop best practice, produce guidance, tools and common standards as well as contribute to improving inspection, permitting, monitoring, reporting and enforcement aspects of EU environmental law;
- develop greater consistency of approach in the interpretation, implementation and enforcement of EU environmental law;
- gather information on experience of implementing and enforcing EU environmental law, from the practitioners point of view;
- provide feedback on better regulation issues with regard to practicability and enforceability as well as provide advice on the practicability and enforceability of new and existing EU environmental law to the European Commission and other EU institutions; and
- explore the use of innovative regulatory and non-regulatory instruments as alternatives or complementary tools to existing regulation.[53]

In crystallising the range of tasks, the IMPEL Statute (2012 version) has built upon earlier efforts to consolidate the association's core objectives.[54]

In terms of its organisational structure IMPEL is serviced by three internal bodies, namely a Secretariat, Board and General Assembly (GA). The association's most important decision-making entity is the GA, which meets at least once a year[55] and determines IMPEL's policy, activities and budgetary decisions.[56] Decisions of the GA are reached by way of two-thirds majority of designated national co-ordinators/representatives. The Board, as executive body, is responsible for the daily management of the association and implementation of GA decisions with the chair and vice-chair being appointed by the GA for a renewable two-year period.[57] The Secretariat provides a supportive administrative role.[58] The association is financed by way of membership subscriptions as set by the GA as well as by third-party sponsorship,[59] notably from the European Commission under the aegis of the EU LIFE Regulation.[60]

11.2.2.2 *Activities*

As far as its activities are concerned, the network has been keen to maintain its focus on supporting projects as the mainstay of its work,[61] whilst organising other activities such as conferences and workshops.[62] Over the years, the association has sponsored and co-ordinated a number of research projects conducted by experts in the domain of environmental law and management. Projects have involved a wide range of subjects, but have usually concerned or touched upon the following areas and issues of EU environmental law implementation and/or enforcement: training of environmental inspectors; establishing minimum criteria for environmental inspections; exchanging experience and information on implementation and enforcement activities; and fielding and relaying views on the coherence and practicality of current and prospective EU environmental legislation. Projects have involved sectoral as well as more general aspects of implementation of EU environment legislation and policy, all of which have been published on the IMPEL website.[63] As a means of assisting with the organisation of project activity, IMPEL has (until most recently) proceeded on the basis of developing clusters,[64] namely fora for discussing and co-ordinating interlinked activities, projects, policy developments and trends. Two clusters were in operation as at 2014 namely: 'Cluster I' (Improving Implementation of EU Environmental Law (Permitting, Inspection, Enforcement and Smarter Regulation)) and 'Cluster TFS' (Transfrontier Shipment of Waste). Whereas Cluster I has been very influential in the area of inspections and permitting, notably in advising the Commission on developing EU-wide minimum criteria regarding environmental inspections (see section 11.3 below), Cluster TFS has focused on analysing issues in relation to the supervision of transboundary waste shipments in accordance with EU waste management legislation. Most recently, in May 2014 IMPEL decided that it will broaden its structure beyond the two clusters (see section 11.2.3 below).

As far as sectoral work is concerned, notable areas of ongoing interest for the IMPEL network have been in connection with detecting illicit trafficking of waste under the auspices of the EU's Waste Shipment Regulation,[65] identifying good practice in permitting systems and compliance mechanisms under the auspices of the (former) IPPC Directive[66] (as now replaced by the Industrial Emissions Directive)[67] and other EU legislation such as that relating to the Union's emissions trading scheme.[68] A notable example of IMPEL project work has been the association's long-standing research (since 2003) into IMPEL members' inspection practices into and detection rates of illegal transboundary shipments of waste within the single market.[69] The most recent project (TFS Enforcement Actions III)[70] involved carrying out in 2012 inspections on waste shipments, knowledge exchange and capacity building in order to harmonise the level of enforcement and expertise within countries participating in the project. For this purpose joint activities were carried out over six inspection periods throughout 2012 in 24 countries. The project report for 2012 identified some 29 per cent of waste shipments inspected by member countries were in violation of the EU waste shipment rules, reflecting ongoing major challenges in tackling criminal and negligent activity in the waste freight sector.

11.2.3 Increasing influence of IMPEL on EU environmental policy

Until relatively recently in its history, the IMPEL network did not have a formal legal connection with the operation of the EU's involvement in environmental protection policy. The 1990s could be characterised mostly as the European Commission and IMPEL aiming to enhance the effectiveness of member state implementation of Union environmental law in separate ways, supranationally and intergovernmentally respectively. However, by the early 2000s it was apparent that IMPEL was becoming more closely involved in the development of EU-level strategies in this area. Specifically, both the Sixth and Seventh EU Environment Action Programmes expressly refer to the need for the Commission to liaise with IMPEL for this purpose.

11.2.3.1 IMPEL and the EU's Sixth Environment Action Programme 2001–12 (EAP6)

The IMPEL network received its first formal legal recognition and a legal basis for its involvement in the development of EU environmental policy in the EU decision concerning the Union's Sixth Environmental Action Programme (2001–12)[71] (EAP6). The role of IMPEL was mentioned in the last indent of Article 3(2) EAP6, a provision which committed the programme to promote more effective implementation and enforcement of EU environmental legislation. Specifically, Article 3(2) required 'improved exchange of information on best practice on implementation including by the European Network for the Implementation and Enforcement of Environmental Law (IMPEL network) within the framework of its competencies'. The Commission subsequently confirmed[72] that IMPEL had another important role to play in connection with a related but distinct requirement in Article 3(2), namely the need to promote 'improved standards of permitting, inspection, monitoring and enforcement by Member States'.

The specific reference to the IMPEL network in EAP6 was both new and significant. First, it established a formal recognition of the involvement of the IMPEL network in the area of implementation and enforcement of EU environmental law. This recognition served to entrench what had been evident in practice since the late 1990s. Notably, the IMPEL network's project work on establishing guidelines for minimum criteria of environmental inspections was relied on substantially by the Commission when proposing a specific policy initiative on the subject, which was adopted by the EU in the form of a soft law (non-binding) 2001 recommendation (namely, Recommendation 2001/331 on environmental inspections)[73] which is discussed later in section 11.3 of this chapter. Secondly, the express reference to IMPEL in the EAP6 signalled recognition on the part of the EU that the European Commission would not necessarily be expected nor required to become (exclusively) politically engaged in supervising the overall approach of national authorities of the EU member states in implementing EU environmental legislative obligations. It became fairly clear, at least within the time span of EAP6, that the Commission had come to view the IMPEL network as the entity best placed to deliver strategies on enhancing the effectiveness of national authorities' performance on supervising the enforcement of EU environmental legislation at national level. The endorsement of the IMPEL network's activities was epitomised at the time by a letter of May 2000 from the former Environment Commissioner Wallström to the IMPEL network, in which she considered it to have a 'key role in the implementation of EU environmental law, a priority for the Commission'.[74]

During the course of the EAP6 period, the IMPEL network began to expand its activities considerably beyond its traditional remit of focusing on issues connected with implementing existing EU environmental legislation so as to engage in policy-oriented work. Specifically, from 2003 onwards the network began openly to engage in appraising ways and means of making better and more simplified EU environmental legislation. This seemingly new dimension to its activities opened the way for IMPEL to provide political opinions on the desirability of new and existing EU environmental legislation. In its Fifth Annual Survey on the Implementation and Enforcement of EU Environmental Law,[75] the European Commission reported on a 2003 IMPEL project entitled 'Impel Better Legislation Project'. The project report's main conclusions were to recommend a number of changes be made to the existing EU legislative process for new legislation, namely that more individuals with practical experience be involved in the law-making process; it should become standard practice to review all related EU legislation, international conventions and CJEU case law prior to launching a legislative initiative; the coherence of legislation should be assessed during the Commission's extended impact assessment of its proposals; an overall, strategic approach be employed to broad sectors of environmental policy; that definitions should be clear and unambiguous, especially in framework legislation and particularly when they determine some key aspect of the scope of a measure or define regulatory requirements; and that IMPEL could be involved in examining drafts at an early stage and commenting from the perspective of enforceability and practicability.[76] A similar broad remit for IMPEL was suggested with respect to appraising existing EU legislation.[77] The Commission's subsequent Sixth Annual Survey on the Implementation and Enforcement of EU Environmental Law[78] revealed that in 2004 the IMPEL network decided to follow up this and other related work by establishing a dedicated working group of members or new 'cluster' to focus actively on the simplification of regulation in the context of environmental policy in the EU.[79] This extension to IMPEL's work appeared to constitute a clear and qualitatively significant departure from its initial brief in the early 1990s.[80] No longer simply concerned with issues connected with implementation issues in terms of the regulatory chain, the network expanded its attention upstream and adopted a political dimension with a view to seeking to influence the specific contents of existing and new EU environmental legislation. On the other hand, this modification of its activities was heralded already some time ago, when the Council in a 1997 Resolution[81] specifically encouraged the IMPEL network to expand its activities to include scrutiny of legislative proposals from the Commission.

11.2.3.2 IMPEL and the EU's Seventh Environment Action Programme
         2013–20 (EAP7)

As with the EAP6, the EU's subsequent Seventh Environment Action Programme (2013–20)[82] (EAP7) also made express reference to the need to include IMPEL in the delivery of part of its agenda. Specifically, the EAP7 specifically refers to IMPEL in relation to two aspects concerning its fourth priority objective[83] of enhancing implementation of Union environmental legislation. First, it foresees a general role for IMPEL in enhancing inter-agency co-operation within the environmental protection sector with a view to facilitating communication of best practice. Specifically, paragraph 63 of the EAP7 decision states:

> 63. The general standard of environmental governance throughout the Union will be further improved by enhancing cooperation at Union level, as well as at international level, between professionals working on environmental protection, including government lawyers, prosecutors, ombudsmen, judges and inspectors, such as the European Union Network for the Implementation and Enforcement of Environmental Law (IMPEL), and encouraging such professionals to share good practices.

Secondly, the EAP7 foresees involvement of the IMPEL network in connection with the development of further EU-level measures relating to environmental inspections.[84] The commitments of the EAP7 towards a strengthening of the existing soft law Union measures on environmental inspections are considered later in section 11.3.

By way of response to the EAP7 as well as to European Commission encouragement, the IMPEL network has recently decided to adjust its strategic objectives. Specifically, in May 2014 IMPEL's GA agreed to terminate the binary cluster approach to develop a single integrated programme involving five thematic areas as regards implementation, namely industry regulation, waste including transfrontier shipment, water and land, nature protection and cross-cutting tools and approaches.[85] Expert teams will develop each of the five thematic areas. IMPEL hopes through these prospective changes to focus on few activities overall so that they will be better funded, involve greater numbers of members and focus more on evaluation of project outcomes and realisation of benefits. An integral part of the changes is for IMPEL to develop a deeper understanding of challenges and gaps in the implementation of EU environmental legislation, in particular through wider consultation of stakeholders (European Commission, EEA, NGEOs, businesses and authorities). IMPEL has identified the following areas that it will be keen to involve itself with more as a means of strengthening implementation of environmental law across its membership, including:

- assisting countries achieve compliance quicker, e.g. by sharing knowledge, skills, good practices and carrying out peer reviews;
- helping environmental authorities use their limited resources more effectively, e.g. by producing technical guidance and promoting the use of risk-based approaches to target effort;

- co-ordinating action between countries, e.g. in the enforcement of rules tack-ling illegal waste shipments;
- facilitating communication between key actors and networks involved in implementation, e.g. prosecutors, judges and ombudsmen); and
- informing policy development/application with practical experience and expertise.[86]

It would appear from the most recent developments initiated at the commence-ment of EAP7 that the IMPEL network is set to seek to entrench and broaden its work in the area of implementation and law enforcement matters. Notably, its recently agreed 2014 strategy foresees a far more materially wide-ranging as well directive role to be assumed by the network than before.

11.2.4 Brief appraisal of IMPEL's impact

The above brief account of the evolution of the IMPEL network underlines that its development has not been uncontroversial. In particular, for a period of time in the early 1990s it was evident that the European Commission and Council of the EU were engaged in a struggle over determining to what extent the Union should become involved in shaping and supervising the implementation of EU environmental legislation by national competent authorities. The IMPEL network represents a model of seeking to enhance effectiveness of application of such leg-islation on the basis of intergovernmental consensus, informality, flexibility and voluntarism. To a limited extent, this model is no doubt of some considerable use. In particular, the exchange of information and experience on practical issues con-nected with implementation of existing EU legislation as well as opportunity to develop cross-boundary partnerships on implementation issues is clearly of ben-efit in terms of promoting a dialogue on best practice and understanding of differ-ent regulatory approaches applicable at national level in the Union. However, the benefits of using this informal intergovernmental approach become far less appar-ent when used as the focus of intra-EU debate on policy issues which are pivotal to ensuring the establishment of an effective application of EU environmental legislation, such as developing minimum standards on inspections or qualification of inspectors or providing opinions on desirability of existing EU environmental legislation. It is at that stage that the work of a body such as IMPEL shifts from a being of a technical, implementation-oriented nature to one which considers broader policy debates, discussions which should feature already in the form of governmental input at the level of Council of the EU.[87] Although admittedly diffi-cult to draw the line in practice, the distinction between technical input and policy appraisal is an important one to seek to apply, not least from the perspective of accountability and transparency.

At the beginning of the 1990s, the European Commission and European Parlia-ment clearly envisaged that the activities of national authorities had to be shaped on the basis of some element of compulsion, such as mandatory independent audit and specific legal requirements on inspections and enforcement. It is evi-dent, though, that over time the more informal and intergovernmental model of co-operation fostered by IMPEL became far more influential by the early 2000s, exemplified by the network's pre-eminent role in crafting the non-binding 2001 recommendation on minimum criteria of environmental inspections[88] (which is considered later in section 11.3). At that stage, the Commission's initial scepticism concerning IMPEL appears to have faded away. With the express incorporation of IMPEL as a supporting actor within the EAP6, the Commission began to actively promote the role of IMPEL as a primary source of advice for analysing and developing EU strategies to enhance implementation of EU environmental policy by competent authorities. The increased prominence of IMPEL also effectively served to quell further discussion within the legislative EU institutions, notably within the European Commission, as to whether an EU-level environmental inspectorate should be established to complement the work of national authorities. The Commission now aligned itself with that of the Council, a long-standing opponent of the idea of a supranational environmental inspectorate.

However, by the time the EAP7 was adopted in 2013, it was also clear that the EU had further evolved its stance on the issue of supranational controls in the area of implementation of EU environmental policy. During the course of the EAP6, there were already number of indications to show that the EU (spearheaded by the Commission) was keen to underpin a Union mandate for shoring up standards at national level on matters relating to implementation, supervision and enforcement. Specifically, the EU adopted a number of legislative initiatives brought to the table by the Commission detailing minimum requirements regarding various supervisory tasks undertaken by national authorities. The most notable examples of EU environmental legislative initiatives requiring national authorities to take specific measures in enforcing EU environmental protection norms include Directive 2004/35 on environmental liability with regard to the prevention and remedying of environmental damage[89] and Directive 2008/99 on the protection of the environment through criminal law,[90] both of which are discussed in turn in the next two chapters. Both measures require member states to designate national authorities to take specific steps of an administrative and punitive nature against persons perpetrating significant violations of EU environmental legislation. This legislation signalled an evolution in the Commission's approach, namely a shift towards subjecting national authority supervision of implementation of EU environmental law to supranational legislative controls, as opposed to more informal means (e.g. information exchange on best practice) as traditionally favoured by IMPEL. This shift reached its clearest confirmation in EAP7, when the EU decided to commit itself to establishing legally binding criteria regarding member state environmental inspections as part of the EAP7 agenda for improving the state of EU environmental legislation (Priority Objective 4).[91] The EAP7 effectively reflects an implicit acceptance by the EU political institutions, notably the Commission, that the voluntarism underpinning IMPEL deliberation and decision-making would not be a suitable model ultimately for ensuring that a common minimum set of standards and benchmarks on inspections would be delivered across all member states. At the same time, it is also fairly evident from the EAP7 that the EU is keen to maintain IMPEL's involvement in the process leading towards crystallisation of legislative requirements on inspections.

In summary, whilst the impact and influence of IMPEL has increased in recent years, it is also fair to add the qualification that the Commission (and the EU as a whole) retains a strong presence in the field of implementation and enforcement matters at national level. In particular, since the mid 2000s the EU has endorsed the development of Union legislation detailing minimum requirements regarding various supervisory operations of national environmental authorities. It will be interesting to see how the relationship between the European Commission and IMPEL unfolds during the EAP7 programme period. In particular, there appears to be potential for overlap between the entities' roles in relation to standard setting which will need to be addressed over time.

11.3 Environmental inspections and EU controls

Without doubt, the subject of environmental inspections lies at the heart of any discussion and appraisal of enforcement of environmental norms. A system of effective inspection brings substantial benefits from both a preventive as well as a sanctioning perspective. Regular and rigorous inspections of installations capable of causing significant environmental damage diminishes the possibilities for instances of serious non-compliance to occur. Inspections are also crucial in terms of garnering vital evidence required to prove culpability of a polluter in the event of an instance of illicit pollution. Without an effective inspection system being present to underpin environmental protection requirements set by law, the writ of those legal requirements is not likely to run. These considerations also apply with regard to the implementation of EU and international environmental law, as they do with national environmental legislation. However, notwithstanding the crucial importance of the quality of inspection controls for the successful delivery of EU environmental law, rather ironically the Union has until relatively recently regarded this area as a matter to be addressed by member states rather than at EU level. For a considerable period, member state concerns about retaining sovereignty on implementation matters such as inspections acted as a barrier to Union intervention. However, by the end of the 1990s the EU has recognised the limits of such an ideologically driven approach and steered towards development of minimum EU-wide standards in the area of environmental inspections.

With the adoption of the EAP6 in 2002, the EU for the first time expressly included the area of environmental inspections as an integral part of the Union's agenda for enhancing environmental protection. The EU's commitments were, though, rather general and vague in nature, characterised by exhortation and reliant upon the force of persuasion. Specifically, the EAP6 called for the 'promotion of improved standards of permitting, inspection, monitoring and enforcement by Member States' as part of its agenda of encouraging more effective implementation of enforcement of EU environmental legislation at national level.[92] The Union's environmental policy programme favoured a clear preference to pursue a route towards non-binding guidance on inspection standards rather the adoption of 'hard law' legislative requirements. Under the aegis of the EAP6, the Union adopting a non-binding recommendation in 2001 providing minimum criteria for environmental inspections (discussed in section 11.3.1 below).

However, the adoption of this soft law measure constituted only the first step towards a strengthening of Union involvement in this area. During the course of the period covered by the EAP6 (2001–12) a number of EU environmental legislative instruments across a range of environmental policy sectors were adopted which, instead of reflecting the 2001 recommendation's soft law approach, stipulated minimum binding requirements regarding inspections. At the same time, evidence was mounting concerning the wide disparity amongst member states regarding the quality of environmental inspection systems.[93] These developments led eventually to a shift in the European Commission's position by the end of the EAP6 programme, namely towards being in favour of legislative harmonisation concerning environmental inspection standards. With the adoption of the EAP7, the Union overtly committed itself to pursuing a path of developing 'binding criteria for effective member state inspections and surveillance',[94] effectively rejecting its earlier policy of soft law persuasion. At the time of writing in 2014, the Commission's services have been actively consulting on the possible contents of a draft general legislative instrument setting minimum environmental inspection standards for member states. The consensual intergovernmentalist-type approach furthered in the EAP6 decision has given way to a harder supranational vision under the aegis of EAP7.

The following sections consider the various phases of development by the Union towards a common policy on environmental inspections. Section 11.3.1 considers the content and impact of the 2001 recommendation, which reflects the first phase of Union's serious interest in engaging in the area. The second phase of EU policy development on inspections is the focus of section 11.3.2, which considers the emergence of legislative requirements regarding inspections in particular environmental sectors. Finally, section 11.3.3 considers the prospective impact of the EAP7.

11.3.1 The first phase: Recommendation 2001/331 on environmental inspections (RMCEI)

Under the aegis of the EAP6, in 2001 the EU adopted its first generic measure on the subject of environmental inspections. Specifically, this was Recommendation 2001/331 providing for minimum criteria for environmental inspections in the member states[95] (hereinafter referred to as the 'RMCEI') which, at the time of writing, is still in force and represents the only general measure at EU level to date addressing itself specifically to responsibilities of national authorities in monitoring compliance with EU environmental legislation. The adoption of a non-binding instrument reflected the EU's thinking at the time that this mechanism was the appropriate means of respecting the principles of proportionality and subsidiarity enshrined in the EU treaty framework.[96] As was mentioned in the previous section, the EU has subsequently adopted a number of legislative instruments that provide for specific inspection-related requirements for national authorities. However, these measures (as discussed in section 11.3.2 below) address themselves rather to specific instances of detected implementation failure and/ or are confined to certain environmental sectors. They do not purport to set out a general framework of the operational responsibilities of national authorities to monitor the due application of EU environmental law.

11.3.1.1 *Scope of the RMCEI*

Whilst the RMCEI is intended to serve as a general guidance instrument on the subject of environmental inspections, it is important to note that its remit is qualified and limited in various ways. In particular, it does not cover all types of inspections of occupational activities with potential for inflicting significant environmental damage and neither does it consider all the key aspects of general operational standards of national environmental inspectorates. Moreover, it does not address itself to the issue of EU-level inspections in relation to the environment.

The RMCEI's material scope covers the inspection of those 'industrial installations, enterprises and facilities whose air emissions and/or water discharges and/or waste disposal or recovery activities are subject to authorisation, permit or licensing requirements under EU law', without prejudice to any specific inspection provisions in existing EU legislation.[97] Accordingly, the RMCEI concerns itself with the inspection of those installations recognised to pose significant risks to the environment and subject to specific legislative controls. These installations, referred to as 'controlled installations'[98] in the recommendation, would include typically industrial production and processing plants, power plants, sewage works and major waste management facilities such as municipal waste incinerators, recycling plants and landfill sites. Accordingly, the material scope of the RMCEI covers a classic and core area of environmental protection authority business, namely the large fixed industrial-related installations. It does not, though, establish an inspection framework for other geographical areas that are also subject to EU legislative control, such as the monitoring of protected wild habitats and species.[99] In addition, the RMCEI does not provide detailed criteria for inspection systems related to illicit trafficking in environmental goods, resources and services regulated by EU environmental legislation, such as the trans-frontier shipment of waste[100] or endangered species.[101] As regards illegal cross-border environmental practices, the RMCEI merely includes a general clause of furthering inter-authority co-operation, urging member states to 'encourage' co-operation with IMPEL the co-ordination of inspections with regard to installations and activities that might have significant transboundary impact.[102]

The RMCEI also has a limited scope in relation to assessing the general aspects of operational standards pertinent to environmental inspectorate systems. In line with the views of the IMPEL network and the Council of the EU at the time of its adoption, the remit of the RMCEI was structured so as to focus on inspection criteria and standards to be followed by national public authorities, as well those entities to which inspection responsibilities may have been delegated.[103] The instrument does not establish criteria specifically regarding the issue of qualifications and training of environmental inspectors, instead inviting the Commission in co-operation with IMPEL and other interested parties to establish minimum criteria on qualifications and training programmes.[104] In 2003, the IMPEL network generated a report on best practices on training and qualification of environmental inspectors.[105] However, IMPEL initiatives of course are not binding and are subject to voluntary take-up by member states. The RMCEI does touch upon the issue of conflicts of interest, specifying that where national authorities decide to delegate tasks of inspections to other persons, they are to ensure that the latter have no personal interest in the outcome of the inspection process.[106]

The RMCEI does not concern itself with issues relating to any EU inspectorates or inspection systems. The exclusive focus on national authority inspection reflects the view underpinning the recommendation at the time that the principles of subsidiarity and proportionality do not warrant an EU-level inspection system.[107] That view has never been convincing, and in any event does not fit with overall EU policy on environmental law enforcement. As was discussed in the first part of this book, the European Commission is vested with specific legal responsibilities to ensure that EU law is applied,[108] which includes, notably, application of the law within the individual member states. To this end, the EU treaty framework has vested the Commission with specific powers to take infringement proceedings against those member states it finds to have been in breach of EU law,[109] and this includes scenarios where a state fails to take action against a person infringing EU legislative requirements. However, very little EU legislation has been enacted in order to assist the Commission specifically in investigating suspected infringements of most sources of EU law concerning environmental protection, notable exceptions being in relation to the common fisheries,[110] civil nuclear[111] and animal testing policy[112] sectors. A weak Commission inspection mandate is contained in the EU's regulation on management of ozone depleting substances,[113] whereby the Commission may with the consent of the national competent authority assist the authority's officials in the performance of their inspection duties. Elsewhere, Union legislation has been passed to provide the Commission with powers of inspection in certain non-environmental sectors of EU policy, including in the fields EU competition law[114] as well as EU food, plant and veterinary health law.[115] As far as the environmental sector is concerned, the Commission could be fairly described as an institution charged with the responsibility of inspection, but without having been vested with effective inspection powers. The RMCEI does not address genuine investigation difficulties that the Commission may well face in the course of following up complaints or own-initiative cases of suspected infringements of EU environmental legislation in the member states, such as refusals to grant it access to documents, witnesses and affected sites without prior notice. This represents a missed opportunity, as the recommendation could have included provisions on co-ordination of inspection work between the Commission and national authorities, with a view to fleshing out in practice the duties owed by member states in respect of Commission enforcement responsibilities under Article 4(3) TEU.

11.3.1.2 *The RMCEI's minimum criteria for inspections*

The RMCEI does set out a range of benchmarks, termed by the instrument as 'minimum criteria', regarding the performance by national authorities of environmental inspections covered by the EU instrument. The RMCE breaks down the minimum criteria for inspections of 'controlled installations' into four main organisational aspects: planning, site visits, reporting and investigations of serious instances of non-compliance with EU environmental legislation. The criteria are intended to provide a clear and comprehensive set of basic procedures to be employed by all member state competent authorities, with a view to ensuring that inspection systems are effective, transparent and are not of such variance across borders so as to represent a factor that may distort conditions of competition within the single market.[116] Most of the criteria are self-evidently straightforward and reflect a common-sensical approach. However, given the wide variety of political stances and effectiveness of administrative systems adopted by the member states in relation to environmental protection policy,[117] the setting out of a common code of standard practice is clearly justified.

PLANNING UNDER THE RMCEI

As regards planning aspects, point IV of the RMCEI sets out some guidelines with a view to ensuring that member states organise inspections in advance in a systematic, comprehensive and transparent manner. The relevant plan(s)[118] for inspections are to ensure that all the territory of the member state is covered as well as the controlled installations located within it. In addition, plans are to be made available to the public in accordance with EU access-to information legislation. The recommendation stipulates that they should be compiled on the basis of a number of general factors and considerations, namely: relevant EU legal requirements; a register of controlled installations within the plan's area; a general assessment of major environmental issues and appraisal of compliance performance by controlled installations in the plan area; information on previous inspections, if available, as well as available information on specific sites and installations; and an assessment of controlled installations' environmental risks and impacts in terms of emissions and discharges.[119] The EU instrument also provides a check-list of minimum requirements to be provided in each plan, namely: definition of plan's geographical coverage; specification of time period for inspections to be carried out; specific provisions for its revision; the identification of sites or types of installation covered; prescription of programmes for routine inspections and procedures for non-routine inspections; and provision for co-ordination between inspecting authorities, where relevant.[120]

SITE VISITS UNDER THE RMCEI

Point V of the RMCEI establishes as a minimum inspection requirement that sites of controlled installations should be subject to visits from national inspection authorities. The provision sets out a number of basic requirements applicable to all site visits, specifically: a check is made to verify compliance with EU legislative requirements; appropriate arrangements are in place to co-ordinate operations where more than one inspection authority is involved; visits are reported; and inspectors have legal rights of access to 'sites and information'.[121] Site visits are divided into two types: routine and non-routine. Routine inspections are defined as those carried out as part of a planned inspection programme, whereas non-routine inspections are defined as site visits carried out in relation to a limited range of special circumstances, namely visits made in connection with either: a response to a complaint; an application for renewal or modification of an existing authorisation, permit or licence; or an investigation into accidents, incidents and occurrences of non-compliance.[122]

In respect of routine site visits, the recommendation stipulates that member states should carry out these 'regularly', a term which is not defined or the subject of any guidance criteria in the instrument. The RMCEI specifies that such (i.e. routine) site visits should be undertaken with a view to inspecting the full range of environmental impacts in conformity, *inter alia*, with EU environmental legislative requirements and with a view to reviewing the effectiveness of existing authorisation arrangements.[123] It also advocates that an educational and informational approach be pursued in connection with routine inspections, so that the opportunity is taken for installation operators' knowledge of EU legislative requirements and environmental impacts of their activities to be enhanced where required.[124] This latter aspect constitutes an interesting application of educational/informational approaches or techniques in connection with the issue of implementation and enforcement.

Under the RMCEI, non-routine site visits are also to be carried out by national inspection authorities. Point V(3) specifies that member states should carry out non-routine site visits in the following circumstances: in the investigation of 'serious' environmental complaints, accidents, incidents and occurrences of non-compliance as soon as possible after being notified[125] and, 'where appropriate', in connection with determinations over the issue, reissue, renewal or modifications of authorisations, permits or licences.[126] The carrying-out of non-routine site visits is obviously important for the purpose of constructing a credible inspections framework. Self-evidently, they represent an important factor in promoting a culture of round-the-clock compliance amongst operators and introduce an element of deterrence against those operators tempted to evade compliance, such as working on the basis of demonstrating compliance solely at the time of routine, planned inspections, of which, most probably, they have received advance warning. The element of deterrence is recognised as a valuable weapon in the armoury of inspection systems by the RMCEI.[127]

However, the provisions in the recommendation on non-routine visits are insufficiently proactive. Notably, the occurrence of such visits is only foreseen in circumstances where the national inspection authority reacts to a specific incident or event, such as a complaint. The limited definition of 'non-routine' is not consonant with the requirements of the precautionary or preventive principles enshrined in the foundational EU treaty framework,[128] which highlight the need to minimise the occurrence of environmental damage where possible. The essence of a genuinely effective non-routine inspection policy should accordingly include a strong element of surprise as well as random selection of target. Such a policy would enhance the factor of deterrence significantly, and accordingly improve the authorities' chances to secure an improved state of compliance. Elsewhere in EU administrative law, national authorities as well as the European Commission have powers to launch own-initiative investigations on a proactive 'surprise' basis in order to enhance compliance.[129]

Another shortcoming with the RMCEI's provisions on site visits is the lack of specificity on the range of powers of investigation that need to be afforded to inspection authorities. The Union instrument contains a general stipulation about the need for authorities to have a 'legal right of access to sites and information',[130] but this is not defined in any detail and left to member states to implement. Specifically, no details are provided about the extent of the right of access and whether this should be subject to any restriction and independent prior scrutiny. No definition is provided of the terms 'site' or 'information'. Yet these factors could prove of crucial importance in particular individual cases of non-compliance in securing evidence.

It is notable and regrettable that the long-standing wide range of investigatory powers afforded to the Commission and national authorities under the auspices of EU competition law was not used as a basis for modelling powers for authorities in the context of environmental inspections.[131] These provide the Commission with powers to investigate cases of suspected non-compliance of EU anti-trust provisions, namely: to request information; to take witness statements; to inspect premises, equipment, books and records, land and means of transport; to seal premises, books or records; to require representatives or staff of an inspected entity to explain facts or documents relating to the subject matter of the inspection; and to inspect in certain circumstances the homes of directors, managers and other members of staff of the inspected entity in certain circumstances where reasonable suspicion exists that relevant information is being stored there.[132] The Commission may require national competition authorities to carry out investigations.[133] The regulation backs up these investigatory powers with powers of the Commission to impose sanctions on persons failing to co-operate with the investigation.[134] In addition, special provision is provided for interim relief in urgent cases.[135] Similar powers are vested in national competition authorities.[136] Some member states, including the UK, have complemented the pecuniary sanctions underpinning the regulation with criminal sanctions.[137] In contrast, the RMCEI does not delineate in any detail the range and depth of legal investigatory powers that it considers should be vested in environmental inspection authorities, a factor that places the criterion of deterrence under considerable strain.

REPORTING UNDER THE RMCEI

The RMCEI contains a number of provisions on reporting by inspection authorities and member states. Point VI of the recommendation concerns reporting by competent authorities on site visits. Specifically, each site visit is to be followed up by a report detailing the inspection data, findings with regard to compliance and evaluation of next steps (e.g. whether enforcement proceedings are required or a decision over authorisation of an activity is to be taken).[138] Such reports are to be made in writing, disclosed to the operator of the controlled installation and made publicly available within two months of the date of the inspection.[139]

Under point VIII of the RMCEI, member states were urged to file reports with the Commission on their experience of the recommendation's operation. These reports fed into the Commission's review of the operation and effectiveness of the RMCEI, which was completed in 2007. The Commission's review is discussed below in section 11.3.1.3.

INVESTIGATIONS OF SERIOUS CASES OF NON-COMPLIANCE UNDER THE RMCEI

Point VII of the RMCEI stipulates that member states should ensure that the investigation of serious accidents, incidents and occurrences of non-compliance with EU environmental legislation is carried out. Specifically, it specifies that investigations should be conducted with a view to: clarifying the causes of the event, the environmental impact and ascertaining responsibility for the event and its consequences; mitigating and where possible remedying environmental impacts through deciding the appropriate action to be taken by operator(s) and/ or authorities; deciding upon action to prevent further adverse events of non-compliance; taking enforcement proceedings, where appropriate; and ensuring that the operator takes appropriate follow-up action.

These particular provisions should now be read in close conjunction with those of the EU's Directive 2004/35 on environmental liability with regard to the pre-vention and remedying of environmental damage,[140] which entered into force on 30 April 2004. This directive, discussed in detail in Chapter 12, vests the compe-tent national authorities with powers and responsibilities to require operators of certain installations found liable for serious violations of specified EU environ-mental legislation to take action in order to fund the prevention of threatened environmental damage and/or the rehabilitation of affected sites. The Environ-mental Liability Directive also empowers the authorities themselves to undertake preventive or restorative measures. Crucially, though, the EU directive does not address the operational aspects of investigatory procedures carried by national authorities; this is a matter devolved to individual member states. Similar consid-erations apply in relation to Directive 2008/99 on the protection of the environ-ment through criminal law,[141] which entered into force on 26 December 2010. This directive, discussed in Chapter 13, also devolves responsibility to the indi-vidual member states to determine operational standards and procedures relating to the investigation of cases of suspected environmental criminal activity.

11.3.1.3 Implementation and review of the RMCEI

The RMCEI bears all the hallmarks of the informal and voluntary approach strongly favoured by several member states and notably the IMPEL network at the time, whose project work on inspections was instrumental in assisting the European Commission construct its contents at draft stage. Given that its provisions are housed within the framework of a recommendation, under EU law, the RMCEI has no legally binding effects.[142] Accordingly, as member states and their authorities are not formally required to adhere to the minimum criteria, there is no possibility for the Commission to take infringement proceedings under Articles 258 and 260 TFEU against a member state that fails to adhere to its minimum recommended standards. Likewise, the non-binding status of the instrument rules out the possibility of any legal action taken by other entities (e.g. NGEOs) with a view to enforcing its standards.

Significantly, the RMCEI is structured so that in practice oversight of the implementation of the EU instrument is in substantial respects managed on an intergovernmental as opposed to supranational basis. Specifically, the instrument encourages a peer support and review process to be set up with a view to enhancing implementation of its objectives and requirements. Specifically, point III(2) of the RMCEI states that 'member states should assist each other administratively' in carrying out the instrument's 'guidelines' by way of information exchange and, where appropriate, exchange of officials. In point III(4) of the RMCEI member states are invited to consider establishing a scheme, in co-operation with IMPEL, under which member states report and offer advice on inspections and inspection procedures in order to promote best practice across the Union. A peer review process has been established via IMPEL under its voluntary IMPEL Review Initiative (IRI) scheme which has led to 17 member country inspectorate systems being reviewed between 2001 and 2013.[143] IMPEL, as an informal inter-agency association, has of course no powers to compel any review upon a state or require practical changes to be made.

Point X of the RMCEI stipulates that member states 'should' inform the European Commission of their implementation of its provisions within 12 months after publication of the instrument, namely by 27 April 2002. Point IX of the RMCEI requires the Commission to review the operation and effectiveness of the EU instrument, this to be completed after member states' had sent it their individual national reports on their operational experience of the recommendation to the Commission. By virtue of point VIII of the RMCEI, national reports were to be notified to the Commission within the first two years of the application of the RMCEI (i.e. by 27 April 2003).[144] The national reports, recommended under RMCEI but not required at the time to be made available to the public, were to include the following information: data about staffing and resources of inspection authorities; the role of the inspection authorities in the setting up and implementation of inspection plans; summary details of inspections carried out, number of site visits made, proportion of site visits made and estimated length of time before all controlled installations by type have been inspected; summary data on degree of compliance as appeared from inspection data; summarised account of actions taken as a result of serious complaints, accidents, incidents and occurrences of non-compliance; and an evaluation of the relative success or failure of inspection plans.[145] The RMCEI provides the possibility of the Commission, if it deems appropriate, bringing forward a legislative initiative in the form of a directive in the wake of the review of the operations of the recommendation.

Given the non-binding nature of the instrument, it was unsurprising that several member states were slow to adopt implementation measures. It has been pointed out that the use of the instrument of a recommendation generally in EU environmental policy has had little if any proven impact on EU or national environmental law.[146] It was not until 2007 that the Commission felt in a position to be able to publish a review of the RMCEI and accompanying report on its implementation by member states.[147]

The Commission's 2007 review document noted that a number of problems had arisen in connection with the EU instrument and was critical of its impact. It identified a number of significant shortcomings, notably in relation to implementation, lack of clarity of certain terminology of the RMCEI, as well as uncertainty on issues relating to access to information and cross-border co-operation. Specifically, it noted that overall the implementation of the RMCEI amongst member states was generally poor. As at 2007, implementation of the instrument was unclear or only partially complete in most member states, with only five countries[148] assessed as having reached a 'high level' of implementation.[149] A notable shortcoming was the fact that the criteria identified in the RMCEI regarding inspection plan coverage had not been implemented in several member states, so that many plans omitted to provide for strategic elements. The Commission also found noted that the RMCEI had been interpreted differently between member states so as create disparities over the types of installations covered and also that the material scope of the instrument was too narrow, excluding a range of activities and sectors with significant impacts on the environment subject to EU legislation (such as waste shipments, protected habitat sites, wildlife trafficking and chemical and hazardous substance use). Moreover, various terms in the RMCEI had been interpreted differently by member states with significant consequences for implementation. For instance, it reported that some member states considered the term 'inspection' meant only direct controls at installations. It also reported confusion over the term 'inspection plan', where some member states considered that this simply required a list of installations to be inspected over time. Information supplied by member states to the Commission was not always comparable and made it difficult at times for it to assess and compare member states implementation of the RMCEI. Whilst the RMCEI refers to routine and non-routine inspections, several member states used different terminology (e.g. reactive/non-reactive, scheduled/non-scheduled) which made it difficult for the Commission to assess and compare the state of implementation regarding inspection planning.

The Commission remarked also on a number of other challenges. A number of member states were unclear of their responsibilities regarding publication of inspection plans and reports, now subject to the Access to Environmental Information Directive 2003/4.[150] Moreover, it noted that member states had interpreted the general clause in the RMCEI encouraging co-operation between member states to prevent illegal cross-border environmental practices in different ways. Overall, implementation was reported as being impossible to assess in light of varying interpretations made at national level. As anticipated in the RMCEI, IMPEL moved to launch a programme of peer review of inspection systems (IMPEL Review Initiative). However, as a voluntary and informal scheme, by 2007 it had only managed to carry out reviews of seven EU member states.

In light of its findings the Commission decided to propose a number of changes to the EU framework on inspections. Specifically, it proposed the following ideas be implemented as a means of improving the national systems of environmental inspections:

- *Revision of the RMCEI*: the Commission proposed that the material scope of the RMCEI be broadened so as to cover all environmentally significant activities, additional criteria should be developed regarding inspection planning and that the reporting system should be simplified so as to provide comparable data on implementation. The Commission rejected the need for the RMCEI to be transformed into legally binding requirements on account of the 'very general and descriptive nature of the criteria'.
- *Development of binding sectoral inspection requirements*: whilst the Commission rejected transforming the RMCEI into a legally binding instrument, it accepted that specifically legally binding requirements on inspection of certain installations and activities should be established in sectoral EU legislative instrumentation. According to the Commission, legally binding requirements were justified to ensure a higher political priority be given to the area of inspections as well as better enforcement. It cited the example of EU legislation on control of major accident hazards,[151] which sets out a harmonised system of minimum inspection standards and requirements according to installation type.
- *Furtherance of inter-state co-operation*: by way of complement to its other two proposals, the Commission also voiced continued support for the work undertaken within IMPEL to produce technical documentation, peer reviews and joint inspection projects.

The Commission was rightly dissatisfied with the existing arrangements at EU level. In the absence of changes to the RMCEI model approach, a fractured state of implementation of the instrument's minimum inspection criteria was likely to continue.[152] The Commission had accepted in essence that inspection requirements stipulated at EU level needed to be contained within a legally binding framework in order to be effective. It preferred, however, to see them crystallised into legislation tailor-made to suit specific activities affecting the environment, whilst being sceptical of the benefits of transforming the RMCEI into a legally binding instrument. At the time, the Commission's proposals received mixed support and reception from other political institutional players. The Union's Economic and Social Committee broadly endorsed the Commission's approach,[153] the European Parliament[154] signalled a strong preference for toughening up the existing EU framework into a legally binding instrument and member states appeared to favour overall main sticking with and developing the contents of the non-binding instrumentation of the RMCEI (albeit with some more detailed criteria on planning and site visits), as reflected essentially in the input from IMPEL into the review process.[155]

11.3.2 *Sectoral development of binding EU environmental inspection standards*

The most significant change in Commission policy to emerge from the 2007 review of the RMCEI was a clear commitment on the part of the EU institution to focus on developing legally binding inspection requirements in particular environmental policy sectors deemed to warrant (the most) immediate EU legislative intervention. Specifically, the Commission instituted the practice of integrating legislative provisions on minimum national inspection requirements within particular Union legislative instruments crafted to shore up environmental protection standards relating to the management of activities considered having significant adverse environmental impact potential.

By 2014, this policy of furthering sectoral development of EU legislative requirements had resulted in the EU having enacted eight environmental statutory instruments stipulating various and varying minimum inspection standards to be applied at national level. The legislative instruments span a considerable range of environmental topics, including measures establishing controls on industrial emissions,[156] major accidents involving dangerous substances,[157] waste management (including specifically in relation to waste shipment, waste electrical and electronic equipment, mining waste and the landfilling of waste),[158] ozone depleting substances,[159] geological storage of carbon dioxide[160] as well regarding the protection of animals used for scientific purposes.[161] Most of these pieces of EU environmental legislation were introduced after 2007; however, a few hail from an earlier date (e.g. inspection provisions relating to controls on major accident hazards[162] and landfill of waste).[163] Each instrument contains a distinct set of environmental inspection obligations – general and specific – as well as powers for national competent authorities applicable to a particular economic activity or set of activities that potentially could have significant adverse environmental impacts unless subject to oversight and controls. Individual instruments are designed to be tailor-made to address the demands of monitoring particular activities. Whilst some instruments contain highly detailed requirements on inspections, others contain more general and briefer provisions. There is no 'one size fits all' approach. All, though, contain a mixture of 'hard' law requirements as well as softer exhortatory provisions, the overall impact of which leaves member states and national competent authorities a considerable margin of discretion over implementation of the inspection frameworks established by the various EU instruments. Table 11.1 at the end of this chapter indicates the various similarities and differences between the key instruments.

Whilst there are some advantages with a strategy on focusing on specific sectors, notably to ensure that requirements are appropriately targeted to addressing identified inspection demands and challenges associated with a particular activity, the result so far has led to a rather piecemeal, fragmented and complex picture at EU level. Some areas have not yet been covered which would warrant legally binding commitments on inspections (e.g. nature protection, wildlife trade, chemicals management). Moreover, no systematic approach has been adopted by the Commission to review whether a common core of legally binding minimum should apply across sectors and, if so, to ensure co-ordinated updating of sectoral legislation containing inspection requirements. To date, no system has been introduced to ensure co-ordinated periodic reviews of EU legislation containing provisions on inspections. The various sectoral instruments containing will be examined briefly in turn.

11.3.2.1 *Industrial emissions*

Undoubtedly the most well-established and well-known set of EU ground rules relating to national environmental inspections has been crafted under the aegis of EU legislation relating to integrated pollution prevention and control (IPPC),[164] as now recast within the Industrial Emissions Directive 2010/75 (IED).[165] The directive's clauses on inspections have been moulded in close association with the work of IMPEL, whose core focus to date has included the IPPC area. The IED contains a consolidated cluster of provisions detailing requirements and powers for national competent authorities regarding the inspection of facilities covered by the directive, namely those industrial installations whose emissions pose significant risks and impacts on the environment. The key provisions, which have provided a basic template for certain other EU environmental legislation instruments containing stipulations on inspections (notably in relation to major accident prevention[166] – see section 11.3.2.3), are summarised below:

- *General national authority duties:*[167] member states must ensure competent authorities organise a system of environmental inspections[168] of installations covered by the IED to examine the full range of their environmental effects.
- *Inspection plan:*[169] member states are obliged to ensure that all installations are covered by an inspection plan at national, regional or local level and ensure its regular review and, 'where appropriate', updating. Each plan must include: a general assessment of relevant significant environmental issues; the plan's geographical area; a register of installations covered; procedures for drawing up programmes for routine and procedures for non-routine inspections as required by Article 23(4)–(5) of the directive; and, 'where necessary', provisions on co-operation between inspection authorities.
- *Inspection programmes:*[170] the member states' competent authorities must regularly draw up programmes for routine inspections, including the frequency of site visits. Routine inspections must take place at least every year for installations posing the highest risks and every three years for those posing the lowest risks, based upon the systematic appraisal[171] of the environmental risks.
- *Non-routine inspections:*[172] member states must ensure that competent authorities carry out 'as soon as possible' non-routine inspections to investigate

complaints, serious accidents and 'near misses', as well as incidents and occurrences of IED non-compliance. In addition, 'where appropriate', non-routine inspections are to be carried out prior to the reconsideration, grant or update of an IED permit.

- *Follow-up to inspections:*[173] within two months after each site visit (whether routine or non-routine), competent authorities must notify the installation operator of the authority's report (to be made publicly available within four-months). Competent authorities must ensure that the operator takes the necessary actions identified in the authority's report within a 'reasonable' period after notification. The competent authority must use any information resulting from monitoring or inspections when reconsidering an installation's permit conditions.[174]

- *Co-ordination:*[175] 'where necessary', provisions on co-operation between inspection authorities are to be set out in the environmental inspection plan.

- *Resourcing:*[176] member states must ensure that operators provide competent authorities with 'all necessary assistance' to enable them to carry out site visits, take samples and gather relevant information needed to perform their IED duties. The preamble to the IED indicates that sufficient numbers of qualified staff should be recruited by member states for the purposes of inspections,[177] but the directive itself does not go into any detail on minimum resource commitments.

Another EU instrument relating to emissions containing inspection provisions is the Union's 2009 Directive on the geological storage of carbon dioxide.[178] Article 15 of the directive contains a mix of general and specific requirements, notably less detailed than those applicable to the IED. In summary the inspection requirements are as follows:

- *General national authority duties:*[179] national competent authorities are required to organise a system of routine and non-routine inspections of storage complexes. Inspections should include visits of surface installations, including injection facilities, assessing the injection and monitoring operations carried out by operators as well as the latter's records.

- *Routine inspections:*[180] routine inspections must be carried out at least annually until three years after site closure, and every five years until transfer to the national authority. Such inspections must examine injection and monitoring facilities as well as the full range of environmental and health effects from the storage complex.

- *Non-routine inspections:*[181] non-routine inspections must be carried out in the following circumstances: if the national competent authority has been alerted to leakages or significant irregularities; reports show insufficient compliance with permit conditions; to investigate serious complaints about the storage site concerning health or the environment; and where the national authority deems it appropriate.

- *Inspection report:*[182] subsequent to each inspection the national competent authority must draw up a report of its findings and indicate whether further action is required. The report is to be communicated to the operator and made public available within two months of the inspection.

11.3.2.2 *Waste management sector*

The environmental sector that has seen the highest number of EU legislative initiatives regarding inspections has been to date the waste management sector. Specifically, provisions have been adopted in relation to the general framework directive on waste, the Waste Framework Directive (WFD)[183] as well as the Landfill Directive,[184] Mining Waste Directive,[185] Waste Electrical and Electronic Equipment (WEEE) Directive[186] and Waste Shipment Regulation.[187]

The overarching instrument applicable to waste management operations, namely the WFD (as recast in 2008), contains a few general inspection obligations on member states devolving to them a considerable degree of discretion. Specifically, under the WFD competent authorities are to subject entities carrying out waste treatment operations, collecting or transporting waste, engaging in brokerage of or dealing in waste, as well as hazardous waste producers to 'appropriate inspections'.[188] Inspections concerning collection and transport obligations must cover origin, nature, quantity and destination of the waste collected and transported.[189] In addition, member states may take account of registrations obtained under the Union's Eco-Management and Audit Scheme (EMAS)[190] when in particular determining the frequency and intensity of inspections.[191]

The Landfill Directive also contains some, if relatively limited, express stipulation regarding inspections of landfill sites. The principal provision requires competent authorities to inspect new[192] landfill sites prior to their disposal operations to ensure that they are compliant with the relevant conditions of the permit as regulated by the directive.[193] The directive also contains a range of obligations for member states to ensure that operators of landfills adhere to minimum standards of safety as set down in the instrument such as regarding waste acceptance standards and procedures, control and monitoring of the site's operational phase as well as closure and after-care procedures.[194] These detailed obligations on site standards implicitly require close and regular monitoring and inspection of waste disposal sites by national authorities; however the instrument does not specify the frequency, nature and intensity of such inspections. The Mining Waste Directive,[195] which regulates the management of waste arising from the operation of onshore mineral extraction installations, also contains some limited inspection requirements for member state authorities. Principally, prior to the commencement of waste deposit operations and at 'regular intervals' thereafter (including during post-closure phase) competent authorities must inspect any mining waste facility covered by the directive in order to ensure that it complies with the relevant permit conditions.[196] Member states determine the frequency of site inspections after site operation commences. A complementary obligation is that member states must require site operators to keep up-to-date records of all waste management operations and make them available for inspection by the competent authority as well as ensure that, in the event of a change of operator, there is an appropriate transfer of relevant up-to-date information and records relating to the waste facility.[197]

The Waste Shipment Regulation (WSR),[198] as amended in 2014,[199] now contains detailed clauses on the inspection role of national authorities. For a number of years, the waste shipment sector has been identified as a sector requiring better standards of inspection to ensure that violations of the environmental and health protection requirements set down in EU legislation relating to the movement of waste are reduced. A number of studies carried out by IMPEL, for instance, have revealed widespread breaches of the WSR in various member states (as noted earlier in section 11.2.2). The high levels of non-compliance undermine the credibility of the legal force of the WSR, which contains vitally important rules needed to ensure that waste generated within the Union is subject to safe and environmentally responsible treatment within the single market area and that the 'Basel Ban'[200] is respected so that Union waste is prevented from being exported to developing countries without appropriate facilities to treat such waste. Whereas the original version of the WSR[201] and its subsequent recasting in 2006[202] contained some general obligations on national authorities to undertake inspections, in 2014 these were significantly enhanced by virtue of further legislative amendment[203] as a response to recognition of divergences and gaps existing in relation to inspections carried out by national authorities.[204] The consolidation of minimum inspection standards, the most recent of which apply as from the beginning of 2016,[205] now contains, *inter alia*, the following key obligations for member states which rank amongst the most specific and detailed legislative provision in the EU environmental policy sector:

- *General national authority duty*:[206] a general duty to provide for inspections of establishments, undertakings, brokers and dealers in accordance with Article 34 WFD as well as for inspections of waste shipments and subsequent treatment (whether recovery/disposal).
- *Inspection plan*:[207] by January 2017 one or more inspection plans must be established covering the entire geographical territory of the member state. Plans are subject a number of detailed requirements and must be reviewed at least every three years. Specifically they must be based on a risk assessment covering specific waste streams and sources of illegal shipment, considering available intelligence-based data from criminal law enforcement agencies. The risk assessment must identify the minimum number of inspections required, including physical checks (on waste entities and shipments). The plan must include the following elements: the objectives and priorities of the inspections, its geographical area; information on planned inspections; inspection authority tasks; co-operation arrangements between inspection authorities; inspection training information and information on human, financial and other resources for the plan's implementation.

- *Inspection of shipments:*[208] the WSR contains a range of duties and powers for national authorities. All inspections must include verification of documents, confirmation of identity as well as, 'where appropriate', physical checking of the shipment.[209] Inspections may take place, 'in particular': at the point of origin, carried out with the waste producer/holder/notifier); at the destination (including interim treatment destinations) carried out with consignee or the treatment facility; at the Union's frontiers; and during the shipment within the EU.[210] The WSR also contains a range of powers for national authorities to determine whether a shipment is waste or non-waste[211] and to verify from the person arranging the shipment that it complies with WSR requirements.[212]
- *Inter-statal co-operation:*[213] member states must co-operate with one another (bilaterally and multilaterally) to facilitate the prevention and detection of illegal waste shipments, including exchanging relevant information in particular via the network of WSR correspondents[214] on shipments, waste flows, operators, facilities as well as sharing knowledge on enforcement measures.[215] The Commission as well as other member states are to be informed of the permanent staff responsible for such inter-statal co-operation as well as the focal point(s) of physical shipment checks.[216] Finally, at the request of another member state, member states are empowered to take enforcement action against persons suspected of illegal waste shipment who are present in their territory.[217]

The WEEE Directive, as recast in 2012 as Directive 2012/19,[218] contains some minimum standards on inspections.[219] Specifically, it obliges member states to undertake 'appropriate' inspections to cover at least the following three aspects: information reported in the framework of the register of producers required to be established by the directive for the purposes of monitoring its compliance; shipments of WEEE (in particular exports) in compliance with the relevant framework EU legislation on waste shipment;[220] and the operation of WEEE treatment facilities (in accordance with the WFD and Annex VII of the directive).[221] Moreover, the WEEE Directive stipulates that member states ensure that used electrical and electronic equipment shipments suspected to be WEEE are carried out in accordance with the minimum verification requirements (Annex VI) and that such shipments are 'monitored accordingly'.[222] Costs of analyses, inspections and storage of used electrical and electronic equipment suspected of being WEEE may be charged to the producers, their agents or persons arranging shipment.[223] The directive also specifically empowers the Commission to develop more detailed rules on inspections and monitoring through implementing acts in order to ensure uniform conditions for the implementation of these provisions.[224]

11.3.2.3 *Major accident hazards*

For a number of years the EU has ensured that detailed minimum inspection requirements are woven into the legal fabric of its legislation setting common rules regarding the control of major accident hazards that might arise from certain industrial activities involving dangerous substances. The latest version of the legislation, namely the 'Seveso III' Directive,[225] contains a wide range of requirements and powers for competent authorities regarding inspections of establishments falling within the directive's scope and is to a certain extent modelled on the approach adopted by the IED (see above section 11.3.2.1). Its inspection provisions are summarised as follows:

- *General national authority duties*:[226] member states must ensure competent authorities organise a system of inspections. Inspections, structured to be appropriate to the particular type of establishment, must be sufficient for a planned and systematic examination of the establishment's systems so as to ensure that: the operator can show that appropriate measures have been taken to prevent major accidents and to limit their on-site and off-site consequences; data and information contained in the establishment's safety report reflects its conditions; and that the public has been notified of relevant information (as contained in Annex V) including notably information on appropriate actions to be taken in the event of an accident.
- *Inspection plan*:[227] member states are obliged to ensure that all establishments are covered by an inspection plan which must include: a general assessment of relevant safety issues; the plan's geographical area; a list of establishments covered including those with so-called 'domino effects';[228] a list of establishments where particular external risks or hazard sources could increase the risk or consequences of a major accident; procedures for routine and non-routine inspections; and provisions on the co-operation between different inspection authorities.
- *Inspection programmes*:[229] the member states' competent authorities must regularly draw up programmes for routine inspections, including the frequency of site visits. Routine inspections must take place at least every year for the most hazardous installations (so-called 'upper-tier' establishments) and three years for others (lower-tier) insofar as the competent authority has not set up an inspection programme based upon the systematic appraisal[230] of major accident hazards of each establishment.
- *Non-routine inspections*:[231] member states must ensure that competent authorities carry out non-routine inspections to investigate complaints, serious accidents and 'near misses', as well as incidents and occurrences of non-compliance with the directive.
- *Follow-up to inspections*:[232] within four months after each (routine/non-routine) inspection, competent authorities must notify the conclusions and necessary actions needed (where applicable) to the operator. Competent authorities must ensure that the operator takes the necessary actions within a 'reasonable' period after notification. Where any inspection has identified an 'important case' of non-compliance with the directive, a further inspection is to be carried out within six months.

- *Co-ordination*:[233] 'where possible', inspections are to be co-ordinated with inspections carried out under other Union legislation (such as the Industrial Emissions Directive 2010/75) and combined 'where appropriate'.[234] Member states must 'encourage' competent authorities to set up systems for exchanging experience and consolidating knowledge, as well as participate in such mechanisms at EU level.
- *Resourcing*:[235] member states must ensure that operators provide competent authorities with 'all necessary assistance' to enable them to carry out inspections and gather relevant information needed to perform their duties under the directive. In particular, this includes assistance to assess the possibility of a major accident, to determine their possible increased probability or aggravation, to prepare an external plan and take account of substances that may require additional consideration. The preamble indicates that sufficient numbers of qualified staff should be recruited by member states for the purposes of inspections,[236] but the directive itself does not go into any detail on minimum resource commitments.

11.3.2.4 Ozone depleting substances (ODS)

Since its inception in 2000, the EU's legislative instrumentation controlling substances that deplete the ozone layer has contained a set of clauses on inspection requirements.[237] The provisions are relatively unusual in an EU environmental policy context, given that they have always envisaged a relatively strong co-ordinating role for the European Commission. The current legislation, housed in the Ozone Depleting Substances Regulation (ODSR) as recast in 2009,[238] contains the following requirements on inspections of undertakings subject to the regulation, notably those undertakings engaged in the production, trade, use and end-of-life treatment of ODS:

- *General member state duty*:[239] member states are obliged to carry out inspections of undertakings covered by the ODSR, according to a risk-based approach. These are to include inspections of imports and exports of controlled ODS as well as products and equipment containing controlled ODS. The RMCEI is indicated as being a source for providing 'guidance' to member states.[240]
- *Inter-statal co-operation*:[241] if requested to do by another member state, a member state may conduct inspections or investigations of undertakings operating on its territory suspected of engaging in illegal movement of controlled ODS.
- *European Commission inspection-related powers*: national competent authorities are obliged to conduct investigations which the Commission considers necessary.[242] The Commission, in performing its ODSR tasks, has the right to obtain all necessary information from member states, competent authorities and undertakings.[243] Subject to the agreement of the relevant investigating national competent authority, the Commission must assist the authority's officials in fulfilling their ODSR duties.[244] The Commission must take action to

promote an adequate exchange of information between itself and national authorities as well as between the latter, whilst taking appropriate steps to protect confidentiality of information obtained.[245]

11.3.2.5 *Protection of animals used for scientific purposes*

The EU has also included some provisions regulating inspections in the sector relating to animal experimentation. Akin to the ODSR mentioned above, the EU's 2010 directive on the protection of animals used for scientific purposes[246] establishes a binary form of inspection regime, specifically foreseeing roles for national authorities as well as the European Commission. The directive's requirements are rather more general in nature than those applicable in relation to installations covered by the IED and major accident instrumentation. Specifically, they comprise in summary the following:

- *General national authority duties*:[247] member states must ensure that competent authorities carry out 'regular' inspections of breeders, suppliers and users of animals used for scientific purposes, including their establishments to verify compliance with the directive's requirements. Inspections are to be carried out on breeders, suppliers and users of non-human primates at least once a year. In respect of other animals, at least one-third of the users must be subject to annual inspection in accordance with a risk analysis formula set out in the directive. An 'appropriate proportion' (undefined) of inspections must be carried out without warning (non-routine).
- *Records*:[248] records of national authority inspections must be retained for at least five years.
- *European Commission inspection-related powers*:[249] when there is 'due reason for concern' the Commission is obliged to undertake controls of the infrastructure and operation of national inspections, taking on board, *inter alia*, the proportion of inspections carried out without prior warning. The member state concerned must give 'all necessary assistance' to the Commission experts, and the Commission must inform the member state of the results of its control. Competent authorities are obliged 'to take measures to take account of' the results of the control.

11.3.3 The impact of EAP7: a trajectory towards general streamlining on inspection standards

By the time the Union came to adopt the Seventh Environment Action Programme (EAP7) in 2013, it was already clear that the European Commission was minded to rethink its approach on regulating environmental inspections. Specifically, in a 2012 Communication[250] the Commission signalled its intention to push for approval for the EU to develop a broadening out and upgrading of the existing EU framework, noting the partial state of coverage of the RMCEI as well as binding sectoral legislation provisions on environmental inspections and surveillance. Key motivations for the Commission for enhanced EU intervention included notably the importance of national inspections and surveillance as means to assist ensuring trust in the requirements set by EU environmental legislation, the demands for securing a level playing field and the need to improve mutual trust and confidence between member states on issues having a trans-frontier character.[251] The Commission considered that improvements could be made by upgrading the existing EU framework, assessing the value of specific inspection and surveillance provisions for all new EU legislative instrumentation as well as appraising options for complementing national inspection and surveillance activities in a targeted way at EU level, including notably considering the possibility for EU-level inspection and surveillance capacity. In its conclusions to its meeting in June 2012, the Environment Council also gave cautious encouragement to the enhancement of inspection regimes, 'where necessary inter alia through guidance for member states, on the basis of experience with existing provisions and avoiding unnecessary administrative burdens'.[252]

The EAP7, as formally adopted in 2013,[253] followed through on the Commission's ideas with a specific commitment on developing binding standards for environmental inspections and surveillance across the span of EU environmental protection policy. Specifically, paragraph 65(iii) of the EAP7 stipulates that, as part of the programme's aim to maximise the benefits of Union environmental law by improving the state of implementation by 2020, this will require:

> (iii) extending binding criteria for effective Member State inspections and surveillance to the wider body of Union environment law, and further developing inspection support capacity at Union level, drawing on existing structures, backed up by support for networks of professionals such as IMPEL, and by the reinforcement of peer reviews and best practice sharing, with a view to increasing the efficiency and effectiveness of inspections.

At the time of writing, no new specific draft proposal had been placed on the table by the Commission in order to revise the current Union legal framework on environmental inspections. Some preparatory work had been undertaken, notably in the form of commissioned studies on possible policy options as well as expert stakeholder meetings.[254] It appears, though, that further Commission work in this area has paused to take account of the change-over to a new Commissioner holding the environmental portfolio for the 2014–19 period.[255] Whether the Commission comes forward with a recrafting of the RMCEI so as to propose a general legislative instrument on inspections with legally binding criteria remains to be seen.

11.4 Implementation, environmental inspections and the EU: some concluding remarks

From the above discussion of the impact of general EU legal obligations incumbent on member states to ensure proper implementation of Union environmental law as well as the policy developments that have materialised at EU level in relation to the areas of environmental investigation and inspection, it appears evident that member state authorities are under a growing range of legally enforceable duties under EU law to ensure that EU environmental legislation is effectively monitored and enforced. However, the growth of EU involvement in these fields, traditionally considered by member states to be matters within their exclusive domain, has been fragmented and uncertain in its development to date.

11.4.1 Implementation duties

Whilst Article 4(3) TEU does establish some general obligations upon member states and their authorities to undertake measures to ensure fulfilment of their obligations under EU law, the extent to which these obligations influence the manner in which national competent authorities set about enforcing EU environmental legislation in practice is in essence unclear. The lack of legal certainty as to the precise manner and extent to which Article 4(3) is relevant in appraising the policy and law on environmental inspections at national level is compounded by the fact that the traditional approach in EU affairs on striking a balance between the supranational interests of the EU and sovereign concerns of member states in the context of implementing common policies of the EU has been to recognise a substantial margin of appreciation for member states in determining how exactly they wish to implement EU legal commitments. The incorporation of the principle of subsidiarity into the EU treaty framework since 1992 by virtue of the TEU was evidently a move on the part of the member states to entrench this approach.

In the environmental policy context, national autonomy in relation to the implementation of EU environmental legislation has been underpinned by the practice on the part of the EU legislative institutions to use the legislative instrument of the EU directive for implementing policy. Article 288(3) TFEU defines them as being binding upon member states as addressees, but leaving the states choice 'over form and method'. This has been taken to mean that member states have, in principle, discretion over the type of legal mechanism used to implement an EU legislative requirement. Where, for instance, EU environmental legislation imposes a minimum environmental standard, member states have usually been endowed with the choice as to how they wish to see it enforced under national law (e.g. using administrative, criminal and/or civil law mechanisms).

That being said, there have been relatively recent developments at EU level which have led to legislative controls over national implementation of EU environmental law. Specifically, the EU has recently adopted legislation to require member states to ensure that national competent authorities render entities liable for the rehabilitation of sites they have subject to serious environmental damage (namely the Environmental Liability Directive 2004/35).[256] This directive is discussed in Chapter 12. In addition, the EU has adopted legislation to require member states to criminalise certain instances of intentional and seriously negligent gross violations of EU environmental law (Directive 2008/99)[257] which is discussed in Chapter 13.

It is true that the CJEU has established some basic ground rules on the relevance of Article 4(3) TEU to the aspect of implementation. Its rulings to date are of rather general import, whose practical value is not yet really well established or recognised generally. However, it is already clear from the existing jurisprudence of the Court that Article 4(3) does impose a general, legally binding obligation upon national implementing authorities to undertake all steps possible to ensure that Union measures are adhered to. However, the treaty provision does not provide national authorities with the requisite powers they may need to set about upholding EU norms. In particular, it does not provide the authorities with any specific or general powers to investigate suspected cases of breaches of EU environmental legislation. These would need to be fleshed out either by distinct Union or national legislation.

Problems also arise when national authorities seek to enforce EU directives against persons breaching their terms, as the CJEU has also developed case law that restricts the abilities of such authorities to rely upon legally binding standards contained in directives against private persons. Specifically, the CJEU's case law on the doctrines of direct and indirect effect serve to restrict the capabilities of national authorities to enforce EU environmental legislation. As was discussed at the beginning of this chapter and in detail in Chapter 6, the CJEU has effectively ruled out the possibility of public authorities being able to enforce a directive either directly or indirectly against persons considered by the authorities to have infringed the requirements contained in the directive. Given that the vast majority of EU legislative instruments are crafted in the format of the EU directive, this means that national authorities' capabilities of enforcing EU environmental law have to a large extent been dependent upon whether and to what extent enforcement powers are conferred to them under national law and to what extent EU environmental legislation has been properly transposed into national law. Enforcement would be much simpler from a legal perspective had the EU chosen to use the form of a Union regulation to implement its common policy on the environment. Regulations are described in Article 288(2) TFEU as being directly applicable in all member states and have general application. The case law of the CJEU has confirmed that, where provisions of regulations meet the criteria of direct effect, they may be enforceable against private persons. However, member states have preferred the EU to use as a rule the instrument of the directive, in order to maximise the role of national governments and legislatures in the construction of legislation based on EU level commitments. The constitutional sensitivities of member states in response to the development of greater EU involvement in regulation of policies, including that concerned with the environmental sector, has resulted in legally complex and evolving set of arrangements between the member states and the EU over delivery of environmental policy.

11.4.2 Environmental inspections

The growth of EU legislative intervention in relation to the subject of environmental inspections has been particularly evident in recent years since the European Commission signalled a clear commitment in its 2007 review of the RMCEI towards developing binding inspection standards across environmental policy sectors and abandoning the RMCEI model of general soft law guidelines. Furthermore, the EAP7 has now signalled a formal commitment on the part of the Union to broaden the reach of EU legislation in relation to the management of inspections.

However, notwithstanding these recent developments, the Union has yet to establish a sufficiently clear and co-ordinated position on the extent to which it should set controls on the manner in which member states ensure that EU environmental legislation is properly monitored. What appears certain is that the Commission will push ahead to continue with its sectoral legislative approach, targeting those areas of EU environmental policy it considers most in need of EU legislative intervention (e.g. nature protection). Whether the Commission will commit to recrafting the RMCEI into a general legislative instrument so as to establish common minimum legally binding requirements on environmental monitoring and inspections is, at the time of writing, unclear. There are strong arguments for a general framework legislative instrument. In particular, such an instrument could serve to act as *lex generalis*, covering activities subject to EU environmental protection requirements but which have not (yet) been subject to EU provisions on inspection controls. Where specific sectoral inspection legislative requirements have been adopted at EU level, these would apply instead (as *lex specialis*). The adoption of a framework legislative instrument (such as in the area of waste management)[258] would serve to reduce the problem of material gaps in coverage of essential minimum standards, pending development and adoption of sectoral instrumentation. Moreover, a framework instrument would assist in co-ordinating the Union's approach across environmental sectors so as to ensure that core common requirements and standards are reflected also in sectoral instruments. Currently, it appears that sectoral instruments diverge widely on basic environmental inspection requirements without it being evident that such divergence is justified. A framework instrument, properly constructed, would assist to ensure that common core requirements were updated as appropriate.

The only general instrument in existence concerning environmental inspections, namely the RMCEI, has a number of notable drawbacks in terms of its ability to deliver improvements in the quality of national systems of inspection. As a soft law instrument, its non-binding nature means that none of its provisions may be guaranteed to be implemented by any or all of the member states, neither can they be enforced by either the Commission or private persons. This is arguably the most significant shortcoming. Such a state of affairs is hardly satisfactory, as it opens up the possibility of member states employing different sets of inspection systems with wide variations in terms of their effectiveness. In addition, most of the instrument's provisions are general in nature with considerable discretion afforded to member states over their precise interpretation. A notable example of this is its brief reference relating to legal powers for inspection authorities in connection with the carrying out of non-routine site visits. Furthermore, the remit of the recommendation is limited to covering inspections of certain installations;

it does not address inspection criteria in relation to other locations vulnerable to adverse environmental impacts and protected under EU environmental legislation, such as protected habitat areas.

Even taking into account the increase in sectoral EU legislative instrumentation in the field of environmental inspections, it is evident that the balance of power between the Union and member states on controlling national inspectorates remains very much with the latter. The sectoral legislative requirements allow a considerable margin of discretion to member states and national authorities on key issues such as resourcing (e.g. minimum numbers of staff and equipment) and frequency as well as intensity of inspections. In most cases, the Commission is not endowed with any powers to assess the quality of national inspectorate systems or issue directions to correct manifest structural shortcomings. Essentially, one could argue that the aspect of implementing and monitoring EU environmental protection legislation at national level remains an area largely shaped by national as opposed to EU decision-making. This reflects the degree of political sensitivity felt by several member states towards moves at EU level to shape the way in which Union environmental legislation is policed within their respective territories.

Member states' concern with subsidiarity and loss of sovereignty has greatly influenced the development of the EU's approach to the organisation of environmental inspections. Although initially disputed by the European Commission and European Parliament as being the appropriate setting for conducting policy discussions and negotiating political strategy on this subject, the intergovernmental network of IMPEL has firmly established itself as a very influential forum for discussions determining the extent and pace of EU involvement in relation to environmental inspection and investigation standards and procedures.

It has been aptly commented that discussions in the past within the EU of creating an environmental inspectorate system at the level of the European Commission have been 'emotionalised as being an intrusion on national sovereignty'.[259] It also reflects the nature of the debate and progress within the EU on the subject of establishing minimum standards on inspection procedures. In accordance with the subsidiarity principle enshrined in the EU Treaty (Article 5(3) TEU), the EU has a legitimate interest in becoming involved in shaping the mode of implementation and enforcement of EU environmental law at national level, to the extent that it is apparent that unilateral national policies are liable not to be able on their own to deliver implementation sufficiently effectively across the Union. The establishment of effective inspection and enforcement systems are obviously central to the delivery of a credible and effective policy of the EU on environmental protection. Environmental standards contained in legislation are virtually meaningless unless backed up by systems able to detect non-compliance adequately and sanction offenders. Experience has shown that the traditional intergovernmentalist approach of allowing member states complete independence to organise their own inspection systems has not been an unqualified success in ensuring effective implementation of EU environmental protection legislation across the Union. Member states have inspection systems of widely diverging quality, which represents a significant challenge to the EU's constitutional commitment of attaining a high level

Table 11.1 Inspection provision in EU environmental legislation

EU legislation→ / Key inspection provisions↓	IED (Dir. 2010/75)	Seveso III (Dir. 2012/18)	WFD (Dir. 2008/98)	Landfill (Dir. 1999/31)	Mining Waste (Dir. 2006/21)	WEEE (Dir. 2012/19)	WSR (Reg. 1013/06)	ODSR (Reg. 1005/09)	CO_2 Storage (Dir. 2009/31)	Animal Experimentation (Dir. 2010/63)
General inspection duty	x	x	x	x	x	x	x	x	x	x
Inspection plan	x	x					x			
Inspection programmes	x	x					x			
Non-routine inspections	x	x					x		x	x
Follow-up inspections	x	x					x		x	
Records of inspections					x					x
Inspection cost charges						x				
Resourcing of inspectorate(s)	x	x					x			
Internal Co-operation	x	x					x			
Inter-statal co-operation	x	x					x	x		
EU Commission inspection/supervisory powers								x		x

of environmental protection.[260] Economic pressures may lead to deterioration in funding for national environmental protection authorities, institutions not considered to be of political priority for several governments and so vulnerable to budgetary cut-backs. Wide variations in quality of inspection systems may also lead to accusations of 'environmental dumping' against member states presiding over ineffective monitoring systems. The key objectives of attaining a high standard of environmental protection and securing appropriate 'level playing field' conditions for the operation of the EU's single market cannot be achieved by unilateral member state action. For these reasons alone, EU legislative action on minimum inspection standards is entirely warranted under the principle of subsidiarity.

In several respects, the particular interpretation of subsidiarity and emphasis on national sovereignty used to justify the predominance of the intergovernmentalist approach in determining progress on intra-EU co-operation with regard to environmental inspections is wearing rather thin. For, most recently, the EU has either proposed or adopted a number of legislative initiatives that specifically address issues of implementation of EU environmental legislation. Specifically, these include the package of measures adopted in order to implement the access to justice and information requirements contained in the 1998 Århus Convention, as discussed in Chapter 8, as well as two measures concerning liability of persons for breaching EU environmental law, discussed in the next two chapters. All of these measures specifically impose legally binding obligations on national authorities in connection with aspects of implementation and enforcement. They underline the point that the application of the subsidiarity principle does not entail a complete exclusion of Union involvement in these particular policy areas.

Notes

1 It should be remembered that Art. 49 TEU stipulates that *any* European state may apply to become a member of the Union, so long as it respects the EU's values as enshrined in Art. 2 TEU and is committed to their promotion. Whereas the EU currently has a membership of 28 countries, the Council of Europe has 47 member states.
2 The reference to 'the Treaties' is defined in the EU treaty framework as meaning the TEU and TFEU (see Art. 1(3) TEU).
3 The former Art. 10 EC (ex Art. 5 EEC) stipulated:

> Member States shall take all appropriate measures, whether general or particular, to ensure fulfilment of the obligations arising out of this Treaty or resulting from action taken by the institutions of the Community. They shall facilitate the achievement of the Community's tasks.
>
> They shall abstain from any measure which could jeopardise the attainment of the objectives of this Treaty.

4 See e.g. para. 26 and para. 8 of CJEU judgments in Case 14/83 *Von Colson and Kamann v Land Nordrhein-Westfalen* and Case C-106/89 *Marleasing* respectively.
5 See e.g. Case 68/88 *Commission v Greece*.
6 See e.g. Case C-354/99 *Commission v Ireland*.
7 See e.g. Case C-365/97 *Commission v Italy*.
8 See e.g. Case 152/84 *Marshall (1)*.

9 See e.g. Case 14/86 *Pretore di Salo* and Case 80/86 *Kolpinghuis*.
10 See e.g. Case C-106/89 *Marleasing*.
11 Case C-168/95 *Luciano Arcaro*.
12 Whether or not authorities may use the doctrine of indirect effect in order to impose civil liability on a private person is not clearly settled by the CJEU's case law. It is unlikely that this could be possible, given that the CJEU has ruled out the use of direct effect to determine criminal or civil liability of individuals. See Ch. 6 for further details on this question.
13 Notable examples include the Waste Shipment Regulation 1013/06 (OJ 2006 L190/1) as amended, CITES Regulation 338/97 (OJ 1997 L61/1) as amended, and the Ozone-depleting Substances Regulation 1005/2009 (OJ 2009 L286/1).
14 OJ 2004 L143/56.
15 OJ 2008 L328/28.
16 See e.g. Case 103/88 *Costanzo SpA v Comune di Milano*.
17 Case C-72/95 *Kraaijeveld*.
18 Directive 2011/92 (OJ 2011 L26/1) as amended (superseding former Directive 85/337 (OJ 1985 L175/40)).
19 See e.g. Case C-435/97 *WWF et al. v Autonome Provinz Bozen*.
20 Case C-201/02 *The Queen, on the application of Delena Wells v Secretary of State for Transport, Local Government and the Regions*.
21 See e.g. Joined Cases C-6 and 9/90 *Francovich and Bonifaci* and Case C-424/97 *Salomone Haim v Kassenzahnärztliche Vereinigung Nordrhein*.
22 OJ 2003 L41/26.
23 OJ 2004 L143/56.
24 See also Art. 6 of the Commission's 2003 Draft Directive on access to justice in environmental matters (COM(2003)624 of 24 October 2003).
25 Former Art. 5(2) EC.
26 Namely, Protocol No. 2 on the application of the principles of subsidiarity and proportionality, as annexed to the TEU/TFEU (OJ 2010 C83).
27 OJ 2004 L143/56.
28 OJ 2008 L328/28.
29 Information on IMPEL may be obtained from its website: http://impel.eu/.
30 Whereas formerly IMPEL's budget, meetings and website were largely supported, hosted and overseen by the European Commission, the association now has assumed full operational and financial independence.
31 See Regulation 17/62 implementing Articles 8[1] and 8[2] of the EU Treaty (OJ Sp Ed 1959–62, 87) as replaced by Regulation 1/2003 on the implementation of the rules of competition laid down in Articles 81 and 82 of the Treaty (OJ 2003 L1/1).
32 See Art. 20 of Regulation 1210/90 on the establishment of the European Environment Agency and the European environment information and observation network (OJ 1990 L120/1), as amended by Regulation 93/1999 (OJ 1999 L117/1).
33 As published in the Official Journal of the EU: OJ 1997 C255/9 and OJ 1998 C123/6.
34 OJ 1997 C321/1. This position was recently endorsed in recital 5 of Recommendation 2001/331 providing for minimum criteria for environmental inspections in the member states (OJ 2001 L118/41).
35 OJ 1993 C138/5, Ch. 9.
36 Temporarily referred to as ECONET (EC Network for the Implementation and Enforcement of Environmental Law) at the end of 1993 before being renamed as the IMPEL network in late 1994.
37 Duncan (2005), p. 5.
38 Ibid., p. 4 as well as SEC(99)592, *First Annual Survey of the Commission on the Implementation and Enforcement of EU Environmental Law 1996–7*, p. 15.
39 For details, see SEC(2000)1041, *Second Commission Annual Survey on Implementation and Enforcement of EU environmental Law*, Ch. II.

40 OJ 1997 C321/1.
41 COM(96)500, of 22 October 1996.
42 Decision 1600/2002 laying down the Sixth EC Environment Action Programme (OJ 2002 L242/1).
43 Decision 1386/2013 on a General Union Environment Action Programme to 2020 'Living Well, within the Limits of our Planet' (OJ 2013 L354/171).
44 Statutes of the EU Network for the Implementation and Enforcement of Environmental Law (IMPEL Statute) (version valid at 6 December 2012 available for inspection on the IMPEL website: http://impel.eu/wp-content/uploads/2013/02/IMPEL-Statute-web-version-06-Dec-2012.pdf).
45 Specifically, the *IMPEL Internal Rules – Organisational Structure and Proceedings of the IMPEL Network (as amended by the IMPEL General Assembly*, 5–6 December 2012) (available for inspection on the IMPEL website: http://impel.eu/wp-content/uploads/2013/02/IMPEL-rules-amended-at-Nicosia-General-Assembly-Dec-06–2012.pdf).
46 This could include e.g. environmental ministries, agencies, regulators and inspectorates.
47 Art. 4 IMPEL Statute.
48 The founding members are based in the following countries: the Netherlands, UK, Czech Republic, Belgium, Portugal, Slovakia, Hungary and France. The Environment Agency for England and Wales is the UK representative in IMPEL.
49 Former Yugoslav Republic of Macedonia.
50 Art. 7 IMPEL Statute.
51 Currently, IMPEL has six observers: the Themis Network (a regional co-operation initiative between the environmental law enforcement units of Albania, Bosnia and Herzegovina, Kosovo: http://themis.rec.org/), Network of Heads of European Environmental Protection Agencies (http://epanet.ew.eea.europa.eu/), Environmental Compliance and Enforcement Network for Accession (ECENA) (http://ecena.rec.org/), Regulatory Environmental Programme Implementation Network (REPIN) for transition economies in Eastern Europe, Caucasus, and Central Asia (EECCA) (http://inece.org/oecdtmp/cd/en/about.html) and International Network for Environmental Compliance and Enforcement (INECE) (http://inece.org/).
52 *Memorandum of Understanding: Core Elements of Future Co-operation between the Commission and IMPEL*, 15 September 2009 (available for inspection: http://impel.eu/wp-content/uploads/2010/01/MoU-EU-IMPEL.pdf).
53 Art. 3(3) IMPEL Statute.
54 Notably, the paper 'The Role and Scope of IMPEL' (November 2002), agreed to by its membership at a plenary meeting in 2002 Santiago de Compostela, Spain.
55 Art. 9 IMPEL Statute.
56 See ibid., Art. 8e.
57 See ibid., Arts. 12–14.
58 Ibid., Art. 15.
59 Ibid., Art. 19.
60 LIFE 2014–2020 Regulation 1293/2013 (OJ 2013 L347/185). See http://ec.europa.eu/environment/life/funding/lifeplus.htm.
61 Art. 10 IMPEL Statute.
62 E.g. in recent years IMPEL has organised a seminar on environmental inspections (2010), as well as conferences on transfrontier shipments of waste (annually), industrial accidents (2011, 2013) and on implementation and enforcement generally (2013). For details see the IMPEL website: http://impel.eu/conferences/?ec3_listing=events.
63 http://impel.eu/category/projects/.
64 Art. 11 IMPEL Statute.
65 Regulation 1013/2006 (OJ 2006 L190/1) as amended.
66 Former Directive 2008/1 (OJ 2008 L24/8).
67 Directive 2010/75 (OJ 2010 L334/17).

68 Directive 2003/87 establishing a scheme for greenhouse gas emission allowance trading within the Community (OJ 2003 L275/32) as amended.

69 Namely the IMPEL projects: *Seaport Projects I-II* (2003–6), *Verification of Waste Destinations Projects I* (2003–6) and *Enforcement Actions Projects I–III* (2008–12). An overview is provided for on the IMPEL website: http://impel.eu/cluster-2/.

70 IMPEL, *TFS Enforcement Actions III: Project Report Year 1 (March–October 2012)*, Enforcement of the European Waste Shipment Regulation.

71 Decision 1600/2002 (OJ 2002 L242/1).

72 See e.g. The Commission's Sixth Annual Survey on the Implementation and Enforcement of EU environmental law (COM(2005)1055), p. 26.

73 Recommendation 2001/331 providing for minimum criteria of environmental inspections in the member states (OJ 2001 L118/41).

74 The letter of 23 May 2000 is accessible from the EU Commission's archive (former website link reference: www.europa.eu.int/comm/environment/impel/wallstrom.htm).

75 SEC(2004)1025, of 27 April 2004.

76 Ibid, section 1.3.2. of Ch. II.

77 Ibid.

78 SEC(2005)1055, of 17 August 2005.

79 Ibid., section 1.3.3. of Ch. II.

80 See comments of Duncan (2000), p. 5 on earlier concerns within IMPEL about the Commission drawing on it for advice about specific policy proposals. Duncan's paper is published on the IMPEL website: www.europa.eu.int/comm/environment/impel/about.htm.

81 OJ 1997 C321/1.

82 Decision 1386/2013 (OJ 2013 L354/171).

83 Priority Objective 4: To maximise the benefits of Union environment legislation by improving implementation (paras. 56–65 of Decision 1386/2013 on EAP7).

84 Ibid., para. 65(iii).

85 See IMPEL document *Better Implementation for the Future – A New Strategic Direction for IMPEL* (August 2014).

86 Ibid., p. 2.

87 See comments of Duncan (2000), p. 5 relaying his concerns about IMPEL falling into the trap of duplicating work of 'national policy-making colleagues'.

88 Recommendation 2001/331 (OJ 2001 L118/41).

89 OJ 2004 L143/56.

90 OJ 2008 L328/28.

91 Para. 65(iii) of the EAP7 in its Priority Objective 4: To maximise the benefits of Union environment legislation by improving implementation (Decision 1386/2013 (OJ 2013 L354/171).

92 See Art. 3(2) of Decision 1600/2002 (OJ 2002 L242/1).

93 See e.g. SEC(2007)1493, *Commission Report on Implementation of Recommendation 2001/331 Providing for Minimum Criteria for Environmental Inspections*, 14 November 2007.

94 Para. 65(iii) of the EAP7 in its Priority Objective 4: To maximise the benefits of Union environment legislation by improving implementation (Decision 1386/2013 (OJ 2013 L354/171).

95 OJ 2001 L118/41.

96 See recital 21 of the preamble to the RCMEI. The principles are housed in Art. 5(3)–(4) TEU (superseding former Art. 5(2) EC).

97 Para. II(1)(a) RMCEI.

98 Ibid., para. II(1)(b).

99 As regulated by the EU's Wild Birds Directive 2009/147 (OJ 2010 L20/7) and Habitats Directive 92/43 (OJ 1992 L206/7) as amended.

100 As regulated by the Waste Shipment Regulation 1013/2006 (OJ 2006 L190/1) as amended.
101 As regulated principally by Regulation 338/97 on the protection of species of wild fauna and flora by regulating trade therein (OJ 1997 L61/1) in conjunction with Regulation 865/2006 (OJ 2006 L166/1) as amended.
102 Point III (3) RMCEI.
103 See in particular ibid., point II(4)(a)–(b).
104 Ibid., point IX(2)-(3).
105 Available for inspection on the IMPEL website: http://impel.eu/.
106 Point II(3)(b) RMCEI.
107 See recital 5 to the preamble of the RMCEI.
108 Art. 17 TEU (ex Art. 211 EC).
109 Arts. 258 and 260 TFEU.
110 See EU Regulation 768/2005 establishing a Community Fisheries Control Agency and amending Regulation 2847/93 (OJ 2005 L347) in conjunction with Regulation 1224/2009 establishing a Community control system for ensuring compliance with the rules of the CFP (OJ 2009 L343).
111 Art. 35 EAEC (Euratom Treaty) states:

> Each Member State shall establish the facilities necessary to carry out continuous monitoring of the level of radioactivity in the air, water and soil, and to ensure compliance with the basic standards. The Commission shall have the right of access to such facilities; it may verify their operation and efficiency.

> The Commission has published the modalities of its nuclear inspections in the following Commission Notice, *Verification of Environmental Radioactivity Monitoring Facilities under the Terms of Art. 35 of the Euratom Treaty – Practical Arrangements for the Conduct of Verification Visits in Member States* (OJ 2006 C155/2).
112 See Art. 35 of Directive 2010/63 on the protection of animals for scientific purposes (OJ 2010 L276/33) which enables the Commission in certain circumstances to initiate controls of the operation of national inspections. However, member states are only obliged to take account of the results of Commission controls carried out (Art. 35(3)).
113 See Art. 28(2) of Regulation 1005/2009 (OJ 2009 L286/1).
114 Regulation 1/2003 on the implementation of the rules on competition laid down in Articles [101 and 102 TFEU] (OJ 2003 L1/1) as amended.
115 See Regulation 882/2004 on official controls performed to ensure the verification of compliance with feed and food law (OJ 2004 L191/1) as amended.
116 See recitals 7–8 to the preamble of the RMCEI.
117 For overviews of and insights into the wide variety of systems of environmental inspections at national level within the EU, see e.g. COWI/ECORYS/Cambridge Econometrics, *Impact Assessment Study into Possible Options for Revising Recommendation 2001/331 – Final Report* (June 2011) (available for inspection on DG ENV website: http://ec.europa.eu/environment/legal/law/pdf/Env%20inspections_report.pdf), SEC(2007)1493, *Commission Report on Implementation of Recommendation 2001/331 Providing for Minimum Criteria for Environmental Inspections*, 14 November 2007 and the 2003 report of the IMPEL Secretariat, *Short Overview of the Organisation of Inspection in the EU Member States, Norway and Acceding and Candidate Countries*.
118 Plans may be national, regional and/or local depending upon the constitutional structure of the member state concerned.
119 See point IV(3)–(4) RMCEI.
120 Ibid., point IV(5).
121 Ibid., point V(1).
122 Ibid., point II(3)(a)–(b).
123 Ibid., point V(2(a) and (c).
124 Ibid., point V(2)(b).

125 Ibid., point V(3)(a)–(b).
126 Ibid., point V(3)(c)–(d).
127 See recital 7 of the preamble to the RMCEI.
128 As enshrined in Art. 191 TFEU.
129 See notably, in the domain of EU competition law, Regulation 1/2003 on the imple-
     mentation of the rules laid down in Articles [101 and 102 TFEU] (OJ 2003 L1/1).
130 Point V(1)(d) RMCEI.
131 Regulation 1/2003 on the implementation of the rules laid down in Articles [101 and
     102 TFEU] (OJ 2003 L1/1).
132 Ibid., Arts. 18–21.
133 Ibid., Art. 22(2).
134 Ibid., Arts. 23–4.
135 Ibid., Art. 8.
136 Ibid., Art. 5.
137 Under the aegis of the UK's Competition Act 1998 and Enterprise Act 2002. For a
     recent assessment by the Commission of the application of these rules by national
     competent authorities, see SWD(2014)231/2 Commission Staff Working Document,
     *Enhancing Competition Enforcement by the Member States' Competition Authorities: Institutional and
     Procedural Issues* (9 July 2014) accessible at http://ec.europa.eu/competition/antitrust/
     legislation/regulations.html.
138 Point VI(1) RMCEI.
139 Ibid., point VI(2).
140 OJ 2004 L143/56. See also Directive 96/82 on the prevention of industrial accidents
     (OJ 1997 L10/13).
141 OJ 2008 L328/28.
142 See Art. 288(5) TFEU which states that recommendations 'shall have no binding
     force'.
143 See IMPEL website for details: http://impel.eu/projects/results-of-the-impel-
     review-initiative-iri/. The IMPEL member countries that have undergone IRI
     projects are: Germany, Ireland, Belgium, France, the Netherlands, Spain, Sweden,
     the UK, Portugal, Romania, Slovenia, Croatia, Latvia, Italy, Finland, Norway and
     Iceland.
144 Point VIII(1) RMCEI.
145 Ibid., point VIII(2)(a)–(f).
146 Krämer (2003), p. 54.
147 COM(2007)707, *Commission Communication on the Review of Recommendation 2001/331 Providing
     for Minimum Criteria for Environmental Inspections*, 14 November 2007 and SEC(2007)1493,
     *Commission Report on Implementation of Recommendation 2001/331 Providing for Minimum Criteria
     for Environmental Inspections*, 14 November 2007. Both documents may be inspected on the
     Commission's DG ENV website: http://ec.europa.eu/environment/legal/law/rmcei.
     htm.
148 Belgium, Germany, Ireland, the Netherlands, Sweden and the UK.
149 See p. 20 of SEC(2007)1493, *Commission Report on Implementation of Recommendation
     2001/331 Providing for Minimum Criteria for Environmental Inspections*, 14 November 2007.
150 OJ 2003 L41/26. See discussion of Directive 2003/4 in Ch. 9 above.
151 At the time, this was former Directive 96/82 (Seveso II) (OJ 1997 L10/13) as subse-
     quently superseded by Directive 2012/18 (Seveso III)(OJ 2012 L197/10).
152 E.g. as confirmed by a 2011 Commission-sponsored study into inspections: COWI/
     ECORYS/Cambridge Econometrics, *Impact Assessment Study into Possible Options for
     Revising Recommendation 2001/331 – Final Report* (June 2011), p. 13 (available for inspec-
     tion on the DG ENV website: http://ec.europa.eu/environment/legal/law/pdf/
     Env%20inspections_report.pdf).
153 EESC Opinion on Commission Communication COM(2007)707, 22.4.2008 (NAT/
     383- CECE 762/2008).

154 EP Resolution on the Review of Recommendation 2001/331, 20 November 2008 (P6_TA (2008)0568).

155 *IMPEL Input for the Further Development of the RCMEI – Final Report* (October 2007) (available for inspection at the following DG ENV website: http://ec.europa.eu/environment/legal/law/rmcei.htm).

156 Directive 2010/75 on industrial emissions (integrated pollution prevention and control) (Recast) (OJ 2010 L334/17) (IED Directive).

157 Directive 2012/18 on the control of major accident hazards involving dangerous substances, amending and subsequently repealing Directive 96/82 (OJ 2012 L197/1) (Seveso III)

158 See Directive 2008/98 on waste and repealing certain Directives (OJ 2008 L312/3), Directive 1999/31 on the landfill of waste (OJ 1999 L182/1), Directive 2006/21 on the management of waste from extractive industries and amending Directive 2004/35 (OJ 2006 L143/56), Directive 2012/19 on waste electrical and electronic equipment (WEEE) (recast) (OJ 2012 L197/38) and Regulation 660/2014 amending Regulation 1013/2006 on shipments of waste (OJ 2014 L189/135).

159 Regulation 1005/2009 on substances that deplete the ozone layer (recast) (OJ 2009 L286/1).

160 Directive 2009/31 on the geological storage of carbon dioxide and amending various Directives (OJ 2009 L140/114).

161 Directive 2010/63 on the protection of animals used for scientific purposes (OJ 2010 L276/33).

162 Former Seveso II Directive 96/82 on the control of major accident hazards involving dangerous substances (OJ 1997 L10/13)

163 Directive 1999/31 (OJ 1999 L182/1).

164 See the general inspection provision Art. 14 of former IPPC Directive 96/61 (OJ 1996 L257/26) and succeeding former Directive 2008/1 (OJ 2008 L24/8).

165 Directive 2010/75 on industrial emissions (integrated pollution prevention and control) (recast) (OJ 2010 L334/17). The earlier IPPC legislation, namely former IPPC Directive 96/61 (OJ 1996 L257/26) and succeeding former Directive 2008/1 (OJ 2008 L24/8), contained only very general provision on inspections (Art. 14).

166 Directive 2012/18 (OJ 2012 L197/1) (Seveso III).

167 Art. 23(1) of Directive 2010/75 (OJ 2010 L334/17) (IED).

168 Art. 3(22) IED defines environmental inspections as meaning 'all actions, including site visits, monitoring of emissions and checks of internal reports and follow-up documents, verification of self-monitoring, checking of the techniques used and adequacy of the environment management of the installation, undertaken by or on behalf of the competent authority to check and promote compliance of installations with their permit conditions and, where necessary, to monitor their environmental impact.'

169 Ibid., Art. 23(2)–(3).

170 Ibid., Art. 23(4).

171 Systematic appraisal must include appraisal of potential and actual impacts on human health and the environment, the establishment's track record of compliance with IED permit conditions as well as the participation of operators in the EU's EMAS (eco-management and audit scheme) under Regulation 1221/2009 (OJ 2009 L342/1).

172 Ibid., Art. 23(5).

173 Ibid., Art. 23(6).

174 Ibid., Art. 23(2).

175 Ibid., Art. 23(3)(f).

176 Ibid., Art. 23(1) second subpara.

177 See ibid., recital 26 of the preamble.

178 Directive 2009/31 (OJ 2009 L140/114).

179 Ibid., Art. 15(1)–(2).

180 Ibid., Art. 15(3).

181 Ibid., Art. 15(4).
182 Ibid., Art. 15(5).
183 Directive 2008/98 on waste and repealing certain Directives (OJ 2008 L312/3) (WFD).
184 Directive 1999/31 on the landfill of waste (OJ 1999 L182/1).
185 Directive 2006/21 on the management of waste from extractive industries and amending Directive 2004/35 (OJ 2006 L102/15) as amended.
186 Directive 2012/19 on waste electrical and electronic equipment (WEEE) (recast) (OJ 2012 L197/38).
187 Regulation 1013/2006 on shipments of waste (OJ 2006 L190/1).
188 Art. 34(1) WFD (OJ 2008 L312/3).
189 Art. 34 (2) WFD (OJ 2008 L312/3).
190 EMAS III Regulation 1221/2009 on the voluntary participation by organisations in a Community eco-management and audit scheme (EMAS), repealing Regulation (EC) No. 761/2001 and Commission Decisions 2001/681/EC and 2006/193/EC (OJ 2009 L342/1).
191 Art. 34(3) WFD (OJ 2008 L312/3).
192 Namely, those landfill sites granted a permit or coming into operation after the Landfill Directive's transposition deadline (16 July 2001 (Art. 18(1)). The directive contains a distinct regime in Art. 14 in respect of landfills in existence prior to the transposition deadline.
193 See recital 18 of the preamble and Art. 8(c) Directive 1999/31 (OJ 1999 L182/1).
194 See notably ibid., Arts. 5, 6, 11–14.
195 Directive 2006/21 (OJ 2006 L102/15) as amended.
196 Ibid., Art. 17(1).
197 Ibid., Art. 17(2).
198 Regulation 1013/2006 (OJ 2006 L90/1) as amended.
199 By Regulation 660/2014 amending Regulation 1013/2006 on shipments of waste (OJ 2014 L189/135).
200 Under the 1989 Basel Convention on the Control of Transboundary Movements of Hazardous Wastes and their Disposal 28 ILM 657 (1989), of which the EU is a contracting party, the parties agreed in 1995 to adopt a comprehensive ban on the export of hazardous waste from OECD to non-OECD parties (Decision III/1) whether for disposal or recovery operations. However, the 'Basel Ban' has yet to come into force as insufficient numbers of parties have ratified the instrument (Art. 17 requires 75% of parties which adopted the amendment to ratify). The EU, however, unilaterally decided from the outset to apply the ban in the WSR.
201 See Art. 30 of former Regulation 259/93 (OJ 19993 L30/1).
202 See Art. 50 of Regulation 1013/2006 (OJ 2006 L90/1) as it stood originally as at its adoption on 14 June 2006.
203 By virtue of Regulation 660/2014 (OJ 2014 L189/135).
204 See recital 1 of the preamble to Regulation 660/2014.
205 Ibid., Art. 2.
206 Art. 50(2) Regulation 1013/2006 (OJ 2006 L90/1) as amended by Regulation 660/2014.
207 Ibid., Art. 50(2a).
208 Ibid., Art. 50(3)–(4a).
209 Ibid., Art. 50(4).
210 Ibid., Art. 50(3).
211 Ibid., Art. 50(4a–b).
212 Ibid., Art. 50(4c–d).
213 Ibid., Art. 50(5)–(7).
214 As established under ibid., Art. 54.
215 Ibid., Art. 50(5).

216 Ibid., Art. 50(6).
217 Ibid., Art. 50(7).
218 OJ 2012 L197/38.
219 The original version of the WEEE Directive (namely former Directive 2002/96 (OJ 2003 L37/24)) contained only a rather vague and general inspection obligation. Specifically, Art. 16 of former Directive 2002/96 simply required member states to 'ensure that inspection and monitoring enable the proper implementation of this Directive to be verified'.
220 Namely Regulations 1013/2006 (OJ 2006 L90/1) and 1418/2007 (OJ 2007 L316/6) as amended.
221 Art. 23(1) (a)–(c) of WEEE Directive 2012/19 (OJ 2012 L197/38).
222 Ibid., Art. 23(2).
223 Ibid., Art. 23(3).
224 Ibid., Art. 23(4).
225 Directive 2012/18 on the control of major-accident hazards involving dangerous substances, amending and subsequently repealing Directive 96/82 (OJ 2012 L197/1) (Seveso III).
226 Ibid., Art. 20(1)–(2).
227 Ibid., Art. 20(3).
228 See ibid., Art. 9.
229 Ibid., Art. 20(4).
230 Systematic appraisal must include appraisal of potential impacts on human health and the environment as well as the establishment's track record of compliance with Seveso III requirements: ibid., Art. 20(5).
231 Ibid., Art. 20(6).
232 Ibid., Art. 20(7)–(8).
233 Ibid., Art. 20(9)–(10).
234 See also ibid., recital 26 of the preamble.
235 Ibid., Art. 20(11).
236 See ibid., recital 26 of the preamble.
237 See Art. 20 of former Regulation 2037/2000 on substances that deplete the ozone layer (OJ 2000 L244/1).
238 Regulation 1005/2009 on substances that deplete the ozone layer (recast) (OJ 2009 L286/1).
239 Ibid., Art. 28(1).
240 See ibid., recital 23 of the preamble.
241 Ibid., Art. 28(5).
242 Ibid., Art. 28(1) final sentence.
243 Ibid., Art. 28(3).
244 Ibid., Art. 28(2).
245 Ibid., Art. 28(4).
246 Directive 2010/63 on the protection of animals used for scientific purposes (OJ 2010 L276/33).
247 Ibid., Art. 34(1)–(4).
248 Ibid., Art. 34(5).
249 Ibid., Art. 35.
250 COM(2012)95 final, Commission Communication, *Improving the Delivery of Benefits from EU Environmental Measures: Building Confidence through Better Knowledge and Responsiveness*, 7 March 2012.
251 See ibid., pp. 7–8.
252 3173rd Environment Council Meeting (Luxembourg, 11 June 2012), *Conclusions on Setting the Framework for a Seventh EU Environment Action Programme*, p. 4.
253 Decision 1386/2013 (OJ 2013 L354/171).

254 See notably BIO Intelligence Service/ECO Logic/IEEP, *Study on Possible Options for Strengthening the EU Level Role in Environmental Inspections and Strengthening the Commission's Capacity to Undertake Effective Investigations of Alleged Breaches in EU Environmental Law – Final Report* (January 2013) and COWI/ECORYS/Cambridge Econometrics, *Impact Assessment Study into Possible Options for Revising Recommendation 2001/331 – Final Report* (June 2011). See more generally the Commission's DG ENV website: http:// ec.europa.eu/environment/legal/law/inspections.htm.

255 At the time of writing, it had been announced that Karmenu Vella, the Maltese nominee, had been proposed by European Commission President-elect Jean-Claude Juncker to serve as Commissioner for Environment, Maritime Affairs and Fisheries for the 2014–19 cycle.

256 Directive 2004/35 on environmental liability with regard to the prevention and remedying of environmental damage (OJ 2004 L143/56) as amended.

257 Directive 2008/99 on the protection of the environment through criminal law OJ 2008 L328/28.

258 Waste Framework Directive: Directive 2008/98 on waste and repealing certain Directives (OJ 2008 L312/3).

259 Krämer (2003), p. 381.

260 See Art. 3(3) TEU and Art. 191(2) TFEU.

12 Enforcement of EU environmental law by national authorities (2)

Environmental civil liability

The subject of environmental liability has only relatively recently emerged as a significant new dimension to the subject of EU environmental law enforcement. Specifically, it is only since the turn of the current century that the EU has passed a legislative instrument on environmental civil liability[1] as well as legislation on environmental criminal liability.[2] Both types of liability instrumentation seek to place national authorities of the EU member states at centre stage in terms of enforcing their requirements, and are designed to enhance existing legal powers afforded to public authorities to hold persons to account who have been found to have caused serious infringements of certain environmental protection requirements under EU environmental law. The aim of this particular chapter will be to assess the extent of the new civil liability framework introduced at EU level,[3] whilst the subsequent chapter will focus on criminal liability.

As is widely recognised, liability regimes are not necessarily suitable instruments for dealing with environmental impairment caused by human activity.[4] They are not, in any sense of the imagination, a panacea for achieving an optimal system of enforcement of environmental protection law. For instance, the frequently diffuse nature of certain types of pollution may make it difficult for authorities or others to determine their sources and therefore individual polluters.[5] In addition, those wishing to use the tool of liability may face tough challenges when seeking to address widespread pollution of the environment where society itself has chosen to tolerate such activity and several actors are clearly responsible (good examples are air pollution and adverse impacts on climate change arising from traffic or urban dwelling emissions). Moreover, liability mechanisms do not usually contain a preventive action dimension, but apply once environmental damage has occurred. Notwithstanding these caveats, the liability regimes introduced by the EU offer some innovative supplementary legal mechanisms that may at least serve to assist in deterring serious instances of illicit environmental pollution and in holding such persons to account for causing or threatening to cause such pollution.

To date, there is no general global agreement on minimum standards regarding civil liability for trans-boundary or non-trans-boundary pollution or damage.[6] There are, though, a number of international conventions in specific environmental sectors that provide for civil liability frameworks,[7] several of which are not yet in force on account of insufficient numbers of states ratifying them. Regional initiatives within Europe have sought to develop greater international co-operation in this environmental policy field. To date, both the Council of Europe and the EU are the only international organisations to have either tabled or agreed to general cross-sectoral international instruments on liability in respect of environmental damage.

12.1 The Council of Europe's 1993 'Lugano' Convention

The Council of Europe's 1993 Convention on civil liability for damage resulting from activities dangerous to the environment[8] (hereinafter referred to as the 'Lugano Convention')[9] constitutes an important milestone in the historical development of European initiatives, including those of the EU, on environmental civil liability.[10]

Although there were a number of international agreements addressing civil liability issues in relation to specific environmental sectors prior to its adoption,[11] the Lugano Convention was the first international instrument of its kind to attempt to set out a comprehensive framework for liability in respect of environmental damage and the first to focus on the need for legal systems to employ environmental protection-oriented sanctions on persons found liable of causing significant environmental damage.

From an EU perspective, though, the Lugano Convention is now largely of historical interest only. A number of EU member states indicated relatively early on that they had serious reservations about acceding to it, notably Denmark, the UK and Germany.[12] The EU member states remained divided over a number of years after the Convention was tabled for signature as to whether to adopt it as an appropriate model for the basis of a common liability framework. Of the nine signatories to the Convention, seven are EU member states.[13] However, no nation state has proceeded to ratify the Convention, and it may not enter into force unless at least three states do so.[14]

More significantly, since the adoption in 2004 of specific EU rules on environmental civil liability in the form of the Environmental Liability Directive 2004/35, as amended,[15] the Lugano Convention is no longer relevant in respect of civil liability issues arising from environmental damage caused and occurring within the territory of the EU. Article 25(2) of the Lugano Convention stipulates that as regards the mutual relations of its contracting parties who are also EU members, EU rules are to apply and not those of the Convention. Whilst the Lugano Convention may theoretically retain some potential relevance in connection with relations between the EU member states and other countries, the current political reality is that the Convention is unlikely to be of much if any significance in this context either, given the long-standing division between EU member states over its utility. Accordingly, given its limited practical influence on current EU law, only a brief reference to the Lugano Convention's core provisions need be provided here. Many of its provisions have provided a useful backdrop to discussions on liability at EU level, and some have effectively been adopted within the Environmental Liability Directive 2004/35.

The Lugano Convention aims to ensure 'adequate compensation' in respect of environmental damage caused by operators in control of specified dangerous activities[16] as well as provide for means of prevention and reinstatement of such damage.[17] The concept of damage is interpreted broadly to include, in addition to the standard heads of damage of personal injury and damage to property, loss or damage by impairment of the environment reflected by the costs of 'reasonable' measures taken by persons to prevent or minimise loss to or to reinstate the environment.[18] Liability of operators is to some extent strict in the sense that a plaintiff need not prove fault or negligence but only that the operator caused damage.[19] However, operators have the opportunity to be exempt from liability if they are able to prove one of a number of specified situations that excuse them from liability, and a number of these are focused on fault-related concepts. The exemptions include damage occurring as a result of acts of war, natural disasters,[20] third-party intervention committed with intent to cause damage, compliance with an order from a public authority, pollution 'at tolerable levels under local relevant circumstances', a dangerous activity taken lawfully in the interests of persons suffering damage or as a result of fault on the part of the victim of damage.[21]

Regarding the issue of causation, whilst the Convention does not specify any particular presumptions of a causal link between damage and defendant to be made by courts, the Convention requires that the burden of proof on the plaintiff is to be varied according to relative risk of the activity. Specifically, courts are required to take into account of the 'increased danger of causing such damage inherent in the particular activity' when considering evidence of causality.[22] This provision is designed to assist victims of damage seeking compensation in discharging the onus of proof, a factor of crucial importance in cases where pollution is diffuse and may be difficult to trace with certainty to a particular source. Liability under the Convention is based on the principle of joint and several liability where more than one operator is involved, with detailed provisions on apportionment so as to afford operators the opportunity to limit liability if they are able to prove that their activities caused only part of the damage.[23]

Liability is also subject to specific temporal limits. In principle, actions for compensation must be brought within three years of the claimant's actual or constructive knowledge of the damage, and no civil litigation may be brought 30 years after the date of the incident causing the damage.[24] In addition, the Convention is structured so that liability is predicated fundamentally upon a non-retroactive footing, in applying to incidents occurring after the Convention's entry into force.[25]

In addition to containing provisions on determining the parameters of liability, the Lugano Convention also incorporates some interesting flanking provisions. One aspect of the Convention that has stimulated protracted discussion is its approach to the issue of financial cover for operators. Specifically, it contains a soft requirement for contracting parties to ensure 'where appropriate' that operators of dangerous activities participate in 'a financial security scheme' or to have a 'financial guarantee up to a certain limit' to cover liability.[26] The issue of whether to impose mandatory financial cover on operators and if so, whether this should be capped, has proved to be a difficult one to resolve, not least within the EU where this has been the subject of ongoing review. The vagueness of the Convention's requirement reflects the degree of political disagreement over this matter between states. On the one hand, an obligation for mandatory financial cover appears to be beneficial in entrenching the 'polluter pays' principle, in seeking to avoid the prospect of general taxpayers being required to pay for the costs of taking measures to rehabilitate contaminated sites where an operator becomes insolvent or cannot be identified. In addition, the imposition of upfront financial security or cover also underpins the principle of prevention in providing an incentive to operators to reduce possibilities for environmental damage accidents arising, in that effective proactive safety measures and lengthier safety records will attract reductions in insurance premiums. On the other hand, a number of stakeholders in this debate have been cautious to accept mandatory cover without at least further reflection, some wary of the relative lack of settled experience with the specific financial markets involved and others sceptical of the prospect of placing caps on liability as being sufficiently in alignment with 'polluter pays'.[27] The Convention also contains a number of provisions on rights to access to information on environmental matters.[28] The provisions on access to information from public authorities have now been effectively succeeded by those in the 1998 United Nations Economic Commission for Europe (UNECE) Århus Convention on access to information, public participation in decision-making and access to justice in environmental matters,[29] as discussed earlier in Chapter 9. However, the Lugano Convention contains an interesting provision, not followed up specifically under the Århus agenda, guaranteeing victims of damage access to specific environmental information held by operators by court order.[30] Finally, the Lugano Convention contains detailed provisions on jurisdiction, recognition and enforcement of court judgments for the purposes of addressing scenarios of environmental damage involving more than one contracting party.[31]

What is particularly evident from the structure of the Lugano Convention is that, in terms of law enforcement, its provisions are predominantly focused on addressing procedural and substantive aspects of civil litigation brought by private plaintiffs. The Convention does not specifically provide for procedures which public authorities may use to remediate environmental damage. Although this is not explicitly expressed in the Convention itself, it is apparent that there is an assumption underlying the provisions of the Convention that it is the private as opposed to the public sector that is to hold operators to account under the aegis of its civil liability framework. This assumption is borne out by Article 18 which provides certain rights to non-governmental environmental organisations (NGEOs). Under this provision, associations or foundations whose statutes aim at the protection of the environment have the right to request the following: the prohibition of an unlawful dangerous activity that poses a grave threat of environmental damage or that the operator be ordered to take preventive measures or measures of reinstatement.[32] The Convention defers to contracting parties to establish the recipient of the request and provide rules on requests that may be deemed by them to be inadmissible.[33] No specific requirements are set down in the Convention on responsibilities of public authorities to investigate or address actual or suspected incidents of environmental damage. The Convention simply offers parties the option of allowing 'competent public authorities' to be heard in relation to a request for action.[34] Accordingly, under the Lugano Convention it is for the parties to determine what action, if any, will be taken by public authorities with a view to requiring an operator, who causes actual or threatened environmental damage, to take preventive or remedial action.

The consequences of the Convention focusing predominantly upon private plaintiffs are that its provisions do not specifically require environmental damage to be addressed where operators are found liable. The outcome of civil litigation in respect of environmental damage, as guided by the Convention's provisions, is very much a matter to be determined by the individual private plaintiff. Contracting parties have the option to structure their domestic civil liability frameworks so as to incorporate an element of public authority enforcement, but this is not specifically required or even addressed in the Convention. As a result of these factors, it is evident that the Lugano Convention contains a clear anthropocentric bias in relation to issues of liability for environmental damage. In practice, the Convention's provisions continue to work with the traditional approach of national and international civil liability systems by focusing legal attention on securing compensation for human victims of environmental damage, specifically in respect of personal injury and/or damage to property. The subject of remediation of adverse effects to the environment is thereby effectively treated as a matter of subsidiary importance within the context of its particular civil liability framework.

As will be explored in the subsequent sections, the focus of the Lugano Convention on providing assistance to private litigants (as victims of environmental damage scenarios) may be contrasted with approach followed in the legislation recently adopted by the EU on environmental liability. Under EU Directive 2004/35, public authorities are placed at the heart of civil liability law enforcement. Legal aspects of civil litigation brought by private persons against polluters are ignored within the EU's rules on civil liability. This reflects the view that assisting with or enhancing existing traditional mechanisms of civil litigation may not be effective in ensuring that instances of serious environmental damage, as perpetrated by identifiable polluters, is in fact rectified.

12.2 Developments of EU environmental policy on environmental civil liability

As mentioned above, it is only relatively recently, namely in 2004, that the EU passed legislation intended to introduce a common EU legal framework on environmental liability. This came in the form of the Environmental Liability Directive 2004/35 (ELD), as amended.[35] Prior to the ELD, discussions on the development of EU rules to harmonise member states' laws on the subject of environmental civil liability may be traced back to the 1970s,[36] but arguably began to gain serious momentum from the mid 1980s onwards, notably in the wake of a major industrial accident in 1986 at the Sandoz chemical plant in Basel, Switzerland, which caused extensive damage to the Rhine. The journey to a legislative outcome at EU level in the form of the EU Environmental Liability Directive in 2004 was both lengthy and difficult to negotiate. The initial focus of the Commission was on introducing harmonising measures of civil liability with regard to the waste management sector, before it began to consider introducing a general environmental civil liability framework in the 1990s. This particular section of the chapter will outline some of the key developments that led ultimately to legislative harmonisation of rules on environmental civil liability at EU level. Space allows but a relatively brief overview.[37]

Subsequent to the incorporation of provisions for a common policy on the environment into the EU Treaty by virtue of the Single European Act 1986, the European Commission was keen to explore ways and means to utilise the concept of civil liability to enhance a number of the key environmental principles woven into the EU's amended foundational treaty fabric (namely, the former European Community (EC) Treaty). Of relevance in this regard are: the principle that preventive action should be taken, that the polluter should pay for costs incurred to the environment, environmental damage should as a priority be rectified at source and the precautionary principle.[38] During the course of the 1990s the Commission spearheaded a debate on the subject of environmental civil liability at EU level. Discussion with member state governments and other stakeholders was substantial and lasted for a considerable period. In May 1993, the Commission published its Green Paper on remedying environmental damage,[39] a document mapping out possible alternative strategies that the EU could follow up. The Commission received feedback from various stakeholders on the Green Paper, including from member states, other EU organs as well as from business and NGEOs. This culminated in the Commission firming up its analysis and views on the possibilities for an EU legislative regime on environmental liability, in a White Paper on environmental liability published in February 2000.[40] In the White Paper, the Commission signalled its preference for a specific and comprehensive EU legal framework in the form of a directive and ruled out other options previously tabled, notably EU accession to the Lugano Convention or a Union regulatory framework limited to cross-border instances of environmental damage.

In ruling out accession to the Lugano Convention, the Commission noted the split amongst EU member states on the regional agreement's utility. A number of member states and several industrial lobby groups considered its provisions to be unduly wide. Other criticisms focused on the unspecific manner in which the terms of the Convention address the issue of environmental damage, in not providing for any criteria in relation to the carrying out of remedial measures. Notably, the Convention does not require evaluation of damage or restorative measures to be undertaken.[41] Those in favour of a limited set of EU rules covering only trans-boundary damage had sought to draw support from the principle of subsidiarity[42] to underpin their arguments. According to this principle, as now enshrined in Article 5(3) of the Treaty on European Union (TEU), the EU is to take action in areas not falling within its exclusive competence only if and insofar as the objectives of the proposed action at EU level cannot be sufficiently achieved by the member states and can therefore, by reason of the scale or effects of the proposed action, be better achieved by the EU. This argumentation was effectively countered by the Commission, which argued convincingly that a framework limited to trans-boundary damage would have failed to take on board the fact that pollution occurring within the territory of a single member state might well have environmental protection implications for the EU region as a whole, such as damage to protected species or habitat. In addition, a multiplicity of liability regimes would serve to undermine the principle of equal treatment of persons carrying out commercial operations within the single market. In effect, the principle of subsidiarity proved to be an argument in favour of the adoption of harmonisation of policy at EU level, given that the environmental policy issues at stake could not adequately be addressed through independent national policies alone.[43]

Although the European Commission's 2000 White Paper was not accompanied at the time by a specific draft proposal for Union legislation, it was clear at that stage that the Commission had formed, at least in part, some ideas of the contours of a liability regime. Several of these were drawn from the Lugano Convention, although some were intentionally different. For instance, the White Paper indicated that a Union legislative initiative would ensure that liability for environmental damage would involve ensuring that compensation obtained would be required to be used specifically for the purpose of restoration of environmental damage.[44] In addition, it opined that liability would be structured on a two-tier basis, targeting two different types of activity causing environmental damage. Specifically, liability would be strict in relation to activities deemed to be an inherent risk to the environment, and based on fault in relation to other activities deemed non-dangerous.[45] Liability for non-dangerous activities would, though, only relate to biodiversity damage. Accordingly, the extent of personal liability envisaged by the White Paper was wider than the Convention, in addressing also the behaviour of operators of non-dangerous activities. The Commission noted that this extended coverage of liability was justified, given the vulnerability of protected species and sites covered under EU environmental nature protection legislation, which could easily be damaged by activities other than those considered inherently risky to the environment.[46] The 2000 White Paper also ruled out mandatory insurance cover, in order to allow a period of experience to develop for markets under any EU legislative framework. It appeared, though, not to rule out the possibility of introducing caps to liability for natural resources damage, although at the same time submitted that this would 'erode' application of the effective application of 'polluter pays'.[47]

After the White Paper, the European Commission submitted a formal proposal[48] for an EU directive on environmental liability at the beginning of 2002.[49] The proposal adopted a radically different approach to the Lugano Convention and, to a considerable extent, from the direction indicated in the White Paper. The Commission's proposal focused on applying the principle of liability to ensure that those found legally responsible for causing significant environmental damage would be required to take or fund the necessary measures to ensure that the damaged environment would be restored as close to its condition prior to the occurrence of damage as is feasible. Aspects to do with harm perpetrated to persons, such as personal injury or damage to property, were not addressed by the legislative initiative, on the grounds that such considerations do not specifically or satisfactorily deal with the issue of addressing and correcting environmental impairments and that national legal systems already had developed civil liability regimes for traditional damage.[50]

In addition, the proposal allocated the primary task of enforcing the proposed civil liability framework to public authorities of the member states. This aspect reflected a convincing practical as well as philosophical perspective underpinning the proposal. From a practical perspective, it is clear that public authorities are in the best position to ensure that the environment is protected, given that they have far greater levels of resources than private litigants to investigate, assess and follow up instances of illicit pollution. From a philosophical perspective, placement of primary enforcement responsibility in the hands of public authorities reflects the view that the environment is a collective good[51] that needs protection for its own sake, and not one that should be allowed to be subject to commodification or valuation on the basis of economic assessment. The environmental protection focus of the legislative proposal was underpinned by provisions requiring national competent authorities to be charged with the ultimate responsibility of ensuring that significant environmental damage be remedied, even where an operator may not be found liable or be capable of funding the costs for such restoration to take place.[52]

During the course of its passage via the legislative process at EU level,[53] the Commission proposal was subject to various amendments, culminating in its promulgation in April 2004. The resulting legislative instrument, the ELD, is subject to detailed discussion in the next sections.

12.3 EU Directive 2004/35 on environmental liability (ELD)

On 21 April 2004, the European Union adopted a legislative instrument on civil liability in relation to environmental damage. The ELD (Directive 2004/35 on environmental liability with regard to the prevention and remedying of environmental damage)[54] entered into force on 30 April 2004.[55] Member states are required under the ELD to have transposed its provisions into national law by 30 April 2007 as well as notify the European Commission of the provisions of the national rules of implementation.[56] The first Union instrument of its kind, the ELD specifies the parameters of civil liability of certain persons whose activities either have caused or are likely to cause imminent environmental damage. It also determines the role and responsibilities of competent public authorities, to be designated by the member states, which are to ensure that its requirements are fulfilled. In addition, the legislative instrument also provides for the possibility for private individuals and entities to become involved in assisting in the task of enforcing its obligations. These particular provisions are discussed in section 8.31 of Chapter 8.

One of the most striking features of the ELD is the specific emphasis and focus it places on addressing the remediation of environmental damage, as opposed to other types of harm such as loss or damage to persons. Earlier international efforts on co-operation in the field of environmental civil liability placed substantial if not equal attention on legal aspects of personal loss that might often be closely connected in situations involving environmental damage. This broader approach to the issue of environmental liability is reflected in the Council of Europe's Lugano Convention as well as the initial discussions within the EU itself on crafting a suitable civil liability framework.[57] However, the ELD specifically excludes from its scope any remediation in respect of harm to persons that may arise from damage caused to the environment, namely personal injury, economic loss and/or damage to private property.[58] In addition, it stipulates that none of its provisions are to give rights to private parties to receive compensation as a consequence of actual or an imminent threat of environmental damage.[59] Rights to obtain compensation or other remedies in respect of anthropogenic loss or damage, as provided under the civil liability rules of the various national legal systems of the member states, are unaffected by the ELD.[60] A related important and novel feature of the ELD is that its requirements apply to environmental resources irrespective of whether or not subject to legal ownership.[61] Accordingly, its breaks through the traditional limitation associated with national civil liability regimes that predicate civil action upon the proof of damage to a plaintiff's legally defined property and/or other assets.

Accordingly, two sets of civil liability rules apply in relation to environmental damage scenarios within the EU: the existing national civil law of obligations of the member states as well as the rules on environmental liability under the ELD. However, the ELD does permit member states to rule out the possibility of a defendant facing financial liability under both systems of civil liability in respect of the same environmental damage, and where the object of civil litigation involves the defence of property interests.[62] Specifically, 'double recovery of costs' may be ruled out in a situation where legal action is brought by a competent national authority to recover costs on preventing or remedying environmental damage under the auspices of the directive at the same time as a civil action is being brought by another party on account of damage sustained to their property rights.

Arguably, there are a number of shortcomings with the narrow approach to environmental civil liability pursued by the ELD. The development of a Union legislative framework on environmental civil liability represented an opportunity for the EU to facilitate the enforcement of its environmental norms with the assistance of the private sector, to the extent that private property interests of individuals and environmental protection goals could coincide with one another. Specifically, the ELD could have provided useful legal assistance to individuals wishing to take civil action to gain judicial relief in respect of personal harm they sustained as a result of instances of environmental damage. Under existing civil laws of several member states, it is evident that private claimants may well face a number of difficult legal hurdles to overcome in proving civil culpability under traditional rules of tortious responsibility in respect of harm sustained to their own person or their physical property (such as goods, fixed assets or territory) caused as a result of damage as diffuse as environmental pollution. Particularly difficult problems may arise in relation to a claimant having to shoulder the burden of proof in having to be able to attribute blame on an individual defendant. Claimants are typically required to prove on the balance of responsibilities that the defendant is the source of activity attributed as causing damage and that the defendant's activities caused the harm sustained. Given the diffuse nature of environmental pollution, this may present a number of significant evidential difficulties. For instance, it may well be difficult from a scientific perspective for a person to identify with certainty the source of harm in terms of its physical properties; the source may well be mixed in environmental media with a combination of possible agents that may or may not be capable of causing harm individually or collectively. The epidemiology of environmental damage may well be highly complex and uncertain. In addition, even if the physical properties of the substance causing harm may be identified scientifically, there may well be difficulties in showing to the satisfaction of a court that its release into the environment has in fact been perpetrated by a specific entity, where the substance may potentially have been emitted from any one of a number of possible locations. Finally, claimants are often faced with other legal hurdles that may make it difficult in practice to prove that a defendant breached a legal duty of care in environmental cases. Specifically, they may have the onus of proof to show that the defendant's conduct is at fault or negligent in some respect. This particular burden presents difficulties and challenges in terms of a claimant's ability, legally and scientifically, to be able to access as well as analyse complex environmental information. Regrettably, the ELD does not address these legal problems and challenges and thus neglects to harness the potential contribution that rules on civil liability in respect of personal harm may bring to bear in terms of assisting in the deterrence and remedying of environmental damage. However, it cannot be ruled out that the EU might, at some point in the future, address itself again to the 'personal damage' dimension environmental liability.

On the other hand, this particular shortcoming should be placed into its proper, limited context. Quite rightly, the ELD focuses on the role of national competent authorities as the principal means of ensuring that operators adhere to their responsibilities to prevent and remediate environmental damage.[63] Given the evidential difficulties raised in attributing liability to specific persons, it is realistic to consider that in practice national public authorities, as opposed to private persons, are in the best position to enforce the directive's requirements. Public authorities are vested with powers and resources that individuals do not usually command. Specifically, public authorities involved in environmental protection matters are vested with powers to inspect sites and premises. In addition, they have access to financial, scientific, information-related and legal resources necessary to carry out investigations as well as to take steps to enforce environmental norms, such as in the form of granting, amending and/or withdrawal of permits or taking legal action (whether criminal or administrative in nature). Moreover, it is not the case that a private civil action will actually serve to secure remediation of environmental damage. The principal if not exclusive focus of civil litigation brought by an individual whose personal legal interests have been harmed is to secure a remedy in respect of the losses or impairments sustained in respect of those particular personal assets.

Whilst improvements to procedural rules concerning private civil litigation may arguably have some deterrent effect on perpetrators of environmental damage, it is clear that the use of tort law in its traditional context may not lead to the remediation of a damaged site from an environmental protection perspective. Instead, a remedy may be provided in the form of monetary compensation, which may not be adequate or in fact used for the purpose of restoring a site to its condition prior to the period it was damaged.[64] The focus of the ELD on the role of public authorities reflects a strong theme of realism that underpins its provisions, namely an intention to enable the maximum degree of practical application of effective environmental liability principles at national level. It has also been commented that the key enforcement role of national authorities under the ELD illustrates its transformation since its origins from a civil to essentially a public law compensation scheme.[65]

The ELD's approach to the subject of environmental civil liability resonates strongly with that adopted at federal level in the USA by the mid 1980s, notably under the aegis of statutes such as the Comprehensive Environmental Response, Compensation and Liability Act (CERCLA) and Oil Pollution Act. The US approach also establishes a public law-led response to the challenge of environmental damage, endowing authorities at federal and state level with powers and responsibility to take action against polluters with a view to ensuring that the latter bear the costs of environmental restorative measures.[66]

A final introductory point to note on the ELD is that, in alignment with the environmental legal framework of the Treaty on the Functioning of the European Union (TFEU),[67] it expressly permits member states to maintain or adopt more stringent provisions than its own in relation to the prevention and remediation of environmental damage as well as extend liability in respect of human activity not covered by its provisions.[68] Accordingly, member states are entitled to apply stricter civil liability rules.

12.3.1 Scope of liability under the ELD

The overall purpose of the ELD is to establish a viable legal framework of environmental liability based on the 'polluter pays' principle.[69] The legislative instrument concerns itself with civil liability of persons causing environmental damage, specifically their financial liability to provide the funds for costs required to prevent or remedy environmental damage for which they are responsible.[70] Under the ELD, the primary degree of legal responsibility for attending to environmental damage is required to lie with the person responsible for damage, taken in the context of the directive to mean the operator of occupational activities specified in the legislative instrument.[71] The position adopted is in accordance with the 'polluter pays' principle, as recognised as an integral part of EU environmental as well as other Union common policies.[72] Accordingly, member states are not, as a matter of principle, entitled to elect to fund the restoration of damaged environmental sites by way of drawing from the public purse. Responsibility for taking appropriate preventive or remedial steps must rest first with the polluter.

State-funded intervention is permitted under the ELD only in certain exceptional circumstances, where the application of 'polluter pays' is not practicable.[73] A complementary aim of the directive is to provide a suitable legal framework to enable national authorities to be in a position to take necessary steps to ensure that persons engaging in particular activities, which cause actual or an imminent threat of environmental damage, are held accountable for their actions.

The scope of liability under the ELD is determined in broad terms. Specifically, Article 3 stipulates that the directive applies in respect of environmental damage caused by certain occupational activities and to instances of imminent threat of such damage occurring arising as a result of such activities. Its application is predicated upon national competent authorities being able to identify and assess actual or prospective damage, the activity and/or substance responsible for such damage as well the polluter(s) involved.[74]

The fact that the instrument seeks to address liability in the context of imminent threats of environmental damage in addition to actual instances of damage reflects a desire to apply the EU environmental principle that preventive measures should be taken.[75] This constitutes recognition of the fact that a liability framework requiring action to be taken only at the stage where environmental damage has materialised falls short of an effective environmental protection response. In particular, this is clear where damage may have irrevocable adverse consequences for the state of the environment in some way, such as permanent loss of a particular ecologically sensitive habitat host to protected species on account of irremediable pollution of environmental media located at the site (e.g. deep subsoil or water resource contamination).

12.3.1.1 *Operators of occupational activities covered by the ELD*

Not all types of anthropogenic activity may give rise to liability under the ELD. The scope of liability is limited to cover activities that are considered to pose the greatest threats to the environment. As a starting point, the directive makes clear that only 'occupational' activities fall within its remit.[76] Such activities are defined broadly to mean 'any activity carried out in the course of an economic activity, a business or an undertaking, irrespective of its public or private, profit or non-profit character'.[77] This broad definition effectively embraces any economic operation carried out by persons, charities, companies or public bodies, whether involving the production or provision of services, goods or works and irrespective of its commercial or non-commercial nature. Accordingly, any activities of individuals carried out in a purely private and domestic capacity outside the public arena of gainful employment or self-employment are not covered by the directive.

The ELD adopts a two-tier approach to liability. In respect of certain types of occupational activity listed in Annex III of the directive, deemed to carry particular serious risks to the environment, liability for actual or threatened environmental damage is strict and covers a wide range of types of damage. In respect of other occupational activities, though, the scope of liability is confined to cover a narrower range of environmental harm and is predicated upon proof of fault or negligence. Specifically, liability is structured under Article 3(1) ELD to cover the following different scenarios of damage to the environment:

(a) environmental damage[78] caused by any of the occupational activities listed in Annex III, and to any imminent threat of such damage occurring by reasons of those activities.

(b) damage to protected species and natural habitats caused by any occupational activities other than those listed in Annex III, and to any imminent threat of such damage occurring by reason of those activities, whenever the operator has been at fault or negligent.

The directive clarifies that this liability formula is subject to any stricter EU rules adopted in relation to regulation of any of the activities falling within its remit[79] and is also subject to any stricter liability rules formulated at national level.[80]

As a result of the delimitation of liability set out in Article 3(1) ELD, it is evident that in practice it is going to be relatively rare for operators of activities other than those listed in Annex III ELD to be subject to environmental liability under the aegis of the Union legislative framework. The coverage in Article 3(1)(b) is usually going to be of immediate relevance to persons professionally engaged in operations closely involved with or located adjacent to protected habitats (such as those professionally engaged in activities involving agricultural, forestry, environmental media or wildlife protection management). Annex III contains a list of 12 categories of occupational activity, which either directly or indirectly inhere substantial risks to the environment if mismanaged. These include: activities of installations subject to permits under the auspices of the (former) IPPC Directive;[81] waste management operations involving waste and hazardous waste, as subject to EU legislative requirements, as well as the trans-boundary shipment of waste requiring an authorisation or which is prohibited under EU legislation;[82] discharges into and manipulation of water resources that require prior authorisation under EU environmental legislation;[83] the manufacture, use, storage, processing, filling, release into the environment and on-site transport of certain dangerous chemical substances and products whose applications are subject to controls under EU rules;[84] transportation by road, rail, inland waterway, sea or air of dangerous or polluting goods subject to EU legislative controls;[85] the operation of installations subject to authorisation under Union air pollution emissions legislation;[86] and any contained use involving genetically modified micro-organisms or any deliberate release into the environment, transport or placing on the market of GMOs as subject to EU legislative restrictions.[87]

The ELD's provisions refer to liability falling on 'operators' of occupational activities covered by Article 3. Specifically, it is the operator who is subject to particular legal obligations under the directive to take preventive or remedial steps arising from actual or an imminent threat of environmental damage[88] and who is financially liable for the costs incurred in meeting these obligations.[89] The definition of 'operator' under the ELD is crafted in a deliberately broad manner, to ensure that it covers persons operating or in control of the activity:

> 'operator' means any natural or legal, private or public person who operates or controls the occupational activity or, where this is provided for in national legislation, to whom decisive economic power over the technical functioning of such an activity has been delegated, including the holder of a permit or authorisation for such an activity or the person registering or notifying such an activity.[90]

It is evident from this definition that there may well be more than one person involved in the pursuit of a particular occupational activity, such as a company in charge of a particular project who subcontracts work to other legal or natural persons. In such cases, the definition of 'operator' indicates that liability is on a joint and several basis. The reference to control may be particularly important in the context of corporate liability for other reasons, as it covers those persons who have legal or *de facto* decisive influence over the occupational activity of a company engaged in a disputed activity. This would certainly include persons having a controlling shareholding in a company as well as persons in charge of a company in administration or the subject of insolvency procedures. It would probably include executive officers in charge of taking strategic decisions over corporate activity (e.g. board of company directors). However, no definition of 'control' is provided in the ELD. However, in line with the aims and objectives of the directive, it is clear that the term should be interpreted broadly so as to encompass all persons involved in making or having the opportunity to exert a decisive influence over decisions on the management of occupational activities of a corporate entity. No doubt this particular aspect of the directive may well be taken up in litigation over the interpretation of 'operator' at some stage in the future.

12.3.1.2 Environmental damage

Liability under the ELD is also delimited according to the types of environmental damage covered by the legislative instrument as well as occupational activity involved. Operators of Annex III activities have a broader duty of care to the environment under Article 3 ELD than persons engaged in other occupational activities.

Annex III operators' liability is triggered in principle by any 'environmental damage' or imminent threat of such damage occurring by reason of their occupational activities. 'Environmental damage' is defined in some detail in Article 2 ELD as covering damage to protected species and habitats,[91] water damage[92] as well as land damage.[93] 'Damage' is defined as meaning any measurable adverse change in a natural resource or measurable impairment of a natural resource service which may occur directly or indirectly.[94] Whilst the Commission's draft legislative proposal indicated its wish to cover damage broadly, namely so as to cover damage to biodiversity, reference to the concept of 'biodiversity damage' was dropped in the adopted legislative instrument.[95] Both Commission and Council did not ultimately wish for the ELD to extend beyond the material scope of existing EU nature conservation legislation, rejecting any attempt to incorporate the broad definition of biodiversity as contained in the UN Biodiversity Convention.[96] The European Parliament and Economic and Social Committee argued unsuccessfully for a broad scope to liability in respect of damage to natural living resources.[97] Accordingly, the ELD came to be structured so as to focus upon the existing remit of EU nature conservation legislation (namely, the Habitats Directive 92/43 and Wild Birds Directive 2009/147) for the purposes of protecting biota. By way of compromise, it was agreed to allow member states to apply the directive's rules to species and habitats not protected by EU legislation.[98]

Whilst the scope of environmental damage is defined relatively broadly in the ELD, the directive also introduces a threshold of 'significance' which attenuates somewhat the extent of liability. Specifically, environmental damage is defined as including: damage to protected species and natural habitats having significant adverse effects on favourable conservation status;[99] water damage that significantly adversely affects the ecological, chemical and/or quantitative status and/or ecological potential of the waters concerned;[100] and land damage that involves any land contamination creating a significant risk of human health being adversely affected as a result of (in)direct introduction of substances, preparations, organisms or micro-organisms in, on or under land.[101] Whilst damage to the environmental medium of air is not directly incorporated within the terms of the definition, it is clear that it would be inaccurate to conclude from this that air pollution falls outside its scope. In particular, liability will arise where air emissions perpetrate damage to water, land or protected species or habitats.[102]

In respect of occupational activities not covered by Annex III the operator's duty of care extends only to 'protected species and protected habitats', as clarified in Article 3(1)(b) ELD. These are defined in Article 2(3)(a)–(c) ELD to mean: species cited in Article 4(2) or Annex I of the (former) Wild Birds Directive 79/409,[103] or listed in Annexes II and IV of the Habitats Directive 92/43;[104] the habitats of species cited in Article 4(2) or Annex I of the Wild Birds Directive, or listed in Annex II of the Habitats Directive; the natural habitats listed in Annex I to the Habitats Directive; the breeding sites or resting places of species listed in Annex IV to the Habitats Directive; and any habitat or species not listed in the above-mentioned Annexes to the Wild Birds and Habitats Directives where a member state has designated them for equivalent purposes. Damage to such species and habitats is defined as meaning damage having significant adverse effects on reaching or maintaining their favourable conservation status,[105] except where such damage has resulted from acts authorised under the auspices of EU nature protection legislation or equivalent national conservation laws.[106] A detailed set of criteria apply in the directive to determine the existence of significant damage.[107]

12.3.1.3 *Causation issues*

Liability under the ELD is predicated upon the ability of member state competent authorities being able to attribute responsibility of environmental damage or an imminent threat of its occurrence to a particular person. Article 4(5) ELD stipulates that the directive's requirements apply only where it is possible to establish a causal link between damage and the activities of individual operators.[108] This requires that national competent authorities, charged by member states with the responsibility to fulfil the duties set out in the EU legislative instrument, have to procure evidence on two crucial issues, namely evidence to identify with sufficient certainty the identification of activities and/or substance(s) causing actual or threatened environmental damage as well as the discovery of individual operators responsible for such activities and/or substances.[109] Given the often diffuse nature of environmental pollution, these procedural hurdles may well prove very significant in denting the enforcement capabilities and strategies of national competent authorities. As the ELD realistically recognises:

> Not all forms of environmental damage can be remedied by means of the liability mechanism. For the latter to be effective, there need to be one or more identifiable polluters, the damage should be concrete and quantifiable, and a causal link should be established between the damage and the identified polluter(s). Liability is therefore not a suitable instrument for dealing with pollution of a widespread, diffuse character, where it is impossible to link the negative environmental effects with acts or failure to act of certain individual actors.[110]

The ELD does not provide any specific guidance on the manner in which evidence is to be garnered or assessed. Notably, it does not expressly make reference to the utilisation of the precautionary principle in determining possible sources of damage. The principle may be of relevance if and when competent authorities are faced with scenarios of actual or prospective environmental damage, where the source is not clearly established from a scientific perspective.[111] The ELD's silence might imply that such evidential issues are to be determined solely in accordance with national rules of civil or administrative procedure, which may or may not have recourse to the precautionary principle in some form. However, it should be noted that under Article 191(2) TFEU Union environmental policy is to be based on the precautionary principle; accordingly, this general principle is also pertinent to the application of the ELD. However, it is unclear to what extent this principle requires national courts to assess evidence offered in relation to the question of attribution of liability in any particular way. Hitherto, institutional discourse at EU level on the precautionary principle has focused on the extent to which its application is relevant to EU legislative decision-making processes.[112] Whether it is acceptable from a subsidiarity perspective for the ELD to tolerate a divergence amongst member states' legal systems on application of the principle in relation to evidentiary issues relating to civil or criminal liability is questionable.

12.3.1.4 *Terms of and exceptions to liability*

FAULT AND NEGLIGENCE

The liability regime employed by the ELD does not impose a single approach to the issue of fault or negligence on the part of operators. Instead, the directive applies a bifurcated approach, applying (in Article 3) a strict-liability model in respect of operators of the most hazardous occupational activities (i.e. carrying out an Annex III activity) and a model that predicates liability upon fault with respect to operators of other occupational activities causing actual or threatened damage to protected species and habitats. There are, though, a number of qualifications and exceptions to liability woven into the legislative fabric which may serve to exonerate an operator's culpability totally or serve to excuse the operator from having to bear the costs for rehabilitating a contaminated site or one threatened with environmental damage. In essence, the ELD applies the onus of proof differently for Annex III operators and other operators, in order to variegate the relative stringency of liability in accordance with the perceived level of environmental risk associated with the particular type of occupational activity.

OPERATORS OF ANNEX III ACTIVITIES

Where actual or imminent threat of environmental damage is caused by an occupational activity of an Annex III operator, namely one listed as being noted as particularly hazardous, it is in principle irrelevant whether the damage is as a result of the operator's fault or negligence. Liability is in essence triggered upon a finding of environmental damage attributable to such an operator irrespective of such factors. Subject to certain limited exceptions, the operator is obliged to take appropriate steps as prescribed in Articles 5–7 ELD either to preserve the site's environmental state or, if that is too late, to rehabilitate any damaged site. Moreover, as a matter of first principle, the operator is obliged to bear the costs of these measures.[113]

However, Article 8 ELD provides certain exemptions for operators in respect of their financial liability to bear the costs of either maintaining or rehabilitating a site subject to actual or threatened with imminent environmental damage. These exemptions place the onus of proof on operators to show that, for particular reasons, they are not to blame for instances of actual or the threat of imminent damage. The onus of proof is set according to the standards normally applicable under national civil procedures,[114] and this is usually based upon a test centred on the balance of probabilities. Specifically, operators are automatically exempted from having to bear preventive or remedial costs in two situations. First, they are exempt where they are able to prove that the damage or threat has been caused by a third party and occurred notwithstanding the application of appropriate safety measures on the operator's part.[115] Secondly, they are also exempt if acting in compliance with a compulsory order or instruction from a public authority other than one consequent upon an emission or incident caused by the operator's activities.[116] In such circumstances, member states are required to ensure that operators are able to recoup costs they have incurred.

Moreover, member states have the option under the ELD to exempt an operator from having to bear the costs of remedial action where the latter is able to demonstrate that they were not at fault or negligent and that the damage was caused by either of the following two scenarios: (1) an emission or event explicitly authorised by national rules implementing EU environmental legislation specified in Annex III

610 Enforcement of European Union Environmental Law

of the directive[117] (so-called 'permit' or 'regulatory compliance' defence') or (2) an emission or use of a product in the course of an activity which the operator demonstrates was not considered likely to cause environmental damage according to the current state of scientific and technical knowledge[118] (so-called 'state of the art' defence). As discussed in section 12.4.1 below, member states have been divided over the justification of Annex III operators companies being able to utilise these defences; just under half of the member states have opted to make use of both defence options with a similar number deciding to rule out recourse to either defence.

It is important to note, though, that it may be difficult in practice for an Annex III operator to discharge the burden of proof, especially in relation to third-party intervention cases. The 'state of the art' defence provides an incentive for operators to acquire technology for the application of their activities that is proven to be least risky to the environment, and thus accords with the general environmental principle underpinning EU environmental policy that the EU should aim to promote a high level of environmental protection.[119] Crucially, the incentive is not weakened by any reference to a caveat of words to the effect 'not entailing excessive costs'; such a caveat would have undermined the impact of the directive considerably.

Member states also have the option to require that their competent authorities take the necessary preventive or remedial measures on affected sites instead of operators where the latter are not required to bear the costs of such measures under the aegis of the ELD.[120] National authorities are also entitled to waive recovery of any costs against an operator incurred in undertaking preventive or remedial steps, where the process to recover such costs exceeds the recoverable sum itself.[121]

OTHER OPERATORS NOT ENGAGING IN ANNEX III ACTIVITIES

The concept of fault and negligence are central features of the liability of operators of occupational activities not covered by Annex III ELD which perpetrate or threaten damage to protected species or habitats. In contrast with the situation applicable to Annex III occupational activities, it is incumbent upon the member state's competent authorities to prove that such operators were at fault or negligent in causing actual or an imminent threat of damage to protected species or natural habitats.[122] In addition, such operators are (like Annex III operators) also entitled to rely upon the particular exemptions relating to prevention and remediation costs set out in Article 8(3)–(4) ELD mentioned above.

EXCEPTIONS TO LIABILITY

In addition to the above-mentioned limitations and qualifications to liability established by various provisions of the ELD, Article 4 of the directive specifies a number of exceptions to the application of its requirements. The exceptions relate to specific instances of *force majeure*, policy areas already subject to international civil liability rules as well as politically sensitive areas involving national security issues. Specifically, the ELD excludes from its remit actual or imminent threats of environmental damage caused by either:

- activities relating to war[123] or activities whose purpose is otherwise to serve national defence or international security;[124]
- irresistible natural phenomena[125] (i.e. natural disaster scenarios) or activities exclusively intended to protect areas from such phenomena;[126]
- incidents covered by international civil liability conventions concerning oil pollution of the marine environment or the carriage of dangerous goods of which member states are contracting parties, as listed in Annex IV of the directive;[127] or
- nuclear risks or activities covered by the Euratom Treaty or international instruments on liability for nuclear related incidents, as listed in Annex V of the directive.[128]

In addition, the ELD's application is without prejudice to the rights of operators to limit their liability in accordance with national laws implementing the 1976 and 1988 Conventions on Limitation of Liability for Maritime Claims and on Limitation of Liability in Inland Navigation respectively.[129] The ELD makes clear that the European Commission must review the exceptions relating to marine and nuclear sectors in the context of its report on the application of the legislative instrument by 30 April 2014.[130] This signals that their continued exception from the EU liability framework may not necessarily be permanent, and will be assessed instead in the light of experience in terms of the effectiveness of existing procedures. At the time of writing, the Commission report had not yet been published and was not anticipated to be completed before the end of 2014.[131]

12.3.1.5 Temporal scope of liability

The ELD limits the scope of liability temporally, from a retrospective as well as prospective sense. First, in concert with the Lugano Convention and in contrast with US 'Superfund' rules on civil liability,[132] the directive rules out the application of its rules retrospectively. Specifically, the application of the ELD does not cover damage caused by an emission, event or incident taking place before the deadline set for its transposition, namely 30 April 2007.[133] Neither does it apply to damage caused by an emission, event or incident which, although taking place after 30 April 2007, derives from an activity that took place and finished prior to that date.[134] Secondly, the directive excludes liability in a prospective sense. Specifically, the ELD does not apply in relation to damage occurring more than 30 years after the relevant emission, event or incident, which caused it to occur.[135]

In addition, Article 10 of the ELD sets a time limit on how long a competent authority is entitled to initiate proceedings in order to recover costs of preventive or remedial measures undertaken in order to address environmental damage. Specifically, the authority has five years to commence recovery proceedings, starting either from the date when the measures have been completed or when the liable operator has been identified, whichever is the later date.

12.3.2 *Extent of liability: an operator's specific obligations*

Another key and distinctive feature of the ELD is the set of obligations it lays down to be performed by operators found to be liable for causing actual or an imminent threat of environmental damage. In contrast with the approach adopted by other international instruments addressing civil liability in respect of harm to the environment (such as the Lugano Convention), the ELD does not use the sanction of monetary compensation. Instead, it obliges liable operators to take certain steps to prevent or remediate damage as well as fund the costs required in order to ensure their due completion. Accordingly, the ELD's approach is fully in line with the 'polluter pays' principle, in the sense that payment procured from the polluter is guaranteed to be targeted at either ensuring that threats to the environment are averted or restoring damaged environs to the condition they were in prior to the time when they were damaged by the activities of the polluter.

The traditional sanction of monetary compensation, as used in civil law systems as the principal means to provide recompense in relation to loss or damage, has a number of deficiencies from an environmental protection perspective. In particular, two major problems arise where monetary compensation is the remedy used to address environmental torts, namely difficulties of ensuring that any level of compensation provided is adequate recompense for damage sustained as well as the absence of any controls as to what purpose compensation will be directed (restoration of the environment as such may not be desired by a claimant with a personal injury claim or claims in respect of loss or impairment to their property interests). The approach adopted by the ELD is intended to avoid the trap of civil liability being reduced to being perceived as a *de facto* tax on occupational activity, namely an inconvenient financial burden as opposed to a genuine deterrence for operators intending to engage in activities that may cause significant damage or an imminent threat of serious damage to the environment.

The provisions of the ELD containing specific environmental protection obligations for liable operators are enshrined in Articles 5–8 of the legislative instrument. The principal obligations concern those in relation to preventive measures (Article 5) and remedial action (Articles 6–7) which apply unless authorised in the public interest under the Articles 6(3) and (4) or 16 of the Habitats Directive 92/43, Article 9 of the Wild Birds Directive 2009/47 or Article 4(7) of the Water Framework Directive 2000/60.[136] A second, complementary duty relates to the operator bearing the costs of preventive and remedial measures (Article 8) subject to certain limited derogations. A particularly notable innovative element of the directive is that the obligations are designed to apply automatically to operators, without the need for prior command from a competent authority to undertake action. This is a subtle but important contribution towards inculcating a greater sense of self-responsibility in business culture in relation to the environment,[137] although its practical application will rely heavily upon corporate management and shareholders instituting its implications. In practice, though, it is anticipated in most instances that the ELD obligations are going to be largely reliant upon competent authorities invoking their powers and responsibilities under the directive to see that its terms are adhered to. In so doing, the ELD obliges them to ensure that a particular operator has caused specific environmental damage or an imminent threat of damage by its occupational activities.

The ELD respects the basic procedural guarantees that would normally be expected in the event of a person being subject to an adverse decision by a public authority. Specifically, it stipulates that any decision taken under its auspices imposing preventive or remedial action is to be notified immediately to the operator concerned.[138] Notification of the decision will include citation of the precise grounds on which it is based as well as information on the legal remedies and the relevant time limits available to the operator under national law.[139]

12.3.2.1 *Preventive measures*

The requirements under the ELD regarding preventive action are relevant in situations where environmental damage has not yet occurred. Specifically, Article 5(1) ELD stipulates that where environmental damage has not yet occurred but there is an imminent threat of such damage arising, the operator (responsible for the threat) must 'without delay take the necessary preventive measures'. 'Preventive measures' are defined in the ELD to mean any measures undertaken in response to an event, act or omission that has created an imminent threat of environmental damage, with a view either to its prevention or minimisation.[140] Operators are to be obliged, as a minimum, by member states to notify the national competent authority forthwith if an imminent threat is not dispelled by preventive measures.[141] Competent authorities are required to ensure that the obligations in relation to preventive action are taken by the operator concerned and have powers to supervise and control the manner of their execution.[142] The ELD does not specifically require competent authorities to be vested with powers to seek injunctive relief from national courts in urgent cases. However, that member states should vest them with such powers is implicit from the provisions of the directive conferring authority on competent authorities to require preventive measures be taken, which in many instances may have to be taken urgently. Unless the competent authority is able to support its decisions by threat of court order, the credibility and effectiveness of their enforcement action will be actually or potentially undermined. Accordingly, it is evident that member states should ensure that emergency judicial or equivalent relief is available, otherwise this will be tantamount to violation of the duties of co-operation on their part contained in Article 4(3) TEU in light of Court of Justice of the European Union (CJEU) jurisprudence.[143] It may well have been wiser, though, from the perspectives of complete transparency and legal certainty for emergency relief provisions to have been set out expressly in the terms of the directive.

12.3.2.2 Remedial measures

Where environmental damage has occurred, operators are obliged under the ELD to carry out measures designed to remedy the effects of the damage. Articles 6–7 and Annex II ELD provide a detailed set of obligations in this regard. Article 6(1) lays out three key duties for operators to fulfil in the event of environmental damage occurring, namely: to notify the competent authority immediately of all relevant details;[144] to take measures to contain the extent of the damage;[145] and to take measures necessary to remediate damage sustained in accordance with Article 7.[146] As is the case with preventive measures, national competent authorities are vested with powers to oversee the performance of an operator to take remedial action.[147]

The ELD's provisions on remediation are constructed with a view to ensuring that remedial measures are carried out in a way that is most suitable to local environmental conditions and requirements. Specifically, safeguards are placed in the directive's legal framework to ensure that a suitably clear, effective and accountable deliberative process is undertaken prior to the instigation of remedial action.[148] These include the following mandatory basic requirements: that a plan is to be drafted on a strategy of action; that the plan accords with minimum standards as set out in the ELD; that the operator must defer to the competent authority (as impartial actor) for final decisions over implementation of restorative measures; and that the implementation of remedial action accords with the ELD's minimum standards. The key stages of this process will be briefly examined below.

The first key stage concerns planning for remediation by the operator and notification of this to the competent authority. In accordance with 'polluter pays', the operator is to draw up an appropriate plan to remediate a contaminated site. Specifically, the operator is obliged to identify potential remedial measures and submit them to the competent authority, unless the latter has already intervened by carrying out remedial work itself.[149] The draft remediation plan is to be in accordance with a detailed set of requirements laid out in Annex II ELD. Annex II lays out a common framework to be followed in determining the appropriate measures to be applied for the purpose of remedying environmental damage. It applies two sets of ground rules, namely one set in relation to the remediation of land damage[150] and the other in relation to scenarios involving damage to water, protected species or natural habitats.[151]

Under Annex II ELD, remediation of damage to water, protected species or natural habitats is to be achieved on the basis of seeking to restore the environment to its 'baseline condition'. The 'baseline condition' is a concept defined as meaning the condition at the time of the damage of the natural resources and related services that would have occurred but for the environmental damage, estimated on the basis of the best information available[152] (namely the *status quo ante*). The restorative principle employed in Annex II is to be achieved by various types of measures, which are designed to ensure that a state of environmental conditions is attained which is as close as possible to the baseline condition: namely, through the use of 'primary', 'complementary' and 'compensatory' measures. Primary measures[153] are the measures deployed in order to return the damaged natural resources and services to or towards the baseline condition, and these measures are to be used as a first priority over complementary measures. Complementary remedial action[154] involves action taken to compensate in the event that primary remediation does not result in fully restoring the natural resources or services. Compensatory remediation[155] concerns any steps (not involving monetary payment to the public) taken to compensate for interim losses of natural resources including eco-system services that occur from the date of damage until primary remediation has achieved its full effect. In terms of identifying remedial measures to be employed, primary measures are to be considered first.[156] Annex II provides a set of criteria and ancillary requirements to assess in individual cases which particular type of remedial options, based on 'best available technologies', should be utilised and when these should cease.[157] Remediation also requires that any significant risks to human health caused by the damage should also be removed.[158]

In terms of remediation of land damage, Annex II stipulates fewer requirements. The central focus of the legal framework here is to ensure that the affected sites no longer pose significant risks to human health.[159] As a minimum, relevant contaminants are to be removed, controlled, contained or diminished with a view to eliminating serious health risks. Scientific risk assessments are to be carried out to ascertain the state of risk, based on analyses of soil and contaminant type and concentrations.

The second key stage of the remediation process involves the competent authority. Under the ELD, it is the national competent authority which is vested with the task of determining the particular remedial measures to be implemented and in what order.[160] In the event of the occurrence of multiple sources of environmental damage which are unable to remedied simultaneously, the authority is charged with the task of deciding which particular aspect of damage is to be addressed first of all. Various factors have to be taken into account in this situation in order to for an evaluation of priorities to be made, namely the nature, extent and seriousness of the instances of damage concerned, possibilities of natural recovery and risks to human health.[161]

As an integral part of its decision-making process, the national authority is obliged to invite observations from persons actually or likely to be affected by the damage. In any event such persons include those whose land would be subject to any remedial action as well as persons having a sufficient interest in environmental decision-making relating to the damage or alleging the impairment of a right as result of the damage.[162] In accordance with the general principle of a fair hearing under EU law,[163] this means that competent authorities are required to afford a genuine opportunity for the public concerned to submit comments prior to remedial action being taken, at the very least in relation to measures designed to effect long-term remediation if not necessarily in relation to urgent containment measures that may well be required to be effected immediately.

12.3.2.3 Operator's financial liability for preventive and remedial action

In accordance with the 'polluter pays' principle, the ELD imposes a general requirement on member states to ensure that an operator (found liable for actual or threatened environmental damage) pays the costs for any preventive and/or remedial measures taken.[164] By way of complement to this obligation, national competent authorities are required as a rule to recover costs that they have incurred in relation to any such action they may have taken in response to the damage.[165] Certain exceptions, however, apply in relation to these fundamental requirements, where the operator is able to prove lack of fault or negligence in specified situations.[166] These have been referred to already in section 12.3.1.4 and need not be repeated.

An important general point to note is that the ELD does not set any caps or ceilings to the financial liability of operators found responsible for damage to the environment. The Commission, when crafting its legislative proposal for a directive on environmental liability in 2002, was sceptical of introducing a liability ceiling, conscious that if a ceiling is set too low it would compromise the 'polluter pays' principle.[167] Whilst the directive itself does not establish a formal cap, it would be inaccurate to suggest that the ELD's framework necessarily requires competent authorities to demand that the operator foot the bill for absolute remediation of the environment. The legislative framework is more nuanced, providing competent authorities with considerable discretion under the aegis of Article 6 in conjunction with the Annex II criteria of the ELD in determining the appropriate range of remedial measures to be taken.[168]

A major shortcoming (may be even an Achilles heel) of the ELD concerns its lack of focus on the element of financial security, notably environmental liability insurance. Under the current version of the ELD, operators are not required to provide for sufficient financial security in the event of the occurrence of actual or threatened environmental damage. The aspect of financial cover was the subject of considerable scrutiny and debate in the preparations leading up to the passage of the directive. It remains a contentious and complex field, requiring careful as well as realistic assessment in terms of its implication for application of the 'polluter pays' principle.[169] An obligation for Annex III operators to secure adequate insurance cover or provide equivalent financial guarantees prior to operations would have significantly reinforced the 'polluter pays' principle underpinning the legislative instrument. Without adequate financial security in place, it is evident that operators might well be unable to meet any extensive financial costs involved required to effect appropriate remediation of serious instances of environmental damage. The financial consequences flowing from the insolvency of a liable operator may well be that any funds needed to clean up environmental damage might not be able to be drawn down (fully or at all) from the residual funds of the polluter. For under insolvency law, the environment is not usually listed as a preferred creditor. In event of a shortfall of funds from the polluter, environmental rehabilitation costs would have to be met in practice from other sources, such as from local and/or general taxpayers, a prospect that would run counter to 'polluter pays'. Moreover, the absence of requirements to establish adequate environmental liability cover makes little economic sense either, given the potential adverse impact on employment and business activity in the event of a significant liability event arising for an operator.

Instead of any specific financial security obligations being incorporated within its legal framework, the approach of the ELD is cautious and facilitative, as was the Commission's 2000 White Paper. Specifically, it contains only a very soft requirement for member states to 'encourage' the development of financial security instruments and markets suitable for providing cover for operators.[170] Under Article 14(2) ELD, the European Commission was obliged to review this area and provide a report by 30 April 2010, with a view to a possibility of it coming forward after that point with proposals for a mandatory system of financial security. In its 2010 report,[171] the Commission considered that lack of experience with member state implementation of the ELD had not provided any sufficient justification for introducing a harmonised system of financial security. It noted that member states had undertaken limited action in this area, 'restricted to discussions with insurers and/or their trade associations'. It was also unsure whether the current capacity of the (re-)insurance industry was sufficiently large to cover ELD liabilities efficiently. The Commission preferred instead to await developments at national level on the emergence of mandatory insurance cover systems, suggesting that where member states opted for compulsory insurance cover, this should be undertaken gradually (e.g. limitation on Annex III operators), with guarantee ceilings (bearing in mind the infeasibility of private insurers offering unlimited liability) and exclusion of low-risk activities.[172]

The 2010 Commission report reflects a rather tepid and unambitious response to this important issue, though, and is effectively devoid of the Union-level institutional leadership it warrants. Simply reacting passively to events that may or may not develop at national level is tantamount to the Commission dampening possibilities for an environmental liability insurance market to develop. It should be remembered that markets, including insurance markets, are constructed and shaped to a large extent by the contours and reach of obligations stipulated by rules of law, including notably public law. Why should any operator be necessarily interested in seeking environmental liability insurance, when they know that other rivals are not obliged to enter into such a contract in the single market? The Commission is due to reassess its position in light of its review of the application of the ELD required to be completed under Article 18 of the directive. This should have been published by 30 April 2014, but is expected to be published belatedly sometime after 2014.

It should also be noted that the EU has taken steps in other environmental instrumentation to ensure that an operator of a hazardous facility provides financial security to cover the event of environmental damage arising. Specifically, the Mining Waste Directive 2006/21[173] requires that national competent authorities must ensure that, prior to the commencement of any operations involving the accumulation or deposit of extractive waste in a waste facility, a financial guarantee (e.g. in the form of a financial deposit, including industry-sponsored mutual guarantee funds) is established so that all the directive's obligations, as included with the waste permit, are discharged and that there are funds readily available for the rehabilitation of the land affected by the waste facility.[174]

The ELD does not provide for specific rules on cost allocation in cases involving multiple sources of environmental damage. Apportionment of liability for costs between operators found to have been jointly responsible for causing a particular instance of environmental damage is a matter devolved to the member states.[175] It is clear, though, from the terms of the ELD that, subject to the rules under national law that may apply on apportionment, each operator found to be liable for damage is so effectively on a joint and several basis. No tiering of liability is made according to the status of a particular operator (e.g. producer, retailer, holder or owner).

12.3.3 Competent authorities: principal enforcers

From a law enforcement perspective, it is important to note that the ELD places member states with central responsibility for overseeing the implementation of its civil liability requirements. A central plank of its legal framework is the predominant role afforded to national authorities in ensuring that operators adhere to their environmental liability obligations. Brans has noted that in effect the ELD has established a particular type of trusteeship in relation to the protection of natural resources.[176] In certain respects, competent authorities may be seen as being endowed with responsibilities akin to that of a trustee, having a remit to protect the environment as beneficiary. Specifically, Article 11(1) ELD requires member states to designate the 'competent authority(ies)' responsible for fulfilling the duties provided for in the directive. Competent authorities are charged with two principal tasks: verification of liability and supervision of remediation.

In terms of verification, competent authorities have the duty to establish which operator has caused actual or threatened environmental damage.[177] In order to fulfil this duty, it is self-evident that such authorities need to be vested with the necessary inspection and investigatory powers. However, the ELD does not specify in detail any particular powers that must be accorded to the authorities involved; this is a matter devolved to the national level. Under general duties of co-operation owed by member states to the EU flowing from Article 4(3) TEU, it is clear from that provision and CJEU jurisprudence that member states are required to ensure that authorities are endowed with effective powers and resources to enable them to fulfil their EU environmental legal responsibilities,[178] in this case of identifying sources of damage. However, it is regrettable that the ELD does not spell out a minimum list of mandatory investigatory powers, given that detection and identification of sources of damage and threats of damage are obviously crucially important to achieve the aims underpinning any environmental liability regime, whether civil or criminal. This would have been beneficial from a number of perspectives. Member states would be left in no doubt as to what is required for the purposes of fulfilling this responsibility (issue of legal certainty). More importantly, there would be reduced scope for possibilities of member states vesting authorities with an inadequate range of investigatory powers (issues of effectiveness and uniformity of application of Union law). To date, the EU has only passed a non-binding recommendation on minimum criteria for environmental inspections,[179] although as discussed in Chapter 11 the Commission is actively considering proposing enhancements to this framework under the aegis of the Seventh EU Environment Action Programme (2013–20).[180]

As far as supervision is concerned, competent authorities are obliged under the ELD to ensure that environmental obligations directed at operators as set out in the directive are in fact fulfilled. Principally, this means that such authorities have responsibility to assess the state of actual or threatened damage and determine any preventive or rehabilitative measures to be taken.[181] As regards assessment of environmental damage, competent authorities may require operators to carry out their own assessment and supply any information or data required.[182] Competent authorities therefore have a central role in directing operators' actions in the event that environmental damage is threatened or arises.

As far as preventive measures are concerned, Article 5 ELD stipulates that member states are to vest competent authorities with a range of specific powers. Whilst the operator has a primary duty under the ELD to take the necessary preventive measures to address an imminent threat of environmental damage,[183] competent authorities are obliged to require that such steps are taken.[184] To assist it in its supervisory role, the ELD provides for certain notification arrangements. Specifically, competent authorities are to have the power to require an operator to provide information to it on any actual or suspected imminent threat of environmental damage,[185] and must be informed by an operator of any failed attempt to dispel an imminent threat as soon as possible.[186] The directive requires that competent authorities be endowed with powers to require the operator to take preventive action and give instructions on steps to be taken.[187] A competent authority may also undertake preventive measures itself[188] or direct third parties to carry out such measures,[189] thereby covering scenarios where an operator fails to comply with its ELD obligations, is unable to be identified or is not required to bear costs under the directive.[190]

As far as remedial action is concerned, Article 6 of the ELD endows competent authorities with similar wide-ranging powers and responsibilities for the purpose of overseeing their proper enforcement. Operators are obliged to inform such authorities of any incidents of environmental damage[191] and are obliged to undertake remedial measures.[192] Competent authorities are charged with a general responsibility to require that remedial measures are carried out by the operator.[193] Under the ELD, competent authorities are to be endowed with a range of powers to assist them in this purpose. Specifically, they may require the operator to provide supplementary information on any damage that has occurred, so as to be properly briefed and updated on the environmental state of the site concerned.[194] Competent authorities may also direct the operator to take steps to contain the situation so as to seek to limit the spread of damage,[195] require the operator to take necessary medial measures[196] as well as give instructions for this purpose. As for preventive measures, under the directive competent authorities may also take the necessary preventive measures themselves[197] or direct third parties to carry out the work.[198] In relation to rehabilitation aspects, Annex II ELD provides a common framework of criteria to be followed by operators, with competent authorities bearing the responsibility to oversee that the most appropriate remediation measures are selected.[199]

From the above, it is apparent that competent authorities have a key role in ensuring that sites threatened with or subject to environmental damage are appropriately protected. However, the ELD provides a degree of flexibility where the authority is faced with difficulties in requiring operators to take action. Specifically, competent authorities are entitled but not required under the directive to take preventive or remedial action themselves or entrust third parties with this work where the operator fails to take action as required, cannot be identified or is not required to bear the costs of preventive or remedial action under the directive (so-called 'orphan damage' scenarios).[200] The original 2002 Commission legislative proposal had foreseen that competent authorities would be required to ensure restorative measures were carried out also in orphan damage cases.[201] The discretion afforded to competent authorities under the ELD arguably falls short of what one might expect to be undertaken by them in these circumstances, from an environmental protection perspective. Accordingly, the ELD leaves open the possibility of environmental damage not being rectified in these circumstances. Competent authorities have no obligation to ensure that a contaminated site is in fact to be rehabilitated if an operator is not liable or able to pay. Such a position is difficult to reconcile with basic environmental protection principles underpinning EU environmental policy, notably attainment of a high level of environmental protection and the 'polluter pays' principle. Under the 'polluter pays' principle, it is clear that persons immediately responsible for causing damage (operators or intervening third parties) should bear, in the first instance, legal duty for clean-up operations. However, where such persons for a particular reason under the ELD do not have legal responsibility, such as on account of absence of fault or a failure to be identified by competent authorities, it is not evident that the rest of society should be exonerated from ensuring rehabilitation of affected sites under 'polluter pays'. In some, albeit indirect, sense, society does bear a degree of (residual) responsibility in having legitimised the practice of occupational activities known to bear certain environmental risks. Viewed realistically, the 'polluter pays' principle involves a chain of responsibility, as opposed to focusing singularly on the particular persons most directly responsible for environmental damage.

Regrettably, the ELD does not reflect the fact that society in general, in addition to individual operators, bears residual responsibility for consequences of environmental damage. A 'chain of responsibility' approach would have required competent authorities to ensure that, where the immediate polluter is unable to pay for the costs of preventive or remedial action, affected sites would in any event be subject to effective environmental protection measures, as appropriate, in order for baseline conditions to be retained or regained as far as possible. As mentioned earlier,[202] the Commission's original legislative proposal for an environmental liability instrument in 2002 did contain a clear legal requirement for member states to ensure that requisite preventive or restorative measures were carried out, irrespective of whether or not a particular operator is found liable and is able to pay for the restorative costs involved.

12.3.4 Cross-border liability scenarios

As would be expected in a supranational instrument of its kind, the ELD contains provisions relevant to scenarios of threatened and actual environmental damage affecting more than one member state in addition to ones located within a single state. Article 15 ELD lays down a general duty on member states to co-operate with one another with a view to ensuring that preventive and/or remedial action is taken in the event of trans-boundary environmental damage occurring, including the requirement to provide information to affected member states.[203] In addition, under this provision member states are entitled to recover costs incurred by them in relation to preventive or remedial measures taken in respect of damage occurring within their borders but not caused within them. In such instances, member states must adhere to the procedural and other requirements set out in respect of recovery of costs under the directive.[204]

The ELD clarifies that its provisions are without prejudice to the existing EU rules on conflicts of laws, namely questions concerning the determination of which member state law on non-contractual obligations is to apply in the event of trans-boundary environmental damage scenarios.[205] The EU legislative rules on jurisdiction in relation to cases of trans-boundary environmental damage, as currently principally contained in the 'Rome II' Regulation,[206] stipulate that the relevant EU member state law relating to non-contractual obligations arising out of trans-boundary environmental damage[207] or damage sustained by persons or property as a result of such (environmental) damage shall be the law of the member state in which the damage occurs (*lex loci damni*) unless the person seeking compensation for damage opts to base their claim on the law of the member state in which the event giving rise to damage occurred (*lex loci actus*). The Union's conflict of laws rules reflect a long-standing preference within most European states to construct a jurisdictional formula as favourable as possible to the victim of cross-border tortious damage, a stance which also serves to complement the 'polluter pays' principle.[208]

12.4 Implementation of the ELD

It is fair to say that implementation of the ELD by member states has so far been a slow process, which has led to substantial delays in the directive's requirements achieving genuinely operative status. The existing Union legal framework has yet to bed down in a number of respects, with a number of terms and concepts contained in the directive yet to receive sufficient clarification either in the form of Commission guidance or definitive CJEU clarification.

12.4.1 The supervisory role of the European Commission

The ELD entered into force on 30 April 2004, with member states being granted a generous three-year period in order to transpose the terms of the directive into national law. However, as at 30 April 2007, the Commission had found that only four member states[209] had adopted transposition legislation on time, which resulted in the EU institution commencing infringement proceedings against 27 member states.[210] Ultimately, infringement litigation over transposition failings led to seven judgments from the CJEU against defaulting member states in 2008–9.[211] The Commission has also recently commenced infringement action against one member state for failing to apply the ELD's remediation requirements in respect of damage caused by an operator of a steel plant.[212]

Full and correct transposition of the ELD is particularly important from a law enforcement perspective, because otherwise it will have limited legal effects at national level. Notably, in the absence of national legislation designed to transpose the ELD's provisions into domestic law of the member states, the obligations contained in the ELD may not be enforced in the national courts directly (under the EU legal doctrine of direct effect) against those operators who are private persons.[213] The position is different for publicly owned entities and other entities deemed to be 'emanations of the state' in the terminology of the CJEU.[214] Moreover, under the CJEU's current jurisprudence on the doctrine of indirect effect of directives, as discussed in Chapter 6, it appears doubtful whether a competent authority may act on the basis that existing national legislation on environmental civil liability should be interpreted in line with the ELD's requirements, where this leads to the imposition or aggravation of liability of operators.[215] In any event, detailed national implementing measures are required to crystallise the ELD powers and responsibilities of competent authorities, the entities envisaged and required to be the principal agents of law enforcement under the ELD's regime. Furthermore, it is doubtful whether NGEOs would be able to harness the state liability doctrine as developed by the CJEU[216] (and discussed in Chapter 7) in order to assist in the enforcement of the ELD. Given that one of the three central requirements for a successful state liability action requires existence of a breach of EU law specifically intended to confer rights on individuals, it is doubtful whether this would be applicable in the context of the ELD, which is deliberately designed to focus on environmental interests as opposed to individual rights protection. This is reflected by the fact that monetary compensation in respect of personal loss or damage is excluded from the ELD's remit, and the directive does not confer procedural rights to individuals to enforce the liability provisions before national courts or tribunals.[217]

In 2010 the Commission issued a report on the implementation of the directive as required by the ELD.[218] Specifically, Article 14(2) ELD requires the Commission to present a report on the effectiveness of the directive in terms of actual remediation of environmental damage as well as on the issue of liability insurance. The Commission issued a single report addressing both elements. Its findings on financial security have already been addressed above and need not be repeated here. The report considered that the belated and slow rate of transposition had resulted in only a limited number of environmental liability cases being processed at national level, some 16 completed by the beginning of 2010 with 50 in total (including ongoing litigation).[219] The activities involved were (unsurprisingly) almost exclusively related to Annex III activities falling mainly under the (former) IPPC Directive 2008/1,[220] waste management operations and dangerous products (chemicals) sector. Regrettably, member states were not obliged under the ELD to provide data for the purposes of the report, with information supplied on a voluntary basis from only half of the member states.

The Commission extrapolated from the available information some tentative findings. Specifically, it was apparent that only a limited number of reported liability cases concerned protected species and natural habitats. This may have some relation to the fact that competent authorities providing data to the Commission considered that amongst the most challenging legal issues were the complex technical requirements concerning economic evaluation of damaged resources and services as well as environmental remediation methods, in addition to the lack of binding parameters regarding certain key concepts in the directive such as 'significant damage'. Only some member states were reported to have developed guidelines on valuation as well as procedures and manuals on risk assessments. The Commission has sought to build on this emerging experience and expertise. For the purpose of assisting implementation of the Annex II criteria, the Commission funded a research project REMEDE (Resource Equivalency Methods for Assessing Environmental Damage in the EU)[221] on economic evaluation methodologies for estimating remediation costs. In addition, it has established stakeholder contacts for the purposes of information exchange (including notably a standing ELD government experts group), as well as the publication of an ELD training manual and information sheets, information concerning methodologies for identifying baseline conditions of biodiversity used in member states in the event of damage to protected species and/or habitats and a number of research studies relating to implementation.[222] The Commission also found in its report that knowledge of ELD obligations amongst the business sector (including the Annex III sector) was generally low, in particular with respect to small and medium-sized enterprises (SMEs). On the other hand, more encouragingly it also acknowledged that those operators found to be aware of ELD obligations tended to set up a mix of environmental insurance arrangements.

Another theme to emerge from the Commission report was the fact that member states' transposition of the ELD had resulted in a wide divergence on a number of key provisions, where member states had chosen differing implementing options available. A notable example related to the ELD provisions concerning the 'permit defence' and 'state of the art' defence.[223] Whereas some (under half) member states determined to allow both defences,[224] others (under half) decided not to allow them at all,[225] with others allowing one or the other defence.[226] On multi-party causation, most but not all member states decided to opt for a system of joint and several liability, with others[227] selecting a liability model based on proportionate responsibility. Only eight member states decided to introduce systems of mandatory financial security,[228] the rest choosing to opt for voluntary insurance for operators. Several member states took advantage of the ELD's option to exempt sewage sludge spreading from the scope of the directive.[229] Some member states decided to implement stricter standards than those envisaged in the ELD, such as widening the personal[230] and material[231] scope of the directive.

The 2010 Commission report concluded that it had received insufficient data to make any definitive appraisal on the effectiveness of the ELD. Instead, it considered that the appropriate stage to consider this issue would be in the context of the Commission's review and report on experience of the ELD foreseen in Article 18 of the directive. Under Article 18(1) member states are obliged to report to the Commission on their experiences gained with respect to the operation of the directive by 20 April 2013, with the Commission being required under Article 18(2) to submit a report by 30 April 2014. As already mentioned, the Commission's report has been delayed and is not expected before the end of 2014.

Useful insights have been gleaned, though, already in relation to the application of the ELD in the form of a 2013 study[232] sponsored by the Commission. The ELD implementation study, which surveyed the implementation and experience of application of the directive in 16 EU member states, notes a number of challenges and recommendations concerning the ELD's operation at national level. Given the wide range of matters relating to liability devolved by the directive, the study comments that the result of implementation to date is 'a patchwork of liability systems for environmental damage across the EU', rendering the directive far from the status of a harmonising legislative instrument.[233] Diversity of approach as regards the implementation of EU directives is neither unusual nor necessarily undesirable, bearing in mind in particular the EU's constitutional principle of subsidiarity[234] and the fact that the EU treaty system foresees choice for member states over form and method of implementing directives' requirements.[235] However, it does appear from the study that the *degree* of discretion provided to member states in relation to a wide range of the directive's legal requirements and options has raised a number of unanswered questions and problems. In a number of respects, a pall of legal uncertainty hangs over certain terms of the ELD, making it more challenging for competent authorities to be able to rely upon its requirements. For instance, the study notes that a number of member state authorities appear unsure as to the determination of the threshold of 'significance' of damage required for the application of the ELD; there appears to be widely differing understandings of the term in general and in particular of the definition of water and biodiversity damage.[236] Another example is that member states appear split as to whether the ELD's defences in Article 8(3)–(4) (i.e. 'permit' and 'state of the art' defences) exonerate an operator from liability or solely for the legal costs of prevention and remediation.[237] The study recommends that EU-wide guidance be issued on these and other areas lacking legal clarity.

Moreover, according to the study, application of the ELD appears fractured in a number of respects. A few notable examples of its findings may be cited here. Some member states, for instance, have taken advantage of the possibility to extend liability beyond that prescribed by the directive or to restrict its application by utilising optional exceptions (notably, the 'permit' and 'state of the art' defences). Experience appears to indicate that the material scope of strict liability of the ELD (i.e. the Annex III list) requires periodic review to ensure that its reach is sufficiently effective to meet the directive's aims.[238] The study has recommended the development of dissemination of greater levels of information, training and guidance on the operation of the ELD, including at EU level, something which the Commission has recently started to develop. In addition, the study also recommends greater focus on ensuring that sufficient resources be provided for competent authorities in respect of ELD investigation assessments in instances where the authority is unsure whether costs for these may be recouped (e.g. where the damage is deemed not to meet the threshold of 'significance' for the purposes of the ELD).[239]

12.4.2 The CJEU

To date the CJEU has had relatively little opportunity to provide clarification on key terms of the ELD, not least on account of the delays of transposition of the directive into national law by several member states. The bulk of the Court's case law so far has centred on failures to enact transposition measures in the context of infringement proceedings. However, the *Raffinerie Mediterranee* litigation,[240] involving two preliminary rulings by the CJEU in 2010 concerning an Italian environmental remediation dispute, has provided some definitive interpretation of certain legal aspects regarding the parameters of the directive. Further litigation on legal questions concerning the correct application of the directive will no doubt ensue, as competent authorities seek to enforce its obligations under the aegis of national implementing rules. Space allows but a brief overview of the factual background to the litigation as well as legal findings of the CJEU.[241]

The litigation in *Raffinerie Mediterranee* concerned a dispute about questions of legal responsibility of certain petrochemical companies for the remediation and further prevention of environmental damage perpetrated to a safe anchorage area of the Sicilian coastline in the Priolo Gargallo Region, the so-called Augusta roadstead. Practically ever since its creation in the 1960s as a major industrial hub of the petrochemical sector, the roadstead had been affected by a number of environmental pollution incidents and was ultimately designated a site of national interest for decontamination purposes. In the wake of an investigation into the condition of the surrounding land, groundwater, sea-bed and coastal sea, the municipal authorities in 2006 required petrochemical operators in the area at their expense to undertake certain remedial measures, including removal of contaminated sediment from the sea-bed up to a depth of 2 metres, reinstatement of the sea-bed as well as construction of a hydraulic dyke to ensure physical containment of the water table. Subsequently, in December 2007–February 2008 the competent authority, assessing that the existing measures were inadequate, decided to supplement them by requiring the companies to erect a dam along the shoreline adjacent to the roadstead. Throughout the process the petrochemical companies disputed the legality of the competent authority's decisions, seeking judicial review via the Italian court system in respect of the original and supplementary remedial requirements. The principal national court involved in adjudicating the dispute (Tribunale amministrativo regionale della Sicilia) referred a number of legal questions to the CJEU regarding, *inter alia*, the interpretation of the ELD.

A primary legal issue concerned whether or not the ELD applied to the particular dispute at hand from a temporal perspective. In particular, it was evident that a substantial part of the environmental damage had originated from industrial activities prior to the transposition deadline applicable to the directive (30 April 2007) and from companies no longer in existence. As noted above (section 12.3.1.5) under the first and second indents of Article 17 ELD, the directive does not apply to damage caused by an emission, event or incident taking place prior to 30 April 2007 or to damage caused after that date which derives from a specific activity that was carried out and finished before that date. Whilst deferring to the national court to apply Article 17 to the facts of the case, the CJEU confirmed that the ELD applied to damage arising from activities taking place after the transposition deadline where such damage derives from activities carried out after that date or from activities which were carried out but not completed by that date.[242] Effectively, this meant that application of the ELD could not be ruled out where similar occupational activities were ongoing in the area subsequent to the transposition deadline; the fact that certain operators no longer existed or operated in the vicinity by that date was irrelevant.

One of the key planks of the companies' defence was the submission that the competent authority had failed to respect the 'polluter pays' principle under Article 191 TFEU and rules of causation under the ELD, in not having carried out an investigation into its causes or having determined a causal link between the operators and damage. The principle of strict liability applied in this case, given that the operators' activities concerned Annex III activities under the directive, thereby eliminating the need for competent authority to prove fault, negligence or intent on the part of the operators. However, the issue of proving causation still needed to be addressed. By way of general point, the CJEU confirmed that the ELD[243] requires a competent authority, prior to imposing remedial measures, to establish in accordance with national rules on evidence which (Annex III) operator is responsible for the environmental damage.[244] In line with previous case law,[245] the CJEU though dismissed the argument that the 'polluter pays' principle enabled individuals to challenge national law, given that it only is directed at Union-level action and the EU had not adopted measures specifically covering the application of the principle at national level.[246] In addition, whilst confirming that in principle the ELD was not applicable to instances of diffuse pollution, the CJEU held that a causal link could be established easily where the relevant pollution is confined to a particular area, period of time and is attributable to a limited number of operators.[247] Given that the directive did not prescribe the rules on causation, according to the CJEU a member state's law may provide that a causal link between operator's activity and damage may be presumed, so long as this is capable of being plausibly justified, such as the fact that the operator's installation is located close to the pollution and that there is a correlation between the pollutants causing the damage and substances used by the operator in connection with his occupational activities.[248] Whilst competent authorities are not required to prove negligence, fault or intent on the part of Annex III operators, the CJEU confirmed that they must, first, carry out a prior investigation into the origins of the pollution concerned, the procedures and duration of which are to be determined under national law.[249] In response to the operators' contention that certain third parties had caused the pollution, the CJEU confirmed that Article 8(3)(a) ELD establishes that an operator will not be liable for the remediation costs where they are able to prove that a third party was responsible for the damage and where the operator had ensured that appropriate safety measures had been put in place.[250] In effect, the Court confirmed that a reversal of burden of proof in the rules of a member state relating to causation was compatible with both the ELD and the 'polluter pays' principle, in providing a mechanism to ensure that Annex III operators take on the burden of remedying pollution to which they have contributed.[251] Reversal of the onus of proof is an exceptionally important legal tool in assisting competent authorities to address scenarios involving multiple tortfeasors, given the potentially very substantial technical and financial challenges involved in being able to identify individual entrepreneurial fingerprints to specific sources of pollutants. Under the ELD, the rules of causation have not been harmonised, though, but remain a matter to be resolved at national level.[252]

In the second of the preliminary rulings the CJEU considered the legal issues arising from the competent authority's decision to institute on its own initiative and without consulting the operators concerned a significant change to the remediation measures required to be undertaken. The CJEU held, by way of a general point, that the terms of the ELD provide competent authorities with the power to alter environmental remediation measures previously adopted, and without having to receive an initial proposal from the operator.[253] Specifically, the Court's conclusion here was based on Articles 6(2) and 7(2) ELD, which establish that competent authorities have power to determine ultimately which remedial measures are to be taken with reference to the Annex II criteria set down in the directive. However, the Court also confirmed[254] that competent authorities must ensure that, prior to determining the means for effective enforcement of the directive, they hear interested parties on the matter in accordance with the EU legal principle of the right to be heard[255] and reflected to an extent in certain provisions of the ELD.[256]

12.5 Environmental civil liability and the EU: some concluding remarks

Given the relatively belated completion of the ELD's transposition by member states and awaited completion of a substantive review on its application by the European Commission, it is arguably premature to draw any definitive conclusions on the operative effectiveness of the directive. However, it is submitted that some comments may be made at this relatively early stage in the ELD's career, specifically on the way in which its legal architecture has been constructed.

In a number of respects, it is clear that the ELD employs a unique and refreshingly pragmatic approach in applying the legal concept of civil liability to an environmental context. Characteristics that one might associate traditionally with a civil liability framework applicable to environmental damage, such as the predominant role of private natural resource owners as plaintiffs in determining whether to bring a suit, the element of fault, onus of proof on plaintiff, as well as focus on monetary compensation as chief form of remedy, thankfully do not feature in the ELD. The traditional principles of civil liability, as developed over centuries within the legal systems of member states, are fundamentally ill-suited to holding polluters to account in respect of harm perpetrated by them to the environment. A traditional civil liability model does not serve to ensure that environmental protection needs are met, but instead focuses on attending to anthropogenic interests of property ownership when undermined by contamination from a third party. A property owner, whose land is subject to environmental damage contrary to their civil law rights, may or may not decide to use a monetary compensation award to reinstate the environment or for a different non-environmental objective. Moreover, orthodox civil law principles place the responsibility of proving legal elements of culpability firmly on the shoulders of the victim property owner, such as causation of damage as well as fault on the part of a defendant which may be technically difficult to prove. In addition, a private plaintiff may also bear the risk of shouldering the legal costs of the defendant as well as their own in the event of losing a civil legal action.

The ELD adopts a radically different approach to the issue of civil liability. In particular, the directive's remedies of preventive and remedial action are targeted at ensuring that actual or threatened environmental damage is rectified. Accordingly the remedies envisaged in the ELD are ends-oriented; it avoids relying on other types of sanctions or penalty mechanisms commonly found in member state civil or even administrative law that may not achieve environmental protection goals (e.g. monetary compensation, cease and desist orders, fines and/or emissions charges).[257] The ELD focuses on tending to the needs of the environment as victim, as opposed to addressing damage to anthropogenic interests. A central role is allocated to competent authorities in enforcing the requirements of the ELD; the traditional reliance on the private plaintiff as principal source for the prosecution of civil litigation does not feature.

These aspects of the ELD are to be welcomed, as they lend a far greater level of credibility to its environmental protection aims being achieved in practice. As far as remedies are concerned, the directive is wholly justified in requiring operators to take action to prevent harm occurring and/or to restore damaged sites as far as possible to the environmental conditions they were subject to prior to the occurrence of damage. Notably, an award of monetary compensation alone to a private plaintiff might be inadequate to attain this task and/or might be directed to other non-environmental purposes. The pivotal role assigned to competent authorities as principal enforcers of the ELD's requirements is justified for a number of reasons. Competent authorities are far better placed than private persons to secure and assess information relating to environmental damage. It is clear that public authorities usually have greater legal,[258] administrative and financial[259] resources as well as specialist knowledge and experience in this regard. In addition, the motivations of competent authorities may be expected to be usually in closer alignment with environmental protection aims than several private litigants seeking redress in respect of damage to their real property interests caused by a (neighbouring) operator of a particular occupational activity. For whilst such a private plaintiff's aim may well be principally to secure financial recompense for damage sustained to their assets,[260] a competent authority's remit is focused on serving the common weal relating to the entire site area affected by actual or threatened environmental damage.

The central involvement of public authorities in enforcing the directive's liability provisions introduces a significant element of public law-type obligations and arrangements into the overall legal framework. As a consequence, the ELD should arguably be described as establishing a set of liability rules based on modern administrative legal principles and practice as opposed to classical principles emanating from the law of civil obligations.[261] The ELD also harnesses the participation of civil society in relation to enforcing its terms, namely vesting private entities such as NGEOs with powers to request intervention by competent authorities as well as subject a refusal to intervene to an independent review process.[262]

Admittedly, though, the ELD does have a number of shortcomings, as is evident from the earlier overview in this chapter of its contents. For instance, the legislative instrument does not require operators to make provision for any specific type or level of financial cover in the event of an environmental incident. Article 14(2) ELD required financial security to be subject to a review by the Commission. The Commission's 2010 report on this issue concluded, though, that more time was required to assess the development of the insurance market in relation to Annex III activities, effectively kicking the can down the road for an undefined period. The Commission's report contrasts with its earlier bolder ambitions for this area, having noted in its Explanatory Memorandum to its 2002 draft proposal for a liability directive that its own research had indicated that clean-up liability is already insurable within the EU and is accordingly available on the open market.[263] It had intimated that it was not minded to introduce compulsory insurance cover based on caps, given that it was wary of setting limits too low to be consonant with 'polluter pays'. Debate remains ongoing on the issue of whether financial security should be made mandatory.[264]

A more significant shortcoming of the ELD is that it does not require competent authorities, acting on behalf of society in general, to ensure that environmental damage is remedied where operators or third parties escape liability. Arguably, this constitutes an omission on the EU's part to hold society to account where immediate polluters are excused from personal liability or cannot be found. A possible reform to the current position, with a view to ensuring as close alignment to the 'polluter pays' principle as possible, could be the introduction of a requirement for compensation fund schemes to be established by industry to cover competent authority costs for preventive and clean-up measures in the event of it being impossible to hold any individual entities legally responsible. Such models are well established in other commercial contexts, such as the motor insurance sector in the UK for which there exists a compensation fund financed by insurance companies to provide compensation in cases in which the driver at fault cannot be identified. Other problems with the ELD include the lack of guidance on evidential issues in cases of scientific uncertainty (i.e. utilisation of the precautionary principle); a misplaced assumption that existing international conventions satisfactorily address certain types of environmental damage and need not be included within the material scope of the ELD (e.g. nuclear pollution);[265] predicating land damage upon there being a risk to human health; as well as the absence of provisions on enhancing the potential complementary enforcement role of civil liability actions brought by private persons. The ELD should have also been drafted in closer co-ordination with other related EU legislation, notably those legislative instruments addressing aspects closely connected with operators requirements to prevent and/or minimise the possibility of serious environmental damage arising – in particular, the former IPPC Directive 2008/1 (now superseded by the Industrial Emissions Directive 2010/75)[266] as well as the 'Seveso' legislative instrumentation[267] on addressing and planning for industrial accidents.

Notwithstanding these points, it would appear that overall the ELD represents a positive contribution in terms of enhancing the existing legal machinery on EU environmental law enforcement. It has established a legal framework that is essentially suited to attend to environmental problems arising from instances of serious actual or threatened environmental damage in accordance with the 'polluter pays' principle. The Commission needs to ensure that the EU legislative framework is further refined as appropriate to ensure that the Union's liability regime is as effective, transparent and fair as possible, in particular taking into account problems arising in light of enforcement experience from competent authorities. Above all, though, it is primarily up to the member states to see that the ELD's provisions are implemented so as to enable the Union to achieve the ELD's environmental protection goals. The extent and manner in which member states invest appropriate levels of resources into their designated competent authorities, in terms of legal, financial, technical and personnel resources, will have a significant bearing on the degree to which the ELD will be effective in practice. The well-known saying goes that 'Rome was not built in a day'.[268] The ELD's enactment represents but the initial crucial step along a journey towards the Union finding an appropriate and workable balance of rights and responsibilities between key stakeholders (including notably operators, national governments, competent authorities and civil society) in ensuring that the threat of serious environmental damage in the EU from industry may be minimised as far as possible and, where it does occur, that environmental damage is rectified as swiftly as is feasible in accordance with the 'polluter pays' principle.

Notes

1 Directive 2004/35 on environmental liability with regard to the prevention and remedying of environmental damage (OJ 2004 L143/56) as amended by Directives 2006/21 on the management of waste from extractive industries (OJ 2006 L102/15), 2009/31 on the geological storage of carbon dioxide (OJ 2009 L140/114) and

2013/30 on safety of offshore oil and gas operations (OJ 2013 L178/66). A consolidated version is available for inspection on the EU's EUR-LEX website: http://eur-lex.europa.eu/homepage.html. For assessments on the impacts of the recent material scoping amendments introduced by Directives 2009/31 and 2013/30 see e.g. Bergsten (2011) and Gordon (2013).

2 Notably, Directive 2008/99 on the protection of the environment through criminal law (OJ 2008 L328/28) and Directive 2005/35 on Ship-source pollution and on the introduction of penalties for infringements (OJ 2005 L255/11) as amended by Directive 2009/123 (OJ 2009 L280/52).

3 For general analyses of the EU Environmental Liability Directive 2004/35, see e.g. Krämer (Ch. 2) in Betlem and Brans (eds.) (2006); Brans (2005); Hinteregger (2008); Winter *et al.* (2008); Krämer (2011), pp. 173 *et seq.*; and Bergkamp and Goldsmith (2013). For a comparative analysis of EU, national and international law on environmental civil liability, see e.g. Wilde (2013).

4 See e.g. Krämer (2011), pp. 173–5 and Daniel (2003), pp. 236–41). See also the European Commission's comments in its White Paper on Environmental Liability (COM(2000)66, p. 11).

5 As underlined in recital 13 of Directive 2004/35. Although appropriate configuration of the rules on onus of proof for liability may be of considerable assistance here.

6 For a recent analysis of public international legal developments on civil liability for environmental harm, see e.g. Boyle (2005).

7 Namely, in the sectors of marine pollution (1977 Convention on Civil Liability for Oil Pollution Resulting from Exploration for and Exploitation of Seabed Mineral Resources; 1992 Convention on Civil Liability for Oil Pollution; 1992 Convention on an International Fund for Compensation Fund of Oil Pollution Damage; 1996 Convention on Liability and Compensation for the Carriage of Hazardous and Noxious Substances by Sea; 2001 Convention on Civil Liability for Bunker Oil Damage); carriage of dangerous goods (1971 Convention on Civil Liability in the Field of Maritime Carriage of Nuclear Material; 1989 Convention on Civil Liability for Damage Caused during Carriage of Dangerous Goods by Road, Rail and Inland Navigation); the nuclear industry (1960 Paris Convention on Third Party Liability in the Field of Nuclear Energy and 1963 Brussels Supplementary Convention; 1963 Vienna Convention on Civil Liability for Nuclear Damage; 1971 Convention on Civil Liability in the Field of Maritime Carriage of Nuclear Material; 1988 Joint Protocol on the Application of the Paris and Vienna Conventions); industrial accidental pollution of transboundary rivers and lakes (2003 UNECE Kiev Protocol on Civil Liability and Compensation for Damage Caused by Transboundary Effects of Industrial Accidents on Transboundary Waters); and shipment of hazardous waste (1999 Protocol on Liability and Compensation for Damage Resulting from Transboundary Movements of Hazardous Waste). For an overview, see e.g. Daniel (2003).

8 European Treaty Series – No.150. The Convention together with an official Explanatory Report of its contents are available for inspection on the Council of Europe's website: http://conventions.coe.int

9 The Convention was opened for signature in Lugano, Switzerland, on 21 June 1993.

10 For other analyses of the Lugano Convention see e.g. Hinteregger (2008), pp. 3–5, and Sands and Peel (2013), pp. 766–70.

11 Such as in relation to marine oil pollution and civil nuclear damage. For an overview and analysis of these agreements, see e.g. Birnie, Boyle and Redgwell (2010), Chs. 7 and 9.

12 As noted in the European Commission's White Paper on Environmental Liability (COM(2000)66, p. 25).

13 Namely, Cyprus, Finland, Greece, Italy, Luxembourg, the Netherlands and Portugal. The non-EU signatories are Iceland and Liechtenstein.

14 See Art. 32(3) Lugano Convention.

15 See n. 1.
16 As elaborated in Art. 2 and Annexes I–II Lugano Convention. These include production and handling of dangerous chemical substances, certain genetically modified organism, genetically modified micro-organisms as well as the operation of waste management installations. Nuclear-related incidents and carriage of goods scenarios are excluded from the scope of the Convention (Art. 4).
17 Art. 1 Lugano Convention.
18 See ibid., Art. 2(7)–(10).
19 Ibid., Arts. 6(1) and 7(1).
20 See comments by Winter *et al.* (2008), p. 172, noting the problem in the ELD in allowing the term 'natural disasters' to include damage caused by anthropogenically driven climate change. The authors advocate making administrative agencies liable for remediation, as originally proposed by the Commission in its draft directive, given the diffuse nature of the causes of the problem. However, the member states rejected this approach on grounds of costs.
21 Arts. 8–9 Lugano Convention.
22 Ibid., Art. 10.
23 See ibid., Arts. 6(2)–(4), 7(3) and 11.
24 Ibid., Art. 17.
25 Ibid., Art. 5.
26 Ibid., Art. 12. Caps or monetary thresholds of liability are employed in certain international conventions on civil liability relating to environmental damage, such as in the context of oil pollution of the marine environment: see the 1992 Conventions on Civil Liability for Oil Pollution Damage and on an International Fund for Oil Pollution Compensation as well as 2001 Convention on Bunker Oil Damage.
27 See e.g. assessment of financial security in the European Commission's White Paper on Environmental Liability (COM(2000)66, pp. 23–4).
28 Chapter III Lugano Convention (Arts. 13–15).
29 2161 UNTS 447.
30 Art. 16 Lugano Convention.
31 Ibid., Arts. 19–24.
32 Ibid., Art. 18(1).
33 Ibid., Art. 18(2)–(3).
34 Ibid., Art.18(4).
35 See n. 1.
36 See notably the Commission's proposal for a directive on dangerous waste (OJ 1976 C194/2). Until the enactment of the EU Environmental Liability Directive 2004/35 in 2004, the Commission also attempted unsuccessfully to introduce other civil liability harmonisation measures and provisions in relation to the waste management sector: Commission proposal for a regulation on the shipment of waste (OJ 1983 C186/3); COM(89)282, Commission proposal for a directive on civil liability for damage caused by waste (4 October 1989), later amended by COM(91)219 of 23 July 1991); and COM(93)275, Amended Commission proposal for a directive on the landfill of waste (5 August 1993).
37 The European Commission's Environmental Directorate-General (DG ENV) provides information on all the relevant policy documents involved in the negotiation of a common EU liability framework: http://ec.europa.eu/environment/legal/liability/index.htm. For overviews of the early evolution of EU policy in this area, see e.g. Krämer (2003), pp. 167–70 and Hedemann-Robinson and Wilde (2000).
38 As enshrined in Art. 191(2) TFEU (formerly Art. 174(2) EC). The precautionary principle was incorporated into the EU treaty framework by virtue of the TEU 1992, whereas the other environmental principles were introduced by virtue of the Single European Act 1986.

39 COM(93)47, Commission Communication, *Green Paper on Remedying Environmental Damage*, 14 May 1993.
40 COM(2000)66, Commission Communication, *White Paper on Environmental Liability*, 9 February 2000.
41 COM(2000)66, p. 25.
42 As enshrined in Art. 5(3) TEU (ex Art. 5(2) EC) and Protocol No. 2 on the Application of the Principles of Subsidiarity and Proportionality annexed to the TEU/TFEU (OJ 2010 C83). The latter replaced the former Protocol No. 30 on Subsidiarity and Proportionality (established by the former amending Treaty of Amsterdam 1997).
43 For a different view on the adequacy of the explanations provided by the Commission in respect of subsidiarity in connection with an EU framework on environmental liability, see Farnsworth (2004).
44 COM(2000)66, p. 21 (section 4.6).
45 COM(2000)66, pp. 16–17.
46 Ibid.
47 COM(2000)66, p. 24.
48 COM(2002)17, Commission proposal for a directive on the prevention and restoration of significant environmental damage, 23 January 2002.
49 For analyses of the Commission's proposal, see e.g. Jones (2002); Lee (2002); Krämer (2003), pp. 167–9; and Farnsworth (2004).
50 COM(2002)17, pp. 16–17.
51 Krämer (2003), p. 168.
52 See Arts.4(5)–(6) and 5(5)–(6) of the proposed directive (COM(2002)17, pp. 8–9).
53 Namely, via the co-decision process under former Art. 251 EC (now superseded by the ordinary legislative process as contained in Art. 294 TFEU) which requires the joint agreement of the European Parliament and Council of the EU.
54 See n. 1.
55 The date of its publication in the EU's Official Journal, as specified in Art. 20 ELD.
56 Art. 19 ELD.
57 See e.g. the Commission's Green and White Papers on environmental liability: COM(93)47 final, Commission Communication, *Remedying Environmental Damage*, 14 May 1993 and COM(2000)66 final, Commission Communication, *White Paper on Environmental Liability*, 9 February 2000, esp. p. 15.
58 See recital 14 of the preamble to the ELD.
59 Art. 3(3) ELD.
60 See recital 14 to the preamble and Art. 3(3) ELD.
61 See recitals 3 and 14 of the ELD. See also Petersen (2009), p. 2.
62 See Art. 16(2) ELD.
63 See recital 15 to the preamble and Art. 11 ELD.
64 See also Lee (2002), p. 192.
65 Winter *et al.* (2008), p. 163.
66 For commentary on the US system on environmental liability, see e.g. Hinteregger (2008), pp. 9–12; Betlem and Brans (eds.) (2006). See also Wilde (2013).
67 Art. 193 TFEU (ex Art. 176 EC).
68 See recital 29 of the preamble and Art. 16(1) ELD.
69 See recital 2 of the preamble and Art. 1 ELD. For a general appraisal of the relationship between the 'polluter pays' principle and the ELD, see e.g. de Sadeleer (ch.4) in Betlem and Brans (eds.) (2006).
70 See recital 2 to the preamble of the ELD.
71 See in particular recital 18 to the preamble and Arts. 5–8 ELD. The definition of 'operator' is in Art. 2(6) ELD and discussed at 12.3.1.1 below.
72 See Arts. 11 and 191(2) TFEU.
73 See Art. 8(2)–(4) ELD.

74 See recital 13 of preamble and Art. 4(5) ELD.
75 Art. 191(2) TFEU.
76 Art. 3 ELD.
77 Ibid., Art. 2(7).
78 Environmental damage is defined in Art. 2(1) ELD. See section 12.3.1.2 below.
79 Art. 3(2) ELD.
80 Ibid., Art. 16(1).
81 Former Directive 96/61 on integrated pollution prevention and control (OJ 1996 L257/26) as consolidated by former Directive 2008/1 (OJ 2008 L24/8) – see para. 1 of Annex III ELD. The IPPC Directive was superseded by the Industrial Emissions Directive 2010/75 (OJ 2010 L314/17) as from 7 January 2014.
82 Paras. 2 and 12 of Annex III ELD. Sewage sludge from urban waste water treatment plants used for spreading operations in agriculture is excluded from Annex III, subject to such waste being treated to an 'approved standard' (this is not defined).
83 Paras. 3–6 of Annex III.
84 Ibid., para. 7(a)–(d).
85 Ibid., para. 8.
86 Ibid., para. 9.
87 Ibid., paras. 10–11.
88 Arts. 5–7 ELD.
89 Ibid., Art. 8.
90 Ibid. Art. 2(6).
91 Ibid., Art. 2(1)(a) defines 'damage to protected species and natural habitats' in the following terms as meaning:

> any damage that has significant adverse effects on reaching or maintaining the favourable conservation status of such habitats or species. The significance of such effects is to be assessed with reference to the baseline condition, taking account of the criteria set out in Annex I;
>
> Damage to protected species and natural habitats does not include previously identified adverse effects which result from an act by an operator which was expressly authorised by the relevant authorities in accordance with provisions implementing Article 6(3) and (4) or Article 16 of Directive 92/43/EEC or Article 9 of Directive 79/409/EEC or, in the case of habitats and species not covered by Community law, in accordance with equivalent provisions of national law on nature conservation.

The 'baseline condition' is defined in Art. 2(14) ELD as meaning 'the condition at the time of the damage of the natural resources and services that would have existed had the environmental damage not occurred, estimated on the basis of the best information available'. For an overview of the impact of the ELD in rendering EU legislative rules on nature protection (i.e. the Habitats Directive 92/43 and Wild Bird Directive 2009/147) more effective, see Petersen (2009).

92 Art. 2(1)(b) ELD defines 'water damage' the following terms as meaning:

> any damage that significantly adversely affects:
>
> (i) the ecological, chemical or quantitative status or the ecological potential, as defined in Directive 2000/60/EC, of the waters concerned, with the exception of adverse effects where Article 4(7) of that Directive applies; or
> (ii) the environmental status of the marine waters concerned, as defined in Directive 2008/56/EC, in so far as particular aspects of the environmental status of the marine environment are not already addressed through Directive 2000/60/EC.

The current definition of water damage in Art. 2(1)(b) ELD was recently amended by Directive 2013/30 on safety of offshore oil and gas operations (OJ 2013 L178/66). It should also be noted that certain exceptions apply under Art. 4 in conjunction with Annex IV ELD in relation to instances of marine environmental damage covered by specific international conventions in force in member states (see section 12.3.1.4 below).

93 Art. 2(1)(c) ELD defines 'land damage' as meaning:

> any land contamination that creates a significant risk of human health being adversely affected as a result of the direct or indirect introduction, in, on or under land, of substances, preparations, organisms or micro-organisms.

94 Art. 2(2) ELD.

95 See Krämer (Ch. 2) in Betlem and Brans (eds.) (2006), pp. 39–40; and Hinteregger (2008), pp. 14–15.

96 (1992) 32 ILM 818. Art. 2 of the 1992 UN Biodiversity Convention defines biodiversity as meaning 'the variability among living organisms from all sources, including *inter alia* terrestrial, marine or other aquatic ecosystems and the ecological complexes of which they are a part; this includes diversity within species, between species and of ecosystems'.

97 See the EP's Resolution T5–0211/2003 of 14 May 2003 (OJ 2004 C67E/186) and the ESC's Opinion of 21 June 2002 (OJ 2002 C151 E/132).

98 See Art. 2(3)(c) ELD. In any event, member states have a power under Art. 193 TFEU to adopt stricter environmental protection measures than those agreed at Union level so long as compatible with the EU founding treaty framework of the TFEU/TEU.

99 Art. 2(1)(a) ELD.

100 Ibid., Art.2(1)(b).

101 Ibid., Art. 2(1)(c). For the purposes of assessing land damage, the use of risk assessment procedures are deemed desirable in the directive to determine likely adverse effects on human health: see recital 7 of preamble to the ELD.

102 As underlined by recital 4 to the preamble of the ELD.

103 OJ 1979 L103/1. Directive 79/409 has been replaced by Directive 2009/147 (OJ 2010 L20/7).

104 OJ 1992 L206/7.

105 Art. 2(1)(a) ELD. 'Favourable conservation status' of natural habitats and species is defined in Art. 2(4)(a) and (b) ELD.

106 See ibid., second para. of Art. 2(1)(a).

107 See Annex I in conjunction with Arts. 2(1)(a) and 2(14) ELD.

108 Rather curiously this clause is housed in Art. 4 ELD which is entitled 'Exceptions'.

109 See ibid., Art. 11(2).

110 Recital 13 of the preamble to the ELD.

111 As the European Commission has noted,'[r]ecourse to the precautionary principle presupposes that potentially dangerous effects deriving from a phenomenon, product or process have been identified, and that scientific evaluation does not allow the risk to be determined with sufficient certainty' (COM(2000)1 final, Commission Communication, *The Precautionary Principle*, 2 February 2000, p. 3).

112 See e.g. COM (2000)1 final and e.g. Case C-157/96 *The Queen v Ministry of Agriculture, Fisheries and Food, Commissioners of Customs & Excise, ex parte National Farmers' Union et al.*; Case C-180/96 *UK v Commission*; Case T-199/96 *Bergaderm v Commission*; and Case T-70/99 *Alpharma Inc. v Council of the European Union*.

113 Art. 8 ELD.

114 In accordance with the CJEU's jurisprudence on the limits to member state's procedural autonomy (see Ch. 7), national rules of procedure intended implement EU legislation must be effective, proportionate and be equivalent to similar procedures applied at national level.

115 Art. 8(3)(a) ELD.
116 Ibid., Art. 8(3)(b).
117 Ibid., Art. 8(4)(a).
118 Ibid., Art. 8(4)(b).
119 Art. 3(3) TEU and Art.191(2) TFEU.
120 See Arts. 5(4) and 6(3) ELD.
121 Ibid., Art. 8(2) second para.
122 Ibid., Art. 3(1)(b).
123 Ibid., Art. 4(1)(a).
124 Ibid., Art. 4(6).
125 Ibid., Art. 4(1)(b).
126 Ibid., Art. 4(6).
127 Art. 4(2) in conjunction with Annex IV ELD. The specific conventions listed in Annex IV are: the International Convention of 27 November 1992 on Civil Liability for Oil Pollution Damage, the International Convention of 27 November 1992 on the Establishment of an International Fund for Compensation for Oil Pollution Damage, the International Convention of 23 March 2001 on Civil Liability for Bunker Oil Pollution Damage, the International Convention of 3 May 1996 on Liability and Compensation for Damage in Connection with the Carriage of Hazardous and Noxious Substances by Sea and the Convention of 10 October 1989 on Civil Liability for Damage Caused during Carriage of Dangerous Goods by Road, Rail and Inland Navigation Vessels.
128 Art. 4(4) in conjunction with Annex V ELD. The specific instruments listed in Annex V are: the Paris Convention of 29 July 1960 on Third Party Liability in the Field of Nuclear Energy and the Brussels Supplementary Convention of 31 January 1963, the Vienna Convention of 21 May 1963 on Civil Liability for Nuclear Damage, the Convention of 12 September 1997 on Supplementary Compensation for Nuclear Damage, the Joint Protocol of 21 September 1988 relating to the Application of the Vienna Convention and the Paris Convention and the Brussels Convention of 17 December 1971 relating to Civil Liability in the Field of Maritime Carriage of Nuclear Material.
129 Art. 4(3) ELD.
130 See ibid., Art. 18(3). For a general overview of the ELD and liability for damage to the marine environment see e.g. Carbone, Munari and Schiano di Pepe (2008).
131 The relevant DG ENV website cites delays in submission of member state reports and the 2014 European parliamentary elections and new round of European Commissioner appointments as reasons for the report's delay: http://ec.europa.eu/environment/legal/liability/index.htm.
132 Organised under the auspices of The Comprehensive Environmental Response, Compensation and Liability Act (CERCLA) 42 USC103. For further discussion on CERCLA and its influence on the European Commission's work, see the Explanatory Memorandum to the Commission's proposal for a directive on environmental liability (COM(2002)17).
133 Art. 17, first indent, ELD.
134 Ibid., Art. 17, second indent.
135 Ibid., Art. 17, third indent.
136 As stipulated ibid., Art. 2(1)(a)–(c).
137 See e.g. Winter *et al.* (2008), p. 169.
138 Art. 11(4) ELD.
139 Ibid.
140 Ibid., Art. 2(10).
141 Ibid., Art. 5(2).
142 Ibid., Art. 5(3)–(4).

143 See e.g. Case 68/88 *Commission v Greece (Greek Maize)* (paras. 24–5 of judgment). See also Case C-326/88 *Anklagemyndigheden v Hansen & Soen* (para. 17 of judgment) and Case C-186/98 *Criminal proceedings against M Nunes and E de Matos* (paras. 9–12 of judgment).

144 Art. 6(1), chapeau, ELD.

145 Ibid., Art. 6(1)(a).

146 Ibid., Art. 6(1)(b).

147 Ibid., Arts. 6(2)–(3) and 7(2)–(4).

148 As contained in Art. 7 in conjunction with Annex II ELD.

149 Art. 7(1) ELD.

150 s. 2 of Annex II ELD.

151 Ibid., s. 1.

152 Art. 2(14) ELD. This approach is, of course, in full alignment with standard principles applied in respect of the remediation of civil wrongs under national civil law systems.

153 See ss. 1(a) and 1.1 of Annex II ELD.

154 See ibid., ss. 1(b) and 1.2.

155 See ibid., ss. 1(c) and 1.3.

156 See ibid., s. 1.2.

157 See ibid., s. 1.3.

158 See ibid., final subpara. of s. 1.

159 Ibid., s. 2. See also recital 7 to the preamble of the ELD.

160 Art. 7(2) ELD.

161 See ibid., Art. 7(3).

162 Ibid., Art. 7(4).

163 See e.g. Case 17/74 *Transocean Marine v Commission*.

164 Art. 8(1) ELD.

165 Ibid., Art. 8(2).

166 Namely, those cited ibid., Art. 8(3)–(4).

167 COM(2002)17, at p. 9.

168 See e.g. Krämer (Ch. 2) in Betlem and Brans (eds.) (2006), p. 33.

169 For an assessment of the impact of financial provision in relation to environmental civil liability, see e.g. Ch. 11 of Wilde (2013).

170 Art. 14(1) ELD.

171 COM(2010)581 final, *Commission Report under Article 14(2) of Directive 2004/35 on Environmental Liability with Regard to the Prevention and Remedying of Environmental Damage*, 12 October 2010.

172 See ibid., s. 4 (Financial Security for ELD).

173 Directive 2006/21 on the management of waste from extractive industries and amending Directive 2004/35 (OJ 2006 L102/15), as amended.

174 Ibid., Art. 16.

175 Art. 9 ELD. See also recital 22 to the preamble of the ELD which indicates that member states might consider imposing differential levels of financial responsibilities on producers than users of products.

176 See Brans (2005), p. 96.

177 Art. 11(2) ELD. Where third parties, as opposed to the operators themselves, are directly responsible for actual or threatened environmental damage, member states are required to endow competent authorities with powers to require such parties to carry out necessary preventive or remedial measures (Art. 11(3) ELD).

178 See e.g. Case C-365/97 *Commission v Italy*.

179 Recommendation 2001/311 providing for minimum criteria for environmental inspections in the member states (OJ 2001 L118/41).

180 See paras. 58 and 63(cc) of Decision No. 1386/2013/EU of the European Parliament and of the Council of 20 November 2013 on a General Union Environment Action Programme to 2020 'Living Well, within the Limits of our Planet' (OJ 2013 L354/171).

181 Art. 11(2) ELD.
182 Ibid., Art. 11(2) final sentence. See also specific powers of competent authorities to require disclosure of information from operators: ibid., Arts. 5(1), 5(3)(a), 6(1), 6(2)(a).
183 Ibid., Art. 5(1).
184 Ibid., Art. 5(4).
185 Ibid., Art. 5(3)(a).
186 Ibid., Art. 5(2).
187 Ibid., Art. 5(3)(b)–(c).
188 Ibid., Art. 5(3)(d).
189 Ibid., Art. 11(3).
190 Ibid., Art. 5(4), final sentence.
191 Ibid., Art. 6(1), chapeau.
192 Ibid., Arts. 6(1)(a)–(b) and 7.
193 Ibid., Art. 6(3).
194 Ibid., Art. 6(2)(a).
195 Ibid., Art. 6(2)(b), which states that the competent authority may 'take, require the operator to take or give instructions to the operator concerning all practicable steps to immediately control, contain, remove or otherwise manage the relevant contaminants and/or any other damage factors in order to limit or to prevent further environmental damage and adverse effect on human health, or further impairment of services'.
196 Ibid., Art. 6(2)(c).
197 Ibid., Art. 6(2)(e).
198 Ibid., Art. 11(3).
199 As set out in Annex II ELD.
200 See Arts. 5(4), 6(3) and 11(3) ELD.
201 See Art. 5(2) of Commission proposal for a directive on environmental liability with regard to the prevention and remediation of damage (OJ 2002 C151 pE/132). See also note by Krämer in Betlem and Brans (eds.) (2006), p. 37.
202 See section 14.2 above.
203 See Art.15(1)–(2) ELD.
204 Ibid., Art.15(3).
205 See ibid., recital 10 of the preamble and Art. 3(2).
206 See recitals 24–5 of the preamble in conjunction with Arts. 4 and 7 of Regulation 864/2007 on the law applicable to non-contractual obligations (Rome II) (OJ 2007 L199/40). See also Regulation 44/2001 on jurisdiction and the recognition and enforcement of judgments in civil and commercial matters (OJ 2001 L12/1) as amended.
207 'Environmental damage' is defined broadly in recital 24 of the preamble to the Rome II Regulation 864/2007(OJ 2001 L12/1) as meaning 'adverse change in a natural resource, such as water land or air, impairment of a function performed by that resource for the benefit of another natural resource or the public, or the impairment of the variability among living organisms'.
208 See recital 25 to the Rome II Regulation 864/2007(OJ 2001 L12/1). For commentary on conflicts of law issues arising in relation to transboundary environmental damage, see e.g. Posch (2008).
209 Italy, Lithuania, Latvia and Hungary.
210 See p. 3 of COM(2010)581. See also Commission RAPID press release IP/08/1025, Brussels, 26 June 2008.
211 Namely, CJEU judgments in Case C-328/08 *Commission v Finland*, Case C-330/08 *Commission v France*, Case C-331/08 *Commission v Luxembourg*, Case C-368/08 *Commission v Greece*, Case C-402/08 *Commission v Slovenia*, Case C-417/08 *Commission v UK* and Case C-422/08 *Commission v Austria*. Infringement proceedings against Ireland

reached the stage of being referred to the CJEU but then subsequently withdrawn (Case C-418/08).

212 Commission RAPID Press release IP/13/866 and MEMO/13/820, Brussels, 26 September 2013. The case concerns the ILVA steel plant in Taranto, Italy.

213 Directives may not be invoked directly against private persons under the EUJ's doctrine of direct effect of EU law, either by other private persons (e.g. Case 152/84 *Marshall (1)*) or by public authorities (Case 14/86 *Pretura di Salo*). The position is admittedly different in respect of public sector operators or those operators deemed to be an emanation of the state (see e.g. Case C-188/89 *Foster*).

214 See e.g. Case C-188/89 *Foster.*

215 See e.g. Case C-168/95 *Arcaro*. At the time of writing, the law on indirect effect leaves substantial doubt as to whether or not the EUJ's case law on limiting indirect effect of directives applies solely to a criminal liability context. See Ch. 6 for details of this particular legal debate.

216 See e.g. Joined Cases C-6 and 9/90 *Francovich.*

217 On the other hand, it is also possible to construe the ELD in a different and broader perspective, namely that it crystallises the EU's commitment of enhancing fundamental rights of citizens: see Art. 37 of the Charter of Fundamental Rights of the Union (OJ 2010 C83/02) which commits the Union, *inter alia*, to attain a high level of environmental protection and improvement to environmental quality in accordance with the principle of sustainable development.

218 COM(2010)581 final, *Commission Report under Article 14(2) of Directive 2004/35 on Environmental Liability with Regard to the Prevention and Remedying of Environmental Damage*, 12 October 2010.

219 See ibid., section 2.3.

220 OJ 2008 L24/8.

221 The REMEDE project studies are available for inspection at: www.envliability.eu/index.htm. In particular, see on the website J. Lipton *et al.*, *Toolkit for Performing Resource Equivalency Analysis to Assess and Scale Environmental Damage* (2008). For general comments on REMEDE see e.g. Aiking, Brans and Ozdeiroglu (2010).

222 Access to these various sources of information is available on the relevant DG ENV website of the Commission: http://ec.europa.eu/environment/legal/liability/index.htm.

223 See Art. 8(4) ELD.

224 Belgium (at regional level), Cyprus, Czech Republic, Estonia (except GMOs), Greece, Italy, Latvia (except GMOs), Malta, Portugal, Slovakia, Spain and the UK (except GMOs in Scotland and Wales). Sweden decided instead to admit both defences as mitigating factors in the decision process.

225 Austria, Belgium (at federal level), Bulgaria, Germany, Hungary, Ireland, the Netherlands, Poland, Romania and Slovenia.

226 Denmark, Finland, and Lithuania decided to allow the 'permit defence', whilst France opted to allow the 'state of the art' defence.

227 Denmark, Finland, France, Slovakia and Slovenia.

228 Bulgaria, Portugal, Spain, Greece, Hungary, Slovakia, Czech Republic and Romania. For an overview of the Spanish system see e.g. Pedraza, de Smedt and Faure (2012).

229 Bulgaria, France, Latvia, Malta, Portugal, Romania, Slovakia, Slovenia and UK.

230 All but one member state decided to apply an extended definition of 'operator', with some member states providing the definition with a particularly broad scope (Estonia, Finland, Hungary, Lithuania, Poland and Sweden).

231 14 member states decided to apply an extended scope to the definition of species and habitats under Art. 2(3) ELD: Austria, Belgium, Cyprus, Czech Republic, Estonia, Greece, Hungary, Latvia, Lithuania, Poland, Portugal, Spain, Sweden and UK. Some member states chose to subject certain activities not mentioned in Annex III ELD

to the strict liability regime: Belgium, Denmark, Finland, Greece, Hungary, Latvia, Lithuania, the Netherlands and Sweden.

232 Bio Intelligence Service, Stephens & Bolton LLP, *Implementation Challenges and Obstacles of the Environmental Liability Directive – Final Report*, 16 May 2013, accessible on the Commission's DG ENV website: http://ec.europa.eu/en/legal/liability/index.htm.

233 Ibid., pp. 6 and 21.

234 Art. 5(3) TEU.

235 Art. 288(3) TFEU.

236 Bio Intelligence Service, Stephens & Bolton LLP, *Implementation Challenges and Obstacles of the Environmental Liability Directive – Final Report*, 16 May 2013, esp. pp. 8 and 59–60.

237 Ibid., p. 62.

238 The study cites the example of the France deciding to legislate in 2012 to ensure that underground oil pipelines would be covered by its implementation of the ELD strict liability regime in the wake of a spill in the *Coussuls de Crau* nature reserve. In order to avoid having to prove the operator's fault or negligence, the French authorities decide to apply pre-existing legislation that only covered the aquatic environs. See ibid., pp. 98–9.

239 Ibid., p. 144.

240 Case C-378/08 *Raffinerie Mediterranee (ERG) SpA et al. v Ministero dello Sviluppo economico et al.* and Joined Cases C-379–80/08 *Raffinerie Mediterranee (ERG) SpA et al. v Ministero dello Sviluppo economico et al.*

241 For commentaries on the *Raffinerie* litigation see e.g. Vogleman (2010) and Reid (2010).

242 Case C-378/08 (paras. 40–1 of judgment).

243 By virtue of recital 13 of the preamble in conjunction with Arts. 4(5) and 11(2) ELD.

244 Case C-378/08 (paras. 54 and 64 of judgment).

245 E.g. Case C-379/92 *Peralta* (paras. 57–8 of judgment).

246 Case C-378/08 (para. 46 of judgment).

247 Ibid. (para. 54 of judgment).

248 Ibid. (paras. 57 and 70 of judgment).

249 Ibid. (para. 65 of judgment).

250 Ibid. (para. 67 of judgment).

251 See Case C-293/97 *Standley et al.* (para. 51 of judgment).

252 Noted by Reid (2010), p. 90.

253 Joined Cases C-379–80/08 (paras. 48–51 of judgment).

254 (Ibid. (paras. 52–4 of judgment).

255 E.g. as confirmed by the CJEU in para. 35 of its ruling in Joined Cases C-439 and 454/05P *Land Oberösterreich and Austria v Commission*.

256 Specifically, recital 24 of the preamble and Art. 7(4) ELD.

257 Winter *et al.* (2008), p. 170.

258 E.g. through the use of investigatory powers established under public law, such as on-site inspections.

259 In terms of funding investigations and litigation.

260 See e.g. Brans (2005), p. 96.

261 See e.g. Jones (2002), p. 6 and Lee (2002), p.196.

262 Arts. 12–13 ELD.

263 COM(2002)17, p. 9.

264 See e.g. differences of approach taken by Bergkamp and Goldsmith (2013), p. 340 and Mackie (2014), p. 83.

265 See e.g. comments by Winter *et al.* (2008), p. 173; Krämer (Ch. 2) in Betlem/Brans (eds) (2006), pp. 41–2; and Brans (2005), p.107. Brans notes, for instance, that the standard approach in international civil liability instruments is to limit reinstatement measures to those of reasonable cost without this being subject to guidance, with limited recourse to complementary remediation measures and no redress for interim losses (compensatory remediation).

266 OJ 2010 L334/17.

267 Seveso III Directive 2012/18 on the control of major accident hazards involving dangerous substances, amending and subsequently repealing Council Directive 96/82/EC (OJ 2012 L197/1), which replaces the Seveso II Directive 96/82 (OJ 1997 L10/13) as from 1 June 2015.

268 See A. Tobler A, *Li Proverbe au Vilan – Die Sprichwörter des Gemeinen Mannes Altfranzözische Dichtung nach den bisher bekannten Handschriften* (Leipzig Verlag, 1895), p. 43 citing the old French version 'Rome ne fus pas faite toute en un jour' dating back to 1190 (now expressed as 'Rome ne s'est pas faite en un jour').

13 Enforcement of EU environmental law by national authorities (3)

Environmental criminal liability

Moves to promote co-operation between states on the use of criminal law as a means to enforce environmental law have only relatively recently emerged onto the international political agenda. This is not that surprising given that decision-making concerning the scope of criminalisation of personal conduct has traditionally been considered by nation states as a matter to be determined at statal rather than inter-statal level. The power of states to impose duties and sanctions on their inhabitants, including notably those under criminal law, has been traditionally viewed as a foundational element of national sovereignty. This viewpoint has also been reflected in international law in various ways, notably in the presumption that implementation of binding international standards (such as environmental protection requirements contained in treaties) within the national legal order should be a matter for each nation state. Whilst various sources of international law have been developed so as to target particular types of serious environmental crime,[1] to date key international discussions and legal developments intended to combat environmental crime have taken place predominantly within a European context.

Within Europe, as is the case internationally, transboundary dimensions to environmental crime have risen in prominence in parallel with the facilitation of increased international trade. The increased dismantling of national frontier controls under the aegis of international trade regimes, including the WTO, EU as well as other bilateral and regional free trade agreements, has made it easier for trans-boundary environmental crime to develop and more challenging for national authorities to combat in isolation. Key examples of trans-boundary environmental crime concern the illicit trade in waste, species of protected flora and fauna and ozone-depleting substances carried out in contravention of international law.[2] Such illicit trade is often extremely lucrative. For instance, in 2000 a US study[3] estimated that the global annual turnover in relation to the illegal trade in these items amounted approximately between $10–12 billion, $6–10 billion and $20–25 million respectively. The elimination of national frontier checks of goods since 1992 within the EU single market has presented particular difficulties and challenges to national law enforcement authorities in controlling illicit traffic in goods contrary to EU and international environmental protection standards. A number of studies and reports have highlighted the significant presence of cross-border environmental crime operating within the Union. For instance, inspection projects carried out by IMPEL[4] between 2004–6 into shipments of waste found that 51 per cent of the waste shipments located at various seaports and 12 per cent of waste otherwise inspected during the various phases of its management contravened EU rules.[5] A more recent IMPEL study in 2009 found that 20 per cent of waste shipments inspected as part of enforcement actions by member states was illegal.[6] Given the context, member state authorities are increasingly becoming more reliant on one another for information and assistance in detecting and prosecuting offenders who may wish and be able to move across national boundaries relatively swiftly. The frequently trans-boundary nature of environmental crime can mean that its commission and effects may appear in two or more jurisdictions, each containing different rules relating the sanctioning of illicit conduct. Studies commissioned by the Commission in connection with its work on developing EU environmental policy on crime have shown that member states have widely varying criminal sanctions for similar environmental offences.[7] Not only does weak criminal sanctioning offer little or no deterrence against intentional or negligent acts of environmental damage, it also constitutes a perverse economic advantage for commercial operators competing for business within the single market.

Notwithstanding widespread awareness of the prominent problem of international environmental criminal activities, Union member state governments have until very recently been reluctant to accept the idea that EU environmental policy should encompass measures to combat trans-boundary environmental crime. The development of a criminal policy dimension to EU environmental law and policy has been a protracted and tortuous affair, characterised by a series of struggles over the issue of legal competence. For several years after the entry into force of the treaties founding the EU, namely the original three European Community treaties,[8] the Union's member states as well its supranational political institutions appeared to subscribe to the view that the area of criminal policy remained a matter essentially outside the remit of EU law. It was only really with the introduction of intergovernmental framework for the development of agreements between member states on promoting certain aspects of police and judicial co-operation in criminal matters by virtue of the 1992 Treaty on European Union (TEU) that member states began to work towards developing legal instrumentation at EU level for the purpose of crafting a trans-boundary strategy on combating environmental criminal activity. At the same time member states remained for the most part fiercely resistant to any genuinely supranational initiative put forward by the European Commission under the aegis of the former first pillar of the EU's legal framework, until the CJEU decided in 2005 in its *Environmental Crimes* ruling[9] that the (former) European Community enjoyed implied competence under the auspices of the provisions of the European Community (EC) Treaty on a common environmental policy to enact measures to combat environmental crime. Once the legal matter of competence had been settled by the Court of Justice of the European Union (CJEU), the member states effectively relented to the Commission's proposition for EU supranational legislation on environmental crime under the first pillar. This led eventually to the adoption of EU Directive 2008/99 on the protection of the environment through criminal law[10] (PECL Directive), containing, *inter alia*, certain minimum requirements regarding the prosecution of environmental offences at national level. It entered into force on 26 December 2010. With the subsequent restructuring of the EU's founding treaties by virtue of the adoption of the 2007 Lisbon Treaty, the EU's legal framework now contains specific provisions enabling the possibility of harmonisation measures to be adopted in the field of criminal policy (as contained in Article 83 of the Treaty on the Functioning of the European Union (TFEU)). Notwithstanding these legal developments, intra-EU co-operation in the field of criminal policy, including environmental crime, remains a politically sensitive area, where the EU's political evolution rubs against the raw nerve of national sovereignty.

This chapter will focus on the impact of various recent political and legal developments that have occurred within the EU generally to promote greater and more formal co-operation between its member states in relation to addressing instances of serious environmental criminal conduct causing actual and potential grave harm to the environment and/or to human, animal and plant health. By way of initial background, reference is first made to the influence of the Council of Europe in stimulating regional co-operation and debate in this area before the remainder of the chapter turns to consider how the EU has developed its remit for and involvement in relation to combating environmental crime.

13.1 1998 Council of Europe Convention on the Protection of the Environment through Criminal Law (PECL Convention)

The Council of Europe Convention on the Protection of the Environment through Criminal Law (CPECL),[11] signed on 9 September 1998, was the first significant attempt at a European level to secure regional co-operation over the combating of environmental crime.[12] The objective of CPECL is both broad and bold in scope, namely the pursuit of a common criminal policy aimed at the protection of the environment.[13] The Convention does not simply focus on enhancing international co-operation with respect to the prosecution of environmental offences of a directly cross-border nature, where law enforcement agencies and jurisdictions of more than one State are involved. It also contains a number of provisions intended to achieve amongst Council of Europe (CoE) member states a common understanding on what would be expected in principle to be a minimum to constitute a criminal offence in respect of conduct perpetrating damage to the environment. As the end of July 2014, only 14 CoE member states had signed CPECL, 13 of which are EU members.[14] CPECL has not yet entered into force, given that only one state (Estonia) has so far ratified the Convention;[15] its entry into force requires at least three states to have ratified or signed without reservation as to subsequent internal ratification, acceptance or approval.[16]

The core structure of CPECL is founded upon two main sections, namely Sections II[17] and III,[18] which seek to address matters pertaining to the prosecution of domestic as well as cross-border environmental crime respectively.[19] Section II contains a range of provisions obliging contracting parties to take a series of measures at national level. These may be divided roughly into different groups, namely provisions concerning: the definition of certain environmental offences; corporate liability; sanctions to be imposed on offenders; and provisions addressing domestic jurisdictional and institutional issues. Each of these groups of provisions will be examined briefly in turn.

An integral part of CPECL is the aim to agree upon a minimum common core of environmental offences applicable within the jurisdictions of the contracting parties. Articles 2–4 of the Convention provide for common definitions for a series of environmental offences. Articles 2–3 identify the most serious of offences causing or very likely to cause damage to the environment and/or human health, and require parties to outlaw them under criminal law. Whereas Article 2 addresses crimes committed intentionally, Article 3 focuses on negligence. The key provision is Article 2 which stipulates:

Article 2 – Intentional offences

1. Each Party shall adopt such appropriate measures as may be necessary to establish as criminal offences under its domestic law:

   a) the discharge, emission or introduction of a quantity of substances or ionising radiation into air, soil or water which:
      i) causes death or serious injury to any person, or
      ii) creates a significant risk of causing death or serious injury to any person;

   b) the unlawful discharge, emission or introduction of a quantity of substances or ionising radiation into air, soil or water which causes or is likely to cause their lasting deterioration or death or serious injury to any person or substantial damage to protected monuments, other protected objects, property, animals or plants;

   c) the unlawful disposal, treatment, storage, transport, export or import of hazardous waste which causes or is likely to cause death or serious injury to any person or substantial damage to the quality of air, soil, water, animals or plants;

   d) the unlawful operation of a plant in which a dangerous activity is carried out and which causes or is likely to cause death or serious injury to any person or substantial damage to the quality of air, soil, water, animals or plants;

   e) the unlawful manufacture, treatment, storage, use, transport, export or import of nuclear materials or other hazardous radioactive substances which causes or is likely to cause death or serious injury to any person or substantial damage to the quality of air, soil, water, animals or plants, when committed intentionally.

2. Each Party shall adopt such appropriate measures as may be necessary to establish as criminal offences under its domestic law aiding or abetting the commission of any of the offences established in accordance with paragraph 1 of this article.

Article 3 CPECL requires parties in principle to criminalise the offences listed in Article 2(1) where committed with negligence. However, this requirement is subject to a number of caveats. First, parties may decide to restrict criminal liability to covering acts committed with 'gross negligence'.[20] Secondly, by virtue of Article 3(3) parties may opt out of criminalising negligence in respect of certain offences.[21]

Articles 2–3 address offences actually or likely to cause damage to the environment or human health and are considered by the Convention to constitute the most serious type of environmental crime (so-called concrete offences). By way of contrast, seven offences defined in Article 4 are considered by the Convention to be less serious in nature in that they involve infringements of environmental law, belonging to a different group of offences (so-called abstract endangerment offences).[22]

Contracting parties are required to provide for sanctions in respect of these particular offences, whether committed intentionally or negligently, although they need not necessarily subject them to the criminal law. Specifically Article 4 refers to certain types of 'unlawful'[23] conduct as belonging to this category, namely the illicit: discharge, emission or introduction of a quantity of substances or ionising radiation into environmental media;[24] causing of noise;[25] disposal, treatment, storage, transport, export or import of waste;[26] operation of plant;[27] manufacture, treatment, use, transport, export or import of radioactive substances or hazardous chemicals;[28] causing of changes detrimental to natural components of a national park, nature reserve, water conservation area or other protected areas;[29] or possession, taking, damaging, killing or trading of or in protected wild flora and fauna species.[30]

A number of features stand out for comment in relation to these particular provisions on the common definition of offences. First and foremost, it is important to note that all offences cited in Articles 2–4 CPECL bar one[31] are dependent upon the offender having perpetrated a breach of domestic law when committing a particular act. Specifically, the vast majority of offences are defined on the basis of an offender acting on an 'unlawful' basis. Consequently, no liability will incurred if a person is carrying out an activity authorised by law or administrative decision of a competent authority.[32] Given that the definition of 'unlawful' depends ultimately upon the parameters set by national rules, this represents a serious qualification to the commonality of standards underpinning the definition of offences. A number of key elements to the definition of offences listed in the Convention are not defined, and therefore effectively defer to contracting parties on how to implement them in practice. This risks a distorted and differentiated application of the Convention amongst parties on various points of law, such as regarding the issue of what constitutes a 'dangerous activity' and 'substantial damage' for the purposes of the offence referred to in Article 2(1)(d) CPECL. It is also noteworthy that there is a strong anthropocentric streak in the way in which the Convention categorises the seriousness of offences. For instance, the only autonomous offence, i.e. in respect of which it is no defence for a person to rely upon the existence of authorisation under national law legitimising their activities, is the one defined in

Article 2(1)(a) CPECL. This provision requires parties to criminalise the release of substances or radiation causing, or that risk causing, human death or serious injury. In contrast, under Article 4 CPECL parties are not required to criminalise illegal trade in wildlife. In addition, neither are they required to criminalise conduct infringing domestic law causing detrimental changes to wildlife habitats where their activities are not specifically caught by Articles 2–3. Accordingly, illicit development projects and hunting activities that interfere with protected nature sites are not required by CPECL to face criminal sanction.

Another notable feature of the manner in which offences are addressed under Articles 2–4 CPECL is that the Convention does not adopt a strong preventive approach to tackling conduct posing a risk to the environment. The way that offences are constructed under the Convention has meant that the factor of deterrence is applied in a relatively modest fashion. Specifically, the Convention rejects the application of a strict liability approach, integrating the element of mental culpability within all of the offences in Articles 2–4 (i.e. either intention or negligence).[33] In addition, it is arguable that CPECL tends to favour a reactive use of criminal law. The only offences covered in Articles 2–3 that are required to be criminalised are based on actual harm having been caused or evidence being present of the defendant's conduct in question having presented a risk of serious harm. Admittedly, the requirement to criminalise based on evidence of a risk of serious harm reflects a precautionary approach to liability,[34] but this is tempered by the fact that the Convention's provisions appear to require proof by the prosecuting authorities that a very high level of threat is being or has been posed by the defendant's illicit activities. Moreover, the conduct covered by Article 4 CPECL, notwithstanding recognition of it posing an unacceptably high risk to the environment, is not required under the Convention to be criminalised, and may instead be subject to other types of sanctions such as administrative penalties.

With regard to the issue of scope of personal liability, CPECL adopts a very flexible as well as mild approach concerning the responsibility of corporations. Article 9(1) CPECL requires that parties are to adopt either criminal or administrative sanctions or measures on legal persons on whose behalf offences under Articles 2 or 3 have been committed. Accordingly, not only does the Convention avoid imposing mandatory criminal liability on legal persons, it envisages that the existence of corporate liability is to be dependent upon the existence of proof of culpability of an individual. The idea of imposing a stricter form of liability at the corporate level as compared with individual level is ruled out. Moreover, there is no provision for corporate responsibility, criminal or otherwise, in respect of offences covered in Article 4. By way of a declaration, parties are entitled to opt out either fully or partially of the general obligation in Article 9(1) to impose sanctions on corporations.[35] The Convention does confirm, though, that the existence of corporate liability may not be used as a defence against the prosecution of natural persons under criminal law.[36]

As far as the general subject of sanctions is concerned, CPECL again is short on detail and generous in terms of granting discretion to contracting parties. With respect to the most serious offences covered by Articles 2–3, the Convention lays down a general and vague requirement that these are to be punished by criminal sanctions which take into account their serious nature. No specific punitive measures must be imposed, but instead parties are required to make imprisonment and pecuniary sanctions 'available' as possible outcomes. The Convention allows parties to determine whether they are to include confiscation measures[37] or reinstatement[38] as supplementary sanctions.

Section II of the Convention also includes various provisions seeking to improve the management of casework within the territories of the contracting parties. Article 5 CPECL lays down the circumstances whereby parties are required in principle to accept jurisdiction over criminal offences. The provision adopts an approach that seeks to maximise individual territorial jurisdiction of the parties. Under Article 5(1), each party is required to accept jurisdiction if an offence is committed either: within its territory,[39] on board a ship or aircraft carrying its flag or registered in it,[40] or by one of its nationals if the offence is punishable under the criminal law where it was committed or if the offence is committed in a place not falling under any territorial jurisdiction.[41] Article 5(2) stipulates that each party is to accept jurisdiction where the offender is present within its territory but is not extradited to another party as requested. A key objective underpinning Article 5 is to assist in minimising if not eradicating legal uncertainty over determining jurisdictional competence as between parties in instances of cross-border environmental crime. Accordingly, this treaty provision has an important bearing on the issue of facilitation of cross-border co-operation. In particular, Article 5(1)(a) clarifies that the so-called principle of ubiquity is to apply in trans-boundary pollution cases, so that wherever a constituent element of an offence or an effect occurs, that is to be considered as the place of perpetration or commission. However, the effectiveness of Article 5 is rather undermined by the fact that the Convention allows parties to opt out of their obligations.[42] Article 10 CPECL contains some limited obligations for each contracting party to ensure that inter-institutional co-operation is enhanced with a view to improving internal public administrative action against environmental crime. Specifically, Article 10(1) specifies that parties are required to ensure that their environmental protection authorities co-operate with the relevant authorities responsible for investigating and prosecuting environmental crime in the form of providing on their own initiative the latter with information they suspect constitutes a commission of an offence under Article 2, as well as providing law enforcement agencies with information upon request. Disappointingly, this information-exchange obligation is rather meek, in the sense that active provision of information must only relate to suspected cases of intentionally committed crime[43] and that parties may decide to opt out of these obligations partially or altogether.[44] Finally, Article 11 CPECL stipulates that parties may declare that they will grant rights to environmental NGOs to participate in criminal proceedings. This provision is largely symbolic, though, given it does not have the status of a treaty obligation.

Whereas Section II of CPECL addresses the internal regulation of environmental crime within each contracting party, Section III seeks to address the subject of international co-operation in relation to cross-border crime. Disappointingly,

Section III contains but a single article with only minimal provision for co-operation between parties involved in the prosecution of environmental crime which concerns more than a single state. Specifically, Article 12(1) CPECL imposes a vague obligation on parties to afford each other 'the widest measure of co-operation' in investigations and judicial proceedings relating to criminal offences established by the Convention, with Article 12(2) making it optional for parties to do the same in relation to the acts specified in Article 4 not covered by the definitions of intentional and negligent offences in Articles 2 or 3. Accordingly, the CPECL fails to address a number of key issues that are liable to arise in relation to the handling of cross-border crime including, amongst others, provision for the exchange and handling of data and other forms of mutual assistance between police forces and prosecutors and recognition and enforcement of judgments on criminal liability. As mentioned earlier, Article 5 addresses to some extent questions in connection with jurisdictional competence in the event of environmental impairment affecting more than one party.

Sixteen years after being opened for signature, the CPECL's entry into force looks remote. Events subsequent to 1998 ultimately led to the gradual emergence of EU legislation on environmental crime. This has had the effect, both politically and legally speaking, of diverting the EU membership's focus away from the Council of Europe as a site for development of policy co-operation. In addition, CPECL has a number of inherent structural weaknesses which have been the subject of substantial comment elsewhere.[45] Several of these weaknesses either do not apply at all or do not appear to be relevant in so marked a fashion with respect to EU legislative instrumentation. In particular, it is apparent that even if the CPECL were to come into force its impact would be liable to be rather uncertain and fractured. Specifically, a number of its provisions are poorly defined or entirely open to interpretation.[46] A number of key provisions are optional rather than mandatory.[47] Moreover, some provisions are open to be subject to unilateral reservations being made by contracting parties,[48] and a party is entitled to denounce the Convention subsequent to ratification.[49] In common with most international treaties, there are no specific legal sanctions against contracting parties who fail to implement CPECL obligations[50] and no rights under the Convention for individuals to be able to rely on its terms in order to enforce it before national authorities and courts. Bearing in mind its limitations, uncertainties and caveats, it is clear that if it ever enters into force the CPECL would offer only a limited way forward towards greater European legal integration in the sphere of environmental crime. As a consequence, it has been rightly commented that the primary value underpinning the treaty's text is state sovereignty, although this is not expressly stated to be the case in the Convention.[51] In many respects, the CPECL reflects an era when intergovernmentalist approaches to addressing international issues of environmental crime at European level were especially dominant.

Nevertheless, notwithstanding its poor prospects of becoming legally binding and numerous legal deficiencies, CPECL represents an important milestone in terms of the development of a substantial European dimension to law and policy on environmental crime. A number of the Convention's provisions have been in practice very influential, serving as benchmarks during the course of political negotiations over a general EU legislative text on environmental crime.

13.2 The origins of EU environmental criminal policy

In order to gain a better understanding of the contemporary nature of the Union's involvement in environmental criminal policy, it is worth first reflecting on how the EU has developed its approach over time towards this policy field.[52] This requires consideration of the former legal framework of the Union prior to the Lisbon Treaty, in particular the impact of the former tripartite pillar structure, prior to analysis of the 2008 PECL Directive in section 13.3.

13.2.1 The initial phases of policy development: the battle over intergovernmental and supranational competence (1957–2007)

Prior to the CJEU's seminal 2005 judgment in *Environmental Crimes* considerable uncertainty existed at EU level as to the nature of the Union's legal competence to enact measures intended to combat environmental crime. The basic problem was that it was not clear whether the first pillar implicitly encompassed the possibility for measures on environmental crime to be adopted under its auspices, and what impact the introduction of the third pillar in relation to the question of legal competence would have.

The former first pillar of the Union's legal framework, in the form of the EC Treaty, provided a broad legal basis for the development of a common environmental policy at Community level since the amendments introduced by the 1986 Single European Act (former Articles 174–6 EC). The first-pillar treaty provisions, just like the contemporary EU treaty provisions on the Union's common environmental policy,[53] were silent as to whether it might be possible for the Community to adopt harmonising measures so as to set minimum standards in the domain of environmental criminal law. Prior to judicial clarification, academic opinion was fairly divided on the extent of implied Community competence in relation to criminal matters.[54] Without an express mandate being granted to the Community, some questioned the democratic legitimacy of the proposition that the Community might have implied competence.[55] Others have appeared to adopt a more nuanced view, submitting that whilst the Community is not vested with powers to approximate national criminal rules it does have implied power to require member states to adopt criminal legislation in order to implement EC obligations.[56] Some commentators though were of the view that the Community did have implied powers to take legislative action on crime, on the basis that criminal law should be considered as a potential instrument to be used to deliver Community policy objectives.[57]

When the EU came to introduce the former so-called second and third pillars to its legal framework under the aegis of the original version of the TEU,[58] namely a common foreign and security policy and co-operation in the field of justice and home affairs, the Union appeared to have established a clear basis in the third pillar for the adoption of legal instrumentation in the area of criminal policy. However, the impact of the amendments made to the EU's legal framework in the 1990s, notably the creation of the third pillar and particular amendments made to the EC Treaty, did nothing to lessen debate relating to the question of Community competence in relation to criminal policy.

A number of commentators were of the opinion that the establishment the third pillar had the effect of confirming that the Community had no legal competence to take measures on crime. Some took the view that the third pillar acted effectively as a *lex specialis* agreement by the member states for discussions on criminal policy at EU level to be held exclusively under the auspices of the third pillar, with the effect of preventing the possibility of first-pillar measures being adopted in the same area.[59] The third pillar is viewed by this school of thought as a *lex specialis* on matters of crime.[60] The specialist working group on freedom, security and justice matters of the European Convention undertaking preparatory work in relation to the construction of the failed 2004 EU Constitutional Treaty expressed the view that approximation of substantive and procedural aspects of criminal law fell under the auspices of the third pillar.[61]

However, a number of other commentators suggested that the amendments made to the EU's constitutional framework in the 1990s did not necessarily have the effect of excluding implied Community legal competence in the area of criminal policy.[62] Notably, specific provision was made within the TEU at the time to guarantee that neither the second or third pillars could be interpreted or applied so as to encroach upon the scope of Community powers.[63] This undermined the view that the third pillar was to be considered as a *lex specialis* in relation to the former EC Treaty. In addition, the third-pillar provisions did not appear to confer comprehensive powers to the Union to address the subject of environmental crime.[64] Accordingly, some questioned whether the third pillar provided an appropriate legal basis for the adoption of all types measures designed to combat environmental crime, namely an area not specifically addressed by nor flagged up for approximation under the third pillar.[65] In addition, it was also argued that the effect of the introduction of Articles 135 and 280(4) into the former EC Treaty, namely provisions incorporated within the EC Treaty by virtue of the Treaty of Amsterdam (ToA) 1997 expressly excluding the possibility of the Community adopting rules on criminal law relating to the common policies of customs co-operation and countering EC budgetary fraud, confirmed that member states did not rule out the possibility of the Community having implied competence to combat crime in other policy fields such as the environment.[66]

Whilst uncertainty existed concerning the issue of competence, the legal as well as political stakes were high. For a number of reasons it mattered greatly as to whether or not an EU environmental crime instrument could be based on the first as opposed to the third pillar. First, the legal basis had an impact on member state influence in policy-making. Under the first pillar, the common policy on the environment could be decided on the basis of qualified majority voting (QMV) within the Council of the EU, but measures decided under the third pillar were determined on the basis of Council unanimity. Hence, if the Community were found to have competence to adopt legislation on environmental crime under the auspices of the first pillar, individual member state governments against such a legislative proposal could be outvoted and be bound under Community law to implement the adopted legislative instrument. Secondly, under the first pillar the European Commission enjoyed greater powers over policy development. Whilst the Commission had an exclusive right to present legislative proposals in the environmental sphere under the first pillar, it shared this power with member states in pillar three.[67] Thirdly, the European Parliament (EP) had greater influence over first-pillar measures. Specifically, the EP had joint decision-making powers with the Council over the adoption of first-pillar environmental measures, but only enjoyed limited consultation rights under the third pillar.[68] Fourthly, the possibility of first-pillar competence would mean traditional statal sources of governance (national and sub-national governments and parliaments) relinquishing their exclusive powers to enact criminal laws vis-à-vis the inhabitants located with the state. Fifthly, the European Commission was vested with certain law enforcement powers in relation to first-pillar measures. Specifically, the Commission had a specific mandate[69] and powers[70] to take infringement proceedings against member states who failed to implement first-pillar legislation correctly, ultimately with the possibility of requesting the CJEU to impose financial penalties in cases of protracted non-compliance. Neither the Commission nor other parties were vested with any enforcement powers in respect of measures adopted under the second or third pillars, member states being effectively solely responsible for their implementation at national level. Sixthly, the legal doctrine of direct effect, whilst applicable to first-pillar norms and capable of being invoked before national courts and authorities, did not apply to the third pillar.[71] Finally, the CJEU only had limited jurisdiction to review third-pillar activities or provide judicial interpretation of third-pillar measures[72] as compared with its powers under the first pillar.[73]

13.2.1.1 The former third pillar

The establishment of the tripartite framework of the EU by virtue of the TEU facilitated a clear possibility of co-operation being developed between EU member states on the subject of criminal policy. Whilst member states declared themselves to be increasing willing ultimately to co-operate over certain aspects of environmental criminal policy, particularly those that proved necessary within the context of elimination of customs frontiers within the single market, it was clear that they wished to entrench the utilisation of intergovernmental as opposed to any supranational mechanisms for developing agreement on common approaches to combating crime. Specifically, this would mean that political agreement would have to be crafted upon the basis of the express consent of each member state and would not be expected to have any legal force other than that attributed to agreements under standard principles of international law. Upon entry into force of the TEU in 1993, for the first time it appeared that the member states had agreed to construct a clear legal basis for the development of a political co-operation over crime at EU level in the form of the third pillar (Title VI EU).[74] The creation of the third pillar served to underpin a widely held view, and one most clearly shared by the Council of the EU, that co-operation on crime at Union level should be and could only be legitimately based on an intergovernmental as opposed supranational basis.

Notwithstanding that the third pillar was constructed at a relatively early stage in the 1990s,[75] it took a number of years before the member states were prepared to make use of its provisions and begin to craft common policies in the sector of crime, including environmental crime. This was in no small part due to the fact that the third pillar's original provisions required subsequent substantial changes by virtue of later amending treaties, principally the ToA[76] and Treaty of Nice (ToN) 2001, before they provided a sufficiently detailed and viable framework for policy development on crime. The original version of the third pillar, entitled Title VI Provisions on Co-operation in the Field of Justice and Home Affairs,[77] cited a range of policy areas as being matters of common interest amongst member states, criminal and non-criminal, for the purpose of achieving the Union's objectives, in particular the free movement of persons. These areas included asylum, immigration, judicial co-operation in civil matters and customs co-operation. It was clear from this that the priority for member states in relation to developing a criminal political dimension to Union affairs would be to focus on security aspects relating to personal cross-border migration, rather than other policy fields such as the environment. Two types of co-operation were addressed. Specifically, 'judicial co-operation in criminal matters'[78] as well as 'police co-operation for the purposes of preventing and combating terrorism, unlawful drug trafficking and other serious forms of international crime, including if necessary certain aspects of customs co-operation'[79] constituted areas that were to be regarded as matters of common interest in criminal policy amongst EU member states. Environmental crime was not specifically addressed. The initial range of policy instruments made available for the purposes of the developing co-operation under the auspices of the third pillar reflected member states' intentions to ensure that any agreements over policy would not have any legal force over and above that expected under international law. Specifically, the range of instrumentation included the classic format of international conventions as well as novel mechanisms of joint positions and joint actions, the legal effects of which were unclear.

The ToA 1997, which entered into force in May 1999, substantially restructured the third pillar so that it would in future focus solely on the sector of criminal policy. In order to reflect the third pillar's new remit, Title VI to the TEU was renamed as containing Provisions on Police and Judicial Co-operation on Criminal Matters.[80] The other elements to the third pillar were transferred to the first pillar,[81] so falling within the supranational competence of the Community. Subject to a few minor amendments[82] that were made by virtue of the ToN 2001,[83] the ToA version of the third pillar remained substantially the same until the tripartite pillar structure's termination by virtue of the 2007 Lisbon Treaty. Whilst the intergovernmental nature of the decision-making and legal status and force of third-pillar norms were not in substance changed by the ToA/

ToN amendments, the contents of the third pillar were expanded substantially, providing far greater detail on the scope, type and intensity of Union policy integration in relation to combating crime. Admittedly, the main political priority for political co-operation on crime post-ToA remained focused on providing a basis for policing increased personal mobility within the emerging single market, specifically to provide citizens with a high level of safety within 'an area of freedom, security and justice'.[84] Moreover, the subject of environmental crime remained unspecified as an area for third-pillar co-operation. However, the fact that environmental crime was not expressly mentioned in the treaty provisions did not exclude it from being addressed under the auspices of Title VI EU; the absence of any specific reference to it as a potential area for intergovernmental discussions merely reflected the relative lack of political priority attached to the field at the time.

The changes made to the original version of the third pillar by the ToA and ToN provided the possibility for the Union to engage in in-depth political co-operation over a broad range of criminal policy matters, covering not only aspects of cross-border co-operation between national institutions involved in the application of criminal law but also the subject of harmonisation of national criminal law. Article 29 of the former Title VI of the TEU (Article 29 EU) set out the broad objectives underpinning the third pillar as well as its material scope:

Article 29 EU

Without prejudice to the powers of the European Community, the Union's objective shall be to provide citizens with a high level of safety within an area of freedom, security and justice by developing common action among the member states in the fields of police and judicial co-operation in criminal matters and by preventing and combating racism and xenophobia.

That objective shall be achieved by preventing and combating crime, organised or otherwise, in particular terrorism, trafficking in persons and offences against children, illicit drug trafficking and illicit arms trafficking, corruption and fraud, through:

- closer co-operation between police forces, customs authorities and other competent authorities in the member states, both directly and through the European Police Office (Europol), in accordance with the provisions of Articles 30 and 32;
- closer co-operation between judicial and other competent authorities of the member states, including co-operation through the European Judicial Co-operation Unit ("Eurojust"), in accordance with the provisions of Articles 31 and 32;
- approximation, where necessary, of rules on criminal matters in the member states, in accordance with the provisions of Article 31(1)(e).

Articles 30–2 EU fleshed out in detail the essential parameters of inter-state co-operation regarding the first two indents of the second paragraph of Article 29

EU. Those first two indents were intended to provide a basis for developing co-operation between member state authorities on addressing the handling of cross-border crime, the major preoccupation of the third pillar. Article 30 EU foresaw a number of steps to be taken as part of a common action in the field of police co-operation between member states[85] and at European level[86] through Europol[87] and the European Judicial Co-operation Unit ('Eurojust').[88] Provision was made for possible collaboration between national police authorities on a number of fronts including: operational co-operation in relation to the prevention, detection and investigation of offences; exchange and management of information held by law enforcement services subject to personal data protection; co-operation and joint initiatives research; and common evaluation of particular investigative techniques used to detect serious forms of organised crime.[89] Article 31(1) EU provided that common action on judicial co-operation in criminal matters at national level between national authorities would include: facilitation and acceleration of co-operation between national authorities in relation to proceedings, enforcement of decisions and facilitation of extradition between member states; ensuring compatibility of national rules where necessary to improve judicial co-operation; prevention of jurisdictional conflicts between member states; and the progressive adoption of measures establishing minimum rules relating to constituent elements of criminal acts and penalties in certain fields of crime.[90] Article 32 EU required the Council to stipulate the conditions and limitations under which national police and judicial bodies might operate in territories of other member states in liaison and in agreement with the authorities of the host state.

In addition to facilitating cross-border co-operation between national authorities, the third pillar envisaged a deeper level of collaboration amongst member states on the subject of crime. Specifically, the third indent of the second paragraph to Article 29 EU envisaged the approximation of national criminal laws, where necessary. Such legal integration was to be conducted 'in accordance' with Article 31(1)(e) EU which provided:

Article 31 EU

Common action on judicial co-operation in criminal matters shall include:

. . .

(e) progressively adopting measures establishing minimum rules relating to constituent elements of criminal acts and penalties in the fields of organised crime, terrorism and illicit drug trafficking.

Whereas the initial version of the third pillar provided for a limited and conservative range of policy instrumentation for implementing its agenda,[91] subsequent treaty amendments by virtue of the ToA made some important changes. Specifically, the ToA introduced the possibility of a broader range of pillar-three measures that might be adopted, namely common positions, framework decisions for the purpose of approximation of member state rules, decisions for pursuing objectives other than approximation and conventions. Of most significance was the innovation of the framework decision, a legislative-type instrument not requiring statal ratification (unlike the format of a convention) as described in former Article 34(2)(b) EU:

Article 34 EU

. . .

2.   The Council shall take measures and promote co-operation, using the appropriate form and procedures as set out in this Title, contributing to the pursuit of the objectives of the Union. To that end, acting unanimously on the initiative of any Member State or of the Commission, the Council may:

. . .

(b)   adopt framework decisions for the purpose of approximation of the laws and regulations of the member states. Framework decisions shall be binding upon the member states as to the result to be achieved but shall leave to the national authorities the choice of form and methods. They shall not entail direct effect.

Whilst the amended third pillar appeared to introduce for the first time in EU history a viable legal framework dedicated to addressing the subject of co-operation between EU member states on aspects of criminal policy, it was not clear what legal impact this would have on the question regarding the extent of the Community's legal competence under the first pillar, if any, to adopt measures to combat crime (including environmental crime). On the one hand, the general intentions of the member states appeared to be clear, namely to house policy discussions on crime under the intergovernmental umbrella of the third pillar. However, the provisions of the TEU had not been crafted sufficiently clearly to exclude the former EC Treaty from having jurisdiction for the adoption of (first-pillar) Community measures in the criminal policy sector. Specifically, provisions in the TEU stated that the second and third pillars were without prejudice to the scope and application of the provisions of the first pillar,[92] including the framework treaty provisions regarding a common Community environmental policy of the Community under former Title XIX to the former EC Treaty (i.e. Articles 174–6 EC). Accordingly, the extent to which the third pillar may be used as a legal framework for the development of EU policy on environmental crime was dependent upon the extent of the competence of the Community to adopt legislative measures on the basis of former Article 175 EC. The question of the extent of Community competence in the criminal policy sector had remained an open legal question when the tripartite pillar structure was introduced. However, it was not until the turn of the millennium that this became a live issue, when the first EU legislative proposal on the subject of environmental crime was placed on the table for negotiation.

13.2.1.2 The Danish initiative in 2000

Whilst it was fairly clear that for the most of the 1990s the Council of Europe appeared to be for many EU member states an appropriate forum to negotiate on developing common approaches with regard to the subject of environmental criminal conduct, it was also evident that by 1998 there was willingness amongst member states to foster co-operation also under the auspices of the third pillar. The European Council first indicated that it wished to develop intra-EU co-operation on environmental crime at its summit in December 1998. It endorsed an Action Plan[93] agreed to by the Council of the EU and European Commission on the implementation of the ToA agenda of realising an area of freedom, security and justice within the Union, specifically recommending that environmental crime, with its 'strong cross-border implications' should be approached in an equally effective manner across the EU.[94] At a later summit in Tampere in October 1999, the European Council called for efforts to focus on obtaining agreement on 'common definitions, incriminations and sanctions' within the area of environmental crime as part of the Union's freedom, security and justice agenda.[95] No specific details of a prospective legislative programme accompanied these political commitments on environmental crime, neither from the European Commission or Council.

In fact it was the Danish government which took the lead on the issue, by proposing independently a specific third-pillar legislative initiative in 2000. In February 2000 the Danish government's proposal for a Council framework decision on combating serious environmental crime was published in the EU's Official Journal.[96] Based upon provisions in the third pillar, specifically former Articles 31 and 34(2)(b) EU, the legislative initiative appeared to be a move to consolidate upon the regional European agreement struck over environmental crime under the CPECL.

In broadly similar vein to the CPECL, the Danish proposal sought to secure broad inter-statal agreement on the means to address the most serious instances of environmental crime. However, its approach to achieving this objective was substantially different from the one adopted by the Council of Europe Convention. Specifically, it did not provide a core list of offences but instead required member states to criminalise 'serious environmental crime'.[97] Serious environmental crime was defined in the draft text as the perpetration of actual or an obvious risk of substantial environmental damage caused by certain acts or omissions under 'aggravating circumstances'.[98] The acts and omissions referred to spanned a relatively narrow range of conduct as compared with CPECL, namely either the pollution of environmental media[99] or the storage or disposal of waste or 'similar substances'.[100] The draft text used the term 'aggravating circumstances' to limit the scope of crime covered by it considerably, defining[101] it to mean that the conduct 'cannot be considered part of the normal, everyday operation of an otherwise lawful activity' and that either the offence would need to be 'major in scale'[102] or that financial gain was obtained or sought. The effect of this restricted the definition of serious environmental crime to cover a very narrow range of organised criminal activity.[103] The Danish initiative was less anthropocentric in its approach as compared with CPECL, choosing to focus on environmental impairment alone, leaving aside questions concerning human health impacts of environmental crime. It also set out as a basic requirement that member states should criminalise serious environmental criminal conduct.[104] Criminalisation was foreseen in the draft to be mandatory, including in cases of offences perpetrated by legal persons.[105]

Notwithstanding these differences and innovations, the Danish proposal did not seek essentially to present itself as a rival international instrument to the CPECL. Instead, in several respects it was designed to serve more as a complementary intergovernmentalist measure. This was underlined, in particular, by the fact that the Danish initiative required member states to take ensure that they proposed to their respective national parliaments ratification of the CPECL by the beginning of 2001 and, as far as possible, without reservations.[106] It also sought to strengthen several CPECL provisions in areas where the Convention merely contained a number of options as opposed to legal requirements for contracting parties.[107] The Danish initiative also went further than CPECL in certain respects, notably in stipulating for disqualification of offenders from activities requiring authorisation or from corporate management where, in particular, there was a risk of recidivism. In addition, member states were to ensure that 'effective compensation rules' covered the criminal activity targeted by the legislative proposal. The Danish initiative also contained a number of general provisions designed to enhance the process of investigation and judicial procedure, both domestically within individual member states[108] as well as between member state authorities engaged in law enforcement.[109] For the most part, though, the Danish proposal substantially reiterated or otherwise underpinned commitments contained in CPECL and in other Council of Europe Conventions related to regional co-operation on counter-crime measures. Innovatively, it envisaged the creation of a centralised pool of data on serious environmental crime to be kept for the mutual benefit for member states, specifically a register of special skills and know-how that would ultimately fall under the auspices of Europol if it became entrusted with dealing with environmental crime.[110]

For just over a year the Danish proposal appeared to be on course to becoming adopted under the auspices of the EU's third pillar. During this period it did not appear that there was any disagreement amongst the EU's legislative decision-making institutions about its prospective promulgation. The Commission initially remained silent on the initiative, which suggested tacitly that it had no disagreement about the legal basis used for the proposal. In July 2000, the EP adopted a resolution in favour of the initiative.[111] However, in early spring 2001 the picture began to change quite radically. In March 2001, on the eve of a substantive discussion within the Council of the EU on the Danish initiative, the Commission decided to publish a separate legislative proposal on environmental crime based upon the first pillar, namely former Article 175 EC, and place this before the Council for legislative negotiation. It submitted that the first and not the third pillar of the EU's treaty framework was the appropriate basis for the promulgation of

EU measures concerning certain aspects of environmental crime, and that a first-pillar measure setting out minimum core offences and sanctions would be significantly more effective than intergovernmental instruments such as the CPECL and Danish initiative. The scene was set for a major inter-institutional battle between Commission and Council over the heart and soul of EU environmental criminal policy, one that would not be resolved between them until some seven years later.

13.2.1.3 *The European Commission's 2001 Draft Directive*

When the European Commission published its first draft legislative proposal for an EC directive on environmental crime in March 2001[112] (hereinafter referred to as the '2001 Draft PECL Directive'), with hindsight this marked the beginning of the end of the high-water mark of hitherto exclusively intergovernmental approaches promoted by member states towards developing a common European policy in the area. As a result of the Commission's intervention, progress on the Danish initiative stalled and Council attention focused on the content and implications of the Commission's first-pillar initiative instead. Whilst the focus of the Council's legislative deliberations changed, its overall fundamental position remained that the outcome of negotiations would not lead to anything other than a third-pillar measure. The 2001 Draft PECL Directive was based on the former first pillar of the EU legal framework (Article 175 EC), and accordingly proposed founding policy development upon a supranational footing. As already mentioned earlier in this chapter, the choice of legal basis mattered a great deal for a number of reasons, political as well as legal.

Before considering the particular provisions of the First PECL Directive, it is useful to take on board the Commission's principal motivations for proposing a first-pillar legislative initiative. It is evident from the documents accompanying the draft legislative text that the prime motivation concerned the need to enhance the effectiveness of EU environmental protection legislation in practice, in particular to achieve a better deterrence of at least the most serious violations of EU obligations. The Explanatory Memorandum prefacing the draft proposal and ancillary Commission Staff Working Paper[113] referred to a number of related points on this front. Notably, the Commission referred to the fact that not all member states criminalised the most serious breaches of environmental law,[114] notwithstanding the fact that well-established CJEU jurisprudence had made it clear already that under the EU treaty framework (at the time by virtue of former Article 10 EC)[115] member states are obliged to impose sufficiently dissuasive and effective penalties on persons perpetrating breaches of EU law.[116] In its Explanatory Memorandum the Commission also referred to criminal sanctions as being in many cases the only genuine means of deterring offenders from perpetrating serious violations of EU environmental law, bearing in mind the relative severity and social stigma that may be attached to and associated with criminal penalties.[117] Moreover, it perceived material advantages in using criminal as opposed to administrative law as the means to take action against serious breaches of law, in that responsibility for investigating and prosecuting offences is usually then under the aegis of authorities independent from those invested with tasks related to permitting activities that impact on the environment. The Commission noted the presence of organised cross-border crime within a borderless EU in a number of environmental sectors, including notably illicit trade in protected flora and fauna, ozone depleting substances and trans-boundary movements of hazardous waste, as a factor in favour of deepening common approaches to tackling such activities.[118] These arguments and others have been subsequently developed and explored by the Commission in order to fortify its justification for supranational legislative involvement in the area of environmental crime.

The element of effectiveness constituted a key feature of the 2001 Draft PECL Directive. Notably, Article 1 specified that the measure's purpose is to ensure a more effective application of Community law concerning environmental protection by establishing a minimum set of criminal offences. These offences were set out principally in Article 3, the core substantive provision of the draft text:[119]

Article 3 – Offences

Member States shall ensure that the following activities are criminal offences, when committed intentionally or with serious negligence, as far as they breach the rules of Community law protecting the environment as set out in the Annex and/or rules adopted by Member States in order to comply with such Community law:

(a)   the discharge of hydrocarbons, waste oils or sewage sludge into water;
(b)   the discharge, emission or introduction of a quantity of materials into air, soil or water and the treatment, disposal, storage, transport, export or import of hazardous waste;
(c)   the discharge of waste on or into land or into water, including the operation of a landfill;
(d)   the possession, taking, damaging, killing or trading of or in protected wild fauna and flora species or parts thereof;
(e)   the significant deterioration of a protected habitat;
(f)   trade in ozone-depleting substances;
(g)   the operation of a plant in which a dangerous activity is carried out or in which dangerous substances or preparations are stored or used.'

From this provision it is possible to note that in certain important respects the approach of the 2001 Draft PECL Directive differed quite substantially from its European intergovernmental predecessors as regards the establishing a common minimum definition of environmental crime. In contrast with the CPECL, the 2001 Draft PECL Directive focused solely on criminalising conduct causing either actual harm or risk of harm to the environment. Anthropocentric concerns relating to human health did not feature in the draft legislative text. Moreover, the 2001 draft required member states to criminalise instances of both abstract and concrete types of offences, without requiring the evidence of an obvious or significant risk having been created. In this sense, the draft proposal adopted a far more preventive approach to environmental damage than its Council of Europe counterpart.[120] It is also evident that the draft legislative instrument avoided several of the traps of legal uncertainty that the CPECL falls into. Notably, it does not allow for options or derogations. Moreover, liability is predicated fundamentally upon the breach of specific EU legislation,[121] thereby avoiding the risk of distorted implementation amongst member states. By way of contrast, CPECL excludes criminal liability attaching to conduct having been authorised at national level, opening the door for contracting parties to adopt substantially differential levels of minimum baseline environmental protection standards for the purpose of criminal prosecution.[122] The 2001 Draft PECL Directive also avoided incorporating any vaguely worded terms within the definition of offences, a factor that could lead to significant distorted application of law enforcement amongst member states.[123]

Whilst the 2001 Draft PECL Directive sought to achieve a more effective application of EU environmental law on the ground through the use of criminal law, it is clear that the Commission's supranational agenda was deliberately limited so as to focus on harmonising those aspects of member states' national criminal laws considered essential for the attainment of EU environmental protection objectives. The Commission was aware from the outset of the need to ensure that its draft legislative text did not affect certain areas of criminal policy falling outside the legal competence of the Community, as required, *inter alia*, by Article 5(1) of the former EC Treaty (and subsequently superseded by Article 5 TEU). Given the fact that the subject of criminal law was not expressly integrated within the first pillar, the Commission considered that Community competence should be considered limited so that first-pillar legislation would not be able to change the fundamental aspects of the national criminal legal systems of the member states. However, for the Commission this did not mean that the Community could not compel member states in general to criminalise certain types of conduct.[124] Secondly, the Commission also recognised that, even where the Community had legal competence in a policy field shared with member states (as in the case of the environment under Title XIX of the former EC Treaty), Community action was subject to compliance with the subsidiarity and proportionality principles.[125] The latter two principles placed the onus on the Community to justify the adoption of first-pillar instrumentation rather than leaving legislative action to the national and/or sub-national levels.

These particular priorities were crystallised in the 2001 Draft PECL Directive in a number of respects. First, the draft proposal was careful not to concern itself with the enforcement of any legislative instrumentation other than Community legislation. Secondly, like CPECL, the draft proposal focused on the most blatantly serious instances of culpable conduct, namely offences committed either intentionally or with 'serious negligence'. Accordingly, the Commission confirmed its wish to require member states to address the most inexcusable acts and omissions, whilst deferring to the latter how they wished to define the parameters of *mens rea* and whether they wished to apply more stringent criminal rules on a strict liability basis. Thirdly, as far as sanctions and the question of corporate liability were concerned, the Commission proposed relatively general obligations with a view to providing a considerable degree of flexibility for member states in implementing their core commitments contained in Article 3 concerning offences. Article 4 of the 2001 Draft PECL Directive on sanctions sought to compel member states to provide for criminal penalties for natural persons caught committing Article 3 offences. However, as the proposal's Explanatory Memorandum made clear,[126] the draft legislative text did not compel states to use criminal sanctions in every case, but merely to include them within the range of available sanctions under national rules. Article 4(2) of the draft proposal required provision of a minimum set of non-penal penalties[127] in respect of corporate offenders, allowing member states the option of applying criminal rules to legal persons.[128] Moreover, the 2001 Draft PECL Directive excluded states and public bodies exercising sovereign rights from its scope, leaving individual member states to determine the degree and availability of criminal sanctions with respect to the conduct of public authorities.[129] Finally, the draft proposal deferred to member states over the type and severity of criminal penalty to be imposed on offenders, merely setting out a general requirement that Article 3 offences are to be punishable by 'effective, proportionate and dissuasive sanctions', thus effectively deferring to the general principles of CJEU case law on the implementation of Community obligations.

The impact of the 2001 Draft PECL Directive at the political institutional level of the EU was marked, but not decisive. The immediate effect on the Council of the EU was to deflect its consideration away from the Danish third-pillar initiative and allow time for consideration of the Commission proposal. However, contrary to the advice of its Legal Service,[130] the Council ultimately refused to accept that the first pillar (former Article 175 EC) would be the correct legal basis for Union legislation on environmental crime and decided not to participate in the co-decision procedure foreseen for the adoption of a Community legislative measure. The political impact elsewhere, however, was more favourable. The EP issued resolutions[131] in support of adoption of a first-pillar instrument, as did the European Economic Social Committee in its advisory capacity.[132] In the absence of the Council submitting a common position on the proposal, the Commission decided to issue a revised version of the 2001 Draft PECL directive in 2002[133] in order to address proposed amendments made by the EP. However, without the participation of the Council in the co-decision legislative process it would not be possible to adopt a Community legislative measure on environmental crime.

13.2.1.4　*The 2003 Framework Council Decision*

By way of reaction to the Commission's supranational initiative, the Council affirmed its intergovernmentalist stance by deciding in March 2003 to complete the legislative cycle by adopting a framework decision on environmental crime under the auspices of the third pillar. The framework decision on the protection of the environment through criminal law[134] (2003 PECL Framework Decision) included a number of provisions in areas covered by the 2001 Draft PECL Directive, notably regarding the definition of offences and sanctions.

The 2003 PECL Framework Decision contained provisions concerning both substantive as well as procedural aspects of the application of environmental criminal law. It was far broader in its scope than the 2000 Danish initiative and was loosely modelled upon the approach adopted by the CPECL. Articles 2–4 of the Framework Decision provided that member states were obliged to establish under their criminal laws a set of common environmental offences, committed or organised either intentionally or perpetrated on account of serious negligence. Article 6 addressed the question of the extent of corporate liability for offences committed for the benefit of legal persons. Articles 5 and 7 of the Framework Decision contained general obligations relating to sanctions to be applied in respect of natural and legal persons. As regards natural persons, Article 5 provided that member states ensure that punishment would be secured through effective, proportionate and dissuasive penalties, with deprivation of liberty enabling the possibility of extradition 'at least in serious cases'. Article 7 was more general in nature, leaving member states to determine whether to impose criminal or non-criminal penalties, so long as the sanctions chosen by them were 'effective, proportionate and dissuasive'. Both provisions set out a list of possible but not obligatory types of non-criminal penalties that might be applied to corporate and non-corporate offenders.[135] In addition, the legislative instrument contained a number of provisions related to facilitating cross-border co-operation on environmental crime,[136] which were accepted by the Commission as properly falling within the remit of the third pillar on the grounds that these were matters more closely connected to the third pillar (police and judicial co-operation on criminal matters) than the first pillar (environmental protection).[137]

As a consequence of the Council's decision to adopt its first-pillar initiative in the form of a third-pillar instrument, the Commission decided to take advantage of the minimal legal powers made available to it under Title VI TEU by bringing an annulment action before the CJEU[138] on the grounds that essentially the framework decision was adopted *ultra vires*, in encroaching upon spheres of Community (i.e. first pillar) legal competence in contravention of EU law. The annulment proceedings, which ultimately led to the seminal 2005 judgment in *Environmental Crimes*, opened up the possibility for the CJEU for the first time to pronounce definitively on the crucial but hitherto unresolved issue relating to the existence of Community legal competence in the domain of environmental crime, and aspects of criminal policy pertinent to the development of other common policies under the auspices of the former EC Treaty.

13.2.1.5 *The Environmental Crimes ruling (Case C-176/03 Commission v Council)*

In the absence of textual clarity on the existence of first-pillar competence in relation to environmental crime and the marked difference of opinions expressed within the EU political institutional set up, it was inevitable that the CJEU would become involved at some point to provide judicial clarification. The decision of the Council of the EU to adopt the 2003 PECL Framework Decision[139] under the auspices of the third pillar and reject adoption of a first-pillar instrument provoked the European Commission into bringing annulment proceedings before the CJEU. The Commission submitted that the Council had acted *ultra vires* in passing the third-pillar instrument, given that the 2003 PECL Framework Decision contained provisions concerning matters upon which the former considered fell within the remit of the first-pillar environmental policy, specifically provisions concerning the definition of offences and sanctions.

The CJEU pronounced judgment on the dispute between the Commission and Council in September 2005,[140] arguably one of the most controversial and important of institutional legal cases in recent times and certainly a seminal moment for the future of EU environmental criminal law. No less than 11 member states intervened in support of the defendant Council of the EU, whilst the EP presented legal counsel in support of the Commission. The judgment has been the subject of substantial comment and analysis elsewhere,[141] some of it very critical,[142] and need only be addressed relatively briefly here. In its ruling in *Environmental Crimes* the CJEU upheld the Commission submission that the 2003 PECL Framework Decision should be annulled on the basis that the decision encroached upon the Community's powers, contrary to (former) Article 47 EU.[143] Whilst the Court confirmed that, as a general rule, neither criminal law nor the rules of criminal procedure fall within the Community's competence, at the same it confirmed that this:

> does not prevent the Community legislature, when the application of effective, proportionate and dissuasive criminal penalties by the competent national authorities is an essential measure for combating serious environmental offences, from taking measures which relate to the criminal law of the member states which it considers necessary in order to ensure that the rules which it lays down on environmental protection are fully effective.[144]

The member states had indicated in the first three recitals to the 2003 PECL Framework Decision that criminal penalties were necessary for combating serious environmental offences, a key factor that the CJEU took into account in affirming that a third-pillar instrument had been agreed to which should have been based upon the EC Treaty under former Article 175 EC.

In its judgment, the CJEU appeared to take a broader view of the scope of the Community's implied powers than the Commission. In holding that the first seven Articles of the PECL Framework Decision were *ultra vires* the Court ruled that the instrument's provisions on sanctions should have been adopted on the basis of Article 175 EC. As already noted, Articles 5 and 7 of the 2003 PECL Framework Decision contained some specific and detailed provisions regarding the type of sanctions adopted at national level by the member states. Specifically, Article 5(1) required that in serious cases punishable conduct must include penalties involving deprivation of liberty which can give rise to extradition. Article 7 contained a list of non-criminal sanctions that member states could select when penalising corporate offenders. The Commission's position with respect to sanctions had been that, whilst the Community could require conduct in breach of Community environmental legislation to be criminalised under national rules, there was no implied powers under the first pillar to stipulate specific types of criminal sanctions. In his Opinion on the case, Advocate General Ruiz-Jarabo Colomer also considered that the Community was not legally competent to provide for specific types or levels of penalties in respect of offences. He considered that Article 5(1) and Article 7 of the framework decision lay outside the scope of first-pillar powers.[145] Given the fact that the CJEU did not endorse the approach taken by the Advocate General, it did appear that the Court had confirmed that the Community had legal competence to prescribe legislative rules on both nature and level of criminal penalties, insofar as the Community legislature determined it essential for the implementation of first-pillar obligations to be enforced by criminal law. The Commission interpreted the Court's ruling in this light. Some have questioned, rather unconvincingly, whether it was reasonable to make such a far-reaching conclusion.[146] The Court did appear in one part of its judgment to consider erroneously that the PECL Framework Decision did not compel the member states to adopt specific types of criminal or other penalties. However, there was nothing of real substance in the judgment to give the Commission real cause for doubting that the Court had adopted a different conclusion to the one opined by the Advocate General.

13.2.1.6 The Commission's reaction: a second first-pillar proposal

The reaction of the Commission to the judgment in *Environmental Crimes* was both swift and potentially far-reaching. The importance attached to the judgment by the Commission was exemplified by the fact that it adopted a Communication[147] a couple of months after the CJEU's ruling in November 2005 for the purpose of setting out its analysis of the judgment's implications for the subsequent development of EU decision-making in relation to criminal policy in general. The Communication considered that, by virtue of the fact that the CJEU had annulled Articles 1–7 of the PECL Framework Decision in their entirety, the CJEU had confirmed the Community was competent to prescribe not only the imposition of criminal penalties and definition of offences but also the nature and level of penalties.

As a consequence, the Commission signalled that it would now take steps to revise existing EU legislative instruments in the field of criminal policy so as to ensure that they accorded with the Court's ruling. It announced that it would end the so-called 'double text' mechanism that the EU legislative institutions had used up until this point, whereby Community measures had been accompanied by third-pillar instruments in order to compel member states to criminalise certain conduct. Typically, a double text approach would involve the EC measure referring to an accompanying third-pillar instrument that stipulated in detail the nature and level of criminal penalties to be applied at national level. In its Annex, the Communication contained a list of proposed and adopted EU policy instruments that were to be ear-marked for legislative revision. These included a first- and accompanying third-pillar instrument adopted in 2005 on ship-source pollution.[148] On the same day as the Communication was published, the Commission decided to bring annulment proceedings in respect of the Council's framework decision on ship-source pollution. That litigation, which ultimately led to another important CJEU judgment in late 2007 addressing the subject of legal competence, is discussed below in section 13.2.1.7.

It was not, however, until early 2007 before the Commission decided to re-grasp the initiative over development on construction of a general EU legislative instrument on environmental crime based on the first pillar. In the wake of the *Environmental Crimes* judgment, it was not immediately apparent where the next legislative move would emerge. The Commission's 2005 Communication appraising the judgment's implications did not specify how the Commission would approach the next stage of inter-institutional negotiations on a legislative text. Technically, it could have been expected for the onus to fall on the Council of the EU to forge a common position on the amended First Draft PECL directive under the relevant first-pillar co-decision procedure,[149] given that it had lost the case. However, the Council of the EU was (and still is post-Lisbon) under no legal obligation to act upon a legislative proposal, and for a considerable period it was not evident that the Council was prepared to participate in the legislative process. In the autumn of 2006 the EP had signalled that it was losing its patience, calling upon the Commission to issue a fresh legislative proposal if the Council did not provide legislative input on the draft directive.[150]

As a move intended to relaunch negotiations over a first-pillar-based legislative text, the Commission published a fresh proposal for an Community directive on environmental crime in February 2007[151] (hereinafter referred to as the '2007 Draft PECL Directive'). As expected, the draft instrument reflected the Commission's understanding on the impact of the *Environmental Crimes* judgment with respect to the subject of sanctions. However, the 2007 PECL Draft Directive did not simply tack on a few provisions onto the original proposal, but crafted a substantially different new initiative which took on board several elements of previously negotiated intergovernmental agreements struck at European level referred to earlier in this chapter, no doubt with a view to making Council participation in legislative negotiations more attractive and realistic.

Notably, its definition of common offences (Article 3 of the draft) was modelled in large part upon the structure and approach adopted in the 2003 PECL Framework Decision[152] and to a lesser extent the 1998 CPECL. The draft's provisions on substantive issues of criminal liability have been discussed elsewhere,[153] and for reasons of space will not be analysed in detail here. In essence, the Commission's proposals here bore fruit ultimately with the 2008 PECL directive which is addressed in section 13.3. A few general comments on them are appropriate here. A number of features were woven into the legislative fabric of the 2007 Draft PECL Directive that were previously spurned by the Commission. Notably, the draft text stipulated a number of significant preconditions and limits attached to the triggering of liability. First, the vast majority of offences defined were not abstract in nature, but focused mostly on concrete situations of damage arising or the causing of a significant risk of damage.[154] Secondly, the 2007 draft instrument reflected anthropocentric concerns and values contained in previous intergovernmental instruments on environmental crime, expressed by its focus on conduct causing or risking serious damage to human health as well as to the environment. The 2007 draft prioritised human health protection over environmental impairment, by virtue of the fact that the only autonomous offence it listed (namely an offence not predicated upon an activity being 'unlawful') related to pollution causing either death of serious injury. Thirdly, a number of concepts relating to the definition of offences were uncertain in scope, such as the requirement for several offences that damage to environmental services had to be at least 'substantial' or constitute 'significant deterioration'. Akin to the structuring used in the 2003 PECL Framework Decision, the majority of offences in the 2007 draft text were predicated on the term 'unlawful'. The 2007 Draft PECL Directive defined 'unlawful' to mean either an infringement of Community law or breaches of national environmental protection rules and decisions of competent authorities.[155] Its focus was, therefore, not simply on Community environmental legislation but also encompassed breaches of national rules aiming at protection of the environment. The draft was also broader in material scope by covering nuclear radiation. By including infringements of Community environmental protection rules within the definition of 'unlawful', the 2007 draft text intended to avoid the risk of defendants relying upon instances of defective transposition of Community legislation at national level.[156] In other respects, the 2007 Draft PECL Directive mirrored elements contained in the 2003 PECL Framework Decision, including in respect of corporate liability and inchoate offences.[157]

As widely anticipated, the 2007 Draft PECL Directive contained substantially enhanced obligations in the area of criminal and non-criminal sanctions. The draft text reflected the understanding that Community legislation could determine both the type and severity of sanction. Articles 5 and 7 of the 2007 draft contained detailed provisions on sanctions, including certain criminal and non-criminal penalties with minimum and maximum thresholds,[158] to be made available to punish both natural as well as legal persons respectively. The nature and level of sanctions were based upon a three-step scale envisaged as a basic guideline for sentencing rules agreed by the Justice and Home Affairs Council in April 2002.[159] Article 5 set out a list of criminal penalties to be applicable by member states to natural persons, tiered according to three general levels intended to reflect the perceived relative gravity of an individual offence. Specifically, it envisaged member states being obliged to make the most serious types of offences causing death or serious personal injury punishable by a maximum of at least between 5 and 10 years' imprisonment, namely certain intentionally committed crimes.[160] In respect of certain offences committed with serious negligence resulting in death or serious personal injury, committed intentionally causing substantial environmental damage or committed by way of organised crime, member states were obliged under the draft to make available for punishment the maximum criminal sanction of at least between two and five years' imprisonment.[161] Finally, member states were required under the 2007 draft proposal to ensure that certain offences causing substantial environmental damage through serious negligence would be punishable by a maximum of at least between one and three years' imprisonment.[162] The tiering of offences reflected strong anthropocentric concerns and values relative to environmental protection. No minimum specific sanctions were foreseen in respect of abstract offences defined in Article 3 of the 2007 Draft PECL Directive, although it contained a general obligation for member states to ensure that such violations would be subject to 'effective, proportionate and dissuasive criminal sanctions'.[163] Accordingly, the approach adopted on sanctions by the 2007 draft proposal reflected a distinct move away from the earlier emphasis on prevention fostered in the 2001 Draft PECL Directive. The 2007 draft text deferred to member states whether to apply a range of non-criminal sanctions to natural persons, namely disqualification from activities, publication of judicial decisions imposing convictions or sanctions or environmental reinstatement.[164]

As regards the sanctioning of corporate offenders, the 2007 Draft PECL Directive adopted a similarly detailed and prescriptive approach. Under Article 7 of the draft, member states were obliged to set fines with maximum and minimum scales for corporate offenders, whilst retaining the choice as to whether to classify the penalties as criminal or non-criminal sanctions.[165] The draft divided corporate offences according to the same three levels of penalties applicable in relation to natural persons under Article 5. Instead of custodial punishment, though, the sanction used for corporate offenders was a fine. Specifically, member states were obliged to stipulate a maximum fine of at least between €750,000 and €1.5 million for the most serious offences, between €500,000 and €750,000 for the next most serious category of offences, and between €300,000 and €500,000 for the least serious category of offences deemed by the draft proposal to warrant a minimum specific figure for a financial penalty.[166] As compared with the EU's approach to fines for corporate entities breaching EU competition law, one might have some cause to argue that the proposed sanctions were relatively lenient.[167] Member states would retain the option to apply a different system of setting levels of fines according to the relative financial strength of the offender,[168] provided that the national system deployed set maximum fines at levels that would be at least equivalent to the minimum thresholds prescribed in the draft proposal.[169] This option effectively confirmed possibilities for member states to apply in practice more stringent fines than the basic model envisaged in the draft text. As in the case for natural persons, the draft text deferred to member states whether they wish to provide for a range of accompanying non-criminal sanctions.[170]

13.2.1.7 Further twists in the competence tale: the Ship-source Pollution *and* Intertanko *CJEU judgments (Cases C-440/05 and C-308/06)*

Just as the 2007 PECL Draft Directive had seen the light of day, its progress through the EU legislative process was checked by the impact of further CJEU clarification on the extent of first-pillar competence in relation to criminal matters. In the autumn of 2007, The CJEU issued another key ruling on the subject of Community competence in the area of environmental criminal policy. Specifically, the Court pronounced judgment in the *Ship-source Pollution* case,[171] another dispute between Commission and Council involving questions of validity relating to a third-pillar instrument that had been adopted in order to combat environmental pollution generated by the marine transport sector. Like the 2005 *Environmental Crimes* judgment, this ruling had the effect of requiring significant adjustments to be made to the contents of the 2007 legislative draft on environmental crime.

The *Ship-source Pollution* judgment and its background, which has been the subject of substantial comment elsewhere,[172] need only be summarised here. As an integral part of its maritime transport safety strategy, the EU legislature decided in 2005 to adopt under the auspices of the first pillar's common transport policy (former Article 80(2) EC) a directive on combating marine pollution from ships (Directive 2005/35).[173] Legislative action had been deemed warranted on the part of the Commission in the light of evidence of persistent failures by the shipping industry to respect prohibitions of discharges of significant quantities of pollutant from vessels into marine environment set down by international agreement in the MARPOL 73/78 Convention.[174] In the wake of the sinking of the *Prestige* oil tanker off the Galician coast in the autumn of 2002, by the end of that year member states were calling for common action to be taken on the subject of ship pollution.[175] As a result, Directive 2005/35 was adopted, requiring member states to take steps to combat the discharge of polluting substances from ships into the aquatic environment that contravene internationally agreed standards set under the auspices of the MARPOL 73/78 Convention, where the discharge is committed either intentionally, recklessly or by virtue of serious negligence. Originally, the Commission had proposed that the first-pillar legislative instrument should contain provisions obliging member states to provide for some specific minimum criminal and non-criminal sanctions for natural and legal persons committing infringements of its terms.[176] However, ultimately the EU legislature decided to use an accompanying third-pillar measure in order to address the subject of applying criminal law (thus using the so-called 'double text' approach). Specifically, in 2005 the Council adopted a framework decision under the aegis of the third pillar (Framework Decision 2005/667/JHA)[177] requiring member states to establish criminal offences and related specific penalties as a means to enforce the first-pillar directive. When adopted, Directive 2005/35 did not contain any specific obligations on the part of member states to adopt criminal offences, but simply cross-referred to the third-pillar framework decision as regarding infringements of its terms as criminal offences.[178] The first-pillar directive contained the standard mantra that member states were obliged to ensure that infringements would be 'subject to effective, proportionate and dissuasive penalties'.[179] However, in the wake of the *Environmental Crimes* judgment the Commission considered that the framework decision in parts unlawfully encroached upon Community competence within the field of transport, and as a consequence brought legal proceedings before the CJEU[180] with a view to seeking an annulment of the third-pillar measure.

The Commission gained what could be described to be a partial or pyrrhic victory in the *Ship-source Pollution* case. The CJEU annulled Framework Decision 2005/667/JHA on the grounds that certain of its key provisions were *ultra vires*[181] in containing obligations that should have been legislated for under the auspices of the first pillar (namely former Article 80 EC). Specifically, these related to requirements on member states to criminalise infringements of Directive 2005/35 for natural persons[182] and to impose either criminal or non-criminal liability on corporate offenders in respect of such infringements committed for their benefit.[183] In these respects the Court confirmed the reasoning it adopted in *Environmental Crimes*. However, supported by the Advocate-General's opinion[184] and contrary to the Commission's view, the CJEU held that decisions over the type and level of the criminal penalties did not fall within the Community's sphere of competence.[185] Accordingly, the provisions contained in the framework decision relating to detailed criminal and non-criminal sanctions fell within the remit of the third and not the first pillar of the EU's constitutional framework. These provisions, imposing minimum imprisonment terms for natural persons and fines for legal persons,[186] were of a similar nature and structure adopted in the 2007 Draft PECL Directive.

The *Ship-source Pollution* judgment accordingly had the effect of determining a major adjustment in legal appraisal of the relative balance of powers between, on the one hand, the Community and, on the other, the Union acting under the aegis of the third pillar in relation to the area of criminal policy in general. The CJEU had confirmed that the Community may, where it deemed this to be essential to fulfil one or more of its policy objectives, require member states to criminalise certain conduct and for that purpose determine in broad terms the parameters of liability such as define common offences and require member states to apply their criminal laws to enforce against offenders effectively, proportionately and dissuasively. However, Community competence did not according to the Court reach beyond these elements, so that in particular matters relating to criminal procedure and specification of type and intensity of sanction should be agreed upon under the legal basis and decision-making arrangements foreseen in Title VI TEU on police and judicial co-operation in criminal matters.

In the wake of the Court's judgment, the Commission took certain steps to adjust its ship-source pollution legislation in line with the CJEU jurisprudence. Specifically, a directive was passed[187] so as to amend Directive 2005/35 so that it now incorporated the provisions considered to have been adopted *ultra vires* in the annulled framework decision. Whilst it was envisaged that a new slimmed-down framework decision would be passed by way of accompaniment, this did not materialise.

Subsequent to the *Ship-source Pollution* case, the CJEU also issued a judgment concerning the validity of Directive 2005/35 which also had wider implications for the future construction of EU criminal policy measures. Specifically, in its 2008 preliminary ruling in *Intertanko*,[188] the CJEU upheld that Directive 2005/35 had been adopted in accordance with EC Treaty requirements. In that case the International Association of Independent Tanker Owners had sought judicial review in the English and Welsh High Court in respect of the validity of the first-pillar instrument, on grounds that it not only contravened the standards set under international law for liability exposure in respect of ship-source pollution (both MARPOL 73/78 and the 1982 UN Convention on the Law of the Sea (UNCLOS)), but also that its use of general undefined concepts with regard to the determination of infringements (e.g. serious negligence) breached the EU legal principle of legal certainty and the closely related derivative principle of *nullem crimen nulla poena sine lege*.[189] The High Court requested a preliminary ruling from the CJEU as to whether the directive had been validly adopted. The CJEU held that, since the Community was a not a party to MARPOL and the relevant provisions on innocent passage rights for vessels under UNCLOS were not sufficiently precise or unconditional, it would not be possible for the directive's validity to be examined in the light of these international rules at the behest of private individuals.[190] Of wider significance, the CJEU also upheld that the directive complied with the requirements of legal certainty. As a general point, it noted that the general principle of legal certainty under EU law requires that rules should be clear and precise, so that individuals may ascertain unequivocally their rights and obligations and take steps accordingly.[191] With regard to the undefined legal concepts used in the directive to determine the extent of liability for infringements of its provisions, the CJEU noted that it was impossible in any event to provide a comprehensive definition to terms such as intent, recklessness and serious negligence. Such concepts were, though, familiar to all national legal systems of the EU member states. The concept of 'serious negligence' could be understood as entailing an unintentional act or omission entailing the commission of a patent breach of a duty of care. Moreover, given that the directive was required under EU law to be transposed into national law, national rules would be required as an integral part of the implementation process to provide for appropriately detailed definitions on liability.[192] As a result, the Court concluded that the rules under Directive 2005/35 had defined the scope of liability for infringements of its provisions with sufficient certainty.

Both the *Ship-source Pollution* and *Intertanko* judgments were relevant to the promulgation of general environmental criminal legislation adopted under the auspices of the EC Treaty. In the wake of the *Ship-source Pollution* judgment it was readily apparent to the EU political institutions that the 2007 Draft PECL Directive's provisions on penalties required amendment. Specifically, its detailed provisions on penalties would have to be removed and transferred to an accompanying third-pillar instrument. The *Intertanko* judgment served to quash any concerns that the general terminology used in the 2007 Draft PECL Directive, notably in relation to the definition of offences, might be legally vulnerable from a legal certainty perspective. After these judgments the course was set fair for the EU finally to enact a directive on environmental crime, which ultimately happened in 2008 in the form of the PECL Directive, which is assessed in the next section.

13.3 EU environmental criminal law comes of age: Directive 2008/99

Subsequent to the inter-institutional turmoil that occurred for the most part of the first decade after the millennium, the EU was finally able to enact its first general piece of supranational legislation in relation to environmental crime towards the end of 2008. Specifically, on 19 November 2008 the EU adopted a first-pillar directive, namely Directive 2008/99 on the protection of the environment through criminal law (2008 PECL Directive).[193] Member states were required to transpose their obligations into national law by 26 December 2010.[194] The 2008 PECL Directive has remained in force subsequent to the EU treaty changes on criminal law policy effected by the 2007 Lisbon Treaty, which have made the possibility of enacting Union criminal legislation subject to much stiffer voting requirements at Council level. The treaty changes are considered in section 13.4.

Subsequent to the CJEU's ruling in *Ship-source Pollution*, the EU legislature managed to negotiate a political agreement on the basis of the Commission's Draft 2007 PECL Directive, with the Commission not needing to produce a third draft legislative initiative. The Council decided to engage in crafting suitable amendments to the 2007 draft via a specialist working party on substantive criminal law operating under the supervision of the Council Presidency.[195] Its former resistance to a first measure had evaporated in the wake of the *Environmental Crimes* ruling. Ensuing consultations with the EP[196] were productive, leading relatively swiftly to political agreement between the two institutions being achieved at first reading stage of the co-decision procedure in May 2008.[197]

For this purpose, it is sufficient to focus on the main aspects of the agreed text. Subject to some changes, the agreed version corresponds in substantial part with the structuring and approach adopted by the Commission's 2007 Draft PECL Directive (minus the draft's provisions on sanctions). Articles 3–4 cover the definition of offences. The core provision is Article 3, focusing on intentionally committed and serious negligent conduct leading to damage to the environment and/or human health:

Article 3 – Offences

Member States shall ensure that the following conduct constitutes a criminal offence, when unlawful and committed intentionally or with at least serious negligence:

(a)   the discharge, emission or introduction of a quantity of materials or ionising radiation into air, soil or water, which causes or is likely to cause death or serious injury to any person or substantial damage to the quality of air, the quality of soil, the quality of water or to animals or plants;

(b)   the collection, transport, recovery and disposal of waste, including the supervision of such operations and the after-care of disposal sites, and including actions taken as a dealer or a broker (waste management) which causes or is likely to cause death or serious injury to any person or substantial damage to the quality of air, the quality of soil, the quality of water or to animals and plants;

(c)   the shipment of waste, where this activity falls within the scope of Article 2(35) of Regulation (EC) No 1013/2006 of the EP and of the Council of 14 June 2006 on shipments of waste and is undertaken in a non-negligible quantity, whether executed in a single shipment or in several shipments which appear to be linked;

(d) the operation of a plant in which a dangerous activity is carried out or in which dangerous substances or preparations are stored or used and which, outside the plant, causes or is likely to cause death or serious injury to any person or substantial damage to the quality of air, the quality of soil, the quality of water or to animals and plants;

(e) the production, processing, handling, use, holding, storage, transport, import, export and disposal of nuclear materials or other hazardous radioactive substances which causes or is likely to cause death or serious injury to any person or substantial damage to the quality of air, the quality of soil, the quality of water or to animals and plants;

(f) the killing, destruction, possession and taking of specimens of protected wild fauna or flora species, except for cases when the conduct concerns a negligible quantity of those specimens and has a negligible impact on the conservation status of the species;

(g) trading in specimens of protected wild fauna and flora species or parts or derivatives thereof, except in cases when the conduct concerns a negligible quantity of those specimens and has a negligible impact on the conservation status of the species;

(h) any conduct which causes the significant deterioration of a habitat within a protected site;

(i) production, importation, exportation, placing on the market or use of ozone-depleting substances.

Whilst there were certain changes made to the Commission's 2007 draft text in order to flesh out in more detail a number of individual heads of infringement and incorporate greater precision into the main provision defining offences, the essence of the final legislative text does not differ that significantly from the 2007 proposal on substantive issues. Article 4 of the PECL Directive stipulates that member states must render incitement, aiding and abetting of intentional conduct referred to in Article 3 as punishable under criminal law.

Two changes perhaps stand out for particular comment here. First, it is noticeable that all offences defined in Article 3 of the directive are subject to the precondition of being 'unlawful', and so none are autonomous. The legislative text limits this term to encompassing breaches of environmental legislation adopted under the auspices of the (pre-Lisbon) EU treaty framework and which are specified in Annexes[198] attached to the directive, or breaches of member state rules or decisions of national competent authorities intended to give effect to such EU environmental legislation.[199] This differs from the approach to scoping adopted in the text of the Commission's 2007 draft proposal, which covered also national rules and decisions of national competent authorities on the protection of the environment. Secondly, it is apparent that Article 3 of the 2008 PECL Directive does not reflect a hierarchical approach regarding the consideration of anthropocentric and ecological interests. Specifically, human health and environmental protection concerns are equally valued. In contrast, the Commission's 2007 draft envisaged creating an offence without the need for proving 'unlawful' behaviour where either death or serious personal injury had been caused as a result of discharge of pollutant materials into environmental media. Article 4 of the 2008 PECL Directive requires criminalisation of the incitement, aiding and abetting of Article 3 conduct that is intentionally committed.[200]

The 2008 PECL Directive also contains particular provisions on the liability of corporations and other legal persons. Article 6(1) of directive requires that legal persons are to be held liable for offences defined in the directive (Articles 3–4) where such offences have been committed for their benefit by any person having 'leading position within the legal person' based on either a power of representation of the legal person, an authority to take decisions on behalf of the legal person or an authority to exercise control within the legal person. In addition, corporate liability is also triggered where lack of supervision or control by a person with a leading position has made possible the commission of an offence for the legal person's benefit by a person under the latter's authority.[201] Article 6(3) stipulates that liability of legal persons shall not exclude criminal proceedings against natural persons found to be perpetrators, inciters or accessories in offences covered by the directive.

As expected, the major changes made to the final agreed and adopted legislative text concerned the subject of sanctions. In line with the CJEU's *Ship-source Pollution* judgment the EU legislature ensured that the 2008 PECL Directive includes no detailed specifications relating to the type and level of sanction for natural and legal persons. Instead, the instrument contains only general obligations on member states to ensure that the penalties they apply are effective. With respect to the issue of sanctions for natural persons, Article 5 simply requires member states to ensure that the directive's offences (as listed in Articles 3 and 4) are punishable by 'effective, proportionate and dissuasive criminal penalties'.[202] Article 7 imposes a similar general requirement in respect of corporate conduct, but with the difference that member states are allowed to determine whether penalties for legal persons should be criminal or non-criminal in nature. The directive does not cross-refer to any accompanying (third pillar) instrument to address other aspects, in particular the severity of penalties, jurisdictional issues, inter-statal co-operation in criminal investigations and judicial procedures. Whilst it was originally anticipated that a third-pillar measure might be adopted, in the event none was passed. Any future moves to legislate on the detail of these aspects would now have to be adopted through the specific EU treaty provisions established by virtue of the 2007 Lisbon Treaty, which are discussed in section 13.4 below.

Notwithstanding the fact that the PECL Directive has made it to the EU statute books, it appears that significant political as well as legal difficulties remain with regard to its effective implementation in the future. A key shortcoming in the directive itself is the absence of monitoring and review provisions normally woven into the environmental legislative fabric as standard. In particular, member states are not required to issue regular reports on the implementation of the experience and the Commission has no specific remit under the directive to engage in any periodic review of the legislative instrument with a view to assessing its current state of effectiveness. In addition, there are no specific procedures foreseen within the instrument for the purpose of enabling the Commission (subject to appropriate legislative scrutiny) to update the non-essential terms of the instrument. In particular, there is no mechanism to enable the lists of EU environmental legislation contained in the Annexes to the directive to be updated. As it stands, any such non-contentious changes need to pass through the full co-decision legislative procedure. The absence of these provisions would appear to indicate that the EU legislature has failed to demonstrate any notable degree of serious political interest in ensuring an active and high-level EU presence in this policy terrain for the future. It is notable also that the EU failed to enact any third-pillar instrument prior to the termination of the tripartite pillar structure in December 2009 by virtue of the Lisbon Treaty to flesh out details on minimum requirements regarding sanctions, reflective also of a distinct lack of interest on the Council's part to engage in this area. Some commentators have also suggested that another shortcoming in the legislative instrument lies in its failure to address the issue of victims' rights.[203] Unlike the Environmental Liability Directive 2004/35, discussed in the previous chapter, the 2008 PECL Directive does not require the voice of persons affected by environmental criminal damage to be taken into account.[204]

The only clear supervisory role for the Commission envisaged by the 2008 PECL Directive is in relation to the transposition of the instrument. Transposition of the directive in national law was required to be completed by 26 December 2010, with member states being obliged to communicate national transposition measures to the Commission.[205] This is the bare minimum of a supervisory role that could be possibly envisaged for the Commission. The task of transposition for member states has not been made straightforward, given that a number of the legal terms in the directive are general and undefined (e.g. 'serious negligence', 'substantial damage') and the Commission has not issued any accompanying soft law guidance.[206] Since the elapse of the transposition deadline, several member states were slow to comply with this basic legislative requirement and the Commission was forced to commence a number of infringement actions under Article 258 TFEU. By October 2011, the Commission was litigating against no less than 11 member states in respect of transposition shortcomings,[207] with one member state being referred to the CJEU in 2012 with a request for imposition of a daily penalty under the accelerated infringement procedure introduced by the Lisbon Treaty (Article 260(3) TFEU).[208] A number of member states were also late with their transposition of the amending Directive 2009/123 on ship-source pollution.[209] However, in the event it appears that all member states have now transposed the EU legislation relating to environmental crime to the satisfaction of the Commission, with no case reaching CJEU judgment stage.

13.4 The impact of the 2007 Lisbon Treaty on the future prospects for EU environmental criminal law

The 2007 Lisbon Treaty made some important changes to the EU treaty framework concerning EU competence to adopt measures combating crime when entering into force in December 2009. As well as eliminating the tripartite pillar structure so as to introduce legal unity to the Union legal order,[210] the Lisbon amendments introduced for the first time express provision for decision-making procedures relating to the promulgation of measures intended to harmonise criminal laws of the member states. The key provision is Article 83 TFEU which is housed within Chapter 4 (Judicial co-operation in criminal matters) of Title V TFEU (Area of Freedom, Security and Justice).[211]

In addition to establishing a more transparent decision-making framework for the development of EU criminal policy, Article 83 TFEU introduces a far more consensual decision-making process at the level of the Council of the EU, with the effect that the principle of unanimity amongst member states ultimately trumps the standard method of QMV in Council decision-making envisaged to apply in relation to TFEU policy matters. It is clear that Article 83 TFEU is intended to serve as the principal provision determining decision-making over criminal policy matters at Union level. The treaty provision should be considered a *lex specialis* to other provisions containing general mandates for Union engagement in policy sectors such as environmental policy (as framed in Articles 191–3 TFEU). Moreover, the TFEU makes it clear that the EP and Council must refrain from adopting acts not provided for by the relevant legislative procedure in the area in question.[212] The effect of these treaty changes would appear to rule out any prospect of Article 192 TFEU, the general legal basis for Union environmental policy decisions (succeeding Article 175 EC), being used as an alternative legal basis in the future for the adoption of EU measures on environmental crime.

Article 83 TFEU contains two potential legal bases for the adoption of EU directives to approximate national criminal laws, namely Article 83(1) and (2). From the perspective of environmental policy, Article 83(2) TFEU is the most significant provision. Both legal bases envisage decision-making at Council level to be governed usually by way of QMV. However, the use of QMV is heavily qualified by a number of derogations which, if deployed, would require Council unanimity before any measure could be adopted. Notably, these include the special procedure contained in Article 83(3) TFEU enabling any member state to force a suspension of QMV. In addition, by virtue of Article 76 TFEU, legislative proposals for both procedures could be introduced formally either by a quarter of member states or by the European Commission, thus ending the latter's traditional monopoly in proposing EU legislative initiatives.

Article 83(1) TFEU provides for the adoption of directives by way of ordinary legislative procedure[213] to establish minimum rules concerning the definition of certain criminal offences and sanctions in the areas of particularly serious crime with a cross-border dimension resulting from the nature or impact of such offences or from a special need to combat them on a common basis. A specific list of the areas of crime covered by the treaty provision is provided, none of which specifically refers to or directly addresses environmental criminal offences. Article 83(1) further provides though that, 'on the basis of developments in crime', the Council of the EU may decide on the basis of unanimity and after gaining the EP's consent to expand the list to identify other areas of crime covered. For a number of reasons, it is not expected that this provision would be likely to be utilised to provide a legal platform for the adoption of Union measures on environmental crime. First, the EU legislature would be faced with having to justify prospective measures on environmental crime on the basis of parameters which may be considered from an environmental protection perspective to be either arbitrary (cross-border dimension) or vague and difficult to satisfy (special need). Secondly, before Article 83(1) could be utilised to enact measures on combating environmental crime, unanimous agreement would have to be obtained at Council level after providing evidence of 'developments in crime' that would warrant such an addition. Thirdly, the alternative legal basis for legislative action contained Article 83(2) offers a much more coherent platform upon which to proceed.

Article 83(2) TFEU provides a legal basis which is based on the broad reasoning utilised by the European Court of Justice (ECJ) in the *Environmental Crimes* judgment to justify environmental crime measures under the auspices of Article 175(1) EC. Specifically, the treaty provision provides a broad and flexible mandate to the EU legislature based on the criterion of essential need in relation to policy implementation:

Article 83[TFEU]

. . .

2.   If the approximation of criminal laws and regulations of the Member States proves essential to ensure the effective implementation of a Union policy in an area which has been subject to harmonisation measures, directives may establish minimum rules with regard to the definition of criminal offences and sanctions in the areas concerned. Such directives shall be adopted by the same ordinary or special legislative procedure as was followed for the adoption of the harmonisation measures in question, without prejudice to Article 76.

This particular legal basis for decision-making would be particularly well-suited for the adoption of measures on environmental crime, not least given that it follows an approach to policy development with which the principal EU institutions and stakeholders are familiar.

As mentioned earlier, Article 83(3) TFEU provides for a special deviation from the standard rule of QMV within the Council of the EU envisaged in the ordinary legislative procedure, and is commonly known as an 'emergency break' procedure providing a safeguard for the preservation of national sovereignty. Specifically, it provides that where a Council member considers that a draft directive based on either Article 83(1) or (2) TFEU 'would affect fundamental aspects of its criminal justice system' the member state concerned may request that the proposal be referred to the European Council, whereupon the ordinary legislative procedure is to be suspended. If within four months there continues to be disagreement amongst member states, the proposal will not be considered any further. However, if at least nine member states wish to pursue its adoption then the measure may be adopted by those Member States on the basis of enhanced co-operation and related decision-making procedures under the auspices of Article 20(2) TEU and Title III TFEU.[214] This would mean that a core of member states could in theory adopt EU measures on environmental crime binding amongst themselves alone, with the other member states remaining unaffected unless and until they might wish to participate in the enhanced co-operation. There is no indication, though, at the moment that this procedure is likely to be triggered any time soon in relation to the area of environmental criminal policy.

Article 83 TFEU has increased substantially the degree of influence and control of individual member states over any moves to enhance Union legislation on combating crime. Notably, it ensures that it would not be possible to force through legislative instrumentation on the supranational basis of QMV. Both legal bases for policy development in Article 83 TFEU are ultimately subject to the principle of Council unanimity being applicable in the event that one member state requires this to happen. In addition, the UK, Ireland and Denmark have additional safeguards, in that their special opt-in arrangements in the field of justice and home affairs apply in relation to the whole of Title V TFEU.[215] As a consequence, from the outset, these three member states will have to provide the EU with specific notification if they wish to participate in the adoption of any measure adopted under Article 83 TFEU.

One should also mention in this context that the Lisbon Treaty 2007 creates specific powers for national parliaments[216] of member states to issue reasoned opinions if they consider an EU legislative proposal to be in breach of the principle of subsidiarity (as now enshrined in Article 5(3) TEU).[217] If at least one-quarter of reasoned opinions from national parliaments is against a particular Commission legislative proposal concerning a criminal policy matter, the proposal must be reviewed by the Commission, which is obliged to justify its response (whether maintaining, amending or withdrawing the proposal).[218] Where a simple majority of national parliamentary reasoned opinions consider that the proposal contravenes the principle of subsidiarity, in addition to being subjected to a Commission review the proposal will also be required to be subject to review by the EP and Council prior to concluding their first reading to assess whether the subsidiarity principle has been breached. If either 55 per cent of the Council members or a majority of EP votes cast consider the proposal to conflict with the principle of subsidiarity, the legislative initiative is to be given no further consideration.[219]

Article 83 TFEU together with the revised Protocol on Subsidiarity and Proportionality are likely to have a profound impact on the prospects for future decision-making processes at EU level in relation to political strategies on environmental crime. In particular, political agreement is far less likely to be forthcoming within the Council of the EU, given that the application of QMV may be resisted by a single member state. National parliaments are likely to scrutinise very carefully whether any legislative proposal has sufficient trans-boundary qualities and elements for the purpose of adhering to the subsidiarity principle. The Lisbon Treaty has effectively shifted political power to the level of the nation state and away from the supranational institutional level. The Lisbon Treaty has essentially transformed the future of decision-making in this EU policy area to be essentially

subject to an intergovernmentalist framework, overriding the practical significance of the CJEU's *Environmental Crimes* judgment.

13.5 Some brief reflections

It is evident in some respects that the EU has made significant legal strides in
developing a clear criminal law dimension to its common environmental policy.
A supranational legislative instrument has been adopted in the form of the 2008
PECL Directive, the culmination of several years of inter-institutional political
battling over the issue of legal competence. The instrument has ensured that
all member states have enacted criminal legislation to tackle the most egregious
instances of environmental crimes committed by natural persons and that corporate entities are held liable for similar conduct.

However, there are a number of significant qualifications involved. In particular, the 2008 PECL Directive has a number of serious limitations, including
notably not envisaging an ongoing role for the Commission in monitoring and
reviewing the legislative instrument or for national authorities in providing periodic reports on their implementation experiences. Updating the material scope
of the directive, so as to be in line with changes to EU environmental protection
legislation, is not going to be straightforward given that the appropriate delegatory
powers to the Commission have not been provided. Moreover, the directive does
not of course stipulate any minimum criminal penalties for specific environmental
offences. Political interest within the Commission in this area appears to have
ebbed away. There appear to be no longer any personnel within the Commission's
Environment Directorate-General dedicated to following up the directive's implementation in a technical capacity. The Commission's website on environmental
crime has been effectively acting for some time now as an archive of information
relating to Commission activities leading up to the adoption of the directive.[220]
The Seventh EU Environment Action Programme (2013–2020) does not foresee
any specific Commission-level work in the area of EU environmental criminal
policy within the context of its (fourth) priority objective on enhancing implementation of EU environmental legislation during the period covered by the programme.[221] Moreover, there appears no intention on the part of member states to
engage in setting any common minimum benchmarks relating to environmental
criminal sanctions. Whether the 2008 PECL Directive will be left to wither in
effective isolation on the legislative vine remains to be seen, but there seems to be
little in the way of political appetite at EU political institutional level currently to
build upon its relatively limited requirements and achievements.

Notes

1 On environmental crimes as sources of international criminal law, see the Statute
of the International Criminal Court 1998 (Art. 8). Regarding international efforts
to require criminalisation under national law of certain environmental offences, see
e.g. the 1973 Convention on International Trade in Endangered Species of Wild
Fauna and Flora (Art. 4), the 1982 United Nations Convention on the Law of the

Sea (Art. 218) and the 1989 Basel Convention on the Control of Transboundary Movements of hazardous Waste and their Disposal (Art. 9). For an overview of developments in international environmental criminal law, see e.g. Boister (2003), Birnie, Boyle and Redgwell (2009), pp. 329 *et seq.*

2 Specifically, the 1989 Basel Convention on the Control of Transboundary Movements of Hazardous Wastes and their Disposal (28 ILM 657(1989)) and the 1973 Convention on International Trade in Endangered Species of Wild Flora and Fauna CITES (993 UNTS 243), as updated and the 1987 Montreal Protocol on Substances that Deplete the Ozone Layer (26 ILM 154 (1987)).

3 US Government commissioned 'International Crime Threat Assessment' of 2000 (available at http://clinton4.nara.gov/WH/EOP/NSC/html/documents/pub45270/pub45270chap2.html#6).

4 EU Network for the Implementation of Environmental Law.

5 IMPEL TFS Seaport and Verification Projects 2004–2006, report available at: http://ec.europa.eu/environment/impel/impel_tfs.html.

6 IMPEL-TFS, *Enforcement of EU Waste Shipment Regulation* (IMPEL-TFS Enforcement Action II, Interim Project Report, 12 October 2009).

7 See studies on DG ENV website: http://ec.europa.eu/environment/legal/crime/studies_en.htm. Faure and Heine, *Criminal penalties in EU Member States' Environmental Law* (2002); Huglo Lepage & Partners, *Study on Environmental Crime in the 27 Member States* (2007).

8 Namely the 1951 European Economic and Steel Community, 1957 European Economic Community Treaty and 1957 European Atomic Energy (Euratom) Treaty. The EEC Treaty was renamed as the European Community (EC) Treaty in 1992, by virtue of the TEU 1992.

9 Case C-176/03 *Commission v Council* [2005] ECR I-7879.

10 OJ 2008 L328/28.

11 1998 CETS 72. The Convention is available for inspection on the Council of Europe's website: http://conventions.coe.int.

12 The official origins of the Convention may be traced to the establishment of a selected committee of experts in 1991, set up in the wake of a 1990 resolution adopted under the auspices of the Council of Europe's Committee of Ministers recommending the development of common guidelines for the purpose of combating environmental impairment. See Resolution No. 1 of the 17th Conference of Ministers of Justice (1990, Istanbul). See Section I (Historical Background) of the Explanatory Report accompanying the Convention, available on the Council of Europe's website. Prior to the 1990 ministerial resolution, the Council of Europe had studied possibilities of developing a criminal dimension to environmental protection, see Selin (2001), p. 106

13 Recital 2 CPECL.

14 Austria, Belgium, Denmark, Estonia, Finland, France, Germany, Greece, Iceland, Italy, Luxembourg, Romania and Sweden. The non-EU signatory state is Ukraine.

15 Estonia ratified on 26 April 2002.

16 Art. 13 CPECL.

17 Ibid., Arts. 2–11.

18 Ibid., Art. 12.

19 Section I (Art. 1) and Section IV (Arts. 13) of CPECL deal with definitions and general obligations pertaining to the legal effects of the Convention respectively.

20 Ibid., Art. 3(2).

21 Specifically offences listed ibid., Art. 2(1)(a)(ii) and Art. 2(1)(b).

22 See Section III (Commentary) of the Explanatory Report regarding Arts. 2–4 CPECL accompanying the Convention.

23 Just like for the majority of offences covered by Arts. 2–3, Art. 4 CPECL makes liability dependent on the defendant acting in breach of domestic rules of law. Accordingly,

if the activity in question is covered by a licence issued by a competent authority, no
offence will be committed under the terms of Art. 4.

24 Art. 4(a) CPECL.
25 Ibid., Art. 4(b).
26 Ibid., Art. 4(c).
27 Ibid., Art. 4(d).
28 Ibid., Art. 4 (e).
29 Ibid., Art. 4 (f).
30 Ibid., Art. 4 (g).
31 Ibid., Art. 2(1)(a).
32 See definition of 'unlawful', ibid., Art. 1(a).
33 Under Art. 3(2) CPECL parties may restrict the criminal penalisation of negligent
    acts to acts committed with 'gross negligence'.
34 See Selin (2001), p. 114.
35 Art. 9(3) CPECL.
36 Ibid., Art. 9(2).
37 Ibid., Art. 7.
38 See ibid., Art. 6, final sentence, and Art. 8.
39 Ibid., Art. 5(1)(a).
40 Ibid., Art. 5(1)(b).
41 Ibid., Ibid., Art. 5(1)(c).
42 Ibid., Art. 5(4)L.
43 Ibid., Art. 10(1)(a).
44 Ibid., Art. 10(2).
45 See e.g. Selin (2001).
46 E.g. Art. 6 CPECL defers to contracting parties as to what criminal sanctions to apply
    in respect of any of the environmental offences defined in the Convention.
47 E.g. Art. 3(2) CPECL allows the contracting parties the option of restricting criminal-
    ising negligence to covering gross negligence. Other examples include Arts. 7, 8 and 9
    CPECL, which provide parties with the option of deciding whether to provide for
    confiscation, reinstatement and criminal corporate liability respectively.
48 Art. 17 CPECL.
49 Ibid., Art. 20.
50 Ibid., Art. 19 makes provision for the settlement of disputes over the interpretation
    or application of the Convention. However, this may be performed by informal con-
    fidential negotiation between disputants and is not required to be carried out by an
    independent third party. Moreover, CPECL does not provide for the monitoring of
    compliance with the Convention by an independent body, in contrast with the posi-
    tion applicable to the TFEU in respect of which the European Commission is vested
    with specific supervisory responsibilities and powers (see notably Arts. 258 and 260
    TFEU).
51 Selin (2001), p. 106.
52 For a detailed analysis of this area see e.g. Hedemann-Robinson (2008a) and (2008b).
53 Namely, Arts. 191–3 TFEU.
54 See e.g. Roger France (1994), p. 354; Delmas-Marty (1998), p. 87; Kaiafa-Gbandi
    (2001), p. 249.
55 See e.g. Corstens (2003), p. 144; Roger France (1994), p. 358.
56 See e.g. Bridge (1976), p. 91; Dine (1993), p. 246; Roger France (1994), p. 354.
57 Wasmeier and Thwaites (2004), p. 614.
58 OJ 1992 C191
59 Albrecht and Braum (1999), p. 302.
60 Some have pointed to the so-called passerelle (or bridging) clause within the former
    (pre-Lisbon) version of the TEU, namely former Art. 42 EU, as evidence in support
    of this interpretation. This particular TEU provision enabled the member states to

transfer third-pillar matters to the first pillar (specifically, Title IV of the former EC Treaty). See e.g. Corstens (2003), p. 136; Kaiafa-Gbandi (2001), p. 42.

61 Final Report of Working Group X, 'Freedom, Security and Justice', to the European Convention (WGX 14 CONV 426/02, 2 December 2002)

62 See e.g. Wasmeier and Thwaites (2004), p. 614.

63 See Arts. 29, first sentence and 47 EU.

64 See e.g. Weyembergh (2005), p. 1568; Wasmeier and Thwaites (2004), p. 628; Krämer (2006b), p. 277. Specifically, upon close inspection of Arts. 29 and 31(1) (e) EU, it appears that the remit for the Union to harmonise national criminal rules under the auspices of the third pillar was limited. These provisions referred only to certain types of crime that may be subject to approximation as part of the third pillar's freedom, security and justice objective, namely: organised crime, terrorism and drug trafficking. The third pillar did, though, specifically provide for the possibility of measures being adopted to facilitate co-operation between investigative, prosecuting and judicial authorities to prevent and combat crime (see former Art. 29 EU, first two indents).

65 Comte (2003), p. 153. See notably former Art. 31(1)(e) EU.

66 Wasmeier and Thwaites (2004), p. 625. However, this particular argument seems rather unconvincing. It appears instead far more plausible that the exclusion clauses were integrated within the framework treaty provisions in these two common policy areas because it was apparent that their objectives directly related to combating particular types of criminal behaviour. No doubt the member states assumed that there was no need to provide for exclusion clauses elsewhere in the first pillar, including in relation to environmental policy, on the grounds that the link between criminal policy and the other Community common policies was too tenuous and remote to consider that criminal policy powers could be legally implied in relation to them.

67 Former Art. 34(2) EU.

68 Former Art. 39 EU.

69 Former Art. 211 EC.

70 Former Arts. 226 and 228 EC.

71 Direct effect was specifically ruled out in relation to legislative-type instruments that might be adopted under the auspices of the third pillar, namely framework decisions and decisions (see former Arts. 34(2)(b)–(c) EU).

72 See former Arts. 33 and 35 EU.

73 See former Arts. 220–45 EC.

74 For an in-depth legal analysis of the evolution of the third pillar which is beyond the scope of this book, see e.g. Peers (2006) and (2012).

75 The TEU entered into force on 1 November 1993, one month after all the member states had ratified the treaty.

76 OJ 1997 C347.

77 Arts. K.1–K.9 EU, original 1992 version.

78 Former Art. K.7 EU.

79 Former Art. K.9 EU.

80 Former Arts. 29–42 EU (replacing Arts K.1–K.14 EU).

81 The areas of asylum, immigration and judicial co-operation in civil matters became incorporated within the provisions of Title IV to the former EC Treaty on Visas, Asylum, Immigration and Other Policies Relating to the Free Movement of Persons (former Arts. 61–9 EC), whilst the sector of customs co-operation was also transferred to the former first pillar (former Art. 135 EC).

82 Specifically, with regard to former Arts. 31 and 40 EU.

83 OJ 2001 C80.

84 The objective of transforming the geographical area of the EU into an area of freedom, security and justice was introduced into the Union's treaty framework by virtue

of the ToA. See notably former Arts. 2, fourth indent and 29(1) EU and former Art. 61 EC.

85 Former Art. 30(1) EU.
86 See Former Arts. 30(2) and 31(2) EU.
87 The European policing body established by the 1995 Europol Convention (OJ 1995 C316/1).
88 Eurojust is an EU agency established to facilitate cross-border co-operation between national prosecutors (OJ 2002 L63/1).
89 See former Art. 30(1) EU.
90 See former Art. 31(1) EU.
91 Former Art. K.6 EU.
92 See former Arts. 29 and 47 EU.
93 Vienna Action Plan (OJ 1999 C19/1).
94 Ibid., Point 18.
95 Point 48 of the Presidency Conclusions of the European Council, Tampere 16.10.1999.
96 Initiative of the Kingdom of Denmark with a view to adopting a Council Framework Decision on combating serious environmental crime (OJ 2000 C39/4).
97 Ibid., Art. 2(1).
98 Ibid., Art. 1(1).
99 Ibid., Art. 1(1)(a).
100 Ibid., Art. 1(1)(b).
101 Ibid., Art. 1(2), first subpara.
102 The draft refers to certain factors to be taken into account in assessing whether the offence is major in scale, specifically whether the crime is systematic or persistent, pre-meditated or has been the subject of attempts of concealment (Art. 1(2), second subpara.)
103 The range of targeted behaviour is narrower than that addressed under CPECL, which is mostly focused on behaviour considered unlawful under national level.
104 Ibid., Art. 2(1).
105 Ibid., Ibid., Art. 2(1)(b).
106 Ibid., Art. 14.
107 E.g. a number of sanctions for offenders were set out as mandatory in the Danish initiative including in relation to the confiscation of equipment, proceeds and assets of criminal activity as well as environmental rehabilitation.
108 Specifically, Art. 3 required member states to ensure law enforcement authorities be endowed with effective investigative powers and Art. 5 obliged them to ensure appropriate co-ordination of national authority activity.
109 Specifically, the Danish proposal sought to provide clarification on territorial jurisdiction (Art. 4), transnational co-operation between agencies involved in investigation and prosecution (Art. 6), exchange of information (Art. 7), transfer of proceedings and enforcement of criminal penalties (Art. 8) and the establishment of national contact points for collection and exchange of information on crime (Art. 9).
110 Ibid., Arts. 10–13.
111 OJ 2001 C121/502.
112 COM(2001)139, Commission proposal for a directive on the protection of the environment through criminal law, 13 March 2001.
113 SEC(2001) 227, Commission Staff Working Paper, *Establishment of an Acquis on Criminal Sanctions against Environmental Offences*, 7 February 2001.
114 COM(2001)139, p. 2.
115 Now Art. 4(3) TEU.
116 See e.g. Case 68/88 *Commission v Greece (Greek Maize)* (paras. 24–5 of judgment). See also Case C-326/88 *Anklagemyndigheden v Hansen & Soen* (para. 17 of judgment) and

Case C-186/98 *Criminal proceedings against M Nunes and E de Matos* (paras. 9–12 of judgment).

117 COM(2001)139, p. 2.

118 SEC(2001) 227, p. 5.

119 Art. 4 of the First Draft PECL Directive also requires member states to criminalise 'participation in or instigation' of Art. 3 offences. The approach of the draft text with regard to addressing inchoate offences is similar to that in the CPECL (see Art. 2(2) of the Convention).

120 The preventive approach of the 2001 Draft PECL Directive accords with EU treaty requirements that the common environmental policy should be based on the principle of preventive action; it also accords with principles of precaution and attainment of a high level of environmental protection, both constituent elements of EU environmental policy (see former Art. 174(2) EC (now superseded by Art. 191(2) TFEU)).

121 Exhaustively cited in the 2001 proposal's Annex.

122 The effect of the CPECL model risks undermining national initiatives adopting relatively high environmental protection systems, as contracting parties may harbour concerns of imposing enforcement regimes that might deflect inward investment towards lowest common denominator jurisdictions.

123 As is picked up by the Commission's Staff Working Paper (SEC(2001)227, p. 2) the problem of ill-defined terminology is a serious flaw of CPECL.

124 See SEC(2001)227 Commission Staff Working Paper, section 2.1; Comte (2005), p. 216.

125 By virtue of former Art. 5(2)–(3) EC. See also the Protocol on the Application of Subsidiarity and Proportionality, as annexed to the EC Treaty by virtue of the ToA.

126 COM(2001)139, p. 4.

127 Specifically: fines, exclusion from public financial assistance, temporary or permanent disqualification from the practice of commercial activities, and judicial supervision or winding up orders.

128 Interestingly, the 2000 Danish initiative was more stringent in this respect in seeking to make compulsory criminal corporate liability in respect of serious environmental crime.

129 By virtue of Art. 2(a) of the draft text concerning on the definition of 'legal persons'.

130 As detailed by Comte (2003), p. 150.

131 EP Resolutions of 9 April 2002 on the 2001 Draft PECL Directive and draft Council Framework Decision (Docs. T-5–0147/2002 and T5–0151/2002 respectively).

132 Draft EESC Opinion (Agriculture, rural development and environment section) of 11 April 2001 (Doc. NAT/114). In the absence of a Council common position stalling progress of completion of the co-decision legislative procedure under former Art. 251 EC, the EESC did not feel it within its formal powers to be able to issue a formal opinion.

133 COM(2002)544 final, 30 September 2002. In the absence of the Council acting, the Commission is entitled to revise its legislative proposals unilaterally (see former Art. 250(2) EC (now superseded by Art. 293(2) TFEU).

134 Council Framework Decision 2003/80/JHA on the protection of the environment through criminal law (OJ 2003 L29/55).

135 Ibid., Arts. 5(2) and 7(a)–(e).

136 Namely, ibid., Arts. 8 (jurisdiction) and 9 (extradition and prosecution).

137 See Commission's early appraisal of the extent of implied powers of the Community under former Art. 174 EC in SEC(2001)227, Commission Staff Working Paper, *Establishment of an Acquis on Criminal Sanctions against Environmental Offences*, 7 February 2001.

138 Former Art. 35(6) EU provided, *inter alia*, that the CJEU had jurisdiction to review the legality of framework decisions in actions brought by the Commission on grounds of lack of competence, infringement of an essential procedural requirement, infringement of the TEU or of any rule relating to its application, or misuse of powers.

139 Council Decision 2003/80/JHA (OJ 2003 L29/55).
140 Case C-176/03 *Commission v Council (Environmental Crimes)* [2005] ECR I-7879
141 See e.g. Ryland (2009); Dawes and Lynskey (2008); Herlin-Karnell (2007); Biondi and Harmer (2007); Jacobs (2006); Krämer (2006b); Tobler (2006); Hedemann-Robinson (2005).
142 Francis Jacobs, former Advocate General (AG) of the CJEU, made the following acerbic comment about the reaction by *The Times* newspaper article 'Legal Trespass' (14 September 2005) at a guest lecture in the UK on the role of the CJEU in environmental protection:

> The judgment, which the British Government called 'disappointing', was according to an editorial in *The Times*, 'as ominous as it is deluded' and a 'transparent attempt at empire-building beyond the boundaries laid down for Europe's bureaucrats'. It was also branded a 'lamentable judgment' which 'strikes at the heart of national sovereignty and Britain's ability to decide the law for itself'. The editorial concluded that 'democracy yesterday suffered a grievous defeat in a court whose contempt for sovereignty verges on the criminal'. However, on arrival today from Luxembourg to give this lecture, I am glad to say that I was not arrested on charges of high treason.

> Extract from his lecture published in Jacobs (2006), p. 202.

143 Former Art. 47 EU stipulated:

> Subject to the provisions amending the Treaty establishing the European Economic Community with a view to establishing the European Community, the Treaty establishing the European Coal and Steel Community and the Treaty establishing the European Atomic Energy Community, and to these final provisions, *nothing in this Treaty shall affect the Treaties establishing the European Communities or the subsequent Treaties and Acts modifying of supplementing them*. [Author's emphasis added]

144 Case C-176/03 (para. 48 of judgment).
145 See paras. 83, 94 and 95 of the AG's Opinion in Case C-176/03 *Commission v Council*.
146 See Jacobs (2006), p. 205; Dawes and Lynskey (2008), pp. 137 *et seq*.
147 COM(2005)583, Commission Communication to the EP and Council on the implications of the Court's judgment of 13 September 2005 (Case C-176/03 Commission v Council), 23 November 2005.
148 Directive 2005/35/EC on ship-source pollution and on the introduction of penalties for infringements and Framework Decision 2005/667/JHA to strengthen the criminal law framework for the enforcement of the law against ship-source pollution (OJ 2005 L255/11 and 164).
149 As foreseen to be the applicable legislative decision-making procedure under Art. 175 EC, the legal basis of the 2001 Draft PECL Directive.
150 Para. 8 of EP Resolution P6_TA(2006)0458 of 26 October 2006 (Use of criminal law to protect the environment).
151 COM(2007)51, Commission proposal for a Directive on the protection of the environment through criminal law, 9 February 2007. See also accompanying Commission press releases on RAPID: IP/07/166 and MEMO/07/50, Brussels, 9 February 2007 (available for inspection on the EU's official website; www.europa.eu.int).
152 As confirmed in the Explanatory Memorandum to the Second Draft PECL Directive, COM(2007)51, section 5.1, p. 7.
153 Hedemann-Robinson (2008b).
154 The only abstract offences in the draft text concerned illicit trade in waste and ozone depleting substances (as set out in Art. 3(e) and (h) Draft 2007 PECL Directive).
155 Ibid., Art. 2(a).
156 This is a fundamental weakness of previous European intergovernmental instruments on environmental crime.

157 Arts. 6 (Liability of legal persons) and 4 (Participation and Instigation), COM(2007)51.
158 It is not clear, though, how the stipulation of a maximum sanction could be reconciled with the principle enshrined in EU treaty provisions relating to a common environmental policy allowing member states to main or introduce 'more stringent protection measures' (see former Art. 176 EC (now superseded by Art. 193 TFEU).
159 See p. 8 of the Explanatory Memorandum of the Second Draft PECL Directive, COM(2007)51.
160 Art. 5(4), COM(2007)51.
161 Ibid., Art. 5(3).
162 Ibid., Art. 5(2).
163 Ibid., Art. 5(1).
164 Ibid., Art. 5(5).
165 Ibid., Art. 7(1).
166 Ibid., Arts. 7(2)(c), (b) and (a) respectively.
167 Fines imposed by the Commission for substantive breaches of EU Competition Law, notably Arts. 101–2 TFEU (ex Arts. 81–2 EC), are required to be calculated on the basis of up to 10% annual global turnover of a defendant (Art. 23 of Regulation 1/2003 (OJ 2003 L1/1)). As a result, fines may be very substantial and have a stronger chance of rendering a deterrent effect. For example, Microsoft was fined in 2004 by the Commission close to €500m in respect of an abuse of a dominant position prohibited under Art. 102 TFEU (Case COMP/C-3/37.792). In 2012 the Commission imposed fine of almost €1.5bn on undertakings participating in a long-standing cartel within the television and monitor tubing sector (COM RAPID press release IP/12/1317, 5 December 2012). The proposed model fining regime contained within the 2007 Draft PECL Directive simply pales in comparison.
168 The draft text refers to turnover or financial gain attained or envisaged by commission of the offence as examples that could be used as the basis for calculation of individual fines.
169 Art. 7(2) final para.; COM(2007)51.
170 Ibid., Art. 7(4) (a)–(g). This provision cited seven additional non-criminal sanctions by way of example: obligations relating to environmental reinstatement or adopting specific measures to eliminate consequences of illegal conduct; exclusion from public financial assistance; disqualification from practising an activity; judicial supervision and winding up orders; and the publication of relevant judicial decisions such as those relating to conviction and/or sanction.
171 Case C-440/05 *Commission v Council*.
172 See e.g. Dawes and Lynskey (2008); Faure (2008); Hedemann-Robinson (2008c); Lowther (2007).
173 Directive 2005/35 on Ship-source pollution and on the introduction of penalties for infringements (OJ 2005 L255/11).
174 1973 International Convention for the Prevention of Pollution from Ships (12 ILM (1973) 1319, as amended by its 1978 Protocol (17 ILM (1978) 546) and subsequently updated.
175 See notably, Transport Council's conclusions on ship safety and pollution prevention of 6 December 2002 and the Presidency conclusions of the European Council, Copenhagen, 13 December 2002.
176 See Art. 4 of COM(2003)92, Commission proposal for a directive on ship-source pollution and on the introduction of sanctions, including criminal sanctions, for pollution offences, 5 March 2003.
177 Council Framework Decision 2005/667/JHA to strengthen the criminal law framework for the enforcement of the law against ship-source pollution (OJ 2005 L255/164).
178 Art. 4 (Infringements) of Directive 2005/35.
179 Ibid., Art. 8 (Penalties).
180 Under former Art. 35(6) EU.

181 Namely, contrary to former Art. 47 EU.
182 Arts. 2 (Criminal Offences) and 3 (Aiding abetting and inciting) of Council Framework Dec. 2005/667/JHA.
183 Ibid., Art. 5.
184 Opinion of AG Mazak in Case C-440/05 *Commission v Council*, delivered on 28 June 2007.
185 See para. 70 of the Court's judgment in Case C-440/05 *Commission v Council*.
186 Arts. 4 (Penalties) and 6 (Penalties against legal persons) of Council Decision 2005/667/JHA.
187 Directive 2009/123 amending Directive 2005/35/EC on ship-source pollution and on the introduction of penalties for infringements (OJ 2009 L280/52).
188 Case C-308/06 *R v Secretary of State for Transport, ex parte International Association of Independent Tanker Owners (Intertanko)*. See case comment by Pereira (2008).
189 This translates roughly to mean no crime or punishment without law to cover the offence in question.
190 Case C-308/06 (para. 45 of the CJEU judgment).
191 Ibid., para. 69.
192 Ibid., paras 71–8.
193 OJ 2008 L328/28.
194 Art. 8(1) of Directive 2008/99.
195 See e.g. Council of the EU Press Release 16183/07 (Press 286) of the minutes of the 2842nd Council Meeting (Environment), Brussels, 20 December 2007.
196 By the beginning of March 2008, the Slovenian Presidency had consulted informally the Rapporteurs of the EP's Committee on Legal Affairs and Committee on the Environment, Public Health and Food Safety (see Council Doc. 6749/1/08 REV1 (DROIPEN 16) of 4 March 2008).
197 As noted in p. 13 of the minutes of the 2874th Council Meeting (Environment), Luxembourg, 5 June 2008 (Council Doc. 9959/08 (Presse 149)).
198 Annex A lists first-pillar environmental legislative measures and Annex B lists certain Euratom legislation.
199 Art. 2(a)(i)–(iii) of Directive 2008/99.
200 In comparison, the Commission's 2007 draft proposal was broader in scope, covering instigation of and participation in serious negligent as well as intentional conduct (Art. 4 of COM(2007)51).
201 Art. 6(2) of the 2008 PECL Directive 2008/99.
202 For a discussion on the meaning of the concept of effective, proportionate and dissuasive penalties, see e.g. Faure (2010).
203 See Cardwell, French and Hall (2011).
204 See Art. 12 of Directive 2004/35 (OJ 2004 L143/56).
205 Ibid., Art. 8.
206 For analysis of this aspect see Faure (2010).
207 EU RAPID press release IP/11/1246, Brussels, 27 October 2011. The member states concerned were Austria, Cyprus, the Czech Republic, Finland, Germany, Greece, Lithuania, Malta, Portugal, Slovenia and the UK.
208 EU RAPID press release IP/12/296, Brussels, 22 March 2012. The member state concerned was Cyprus, with the Commission requesting a daily penalty of €5,909.
209 EU RAPID press release IP/11/739, Brussels, 16 June 2011. In June 2011, the Commission commenced infringement action against eight member states over failures to transpose Directive 2009/123 on time: Czech Republic, Finland, Greece, Italy, Lithuania, Portugal, Romania and Slovakia.
210 See Art. 1 TEU and Art. 1(2) TFEU.
211 Arts. 67–89 TFEU. Effectively, Title V of the TFEU is based upon a merging as well as expansion of the policy fields covered by Title IV of the former EC Treaty (on Visas, Asylum, Immigration and other Policies Related to Free Movement of Persons)

and those policy areas addressed in Title VI of the pre-Lisbon version of the TEU (on Police and Judicial Co-operation in Criminal Matters).

212 Art. 296(3) TFEU.

213 The TFEU introduced the 'ordinary legislative procedure' by way of replacement to the former co-decision procedure currently used in the former EC Treaty. The ordinary legislative procedure is set out in Art. 294 TFEU and is similar to the co-decision procedure in requiring both the EP and Council to give their consent before a measure may be passed.

214 Arts. 326–34 TFEU, notably Art. 329 TFEU.

215 See Protocol (No. 21) on the position of the UK and Ireland in respect of the Area of Freedom, Security and Justice (OJ 2008 C115/295; OJ 2007 C306/185) and Protocol (No. 22) on the position of Denmark (OJ 2008 C115/299; OJ 2007 C306/187), annexed to the TEU and TFEU as amended by the Lisbon Treaty 2007. Both protocols are contained in the consolidated versions of the TEU and TEFU, as amended prospectively by the Lisbon Treaty 2007, published in the EU Official Journal (OJ 2008 C115).

216 See the Protocol (No. 2) on the Application of the Principles of Subsidiarity and Proportionality, as adopted by the Lisbon Treaty (OJ 2010 C83). (The Protocol replaced the former 1997 Protocol of the same title.)

217 Art. 5(3) TEU states:

> Under the principle of subsidiarity, in areas which do not fall within its exclusive competence, the Union shall act only if and so far as the objectives of the proposed action cannot be sufficiently achieved by the Member States, either at central level or at regional and local level, but can rather, by reason of the scale or effects of the proposed action, be better achieved at Union level.

218 Art. 7(2) Protocol (No. 2).

219 Ibid., Art. 7(3).

220 See relevant DG ENV website: http://ec.europa.eu/environment/legal/crime/index.htm.

221 See *Priority Objective 4: To Maximise the Benefits of EU Environmental Legislation* of Decision No. 1386/2013/EU of the European Parliament and of the Council of 20 November 2013 on a General Union Environment Action Programme to 2020 'Living Well, within the Limits of our Planet' (OJ 2013 L354/171).

14 EU environmental law enforcement

Reflections

As part of its analysis of the various EU legal arrangements that provide the framework for the enforcement of EU environmental law, this book has sought to reveal the extent to which this framework is adequate in harnessing the primary actors interested in enforcement work. Specifically, its exploration of the field has considered the roles of the European Commission, private persons and member state national authorities. During the early years of the Union's development of an environmental dimension to its policy objectives in the 1970s and 1980s, the European Commission shouldered a considerable degree of responsibility for overseeing that implementation of EU environmental law was carried out at national level. The Commission utilised its powers to prosecute member states under the infringement procedures (as enshrined in Articles 258 and 260 of the Treaty on the Functioning of the European Union (TFEU)) to cover a wide variety of non-compliance scenarios. Subsequently, it is evident that supervisory responsibility and power has become more widely dispersed. In particular, since the early 2000s the EU has adopted a range of legislative and non-legislative initiatives to facilitate increased involvement for both civil society as well as national authorities in law enforcement work concerning EU environmental legislation. This shift in terms of power and responsibility is to be welcomed, as it has always been highly unrealistic as well as conceptually problematic to assume that the Commission on its own would be both capable or suited exclusively to fulfil the challenging task of ensuring due application of EU environmental legislation throughout the territory of the European Union.

The Commission continues to play a very significant role in the enforcement of EU environmental law, notwithstanding relatively recent changes to enhance the law enforcement position of other actors. There are good reasons to support the view that this should remain the case. In particular, given its supranational and therefore central institutional status within the polity of the EU, the Commission is well-suited to playing a crucial role in ensuring that EU member states' national laws accord with their EU environmental obligations. The system employed by the Union to require member states to notify the Commission of their national legislation intended to implement EU directives in advance of the relevant deadline for transposing a directive's provisions into national law is both logical and effective. The Commission's services are in a good position to supervise and ensure that the transposition of EU environmental directives is carried out fully and on time. Independent from member state interests, the Commission's role of scrutinising national transposition legislation gives states confidence that supervision will be carried out on the basis of equal treatment and more effectively than would be the case under a system of peer review. The Commission is the only political Union institution whose remit is exclusively tied to serving the EU interest. However, the Commission's law enforcement function faces a number of problems and limitations.

From a practical perspective, it is clear that the powers afforded to the Commission under the infringement procedures contained in Articles 258 and 260 TFEU are not as effective as they might be. In a number of respects, one could say that the Commission is effectively being required to operate with one hand tied behind its back. Notably, the infringement procedures are still relatively cumbersome and slow to take effect in practice, notwithstanding recent changes made by way of treaty amendment under the 2007 Lisbon Treaty. Member states are effectively provided with too much time after transposition deadlines to ensure that their national legal system complies with Union legislative obligations. The pre-litigation phase under the aegis of Article 258 TFEU is overly deferential to the defendant member state, in requiring the Commission to issue the defendant with two formal written warnings before an application may be made to the CJEU. In practice, this often transpires to be three warnings with the issuing of an informal 'pre-letter of formal notice' by the Commission prior to the commencement of the infringement procedure. Only one warning should be required. In non-conformity cases this is underlined by the fact that the member states have already had a considerable period of time granted by each EU directive to allow for transposition to take place (typically two years but sometimes significantly longer). One positive development to note has been the Lisbon Treaty amendment[1] enabling the Commission to request the Court of Justice of the European Union (CJEU) to impose financial penalties already in first-round infringement proceedings involving the failure by a defendant member state to take sufficient measures to transpose EU directives into national law on time. This eliminates the need to go through two rounds of infringement proceeding for this type of case.

Another significant problem concerning the infringements procedure is that the Commission is not vested with any general powers to carry out on-site investigations into suspected cases of bad application of EU environmental law. As a consequence, its legal services are wholly reliant upon evidence supplied to them by the public or national authorities before they will usually be in any position to assess whether a case should be brought under Article 258 TFEU. This is unsatisfactory, given that civil society (notably members of the public and non-governmental organisations (NGEOs)) will not usually be vested with any legal powers to inspect sites and it may be the case that national authorities may, for various reasons (e.g. political, resource-related), be reluctant to intervene. The conferral of investigative powers to the Commission for environmental casework, along the lines granted to its services in other Union policy sectors, such as fisheries and competition, is long overdue. A Commission power to undertake surprise inspections of installations and other sites suspected of being the locus for EU environmental law infringements would lend the current system of law enforcement a much needed element of deterrence and credibility.

The Commission's services dealing with environmental infringement casework remain understaffed, with usually no more than two lawyers (if lucky) attending to all infringements for each member state. One has to bear in mind here that complaints against member states in connection with implementation of EU environmental legislation number amongst the highest for any policy sector (around 19 per cent between 2009 and 2012).[2] Unless the situation regarding human resources is radically improved, which appears unlikely, the Commission will continue to be overstretched in dealing with its infringement casework. The Commission has also taken steps to reduce the number of bad-application complaints it investigates and to concentrate on non-conformity cases through internal reforms introduced in 2007–8. One could say that it has cut its cloth according to the administrative and legal resources placed at its disposal. Such a development has been regressive, bearing in mind the often very considerable financial and legal obstacles that complainants may face in taking legal action at national level and the possibility that national authorities might not be in a position to take enforcement action themselves in certain cases (due to incapacity or reluctance to take action).

The limitations inherent in supranational supervision of EU law should not be overlooked either. It is obviously not realistic to expect the Commission to intervene in all bad-application cases throughout the EU, at the time of writing numbering 28 member countries and likely to expand its membership further over time. In terms of bad-application cases, the Commission's role should be confined sensibly to addressing those infringements on the ground which lend themselves to being addressed at EU level. These could include cross-border pollution scenarios, precedent-type cases involving important unresolved issues of EU environmental law, cases involving gross violations of EU environmental legislation and cases where it is evident that no legal enforcement action is likely to be taken at national level by competent authorities.

The impact of the 'second-round' infringement action under Article 260(2) TFEU has been relatively modest, and this is down to the structuring of the enforcement procedures themselves. From a positive perspective, the introduction of financial penalties for breaches of EU obligations under this provision in 1992 and subsequently amended by virtue of the 2007 Lisbon Treaty offers a far more effective form of sanction to be applied in respect of breaches EU environmental law than simply the traditional judicial declaration of illegality from the CJEU. Declarations of illegality do not in practice cut much ice, at least in the short to medium term after a judgment has been handed down by the Court. Experience shows that the imposition of financial sanctions is far more likely to concentrate the minds of national governments than international court judgments on the rule of international law. Minds were certainly concentrated, for example, with the CJEU's judgment in *French Fishing Controls (2)*[3] on the application of Article 260(2) TFEU. The Court imposed on France a daily penalty of some €57 million for each six months it continued to fail to adhere to an earlier 'first-round' judgment against it relating to implementation of EU measures requiring the imposition of conservation measures in the fishing industry and a lump sum fine of €20 million. No fewer than 16 member states elected to make observations to the CJEU in this case.

However, behind the headline figures lie some real concerns with this procedure. For instance, the onus of proof in second-round proceedings is on the Commission to prove non-compliance with a first-round judgment. This confers an unwarranted benefit on defendant member states, which should instead have the burden to demonstrate compliance with a first-round judgment. In addition, the penalties applicable under the Article 260(2) procedure may only be set in relation to the time after first-round judgment, not after the date when it was found by the CJEU that an infringement of EU environmental law had occurred. In addition, it appears fairly clear that member states have been guilty of taking advantage of the weaknesses of the system, in stringing out second-round proceedings to the last minute until the passing of the deadline for responding to the second-round reasoned opinion. If they comply before that deadline, no sanctions may be imposed even though a lot of unnecessary environmental damage may have been perpetrated as a result of the state's non-compliance until that point. Given these and other structural weaknesses in the second-round procedure, further reform of the infringements procedures is required. Specifically, the first-round procedure under Article 258 TFEU must be made more robust in providing for the possibility of financial sanctions being applied in every type of case, not just in respect of non-communication of directives as is the position currently. Such a change would render the second-round infringement procedure otiose.

The institutional structure of the European Commission also presents problems from a law enforcement perspective. From the discussion in Chapter 5, it is evident that the multiplicity of tasks incumbent upon the Commission may serve on occasion to clash with its duty to ensure the application of EU law under Article 17 TEU. Specifically, alongside its law enforcement role, the Commission is charged with political and legislative responsibilities under the EU's founding treaties. Since the inception of the EU, it has been vested with exclusive power to propose EU legislation in the vast majority of common policy sectors of the Community. It also has powers to exercise a notable influence on the EU legislative process itself. Specifically, it may force the Council of the EU to decide on the basis of unanimity if it disagrees with European Parliament amendments made to environmental legislative proposals adopted under the ordinary legislative procedure, as set out in Article 294(9) TFEU. These and other factors have come to entrench the Commission's central position of influence with respect to decisions over policy development within the Union. Occasionally, for a variety of reasons, the dual functions of policy development and law enforcement may conflict with one another. For instance, the Commission may be placed in the position of having to decide whether to undertake legal action against a member state based on the legal merits or to abstain from launching proceedings on account of a need to garner support from the particular member state, such as secure its votes in the Council of the EU with respect to another (related or unrelated) policy measure.

These sometimes conflicting pressures may be felt at every level of the Commission, both within the Commissioners' College as well as at departmental level. Although rare, such a conflict of interests may come to be felt in crucially important cases, enough to undermine the credibility of the Commission to deliver justice impartially when most wanted.

For this reason, the current position of the Commission's law enforcement role needs to be reviewed. At the very least, the Commission must be required to organise its legal teams dealing with infringement actions in a viable independent setting. That could mean, for instance, creating a separate Directorate-General (DG) for Infringements or merging the infringement teams with the Commission's Legal Service, which is mainly responsible for representing the Commission before the CJEU and delivering binding internal legal opinions in the event of a dispute over the interpretation of EU law between two DGs. In addition, it might well mean that the Commission President, under whose immediate authority the Commission's Legal Service operates within the Secretariat General, has to provide an undertaking publicly that Legal Service work is not to be subject to the presidency's political influence and that the College of Commissioners is to adhere to legal analysis supplied by the Legal Service. Formally, though, the College would still take the decisions on infringement cases. Alternatively, and perhaps a more satisfactory solution from a theoretical perspective, would be to divest the Commission of its responsibilities for environmental law enforcement work and to confer this to an independent Union organ, such as the European Environment Agency. The first suggestion to stick with the Commission's law enforcement function is more practicable than the second, in the sense that no specific EU treaty changes would need to be made. Currently, the EU founding treaties do not empower the Commission to delegate its decision-making in law enforcement matters. A treaty amendment to allow this would require the unanimous consent of and ratification by the member states. The first suggestion would involve restructuring the internal working arrangements of the Commission services onto a footing that would better reflect the existing and long-standing EU constitutional position which places responsibility on the Commission to ensure that EU law is duly applied.

The role of civil society in enforcing EU environmental law has until relatively recently received little serious attention from the EU institutions and member states. For several years during the early phases of the Union's history, the Commission acted *de facto* as the primary representative of the public in taking steps to ensure that EU environmental legislation would be correctly implemented at national level. Over time, though, private persons have acquired a significant range of rights under Union law for the purposes of seeking to ensure the proper implementation of EU environmental legislative norms within member states. The role of the CJEU has been influential in this respect, with its development of various general doctrines and principles such as direct and indirect effect[4] that have enabled individuals to invoke and to some extent enforce EU environmental norms.

Certain Union institutional organs have also been of assistance to civil society in addressing breaches of EU environmental law other than the European

Commission, notably the European Ombudsman and European Parliament (EP). The possibility of recourse to the European Ombudsman, whose remit is to tackle instances of Union institutional maladministration, has offered some inroads for the public to force the European Commission to review its decisions not to prosecute member states under the infringement procedure. The right of petition to the EP has also opened up opportunities of challenging Commission decision-making in relation to enforcement. These review channels, which although do not lead to any legally binding outcome, remain in practice significant, not least given the absence of any formal right for the public to seek judicial review of Commission decisions on whether to utilise the infringement procedures under Articles 258 and 260 TFEU against member states.

However, it has been the recent adoption since the mid 2000s of various legislative initiatives at EU level designed to implement the 1998 Århus Convention on access to information, public participation in decision-making and access to justice in environmental matters which has transformed the legal position of private persons, particularly NGEOs, wishing to engage in supervision of EU environmental law. Specifically, private persons have acquired a substantial range of important rights to access justice and environmental information at national and Union levels. As discussed in Chapter 8, various EU legislative instruments have been adopted containing provisions specifically intended to shore up rights of individuals taking legal action before national courts of the member states with a view to enforcing EU environmental protection statutory requirements, including notably Directive 2003/35 on public participation in respect of the drawing up of certain plans and programmes relating to the environment,[5] the Environmental Liability Directive 2004/35,[6] the Environmental Impact Assessment Directive 2011/92[7] and the Industrial Emissions Directive 2010/75.[8] Whilst a general access to justice instrument still eludes the EU, although the Seventh Environmental Action Programme (EAP7) has now signalled this to be forthcoming. In addition, the EU has also adopted legislation to secure an individual right of access to environmental information at national level.[9] As discussed in Chapters 9–9A, the Union has also taken steps to ensure that civil society is invested with certain rights to seek review of EU decision-making with respect to the environment as well as access environmental information, in the form of the Århus Regulation 1367/06,[10] which represent a substantial improvement on the very limited rights of action available to individuals vis-à-vis Union activities.

Notwithstanding the fact that these legislative changes represent a significant boost to the role that civil society may play in assisting in the enforcement of EU environmental law, there is also room for considerable improvement. First, the post-millennium arrival of EU legislative provision on access to environmental justice to date does contain some flaws. In particular, private persons are not vested with any rights under the legislation (specifically, under Århus Regulation 1367/06) to seek judicial review of a Commission decision not to take up infringement proceedings against a member state under Articles 258 and 260 TFEU as requested by a complainant. This is unsatisfactory and arguably an omission in contravention of the 1998 Århus Convention (Article 9(3)). The multiplicity of tasks which the Commission is charged to fulfil underlines the need to ensure that civil society has a possibility at the very least to seek independent review of a failure on the Commission's part to take infringement action. There is an element of double standards here, given that the Environmental Liability Directive 2004/35 provides private persons with certain rights to challenge omissions on the part of national authorities to take legal action against persons liable for disrespecting the requirements of EU environmental protection rules. Secondly, whilst the increase in range and depth of supervisory rights for NGEOs and other private persons under EU law is to be welcomed, they should not be perceived as a panacea for ills in the current system of EU environmental law enforcement. It should always be recognised that the capabilities of the private sector to engage in environmental law enforcement are going to be relatively limited, both from a legal and financial perspective. Specifically, the absence of investigatory powers for private persons to inspect premises as well as difficulties in acquiring legal standing at national level to take action directly against private polluters are examples of considerable legal obstacles often faced by NGEOs when contemplating public interest litigation in relation to bad-application cases. The burden of shouldering legal costs may also prove a significant a barrier, although as seen in Chapter 8 the EU has made some significant inroads into addressing this particular issue in line with the Århus Conventions requirements against prohibitively expensive legal costs. Realistically, the most effective form of enforcement action that NGEOs and other private persons can undertake is to place pressure on the relevant authorities at national and international level to take action. In several respects, the various EU legislative instruments concerning access to environmental justice and information take this factor on board in constructing various review mechanisms to be made available to private persons and, in particular, certain types of qualifying NGEOs.

Just as in the case of civil society, the enforcement role of member state authorities has been substantially underplayed at Union level with respect to EU environmental legislation. A general legal responsibility of member states to implement EU law, including EU environmental legislation, is enshrined as a cornerstone of the EU treaty framework[11] and has existed since the inception of the EU. However, member states have been slow and in some cases reluctant to accept the legal reality that the duty to ensure proper, full implementation of EU law at national level includes a duty to ensure that it is applied in practice as well as being incorporated formally within the body of national rules of law. Whilst the CJEU has clarified this to be a well-established principle of EU law,[12] the Union did not seek to crystallise this obligation into detailed legislative form. However, since the early 2000s the position has changed quite radically. As discussed in Chapter 11, the Union has adopted a series of measures stipulating minimum standards in relation to the area of environmental inspections. Whereas initially the Union pursued a soft law approach with the adoption of a general non-binding recommendation in 2001, namely Recommendation 2001/331 on minimum criteria for environmental inspections (RMCEI),[13] it has steadily moved towards entrenching inspection benchmarks in legally binding legislative form during the latter stages of the EAP6 and now EAP7. In addition, the EU has adopted instruments that directly concern the manner in which national authorities enforce EU environ-mental protection law. Measures such as the Environmental Liability Directive 2004/35 and Directive 2008/99[14] on the protection of the environment through criminal law are notable in this regard. Both legislative instruments impose spe-cific binding obligations on authorities designated by the member states to take legal action, civil as well as criminal, in the event of persons breaching EU envir-onmental protection rules. These are welcome developments, because they spe-cifically require member states to internalise their EU environmental obligations into their respective national legal orders with a view to ensuring that the obli-gations are adhered to in practice. That being said, there remains considerable room to develop further enforcement-related obligations on national authorities. In particular, the EU's instrumentation on inspections is partial in its coverage and requires better co-ordination. The RMCEI providing for minimum criteria of environmental inspections in member states is non-binding and lacks sufficient precision and coverage, and needs to be firmed up into binding legislative form.

It is apparent that in recent times the EU has been moving closer to a situation in which it recognises the importance of ensuring that the task of ensuring adher-ence to its rules on environmental protection should be spread widely amongst interested parties. The traditional over-reliance upon the European Commission as 'guardian' of EU environmental norms has become gradually overtaken by a welcome, albeit rather belated, sense of realism that both civil society and, in particular, national authorities of member states have major enforcement roles to play. The EU's moves towards enhancing a three-dimensional perspective to environmental protection supervision constitute a significant advance in terms of adding credibility as well as democratic accountability to decisions taken in the area of EU environmental law enforcement. The three-dimensional perspective involves the harnessing of three key resources to assist in law enforcement: Euro-pean Commission, civil society and member state authorities involved in environ-mental protection.

A number of positive features emerge from the enhancement of a tripartite system of supervision. First, it is clear that each enforcement actor is able indepen-dently to contribute significantly to the work required to supervise implementation of EU environmental law. The Commission is particularly well positioned to over-see that member state governments implement their legally binding EU environ-mental obligations into law. Without being endowed with legal powers and other resources to carry out investigatory work, its role in bad-application casework will remain limited and heavily dependent upon the supply of information and evi-dence from either civil society or national authorities. Private persons, in particular NGEOs, are particularly well positioned to monitor compliance with EU environ-mental law at national level in areas of environmental protection regulation that are subject to public consultation (e.g. project development) or where evidence of illicit pollution may be accessible to public scrutiny or otherwise readily apparent (e.g. illicit waste deposition, or illicit interference with protected nature sites). Pri-vate persons may be able to draw public authorities' attention (whether national environmental protection authorities or the Commission) to such instances of bad application. They also may be able to monitor alongside the Commission the current state of transposition of EU environmental legislation and place political pressure on national governments as well as the Commission to act where needed. Member state authorities charged with environmental protection responsibilities under national law have an especially important role to play in terms of enforcing EU environmental law. Usually, given their financial resources and legal powers to investigate sites and prosecute offenders, they are best placed to tackle instances of bad application of EU environmental law. Secondly, the tripartite nature of this enforcement framework involves an interactive and constructive relationship between all three parties. Each of them may decide to take unilateral action in respect of infringements and/or engage in co-operative strategies or partnerships with the others. In addition, each party may be able to engage in some form of useful supervision of the others' performance in law enforcement work (e.g. NGEOs in relation to Commission decisions on infringement cases in relation to Article 258/260(2) TFEU, the Commission in relation to decisions by member state authorities). The interactive and interdependent nature of the agents engaged in EU environmental law enforcement work may be usefully depicted in diagrammatic form:

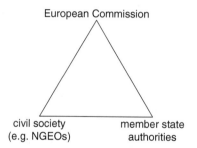

European Commission

civil society
(e.g. NGEOs)

member state
authorities

Each law enforcement agent is represented as a point in the triangle, signifying their integral value and importance to the overall legal framework for supervising compliance with EU environmental law as well as indicating the significance of interaction between the constituent agents in terms of enhancing their individual performance as well as degree of accountability in taking key decisions in the field. Above all, each agent is linked to one another by a common interest, namely to ensure compliance with EU environmental protection standards.

Before ending this book, it is perhaps apt to make at least a few remarks on how the role of law should be perceived to fit within the broader contemporary debates in the EU and elsewhere about selecting the best means to secure ever better compliance with accepted minimum environmental standards. Within various academic and professional circles involved in environmental politics, it is not uncommon to hear the view that the use of centralised mechanisms to secure societal compliance with environmental protection goals, such as law enforcement and regulation, represents an outmoded and in practice ineffective approach to governance. The use of market instruments, such as economic incentives in the form of fiscal measures, are proffered as superior and even substitute mechanisms over 'command and control' approaches in influencing society's behaviour towards the environment. It is important to stress here that these two types of technique of governance should be seen as complementary to one another and not as alternative strategies for environmental protection policy. Lawyers would be the first to admit that recourse to law to uphold environmental protection standards is not necessarily the most efficient or effective mechanism at society's disposal to protect the environment. For, notwithstanding that the threat of law enforcement may, if structured effectively, contain an element of deterrence and therefore have some preventive impact, its application is usually undertaken as a means of last resort in order to respond to illicit conduct that has already transpired which may already have had profound and even irremediable effects on the state of the environment. It is clear that other enforcement strategies geared to promote the prevention of environmental damage should also be fostered alongside legal initiatives, such as educational guidance and other culturally based initiatives. The roles of education and public awareness have so far not been taken as seriously as they might at EU level.

At the end of the day, though, law enforcement represents the most important and fundamental component in any strategy to secure effective implementation of environmental protection policy, not least given that markets contain no inherently dominant and stable long-term economic interests to safeguard the state of the environment. In any event, as far as the enforcement of EU environmental law is concerned, its use in the past has been hampered by an unduly narrow vision as to who should undertake the law enforcement role. The wave of EU legislative initiatives adopted since the turn of the millennium according civil society and national authorities far more opportunities and responsibility in this regard seem set to improve matters significantly. It will, though, take a considerable period yet for these measures to bed down into legal practice so as to be able to provide the requisite assistance to delivering and safeguarding EU environmental protection obligations. Overall, the EU's approach to the challenge of securing enforcement of its environmental protection obligations appears positive. It needs to stick with the course of providing effective support to the tripartite matrix of actors (namely Commission, civil society and national authorities) which it has rightly identified can make the difference between good and poor adherence to EU environmental law, and consequently to the state of environmental protection within the Union.

Notes

1 Art. 260(3) TFEU.
2 The average is drawn from the European Commission's 27th–30th annual reports on monitoring the application of EU Law for the years 2009–12 , as compiled by the Commission's Secretariat General, which may be accessed from the following EU website: http://ec.europa.eu/eu_law/infringements/infringements_annual_report_en.htm. See also Table 5.1 in Chapter 5 above.
3 Case C-304/02 *Commission v France (French Fishing Controls (2))*.
4 See e.g. notably CJEU rulings in cases such as Case C-72/95 *Kraaijeveld* and C-201/02 *Delena Wells* and discussion of the CJEU case law in Chapter 6.

5   OJ 2003 L156/17.
6   OJ 2004 L143/56.
7   OJ 2011 L26/1, as amended by Directive 2014/52 (OJ 2014 L124/1).
8   OJ 2010 L334/17.
9   Directive 2003/4 on public access to environmental information and repealing Directive 90/313(OJ 2003 L41/26.
10 OJ 2006 L264/13.
11 See Art. 4(3) TEU (formerly Art. 10 EC/Art. 5 EEC).
12 See e.g. Case C-431/92 *Commission v Germany*.
13 Recommendation 2001/331 (OJ 2001 L118/41).
14 OJ 2008 L328/28.

Bibliography

Aiking, H., Brans, E., Ozdemiroglu, E. (2010) 'Industrial Risk and Natural Resources: The EU Environmental Liability Directive as a Watershed?', 1 *Env Liability* 3.

Albors-Llorens, A. (1998) 'Locus Standi of Private Parties in Environmental Cases', 58 *CLJ* 33.

Albrecht, P.-A. and Braum, S. (1999) 'Deficiencies in the Development of European Criminal Law', 5(3) *ELJ* 302.

Anagnostaras, G. (2001) 'The Allocation of Responsibility in State Liability Actions for Breach of Community Law: A Modern Gordian Knot?', 26 *EL Rev* 139.

Arnull, A. (1999) 'Editorial: The Incidental Effect of Directives', 24(1) *EL Rev* 1.

Arnull, A. (2011) 'The Principle of Effective Judicial Protection in EU Law: An Unruly Horse?', *EL Rev* 51.

Audretsch, H (1987) 'Supervision in the EEC, OECD, and Benelux: A Difference in Degree, But Also in Kind?', 36 *ICLQ* 838.

Balthasar, S. (2010) '*Locus Standi* Rules for Challenges to Regulatory Acts by Private Applicants: The New Article 263(4) TFEU', 35 *EL Rev* 542.

Barav, A. (1975) 'Failure of Member States to Fulfil their Obligations under Community Law', 12 *CML Rev* 369.

Bell, S. and McGillivray, D. (2000) *Environmental Law*, 5th edn (Oxford: Blackstone Press).

Bell, S., McGillivray, D. and Pedersen, O. (2013) *Environmental Law*, 8th edn (Oxford: Blackstone Press).

Bergsten, M. (2011) 'Environmental Liability Regarding Carbon Capture and Storage (CCS) Operations in the EU', 20(3) *EEEL Rev* 108.

Berrod, F. (1999) 'Case Note on *Stichting Greenpeace*', 36 *CML Rev* 635.

Betlem, G. and Brans, E. (eds.) (2008) *Environmental Liability in the EU: The 2004 Directive compared with US and Member State Law* (London: Cameron May).

Biernat, E. (2003) 'The Locus Standi of Private Applicants under Article 230(4) EC and the Principle of Judicial Protection in the European Community', Jean Monnet Working Paper 12/03, The Jean Monnet Program, New York University School of Law.

Biondi, A and Harmer, K (2007) '2005 in Luxembourg: Recent Developments in the Case Law of the Community Courts', 13(1) *EPL* 33.

Birnie, P. and Boyle, A. (2002) *International Law and the Environment*, 2nd edn (Oxford: Oxford University Press).

Birnie, P., Boyle, A. and Redgwell, C. (2009) *International Law and the Environment*, 3rd edn (Oxford: Oxford University Press).

Bonnie, A. (1998) 'Commission Discretion under Art. 171(2) EC', 23(6) *EL Rev* 537.

Bonnor, P. (2000) 'The European Ombudsman: A Novel Source of Soft Law in the EU', 25 *EL Rev* 39.

Borzsák, L. (2011) *The Impact of Environmental Concerns on the Public Enforcement Mechanism under EU Law: Environmental protection in the 25th Hour* (The Netherlands: Wolters Kluwer).

Bossche van den, P. (1996) 'In Search of Remedies for Non-compliance: The Experience of the European Community', 3 *MJ* 371.

Boyle, A. (2005) 'Globalising Environmental Liability: The Interplay of National and International Law', 17(1) *JEL* 3.

Brans, E. (2005) 'Liability for Damage to Public Natural Resources under the 2004 EC Environmental Liability Directive: Standing and Assessment of Damages', 7 *Env LRev* 90.

Bridge, J. (1976) 'The European Communities and the Criminal Law', *Crim LR* 88.

Brown Weiss, E. and Jacobsen, H. (eds.) (2000) *Engaging Countries: Strengthening Compliance with International Environmental Accords* (Cambridge, MA: The MIT Press).

Carbone, S., Munari, F. and Schiano de Pepe, L. (2008) 'The Environmental Liability Directive and Liability for Damage to the Marine Environment', 1 *Env Liability* 18.

Cardwell, P., French, D. and Hall, M. (2011) 'Tackling Environmental Crime in the EU: The Case of the Missing Victim?', 1 *Env Liability* 35.

Colgan, D. (2002) 'Triangular Situations: The Coup de Grâce for the Denial of Horizontal Direct Effect of Community Directives', 8(4) *EPL* 545.

Comte, F. (2003) 'Criminal Environmental Law and Community Competence', 12 *EEEL Rev* 147.

Comte, F. (2004) 'Protection of the Environment through Criminal Law: Destiny of the Various European Union's Initiatives' in Onida, M. (ed.), *Europe and the Environment: Legal Essays in Honour of Ludwig Krämer* (Groningen: Europa Law Publishing).

Comte, F. (2005) 'European Environmental Criminal Law: Recent Developments', 4 *YEEL* 209.

Corstens C. (2003) 'Criminal Law in the First Pillar?', 11(1) *Eur J Crime, Crim L & Crim Justice* 144.

Craig, P. (1993), '*Francovich*, Remedies and the Scope of Damages Liability', 109 *LQR* 595.

Craig, P. (1997a) 'Once More Unto the Breach: The Community, the State and Damages Liability', 113 *LQR* 67.

Craig, P (1997b) 'Directives: Direct Effect, Indirect Effect and the Construction of National Legislation', 22(6) *EL Rev* 519.

Craig, P. (2003) 'Standing, Rights, and the Structure of Legal Argument', 9(4) *EPL* 493.

Craig, P. and de Búrca, G. (1998) *EU Law: Text, Cases and Materials*, 2nd edn (Oxford: Oxford University Press).

Craig, P. and de Búrca, G. (2003) *EU Law: Text, Cases and Materials*, 3rd edn (Oxford: Oxford University Press).

Craig, P. and de Búrca, G. (2011) *EU Law: Text, Cases and Materials*, 5th edn (Oxford: Oxford University Press).

Daniel, A. (2003) 'Civil Liability Regimes as a Complement to Multilateral Environmental Agreements: Sound International Policy or False Comfort?', 12(3) *RECIEL* 225.

Dashwood, A. and White, R. (1989) 'Enforcement Actions under Articles 169 and 170 EEC', 14(6) *EL Rev* 388.

Davies, P. (2004) *European Union Environmental Law: An Introduction to Key Selected Issues* (Aldershot: Ashgate Publishing Ltd).

Dawes, A. and Lynskey, O. (2008) 'The Ever-longer Arm EC Law: The Extension of Community into the Field of Criminal Law', 45 *CML Rev* 156.

Deards, E. (1997) ' "Curiouser and Curiouser"? The Development of Member State Liability in the Court of Justice', 3 *EPL* 117.

Delmas-Marty M. (1998) 'The European Union and Penal Law', 1 *ELJ* 88.

Delnoy, M. (2011) 'Implementation of the Aarhus Convention in Belgium: Some Elements', in Pallemaerts, M. (ed.) *The Aarhus Convention at Ten: Interactions and tensions between Conventional International Law and EU Environmental Law* (Groningen: Europa Law Publishing).

Demmke, C. (2001) 'Towards Effective Environmental Regulation: Innovative Approaches in Implementing and Enforcing European Environmental Law and Policy', Jean Monnet Working Paper 5/01, The Jean Monnet Program, New York University School of Law.

Demmke, C. (2003) 'Trends in European Environmental Regulation: Issues of Implementation and Enforcement', 3 *YEEL* 329.

Dette, B. (2004) 'Access to Justice in Environmental Matters: A Fundamental Right' in Onida, M. (ed.), *Europe and the Environment: Legal Essays in Honour of Ludwig Krämer* (Groningen: Europa Law Publishing).

Dine, J. (1993) 'European Community Criminal Law?', *Crim LR* 246.

Duncan, A. (2000) 'The History of IMPEL', paper published on the EU's Network for the Implementation of Environmental Law (IMPEL): www.europa.eu.int/comm/environment/impel/about.htm.

Ebbesson, J. (2001) 'Access to Justice at National Level: Impact of the Aarhus Convention and EU Law' in Pallemaerts, M. (ed.), *The Aarhus Convention at Ten: Interactions and tensions between Conventional International Law and EU Environmental Law* (Groningen: Europa Law Publishing).

European Commission, http://ec.europa.eu/environment/legal/crime/studies_en.htm.

Evans, A. (1979) 'The Enforcement Procedure of Article 169 EEC: Commission Decision', 4 *EL Rev* 442.

Farnsworth, N. (2004) 'Subsidiarity: A Conventional Industry Defence. Is the Directive on Environmental Liability with Regard to Prevention and Remedying of Environmental Damage Justified under the Subsidiarity Principle?', 13(6) *EEEL Rev* 176.

Faure, M. (2004) 'European Environmental Criminal Law: Do We Really Need It?', 13(1) *EEEL Rev* 18.

Faure, M. (2008) 'The Continuing Story of Environmental Criminal Law in Europe after 23 October 2007', 17(1) *EEEL Rev* 68.

Faure, M. (2010) 'Effective, Proportional and Dissuasive Penalties in the Implementation of the Environmental Crime and Ship-source Pollution Directives: Questions and Challenges', 19(6) *EEEL Rev* 256.

Faure, M. and Heine, G. (2002), 'Criminal penalties in EU Member States' Environmental Law' (Maastricht: Maastricht European institute for transnational legal research).

Gaffney, J. (1998) 'The Enforcement Procedure under Article 169 EC and the Duty of Member States to Supply Information Requested by the Commission: Is There a Regulatory Gap?', 25(1) *LIEI* 117.

Gáspár-Szilági, S. (2013) 'EU Member State Enforcement of 'Mixed' Agreements and Access to Justice: Rethinking Direct Effect', 40(2) *LIEI* 163.

Gillespie, A. (1997) *International Environmental Law: Policy and Ethics* (Oxford: Oxford University Press).

Grant, W., Matthews, D. and Newell, P. (2000) *The Effectiveness of European Union Environmental Policy* (Basingstoke: Macmillan Press Ltd).

Gray, C. (1979) 'Interim Measures of Protection in the European Court', 4 *EL Rev* 80.

Grohs, S. (2004) 'Commission Infringement Procedure in Environmental Cases' in Onida, M. (ed.), *Europe and the Environment: Legal Essays in Honour of Ludwig Krämer* (Groningen: Europa Law Publishing).

Hallo, R., 'Access to Environmental Information. The Reciprocal Influences of EUI law and the Aarhus Convention', in Pallemaerts, M. (ed.), *The Aarhus Convention at Ten: Interactions and tensions between Conventional International Law and EU Environmental Law* (Groningen: Europa Law Publishing).

Harding, C. (1997) 'Member State Enforcement of European Community Measures: The Chimera of 'Effective' Enforcement', 4 *MJ* 5.

Hart, D. (2012) 'Case Commentaries: The CJEU on "Prohibitively Expensive" and the New Protective Costs Order Regime', 6 *Env Liability* 257–8.

Hartley, T. (2003) *The Foundations of European Community Law*, 5th edn (Oxford University Press).

Hartley, T. (2014) *The Foundations of European Union Law*, 8th edn (Oxford: Oxford University Press).

Hattan, E. (2003) 'The Implementation of EU Environmental Law', 15(3) *JEL* 273.

Hedemann-Robinson, M. (2003), 'Uncharted Waters for EU Law Enforcement: EU Waste Management Law and the Marine Environment: Liability Issues Arising from the Prestige Oil Tanker Disaster', 11(3) *Env Liability* 89.

Hedemann-Robinson, M. (2005) 'The EU and Environmental Criminal Liability: A Legal Analysis in the Light of the Recent Ruling of the ECJ on EC Competence (Case C-176/03)', 6 *Env Liability* 149.

Hedemann-Robinson, M. (2006) 'Article 228(2) EC and the Enforcement of EC Environmental Law: A Case of Environmental Justice Delayed and Denied? An Analysis of Recent Developments', 15(11) *EEEL Rev* 312.

Hedemann-Robinson, M. (2007) *Enforcement of EU Environmental Law* (London: Routledge Cavendish).

Hedemann-Robinson, M. (2008a) 'The Emergence of European Union Environmental Criminal Law: A Quest for Solid Foundations: Part I', 16(3) *Env Liability* 71.

Hedemann-Robinson, M. (2008b) 'The Emergence of European Union Environmental Criminal Law: A Quest for Solid Foundations: Part II', 16(4) *Env Liability* 111.

Hedemann-Robinson, M. (2008c), 'The EU and Environmental Crime: The Impact of the ECJ's Judgment on Framework Decision 2005/667 on Ship-Source Pollution', *JEL* 1.

Hedemann-Robinson M. (2010) 'Enforcement of EU Environmental Law and the Role of Interim Relief Measures', 19 *EEEL Rev* 204.

Hedemann-Robinson, M. (2012) 'EU Enforcement of International Environmental Agreements: The Role of the European Commission', 21(1) *EEEL Rev* 2.

Hedemann-Robinson, M. and Wilde, M. (2000) 'Towards a European Tort Law on the Environment? European Union Initiatives and Developments on Civil Liability in Respect of Environmental Harm' in Lowry, J. and Edmunds, R. (eds.), *Environmental Protection and the Common Law* (Oxford/Portland, OR: Hart Publishing).

Herlin-Karnell, E. (2007) 'Commission v Council: Some Reflections on Criminal Law in the First Pillar', 13(1) *EPL* 69.

Hilson, C. and Downes, T. (1999), 'Making Sense of Rights: Community Rights in EC Law', 24 *EL Rev* 121.

Hinteregger, M. (ed.) (2008) *Environmental liability and Ecological Damage in European Law* (Cambridge: Cambridge University Press).

Holder, J. (1996) 'A Dead End for Direct Effect? Prospects for Enforcement of European Community Environmental Law by Individuals', 8(2) *JEL* 313.

Ibáñez, A. (1998a), 'A Deeper Insight into Article 169', Jean Monnet Working Paper 11/98, The Jean Monnet Program, New York University School of Law.

Ibáñez, A. (1998b) 'Commission Tools for the Supervision and Enforcement of EC Law other than Article 169 EC Treaty', Jean Monnet Working Paper 12/98, Jean Monnet Program, New York University School of Law.

Jack, B. (2011) 'Enforcing Member State Compliance with EU Environmental Law: A Critical Evaluation of the Use of Financial Penalties', 23(1) *JEL* 73.

Jacobs, F. (2006) 'The Role of the ECJ in the Protection of the Environment', 18(2) *JEL* 202.

Jans, H. (1996) 'Legal Protection in European Environmental Law: An Overview' in Somsen, H. (ed.), *Protecting the European Environment: Enforcing EC Environmental Law* (London: Blackstone Press Ltd).

Jans, H. (2000) *European Environmental Law*, 2nd edn (Groningen: Europa Law Publishing).

Jans, H. and Vedder, H. (2008) *European Environmental Law*, 3rd edn (Groningen: Europa Law Publishing).

Johnson, S. and Corcelle, G. (1995), *The Environmental Policy of the European Communities*, 2nd edn (London/The Hague/Boston: Kluwer Law International).

Jones, B. (2002) 'European Commission: Proposal for a Framework Directive on Environmental Liability', 14(1) *ELM* 5.

Kaiafa-Gbandi, M. (2001) 'The Development towards Harmonisation within Criminal Law in the EU: A Citizen's Perspective' 9(4) *Eur J Crime, Crim L & Crim Justice Eur J Crime, Crim L & Crim Justice* 249.

Kilbey, I. (2007) 'Financial Penalties under Article 228(2) EC: Excessive Complexity', 44 *CML Rev* 753.

Kingston, S. (2011), 'Mind the Gap: Difficulties in Enforcement and the Continuing Unfulfilled Promise of EU Environmental Law', paper presented at the 14th Annual Conference of the Irish European Law Forum: *Frontiers in European Environmental Law and Governance*, University College Dublin School of Law.

Koufakis, J. (2001) 'Case C-387/97: Commission of the EC v Hellenic Republic (Crete Case II)', *EEL Rev* 120.

Koutrakos, P. and Hillion, C. (eds.) (2010) *Mixed Agreements Revisited: The EU and its Member States in the World* (Oxford: Hart).

Krämer, L. (1991) 'The Implementation of Community Environmental Directives within Member States: Some Implications of the Direct Effect Doctrine', 3(1) *JEL* 39.

Krämer, L. (1993) *European Environmental Law Casebook* (London: Sweet & Maxwell).

Krämer, L. (1996a) 'Direct effect of EC Environmental Law' in Somsen, H. (ed.), *Protecting the European Environment: Enforcing EC Environmental Law* (London: Blackstone Press Ltd).

Krämer, L. (1996b) 'Public Interest Litigation in Environmental Matters before European Courts', 8(1) *JEL* 1.

Krämer, L. (2002a) *EU Casebook on Environmental Law* (Oxford/Portland, OR: Hart Publishing).

Krämer, L. (2002b), 'Thirty Years of EC Environmental Law: Perspectives and Prospectives', 2 *YEEL* 155.

Krämer, L. (2003) *EC Environmental Law*, 5th edn (London: Sweet & Maxwell).

Krämer, L. (2006a) 'Statistics on Environmental Judgments by the EC Court of Justice', 18(3) *JEL* 407.

Krämer, L. (2006b) 'Environment, Crime and EC Law', 18(2) *JEL* 277.

Krämer, L. (2011) *EU Environmental Law*, 7th edn (London: Sweet & Maxwell).

Lackhoff, K. and Nyssens, H. (1998) 'Direct Effect in Triangular Situations', 23 *EL Rev* 397.

Lange, F. de (2003) 'Beyond *Greenpeace*, Courtesy of the Aarhus Convention', 3 *YEEL* 227.

Lee, M. (2002) 'The Changing Aims of Environmental Liability', 14(4) *ELM* 189.

Lee, M. (2005) *EU Environmental Law: Challenges, Change and Decision-Making* (Oxford/Portland, OR: Hart).

Lee, M. (2014) *EU Environmental Law, Governance and Decision-Making*, 2nd edn (Oxford/Portland, OR: Hart).

Leeuw, M. de (2003) 'The Regulation on Public Access to European Parliament, Council and Commission Documents in the European Union: Are Citizens Better Off?', 28(3) *EL Rev* 324.

Lenaerts, K. and Gutiérrez-Fons, J. (2011) 'The General System of EU Environmental Law Enforcement', 30(1) *YEL* 3.

Lenz, M. (2000) 'Horizontal What? Back to Basics', 25(5) *EL Rev* 509.

Lowther, J. (2007) 'Case Law: EC Law Criminal Penalties Case (C-440/05)', 19 *ELM* 305.

Macrory, R. (1992) 'The Enforcement of Community Environmental Laws: Some Critical Issues', 29 *CML Rev* 347.

Macrory, R. and Purdy, P. (1997) 'The Enforcement of EC Environmental Law against Member States in Holder, J. (ed.), *The Impact of EC Environmental Law in the United Kingdom* (Chichester: John Wiley & Sons).

Macrory, R. and Westaway, N. (2011) 'Access to Environmental Justice: A UK Perspective' in Pallemaerts, M. (ed.), *The Aarhus Convention at Ten: Interactions and tensions between Conventional International Law and EU Environmental Law* (Groningen: Europa Law Publishing).

Marsden, S. (2012) 'Direct Public Access to EU Courts: Upholding Public International Law via the Aarhus Convention Compliance Committee', 81 *Nordic JIL* 175.

Maselis, I. and Gilliams, H. (1997) 'Rights of Complainants in Community Law', 22(2) *EL Rev* 103.

Mastroianni, R. (1995) 'The Enforcement Procedure under Article 169 of the EC Treaty and the Powers of the European Commission: *Quis Custodiet Custodes?*', 1(4) *EPL* 535.

Mathiesen, A. (2003) 'Public Participation in Decision-making and Access to Justice in EC Environmental Law: The Case of Certain Plans and Programmes', 12(2) *EEEL Rev* 36.

Maurici, J. and Moules, R. (2013) 'The Influence of the Aarhus Convention on EU Environmental Law: Part 1', *J Pl & Env Law* 1496.

Maurici, J. and Moules, R. (2014) 'The Influence of the Aarhus Convention on EU Environmental Law: Part 2', *J Pl & Env Law* 181.

Mertens de Wilmars, J. and Verougstraete, I. (1970), 'Proceedings against Member States for Failure to Fulfil their Obligations', 7 *CML Rev* 385.

Morghera, E. (2014), 'Environmental Law' in Barnard, C. and Peers, S, (eds.), *European Union Law* (Oxford: Oxford University Press).

Nadal, C. (2008) 'Pursuing Substantive Environmental Justice: The Aarhus Convention as a 'Pillar' of Empowerment', 10 *Env LRev* 28.

O'Keeffe, D. and Schermers, H. (eds.) (1983) *Mixed Agreements* (Deventer: Kluwer)

Onida, M. (2004) 'Environmental Protection by Product Policy; Focus on Dangerous Substances' in Onida, M. (ed.), *Europe and the Environment: Legal Essays in Honour of Ludwig Krämer* (Groningen: Europa Law Publishing).

Pallemaerts, M. (ed.) (2011) *The Aarhus Convention at Ten: Interactions and tensions between Conventional International Law and EU Environmental Law* (Groningen: Europa Law Publishing).

Pedersen, O. (2011) 'Price and Participation: the UK before the Aarhus Convention's Compliance Committee', 13(2) *Env LRev* 115.

Pedraza, J., de Smedt, K. and Faure, M. (2012) 'Compulsory Financial Guarantees for Environmental Damage: What Can We Learn from Spain?', 6 *Env Liability* 227.

Peers, S. (2006) *EU Justice and Home Affairs Law*, 2nd edn (Oxford: Oxford European Union Law Library).

Peers, S. (2012) *EU Justice and Home Affairs Law*, 3rd edn (Oxford: Oxford European Union Law Library).

Peers, S. and Costa, M. (2012) 'Judicial Review of EU Acts after the Treaty of Lisbon', *Eur Const L Rev* 82.

Pereira, R. (2008) 'On the Legality of the Ship-source Pollution 2005/35/EC Directive: The *Intertanko* Case and Selected Others', 17(6) *EEEL Rev* 372.

Petersen, M. (2009) 'The Environmental Liability Directive: Extending Nature Protection in Europe', 11(1) *Env LRev* 5.

Posch, W. (2008) 'Some Observations on the Law Applicable to Transfrontier Environmental Damage' in Hinteregger, M. (ed.), *Environmental liability and Ecological Damage in European Law* (Cambridge: Cambridge University Press).

Prechal, S. and Hancher, L. (2002) 'Individual Rights: Conceptual Pollution in EU Environmental Law?', 2 *YEEL* 89.

Prete, L. and Smulders, B. (2010) 'The Coming of Age of Infringement Proceedings', 47 *CML Rev* 9.

Ragolle, F. (2003) 'Access to Justice for Private Applicants in the Community Legal Order: Recent (R)evolutions', 28(1) *EL Rev* 90.

Rawlings, R. (2000) 'Engaged Elites Citizen Action and Institutional Attitudes in Commission Enforcement', 6(1) *ELJ* 4.

Reid, C. (2010) 'Case Comment on Case C-378/08', *Scottish Planning & Environmental Law Journal* 90.

Reid, C. (2011) 'Case Comment on Case C-240/09', *Scottish Planning & Environmental Law Journal* 89.

Roger France, E. (1994) 'The Influence of EC Law on the Criminal Law of the Member States', 2 *Eur J Crime, Crim L & Crim Justice* 324.

Roller, G. (2011) '*Locus Standi* for Environmental NGOs in Germany: The (Non-) Implementation of the Aarhus Convention by the Umweltrechtsbehelfsgesetz: Some Critical Remarks' in Pallemaerts, M. (ed.), *The Aarhus Convention at Ten: Interactions and tensions between Conventional International Law and EU Environmental Law* (Groningen: Europa Law Publishing)

Ryall, A. (2004) 'Implementation of the Aarhus Convention through Community Environmental Law', 6(4) *Env LRev* 274.

Ryland, D. (2009), 'Protection of the Environment through Criminal Law: A Question of Competence Unabated?', 18(2) *EEL Rev* 91.

Sands, P. and Peel J. (2012) *Principles of International Environmental Law*, 3rd edn (Cambridge: Cambridge University Press).

Schrauwen, A. (2006) 'Fishery, Waste Management and Persistent and General Failure to Fulfil Control Obligations: The Role of Lump Sums and Penalty Payments in Enforcement Actions under Community Law', 18(2) *JEL* 289.

Schermers, H. (1974) 'The Law as it Stands against Treaty Violations by States', 2 *LIEI* 111.

Scott, J. (1998) *EC Environmental Law* (Harlow: Addison Wesley Longman Ltd).

Selin, C. (2001) 'Your Money of Your Life; A Look at the Convention on the Protection of the Environment through Criminal Law', 10(1) *RECIEL* 106.

Smith, M. (2009) *Centralised Enforcement, Legitimacy and Good Governance in the EU* (London: Routledge).

Snyder, F. (1993) 'The Effectiveness of European Community Law: Institutions, Processes, Tools and Techniques', 56 *MLR* 19.

Somsen, H. (ed.) (1996) *Protecting the European Environment: Enforcing EC Environmental Law* (London: Blackstone Press Ltd).

Somsen, H. (2001) 'The Private Enforcement of Member State Compliance with EC Environmental Law: An Unfulfilled Promise?', 1 *YEEL* 310.

Somsen, H. (2003a) 'Current Issues of Implementation, Compliance and Enforcement of EC Environmental Law' in Krämer L. (ed.), *Recht und Umwelt; Essays in Honour of Professor Dr Gerd Winter* (Groningen: Europa Law Publishing).

Somsen, H. (2003b) 'Discretion in European Community Environmental Law: An Analysis of ECJ Case Law', 40 *CML Rev* 1413.

Steiner, J. (1998) 'The Limits of State Liability for Breach of European Community Law', 4(1) *EPL* 69.

Stone, C. (2010) *Should Trees Have Standing? Law, Morality and the Environment* 3rd edn (Oxford: Oxford University Press).

Sunkin, M., Ong, D. and Wight, R. (2002) *Sourcebook on Environmental Law*, 2nd edn (London/Sydney: Cavendish Publishing Limited).

Tanzi, A. and Pitea C. (2011) 'The Interplay between EU law and International Law Procedures in Controlling Compliance with the Aarhus Convention by EU Member States' in Pallemaerts, M. (ed.), *The Aarhus Convention at Ten: Interactions and tensions between Conventional International Law and EU Environmental Law* (Groningen: Europa Law Publishing).

Tesauro, G. (1992) 'La Sanction des infractions au droit communautaire', 32 *Rivista di Diritto Europeo* 477.

Theodossiou, M. (2002) 'An Analysis of the Recent Response of the Community to Non-compliance with Court of Justice Judgments: Article 228(2) EC', 27(1) *EL Rev* 25.

Tobler, C. (2006) 'Case Comment on Case C-176/03', 43 *CML Rev* 835.

Toth, A. (1975) 'The Law as it Stands on the Appeal for Failure to Act', 2 *LIEI* 65.

Tridimas, T. (1994) 'Horizontal Effect of Directives: A Missed Opportunity', 19(6) *EL Rev* 621.

Tridimas, T. (2001) 'Liability for Breach of Community Law: Growing Up and Mellowing Down?', 38 *CMLRev* 301.

Tsadiras, A. (2007a), 'Navigating through the Clashing Rocks: The Admissibility Conditions and the Grounds for Inquiry into Complaints by the European Ombudsman', 26 *YEL* 157.

Tsadiras, A. (2007b), 'The Position of the European Ombudsman in the Community System of Judicial Remedies' 32 *EL Rev* 607.

Tsadiras, A. (2008) 'Unravelling Ariadne's Thread: The European Ombudsman's Investigative Powers', 45 *CML Rev* 757.

Tsadiras, A. (2013a), 'The European Ombudsman's Remedial Powers: An Empirical Analysis in Context', *EL Rev* 52.

Tsadiras, A. (2013b) 'Environmental Protection through Extra-judicial Means: The European Ombudsman's Contribution', 22(4) *EEEL Rev* 152.

Usher, J. (2003) 'Direct and Individual Concern: An Effective Remedy or a Conventional Solution' 28(5) *EL Rev* 575.

Vedder, H. (2010) 'The Treaty of Lisbon and European Environmental Law and Policy', 22(2) *JEL* 285.

Vogleman, V. (2012), 'The European Court of Justice Rules on the Environmental Liability Directive', 2 *Env Liability* 39.

Wägenbaur, R. (1990–1), 'The European Community's Policy on Implementation of Environmental Directives', 14(2) *Fordham Int. LJ* 455.

Ward, A. (1995), 'Effective Sanctions in EC Law: A Moving Boundary in the Division of Competence', 1(2) *ELJ* 205.

Ward, A. (2001) 'Judicial Review of Environmental Misconduct in the European Community: Problems, Prospects and Strategies', 1 *YEEL* 137.

Wasmeier M. and Thwaites, N. (2004) 'The "Battle of the Pillars": Does the EC Have the Power to Approximate National Criminal Laws?', 29(5) *EL Rev* 613.

Wates, J. (2011) 'The Future of the Aarhus Convention: Perspectives Arising from the Third Session of the Meeting of the Parties' in Pallemaerts, M. (ed.), *The Aarhus Convention at Ten: Interactions and tensions between Conventional International Law and EU Environmental Law* (Groningen: Europa Law Publishing).

Weatherill, S. and Beaumont, P. (1999) *EU Law*, 3rd edn (London: Penguin).

Wennerås, P. (2006) 'A New Dawn for Commission Enforcement under Articles 226 and 228 EC: General and Persistent (GAP) Infringements, Lump Sums and Penalty Payments', 43 *CML Rev* 31.

Wennerås, P. (2007) *The Enforcement of EC Environmental Law* (Oxford: Oxford University Press).

Wennerås, P. (2012), 'Sanctions against Member States under Article 260 TEU: Alive, But Not Kicking?', 49 *CML Rev* 145.

Weyembergh, A. (2005) 'Approximation of Criminal Laws, the Constitutional Treaty and the Hague Programme', 42 *CML Rev* 1571.

Wilde, M. (2013) *Civil Liability for Environmental Damage: Comparative Analysis of Law and Policy in Europe and the US*, 2nd edn (Netherlands: Wolters Kluwer).

Williams, R. (1994) 'The European Commission and the Enforcement of Environmental Law: an Invidious Position', 14 *YEL* 351.

Williams, R. (2002) 'Enforcing European Environmental Law: Can the European Commission Be Held to Account?', 2 *YEEL* 271.

Winter, G. (1996) 'On the Effectiveness of the EC Administration: The Case of Environmental Protection', 33 *CML Rev* 689.

Winter, G. (2002), 'Constitutionalizing Environmental Protection in the EU', 2 *YEEL* 67.

Winter, G. *et al.* (2008), 'Weighing Up the EC Environmental Liability Directive', 20(2) *JEL* 163.

Wyatt, D. (1998) 'Litigating Community Environmental Law: Thoughts on the Direct Effect Doctrine', 10(1) *JEL* 9.

Index